B R A I N T R E E   S T.

S P R I N G   St

BUILDING OLD CAMBRIDGE

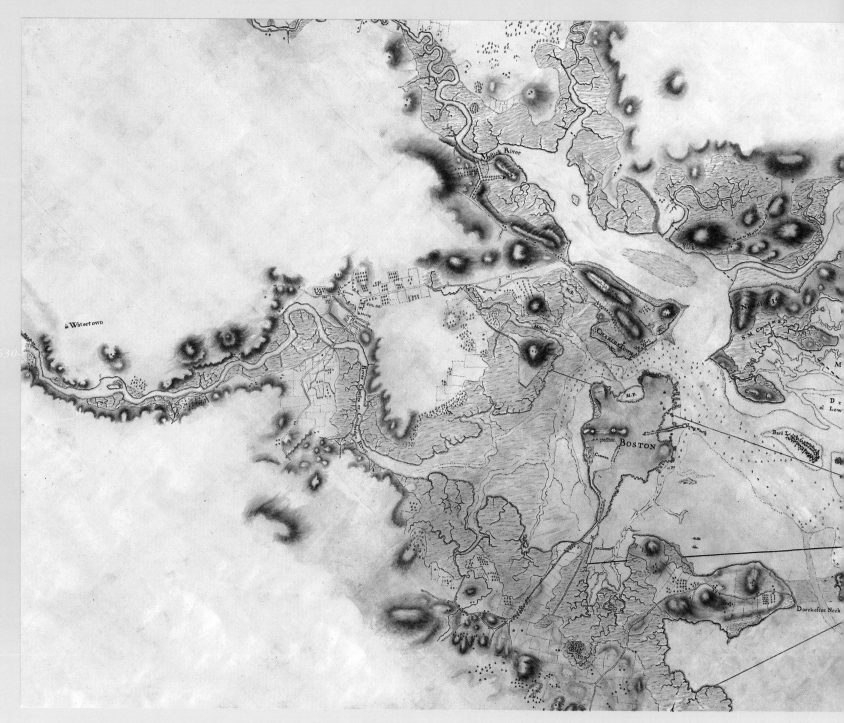

FRONTISPIECE: Cambridge, Charlestown, and Boston in the early 1770s. This appears to be the most accurate of several early depictions of the region by British military cartographers, perhaps because it was made before the Siege of Boston, when access to the countryside was still possible.

BUILDING OLD CAMBRIDGE

ARCHITECTURE AND DEVELOPMENT

Susan E. Maycock and Charles M. Sullivan

The MIT Press   Cambridge, Massachusetts   London, England

This book was set in Adobe Garamond by the MIT Press.

Printed and bound in Canada.

Library of Congress Cataloging-in-Publication Data

Names: Maycock, Susan E., 1943- author. | Sullivan, Charles, 1940- author. | Cambridge Historical Commission.

Title: Building old Cambridge : architecture and development / Susan E. Maycock and Charles M. Sullivan.

Other titles: Survey of architectural history in Cambridge.

Description: Cambridge, MA : The MIT Press, 2016. | An addition to the Survey of Architectural History in Cambridge; expands the scope and physical area of the Commission's 1973 Report Four: Old Cambridge. | Includes bibliographical references and index.

Identifiers: LCCN 2016036114 | ISBN 9780262034807 (hardcover : alk. paper)

Subjects: LCSH: Architecture--Massachusetts--Cambridge--History. | Architecture and society--Massachusetts--Cambridge--History. | Cambridge (Mass.)--Buildings, structures, etc. | Cambridge (Mass.)--History.

Classification: LCC NA735.C28 M39 2016 | DDC 720.9744/4--dc23 LC record available at https://lccn.loc.gov/2016036114

10 9 8 7 6 5 4 3 2 1

Harvard Yard, looking north from the attic of Wadsworth House in 1821.
Massachusetts Hall is at left, Holworthy is in the center, and University Hall
is on the right.
Harvard Art Museums/Fogg Museum. Alvan Fisher, "College Yard: A View
from the President's House," 1821, presented for the use of Harvard College
by Henry Pickering, 1823. Harvard University Portrait Collection, 1823, L3.
Photo: Imaging Department © President & Fellows of Harvard College

Harvard Square in 1912, after completion of the subway. See figure 2.46.

Contents

Edwin D. Mellen house (Greycroft), 1590 Massachusetts Avenue, ca. 1899.
See figure 4.180.

FOREWORD

The house where I live in Cambridge was first owned by a woman named Bridget Sarah Coon. Her husband had been a brick mason, and four of her sons were masons, too. One of them built the Cambridge Mutual Fire Insurance Company, on the corner of Inman Street and Massachusetts Avenue, in 1889.

Three generations of Coons lived in my house at the same time. Once, when my house was being renovated, workers found a book under a floorboard, a children's magazine published in 1886, *The Golden Library of Choice Reading for Boys and Girls*. More than once, when I've been digging in my backyard, pulling up dandelion roots and Englishmen's foot, I've come across bits of history: ceramic beer bottles, mostly. One day, when I knocked down a lath-and-plaster wall, I found a glass jar tucked behind the horsehair. I keep these things on a shelf as relics. I think of them as The Remains of the Builders.

Every city is a city of buildings and every building houses a history within its walls. But very few cities are so lucky in their history as Cambridge. That's because of the work of the Cambridge Historical Commission, and, in particular, that's because of the work of Susan Maycock and Charles Sullivan. Some of that work has involved preservation. (The house where I live would have been demolished in the nineteen seventies, if the neighborhood hadn't gotten together to save Garfield Street, work that is now done by the Cambridge Historical Commission.) But the great bulk of it is documentary, a kind of civic-scholarship that

is as valuable as it is rare. In *Building Old Cambridge*, Maycock and Sullivan have continued the Commission's extraordinary work in surveying and documenting every single structure in the city. But the book is far more than an inventory. It's a rich and dazzling history, full of quirky characters, noble ambitions, and distressing shortcomings. There are swamps and plinths, parks and subways, schools and turrets. You can walk across Old Cambridge in an afternoon, and you should. But you ought, on many afternoons, to walk across the Cambridge Common and head over to the Cambridge Public Library, on Broadway, find a chair, and sit and read *Building Old Cambridge*, within the walls of a building that first opened in 1889 and then, in 2009, opened again, with a whole new wing, making it, like much else in Old Cambridge, young again.

Jill Lepore
Cambridge, December 2015

Winthrop Square as seen from Mt. Auburn Street, ca. 1889. See figure 3.7.

PREFACE

This comprehensive book, many years in the making, forms an appropriate complement to the Cambridge Historical Commission's five-volume Survey of Architectural History in Cambridge, which the staff began over fifty years ago and completed in 1977. In the ordinance establishing the Commission on June 24, 1963, the City Council instructed it "to conduct a survey of Cambridge buildings for the purpose of determining those of historic significance architecturally or otherwise, and pertinent facts about them," to advise owners of historic buildings in Cambridge on issues of preservation, and to collaborate with other city agencies. The comprehensive inventory of every structure in the city was carried out from 1964 to 1975 and has been updated and strengthened by documentary research and the discovery of historic images over the past forty years. The inventory continues to provide an invaluable basis for addressing the Commission's goals, as well as informing all its publications.

Building Old Cambridge presents the results of significant new research and greatly expands the scope and physical area of the Commission's 1973 *Report Four: Old Cambridge*. Both authors of this new book have long associations with the city and the Commission. Trained as a city planner, Charles Sullivan became the Cambridge Historical Commission's Executive Director in 1974. He has been responsible for initiating many new programs to enhance the public's understanding of the city's rich history and to encourage preservation of its built environment.

His impressive familiarity with all phases of Cambridge history and development underlies his frequent and popular public presentations and walking tours, as well as the current volume. Architectural historian Susan Maycock originally came to the Commission in 1968 as Survey Associate while still a graduate student. She returned in 1980 to become Survey Director and to advise owners on the appropriate historic paint colors for their buildings. She wrote a new book on East Cambridge, published in 1988, before beginning research and writing for *Building Old Cambridge*.

In addition to its publications, the Commission has pioneered a number of preservation tools to address the needs of this ever changing city; some of these have become models for other communities. The 1963 ordinance created Cambridge's first historic districts and gave the Commission administrative authority over properties in them. Protecting these districts continues to be a principal responsibility, but the number of buildings they include has greatly increased. The present Old Cambridge Historic District is the result of the consolidation of four earlier districts and subsequent expansions in 1976, 1986, and 1996 to include additional streets. This enlarged area now forms a major part of the focus of *Building Old Cambridge*.

Through the years overdevelopment and demolition have threatened many neighborhoods and buildings considered worthy of preservation but which were not appropriate candidates for historic districts or designation as landmarks. In 1979, at the Commission's urging the City Council adopted a citywide demolition delay ordinance to slow down the increasing number of demolitions of buildings not in protected areas and to provide time to explore possible alternatives. This ordinance allows the Commission to place a six-month delay on the proposed demolition of any property over 50 years old that it determines is significant and preferably preserved. Similar measures have since been adopted by almost 150 other Massachusetts cities and towns.

The Commission also originated a new type of regulated district with less stringent restrictions that could be tailored to the specific characteristics of each designated area. In 1983 the City Council adopted an ordinance providing for the establishment of neighborhood conservation districts (NCDs) and protected landmarks. Each NCD and landmark is designated by the City Council based on the Commission's detailed study of the area or property and its specific preservation goals. The Commission currently oversees more than 3,000 buildings in two historic districts, four NCDs, and thirty-seven city landmarks.

In addition to these preservation tools, the Commission staff supports homeowners, investors, and local institutions with advice on maintaining or restoring old buildings and on historic paint colors. The Commission contributes to neighborhood revitalization through a program of Community Preservation Act grants for non-profit owners of significant buildings, low- and moderate-income owners, and affordable housing agencies. An annual preservation awards program honors individuals and institutions for their outstanding historic preservation projects. Of particular significance in the preservation of many buildings in Old Cambridge is the 1986 protocol with Harvard University, under which the university regularly consults with Commission staff about exterior changes to its buildings listed on the National Register of Historic Places. The Commission has recently entered into a similar arrangement with the Massachusetts Institute of Technology.

Throughout its existence the Cambridge Historical Commission and its programs have benefitted from the active support of the City Manager and the City Council. Times and priorities have changed, from the days of blight, urban renewal, and massive highway proposals through rent control and excessive infill to adaptive reuse of industrial buildings and the development of a new biotech and innovation economy at Kendall Square. As Cambridge faces the continuing challenges of balancing the growth and renewal needs of the city with appreciation and protection of its rich historical assets, the Cambridge Historical Commission's education, publication, and preservation programs that celebrate the city's history seem even more crucial now than when it was established. *Building Old Cambridge* is a welcome addition to these important ongoing programs.

William B. King
Chair, Cambridge Historical Commission
September 8, 2015

The Botanic Garden House and Thayer Herbarium, 1867. See figure 5.85.

INTRODUCTION

Building Old Cambridge: Architecture and Development continues the publication program begun by the Cambridge Historical Commission in 1965 with *Report One: East Cambridge* of the Survey of Architectural History in Cambridge. *Report Four: Old Cambridge* appeared in 1974, and the series concluded in 1977 with *Report Five: Northwest Cambridge*. Since then, the Commission staff has substantially deepened its knowledge of Cambridge history, collecting thousands of historic photographs and delving increasingly into primary sources. By the 1980s the early volumes, which had been applauded for their innovative exploration of urban growth and vernacular architecture, began to seem dated. A second series was launched in 1988 with the publication of Susan Maycock's *East Cambridge*, which ranged beyond architecture to explore the social history, immigrant experiences, and long-vanished industries of that early planned village. The book set a new standard for the series, and a few years later we began work on a comprehensive history of the architecture and urban development of Old Cambridge.

Old Cambridge originated as an early colonial village that served briefly as the capital of Massachusetts Bay and grew up around Harvard College. It was the only village in the First Parish from 1630 until shortly after the West Boston Bridge opened in 1793, when new settlements in Cambridgeport and East Cambridge began to outstrip it. The term "Old Cambridge" came to represent not only a distinct place but also a state of mind identified with the conservative heritage of Tory Row and the elitist character of the university.

Neighborhood boundaries in Cambridge have proved quite elastic over the years. This book includes areas that were tributary to Harvard Square in the 19th and early 20th centuries, even though some of these appeared in the Commission's earlier *Mid Cambridge* and *Cambridgeport* volumes. The current study area encompasses the Agassiz neighborhood, the Shady Hill estate, the professors' houses on Kirkland, Ware, and Prescott streets, and the Greek Revivals on Sumner Road. Avon Hill is included, although the city once considered everything north of Shepard and Sacramento streets to be part of North Cambridge. The north slope of Reservoir Hill in West Cambridge is contrasted with the south-facing slope behind Tory Row. On the western edge, we included Mount Auburn Cemetery, Cambridge Cemetery, Coolidge Hill, and Larchwood, but not Aberdeen Avenue and Strawberry Hill, which were well covered in *Northwest Cambridge*. We also discuss riverfront activities and institutions, such as The Riverside Press, that were culturally and economically tied to Old Cambridge.

Beginning in the late 19th century, reform-minded citizens sought to erase the neighborhood distinctions that they believed contributed to sectarian rivalries among the city's diverse communities. They finally succeeded when the city adopted new planning areas for the 1950 census, arbitrarily dividing Old Cambridge into five sub-areas. Given the rapid turnover of population in a university town, few people today remember Cambridge's traditional neighborhood boundaries. In 2010 the Census Bureau determined that 30% of owner-occupants and over 70% of renters had arrived within the previous five years, while only 17% of owner-occupants and 2% of renters had lived here for more than twenty years.[1] As a result, Cambridge in the 21st century is a community in danger of losing its collective memory.

The first five volumes of the Survey of Architectural History in Cambridge were intended to be planning and preservation tools, as well as a means of deepening the public's interest in the history of this many-layered city. The purpose of this new book is to be an owner's manual for all Cantabrigians. By describing in detail the architectural and physical development of Old Cambridge from presettlement times to the present, we hope to impart a greater understanding of how the city evolved to its present form and what elements, both physical and cultural, are important to preserve.

Building Old Cambridge may not satisfy those looking for a detailed social or political history. It focuses instead on the physical form of the city and considers aspects of its social, economic, and political history as they illuminate its physical development. The town's colonial history, briefly summarized in chapter 1, sets the stage for the city's 19th-century urban development. This chapter is based on Robert H. Nylander's exhaustive primary source documentation of nearly every significant property transfer and probate record before 1775. The town's early political and social history is drawn largely from secondary sources, and we hope that this period will receive fuller treatment in the future. (For those interested in greater detail we recommend John D. Burton's dissertation, "Puritan Town and Gown: Harvard College and Cambridge, Massachusetts, 1636–1800.") The next two chapters describe Cambridge after 1793, when bridges began to open the colonial landscape to development. Chapter 4 uses extensive deed, map, and genealogy research to explore changing ownership and land use in the residential neighborhoods that make up Old Cambridge, while chapter 5 focuses on parks and open space. Chapter

6 describes the progression of architectural styles in the area's residential buildings, including the development of apartment living. Chapters 7 and 8 present the area's civic, religious, educational, and commercial architecture, and chapter 9 explores the influence of transportation and industry. The book concludes with a chapter on the physical evolution of Harvard University and its changing relationship to Cambridge since 1636.

We have drawn on many sources to complete this work. The Cambridge Historical Commission's inventory of all 13,000 Cambridge buildings was initially compiled in a field survey conducted between 1964 and 1975. Decades of subsequent research have yielded countless historic photographs and newspaper articles, as well as deeds, assessors' records, surveys, and correspondence, all cross-indexed to the inventory files. In addition, the Commission has assembled an extensive collection of early maps, atlases, and city directories, as well as files on architects and builders, individual citizens, groups, voluntary organizations, institutions, and businesses of all sorts. The recent digitization of Cambridge newspapers since 1846 provided a rich trove of new information. These sources were too numerous and complex to be fully referenced in footnotes, but they are available to the public in the Commission's archive, where full-time staff will assist researchers. A forthcoming project to digitize the Commission's files will facilitate access.

A special note is in order concerning the Commission's practice for dating buildings. The year the building was designed is considered to be definitive, not the year it was constructed or completed. The architect's work is an act of creation that takes place at a specific time; when a building is completed, sometimes years later, it may already be considered out of date. In practical terms, we determine a building's date from contemporary sources, such as newspaper articles; for buildings constructed after 1886 we use the building permit date. A completion date will sometimes be cited if nothing else is known about the structure.

Charles M. Sullivan, Executive Director
Cambridge Historical Commission

Civil War veterans parading on Chauncy Street, April 17, 1886. See figure 4.138.

ACKNOWLEDGMENTS

A project this complex could not have been brought to completion without the support of generations of Cambridge Historical Commission staff members and interns, volunteer readers, librarians and archivists at multiple institutions, the Cambridge City Council, and the city administration. The authors are extremely grateful for their help over many years.

Current staff members whose involvement has been critical for completing this project are Assistant Director Kathleen (Kit) Rawlins, our eagle-eyed copy editor, who faithfully read and commented on each version of the manuscript, flagged inconsistencies, and kept her sense of humor throughout, and Archives Assistant Anthony Zannino, who diligently tracked down and organized hundreds of digital image files and obtained permissions to reproduce them. Among the many former staff members who contributed significantly were Sally Zimmerman, who prepared a first draft of the section on apartment buildings; Therese Alduino, whose undergraduate thesis on the Cambridge Park Commission supported chapter 5; Ann Clifford, a crackerjack researcher who rediscovered the history of Lewisville and many other aspects of Cambridge history; and Sharon Cooney, who investigated the activities of the Harvard Riverside Associates, the Harvard clubs, and the Gold Coast dormitories. Jill Sinclair researched several landscape architects and their projects in Old Cambridge; her essays will be published on the Commission's website as a supplement to this book. Little could have been accomplished in the last few years without the support of Preservation Planner Sarah Burks, who shouldered most of the regulatory activities of the commission so the Executive Director could pursue his passion for Cambridge history. Preservation Administrator Samantha Paull's sunny personality helped keep the office on an even keel. Rafael Morales and Rachel Williams of Cambridge's Information Technology Department rendered assistance at critical moments.

Eliza McClennen and Herb Heidt of MapWorks in Harwich, Massachusetts, provided the cartography for this volume. As they had done for *East Cambridge,* Eliza and Herb transformed complex plans and scribbled notations into beautiful maps that clarify the development of Old Cambridge.

The process of gathering the images reproduced here also involved many people. Maria Muller restored and printed many historic negatives; Bonnie Orr Miskolczy, a staff photographer in 1966–73, donated her Cambridge negatives and prints to the commission in 2014; and Daniel Reiff, a survey associate in 1967–69, allowed us to digitize his collection of color slides. We also relied heavily on the work of Richard Cheek, a staff photographer in 1968-75. Several Wellesley College interns, including Louren Hernandez, Francesca Gobeille, Laura Barrett, and Katherine Scafuri, initiated the process of retrieving and scanning images, work that Anthony Zannino carried to completion. Megan Schwenke developed a database for tracking the status of each image. John Dalterio, a student at Lesley University's College of Art and Design, digitally processed almost every image with remarkable skill and was assisted in the final crunch by Danielle Tolman.

Readers of early drafts included historical commission members Robert G. Neiley, Charles W. Eliot 2nd, William B. King, Dorothy LeMessurier, and Mrs. Suzanne Green, as well as Roger Boothe and Les Barber of the Cambridge Community Development Department. John DiGiovanni and Karen Sommerlad provided useful comments on chapter 3, while Karl Haglund, Bill Clendaniel, Shary Berg, and Janet Heywood reviewed chapter 5. Kathy Spiegelman and the staff of what was then Harvard Planning + Allston Initiative commented on an early draft of chapter 10. Jill Lepore, David Woods Kemper '41 Professor of American History at Harvard University, read the earliest complete draft in its entirety and offered many perceptive comments. Readers of the final draft in 2014–15 included Dr. Jo Solet, Heli Meltsner, and Michael Kenney.

Denys Peter Myers, Donald York, Cynthia Zaitzevsky, Roger Reed, Jim Shea, Arthur Krim, and Gavin Kleespies provided general advice and encouragement as far back as the early 1990s. Transit historian Frank Cheney supplied many illustrations, particularly for chapter 9. Arleyn Levee provided correspondence regarding several Cambridge projects of the Olmsted firm of landscape architects. Emily Mueller De Celis, Associate Principal of Michael Van Valkenburgh Associates, Inc., shared an obscure but telling quote she found in the Josep Lluis Sert archives, and David Armitage of the Harvard Planning Office found an important document describing the choice of Georgian Revival over Scottish Gothic for Harvard's Gore Hall in 1913. Annette LaMond offered useful insights relating to the Cambridge Skating Club and the Cambridge Plant & Garden Club. Roger Thompson, emeritus professor of American Colonial History at the University of East Anglia, gave us many valuable insights into the personalities and character of First Period Cambridge.

Staff members at many Harvard facilities have been very generous with their time and resources. Robin McElheny, Harvard's Associate University Archivist for Collections and Public Services, has been a mainstay throughout this project and she was well supported by colleagues Brian Sullivan and Michelle Gachette, among others. Similarly, Radcliffe Archivist Jane Knowles responded promptly to our many requests from her base at the Schlesinger Library. Other helpful Harvard staff have included Megan Schwenke, Archivist, and Isabella Donadio, Permissions and Image Research Coordinator, both of the Harvard Art Museums; Emily Una Weirich, Access Services Coordinator at Harvard's Fine Arts Library; Mary Haegert at the Houghton Library; William L. Graves at the Gordon McKay and Blue Hill Libraries at the John A. Paulson School of Engineering and Applied Science; George Clark and Scott Walker at the Harvard Map Collection; Diana Carey at the Schlesinger Library; and Janina Mueller, Ines Zalduendo, and Johanna Kasubowski at the Frances Loeb Library of the Graduate School of Design. David Remington, Manager of Harvard Digital Imaging and Photography Services, and his staff Tom Lingner and Yuhua Li expeditiously processed our many requests for reproductions.

We received essential assistance from librarians and archivists of many regional libraries and archives. Historic New England has the premier collection of material on New England history, and Lorna Condon and Jeanne Gamble were unstinting in their support. Mark Vassar, archivist of the Cambridge Historical Society, cheerfully responded to our many requests for scans, as did Alyssa Pacy, archivist at the Cambridge Public Library, Meg Winslow at Mount Auburn Cemetery, Sally Pierce and Patricia Boulos at the Boston Athenaeum, Diana Yount at the Andover-Newton Theological School, Anita Israel and Christine Wirth at the Longfellow House-Washington's Headquarters National Historic Site, Aura Fluet at Episcopal Divinity School, Anna Clutterbuck-Cook at the Massachusetts Historical Society, Kate Judd and Christine Reynolds at First Church in Cambridge, Congregational, UCC, Kittle Evenson at Buckingham, Browne & Nichols, and Jaclyn Penny at the American Antiquarian Society. Joyce Connolly gave us access to many plans held by the Frederick Law Olmsted National Historic Site before they were removed for safekeeping during their recent restoration project. Staff of the Southwest Harbor Public Library in Maine allowed us to copy Henry L. Rand's images of the Shady Hill neighborhood. Bob Cullum, on behalf of the family of photographer Leslie R. Jones, granted permission to reproduce images held at the Boston Public Library. Steve Rosenthal facilitated the reproduction of several of his magnificent photographs. Donald Friary, president of the Colonial Society of Massachusetts, expedited the reproduction of the portrait of Stephen Higginson so it could be included in this volume.

Finally, we could not have brought this project to completion without the extraordinary staff of the MIT Press, including Ellen Faran, who retired as director in 2015, editorial director Gita Devi Manaktala, acquisitions editor Susan Buckley, managing editor Michael Sims, design manager Yasuyo Iguchi, and production manager Janet Rossi. Michael and Yasuyo in particular seemed to give our project their full and undivided attention over many months, and the book has benefitted from their commitment to excellence. We offer our sincere thanks to all of you.

Susan E. Maycock
Charles M. Sullivan

FIGURE 1.1 A reconstructed plan of Cambridge and its environs in the 17th century, drawn by Edwin Raisz of Harvard's Institute for Geographical Exploration for Samuel Eliot Morison in 1935. The road system is based on data compiled by City Engineer L.M. Hastings in 1920. The map is somewhat fanciful but accurate enough at this scale to convey the character of the region.

I EARLY SETTLEMENT AND DEVELOPMENT, 1630–1793

On the tide of this River is built Newtowne, which is three miles by land from Charles Towne, and a league and a halfe by water. This place was first intended for a City, but upon more serious considerations it was not thought so fit, being to farre from the Sea; being the greatest inconvenience it hath. This is one of the neatest and best compacted Townes in New England, having many faire structures, with many handsome contrived streets. The inhabitants most of them are very rich, and well stored with Cattel of all sorts; having many hundred Acres of ground paled in with one generall fence, which is about a mile and a half long, which secures all their weaker Cattle from the wilde beasts. On the other side of the River lieth all their meadow and Marsh-ground for Hay. (William Wood, *New Englands Prospect*, 1634)

THE LAND

The natural landscape of Massachusetts Bay was shaped by glacial action and the gradually rising sea. The first Europeans encountered steep hills and islands, vast salt marshes, and shallow tidal streams meandering deep into the hinterland. This well-watered region supported a seasonal population of Algonquians who harvested shellfish and game, cultivated crops, and established footpaths connecting river crossings, settlements, and hunting grounds.

The location chosen for Newtowne, as the English settlers first called Cambridge, was a low drumlin rising from the tidal marshes on the north side of the Charles River.[1] In the immediate vicinity were some small outlying hills, springs, brooks, and a pond. The long reach of the river to Captain's Island was fully in view, and from the top of the drumlin it was possible to see across the marshes of the lower Charles, Back Bay, and Boston Neck into Boston Harbor.

According to Captain Edward Johnson, who wrote the first history of New England in 1654, the village was bordered by "a spacious plain, more like a bowling green than a Wilderness" (*Wonder Working Providence*, 201).[2] On the east, the ground rose gradually to the crest of a long north–south ridge (now traversed by Dana Street), the southern end of which terminated in an escarpment rising about 40 feet above the marshes that penetrated as far as today's Green Street. Beyond this moraine nothing interrupted the sweep of marsh and bay along the lower Charles River except the isolated drumlin that is now East Cambridge, where Thomas Graves had settled in 1629. To the north, beyond a pine swamp, more drumlins in what is now Somerville separated the Mystic River watershed from that of the Charles. To the northwest the plain gave way to a ridge, the Fresh Pond moraine, rising near present Porter Square. This chain of hills ran southwest into Watertown, separating Fresh Pond from the Charles River. The level of the pond was only a foot or two above high tide, and its sluggish drainage through Alewife Brook to the Mystic River created a huge freshwater marsh and extensive meadows.[3]

Newtowne was rich in wildlife but poor in building materials. Early writers remarked on the abundance of edible birds and shellfish and the many wolves and rattlesnakes around Massachusetts Bay. It is not known to what extent the town was forested, but sixteen years after settlement the selectmen were issuing licenses to cut trees for building projects and restricting firewood harvesting to the swampy areas near Fresh Pond, where no useable timber grew. The glaciated landscape afforded some well-drained sites to early builders but also much peat and clay that beset homeowners when the city began to fill up two centuries later. The till and clay that predominated in Newtowne offered few boulders to obstruct farmers' plows but provided little stone good for building. Outcroppings of argillite in Somerville were quarried for Cambridge foundations until the 20th century. Boulders—glacial erratics—were gathered from Boston's harbor islands and from Menotomy Rocks in Arlington, and puddingstone was quarried in Roxbury, as can be seen in the retaining wall along the Town Creek, between today's Winthrop and Eliot streets (see chapter 4). Clay deposits were prevalent, so bricks could be fired near most building sites. Commercial brickmaking was first recorded in 1672, when a man was permitted to build kilns on common land, but large-scale production did not begin until the railroad reached Cambridge in the 1840s; the town retained its tradition of building in wood until recent times.

Disease and tribal warfare had decimated the native population before the colonists arrived. The few remaining Algonquians did not contest the preemption of their lands, but the colonists nevertheless were careful to secure a deed from the widow of Nanepashemet, the last chief of the Massachusett tribe, who was living near the confluence of Alewife Brook and the Mystic River. In 1640 the General Court ordered that she be paid about £23 for the land occupied by Cambridge and Watertown, "and also Cambridge is to give Squa-Sachem a coate every winter while she liveth" (Paige, 384; figure 1.2 and *Report Five: Northwest Cambridge*, figure 7).

Although the Native Americans had nearly disappeared from the immediate vicinity of Cambridge, their long occupation of

FIGURE 1.2 The Winthrop-Woods Map of Massachusetts Bay, ca. 1633–37 (detail). As with many early maps, the coastline is fairly accurate, but topographical features (such as the hills surrounding the Boston Basin) are drawn as they were seen from a distance. The villages of Newtowne and Watertown (the latter in its original location near today's Gerry's Landing) are clustered on the north bank of the Charles River, less than a mile apart, while Boston and Charlestown face each other across the mouth of the river, past Back Bay. Fresh Pond ("40 fathoms" deep) is shown in its correct location, but with its shoreline reversed. The village of the so-called Squaw Sachem, the widow of Nanepashemet, is shown at the confluence of Alewife Brook and the Mystic River.

Massachusetts Bay prepared the land for English settlement. Their agricultural methods involved succession cropping of corn and squash followed by a fallow period and then burning to eliminate brush and fertilize the ground for the next planting. This left a landscape that was easily adapted to the English practice of mixed husbandry (although the colonists soon discovered that the soil had little natural fertility and was best suited for pasture). The "spacious plain" north of the village observed by Johnson may have been a fallow cornfield. Wigwam Neck, a finger of land just downstream from the village, was most likely a seasonal Algonquian encampment adjacent to the rich fowling and fishing grounds along the river. It is generally accepted that the early path between Charlestown Neck and Watertown was an Indian trail, and it seems likely that the river crossing at Newtowne had also been used in precontact times.

THE PERIOD OF SETTLEMENT

Cambridge had a special character from its inception because it was intended to be the capital of the Massachusetts Bay colony, a community of Puritans who dissented from England's established Anglican Church. Conceived as a fortified town, the only one in the colony, the capital had to meet specific criteria: accessibility to oceangoing vessels, protection from assault by sea and land, adequate drinking water, good agricultural land, and a location central to the other Massachusetts Bay plantations. However, the actual founding of Newtowne was a rather haphazard enterprise.

The Massachusetts Bay Company had obtained a royal charter in March 1629 from King Charles I, giving it title to all the land from three miles north of the Merrimack River to three miles south of the Charles. The colonists intended to establish a Christian commonwealth in the new world, but their initial form of organization was that of a joint-stock company, a type of partnership whose investors (the colonists) could transfer their shares by sale or inheritance without consent of the rest; the territory it had been granted by the king constituted most of the company's capital, and subsequent grants to individuals served as dividends that were proportional to their investment and status in the community. The colony would be ruled by a governor, deputy governor, and assistants, whose administrative sessions, called a Court of Assistants, would become the General Court, as the Massachusetts legislature is called today. Elected

representatives were added in 1634.[4] Exceptionally, the charter did not establish the company's headquarters in London, so its officers were free to take it with them to America (figure 1.3). Possession of this document was essential to the Puritans' independence, and they were determined to protect it from the possibility of seizure by the English government.

The members of the Massachusetts Bay Company agreed in August 1629 to remove to America, elected John Winthrop governor in October, and set sail the following March. Arriving in Salem on June 12, 1630, the governor and his party stayed only a few days before setting out overland for Charlestown, intending

FIGURE 1.3 The Massachusetts Bay Colony charter of 1629. Two copies were signed by King Charles I; one was taken to Salem by James Endicott, the first governor, and the other traveled separately to America. The charter remained the basis of colony government until it was annulled in 1684, when Charles II consolidated all the New England colonies under the administration of Sir Edmund Andros. In 1691 a new charter united the Massachusetts and Plymouth colonies as the Province of Massachusetts Bay and extended voting rights beyond members of the Puritan sect.

to make that the capital. The governor convened the first Court of Assistants on August 23 and "ordered his house to be cut and framed there" (Winsor, 115).

The Massachusetts coast had been known to European traders and fishermen for many years, but the first permanent settlement in Massachusetts Bay was not made until Sir Ferdinando Gorges's company, the Council for New England, spent the winter of 1623–24 at Weymouth. Finding it to be a poor location for a town, some of the principals dispersed: the Reverend William Blackstone to the Shawmut peninsula, where he became the first resident of Boston; Samuel Maverick to Noddles Island (East Boston); and Thomas Walford to Charlestown. All were probably the first European settlers in these locations.

The Massachusetts Bay Company retained Thomas Graves, an engineer from Gravesend in Kent, to go to New England and lay out a town. Graves arrived in June 1629, laid out the village at Charlestown, and supervised the construction of a "great house" that became its first meetinghouse; he built his own house at what would be called Lechmere's Point, becoming Cambridge's first European settler. When poor water in Charlestown caused many of Winthrop's group to fall ill, the governor decided to look for a more suitable location. At Blackstone's invitation, the majority of the company moved across the Charles to Boston in September 1630, taking the unfinished frame of the governor's house with them. Others dispersed to Medford, Watertown, Roxbury, Saugus, and Dorchester.

Still seeking a site for a capital, Winthrop and the assistants considered Roxbury Neck and Watertown but were unable to agree. (Boston and Charlestown had incomparably better harbors but were disqualified by their exposure to attack by sea.) They reconvened at Watertown (then at its original location at Gerry's Landing) on December 21, 1630, "and there, upon view of a place a mile beneath the town, all agreed it a fit place for a fortified town, and we took time to consider further about it" (Winthrop, 46). On December 28, Lieutenant Governor Thomas Dudley reported, "we grew to this resolution, to bind all the Assistants … to build houses [there] the next year; that so by our examples,

and by removing the ordnance and munition thither … a fortified town might there grow up, the place fitting reasonably well thereto" (Young, 320). This place would be called Newtowne.

In 1654 Edward Johnson described the reasoning behind this decision, in which the governor and assistants balanced the possibility of a punitive expedition by an English government still intolerant of dissent against the danger of Indian attack:

> At this time those who were in the place of civill Government … began to think of a place of more safety in the eyes of Man, then the two frontier towns of Charles Towne and Boston. … Wherefore they rather made choice to enter farther among the Indians, then hazard the fury of malignant adversaries, who in a rage might pursue them, and therefore chose a place scituate on Charles River, between Charles Towne and Water-Towne, where they erected a Town called New-Towne, now named Cambridge. (*Wonder-Working Providence*, 61)

The chosen site was a low drumlin on the north bank of the Charles River, a topographic feature that is still evident today. The hill overlooked a creek almost seven miles upstream from Boston's original settlement on the harbor. Here the river was deep enough at low tide to accommodate the era's oceangoing ships, yet the marshes and tidal flats made passage difficult for those unfamiliar with the winding channel. Other advantages included another nearby hill that could be fortified to command the landing and a low rise farther inland where a watch house could protect the land approaches. A short distance upstream, a drumlin at the foot of today's Ash Street could accommodate a landing and a windmill. The site was well drained, a spring promised adequate water, and the surrounding countryside seemed suitable for agriculture.

Thomas Dudley was Newtowne's patron. Although Governor Winthrop and all but two of the assistants had agreed to build houses in Newtowne in the spring of 1631, only Dudley and Simon Bradstreet actually did so. Two assistants returned to England, and the other six remained in their respective towns. Winthrop put up a house but had it taken down and re-erected in Boston. In August 1632 he defended himself against Dudley, noting that he had promised those who had settled with him in Boston that he would not relocate unless they could accompany him.

Although Winthrop and most of the assistants never lived in Newtowne, they still promoted it as the seat of government at the expense of other settlements. In 1631 all the towns were assessed to pay for dredging and widening the Town Creek "to make a passage from the Charles River to the Newtowne, twelve foot broad and seven foot deep," and early the next year they were assessed for the cost of a palisade around the village (Shurtleff, June 14, 1631). The first meetinghouse, which would also accommodate the Governor and the Court of Assistants, was completed in December 1632.

Only about eight families settled in Newtowne in 1631, however, and in 1632 the Court of Assistants directed a recently arrived group of twenty families to move there from Mount Wollaston in Braintree (now Quincy). By February 1635 there were eighty-two families living north of the river, including forty in the village. However, these followers of Reverend Thomas Hooker were dissatisfied with the lack of pasture for their cattle and the strictness of Winthrop's leadership (or, more likely, the lack of opportunity for Hooker to become a leader himself). In July 1634 six Newtowne men went by ship to explore the Connecticut River, and although the court offered to transfer the Muddy River district (now Brookline) to Newtowne, more than fifty families followed them in the summer of 1635. On May 31, 1636, Winthrop reported that "Mr. Hooker, pastor of the church at Newtown, and the most of his congregation went to Connecticut. His wife was carried in a horse-litter, and they drove 160 cattle and fed of their milk by the way" (Winthrop, *Journal,* 95). Hooker's settlement of Hartford is considered the beginning of the Connecticut Colony.

The eleven households remaining in Newtowne were joined by a new contingent of about thirty families who arrived in Boston in October 1635 under Reverend Thomas Shepard. This party soon visited Newtowne and arranged to purchase the houses and furnishings of those who were leaving. Shepard became the minister of Newtowne and remained so until his death in 1649.

The Court of Assistants finally met at Newtowne when Thomas Dudley was elected governor in May 1634. At that time the colony established a representative General Court consisting of twenty-five delegates, with two or three from each town. The new legislature convened at Newtowne during the terms of Dudley and John Haynes, a Newtowne man who succeeded him. When Winthrop was reelected governor in May 1636, the General Court moved back to Boston. It met in Newtowne again only between April 1637 and September 1638, when the Antinomian heresy of Anne Hutchinson and her followers threw the Puritan hierarchy into such turmoil that they moved the sessions out of Boston to avoid a confrontation with her followers.[5]

Civil and ecclesiastical matters were inextricably combined in the administration of the colony. The Puritans formed towns and gathered churches by entering into covenants. A civil covenant bound the inhabitants to a town, and a church covenant bound those admitted to membership to each other and to God.[6] Until February 1634, the civil affairs of Newtowne were administered by a monthly meeting open to all legal voters. "The whole business of the town" was then delegated to seven men, at first called Townsmen and later Selectmen, who were elected by the town meeting (Town Records, 11). The inhabitants of Massachusetts were taxed to support the ecclesiastical establishment (known as the Standing Order) until 1833. For generations, meetinghouses were used both for town meetings and for worship.

Newtowne differed from other Massachusetts communities in its well-ordered appearance, which reflected its intended status as a capital. The network of streets laid out in the spring of 1631 constituted the earliest grid-plan town in New England, preceding New Haven (1640). The plan may have been the work of Thomas Graves, who was still living at Graves' Neck, although his earlier plan for Charlestown was based on an ellipse that followed a contour line around a low hill near the harbor. One historian noted that "in its scale and the clear definition between village and countryside the Newtowne plan resembles the tiny bastide towns of southern France or the similar settlements in Britain like Winchelsea, Flint, Salisbury, or Hull" (Reps, 126).

The streets of Newtowne were arranged in a slightly irregular grid. The three principal streets ran down to the river; their orientation, approximately 45° from true north, may have been chosen to maximize the southern exposure of the sixty-four house lots, which ranged from an eighth to three-quarters of an acre (compared to two acres in Charlestown). The village was bounded on the west by the Town Creek, which ran around the base of the hill through the present Eliot, Brattle, and Harvard squares, on the north by the open expanse of the future Harvard Yard, and on the east by another brook crossed by lanes that led to the planting fields and oyster banks east of town (figure 1.4).

William Wood described Newtowne as "one of the neatest and best compacted Townes in New England," which was the result of decisions made by the town meeting (43). An order adopted in January 1633 provided that "no person whatever [shall set] up any house in the bounds of this town [without] leave from the major part," and that "by a joint consent [the] town shall not be enlarged until all [the vacant] places be filled with houses." Uniform setbacks were enforced by a provision "that all [the houses shall] range even, and stand just six [feet on each man's] own ground from the street." Another order required that "all the houses [within] the bounds of the town shall be covered [with] slate or board, and not with thatch" (Town Records, 4).[7] Perhaps the earliest house to be described in its original state was built in 1634 by Nathaniel Hancock on Dunster Street; its tall narrow gables and upper story projecting three feet over the street gave it a distinctly medieval appearance (figure 1.5). Governor Haynes's "slate house," with its presumably exceptional roof, stood on the west side of the market square; it had the only courtyard of all the houses listed in a 1635 inventory (*Proprietors' Records, 3*).

Water (now Dunster) Street led to the town landing and during the early decades was the principal street of the village; the ferry established in 1635 was a link in the overland route to Boston. The first meetinghouse was built on the corner of Dunster and Mt. Auburn streets in 1632. Dunster Street had the town's first tavern and by 1662 had thirteen of the village's fifty-seven known houses (see figure 1.12).

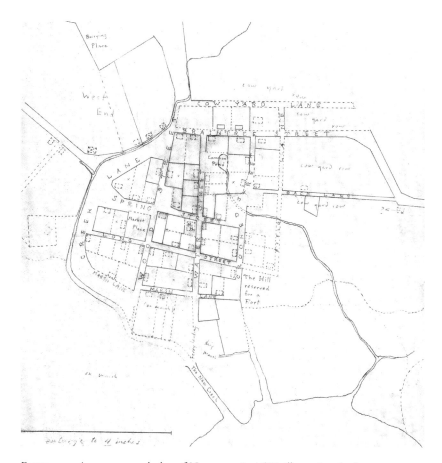

FIGURE 1.4 A reconstructed plan of Newtowne in 1635, illustrating the "contrived streets" and "faire structures" described by William Woods in 1634. The meetinghouse stands in the center of the village at the corner of today's Dunster and Mt. Auburn streets. The Cambridge Historical Commission's historian, Robert H. Nylander, compiled this and the following plans of the village by searching all the deeds and property descriptions back to the beginning of settlement. Solid lines show building footprints known from archeological evidence and property boundaries that exist today; dashed lines show boundaries and footprints derived from descriptions in deeds and probate records.

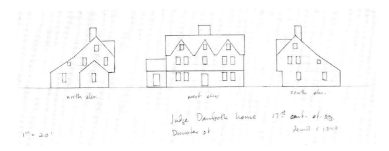

FIGURE 1.5 A conjectural drawing of the 1634 Nathaniel Hancock house, which stood on the east side of Dunster Street about a hundred yards from Harvard Square. Later the home of Judge Samuel Danforth, it survived until 1849.

FIGURE 1.6 The Hooker-Shepard-Wigglesworth house on Massachusetts Avenue opposite Holyoke Street (ca. 1633). The house was rebuilt ca. 1695 and altered ca. 1730; this view represents its appearance before it was demolished in 1843.

Winthrop Square was the other early focal point of the village. When Sir Richard Saltonstall returned to England in 1631, he forfeited the half-acre lot assigned him, and the town set it aside as the market square. Of the fifteen Massachusetts settlements in 1635, Newtowne was one of four designated as a market town. There are no descriptions of activity at the market, but town records refer to it as late as 1699, and the square was still known by that name in the 19th century (see chapter 5).

John F. Kennedy Street became the principal road through the village after the completion of the Great Bridge in 1660. The marketplace and (after 1681) the county jail occupied the high ground at the top of the hill. On the south-facing slope, the block bounded by Winthrop, Kennedy, and Eliot streets (Long, Wood, and Creek streets) had been divided in 1635 into six lots. George Cook, the first captain of Cambridge's militia, acquired three on Eliot Street but returned to England in 1645 to join Cromwell's army. Elizabeth Sherburne, a single woman who had hidden the Reverend Thomas Shepard and his family from the authorities in London before their embarkation in 1635, and John Scill, one of the few first settlers who did not follow Reverend Hooker to Hartford, occupied the other corners (see figure 3.6).

North of the marketplace the land fell off toward the Town Creek. John Stedman, Elizabeth Glover's steward, acquired three of the four lots on the west side of Kennedy Street soon after his arrival in 1638. He kept a store in his house and in 1658 held a

monopoly on the fur trade in Cambridge. A small separate lot at the intersection with Brattle Street was occupied by a house and blacksmith shop after about 1684. Simon Bradstreet, one of the founders of the town, lived on the east corner with his wife, Anne, who is known as America's first woman poet and published author; they moved to Ipswich about the time Hooker's party left for Hartford.

Just north of the village, the families who arrived with Thomas Shepard laid out Braintree Street (now Massachusetts Avenue between Quincy and Harvard squares) and built several houses there. Behind them was Cow Yard Row, a series of pens for the village cattle. These were drained by the Town Creek, which flowed through a swale that separated the village from the Charlestown–Watertown path. On one side of the creek was Watch House Hill, and upstream, on the other side, was the town cemetery.

The General Court voted to establish "a schoale or colledge" in the colony on October 28, 1636, and a year later directed that "the Colledg is … to bee at Newetowne" instead of at Salem, the other contending location (Morison, *Three Centuries,* 6). The selection of Newtowne recognized the vigilant Puritan orthodoxy of Reverend Shepard, who wrote in his autobiography that "because this town … was thorow gods great care and goodnes kept spotles from the contagion of the opinions [of the Antinomians] … the court for that and sundry other reasons determined to erect the Colledge here" (Morison, *Founding,* 182). Two years later the General Court ordered "that Newetowne shall henceforward be called Cambridge," recalling the university town in England where many of the leading settlers had studied (Paige, 43).

The Board of Overseers engaged Nathaniel Eaton, a contemporary of Reverend John Harvard at Cambridge University, as the first master of the college, and by June 1638 he was settled in a house purchased from William Peyntree, who had relocated to Connecticut in 1635. This was one of three houses on the north side of Massachusetts Avenue in the present Yard; each stood on an eighth-of-an-acre lot with an additional one-acre plot behind in Cow Yard Row (figure 1.7). Construction of the first college building began during the summer of 1638 in one of the former cow pens behind the Peyntree house. By the time it was completed in 1642 it had cost about £600 and was thought "to be too gorgeous for a Wilderness and yet too mean … for a Colledg" (Johnson, 201). Students who had been dispersed in the village could now be accommodated at the school, the first of many changes in college housing policy to affect the town (see figure 10.3).

Soon after settlement it became apparent that Newtowne would never become the principal town of the colony, even if it remained the capital. The windmill failed to operate satisfactorily and was moved to Boston in 1632. Ships grounded in the Town Creek at low tide. Charlestown, the largest settlement in Middlesex County, had a port that rivaled Boston's and "a market [that] was kept constantly on the sixth day of every week" (Winsor, 392). As early as 1640 "there were in [Charlestown] tailors, coopers, rope-makers, glaziers, tile-makers, anchor-smiths, collar-makers, charcoal burners, joiners, wheelwrights,

FIGURE 1.7 The Peyntree-Eaton house was removed in 1645. Its foundations and those of Edward Goffe's house next door were discovered during construction of the subway in 1910 and are commemorated by two pairs of brass plaques in the middle of Massachusetts Avenue, between Wadsworth House and Holyoke Center.

blacksmiths; there was a brew-house, a salt pan, a potter's kiln, a saw pit, a wind mill, a water mill near Spot Pond and (certainly in 1645) the old tide mill at the Middlesex Canal landing," in sharp contrast to Cambridge's handful of tradesmen, farmers, and innkeepers (Frothingham, 103). Even though Newtowne shared with Charlestown the quarterly court sessions that were established in 1636 and became a shire town when Middlesex County was created in 1643, only the college distinguished it from other rural communities.

The college attracted Cambridge's earliest and once most characteristic industry, printing and publishing. In 1638 Reverend Jose Glover emigrated from England with several servants, a stock of merchandise, and a press. He died on the voyage, and his widow, Elizabeth, came (or was directed) to Cambridge, where she bought Governor Haynes's house on the west side of Winthrop Square. John Stedman, her steward, opened a store, and Stephen Daye, another servant, set up Glover's press, the first in New England. Mrs. Glover married President Dunster of Harvard in 1641, and when she died two years later the press became his property. Dunster eventually gave the press to the college, which operated it until about 1692 (see chapter 9).

FIGURE 1.8 A reconstructed plan of the town in 1642, after the departure of Hooker's company. The town has contracted slightly. Cow Yard Lane has been given to the college, and Field Lane has disappeared. Water (now Dunster) Street continued to be the village high street until the construction of the Great Bridge in 1662.

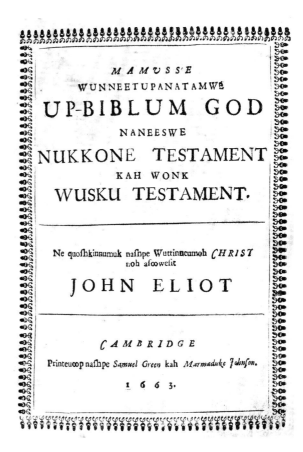

FIGURE 1.9 The press at Cambridge printed religious tracts, almanacs, and government documents from 1640 until 1692, when Harvard switched to commercial printers in Boston. Among the many significant works printed in Cambridge was a Bible translated into the Massachusett language by John Eliot in 1663.

As the capital, Newtowne was intended to be the only systematically fortified town in the colony, and the inhabitants of other settlements were supposed to take refuge there in case of attack. In 1631–32 a mile-and-a-half-long stockade (known as the "pallysadoe") composed of stakes, willows, and a trench was built in an arc from the river at Windmill Hill to the junction of Oxford and Jarvis streets and then back to the Charles southeast of the village. A brook that ran along Follen and across Berkeley and Brattle streets to the river near Willard Street may have been incorporated into this fortification. All twelve Massachusetts settlements were taxed for the project; since Newtowne was charged with the maintenance, its share was only one twentieth of the £60 assessment.[8]

In 1632 the town built an enclosure called the Common Pales from a point on the palisade near Widener Library toward Inman Square and then across the Neck to Gibbon's Creek (now Millers River) along the present boundary with Somerville. Gates at the principal entrances were maintained at least until 1686, when the town records referred to one at Menotomy Bridge over Alewife Brook on today's Massachusetts Avenue. The pales and gates were intended to prevent cattle from straying and wild beasts from entering the settlement, since the colonists believed that wolves would not cross even a rudimentary man-made barrier.

Defense construction in the village was never completed. The proposed site of a fort near today's Lowell House was assigned to an adjoining householder in 1637. As late as 1638 the General Court fined the town ten shillings because it lacked a watch house, pound, and stocks. After the seat of government was shifted to Boston defense became a local matter, and citizens were allowed to live outside the palisade. A 1640 reference to Watch House Hill may imply that such a structure had been erected, but ten years later the site (at the southwest corner of Harvard Yard, where Lehman Hall now stands) was appropriated for a new meetinghouse.[9] The possibility that the Crown might forcibly retrieve the colony's charter ended with the beheading of Charles I in 1649. Indian tribes were not a serious threat until the beginning of King Philip's War in 1675, when a new stockade was commenced but never finished.

The early boundaries of Newtowne were somewhat indefinite. The original allocation of land was characterized as "like a list [strip] cut off from the Broad-cloath" of Watertown and Charlestown; Graves' Neck (East Cambridge) originally belonged to Charlestown, and the city line northwest of Inman Square was originally Charlestown's boundary with Watertown (Johnson, 90). In 1632, when Hooker's company of settlers arrived, the town comprised 1,000 acres enclosed by the palisade and common pales. Hooker was not alone in complaining that this was too small to maintain the community's cattle, and between 1632 and 1636 Newtowne was granted additional land comprising present-day Brighton, Newton, Arlington, and Lexington, and parts of Lincoln and Bedford. A final grant confirmed in 1644 carried the boundaries to the Merrimack River (figure 1.10).

Hardly had these limits been attained when a process of contraction set in. When enough families had gathered in the remote parts of town to support a parish and meetinghouse of their own, they naturally wished to avoid compulsory attendance at the Cambridge meetinghouse, although they continued to participate in town meetings and elect selectmen until they were set

FIGURE 1.10 The boundaries of Cambridge at its greatest magnitude, 1642–55. Cambridge extended some thirty-five miles from Billerica to Newton, in the form of an irregular Y that was only one mile wide at the village.

off in separate towns. The farmers who settled in Shawshine in 1652 separated as Billerica in 1655. Cambridge Village, settled as Southside as early as 1638, was sufficiently populated to have its own meetinghouse by 1664 and became the town of Newton in 1688. Cambridge Farms, settled in the 1630s, was permitted to organize as a parish in 1696 and became the town of Lexington in 1713. Menotomy, settled in 1638, became the Second Parish of Cambridge in 1732; it was set off as the town of West Cambridge in 1807 and renamed Arlington in 1867. South of the river, Little Cambridge became the Third Parish of Cambridge in 1779 and was incorporated as the town of Brighton in 1807.

Early roads always sought the path of least resistance, following the topography and staying on dry ground as much as possible. Massachusetts Avenue, which runs due north to avoid Avon Hill before heading west toward Arlington and Concord, was the only road laid out as a proper highway, 33 yards wide in the English tradition (see chapter 4). Charlestown, five miles to the east, and Watertown, then only one mile to the west, were linked by a pre-settlement footpath that became Kirkland, Mason, and Brattle streets and Elmwood Avenue.[10] Boston could be reached by road and ferry through Charlestown or by road through Brookline Village and Roxbury. Watermen plied the river from the village to Boston, but there was no regular service on this route.

Several roads were laid out in 1632 to newly granted areas of land. The way to the Neck (modern Bow and Arrow streets and Massachusetts Avenue toward Central Square) led past the fields on Dana Hill to pastures near present Central Square, avoiding both the summit of the hill and the marsh south of Green Street. Paths branched off to the oyster banks and salt marshes on the Charles River and to Pelham's Island. Lanes that crossed the saddles in the glacial moraine separating the village from Fresh Pond and the Great Swamp became Garden and Sparks streets. Cambridge's system of trails and river routes radiating from the village made sense to early settlers, if not to a person trying to cross town in an automobile.

Although conceived as a seat of government, Newtowne was by necessity an agricultural community, and land and cattle were its most significant sources of capital. The original concept of land distribution involved three kinds of holdings: house lots in the village with space for a kitchen garden, privately owned fields for cultivation or pasture outside the village (including an allotment of salt marsh), and a reserve of land held for common use. This system perpetuated the pattern of land use in medieval England. East of the village but inside the Common Pales, cultivated fields lay on the slopes of Butler's Hill in three sections:

the "Planting Field," "Small Lots," and "Great Lots," with present Dana Street separating the first two. The "Small Lots" varied from 2 to 5½ acres, and "Great Lots" from 6 to 63 acres. The amount of land granted to each settler differed considerably and was determined by his wealth and standing in the community. Investors in the Massachusetts Bay Colony were entitled to receive 200 acres for each share they held. Colonists who paid their own passage were eligible for 50 acres, and every freeman had the use of at least four acres. Servants were not permitted to own land until they had finished their seven-year indenture. Later grants of common land were essentially dividends on the recipient's investment in the settlement. Many profited by selling their grants to others who would do the hard work of preparing the land for grazing or planting.

Two new regions were opened for settlement to accommodate the twenty families that arrived with Hooker in 1632 and an equal number from elsewhere in the colony and abroad: the West End, between present Brattle Square and Sparks Street, and the West End Field, between Raymond Street and Vassal Lane on the Fresh Pond moraine. These forty-one lots were considerably larger—up to four acres—than those in the village. When Shepard's followers replaced most of these families in 1635–36, more of the original common fields were divided among them. The division of the New Ox Pasture in 1636 afforded several six-acre homesteads, and the division of the New West Field in 1638 partitioned the moraine east of Raymond Street into twenty-four small farms. These grants were outside the palisade and modified the original scheme that separated dwellings and fields.

In accordance with an act of the General Court ordering each town to account for the land granted to its settlers, in February 1635 the town meeting designated five men as the Proprietors of Common Lands, to "survey the town lands, and enter [the same] in a Book appointed for that purpose," *The Registere Booke of the Lands and Houses in the New Towne* (Paige, 21). The Proprietors had jurisdiction over all the ungranted land in Newtowne, which they administered for public use until they saw fit to allocate tracts to individuals. Land suitable for cultivation

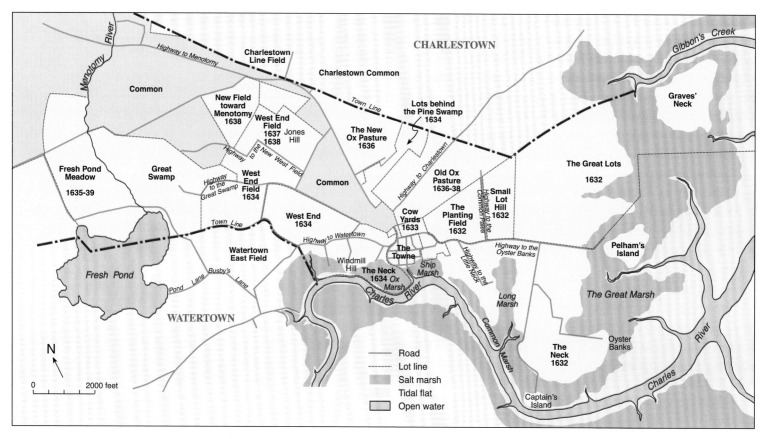

FIGURE 1.11 Public ways and land distribution up to 1639. As the community expanded, tracts with the greatest agricultural value were generally granted first. The extent of common land reflected the community's practice of grazing their cattle together under the eye of a herdsman paid by the town.

and marshes valuable for salt hay were quickly distributed, but grazing lands were initially held in common for the benefit of the townsmen, whose cows, goats, and swine were overseen by specially appointed keepers. The Proprietors managed the distribution of the town's common land until 1829, when the last small tracts were granted.

By far the greatest amount of land was initially held in common; as late as 1647, only 2,618 acres (776 of them arable) had been assigned to individuals out of the tens of thousands controlled by the Proprietors of Common Lands. The pattern of ownership evolved rapidly as the original grantees relocated and the more prosperous colonists consolidated their scattered holdings. One such opportunity came when Hooker's company moved to Hartford; another followed the severe economic conditions of 1640, when land values fell to a fifth of their former level. Edward Goffe bought up all the Planting Fields, and Herbert Pelham bought four of the twelve Great Lots to make a 118-acre farm that later became the Ralph Inman estate. With fewer people controlling the land, more villagers supported themselves as tradesmen and craftsmen. Others petitioned for grants in remote areas. These allocations so diminished the reserve of common land that by 1670 the common pasturage convenient to the village had been reduced to 260 acres, although common woodlands and meadows were still present in Arlington and Lexington.

After hard times in the 1640s, a burst of activity in the village produced several public buildings and many improvements. The town built a new meetinghouse on Watch House Hill in 1650, a schoolhouse on Holyoke Street in 1669, and a parsonage next to the college in 1670.[11] Harvard built the Indian College in 1654–56 and the second Harvard Hall in 1674–82 (see figure 10.2). In 1681 Middlesex County purchased the old Glover house and erected a jail next to the marketplace. On the west side of Harvard Square, only a single house stood on a 2½-acre field that stretched along Massachusetts Avenue from the Burying Ground to the corner of Brattle Street. To the east along present Massachusetts Avenue as far as Holyoke Street were four tradesmen's houses, including, in 1656, a "beer and bread shop" catering to Harvard students (Paige, 244).

The town constructed a new wharf near the ferry landing in 1651, and townsmen built several warehouses nearby; water traffic was substantial, especially for cargoes such as building material, firewood, and farm produce (see chapter 9). The most important development was the construction in 1660–62 of the Great Bridge over the Charles River, on the site of today's Anderson Bridge, financed by a general levy on Massachusetts Bay towns. Since this was the only river crossing below the falls at Watertown (and until 1786 the closest bridge to the mouth of the river), everyone seeking a land route to Boston from the north traveled along Wood (now Kennedy) Street, which superseded Water (now Dunster) Street as the town's principal thoroughfare.

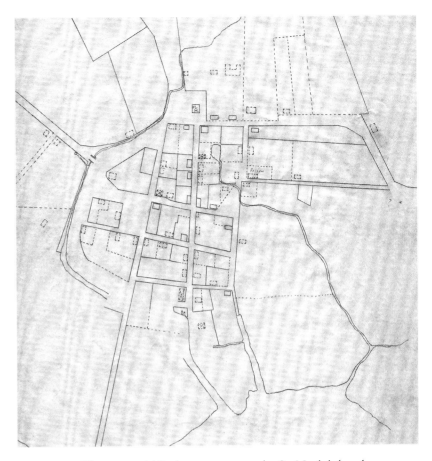

FIGURE 1.12 The town in 1662. A causeway across the Ox Marsh led to the Great Bridge, making Wood (now John F. Kennedy) Street the main thoroughfare. The new meetinghouse, placed adjacent to the college on Watch House Hill, shifted the center of the village to what would be called Harvard Square two centuries later.

FIGURE 1.13 The first known view of Cambridge, a "Bourgade de 80 Maisons C'est une université," published in 1693 but perhaps based on information gathered by a Jesuit who visited Massachusetts on a diplomatic mission in 1650–51. The building on the left is clearly Harvard Hall I (extant 1638-1686), shown from the north with its wings flanking a courtyard; the many-gabled structure to the right of it may be the Indian College (1656), or Harvard Hall II (1682). The meetinghouse appears on the right (see figure 7.1). The perspective is confused; the major buildings were probably sketched separately and assembled into a single view by the cartographer, Jean-Baptiste Franquelin of Montreal.

A 17th-century view of the town, the earliest known, shows a dense settlement of gabled houses grouped around the college and the Second Meetinghouse (figure 1.13). A Dutchman who visited Cambridge in 1680 was not impressed.

> It is not a large village, and the houses stand very much apart. The college building is the most conspicuous among them. We went to it, expecting to see something curious, as it is the only college, or would-be academy of the Protestants in America, but we found ourselves mistaken. … We passed by the printing office, but there was nobody in it; the paper sash however being broken, we looked in; and saw two presses with six or eight cases of type. There is not much work done there. Our printing office is well worth two of it, and even more. (Dankers, 384)

CAMBRIDGE IN THE EIGHTEENTH CENTURY

The last distant settlement was set off as Lexington in 1713, but Cambridge expanded again in 1754 when several Watertown farmers petitioned to join the town because their new meetinghouse was no longer convenient for worship (figure 1.14). The original Watertown meetinghouse was located at Gerry's Landing, but since that town included present-day Waltham, Weston, and parts of Lincoln this location was impossibly remote for later settlers. Watertown built successive meetinghouses further west in 1635, 1723, and 1754, until farmers in the eastern part of town complained that they had been left behind and petitioned the General Court to be "set off to the town of Cambridge, as well as to the First Parish" (Bond, *Watertown,* 992). The boundary was moved west from present Sparks Street to Coolidge Avenue, but within a few years most of these new parishioners had sold their farms to wealthy loyalists. Well-landscaped estates soon bordered the Watertown road, now Brattle Street. The new families differed in religion, class, and outlook from the descendants of the Puritans, and their arrival fundamentally changed the character of Old Cambridge.

The village itself remained a compact settlement with fields and pastures nearby, but many vacant lots signaled that it had still not reached the potential envisioned in the previous century. The town built its third meetinghouse in 1706, and the county put up a courthouse facing it in 1708. The meetinghouse faced south, and presumably the courthouse faced east, making a square within a square and allowing traffic to flow freely between and around them (figure 1.15).

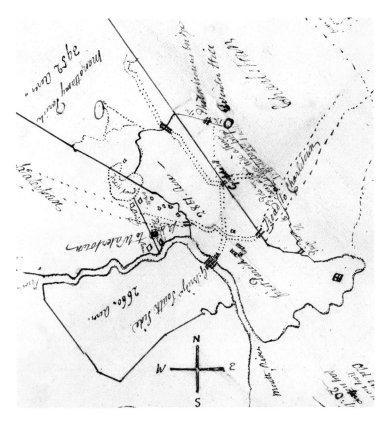

FIGURE 1.14 A plan prepared for the legislature in 1754 showing land in Watertown and Charlestown whose owners wished to be set off to Cambridge. The plan describes the three parishes of Cambridge and the proposed new boundaries. The General Court accepted only the petition of the seven Watertown families, "the farthest abt. 1½ [miles from the Cambridge meetinghouse] but 2½ in Watertown." If accepted, the petition of about twenty Charlestown families would have given Cambridge about a third of present-day Somerville, running from Alewife Brook to the Millers River along the south slopes of Winter and Prospect hills.

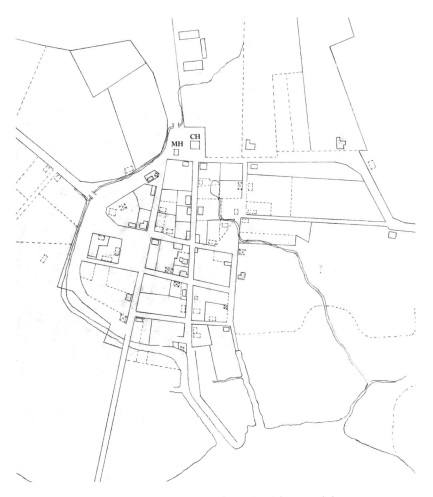

FIGURE 1.15 The town in 1720. A new courthouse (CH) has joined the meetinghouse (MH) in the future Harvard Square. There are still many vacant lots, sixty years after the construction of the Great Bridge.

Harvard College at this time began to lay out the first of a series of quadrangles beyond the meetinghouse, along the public road that is now Peabody Street.[12] While these buildings were close to the village by today's standards, they remained visually and functionally separate and contrasted strongly with it. Only the president's house, the finest residence in town when it was built for Benjamin Wadsworth in 1726, faced the village.

A traveler who visited in 1750 noted that although the town was "well scituated" on a navigable river near "a very good wooden bridge," its inhabitants were dependent on the courts and the college. The town had no trade because it was too near Boston, and "for want of trade one 4th part of it is not built" (Birket, 18–19). Over the next few years, though, new construction almost surrounded the square. The Fourth Meetinghouse,

FIGURE 1.16 The earliest surviving map of the village, ca. 1748.

Pelham's 2½-acre pasture on the southwest corner of Harvard Square paid handsome dividends. After he built a gambrel-roofed house for himself about 1750, he sold a lot to Middlesex County for a new court house in 1756 and then four more lots before his death in 1772 (figure 1.17).

Every July life in Puritan Massachusetts was enlivened by the raucous public holiday that celebrated Harvard's commencement week. People from miles around converged on Cambridge for festivities that had a decidedly nonacademic character.

> About ten days before [commencement], a body of Indians from Natick … commonly made their appearance in Cambridge, and took up their station around the Episcopal Church, in the cellar of which they were accustomed to sleep, if the weather was unpleasant. The women sold baskets and moccasins; the boys gained money by shooting at it, while the men wandered about and spent the little that was earned by their squaws in rum and tobacco. Then there would come along a body of itinerant negro fiddlers, whose scraping never intermitted during the time of their abode.
>
> The Common, on Commencement week, was covered with booths, erected in lines, like streets, intended to accommodate the populace from Boston and the vicinity with the amusements of a fair. In these were carried on all sorts of dissipation. Here was a knot of gamblers, gathered around a wheel of fortune. … There was dancing on this side, auction-selling on the other; here a pantomimic show, there a blind man, led by a dog, soliciting alms; organ-grinders and hurdy-gurdy grinders, bears and monkeys, jugglers and sword-swallowers, all mingled in inextricable confusion.
>
> In a neighboring field, a countryman had, perchance, let loose a fox, which the dogs were worrying to death, while the surrounding crowd testified their pleasure at the scene by shouts of approbation. Nor was there any want of the spirituous; pails of punch, guarded by stout negroes, bore witness to their own subtle contents … [and to] the drunkard, reeling, cursing and fighting among his comrades. (Bartlett, 61)

The pandemonium of commencement week became a byword in the colonies; historian Jeremy Belknap reported that

built in 1756, stood further back from Massachusetts Avenue (approximately on the site of Lehman Hall) and faced south, with its front facade almost in line with the rear wall of Wadsworth House. Along the east side of Peabody Street three new college buildings created a second quadrangle next to the first (see figure 10.6). On the west side of the square, cordwainer (shoemaker) Caleb Prentice's strategic 1747 purchase of Edward

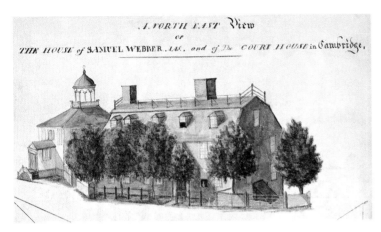

FIGURE 1.17 The Middlesex County Courthouse (1758), on the site of today's Harvard Cooperative Society, and the Prentice-Webber house (1750). Caleb Prentice's house was purchased by the College in 1790 and was the home of Hollis Professor of Mathematics Samuel Webber until he became president in 1806. The Harvard Law School held its first classes here in 1817; it was razed in 1844. View 1796.

FIGURE 1.18 A view of the village from the north, with Massachusetts Hall and the Fourth Meetinghouse in the foreground, as shown on a model of Cambridge in 1776. This model was based on original research by Robert H. Nylander. Property lines, roads, orchards, and gardens, where shown, were fully supported by documentation. Buildings known only from land titles are rendered schematically; buildings known from descriptions are shown in detail. The model was installed on the third floor of City Hall to commemorate the Bicentennial.

the Siege of Louisburg in 1745 was conducted "in a tumultuary, random manner, resembling a Cambridge commencement" (Belknap, II, 170). After the Revolution the public celebration was gradually subsumed by the Fourth of July holiday, but there was still sufficient disorder that the college supported the enclosure of the Common in the 1820s (see chapter 2).[13]

According to the provincial census of 1765, the adult population of the First Parish, which corresponded to present-day Cambridge, was 785; the college added another 160. The Second Parish, Menotomy (Arlington), had 524, and the Third Parish, Little Cambridge (Brighton), 262. Although the town had grown moderately since the late 17th century, there had been little fundamental change in its economy. The same trades were represented in 1765 as a century earlier, though in slightly larger numbers: blacksmiths (two), carpenters (five), and shoemakers, tailors, and tanners (three each). New occupations included barber, brickmaker, cooper, currier, distiller, glazier, hatter, and saddler. The number of shops had grown to nineteen, and there were now a counting house, a distillery, and three law offices.

Commercial activity occurred primarily along Kennedy Street, which in 1770 contained seven shops, an office, a tavern, and two tradesmen's houses (figure 1.18).

John Bradish acquired George Cook's old homestead on Eliot Street in 1701 and built a substantial new house on the strength of his income as Harvard's glazier—always a profitable occupation in a college town. The northeast corner of the block belonged to Peter Towne, a cooper, who died in 1705.[14] Bradish acquired this property also but sold it to William Manning, a cordwainer, in 1725. Manning built a three-story house overlooking the marketplace where his son Samuel lived until his death in 1825 (see figure 3.7). Toward the end of the century the block was a tradesman's quarter occupied by William Angier, a tanner, Samuel Whittemore, a currier, and Isaac Bradish, a blacksmith who was keeper of the county jail until it closed in 1814.

Professor John Winthrop acquired a "small and lovely" house on Mt. Auburn Street in 1746, "facing south [across Winthrop Square] with a view of the river and the hills beyond." Winthrop, "the greatest American scientist of the Colonial period," became Hollis Professor of Mathematics in 1738 at age 23. In 1756 he married Hannah Fayerweather Tolman, "a woman of prodigious energy," who encouraged him to stand for election to the Provincial Council in 1774 (Sibley IX, 240–64). Their son, James, an eccentric and intemperate bachelor, lived at home until his death in 1821. Although James thought of himself as a scholar (he remodeled the original building of the Blue Anchor tavern for his considerable collection of books), he was often disappointed in his ambitions. He served as college librarian until it became clear that he would not be named to his father's chair. Governor Hancock appointed him a county judge in 1790, but he was removed in 1812 when the General Court decided that jurists should have legal training. Winthrop's forty-two-year career as Register of Probate ended when the county offices relocated to Lechmere's Point in 1817 (see *East Cambridge*, 27).

Joseph Bean, a Boston innkeeper, took over the Blue Anchor Tavern at its original site on the northeast corner of Kennedy and Mt. Auburn streets in 1731 and in 1737 moved it into a house at 17 Kennedy Street built in 1699. The Blue Anchor hosted the monthly meetings of the selectmen, and "their patronage of the bar … probably paid for the use of the rooms" (Paige, 225). Israel Porter, Bean's bartender, bought the place in 1796 and in 1820 built a brick house on the corner facing the Square. The Blue Anchor closed after Porter died in 1837, and part became a notorious tenement that was "successfully fired by an incendiary" in 1850 (*Chronicle,* Jan. 8, 1850).[15]

Apart from the college, farming was the most important activity in 18th-century Cambridge. In 1781 the assessors enumerated 777 acres of tillable land, 1,402 acres of marsh and meadow, 1,446 of mowing fields, and 3,523 of pasture in all three parishes.

As in most of Massachusetts, Cambridge farmers practiced a system of mixed husbandry, in which cattle were the basic resource. The pastures supported livestock, which provided manure for the tillable land, and hayfields provided basic subsistence for cattle in the winter and a cash income to the farmer; the thin soil could not otherwise have sustained crops. The salt hay harvested from the marshes that bordered the Charles was the community's most valuable agricultural product, and over time the marsh lots, many of them owned by inhabitants of the second and third parishes, were subdivided into hundreds of narrow parcels that extended from the upland to the water.

For the first hundred years after settlement, Cambridge's agricultural landscape evolved under successive generations of farmers like the Marretts, the Frosts, and the Coopers who settled the plain north and west of the village (see chapter 4). As early as the 1720s, however, wealthy Boston gentlemen began to buy Cambridge farmsteads for country retreats. This trend accelerated after 1750, when West Indian planters began acquiring land with scenic views of the river or of Boston. These men were most interested in the recreational value of their country properties and directed their tenant farmers to plant strawberry beds and drain low-lying meadows to accommodate horses rather than cattle. The descendants of the Puritans held sway in the back lands and along the road to Arlington, where they continued to farm in the old way until the suburban era arrived in the 1840s.

On the eve of the Revolution, when Cambridge was about to play its most conspicuous role in colonial history, Yankee and loyalist societies were living in close proximity, supported by a small number of black servants and slaves. Descendants of the Puritan settlers constituted more than 90 percent of the population. These were mostly farmers, artisans, and tradesmen who relied on their own labor and local resources for their livelihoods, although some had risen through the professions. Others depended on the college, but their outlook was equally parochial. When the political crisis arose, almost all opposed the Crown, with the notable exception of John Nutting, a master builder who actively supported the British side. The president,

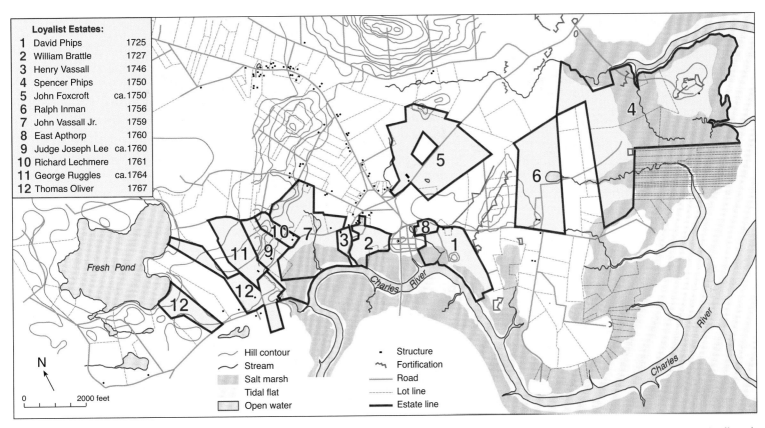

Loyalist Estates:

1 David Phips   1725
2 William Brattle   1727
3 Henry Vassall   1746
4 Spencer Phips   1750
5 John Foxcroft   ca.1750
6 Ralph Inman   1756
7 John Vassall Jr.   1759
8 East Apthorp   1760
9 Judge Joseph Lee   ca.1760
10 Richard Lechmere   1761
11 George Ruggles   ca.1764
12 Thomas Oliver   1767

Fresh Pond

N

0   2000 feet

Hill contour
Stream
Salt marsh
Tidal flat
Open water

Structure
Fortification
Road
Lot line
Estate line

Charles River

FIGURE 1.19 The mature colonial landscape of Cambridge in 1776. All roads lead to the village, following the path of least resistance around the hills and marshes. The fortifications were erected by the American Army during the Siege of Boston in 1775–76. Much of the town is occupied by Loyalist estates.

professors, and tutors of the college were a small minority, and only a few participated in public affairs.

Blacks had been present in Cambridge since the earliest days of settlement, although the records are sparse and inconsistent. Nathaniel Eaton, the first master of Harvard College, owned at least one slave in 1639. Peter Towne, a cooper, gave his three slaves their freedom on his death in 1705 (Paige, 671). Harvard president Benjamin Wadsworth had two slaves when he moved into the new President's House in 1726. In 1749, just before the influx of West Indian planters, Cambridge assessors identified twelve slave owners among the 208 taxpayers in the First Parish.[16] All had a single slave except for Henry Vassall, who had four. A 1754 provincial census tallied fifty-six blacks in all three parishes of Cambridge. By 1765 there were ninety, but the total fell to sixty in 1790; many African Americans moved to Boston after slavery ended in Massachusetts in 1783.

The loyalists who left Massachusetts during the Siege of Boston took most of their slaves with them but typically left a few behind to look after their properties. At least three black men served in Cambridge militia companies in April 1775, and the census of 1777 listed nine in the First Parish who were sufficiently established to pay a poll tax. All remaining slaves in Massachusetts were considered free after a 1783 court decision.

The elite of Cambridge were the loyalist, oligarchic, and Anglican families that became known as Tories in the years leading up to the Revolution.[17] Consisting of hardly more than a dozen households, this circle lived apart from village affairs. A few, like the Brattles and the Foxcrofts, were descendants of 17th-century Cambridge families that had become wealthy and fallen out of sympathy with Puritan customs; others, like the Phipses and Vassalls, arrived in the second quarter of the 18th century. Once these families had established a social order in Cambridge, others like the Inmans naturally followed. All relied on outside income, whether profits from West Indies plantations or Boston mercantile houses, or stipends for service to the colonial government. United by religion, class, politics, and marriage, they built elaborate houses and affected manners and attitudes that grated

TABLE 1.1 SLAVE OWNERS IN THE FIRST PARISH OF CAMBRIDGE, 1749

	Probable Occupation	Number of Slaves Aged 12–50
William Angier	tanner	1
Moses Bordman Jr.	tanner	1
Francis Foxcroft	judge	1
Elizabeth Nutting	unmarried	1
Stephen Prentice	cordwainer	1
Jonathan Sprague	?	1
Lieut. [Ebenezer] Stedman	innkeeper	1
Edmund Trowbridge	judge	1
Henry Vassall	merchant	4
[Mrs. John] Vassall	widow	1
Abraham Watson	tanner	1
Deacon [Samuel] Whittemore	storekeeper	1
		15

Sources: Town of Cambridge Tax Valuation Sheet, 1749; Paige, *History of Cambridge*, 1877; Massachusetts Vital Records.

on less-favored neighbors whose simpler tastes derived from their roots in New England's Puritan heritage.[18] Most were closely bound by marriage; three of the matrons were originally Vassalls, and three were the daughters of Governor Spencer Phips. The Baroness Frederika Riedesel, who was interned with her husband in the Lechmere-Sewell house on Brattle Street during the winter of 1777–78, described the social scene:

> Never had I chanced upon such an agreeable situation. Seven families, who were connected with each other, partly by ties of relationship and partly by affection, had here farms, gardens and magnificent houses, and not far off plantations of fruit. The owners of these were in the habit of daily meeting each other in the afternoon, now at the house of one, now at another, and making themselves merry with music and the dance—living in prosperity, united and happy, until, alas! this ruinous war severed them and left all their houses desolate, except two, the proprietors of which were also soon obliged to flee. (Paige, 168–69)

FIGURE I.20 Ralph Inman (1713–88), a Boston merchant and a founder of Christ Church, owned one of Cambridge's great Tory estates. He married Susannah Speakman in 1746 and purchased 180 acres on the east slope of Dana Hill ten years later. Their portraits were painted by Robert Feke in 1748. Mrs. Inman died in 1761, and Ralph married Elizabeth Murray in 1771.

FIGURE I.21 Susannah Speakman Inman (1727–61).

FIGURE 1.22 The model of Cambridge in 1776, viewed from the west with the Richard Lechmere estate at the intersection of Sparks and Brattle streets in the foreground and the village in the distance.

Seven loyalist families lived on estates west of town along Brattle Street, while four resided east of the village. Along Tory Row the estates ranged from Henry Vassall's 9 acres to John Vassall's 100; the Lee, Ruggles, and Oliver estates had 35 to 40 acres. The Ralph Inman and Francis Foxcroft estates east of town comprised 180 and 120 acres, respectively, while Spencer Phips owned 326 acres in East Cambridge, 138 of which passed to Richard Lechmere through his daughter Mary. These properties were cultivated by tenant farmers or slaves but were not productive enough by themselves to support life on a grand scale (see chapter 4).

The houses that the Tories built in the 1750s and '60s were some of the largest and most sophisticated buildings in New England. John Vassall, an heir to substantial plantations in Jamaica, was still an adolescent when he built his country residence on

Brattle Street in 1759. A distinguished example of High Georgian taste sitting prominently on a terraced rise well back from the street, Vassall's house created an appropriate setting for his opulent way of life (figure 1.23). Equally imposing are the mansions built in the 1760s by George Ruggles, Thomas Oliver, and East Apthorp (see figures 6.24, 6.25, and 4.270). Cambridge was the principal residence of most of these families, and they erected their own house of worship, Christ Church, facing Cambridge Common midway between their estates (figure 1.24; see chapter 7). William Brattle, John Vassall, and Richard Lechmere also kept houses in Boston. Some Cambridge loyalists owned plantations in the West Indies, but the islands were unhealthy, and most settled in England after 1776.

FIGURE 1.23 John Vassall Jr. house, 105 Brattle Street (1759). This view was made in 1815, after Andrew Craigie added the side porches.

FIGURE 1.24 Christ Church, Zero Garden Street (Peter Harrison, 1759). Christ Church represented the aspirations of Cambridge loyalists for affiliation with the Church of England, which supported the enterprise with a grant to its first minister, Reverend East Apthorp. Almost all the founding families left Cambridge during the Revolution; most forfeited their estates and never returned.

FIGURE 1.25 Joseph Hicks house, Wood Street corner of South Street (64 Kennedy Street, ca. 1693-1715; demolished ca. 1900). The house was typical of the modest vernacular structures built in the village in the 18th century. It was purchased by the town in 1779 and served as an almshouse until 1786. Photo ca. 1900.

Ordinary Cambridge dwellings were small and unostentatious and contrasted sharply with the opulence of the Vassall and Oliver houses built in the same decades. In 1770, approximately a quarter (twenty-three) of the houses within the dozen square blocks of the village dated from the 17th century. None survive, but the Joseph Hicks house (ca. 1693–1715) lasted long enough to be photographed (figure 1.25). Middle-class houses such as Aaron Hill's, built ca. 1755 and now at 17 Brown Street, and the John Hicks house, built in 1762 and now at 64 Kennedy Street, are modest Georgian homes with gambrel roofs, a type initiated thirty years earlier with the houses of Benjamin Wadsworth and William Brattle (see figures 6.5 and 6.7). Others, such as Edward Marrett's at 77 Mt. Auburn Street, incorporated shops without sacrificing their domestic scale and appearance (figure 1.26; see also figure 6.29).

FIGURE 1.26 Edward Marrett house, 77 Mt. Auburn Street (1760). The Marretts arrived in Cambridge in 1638, and successive generations became shoemakers, brickmakers, farmers, and glaziers while accumulating considerable wealth and land. Edward Marrett, a tailor, sold the family farm on Brattle Street to John Vassall in 1759 and probably built this house with the proceeds. The house was disassembled and moved to Manchester, Massachusetts, in 1926. Photo ca. 1926.

The town of Cambridge is about six miles from Boston, and was the country residence of the gentry of that city; there are a number of fine houses in it going to decay, belonging to loyalists. The town must have been extremely pleasant, but its beauty is much defaced, being now only an arsenal for military stores. (Anburey, II, 41 [Nov. 30, 1777])

Cambridge participated in the general unrest that led up to the Revolution, but few could have foreseen that it would become headquarters for the first military campaign of the war. The town meeting joined the protests against the Stamp Act in 1765 and repeatedly instructed its representatives to the General Court to support the independence of the colonies, while pledging allegiance to the king. When a new General Court was summoned in 1768, Cambridge chose as representatives Captain Samuel Whittemore, who would serve as a minuteman on April 19, 1775, and Thomas Gardner, who died at Bunker Hill.

On December 14, 1772, the town voted to appoint its own Committee of Correspondence to support the one that Boston's town meeting had established six weeks before. The decision of Parliament in 1773 to retain a tax on tea imported by the East India Company set off a fury of discussion. The committees of correspondence of Boston, Cambridge, Brookline, Dorchester, and Roxbury met daily in Faneuil Hall, culminating in the famous tea party of December 16, 1773. Parliament responded in May 1774 by nullifying the Massachusetts charter of 1682. The Massachusetts Government Act replaced the elected Governor's Council with a Mandamus Council appointed by the Crown, authorized the governor to appoint judges and sheriffs to select jurors, and limited towns to one meeting a year.[19] The Cambridge loyalists who accepted appointments under the new regime, Lieutenant Governor Thomas Oliver, Attorney General Jonathan Sewell, and Mandamus Council members Joseph Lee and Samuel Danforth, became objects of popular hostility.

Feelings boiled over on September 1, 1774, when 260 British troops guided by Middlesex County sheriff David Phips

confiscated the contents of the powderhouse in Somerville and two field pieces from the Cambridge militia. That evening "some thousands" of armed men converged on Cambridge, and patriot mobs began to threaten loyalists in the countryside. One group, "mostly boys and negroes," surrounded the house of Attorney General Jonathan Sewell (145 Brattle Street; *Boston Gazette*, Sept. 5, 1774, in Paige, 154). John Colman, a young friend of the family, wrote an eyewitness account:

On Thursday evening September 1 there was a riotous assembling of about 40 or 50 men & boys in the Town of Cambridge. … Being alarmed with the noise of their coming, & having secured the windows and doors as well as we could, we repaired to Mrs. Sewall's chamber; they came shouting and blowing a horn & Mrs. Sewall threw up the window when they had got to the house & asked them what they would have. They replied Mr. Sewell. She told them he was not at home, but had gone to Boston in the morning and had not returned since; on which they exclaimed that she was a damned liar and that he was in the house and they would search the house for him and have him. … Finding they had entered and hearing them below, Mr. Chipman, Mr. Coffin and myself together with a servant of Judge Sewall's being all the males that were in the house, ran downstairs, attacked them, and by an active and vigorous application of the Argumentum Baculinum drove them out.[20] … [They finally] told us we had fought like brave fellows & if we would give them something to drink they would not go to Judge Lee's as they intended but would disperse which they did after drinking a few glasses of wine and cordially bid each other good-night. (Colman, 7627–28)

The next morning the committees of correspondence of Boston and Charlestown came out to join their local counterparts and found "some thousands of people assembled round the court-house steps" demanding that the new officials resign. Councilors Danforth and Lee appeared in person to renounce their appointments, and Sheriff Phips apologized for his actions. After a false alarm of British troops on the move, the crowd marched on Lieutenant Governor Oliver's house on the Watertown Road (now 33 Elmwood Avenue). Oliver agreed to the

TABLE 1.2 POLITICAL STATUS AND PROPERTY DISPOSITION OF CAMBRIDGE'S FIRST PARISH LOYALISTS

Name, Address	Political Status*	Outcome	Property Status	Property Disposition	Buyer
John Borland, merchant 10 Linden Street	Absentee	d. Boston, 1775	Seized, occupied, leased by CCC	Returned to heirs	-
Gen. William Brattle	Absentee, Proscribed	d. Halifax, 1776	Sold to Thomas Brattle, 1774	-	-
Thomas Brattle, merchant 42 Brattle Street	Absentee	d. Cambridge, 1801	Seized, occupied, leased by CCC	Returned to owner	-
Judge Samuel Danforth 22 Dunster Street	To Boston	d. Boston, 1777	Undisturbed	-	-
John Foxcroft, Register of Deeds Kirkland cor. Oxford Street	Remained	d. Cambridge, 1802	Occupied, burned 1777	-	-
Ralph Inman, merchant 11 Inman Street	Boston, arrested 1776	d. Cambridge, 1788	Seized, occupied, leased by CCC	Returned to owner	-
Richard Lechmere, distiller Lechmere's Point	Absentee Proscribed	d. England, 1814	Seized, occupied, leased by CCC	Confiscated and sold (144 acres)	Andrew Cabot, Salem, 1779
Judge Joseph Lee 159 Brattle Street	Boston, returned unmolested	d. Cambridge, 1802	Undisturbed	-	-
John Nutting, carpenter 1541 Mass. Avenue	Proscribed	d. Nova Scotia, 1800	Foreclosed	Sold by creditors	-
Lt. Gov. Thomas Oliver 33 Elmwood Avenue	Absentee, Proscribed, Conspirator	d. England, 1815	Seized, occupied, leased by CCC	Confiscated and sold (96 acres)	Andrew Cabot, Salem, 1779
Col. David Phips, Sheriff 24 Arrow Street	Absentee, Proscribed	d. England, 1811	Seized, occupied, leased by CCC	Confiscated and sold (50 acres)	Isaiah Doane, Boston, 1781
Capt. George Ruggles 175 Brattle Street	Absentee	Unknown	Sold to Thomas Fayerweather, 1774	-	-
Atty. General Jonathan Sewell 145 Brattle Street	Absentee, Proscribed, Conspirator	d. New Brunswick, 1786	Seized, occupied, leased by CCC	Confiscated and sold (44 acres)	Thomas Lee, Pomfret, Conn., 1779
Penelope Vassall, widow 94 Brattle Street	Absentee	d. Boston, 1800	Seized, occupied, leased by CCC	Returned to owner, sold by creditors	Nathaniel Tracy, Newburyport 1782
Col. John Vassall 105 Brattle Street	Absentee, Proscribed	d. England, 1797	Seized, occupied, leased by CCC	Confiscated and sold (116 acres)	Nathaniel Tracy, Newburyport 1781

*Political Status during and after the Siege of Boston: Absentee: Designated by the Cambridge Committee of Correspondence (CCC) in 1775; Proscribed: Named in the Massachusetts Banishment Act, Ch. 24 of the Acts of 1777–78; Conspirator: Named a "notorious conspirator" in Ch. 48, Acts of 1779.

Sources: Paige, 167–71; Maas, *Divided Hearts.*

resignation prepared for him by the committee but added this disclaimer: "My house at Cambridge being surrounded by about four thousand people, in compliance with their command I sign my name" (Paige, 152, 155). The same edition of the *Boston Gazette* that described these events contained a copy of a letter written by General William Brattle to the British General Gage in Boston, informing him of militia activities in the countryside. By the time Brattle's apology appeared a week later he had already been driven out of Cambridge.

Loyalists were intimidated by the violent actions of the patriots, which preceded by many months official moves against them. Most left Cambridge about this time, and those that remained were frightened into passivity. In 1777 the General Court called on town meetings to identify disaffected persons for arrest and trial; by the time it adopted the Banishment Act of 1778 most of the 300 named individuals had left the area. Another act named twenty-nine "notorious conspirators," including Thomas Oliver and Jonathan Sewell, who were deemed to have forfeited "all their property, rights and liberties" (Ch. 48, Acts of 1779).

In June 1775 the General Court authorized local committees of correspondence to take possession of absentee estates and find renters for them; the Cambridge committee administered ten estates and received £406 from tenants in 1776, although many properties had been seized by the state for military use.[21] A few loyalist women stayed behind to protect their homes. Elizabeth Murray Inman remained in residence at the beginning of the Siege, but her husband's estate east of town was too important to be left in loyalist hands. Katherine Brattle Wendell successfully retained her father's property by acting as hostess to the American officers billeted there.

Meanwhile, Cambridge continued on its revolutionary course. A town meeting on October 3, 1774, authorized the selectmen to purchase powder, shot, and a cannon, and to equip and pay fifers and drummers. On the night of April 18, 1775, when Paul Revere rode through Charlestown toward Lexington and Concord to warn of the British advance, William Dawes carried the alert to Roxbury and Cambridge. A British supply train was delayed by the removal of planks from the Great Bridge but passed peacefully through the village on the morning of the 19th. That afternoon the redcoats' retreat was opposed by a militia company of seventy-seven Cambridge men, including three students from the college and two black men. John Hicks, Moses Richardson, and William Marcy, were killed in a skirmish near the junction of Massachusetts and Rindge avenues in North Cambridge; they lie in the Old Burying Ground under a granite marker erected in 1870 (see chapter 5).

Militia companies throughout New England gathered in Cambridge, where they formed the nucleus of an American army that occupied the town for the next eleven months. They immediately began to fortify Roxbury Neck and Prospect Hill in Somerville. General Artemas Ward, the first American commander, lived in Jonathan Hastings's house, and several loyalist mansions were used as hospitals or officers' quarters. Crude barracks were constructed on the Common (see figure 5.2). Harvard students were dismissed and the library sent to Andover in Essex County for safekeeping while troops occupied the college.

On July 2, 1775, two weeks after the Battle of Bunker Hill, George Washington arrived to take command. He was first quartered in the Harvard president's house but soon relocated to John Vassall's mansion, today's Longfellow House-Washington's Headquarters National Historic Site. Washington designed additional fortifications to confine the British within Boston. In Cambridge, an inner defensive line, running from Fort No. 1 on the Charles River at River Street to Fort No. 3 near Union Square in Somerville, was anchored by earthworks across Butler's (now Dana) Hill that commanded the level ground running down to the river. An outer system included a major fortification at Lechmere's Point and several small forts along the river, including today's Fort Washington in Cambridgeport (see figure 1.19).

During the winter of 1775–76, about 6,000 troops were quartered in Cambridge. After the successful conclusion of the Siege of Boston in March 1776, the army departed, leaving behind considerable devastation. "Who would have thought," wrote the army chaplain, Reverend William Emerson of Concord, on July

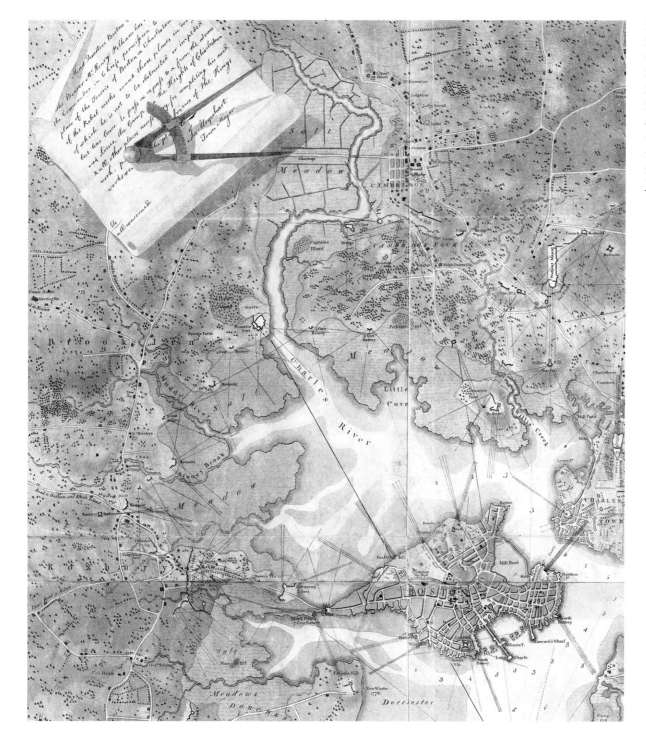

FIGURE 1.27 Boston and vicinity during the Siege of Boston, 1776, showing Cambridge and its fortifications. British mapmakers of this period were hampered by the army's confinement in Boston. The military works are assumed to be accurate, but the plan of the village is heavily distorted. The cartographer, Henry Pelham, was a Boston native and a half-brother of artist John Singleton Copley.

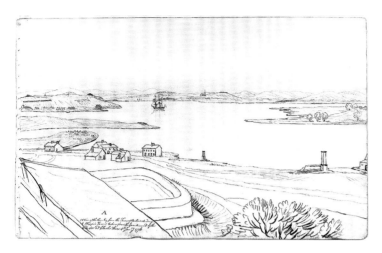

FIGURE 1.28 British Army engineers made detailed drawings of the country-side around Boston. These sketches, part of a panorama drawn by Lieutenant Archibald Robertson at the British fort on Bunker Hill, were made on January 4, 1776. Beacon Hill is at left. A warship is guarding the mouth of the Charles River, and the Roxbury Meetinghouse can be seen in the distance, in the center of the view. The three trees on the right are on Lechmere's Point.

FIGURE 1.29 A continuation of Robertson's panorama. From left to right are the American forts on Lechmere's Point and Cobble Hill, with the village of Cambridge in the distance. The landscape of Cambridge was almost completely open; American troop movements took place at night to avoid detection by the British.

FIGURE 1.30 The Cambridge meetinghouse and Harvard College as seen from the British citadel in Charlestown. The long structure left of the meetinghouse was an earthwork defending the village.

7, 1775, "a twelve month past that all Cambridge and Charlestown would be covered over with American Camps, and cut up into Forts and Entrenchments, & all their Lands, Fields & Orchards laid common, ye Horses & other Cattle feeding in ye choicest mowing Land,—whole fields of Corn eat down to the Ground. Large parks of well regulated Locusts cutt down for fire wood & other public uses" (Emerson, 79).

Ralph Inman's niece lamented his ruined estate, which had been occupied by General Israel Putnam and 3,000 troops after the Battle of Bunker Hill: "Oh! that imagination could replace the wood lot, the willows round the pond, the locust trees that so delightfully ornamented the roads leading to this farm … every elegance which it cost years of care and toil bringing to perfection, is laid low. It looks like an unfrequented desert, and this farm is an epitome of all Cambridge, [once] the loveliest village in America" (DAR, 176; figure 1.31).

The last episode of the war in Cambridge began in November 1777, when British troops under the command of General John Burgoyne, which had been defeated at Saratoga the month before, arrived as prisoners of war. The enlisted men were housed in the old American barracks in Somerville, but the officers, including Generals Burgoyne and Riedesel, were billeted in private homes.[22] Local residents considered this an intolerable burden, given the destruction the town had already suffered and the general deprivation in the region, and there were several unpleasant incidents before the prisoners left for Virginia a year later. On September 1–7, 1779, a Convention of Delegates convened in the Cambridge meetinghouse to draft a new constitution for Massachusetts. After another two-week session that fall and additional meetings in Boston between January and March 1780, the convention adopted a document that is the oldest written constitution still in effect.

After the peace treaty was concluded in 1783 some banished loyalists were allowed to return, although their reception varied. Thomas Oliver and Jonathan Sewell were permanently excluded because they were among the twenty-nine "notorious conspirators" whose properties were seized by the General Court

FIGURE 1.31 Ralph Inman built this elaborate three-story mansion on 180 acres of pasture and woods east of Dana Hill in 1756. Inman and his wife, Elizabeth, remained in Massachusetts during the war, so the property escaped confiscation, and they were allowed to return after the Siege. The house was moved from 15 Inman Street to Brookline Street in 1873 and demolished in 1961 (see *Report Three: Cambridgeport*, 15–16). View in 1859.

FIGURE 1.32 The earliest accurate view of the village was drawn by a Harvard undergraduate in 1780–81. This panorama from Dana Hill, about half a mile east of the meetinghouse, recorded what is possibly the John Hicks house and its neighbors on the extreme left; Spencer Phips's "very large new built barn" (see chapter 4); the Apthorp-Borland house with its barn; the Fourth Meetinghouse, behind the Wadsworth, Hooker-Shepard-Wigglesworth, and Stephen Sewell houses; and the parsonage, with Christ Church in the distance. The Harvard buildings include Massachusetts Hall (behind the parson's barn); Stoughton I; Harvard Hall III, still without a cupola; and Hollis Hall, behind the college brewhouse.

in 1779 (Ch. 48, Acts of 1779). Thomas Brattle had difficulty gaining permission to return, despite his service to American prisoners of war in Britain; others found acceptance through former friends and relations. The few loyalists who reclaimed their properties were able to live out their days unmolested, but none regained their former wealth or influence. Their places in the new republic were taken by the former revolutionaries, who demonstrated a spirit of entrepreneurship that gave rise to all kinds of internal improvements. The Siege had highlighted the strategic value of the empty fields between the village and the river, and in 1793 the West Boston Bridge (on the site of today's Longfellow Bridge) established a new spatial relationship between Cambridge and Boston.

FIGURE 2.1 Harvard College and the village at the dawn of the turnpike era, seen from the northwest in 1796 with Cambridge Common in the foreground. The Charlestown Road (Kirkland Street) enters the Common on the left; Broadway and Cambridge Street do not yet exist. The Fourth Meetinghouse stands on the site of today's Lehman Hall. Dana Hill rises in the background.

2 BECOMING MODERN CAMBRIDGE, 1793–2016

Cambridge began to urbanize soon after the Revolution. The strategic position of the meadows and marshes east of the village had become apparent during the Siege of Boston, and returning prosperity revived old schemes to link Boston to its hinterland. The bridges built in 1793 and 1809 set off waves of speculation and road construction. The rapid growth of Cambridge-port and East Cambridge triggered a momentous realignment of political power among the villages. Deprived of the courthouse in 1816 and the meetinghouse in 1831, Old Cambridge tried to establish itself as a separate town in 1842, 1846, and 1855. The incorporation of Cambridge as a city in 1846 papered over neighborhood rivalries that still resonate today.

After the bridges opened Cambridge to suburban development, succeeding generations of "improvers" created parks, laid out streets and subdivisions, and established civic enterprises that provided transportation, water, and illuminating gas. At the end of the century the rapidly industrializing municipality secured the entire riverfront for public use. The completion of the subway in 1912, the forceful expansion of Harvard University under Presidents Eliot and Lowell, and the arrival of the Massachusetts Institute of Technology in 1916 helped make Cambridge a modern city. At the beginning of the 21st century Harvard shifted its focus toward developing a new campus in Allston, opening another chapter in a vital but often tempestuous relationship with Cambridge.

VILLAGE TO CITY, 1793–1846

> It is generally conceded, that this town eminently combines the tranquility of philosophic solitude, with the choicest pleasures and advantages of refined society. (Abiel Holmes, *The History of Cambridge,* 1801)

Prosperity returned slowly to Cambridge after the Revolution. The First Parish, located between the Charles River and Alewife Brook and comprising all of present Cambridge, had approximately 1,000 people and 135 dwellings, about 90 of which were in the village. The parish included the college, some farms and homesteads along the Menotomy road (now Massachusetts Avenue toward Arlington), and "several elegant seats, which attract the notice, and delight the eye" on the Watertown road, now Brattle Street (ibid., 6). East of the village was the Neck, a vast expanse of pasture and marsh between the Charles and Millers rivers that contained only five farms. Cambridge was rural, but the soil was not naturally productive, and most farmers grew hay and raised cattle to fertilize their fields. In the absence of water-power commerce was limited to cottage trades such as tanning and shoemaking. A few taverns catered to the public business of the town and served travelers on the eight-mile-long road to Boston over the Great Bridge via Brighton, Brookline, and Roxbury. Everyone lived and worked in the town, where a limited economic base meant that only the oldest sons could remain; the rest had to seek opportunities elsewhere.

The population of Cambridge was more homogeneous than it had been before the war. Only two of the sixty-two founders of Christ Church remained in town, and just a handful of the proscribed loyalists were allowed to return. The Committee of Correspondence had seized most of the loyalists' estates on the Watertown Road and all those east of the village. Some absconders left a trusted slave in charge, but only a few blacks remained after slavery ended in 1783. American war profiteers purchased several of the confiscated properties.

Harvard College was recognized as a university in the Massachusetts Constitution of 1780. The medical school was established in Cambridge in 1793 and the law school in 1817. The institution was still very small, however, with only twelve professors and 188 students in 1809–10. Between 1810 and 1820 the number of students from outside New England increased from 11 to 27 percent of the total, a measure of its growing national appeal. In the 1820s the faculty doubled in size, and the number of students rose to more than 400 (including medical students, who by then studied in Boston).

Most Harvard faculty and administrators had strong personal ties to Cambridge. From 1726 until 1849 presidents lived in Wadsworth House in the heart of the village, and until 1851 the Overseers included ministers from Cambridge, Boston, Charlestown, Watertown, Roxbury, and Dorchester. Faculty members were required to live in Cambridge, and the university provided house lots and mortgages to senior professors. In 1820 the legislature went so far as to adjust the boundary with Charlestown to accommodate one professor's purchase of a house there (see chapter 4). Most administrators and employees came from local families, and some positions were practically hereditary.

Beginning with Reverend Samuel Webber (1806–10), Harvard's presidents for many years were both Unitarians (religious liberals) and Federalists (political conservatives). John Kirkland (1810–28) solidified the university's association with Boston's mercantile elite and brought the first European-trained professors to Cambridge. Kirkland and his chief administrative officer, college steward Stephen Higginson, landscaped the Yard and supported civic improvements such as the enclosure of the Common. Former Boston mayor Josiah Quincy (1829–45), the first lay president, commissioned the first accurate survey of Old Cambridge and completed the acquisition of the Yard (see figure 3.3 and chapter 10).

Bridges, Turnpikes, and Speculators

The new Massachusetts elite were ambitious men who belonged mainly to the dominant Federalist Party. Many had profited handsomely from their service to the republic and now speculated in land, the country's most abundant natural resource. Massachusetts offered many opportunities for gain. Connected to the mainland by a narrow neck, Boston was isolated from Middlesex and Essex counties by the Charles and Mystic rivers, which were crossed by ferries to Charlestown and Winnisimmet (Chelsea). The rivers had originally been important links to surrounding settlements, but after the Revolution they began to be seen as barriers to overland commerce.

Reverend Abiel Holmes, writing in 1814, recalled the Cambridge shore opposite Boston as "sort of an insulated tract, detached from any other … chiefly valued for the abundance of hay and forage, which the salt marshes furnished. These marshes, extending far out from the banks of the river, comprised the principal part of those lands. The situation was very uninviting. The grounds lay low. There were no roads. Access could not be had to the capital, except by boats, only by the circuitous route of Roxbury or Charlestown" (*Memoir*).

The possibility of a bridge between Boston and Charlestown was discussed in 1713, but it was difficult to find investors for such an expensive project; Harvard feared the loss of income from the ferry, which the General Court had granted it in the 1650s. In 1738 Harvard blocked a proposed bridge between Cambridge and Boston, claiming:

> that any nearer and more ready Passage, over s^d River and especially by a Bridge, will cause such an increase of Company &c at the College, that thereby the Scholars will be in danger of being too much interrupted in their Studies and hurt in their Morals. (quoted in Tourtellot, 233)

In 1785 the General Court received petitions from Thomas Russell, a wealthy Boston merchant, to build a bridge to Charlestown and from Andrew and John Cabot, speculators who had purchased many Cambridge estates, to build a bridge to Lechmere's Point. The Charlestown party prevailed after the legislature granted Harvard a share of the tolls, and the Charles River Bridge opened in 1786. The new bridge diverted traffic away from Cambridge and motivated local interests to pursue their own charter.

Chief Justice Francis Dana played a key role in bringing a bridge to Cambridge. Dana had inherited about 100 acres east of today's Ware Street in 1772, bought additional acreage after 1777, and built a mansion on Dana Hill with a commanding view of Back Bay in 1785 (see figure 4.242). He continued to accumulate property and eventually owned much of the Neck south of Massachusetts Avenue. Colonel Leonard Jarvis of Boston, who bought Ralph Inman's estate in 1792, became Dana's informal collaborator in the development of Cambridgeport.

On November 30, 1791, the *Columbian Centinel* published a notice that John Cabot and a group of Boston men planned to construct a bridge from Boston to Lechmere's Point. Five weeks later, on January 7, 1792, Justice Dana and some associates announced a rival proposal in the same paper.

WEST BOSTON BRIDGE.

As *all* citizens of the United States have an *equal* right to propose a measure that may be beneficial to the publick or advantageous to themselves, and as no body of men have an *exclusive* right to take to themselves such a privilege, a number of gentlemen have proposed to open a new subscription, for the purpose of building a BRIDGE from West Boston to Cambridge—at such place as the General Court may be pleased to direct.

The promoters alleged that the route by way of Pelham's Island (the present Main Street and Longfellow Bridge) would "shorten the travel from the western part of the state to Boston [by] one mile and one hundred and forty-six rods." Opponents charged that a few rich gentlemen would destroy the trade of Charlestown and the North End just to gain access to their Cambridge

FIGURE 2.2   The West Boston Bridge in 1797, looking toward Boston. The State House is on the right and the North Church on the left.

estates. One predicted a decline in the morals of the Harvard students: "that [the city] is already too near, has been a serious complaint" (ibid., Jan. 21, 1792).

The subscription for Dana's bridge was filled within three hours. Only nine of the 112 shareholders were Cambridge residents, but they provided 25 percent of the capital. The General Court incorporated Dana, James Sullivan, and Mungo Mackay of the West Boston group and Oliver Wendell, Henry Jackson, and William Wetmore of the Lechmere's Point party as the Proprietors of the West Boston Bridge. Of the twelve directors, only Dana and James Winthrop were Cambridge men; the rest were Boston merchants, entrepreneurs, and politicians.

Construction began in July 1792, and the completed timber-pile structure, which extended 3,500 feet across the river and continued another 3,300 feet on a causeway across the marsh to Pelham's Island, opened for travel on November 23, 1793. The bridge reduced the distance from the State House to the Cambridge meetinghouse from eight to a little over three miles. Reverend Holmes noted in 1801 that "the erection of this bridge has had a very perceivable influence on the trade of Cambridge, which formerly was very inconsiderable. By bringing the travel from the westward and northward through the centre of the town, it has greatly invigorated business there" (*History,* 4).

The bridge spawned many new roads, all of which bypassed the old village center and dampened its brief burst of prosperity. Between 1803 and 1810, the legislature chartered ten turnpikes in Middlesex County; four (Hampshire Street, Concord Avenue and Broadway, River Street, and Western Avenue) passed through Cambridge to reach the West Boston Bridge. Other investors built Cambridge and Harvard streets to open their lands for development. Towns and counties also built roads, and rival parties struggled to elect selectmen and delegates to the Court of Sessions (county commissioners), seeking to short-cut or block their competitors. The boom ended with the trade embargos that preceded the War of 1812.

The federal government sold Colonel Jarvis's property in 1798 to satisfy a judgment against him, and some of the new owners tried to enhance the value of their property by building Harvard Street as a more direct way from the meetinghouse to the West Boston Bridge. Justice Dana, concerned that the road would intrude on his privacy and bypass the nascent village he was promoting at Lafayette Square, built the "Opposition House" on his property line to block the intended route. Although the house was soon moved to its present site on Hancock Place, the climb over Dana Hill discouraged travelers, and the new road never became a major thoroughfare (see figure 4.243).

Colonel Jeduthun Wellington, a farmer in the Second Parish and a Cambridge selectman, organized the Cambridge & Concord Turnpike Corporation to construct Concord Avenue as a toll road in 1803. The other investors were farmers and merchants in outlying towns. Like turnpike promoters everywhere, they were obsessed with creating the shortest possible route. In 1805 the legislature authorized the company to extend the road from Garden Street across the Common to the West Boston Bridge, on the condition that Broadway stay 90 feet from Stoughton Hall, creating a slight detour and establishing the northern boundary of Harvard Yard (see chapter 10). Both this toll-free extension and Hampshire Street, which the Middlesex Turnpike Corporation

FIGURE 2.3 The milestone was rescued from a stone crusher by antiquarian William A. Saunders and placed in the Old Burying Ground about 1900. Carved by Abraham Ireland in 1734, it indicates on one side, accurately, "Boston eight miles" via the road over the Great Bridge and through Brookline and Roxbury. In 1794 the reverse side was misleadingly inscribed "2½ miles" to Boston via the West Boston Bridge; the actual distance is 3.4 miles. Photo 1938.

laid out in 1805 to reach the Second New Hampshire Turnpike at Tyngsborough, dampened commercial activity in the village by sending traffic directly to the bridge (figure 2.4).

The success of the West Boston Bridge prompted another old revolutionary, Andrew Craigie, to begin a vast speculation at Lechmere's Point that ultimately deprived Old Cambridge of its status as a county seat (see *East Cambridge*). Craigie, a Boston

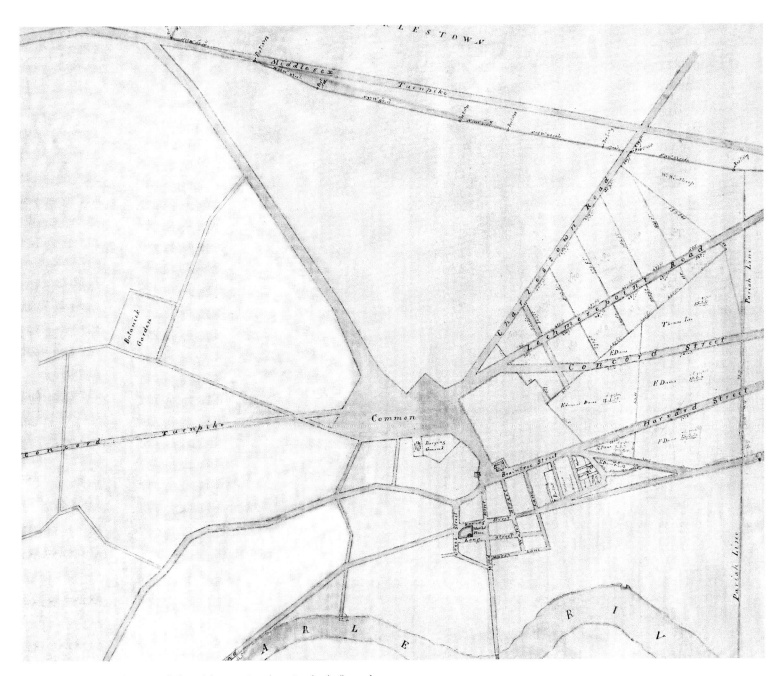

FIGURE 2.4 Peter Tufts's 1813 "Plan of the First Parish in Cambridge" was the first accurate survey of Old Cambridge. Mt. Auburn Street (labeled "New Brattle Road") offered a convenient short-cut for travelers. The new roads entering the village from the east—Cambridge Street ("Lechmere Point Road"), Broadway ("Concord Street"), and Harvard Street—already show real estate activity.

native, served as apothecary general of the American army before acquiring the Vassall estates on Brattle Street and moving to Cambridge in 1792. While the West Boston Bridge and the development of Cambridgeport were to some extent local ventures, Craigie and his investors had no strong ties to Cambridge, and his Federalist Party connections often enabled him to prevail against the wishes of the town.

Beginning in 1795 Craigie secretly acquired nearly all of Lechmere's Point, as well as large tracts east of Fayette Street and north of Broadway. He received a charter from the General Court in 1805 and opened the Craigie Bridge on August 30, 1809. His extension of Cambridge Street to Cambridge Common triggered another episode of strategic road building.

In 1805 the selectmen petitioned the county court of sessions to "establish [a road] from the garden of the Hon. Elbridge Gerry to the garden of the late Thomas Brattle, Esq." (Mt. Auburn Street from Elmwood Avenue to Brattle Square) in order to bypass Brattle Street and shorten the distance from Watertown to the West Boston Bridge (Paige, 203). Craigie proposed an alternate route leading to his bridge at Lechmere's Point by way of Mason and Cambridge streets. His offer to pay part of the cost persuaded the selectmen to approve his plan in 1807, but the next town meeting reverted to the original proposal, which favored the Cambridgeport faction. Craigie continued to file petitions to block the new road, and on May 16, 1808, he and thirty-five others so violently protested the laying out of Mt. Auburn Street that the town meeting authorized the selectmen to prosecute "Andrew Craigie and others, for trespasses committed … upon the road" (ibid., 204). Mt. Auburn Street opened for travel in 1809, but in 1812 Craigie's Federalist friends on the court of sessions evened the score by extending Brattle Street from Fayerweather Street to Mt. Auburn, short-cutting the circuitous route through Gerry's Corner and Elmwood Avenue.

So great was the public interest in these matters that in 1821 surveyor John G. Hales published an evaluation of the major highways within 15 miles of the Old State House. There were only trivial differences between the competing Cambridge roads:

TABLE 2.1 DISTANCES FROM THE OLD STATE HOUSE IN BOSTON TO OLD CAMBRIDGE

	Miles	Furlongs	Rods	Total
West Boston Bridge via:				
Main St. and Massachusetts Avenue to Cambridge Meetinghouse	3	3	9	3.40
Harvard Street to Cambridge Meetinghouse	3	2	20	3.31
Broadway to N.W. corner Harvard Yard	3	2	9	3.28
Craigie Bridge via:				
Cambridge Street to N.W. corner Harvard Yard	3	3	23	3.45

Source: John G. Hales. *A Survey of Boston and its Vicinity, Showing the Distances from the Old State House … to All the Towns and Villages Not Exceeding Fifteen Miles Therefrom …* Boston, 1821.

The most preferable of these roads as to bottom is that of Craigie's [Cambridge Street] though the greatest in point of length, yet its other advantages are more than a compensation for the trifling difference in distance. Next to Craigie's the one most used is that through Cambridge Port [Main Street and Massachusetts Avenue], but some part of this road is soft and muddy after rain, and in dry seasons so dusty, as to make the traveling very unpleasant. The Concord Turnpike [Broadway] is sandy and often out of repair. (Hales, *Survey*, 31)

The decrepit state of the 1756 courthouse provided Craigie and his investors another opportunity to promote East Cambridge at the expense of Old Cambridge. The voters of Middlesex County had recently decided to move the court to Concord, which was more centrally located, while the court of sessions preferred to remain in Cambridge. Craigie's Lechmere Point Corporation offered to help the county build a new courthouse and jail in East Cambridge, but the townspeople argued that they had paid a third of the upkeep of the courthouse for more than a century and should have a say in any new location. A Federalist victory at the polls and a $24,000 donation from the Lechmere Point Corporation won over the court of sessions in 1813. When the new courthouse and jail were completed in

1816, James Winthrop, the register of probate for forty-one years, resigned rather than move to East Cambridge. The old building then became the town hall (see chapter 7).

The result of all this activity was a radical shift in the balance of power among the villages. After the Second and Third parishes became West Cambridge (now Arlington) and Brighton in 1807, Old Cambridge was surpassed by the growing settlements in Cambridgeport and East Cambridge. In 1816 Abiel Holmes contrasted "the old town, the inhabitants of which are principally husbandmen, or gentlemen who have retired from business, and live on their income," with Cambridgeport, where "trade and manufactures unitedly flourish."

In 3 years, from 1804 to 1807, more than 120 houses and stores, many of them brick, were constructed in that village. It now contains 195 dwelling houses, … 29 large stores and warehouses, generally 3 stories high, and principally occupied in the sale of West India goods, iron, salt, crockery ware, and all kinds of heavy merchandize, together with beef, pork, butter, cheese etc. There are also about 30 shops and other buildings occupied by various mechanics [and] one druggist and apothecary. Soap and candle manufacturers, leather dressers, cabinet and chair makers, hatters, shoe makers, wheelwrights, blacksmiths, book binders and harness makers; also 2 manufacturers of printers ink, which furnish a large supply to this and the adjacent states, as nearly to exclude importation. There are 3 lumber wharves, which are supplied with timber, boards, shingles, clapboards, lime etc. from the eastward, and furnish the towns, for about 25 miles to the westward, almost entirely, with these articles. … Cambridgeport is very advantageously situated, as a place of trade between the capital and the country, and is already a place of much business and resort. (Holmes, "Description")

For some years, Old Cambridge men like Levi Farwell remained active in Cambridgeport enterprises such as the First Baptist Church and the Cambridge Bank, but the new villages quickly became self-sufficient. Old Cambridge became ever more dependent on the university as a source of distinction and economic opportunity.

FIGURE 2.5 Cordwood on a cart passing Cambridge Common and the Hastings-Holmes house (right), ca. 1850.

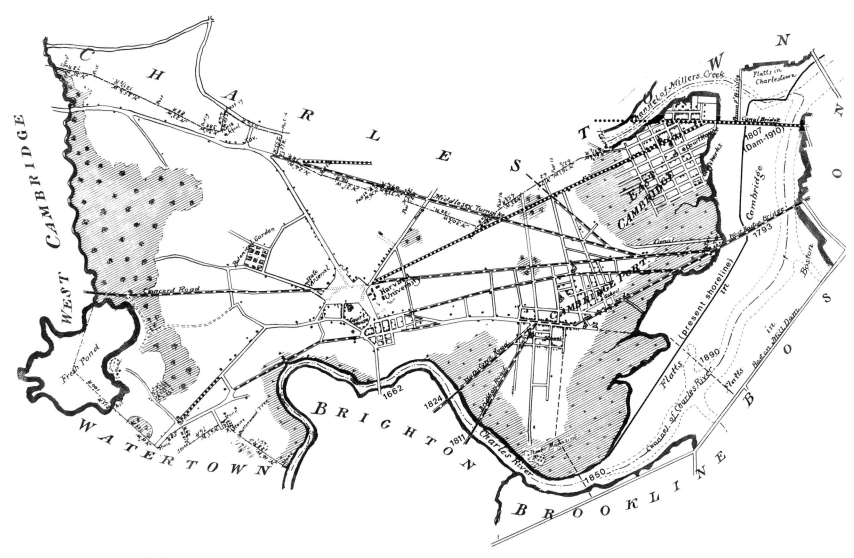

FIGURE 2.6   Cambridge in 1830, showing roads built in conjunction with the West Boston Bridge (dashed lines) and the Craigie Bridge (dotted lines). The arrow-straight turnpikes radiating from Boston were superimposed on a colonial landscape where roads typically wound through the countryside along the gentlest grades. With the exception of Kirkland Street and parts of Massachusetts Avenue and Pleasant Street, all the roads east of the village were constructed after 1793. The modern shoreline and dates of the bridges have been superimposed on the original map.

FIGURE 2.7 Cambridgeport about 1825, looking east toward the intersection of Massachusetts Avenue and Main Street. A tavern, blacksmith shop, watering trough, and hay scale served travelers on the road to Boston. The substantial residence of Nathaniel and Isaac Livermore (1800), the First Universalist Church (1822), and Francis Dana's brick South Row (1806) all faced Lafayette Square.

The Enclosure of Cambridge Common

Cambridge Common achieved its present dimensions in 1724, and the Proprietors of Common Lands deeded it to the town in 1769. For two centuries it had been the scene of public gatherings, military drills, and the boisterous public celebrations that accompanied Harvard commencements. The college as well as nearby householders disliked these riotous occasions and objected to overnight stays by upcountry drovers. In 1823 the town meeting defeated a petition from a group seeking permission to enclose the Common at its own expense, but in 1830 petitioners with strong connections to the college bypassed the town and received approval from the General Court to fence and landscape it as a public park (see chapter 5; figure 2.8).

FIGURE 2.8 Cambridge Common in 1821, with Harvard Yard and the village. This view from Benjamin Waterhouse's residence on Waterhouse Street shows the Harvard Yard fence and elms placed by Stephen Higginson. Christ Church is visible at the extreme right, with the steeple of the Fourth Meetinghouse beyond.

The enclosure infuriated country folk, who had been deprived of their ancient rights to the Common. The proprietors of the Concord Turnpike and the towns of West Cambridge, Lexington, Waltham, and Watertown petitioned the legislature, claiming that the detour forced travelers "to pass said Common, in their travel to and from the city of Boston, by a circuitous route, considerably increasing the distance," and that their rights were "impaired … to gratify the taste for ornament of a few individuals." The Senate, however, observed that:

> it is deeply to be regretted, that a controversy of so trifling a value … [as] the diversion of at most four rods [64 feet] in one case, and fifteen [240 feet] in another, in two roads of no great travel, should frustrate or even hazard the gratification of an ambition so laudable. (Mass. Senate 23, 1832, 11)

The Supreme Judicial Court upheld the enclosure in 1835, and the townspeople "thus secured in perpetuity, for themselves and their descendants, a spacious and pleasant park, rich in historical associations" (Paige, 238).[1]

Meetinghouse and Town Hall

The controversy over the enclosure of the Common reshaped the political geography of the town. In October 1830 a contentious meeting called to discuss the enclosure of the Common overflowed the old courthouse and adjourned to the meetinghouse. After this experience, some members of the parish "expressed a natural unwillingness to have their house of worship used for the transaction of secular business, and especially for the indulgence and expression of angry passions" (ibid., 239). A warrant was placed before the next town meeting, and a committee representing each of the villages reported in March 1831 that a town hall should be erected in Cambridgeport.[2]

Having lost the courts to East Cambridge and the town government to Cambridgeport, Old Cambridge next lost its meetinghouse. For some years the First Parish had been in turmoil. Doctrinal differences and the growth of other denominations had diminished the status of the Congregational church, the descendant of the old Puritan communion that once embodied both religious and secular government. Reverend Abiel Holmes, a strongly orthodox Trinitarian, had served the First Parish since 1792, but after 1800 the more liberal Unitarians were in ascendance. In 1829 the parish separated into two parties. Following the precedent set by the Supreme Judicial Court in a Dedham case in 1820, the legal continuity of the Cambridge church was judged to be with the Unitarian members who remained with the parish, and their deacons retained title to the church silver, the poor funds, and the meetinghouse. The theologically more conservative Trinitarian or Congregational faction, consisting of Reverend Holmes and two-thirds of the members, was held to have withdrawn on principle. The repercussions of this schism were felt in Old Cambridge for generations.

The remaining members of the now Unitarian First Parish decided to give up the old meetinghouse. Although Harvard had established its own church in University Hall in 1814, the university maintained a one-seventh share and held commencements there. President Quincy offered $11,900 to build a new meetinghouse next to the burying ground if the parish would deed the old meetinghouse and parsonage to Harvard. Quincy eulogized the building before razing it in 1833: "In this edifice all the public Commencements and solemn inaugurations, during more than seventy years, were celebrated; and no building in Massachusetts can compare with it in the number of distinguished men, who at different times have assembled within its walls" (Quincy, *History*, 463).

Old Cambridge in the Early Nineteenth Century

The old village seemed dilapidated and dingy, especially in comparison to the booming communities of Cambridgeport and East Cambridge. Yale president Reverend Timothy Dwight observed that "the houses exhibit every gradation of buildings, found in this country, except the log-hut. Several handsome villas, and other handsome houses are seen here, a considerable number of decent ones, and a number, not small, of such as are ordinary and ill-repaired" (*Travels,* I, 479).[3] The residents included many intermarried descendants of the old Puritan families, then being diminished by the Western migration; some ambitious Yankee shopkeepers from upcountry towns; a handful of African Americans; and a few wealthy merchants who anticipated the suburban movement. "College people and those who had come to Cambridge to educate their sons" were "a more distinct gentry" (T.W. Higginson, in Gilman, *1896,* 40).

The Danas were the most prominent family in early 19th century Cambridge. Their roots went back to Edward Goffe, whose farm was northeast of the village, but it was Francis Dana (1743–1811) who founded the dynasty in Cambridge. Dana grew up in Boston; after graduating from Harvard College in 1762, he studied law in Cambridge with his uncle, Judge Edmund Trowbridge. In 1773 he married Elizabeth Ellery, a granddaughter of Judge Jonathan Remington. Dana was a delegate to the Continental Congress from 1776 to 1780 and served as American minister to Russia from 1781 to 1783. John Hancock appointed him to the Supreme Judicial Court of Massachusetts in 1785, and he became chief justice in 1791. Dana was a dominant figure in the development of Cambridgeport and encouraged his children to settle there; daughter Martha settled on Auburn Street in 1830 with her husband, the painter Washington Allston, and sons Edmund and Richard lived nearby on Green Street. Life in the dusty new village had few attractions for an educated man, however, and after Justice Dana died in 1819 Richard retreated with his family to Old Cambridge (figure 2.9).

A new class of self-made merchants and tradesmen, many of whom had arrived during the boom years before the War of 1812, achieved prominence in town and college affairs. Levi Farwell (1784–1844), who came from Fitchburg about 1808 apparently without property or family connections, became the largest retailer in the village by marrying Richard Bordman's widow, Prudence, and taking over his dry-goods store. He was president of the Cambridge Bank, the Charles River Bank, and the Cambridge Mutual Fire Insurance Company, chairman of the

FIGURE 2.9 Chief Justice Francis Dana, ca. 1800.

Cambridge Savings Bank, a founder, deacon, and benefactor of the First Baptist Church in Central Square, a trustee of the Newton Theological Institute, and steward of Harvard College (figures 2.10–2.11). House painter Jacob Hill Bates (1788–1861), from Weymouth, succeeded Farwell as president of the Cambridge Savings Bank, and housewright William Saunders (1787–1861), who came from Quincy in 1801 at age 14 or 15, became a selectman and alderman. All five of Saunders's sons established themselves as merchants in Boston and Cambridge; three served as elected officials, and two built impressive houses on Massachusetts Avenue.

FIGURE 2.10 Deacon Levi Farwell (1784–1844), storekeeper, bank president, and steward of Harvard College.

FIGURE 2.11 Prudence Farwell (1775–1847). Prudence Dockham's first husband was Richard Bordman, a trader and bricklayer. She married Levi Farwell in 1818 and with him was a benefactor of the Newton Theological Institution, a Baptist seminary that became the Andover-Newton Theological School.

College people included faculty members and their families, students, employees, and hangers-on. The prominence of Professors Joseph Story, George Ticknor, and Edward Channing, coupled with Harvard's involvement in enclosing the Common and maintaining public order, brought a sense that the university was superior to the town, in spite of the continuing presence of "ancient resident graduates who had become waterlogged on their life voyage" (Peabody, *Reminiscences,* 211). Townswomen known as *goodies* (a contraction of goodwife, considered "a low term of civility or sport") were employed to take care of the students' rooms (Bartlett, 147). Undergraduates constantly engaged in mischief; many local barns went up in smoke, and the college glaziers and carpenters were fully employed. In the village, barbers and tailors prospered from the student trade, and a few immigrant peddlers became student mascots.

Among the old families that dispersed at this time were several descendants of William Manning, who had settled on South Street in 1638 and sired five generations of watermen and shoemakers. In the sixth generation, Samuel Manning graduated from Harvard College in 1797 and became a physician;

FIGURE 2.12 Thirteen Goodies gathered outside Harvard Hall for a portrait in 1862. Little is known about the lives of these women, who were employed by the college to serve students by making beds, laying fires, and cleaning rooms.

four of his children moved to the booming port of Baltimore about 1822. Many Coopers and Frosts gave up farming for trade or moved west, but some descendants of Nicholas Wyeth, who had started a farm on Garden Street in 1645, found reasons to stay. His great-grandson Jacob Wyeth established the Fresh Pond Hotel in 1796 at what is now Kingsley Park, and it remained a popular summer resort until the 1880s; his son Nathaniel, "one of the most active and energetic men ever born in Cambridge," developed techniques for mechanically harvesting and storing ice (Paige, 705). In 1832 he led an expedition to Oregon with three boat-shaped wagons of his own design, with iron parts

forged by Dexter Pratt, Longfellow's village blacksmith. Wyeth founded trading posts on the Snake and Columbia rivers before returning to the ice business in Cambridge in 1836.

Prosperous Boston merchants such as John Phillips, Nathaniel Ireland, and William Gray found Cambridge a pleasant place to live, especially in the summer. They acquired former Tory estates or created new ones with ample houses like Shady Hill (1806), Fay House (1807), and the Larches (1808), and joined the few loyalist families like the Lees whose properties had escaped confiscation (see chapter 4). The outer reaches of Brattle Street were quite isolated. Schoolmaster William Wells described it in the

1820s: "a mere lane, with neither pavement nor sidewalk, and for the great part of the year a continuous quagmire, with no means of communication with the outside world except by a two-horse stagecoach twice a day" (A. Peabody, *Harvard Graduates,* 64). Sites east of the village were more convenient, and William Winthrop put up a substantial house in 1818 on Arrow Street on the site of Spencer Phips's 18th-century mansion. Josiah Coolidge and George Brimmer in the 1820s and John Palfrey in 1831 acquired large tracts of farmland and created new estates not associated with the Tories (see chapter 4).

About this time the town replaced the descriptive street names of the 17th century with names that recalled historical associations. Crooked Street was straightened in 1800 and renamed for President Holyoke of Harvard. Water Street became Dunster in 1838, and Wood Street became Brighton (then Boylston in 1882, and finally John F. Kennedy Street in 1981). The old order definitively ended on February 19, 1829, when the Proprietors of Common Lands recorded their last meeting in *The Registere Booke of the Lands and Houses in the Newtowne,* which had chronicled their activities since 1634.

The Movement for Separation

Deteriorating relations between the villages in the 1830s culminated in several attempts by Old Cambridge to become a separate town. East Cambridge remained isolated on its salt-marsh island until the end of the century, and Cambridgeport was separated from Old Cambridge by Francis Dana's estate, which his heirs kept off the market until 1835. Socially, the villages were very different from one another. In the 1830s East Cambridge was an industrial community, full of young male English and European glassworkers. In 1820 Cambridgeport's population reached 1,360, exceeding that of Old Cambridge for the first time and replacing it as a place of opportunity for ambitious young farmers and tradesmen from rural New England.

Village rivalries abounded. Newcomers chafed at the reluctance of Old Cambridge voters to allow them schools and services, while Old Cambridge people felt humiliated by the loss of the courts and the town hall. Influential Old Cambridge families reflected the prejudices of Harvard and its constituency, the mercantile elite of Boston. Politically, the community was strongly conservative and Federalist long after the party had faded from the national scene. It then became a Whig stronghold and opposed the nativist democracy of the new villages. Tensions were exacerbated by a series of incidents involving Harvard students, whose arrogance was bitterly resented by the townsmen they called "Port chucks" and "Pointers." In 1833 President Quincy broke up a bloody melee between students (who in this period were often led by quarrelsome Southern aristocrats) and men building the new Unitarian church. More altercations followed.

Matters came to a head in 1842, when Old Cambridge residents petitioned the General Court that "in consequence of the rapid increase in population in those parts of town being nearest to Boston and called Cambridgeport and East Cambridge, the town in fact consists of three distinct and separate communities, which are generally known to the public by those names, and each of which has a Post Office. … The time cannot be far distant, when a division of the town … will be deemed as necessary as it ever has been at any former period of its history" (Paige, 242). The proponents included many of the same men who had sought to enclose the Common in 1830, as well as the Unitarian and Congregational ministers and Professors Joseph Story and Simon Greenleaf of the law school. They wished to divide the town at Lee Street and to retain the name of Cambridge. In January 1844, however, the town meeting resolved that division "would be not only inexpedient, but greatly and permanently prejudicial to the true interests and the legitimate weight and influence of the town" (ibid., 243).

At the next town meeting in March, James D. Green, a flinty East Cambridge minister who had retired to Old Cambridge, urged voters to support candidates who pledged to reform town government and reduce spending. When no satisfactory measures were taken, the following meeting instructed the selectmen to petition the legislature for a city charter. Old Cambridge forces made another attempt at separation, but on March 17, 1846, the town adopted city government by a vote of 645 to 244 and a month later elected Reverend Green its first mayor.[4]

The separatists asked again in 1855 that Old Cambridge be "set off and incorporated into a town by the name of Cambridge, and that the remaining portion of the territory of said city be called Cambridgeport, or such other name as may seem fit" (ibid., 245; see figure 2.19). Lucius Paige, who was town and city clerk throughout this period, pointed out "the extraordinary fact, that the petitioners, like their predecessors of 1844, did not ask to be set off from Cambridge, but to be incorporated as Cambridge,— an unprecedented request" (ibid., 245n). These repeated petitions cemented Old Cambridge's reputation as a self-centered community with little sympathy for its neighbors.

The form of city government established in 1846 served, with some variations, until 1916. There was a popularly elected mayor, a six-member board of aldermen elected at large, and a twenty-member common council elected by wards in proportion to their population: five from Old Cambridge (Ward I), nine from Cambridgeport (Ward II), and six from East Cambridge (Ward III).[5] The aldermen oversaw the police and fire departments, issued licenses, and prepared voting lists, while the common council initiated bylaws and appointed the city clerk and treasurer. The mayor presided over the board of aldermen, the school committee, and the overseers of the poor but had little executive power until a reform measure was adopted in 1892.

SUBURBAN LIFE IN OLD CAMBRIDGE, 1846–90

> Our City, Gentlemen, is advancing with a rapid, and, we trust, a healthy growth. There is no spot more eligible for a dwelling place;—none where greater privileges are to be enjoyed;—none where more is doing or contemplated, to promote the mental and moral improvement, the social well-being, and the domestic and personal comfort of the citizen. We cannot but feel satisfaction and thankfulness at the numerous indications of prosperity, which we see around us; and we should extend encouragement to those en-

terprises, which contemplate a further addition to our comforts, by furnishing to our streets and dwellings a better light, supplying every part of the city with an abundance of pure water, and increasing our facilities of communication with the neighboring metropolis. (Inaugural Address of Mayor James D. Green, Cambridge *Annual Documents,* 1853, xvii–xviii)

By the 1840s it was apparent that Cambridge could not rise above its rural roots without efficient public transportation and a reliable supply of water and illuminating gas. Within a few years local investors built a railroad, a street railway, a water works, and a gas works, while subdividing old farms and estates. Their efforts paid off handsomely, as the *Chronicle* noted:

> At no time since Cambridge was first settled, has there been a time when the evidence of material prosperity was so apparent as now. In every part of the city is heard the sound of the hammer, the trowel, and the spade. Cellars are dug, frames are up, covered and completed as if by magic.—Where but yesterday we saw a vacant lot, today is an occupied house. The houses which are built are mostly of the better sort, many of the first class, built by those who propose to occupy them, and are paid for in cash down; showing that our [prosperity] is real, not bogus; substantial and natural, not forced. (May 15, 1869)

Old Cambridge remained a distinct entity until well after the Civil War, with recognizable limits where the village tapered off to fields or marsh. The western edge of town was the most clearly defined, with little building beyond Ash Street. Observatory Hill was a distant outpost, and North Cambridge was recognized as a separate village when a post office opened in Porter Square in 1853. The northeastern limit was the ancient Pine Swamp, a low, damp region in the neighborhood of Oxford and Jarvis streets. Professors Row on Kirkland Street ended at Charles Eliot Norton's estate, Shady Hill, and the land between Prescott Street and Dana Hill was still only thinly settled. The riverfront was dotted with wharves where schooners unloaded coal, granite, firewood, and lumber. The marshes above and below the village began to develop as Irish workingmen's districts in the late 1850s.

FIGURE 2.13   A suburban scene at Porter's Station in North Cambridge, ca. 1856–69. At left a horsecar passes the Cambridge Railroad's stable on Massachusetts Avenue, while a Fitchburg Railroad train pauses at Porter's Station. The Allen Street Congregational Church (1851, now a row house at 14–20 Allen Street) is in the center of the view. The Pine Island Cottage (right) faced Elm Street in Somerville; the pond in the foreground appears in figure 4.189. Twenty-eight houses on Holyoke Road now occupy the site. The railroad station was moved to the corner of Cedar and Dudley streets in 1888 and raised to two stories; it now comprises the center section of the building at 54–60 Dudley Street.

STAGES AND OMNIBUSES

The paramount factor in Cambridge's development as a suburb was dependable and inexpensive access to Boston. The first stagecoach, said to be "capable of holding eight persons besides the driver," crossed the West Boston Bridge in the spring of 1795 (*Cambridge Chronicle,* June 12, 1852). The original Cambridge terminus was a tavern at the northeast corner of the Common, but in 1797 a stop near the courthouse was deemed more convenient; the fare was 25¢, a large sum for the time.

The stage made two trips a day until 1826, when Ebenezer Kimball, who kept a tavern on Pearl Street, began to run a coach from Cambridgeport to Boston every two hours. He bought the

FIGURE 2.14 A Harvard Street omnibus of the type built by Charles Davenport
passing Dane Hall in 1852. This view of Dane shows a transverse wing designed
by Isaac Melvin in 1844.

Old Cambridge coach in 1828 and expanded the service. Kimball entered the coach-building business in 1832, when he bought a Cambridgeport carriage shop and acquired the services of Charles Davenport, who had apprenticed there. In 1834 Davenport built the first center-aisle passenger car in the United States for the Boston & Worcester Railroad and the first omnibus in New England. Omnibuses were the earliest mass transit vehicles; in contrast to stagecoaches, they had elongated bodies with rear entrances and seats that ran lengthwise, facing each other. Drawn by two or four horses, they could carry twenty or more passengers.[6]

In 1839 Abel Willard, an Old Cambridge tavernkeeper, formed the Cambridge Stage Company and purchased Kimball's line. By this time coaches ran every half hour along the Massachusetts Avenue-Main Street route through Cambridgeport to Boston. Service expanded to Harvard Street and Broadway in 1843. In the same year, Joseph Tarbox, a former driver for Kimball, started the New Line and by 1845 was also running coaches to Boston every half hour. In 1847 omnibuses ran every fifteen minutes from 6:30 a.m. to 7:00 p.m.; the last one left Boston at 10:00 p.m. A single fare was 15¢, but commuters could buy a quarterly pass that reduced the cost to less than 6¢. The fifty-two daily departures from Old Cambridge had a nominal capacity of about 1,000. By 1852 the companies had merged and were operating sixteen omnibuses with 180 horses.

This level of service made Cambridge accessible to Bostonians seeking a suburban environment but at the same time diminished its trade and sense of community. Long-distance highway traffic evaporated when the railroads arrived, and merchants now suffered further. "Daily do [the omnibuses] convey to Boston a large portion of the trade, and much of the property of the town" (*Cambridge Palladium,* Sept. 2, 1843).

> Why is it that our business decreases as our population increases? … Our village affords a delightful retreat from the noise, confusion, and … heat of the city. Our rents are lower; our schools are excellent; our society is generally considered good; and our communication with Boston is cheap and expeditious. These various inducements bring amongst us a large number of individuals, whose business, interests,

> [and] sympathies lie wholly in Boston. Their interests with us are few. … With so little public spirit, so great carelessness in regard to the prosperity of the place, what ground do we have for hope or encouragement in the matter? (Ibid., Aug. 26, 1843)

Steam Railroads

At mid-century, Cambridge lamented that it was the only major Massachusetts town with no railroad service in its two principal villages. There were passenger stations in East Cambridge on the Boston & Lowell; at Park Street (Somerville), Porter's, and West Cambridge (Sherman Street) on the Fitchburg Railroad; Fresh Pond and Mount Auburn on the Watertown branch; and Cottage Farm and Brighton on the Boston & Albany. Progressive citizens were frustrated by the lack of direct service to Cambridgeport or Old Cambridge.

In 1827 a state-funded survey of northern and southern railroad routes across Massachusetts envisioned that both lines would cross Cambridgeport and enter Boston on alignments parallel to the West Boston Bridge. This would have required crossing the Charles River twice, and in 1831 speculators lured the Boston & Worcester Railroad to South Cove instead. The Boston & Lowell Railroad built across the northern edge of East Cambridge in 1835. The Charlestown Branch Railroad surveyed several routes across Cambridge in 1837, including one near Old Cambridge and another through Central Square, in order to connect with the Boston & Worcester in Brighton.[7] In 1841 the company laid a track from East Cambridge through Somerville and around the north side of Avon Hill to carry Fresh Pond ice to the Charlestown wharves for export; when the Fitchburg Railroad built a parallel line in 1843, it precluded the possibility of a mainline railroad through other parts of the city. In 1849 it was observed that "the numerous railroads running from Boston, all of which by some fatality seem to avoid Cambridge, have almost annihilated the extensive trade which was formerly carried on between 'the Port' and the country towns, even as far back as the borders of Vermont and New Hampshire" (*Cambridge Directory,* 5; figure 2.15).

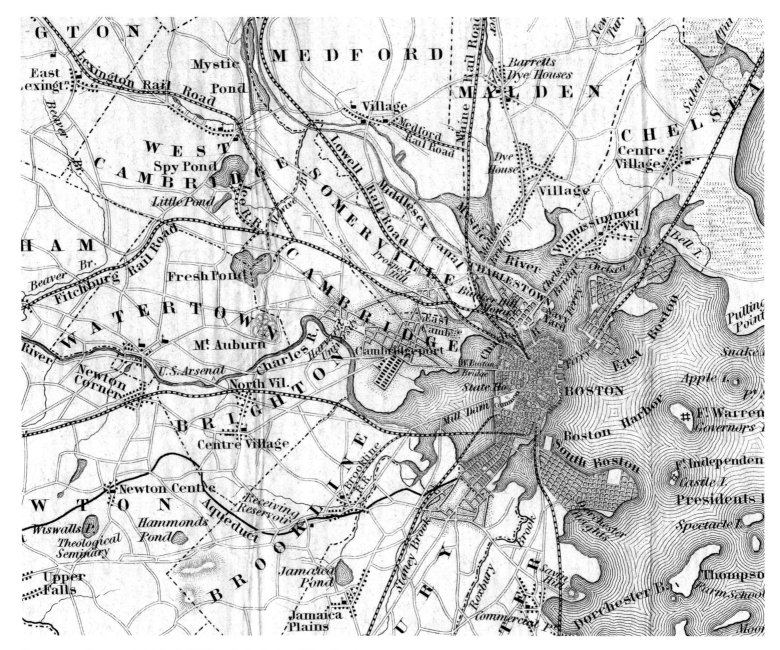

FIGURE 2.15 Boston and vicinity in 1848, at the beginning of the railroad era. The Boston & Lowell, Fitchburg, and Boston & Albany lines surround the city; the Grand Junction and Watertown branch lines have yet to be constructed.

The Charlestown Branch began passenger service between North Cambridge and Charlestown in January 1842 with a coach attached to a train of ice cars; by June the company was running seven round trips a day, stopping at Porter's Station on Massachusetts Avenue. The Fitchburg Railroad absorbed the Charlestown Branch in 1846 and, through connecting roads, soon reached western Massachusetts, Vermont, northern New York, and Canada, bringing long-distance travel and freight service to North Cambridge. North Avenue (Massachusetts Avenue north of the Common) became a prestigious address for Boston commuters, and Porter's became the nucleus of a new suburban village (see chapter 4 and *Report Five: Northwest Cambridge*).

Two newcomers to Old Cambridge actively promoted the public improvements that facilitated suburban growth. Dr. Estes Howe (1814–87) and Gardiner Greene Hubbard (1822–97) founded the Harvard Branch Railroad (1849), the Cambridge Gas-Light Company and the Cambridge Water Works (1852), the Cambridge Railroad (1853), the Union Railway (1855), and the East Cambridge Land Company (1861). Typically, Hubbard was president and Howe was treasurer or clerk of these ventures.

Estes Howe was the son of a distinguished attorney in Worthington, Massachusetts. His widowed mother opened a student boarding house on Dunster Street when Howe entered Harvard at 14; she later operated similar establishments on Appian Way and Garden Street. Howe married and moved to Ohio after graduating from Harvard Medical School in 1835 but returned to Cambridge around 1844. A widower by 1848, he married Lois White, a sister of James Russell Lowell's first wife, Maria. Their daughter, Lois Lilley Howe, was one of the first woman architects to graduate from M.I.T. (see chapter 6).

Gardiner Hubbard, grandson of Boston aristocrat Gardiner Greene, studied law at Harvard and was admitted to the bar in 1843. With a substantial practice in Boston, he began to develop suburban real estate and became a corporate promoter and financier. In 1849 he bought a 45-acre meadow from the Craigie estate, subdivided part of it, and built his own house on the remainder. Showing characteristic optimism, he had his

FIGURE 2.16 Dr. Estes Howe (1814–87).

FIGURE 2.17 Gardiner Greene Hubbard (1822–97).

new house piped for gas in 1850, two years before he founded the gas company. His daughter Mabel, who was deaf, married her teacher, Alexander Graham Bell, in 1877, shortly after Hubbard organized the Bell Telephone Company. Hubbard moved to Washington, D.C., in 1873 but remained active in the development of his estate (see chapter 4).

Frustrated that more distant towns had better access to Boston, Howe and Hubbard petitioned the General Court in 1848 to charter the Harvard Branch Railroad. The *Cambridge Chronicle* endorsed the venture:

> The citizens of Old Cambridge, in the way of communication with the City of Boston, are a quarter of a century "behind the times"; and, comparatively speaking, much further from that Metropolis than towns on Railroad lines at a distance of ten or fifteen miles. … [We] are under most favorable circumstances from 30 to 50 minutes making the passage from [the] University to Boston. … Now the citizens of Watertown, Newton, Waltham, Lexington, Dedham, [and] Lynn … can reach Boston quicker and at half [the] expense per annum. (Feb. 1, 1849)

The charter granted on April 17, 1849, authorized Samuel Batchelder, Oliver Hastings, and William L. Whitney to lay three-quarters of a mile of track from the Fitchburg Railroad near Park Street, Somerville, across Beacon and Oxford streets to a station near the Common. Batchelder, an early cotton manufacturer in Lowell and an associate of Nathan Appleton, had retired to Cambridge and purchased the Henry Vassall house (now 94 Brattle Street) in 1841. Hastings was an upwardly mobile contractor, lumber dealer, and self-trained architect who lived near Batchelder on Brattle Street. Whitney was a Harvard Square businessman and treasurer of the Cambridge Savings Bank.

Construction of the Harvard Branch Railroad began in the summer of 1849. The company built a station on Holmes Place (on the present site of Austin Hall) and began operation on December 31 with six trains daily in each direction pulled by a small locomotive, the "Tudor."[8] In its first year, the line logged 101,000 10¢ fares (or about 160 round trip tickets per day) to the Fitchburg depot on Causeway Street.

FIGURE 2.18 Schedule of Harvard Branch trains between Cambridge and Boston, 1852.

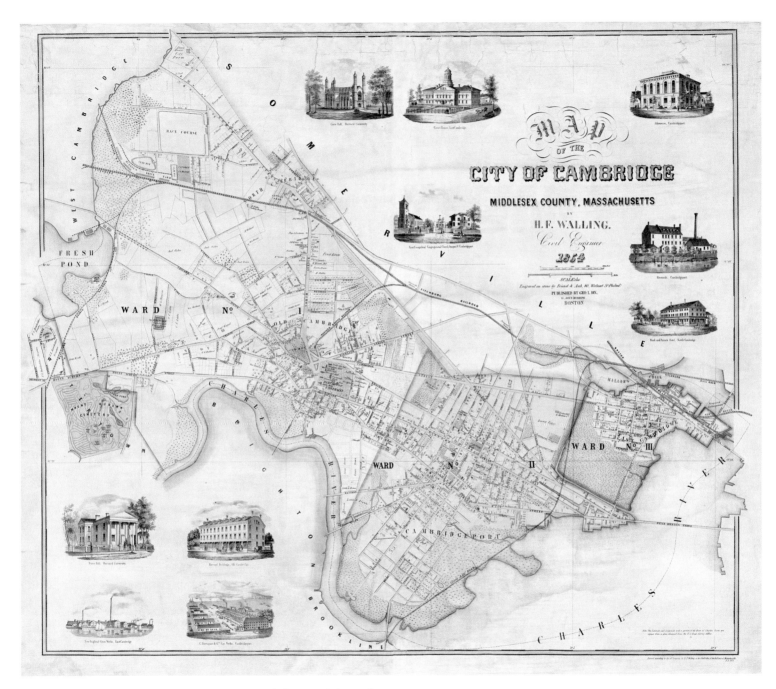

FIGURE 2.19 Cambridge in 1854. A comparison with figure 2.6 shows the extraordinary growth of Cambridgeport since 1830. The division between Ward I—Old Cambridge—and the rest of the city was a line along Dana Street, extended to the river and the Somerville line; this differed from the Lee Street boundary proposed by the secessionists in 1846.

In 1850 the *Chronicle* complained that the new service was too remote and expensive for most of the town. Saddled with a venture that was unprofitable from the start, the directors discussed extending the line to Fresh Pond or building a connection with the Fitchburg's competitor, the Boston & Maine. When the Fitchburg declined a rent-free lease of the line, the Harvard Branch became the first railroad ever abandoned in Massachusetts. In September 1855 John Holmes reported:

> Poor little Harvard Branch was sold up about two months since—Wm. L. Whitney bought it, $10,500, and he has resold it in the most thorough manner—land (most of it), rails, turntable-stones. … I should not omit the station house, which was sold in lengths like tape. (Holmes, *Letters,* 17)

Steam railroad schemes proliferated despite the demise of the Harvard Branch. In 1855 the New York & Boston Air Line Railroad, which had recently acquired a route through Newton and Brookline that is part of today's Riverside line of the MBTA, applied for a charter to bridge the Charles near the Riverside Press and tunnel under Dana Hill to connect with the Fitchburg Railroad in Somerville. As late as 1881, the Fitchburg Railroad was said to be interested in reviving the Harvard Branch and building a tunnel under Cambridge Common, probably in connection with a proposal to relocate the Watertown Branch to run from Mount Auburn station across Old Cambridge in front of Longfellow's house. At about the same time the Boston & Albany projected a branch across the river near Captain's Island, serving Harvard Square with a station on Kennedy Street and paralleling Mt. Auburn Street before rejoining its main line near Newton Corner.

Public Utilities

Gardiner Hubbard and Estes Howe launched the Cambridge Gas-Light Company in March 1852 and the Cambridge Water Works two months later. The promoters offered to install gas lights on Main Street and across the West Boston Bridge if

FIGURE 2.20   The Cambridge Gas-Light Company's gasholder at the foot of Ash Street (1852; demolished 1900). The circular brick structure enclosed an inverted iron tank that rose and fell in a water seal. The enclosure protected the water from freezing, and the weight of the tank pressurized the gas and forced it through the mains. The Cambridge Casino (1882) is at left. The gasholder was razed in 1900 and apartment buildings began to occupy the site in 1914. See also figure 9.6. Photo ca. 1890.

investors responded. The extension of service throughout the city would depend on how much stock was purchased by the residents of each ward. Old Cambridge subscribed heavily, and in July mains were already being laid in Brattle Street.[9]

Illuminating gas was produced by heating coal in a sealed retort. The company secured a site on Windmill Hill next to the Brick Wharf at the foot of Ash Street, where coal could be delivered by water, and erected a retort house and a cylindrical brick gasholder (figure 2.20). Additional gasholders were built in East Cambridge in 1854 and in Cambridgeport in 1856. The Old Cambridge gas works operated until 1873, when the company built a larger facility on the Broad Canal.

The gas company paid an 8 percent dividend as early as 1856, but the water works never made money. In 1853 Cambridge voters agreed to lend the company $50,000, but capital was scarce and construction did not begin until 1855. Nathaniel Wyeth, acting on behalf of the ice companies, unsuccessfully challenged the company's right to take water from Fresh Pond and claimed that fisheries "worth $100,000" would be ruined (Holmes, *Letters,* 17). The water works included a pumping station at Fresh Pond and a granite storage basin on Reservoir Hill, 73 feet above the pond. The company first distributed water in December 1857 but by the end of 1861 had laid only 23 miles of pipe out of the 105 miles required to serve every street. The city acquired the water works in 1865, and in 1868 it doubled the size of the reservoir and added a standpipe to provide additional pressure (figure 2.21).[10]

Initially, the town built sewers where natural drainage was inadequate; parts of the Town Creek ran in the open through Harvard and Brattle squares until it was placed in a continuous drain in 1853. Systematic construction of sanitary sewers began in the 1860s, but most householders relied on privies or cesspools; night-soil men removed the solid waste and sold it to local farmers. A landowner diverted a brook along Willard Street into a covered drain in 1854–57, but houses nearby were not connected to a sewer until 1891–92.

The next major advance was the introduction of electricity in 1887. Cambridge was a laggard in this regard. Arc lights were first installed on Broadway in Manhattan in 1880. By 1885 there were 600 lighting companies across the country, with thirteen in Boston alone. The *Chronicle* complained that other places in Massachusetts—"even the little insignificant city of Newton"—were ahead of Cambridge (Apr. 30, 1887). Some residents could not wait: Walter Briggs had his new house at 878 Massachusetts Avenue wired for electricity in 1882. Finally North Cambridge bank president Chester Kingsley, iron dealer Robert Fuller, and Mayor J. Warren Merrill invested $60,000 to found the Cambridge Electric Light Company in 1886. A small generator in a rented building in Kendall Square served street lights on Main Street, and in 1888 the company built its first permanent power station on the Charles River near the Riverside Press (see figure

FIGURE 2.21 Cambridge Water Works reservoir and standpipe, with 27 Reservoir Street at left. The original basin, emptied for maintenance, is in the foreground. Photo 1896–97.

9.33). In 1887 arc lights appeared in Harvard Square, and forward-looking builders began wiring new houses in anticipation of electric service.[11] Electricity quickly supplanted gas for street lighting, but many new houses were equipped for both, and the gas company promoted advanced methods of lighting as late as 1921. The Cambridge Gas and Electric Light companies were acquired by the New England Gas & Electric Association in 1926–27, but they maintained a local identity until 2000.

STREET RAILWAYS AND SUBURBAN GROWTH

Hubbard organized Cambridge's first street railway company in 1853 while still president of the Harvard Branch. His partners in this venture were Charles C. Little, a principal in Little, Brown & Company, who had extensive interests in local real estate, and Isaac Livermore, a former state representative and senator from Cambridgeport. The Cambridge Railroad was the first street railway in New England and only the third in the United States. The population of Cambridge had increased from 8,409 in 1840 to 15,215 in 1850 (compared to Boston's 136,881) and demand exceeded the capacity of the omnibus system. The Harvard Branch was failing, but rail technology held great promise. Horse-drawn streetcars offered unparalleled comfort and speed to more people at lower cost. Although laborers could not afford to ride, commuting would no longer be the exclusive province of the well-to-do. Street railways were indispensable to the growth of Old Cambridge as a middle-class suburb.

The city granted the Cambridge Railroad a right-of-way in December 1854. The demise of the Harvard Branch and the capital requirements of the utility companies discouraged potential investors, and the line was built by a contractor who agreed to be paid in securities. The capitalization of the company was inadequate to operate it, so Howe and Hubbard formed the Union Railway, which leased the Cambridge Railroad and acquired the horses and omnibuses of the Cambridge Stage Company. As one participant put it: "People who declined to furnish money to build the road were found willing to take stock in a company to equip it. There was something tangible about horses, cars and real estate" (Muzzey, in Palmer, 82).

The horsecars ran from Bowdoin Square in Boston on a double track down Cambridge Street and across the West Boston Bridge, then along Main Street and Massachusetts Avenue to Harvard Square. A single track continued out Brattle Street to Mount Auburn Cemetery; in 1857 a track was also laid on Concord Avenue and Craigie Street. Another line went up Massachusetts Avenue to Porter's Station. Carbarns and stables were built at the corner of Upland Road, on Mt. Auburn Street opposite the cemetery, and on Dunster Street in Harvard Square (see chapter 9). Soon after service began, a report noted that "fifty persons can be drawn in a car, by two horses, with more ease and comfort than can half that number in an omnibus, drawn by four horses" (*Chronicle,* Mar. 29, 1856). John Langdon Sibley wrote in his diary that the horsecars carried 25,000 passengers on July 4, 1859.

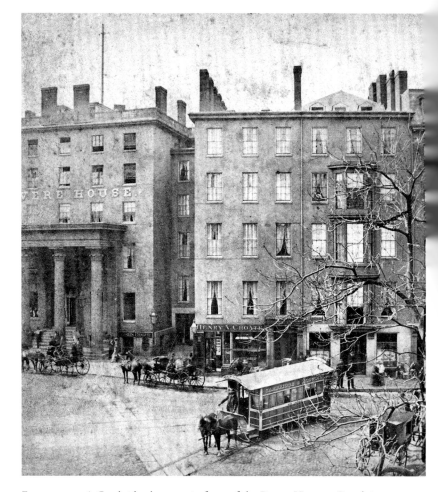

FIGURE 2.22 A Cambridge horsecar in front of the Revere House at Bowdoin Square, Boston, ca. 1865.

The horsecars helped Cambridge's population grow from about 20,500 in 1855 to 47,800 in 1875. New houses rose on the main thoroughfares almost as soon as tracks were laid. Speculators subdivided tracts of land as soon as they acquired them, laid out side streets, and sold the lots at auction. Builders concentrated on lots close to the car lines, leaving stretches of empty

FIGURE 2.23 Harvard Square became a major terminus and transfer point for lines running to the northern and western suburbs. In this 1869 image, a Union Railway car waits to begin its run to Boston via Cambridge Street. Farwell's store is at left center, behind the tree, and Lyceum Hall is on the right, on the site of today's Harvard Cooperative Society.

land between the arteries. Low or swampy areas were occupied later with less expensive houses. Since the main roads were not parallel, the street pattern was irregular. Local streets spread out until they came to some natural obstacle or other landholding; communication between neighborhoods was often roundabout and remains so today.

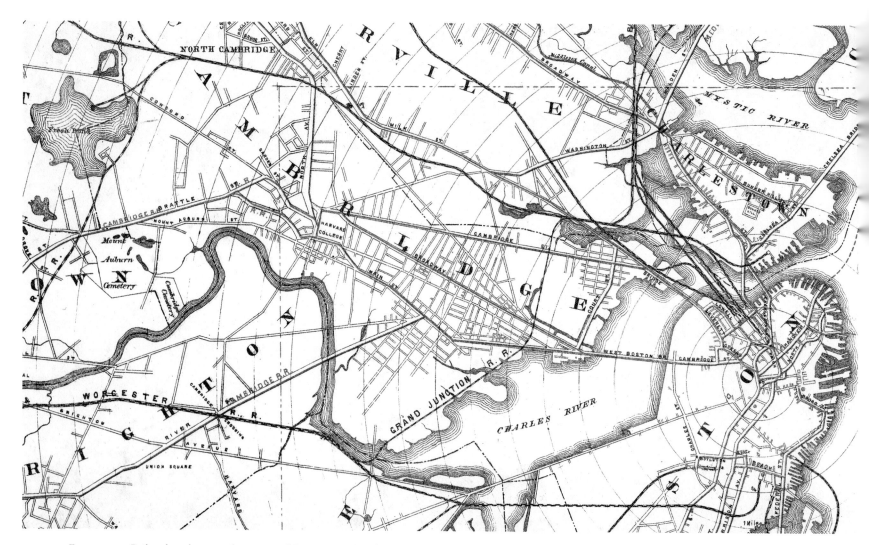

FIGURE 2.24 Railroads and street railways around Boston in 1865. Through the 1870s, horsecar fares were 8¢ from Boston to Cambridgeport, 10¢ to Old Cambridge, and 15¢ to Mount Auburn. Commuting became more affordable when the Cambridge Railroad reduced the basic fare to 5¢ in 1887, although free transfers did not come into general use until about 1903. Steam railroads offered a competitive service until about 1900, when electrification made the street railways faster and cheaper for short distances.

TABLE 2.2 CAMBRIDGE POPULATION, 1765–2010

Year	Household Population*	Group Quarters**	Total Population
1765	1,582		1,582
1790	2,115		2,115
1800	2,453		2,453
1810***	2,323		2,323
1820	3,295		3,295
1830	6,073		6,073
1840	8,409		8,409
1850	15,215		15,215
1860	26,060		26,060
1870	39,634		39,634
1880****	52,860		52,860
1890	70,028		70,028
1900	91,886		91,886
1910	104,836		104,836
1920	109,694		109,694
1930	113,643		113,643
1940	110,879		110,879
1950	107,676	13,064	120,740
1960	95,778	11,938	107,716
1970	88,502	11,859	100,316
1980	82,888	12,434	95,322
1990	81,769	14,033	95,802
2000	86,692	14,663	101,355
2010	88,066	17,162	105,162

*Excludes students, prisoners, and others living in group quarters. Reports before 1950 may not consistently define characteristics of persons enumerated.

**Separately enumerated beginning in 1950. "In accordance with the Census practice dating back to 1790, each person enumerated in the 1950 census was counted as an inhabitant of his usual place of residence. … College students were enumerated in 1950 as residents of the communities in which they were residing while attending college, whereas in 1940, as in most previous censuses, they were generally enumerated at their parental homes" (U.S. Census of Population: 1950).

***West Cambridge (Arlington) and Brighton set off as separate towns in 1807.

****Strawberry Hill and Cambridge Highlands annexed from Belmont in 1880.

Sources: 1765, Benton, *Early Census Making in Massachusetts*; 1790–1860, Handlin, *Boston's Immigrants*, Table II; 1870–1900, U.S. Census, *Statistics of the Population of the United States*; 1910–40, Loring, "The Residential Population of Cambridge" (1957); 1950–2000, Cambridge Community Development Department, "Demographic & Socioeconomic Statistics" (2001); 2010, Cambridge Community Development Department, "City of Cambridge Statistical Profile" (2011)

NOSTALGIA VS. MODERNITY: THE EMERGING IDENTITY OF OLD CAMBRIDGE

Cambridge's prospective character as a suburb of Boston was intensely debated. The *Chronicle* engaged in unashamed boosterism:

Cambridge is out of doors. Bordered north, west and south, by the country—the home of the farmer—the region of rock and hill and running stream, of forest and field—its streets are scented by the fragrance of orchards, and its air stirred with the sounds of rural industry. Green fields, and salubrious air, and fine gardens, and clustering trees, and the notes of wild birds, and groups of little children carelessly at play,—are attractions which the human heart cannot, or ought not, dispense with and be contented. (July 19, 1856)

Guidebooks touted the city's colonial past, while Henry Wadsworth Longfellow and James Russell Lowell extolled Cambridge's idyllic character even as they mourned the passing of its rural scenes. The image of Old Cambridge as a historic place, somehow existing out of time, became popular as early as 1851:

Let the stranger stroll along the old road to Watertown,—the Brattle Street of the moderns. Leaving the venerable Brattle mansion on the left … and passing beyond the more thickly settled part of the village, he will find, on each side of the way, spacious edifices, belonging to some former day and generation; extensive gardens, farms and orchards, evidently of no modern date; and trees, whose giant forms were the growth of years gone by. Who built these stately mansions … with their spacious lawns, shaded by noble elms, and adorned with shrubbery? Who were the proprietors of these elegant seats, which arrest the attention and charm the eye of the passing traveler? Who were the original occupants of these abodes of aristocratic pride and wealth? … A race of men which has passed away forever! (Homans, 92)

After the centennial of 1876, the Tory mansions occupied by Longfellow and Lowell became icons of American history. Their images were widely published, and copies were built in suburbs across the country. Nostalgia was transformed into activism, and

Figure 2.25 The garden of Craigie House, 105 Brattle Street, ca. 1845.

Figure 2.26 Henry Wadsworth Longfellow, Frances Appleton Longfellow, and their sons Charles and Ernest. Photo ca. 1849.

private citizens sought to preserve some of the old landmarks. When Lowell's heirs put his house on the market in 1896, the *Chronicle*, quoting the *Boston Herald*, called it one of the "notable antiquities of Cambridge."

> It belongs to that class of objects which have given Massachusetts a unique hold upon the enthusiasm of the American people. More and more persons are every year coming to Boston to see the antiquities of America, and it is for them quite as much as for Cambridge that these historical localities should be preserved. (Feb. 29, 1896)

Henry Wadsworth Longfellow (1807–82) was appointed to teach modern languages and literature at Harvard in 1836. He rented Washington's former study from Andrew Craigie's widow in 1837, and when he married Fanny Appleton in 1843 his father-in-law bought the Vassall-Craigie house for them (see chapters 4 and 6; figure 2.26). By mid-century Longfellow was an immensely popular figure whose poems about the village

smithy and the gleaming waters of the Charles gave Old Cambridge a romantic aura. Longfellow tried to preserve his house and its setting as Washington had known it. In 1868 he and a few others purchased 70 acres of the Brighton marshes that were in danger of being "filled with the intolerable slaughter-houses which render that town uninhabitable" (Longfellow, *Letters,* V, 311). Two years later, he gave the land to Harvard, to be protected as open space forever. In 1872, during an epizootic that crippled the horsecar companies, he wrote:

This influenza … has thrown Cambridge back to where it was forty years ago. Our City has become once more a remote and quiet village. To me the feeling is delightful. I think of the army of invaders, unable to cross the bridge, and enjoy their discomfiture, and my repose. Alas! It is only a momentary triumph. (Ibid., 609)

Longfellow, despite his international prominence, remained accessible to the Cambridge community. He walked back and forth to Boston, often visited Washington Allston in Cambridgeport, and strolled down to the Riverside Press to read proofs. He attended a function at Isaac Livermore's house near Central Square, a lecture by Emerson on the fugitive slave law at Cambridge City Hall, and "a sumptuous game dinner at Porter's in [North] Cambridge [with] Lowell, Emerson, Holmes, Quincy, Parkman, Dr. Estes Howe" (Paterson II, 351). He entertained constantly; Charles Dickens was one of his more prominent guests. While he disliked the Irish, he was sympathetic to African Americans. He received Josiah Henson, who sought assistance for the Dawn settlement in Ontario, escaped slave and author Lunsford Lane, "and old Mr. [Darby] Vassall (born a slave in this house in 1769)" (Paterson II, 243).

Several prominent writers of Longfellow's generation were born in Cambridge and attended local schools; some wrote extensively about the town. Richard Henry Dana Jr. (1815–82), the author of *Two Years Before the Mast,* returned from his voyage to graduate from Harvard in 1837. He practiced law in Boston and became known for defending the rights of oppressed sailors and fugitive slaves. Dana was the prototype of the aristocratic liberal reformer, which limited his opportunities in politics; his enemies in the legislature called him "the Duke of Cambridge," and despite his early experience as a sailor he was more suited to represent Old Cambridge than Cambridgeport (Perry, *Dana,* 13).

John Holmes (1812–99), brother of famous physician and author Oliver Wendell Holmes, wrote some of the earliest accounts of life in the village. Holmes graduated from Harvard Law School in 1839, but he never practiced and rarely left the village. His more cosmopolitan friends felt that he represented

FIGURE 2.27   Oliver Wendell Holmes, his wife, Amelia, their son Oliver Wendell Holmes Jr. (the future Supreme Court justice), and Oliver Senior's brother, John, on the lawn of the Hastings-Holmes house, ca. 1862. "The Autocrat of the Breakfast Table" made his childhood home famous before it was demolished for Austin Hall in 1883 (see chapter 10). Photo by Oliver Wendell Holmes Jr.

the traditional values of Old Cambridge and published his nostalgic letters in 1904 (figure 2.27).

James Russell Lowell (1819–91), who lived at Elmwood when not serving in diplomatic posts abroad, wrote about the Cambridge he knew as a child:

Boston was not yet a city, and Cambridge was still a country village, with its own habits and traditions, not yet feeling too strongly the force of suburban gravitation. Approaching it from the west by what was then called the New Road [Mt. Auburn Street] … you would pause on the brow of Symonds' Hill to enjoy a view singularly soothing and placid. In front of you lay the town, tufted with elms, lindens, and horse-chestnuts. … Over it rose the noisy belfry of the College, the square, brown tower of the church, and the slim, yellow spire of the meetinghouse. … On your right, the Charles slipped smoothly through green and purple salt-meadows. … Over these marshes, level as water, … the eye was carried to a horizon of softly-rounded hills. To your left hand, upon the Old Road, you saw some half-dozen old houses of the colonial time, all comfortably fronting southward. (Lowell, *Fireside Travels,* 17–19)

CAMBRIDGE IN 1824

Rumford Professor Eben Norton Horsford (1819–93) added another dimension to Cambridge's reputation. Horsford developed a passion for the Norse sagas that were first published in translation in America in the 1870s and became obsessed by the idea that Leif Erikson had founded Vinland on the Charles River in 1000 B.C.E. He placed a plaque at an old foundation at Gerry's Landing that he thought represented a Norse settlement and built a stone tower upstream to commemorate the legendary city of Norumbega. Horsford's theories excited the popular imagination but did not impress the scientific community.[12]

Thomas Wentworth Higginson (1823–1911), the tenth child of Stephen Higginson, the steward of the college, grew up on Kirkland Street and graduated from Harvard in 1841. He became a radical abolitionist and commanded a regiment of black troops in the Civil War. Higginson built a house in 1880 on fashionably suburban Buckingham Street (see figure 6.120). In later life he was well known as a writer, publishing more than 500 essays, articles, and poems, including his popular reminiscence, *Old Cambridge* (1899). Today he is best remembered as a mentor to Emily Dickinson, who never left Amherst to meet him.

Lucius Paige (1802–96) provided a dry counterpoint to the gauzy prose so popular at the time. He based his encyclopedic 1877 *History of Cambridge* on the records to which he had access when he served as town and city clerk between 1839 and 1855. He noted "the almost entire absence of legendary lore" in his book; having come to Cambridge as an adult, "I had no opportunity in the first thirty years of my life to gather the local

FIGURE 2.28 The view from Symonds's Hill, 1824. Ten years later, the drumlin disappeared. "It was bought as speculation, the trees cut down, the hill leveled, great gashes made in the slopes, and now what might have always been a delight to the eye is a level piece of gravel, with scarcely a piece of vegetation. The gravel … was sold for more than the land cost, and the owners have been complimented on their prudence and sagacity" (Scudder, "St. George's Company"). Mount Auburn Hospital now occupies the site.

traditions, which so deeply impress the youthful mind, and which tinge the facts of history with such a brilliant, though often deceptive light" (vi). Reverend Paige received an honorary degree from Harvard in 1850.

Newcomers William Dean Howells (1837–1920) and Henry James (1843–1916) described Cambridge without sentimentality. A native of Ohio, Howells and his wife, Elinor Mead, settled at 41 Sacramento Street in 1866 when he became assistant editor of *The Atlantic Monthly* (figure 2.29; see also figure 4.207). He disguised Cambridge as "Charlesbridge" and Sacramento as "Benicia Street":

> The neighborhood was in all things a frontier between city and country. The horse-cars … went by the head of our street … while two minutes walk would take us into a wood so wild and thick that no roof was visible through the trees. We learned … to know the voices of the cows pastured in the vacant lots, and … to distinguish the different whistles of the locomotives passing on the neighboring railroad. All around us carpenters were at work building new houses. (*Suburban Sketches*, 12–14)

To Howells, Old Cambridge had "a charm quite independent of beauty." There was "less intellectual vulgarity … than anyplace else in the world. And yet it's a hard place to live in, expensive, inconvenient, and at times quite desolate" (Howells to Henry James, June 26, 1869, in Anesko, 65).

Henry James viewed Cambridge from a more cosmopolitan perspective. Having grown up in Manhattan and in Europe, his first exposure to Cambridge was in 1862–63, when he roomed with his brother William in an old house on Winthrop Square and briefly attended Harvard Law School. The *North American Review* published his first short story in 1864, and about this time he joined Howells in the literary circle of Charles Eliot Norton. Although brother William had a distinguished career at Harvard, Henry was never more than a visitor in Cambridge; he was already 23 when his parents settled on Quincy Street in 1866 and lived there for only six years (see figure 4.250). In *The Bostonians* (1885), James characterized suburban Cambridge as a

FIGURE 2.29 William Dean Howells and Elinor Mead Howells in Paris, 1862.

dreary place of "little wooden houses … [that] looked as if they had been constructed by the nearest carpenter and his boy." He described a suburban thoroughfare, probably North Avenue (see figure 4.171):

> fringed on either side with fresh villas, offering themselves trustfully to the public, [with] the distinction of a wide pavement of neat red brick. The new paint on the square detached houses shone afar off in the transparent air; they had, on top, little cupolas and belvederes, in front a pillared piazza, made bare by the indoor life of winter, on either side a bow window or two, and everywhere an embellishment of scallops, brackets, cornices, wooden flourishes. They stood, for the most part, on small eminences, lifted above the impertinence of hedge or paling, well up before the world. (218)

Before Howells, there was little in literature about the enormous social changes brought by immigration from Ireland. Earlier in the century, the population of Massachusetts had been almost entirely native-born and Protestant; the few immigrants, typically from Great Britain, Canada, or Germany, tended to be skilled craftsmen and mechanics. Between 1835 and 1840, when crop failures began to displace thousands of rural Catholics, only 443 people arrived in Boston from Ireland, but the next five years brought 10,157. Many settled in the North End and Fort Hill in Boston, displacing the inhabitants to Roxbury, Dorchester, and Cambridge, but others sought opportunities further afield. In 1843 the *Cambridge Palladium* reported: "we have noticed during the past week, a large number of wagons loaded with furniture, women, children, etc., to pass our window, journeying we know not whither. They appeared to be mostly emigrants from Ireland. We fear they will wish themselves in their own 'swate countrie' again ere long" (May 27).

FIGURE 2.30 The Harvard Observatory (1845) and St. Peter's Church (1848) bracket the Concord Turnpike where it crosses the Fresh Pond moraine, as seen in 1851. St. Peter's was the second Roman Catholic house of worship in Cambridge and a beacon for Irish immigrants.

Between 1846 and 1855, 129,387 people arrived in Massachusetts directly from Ireland, and many more came by way of Canada. By 1855 almost 30% of the inhabitants of Boston were Irish-born, as were 22% in Cambridge (26% in Old Cambridge). The removal of tolls on the Charles River bridges in 1858 opened more opportunities for working people to live outside Boston, and between 1855 and 1865 the number of Irish in Cambridge increased by over 20%. Of all the outlying towns, only Roxbury had a larger Irish community. Cambridge experienced no significant immigration from other European countries until well after the Civil War; the 1865 census counted 5,588 Irish, but only 347 Germans, 73 French, and 3 Italians.[13]

Some of the less fortunate Irish squatted on waste ground on the margins of settled areas. In 1851 a traveler noted the "innumerable cabins, of mushroom growth, the unmistakable lurking places of the Irish" in the marshes near Kendall Square (Homans, 28). The first permanent Irish settlement in Old Cambridge was near the top of Observatory Hill, where St. Peter's Church was founded in 1848 to serve laborers in the nearby brickyards. Irish families populated new neighborhoods near the village known as the Upper Marsh (between Foster and Mt. Auburn streets) and the Lower Marsh (between Holyoke and Banks streets, later Kerry Corner). The residents of these areas were primarily laborers, carpenters, and tradesmen, but by the 1880s some had better jobs at the Riverside and University presses. In 1875, 27% of the population of Old Cambridge was foreign born, only slightly less than the city's total of 31%.

Howells vividly described the impact of the Irish. On a walk from his home to Dublin, the brickyard settlement on Sherman Street, he saw "more than one token of the encroachment of the Celtic army, which had here and there invested a Yankee house with besieging shanties on every side. … Where the Celt sets his foot, there the Yankee … rarely, if ever, returns. The place remains to the intruder and his heirs forever" (*Suburban Sketches*, 71). Ironically, he found Dublin "as fearful of the encroachment of the French, as we, in our turn, dread the advance of the Irish."

We must make a jest of our own alarms, and even smile—since we cannot help ourselves—at the spiritual desolation occasioned by the settlement of an Irish family in one of our suburban neighborhoods. The householders view with fear and jealousy the erection of any dwelling of less than a stated cost, as portending a possible advent of Irish; and when the calamitous race actually appears, a mortal pang strikes to the bottom of every pocket. … None but the Irish will build near the Irish; and the infection of fear spreads to the elder Yankee homes about, and the owners prepare to abandon them. (Ibid., 70–71)

William and Elinor themselves moved to Concord Avenue after a large Irish family arrived on their block in 1870 (see figure 4.123).

The African American community of Cambridge was quite small. A 1755 census found 56 slaves over the age of 16. There were 90 blacks (both slave and free) in 1765, but with the departure of slave-holding loyalists they declined to only 25 in 1800.[14] Their number stood at 77 in 1840, 141 in 1850, and 278 in 1855, but blacks barely exceeded 1% of the total population in this period. Boston had much larger numbers—1,174 (4.6%) in 1800 and 2,284 (1.7%) in 1860—but an 1848 decision upholding segregation in its public schools caused some families to leave the back slope of Beacon Hill for Cambridge, where schools were never segregated. By 1860 the black population of Cambridge rose to 354, perhaps because of an influx of escaped slaves, and a small community began to coalesce in the Port. The citywide population grew to 848 in 1870 and 1,504 in 1880, with most African Americans living east of Windsor Street.[15]

Many of the thirty-seven African Americans in Old Cambridge in 1860 lived in Lewisville on Garden Street in the Lower Common (see chapter 4). The residents were members of the extended family of Peter and Minor Walker Lewis, of Cambridge and Barre, Massachusetts.[16] Several of their children were active in the broader African American community. Adam relocated to the colony of escaped slaves founded by Joshua Henson at Dawn, Ontario. Simpson and Walker held prominent positions in the African Humane Society, the Massachusetts General

FIGURE 2.31 Workmen at George O. Rollins's blacksmith shop, 23–25 Church Street, ca. 1875.

Colored Association, the Boston Vigilance Committee, the African Baptist Church, and the First Methodist Episcopal Zion Church. Enoch, the eldest, with "some of the most respectable colored persons among us" founded the Cambridge Liberian Emigrant Association in 1858 (*Chronicle,* July 10).[17]

Encouraged by Dana and the Massachusetts Colonization Society, fifty-one emigrants sailed from Baltimore for Liberia in November 1858. Of the twenty-three from Cambridge, fourteen were descendants of Peter Lewis. Dr. Daniel Laing, who had been one of the first blacks admitted to the Harvard Medical School, reported on the settlement in Clay-Ashland on the St. Paul's River. In 1859 he wrote: "We have a company of emigrants from Cambridge who have taken quarters back of us in the little cottage receptacle brought out by Mr. Cowan" ("From Liberia," *The African Repository,* June 1859). Two months after this promising start, Laing reported the deaths of Enoch and his wife, Azubah, "from dysentery brought on by imprudence. … He was an enterprising and intelligent man, and would, had he lived, be one of our most valuable citizens" (ibid., Nov. 1859).

FIGURE 2.32 African American waiters outside Memorial Hall, 1875. The waiters formed a distinct community of single men, some of whom lived upstairs in the former Harvard Branch Railroad station. They had a sometimes contentious relationship with the students and occasionally went on strike for better working conditions; President Lowell replaced them with white waitresses in 1924.

The number of blacks in Old Cambridge rose to eighty-six in 1870 and continued to increase as Harvard employed many African Americans waiters in Memorial Hall (figure 2.32); others worked mainly in menial positions. A few rose to positions of responsibility and respect, including Enoch Lewis, who retired as Superintendent of Rooms, Francis Cleary, a preparator in the Chemistry Department, and George Washington Lewis, steward of the Porcellian Club (figure 2.33). Toward the end of the 19th century a community began to develop in Riverside, but there were no black churches or other institutions in this area until Barbadian immigrants began to arrive before World War I.

After the Civil War, Cambridge developed a significant industrial sector that attracted many immigrants. Old Cambridge, however, lacked the rail transportation, cheap land, and proximity to Boston that drew manufacturers to East Cambridge and Cambridgeport. The most significant industries in the village were printing, publishing, and bookbinding (see chapter 9). Apart from the university and the horsecar companies, only building tradesmen and a few carriage builders, stables, and blacksmith shops on Church and Palmer streets offered much working-class employment, although women easily found places as servants.

Immigration had important ramifications for Cambridge's political life. Beginning in the 1840s, the temperance movement seemed to grow in proportion to the swelling population of foreigners. Clergymen preached self-restraint because of the social costs of over-indulgence, but after the Civil War temperance became a secular method of controlling the public behavior of workingmen and immigrants. In the 1880s prohibitionists allied

FIGURE 2.33 George Washington Lewis (1848–1929), steward of the Porcellian Club for forty-five years, shown here with Nancy Lewis in front of their house at 47 Parker Street. Lewis's funeral at Christ Church was attended by some of Harvard's most illustrious graduates.

FIGURE 2.34 Motormen and conductors at the Boylston Street car house, ca. 1892. In the center is Harry Havelock Hanson (1867–1952), a Nova Scotia native who first worked as a conductor for the West End Street Railway in 1889 and rose to become district superintendent for the Boston Elevated Railway in Cambridge; in 1919 he became superintendent of the Middlesex & Boston Street Railway.

with Old Cambridge-based nonpartisan reformers in their concern with the influence of immigrants—predominantly Irish—on morals and politics.

Most of the eighty-five liquor dealers and saloons in the city in the mid-1880s were in East Cambridge, but one Old Cambridge establishment was considered a particular threat to the social order. Charles Eliot Norton, who had been sympathetic to workingmen in his youth, was outraged by the opening of Dewire's Tavern at 98 Kirkland Street, conveniently adjacent to the dry community of Somerville but gallingly close to his house. With Norton's enthusiastic support, groups such as the Home Protection League agitated to end the sale of alcoholic beverages. Their efforts culminated in the passage of a "No-License" referendum in 1886, and Cambridge remained dry until the repeal of Prohibition in 1933.

FIGURE 2.35 Housemaids at the home of Professor Epes Sargent Dixwell, 58 Garden Street, ca. 1885. In 1880 the census taker enumerated three servants at the Dixwells: Julia Sullivan, 30; Sarah Cohen, 28; and Ellen Stockwell, 21. Sullivan and Cohen were Irish; Stockwell was from St. Lawrence County, New York.

METROPOLITAN CAMBRIDGE, 1890–1940

In 1890, 70,000 people lived in Cambridge. Since 1840 the population had doubled about every sixteen years, an increase spurred as much by industrial expansion as by suburban development. In 1894, shortly after the opening of the Harvard Bridge, Massachusetts Avenue was created by renaming West Chester Park in Boston, Front Street, parts of Main and Harvard streets and North Avenue in Cambridge, and the latter's continuation in Arlington and Lexington. Electrification of the horsecar lines beginning in 1889 and completion of the subway in 1912 tied Cambridge closely to nearby cities and towns. Fast trains linked Boston with New York, making weekend visits—even day trips— possible. Home delivery of mail, instituted in 1866, occurred three times daily—four times for businesses. The telephone became usual in middle-income households, and long-distance service was increasingly available.[18] Even as Old Cambridge was entering the metropolitan era, some old ways persisted:

> It is no uncommon sight to see a drove of cows passing through the streets of a morning or afternoon. They can be seen not only on [Massachusetts] avenue, but in such a highly select section as Sparks street, where a large herd was being driven at a quick gait on Thursday afternoon. Many are the property of the drovers who purchase at the Brighton yards and want to get the cows home by the shortest route. (*Chronicle,* Oct. 9, 1897)

These decades brought several determined attempts to annex Cambridge to Boston. As the *New York Times* put it in 1892, twenty years of unbridled expansion had left Cambridge "more and more entangled in financial embarrassments. Property is exorbitantly assessed, and the extremely high tax rate is a grievous burden" (Mar. 27). The city faced a steep assessment for the metropolitan sewer and was under pressure to construct parks and expand its water supply. About this time a bill was introduced in the legislature calling for the consolidation of all municipalities within eleven miles of Boston City Hall. Cambridge was determined not to follow the formerly separate municipalities of Brighton, Charlestown, Dorchester, and Roxbury into union with Boston but found itself "in much the position of a poor but proud maiden whose guardians are agitating a matrimonial alliance toward which her independent spirit rebels, yet to which her judgment and sense of policy incline" (ibid.). One real estate man thought that "the value of real estate here would triple" if annexation were accomplished (*Cambridge Tribune*, Sept. 24, 1892). State senator John Read, an Appleton Street resident, helped defeat the measure, and in January 1893 a newly empowered mayor, William A. Bancroft, took office under a revised charter and moved ahead with a broad program of municipal improvements. The appeal of annexation gradually faded, but the city still guards its independent water supply and entrusts only its sewage to the regional water authority.[19]

Transportation enhancements made Old Cambridge a more attractive location for suburban homes. Electrification speeded travel, and in 1894 a new line on Huron Avenue created the streetcar suburb of West Cambridge. After World War I the last subdivisions in Old Cambridge—Coolidge Hill, Shady Hill, and Gray Gardens—were the first to accommodate the automobile (see chapter 4). Mandatory residence in college dormitories reduced the number of families moving to Old Cambridge while their sons attended Harvard, but apartment houses attracted office workers and young professional families. Descendants of Irish immigrants filled two-family houses and three-deckers along the car lines. The city responded by expanding its water supply to Stony Brook in Waltham in 1887, joining the Metropolitan Sewer District in 1889, creating the Cambridge Park Commission in 1892, and accepting the Boston Elevated Railway's plans for a subway in 1909.

The physical fabric of modern Cambridge was essentially complete by 1925. Streets had been widened, paved, and lighted, curbs and sidewalks installed, water and sewer lines extended to every neighborhood, the subway opened, and the park system completed. By 1916 almost every house was connected to a sewer, and only a handful still relied on private wells. Much of this work was accomplished during a long period of

nonpartisanship that ended in 1902 with the inauguration of the city's first Irish-American mayor, John H.H. McNamee (see figure 2.54). The goals of city government then shifted to providing services such as education, playgrounds, and health care that were desperately needed in working-class neighborhoods.

Harvard University was still Old Cambridge's primary economic engine, and Charles W. Eliot (1834–1926), a lifelong resident, was the city's most important public figure (figure 2.36). Eliot, who served as president from 1869 until 1909, was an indefatigable participant in public affairs. He had represented Old Cambridge on the common council in 1866 and frequently testified before the board of aldermen. He served as president of the Cambridge Club, helped found the Prospect Union (an adult education agency in Central Square), and encouraged faculty to run for local office. Eliot was sensitive to local concerns and directed Harvard's growth away from the village. A notable egalitarian, Eliot was a highly visible spokesman for equal access to higher education.

Figure 2.36 Charles W. Eliot (1834–1926), Harvard's longest-serving president, took office in 1869, when he was 35, and served until 1909. At the time of this portrait Eliot was about 40. He had a prominent port-wine birthmark and was always photographed from his left side.

A. Lawrence Lowell, who became president in 1909, directed a massive expansion of the university along the river (see chapter 10). By the 1920s, however, Harvard was no longer the center of Cambridge's universe. Historian Orra Stone characterized the city as "an industrial boom town [like] Akron, Ohio or Detroit, Michigan," while the *Crimson* observed that the university had been "swallowed up in a city extraordinarily occupied with industry" in which "the boosters are in control. ... The calm that surrounded the nineteenth century giants of Cambridge is gone, and the student of the present must piece out an education as best he can amid the clang of streetcars and the whirr of machines" (Stone, 773; *Crimson,* Mar. 9, 1928).

THE DEVELOPMENT COMMUNITY: SURVEYORS, BUILDERS, ARCHITECTS, AND INVESTORS

A growing 19th-century city like Cambridge depended on a constantly evolving cast of surveyors, land owners, attorneys, and real estate agents, some of whom became property developers; builders, carpenters, and housewrights, some of whom proclaimed themselves architects; academically trained architects, some of whom became developers and property managers; and building-material suppliers, some of whom offered design advice and prefabricated kits for new homes. Nor was community building limited to those fields; merchants, attorneys, shopkeepers, tradesmen, widows, boardinghouse keepers, and ordinary homeowners all invested in property development, which was one of the best avenues for capital formation during boom times.

The orderly growth of Cambridge would have been impossible without generations of surveyors and civil engineers who had to learn the suitability of the land to sustain development. At first, the wilderness had to be carved up into manageable tracts of common land, which were parceled out in field divisions. Much later, the fields had to be separated into parcels that could be efficiently subdivided into building lots. In the 19th century a successful developer needed to balance the qualities

and value of the land against the demands of the marketplace and necessarily relied on a surveyor to realize his vision. After 1866 the city engineer, a public employee, influenced development decisions by establishing street grades, designing drains and sewers, advising the city council on street acceptances, and clearing away encroachments on public rights of way. There was no central planning until the park commission and the city engineer began to exercise that function in the 1890s.

Ensign David Fiske (ca. 1623–1710/11), a wheelwright who arrived from Watertown in 1646, was Cambridge's earliest designated surveyor. Surveying was not a full-time occupation until well into the 19th century. Osgood Carleton (1741–1816), the Boston polymath, conducted many local surveys, the earliest being a plan of land needed for the causeway to the West Boston Bridge. Peter Tufts Jr. (1774–1825), keeper of the powder magazine at Somerville, took over the Cambridge powder house in 1818 and prepared the first detailed plans of Old Cambridge in 1813 and Cambridgeport in 1824. Alexander Wadsworth (1806–98), one of the earliest professional surveyors, prepared the first plans of Mount Auburn Cemetery (1831) and Old Cambridge (1833), as well as subdivision plans for the Craigie and Fayerweather estates. After 1789 Harvard undergraduates produced mathematical theses that often demonstrated their knowledge of surveying. Professor James Hayward (1786–1866) of the class of 1819 was one of the first to put his skills to practical use, making a survey of the town's roads in 1838 and laying out Oxford, Wendell, and Mellen streets in 1847 (see chapter 4).

Cambridge's preeminent surveyor for much of the 19th century was William A. Mason (1815–82). Born in Cambridgeport, he trained in Hayward's office before setting up an independent practice in 1839. After his death, the firm continued as William A. Mason & Son until after World War II. Accumulating a vast library of notes and plans by other surveyors, the firm worked in many surrounding towns, reestablishing old boundaries and making new ones, preparing subdivision plans, writing specifications for streets and utilities, and laying out foundations for new buildings. Both William and his son Charles developed land on

FIGURE 2.37 William A. Mason's advertisement depicts a survey team near the foot of Avon Hill, with the Somerville High School on Central Hill at left, Memorial Hall's tower in the middle distance, and the factory chimneys of East Cambridge a comfortable distance away.

their own account, including Bellevue Avenue behind the family home on Avon Hill.

Cambridge appointed a city engineer in 1866 to bring order to the chaotic process of urbanization. The engineering staff was responsible for the design and construction of the city's reservoirs, pumping station, and distribution system; when Fresh Pond proved inadequate, city staff planned the Stony Brook reservoir and aqueduct in Weston and Waltham. The city engineer monitored rainfall for decades so that sewers would be correctly sized and analyzed runoff and topography so they would drain properly; several low-lying city blocks were raised a number of feet to ensure drainage. The staff recorded the metes and bounds of every property in the city and surveyed hundreds of buildings annually to keep the assessors informed of new construction. They evaluated private streets for acceptance as public ways, planned the extension of Huron Avenue, coordinated

projects with the Cambridge Park Commission and the Boston Elevated Railway, and designed many bridges. Lewis M. Hastings (1853–1936), the greatest of the city's engineers, joined the department in 1871 and was appointed to the top position in 1889. He served for sixty-one years, during which the population of Cambridge nearly tripled. After his retirement in 1932 the city's infrastructure was not materially improved until the late 20th century.

The boom in residential construction produced a vigorous community of housewrights, architects, property developers, promoters, and civic boosters. Most of these men were immigrants or migrants from elsewhere in New England. The high end of the market operated in a still-familiar way: a well-to-do family would buy a lot in a well-drained area on the sunny side of a main street, hire an architect, find a builder, and erect its dream home. At the middle of the market, housewrights bought small parcels, subdivided them if possible, and built one or two houses at a time on speculation, often living in them until they could be sold. These vernacular buildings were often side-hall-plan homes executed with Italianate, Second Empire, or Queen Anne details in the style of the day. At the low end, workers' cottages were often built by the occupants using salvaged materials, their typical high basements reflecting the poor drainage qualities of inexpensive land. Houses were often relocated when their sites were needed for other purposes; the city issued as many as seventy permits for moving buildings each year in the early1890s.[20] At all income levels, wood was the material of choice; as the *Tribune* noted:

> For a city that produces so many millions of brick every year, it is surprising that Cambridge has so few brick houses. … Wood is equally the material of the man who builds a cottage on the humblest street in the city, or a twenty thousand dollar mansion on North Avenue or Brattle Street. (Aug. 6, 1887)

After the Civil War some Cambridge housewrights became known for the quality of their vernacular designs and began to advertise as architects. This trend was reinforced in 1886 when the city began requiring that plans be filed with applications for building permits. James Fogerty (1830–89) was among the most prolific of these men. He was born in Nova Scotia and rose to become a foreman under Cambridgeport housewright James Sparrow. In 1872 he began to practice as an architect; in the course of his career he designed eight public schools, several fire stations, and more than one hundred houses. George Fogerty (1860–1905) entered his father's office as a 13-year-old and is credited with designing more than 160 buildings in Cambridge, including the first Peabody School (1888) and Claverly Hall (1892).

Other tradesmen followed a similar path. Charles H. McClare (1861–ca. 1940), another Nova Scotian, arrived in Cambridge in 1881 and worked as a box maker and carpenter before advertising as an architect in 1888. McClare was also highly prolific, with 157 buildings to his credit, mostly residences but also many

FIGURE 2.38 Cambridge directories listed dozens of carpenters and tradesmen in 1889. Frederick Furbish was a well-known builder in Old Cambridge between 1885 and 1918; both he and William Holt had their workshops in the tradesmen's quarter on Church and Palmer streets. "Architect, Contractor, and Builder" Albert Hopkins is credited with about thirty vernacular houses in a variety of styles, most within a few blocks of his home on Pearl Street.

apartment buildings, schools, and churches. The nature of his training is unknown, but he worked primarily in the Queen Anne style. Most men who made the transition to architect at this time learned the profession from an established practitioner; opportunities for formal training were scarce until Cambridge architects H. Langford Warren and Clarence Blackall founded the Boston Architectural Club in 1889, which offered evening courses to the members' draftsmen.

Cambridge men (and one notable woman) began to seek academic training in architecture in the 1890s. While most maintained offices in Boston, much of their work was in Cambridge. Lois Lilley Howe (1864–1964), the daughter of Estes Howe, the utility investor, was one of the first women to attend M.I.T.'s School of Architecture in 1888–90. Establishing her practice in 1894, she and her firm executed forty-six residential commissions in Old Cambridge by 1929. Edward T.P. Graham (1872–1964), whose father was a stonemason, grew up in East Cambridge and graduated from Harvard's Lawrence Scientific School in 1900. After short stints with Willard Brown and Shepley, Rutan & Coolidge and a two-year fellowship in Europe, he became well known as an architect of hospitals and churches, including St. Paul's on Arrow Street. Graham's contemporary Charles Greco (1874–1963) was a barber's son who took four years of drafting during high school. He worked briefly at Peabody & Stearns and set up his own practice after winning a competition for a new firehouse in Lafayette Square in 1893.[21] Greco executed seventy-two commissions in Cambridge between 1893 and 1939 and developed a broad institutional practice involving schools, courthouses, and churches, as well as many houses in West Cambridge. Greco's testimony about kickbacks helped send Mayor John Lyons to jail in 1942.

Albert Blevins (1874–1946) was an academically trained architect who took a different direction. He grew up on Putnam Avenue, the son of a slate roofer, graduated from Harvard in 1898, and worked for Nathaniel Bowditch before partnering with Lewis C. Newhall (1869–1925), a Malden native who graduated from M.I.T. in 1891. Newhall & Blevins designed several important commercial buildings but specialized in apartment houses in which the firm also invested. When the partnership dissolved in 1917 Blevins left architecture to manage the buildings he had helped design.

Langdon Street resident Hamilton Harlow (1889–1964) graduated from M.I.T. with a degree in architecture in 1914 and opened a Cambridge development office with his father, Boston lawyer Frank S. Harlow, in 1921. Harlow designed twenty-three large brick apartment buildings in Old Cambridge between 1914 and 1931, and while few are distinctive architecturally, the "Harlow building" became a recognized type. In the 1960s Harlow Properties managed seventeen apartment buildings in Cambridge.

William L. Galvin (1902–1983) moved to Cambridge to prepare for Harvard and graduated in 1924. During a two year suspension he worked with a Harvard Square builder-turned-architect and real estate agent, Nova Scotia native R. Currie Grovestein (1866–1941). Inspired, Galvin began dealing in property while still a student and announced his ambition to become a "promoting architect" (*Class of 1924, Second Report*). Unlike most of his classmates, he never left Cambridge. With experience in real estate and a master's degree from the School of Architecture he often designed projects on land that he had sold to his clients. He was surprisingly successful during the Depression, when his buildings changed the face of Brattle Square (see figures 8.33, 8.38, and 8.53). Stylistically, Galvin advanced from the clumsy Georgian Revival projects of his younger days to a sleek Art Moderne. He never embraced the International Style, and many of his postwar projects were banal. He served six terms as president of the Harvard Square Business Association and twenty-two years as chair of the Board of Zoning Appeal.

Building materials suppliers were an important part of the development scene. While quarries in Somerville provided ledgestone for foundations, and bricks could be locally sourced from North Cambridge, most materials originated elsewhere. In the early 19th century white pine and spruce lumber began to arrive from the Merrimack Valley via the Middlesex Canal and by coastal schooner from Maine, landing at wharves on the Millers River, the Broad Canal, and near Harvard Square; later, schooners brought yellow pine lumber from Southern ports, a trade that continued until the Depression. After about 1870 New England's coastal forests became depleted, and railroads increasingly dominated the lumber trade.

The Dix Lumber Company on Harvey Street became the most important dealer serving Old Cambridge after the park commission took Harvard Square's lumber wharves in 1892. Maine native Ervin Dix (1867–1948) was 27 when he obtained his first Cambridge building permit in 1894. At first he operated in the 19th-century tradition of the speculative housewright, buying lots and putting up one or two houses at a time. By 1912, when he stopped pulling permits in his own name, he had completed seventy-five houses in North Cambridge, almost all two-families and three-deckers. Dix established a lumber yard along the Central Massachusetts branch of the Boston & Maine Railroad around 1900 and began selling building materials to the public about 1913. In 1925 he founded the Home Service Company to attract clients seeking to build houses from a catalog of plans and opened a storefront at 2420 Massachusetts Avenue where a saleswoman met customers who might be intimidated by the lumberyard clerks. One historian cites this aspect of Dix's operation as a precursor of the home improvement stores that sprang up after World War II (R. Harris, 705; figure 2.39). Dix's firm became the Cambridge Lumber Company in 1948 and continued in business until 2011.

Real estate agents emerged in Cambridge about 1860. Acting as intermediaries between sellers and buyers, they facilitated the operation of the market. Some moved into property development, which became a recognized occupation in the early 20th century. For example, August Hederstedt (1872–1949) arrived from Sweden in 1890. After a dozen years as a broker for Theodore H. Raymond in Central Square he became a speculative builder, obtaining designs from William H. Mowll for about twenty-five two-family houses on Huron Avenue, Fresh Pond Parkway, and Larch Road in 1911–14 (see chapter 4).[22]

FIGURE 2.39 The Dix Lumber Co. and the Home Service Co. built over sixty homes on company-owned lots on Fresh Pond Parkway, Aberdeen Avenue, Chilton Street, and the outer reaches of Fayerweather Street, mostly in 1927–28 but continuing as late as 1941. Dix and Home Service also put up houses in Arlington, Medford, and Brighton.

John J. Shine (1893–1983) was one of many ambitious young men who played the real estate game in the booming 1920s. The son of an Irish laborer, Shine grew up near St. Peter's Church on Observatory Hill and purchased his first property soon after graduating from high school. In 1917 he completed an unfinished 32-unit apartment building at 72–74 Kirkland Street, and in 1923 he built nine two-family houses on Longfellow Road. A year later he put up the 32-unit "John Harvard" at 1636 Massachusetts Avenue in thirty-four working days, followed by the "Dean Howells" on Craigie Street and the seven-story Commander Hotel on Garden Street (1926). Shine also built the Ambassador Hotel on Cambridge Street (1926), the Continental Hotel on Garden Street (1929), and an 83-unit building at 15–17 Everett Street (1937) before exiting the scene during World War II (see figures 8.5 and 8.7).

William Rogers Ellis founded the Ellis Real Estate & Insurance Company in Harvard Square in 1888. When Cambridge native Robert Melledge joined, it became Ellis & Melledge. In 1903 Ellis died, and Melledge extended a partnership to Ellis's son, Benjamin. Melledge passed away in 1917, and the firm became Ellis & Andrews in 1920 when real estate veteran Edward A. Andrews came on board. After Andrews died in 1936 the firm became Ellis & Bowditch, but when his son Dwight (1908–88) returned after World War II, the firm again became Ellis & Andrews. In 1979 realtor Helen Moulton bought the agency, which merged with another firm in 1994.[23] Primarily a brokerage, Ellis & Andrews was widely patronized by the academic community.

Another piece of the development puzzle involved finance. In the early days of the colony capital existed in the form of land, and preservation of real property was one of the first principles of inheritance. Merchants made secured loans on real estate, but tradesmen and the like had few opportunities to accumulate capital safely. The Cambridge Savings Bank, founded in 1834, was the first institution offering thrift services in Old Cambridge, but its clients were mainly middle-income or higher. Beginning in the 1880s socially conscious individuals founded cooperative banks to encourage home ownership; for example, General Edward Hincks, James G. Thorpe, and a few other progressives organized the Reliance Co-operative Bank in Harvard Square in 1889 to encourage thrift and make property loans to working-class families.[24] By the beginning of the 20th century commercial banks and real estate investors recognized their common interest; Albert Blevins's position on the board of the Harvard Trust Company symbolized this relationship. Some banks were founded specifically to promote development. William L. Galvin, the architect, helped organize the Cambridge Federal Savings & Loan Association in 1938. In 1965 Cambridge developer John Briston Sullivan joined City Councillor Walter J. Sullivan, two state representatives, and several local businessmen to found the Charlesbank Trust Company, which invested in the rehabilitation of a former carriage factory in North Cambridge and a box factory in Kendall Square before being acquired by a regional holding company in 1982.

Cambridge's local newspapers consistently supported urban development as a way of increasing circulation and advertising. Several short-lived papers were published in Cambridge beginning in 1839, but it took the establishment of city government in 1846 to convince Andrew Reid, a Scottish immigrant printer, that there would be sufficient interest to support a weekly paper.[25] The *Cambridge Chronicle* was published in Central Square and assumed a role as the city's newspaper of record, but it was politically conservative and pro-temperance, and it rarely displayed much patience with municipal officeholders. The *Cambridge Press*, founded in 1866 by former mayor Hamlin Harding and fire chief Patrick H. Raymond, presented opposing views until it was acquired by the *Chronicle* in 1900; it published until 1904. The *Chronicle*'s most significant competitor, the *Cambridge Tribune*, was founded in 1878 to protest municipal corruption, most notably the City Building recently erected in Eliot Square; it was published in Harvard Square until 1941 and represented the interests of Old Cambridge and Harvard University. The *Cambridge Sentinel*, a Democratic Party organ, published from 1903 until 1947. These papers and many others were weeklies.

In 1880 the *Chronicle* attempted a greater frequency with the *Cambridge Daily Telephone* but gave it up after a week.

All the papers celebrated development, with much attention paid to new houses and commercial blocks, street railway matters, and municipal infrastructure. The *Tribune*, whose founder was real estate man D. Gilbert Dexter, was the first to run woodcuts illustrating new houses; soon after the city began requiring building permits in 1886 both the *Tribune* and the *Chronicle* started publishing semiannual real estate editions with detailed descriptions of new buildings. Other newspaper owners also invested in real estate; Linn Boyd Porter, who owned the *Chronicle* from 1873 until 1886, erected six apartment houses on Austin and Norfolk streets in 1884–89 and Ware Hall, a private dormitory on Harvard Street, in 1893.

THE REGULATORY FRAMEWORK FOR BUILDING

By the 19th century the ancient bylaws that prohibited thatched roofs and wooden chimneys and established a six-foot setback from the street had long been forgotten. The only standards for building construction were occasional deed restrictions imposed by sellers of real estate. Private restrictions could prohibit noxious trades, establish setbacks, set a minimum value for new houses, or, rarely in Cambridge, stipulate that properties could not be sold to minorities.[26] Stables, tanneries, and workshops were among the activities considered undesirable in the mid-19th century; later, three-deckers, apartment houses, and commercial garages also provoked calls for relief. Cambridge's 1924 zoning ordinance supported prevailing development patterns; apartment buildings and business uses were largely prohibited in West Cambridge but were allowed along almost every car line as well as in some built-up areas close to Harvard Square.

Cambridge's first building ordinance was enacted in 1863 and addressed structures encroaching on public ways or not conforming to the street grades being established to promote drainage. This measure was administered by the city engineer, as was an 1877 ordinance regulating the thickness of walls and the provision of fire escapes. As in many American cities, the reach of building codes was related to a slowly expanding conception of public welfare, beginning with protecting property through fire prevention and later introducing requirements for light and air and sanitary conditions to prevent the spread of disease and protect the public at large. Cambridge did not adopt a comprehensive building code until 1885, thirteen years after the great Boston fire of 1872. The building department began recording permit applications on February 26, 1886, listing architects and other information useful to historians.

Cambridge's building ordinance was amended several times to enhance fire safety before it was completely rewritten in 1897 to incorporate recently enacted state laws.[27] The height of buildings everywhere was limited to 125 feet (twelve stories), although the tallest buildings in Cambridge—the Montrose and the Dunvegan at 1648 and 1654 Massachusetts Avenue (1898)—had only six stories (see figure 4.182). Fire limits were established, first within three miles of City Hall, and then, in 1895, along major thoroughfares. Within these districts, all buildings above three stories had to be built of incombustible material (designated as first- and second-class construction), and dwellings above three stories had to have both front and rear porches. Balloon frames were outlawed. Wooden buildings above three stories (four-deckers) were banned. Iron and steel were permitted if covered with brick, terra-cotta, or plaster, and an amendment allowed flat tar-and-gravel roofs. The 1897 code put further restrictions on buildings above 70 feet and required that ceilings in tenements and lodging houses be no lower than eight feet. The 1908 code maintained the 125-foot height limit but stipulated that a building could be no higher than two-and-a-half times the width of the street it faced. It also established yard requirements for tenements. Reinforced concrete construction was recognized, although such structures had been allowed at the discretion of the building inspector at least since the construction of the University Press in 1895 (see figure 9.41).

During this period progressives realized that building code reform addressed only the symptoms of overcrowding and disease; a broader approach was necessary to promote public welfare. The nascent field of city planning attracted several pioneers to Harvard. John Nolen (1869–1937) came at age 34 to study under Arthur Shurtleff and Frederick Law Olmsted Jr. Graduating with honors in 1905, he opened an office in the Abbot Building in Harvard Square. At his death in 1937 his firm had completed over 450 public projects and landscape commissions, including comprehensive plans for Madison, Wisconsin (1911), San Diego (1926), and Philadelphia (1931). Nolen was one of the founders of city planning in the United States, and it is surprising that his only local public project was a 1911 report to the Cambridge Playgrounds Commission. Nolen believed that planning based on civic surveys and public participation could be a vehicle for social change, an approach that took into account the character and history of the landscape. His ideas were reflected in the naturalistic subdivision plans of Larchwood and Coolidge Hill, as well as in the early holistic approach of the Cambridge Planning Board.

Old Cambridge residents were deeply involved in housing reform, public health, and the parks movement. In 1911–12 the Cambridge Housing Association, whose members included James W. Ford, a future professor of social ethics, architect William L. Mowll, and architecture professor Charles W. Killam, documented shocking conditions in Cambridgeport and East Cambridge and led the fight for statewide legislation to regulate tenement construction. The spread of inexpensive multifamily housing was among the most controversial issues facing Cambridge at this time; in Old Cambridge, the new streets off Huron Avenue seemed particularly vulnerable. The Cambridge Anti-Tuberculosis Association and the Municipal Art Society opposed three-deckers, and the building inspector decried "street after street of so many three-flat wooden houses, resembling as many dry goods boxes standing on end" (*Chronicle*, Sept. 27, 1913). Ford noted that seventy-seven three-deckers were built in Cambridge in 1915 alone. Since they could legally be as close as three feet from a lot line, they contributed to the conditions that had characterized Chelsea before its great fire in 1908. They were

sold to "small Cambridge capitalists, who vainly try to meet the very heavy carrying charges. They are shoddily built and won't last long, as the owners can't afford to repaint them" (*Boston Globe,* May 6, 1916).

In 1911–13 the General Court passed tenement-house acts that allowed municipalities to prohibit three-deckers and regulate setbacks in residential districts.[28] Although the rationale was fire prevention, the acts reflected a national movement to limit the spread of multifamily housing on moral grounds (which in itself was code for keeping immigrants out of established neighborhoods). Ownership of a single-family home was the ideal. Developers countered by promoting "respectable" tenements as "apartment hotels," of which there were 170 in the 1925 city directory, including fifty in Old Cambridge.

Cambridge adopted the tenement-house act in 1916, but Mayor Edward Quinn (1918–29) believed that multifamily housing was necessary to address a postwar housing shortage and to allow continued growth: "While the tracts of vacant land for residential purposes are limited, there are sections of our city which were built up many years ago, largely with single houses that are fast declining in usefulness. These houses occupy for the most part large land areas, which could be utilized to a much greater taxable advantage for apartment house construction" (Cambridge *Annual Documents,* 1919–20, 7–8). Two years later, Quinn noted that three-deckers "with rational restrictions" were "one of the best means of solving our housing problems" (ibid., 1921–22, v). By this time only Boston and Somerville were allowing new three-deckers, but in 1922 Cambridge proposed permitting them again if they were covered with stucco or some other fireproof material.[29] After a six-year hiatus three-decker construction resumed in 1923, although at a much slower pace after zoning went into effect—79 in 1924–28, versus 315 in 1912–16. The last building permit for a three-decker in Cambridge was issued in 1930 for one at 139 Magazine Street (figure 2.40).

In 1913 the legislature mandated that every municipality with a population over 10,000 establish a planning board "whose duty it shall be to make careful studies of the resources,

FIGURE 2.40 In the first three decades of the 20th century three-deckers and two-family houses filled the streets north of Huron Avenue from Chilton Street (foreground) to Lexington Avenue. Several went up as late as 1927–28 on Chilton, Standish, and Walden streets. Photo 1929.

possibilities and needs of the city or town, particularly with respect to conditions which may be injurious to the public health or otherwise injurious in and about rented dwellings, and to make plans for the development of the municipality with special reference to the proper housing of its people" (Ch. 484, Acts of 1913). Mayor Timothy Good appointed a five-member board that elected John Nolen as its first chair and retained Arthur C. Comey as a consultant.[30]

Arthur Comey (1886–1954) was a native of Cambridge who graduated from Harvard with a degree in landscape architecture in 1907. A protégé of Frederick Law Olmsted Jr., he returned to Cambridge in 1911 and became a city planning consultant. Comey's design for the 1912 Canberra competition earned favorable comment, and by 1914 he had won commissions in Detroit and California. The Cambridge Planning Board's first annual report contained his expansive definition of city planning as "the co-ordination of all the activities of the city in a unified organic whole, planned to produce a healthful, convenient and beautiful city" (*Annual Documents*, 1914–15, 505). In his first year Comey compiled forty-five maps documenting every aspect of the city's land use, intending to distill them into a master plan on one 200 scale sheet. He also reported on rapid transit, removal of overhead wires, mosquito control, playgrounds, traffic conditions, and public toilets. Some of his recommendations were far-fetched; for example, in 1916 he proposed that Cambridge merge with Somerville, Medford, Belmont, Arlington, and Watertown to create a "great Middlesex city" of 265,000 people (*Boston Globe*, Nov. 15, 1916).

Progressives started to focus on the rationalization of urban land use at the beginning of the 20th century. The movement gained momentum after New York adopted the first citywide zoning code in 1916; Massachusetts passed an enabling ordinance in 1920. Zoning was seen as a way of keeping incompatible activities out of established neighborhoods. In Old Cambridge, neighborhoods with spacious lots and large homes attracted developers of apartment houses. Residents fought buildings like Wadsworth Chambers at 83 Brattle Street (1908) and the Longfellow Park

apartments at 41 Hawthorn Street (1911), but until zoning was enacted in 1924 they had little recourse unless, like the residents of Arlington Street in 1896, they bought out a prospective apartment builder (see chapters 4 and 6). Conflicts became more frequent with the proliferation of automobile filling stations and commercial garages. These came under the jurisdiction of the license commission, which regulated the storage of gasoline, but that body was singularly disinclined to consider quality of life issues; as the *Chronicle* noted, "their slogan seems to be, 'Oil's well' with regard to 'Gassachusetts Avenue'" (Aug. 22, 1925).[31]

The initial draft of the Cambridge zoning code that the planning board sent to the city council in 1922 proposed three use districts—business, residential, and unrestricted (industrial)—and four bulk districts which allowed building heights from 40 to 80 feet (two-and-a-half to six stories). Except for Harvard Square, all of Old Cambridge would be zoned primarily for residential uses, as well as for hotels, clubs, churches, schools, and philanthropic institutions. The reaction was predictably intense. The city council held its first public hearing in November but then disappeared behind closed doors for thirteen months while "every request and every amendment made by any member of the council [was] favorably acted upon" (*Chronicle*, Dec. 15, 1923). The ordinance adopted on January 5, 1924, differed considerably from the draft. Massachusetts Avenue now had a patchwork of use districts. The height limit for the least restrictive districts—Harvard Square and Massachusetts Avenue as far as Alewife Brook Parkway—remained 100 feet as already permitted under the building code. Both business and residential uses were allowed north of Wendell Street. Four-story buildings were permitted throughout the Lower Common, up to Linnaean Street. West Cambridge, Avon Hill, and Shady Hill remained in the most restrictive district. Despite predictions, construction boomed after the ordinance went into effect, making 1925 a record year for housing starts (see table 2.3).

The adoption of zoning did not end controversies over land use. Within a month the council began to grant requests for relief, and most planning board members who had worked on

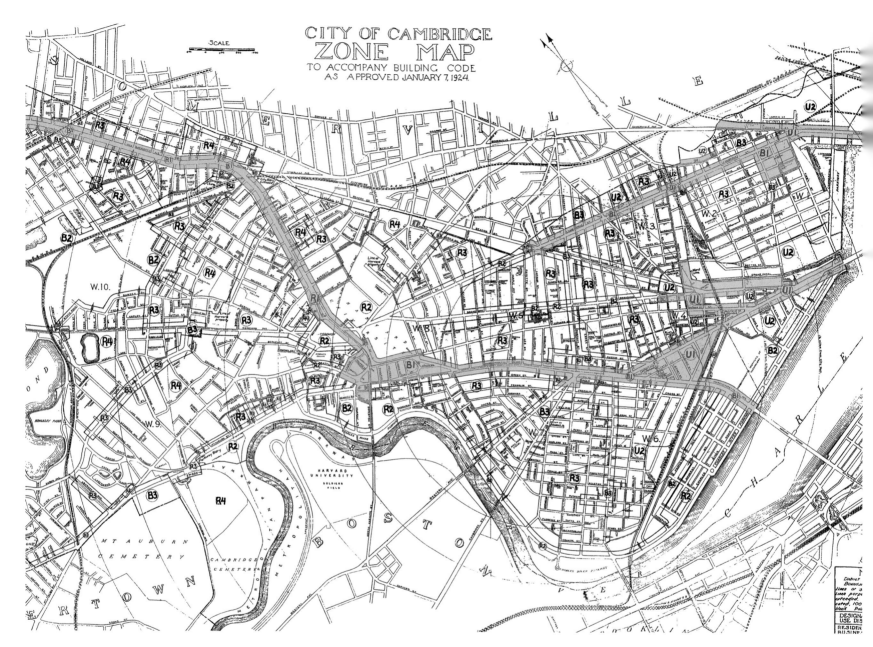

FIGURE 2.41 Cambridge's first zoning map, 1924. Most of Old Cambridge was zoned for single family houses, but builders of apartment houses found variances easy to obtain. The highest density business, residential, and unlimited-use districts (shaded) carried a 100-foot height limit; see figure 2.59 for the districts with no height limits allowed in the 1962 code.

TABLE 2.3 KEY TO 1924 ZONING MAP

District	Permitted	Prohibited	Height	Stories
R-1	Dwellings, hotels, churches, clubs, churches, schools, philanthropic institutions, greenhouses and gardening, with customary incidental accessory uses including garage for not more than two cars	Business and industry of all sorts	100′	
R-2	Same	Same	80′	6
R-3	Same	Same	60′	4
R-4	Private and two-family dwellings, clubs, churches, schools, greenhouses and gardening, with customary incidental accessory uses including garage for not more than two cars	Business and industry of all sorts, carbarns, amusement parks, hospitals, hotels and multiple dwellings	40′	2½–3
B-1	Residence, business, light and other non-noxious industries	Industries emitting noxious odors, dust, smoke, gas or noise	100′	
B-2	Same	Same	80′	6
B-3	Residence, business, light manufacturing chiefly for sale at retail and similar uses supplying local needs	Heavy and general industry	60′–80′	4
B-4	Same	Same	40′	2½
U-1–U-4	All uses now permitted	No uses prohibited	40′–100′	3+

the original draft soon resigned. New members included Charles Killam and Harvard city planning professor Bremer Pond, but in 1929 the entire membership resigned to protest the city's indifference to its recommendations. Cambridge functioned without a planning board until Mayor Richard M. Russell made new appointments in 1930. The Depression halted almost all construction, and municipal interest in planning did not resume until after World War II.

ADVANCES IN SURFACE TRANSPORTATION

In the era before automobiles public transportation was essential for sustained urban growth, and its quality, speed, and cost were issues of widespread concern. The street railway companies were privately owned but subject to public scrutiny and potentially ruinous competition. In 1863 the Union Railway absorbed one rival, the Broadway Railroad, which was promoted by local people who objected to high fares and overcrowding, but in 1881 it faced another, the Charles River Railroad. The new company established routes on Brookline, Hampshire, and Kirkland streets, but the Union Railway forced it to operate mostly on side streets between Harvard Square and Boston. In 1882 the Cambridge Railroad bought out the Union Railway, acquiring 231 cars, 1,486 horses, and all its real estate. Four years later it acquired the Charles River Railroad. In 1887 it was about to merge with Boston's Metropolitan Railroad when all four major Boston-area street railways were consolidated into the West End Street Railway under the direction of Henry M. Whitney, a Brookline real estate developer.

The West End became the largest street railroad in the world, with almost 1,000 cars, 10,000 horses, and more than 200 miles of track. Dissatisfaction with the speed and capacity of horsecars led the company to explore other means of propulsion, including a cable mechanism similar to San Francisco's.[32] Instead, the West End inaugurated an overhead electric system on a route in Brighton on January 1, 1889. Six weeks later twenty electrified horsecars began running between Boston and Harvard Square

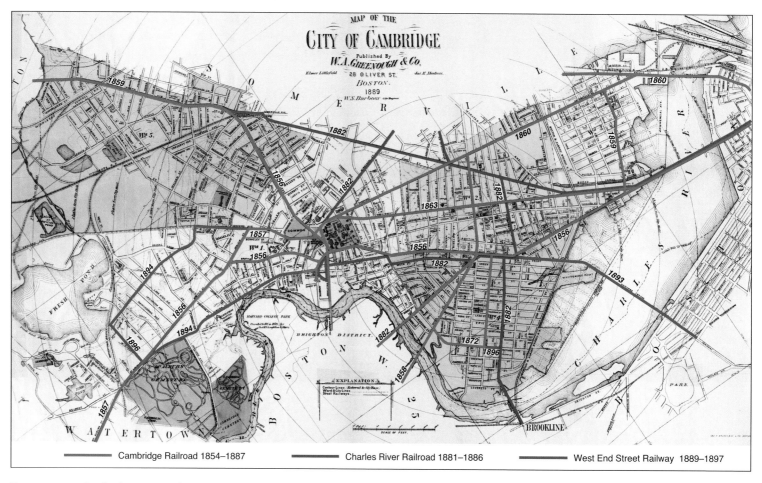

━━━ Cambridge Railroad 1854–1887   ━━━ Charles River Railroad 1881–1886   ━━━ West End Street Railway 1889–1897

FIGURE 2.42   Cambridge street railway routes, 1882–94. The Cambridge Railroad forced the Charles River Railroad to adopt a ruinously circuitous route from Harvard Square to Boston via Mt. Auburn Street, Green Street, Columbia Street, and Broadway. The Cambridge Railroad tore up most of these tracks soon after it acquired the Charles River company in 1886. The West End Street Railway abandoned the Brattle Street line in favor of new routes along Mt. Auburn Street and Huron Avenue in 1894. This map also shows Old Cambridge as it was defined after North Cambridge became a separate ward in 1857, with a boundary running along Sacramento and Shepard streets.

(figure 2.43). Wires soon extended up North Avenue, and within two years all the Cambridge routes except the Brattle Street line had been converted to trolley operation.

The electrification of street railways had far-reaching effects. Time-distance-cost relationships improved, and property values, population density, and neighborhood character changed accordingly. Electric propulsion eliminated horses along with their stables and waste but required more land for carbarns and generating stations. Unsightly overhead wires and the noise and speed of electric streetcars made living on their routes unappealing. Until the 1890s the thoroughfares of Old Cambridge were also the homes of its suburban elite. North Avenue was one of

FIGURE 2.43 Recently electrified streetcars in Harvard Square, looking east on Massachusetts Avenue. The former horsecar at left has received a new Thomson-Houston trolley pole and traction motors, while its mate is an unpowered trailer. Photo 1890.

FIGURE 2.44 A horsecar traveling eastbound on Brattle Street passes the corner of Riedesel Avenue, ca. 1890.

the city's most important residential streets when its car line was electrified. A plan to rebuild the avenue as a boulevard was never implemented, and without effective land use controls apartment houses and stores soon replaced many residences (see chapter 4).

One neighborhood successfully opposed electrification. Brattle Street, the most prestigious address in Cambridge, was the main route to the western suburbs. Bishop William Lawrence at the Episcopal Divinity School complained about the roar of electric cars on Massachusetts Avenue, half a mile away. When residents resisted conversion, Henry Whitney called their bluff by maintaining through service for Brattle Street horsecars all the way to Boston, impeding electric cars using the same track.

By 1893 the public was clamoring for electrification, and the opponents were portrayed as "selfishly standing in the way of the interests of the entire city" (*Chronicle,* June 3, 1893). A proponent said that "the time had gone by when a few old landmarks could hold back the progress of Cambridge," while an opponent replied that "some people would take delight in torturing the people of Brattle Street by putting the trolley system through whether they wanted it or not" (June 24, 1893). The controversy had clear class and sectional overtones. The *Chronicle,* which was published in Central Square, vigorously supported conversion and recalled old antagonisms: "It used to be said, when all the cars came out from Boston through [Cambridgeport], that a 'person had to pass through the abomination of desolation' to get to Harvard" (July 15, 1893).

On August 1, 1893, the aldermen voted for electrification on Brattle Street. Work did not begin at once, however, and the *Chronicle* reported that several leading citizens had returned from their summer homes to plan a new strategy. In November the state Board of Railroad Commissioners voted "to over-ride the wishes of the people," as the *Chronicle* put it, finding that an electric line:

> would materially change the character of that street. ... Shops and blocks of buildings erected for new uses would gradually encroach upon [it]. Trees, turf, shrubbery and open spaces would disappear. Engineering skill can lay out and money can build more magnificent avenues, but neither can make another Brattle Street. ... Cambridge is fortunate, most fortunate, in the possession of this street. No other city holds in trust for its own inhabitants, for the commonwealth and for the nation, a street so beautiful in itself and so enriched by its memories. (Nov. 4, 1893)

The aldermen accused Governor William Russell, a Brattle Street resident and former attorney for the West End Company, of influencing the railroad commissioners. The *Chronicle* ranted that it was "the same old story, Brattle Street, Brattle Street, everything for the favored few on Brattle Street! To the others ... 'Why, get off the earth. Why encumber you the ground?'" (ibid.). Eventually the aldermen recognized that they had no choice but to grant the other locations, but Watertown passengers on electric cars had to break their journey to ride the horsecars to Harvard Square until the new Mt. Auburn Street service began on May 17, 1894. The Concord and Huron Avenue line was

supposed to open in July, but electric service there was blocked by Edwin H. Abbott, one of Cambridge's largest taxpayers, who contended that electric cars were like steam trains and should not be permitted without payment of damages to abutters along the route. The West End ended horsecar service on Brattle Street on July 28 and transferred the cars to the Huron line. The court challenge failed, and the electrics began operating out to Fresh Pond Lane on November 17.[33]

Five years later, the *Chronicle* reprinted an editorial from the *Boston Herald:*

> Several years ago, when Brattle Street nearly had a fit because it was proposed to send the electric cars through it to Watertown, Mt. Auburn Street was a third-rate road filled with semi-suburban houses and mud. Brattle Street's objections to the electrics have been the means of transforming it into a thoroughfare of importance, if not of actual beauty. ... The regeneration of the flats, the work on the Charles River embankment, the beautification of the little parks and the gradual improvement of the real estate have all conduced to make Cambridge proud of its own foresight and to thank aristocratic Brattle Street for having been so disobliging. (Oct. 10, 1898)

THE CAMBRIDGE SUBWAY

The first successful rapid transit in America was a double-track elevated railroad powered by steam locomotives that opened in Manhattan in 1871. In 1880 the General Court chartered a similar line, the Cambridge & South Boston Railroad, to run from Mount Auburn through Harvard Square to City Point. That charter lapsed, and in 1884 the legislature authorized inventor Joe V. Meigs to build an elevated steam-powered monorail between Boston and Harvard Square (see *East Cambridge,* 78–81). Meigs was stymied by sabotage and lack of funds, and in 1894 the legislature incorporated the Boston Elevated Railway to build monorail lines in Boston and several surrounding cities. The Cambridge routes would have run from Brattle Square to Roxbury Crossing via Mt. Auburn, Green, and Main streets; from Central Square to Brighton via River Street; and from Union Square, Somerville, to Hyde Park via Webster Avenue, Cambridge Street, and the Craigie Bridge. Unable to raise the money themselves, Meigs's backers sold the company and its franchise in 1895 to a syndicate led by J.P. Morgan. The Boston Elevated then acquired the West End Street Railway.

In 1897 the General Court authorized the Elevated to build a conventional rapid transit system with trains propelled by electricity. At the request of the Cambridge authorities, the legislature required the company to subsidize a replacement for the West Boston Bridge and build a line between Harvard Square and Boston. This was initially assumed to involve trains running on a steel structure down the middle of Main Street and Massachusetts Avenue, but the *Chronicle* predicted that it was "by no means certain that Cambridge will have an elevated, for considerable effort will probably be made … to have a subway provided, to avoid the noise which the Boston people are undergoing."

Prophetically, the *Chronicle* added, "there is time enough for creating considerable agitation on the matter" (Sept. 28, 1901). The Elevated agreed that the line could run along Green Street to Putnam Avenue and jog over to Mt. Auburn Street, but then owners of the new buildings on the Gold Coast, which would become entirely unsuitable as dormitories, agitated for an "across lots" route on an extension of Green Street (*Chronicle,* Mar. 2, 1901).

Former mayor William A. Bancroft, the Elevated's president from 1899 to 1916, directed its expansion in Cambridge. An attorney and an officer in the Massachusetts Volunteer Militia, General Bancroft had been superintendent of the Cambridge Railroad in 1885 and the first roadmaster of the West End Street Railway. For many years a private streetcar picked him up each morning on Broadway near his house at 12 Ware Street (see figure 4.253). Bancroft's political experience served him well in the melee of rapid transit planning, but public sentiment was

FIGURE 2.45 The proposed elevated line crossing Massachusetts Avenue at Lafayette Square. Initially the elevated was to run above Main Street and Massachusetts Avenue to Harvard Square; this sketch was prepared by the Boston Elevated Railway to illustrate the effect of a diversion via Green and Mt. Auburn streets. See figures 3.40–3.41 for the proposed terminal in Harvard Square.

overwhelmingly against an elevated. The aldermen debated alternatives, including an open cut along Main, Green, and Mt. Auburn streets, and in 1904 proposed that the city itself construct a subway, as the Boston Transit Commission had done in Boston. Bancroft rejected this offer, and in 1906 Cambridge secured an act that required the company to build a subway as well as the present viaduct over the Charles River to Lechmere Square.

Locating stations consumed another three years. The Elevated wanted a high-speed line from Park Street to Harvard Square, with one station at Central. The city hired New York engineer William Barclay Parsons to study possible stops at Dana Street, Lafayette Square, Portland Street, and Kendall Square. Parsons thought the plan would "concentrate development, with congested conditions, about [Central and Harvard] squares, while if a station

was located midway between, development would be more evenly spread" (Parsons, 24). The company agreed to build a station at Kendall but refused to add a stop between Central and Harvard.

The Hugh Nawn Contracting Company finally started work at the corner of Bay Street and Massachusetts Avenue on May 24, 1909. Tunneling began July 17, and ground was broken in Harvard Square on August 5. From the Longfellow Bridge to Inman Street and from Putnam Square to Bennett Street the contractors excavated a trench and roofed it over so traffic could continue overhead. From Inman Street to Putnam Square, a shield propelled by hydraulic jacks bored a tunnel. With 4,000 men working 12-hour shifts construction went rapidly, and on January 23, 1911, Bancroft led an automobile procession through the tunnel from the Longfellow Bridge to the Bennett Street

FIGURE 2.46 Harvard Square in 1912, after completion of the subway. The new headhouse was initially considered to be an ornament to the Square, but the design was hazardous to pedestrians, and it was replaced in 1928. Some car lines were rerouted into a streetcar subway, but others continued to run on the surface.

yards. The first test trains ran in January 1912, only two and a half years after work began. Regular service began on March 23, and from all reports, the public was delighted.

> Trains do in fact run from Harvard Square to Park Street in eight minutes. It is possible to leave one's house in North Cambridge … and be in the heart of the great city in twenty minutes. … The subway has become an asset of Cambridge, in which our citizens may justly take pride, and to which they may look with confidence for a stimulus to growth along the most desirable lines. (*Chronicle,* Mar. 30, 1912)

The Elevated's 5¢ fare and easy underground transfer from streetcar lines to the subway brought a significant shift away from railroad travel. In the early 1920s the Boston & Maine Railroad closed most of its local stations and drastically reduced commuter service on the Watertown and Lexington & Arlington branches; by 1923 only the Porter Square station was still attended by an agent. The subway not only brought outlying towns into the orbit of Harvard Square but also made them more attractive to Cambridge residents seeking suburban homes. The trip from Boston to Arlington Heights was reduced from 49 minutes to 34 and to Watertown from 40 minutes to 25. Arlington had hoped to become an upper-middle-class community, but was unable to prevent tract development along its car lines until it outlawed three-deckers in 1926. Belmont was better prepared; the Fitchburg Railroad had served the town since 1843, but there were no car lines until 1898. Colonized by upper-class Boston families, Belmont outlawed tenements in 1912, and one new subdivision was "carefully restricted so that each owner is assured a delightful neighborhood" (*Belmont Tribune,* June 1, 1912).

Automobiles became a significant presence even as the subway was under construction. Traffic soon became unbearable, and highway schemes proliferated. The Metropolitan Improvement Commission advocated circumferential roadways as early as 1909. Memorial Drive, completed in 1914 as a parkway, quickly became clogged with commuters from outlying towns, and in 1921 Brattle Street residents convinced the city council

Figure 2.47 Charles Eliot (1859–97), landscape architect.

to ban heavy trucks, effectively shifting them to Mt. Auburn Street. Relief did not arrive until after World War II, when the metropolitan parkways were linked to divert traffic away from residential neighborhoods.

CHARLES ELIOT AND THE PARKS MOVEMENT

The parks movement in Massachusetts emerged during the Progressive Era largely as a means of addressing acute overcrowding on Boston's narrow peninsula and became associated with the ideal of regional planning. With the exception of the metropolitan sewer, regional cooperation was anathema to Cambridge leaders. Park advocates had to convince the city to invest in parks for its own sake, without appearing to unduly benefit Boston.

The notion that local governments could acquire land to create taxpayer-supported public open spaces took a long time to gain acceptance in Cambridge, in part because individuals continued to be generous in this regard. The privately supported enclosure of Cambridge Common and Winthrop Park in 1830 and 1834 was followed by the creation of three parks in Cambridgeport in 1856–57 by the heirs of Justice Francis Dana. While some mayors, notably Sidney Willard (1848–51), John Sargent (1856–60), Charles H. Saunders (1868–70), and Hamlin Harding (1870–72), foresaw the need for parks in their rapidly urbanizing city, each of their successors had more constricted views. Mayor Henry O. Houghton (1872–73) saw public parks as an unnecessary expense, at least in part because private citizens had once been so generous.

> There seems to have been in the last two or three years in many of our cities what may be denominated a park epidemic, and Cambridge has not escaped its symptoms, although it has, so far, its ravages. Most if not all of our public parks have been given to the city by liberal and wealthy citizens, who by so doing have not only made their memories fragrant, but have in the most substantial way benefited their own estates. I commend their example to those who are now trying to increase the number of our public parks. (Cambridge *Annual Documents,* 1872)

The alternation between fiscal conservatives and urban visionaries continued even as the parks movement gained wide public support. Finally Mayor Alpheus Alger (1891–93), with the assistance of Councillor John H. Ponce of East Cambridge, secured legislative authority to appoint a park commission and sell bonds for park purposes. The city then moved with unprecedented alacrity to capture essential territory and establish a park system.[34] Working in parallel with the Metropolitan Park Commission and with the advice of their common landscape architect, Charles Eliot, the Cambridge Park Commission transformed the Charles River into the centerpiece of a vast regional system of public open spaces.

Charles Eliot (1859–97) achieved many of the goals of the parks movement in a short period of vigorous activity. He grew up on Kirkland Street next to Norton's Woods, the 35-acre Shady Hill estate of his uncle, Charles Eliot Norton, and was 10 when his father became president of Harvard.[35] After graduating from Harvard in 1883, Eliot worked two years for Frederick Law Olmsted in Brookline and studied abroad before opening

an office in Boston in 1886. Encouraged by Olmsted to write about landscape issues for the popular press, Eliot published an article in 1889 suggesting that a voluntary association could purchase natural areas and historic sites to preserve them from destruction. This notion resonated widely, and "almost immediately it became clear that the precise work to be done was to give effect to a public sentiment already in existence" (Eliot, *Charles Eliot,* 322). In April 1890 open space advocates organized The Trustees of Public Reservations (now The Trustees of Reservations) with Dr. Henry P. Walcott of Cambridge as interim chair and Eliot as secretary. Walcott, for many years president of the Massachusetts Board of Health, reinforced Eliot's belief that the physical and moral well-being of the urban public depended on fresh air, clean water, and natural beauty.

It soon became apparent that no private organization could provide enough parkland for the one million people living within twelve miles of the State House. In December 1890 Eliot took advantage of a "long acquaintance, and of friendly relations between the two families" to suggest to Governor Russell that Walcott's board prepare "a plan or scheme for a metropolitan system of public reservations" (ibid., 357). The governor responded by appointing Eliot to the new Charles River Improvement Commission. Its first report, completed by Eliot in February 1892, called for private enterprises to continue constructing seawalls along the lower basin, public authorities to take the banks upstream from Captain's Island by eminent domain, and "legislation enabling towns and cities to cooperate in securing and eventually improving public open spaces lying in more than one city" (ibid., 569).

Cambridge signaled its ambivalence by boycotting the December 1891 meeting of municipal park commissions convened by the Trustees to explore the need for regional cooperation, and the city was not represented on the temporary Metropolitan Park Commission (MPC) appointed by Governor Russell in June 1892 (although it was included in the metropolitan district for planning purposes). Eliot's January 1893 report (with journalist Sylvester Baxter) mapped out the future regional park system. He urged the Commonwealth to purchase huge

FIGURE 2.48 The degraded marsh between Mt. Auburn Street and the Charles River in 1887. The Irish immigrant neighborhood known as the Upper Marsh is at left.

tracts in the Middlesex Fells and the Blue Hills, Prospect Hill in Waltham, beaches in Revere, Lynn, Nahant, Winthrop, and Quincy, and the banks of the Neponset, Mystic, and Charles rivers. On August 1, 1893, the General Court established the MPC as a permanent commission with powers of eminent domain in thirty-six cities and towns around Boston. Eliot, now a partner in the firm of Olmsted, Olmsted & Eliot, was appointed consultant to a joint board of the MPC and the state board of health examining improvements to the Charles River.[36]

Cambridge was rapidly running out of undeveloped land, and its population was projected to double to 140,000 by 1910. The need for comprehensive sanitary measures and public open spaces was becoming urgent, especially in Cambridgeport and East Cambridge.[37] A new charter adopted in 1892 enabled nonpartisan mayor Alpheus Alger to appoint a temporary citizens' park committee chaired by General Edward W. Hincks, a decorated veteran from Maine who had lived on Brattle Street since 1883. Hincks had no experience with parks, but he had served on the board of aldermen in 1886–88 and was a respected administrator.

Hincks's committee, with Charles Eliot as consultant, held twenty public hearings and toured the proposed metropolitan parks, as well as every Cambridge neighborhood. Two of the five wards had no parks at all, and the city would have to acquire 38 acres (not counting the riverfront and Fresh Pond) to reach an acceptable standard. The committee decided to make reclamation of the river banks its highest priority; inland parks would serve their immediate surroundings, but a riverfront park would benefit the entire city.

> Here is a total of eight hundred acres of permanently open space provided by nature without cost to Cambridge. All of this area was, until lately, unavailable for purposes of public recreation, and, except by boats, most of it remains so … these priceless spaces still lie unused, like money hoarded in a stocking, yielding no return to their owners. If Cambridge is to invest money in public recreation grounds, a just economy demands that such money shall first be placed where it will bring into use for public enjoyment, these now unused and inaccessible spaces with their ample air, light, and outlook. (C.W. Eliot, 423)

Mayor Bancroft secured legislation authorizing a permanent park commission and an appropriation of $500,000 for land purchases. The new commissioners—Henry Yerxa, a wealthy businessman, George Howland Cox, an engineer, and Father John O'Brien, pastor of Sacred Heart Church in East Cambridge—took office in July 1893, and in January 1894 the city used its power of eminent domain to acquire the entire riverfront from the Watertown line to today's Museum of Science. The commission retained Olmsted, Olmsted & Eliot to plan and supervise construction of the new park (see chapter 5). With the firm's advice, the commission also developed large inland parks at Rindge Field and Cambridge (now Donnelly) Field, rejuvenated Broadway Common and Winthrop Square, and proposed boulevards to link parks and major squares (figure 2.49).[38]

After ten years of vigorous activity the park commission lost momentum when the nonpartisan era ended in 1902. Mayor McNamee reduced expenditures and appointed new members to the board, and park construction nearly stopped until Charles Thurston took office in 1906. Reformers led by President Eliot, Old Cambridge attorney Stoughton Bell, and city planner John Nolen gained new energy and in 1910 secured a ballot initiative

in which Cambridge voters favored playground construction by 10,131 to 860. The city's attention then shifted so quickly to building playgrounds and running recreational programs that it reminded a protesting alderman of the era when the city was "park mad" (*Chronicle,* June 11, 1911).

A citizens' lobby, the Cambridge Municipal Art Society, tried to ensure that future public and private improvements would be well designed. Founded in 1904 "to encourage and develop whatever will improve the external aspect of the city, and to oppose whatever seems likely to mar its beauty," the society grew out of conversations between Clarence Blackall, a Boston architect who had lived in Cambridge for many years, and H. Langford Warren, chairman of the Department of Architecture at Harvard (*Chronicle,* Dec. 31, 1904). An advisory committee included President Eliot and Frederick Law Olmsted Jr. In its first year, the society reviewed a new monument on the Common, the Washington Court apartments at 51 Brattle Street, and the Cambridgeport Savings Bank building in Central Square. In 1907 it lobbied effectively for an appropriate replacement for the old wooden Great Bridge at the foot of present Kennedy Street (see chapter 5).

The successful reclamation of the river banks in 1892–1914 linked Cambridge inextricably with the landscape of metropolitan Boston. The city now faced outward, instead of inward to the old village centers. The park commission imposed deed restrictions to ensure that properties on the parkway would be appropriately developed. Harvard alumni began buying land near the river and made grandiose plans for a new academic precinct (see chapter 10). The Massachusetts Institute of Technology's 1911 decision to build a new campus in Cambridge was a magnificent validation of the city's vision.

The movement for municipal beautification scored a further victory in 1922, when the General Court gave municipalities a ten year window to order utilities to remove overhead wires from major thoroughfares. Wires were buried on Massachusetts Avenue in 1923, Cambridge Street in 1924, Brattle Street and Western Avenue in 1925, Main, River, Magazine, Kennedy, and

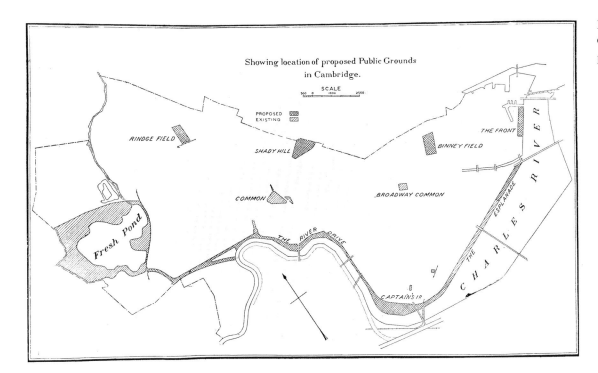

Showing location of proposed Public Grounds in Cambridge.

Garden streets in 1926, Broadway, Kirkland, Mt. Auburn, and Putnam in 1927–28, and Beech and Hampshire streets in 1931. This resolved a controversy that had been brewing since the 1870s, when telegraph wires first began to proliferate. Little has been accomplished in this regard since 1932 because the immediate customers must bear the cost.

City Life in the Metropolitan Era

The generation that came of age at the turn of the century found Cambridge becoming a modern city. Running water and gas service were nearly universal, and sewers had almost eliminated the backhouse and the night-soil carrier. Electricity was introduced in 1887, but most people preferred gas for illumination. Telephone service began about 1878, and by 1900 the Old Cambridge exchange had 1,200 subscribers. The extension of electric railways and the availability of inexpensive bicycles greatly facilitated travel.

Socially, Cambridge was becoming more inclusive. Many intelligent and well-educated women—often the wives and daughters of professors—lived in Old Cambridge, but the community had a mixed record on women's rights. Women achieved greater independence in Massachusetts after 1841, when the legislature reformed their common law status, "under which every article of the wife's property, and all which came to her afterward, real or personal, became the property of her husband; all her earnings were his; she was incapable of making a legal contract; she had no legal control over her children; and her husband had a legal right to confine her to the house 'in a reasonable manner'" (Thomas Wentworth Higginson, *Chronicle*, Oct. 26, 1895).

Women began serving on school committees in Massachusetts in 1868, but none were elected in Cambridge until the legislature specifically allowed it in 1879. Phoebe Mitchell Kendall (1828–1907) served until 1894 and Sarah Sprague Jacobs (1813–1902) until 1885; both were residents of Cambridgeport.[39] Sarah

Burnham, a retired teacher from East Cambridge, apparently declined to serve. An 1895 nonbinding referendum on suffrage in municipal elections received less support in Cambridge than in Massachusetts as a whole, with 93% of women and 27% of men in favor, versus 96% and 3% across the state.[40] Old Cambridge provided some strong advocates on both sides: Ellen Batelle Dietrick of Lowell Street demolished a correspondent who compared women to "idiots, infants, paupers and criminals," while Mary McIntyre of North Avenue claimed in public debates that women had no natural right to vote (*Tribune,* June 15, 1895).

Elizabeth Cabot Cary Agassiz (1822–1907), the wife of Professor Louis Agassiz, operated a girls' school in their home at 36 Quincy Street from 1855 to 1863 and engaged Harvard professors to lecture on science, mathematics, and languages. Mrs. Agassiz and Arthur Gilman adapted this model when she and six other women helped found the Society for the Collegiate Instruction of Women, later Radcliffe College, in 1879 (see chapter 10). LeBaron Russell Briggs, the second president of Radcliffe, recalled that "at a time when the collegiate instruction of women was unfashionable, these women, who had not known it themselves, and who might be regarded as evidence that it is not needed, threw into the scale with it their energy, their culture, and their unquestioned social position" (Howells, *A Century to Celebrate,* 1–3).

Melusina Fay Peirce (1836–1923) lived on Arrow Street with her husband, philosopher and mathematician Charles Peirce. Mrs. Peirce wrote a series of articles for *The Atlantic Monthly* in 1868–69 suggesting that women should be paid to manage their households. She formed a cooperative housekeeping association in 1870, but the experiment failed when members' husbands objected. In *Co-operation* (1876) she promoted a communitarian vision for women, and in 1903 she patented a model apartment-house plan that included a communal kitchen, a concept that was reflected in some apartment hotels of the period.[41]

The leaders of Cambridge society at the beginning of the 20th century were Henry Wadsworth Longfellow's daughters,

WOMEN DEPOSITING THEIR BALLOTS AT THE POLICE COURT POLLS, CAMBRIDGE.

FIGURE 2.50 Voting at the municipal building in Brattle Square on December 2, 1879. Massachusetts women won the right to vote in school committee elections in 1879 but could not vote in general elections until universal suffrage was adopted in 1920.

Alice (1850–1928), Edith Dana (1853–1915), and Anne Allegra Thorp (1855–1934), as well as the younger Howes, Eliots, Bowens, and Batchelders. They were all deeply rooted in Cambridge and created a web of relations almost as complex as those Baroness Riedesel described among the Tories. They and their husbands commissioned residences that represented significant evolving trends in American architecture (see chapters 4 and 6).

"Grave Alice" (as her father described her in "The Children's Hour") never married and lived her entire life at Craigie House, as her family called it. She attended Lyman Williston's school on Berkeley Street and was a generous benefactor of Radcliffe College (see chapter 10). She was elected to the Cambridge School Committee in 1887 and supported the Cambridge

Neighborhood House and the Cambridge Homes for Aged People. She became vice regent of the Mount Vernon Ladies Association in 1880, helped found the Cambridge Historical Society in 1905, and joined her cousin William Sumner Appleton as an incorporator of the Society for the Preservation of New England Antiquities in 1910. With another cousin, architect Alexander Wadsworth Longfellow, she modernized Craigie House and prepared it for public life as a historic site (figure 2.51).

Alice's sisters settled close by in 1887. Edith and Richard Henry Dana III built a Queen Anne house at 113 Brattle Street, while Anne Allegra and her husband, lawyer Joseph G. Thorp Jr., built a Colonial Revival at 115 (see figure 4.28; see also figures 6.127 and 6.158). The families had eleven children between them, which was sufficient reason for their fathers to organize the Cambridge Skating Club on Mrs. Thorp's flooded meadow in 1898 and to found the Cambridge Boat Club in 1909 (see chapters 5 and 7).[42]

Richard Henry Dana III (1851–1931) grew up on Berkeley Street with Longfellow's children, the budding ornithologist William Brewster, and Brewster's close friend, the future sculptor Daniel Chester French. Dana graduated from Harvard Law School in 1877 and married Edith Longfellow a year later. He was as devoted to reform as his father and advocated for civil service and the secret ballot. Although he served on commissions that built the Charles River Dam and the Longfellow Bridge, the greatest part of his public service was performed as a trustee of organizations ranging from the Episcopal Theological School to the Cambridge Boat Club.

The last Longfellow descendant to play a prominent part in Cambridge was Richard and Edith's son, Henry Wadsworth Longfellow Dana (1881–1950). Harry Dana received a doctorate in philosophy from Harvard in 1910 but was dismissed by Columbia University in 1917 for antiwar activities. He returned to live at the Longfellow house and became a strong supporter of progressive causes, visiting the Soviet Union five times in 1927–35. Dana was deeply interested in local history and made the house a repository for the family archives that he actively collected.

FIGURE 2.51 Alice Longfellow (1850–1928), the oldest daughter of Fanny and Henry Wadsworth Longfellow. Photo ca. 1900.

Many social circles coexisted in Old Cambridge. While successful Boston capitalists preferred to settle in Brookline or Weston, lawyers and merchants were drawn to Cambridge. Some Cambridgeport businessmen like Edwin D. Mellen, who sold his soap business to Lever Brothers in 1898, and Frank A. Kennedy, whose bakery became part of the National Biscuit Company, built substantial mansions in the 1890s and became leaders of a growing upper-middle class. Faculty families entertained at home, while eligible college men were in great demand among Back Bay hostesses. Sons of eastern capitalists replaced Southerners as the university elite, and palatial private dormitories competed for the Vanderbilts, Roosevelts, and Morgans who set the social standard for undergraduates. Some of these men lived in Cambridge after graduation; Arthur Astor Carey '79 returned in 1882 and built a precedent-setting Colonial Revival house at 28 Fayerweather Street (see figure 6.154).

At the end of the century, the older men who made up the city's power elite belonged to the Cambridge Club, founded in 1879, while the Colonial (1890) and Newtowne clubs (1893) emphasized social activities for the rising middle class.[43] Upper-class families and young adults of both sexes joined the Cambridge Casino (1882), the Cambridge Social Dramatic Club (1891), the Old Cambridge Photographic Club (1892), the Cambridge Skating Club (1898), and the Cambridge Boat Club (1909), most if not all of which were limited to a certain number of elected members. That so many of these clubs survived the enthusiasms of their founders is evidence of the cohesiveness and stability of the Old Cambridge elite.

Some early women's clubs were quite small and limited in purpose at first, but grew to have a wider influence. The professor's wives and daughters who founded The Bee (1861–1931) gathered weekly to knit socks and make shirts for Union soldiers; their successors met as a social club but rallied again during the First World War. Mrs. Estelle Merrill, a journalist residing on Bellevue Avenue, founded the Cantabrigia Club, a women's service organization, with about 150 members in 1892. At its "christening party" she explained that the club would pursue a progressive "social, intellectual and humanitarian" agenda; although she considered herself a resident of North Cambridge, she hoped to unite women from across the city (*Chronicle*, Oct. 29, 1892). The Cantabrigians occupied the Torrey Hancock house at 53 Church Street until they built a brick clubhouse on Winthrop Square in 1929.

Many members of the Cambridge Plant Club (1889) had an academic bent and often met at the Botanic Garden, occasionally venturing to the Arnold Arboretum and other horticultural destinations. The club's civic work began at the Margaret Fuller House and the Cambridgeport Neighborhood House around 1910 and continued for decades. In 1931 the club began a twenty-year project to plant a shrub border around Cambridge Common. A limit on the membership of the Plant Club led to the founding of a sister club, the Cambridge Garden Club, in 1938. The two clubs undertook joint projects, such as the installation of a garden at the Cambridge Community Center (with plant material from the Botanic Garden) and the reclamation of Blacks Nook at Fresh Pond, a project that led to their merger in 1966. Other projects included the garden at the Hooper-Lee-Nichols house (a fifty-plus year project); the Longfellow house garden (before the property was acquired by the National Park Service); and the planting of trees along streets and in parks.

The Hannah Winthrop Chapter of the Daughters of the American Revolution became a major force for historic preservation in the early 20th century. The national organization was founded in 1890 by women seeking to promote American values during a period of high immigration. By 1895 the Cambridge chapter had dozens of members who claimed descent from Revolutionary servicemen. In addition to public programs and civics classes, the chapter initiated an index of Lucius Paige's *History of Cambridge* in 1904 and published the critically acclaimed *Historic Guide to Cambridge* in 1906. The chapter also arranged for a restoration of Fort Washington in 1904 and the erection of the memorial flagstaff on Flagstaff Park in 1913.

Local historical societies flourished in this period. Francis Gilman founded the Shepard Historical Society "for the study of the history of his church" (now the First Church in Cambridge, Congregational; *Chronicle,* Dec. 18, 1889). The Shepard society was very active for a decade, but its focus was limited to the earliest days of settlement. The *Chronicle* soon noted that while Medford, Arlington, and Somerville had formed townwide historical societies, Cambridge, "with a better field than any of its neighbors," had so far failed to do so (Nov. 20, 1897).

Thomas Wentworth Higginson, Richard Henry Dana III, and Reverend Alexander McKenzie, minister of the First Church, founded the Cambridge Historical Society in 1905. Cambridge had marked its fiftieth anniversary as a city in 1896 with a proud celebration and a substantial commemorative volume that described its prospects as enthusiastically as its glorious past.[44] In 1905 the prospects for America seemed darker, and Dana called on the society to honor "the character of our ancestors" and promote the idea of "plain living and high thinking" that characterized Old Cambridge (CHS *Proceedings*, I, 25–27). President Eliot described Cambridge as a good place to teach Americanism:

> We cannot help but look forward with some anxiety to the future of Cambridge, because of the prodigious change in the nature of its population. The Puritans no longer control Cambridge; the suffrage is no longer limited to members of the Puritan church. Many races are mixed in our resident population. … They look back to various pasts, but may look forward to one and the same future of public freedom, justice, and happiness. (Ibid., 41–42)

Over the next century historical society members filled the *Proceedings* with valuable articles on Cambridge history. Mary I. Gozzaldi completed the index of Paige's *History*; Samuel Batchelder debunked the Washington Elm tradition; Harry Dana documented the history of his family and their slaves; and Lois Lilley Howe helped preserve the John Hicks house. The society limited itself to 200 elected members until the mid-1980s, when it amended its bylaws and began reaching out to other neighborhoods from its headquarters in the Hooper-Lee-Nichols house on Brattle Street.

The 1890s were a high-water mark for Old Cambridge political interests, which were characterized by a liberal progressivism described as "the Cambridge Idea." The extraordinary wave of greed and corruption that overtook America after the Civil War caused many educated men, including President Eliot and his cousin, Charles Eliot Norton, to bolt the Republican Party during the presidential election of 1884. In Cambridge, these Yankee progressives—taunted as "mugwumps" for having their mugs on one side of the political fence and their wumps on the other—joined adherents of the No-License (temperance) movement, the Civil Service Reform League, and emerging Irish politicians to find common cause in the Democratic Party. Cambridge "oversubscribed its quota of cranks … but it supplied, along with its group of crusaders, some very level-headed organizers" (Chase, 28). Progressives favored nonpartisan elections, professional administration, and municipal improvements. They succeeded in amending the city charter in 1891 to concentrate power in the mayor at the expense of the aldermen, who tended to be captives of ward interests.

The inauguration of William E. Russell as mayor in 1885 initiated a period of nonpartisanship that lasted until 1902. Russell (1857–96), who grew up on Sparks Street and whose father, Charles Theodore Russell, had been mayor in 1861–63, was elected to the common council a year after finishing law school in 1880. Known as the "boy mayor," he stressed efficiency and professionalism in city government; he was instrumental in securing the public library, manual training school, and city hall as gifts from his schoolmate, the philanthropist Frederick Hastings Rindge (1857–1905). Massachusetts was a Republican stronghold, but after two attempts Russell was elected governor in 1890 and served until 1894. His connections through the Irish Democrats of East Cambridge to Martin Lomasney in Boston's West End enabled him to tap the votes of immigrants and labor. In 1892 Russell was the only Democrat elected to statewide office. His success brought him national attention and talk of a vice-presidential nomination. However, William Jennings Bryan defeated the progressives at the 1896 Democratic convention, and Russell's untimely death a few weeks later deprived the party of a candidate who united the reformers and the ethnic politicians. Without Russell, the Irish deserted, and in the local election of 1901 party toughs broke up nonpartisan rallies in East Cambridge.

William A. Bancroft was elected mayor in 1893 and staked his claim for reelection on the progress Cambridge had made under nonpartisan administration:

> During the past 20 years, [the city] has doubled in population, having now upwards of 84,000 people, and has attained to a degree of moral and material prosperity which at the beginning of the period could hardly have been anticipated. With ... ample and suitable public buildings, with the best of schools, with efficient police and fire departments kept adequate in size and equipment, with a sewerage system unexcelled in the state, with a water supply soon to be adequate for 160,000 people, with an extensive and beautiful park system well under way, with approaches and streets well lighted, immeasurably better than they were even six years ago, ... with the large areas adapted to resident building in the southeastern and western sections of the city, recently supplied with the best of transportation facilities, with a decreasing tax rate, and for nearly eight years without an open saloon within her borders ... Cambridge has no reason to feel ashamed of her standing in the community. (*Chronicle,* Dec. 8, 1894)

During this period African Americans found acceptance at Harvard and success at the ballot box—a progressive trend that was reversed in the 20th century. Escaped slaves had begun arriving in the 1840s; Mary Walker and Harriet Jacobs settled at either end of Story Street, Walker in the Blacksmith House and Jacobs at the corner of Mt. Auburn, where they ran boardinghouses and became notable members of the community. Cambridge elected J. Milton Clarke as its first black common councilman in 1870, the same year that Harvard graduated its first African American, Richard T. Greener. By 1903, when the *Chronicle* published a self-congratulatory article headed "Color Line Not Drawn and Merit Recognized," Cambridge had elected one black man to

FIGURE 2.52   William E. Russell (1857–96), the "boy mayor" of Cambridge, was a contemporary of landscape architect Charles Eliot and philanthropist Frederick Hastings Rindge. The city commissioned this 1907 portrait by William Morton Rice following widespread discontent over an earlier effort by Charles Hopkinson, President Eliot's nephew. The Hopkinson portrait now hangs in the Social Law Library at the John Adams Courthouse in Boston.

the board of aldermen, seven to the common council, and two to the legislature. An African American woman, Maria Baldwin, was master of the Agassiz School (now called the Baldwin School). Several other black Cantabrigians had distinguished careers: President Taft appointed William H. Lewis, a graduate of Harvard Law School, as an assistant attorney general in the Justice Department in 1911, while Clement Morgan, another law graduate, joined Emery Morris and W.E.B. Du Bois to found the Niagara Movement in 1905 (figure 2.53).[45]

The inauguration of John H.H. McNamee in 1902 began a new era in Cambridge politics (figure 2.54). The progressives, who were well aware of Boston's mixed experience with Irish-American politicians, contested McNamee's candidacy. The son of immigrants, McNamee owned a book-bindery in Harvard Square. He held office for only one term, but his election presaged an era of fierce partisanship. In 1915, a grand jury, "acting on complaints by local politicians that many men connected with the university had not qualified legally for registration," returned forty-two indictments against nine professors and students charged with conspiracy and making false statements about their residence in Cambridge; proceedings were halted after President Lowell sent Professor Felix Frankfurter to confer with the district attorney (*New York Times,* Dec. 8, 1915). The Red Scare of 1920 and the brief emergence of the Ku Klux Klan in North Cambridge in 1922 presaged a darker, less tolerant time

in local politics. In 1924, aldermen mocked former President Eliot when he suggested ways to make Cambridge a more livable city and rejected Old Cambridge architect Allen Jackson's nomination to the planning board because they claimed that he had insulted Éamon de Valera, the president of the Irish Republic. As in Boston, where the demagogue James Michael Curley was mayor four times between 1914 and 1950, the principal focus of politicians was patronage. Ward-based Democratic Party politicians controlled the city, and Richard M. Russell, William's son, who served as mayor from 1930 to 1936, was unable to reestablish his father's standard of good government. In 1942 Curley ran for Congress and defeated the incumbent, Cambridge's own

FIGURE 2.53 William H. Lewis (1868–1949) was one of several African Americans who found a sympathetic community in Cambridge in the late 19th and early 20th centuries. Lewis graduated from the Law School in 1895, built a house at 226 Upland Road in 1899, and sat on the Common Council in 1899–1901. He served as an Assistant U.S. Attorney and Assistant Attorney General in the Theodore Roosevelt and Taft administrations. When Woodrow Wilson forced out black officeholders after 1913 he returned to Cambridge, where he gained a reputation as an effective advocate and trial lawyer. Photo 1899.

FIGURE 2.54 John H.H. McNamee, Cambridge's first Irish-American mayor. His election as a Democrat in 1902 ended the era of nonpartisanship in local elections.

Thomas Hopkinson Eliot, the grandson of the Harvard president, in a brutal campaign. Echoes of this harshly competitive political climate persisted for decades after city government was reorganized in 1942.

THE ADOPTION OF PLAN E

Good government advocates—mocked as "goo-goos" by the *Chronicle* and the *Cambridge Sentinel*, a paper that favored Irish-American candidates—fought Democratic administrations for thirty years to bring back nonpartisanship, scoring their few successes under the occasional reform-minded mayor. Campaigning with Mayor Walter Wardwell, a nonpartisan candidate, in 1907, George Wright, Richard Henry Dana III, and Stoughton Bell of Old Cambridge got city elections moved to March and the school committee reduced from thirty-three to five members. The election of Democrat J. Edward Barry in 1911 coincided with the failure of reformers led by Harvard engineering professor Lewis Jerome Johnson to secure a charter that would have replaced elected officials with a five-member commission chosen by preferential voting. In 1916, with the election of Citizens' Party candidate Wendell Rockwood, a new charter strengthened the mayor, abolished the common council, and restructured the board of aldermen as a salaried city council elected partly by wards and partly at large.[46] All subsequent mayors until 1940 were Democrats. Professor Johnson continued to advocate for preferential voting, and in 1938 Cambridge reformers secured legislative approval of a new form of municipal government, Plan E, in which a city is governed by a council elected at large by proportional representation; the councilors elect a mayor from among themselves and appoint a city manager as chief executive.[47] The objective was to place municipal affairs under professional administration and to empower marginal interest groups by minimizing the effects of party affiliation.[48]

Ignoring a 1938 petition signed by 11,000 Cambridge voters, Cambridge's mayor and council refused to hold a referendum on Plan E until the Supreme Judicial Court ordered them to do so.

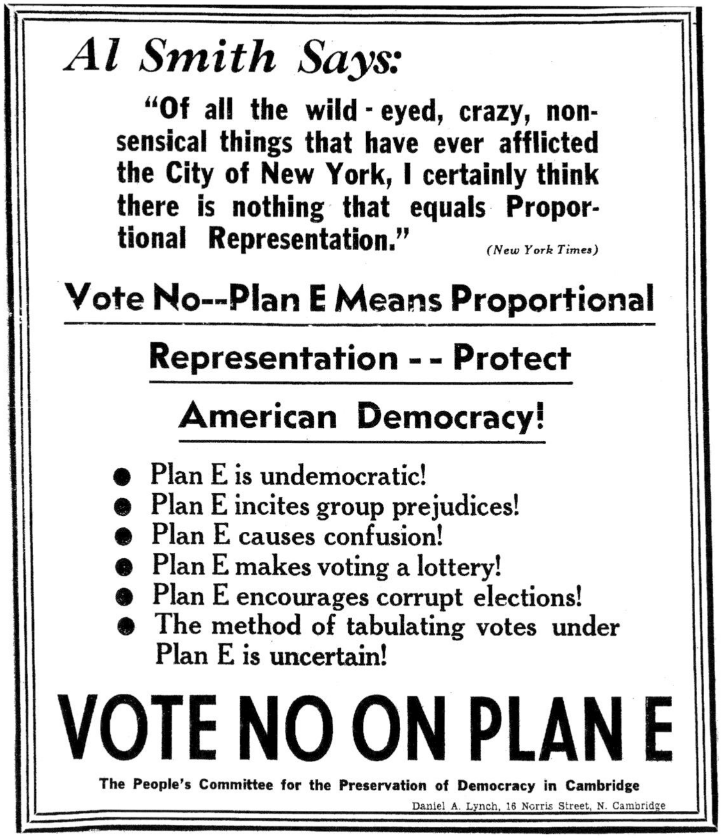

FIGURE 2.55 The opponents of Plan E called it un-American and undemocratic. Both sides invoked national figures in their campaigns.

The Cambridge Committee for Plan E, chaired by Harvard Law School dean James E. Landis, included the industrialist Charles Almy Jr., *Cambridge Chronicle* editor Eliot Spaulding, and attorney Henry Wise, all residents of Old Cambridge. Politicians charged that Plan E was a Harvard plot, that the River Houses concentrated students who should not be allowed to vote, and that the new Littauer School of Public Administration would use Cambridge as a "guinea pig." In October 1938, Councillor

John J. Toomey called for Harvard to be set off as a separate municipality. In a mocking response, brown-shirted members of the Harvard Lampoon goose-stepped down Massachusetts Avenue in a "Sudeten burlesque," and M.I.T. students sought "Anschluss" with Radcliffe, Simmons, Wellesley, and Katherine Gibbs (*Boston Globe,* Oct. 21, 1938; figure 2.56).

Plan E was defeated by a small margin in 1938, but subsequent events ensured its passage. The administration of Mayor John W. Lyons was ostentatiously inefficient and corrupt. A 17 percent tax increase in the spring of 1940 raised a furor, and voters adopted Plan E by a large majority in November. Eighty-two candidates entered the nine-member city council race in 1941; the results were announced after the seventy-eighth tabulation, two weeks after the polls closed. Six members of the old council were reelected, which denied the reform candidates a majority and determined the outcome of a key issue in the campaign, whether the city manager should be a local resident or an outside professional. The new council appointed Colonel John B. Atkinson, a shoe manufacturer and importer who lived on Fresh Pond Parkway, as manager and elected Central Square merchant John B. Corcoran as mayor.

Two weeks after the election, District Attorney Robert M. Bradford indicted Mayor Lyons and contractor Paul Mannos of Brookline on charges of soliciting bribes. Charles Greco, the architect of a public works garage and a 1939 addition to the high school, testified that he gave $21,000 in cash—one-third of his fees—to an intermediary. Lyons was sentenced to four years in prison in 1942; Bradford, a resident of Coolidge Hill, was elected lieutenant governor in 1945 and governor in 1947.

While Cambridge boomed in the 1920s, the Great Depression and World War II froze most construction until 1946. Excluding Harvard's expenditures on the River Houses, the value of all construction activity in Cambridge fell from $6.6 million in 1928 to $602,321 in 1934, and housing production fell from 863 units to six—four single-family houses and one two-family. Ordinary maintenance suffered, and Cambridge acquired a dreary appearance that persisted into the 1960s.

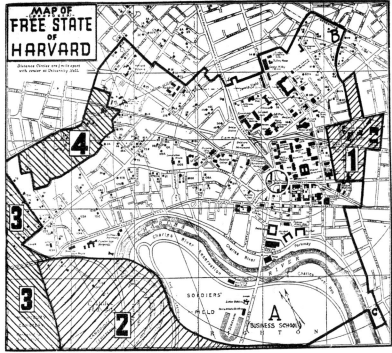

(Copyright, 1938, by the Transcript)

KEY TO HARVARD FREE STATE MAP

1—Proposed buffer State, containing Rindge and Cambridge Latin schools, to be settled by a plebiscite.

2—Coolidge Hill sector, designated a plebiscite area for strategic and cultural reasons, containing Shady Hill and Browne & Nichols schools.

3—(Two areas) Mount Auburn Cemetery, planned as a demilitarized neutral area. No plebiscite considered necessary.

4—Minority group area. Agenda are being drafted for an exchange of populations in this area.

A—Soldiers' Field, Stadium, and Business School Treaty negotiations to be undertaken with city of Boston, to include right of free navigation on the Charles.

B—Shady Hill, home of the late Charles Eliot Norton, and therefore considered a center of ethic culture, difficult to defend.

C—Riverside Press, also held difficult of defense

The circle denotes Harvard square, key to the Boston tunnel, an important line of communication.

FIGURE 2.56 Students invoked current events in Europe to characterize the city council's proposal to cast out Harvard. *The Boston Transcript* imagined the boundary issues that would face a hypothetical "Free State of Harvard."

TABLE 2.4 RESIDENTIAL CONSTRUCTION IN CAMBRIDGE, 1925–40

Year	One-family Houses	Two-family Houses	Multifamily Buildings	Number of Dwelling Units	Estimated Cost*
1925	42	139	37	844	$4,620,840
1926	34	110	28	662	$4,063,950
1927	35	124	42	642	$3,046,150
1928	46	115	17	863	$3,681,500
1929	22	35	16	788	$3,698,400
1930	13	50	4	160	$791,143
1931	16	20	3	137	$674,850
1932	10	1	1	52	$160,000
1933	7	1	-	9	$42,000
1934	4	1	-	6	$32,800
1935	10	-	-	10	$73,000
1936	15	-	-	15	$101,500
1937	14	-	3	122	$392,750
1938	9	3	3	71	$245,600
1939	17	-	3	20	$114,300
1940	19	2	12	315	$843,600

*According to the Bureau of Labor Statistics CPI Inflation Calculator, $1.00 in 1934 had the same buying power as $17.40 in 2013.

Source: Cambridge Annual Documents, 1925–40

CAMBRIDGE U.S.A., 1940–2016

Some months ago I came back to live in Cambridge, Mass., after a fourteen-year absence. I saw new defense plants that had shot up in Cambridge and its environs, attracted by the scientists of M.I.T. I saw more Indians, Africans, and other strangers in town than I had seen of old, and I learned that the Cambridge professors themselves were more global in their interests; they were orbiting round the world more and exerting more influence on foreign lands. … I learned that some of the social sciences were also booming: that a combination of new money and new technology had given them a new hold on life, and a new approach to it. Soon I decided that I had found a renaissance in Cambridge. (Christopher Rand, *Cambridge U.S.A.* [1946])

By the 1940s Boston had become "a hopeless backwater, a tumbled-down has-been among cities" plagued by closed factories, pervasive unemployment, public corruption, and class warfare (*Boston Sunday Globe,* Sept. 22, 1985, in O'Connor, 72). During World War II, however, Cambridge institutions entered into a new relationship with the federal government that prefigured the city's late 20th century adoption of a science-based economy. Wartime research on radar at M.I.T. and on computers at Harvard led to major defense contracts during the Cold War, and Cambridge spun off new enterprises that made Route 128 "America's Technology Highway" in the 1960s. For a while, the city declined as residents left in droves for the suburbs, and old industries withered or were pushed out faster than they could be replaced by new ones. The loss of population, jobs, and economic base panicked city hall into a mentality of encouraging development at all costs. This mindset prevailed until the 1980s, when the technologies developed during the war began to provide a new basis for the local economy. Manufacturing had all but ceased in Cambridge by the end of the 20th century, but by that time a sustained boom in technology enterprises provided a gusher of tax revenue to sustain affordable housing and neighborhood stabilization programs.

The adoption of Plan E in 1942 revived the ideal—if not the—reality of nonpartisanship and rescued Cambridge from

FIGURE 2.57 Harvard Square retained a modest prosperity during the Depression and after World War II rebounded as the retail center for Old Cambridge. One-penny meters were installed on Brattle Street in 1947 to make parking available to suburban shoppers. Photo ca. 1950.

the worst excesses of the old system. Small blocs of voters found it relatively easy to gain representation on the city council, and a new progressive group, the Cambridge Civic Association, was so effective at endorsing candidates that critics accused it of becoming a machine itself. Colonel Atkinson, the first city manager, was a gifted administrator who reduced the city's payroll by a third (approximately 1,000 positions), so that in 1951 Cambridge was the only city in Massachusetts with a lower tax rate than in 1941. *The Crimson* headlined "Town-Gown War End," and in 1951 Harvard awarded Atkinson an honorary degree with the citation "master of the art of government, Cambridge has flourished under his genial management" (*Crimson,* Dec. 13, 1950; *Boston Globe,* June 22, 1951).

In Old Cambridge the vitality of the academic community dampened postwar flight to the suburbs. Until 1941, Brattle

Street and its vicinity had been slowly losing ground as well-to-do householders moved farther from Boston. Restrictions on automobile travel during World War II checked this migration, and rapid increases in building costs and growing congestion after the war persuaded many people to remain in the city. Mansions were updated, and some that were too large for single-family occupancy were divided; rooming houses were reclaimed or converted into apartments; and small houses that once served low-income families were eagerly bought up and improved. Some former working-class areas, like lower Sparks and Foster streets, were almost entirely gentrified. Conditions elsewhere were much less hopeful, and some viewed the city's situation as desperate. The 1955 Massachusetts census showed that 22,000 residents had left since 1945, and manufacturing was fading rapidly. The need for modern housing and commercial development to shore up the tax base became paramount. However, much of Cambridge was owned by the universities, and everything between them was threatened by the Inner Belt, a circumferential highway that at various times between 1948 and 1971 was planned to follow Lee Street through Mid Cambridge, Brookline Street through Central Square, and the Grand Junction Branch past M.I.T. (figure 2.58).

Many postwar projects favored the automobile. The Metropolitan District Commission met some resistance when it extended Memorial Drive from Ash Street to Fresh Pond Parkway in 1947, but the writer Bernard DeVoto and others bitterly opposed further construction through "Hell's Half Acre" to Arsenal Street in Watertown. In 1962 the MDC was authorized to rebuild Memorial Drive as a limited-access highway like Storrow Drive, with underpasses that would have destroyed most of the London plane trees the city had planted in 1897 (see chapter 5). At about the same time, the Massachusetts Parking Authority proposed a 3,000-car underground garage for Cambridge Common. Planners sketched new bypass roads around Harvard Square and suggested putting major arteries underground (see figures 3.77 and 10.81). The community successfully resisted all these projects except for the Watertown extension of Memorial Drive.

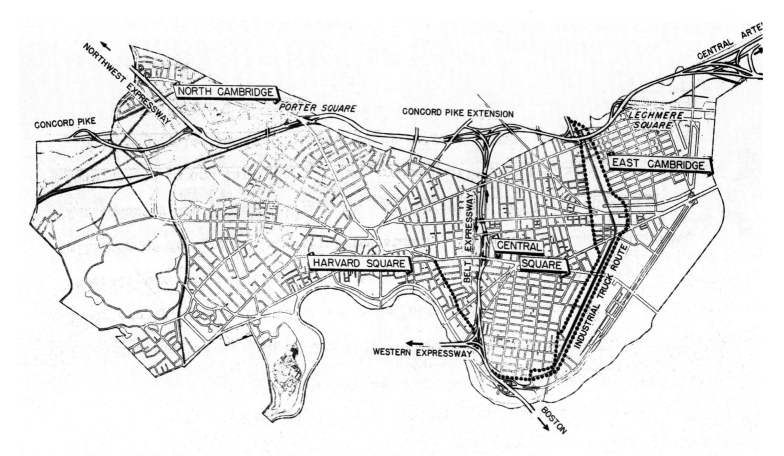

ROUTES OF THE METROPOLITAN HIGHWAY PLAN passing through Cambridge – part of a master plan for the whole metropolitan area prepared in 1948 by a joint committee representing the State Planning Board, the State Department of Public Works, and the Metropolitan District Commission. The Cambridge Planning Board collaborated on local needs. The Concord Pike Extension and the Industrial Truck Route are badly needed to relieve present-day traffic jams. The Belt Expressway and the Northwest Expressway need further study in terms of location and effect upon Cambridge.

19

FIGURE 2.58 The planning board endorsed the state's 1948 metropolitan highway plan, while acknowledging that the Lee Street route of the proposed Inner Belt needed "further study." The board and the state department of public works supported a Brookline-Elm Street alignment until the project was scuttled by Governor Francis Sargent in 1971.

Cambridge gained greater renown with the election of President John F. Kennedy in 1960. Harvard claimed other presidents, including both Theodore and Franklin D. Roosevelt, but Kennedy represented a unique blend of Irish-American and patrician traditions. Many faculty members joined his administration, including Arthur Schlesinger Jr., McGeorge Bundy, Henry Kissinger, and John Kenneth Galbraith. These and other well-known figures established a close connection between Cambridge and Washington and increased the prestige of the university. The bitter controversy over Kennedy's presidential library and the violence that accompanied antiwar protests in the 1960s and '70s extinguished the glow of this era (see chapter 3).

Postwar Planning

The decline of American cities after 1929 encouraged radical solutions. New Deal slum clearance programs expanded, and planning principles devised in the 1920s by the French architect Le Corbusier were widely adopted. His profoundly antiurban concept for the redevelopment of two square miles of Paris, a *Ville Radieuse* of isolated towers surrounded by parks and limited-access highways, was refined at the Bauhaus and transplanted to Cambridge by the charismatic German architect Walter Gropius, who arrived at Harvard's Graduate School of Design in 1937 (see chapter 10). These Modernist principles guided the Newtowne Court "slum-clearance" project in Cambridgeport in 1936–37, inspired urban renewal projects in the 1950s, and provided the theoretical basis for Cambridge's 1962 zoning ordinance.

Cambridge was one of the first cities in New England to take advantage of the U.S. Housing Act of 1949, under which the federal government subsidized two-thirds of the cost of taking blighted urban areas by eminent domain and preparing the cleared land for sale to private developers. The city council embraced urban renewal as "the only way to keep Cambridge from becoming a ghost town" (*Crimson,* Dec. 20, 1955). Department store merchant Paul Corcoran suggested that the first target for clearance should be "the entire area between the [Harvard] houses and Central Square," so that the university could expand along the Charles "and prevent demolition of still-usable buildings in other areas" (ibid., Nov. 30, 1955).

The first actual project undertaken by the Cambridge Redevelopment Authority involved the demolition of the Rogers Block on Main Street in 1957; M.I.T. and a private developer built Tech Square, an office park, on the site. The planning board called for urban renewal in Harvard Square in 1963, but apart from the 1959–62 Riverview project on Mt. Auburn Street the CRA had little involvement in Old Cambridge until it was asked to prepare a master plan for Harvard Square in 1967 (see chapter 3). By this time Cambridge residents could see the effects of urban renewal in Boston's West End (1960), Government Center (1963), and nearby Barry's Corner in Allston (1969), and wanted no part of it. After about 1965 the CRA confined itself to the redevelopment of Kendall Square.

Cambridge also pursued zoning reform as a way of expanding its tax base. The city's 1924 code permitted buildings up to 100 feet tall (ten stories) along Massachusetts Avenue and in Harvard and Brattle squares, and a revision in 1943 maintained the same limits in a smaller area. In the late 1950s the planning board, chaired by Harvard's chief planner, Dean Josep Lluis Sert of the Graduate School of Design, prepared a new code that encouraged growth along Modernist principles. The measure introduced dimensional requirements, including setbacks, minimum lot sizes, and a bulk calculation known as the Floor-Area Ratio (FAR) that tied building volumes to lot sizes.[49] The new code abolished height limits in Harvard Square and on most of the Harvard campus, as well as in the Agassiz, Observatory Hill, and Riverside neighborhoods where the university was actively expanding. The city council, perhaps sweetened by the university's commitment to sell Stillman Infirmary to the developer of a taxable apartment building, 1010 Memorial Drive, instead of to Mount Auburn Hospital, adopted the measure in February 1961. Cambridge became a test-bed for Modernist planning ideas but then spent the rest of the century seeking a better balance between development and neighborhood protection.

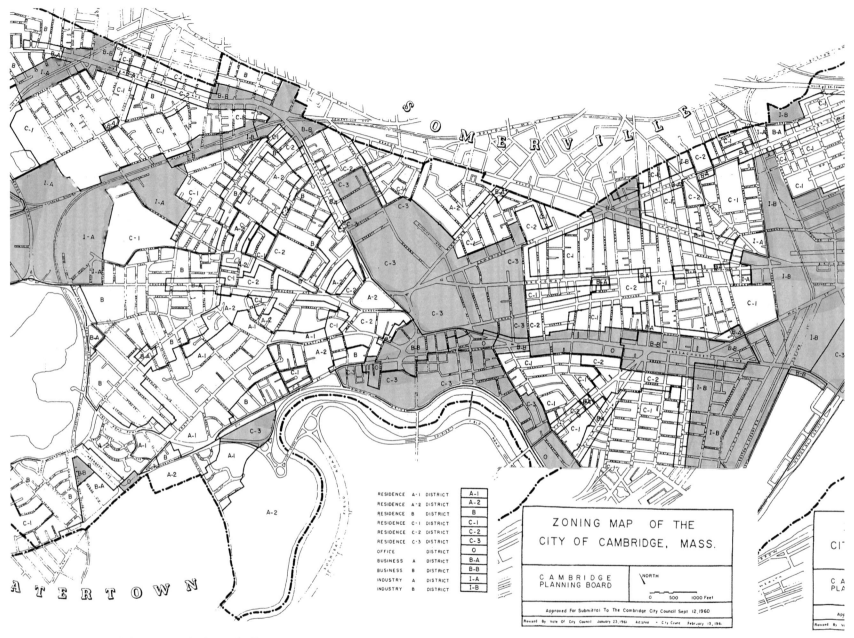

FIGURE 2.59 The zoning code that took effect in 1962 abolished height limits across much of Cambridge (shaded areas). In Old Cambridge, William James Hall (1963), Peabody Terrace (1963), and Mather House (1967) conformed to the new code. By 2009 many neighborhoods had been downzoned; heights were capped at 85 feet in older, settled areas, and 120 feet on the periphery of the city.

TABLE 2.5 KEY TO 1962 ZONING MAP

District	Permitted	Minimum Lot Size	Height	FAR
Residence A-1	Single-family dwellings	8,000	35'	0.5
Residence A-2		6,000	35	0.5
Residence B	Two-family dwellings	5,000	35	0.5
Residence C-1	Multifamily dwellings (hotels, apartment houses, dormitories)	5,000	35	0.75
Residence C-2		5,000	85	1.75
Residence C-3		5,000	None	3.0
Business A	Local and drive-in retail	None	35	1.0
Business B	General business	None	None	4.0
Industry A	Warehouse, storage, light mfg.	None	None	2.0
Industry B	Heavy industry	None	None	4.0
Office	Business/professional offices and multifamily dwellings	5,000	None	3.0

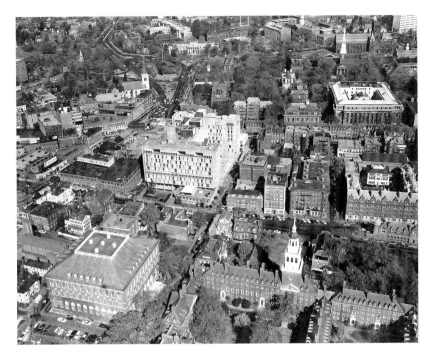

FIGURE 2.60 Holyoke Center represented the Modernist principles in vogue when the 1962 zoning code was adopted. Architect Josep Lluis Sert was Harvard's chief planner and chair of the Cambridge Planning Board during this period. Photo 1966.

Cambridge experienced a preview of the Modernist principles behind the new zoning when Harvard announced plans to build Holyoke Center in 1957 (figure 2.60). The first proposals after the new rules took effect in January 1962 were for a nine-floor office building at 22–26 Kennedy Street and a 23-story hotel in Eliot Square in 1964. At 250 feet, the hotel would have been more than twice as tall as any building in Cambridge (see figure 3.84). Meanwhile, the legislature moved to prohibit communities from restricting the use of land for educational or religious purposes. In 1958 Harvard University tested the validity of the so-called Dover amendment by assigning its lawyers to help the Holy Trinity Armenian Church obtain a permit for a 60-foot high building on Brattle Street in a district with a 35-foot limit. The Superior Court ruled in favor of the church, interpreting the statute in such a way that "Harvard can build as high as it wishes on any of its own land" (*Crimson*, Oct. 22, 1959). Because it had "always been university policy to behave as if Harvard were subject to the zoning ordinances," the university applied to rezone the Holyoke Center site rather than rely on the Dover amendment (ibid., Oct. 30, 1959).

The Armenian church controversy was a catalyst for the creation of a historic district on Brattle Street, where people were still upset by the construction of the Latter-Day Saints church on Longfellow Park in 1955. The legislature had created historic districts on Beacon Hill and Nantucket in 1955. In 1956 Charles W. Eliot 2nd (1899–1993), a grandson of President Eliot who had recently returned to Cambridge after working as a planner in Washington, D.C., and California, petitioned the legislature for a general act to enable cities and towns to establish historic districts on their own. When that approach failed, he proposed a special-act Brattle Street district in 1957 and 1958. These bills were put aside when Governor Foster Furculo signed a general enabling act, Chapter 40C of the General Laws, in 1960.

In 1961 Albert B. Wolfe (1909–98), a West Virginia native and Harvard Law School graduate who specialized in real estate law, secured the appointment of an historic district study committee that also included Dwight Andrews, the Harvard Square realtor, Walter Campbell, an architect, and Rosamund Howe of Coolidge Hill (all Old Cambridge residents), with John Briston Sullivan, the developer, William Edmunds, head of the history department at Cambridge High & Latin, and Hugh Lyons, an East Cambridge history buff. Their report, submitted to the council in 1962, called for establishing four separate districts to protect the surroundings of Cambridge Common, the Longfellow house, the Fayerweather and Lee houses, and Elmwood, all Revolutionary monuments.

The success of the preservation movement in Cambridge can be attributed to Abe Wolfe's energy and political acumen. Eliot (who was not a study committee member) advocated for a continuous district that would include many buildings belonging to Harvard and the Episcopal Divinity School, but Wolfe's strategic approach protected the obvious landmarks and avoided objections from these influential institutions. From its first meeting on November 13, 1963, the Cambridge Historical Commission moved cautiously under Wolfe's leadership, permitting two houses to be demolished for parking lots, one on Appian Way next to Larsen Hall and the other next to the Commander Hotel on Garden Street—actions that probably would not have been allowed a few years later (figure 2.61).

The Cambridge Historical Commission ordinance also directed the Commission to "conduct a survey of Cambridge buildings for the purpose of determining those of historic significance architecturally or otherwise, and pertinent facts about them" (Cambridge Municipal Code, §2.78.020.A). The idea of a comprehensive architectural inventory as a basis for preservation planning was based on a College Hill neighborhood survey conducted by the Providence Preservation Society in 1958–59. Wolfe assembled an advisory committee that included Antoinette Downing, author of the Providence study, and secured a generous budget from John Corcoran, the city manager. In 1964 he hired Professor Bainbridge Bunting of the University of New Mexico, author of an influential dissertation on the houses of

FIGURE 2.61 Progressive real estate interests in Old Cambridge founded the Cambridge Heritage Trust in 1964 to preserve early houses threatened by development. In 1965 the Trust worked with preservationist Roger Webb to dismantle the 1757 Daniel Watson house in North Cambridge and reerect it at 30 Elmwood Avenue (see chapter 6). Dwight Andrews, trust secretary and principal of the Ellis & Andrews real estate firm, Mrs. Harding Greene, representing the trust president, and George A. Macomber, president of the Cambridge Trust Co., convene on the lawn of the restored house. Photo 1966.

Boston's Back Bay, to head a seasonal team of architectural historians that included Robert Rettig, a PhD candidate at Harvard, and Robert Nylander, a recent graduate of the University of Virginia. Wolfe shrewdly directed the team to begin with a survey of East Cambridge, knowing that if Old Cambridge were treated first the other neighborhoods would receive short shrift. Wolfe directed the Commission for ten years, yielding to a new chair and a permanent staff in 1973. The comprehensive inventory of all 13,000 Cambridge buildings that concluded in 1975 and the resulting publications on neighborhood architecture and history constituted a powerful planning tool that became the basis for an expansion of the Commission's authority in the 1980s.

The city's declining population and tax base after World War II caused its leaders to adopt an all-out strategy favoring economic development. In 1951 two members of the CCA coalition—Edward A. Crane and John DeGuglielmo—broke with their colleagues and had City Manager Atkinson dismissed on the grounds that his neglect of capital improvements was holding back the city. The council replaced him with the more tractable John J. Curry, a Longfellow Road resident who had been master of the Roberts elementary school.

Eddie Crane (1914–82), the imposing son of a Cambridge policeman, graduated from Harvard in 1935 and served on the city council from 1939 until 1971. A founder of the Cambridge Civic Association and a dominant figure in city government, he was known as a coalition-builder whose primary interest was "keeping taxes down and forcing unrestrained development." His "fiefdom," which he shared with "politicians, bankers, developers and a university," stretched "from the kiosk to the point where you couldn't get a *New York Times* at a corner newsstand" (*Crimson*, Feb. 7, 1975). Crane worked successfully with M.I.T. president James Killian to promote the redevelopment of Kendall Square but also supported developers John Briston Sullivan and Max Wasserman (figure 2.62).

John Briston Sullivan (1923–2012) burst on the public consciousness in 1957 with a grandiose scheme to fill 39 acres of former tidelands in the Charles River Basin near M.I.T.[50] In 1959 he built a 73-room hotel on stilts over a city-owned parking lot in Eliot Square. A year later, he asked the city to sell him Flagstaff Park so he could build another stilt building, a 15-story office tower with a bus station on the ground level (figure 2.63). The city council and the legislature agreed, but Governor John Volpe vetoed the measure in 1961 after receiving a call from President John F. Kennedy, presumably at the prompting of Harvard president Nathan Pusey. Sullivan also promoted an underground garage for Cambridge Common and challenged the city to undertake a comprehensive program of urban renewal similar to New Haven's.

FIGURE 2.62 Mayor Edward Crane (right) and real estate developer Gerald Blakely (center) greet Governor John Volpe at the groundbreaking for Tech Square on October 9, 1961.

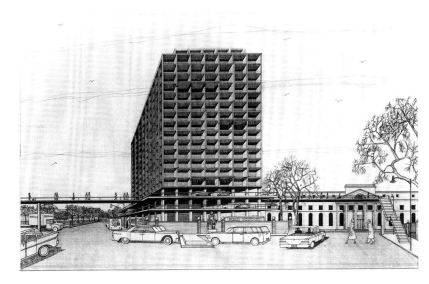

FIGURE 2.63 The proposed fifteen-story tower for Flagstaff Park included a bus station on the ground level. Developers John Briston Sullivan and William J. Chase had Paul Feloney, a young Harvard-trained architect, design this building in 1960.

Max Wasserman (1914–86) was an engineering graduate of M.I.T. who developed the Fresh Pond Shopping Center in 1962 and Rindge Towers in 1968–70. In 1970 Wasserman acquired the real estate holdings of the legendary Bertha Cohen (1898–1965), whose forty-one buildings in greater Boston included twenty-eight in Cambridge. Cohen, a Polish immigrant who worked as a milliner after her arrival in Roxbury in 1905, purchased her first building, Strathcona Hall on Memorial Drive, in 1920. When she died intestate in 1965 she owned two corners of Kennedy and Mt. Auburn streets in Harvard Square, Quincy Hall at 1218 Massachusetts Avenue, and fifteen properties along Massachusetts Avenue between Putnam Avenue and Lancaster Street. Wasserman's acquisition of these buildings initiated the gentrification of the square. He drastically increased rents, in one case from $400 to $2,000 per month, causing an exodus of small shops and restaurants to outlying areas. High-rise buildings replaced Cohen's small storefronts at 1105 (1972), 1050 (1973), and 1100 Massachusetts Avenue (1978). Wasserman upgraded some small properties in the vernacular of the day and converted a garage at Kennedy and Mt. Auburn streets into an indoor mall (see figures 3.63–3.64).

Crane remained a kingmaker until 1966, when a new coalition forced Curry out and installed DeGuglielmo as city manager. Crane's loss of power coincided with an era of instability in city hall. The balance between CCA-endorsed councillors and the so-called independents shifted frequently, with one independent—usually Walter Sullivan of Kerry Corner or Alfred Vellucci of East Cambridge—acting as the swing vote between factions.[51] In this volatile atmosphere DeGuglielmo lasted only two years before he was dismissed in January 1968. After a nine-month interregnum during which the CCA-majority councillors led a fruitless nationwide search for an outside professional, a new coalition hired James Leo Sullivan, a Somerville native who had been town manager of Milton. Sullivan—the first manager to attend council meetings regularly—quickly developed his own power base, but in 1970 an Independent majority replaced him with city purchasing agent John H. Corcoran. Another CCA-led

FIGURE 2.64 Putnam Square contained the largest concentration of properties owned by Bertha Cohen, which were mostly one-story commercial blocks tenanted by small retail stores and services. Photo 1951.

FIGURE 2.65 Putnam Square in 2009. All three former Bertha Cohen properties at Putnam Square were redeveloped between 1972 and 1978. At 1105 Massachusetts Avenue (center, 1972), the architects took advantage of the Modernist 1962 code, which allowed split-level retail and towers set back from the street; at 1100 Massachusetts Avenue (left, 1978) the design reflected amendments that allowed buildings to be built out to the sidewalk and encouraged ground-level retail (Hugh Stubbins & Associates, both buildings). The 1925 store block in the center foreground was replaced by an apartment house in 2011 (see figure 6.243). Photo 2009.

nationwide search in 1972 failed to find an acceptable candidate, and Sullivan was reappointed in 1974. Crane, no longer a top vote-getter, declined to run for reelection in 1971.

The turmoil in city hall reflected the intense controversies that roiled Cambridge in the 1960s and '70s. Since 1946 Harvard and Radcliffe had undertaken more than one major construction project each year. Many entailed relocation of residents and loss of cherished open space. Leverett and Quincy houses (1958), Peabody Terrace (1963), and Mather House (1967) further diminished the Kerry Corner neighborhood. By 1970 Harvard and Radcliffe owned about 120 residential properties that they had purchased for redevelopment since 1953, and Harvard was actively planning high-rise projects at Observatory Hill and Sacramento Field. In 1956 City Councillor Alfred Vellucci repeated the old threat to set Harvard off as a state of its own like the Vatican, but realistic solutions were elusive. Opposition reached a crescendo in 1970, when Riverside residents occupied commencement (figure 2.66). Harvard announced a temporary moratorium on land acquisition in 1972 and published a long-range plan in 1974, its first since the 1920s. The university's relationship with its neighbors slowly improved after the Kennedy Library proposal was withdrawn in 1975, but projects proposed for Riverside, Mid Cambridge, and Agassiz set off new controversies in the 1990s (see chapter 10).

University expansion was just one of many issues that consumed residents and lawmakers. From 1948 to 1972 the Inner Belt threatened to divide the city and displace 1,500 families. Student-led antiwar protests caused widespread property damage and brought the State Police and the National Guard to restore order (figure 2.67). In Old Cambridge, opponents of the proposed Kennedy Library were accused of disrespect toward the late president, while opponents of a plan to convert the Russell School on Larch Road to affordable housing were accused of racism (see chapters 3 and 4).

Perhaps the greatest crisis in modern Cambridge history was precipitated by the postwar housing shortage and the consequent

FIGURE 2.66 On June 11, 1970, community members led by future city councillor Saundra Graham (with bullhorn) invaded Harvard's 319th commencement to protest the university's intrusion into the Riverside neighborhood.

FIGURE 2.67 Antiwar riots and marches between Harvard Square and Boston in 1970 drew national attention.

pressure on the community's stock of affordable housing. A 1968 Harvard study reflected popular views:

> Persons connected with the university, or seeking to live in its shadow, have bid up the price of housing at an astronomic rate. Partly this is the result of … faculty members able and willing to pay higher prices than most other Cambridge residents for existing housing; partly it is the result of the influx of affluent business and professional persons who buy or rent that which even professors can no longer afford; and partly it is the consequence of students and others who … are prepared to join together in groups of three, four or more to rent an apartment at prices far higher than one family can afford. Landlords, once reluctant to rent to students, have in growing numbers been prepared to raise their rents in order to drive out family tenants. ("Preliminary Report of the Committee on the University and the City," 33–34)

A survey of 2,000 elderly residents found that most paid "more than one half of their income for rent and heat. … Given these conditions, it is little wonder that many local citizens feel despair at, and seek explanations for, their predicament" (ibid., 35).

Reported instances of landlords displacing families with rent increases of as much as 400 percent precipitated the reintroduction of rent control in 1970.[52] This stabilized the rental market but discouraged investment in multifamily housing while exempt one-, two-, and three-family owner-occupied houses increased in value. Strict controls on rates of return and restrictions on condominium owners occupying their rent-controlled apartments eventually caused a backlash, and the still locally popular measure was abolished by a statewide referendum in 1994.

The quality of Cambridge's municipal administration improved during this period. State legislation removed the traffic department from political control, so the city council no longer had to approve each stop sign, traffic signal, and one-way street.[53] Massachusetts enacted a uniform building code in 1972, preempting another area that used to distract elected officials. Joseph DeGuglielmo hired the city's first professional planner, M.I.T.-trained Justin Gray, and established an Office of Community Development to prepare a master plan, fight the Inner Belt, and seek federal grants for affordable housing and a Model Cities program. Harvard- and M.I.T.-trained architects and planners staffed the Community Development Department over the following decades, enhancing the city's ability to deal with developers and the universities. During James Leo Sullivan's second term as manager Cambridge adopted a growth strategy that focused on the periphery of the city, somewhat relieving development pressures on Harvard Square.[54] The financial stability and professionalism that characterized the administration of Robert W. Healy, who replaced Sullivan in 1981 and served until 2013, brought Cambridge extraordinary success, balancing economic development with affordable housing production to maintain a diverse population after rent control ended in 1995.

THE ALEWIFE EXTENSION

The transit lines that served Cambridge in 1912 remained intact until the 1980s, although buses began to replace streetcars in the 1920s. In Old Cambridge, buses started running on Huron Avenue in 1933. Trackless trolleys superseded streetcars between Harvard and Lechmere squares in 1936, were introduced on Huron Avenue in 1938, and plied Massachusetts Avenue between Dudley and Harvard squares after streetcar service ended in 1949. Streetcars continued to run on Mt. Auburn Street and Massachusetts Avenue until 1958, when they were needed to equip the new Riverside line. Trackless trolleys survived on these routes because the transit authority was reluctant to run diesel buses through the tunnels at Harvard Station.

Calls to extend the subway came as early as 1920. Governor Charles F. Hurley, a West Cambridge resident, recommended an extension to North Cambridge in 1938. In 1945 the state proposed a surface route from Harvard Square along the river to the Boston & Maine Railroad at East Watertown, then along the Lexington Branch to Arlington Heights. Conflicts over construction methods and station locations stymied proposals in 1956 and 1966, but

Governor Francis W. Sargent's 1974 cancellation of plans to build Route 2 through North Cambridge and the Inner Belt through Cambridgeport allowed the state to match a $381 million federal appropriation obtained through the influence of U.S. House Speaker Thomas P. O'Neill Jr. A commitment to build the subway, known since 1965 as the Red Line of the Massachusetts Bay Transportation Authority (MBTA), was announced in 1976.

The Boston Elevated Railway's plans for Harvard Station had not anticipated that the subway might someday be extended. The orientation of the tunnel toward the river meant that the new line would have to diverge under Brattle Square, an inconvenient point to begin a tunnel leading north or west. The route to Alewife was also controversial (figure 2.68). One alternative ran under Garden Street with no intermediate stations. A route under Massachusetts Avenue with a station at Porter Square was more popular, but merchants opposed cut-and-cover construction, and North Cambridge residents did not want trains running on the surface along the Fitchburg Division tracks. Planners instead chose to demolish the Harvard Square station and dig a tunnel as far as Davis Square in Somerville. Work began in November 1977, when the MBTA relocated the subway repair shops to South Boston and built a temporary station in the Eliot Square yards (see chapter 3). Flagstaff Park was excavated to a depth of 55 feet to give access to a tunnel driven through bedrock at depths ranging from 75 to 130 feet. Spoil was transported by rail to the former city dump on Sherman Street, where the 55-acre Danehy Park was completed in 1990.

Harvard Station reopened in September 1983. Stations at Porter and Davis squares were finished in 1984 and 1985, and the line opened to Alewife in 1986. As in 1912, surface routes were relocated to feed the subway. One important change—the closure of Massachusetts Avenue in front of the Cambridge Savings Bank to accommodate a new station entrance—diverted westbound traffic from Mt. Auburn to Brattle Street. Tory Row residents, no longer much engaged in local affairs, awoke one morning in 1978 to find that they were living on a truck route.

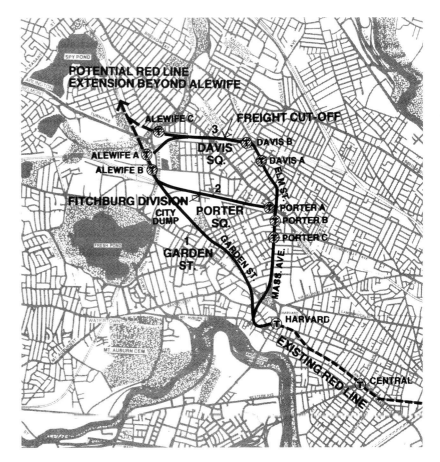

Figure 2.68 Red Line Extension alternate routes and station locations, as proposed in 1973.

Old Cambridge at the Turn of the Twenty-first Century

In the 1980s Old Cambridge began to be threatened by its own success. Harvard Square's vitality stood out against the disintegration of Cambridge's traditional downtown, Central Square. Stores serving a younger clientele displaced markets, variety stores, and cafeterias to outlying areas, revitalizing Inman Square and occupying vacant storefronts well into Somerville. Commercial and institutional construction continued until the surrounding neighborhoods rebelled.

FIGURE 2.69 Indiscriminate demolition of older houses provoked several notable episodes that drew the attention of the city council and facilitated the passage of an ordinance regulating demolition in 1979.

Cambridge Chr[onicle]

THURSDAY, MARCH 2, 1978

CAMBRIDGE (MA

Buildings razed, councillors enraged

By Tom Nutile

"I really felt our cumulative impotence," said City Councillor Mary Ellen Preusser.

"It's as if they came riding into Cambridge shooting off their six-guns," an Arsenal Square resident said.

A bulldozer began to demolish two Arsenal Square buildings at 42 Garden St. and 21 Concord Ave., on Monday, just hours before the City Council voted to favor a moratorium on building and demolition there. The final vote will come on March 13.

Neighbors had a building moratorium petition before the City Council, and had assurances from city councillors and city officials that the demolition wouldn't take place. At least not until after the Council spent several weeks on the issue.

City councillors and city officials thought they had an assurance from a lawyer for the lot's owner that the demolition wouldn't take place on Monday.

Haven O'More, identified as the [...]

Morning meeting

City officials and neighbors, along with police, met at the site 6 a.m. Monday morning in order to stop the proposed demolition.

Robert Jones, an attorney for owner Haven O'More, told the group he would do what he could to stop the demolition. He would call Assistant City Manager for Community Development David Vickery if he could not stop it. Neighbors and officials left the site to one police officer, who was to guard against the demolition.

"We had assurances from everyone, including the workmen, that nothing would happen," Preusser said.

According to varying versions of the story, the police officer was either down the street directing school children, or on the Garden Street side of the lot when the bulldozer came through from Concord Avenue about 2 p.m.

The Duane Co. bulldozer on Monday afternoon pushed in the corners of the two [...]

car. When she arrived, she found another lawyer for O'More there, taking pictures as the bulldozer destroyed.

"I went up the driveway yelling 'Stop that action! Stop that action!! and he turned and laughed at me."

Permit revoked

The demolition permit was yanked by the city because the Duane Co. had gone over the sidewalk and had not notified the Fire Department. Both actions violate city ordinances.

But the damage had been done. The buildings were irreparable.

City officials and Arsenal Square residents consider the incident a case of missed cues, botched communication and misplaced trust.

Over a week ago, Vickery asked Building Supt. Charles Sprague to withhold a permit for demolition because the moratorium was pending.

Vickery said he found out the permit had been granted on late Friday afternoon. The [...]

Zoning was gradually tightened after the city won an exemption from the Dover amendment in 1981. The incorporation of the four original historic districts into the Old Cambridge Historic District in 1976 (and its enlargement in 1986 and 1998) protected all of Brattle Street from Mason Street to Fresh Pond Parkway. In the 1970s and '80s, the intense demand for condominiums led to the demolition of some significant houses in Old Cambridge, such as 42 Garden Street in 1978 and the Greycroft at 1590 Massachusetts Avenue in 1979 (figure 2.69). These losses, as well as the oppressive density of some of the new apartments and townhouses, led the city council to enact ordinances regulating demolition of significant buildings in 1979 and enabling designation of neighborhood conservation districts in 1983. Downzoning campaigns blocked institutional expansion in Agassiz, Observatory Hill, and the Lower Common, while Harvard continued to push into Kerry Corner and

Riverside until it was forced into an accommodation with those neighborhoods in 2004 (see chapters 4 and 10).

In the 1980s a gold-rush mentality overcame the Cambridge real estate market. The extension of the Red Line and the success of development efforts on its periphery contributed to rising property values. In 1986 the *New York Times* reported that "the fashionable streets near Harvard Square are being peopled by wealthy lawyers, doctors, real estate developers, and founders of computer software companies" (Nov. 28). Harvard professors could not afford homes in the city unless they were independently wealthy. The end of rent control in January 1995 contributed to a further turnover of population as longtime residents were forced out by condominium conversions or had to relocate to less expensive areas.[55] The Cambridge Civic Association, the progressive descendant of the Committee for Plan E, disbanded after losing on this key issue, which had energized

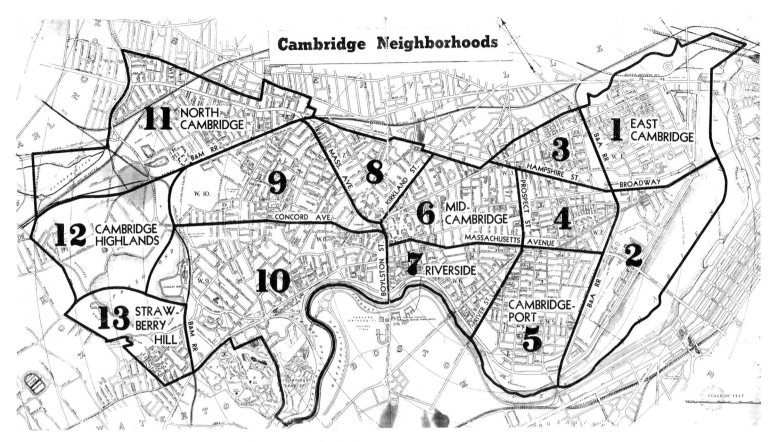

FIGURE 2.70 The planning board prepared for the 1950 census by dividing Cambridge into demographic areas that abolished traditional neighborhood designations.

its base for twenty-five years. Wealthy families poured money into modernizing old houses, sometimes destroying significant original fabric to create luxurious accommodations. Property values skyrocketed to as much as twenty times the levels of the mid-1970s.[56]

During this period the traditional notion of Old Cambridge as a distinct neighborhood was lost to memory. The nonpartisan movement had sought to erase the sectional differences that plagued Cambridge in the 19th century. Post offices had been stripped of their village designations in 1895 and became

Cambridge A, Cambridge B, and so on. Ward boundaries were repeatedly adjusted. Old Cambridge disappeared as a recognized neighborhood in 1949 when the planning board divided the city into thirteen districts, five of which met at Harvard Square (figure 2.70). New residents adopted these artificial designations, while the more stable communities of East Cambridge, Cambridgeport, West Cambridge, and North Cambridge largely retained their traditional identities. Harvard Square remains a distinct entity, but the planning areas around it bear little resemblance to the community once known as Old Cambridge.

FIGURE 3.1 Harvard Square in 1833. The Fourth Meetinghouse occupies the site of today's Lehman Hall. In the background are Bordman's brick store of 1822–23 on the corner of Dunster Street and Willard's Tavern of 1797. The small building surrounded by a rail fence is the market house, on the site of today's kiosk.

3 HARVARD SQUARE

[This scene] seems at first sight to have absolutely nothing to do with the Harvard Square of the present day, but to belong rather to some small hamlet of western Massachusetts. Yet it recalls with instantaneous vividness the scenes of my youth, and is the very spot through which Holmes, and Lowell, and Richard Dana, and Story the sculptor, and Margaret Fuller Ossoli, walked daily to the post office, or weekly to the church. (Thomas Wentworth Higginson, "Life in Cambridge Town," *The Cambridge of 1896,* 35)

The opening of the West Boston Bridge in 1793 produced a brief burst of activity in Harvard Square, but it was followed by a long period of relative decline during which the new settlements of East Cambridge and Cambridgeport gained preeminence and stripped Old Cambridge of its ancient authority as town center and county seat. Commencements ceased to be public spectacles, and apart from the college there was little to attract visitors. The sleepy village known to Higginson, Fuller, Oliver Wendell Holmes, James Russell Lowell, Richard Henry Dana II, and William Wetmore Story in the 1830s and '40s bore a closer resemblance to the colonial settlement of the previous century than to the metropolitan center of the 1890s that was only fifty years in the future. Freestanding 18th-century homes occupied the streets near Winthrop Square, while an ancient inn, the Blue Anchor Tavern, endured on today's John F. Kennedy Street. Schooners discharged their cargoes at the foot of Dunster Street, droves of cattle made their way to the Brighton slaughterhouses, and in winter heavy teams hauling firewood and ice passed constantly down Concord Avenue and Broadway on their way to Boston. Carriage builders and blacksmiths plied their trades in the back streets, and printing was becoming an important industry. The name "Harvard Square" came into use around the middle of the century; before that it was called the "Market-place," or simply "the Village" (Holmes, *Letters*; Howe, 1944). After 1870 investors built fine new residences for students desiring steam heat and running water, amenities not provided in all college halls until 1908. Students and alumni remodeled old houses or built elaborate clubhouses, making the "Gold Coast" along Mt. Auburn Street an attractive precinct for wealthy undergraduates.

In 1901 alumni began to acquire large tracts between the village and the newly reclaimed riverfront, where between 1913 and 1931 the university razed dozens of homes to construct the River Houses. The impending Cambridge Subway encouraged new construction that by 1924 brought parts of the business district up to the architectural standards of the university. For most of the 20th century, however, older buildings were more likely to be adapted to new uses than replaced. Homes became stores, boarding houses, or undergraduate clubs, stables were turned into restaurants, garages, theaters, or department stores, and factories were adapted to offices or reduced to one story. After World War II, Modernist principles threatened wholesale redevelopment, but this vision was realized only at Holyoke Center. The Square's cheerfully shabby and diverse character, so offensive to postwar planners, became its most appealing feature. In subsequent decades the community fought avidly to preserve its diverse character, resisting university expansion, overdevelopment, and commercial gentrification. Harvard Square at the beginning of the 21st century is a richly layered, complex urban fabric that displays elements from every era, from its 17th-century street layout to contemporary office buildings.

HARVARD SQUARE IN THE NINETEENTH CENTURY

When the West Boston Bridge was completed in 1793, the colonial village was still surrounded by the estates of the wealthy and powerful (figure 3.2). Most commercial activity occurred on Wood (now Kennedy) Street leading to the Great Bridge, and Harvard Square proper was the municipal center.[1] From 1793 until 1805–8, when Hampshire Street, Broadway, and Mt. Auburn Street opened, all Boston traffic passed by the meetinghouse on Massachusetts Avenue, giving a brief but decisive burst of energy to the future commercial center of the village.

Growth in the early 19th century was slow, if not glacial; there was none of the explosive, sprawling development that Cambridgeport experienced. In 1798 Jonathan Simpson Jr., owner of the Apthorp-Borland estate, straightened Crooked Street (renamed Holyoke Street in 1850) and started selling house lots. His successor laid out two new streets, Linden and Plympton, that today seem indistinguishable from the colonial grid. On the other side of the village, William Brattle's executors platted Appian Way in 1800 and began to subdivide his estate in 1806. Thirty years later, former Harvard librarian Charles Folsom laid out Holyoke Place and put eight building lots on two acres of Joseph Cook's 17th-century holdings. The first significant real estate activity near the village did not take place until 1857, when the Phips-Winthrop estate, which ran from the foot of Holyoke Street downriver to Western Avenue, was subdivided to serve the growing tide of Irish immigrants (see chapter 4).

In 1812 twenty-four shareholders, many engaged in businesses near the meetinghouse, formed the Proprietors of the Market to provide "a convenient market-stall, sufficiently capacious to admit meat and other articles to be exposed for sale" (Paige, 230). The one-story market house, 34 feet long and 25 feet wide, was built in the middle of the Square and had stalls that were let to butchers, fishmongers, and grocers (see figure 3.1). The 46-by-46-foot lot was owned by the Proprietors of Common Lands and had been occupied by the courthouse until 1758. Several years later the town tried to displace the market: the site had been vacant for some fifty years following the demolition of the courthouse, and the town now claimed the structure was illegally occupying a public way. The real objection was probably revealed in the terms of an 1816 lease to an oyster dealer: "no kind of tippling, gambling or riotous behavior" would be allowed on the premises (Paige, 231, n. 1). Tavern keeper Israel Porter found it profitable to pay half the annual rent of the market for two nights' use during commencement week, a raucous public holiday that was widely thought to be getting out of hand. Although the market's lease ran until 1833, the town seized the opportunity to oust it in 1826, when the Proprietors of Common Lands were winding up their affairs. After a lengthy lawsuit the building was razed in 1830.

Boston surveyor Alexander Wadsworth's *Plan of the Village in Old Cambridge*, completed in January 1833, captured Harvard Square as it was about to assume its modern form (figure 3.3). On the map, the Fourth Meetinghouse still stands at the northeast corner of the Square in the present Harvard Yard, with the courthouse opposite on the site of the Harvard Cooperative Society. Harvard University has just completed the first section of College House, a law school dormitory that also housed the omnibus office and the Harvard Bank, but has not yet razed the houses next to the cemetery to prepare the site of the Fifth Meetinghouse, the present First Parish Church (see chapter seven). Church Street is a dead-end court off Brattle Street, Palmer Street has not been laid out across John Palmer's pasture, and Brattle Square is still a residential quarter. Below Long (now Winthrop) Street the houses thin out toward the river.

FIGURE 3.2 This view illustrates the open landscape of presuburban Cambridge, ca. 1825–39. The 1670 parsonage of the First Parish was on Massachusetts Avenue, just east of Wadsworth House facing Plympton Street. The house in the background on the right was Judge Francis Dana's 1785 mansion on Dana Hill, which burned in 1839. Harvard acquired the parsonage in 1833 and razed it in 1843. The watercolor is unattributed, but the style is that of Eliza Quincy (1798–1884), a daughter of Harvard president Josiah Quincy, who lived in Wadsworth House in this period.

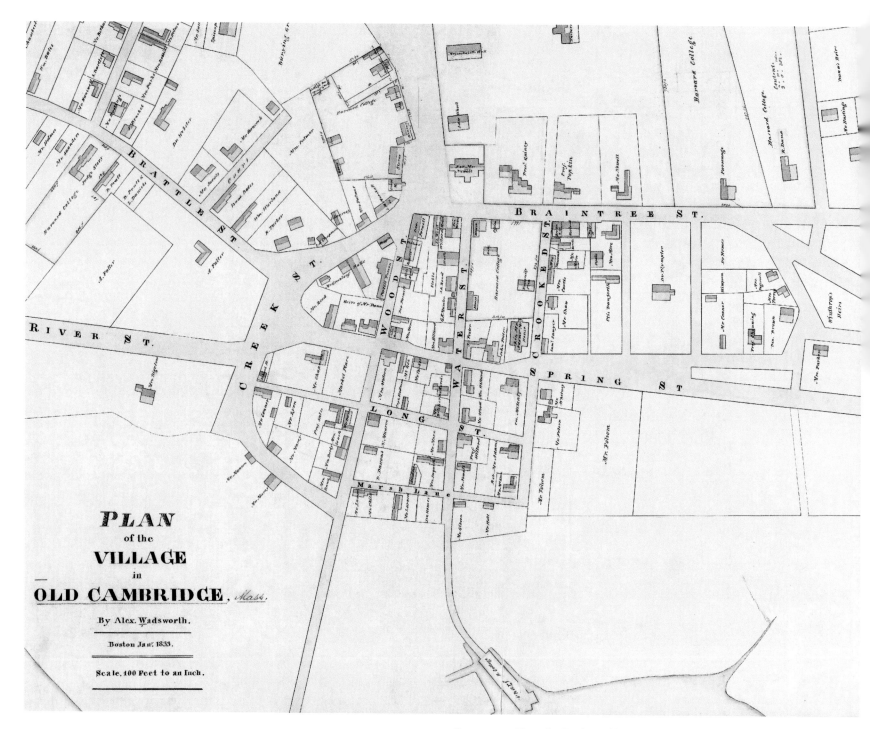

FIGURE 3.3 Alexander Wadsworth's 1833 plan of the village is the earliest accurate map of Harvard Square.

Farwell's Store occupies the corner of Wood (Kennedy) Street, while Israel Porter's Blue Anchor Tavern sits opposite, halfway down the west side of the block. Professor John Winthrop's house faces the marketplace, while Dr. John Kneeland's ca. 1748 gambrel is still the only house on land that was occupied by the Middlesex County jail until about 1817 (figure 3.4). A tiny house built by carpenter Joseph Hicks sometime between 1693 and 1715 stands on the corner of Marsh Lane (now South Street) (figure 3.5).

West of Kennedy Street, the block bounded by Winthrop (Long) and Eliot (Creek) streets shows how the complex layering of history informs land use in present-day Harvard Square (figures 3.6–3.7). The block emerged from the 18th century with scattered houses owned by substantial tradesmen, but it soon became the focus of a major development project with an uncertain goal. During the period of intense speculation caused by the completion of the West Boston Bridge in 1793 and the opening of the Middlesex Canal ten years later, unknown parties built the 10-foot-high dry-laid granite and Roxbury puddingstone wall and created level land adjacent to the Town Creek (Eliot Street). Thomas Brattle acquired all the lots that now adjoin the wall between 1794 and 1797, perhaps meaning to dredge the creek to create a canal like those near Kendall Square. Francis Dana Jr., son of Chief Justice Dana, promoter of the West Boston Bridge, and sixteen investors purchased the lots after Brattle's death in 1806. This group could have built the wall, or they could have been acting preemptively, to prevent development of a wharf that would adversely affect their interests in Cambridgeport (much as they were engaged in struggles with Andrew Craigie over roads). In any event, Dana and his associates began to sell out in 1811, leaving the wall to mystify future historians.

Two Winthrop Street houses on the 1833 plan remain today. The Cox-Hicks house at 98 is "Cambridge's only surviving relic of minimal housing … such as the poor or victims of circumstance might [occupy]" (Robert H. Nylander, CHC survey). Israel Porter bought the lot from Brattle's executors in 1806 and built the house for Susannah Cox, a widow. Elizabeth Hicks,

FIGURE 3.4 Morse-Kneeland house (ca. 1748), 100 Mt. Auburn Street. John Morse, a periwig-maker, exchanged land with Middlesex County and built this house as an inn. After passing through several hands, it was purchased by Dr. William Kneeland, who kept an apothecary shop. It was demolished in 1868. Photo ca. 1865.

FIGURE 3.5 Joseph Hicks house, 64 Kennedy Street at the corner of South Street (ca. 1693–1715). The town established its first almshouse in this house in 1778 but sold the property back into private ownership in 1786. It was taken down before 1903, and Harvard moved the John Hicks house to this site in 1928 (see figure 3.47). Photo ca. 1900.

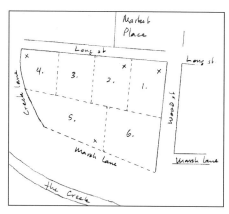

A. 1635. Probable arrangement of earliest lots; x = probable location of houses.

1. Edmund Gearner
2. John Arnold
3. Thomas Carpenter
4. William Kelsey
5. Andrew Warner in 1635
6. Matthew Allen

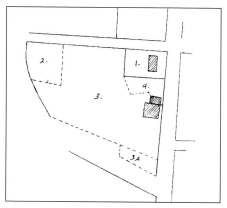

B. 1746. Probable arrangement of lots c. 1747 – c. 1770.

1. William Manning
2. William Brattle
3. Rebecca Oliver to W. Angier, 1746, to S. Whittemore, 1765, to N. Mason and Z. Bordman, 1767, and then to William Angier, 1770
4. R. Oliver to Issac Bradish, 1762

FIGURE 3.6 The evolution of the Winthrop-Kennedy-Eliot block, 1635–1806. Solid property lines and building outlines are firmly documented or survive to the present; dashed lines are inferred from property descriptions. Complete documentation is on file at the Cambridge Historical Commission.

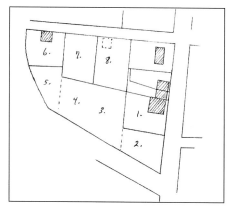

C. 1806. Sale of Thomas Brattle's Estate. Present site of wall indicated.

1.   To Samuel Child, Jr.
2–5. To Francis Dana, et al.
7.   To William Gamage
8.   To Samuel Manning

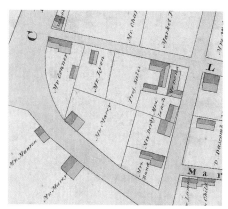

D. 1833. Alexander Wadsworth, *Plan of the Village in Old Cambridge* (detail), with streets widened between 1869 and 1873.

FIGURE 3.7 Winthrop Square as seen from Mt. Auburn Street, with Kennedy Street on the left. William Manning's three-story hip-roof house at 80 Winthrop Street (1725) faces the other side of the park. It was razed about 1911 and replaced by a filling station. Photo ca. 1889.

FIGURE 3.8 The Cox-Hicks house, 98 Winthrop Street, ca. 1806, before conversion to a restaurant in 2002, with the stone retaining wall in the foreground. Photo 2002.

widow of Minuteman John Hicks, lived there until 1825 (figure 3.8). The low house at 106 Winthrop near the corner of Eliot Street was erected by Thomas Brattle about 1800; it housed a dame (primary) school that James Russell Lowell attended in the 1820s. Maurice Connor, an Irish tallow merchant, built the attached house on Eliot Street in 1832–33 (figure 3.9).[2]

Water (now Dunster) Street was the early high street of the village, but on the 1833 plan it is entirely residential except for the stable behind Willard's Hotel. Andrew Bordman's house of ca. 1656 stands on the east corner of Dunster Street and Massachusetts Avenue, but the west corner of Holyoke Street, acquired by President Dunster about 1651, is still vacant. Harvard had bought the adjoining properties in 1794–95, possibly as a site for its new medical school, but in 1810 the faculty left its temporary quarters in Holden Chapel and decamped to Boston. Edward Marrett's ca. 1760 house and Reverend Holmes's new

FIGURE 3.9 From left to right, the Maurice Connor house, 8 Eliot Street, 1832–33; the dame school, 106 Winthrop Street, ca. 1800; and the Winthrop Street wall, probably constructed between 1797 and 1806 to create level land along the Town Creek. Photo 1909.

Congregational meetinghouse occupy the Spring (now Mt. Auburn) Street frontage. Closer to the river, John Hicks's house is at its original location on the southeast corner of Dunster and Winthrop streets (figure 3.10).

East of Crooked (now Holyoke) Street a new cluster of businesses included William Hilliard's bookstore and Thomas Warland's brick and granite mercantile block, which introduced this style of commercial architecture to the Square in 1829 (see figure 8.13). Professor Sewell's house (mislabeled "Mr. Newell") and the parsonage sit next to the President's house on the edge of Harvard Yard, while the Apthorp mansion occupies an entire block (see figure 4.270). Mt. Auburn Street, which penetrated the original village grid in 1808, follows Spring Street until it diverges across the Winthrop farm, shortcutting Bow and Arrow streets on its way to the West Boston Bridge and creating today's broad intersection in front of the Harvard Lampoon.

FIGURE 3.10 Dunster Street, looking from the corner of Winthrop Street toward Richardson & Bacon's coal sheds on the College Wharf, ca. 1895. The John Hicks house (1762) is seen in its original location at 64 Dunster Street.

FIGURE 3.11 The earliest known photograph of Harvard Square, taken before College House was extended to the corner of Church Street in 1859. Willard's Tavern, the Joseph Read house (ca. 1792–1800), and the broad-gabled Farwell's store (ca. 1792–1800, remodeled ca. 1855) occupy the center of the view; then, from left to right, are College House (1832–45), the rear of Lyceum Hall (1841), the cupola of the relocated courthouse (1758, moved in 1841), and the Fifth Meetinghouse (1833).

The village shown on Henry Walling's 1854 *Map of the City of Cambridge* had grown only slightly in the previous twenty years (figure 3.12). Harvard Square proper began to assume its modern form when President Quincy razed the old meeting house in 1833 and rounded off the corner of the Yard where Lehman Hall now stands. The Square achieved its current configuration in 1841, when Lyceum Hall replaced the old courthouse and filled in an awkward jog in the curb, easing the flow of traffic but erasing the last trace of the Square's once-rectangular geometry (figure 3.13). By 1854 Harvard had completed the first expansion of College House in the latest Boston mercantile style (see figure 8.15). Across the Square, President Quincy had Alexander Wadsworth survey a 5½-acre parcel between Dunster and Holyoke streets into nineteen impossibly small lots in 1842. Charles C. Little bought four to put up Little's Block, Cambridge's first (and for two decades, only) private dormitory (figure 3.14).

FIGURE 3.13   College House (1832, right), Lyceum Hall (1841, center), and Thomas Russell's store (1847, left) gave Harvard Square an up-to-date appearance. The frame building to the left of Russell's store was moved in 1868 and now stands at 12 Bow Street. Photo ca. 1865.

FIGURE 3.12   Henry Walling's 1854 map of Cambridge shows many vacant tracts immediately adjacent to the village, including William Winthrop's farm to the southeast and the Ox Marsh below Spring (Eliot) Street. Harvard's subdivision of its Dunster Street property is still mostly vacant, and College House has not yet been extended to Church Street.

FIGURE 3.14   Harvard acquired the frontage between Dunster and Holyoke streets in 1651 but leased it to successive generations of the Bordman family until selling most of it in 1842. From right to left, Little's Block (1854, William Sparrell) was erected by Charles C. Little; Forbes Plaza now occupies this corner. Harvard built Holyoke House (Ryder & Harris) in 1870; Thomas Warland's block at the corner of Holyoke Street (1829; see figure 8.13) is at left. Photo ca. 1875.

West of the center, Brattle Street remained a tradesmen's quarter long after the enormous Brattle House hotel went up on Brattle Square in 1849 (figure 3.15; see also figure 8.2). Palmer and Church streets were the favored location for stables, blacksmiths, carriage shops, and building tradesmen for more than a century after Harvard relocated its wood yard to the College Wharf in 1840 (figure 3.16). Even after 200 years there were still building sites in the heart of the village. Three Greek Revival houses along Winthrop Street—City Marshal Abraham Edwards's at Winthrop and Dunster streets (1841), Joseph Stacy Read Jr.'s at 41 (1845), and Oliver Hastings's at 96 (1846)—are important survivors from this period. No houses stood east of Holyoke Place; although Walling's map shows a projected grid of streets across William Winthrop's farm, nothing materialized there until the late 1850s. North of Mt. Auburn Street, houses had filled the east side of Chestnut (now Plympton) Street, as well as the triangular block cut off from the Dana estate by the construction of Massachusetts Avenue between Putnam Avenue and Quincy Square about 1793 (see chapter 4).

The advent of the street railway in 1856 had an immediate effect on the village. The Union Railway bought the stable behind Willard's Tavern and built carbarns, repair shops, and more stables on both sides of Dunster Street (see chapter 9). Mayor Green complained that "one of our most beautiful squares—hitherto cherished as an ornament to our city—[has been] appropriated almost exclusively as a station for cars and horses" (*Cambridge Chronicle,* Jan. 7, 1860). Horsecar service hurt some merchants by making it easier to shop in Central Square, and the Brattle House failed in part because it became easier for travelers to stay in Boston.

The 1873 Cambridge atlas shows how extensively the Winthrop farm developed after 1854, when George Meacham sold the first lots on Charles River (now Plympton) Street (see chapter 4; figure 3.17). Two years later Solomon Sargent built a wharf and a dike at the foot of the street to exclude the tides, which averaged nine feet above mean low water but regularly crested two feet higher.[3] Within twenty years, Irish immigrants

FIGURE 3.15 Brattle Square before 1868, when it was a tradesman's quarter. The brick building at right is Thomas Russell's 1848 store (see figure 3.13). The building now at 12 Bow Street is in the center; beyond it are workshops occupied by tinsmiths, paper hangers, painters, and furniture dealers. The Brattle House is in the background.

FIGURE 3.16 Church Street looking east, ca. 1857–64. The town's Cambridge 1 fire house (1834) is in the center. Andrew Jones's four-story carriage factory at right still stands at the corner of Palmer Street (see figure 9.17).

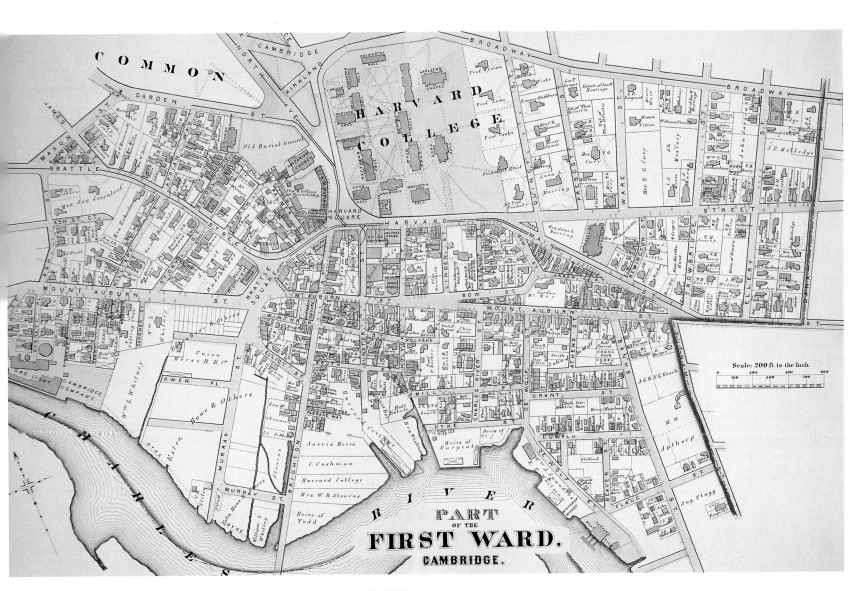

FIGURE 3.17 Harvard Square in 1873. Growing prosperity after the Civil War saw almost all the vacant lots occupied; only the marshes along the river remained undeveloped.

occupied about 150 cottages and tenements on the old farm. Irish families also bought some of the older houses nearby, causing a noticeable demographic shift as former residents moved away. By the 1870s the village was no longer desirable to middle-class families. New buildings were often tenements like the row that builder John Wilson put up as an investment at 10–14 Eliot Street in 1869 (see figure 8.3). Three-deckers appeared on Kennedy and Eliot streets in the 1890s (figure 3.18).

By this time Harvard Square was beginning to develop an industrial sector. Printing, the earliest and most distinctive trade in the village, was reestablished by William Hilliard at the beginning of the 19th century, and in the 1840s several firms settled nearby to process the raw material generated by an academic community—fresh manuscripts to be set in type, proofed, printed, bound, and shipped. Irish men and women became prevalent in these trades; Harvard librarian John Langdon Sibley hired a succession of promising Irish boys in the 1850s, some of whom became skilled bookbinders. A generation later John H.H. McNamee, who lived on Athens Street, established a bindery in Harvard Square before becoming Cambridge's first Irish-American mayor in 1902. The Union Railway employed dozens of drivers, stable hands, mechanics, and car builders. Small enterprises—coal dealers, carriage builders, wheelwrights, and an ice tool factory—served local customers, while one firm manufactured paper shirt collars on Arrow Street for a national market (see chapter 9).

Often beginning as neighborhood grocers, some Irish shopkeepers became provision dealers, selling fresh and prepared meats. In 1900 nine provisioners and three grocers operated in the Square; the nearby Banks Street neighborhood had one provision dealer and twelve grocers. In 1900, when about 14 percent of Cambridge's population was Irish, over 30 percent of the city's grocers were of Irish descent. The last firm of this nature was the Harvard Provision Store, which Philip Rowe established at 96 Mt. Auburn Street in 1895. The "Harvard Pro" gave up groceries after the Depression and sold beer and wine to generations of students until the building was razed in 2003.

FIGURE 3.18 The Winthrop-Kennedy-Eliot block filled with three-deckers at the end of the 19th century. Jennie Packard put up 14A Eliot Street (left, T.F. Haley, architect) as an adjunct to the Hotel Packard in 1900 (see figure 8.3). The historic stone retaining wall can be seen at the end of the alley. Photo 1909.

FIGURE 3.19 The Palmer Street saloon served workingmen until Cambridge went dry in 1882.

Brattle Square continued its halting course of development when the city built a massive police and fire station on Mt. Auburn Street in 1874 (see figure 7.37). A year later, furniture dealer, investor, and banker William Whitney partnered with hardware dealer Ivory Estes to replace Francis Chapman's carriage sheds with a four-story office and store at 13–25 Brattle Street. The first large retail and office building outside Harvard Square proper, it housed the offices of the Union Railway, a meeting hall, and the Pi Eta Club. Grocer Thomas Brewer's

imposing Second Empire block stood across the street on the eastern corner of Brattle Square. The Panic of 1893 halted commercial development for a time; when conditions improved both local and out-of-town investors began to pour money into private dormitories for Harvard students. The University Press (in the former Brattle House) was razed in 1896, but a plan to construct "the most palatial [private] dormitory yet" never materialized, and the site remained underutilized until One Brattle Square was completed in 1991 (*Chronicle,* Jan. 28, 1899).

FIGURE 3.20 Brattle Square from the south, showing Brewer's Block (1868) on the right and Whitney's brick office building (1875) opposite (see figures 8.18 and 8.21). The truncated Mansard in the left center of the view housed the "Sanatory Gymnasium" of Dr. Dudley Sargent's Normal School of Physical Education (see pages 667–668). Photo 1910.

Harvard Square's possible future as an immigrant neighborhood dependent on light manufacturing and service employment was averted by university expansion and a growing demand for off-campus housing. Harvard's enrollment in Cambridge rose from 754 in 1870 to 3,364 in 1909, but college accommodations remained severely limited. After 1870 Harvard built no student housing for almost twenty years. Dormitories were not fully equipped with modern bathrooms until 1898 or with central heating until 1908. The Yard was reserved for seniors, and all others had to commute from home or seek accommodations in the village. By 1900 only 27 percent of undergraduates lived on campus. Investors, recognizing that wealthy families would pay for superior housing, constructed about twenty-five private dormitories around the Square between 1876 and 1904. Most offered steam heat, electricity, and private bathrooms, a level of luxury unprecedented in Cambridge and not widely matched in Boston. Student-oriented boarding houses, restaurants, billiard halls, and retailers proliferated.

The new era in student housing began in 1869–70, when Charles C. Little extended Little's Block, merchant tailor Richard Dolton put up a similar building at the corner of Plympton Street, and Harvard erected Holyoke House, all on vacant lots opposite the Yard on Massachusetts Avenue. These buildings had Mansard roofs, like contemporary commercial buildings in Boston, with stores on the ground floor and student rooms above (see figure 8.19). Luxury housing began to appear in 1876, when Anna Moëring constructed Beck Hall on an open lot facing Quincy Square known as Beck's Lawn (see figure 10.39). This engendered one of the first debates about development; as the *Chronicle* put it: "the large flat-iron piece between the Baptist Church and Quincy Street, has always been considered almost sacred ground by the Ward One [Old Cambridge] people, and the appropriation of land for any purpose has seemed to them as impossible as building on the common" (May 27, 1876). The construction of Claverly Hall in 1892 was the catalyst that

FIGURE 3.21 By the end of the 19th century, private dormitories (apartment buildings designed for students), undergraduate clubs, and exclusive stores lined Massachusetts Avenue opposite the Yard. The buildings in the center of the view occupied the block between Holyoke and Dunster streets, the present location of Holyoke Center and Forbes Plaza; they include Little's Block (1854, here as remodeled ca. 1885) and Holyoke House (1870). Photo November 15, 1910 (detail).

brought ten luxury dormitories and more than a dozen undergraduate clubs to Mt. Auburn Street between Winthrop Square and DeWolfe Street, an area that, after the beginning of the century, became known as the Gold Coast (see chapter 10).[4] Private dormitories began to disappear after 1914, when Harvard required freshmen to live on campus. Several were acquired by the university, and others became apartment houses.

The inception of the Gold Coast set off a wave of gentrification and redevelopment, but many archaic buildings remained for decades. The streets surrounding today's Holyoke Center were more varied than most. Holyoke House and Little's Block took up the Harvard Square frontage, but behind them horsecar stables and workshops filled Dunster Street until the West End

FIGURE 3.22 Dunster Street became an extension of the Gold Coast. Dunster Hall replaced a Union Railway workshop in 1895, and the Dunster Café occupied a remodeled car barn; both were demolished for Holyoke Center in 1960–64. The railroad's stable still stands at the corner of Mt. Auburn Street (see figure 9.29). Photo ca. 1907–8.

FIGURE 3.23 The Dunster Café opened in the refurbished Union Railway car barn in 1905; 400 patrons could dine on the ground floor and enjoy the bowling alleys upstairs. From 1942 until 1960, it was the original location of Cronin's, a popular student bar.

Street Railway relocated to Eliot Street in 1889. Dunster Hall, one of the most elaborate private dormitories, replaced a car shop in 1895, and the Cambridge Savings Bank razed a stable to build Dana Chambers, a mixed-use dormitory, in 1897 (see figures 10.43 and 8.51). The remaining railroad buildings were adapted for new uses (figures 3.22–3.23). On Holyoke Street the Hasty Pudding Club (1886) and Apley Court (1897) coexisted with a seedy student lunch counter (figure 3.24).

Well-to-do students boosted the economy of the square. The Boston firm of Kidder, Peabody & Co. had a storefront brokerage in Little's Block. Tobacconist Leavitt & Pierce opened in Fairfax Hall in 1883, and clothier James August opened below the Porcellian Club in 1901; both continue in their original locations. The 1907 Art Nouveau storefront at 1304 Massachusetts Avenue, designed for Coes & Young, a Boston shoe store, reflected

FIGURE 3.24 Jimmie's Lunch, 8 Holyoke Street (1909). Jimmie's, a stand-up lunchroom, was said to serve 1,200 students a day. When the building was razed in 1927, Jimmie's moved to the basement of the Lampoon.

the luxurious aesthetic of the time (figures 3.25–3.26). The traditional retail district remained in Harvard Square proper, where small stores served householders as well as commuters changing streetcars. Some shopkeepers moved to Brattle Street, although carriage builders (then being succeeded by garages) and carpenters' workshops still predominated on Church and Palmer streets. Old-fashioned village shops contrasted with the modern establishments that catered to students (figures 3.27–3.28).

FIGURE 3.26 Coes & Young storefront, 1304 Massachusetts Avenue (1907, Coolidge & Carlson, architects). An Art Nouveau composition in varnished oak, the storefront displays ovoid shop windows, a comma-shaped transom surrounded by floral carvings, and an entrance with a ribbed, coved ceiling. The storefront was saved from demolition in 1971; preservationists arranged for the Museum of Fine Arts to accept it but then convinced Harvard University, the owner, to restore it instead. Photo 2009.

FIGURE 3.25 Fairfax Hall, 1300–1316 Massachusetts Avenue. When this photo was taken about 1914 the storefronts were occupied by Leavitt & Pierce (a tobacconist), the Durant Company (a haberdashery), Samuel Ramsden's restaurant ("Rammy's Dairy Lunch"), Coes & Young (a shoe store), a bookstore, and a jeweler.

FIGURE 3.27 Stores on Brattle Street differed sharply from the student-oriented shops opposite the Yard. Moore & Hadley's hardware store and Wah Kee's laundry occupied an 1871 building on the corner of Palmer Street, and by the turn of the century they looked cluttered and old-fashioned. The building was removed by the Boston Elevated Railway in 1910 and replaced by 1–8 Brattle Street in 1913 (see figure 8.27). Photo March 3, 1909.

Gold Coast residents adopted the automobile with enthusiasm. Robert Goelet of Claverly Hall had both a steamer and an electric car, and Arthur Iselin, son of the commodore of the New York Yacht Club, had three steamers, including a racer built for him by a mechanic on Mt. Auburn Street. In 1902 undergraduates owned two-thirds of the cars kept at the Harvard Motor Company on Palmer Street; four years later the firm moved into the University Associates' convenient new garage at 1230 Massachusetts Avenue (see figure 9.20). In 1911 the Viking Company on Kennedy Street advertised that it would manufacture "automobiles, aeroplanes, hydroplanes, [and] trucks" to order (*Cambridge Directory*, 1911, 591; figure 3.29).

FIGURE 3.28 Kennedy Street at the corner of Mt. Auburn in 1918. James Winthrop probably erected or rebuilt the building on the corner at 40 Kennedy Street soon after he bought the property in 1787; the storefront dates to 1902. The Sarah Chadbourne store at 34 Kennedy (left) may have dated to 1794. Both were replaced by the Harvard Square Garage in 1923.

FIGURE 3.29 The Viking Company on Kennedy Street styled itself as "manufacturing to order automobiles, aeroplanes, hydroplanes [and] trucks." The biplane was the "Harvard I," which members of the Harvard Aeronautical Society built in Viking's workshop. Club members attempted to fly it from Soldiers Field in June 1910 and again at the Harvard-Boston Aero Meet at Squantum that September, but apparently the machine never got off the ground.

The city's 1892 acquisition of the riverfront for park land excited great interest in the university community. By the 1890s the predominantly Irish neighborhood on the old Winthrop farm had merged almost indistinguishably with the village, where four or five blocks along Mt. Auburn, Winthrop, and South streets were occupied by tradesmen, shopkeepers, and laborers. (figure 3.30). Some Harvard alumni thought the neighborhood near the new riverfront park would make a splendid setting for the university, and in 1901 they began secretly buying land between Mt. Auburn Street and Memorial Drive. After A. Lawrence Lowell became president in 1909, Harvard took title to these privately owned properties, built the River Houses, and acquired several Gold Coast dormitories on favorable terms. After 1930, when the university required undergraduates to live in college dormitories and eat in dining halls, the student-dependent economy of Harvard Square contracted markedly.

Years later, City Councillor John J. Toomey mourned the old Harvard Square and described what had been lost when students were required to live in college dormitories and could no longer eat in local restaurants:

We all remember when many of the streets leading from Harvard Square … were devoted to the housing of the students of the university, as well as to small businesses depending on student patronage. … But within the lifetime of each of us, we have seen a gradual process followed by the university officials whereby these lodging houses, the sites of these small businesses and even public streets were destroyed so that they might set up gigantic and lavish house plans in which students are required to live. (*Boston Traveler*, Oct. 19, 1938)

FIGURE 3.30 A view of Harvard Square in 1897 shows a densely settled residential area along South and Winthrop streets (foreground) that crowds the stables and carbarns on Dunster Street, where newly constructed Dunster Hall (renamed Dudley Hall in 1930) gleams in the sunlight. Kennedy Street, on the left, runs past the cellar hole of the William Manning house (figure 3.7) and the recently redesigned Winthrop Square Park. This view was taken from the chimney of the Boston Elevated Railway's power station on Memorial Drive (see figures 5.41 and 9.32).

Harvard Square has not yet become so full of metropolitan rush and glitter but that now and then there is to be seen there some sight more suggestive of life in the rural districts. Sometimes it is the contented rustic, driving his load of hay, sometimes the market gardener, jogging along with a load of "garden stuff," but for a downright, genuine reminder of the country there is nothing that passes through the square more intensely rural than the occasional drove of cows hustled over the ground as fast as possible by two or three shouting swains, and generally accompanied by a dog, which ki-yi's and darts this way and that to add to the general confusion. … Students, small boys, and canines of the "yaller" stripe seem to enjoy the excitement, but it strikes sudden and sure consternation among the feminine portion of the lookers on, likewise among those sober, brain-weighted gentlemen who wear eyeglasses and carry books under their arm—not to mention many who don't like to be disturbed in such a vulgar manner. (*Chronicle,* May 5, 1900)

HARVARD SQUARE.

FIGURE 3.31   The practice of driving cattle through Harvard Square to the Brighton abattoir, depicted here in 1870, continued well into the 1920s.

FIGURE 3.32   Harvard Square on Class Day, June 22, 1906. A returning member of the class of 1856 would recognize almost every feature of this scene.

At the end of the 19th century, when Gold Coast dormitories and undergraduate clubs were transforming its outskirts, Harvard Square seemed dowdy and ramshackle. Property owners were reluctant to modernize, but the city forced the issue when it widened Kennedy and Eliot streets from 50 to 60 and 70 feet, respectively, in 1896. A collective vision emerged in 1913 when the Harvard Square Business Men's Association responded to the completion of the Cambridge Subway. The city established a planning board in 1914 and adopted a zoning code in 1924, but the business district evolved without much constraint until institutional forces came into play after World War II.

Among the buildings whose fronts were lost in street-widening projects were three ancient structures on the south side of Massachusetts Avenue (figure 3.33). Postmaster Joseph Read had built a three-story house and shop facing the meetinghouse about 1782. Levi Farwell put up the brick store at 10–14 Kennedy Street about 1820, remodeled the corner store about 1830, and acquired the Warland store that stood between them in

1841 (see figure 8.12). When Read's grandson William acquired the property in 1855 the *Chronicle* described it as "the most valuable lot of land of its size in the city" (Sept. 15). After he died in 1884, his executors were reluctant to sell or modernize the premises, and they resisted the city's plan to widen Harvard Square until the mayor threatened to have city crews remove the encroachments. Rather than redevelop the site, the executors hired an architect to unify the truncated structures. The *Chronicle* reported: "Read's Block in Harvard Square has been greatly improved since the front was cut off. The plate glass windows, the graceful sweep of the circular corner, and the graceful addition of a story, really make a wonderful change" (Sept. 5, 1896; figure 3.34). They finally sold the property in 1917. A New York syndicate intended to put up a vaudeville house for the Loew's chain in 1920 but was stymied by material shortages after World War I. The Read Block survived thereafter because its leases did not expire until the Depression, when redevelopment was impossible, and because ownership passed to a real estate trust,

FIGURE 3.33 The structures that were combined into the Read Block in 1896. From left to right, the William Brown store at 1372 Massachusetts Avenue (ca. 1816); Willard's Tavern (1797), here as remodeled into the West End Street Railway's waiting room; the Joseph Read house (ca. 1782–90); and the Read-Farwell store (ca. 1792–1800). Photo 1896.

FIGURE 3.34 The Read Block as remodeled in 1896 (Joseph R. & William P. Richards, architects). The distinctive Neoclassical facade and plate glass windows helped it survive threatened demolition a century later. Photo 1907.

an inherently conservative form of ownership that contributed to the longevity of many Harvard Square properties.[5]

The city's street-widening program also affected the other side of Kennedy Street, where the block bounded by Brattle and Mt. Auburn streets was evolving from a hodge-podge of stables, houses, and shops into a modern commercial district (figures 3.35–3.36). In the early days this was the edge of the village, back of the hill from the landing and the First Meetinghouse, bounded on the northwest by the Town Creek. For over a hundred years the block's principal feature was the Blue Anchor Tavern and its stable (see figure 8.1). John H.H. McNamee, bookbinder and future mayor, began a decade-long campaign of acquisition and improvement when he built a four-story store and bookbindery at 18–24 Brattle Street in 1894 (see figure 8.24). After the city widened Kennedy Street, he bought the corner lot and wrapped the remnants of the old buildings in a new facade similar to that of the Read Block (see figure 3.37).

McNamee's principal objective was an 1871 stable on the tavern property that ran through from Kennedy to Brattle streets and was widely regarded as a nuisance. He acquired the structure in 1904 after the board of health refused to renew its license and commissioned architects George S.R. McLean and Edward T.P. Graham to remodel it with stores on the ground floor and offices above. McNamee moved to Roxbury after he failed to win reelection in 1903 and sold the property to Edwin Hale Abbot, who put up the Abbot Building in 1909 (see figure 8.26). Stores, a garage, and a print shop supplanted the remaining houses on Mt. Auburn Street around 1920, and Brewer's grocery, the last element of the 19th-century streetscape, was replaced in 1930 by an ungainly Georgian Revival building that burned in 1972 (see figures 8.18 and 8.33).

The introduction of electric streetcars in 1889 upended the Square. The *Boston Herald* reported that "the turmoil in Harvard Square these days is sufficient to send a good portion of

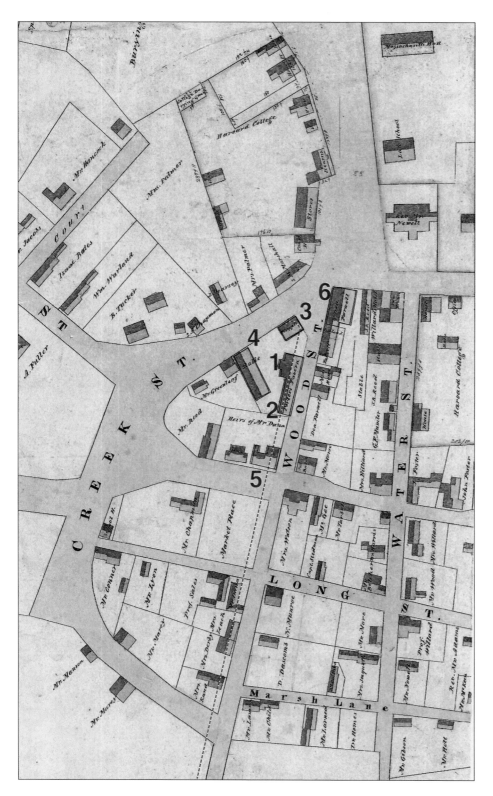

FIGURE 3.35 Harvard Square and the Brattle-Kennedy-Mt. Auburn block in 1833. The dotted line shows the street widening of 1896. See figure 3.38 for the configuration of the block in 1900.

1. Blue Anchor Tavern (1699; partly burned 1850);
2. Israel Porter's tavern addition (1800; demolished 1896); 3. Israel Porter's brick house (ca. 1820; last portion demolished 1909);
4. Porter's stables (demolished 1871);
5. Professor James Winthrop house (ca. 1712; demolished 1896–1921);
6. Farwell's Store (ca. 1830; remodeled 1896).

FIGURE 3.36 Israel Porter's brick house stood on Brattle Street near the corner of Kennedy Street, and Ivory Estes's triangular one-story hardware store faced Harvard Square. Porter's heirs converted the Blue Anchor's ballroom into stores and rebuilt the old stable in 1871. All these structures were taken down, moved, or truncated in 1896, when the city widened Kennedy Street by about 15 feet. Photo 1873.

FIGURE 3.37 Two bays of Israel Porter's brick house survived Mayor McNamee's remodeling project at the corner of Kennedy and Brattle streets (1897, George Fogerty, architect). The small gable-roofed building housed the Holly Tree Café; beyond it are the recently remodeled Porter Stable (1904, McLean & Graham) and McNamee's four-story bindery (1894, George Fogerty; see figure 8.24). Photo 1907.

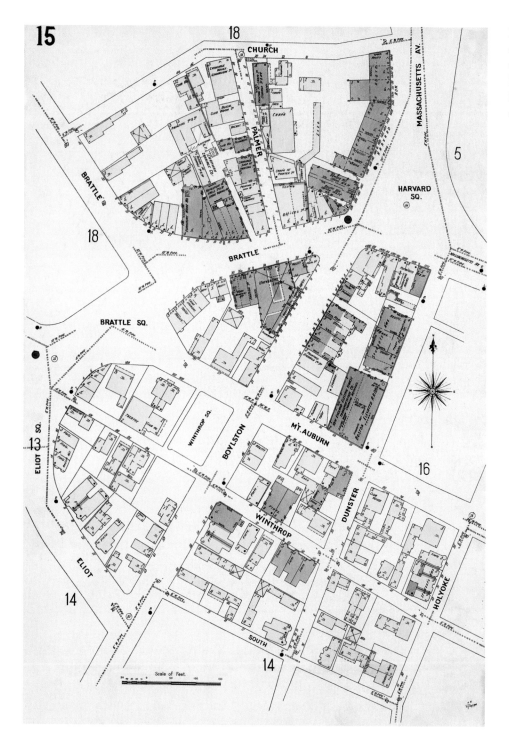

FIGURE 3.38 Harvard Square in 1900. Brick buildings are shown in red; frame buildings are in yellow. This detail from an insurance atlas describes the height of buildings (in number of stories); their use (D=dwelling, S=store); and in some cases, the tenants or the activities carried on there.

FIGURE 3.39 Some streetcar passengers preferred to wait outdoors rather than in the company's fetid waiting room. Photo January 14, 1898.

Cambridge citizens to the lunatic asylum. … It is confusion worse confounded, and amid it all is the knowledge that 'the square' has been made as ugly a terminus as can be found in a day's journey" (*Chronicle,* July 7, 1894). Despite the recent street widening, conditions deteriorated when routes were reorganized after the completion of the Tremont Street Subway in 1897. Some Boston trolleys continued out Massachusetts Avenue and Mt. Auburn Street, but the East Cambridge, Broadway, Watertown, and Newton lines all terminated in the Square. On summer Sundays as many as 20,000 people changed cars, and football games might bring twice that number. The *Boston Transcript* described the scene:

The bleak winds of winter are beginning to blow; slush and snow delusively cover pools of mud in Harvard Square; the cars are crowded, the days are short; bicycles, express teams, furniture wagons dispute with the waiting patrons of the road that one tiny place left free from a labyrinth of tracks in the middle of the square—that little oasis, where thousands … stand shelterless every day. (Nov. 3, 1897)

Some startling proposals were made to alleviate this situation. An alderman proposed a streetcar subway with ramps at Putnam Square, Brattle Square, Garden Street, and Massachusetts Avenue. Another suggested "an ornamental building, with pitch roof, two stories high" as a transfer station on the lower end

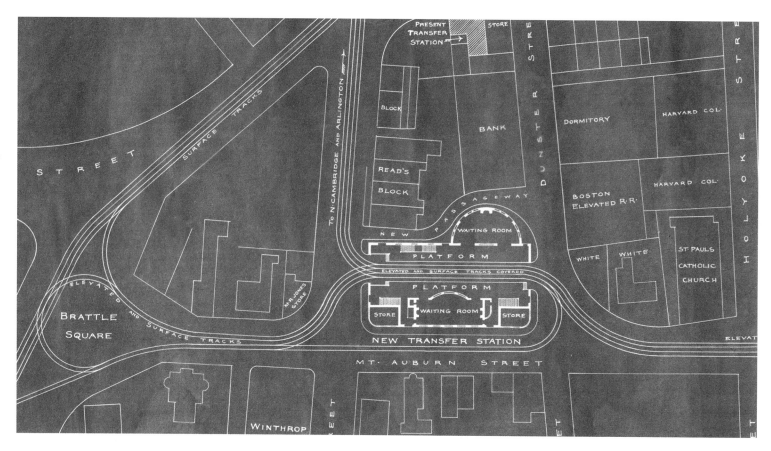

FIGURE 3.40 Proposals for a Harvard Square terminal proliferated after the legislature mandated construction of an elevated rapid transit line in 1897. The authors of this plan had no official standing, but their proposal was dubbed "Best Plan Yet Prepared" by the *Chronicle* (Feb. 5, 1898). Both surface and elevated lines would run on Mt. Auburn Street into a two-story transfer station, from which surface lines would continue toward Arlington and Watertown.

of Flagstaff Park; its remoteness would be balanced by its location "in a beautiful open space, where everybody from a distance could see it" (*Chronicle,* Feb. 19, 1898). President Eliot, concerned about the elevated rapid transit line mandated by the legislature in 1897, favored a station located on Mt. Auburn Street (figures 3.40–3.41).

The Boston Elevated Railway moved quickly once the decision had been made to construct a subway rather than an elevated.

The Hugh Nawn Construction Company broke ground in Harvard Square in August 1909; surface work was completed in October 1911 (figure 3.42). When the line opened the following March, just the Massachusetts Avenue, Broadway, and Cambridge Street lines stopped on the street to transfer passengers to the subway, and congestion was alleviated until automobiles proliferated after World War I. Only the shopkeepers who had profited from the free transfers that allowed commuters fifteen minutes to change cars regretted the improvements, because subway passengers could not come to the surface without paying an extra fare.

Compared with their better-organized brethren in Central Square, local businessmen found themselves at a disadvantage in their dealings with the Elevated. In 1910 they got together

FIGURE 3.41 The proposed Harvard Square transfer station would have resembled the Boston Elevated Railway's station at Dudley Square in Roxbury, which was designed by A.W. Longfellow in 1901. Photo before 1906.

FIGURE 3.42 Subway construction in Harvard Square, 1910. Pedestrians traverse a temporary sidewalk while an open trolley negotiates a temporary track on Kennedy Street. An electric hoist works an excavation in front of the Read Block. Only two buildings were taken down, but the surface of Eliot Street had to be raised as much as seven feet to clear the top of the tunnel. Photo September 30, 1910.

"to promote the commercial and industrial interests of Harvard Square" (*HSBA Bulletin,* Apr. 1911). Under the leadership of George C. Wright, an insurance man, and John Nolen, a landscape architect, the Harvard Square Business Men's Association petitioned the mayor to ask President Lowell to convene a "committee of its experts 'to prepare a plan or plans as a basis for the present and future development of Harvard Square.'" Lowell tapped two architects and a landscape architect, Professors H. Langford Warren, John Humphrey, and Henry Hubbard, and agreed to pay Professor Eugene J.A. Duquesne to prepare drawings. Their report contrasted Central Square, "the natural business centre of Cambridge," and Harvard Square, "the natural centre of a more expensive residence district, with such shops as serve the neighborhood tributary to it." In an ideal metropolitan area, the "collegiate square" and the "centre of a high-class residence district" should be "quickly reached from the city, but … quiet in use and appearance." Harvard Square "was already, in many ways, admirably fitted for its relations to the four main factors in its development—shopping, residence, traffic, and the activities of the College." The committee advocated a uniform architectural style to reflect "the dignified Colonial buildings of Harvard College … by preserving and emphasizing these admirable architectural traditions of Colonial and Georgian architecture, Harvard Square might win a character and an attractiveness which would be unique" ("Committee Appointed by the President …").

The *Boston Evening Transcript* summarized the committee's recommendations:

> Harvard Square would be redeveloped with a modern and commodious hotel where College House now stands, a large convention hall in Palmer Street, a building for a school of dramatic art, a wider [Kennedy] Street, a wider Massachusetts Avenue between Harvard and Central squares, shops with arcades between Harvard and Quincy squares, [and] a boulevard from Quincy Square to the Charles River. (Feb. 25, 1913; figure 3.43)

The mayor disregarded the committee's recommendation for a "permanent expert commission with advisory powers" to review projects in the Square, deferring instead to the city's new planning board (see chapter 2). In 1920 the board observed that "the square has ceased to be the trading center it was before the subway took traffic underground, and since Harvard College has become a great democratic institution lavish expenditure on the part of students has ceased to prevail," but it offered few realistic suggestions and did not assume a design advisory function for new buildings until 1979 (*Cambridge Annual Documents*, 1920–21, 571).

Modernization of the commercial district resumed once the subway was finished. In 1913 George Dow, a Central Square real estate investor, purchased lots that had been cleared for subway construction and erected 1–8 Brattle Street, an office building in the Georgian Revival style that was hailed as the first tangible response to the committee's design recommendations (see figure 8.27). Three years later, the Charles River Trust Company demolished two bays of College House and put up a diminutive Georgian bank next to Lyceum Hall (figure 3.44). When prosperity returned after the war, the Cambridge Savings Bank built its substantial headquarters directly on the Square. In 1924 the Harvard Cooperative Society demolished Lyceum Hall

FIGURE 3.43 Professor E.J.A. Duquesne's rendering of Harvard Square reimagined in the Art Nouveau style. The *Boston Transcript* noted: "Professor Duquesne has come recently from France," and observed that his "not exactly typical" plans would give the Square a distinctly Parisian cast (Feb. 25, 1913).

FIGURE 3.44 After 1912 Harvard Square settled into a brief period of calm until growing automobile traffic began to endanger trolley passengers waiting in the street. From left to right, the original subway headhouse (1912); the Abbott Building (1912); Lyceum Hall (1841); and the Charles River Trust Co. (1916). Photo ca. 1917.

and erected a store that complemented the new Georgian dormitories cloistering Harvard Yard (see figure 8.30). The opening of the 2,000-seat University Theater behind College House in 1926 completed the makeover (figure 3.45).

The university's vigorous expansion during this period attracted speculators, some of whom raised the stakes by proposing objectionable projects. Alumnus Maurice Wyner acquired the former site of St. Paul's Church on the corner of Mt. Auburn and Holyoke streets and in 1925 announced plans to build a hotel in the midst of the Gold Coast. "Immediately a storm of protest arose from all quarters. Prominent alumni urged the university to acquire the property to prevent the district from being marred." Charles Chauncey Stillman bought him out to keep the property "in hands friendly to Harvard" (*Harvard Crimson,* May 11, 1925). When Samuel Lebowitch of Boston threatened to raze Beck Hall for a hotel or a movie theater, Stillman again came to the rescue. By the time Israel Petkin of Roxbury announced in 1927 that the stores he was building at the corner of Mt. Auburn and Dunster streets had been engineered to support a six-story, 250-room hotel, Stillman was dead, but President Lowell squelched this and later schemes by recognizing that patience could often gain favorable terms.

Stillman's executors sold Beck Hall to a group of alumni who in 1928 announced plans to erect a ten-story Georgian Revival apartment house with shops on the ground floor and offices on the second; with 250 suites of two to six rooms it would have been one of the largest in the Boston area (figure 3.46). The proponents overcame university opposition to a zoning variance but sold the property in 1930. The new owners, Roxbury investors Harris and Sumner Poorvu, let it revert to the mortgage holder in 1938. The Gulf Oil Co. acquired Beck in 1940 and replaced it with a service station. Harvard finally purchased the property in 1979 and built The Inn at Harvard in 1988 (see figures 8.8 and 9.24).

In this period of rapid change only one building in Harvard Square was saved because of its historic associations. John Hicks, a Minuteman killed during the British retreat from Concord, built a house at Dunster and Winthrop streets in 1762 (see

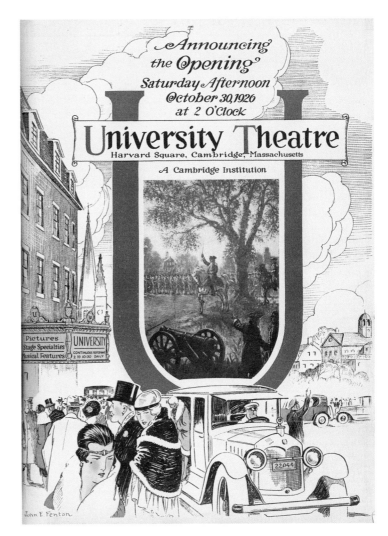

FIGURE 3.45 The opening of the University Theatre in 1926 brought the first permanent entertainment venue to the Square.

FIGURE 3.46 Beck Hall II (proposed), 1201 Massachusetts Avenue (1928, Blackall, Clapp & Whittemore, architects). Rendering 1928.

FIGURE 3.47 John Hicks house (1762) in its new location at 64 Kennedy Street before the construction of Bryan Hall in 1933. Photo ca. 1929.

FIGURE 3.48 Edward Marrett tenant house, 20 South Street (ca. 1760; demolished 1933). The Dunster House Book Shop occupied this site for a few years after its former space at 26 Holyoke Street was razed in 1927 (see figure 10.36).

figures 3.10 and 6.31). A carpenter who served as constable and tax collector, Hicks lost the property in 1773 after being unable to repay John Foxcroft £212 he had borrowed against taxes he could not collect in hard times. An alumnus acquired the place for Harvard in 1903, and in 1922 the university rented it to Cecil and Esther Stevens Fraser. Esther was an ardent preservationist, and when Harvard wanted the site in 1928 for the Indoor Athletic Building (Malkin Center), she mobilized the Cambridge Historical Society and the Society for the Preservation of New England Antiquities to help move the house to Kennedy Street.[6] In 1931 the university remodeled it as a library for Kirkland House. An almost identical gambrel at 20 South Street was taken down without discussion in 1933 (figures 3.47–3.48).

The remaining houses on Dunster and South streets are a fragment of the urban fabric that was lost when Harvard constructed the River Houses (figure 3.49). At 17 South, Ebenezer and Samuel Stedman, sons of postmaster and tavernkeeper

FIGURE 3.49 Surviving houses on South Street. From left to right, Ebenezer Stedman & Co.'s ice house and residence, 17 South Street (1817–26); William Russell's tenement, 71–77 Dunster Street (1894); the Stedman brothers' house, 69 Dunster Street (1832, Oliver Hastings, housewright). All are now owned by Harvard University. Photo 2009.

Business Men's Association mounted a campaign for redress. The Boston Elevated Railway was uncooperative, but Cambridge prevailed in the legislature, and the kiosk was replaced in 1928. Filling stations, garages, and parking lots proliferated. Hundreds of Harvard men brought cars to Cambridge, and heated garages replaced livery stables on Bow and Church streets in 1907 and 1912 (see chapter 8). Garages displaced houses on Kennedy Street in 1911 and 1920 and on Mt. Auburn in 1921 and 1925; the sites of the Shepard Memorial Church and the old City Building were paved for parking in 1924 and 1936. The area's first underground garage opened at Eliot Square in 1930. Filling stations favored Kennedy Street, opening on the corner of Memorial Drive in 1922, at Eliot Street in 1929, and at Winthrop Street in 1939 (figure 3.50). There were at least seventeen auto-related businesses in and around Harvard Square by 1931, including six garages, eight repair shops, two gasoline stations, and a Ford dealership at 1230 Massachusetts Avenue.

Ebenezer Stedman of Mt. Auburn Street, dug a cellar 16 feet deep in 1817 in which to store ice cut from local ponds until it could be shipped to market from the College Wharf. In 1826 the brothers borrowed $600 from Jonas Wyeth to build a cottage over the cellar. Perhaps finding the premises a little damp, the Stedmans put up 69 Dunster Street next door in 1829. When Ebenezer Stedman & Co. failed in 1832, the Wyeths foreclosed, and the property passed in 1867 to Aaron Molyneaux Hewlett, a physical education teacher who was Harvard's first African American instructor. Hewlett died in 1871, and ten years later his daughter Virginia, who had married Frederick Douglass Jr., sold the place to Harvard Square grocer William Russell. Russell rented his new house on the corner to middle-class Irish-American families, while 17 South became the longtime residence of William McGowan, an Irish laborer, and his descendants.

In the 1920s Harvard Square merchants and shoppers became obsessed with traffic, parking, and pedestrian safety. The original subway headhouse had no sidewalks or safety zones, and the

FIGURE 3.50 The Harvard Square Garage began with a conversion of the Union Railway stable on the corner of Mt. Auburn and Dunster streets in 1917 (see figure 9.29). In 1923 the owners added a new three-level structure on Kennedy Street that offered parking for 325 cars.

The evolution of Brattle Square into a modern shopping district began in 1919, when the Business Men's Association orchestrated the construction of a new post office at 38B Brattle Street (see figure 8.28). The Sage family replaced the Jacob Bates house with a Georgian-style market in 1926 (see figures 6.40 and 8.29). George Dow and a partner, Harry Stearns, owned a motley collection of stores along Brattle between Palmer and Church streets. Stearns died in 1930, and in the midst of the Depression Dow set out to develop Brattle Square as a suburban shopping center with modern buildings, plentiful parking, and an attractive array of retailers. Richard (Tony) Dow graduated from Harvard in 1935 and went to work for his father. They first removed the unproductive upper stories of 17–25 Brattle Street and gave the entire row an up-to-date Moderne facade in cast stone (figures 3.51–3.52; see also figure 8.38). They assembled a mix of retailers that would appeal to Old Cambridge housewives and made overtures for a Filene's department store that opened instead in Belmont in 1956. Cambridge architect William L. Galvin's 1937 Federal Savings & Loan building completed the ensemble of Depression-era architecture and screened the parking lots and subway yards that dominated Eliot Square after the municipal building was razed in 1936 (see figure 3.74).

POSTWAR PLANNING AND DEVELOPMENT

After World War II cities across America saw their populations plummet, manufacturing employment and tax bases erode, and business districts disintegrate. Elected officials at all levels desperately sought remedies in slum clearance, highway construction, economic development, and new theories of urban planning. Cambridge's traditional downtown, Central Square, began a decades-long decline, but Harvard Square maintained a modest prosperity that tantalized politicians desperate for taxable development (figures 3.53–3.54).

The city tried to spur growth by relaxing the zoning code and repurposing underutilized public land. The surge of automobile ownership after the war stimulated efforts to provide parking,

FIGURE 3.51 Brattle Square in 1927. The 1875 Estes and Whitney buildings at 13–15 and 17–25 Brattle Street (right) were separately owned, although they shared a common facade. George Dow removed the upper stories of 17–25 in 1936; the Estes building survives today.

FIGURE 3.52 Brattle Square, ca. 1942. Dow's Brattle Square shopping center combined new construction with older stores rebuilt behind a unified Moderne facade. In the foreground, a new facade was applied to a one-story remnant of the Whitney building in 1936 (see figure 8.21). The centerpiece was the impressive new building designed by Graton & Born in 1941. Photo ca. 1942.

FIGURE 3.53 Brattle Street in 1946, looking from Harvard Square toward the Cambridge Federal Savings bank in Brattle Square. Streetcars and trolley buses shared the street with two-way automobile traffic.

FIGURE 3.54 McNamee's Block, 13–25 Kennedy Street and 22–24 Brattle Street (1871, remodeled 1904, Graham & McLean, architects). In 1948 the Dows evicted a dozen small shops from the former Porter's stable on Kennedy and Brattle streets so the building could be remodeled as a branch of Corcoran's, a Central Square department store. Young Lee's restaurant relocated to Church Street and Olsson's moved to Brattle Square; the laundry, the paint store, and the appliance shop closed. Photo ca. 1946.

speed traffic, and alleviate conflicts with pedestrians. Cars competed with streetcars, buses, and pedestrians (the latter comprising an estimated daily volume of 10,000 students and 70,000 commuters in 1949). Even though Cambridge prohibited all-night street parking, 3,800 Harvard students had cars in 1955.[7] The city installed the Square's first parking meters in 1947 to make spaces available to shoppers at 5¢ per hour, and in 1950 created metered lots in Eliot Square and on the west side of Flagstaff park. In 1951 the Cambridge Traffic Board proposed paving the Common for surface parking, and in 1958 the city council funded a study of an underground garage (see chapter 5).

Traffic control in the Square was accomplished "by officers who could mix insults with instructions" and who controlled signals from a wooden booth installed in 1936 (*Crimson*, Sept. 30, 1949). A permanent structure went up in 1951 (see figure 3.87). After streetcar service ended between Harvard Square and the Back Bay in September 1949, the city experimented with rotary traffic around the kiosk.[8] In 1959 and 1962, new building lines foresaw widening the north side of Mt. Auburn Street and the east side of Kennedy, in both cases to 65 feet.[9] A traffic study sponsored by Harvard University recommended creation of a new one-way connector between Garden Street and Memorial Drive by widening Appian Way and Hilliard Street. Beginning in 1962, the city's new traffic director, Robert Rudolph, made most streets in the Square one-way (figure 3.55).

FIGURE 3.55 Harvard Square in 1961, after the streetcar tracks were paved over and pedestrian crosswalks introduced. The light-colored oval around the kiosk reflected a brief experiment with a rotary; two-way traffic on all three sides of the kiosk was still in effect. Red Line construction in 1978–85 closed Massachusetts Avenue in front of the Cambridge Savings Bank and eliminated the information booth and public parking in the foreground.

Many people at this time perceived Harvard Square as undistinguished, overburdened, obsolete, and chaotic. Architect Josep Lluis Sert, Harvard's chief planner, warned an audience that "a few steps away, there is a gateway that opens to Harvard Square and like Dante's door to hell, could carry over it the inscription 'Abandon all hope,' meaning all hope of finding these elements that make our environment human, because across the gate there is noise, disorder, lack of visual balance and harmony" (Sert, 1956). One journalist called the Square "an unmitigated mess" (*Boston Sunday Herald,* Dec. 11, 1966). Others found it cosmopolitan and charmingly eclectic, reflecting the debate between the prevailing planning orthodoxy of Corbusian Modernism and the humanistic principles espoused by Jane Jacobs. Harvard put Sert's Modernist principles into practice when it razed an entire city block to build Holyoke Center in 1960–67. Although its storefronts were a welcome contribution to the side streets, its empty plaza and harsh exterior contrasted sharply with the brick buildings and small shops that once populated this corner (figures 3.57–3.58).

The zoning code adopted in 1962 relaxed or eliminated most height limits and encouraged construction of hotels, apartment houses, and office buildings. Debates over the future of the Square soon became contentious. Community activists fought pitched battles against new buildings, fast-food restaurants, and the proliferation of liquor licenses. Harvard Square ceased to be a neighborhood shopping area for Old Cambridge and began attracting visitors from around the world.

RETAIL TRENDS AND SOCIAL LIFE AFTER 1945

[Before World War II] there were twenty-two restaurants, most of them small and inexpensive. ... For "gourmet" cooking one had to go outside the Square to tea-room type establishments housed in basements of nearby apartment houses. The most numerous group of retail stores was devoted to men's clothing and catered to students. The sole "art" store was a genteel picture-framing shop which also carried gifts; the first exotic shop did not appear until 1939 when refugees from Nazi-dominated Austria opened a tiny

FIGURE 3.56 Harvard Square in 1962.

FIGURE 3.57 Little's Block at the corner of Massachusetts Avenue and Dunster Street accommodated a number of small shops until Harvard razed it in 1964; the corner is now occupied by Forbes Plaza. Holyoke House (occupied by Brine's sporting goods store) survived one more year. Photo ca. 1958.

FIGURE 3.58 Forbes Plaza, Holyoke Center. The haberdashery occupying the store behind the plaza was replaced by a cafe, Au Bon Pain, in 1983. Photo ca. 1968.

cooperative shop in a second floor "window" on Church Street. There were seven bookshops, along with the usual assortment of hardware, grocery, dress, apothecary, and barber shops, and several banks. … There was generally a place to park one's car, and shopkeepers knew their customers. (Bainbridge Bunting, *Report Four: Old Cambridge*, 26–27)[10]

Avant-garde movements in design and entertainment that emerged in the 1950s radically altered the Square. In 1953 Cyrus Harvey and Bryant Haliday converted the Brattle Theater into a movie house showing European films rarely seen in America and began an annual Humphrey Bogart film festival that became a tradition during Harvard reading periods. Club 47, a coffeehouse that introduced many to modern folk music, opened at 47 Mt. Auburn Street in 1958 (figures 3.59–3.60). Benjamin Thompson, an associate of Walter Gropius at The Architects Collaborative (TAC), founded Design Research (D/R) in a corner of his office in 1951. His retail store, which opened two years later, introduced modern Scandinavian furnishings and textiles to American consumers and "forever changed the way America bought design" (*New York Times,* Oct. 12, 2003; figure 3.61). By the early 1960s a number of establishments catered to sophisticated tastes. Nearby houses and apartments, factories, and garages became specialty shops and architects' offices, and young adults began to flock to the Square on weekends.

The ambience of prewar Harvard Square survived well into the 1960s, thanks to the conservatism of local property owners, the indifference of the university toward local commercial property, and the good management of the Dow-Stearns properties. Dow tenants in the 1960s included an A&P supermarket, two florists, two jewelers, clothing stores, an appliance store, and a dry cleaner. Tony Dow, who managed the trust until his death in 1988, maintained elements of this mix as a matter of principle, even when market forces favored high-volume, mass-market chain stores, and boutiques.

The retail character of Harvard Square varied from the Dow family's well-kept shops in Brattle Square to Bertha Cohen's shabby storefronts (figure 3.62). The Dows frequently upgraded

FIGURE 3.59 The Brattle Theater, which the Cambridge Social Union opened as Brattle Hall in 1889, received a new facade designed by Charles Cogswell in 1907 and became a movie theater in 1953 (see figure 7.43). The poster reads, "Opening Soon! New England's Finest Showcase for Foreign Films." After a renovation in 1991 the theater occupied only a portion of the original hall. Photo February 1, 1953.

their buildings, but Cohen, the Square's largest individual property owner, left maintenance to her tenants and kept the rents low. Her death in 1965 created sudden opportunities for investors and turmoil in the retail community. When Max Wasserman purchased all her buildings in 1970, he raised rents as much as 400 percent and displaced colorful (or, to some, seedy) small shops. He remodeled a few storefronts in a contemporary vernacular, but his most visible project was the adaptive reuse of the parking garage at Kennedy and Mt. Auburn streets as The Garage, an indoor mall organized around the building's interior ramps (figures 3.63–3.64).

FIGURE 3.60 The folk scene in Harvard Square attracted performers from all over New England. Joan Baez, a Belmont native shown performing behind the subway kiosk in 1959, used this picture on the cover of her first album.

FIGURE 3.61 Benjamin Thompson's original Design Research store opened at 57 Brattle Street in 1953 and soon became a magnet for consumers. After the firm moved to its new building at 48 Brattle in 1970 Harvard razed the old store for Gutman Hall. Photo ca. 1968.

FIGURE 3.62 Bertha Cohen's storefronts at 29–41 Kennedy Street (1921, S.S. Eisenberg, architect). Many of Cohen's buildings were single-story retail blocks built in the 1920s that she purchased cheaply in the 1930s and '40s. Rooftop billboards brought additional income. This building on the corner of Mt. Auburn Street was razed in 1971. Photo 1965.

FIGURE 3.63 Max Wasserman remodeled 47–49A Mt. Auburn Street in 1971, employing contemporary graphics to attract customers. Photo 1973.

FIGURE 3.64 Wasserman remodeled the Harvard Square Garage at 34–40 Kennedy Street into an indoor mini-mall in 1972. An early example of adaptive reuse, The Garage was an instant success. Photo 1973.

This period of modest prosperity, in which new stores coexisted with traditional retailers and services, ended abruptly with the social unrest that accompanied the Vietnam War. In the summer of 1968 hundreds of teenagers from around the country "who heard that Cambridge was where the dope and music were," begged in the streets and slept on the Common (*Crimson,* Sept. 21, 1970). Political demonstrations replaced previously tolerated student panty raids and riotous celebrations of athletic victories. Tensions rose when hundreds of state and local police mustered in Harvard Square during the student occupation of University Hall in the spring of 1969. Although 10,000 people marched through Cambridge without incident on October 15, 1969, the next academic year was filled with violence. On April 15, 1970, a peace rally on Boston Common ended with a planned "trashing" in Harvard Square, when 3,000 demonstrators broke windows,

set fires in the street, and threw flaming debris into the Coop and the Northeast Federal Savings Bank. Stores were looted, and all the ground floor windows in Holyoke Center were broken. As many as 1,200 policemen engaged in pitched battles with the demonstrators, countering volleys of bricks with tear gas and beatings; 2,000 National Guardsmen stood in reserve. Retreating demonstrators caused extensive damage in Central Square on their way back to Boston (figure 3.65).

Another violent demonstration on May 8th followed the bombing of Cambodia and the killings at Kent State. During the summer, runaway youths were augmented by anarchists who used political protest as a pretext for continued trashing and looting. The daily floating population of Cambridge was estimated at 4,000, and social workers thought that "one out of six street freaks sitting at Forbes Plaza was on heroin" (*Crimson,* Sept. 21, 1970). Rioters overturned a bus on July 25th and again looted stores in Holyoke Center. Another disturbance on August 5th was quelled by an overwhelming police response.

By this time Harvard Square businesspeople were reeling. Although occasional rioting continued until 1972, 1970 was a watershed year. Suburban customers were frightened by news reports and offended by aggressive panhandlers. The merchants had lost their dream of the Square as a "quaint, pleasant place to shop, where anyone can feel comfortable." One reported that shoplifting had doubled, and "nobody who doesn't live here will come in to shop." Harvard Square was in danger of "becoming another Berkeley, a city too risky for high-class businesses" (*Crimson,* July 31, 1970). Boutiques and service businesses that depended on affluent suburban customers failed. The steel grates that merchants installed to protect their windows at night gave the streets a menacing appearance. Police harassed panhandlers and street vendors, raided the Common, and became a constant presence. Felix's newsstand, which sold radical journals in a Harvard-owned storefront, was evicted, and the all-night Hayes Bickford's cafeteria, thought to be a magnet for militants, was forced to close in 1970 when the landlord doubled its rent (figures 3.66–3.67).[11]

FIGURE 3.65 The 1969–70 academic year was marked by repeated violence. On April 15, 1970, antiwar protestors rioted in Harvard Square, setting fires and trashing storefronts despite a massive police presence.

FIGURE 3.66 Felix's Newsstand at 1304 Massachusetts Avenue was evicted in 1970 "because of an unhappiness with some of the books and magazines" it sold (*Crimson,* June 11, 1970). Felix Caragianes had been arrested in 1926 by agents of Boston's Watch & Ward Society for selling copies of H.L. Mencken's allegedly obscene literary magazine, *The American Mercury*; Mencken himself came to Boston to be arrested on the same charge but was acquitted. Felix's nephew Angelo was arrested twice in the 1960s for similar reasons. Photo September 20, 1970.

FIGURE 3.67 Hayes Bickford's was a regional chain of inexpensive cafeterias that operated from 1924 until 1977. The Harvard Square outlet at 1326 Massachusetts Avenue was one of three in Cambridge that fueled students and working people around the clock until 1967, when it began to close between 4:00 and 5:00 a.m. Photo ca. 1962.

FIGURE 3.68 Merchants greatly disliked Brattle Walk, an early experiment in traffic calming; one observed: "it looks lousy, the implementation was poor, and it's just a little place that doesn't go anywhere" (*Crimson*, Mar. 11, 1972). The project was abandoned after a short time, but the concept was revived more successfully by the Red Line improvements in 1978–86. Photo August 17, 1972.

Eventually the scene mellowed. The city tried to help by installing temporary landscaping in the center of Brattle Square in 1971 (figure 3.68). In 1973 a student journalist noted that political activism was already a memory, but hippie craftspeople still sold their wares on the sidewalks, street people panhandled, and freaks made music on Forbes Plaza. Businesspeople tolerated sidewalk musicians and Hare Krishnas as attractions for visitors. Street people aged, and some became homeless adults. Young people flooded into the Square, and the generation that protested the war so violently became an economic force in its own right.

During the 1970s merchants struggled for a footing in a changing demographic environment. The *Crimson* reported that "retail chains have replaced some of the older smaller storefronts," striking a theme that would be repeated constantly in years to come (July 2, 1973). Nostalgia became a staple of news reports about the changing Square; J.D. Pollock, co-owner of the Brattle Theater, reminisced that "what you love about the Square is how you saw it the first time. That is the way you think it should be, and you are resistant to any other view of it." Neil Miller, a journalist,

explained that "for those of us who first came to Cambridge in the '60s and '70s, its charm lay in its basement bookstores and cafes, in its tiny alleyways, in the vaguely bohemian and Continental atmosphere it had at a time when the only croissant to be found in the Western Hemisphere south of Montreal and north of Guadeloupe was at the Patisserie Française, on … J.F. Kennedy Street" (*Boston Phoenix*, Feb. 19, 1985).[12]

Local department stores could no longer compete with chain stores, and some landlords upgraded their properties at the expense of stores selling everyday necessities. Woolworth's five-and-dime store lost its lease at 15 Brattle Street in 1978 and was replaced by The Gap, a chain selling inexpensive clothing. Corcoran's, which sold home furnishings and clothing, gave up its lease on the old Porter stable in 1987; its replacement, Urban Outfitters, sold many of the same articles, but targeted adolescents and college students. Three other chain stores opened in One Brattle Square in 1991, leading to a new round of laments that the Square was becoming "mallified" (*Crimson*, Nov. 21, 1991). The Coop (which had become a department store in the

FIGURE 3.69 Harvard Square mellowed in the early 1970s. The caption of this postcard reads, "This is our scene. … Try to get in it." Postcard ca. 1972.

1930s) sold clothing, records, housewares, appliances, and stationery until 1995, when it gave up half its main selling floor and closed all its departments except a Harvard-themed souvenir shop and a bookstore managed by Barnes & Noble, a national chain. The displacement of middle-income families and students after the end of rent control in 1995 also had a significant impact on the Square's customer base.

Stand-alone stores are always vulnerable to market trends, escalating rents, and life-changing events. Many family-run operations closed when their owners retired or died: the Bicycle Exchange (1991), Olsson's framing and art store (1992), Tommy's Lunch (1992), Cambridge Camera & Marine (1994), Elsie's Lunch (1995), Cahaly's men's clothing (1996), Ferrante-Dege's camera store (2006), and Bob Slate stationery (2011). The Tasty (1997) and the Harvard Provision Store (1999) were evicted for redevelopment. Stores like Sage's Market (2000) could no longer pay competitive rents. Chain stores offered wider selections and lower prices, leading to the closing of Briggs & Briggs, a music store (1999), Billings & Stover's pharmacy (2000), and Brine's

sporting goods (2004). As property owner John DiGiovanni noted: "You really have to be on top of your business because of the competition for your space" (*Crimson,* Feb. 9, 1999).

Changes in American society at the turn of the 21st century struck the Square's bookstores with particular force. Aging baby-boomers (Harvard Square's key demographic for three decades), the ease of Internet shopping, and the rise of electronic readers fatally changed the relationship of many bookstores with their customers. In 1990 there were at least twenty-five sellers of new and used books in the Square. None were national chain stores, and six—the Coop, the Harvard Bookstore, Cambridge Booksmith, Reading International, WordsWorth, and Barillari Books—carried a wide selection of new books and journals.[13] Smaller stores specialized in poetry, foreign languages, architecture, travel, Asia, or leftist politics, while others bought and sold the used books that the academic community traded in profusion. Bookstores were subject to the same forces as other small businesses. Cambridge Booksmith closed in 1992, Reading International in 1993, and Barillari in 1994. By 1998 the

FIGURE 3.70 Sheldon Cohen succeeded his father as a newsboy in 1947 and opened the first Out of Town News stand next to the subway kiosk in 1955. He quickly built a succession of ever-larger freestanding newsstands. The "zipper" sign on this 1966 structure operated from 1976 until the MBTA began construction on the Red Line Extension in 1980. Photo 1976.

remaining stores were under pressure from online vendors and rising rents. When WordsWorth Books closed in 2004 it left only two general bookstores and three specialized booksellers in the Square, the lowest number since the 1930s. As the *Crimson* observed: "a more intellectual customer base with a lower income once sustained a group of stores that now struggle to find a niche" (Feb. 9, 1999). Confirmation of these trends came in 2011, when two more bookstores closed and Amazon.com announced that Cambridge was first among the nation's large cities for per-capita sales of books online. By this time, stores selling recorded music had disappeared from the Square.

The same trends affected newsstands. Sheldon Cohen, who began selling papers as a newsboy in the 1940s, opened Out Of Town News in 1955. A few years later he built a small newsstand next to the kiosk and in 1966 replaced it with a prefabricated structure that sported an illuminated 'zipper' sign like those

in Times Square (figure 3.70). About this time his stand was reputed to stock 3,000 periodicals and newspapers from forty countries. Out Of Town News moved into the refurbished 1927 subway kiosk in 1984, but demand slackened with the rise of the Internet and Cohen sold the business to a new operator in 1994.

REDEVELOPMENT OF THE SOUTHWEST SECTOR

After World War II, the Bennett Street yards of the Metropolitan Transit Authority were considered ripe for development. Harvard coveted them for undergraduate housing, while the city hoped to maximize taxable private construction. The Kennedy family's choice of the yards as the site of a presidential memorial and library in 1964 pitted the community against the city, the university, and the memory of the dead president. Speculators acquired adjoining industrial properties, betting that the expected crowds would demand hotel rooms and places to park and shop. Concerns about overdevelopment and excessive commercialization articulated during this period governed future attitudes toward change in Harvard Square.

The John F. Kennedy Presidential Library and Museum

The ancient Ox Marsh west of Kennedy Street near the Great Bridge saw little activity until Estes Howe and some associates subdivided a tract along Mt. Auburn Street and sold part of it to the city for a municipal building in 1873 (figure 3.72). The lower reaches were subject to flooding, and only a few workshops, stables, and tenements were built there. The Union Railway erected a horsecar storage barn on Bennett Street in 1871, and the West End Street Railway put up several more in the 1880s and '90s. In 1909–12 the Boston Elevated Railway excavated the entire west side of Kennedy Street from Eliot Street to Memorial Drive for subway yards and a repair shop; the rest of the 12.2 acre site, bounded by Memorial Drive, Kennedy Street, Bennett Street, and University Road, was occupied by layover tracks, carbarns, and workshops for streetcars.

FIGURE 3.71 Harvard Square and the southwest sector in 1957. CHC.

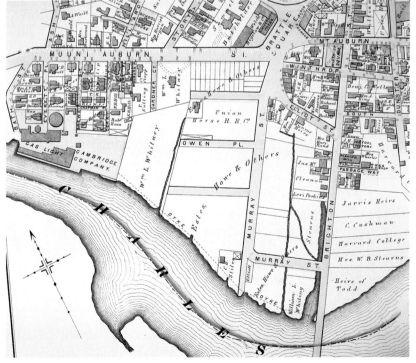

FIGURE 3.72 After the Civil War speculative owners built a dike to exclude the tides from the old Ox Marsh, but the area lay mostly vacant until the street railway companies needed land for carbarns and workshops in the late 19th century.

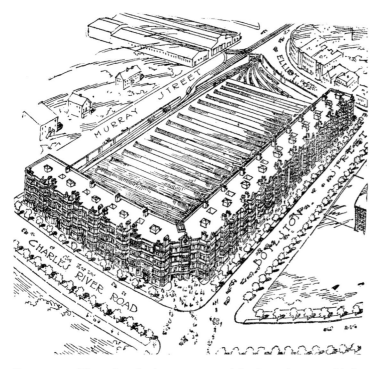

FIGURE 3.73 The earliest development proposal for the yards appeared before the subway was completed. In 1910 Robert S. Peabody, consulting architect for the Boston Elevated Railway, showed how a building containing 125 apartments could be built on a platform over the yards.

The development potential of the yards was obvious as early as 1910, when Robert S. Peabody sketched an apartment house complex on air rights (figure 3.73). In 1925 the Elevated investigated the possibility of building a seven-story garage and opening Stadium Station to regular use. The planning board flagged the site for development in 1950, but the Metropolitan Transit Authority (which succeeded the Boston Elevated in 1947) could not leave until it had a replacement repair facility. After 1958 the change from streetcars to buses made some land surplus, and in 1960 the MTA agreed to sell 11½ acres to Harvard University for about $3.5 million. Harvard planned to use half the site for undergraduate housing and sell the rest for development, but the deal fell through when elected officials opposed a private sale. After a consortium of Philadelphia insurance companies offered

to build five twenty-story apartment buildings, City Councillor Daniel Hayes suggested that the Cambridge Redevelopment Authority (CRA) take the site by eminent domain as it was "the most valuable undeveloped land in Cambridge and could become Cambridge's Prudential Center" (*Crimson,* Feb. 6, 1962).

The MTA tried to auction off the land in 1962. Boston attorney Samuel Coffman bid $2 million on behalf of a syndicate that proposed three 20-story apartment buildings, two 12-story office buildings, a 200-room motel, a 300,000 square foot shopping center, and a 2,800-car parking garage. John Briston Sullivan bid $4 million and said he would build "a 50-story star-shaped office building," a hotel, and a 400-unit apartment house. Harvard offered $5 million and proposed two undergraduate houses and 1,000 apartments in taxable buildings. The planning board suggested that the redevelopment authority should create a "superblock" running from Harvard Square to the river to accommodate a convention center, hotels, and medical offices (*Crimson,* May 2, 1963).

FIGURE 3.74 Beyond Brattle Square, the landscape was cluttered with parking lots, filling stations, and the terminal facilities of the Metropolitan Transit Authority. Every vacant lot and almost every building in this view was redeveloped before the end of the 20th century. Photo 1949.

The assassination of President Kennedy on November 22, 1963, halted all negotiations and precipitated a conflict over the southwest sector that reverberated for a generation. The idea of establishing Kennedy's presidential library at Harvard had been discussed as early as 1961, and in 1963 the president himself selected a two-acre site in Allston next to the Business School. After his death, the president's family decided instead to construct the facility in Cambridge. The congressionally chartered

FIGURE 3.76 Pei's pyramidal skylight for the Kennedy Library was rejected in 1974, but he used a similar structure for the visitor's center at the Louvre that was announced in 1984 and completed four years later.

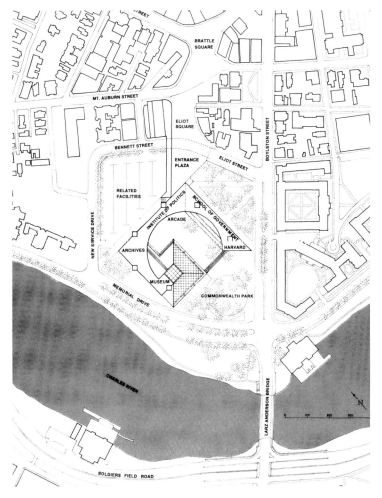

FIGURE 3.75 I.M. Pei's 1973 plan for the Kennedy Library included Harvard's Institute of Politics and School of Government in the same complex as the museum and the presidential library.

nonprofit Kennedy Library Corporation (KLC) selected I.M. Pei & Partners of New York as architects in December 1964, and in 1965 the General Court authorized the MTA to convey the yards to the federal government.

The library corporation planned to build an archive for the president's papers, a museum of his life and presidency, a public park, and a garage on 5.3 acres of the site. Tax-producing buildings owned by the corporation would cover another three acres, and the university would receive 2.2 acres for the Kennedy School of Government. The KLC predicted that the complex would attract up to 1.25 million visitors a year, with daily peaks from 15,000 to 20,000, requiring parking for 700 to 1,000 cars and 35 buses; later estimates rose to two million visitors. Pei envisioned building a glass pyramid 105 feet high next to a marble-clad, 225,000 square foot, 155-foot-high library and archive (figures 3.75–3.76).

At the city council's request, the Cambridge Redevelopment Authority in 1968 released an urban design plan drafted by a San Francisco architectural firm, Okamoto/Liskamm.[14] Tunnels under Massachusetts Avenue, Kennedy, and Mt. Auburn streets would eliminate through traffic, much as Harvard's planners had proposed in 1960, and the subway would be diverted to a new station under Brattle Square, where four sixteen- to twenty-story office buildings would surround a plaza and shopping mall. One scheme placed glass canopies over pedestrian spaces; another combined open plazas with underground arcades. Ten-story apartment houses would rise on Church and Dunster streets. The entire project would produce 1.3 million square feet of office space, 584,000 square feet of retail, 855 apartments, 185 town houses, 400 hotel rooms, and 2,030 parking spaces (figures 3.77–3.78). The community was horrified, and the city council took no further action.

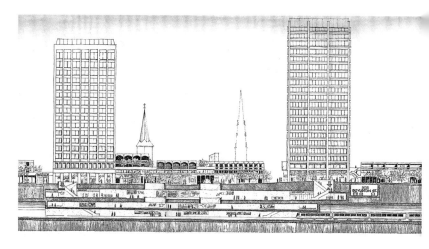

FIGURE 3.78 A sectional view along Mt. Auburn Street looking north shows a relocated subway station in a tunnel under Eliot Square and Kennedy (Boylston) Street. The steeples of the First Parish Church and Memorial Church are visible in the background.

VIEW LOOKING SOUTH FROM HARVARD SQUARE TOWARD CHARLES RIVER

FIGURE 3.77 Okamoto/Liskamm's proposal for the Cambridge Redevelopment Authority involved complete redevelopment of the southwest sector with buildings resembling Holyoke Center.

The KLC had hoped to open the library in 1970, but the Massachusetts Bay Transportation Authority (which replaced the MTA in 1964) did not find a new site for its repair shops until the end of 1969. By that time, the KLC's budget had been eroded by inflation, and the program was reduced to accommodate 600,000 visitors per year and 400 parking spaces. Pei's 1972 design was scaled down to 85 feet in height and 140,000 square feet. The "lively, variegated commercial district of small shops, restaurants, and bookstores" that Mrs. Kennedy hoped would accompany the museum was eliminated (*Crimson*, Sept. 29, 1966).

The Kennedy Library project generated a furious response from some members of the community. Opponents pointed out that four million people were visiting Kennedy's grave at Arlington National Cemetery each year; they feared that the library would turn Harvard Square into "an ugly fusion of traffic jams, parking lots, and tickey-tac, thereby destroying … whatever remains of [its] college-town atmosphere" (*Crimson*, Sept. 1, 1972). In April 1974 the KLC eliminated the pyramid, substituted brick for marble, and cut the height to 49 feet; two months later it proposed reducing the remaining floor space by moving most of the documents off site. City Councillor Barbara Ackermann noted that the new design "splits the library from the museum but does not, as Cambridge residents have asked, split the museum from the library" (*Crimson*, June 12).

The Neighborhood Ten Association, which represented a substantial portion of Old Cambridge, challenged the project in federal court in January 1975. In February the KLC announced that only the library would be built in Cambridge. The opponents were unmoved, and in May the corporation capitulated: it would withdraw from Cambridge and build the entire facility at Columbia Point in Dorchester. Harvard was eager to retain the archive and suggested that the museum might be located in Allston or Watertown, at Faneuil Hall, or at the Kennedy Center for the Performing Arts in Washington, D.C. The KLC was not interested in these alternatives, and early in 1976 it suggested that part of the yards be allocated to Harvard for the

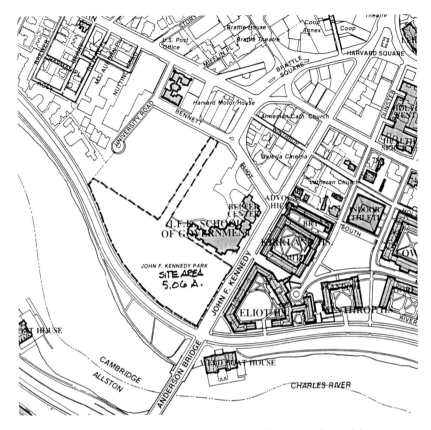

FIGURE 3.79 The three-way division of the MBTA yards in 1976 allocated five acres for a memorial park, three acres to Harvard for the Kennedy School of Government, and 4.2 acres, known as Parcel 1B, to be sold to the highest bidder.

Kennedy School of Government, part become a park, and the remainder—a tract called Parcel 1B—be sold for development. The first $2 million of the proceeds would support construction at Columbia Point, and the balance would fund the park. This plan was quickly ratified by Congress and the General Court (figure 3.79).

The Kennedy Library controversy was a uniquely Cambridge event of almost seismic proportions. Kennedy partisans, who were numerous at Harvard and among the city's independent Democrats, saw the memorial as a sacred cause as well as an opportunity to rebuild Harvard Square. Skeptics, while

In the midst of the debate the council asked the city planning staff "to set forth in specific goals and policies the community consensus on the development policies for the Harvard Square area" (City of Cambridge, "Status of Kennedy Library," 1972). The most useful element of the 1976 "Harvard Square Comprehensive Policy Plan" was an urban design analysis by Monacelli Associates. Earlier studies had viewed the Square as a flawed environment; this one focused on its positive features and presented the status quo as a starting point for gradual improvements. Although the zoning was left untouched, proposals for smaller-scale projects and pedestrian amenities acknowledged community concerns. The plan established guidelines for development of the southwest sector and encouraged construction of parking garages, to the great satisfaction of the business community.

Parcel 1B and the Rise of the Harvard Square Defense Fund

The firm of Carpenter & Company won a competition to acquire Parcel 1B in December 1978 with a proposal for an enclosed mall with stores, cinemas, offices, a hotel, and a seven-story, 850-car garage. This reignited the controversy over development, and the coalition of neighborhoods that had opposed the Kennedy Library brought suit in January 1979 to force compliance with the comprehensive policy plan. Activists formed the Harvard Square Defense Fund (HSDF), which negotiated a reduction in the planned retail space from 126,000 to 45,000 square feet and a corresponding increase in housing. The theaters were eliminated, parking was placed underground, and an open courtyard replaced an atrium. The community's preference for red brick over the precast concrete favored by the architects became a universal concession to activists for the next two decades (figure 3.81).[15] Developer Richard Friedman remarked that the approval process had taken seven years and required "more than 360 public hearings, nine votes of the City Council, and two special acts of the legislature" (*Boston Phoenix*, Feb. 19, 1985).

All this activity stimulated interest in nearby properties. Industrial buildings on University Road occupied about three acres of

FIGURE 3.80 After the election of Ronald Reagan, City Councillor Alfred Vellucci moved to rename Boylston Street because he imagined that Harvard would seek political advantage by changing the name of the John F. Kennedy School of Government. Photo October 1981.

respecting the late president, feared that tourists would overwhelm the Square with traffic, souvenir shops, and fast-food restaurants. Harvard brought all of its considerable influence to bear on city hall, the state house, and Washington but suffered an unprecedented defeat on fields it once dominated. The victorious neighbors learned that court challenges were an effective way to influence debate. The issues raised by the opponents, the intensity of the discussion, and the diversity of the participants were new factors in local policy debates (figure 3.80).

FIGURE 3.81 The ten-story, red-brick Charles Square development included a 300-room hotel, 86 condominiums, 45,000 square feet of retail space, 117,000 square feet of offices, and a 700-car underground garage (1984, Cambridge Seven Associates, architects). Photo 1985.

FIGURE 3.82 West of Charles Square (which occupied the carbarn and bus storage area in the foreground) were several blocks of factories and garages surrounding Craigie Hall. The zoning district there and in the adjoining residential neighborhood allowed the highest possible density under the 1962 code. Photo ca. 1950.

the former Ox Marsh just west of the carbarns. In the 1870s the tract had been owned by Harvard Square merchant William L. Whitney, whose 1860 mansion became a prominent student boarding house in the 1890s. Investors put up several private dormitories nearby, but after the University Press built a three-story printing plant in 1895 the area developed as an industrial and service district adjacent to the Bennett Street yards (figures 3.82–3.83). Harvard professor Walter Baird rented space from the press in 1936, and his scientific instrument company, which became Baird-Atomic, Inc., in 1956, took over the entire building in 1966. The company began marketing the site for development before it moved to Bedford in 1969.

In 1968 Boston developer Daniel J. Rufo applied for a zoning amendment to allow a mixed-use complex with an FAR of 7, "twice as massive as Holyoke Center" (*Crimson,* Oct. 3, 1968).[16]

FIGURE 3.83 University Road looking south from Bennett Street. The carbarns are at left. The buildings on the right include the 1909 factory of the Auto Wind Shield Co. and a 1927 parking garage. The University Press complex began at the far end of the street on the right (see figures 9.41–9.42). Photo 1969.

FIGURE 3.84 The Kavanos proposal for an eighteen-story Holiday Inn on the Baird Atomic site threatened to dwarf the Kennedy Library complex. In this model view, the Brattle Theatre is in the foreground; St. John's Church and the monastery are in the background. Photo 1972.

A compromise measure reflective of the CRA's urban design plan failed to pass the city council. A building permit was finally issued in 1972 for an as-of-right 18-story Holiday Inn (figure 3.84). A new developer, Kanavos Enterprises, began pouring foundations, but halted when the city and the Neighborhood Ten Association agreed to support a lower though denser eight-story complex containing hotel rooms, parking, and commercial space. Construction began in October 1974, but work stopped again after the Kennedy Library project was canceled.

The resolution of the years-long Parcel 1B controversy hardened the activists' determination to tighten up the zoning and reform the way development decisions were made in the Square. In 1979 the city council adopted a zoning overlay district that limited heights to 110 feet and allowed the Planning Board to critique large projects as part of a special permit process. The new district incorporated the goals expressed by the Comprehensive Policy Plan and "set height limits where none had existed, created a rudimentary design review process, and encouraged what were thought to be desirable design features for the Square as a whole" (Boothe, 1990). It was a step away from the purely dimensional application of the zoning code, but activists continued to attack most new projects. Concurrently, the city encouraged development near mass transit stations at Lechmere and Alewife and at University Park in Cambridgeport, which reduced some of the pressure on the Square.

The Harvard Square Defense Fund was founded in 1979 by members of the Neighborhood Ten Association who had fought the Kennedy Library. Organizers included Dean Johnson, Jill Strawbridge, Olive Holmes, Priscilla McMillan, John Moot, Paul Lawrence, and Gladys (Pebble) Gifford—two planners, an interior designer, a writer, a businessman, a business school professor, and a housewife, most of whom were relatively new to Cambridge. Initially the members were concerned about proposals for Parcel 1B, an "issue so big, it needed a group to focus exclusively on it" (*Crimson*, Mar. 8, 1983). Later, it aimed "to protect and enhance the unique urban fabric of the Harvard Square community through an open, participatory planning process, using as our guide the Harvard Square Comprehensive Policy Plan which was developed through the considerable efforts of several of our founding members" (HSDF, University Place position paper, ca. 1980).

With a peak membership of 600, the Defense Fund soon became the most powerful community group in the city. The organizers had learned during the Kennedy Library controversy that the threat of legal action gave them enormous leverage. Among the proposals they successfully challenged were One Brattle Square (redesigned); the Inn at Harvard and the Harvard Hillel Center (reduced in scale); and Zero Arrow Street, 10–18 Eliot Street, and the Eliot Square Office Building (abandoned). The developers of other projects, including University Place/ University Green, 1280 Massachusetts Avenue, One Bow Street, and One Winthrop Square, were allowed to proceed with less than the maximum allowable densities.

The Defense Fund secured a zoning amendment limiting fast-food restaurants and went to court to have it enforced. Claiming the Square had become "a den of iniquity," the group convinced the city to stop issuing new liquor licenses (*HSDF Newsletter,* Spring 2001). Developers learned to request an audience before approaching city agencies. Pebble Gifford, president during most of the 1980s and '90s, earned a law degree so she could more effectively represent the fund, asserting: "We're tough. We don't care what anyone thinks" (*Boston Globe,* Oct. 9, 1994).

The Defense Fund's nemesis during much of this period was Louis DiGiovanni. One of ten children of an Italian immigrant family, DiGiovanni was an attorney and a professor at Boston University's school of management for twenty-four years. He began buying property in Harvard Square in 1961 and by about 1970 owned seven restaurants as well as the buildings they occupied. In 1978 he evicted Woolworth's and redeveloped the Estes building and an old storage warehouse into The Atrium, a mall with entrances on Brattle and Church streets; One Mifflin Place followed in 1982. He bought The Garage at a foreclosure sale in 1983 and in 1985 built a 220-car parking garage on Kennedy Street. DiGiovanni was a target of the Defense Fund in part because he closed several popular stores and restaurants, but also because he was determined to operate independently of community input. Like the Dows and the Poorvus, he founded a family real estate business that continued after his death in 2004.

DiGiovanni's greatest battle involved the Baird-Atomic site and some adjoining properties on Nutting Road and Revere Street, where he intended to put up an office building next to the proposed Holiday Inn. In 1976 he bought the Kanavos property and projected two twenty-story office buildings with 25,000 square feet of retail, 150 town houses, and 950 parking spaces. This brought the southwest sector development controversy to a fever pitch, but community activists were already engaged in trench warfare over the Charles Square project and had little energy to spare. Mayor Francis Duehay reached out to Harvard president Derek Bok, and the university bought most of DiGiovanni's property in 1980. Developed by the Gerald Hines interests of Houston, Harvard's project was not unlike the final version of the failed Kanavos project, with an office

FIGURE 3.85 The University Place office building (1983) and the University Green condominiums (1984, both Skidmore Owings & Merrill—Chicago, architects) flank a garden designed by Carol R. Johnson & Associates in 1985. The houses at right, 134 Mt. Auburn Street (1842) and 3 Mt. Auburn Place (1856), were preserved; the house at left, of which this is not an accurate rendering, was built as a replica of an 1839 Greek Revival house at 8 Ellery Street (1986, Hammer, Kiefer & Todd).

building, University Place, on the Baird Atomic parcel, and a condominium complex, University Green, on DiGiovanni's land. Three three-deckers on Nutting Road were lost, but Harvard agreed not to raze Craigie Hall, the former private dormitory later known as Chapman Arms.

Plans for University Place/University Green were developed in consultation with the Defense Fund and were nearing approval when the Cambridge Historical Commission moved to protect two significant houses on the site. Hines and Harvard restored them and built a replica Greek Revival house in the landscaped forecourt of University Green (figure 3.85). This project was considered a great success. The design review process had accommodated a large project in two years, compared with six to resolve the Parcel 1B free-for-all. The involvement of the university with the community produced an improved design that created a permanent buffer against commercial expansion into the adjoining residential neighborhood.

The southwest sector saga concluded on a different note. Early on the morning of May 17, 1982, a contractor arrived to raze two houses at 5 and 7 Revere Street where DiGiovanni intended to build a ten-unit condominium. A neighbor, Robert Withey, leapt on the moving bulldozer and removed the keys from the ignition. Within minutes the area filled with city officials, who determined that DiGiovanni lacked the required permits. The quarrel was resolved when Harvard acquired, repaired, and sold the two houses and built three compatible town houses to create a buffer along Gerry Street. The area was secured against further development in 1984 when the city council designated it as the Half Crown Neighborhood Conservation District (see chapter 4).

A new vision for Harvard Square began to take shape with the federally funded extension of the subway in 1976. Extensive surface improvements produced a pedestrian-oriented environment between Holyoke Street and Eliot Square. Traffic patterns were altered when the kiosk island was extended to make room for a new headhouse in front of the Cambridge Savings Bank. The kiosk was adaptively reused as a newsstand, and Harvard and Brattle squares acquired plazas designed for impromptu public performances (figure 3.86). By the time construction ended, the gentle hippie days were over, and the sunken plaza behind the headhouse—which became known as "the pit"—became a hangout for disaffected teenagers.

Completion of the Harvard Square improvements in 1984 coincided with the end of another recession. Development pressure intensified, and the community responded assertively. In 1988 alone, the planning board approved 233,500 square feet of new construction that would have nearly doubled the amount of office space in the Square. Developers were bullish; one said: "There's literally no space available in Harvard Square right now" (*Boston Business Journal*, Apr. 18, 1988). Meanwhile, the city continued to tinker with the zoning ordinance. Some of the incentives in the 1962 code that earned a developer additional

FIGURE 3.86 Proposed Harvard Square redesign (1978, Skidmore Owings & Merrill–Boston, architects). Surface improvements planned by the MBTA and the City of Cambridge included a complete reworking of traffic patterns in the Square. Once the kiosk island was joined to the sidewalk in front of the Cambridge Savings Bank it was no longer possible to drive from Massachusetts Avenue to Brattle and Mt. Auburn streets. MacArthur Park (foreground) replaced a public parking facility.

density, such as the split-level commercial frontage at 1105 Massachusetts Avenue (1972) and 28–36 Brattle Street (1974), came to be considered undesirable in the 1980s. Graduate School of Design Professors François Vigier and Christopher Chadbourne refined the 1976 Monacelli report by examining the distinctive qualities of the Square's sub-areas. The amended overlay district, enacted in 1986, established an advisory committee with guidelines that encouraged diversity in design and respect for context. The height limit was reduced from 110 to 85 feet, although the FAR remained at 4.0. Developers could pay a fee to eliminate required parking and earn a density bonus by preserving significant buildings. One-size-fits-all dimensional requirements were loosened, and the allowable density on the Gold Coast was reduced to alleviate development pressure. Two years later, most of the overlay district was placed on the National Register of Historic Places.

The Defense Fund was not satisfied with the amended zoning and fiercely criticized subsequent projects. The university reduced the height of the Inn at Harvard after the city council overruled the planning board and adopted a citizens' downzoning petition. The Fund delayed One Brattle Square for six years and blocked two major projects on Eliot Street. Harvard, which had supported the 1986 amendments, used its status as owner of more than 20 percent of the Square's property to prevent a reduction of allowable density in 1988. This led Gifford to threaten that "Harvard is on a collision course with the community. Glasnost is over" (*Crimson,* Dec. 6, 1988).

The recession that began in 1989 was felt later in Cambridge than elsewhere. Except for Holyoke Center, most construction up to this time had taken place on the periphery of the Square. Beginning with the 1983 Coolidge Bank Building at 104 Mt. Auburn Street, developers began to focus on underutilized sites in the old village. When prosperity returned in 1992, older buildings close to the Square were again at risk. The stage was set for another battle when the Read Block went on the market in 1993. Owned since 1945 by a real estate trust, the building supported an eclectic collection of stores, offices, and restaurants, including the Wursthaus, a German-themed restaurant beloved of postwar undergraduates, and The Tasty, a nine-stool lunch counter. In 1994 the Cambridge Savings Bank outbid a concert promoter for the property and announced plans to put up a four-story office building (figure 3.87).

The Cambridge Historical Commission voted to preserve the Read Block as a landmark in 1997 because it contained significant parts of the city's three oldest commercial buildings as well as remnants of an 18th century residence. The 1896 facade, although only a century old, was considered significant in its own right as an ingenious solution to the problem of unifying four (originally six) structures and adapting them for modern commercial purposes. The building's multiple entrances and small scale imparted a desirable complexity to the urban environment. However, most public debate focused on the fate of The Tasty. Once mainly patronized by shift workers, policemen, and idlers, The Tasty was said to represent the "real" Square of days gone by: colorful, unpretentious, and somewhat shabby. Dozens of supporters turned out for hearings, but the commission had no power over tenancy; after The Tasty closed in 1997 many felt there was no longer anything left in the Square worth defending. Symmes Maini & McKee Associates finally devised a plan to preserve the Read Block's facade by inserting a new structure 20 feet behind it. Although the tenants were permanently displaced, the building's exterior was meticulously restored (figure 3.88).

The Read Block controversy heightened public awareness of the fragility of Harvard Square's older buildings and sharpened the debate about the meaning and limitations of historic preservation. The commission decided that the few remaining wood-frame buildings in the Square should be preserved. Built mostly as residences, they offered flexible, inexpensive space for retailers, services, and professional offices. They contributed to the area's diverse character but were vulnerable to redevelopment because they could not attract premium rents and had a low value relative to the land they occupied. Many had already disappeared; between 1966 and 1989, eleven were razed on the Mt. Auburn-Brattle-Story streets block alone.

FIGURE 3.87 Read Block, 1380–1392 Massachusetts Avenue. The Tasty and the Wursthaus are to the right of the traffic control booth. The most effective instrument of the officer in charge was an amplified warning: "Hey, you in the white bucks, get back on the curb!" Photo 1968.

FIGURE 3.88 The restored Read Block. The ground floor tenants were initially replaced by a chain store marketing expensive clothes to teenagers, which was succeeded by a bank and then a chain drugstore. Photo 2015.

During the Read Block debate, Intercontinental Developers, a Boston firm, announced that it intended to clear the remainder of the block bounded by Winthrop Park, Mt. Auburn, Eliot, and Winthrop streets, where it had put up the Coolidge Bank building in 1983. This site in the old village contained four buildings of varying significance. The proponents quickly agreed to restore the 1908 former Pi Eta Club at 91 Winthrop Street. After further negotiations, the commission agreed that the developer could raze the Pi Eta Theater (1896) and the former Cantabrigia Club (1929) if it moved the 1869 Chapman heirs' house to face Winthrop Square. The Defense Fund supported the developers' request for zoning relief, and their residential condominium project was approved in 1996 (figure 3.89).

FIGURE 3.89 The Winthrop Square project (1998–2000, Tsoi Kobus Associates, architects). The Chapman Heirs' house (foreground) was relocated and turned to face the park. The former Pi Eta Club (left) was restored, and Intercontinental Developers was allowed additional density for the One Winthrop Square condominium. Photo 2009.

Renewal of the Brattle Square Block

In contrast to the contentious undertakings in the southwest sector, several loosely coordinated, privately financed projects redeveloped the block bounded by Brattle, Story, and Mt. Auburn streets over a period of thirty-five years, with only one instance of significant opposition. The block was mostly residential until the mid-1960s, although the Brattle House site, which had been cleared in 1896, supported a ramp into the subway station, a former post office (remodeled in 1954 into a Touraine's department store), a bank (1940), and a service station (1941). Two private dormitories, Waverly and Belmont halls, faced Mt. Auburn Street, and the William Brattle house (1727) and the Brattle Theater (1889) anchored the south side of Brattle Street (figure 3.91). Many homes on Story Street had become rooming

FIGURE 3.91 Brattle Street in 1964. From left to right, the Brattle Theatre; the William Brattle house; 44 Brattle Street (1890, Cabot Everett & Mead, architects; demolished 1971); and the Brattle Inn (1863; demolished 1969). Photo 1964.

FIGURE 3.90 Until the 1960s the Brattle-Story-Mt. Auburn Street block was almost entirely residential. By the end of the century only the William Brattle house, the Brattle Theater, Waverly Hall, and one three-decker remained. Photo 1946.

houses, but its character was similar to that of Hilliard, Revere, and Gerry streets. Mifflin Place, in the center of the block, was a cul-de-sac of three-deckers.[17]

In the 1960s and '70s the block became the epicenter of the architectural profession in New England. Design firms built six concrete and glass office buildings on Story Street and Mifflin Place between 1966 and 1971, primarily for their own use (see chapter 8). In 1946 eleven of Cambridge's thirteen architectural practices were located in Harvard Square, and of these, seven—including The Architects Collaborative, Walter Bogner, Marcel Breuer, Walter Gropius, and Hugh Stubbins Jr.—had offices in College House. Eight years later many firms had regrouped at 1280 Massachusetts Avenue and 92 Mt. Auburn Street, over the Harvard Provision Store. By 1965 the city directory listed forty-five firms and sole practitioners, almost all in Old Cambridge. Eleven years later, there were thirty-six in Harvard Square alone.[18]

In 1966 Walter Gropius's firm, The Architects Collaborative, razed two rooming houses at 4 and 6 Story Street and built an office building with an interior courtyard that became the

FIGURE 3.92 Brattle Street at the corner of Story Street in 1972. From left to right, the Brattle Theatre; 44 Brattle Street (1970–72, Sert, Jackson & Associates, architects); Design Research (1969, Benjamin Thompson Associates); and TAC I (1966, The Architects Collaborative).

FIGURE 3.93 The Brattle Arcade, however inadvertent at the beginning, lent a human scale to the adjoining Modernist buildings. Photo 2012.

nucleus of the Brattle Arcade, which years later linked Brattle Street with Mt. Auburn Street. Benjamin Thompson left TAC in 1966 to found his own firm, and in 1969 put up a new store for Design Research at the corner of Brattle and Story streets, replacing the Brattle Inn (figure 3.92). The D/R Building, with additional buildings designated TAC 2 (1968) and 14 Story Street (1970, Earl Flansburgh & Associates), formed the west side of the arcade. Buildings designed by Sert, Jackson & Associates for their own use in 1970 and 1971 enclosed the east side, but initially the passageway only reached Mt. Auburn Street through Mifflin Place. The arcade gave human scale to a mostly unexceptional collection of buildings; it was institutionalized in subsequent zoning and became a well-known model for urban design in the Modernist period (figures 3.93–3.94).

Between 1987 and 2001 four more buildings were linked to the arcade by pedestrian passageways. The arcade reached Mt. Auburn Street in 1987-88 after Louis DiGiovanni constructed a five-story office building called One Mifflin Place on the site of Belmont Hall, a former private dormitory. In the mid-1980s the owners of the Brattle Theater and the Touraine's store devised a complex plan to rebuild both parcels using air rights over the bus ramp while sharing an underground garage. One Brattle Square was completed in 1991 (figure 3.95). The Poorvu family restored the Brattle Theater in 1990–91 but did not complete their small office building on Mifflin Place until 2002. The last site on the arcade was redeveloped in 2001, when the Poorvus replaced the 1954 post office on Mt. Auburn Street with a five-story office building (see figure 8.46).

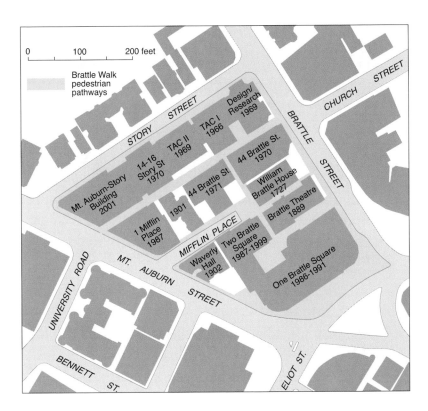

FIGURE 3.94 The Brattle Arcade was gradually extended between 1969 and 2001 to provide a network of pedestrian paths through and between buildings.

FIGURE 3.95 One Brattle Square (1990, Donham & Sweeney, architects). Litigation over the building's height and bulk was unsuccessful, and the project as built differed from the architect's original conception mainly in the increased setbacks of the upper floors. Photo 2014.

HARVARD SQUARE AS A CONSERVATION DISTRICT

During the debate over the Read Block and Winthrop Square the city council asked the historical commission "to preserve and protect all remaining historical buildings in Harvard Square" (CHC, *Final Report,* 23). Two and a half years and fifty-two public meetings later, the council adopted the Harvard Square Conservation District in December 2000. The new district protected the Square's commercial vitality as "a pedestrian-friendly, accessible, human-scale, mixed-use environment that complements nearby neighborhoods and maintains the history and traditions of its location." The measure could be more stringent than zoning, but it kept the property owners' cherished 4.0 FAR, offered retailers flexibility to devise creative signs and storefronts, and satisfied the community's interest in preserving the physical character of the Square.

Although the real estate boom of the 1990s had peaked, a few new projects came under district review. The historical commission approved a replacement for the Harvard Square post office, but in 2001 it rejected a design by the Austrian architect Hans Hollein for a Harvard paper conservation laboratory at 90 Mt. Auburn Street as inappropriately bulky and contemporary for its surroundings (see figure 10.96). A more modest proposal was approved two years later. The commission also approved the adaptive reuse of the 1907 Harvard Automobile Co. garage at 1230 Massachusetts Avenue (completed in 2002) and a theater at Zero Arrow Street (completed in 2005). A project to redevelop Trinity Hall and the Conductors Building on Mt. Auburn Street was approved in 2008 but because of economic conditions did not get underway until 2013.

By this time the influence of the Harvard Square Defense Fund was beginning to wane. Its membership was aging, and it no longer had the resources to oppose a liberalization of the city's licensing laws in 2006 allowing outdoor consumption of alcohol. The historical commission's qualitative review of development projects began to substitute for the Defense Fund's rigorous prescreening of projects, although its members were not always satisfied with the results.

In 2005 the city began planning a major enhancement of the Square's public spaces, based on an initiative by John DiGiovanni, Louis's son and successor in the family business, who with other property owners commissioned an urban design study from the architectural firm Arrowstreet. Released in 1997, the study called for building pedestrian-friendly sidewalks, crosswalks, and streetlights to update the work carried out during Red Line construction in 1978–84. The project began on Palmer Street, where the city replaced the narrow sidewalks, curbs, and cobblestone pavement (installed in 1966 after an epic battle between property owner Sheldon Dietz and the Harvard Coop) with decorative paving and internally illuminated "Palmer blocks" as street furniture.

*

Harvard Square continues to attract crowds as well as doomsayers. In the 1950s, '60s, and '70s the Square was a unique place in America: a vibrant urban center flooded with fresh faces every fall, tolerant of different lifestyles, whose many bookstores fed every intellectual interest. Mo Lotman's *Harvard Square: An Illustrated History Since 1950,* published in 2009, lovingly details this era. The strong emotions that Harvard Square stirred in young people then did not exist before and may depart with that generation.

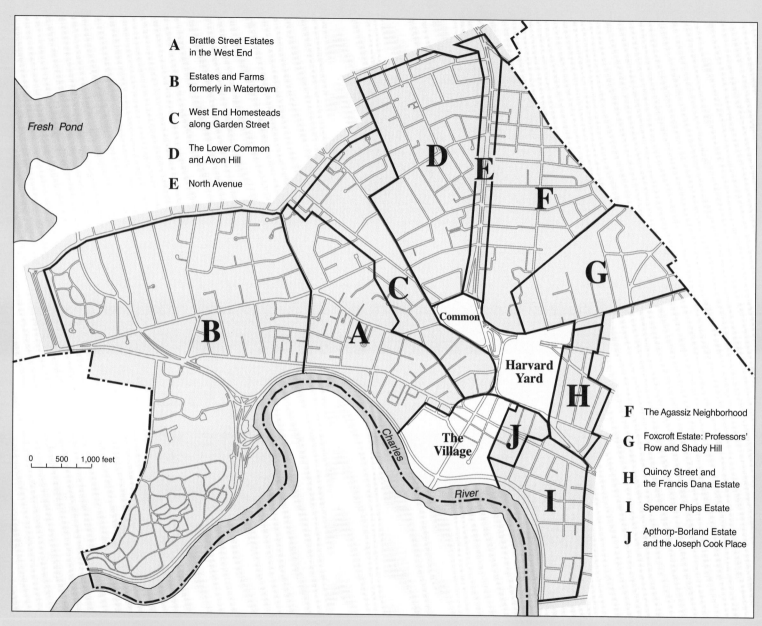

FIGURE 4.1 The neighborhoods of Old Cambridge described in this chapter.

4   Residential Neighborhoods

The neighborhoods that surround the original settlement at Harvard Square all developed differently, depending on the qualities of the terrain, their proximity to the village, the river, and major roads, the ambitions and resources of their property owners, and prevailing economic conditions (figure 4.1).

The initial determinants of land use were topography, soil quality, drainage, and accessibility. Settlers found well-drained deposits of glacial till to be most desirable for building purposes and avoided poorly drained areas if at all possible. The earliest settlers and suburbanites populated the outwash plain around the village. The hillsides attracted developers in the 1850s, and in the 1860s immigrants settled on cheap building lots laid out over partially reclaimed salt marshes. Clay lands were excavated and backfilled with ashes and rubbish before being sold for residential development in the 1890s, while swamps, kettle-hole ponds, and peat bogs were built over when other possibilities had been exhausted, causing future problems with subsidence.

European settlers soon exhausted the natural fertility of the glacial moraines and outwash plain underlying Old Cambridge. The best use of most land was for subsistence farming, which kept the countryside open until urbanization began. Whether owners or tenants, most people with access to land kept cattle on their pastures, grew hay and corn for fodder, and raised small quantities of vegetables and fruits for which the college provided a steady market. These activities gradually diminished, and by the early 20th century only the Coolidge farm, which occupied a rich meadow along the Charles near Gerry's Landing, still engaged in commercial agriculture.[1]

In the 1740s Cambridge's beautiful and healthy landscape began to attract wealthy Boston merchants and West Indian planters who consolidated some of the best farms into estates that formed the framework for suburban development (see chapter 1). Most were on Tory Row, where they occupied south-facing slopes with generous views, but comparable domains were assembled by Francis Foxcroft on Kirkland Street, Spencer Phips and Ralph Inman east of the village, and Richard Lechmere in East Cambridge. After the Revolution wealthy patriots acquired the confiscated Tory estates, but none persisted for more than a generation. Both pre- and post-Revolutionary owners took good care of their properties, and when they subdivided them the new streets were usually orderly and spacious. In contrast, the many smallholdings created by the Proprietors of Common Lands when they divided the Lower Common in 1724 evolved into today's somewhat cramped and heterogeneous neighborhood. The low-lying, narrow fields east of Massachusetts Avenue resisted consolidation, giving each street there a distinct identity.

BRATTLE STREET ESTATES IN THE WEST END

The earliest settlement upstream from the village occurred in the West End, which was divided in 1634 into lots ranging from a quarter of an acre to eight acres in size. As originally defined, the

West End ran from the north side of Harvard Square to the old Watertown line at Sparks Street and from Garden Street to the Charles, excluding the Ox Marsh west of John F. Kennedy Street. Unlike the first settlers, who were required to build houses in the village, those who received grants in the West End were allowed to live there. Only two became permanent residents; twelve left for Connecticut with Reverend Hooker in 1635 (see chapter 1).

By the late 17th century, most of the grants had been consolidated into tightly interwoven smallholdings that contrasted with the large lots west of Sparks Street in what was then Watertown. Boston merchants and West Indian planters began to acquire some of these farms in the 18th century. William Brattle built the first mansion in the West End in 1727. He was followed by Henry Vassall, who remodeled an older house about 1748, and John Vassall in 1759. After Cambridge annexed part of Watertown in 1754, Richard Lechmere (1761), Judge Joseph Lee (ca. 1760), George Ruggles (ca. 1764), and Thomas Oliver (1767) followed suit (figure 4.2).

Brattle Street was laid out from Brattle Square to Mason Street when the West End was opened to settlement. Between Mason and Fayerweather streets it followed the Charlestown-Watertown path, which existed before Newtowne was founded. The road continued by way of Elmwood Avenue to the first Watertown meetinghouse and then followed Mt. Auburn Street west toward Connecticut along today's Route 20. (The section of Brattle between Fayerweather and Mt. Auburn streets was a shortcut opened in 1812.) Until 1809 Brattle Street was known as "the Watertown road," and then, to distinguish it from Mt. Auburn Street, as "the upper road from Mount Auburn." It was called Brattle Street as early as 1833. The nickname "Tory Row" alludes to the political sympathies of those who assembled estates there before the Revolutionary War.

The seven loyalist estates on Tory Row determined the present character of Brattle Street and Elmwood Avenue, comprising a rare urban neighborhood that has never fallen out of fashion. New houses could be built only when the estates were broken up. Much of this activity took place at a high level of

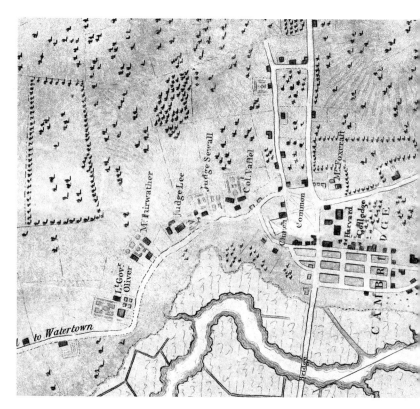

FIGURE 4.2 The Tory Row estates about 1775, drawn from memory by the loyalist cartographer Henry Pelham (see figure 1.27).

investment, and the street today presents an impressive range of high-style domestic architecture, from Georgian mansions to Modern homes built in the 1960s and '70s. The city enacted a historic district ordinance in 1963 to protect the oldest houses. By 1996 the Old Cambridge Historic District included both sides of Mason and Brattle streets from the Common to Fresh Pond Parkway, as well as Follen and Berkeley streets and the south side of Craigie Street.

WILLIAM BRATTLE ESTATE

The estate of General William Brattle, now represented by his 1727 house at 42 Brattle Street, once extended from Brattle Square to Ash Street and from the river almost to Cambridge Common. The earliest owner of Brattle's house lot was William Spencer, who left for Hartford in 1639. When a later owner, rope maker David Deming, moved to Boston in 1707 he sold a house "nearly if not exactly on the spot occupied by the Brattle mansion" and seven acres to Reverend William Brattle, the general's father, and the rest of his land to Boston merchant Andrew Belcher (Paige, 644). Brattle had graduated from Harvard in 1680, but remained in residence as a tutor until he was ordained the fifth minister of the Cambridge church in 1696; his acquisition of Deming's place coincided with his appointment as a Fellow of the college. He retained most of his purchase as open land, but sold the house and three-quarters of an acre to a family that kept it as a tavern.

Reverend Brattle died in 1717. When William Jr. came of age in 1727 he married Governor Gurdon Saltonstall's daughter Katherine, repurchased the Deming property, and built the mansion now occupied by the Cambridge Center for Adult Education (see figure 6.7). Between 1728 and 1746 he expanded his estate to about 18 acres. His largest acquisition was the seven-acre "Half Crown Lot," which included Windmill Hill and about 800 feet of river frontage between the foot of Hawthorn Street and a canal that marked the western edge of the Ox Marsh.

William Brattle had a varied career as "successively preacher, physician, and lawyer," and served in almost every available public office (figure 4.3). Paige remarked that "an inordinate love of popularity seems to have been one of his most striking characteristics; and his taste was abundantly gratified." Brattle long favored "popular rights," but when he was denied his accustomed place on the Governor's Council in 1769 "he received new light concerning the matter in dispute between the Provinces and Great Britain, and was allowed to resume his seat" (Paige, 500). Governor Hutchinson made him major general of the provincial militia in 1771, but his presence in Cambridge became objectionable, and he fled to Boston in 1774. His daughter, Katherine Wendell, widow of the patriot John Mico Wendell, stayed in the house and protected it from confiscation. According to Sibley, "George Washington personally assured her that she had nothing to fear

FIGURE 4.3 William Brattle Jr. (1706–76), painted by John Singleton Copley in 1756 in the uniform of a Major of the Massachusetts Militia.

for her safety" (XII, 219). Major Thomas Mifflin, the commissary-general of the Continental Army, was billeted there from July 1775 to March 1776. General Brattle deeded the property to his son shortly before he died in Halifax in 1776, but Thomas was in England and could not return until the Revolutionary proscription against him was rescinded in 1784.

Once Thomas Brattle gained possession he expanded the property to 22 acres south of Brattle Street and about three acres north of it. A kind and humane man who was interested in horticulture, he opened his garden to Harvard students and built a bathing facility for them at Windmill Hill.[2] English lindens, probably planted by his father, surrounded the house. The old town spring fed a water garden with canals, ponds, and a marble grotto, and a grassy mall ran down to the river. A description in 1792 by a Salem diarist, Reverend William Bentley, revealed the scope of his improvements:

> We first saw the fountain and canal opposite to his House, and the walk on the side of another canal in the road, flowing under an arch and in the direction of the outer fence. There is another canal which communicates with a beautiful pool in the park and place for his wild fowl. The garden is laid out upon a very considerable descent and formed with terrace walks, abounding with Trees, fruits, and the whole luxury of vegetation, and is unrivalled by any thing I have seen of the kind. … The dairy room was the neatest I ever beheld. It was in stone and on the sides surrounded with a beautiful white Dutch tile, in the excess of neatness. The Repositories for the several fruits were in fine order, the barns, yards, and all agreed with the same good order. (Oct. 4, 1792)

Thomas Brattle never married and left no direct descendants. After his death in 1801 his executors subdivided the estate, except for a house near Appian Way that he left to his housekeeper.[3] The mansion and 5¾ acres of land between Brattle and Mt. Auburn streets that they sold in 1807 passed through several owners until Abraham Fuller, a wealthy Boston lawyer, acquired them in 1825. Abraham was an uncle of Margaret Fuller, the transcendentalist and feminist author, whose father, Timothy, was a lawyer and elected official. She was born in 1810 in Cambridgeport and attended school with Richard Henry Dana Jr. and Oliver Wendell Holmes. The family lived in the Francis Dana mansion from 1826 until 1831, when Timothy sold it and began looking for another residence. They lived with the dictatorial Abraham for a year and a half; although Margaret considered her uncle's house a "prison," it turned out to be preferable to exile on the Groton farm her father bought in 1833 (von Mehren, 47). Timothy died in 1835, and Margaret's sisters eventually settled on Story Street.

Edmund Chapman, a chaise maker, and Adam Cottrell, a housewright, acquired the Fuller place and laid out Story Street in 1844. In 1846 they sold the Brattle house and almost 900 feet of frontage on Brattle Street, Brattle Square, and Mt. Auburn Street to Samuel Batchelder, a retired textile manufacturer who had purchased the Henry Vassall estate a few years before. While he may have appreciated the Brattle house for its historical associations, Batchelder understood the potential of its large open lot near the village. In 1847 he erected a Gothic Revival house directly behind the Brattle mansion, and in 1849 he sold about 31,000 square feet on the square to Lyman Willard of Dorchester, who erected the Brattle House hotel (see figure 8.2). Although Edward Everett praised the beauty of the estate and predicted that "[Thomas Brattle's] name is likely to be perpetuated, and his liberal hospitality kept up, on a much enlarged scale in the Brattle House," the venture failed, and the building became a law school dormitory before it was converted to a printing plant in 1863 (Everett III, 37; see figure 9.40).

Samuel Batchelder left the Brattle house to his children, John Batchelder and Isabella James, in 1879. In 1889 James M. Hilton converted the Gothic cottage to a tenement and subdivided the property into seven lots; other developers put up Waverly Hall (1902) and Belmont Hall (1903) as private dormitories. Isabella sold the Brattle house to the Cambridge Social Union, which adapted it for classes and meeting rooms.

Thomas Brattle's executors sold three small lots west of the house in 1807. Torrey Hancock, a blacksmith, built a house and a forge at 54 Brattle Street in 1808. In 1827 he moved across the street and sold his establishment to Dexter Pratt of Framingham. They continued in business together for a few years, and both claimed to be the subject of Longfellow's 1839 poem, "The Village Blacksmith." Longfellow sketched the shop in 1840, and the "spreading chestnut tree" survived to be photographed after Brattle Street was widened in 1870–71 (figure 4.7; see also figure 4.108). From 1870 to 1912 the Hancock-Pratt house was owned by Mary Walker, an escaped slave, and her children. The building became a tea-room in the 1920s, and in 1946 it was

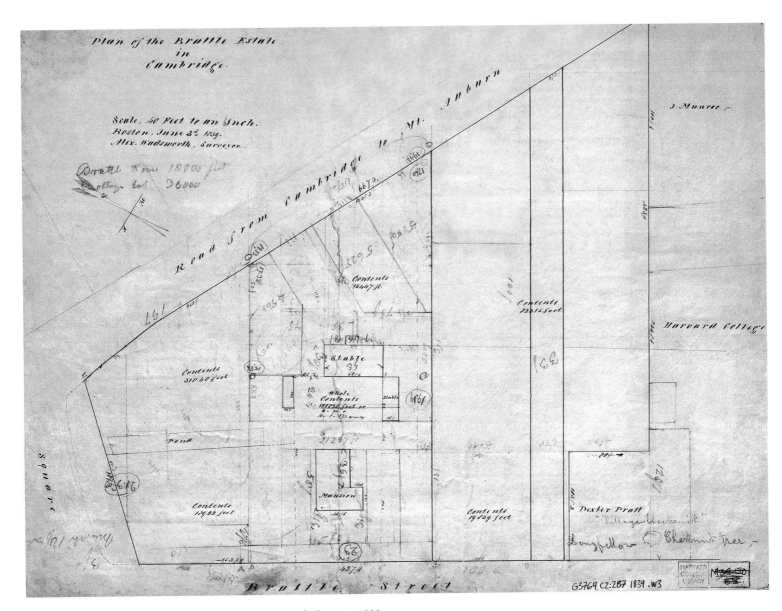

FIGURE 4.4 Plan of Thomas Brattle's former estate on Brattle Street in 1839, showing the house, pond, and stables. Alexander Wadsworth, surveyor.

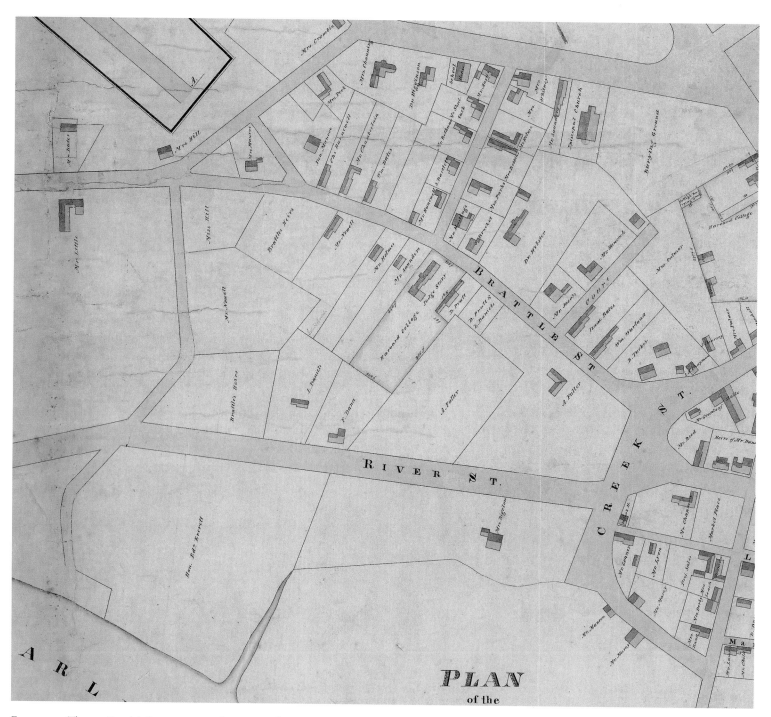

FIGURE 4.5 Thomas Brattle's former estate and its surroundings in 1833.

acquired by The Window Shop, which assisted European refugees of World War II. The board of zoning appeal fortunately blocked a plan to build a store in the front yard, and it serves today as the Blacksmith House of the Cambridge Center for Adult Education.

In 1809 William Hilliard, the printer and bookseller, built a brick house west of Hancock's forge (figure 4.8). In 1829 Harvard bought the property and rented it to law professor Joseph Story, who also served as a justice of the U.S. Supreme Court from 1811 until his death in 1845. Samuel Batchelder bought the Story house in 1854 and rented it to generations of law students; the apartment building at 60 Brattle replaced it in 1945. Simeon Withey's 1868 Mansard on the west corner of Story Street was razed for an office building in 1958 (figure 4.9).

There were no more sales until 1823–25, when Brattle's heirs had reached their majority and the local economy had recovered from the War of 1812. They sold three lots beyond Hilliard's house to William Saunders, Joseph Holmes, and Henry Nowell. Nowell, a "husbandman," had Saunders put up a Federal style house and barn the following year (Middlesex Deeds 261/228). Law professor Simon Greenleaf acquired the Nowell place in 1851 and shared it with his son, James, and daughter-in-law, Mary Longfellow Greenleaf, a sister of the poet. James Greenleaf was a cotton merchant, and he and Mary spent half the year in New Orleans until the Civil War. In 1858 he moved his father's house to 19 Ash Street and commissioned a Mansard that was originally covered with stucco scored in imitation of ashlar masonry (see figure 6.83). After Mrs. Greenleaf died in 1902, Richard Henry Dana III advised her heirs to subdivide the land for development "on the plan of Mercer Circle or Hubbard Park" (Ellis & Andrews Correspondence, Dana to R.J. Melledge, Mar. 19, 1903). In 1905 the heirs organized the Greenleaf Land Trust to "fill, grade, survey, and plot the lands … to locate, lay out, grade and pave streets, sidewalks, ways, parks, squares and the like … to lay gas, water, and sewer pipes, and to set edge stones and curbing … [and] to remove, demolish, repair or rebuild any buildings," but sold the property to Radcliffe College instead

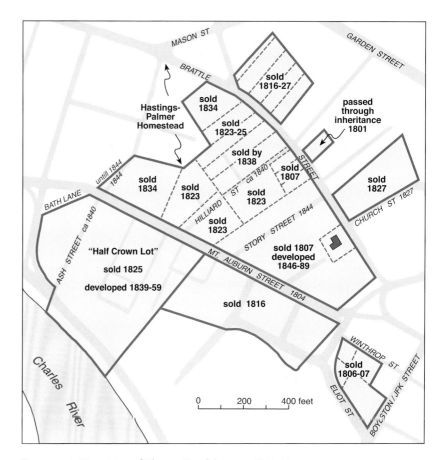

FIGURE 4.6 Disposition of Thomas Brattle's estate, 1801-38.

FIGURE 4.7 Henry Wadsworth Longfellow's 1840 sketch of Dexter Pratt's forge and the spreading chestnut tree at 54 Brattle Street.

FIGURE 4.9 Simeon Withey house, 52 Brattle Street (1859). The Withey house sat on the west corner of Story Street; Longfellow's spreading chestnut tree is visible at right. A corner of the Hancock-Pratt house and the side porch of the Hilliard-Story house are visible at right. Photo before 1870.

FIGURE 4.8 Hilliard-Story house, 60 Brattle Street (1809, Josiah Moore, house-wright). The building was still a boarding house for law students when it was demolished in 1945 for Brattle Arms, a thirty-nine-unit apartment building. Engraving ca. 1855.

(Middlesex Deeds 3150/230). Radcliffe made the house a residence for its president and built the Cronkhite Center on the corner of Ash Street in 1955–59 (see below and chapter 7). The houses that William Saunders and Joseph Holmes built on the corner of Hilliard Street in 1834 and 1839 were removed in 1959 for the Loeb Drama Center (see figure 6.42).

William Bascom, husband of Thomas Brattle's niece Catherine, sold large parcels along Mt. Auburn Street to George King, Stephen Wyeth, and Edward Everett in 1823–25. Wyeth built the Federal style house at 5–7 Hilliard Place in 1824, where it would have had a clear view of the river, but lost it to a creditor in 1829 (figure 4.10). In the early 1840s the next owner, wheelwright Leonard Daniels, his neighbor James Munroe, and housewright William Saunders laid out Woodbine Lane (later Hilliard Street) along their property lines. In 1845 they asked Harvard for an additional 15-foot-wide strip west of Justice Story's house to complete a public passage between Mt. Auburn and Brattle streets. The petitioners noted that Hilliard was 30 feet wide at Mt. Auburn but narrowed to 15 as it approached Brattle. Even this, they claimed, had "become a thoroughfare for omnibuses and other carriages, and is the most direct route for the children of at least twelve families to all the Public Schools in this village" (College Papers XII, 2nd series, 218).

The early houses on Hilliard Street were built for tradesmen, but in 1867 Samuel Batchelder Jr. built a large Mansard at 8 Hilliard in the backyard of the Story house. Twenty years later he put up the stylish Queen Annes at 10 (1884) and 6 (1888). Some of Timothy Fuller's descendants also played an important part in the history of the street. A few years after Fuller died in Groton in 1835, the family settled at 8 Ellery Street while Margaret's brothers, Richard and Arthur Buckminster Fuller, attended Harvard. The brothers married sisters Addie and Emma Reeves. After Arthur was killed at Fredericksburg in 1862, his widow, Emma, bought 11 Hilliard and lived there with her four children; later, Richard's widow, Addie, and her seven children joined them. The household gradually thinned out, but Arthur's daughter, Edith Davenport Fuller, remained to care for her mother and aunt

FIGURE 4.10 Stephen Wyeth house, 5–7 Hilliard Place (1824). Photo 1968.

while working as a librarian and investing in real estate. Edith built the Queen Anne house at 9 Hilliard in 1888 and in 1911 put up 12–20 Hilliard Street on the site of the Holmes elementary school (figure 4.11). Described as a "carefully designed row of instructor's houses," Fuller's project was seen as a beneficial social experiment (Cambridge Chronicle, Apr. 24, 1915). By 1916 she owned seven buildings on Hilliard Street, Hilliard Place, and Fuller Place, and her brother owned two more; together with Marianna Batchelder they controlled the entire block.

Bascom sold Windmill Hill, which Mt. Auburn Street had separated from the rest of the estate, to the recently married Professor Edward Everett in 1825. Everett had purchased part of the old Pine Swamp off Kirkland Street in 1824 but may have wanted a healthier and more dramatic site for a grand estate. He never built on either property and had to leave Harvard when he entered Congress in 1825.[4] George Meacham, a real estate broker, bought Everett's land in 1835 and sold the corner near Revere Street in 1839. He hired Alexander Wadsworth to lay

FIGURE 4.11 Edith Fuller houses, 12–20 Hilliard Street (1911, Newhall & Blevins, architects). Photo 2009.

FIGURE 4.12 The Half Crown neighborhood, ca. 1935. 1–3 Chapman Place (1855) is in the immediate foreground, and 12 Gerry Street (1877; demolished 1981) is at right center. The rear porches of 2, 4, and 6 Nutting Road (1914; demolished 1984 for University Green) are visible in the middle distance.

out Everett Place (now Ash Street south of Mount Auburn) and sold all the lots to George Nichols, a Cambridge bookseller, who quickly resold them for development. Meacham laid out the remainder of the property in 1849 with sixteen lots on Gerry and Brewer streets. Over the next fifty years the neighborhood filled with small vernacular houses inhabited by carpenters, mechanics, and tradesmen, and was infilled with three-deckers as late as 1914 (figure 4.12).

Bascom's final sales in 1833–34 were in a period of greater prosperity, and the buyers, civil engineer James Hayward and housewrights William Saunders and Joseph Holmes, soon developed these tracts. Hayward purchased a 1¼-acre tract at Ash and Mt. Auburn in 1834. He sold part of it to James Childs, who built a singular 1½-story cottage at 145 Mt. Auburn Street in 1837. A gifted housewright, Andrew Waitt, who became the superintendent of college buildings in 1856, bought the remainder after the town relocated the lower end of Ash Street in 1844 to meet Mt. Auburn at a more convenient angle. Waitt put up a house for himself at 18 Ash in 1845 and built three important Italianates at the intersection on Mt. Auburn Street: 151 (1851),

154 (1852), and 156–158 (1856). In the 20th century 18 Ash became the residence of Martin Mower, a lecturer in fine arts at Harvard. He engaged Fletcher Steele to landscape the grounds and Lois Lilley Howe to design an addition that included a fine paneled room possibly taken from an Asher Benjamin house that was razed for the Fogg Museum in 1924.

The Cambridge Gas-Light Company acquired the riverfront of Windmill Hill between 1852 and 1869 and built a retort house that heated coal to produce illuminating gas and a gas-holder at the Brick Wharf (see figure 2.20). This facility blighted the neighborhood until it was razed in 1900. The five apartment buildings built on the gasworks site between 1914 and 1924—the Strathcona, Barrington Court, Hampstead Hall, Radnor Hall, and the Allwyn—now divide the neighborhood from the river (see chapter 6). Since 1984 this area has been protected by the Half Crown-Marsh Neighborhood Conservation District.

Hastings-Palmer Homestead

A property on the east corner of Ash Street—an ancient way around the west side of Windmill Hill to the Brick Wharf—was the only tract on the river side of Brattle Street that was never incorporated into a loyalist estate. It originated as the homestead of Thomas Brigham about 1635. His widow moved to Marlborough in 1653 and sold the place to John Hastings, a tanner from Braintree. John's oldest son, Walter, moved to his wife's house near the Common, and the homestead was conveyed to Stephen Palmer, another tanner, in 1734.

Palmer's great-granddaughter, Lucy Ann Jones, inherited the homestead in 1836. She married William L. Whitney, a furniture dealer, who laid out Ash Street Place and built a house on the north corner in 1837 (figure 4.13). Four of the five houses on the south side went up between 1838 and 1852. Of these the most notable is the Gothic cottage begun in 1848 by Peter Nye, a carpenter under contract to Oliver Hastings, which sold before completion to manufacturer James Hunnewell (see figure 6.65).

Later, the modest house at number 12 was the residence of landscape architect Paul Frost (1883–1957). Frost was born in

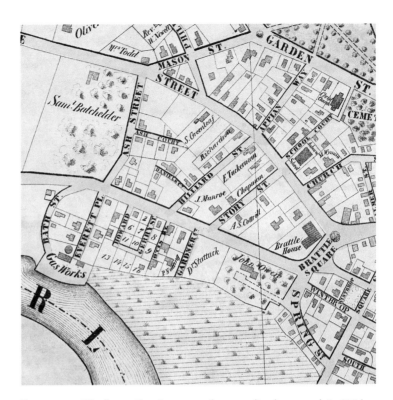

FIGURE 4.14   The former Brattle estate and surrounding homesteads in 1854.

FIGURE 4.13   William L. Whitney house, 10 Ash Street (1837). Whitney's broad-pilastered Regency style house on the corner of Ash Street Place was demolished by Radcliffe College in 1930. Photo ca. 1930.

Cambridge and attended Harvard with the class of 1907, then worked with Charles Platt in New York, the Olmsted Brothers in Brookline, and the Metropolitan Park Commission in Boston. In 1914 he opened an office in Harvard Square that he shared with Arthur Comey, the city planner. Frost's projects include a garden at 7 Berkeley Place (1914) and the redesign of Longfellow Park (1915), but his masterpiece was surely the "horticultural laboratory" on the grounds of his own house (figure 4.15). Frost "divided the tiny property into nine segments and developed each to its maximum potential" (Zaitzevsky, JNEGHS, 16). When space ran out he appropriated the private way in front, leaving a brick walk to connect to Fuller Place. Bainbridge Bunting wrote that the landscape was "a model of what can be done ... to humanize the tyrannical monotony of a city street" (CHC inventory, 1967).

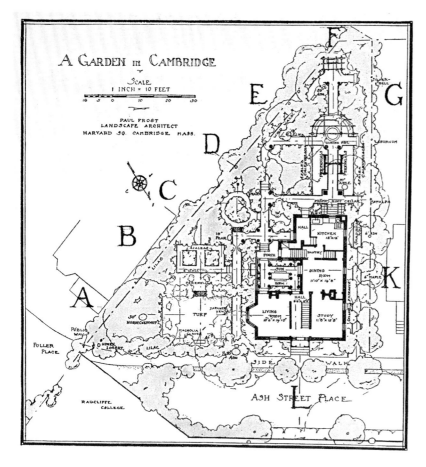

FIGURE 4.15 Paul Frost's garden at 12 Ash Street Place was an intensively culti-vated horticultural laboratory whose design was governed by the site's micro-climates. This plan was published in 1924, before he landscaped the private way in front.

HENRY VASSALL ESTATE

The nine-acre Henry Vassall estate, the smallest on Tory Row, originated as a two-acre grant just inside the Common Pales. William Adams built a house there in 1637 or 1638 but soon moved to Ipswich. In 1682 Lieutenant Jonathan Remington sold the place to his wife's nephew, Andrew Belcher, son of a tavern-keeper who became "one of the most enterprising and wealthy merchants in the Province" (Paige, 486). Jonathan Belcher, the future royal governor of Massachusetts, inherited the property in 1717 and two years later sold it to Boston merchant John Frizzel.

John Vassall, a wealthy young man with roots in Massachu-setts and the West Indies, bought seven acres with a house, barn, and various outbuildings from Frizzel's heirs in 1736. John's grandfather, William Vassall, had settled in Roxbury in 1635, but as an Anglican in a Puritan community he found it pru-dent to relocate to Barbados in 1648; he obtained a plantation in Jamaica after it was taken from the Spanish in 1655. Wil-liam's son Leonard settled in Quincy when his oldest son, Lewis, entered Harvard with the class of 1728.[5] John, Leonard's second son, acquired first rank in the class of 1732 "at the cost of dou-ble tuition and a silver tankard which the college still has" (Sib-ley, IX, 229).[6] Two years after graduating he married Elizabeth Phips, whose father, Lieutenant Governor Spencer Phips, owned an estate east of the village (see below). John borrowed £3,000 from his father in anticipation of an inheritance and used it to acquire the Belcher-Frizzel place.

Governor Belcher appointed John a major, like his father. He settled down convincingly enough to be elected selectman and representative to the General Court in 1739, although "deputy sheriff Samuel Whittemore remarked that the Major was no more fit to be a Selectman of Cambridge than was the horse he rode." Vassall sued Whittemore for £1,000 "on the grounds that he had been brought into great contempt and was much 'damnifyed' by his remark," but Whittemore won a judgment in return "and had the great pleasure of serving the writ on the Major as he presided at an elegant dinner party in his mansion" (Sibley, XIV, 231).

Although he was reelected in 1740, John Vassall announced that he was moving to Jamaica and offered to sell his house and "about forty Acres of Land, the greatest part of it being fine mowing Land, and chiefly fenc'd by the River and a Creek" (*New England Weekly Journal,* Nov. 18, 1740). In fact, he was involved in a scheme with Governor Belcher to become governor of New Hampshire and traveled to London with that object. He failed, as a contemporary recalled, "owing to a feeble mind, the want of Proper address and application to business, and the giving himself up to Pleasure" (Sibley, XIV, 234).

Henry Vassall, who was about to marry Penelope Royall, daughter of the wealthy Isaac Royall of Medford, bought his brother's place for £9,000. His advantageous match brought him a rich prize: Penelope's life interest in the Royall plantation on Antigua. Even this, however, could not support their profligate lifestyle, which involved entertaining, gambling, and so many horses that he had to hire stabling for them. Henry borrowed from his mother-in-law, appropriated his daughter's trust fund, sold his plantation in Jamaica, sold his wife's life interest in her plantation, and executed at least four mortgages on his Cambridge property between 1748 and his death in 1769. Penelope Vassall tried to pay off his debts, but in 1774 she grew frightened of the rebels and fled to Antigua. This made her property subject to confiscation, and during the Siege of Boston her house served as a hospital and a prison for the traitor Dr. Benjamin Church. She hoped to return to Cambridge after the war, but her husband's creditors sold the property in 1782 to Newburyport merchant Nathaniel Tracy (see figure 6.12).

At Henry Vassall's death his slaves included Tony, Dick, James, Dorinda, and Cuba; according to his biographer, Samuel F. Batchelder, about four times as many slaves appeared in his papers at different times. Tony (later known as Anthony) was Vassall's coachman; he was born about 1713 and may have been among the slaves that Penelope brought from Medford in 1740. She kept Tony when she sold his wife, Cuba, and their children across the road to John Vassall Jr. in an attempt to clear her husband's debts. She must have freed him before she left in 1774, because he appears as "1 poll" on the Cambridge assessor's list of 1777.[7]

During the Siege Tony and his family lived on John Vassall's estate in a house "east of the Garden" (Batchelder, "Col. Henry Vassall," 69). In 1778 Tony petitioned the legislature for title to this portion of the property, claiming "that though dwelling in a land of freedom, both himself and his wife have spent almost

FIGURE 4.16 Colonel Henry Vassall (1721–69), attributed to John Singleton Copley, ca. 1750.

FIGURE 4.17 Penelope Royall Vassall (1724–1800), attributed to John Singleton Copley, ca. 1750.

sixty years of their lives in slavery … yet they have ever lived a life of honesty and been faithful in their master's service" (ibid., 70). The legislature instead granted him £12 a year to keep his family off relief. Tony convinced a Commonwealth agent that he should be compensated for supporting his wife and two children, who were still slaves, and received the extraordinary sum of £222. With this he purchased a house on a quarter acre of land on Massachusetts Avenue in the Lower Common.

Anthony died in 1811 at 98 and was buried in the Vassall family tomb under Christ Church. Cuba lived only another year, but their son, Darby, born in 1769, survived them by half a century. An anecdote has Darby swinging on the gate at John Vassall's house when General Washington arrived in July 1775. The general proposed to take him into service, but, as Darby recounted, "General Washington was no gentleman, to expect a boy to work for no wages" (ibid., 75). Darby died a pauper in 1861, still in possession of a "pass" from Henry Vassall's granddaughter that allowed him to be buried with the family.

Andrew Craigie acquired the Henry Vassall estate in 1792 and granted lifetime occupancy to his sister and brother-in-law, Bossenger Foster, "a gentleman of leisure" who was his best friend and agent. Craigie's niece, Elizabeth Haven, sold it to Samuel Batchelder (1784–1879) in 1841. A native of New Ipswich, New Hampshire, Batchelder was hired by his townsmen, Nathan and Samuel Appleton, to superintend their cotton mills at Lowell and Saco. Income from inventions made him wealthy, and although he claimed to be retired he kept an office in Boston for the remaining thirty-eight years of his life. A prolific editorialist and pamphleteer, Batchelder was a member of the first board of aldermen in 1846. His son, attorney Samuel Batchelder Jr. (1830–88), graduated from Harvard in 1851, and his daughter Isabella married Thomas James of Philadelphia. His grandson Samuel F. Batchelder (1870–1927) became one of Cambridge's most productive historians, while Isabella's daughter Mary (1852–1935) married an Austrian count, Silvio de Gozzaldi, edited the DAR's *Historic Guide to Cambridge* (1907), and compiled the *Supplement and Index* to Lucius Paige's *History of Cambridge* (1930).

Batchelder modernized the Belcher-Frizzel-Vassall house with a Greek Revival porch across the east front that faced a "Broad Walk" bordered with flowers and shrubs; the south side of the house faced a boxwood garden from which led a "Long Walk" through fruit trees, grapevines, a vegetable garden, and cornfields to Mt. Auburn Street (figure 4.18). He erected the present concrete block wall in front of the house after the city destroyed nearly a hundred acacia trees to widen Brattle Street in 1871. This was one of the first uses of architectural concrete in Cambridge; a similar wall stands at the junction of Brattle and Craigie streets.

Batchelder began to develop his estate in 1858, when he allowed Simon Greenleaf to move the 1824 Nowell house from Brattle Street to 19 Ash Street. Ten years later he had William A. Mason draft a subdivision plan and rather improbably sold the first lot to George Lyon, the owner of a billiard hall in Harvard Square, subject to the usual conditions on setbacks and the minimum cost of construction. Lyon sold his large new Mansard at 13 Ash to Lucia Ela, a widow who arrived in Cambridge just as her sons Richard and Alfred were graduating from Harvard. They became proprietors of the Standard Turning Works in Cambridgeport, which acquired the property in 1886. After

Figure 4.18 The Henry Vassall mansion at 94 Brattle Street may contain some of the oldest building fabric in Cambridge. This view shows the east front and gardens after Samuel Batchelder added a Greek Revival porch in the 1840s. Photo ca. 1870, before the widening of Brattle Street.

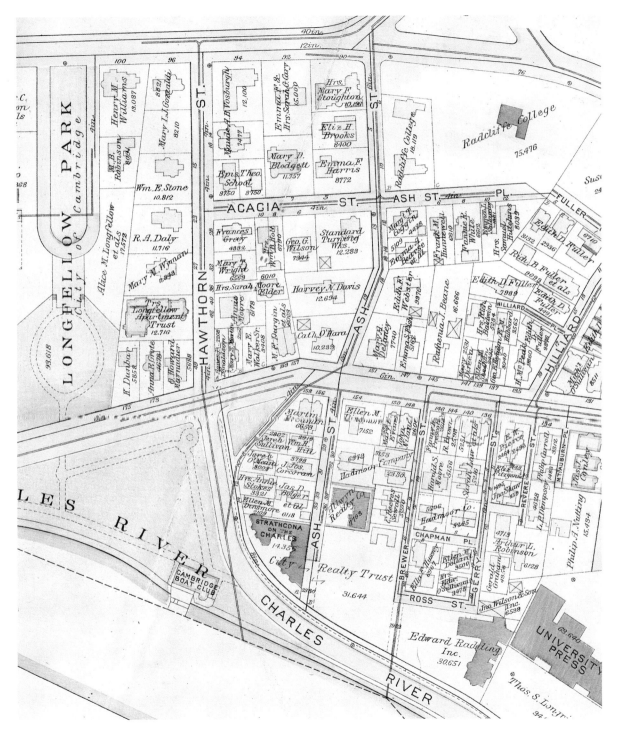

FIGURE 4.19 The former Vassall-Batchelder estate in 1916. The area evolved somewhat haphazardly in the absence of a carefully thought-out subdivision plan or controls on the sequence and quality of construction.

FIGURE 4.20 Mary Isabella de Gozzaldi house, 96 Brattle Street (1881, Peabody & Stearns, architects). In 1954 the Church of Jesus Christ of Latter-Day Saints razed the Gozzaldi house and moved 98 Brattle from the corner of Longfellow Park to 15 Hawthorn Street to make way for the present church. Photo ca. 1938.

the last brother died in 1924 neighbors purchased the house to protect themselves from a possible apartment building.

In 1872 Batchelder or his son laid out Hawthorn Street (named for a hedge that ran along his property line) through the paved court on the west side of the house and Acacia Street (named for the lost trees) at the foot of the garden. Three houses were built before the Panic of 1873, but most construction took place between 1880 and 1900. Longfellow Chambers, one of the few apartment buildings to penetrate the area in the years before zoning, shocked the neighborhood when it went up at 41 Hawthorn in 1911. Prominent Federal houses now mark both ends of Hawthorn Street: the 1813 Jacob Hill Bates house at 11, moved from 45 Brattle Street in 1926, and the handsome Federal Revival at 49, designed in 1900 by Lois Lilley Howe.

Samuel Batchelder's executor sold his Brattle Street lots in 1881–82. Isabella James built a house on the west corner of Hawthorn Street for her daughter, Mary de Gozzaldi (figure 4.20). Sallie and Emma Cary, unmarried sisters of Radcliffe

founder Elizabeth Cary Agassiz, put up a Stick Style house at 92, while historian John Fiske had H.H. Richardson design a house for his mother, Mary Fisk Stoughton (see figures 6.106 and 6.144). Mrs. Stoughton's son-in-law, mining executive John Brooks, built a Colonial Revival house next door on Ash Street. The Vassall-Batchelder house remained in the family until 1973, when new owners divided it and returned the east front to its Georgian appearance by removing the Greek Revival portico.

JOHN VASSALL ESTATE

John Vassall (1713–47) and John Vassall Jr. (1738–97) assembled an estate of 87 acres, the largest on Tory Row during the colonial era, over a period of twenty-eight years. John Vassall Sr. purchased 94 Brattle Street, his first house in Cambridge, in 1736, but sold it to his brother Henry in 1741. When he returned to Cambridge in 1746 he bought the adjoining Marrett homestead, which encompassed 6½ acres north of Brattle Street and 50 acres between the road and the river.

The Marretts typified the Puritan descendants who yielded to the loyalists but ultimately outlasted them. Thomas Marrett, a shoemaker, arrived in the village in 1638. His grandson, Lieutenant Amos Marrett, a wealthy farmer and brickmaker, settled on a 10-acre homestead on the north side of the Watertown road in 1704. Lieutenant Marrett's nephew Amos, a glazier and farmer, inherited the property in 1739 and sold most of it to John Vassall Sr. in 1746.[8] A sixth-generation descendant, Daniel Marrett, was the first in the family to graduate from Harvard, and by the 1830s some of his children had joined Cambridge's urban middle class. The wealthy Vassalls, by contrast, arrived a century after the Marretts, steeped in a plantation culture based on slavery, conspicuous consumption, and pride of place. Resentment of their privileges was amplified by political events and led to their expulsion four decades later.

When John Vassall died in 1747 his executors placed John Jr. in the care of his grandfather Spencer Phips. John probably began to receive his father's possessions when he was about 15 and preparing to attend Harvard:

FIGURE 4.21 John Vassall's coat of arms, displayed on his bookplate. The Vassalls descended from a French Huguenot refugee, John Vassall (1544–1625), who was honored by Queen Elizabeth for outfitting ships for the fleet that repelled the Spanish Armada in 1588. The blazing sun and chalice appear on the Vassall tomb in the Old Burying Ground.

His library, watch, sword, and arms, a velvet coat laced, an embroidered jacket, silk breeches, a blue velvet coat with gold lace, a camblet coat, a flowered silk coat and breeches, a [silk] waistcoat and breeches, scarlet breeches, a scarlet coat, a fustian coat, … a pair of pocket pistols, holsters, and caps, saddlegirt, brass stirrups, a silver hilted sword, a gun, riding pistols, a silver watch. (Paige, 675n1; figure 4.21)

John graduated in 1757 and inherited the family's sugar plantations in Jamaica when he came of age in 1759. He immediately built an ostentatious High Georgian mansion behind the Marrett house, which was taken down or moved away.[9] In 1760 his sister Elizabeth married Thomas Oliver of Dorchester, the future lieutenant governor, and a year later John married Oliver's sister, also named Elizabeth; they had eight children, all but the last born in Cambridge. John expanded the property with purchases of meadow, pasture, and salt marsh, encompassing a landscape that extended from the river to the summit of Observatory Hill (figure 4.22). His claim to the British government after his holdings were confiscated in 1778 described it as "containing 105 Acres of Meadow & Orcharding [and] a large Dwelling House with very extensive Gardens and Stabling and three other houses" (Public Record Office, AO 13/90, 485).[10] He reported an annual income of £150 from the farm and itemized its "sundry stock" and slaves:

A Negro woman, Cuba £40
A Mulatto Man, Malcolm £50
A Mulatto Boy, James £30
A Negro Man, William £20
A Negro Woman, Dinah £30
Two small Boys £30

Two yoke of oxen £50
Six cows £24
A Pair Steers £6
Two heifers £5
Two Yearlings £3
A Bay Mare paid sheriff for £40
A Bay Mare £10
Two horses from England £100
Four colts £25
Five Hogs £5
Forty tons of hay at 40/ per ton £60
Cider £5
Roots £5

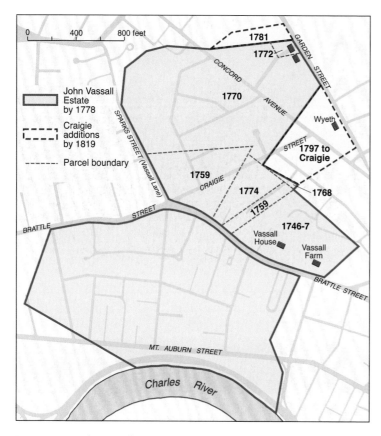

FIGURE 4.22 John Vassall's holdings at the time they were confiscated in 1778.

The Vassalls fled to Boston in 1774 and then to England, where John died in 1797. His house became George Washington's headquarters during the Siege of Boston.

In 1781 the Commonwealth sold the Vassall property to Nathaniel Tracy, a wealthy Newburyport merchant and Revolutionary privateer who had "developed the hobby of collecting country estates with such enthusiasm that it was said that he could travel from Newburyport to Virginia, sleeping in his own house every night" (Sibley, XVII, 249). Tracy held extravagant parties in Cambridge but soon went bankrupt and in 1786 sold the estate to Thomas Russell, president of the Bank of the United States in Boston. Andrew Craigie, the former apothecary general of the American army, purchased it in 1791.

ANDREW CRAIGIE'S MANSION AND FIELDS NORTH OF BRATTLE STREET

A wealthy speculator known for his social pretensions and sharp business practices, Craigie directed his kinsman Bossenger Foster to furnish the mansion and improve the grounds before he moved from New York to Cambridge in 1792. Foster repaired the outbuildings, hired a gardener, and purchased trees, carriages, horses, and a flock of chickens. Craigie added an ell and side porches to the house, built a greenhouse, excavated an ornamental pond, and brought piped water from a spring near the summerhouse that Nathaniel Tracy had put up on Observatory Hill (figure 4.23; see also figure 4.118). He joined the Massachusetts Society for Promoting Agriculture, an organization of gentlemen farmers, and donated land for Harvard's Botanic Garden. He planted a hundred fruit trees, sixty-two fashionable Lombardy poplars, and numerous elms along Sparks Street.

Always eager to expand his domain, Craigie acquired several adjoining Brattle Street properties, including Henry Vassall's estate in 1792 and Richard Lechmere's in 1819.[11] The former became Bossenger Foster's residence, and the latter he rented to Bossenger's brother Joseph. In 1795 Craigie began accumulating acreage on Lechmere's Point, which he developed in the early 19th century. His efforts to build roads and inflate the value of his investment by stripping the village of its courthouse kept Cambridge in turmoil for many years (see *East Cambridge*).

Craigie died intestate and bankrupt in 1819. Bossenger Foster's children contested the division of his property, and only after much delay did the widow Craigie receive the mansion, 41 surrounding acres, "42½ acres of arable and salt and fresh meadow in front of the mansion house," and the 13-acre Richard Lechmere estate (Middlesex Probate 5303). The Fosters received his other Cambridge parcels, including the Henry Vassall estate and the summerhouse and aqueduct lots (figure 4.24).

Elizabeth Shaw of Nantucket had married Craigie in 1793, when he was 39 and she was 21, and survived him by two decades. After his death she scrimped to pay off his debts but

Figure 4.23 John Vassall house, 105 Brattle Street (1759), shown ca. 1845 with the side porches added by Andrew Craigie in the 1790s.

did not sell her land. She reduced her servants from twelve to two and moved into the back of the house with them so she could rent the front rooms. Her boarders included at least two future Harvard presidents, Edward Everett and Jared Sparks. In 1837 a young professor of modern languages, Henry Wadsworth Longfellow, rented two upstairs rooms, where he lived in George Washington's chambers "like an Italian Prince in his villa" (HWL to Anne Longfellow Pierce, Sept. 21, 1837, in Paterson I, 25). After Madam Craigie died in 1841, the lexicographer Joseph Worcester and his wife rented the house. Longfellow stayed on and was still there in May 1843 when he became engaged to Fanny Appleton, whose father, Nathan, was the great Boston cotton manufacturer and cofounder of Lowell.

After Mrs. Craigie's death her property was partitioned among the Fosters and their cousins, the Havens, except for 32 acres west of the house and the 13-acre Richard Lechmere estate, which her executors put up for sale. The Fosters divided the remaining land north of Brattle Street and in 1843 sold the farmhouse and four acres east of the mansion to Oliver Hastings, a prosperous housewright and lumber dealer. Nathan Appleton purchased the Craigie mansion, and Joseph Worcester acquired the remainder.

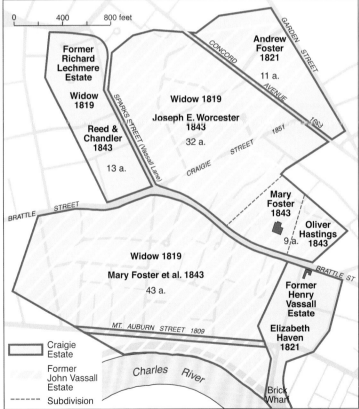

Figure 4.24 The division of Andrew Craigie's estate, 1819–21, and after the death of his widow in 1841.

Henry Wadsworth Longfellow Estate   Henry Wadsworth Longfellow loved living at Craigie house, as he called it. Fanny too became enthralled and wrote that "we have decided to let father purchase this grand old mansion if he will." Their friend George Washington Greene "reminded us how noble an inheritance this is—where Washington dwelt in every room." A few days later, she rhapsodized about the view—"how gracefully the Charles loiters to the sea through green meadows and how large vessels sometimes glide with him and at full tide how lake-like he becomes." She urged her father to purchase the land across the road, "for the view would be ruined by a block of houses" (Fanny to Tom Appleton, Matilda Leiber, and Nathan Appleton, Aug. 30–Sept. 4, 1843, in Paterson I, 199–200).

Nathan Appleton gave Fanny the house and five acres as well as 3½ acres of field and meadow across Brattle Street as a wedding gift. Longfellow immediately began to landscape the grounds, planting an avenue of lindens and, in his enthusiasm, some acorns. In January, Alex Longfellow (Henry's nephew and an apprentice surveyor) reported that "we are very busy laying out the grounds ... the house is to be repaired but not essentially altered, the old outbuildings to be removed, trees planted, a pond [dug] and a rustic bridge [built]" (to Sam Longfellow, ibid., 211). In April Henry confirmed the principle that guided his stewardship: "[George M.] Dexter, the architect, comes out to look upon the field of battle and contemplate the pulling down of old barns and general changes of house and grounds. In the repairs I shall have done as little as possible. The Craigie house is decidedly conservative and will remain as much in its old state as comfort permits" (*Journal,* Apr. 9, 1844, ibid., 228). He built a new barn in 1845 but otherwise made few changes (figure 4.25).

The only cloud on the horizon was Oliver Hastings. Fanny described him as "a driving Yankee neighbor, with a face like a wedge, building too near our left shoulder but as he is to put up a well-looking house and not some diseased Temple & will not sell the land for any Christian sum, we try to resign ourselves with the hope of getting in time an effectual screen of

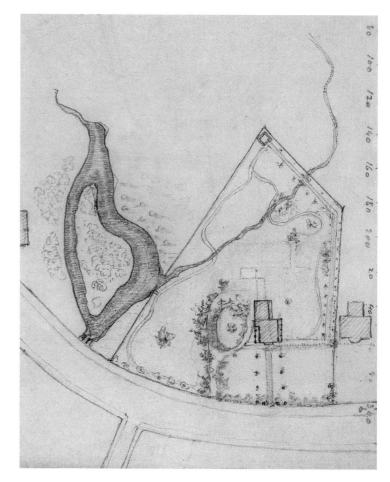

FIGURE 4.25   Alexander W. Longfellow's sketch of the Longfellow house grounds, showing Dictionary Lake (also known as Craigie's Pond) on the left and Oliver Hastings's house on the right. Undated, but ca. 1844.

trees & hedge" (to Tom Appleton, Nov. 1843, ibid., 211–12). Their friend George Hilliard thought it was "a vulgar, impudent looking house ... which I want to kick over every time I see it" (ibid., 220; see figure 6.62). Across the road, the Fosters had "already staked out lots [on Willard Street] besides planting any quantity of bean poles by the road which they intend by some miracle to convert into trees" (ibid., 234). As Fanny feared, these houses blocked their view of the great bend in the river at Gerry's Landing (figure 4.26).

FIGURE 4.26 Ten-year-old Ernest Longfellow's sketch of the Charles River from the second floor of 105 Brattle Street, June 12, 1855. The field between the house and the river is now the site of Longfellow Park. The gardener's cottage (1846, now 7 Longfellow Park) occupies the center of the view.

The Longfellows made a considerable impact on the neighborhood. The poet built houses for his son Ernest at 108 Brattle Street in 1871 and at 12 Berkeley Street in 1882, while daughters Edith and Anne built at 113 and 115 Brattle Street in 1887 (figures 4.27–4.28). After his death they gave two acres across the street to the Longfellow Memorial Association to preserve the view. Alice, who never married, helped establish the Longfellow House Trust in 1913, giving descendants the right to live in the house until twenty years after the death of Henry's last grandchild. Henry Wadsworth Longfellow Dana, a grandson, lived in the house and was deeply concerned about its future. He rebuffed overtures from the Cambridge Historical Society and the Society for the Preservation of New England Antiquities, and after he died in 1950 the trustees offered it to the federal government.

The National Park Service took possession in 1973 and initially continued the operating procedures of the Longfellow Trust. In 1998 the staff decided to interpret the house as of 1928, the year of Alice's death, and completed a $1.6 million restoration in 2003. Harry Dana's enthusiasm for accumulating

FIGURE 4.27 Ernest Longfellow house, 108 Brattle Street (1871, Peabody & Stearns, architects). The Stick Style exterior was covered with stucco in 1925 but could easily be restored to its earlier appearance. Photo 1962.

FIGURE 4.28 Longfellow's daughters Anne and Edith built houses at 115 and 113 Brattle Street next to Craigie House in 1887 (see figures 6.127 and 6.158). Photo ca. 1895.

family papers yielded enormous dividends, and archivists found many treasures that remained after Harvard acquired the poet's manuscripts in 1954. In addition to Henry's art and furnishings, the house contains Charles Longfellow's Asian collections, a 14,000-volume library, 11,500 photographs, and a manuscript collection of over 750,000 items that includes the papers of the extended Appleton, Dana, Longfellow, and Wadsworth families.

Joseph Worcester Estate   Longfellow's fellow tenant at Craigie House, Joseph Worcester, bought 32 acres of Craigie's estate north of Brattle, including Craigie's Pond, and put up a grand, broad-pilastered Regency style house at 121 Brattle Street (see figure 6.61). A friend wrote to the absent poet in 1843:

> You will … be glad to hear that Castle Craigie is still standing and that Worcester Hall is now rising. The Castle and the Hall are not remarkably congruous, but the trees on the border of Dictionary Lake and Atlantic Stream will screen you from the full blaze of the new architectural wonder. (Howe, "Lost Brook," 58)

By 1852 Worcester had laid out Craigie Street and the west end of Berkeley and was selling lots with deed restrictions to ensure spacious settings and expensive houses.[12] The first house on Craigie, designed in 1854 by Henry Greenough for Professor Arnold Guyot, was probably just what he envisioned. At 3 Craigie near Concord Avenue, the housewright Isaac Cutler built a much simpler house with a monitor roof for William Porter, a clergyman, in 1854. The exceptionally large Mansard that Judge Joel Parker put up at 5 Craigie Street in 1856 was replaced by apartment buildings on Craigie Circle in 1917–20 (see figure 6.82).

The residence built in 1868 by Albion K.P. Welch, proprietor of the University Press, dominates the intersection of Craigie and Brattle streets and is the best-preserved academic Second Empire house in the city (figure 4.30; see also figure 6.86). For many years this was the home of Denman Ross (1853–1935), a painter, teacher, and art collector who added a studio wing along Craigie Street. His heirs divided the property in 1970 and placed it under the protection of the Cambridge Historical

FIGURE 4.29   The Joseph Worcester estate in 1854. The original course of Sparks Street is visible in the curved property line at the top of the hill. The brook that crossed the back of Longfellow's yard has been placed in a drain. Berkeley Street was laid out across the Wyeth and Worcester lands in 1851–52.

Commission. Two families now share the house, while a Modern dwelling at 133 Brattle occupies the south lawn (see figure 6.212).[13]

Welch put up a "stone fence" around his property in 1870 (*Chronicle,* July 16, 1870). This use of concrete (or cast stone) in discrete masonry units—marketed as "Stone Brick" by the Union Stone Co. of Boston—occurred only two years after the technology was imported from France, making Welch's wall and Samuel Batchelder's at 94 Brattle Street among the oldest examples of concrete construction in New England. A restored portion encloses a fountain donated to the city by the Ross heirs in 1971 (see figure 5.60).

FIGURE 4.30 Brattle and Craigie streets, looking east. The Guyot Hurlbut house (27 Craigie Street, 1854) is at left; the Denman Ross house (24 Craigie Street, 1869) is at right. Photo after 1870.

Worcester's land extended up Sparks Street to the saddle between Observatory and Reservoir hills. He and an adjoining landowner, George Meacham, straightened the curve just below Huron Avenue, which allowed Boston merchant Charles Deane to build a large Mansard in 1858 that probably had one of the finest views in Cambridge (figure 4.31). With 650 feet of frontage along Sparks Street, Deane set off three large lots below his house that attracted some notable residences, including Edward S. Dodge's brick and shingle Queen Anne at 70 (1878; see figure 6.114), nestled in a hollow 160 feet back from the street, and Lucy Dexter's 1886 Shingle Style house at 76 (1886, William R. Emerson, architect). George Clement Deane laid out Clement

FIGURE 4.31 Charles Deane house, 80 Sparks Street (1858) and stable (1867). Landscape architect Arthur Musgrove gave this house a brick veneer in the Georgian Style in 1932; it became the Buckingham School in 1949. Photo after 1867.

Circle behind his father's house in 1898, and six large homes were crowded onto the cul-de-sac by 1922.

Worcester laid out a new street from Craigie Street to Concord Avenue in 1855 and sold the first two lots to housewrights Oliver Hastings and Albert Stevens. Hastings built 23 Craigie Street for his daughter Caroline on the occasion of her marriage to chemist John Andrew Henshaw (see figure 6.84). Stevens put up a house around the corner and sold it in 1857 to Ellen and Lucy Buckingham, the unmarried daughters of Joseph Buckingham, a retired newspaper publisher who had just sold his place on Quincy Street; Worcester named the new street in his honor. Notable surviving houses include number 13, a Mansard designed for attorney Henry Muzzy by Newburyport architect Rufus Sargent, 23, an elaborate Stick Style dwelling built in 1878 for Professor James Laughlin, and 29, an early Queen Anne house built in 1880 for the abolitionist Thomas Wentworth Higginson (figure 4.32; see also figures 6.104 and 6.120). The east side of the street falls off to a lower elevation and contains smaller lots laid out in 1872; the Stick Style houses at 60 (1879) and 34 (1882) and the Queen Anne at 50 (1884) are modest in scale but fine examples of the period (see figure 6.125).

Parker and Healy streets also occupy Worcester land. "The Hollow" was the source of a brook that fed Craigie's Pond; it was recalled as "a pretty open marshy place where the neighborhood children picked wild flowers as late as the eighties of the nineteenth century" (Howe, "Lost Brook," 53). In 1890 Somerville builder Suther Blaikie put up seven Queen Annes on Parker Street, some of which he sold to unsuspecting African American families. Several had inadequate footings for the peat that underlay the area and settled badly, requiring expensive new foundations. Number 47 was the home of George Washington Lewis, steward of the Porcellian Club and a descendant of the family that had settled nearby Lewisville (figure 4.34).

David Tower, a teacher and textbook author, acquired the Buckingham house in 1865. His widow laid out Buckingham Place with six house lots in 1892. Emily Thackeray, a teacher, built a gambrel cottage at 4, and next door Jeanette Markham

FIGURE 4.32 Henry Muzzey house, 13 Buckingham Street (1862, Rufus Sargent, architect). The original roof and decorative dormers were destroyed in a 1919 fire and replaced with the present hip roof. Photo ca. 1875.

put up a small schoolhouse with the assistance of a neighborhood mother, Edith Longfellow Dana; this became the Buckingham School in 1902 (see chapter 7). The houses at 5, 7, and 10, designed in 1892–93 by William Griswold, a journalist and amateur architect who lived at 25 Craigie Street, led the *Tribune* to declare the street "an exceedingly pretty place" (Apr. 28, 1894). Number 6 was originally Arthur Astor Carey's studio, moved from 10 Fayerweather Street in 1897. An important early Modern house designed by Carl Koch for his parents replaced the Buckingham house in 1937 (see figure 6.194).

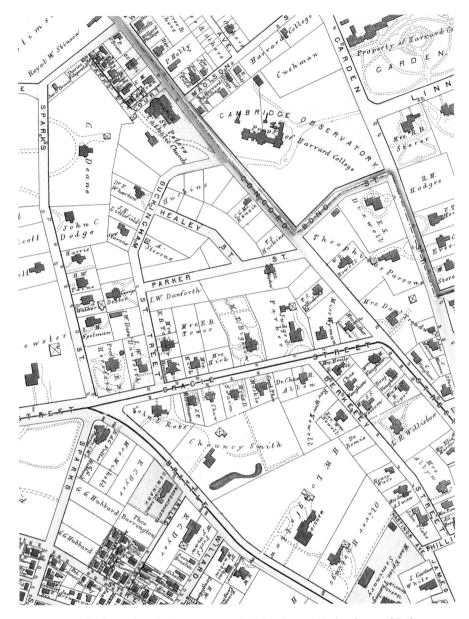

FIGURE 4.33 The former Joseph Worcester estate in 1873, showing Buckingham and Parker streets.

FIGURE 4.34 George Washington Lewis family at 47 Parker Street (1890). Photo ca. 1900.

After Mrs. Craigie's death in 1841, the Foster heirs sold her 42½ acres of fields and meadows south of Brattle Street. Longfellow bought 3½ acres between Hawthorn and Willard streets from his father-in-law in 1849, and in 1853 he purchased a cottage on Willard Street Court as a residence for his gardener (figure 4.35). He built 108 Brattle Street for his son Ernest in 1871 but kept the rest of the land open to preserve his view of the river and the Brighton Hills. After his death in 1882 his children set aside some of this land as a private park, and in 1888 they divided the balance among themselves (figure 4.36; see chapter 5).

After the death of Charles Longfellow in 1893, Alice Longfellow owned all the east side of the park. She sold the corner to Henry Williams, a Boston lawyer, who put up a house at 100 Brattle Street in 1896. John Brooks of 5 Ash Street commissioned Alexander Wadsworth Longfellow to design a Colonial Revival at 6 Longfellow Park for his daughter Margaret in 1901.

FIGURE 4.35 Longfellow gardener's cottage, 7 Longfellow Park (1846; moved and remodeled 1914). Architect Alexander Wadsworth Longfellow Jr. made this sketch in 1914.

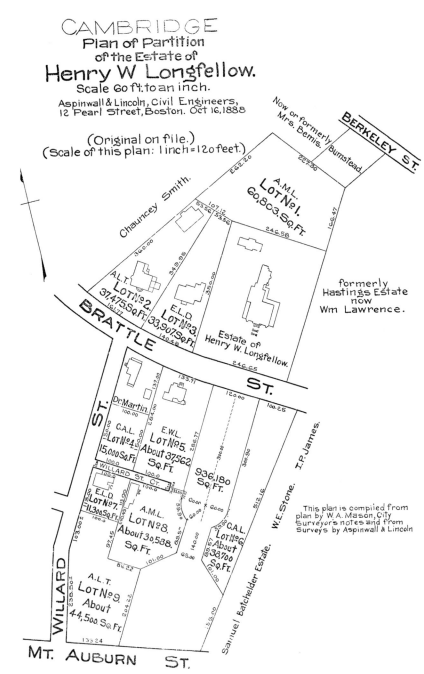

FIGURE 4.36 Disposition of the Longfellow estate in 1888. Initials designate the heirs: AML, Alice M. Longfellow; ALT, Annie Longfellow Thorp; ELD, Edith Longfellow Dana; EWL, Ernest W. Longfellow; and CAL, Charles A. Longfellow.

In 1914 Alice had the gardener's cottage moved forward and modernized, and her sister Anne Thorp had their cousin Alexander design a Georgian Revival house next door. Alice's heirs sold her remaining lots after she died in 1928; one of the two houses built in 1935 is a notable early Modern design by Cambridge architect Eleanor Raymond (see figure 6.193). In 1936 the Boston Society of Friends acquired the Thorp property and added a domestically scaled meetinghouse designed by Duguid & Martin. The Church of Jesus Christ of Latter-Day Saints moved the Williams house to 15 Hawthorn Street and built the present chapel in 1954 (see chapter 7).

The land west of Longfellow's as far as Lowell Street passed in 1843 to George, Samuel, and James Foster, all of whom lived in New York. George, a broker, soon moved to Boston. Acting as trustee for his brothers, he laid out twenty-two lots, mostly along Brattle Street, as well as Lowell Street and Liberty and Union streets (renamed Willard and Foster by 1850), but sales were painfully slow. In 1844 housewright Stephen Brown of Cambridgeport bought two of them, subject to a restriction intended to maintain the social tone of the neighborhood:

> No building which may be erected on the premises herein granted shall be used for the business of a Taverner, Carpenter, Cordwainer, Cabinet Maker, Butcher, Soapboiler, Brewer, Distiller, Tallow Chandler, Sugar Baker, Brazier, Tinsman, Dyer, Foundry Smith, Brickmaker, or for any other nauseous or offensive business. Nor shall any building that may be erected as aforesaid be leased or occupied by any Negroes or other persons of color. (Middlesex Deeds 448/429)[14]

The house at 112 Brattle that Brown built on speculation is one of the finest examples of the vernacular Greek Revival in Cambridge (see figure 6.57). A double house on the west corner of Willard Street that Foster put up in 1845 was probably similar, while a third, the home of Daniel Brown, a real estate broker, made a brave attempt at creating an ensemble. The only other house to appear in this period was George Foster's own place at 19 Lowell Street (figure 4.37).

FIGURE 4.37 George Foster house, 19 Lowell Street (1849, George M. Dexter, architect). Photo 1970.

In October 1849 Samuel Foster sold the heirs' remaining 36 acres to Gardiner Greene Hubbard (1822–97), a lawyer who became deeply involved in civic improvements as the founder of the Cambridge Gas-Light Company, the Cambridge Water Works, and the Cambridge Railroad. According to Hubbard's daughter, "it was a bare uninviting place … just fields of run-down land supporting a meager crop or pasturage with one or two old apple trees" (Bell, "Reminiscences"). A year later, he staked out sixty-seven parcels for auction (figure 4.38). The largest faced Brattle Street and ranged from 100 to 123 feet in frontage and 196 to 367 feet in depth; the marsh lots along Mt. Auburn Street were at least 90 feet wide.[15] The *Chronicle* advised that it would be an excellent opportunity "to exchange the fetid, pent-up limits of the city, for the fresh air and rural comforts of a suburban residence," with prices ranging from 2½ to 6¾ cents per square foot (June 29). Fewer than half sold, and the following year Hubbard auctioned the thirty-eight remaining lots, describing some as "desirable residences for gentlemen and

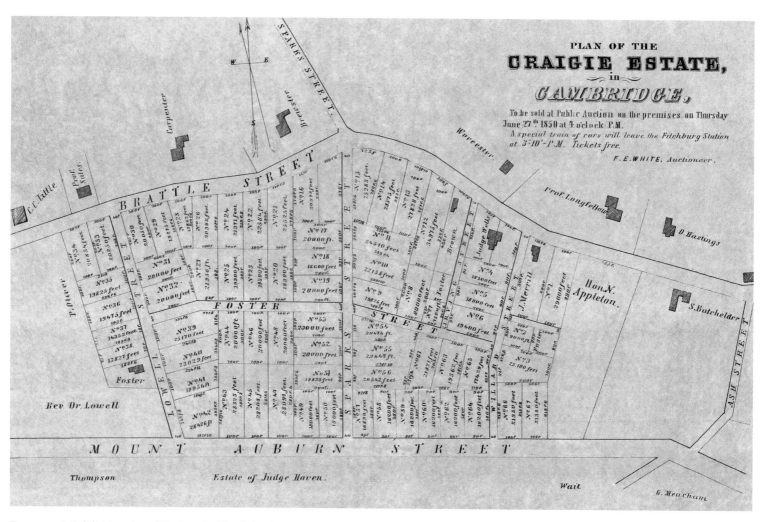

FIGURE 4.38 Subdivision plan of Gardiner Hubbard's land, showing sixty-seven lots to be sold at public auction on June 27, 1850.

merchants," and others as "eligible locations for mechanics and mechanical pursuits" (ibid., June 14, 1851).

This was not Hubbard's first venture in Cambridge—he and a partner had laid out Wendell, Everett, and Mellen streets in 1847—but in this case he retained about six acres for his own use, lived there for twenty-five years, and personally controlled its design and development until his death in 1897:

In the year 1849 I came to this city from Boston, and purchased forty [sic] acres of unimproved land at $1000 an acre … there was not a house, and scarcely a tree on it all. Since that time I have opened Sparks Street, Foster Street, Mercer Circle, and two or three courts, and have been the means, directly or indirectly, of erecting a good many houses. … All the trees on this lot, and on the entire tract, I have planted and have seen grow up to their present size. (*Cambridge Tribune,* Aug. 14, 1886)

The Marsh

Hubbard's development fell into two parts: the high ground near Brattle Street, where large dwellings sat on spacious lots, and the low land toward the river, which became a neighborhood of Irish laborers known as the Marsh (or sometimes the Upper Marsh, to distinguish it from the Kerry Corner neighborhood). Successive owners created a maze of narrow cul-de-sacs lined with closely built houses (figure 4.39). From the perspective of Buckingham Street, Thomas Wentworth Higginson characterized the neighborhood as "poorly settled. When any man in Cambridge has an old house that he wants to get rid of, he sells it at auction for three or four dollars, and it is moved down there on 'the marsh'" (Charles River Ry.

I, 53). By the 1920s the convenient location of the Marsh made it attractive to young academic families, and it became the first working-class neighborhood in Cambridge to experience gentrification.

Brown Street includes characteristics of Brattle Street and the Marsh in one short block. Tenements and workers' cottages filled the lots near Foster Street in the 1850s, while new houses were built closer to Brattle Street in the early 20th century. James Quigley, a laborer, moved the ca. 1754 Aaron Hill house from 99 Brattle to 17 Brown in 1867, raised it, and inserted the present first story (figure 4.40). Of the two Greek Revival houses from the Foster era that once bracketed the corner of Brattle Street, Daniel Brown's was moved from 128 Brattle to 7 Brown in 1890–91, while in 1902 Giles Taintor, an attorney-developer

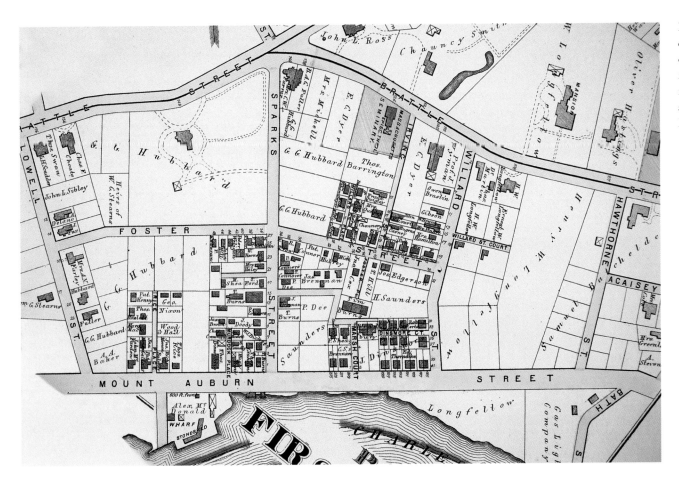

FIGURE 4.39 Hubbard's development in 1873, a quarter-century after his initial auction. Hubbard felt no urgency about selling his more desirable land once he had disposed of the marsh lots.

who specialized in carving up large lots to build stylish but cheaply constructed houses, replaced the other with three houses that turn their backs on Brown Street.

Willard Street, which the Foster heirs laid out east of the brook that drained Craigie's Pond, illustrates the proximity of different classes that was tolerated in this period and the way that social boundaries changed over time.[16] The west side has several modest workers' cottages from the 1850s. Their presence did not inhibit art editor Winthrop Scudder from putting up an elegant Federal Revival at 4 Willard in 1904, nor discourage antiquarian John C. Runkle from moving the ca. 1765 Hill-Munroe house from 83 Brattle Street to 8 Willard in 1908 (see figures 4.112 and 6.174). By the 1950s all the cottages were occupied by academic and professional families who had remodeled most of them beyond recognition.

The blocks defined by Willard, Mt. Auburn, Sparks, and Foster streets are the core of the Marsh. In 1850 Hubbard sold eleven of the twelve original tracts to John C. Martain of Charlestown. Two years later, twelve households occupied Foster Street and its tributaries. In 1860 at least one adult in every family was born in Ireland; half the wage earners were laborers, and the others included carpenters, teamsters, and stonecutters. The typical workers' cottage of this era was the familiar center-hall house set on a high basement that can be found in poorly drained areas throughout Cambridge (see *Report Five: Northwest Cambridge*, 71–73; figure 4.41).[17] After the Civil War, new owners subdivided again. James Dinsmore built twelve Mansard tenements on a 32,000 square foot parcel on Willard Street, Dinsmore Court, and Mt. Auburn Street in 1870. Despite the spring tides and poor drainage, the sewers that the city built on Willard and Sparks streets in 1854 and 1857 did not reach Foster Street until 1885; residents of Dinsmore Court used privies until 1892.

In 1873 Hubbard laid out Gibson Street and part of Kenway through the only land that he retained below Foster Street; the former street he named for his gardener, John Gibson, and the latter for architect Herbert Kenway, who designed at least three houses in Hubbard Park as well as Hubbard's house in

FIGURE 4.40 Hill-Quigley house, 17 Brown Street (1754; moved from 99 Brattle Street, 1867). James Quigley raised the house one story and expanded it from a one-room-deep gabled house to a two-room-deep gambrel; the original outline is shown in a lighter shade. Examination of the framing during a restoration in 2005 revealed that the original house once had a salt-box shape like the 1685 Cooper-Frost-Austin house at 21 Linnaean Street (see figure 4.153).

Washington, D.C. By 1894 the lower half of Gibson was filled with modest houses; the rest, which Hubbard still owned, had been redesigned with a gentle curve and landscaped like Mercer Circle.[18] In 1926 the Harvard Housing Trust (a private venture allied with the university) built Shaler Lane for forty-three married graduate students on a large lot behind 255 Mt. Auburn Street and followed that with another eighteen units on Gibson Street in 1928 (see figure 6.234). The gentrification of the Marsh was facilitated by the four affordable cottages that William and Mary Duguid designed around a central court at 59–65 Foster Street in 1927; these replaced a stable that belonged to one of Hubbard's houses on Mercer Circle and were mostly taken up by Harvard students and recent graduates (figure 4.42).

FIGURE 4.41 Peter Nelligan house, 96 Foster Street (1859). Nelligan, a carpenter born in Ireland about 1824, built this typical center-entrance, three-bay, four-room house once known as a "16-footer" for the width of its footprint. The original high basement was submerged by changes in grade around the house. The bay window and bracketed entrance hood were added ca. 1875. Photo 2009.

FIGURE 4.42 Marsh Associates houses, 59–65 Foster Street (1927, William and Mary Duguid, architects). Photo 1969.

Mt. Auburn Street between Hawthorn and Sparks was originally a narrow causeway over the marsh, desirable only for the poorest sort of houses or for urban fringe activities. Alexander McDonald, who owned a wharf and stone yard on the river, held the corner of Sparks and Mt. Auburn streets until the turn of the century, when he laid out several small lots along a narrow cul-de-sac. These proved unsalable, and in 1914 subsequent owners put up an auto repair shop and garages for forty cars instead (figure 4.43). In 1962 the Cambridge Redevelopment Authority condemned 2½ acres on this corner, relocated twelve families and five businesses, and sold the site to Boston developer Max Kargman, who constructed townhouses on Bradbury Park and the Riverview apartment building at 221 Mt. Auburn Street (see figure 6.239).

FIGURE 4.43 Charles River Garage, 233 Mount Auburn Street (1914, Wate & Copeland, architects). This facility was built to serve wealthy residents of the new Memorial Drive apartment buildings and the middle section of Brattle Street. Photo ca. 1955.

Gardiner Hubbard reserved for himself most of the land on Brattle between Sparks and Lowell streets. In 1850 he commissioned Melvin & Young to design his house at 146 Brattle Street and hired Erie Stewart, a Somerville housewright, to build it. The handsome Italianate dwelling faced Brattle but was set well back from the street in the midst of a six-acre park-like estate (figure 4.44; see also figure 6.76). Hubbard moved to Washington in the 1870s to promote the telephone, newly invented by his son-in-law, Alexander Graham Bell, but he retained his estate and residence, two acres east of Sparks Street, and several acres south of Foster.

Hubbard began to develop the land around his house in 1885. The Boston architectural firm of Allen & Kenway laid out the park-like site with curving, picturesque streets, preserving almost all the mature trees that he had set out in the 1850s. His first project was Mercer Circle, which he initially called Telephone Street but on reflection named for his wife, Gertrude Mercer Hubbard. He described his intentions to a journalist:

> While I don't pose as a philanthropist, I really did intend to open a street which should afford some of the best and most desirable homes in the city. It cost me something like $300 to macadamize and grade [it]. I filled in the lots and then I planned for nine houses, all of which should be unique in architecture, handsome and convenient in design, thorough in construction and absolutely perfect in sanitary arrangements. … It is my intention to rent the houses for the present … and at some future day, when the right sort of people occupy them, to sell them on such terms as will enable the tenants to pay for them very gradually. (*Tribune,* Aug. 14, 1886)

Hubbard also had plans for his own six-acre grounds, which he called Hubbard Park:

> My own home is now in Washington, and there is very little time each year for me to enjoy my Cambridge residence. … I intend, therefore, to gradually fill up the greater part of the six acres with first-class residences. … The full completion of my plans will hardly be attained until after I have passed away, but it will, I am sure,

FIGURE 4.44 The rear of Gardiner Hubbard's house, 146 Brattle Street (1850, Melvin & Young, architects). Photo ca. 1873–94.

guarantee the permanent value of the real estate in this vicinity, and secure for a great many years to come a high class of residents. (Ibid.)

An 1889 plan shows Hubbard's house surrounded by twelve irregular lots with 12- and 16-foot-wide drives that curve picturesquely through the property (figure 4.45). Hubbard hired Cabot & Chandler to design the large, elegant houses at 3 Hubbard Park (1887), 152 Brattle Street (1887), and 8 Hubbard Park (1888). The "high class of residents" included the widow of Boston merchant James Melledge, who moved from 126 Brattle Street; the widow of Richard Henry Dana Jr.; and Mrs. Morris Morgan and her son, a Harvard instructor, who moved from the former William Dean Howells house on Concord Avenue. Hubbard rented Allen & Kenway's "very handsome and striking" 1889 house on the corner of Brattle and Sparks to a series of Harvard professors (*Tribune,* Jan. 8, 1887; figure 4.46). The feeling of Hubbard Park as an estate with outbuildings, tennis courts, and gracious, late 19th century "cottages" began to diminish in 1892, when Hubbard razed some greenhouses and moved his gardener's house to 114 Foster Street. The elegant Colonial Revival residences by Longfellow, Alden & Harlow

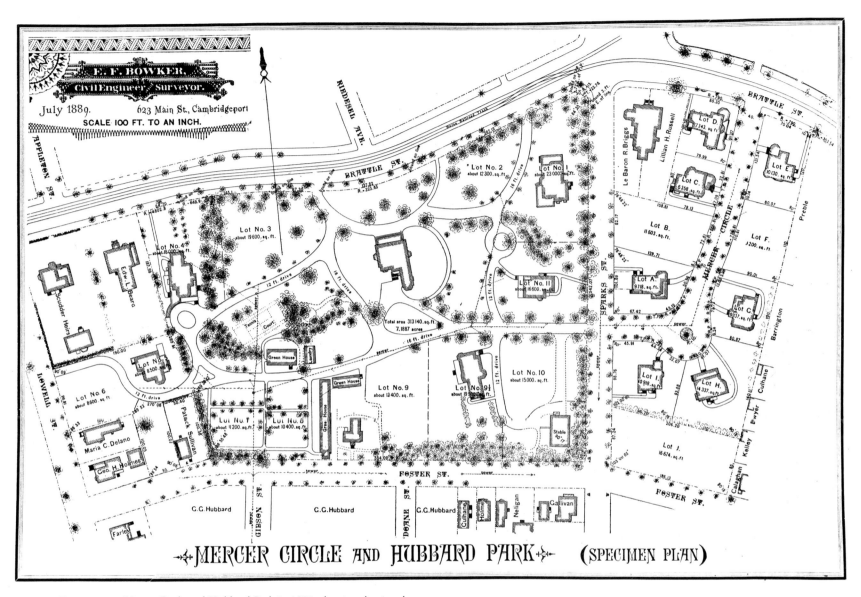

FIGURE 4.45 Mercer Circle and Hubbard Park in 1889, showing the site plan designed by Allen & Kenway and the twelve houses constructed since 1884. Hubbard's own house is in the center, opposite Riedesel Avenue.

FIGURE 4.46 Gardiner Hubbard rental house, 49 Sparks Street (1889, Allen & Kenway, architects). Later owners carved three small lots out of the yard and built new houses at 138 Brattle (left), 140 Brattle, and 47 Sparks Street (right). This house was razed in 1944. Photo ca. 1938.

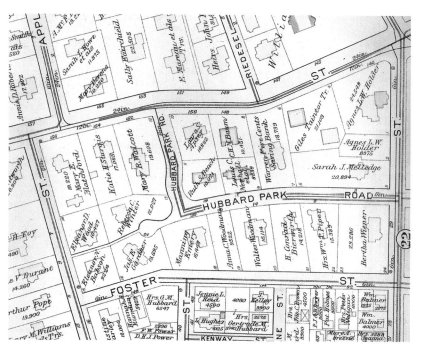

FIGURE 4.47 Draper and Dowling's revised plan for Hubbard Park, 1907. The original twelve building sites were resurveyed into twenty-four lots, some created by relocating older houses on the corner of Foster and Lowell streets.

erected in their place at 14 and 20 began to define a more regular layout along the south side of the street (see figure 6.165).

Hubbard's widow sold Hubbard Park and all its houses to Boston investors J. Sumner Draper and Mark Dowling in 1907. The *Chronicle* noted the rarity of the event:

> No sale of real estate in Cambridge for a number of years means so much as does this one, owing to the fact of its situation in the exclusive section, and because of the great street frontage and the topography of the land. Everything about the surroundings is as near perfect as an up-to-date landscape architect can make it. (Oct. 5, 1907)

The new owners developed Hubbard Park more intensively. They doubled the number of lots and replaced Hubbard's narrow winding drives with a more conventional L-shaped street (figure 4.47). Within a year, most of the old houses had been sold to "Harvard professors, well known literary men, and other representative people," and at least one new house was under construction (*Tribune*, July 25, 1908). Some of the new houses,

such as the stucco examples at 15 (1914, Newhall & Blevins, architects) and 19 (1913, Allen Jackson, with landscaping by Olmsted Brothers), continued Hubbard's tradition of elegance, although on much smaller lots. Hubbard's house occupied the center of the development until 1939, when it was replaced by a two-story copy of the Hooper-Lee-Nichols house framed by Hubbard's magnificent beech trees (see figure 6.191).

The integrity of Hubbard Park began to fray when the extensive grounds of 49 Sparks Street were broken up in 1929. Cambridge realtor Frank Harlow built two modest suburban houses at 45 and 47 Sparks, and Harold Goldenberg put up two bland neo-Federal houses at 138 and 140 Brattle. The original house was demolished in 1944. A 1908 house at 12 Hubbard Park, remodeled in 2011–12 to resemble the 1867 Mansard at 8 Hilliard Street, is a startling anachronism in the neighborhood.

On higher ground than Sparks or Willard, Lowell Street had larger lots and more substantial houses. George Foster built the first one in 1849 on a remnant of Symonds' Hill, a drumlin cut down in 1808 to build the causeway that carried Mt. Auburn Street across the marsh (see figure 2.28). The house at 7 Lowell (1850), designed by Melvin & Young for Boston merchant Moses Rice, originally stood on Brattle Street. In 1884 Boston lawyer Woodward Emery bought the property, moved the house to the rear of the lot, and subdivided the frontage. He sold the corner to his Portsmouth, New Hampshire, townsman and brother-in-law, Charles E. Wentworth, and they put up a pair of fine houses at 158 and 160 Brattle (figure 4.48; see also figure 6.157). Closer to Mt. Auburn Street, two modest Queen Annes built by Suther Blaikie in 1891 face a three-decker built in 1908. The Lowell School (1883) was the last wooden school built in the city.

The last piece of the Vassall-Craigie estate was a two-acre parcel that remained after the Fosters laid out Lowell Street. Publisher Charles C. Little acquired it in 1851, protecting the view toward the river from his home in John Appleton's 1810

FIGURE 4.49 Joseph G. Thorp house, 168 Brattle Street (1888, Arthur Little, architect). Photo ca. 1890.

FIGURE 4.48 Woodward Emery house, 160 Brattle Street (1884, Peabody & Stearns, architects). Photo 1919.

mansion at 163 Brattle Street (see below). Little built a house at 164 Brattle in 1868 that he sold to Cambridgeport coal dealer Newell Bent. Twenty years later, Bent's heirs divided the frontage and sold the west part with over an acre of land to Joseph G. Thorp, a lumberman and politician from Eau Claire, Wisconsin, who had rented Elmwood while his son was at Harvard. When James Russell Lowell returned from Europe, Thorp hired Boston architect Arthur Little to build an ostentatious Colonial Revival at 168 Brattle Street for himself and his widowed daughter, Sara (figure 4.49; see also figure 6.163).

Many families settled in Cambridge while their sons were at school, but the Thorps made a greater impression than most. Sara Thorp married the Norwegian violinist Ole Bull, a friend of Henry Wadsworth Longfellow, in 1870, and her brother, Joseph Thorp Jr., married Anne Allegra Longfellow in 1885. Mrs. Bull became a follower of the Swami Vivekananda and promoted his Vedanta philosophy through the Cambridge Conferences, a lecture series "for the comparative study of ethics, religion and philosophy" that she organized in 1896–97 (Bull, 3). Sara Bull and a few of her friends, including Julia Ward Howe, introduced the practice of yoga to the United States.

After Mrs. Bull's death in 1911 the house was sold to Edwin Grozier, publisher of the *Boston Post.* By the time Grozier died in 1924, he and his wife also owned the back yard of the Bent house as well as the corner lot on Channing Street, totaling a little over two acres in the heart of Old Cambridge. The Episcopal Theological School acquired the property after World War II, and in 1969 planned to put up four two-story garden apartment buildings with twenty-eight units for married students. The neighbors blocked this plan, and the property was eventually subdivided. Sara Bull's house went back into private ownership, and the Divinity School moved a house from 2 Phillips Place to the corner lot in 1965. In 2003 Cambridge architect Graham Gund completed a new house on the 1.6-acre, nearly landlocked parcel that remained (see figure 6.213).

ESTATES AND FARMS FORMERLY IN WATERTOWN

Sparks Street and Vassal Lane, the ancient cartway to Fresh Pond, formed the original boundary between Cambridge and Watertown.[19] Cambridge's annexation of some of this territory in 1754 may have had as much to do with real estate values as convenience of travel on Sundays. The farms were described as "sandy, poor, and barren," but were snapped up by wealthy Bostonians looking for scenic country retreats and became the Lechmere-Sewall, Lee, Ruggles-Fayerweather, and Oliver estates (Convers Francis, 147). Their long, narrow fields crossed over Reservoir Hill, the ridge that lies between Brattle Street and Huron Avenue, and descended to Vassal Lane or Fresh Pond (figure 4.50).

These estates were subdivided at different times in the 19th century, with each owner running a single street—Appleton, Fayerweather, Lake View, Lexington, Grozier, and Larch—up the length of his holdings, connecting only with Vassal Lane until the city opened Huron Avenue in 1893. Bends in the other east–west streets, Highland and Brewster, marked estate boundaries. Gurney and Reservoir turned to stay within an estate.

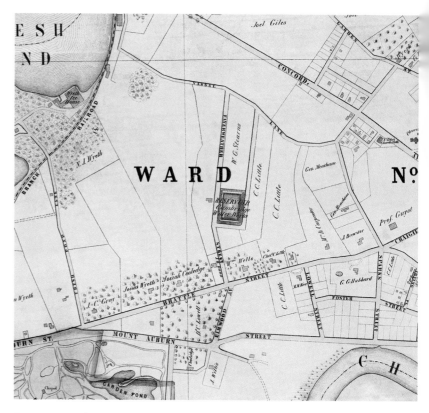

FIGURE 4.50 The Brattle Street estates as shown on Henry Walling's 1854 map of Cambridge. Walling incorrectly placed the Reservoir, which was actually east of Reservoir Street, on C.C. Little's land (see figure 4.65).

Cul-de-sacs such as Dunstable and Wyman roads and dead-end streets such as Appleton Road were built in the 20th century when large suburban-era properties were themselves subdivided. Today, Reservoir Hill is the social watershed that divides Tory Row from the West Cambridge suburb made possible by the Huron Avenue trolley line.

RICHARD LECHMERE ESTATE

The 13-acre Lechmere estate lay between Sparks Street and Riedesel Avenue and incorporated fields that had been owned since the 1600s by Cambridge's Fessenden family. At his death in 1756 William Fessenden passed his eight acres of pasture and "cornyard" on the Watertown Road to his son-in-law, John Hunt. Richard Lechmere, a wealthy Boston distiller who had married Mary Phips, the tenth child of Lieutenant Governor

Spencer Phips, purchased the property in 1761 for £100 along with 3¾ adjoining acres from Amos Marrett for £49. Lechmere built a mansion facing the main road not far from Mary's sister Rebecca, who lived in the Hooper house with her husband, Judge Joseph Lee. In 1771 Lechmere sold the place to fellow loyalist Jonathan Sewall for £2,133 and moved to Boston, retaining his farm on Lechmere's Point. The Lechmeres left for Halifax with the British army in 1776, and all their remaining land was confiscated.

FIGURE 4.51   The Lechmere-Sewall-Riedesel house, now 149 Brattle Street (1761), looking west from its original location at the corner of Sparks Street toward the Joseph Lee mansion (153 Brattle Street; see figure 4.54). Photo before 1869.

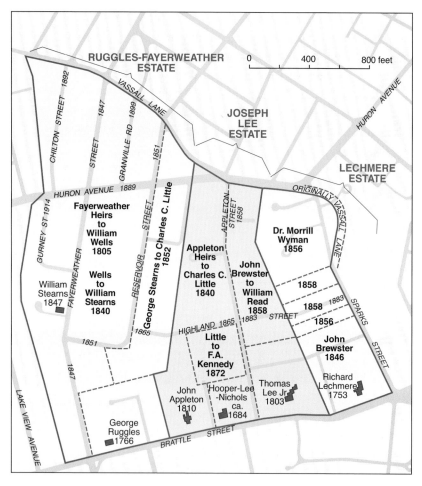

FIGURE 4.52 Disposition of the Lechmere, Lee, and Ruggles-Fayerweather estates.

Sewall, a 1748 Harvard graduate, was an intimate friend of John Adams and related by marriage to John Hancock. An attorney, "he had a soft, smooth insinuating eloquence, which glided into the minds of a jury and gave him as much power over that tribunal as any lawyer ought ever to possess" (DAR *Guide,* 105). Governor Hutchinson appointed him to the new office of solicitor general to ensure his commitment to the loyalist cause and in 1767 made him attorney general of the province. On September 1, 1774, a revolutionary mob threatened Sewall's house, and he fled to Boston (see chapter 1). After educating his children in England, he ended his career as a judge of admiralty for Nova Scotia and New Brunswick.[20]

The captured Hessian general Baron Friedrich Adolf Riedesel and his wife were quartered in Sewall's confiscated house in 1778–79 (see chapter 1). In 1779 the Commonwealth sold the estate to Thomas Lee, who became known as "English Thomas" to distinguish him from his neighbor, Thomas Lee Jr. of Salem. Lee was born in England about 1707 and became a merchant in Boston. Like Judge Joseph Lee, he passed through the Revolution without taking sides, living in comfort and riding to the hounds in Pomfret, Connecticut. His is one of the most elaborate tombs in the Old Burying Ground; the epitaph, now effaced, celebrated his "ample fortune" and lauded his "affability, benevolence, and hospitality, humanity, charity, and beneficence … conjugal attention and tenderness, filial duty and piety, fraternal affection and goodness, [and] gentleness and kindness to domestics" (Harris, 150).

Mrs. Lee, an eccentric woman who was said to have "hoarded gold … in the cellar and cupboards," lived until 1807 (DAR *Guide,* 107). The estate went to her husband's nephew, another Thomas Lee, the son of a former Royal Navy officer living in Medford, but just before he came of age in 1819 his father and guardian sold the place to Andrew Craigie, who rented it to his brother-in-law, Joseph Foster. At this time the estate included the 13-acre homestead, 26 acres near Fresh Pond, 6½ acres across the road, and salt marshes on both sides of the river. When Mrs. Craigie died in 1841 it came into the hands of Boston merchants

Caleb Reed and Theophilus Chandler as trustees for Craigie's heirs. They divided the homestead into thirds and sold it off in 1846 (figure 4.52).

John Brewster, a Boston banker, bought the southern third of the property and twelve years later acquired land on the east side of Appleton Street from the neighboring Joseph Lee estate. He lived in the Lechmere house and cultivated the fields until the 1870s. His son William (1851–1919), an ornithologist, described the property in *The Birds of the Cambridge Region,* a comprehensive natural history:

> [Until] the year 1873 our home place in Cambridge comprised about six acres of smooth, gently sloping land [bordered] by rows of tall elms growing just within the enclosing fences, while a dozen German lindens of the largest size, and probably more than a century old at the date of my birth, were grouped about the front of the house. … The rear of the house was embowered in purple and white lilacs behind which was an old-fashioned flower garden. Still further back were orchards of apple, pear and peach trees, besides rows of raspberry, blackberry, currant and gooseberry bushes. The unshaded portions of the grounds were devoted chiefly to mowing fields, although a generous space was always set aside for the vegetable garden; there was also a small pasture for the cows and horses. Several of the neighboring estates were similar in character and of equal extent, while most of those scattered along the northerly side of Brattle Street, in the direction of Mount Auburn, backed on a wide expanse of open, farming country which stretched west and north to Fresh Pond and the Concord Turnpike. (11)

John Brewster built an incongruous row of four brick houses, known as the Brewster Block, at 61–67 Sparks Street in 1875 (see figure 6.111). A resident recalled this event:

> I remember very well the disappointment felt … by the residents of the street when Mr. John Brewster built this block. The view of beautiful sunsets [was] entirely cut off from the houses on the east side there; but also I often heard the concluding remark, that they supposed that some day the whole street would be all built up closely on both sides, "just like Boston." (Proell, 50)

Brewster laid out the east end of Brewster Street and built the more appealing four-unit Queen Anne row at 29–35 in 1883. By 1885 he had put up 17–19 and 23–25 Brewster and, having acquired a triangle of land east of his house, single-family houses at 5, 7, and 9 Riedesel Avenue, all of which he rented (figure 4.53; see also figure 6.126). The poet Robert Frost, who called the neighborhood "Brewster Village," spent winters at 35 Brewster Street from about 1941 until his death in 1963.

William Brewster built five houses on the east side of Riedesel Avenue after his father died in 1886. He moved the Lechmere mansion to the west corner of Riedesel Avenue so he could build a new house and an ornithological museum that replaced an earlier "museum of natural history and hall" that his father gave him in 1874 (*Chronicle*, Dec. 26, 1874; figure 4.54). The yard east of the house remained open until the Holy Trinity Armenian Church went up in 1960 (see figure 7.33).

George Meacham bought the upper two-thirds of the Lechmere estate in 1850 and built 2 Highland Street in 1852–53. He sold about four acres up the hill to Dr. Morrill Wyman (1812–1903), first president of Mount Auburn Hospital, who built a large house with a curving drive at 77 Sparks Street in 1860 (figure 4.55). Wyman built another house in 1877 at 85 Sparks Street that he rented to Charles Walcott, a Boston lawyer. By 1916 Walcott's widow and son Charles, a physician, owned all of Wyman's property and occupied both houses. The later one survives at the entrance to Wyman Road, a cul-de-sac built up with six simple Georgian Revival houses in 1926–27. In 1937 Dr. Walcott built 9 Hemlock Road on a new cul-de-sac that followed Dr. Wyman's drive, and in 1945 he razed the original Wyman house; four new houses followed in 1948–56.

A later owner laid out Highland Street from Sparks to Appleton Street in 1887 and created lots for six houses.[21] The Queen Anne and Colonial Revival houses here were markedly larger and more expensive than Brewster's many smaller houses at the bottom of the hill, reflecting the desirability of the location and the growing prosperity of the 1880s. The superb Colonial Revival that Longfellow, Alden & Harlow designed at 1 Highland Street for James

FIGURE 4.53 The view up Brewster's new street, with 5, 7, and 9 Riedesel Avenue on the left and 17–19 and 23–25 Brewster Street in the background. Photo 1885–87.

FIGURE 4.55 Dr. Morrill Wyman house, 77 Sparks Street (1860; demolished 1945). Photo ca. 1938.

FIGURE 4.54 The Lechmere-Sewall-Riedesel house on its original site at 145 Brattle Street, after John Brewster raised it and inserted a new ground floor in 1869. In 1886 William Brewster removed the original top story and moved the house to its present location at 149 Brattle. Photo 1885.

and Constance Winsor Noyes in 1894 reflected the appeal of this elevated location for forward-looking, affluent young families who wished to live near the university (see figure 6.166).

JOSEPH LEE ESTATE

Judge Joseph Lee's 25-acre estate, just west of Richard Lechmere's, also ran back to Vassal Lane. The present Hooper-Lee-Nichols House at 159 Brattle Street was built for Dr. Richard Hooper of Hampton, New Hampshire, soon after 1684, when he purchased 12 acres in Watertown's East Field and half an acre of salt marsh from John Holmes. At Hooper's death in 1691, the property contained a one-room-wide, two-story house, a barn, and a six-acre orchard. After his destitute widow died in 1701 the house was apparently abandoned until young Dr. Henry Hooper reached his majority and made some repairs about 1717. In 1733 he sold the property, with 16½ acres north of the road and 28 acres abutting the Watertown landing, to Cornelius Waldo, a Boston merchant who had grown up in Watertown. Waldo further embellished the house and probably used it as a seasonal retreat until his son Joseph graduated from Harvard in 1741, when he offered it for rent:

> a farm in Watertown near the Charles River together with back part of Dwelling house thereon to a good husbandman, and front part of said house with gardens and other Accommodations to a gentleman for a country seat being pleasantly situated & but 4 miles from Charlestown Ferry. (*Boston News Letter,* Mar. 11, 1742)

In 1758 Waldo's widow sold the property to Joseph Lee (1709–1802), who remodeled the house into its present form about 1760 and acquired an additional 3¾ acres from Amos Marrett in 1768 (see figure 6.11). The son of a shipbuilder, Lee was a 1729 Harvard graduate who became a member of the Tory aristocracy through his marriage to Rebecca Phips and was thus related to all the prominent Cambridge loyalist families. He was also an incorporator of Christ Church and a judge of the Middlesex Court of Common Pleas. Lee accepted Governor Hutchinson's appointment to the hated Mandamus Council but resigned in 1774 at the first sign of trouble. During the Siege he lived in Boston and New Jersey, but he was allowed to retain his property and bought an additional 4¾ acres in 1783. An avid horticulturist, Judge Lee was renowned for the strawberry parties he gave each June. In 1802 he bequeathed the property to his nephews, North Shore merchants Joseph and Thomas Lee Jr., and provided for Caesar, a former slave he had inherited from his father.

Mark Lewis, a well-known African American in post-Revolutionary Cambridge, was probably another of Judge Lee's slaves; one document noted that he was "otherwise called Mark Lee" (Middlesex Deeds 155/407). Lewis first appears in the records in 1786 when he bought a house in the West Field, on the east side of Sparks Street near the top of the hill. The quarter-acre property cost him £43 7/6, more than twice what Aaron Hill had paid for it a year before. In the next three years he made three more purchases, and in 1792 he and his wife, Juno, sold nine acres to Andrew Craigie for £200 and moved to Sherborn, where Judge Lee owned a farm. Mark and Juno returned to Cambridge a few years later; he was taxed in 1798 for a house, barn, and a quarter-acre of tillage, and in 1799 for 29 acres of mowing, tillage and pasture he rented from Craigie. The records suggest that they were living in "the little house on the hill" they had sold to Craigie in 1792 (Craigie to Foster, July 19, 1795, Craigie papers, AAS). Lewis farmed Craigie's 29 acres until his death in 1808.

In 1803 Thomas Lee Jr. bought out his brother and built a house in the High Georgian style at 153 Brattle Street. Five years later, he divided the property into two long parcels that extended back to Vassal Lane and sold the Hooper-Lee house and the western half of his land to John Appleton, another Salem merchant.[22] Appleton had served as a U.S. consul in France until 1807, when he married a daughter of Thomas Fayerweather of 175 Brattle Street. He built a Federal mansion at 163 Brattle in 1810 and in 1814 sold the Hooper-Lee house and 1¾ acres to Benjamin Carpenter, also of Salem. Carpenter married Thomas Lee's daughter Deborah in 1823; when he died only two months later she moved back in with her father and rented out the Hooper-Lee house until her death in 1860.

John Appleton died in 1829, and in 1840 his son sold 163 Brattle Street and the remaining 12 acres to Charles C. Little, a founder of the Boston publishing firm of Little & Brown, who was active in several Cambridge real estate ventures (see chapter 9). He laid out Appleton Street in 1858 along the dividing line between his property and that of Deborah Carpenter, who had sold the upper portion of her land to John Brewster. William Read, a Boston hardware merchant, built the first house there in 1859. In 1861 Little sold an orchard on the crest of the ridge to William Read Jr., who built a towered Mansard house overlooking his father's at 89 Appleton Street (figure 4.57). William Cook, an instructor of German at Harvard, bought land from Read in 1874 and the next year commissioned W.P.P. Longfellow to design an important Ruskinian Gothic house at 71 (see figure 6.109).

In 1852 Little bought all the lots on the east side of Reservoir Street on the old Fayerweather estate. He laid out Highland Street across the two properties and erected a Mansard house at 48 in 1863. Frank A. Kennedy, who had inherited his father's Cambridgeport bakery in 1861, purchased the place in 1872 and greatly enlarged it about the time he sold the business to a predecessor of the National Biscuit Company in 1889. A passageway off Brattle Street that led to his stable became the present Kennedy Road. Harvard engineering professor Edward V. Huntington razed the Kennedy house in 1926 and replaced it with a Tudor designed by Allen W. Jackson (see figure 6.188).

In 1860 Mrs. Carpenter's executors sold the Hooper-Lee house to George Nichols, an editor at The Riverside Press, who had been renting it since 1850. Susan Nichols remembered that "in the rear of the mansion were clustered every variety of subordinate building and office essential to an extensive farm," but her father cleared it all away except for the barn (Amory, *Old Cambridge and New*, 29, 31–32). A highly decorated Civil War veteran, General Edward W. Hincks (1830–94), moved in with his new wife, Elizabeth Nichols, in 1883 but left for a new house on Huron Avenue after she died in 1890. In 1916 Austin White, a grandson of George and Susan Nichols, hired preservation architect Joseph Chandler to renovate the old house (see

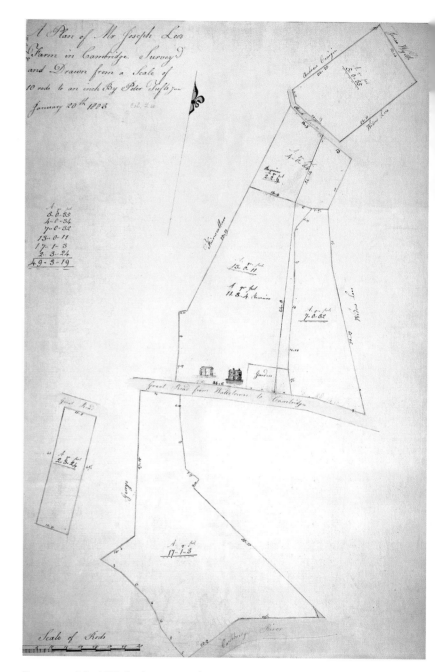

FIGURE 4.56 In 1803 the 49-acre Joseph Lee estate included a 3-acre field north of Vassal Lane and 17 acres with river frontage south of the "Great Road from Watertown to Cambridge."

FIGURE 4.57 William Read Jr. house, 89 Appleton Street (1863). Photo 2010.

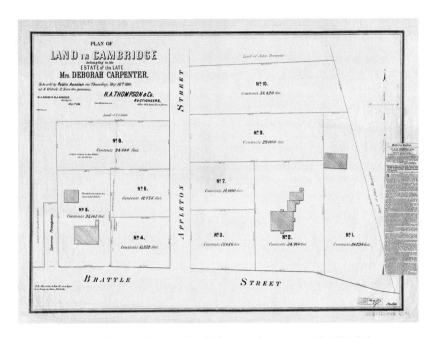

FIGURE 4.58 The division of Mrs. Deborah Carpenter's estate in 1861. "English Thomas" Lee's house and barn at 153 Brattle Street are at right; the Hooper-Lee-Nichols house at 159 Brattle is at left. Charles Choate bought all six lots east of Appleton Street but left them undeveloped until 1887.

chapter 6). It became the headquarters of the Cambridge Historical Society in 1957.

Deborah Carpenter's executors sold Thomas Lee Jr.'s 1803 house at 153 Brattle Street and about three acres to Charles Choate, a Boston lawyer, in 1861 (figure 4.58). The property remained intact until 1887, when Choate, by then president of the Old Colony Railroad, extended Brewster Street to Appleton and began to sell off lots. Dr. Estes Howe's widow and her sister, Mrs. Arthur L. Devens, built adjoining houses at 2 Appleton and 155 Brattle in 1887–89, antiquarian Andrew McFarland Davis built 10 Appleton in 1887, and two more houses appeared on the west end of Brewster Street in the 1890s.

In September 1889 the city projected a new street that would open the north-slope pastures of the Tory Row estates to suburban development. Huron Avenue incorporated the east end of

Vassal Lane and initially ran from Concord Avenue to the Watertown Branch of the Fitchburg Railroad, near Fresh Pond. The city graded and paved the right-of-way as far as Reservoir Street, and the abutters completed the balance. The new car line that opened in 1894 made the north slope a classic streetcar suburb that became known as West Cambridge.[23] Tract builders sold large numbers of nearly identical two-family houses to upwardly mobile families with modest incomes. On the Joseph Lee estate, Enos Comeau acquired 57,000 square feet at the corner of Appleton Street from the heirs of John Brewster, laid out Louisa Street (now Appleton Road), subdivided the land into twelve lots, and in 1915–16 built six two-family houses ranging in price from $5,000 to $7,000. Similarly, builder Jacob Sorkin put up four houses near the corner of Appleton and Huron in 1917. Dunstable Road, which Cambridge architect William Duguid

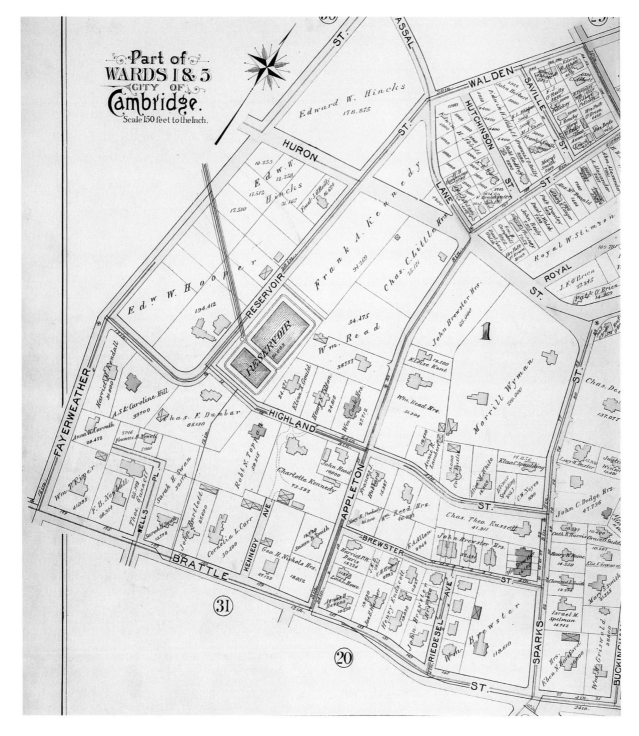

FIGURE 4.59 Development on the former Lechmere-Sewall and Joseph Lee estates in 1894.

developed just below the crest of the hill in 1922, contains six somewhat more expensive houses and separates the utterly different neighborhoods on the north and south slopes of the hill.

John Appleton's 1810 mansion at 163 Brattle Street was nearly derelict when Lucien Carr, an anthropologist and assistant curator of the Peabody Museum, acquired it in 1891. Carr's wife, Cornelia Crow Carr, the daughter of a wealthy St. Louis businessman, was a friend and biographer of Harriet Goodhue Hosmer, one of America's most distinguished female sculptors. The Carrs left the front part of the house intact but retained Rotch & Tilden to design a ballroom in place of the ell (figure 4.60). In 1900 they divided the property so that their daughter and her husband could build 11 Kennedy Road. Heirs divided the property again about 1930, so that a third generation could build at 161 Brattle. Edwin Land, founder of the Polaroid Corporation, acquired the Appleton-Carr house shortly after World War II and lived there until his death in 1991; his wife, Helen Land, hired landscape architect Fletcher Steele in 1947 to build the high wall and sunken garden that gave the couple privacy from the street. Steele's landscape survived the fire that destroyed the Appleton house in 2005.

Ruggles-Fayerweather Estate

The Ruggles-Fayerweather estate west of Joseph Lee's originated in a 40-acre farm that Amos Marrett bought in Watertown after he sold his homestead to John Vassall Sr. in 1746. In 1764 Captain George Ruggles, a Jamaican planter who had married Vassall's sister Susannah in 1742, acquired the place and built the Georgian mansion that is now 175 Brattle Street. Ruggles suffered reverses, and in 1771 his London creditors seized the property. After his Tory neighbors paid off the mortgage in 1774, Ruggles traded it to Thomas Fayerweather for his house in Boston. Fayerweather, a prosperous Boston merchant involved in shipping and land speculation, traveled in both loyalist and patriot circles. He sent his family away during the Siege but remained in possession while the house was used for officers'

quarters and as a military hospital. When he died in 1805, his assets included the mansion, a farmhouse (perhaps dating from Marrett's ownership), and more than 50 acres of upland, salt marsh, meadow, and orchard. His heirs sold the property to William Wells, master of a boys' preparatory school, in 1827. Wells sold the 40-acre back pasture, which ran over the hill to Vassal Lane, to William G. Stearns of Brighton in 1846 but retained most of the frontage to protect himself from the development that was certain to follow.

Longfellow visited the hilltop with a friend and prospective purchaser, Boston attorney George S. Hilliard, and his architect:

> Toward sunset Hilliard and [Isaiah] Rogers called for me with Stearns, of whom they think of buying land for a home in Cambridge. We strolled up the green lane [Sparks Street], over the upland, down the old country, now grass-grown road [Vassal Lane] toward Fresh Pond. Then striking across the fields ascending the

FIGURE 4.60 Appleton-Carr house, 163 Brattle Street (1810; addition by Rotch & Tilden, 1891). The house was being renovated when it burned to the ground on December 6, 2005; the owners replaced it in 2007 with a neo-Federal style house designed by Peter Pennoyer of New York. Photo 1968.

FIGURE 4.61 The coat of arms of the Fayerweather family displays an American beaver with a fish in its mouth surmounting a medieval English helmet and shield. Carved and polychromed wood, probably made in Boston ca. 1760.

rising ground toward the river and the town, directly behind Mr. Wells's. This is the spot, and a lovely secluded place it is, with glimpses of the river—the town southward and the pond westward and all around the waving horizon of the low hills. Near at hand you look down into gardens and see roofs and chimneys rising from among the trees. A retired delicious spot. But as Hilliard must go to Boston every day, will it not grow wearisome, the constant, endless going to and fro? (June 6, 1846, in Paterson I, 302)

Hilliard built a summer place at Longwood in Brookline, leaving Stearns, who had been appointed steward of Harvard College in 1844, to lay out Fayerweather Street in 1847 and build a house on the hilltop himself. He sold the corner lot to John Dana, cashier of the Charles River Bank, who built a Greek Revival house partway up the hill with a long side porch facing Brattle Street (see figure 6.72). Stearns also laid out Reservoir Street and divided the rest of his land into sixty-three lots in preparation for an auction in 1852 (figure 4.63). The lots along Reservoir and the east side of Fayerweather were a fairly uniform 100 by 175 to 200 feet, but the west side of Fayerweather contained much larger, irregular parcels, and these attracted the first houses. Stearns himself moved to Lowell Street about 1857 and continued as steward of the college until 1870. In 1871 he was declared incompetent, and a guardian sold his remaining land.

Charles C. Little purchased all of Stearns's lots on the east side of Reservoir Street (behind his own house at 163 Brattle) in 1852. He sold the top of the hill to the Cambridge Water Works (a private utility of which he was a director), which broke ground in 1855 for the city's first reservoir, a granite structure that held two million gallons of water. Remnants of its foundation can still be seen along Reservoir Street.[24] The hilltop also attracted several distinguished academics. In 1860 Little built a handsome Gothic Revival house at the bend of Reservoir Street that he sold to professor of political economy Charles Dunbar in 1863; seventeen years later, professor of rhetoric and oratory Adam Sherman Hill put up the brick Ruskinian Gothic house at 12 Reservoir, one of the few houses of this style in the city (figure 4.64; see also figure 6.112).

FIGURE 4.62 Thomas Fayerweather house, 175 Brattle Street (1764). Painting
by unknown artist, ca. 1880.

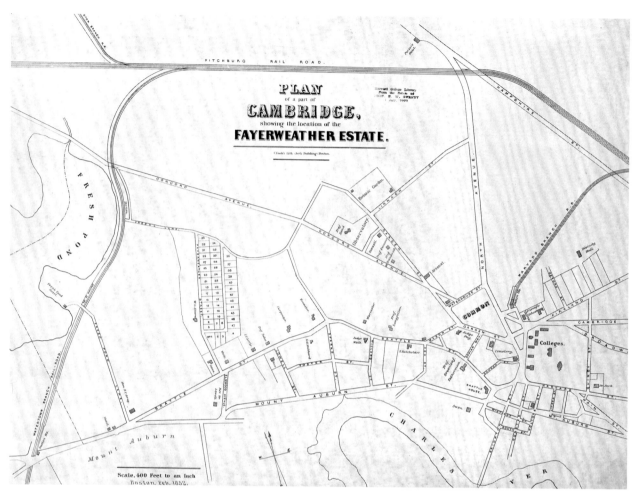

Figure 4.63 William G. Stearns's subdivision of the Fayerweather estate, 1852. Alexander Wadsworth's plan shows how remote the lots were from the settled parts of town. Only Fayerweather Street could go straight through to Brattle; Reservoir had to bend to avoid Wells's land and the steep slope behind his house.

Figure 4.64 Professor Charles H. Dunbar house, 64 Highland Street (built by Charles C. Little, 1860; demolished 1963). Photo 1949.

In 1868 philosophy professor (later Dean) Ephraim Gurney married Ellen Hooper of Boston and the next year purchased the corner lot at Fayerweather and Reservoir streets. Gurney oriented his house due south instead of aligning it with the street and placed the entrance on the north side. Ephraim's in-laws, Harvard treasurer Edward Hooper and his wife, Fanny, bought the lot next door in 1871 and commissioned Sturgis & Brigham to design a house, now 25 Reservoir, aligned with Gurney's (figure 4.65; see also figure 6.100). The Gurneys, who had no children of their own, helped care for the five Hooper daughters after Fanny died of consumption in 1881. Dean Gurney passed away in 1886; his widow, Ellen, committed suicide the next year.[25] Mr. Hooper then moved the Gurney house to Reservoir Street and attached it to his own with a short passageway for the convenience of the combined households. After Hooper died in 1901 Reverend Samuel Eliot, President Eliot's only surviving son, acquired the Hooper house, severed the link with Gurney's, and hired Lois Lilley Howe to modernize it in the Colonial Revival style.

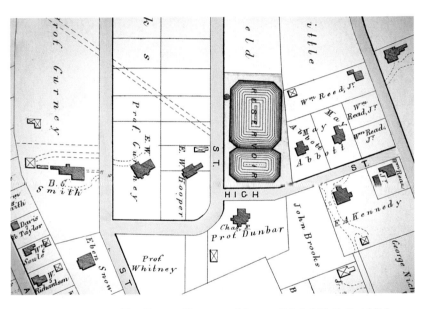

FIGURE 4.65 The Gurney, Hooper, and Stearns (labeled "B.G. Smith") houses in 1873, as originally sited. With William Read Jr.'s, these houses traced the top of the ridge dividing the Brattle Street estates from the back slope fields and pastures. The Cambridge Water Works constructed the smaller basin of the reservoir in 1856; the city added the larger one in 1868. Professor Dunbar's house stood at the corner of Highland and Reservoir.

FIGURE 4.66 Highland Street ca. 1895, looking east with the reservoir at left and 54 Highland on the right. Katherine Copeland Dunbar's husband, William, was a law partner of Louis Brandeis; the couple built number 58 in 1898 but lived for many years in his parent's house at 64. Photo ca. 1900.

The top of the hill changed rapidly after 1900. A new high-storage basin in Belmont made the reservoir obsolete, and in 1901 the property reverted to Little's heirs. Former mayor Alvin F. Sortwell bought the site and built a large Colonial Revival residence at 61 Highland Street (figure 4.67). The same year, Nathaniel Nash, president of the Cambridge Safe Deposit & Trust Company, built an idiosyncratic thirty-room house at the corner of Reservoir and Fayerweather streets on the former site of the Gurney house (figure 4.68). The *Chronicle* remarked that "the section of the city including Reservoir, Fayerweather and Highland streets has become one of the most beautiful residential sections to be found anywhere in Cambridge" (Nov. 4, 1903; figure 4.69).

Reservoir Hill was one of the few neighborhoods of Old Cambridge to see much construction after 1929 and became a notable enclave of Mid-Century Modern houses. In 1940 Harvard mathematician Garrett Birkhoff bought the lot once occupied by William Stearns's house and built an International Style brick residence designed by Walter Bogner (see figure 6.197). After the war, the hilltop lots (but not the drafty old houses on them) attracted affluent, downsizing, older residents and modernist architects. Mayor Sortwell's heirs razed his house at 61 Highland Street in 1948 and subdivided the lot for three new houses at 30 Reservoir (1954, Walter L. Hill, architect), 26 Reservoir (1955, Frederic S. Coolidge), and 61 Highland (1958, William Wainwright; figure 4.70). The foundation of the Sortwell house became a sunken garden, and its stable was remodeled as a residence and nursery school. Modern houses at 18 Reservoir (1949, Gordon Northrup) and 64 Highland (1963, Frederick Bruck) replaced Charles C. Little's house, and 46 Fayerweather (1968, William Wainwright) went up on the site of the Gurney and Nash houses. Houses at 11 Reservoir (1968, Kenneth Redmond) and 14 Reservoir (1983, David Schwartz) were built in the side and front yards of older homes (see chapter 6). Many of these houses proved to be remarkably ephemeral. The owner of 51 Highland Street razed 61 Highland in 2003, while the owner of 12 Reservoir razed adjoining houses in 2006

FIGURE 4.67 Alvin F. Sortwell house, 61 Highland Street (1902, E.S. Child, architect; demolished 1948). Photo 1903.

FIGURE 4.68 Nathaniel C. Nash house, 1 Reservoir Street (1902, G.A. Moore, architect; demolished 1964). Photo ca. 1920.

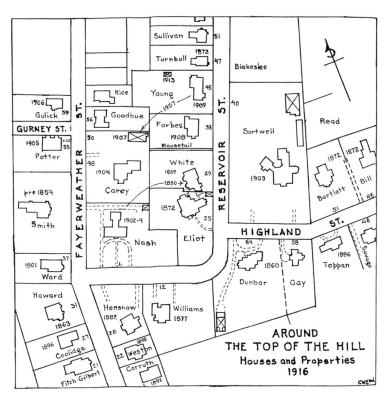

FIGURE 4.69 Houses on Reservoir Hill in 1916

FIGURE 4.70 William Wainwright house, 61 Highland Street (1958, William Wainwright/Geometrics, Inc., architects; demolished 2003). This view of the rear shows the foundation of the Alvin Sortwell house, which remained as a landscape feature after the site was cleared in 2003. Photo ca. 1960.

FIGURE 4.71 General Edward Hincks house, 333 Huron Avenue/81–83 Fayerweather Street (1892, Wilfred A. Norris, architect). The photographer was standing near the intersection of Reservoir Street and Huron Avenue, looking northwest. Photo ca. 1895.

and 2010 to create an elaborate landscape of lawns, terraces, and water features designed by Morgan Wheelock. In 2007, 46 Fayerweather was replaced by a "farmhouse" designed by Robert Augustine, and in 2014, 26 Reservoir fell to a neo-Craftsmen style house by Charles R. Myer & Partners.

The north end of the Fayerweather estate, including several clay pits near Vassal Lane, had been subdivided for over twenty years when General Edward Hincks bought thirty-five vacant lots from William Stearns's guardian in 1872. Hincks retired from public life when he lost the mayoral election of 1886, and after the death of his second wife he built a new house in 1892 on the corner of Fayerweather and Huron Avenue (figure 4.71).

FIGURE 4.72 Auction of lots formerly owned by General Hincks and later built up by Bernard Rice with houses at 306, 312, 316, and 320 Huron Avenue in 1896.

Edward Hooper's heirs laid out Gurney Street in 1904. Although its intersection with Fayerweather was marked by a substantial house, the rest of the land down to Huron was filled between 1909 and 1916 with closely spaced, almost identical two-family houses by builder Bernard A. Rice, who broke a covenant to build a community garage that decades later became the Fayerweather School (figure 4.72; see chapter 7). Similarly, Blakeslee Street (laid out in 1921) and the rest of Reservoir down to Huron Avenue were densely built up by 1930 (figure 4.73; see *Report Five: Northwest Cambridge,* 48–50). The block of eight stores that Forris Norris built at the foot of Gurney in 1912 evolved into a neighborhood shopping district that was enshrined by the zoning code in 1924 (figure 4.74).

The Ruggles-Fayerweather house remained the property of William Wells until he died in 1873. His heirs laid out Channing Place in 1883 and sold the east corner to architect Henry Van Brunt, who put up a Queen Anne house for himself at 167 Brattle (see figure 6.121). Frances Newell, Wells's daughter, commissioned Van Brunt to design 10 Channing Place in 1892. The unusually large and well-detailed Colonial Revival at 3–5 was built in 1893 by Thomas Gannett, superintendent of the Revere Sugar refinery in East Cambridge (see figure 6.168). The Wells heirs sold the old house in 1907 to historian Roger Merriman, who added some modern amenities and erected its elaborate Federal Revival fence.

FIGURE 4.73 Two-family houses on Huron Avenue and Reservoir Street in 1924. Future governor Charles F. Hurley brokered the sale of two acres of the old Fayerweather estate belonging to Frank A. Kennedy in 1921. New houses included, from left to right, 294 Huron Avenue and 60, 58, 56, 54, 48, and 46 Reservoir Street (all 1921–23, William J. Beecher, builder).

FIGURE 4.74 Forris Norris stores, 342–356 Huron Avenue (1912, William L. Mowll, architect). Photo 1939.

The westernmost Tory holding in Cambridge was the estate of Lieutenant Governor Thomas Oliver, the last Royal Lieutenant Governor of Massachusetts. Born in Antigua in 1733, he studied law after graduating from Harvard in 1753 but gave it up to manage the West Indian plantations that he inherited from his grandfather and great-uncle. He allied himself with the planter aristocracy of Jamaica and with most of Cambridge's loyalist families when he married Elizabeth Vassall, the daughter of Colonel John and Elizabeth (Phips) Vassall, in 1760, and his sister Elizabeth married John Vassall Jr.

In 1766 Oliver purchased 21 acres from Christopher Grant, a descendant of one of Watertown's first settlers, and built a house almost as opulent as John Vassall's at a bend in the Watertown Road overlooking the river landing (figure 4.76). Among its attractions was the sweeping view of "a part of Boston … a long curve of the Charles, and the wide fields between me and Cambridge, and the flat marshes beyond the river, smooth and silent" (Lowell, in Paterson I, 299). Later called Elmwood, it became the home of two important figures in 19th-century American politics and literature, Vice President Elbridge Gerry (1744–1814) and poet and diplomat James Russell Lowell (1819–91); today it is the residence of the president of Harvard University.

Oliver, who had no previous political experience, was made lieutenant governor and president of the Mandamus Council in 1774. When angry patriots surrounded his house on September 2, he wrote an addendum to the resignation letter they prepared for him: "My House at Cambridge being surrounded by about four Thousand People, in Compliance with their Commands I sign my Name" (Elton, CSM 38, 51). He then fled to Boston with his wife and daughters and ultimately sailed to England. His property was confiscated and his house used as a hospital during the Siege of Boston. Many of those wounded at Bunker Hill on June 17, 1775, were buried in the field across the road.

Thomas Oliver's petition to the Loyalist Claims Commission described the second-largest estate in Cambridge. Writing from

FIGURE 4.75   Thomas Oliver house, Elmwood, 33 Elmwood Avenue (1767). Photo ca. 1912.

FIGURE 4.76 Thomas Oliver's house, flanked by a stable, gardens, and a large parterre as drawn from memory during the Siege of Boston (see figure 1.27). The cartographer, Henry Pelham, demonstrated first-hand knowledge in his depiction of the abandoned Tory estates in Cambridge.

exile in Bristol in 1783, Oliver declared the loss of 96 acres "of excellent Lands highly improved … a handsome large new built Dwelling House … with large barns Coach House Stables and other out offices, a wharf on Charles River, a large garden well stocked with the best fruits" (PRO, AO 13/48). In addition to horses, carriages, cattle, and equipment, Oliver also reported the largest single holding of slaves in Cambridge:[26]

Buff a Blacksmith let at £20 lawful per annum £100
Cato a Farmer and Gardener £50
Jerry a Coachman and Groom £60
Jeoffrey a Cook £50
Samuel a Footman now with me but to whom I pay wages as free by
    the Laws of England £50
Mira a Cook £30
Jude a young House Maid £40
Sarah a Sempstress and Waiting Maid £45
Jenny a young Girl £20
Violet ditto £20
Young Jerry, a small boy £15

In 1779 the Commonwealth sold Oliver's property to Andrew Cabot of Salem, who in turn sold it in 1787 to Elbridge Gerry, the son of a self-made merchant in Marblehead. Gerry graduated from Harvard in 1762 and grew wealthy as an importer of war matériel and a speculator in securities. He was a contentious, mercurial, and self-contradictory anti-Federalist with elitist tendencies who was so fearful of centralization that he was one of only three delegates who refused to sign the U.S. Constitution adopted in Philadelphia in 1787. He was deeply unpopular with his Federalist peers, but he adhered to his principles and ran for governor four times before attaining the office in 1810.[27]

In 1786 Gerry married Ann Thompson, a cosmopolitan young woman from New York who disdained the fishing village of Marblehead; a year later they settled into a more fashionable life in the Oliver house. In 1793 he purchased 52 acres south of the landing and an isolated 17-acre field on Vassal Lane from the Thacher family, giving him a total holding of 142 acres. Tenant farmer Benjamin Prentice, who probably lived in the old Thacher house on the landing road, farmed 98 acres and kept the Stratton Tavern on Mt. Auburn Street, while William Packard rented the remainder; in 1798 their houses were valued at $270 and $425, while Gerry's was assessed at $5,370. Gerry would not allow his tenants to plow the field opposite the house out of respect for the soldiers buried there.[28]

Gerry was James Madison's vice president when he died property-rich and cash-poor in 1814. The government attached some of his land in default of a debt, and Congress left his widow destitute by refusing to pay his remaining salary. Nevertheless, Ann Gerry was the high bidder on the mansion when her husband's executor began to sell off his holdings in 1815. The 43 acres north of Brattle Street (which the county extended across the estate in 1812) went to local farmer Joshua Coolidge, while Jeduthun Wellington bought most of the land east of Elmwood Avenue (figure 4.77).

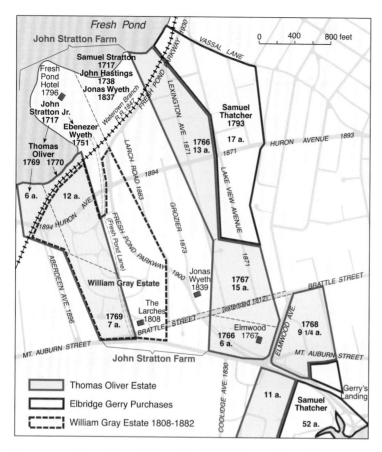

FIGURE 4.77 Formation and disposition of the Thomas Oliver-Elbridge Gerry estate, 1766–93, and the formation of the William Gray estate, 1808–81.

Elmwood

In 1818 Ann Gerry sold the mansion and 8¾ acres to Reverend Charles Lowell, pastor of the West Street Congregational Church in Boston. Lowell named the Oliver-Gerry house "Elmwood" and gradually reassembled the estate. In 1827–29 he purchased the corner of Brattle and Elmwood from William Wells, four acres of the former Gerry holdings across the road from Jeduthun Wellington, and all five parcels belonging to the U.S. government.

James Russell Lowell was born at Elmwood in 1819. He graduated from Harvard in 1838, and after he married Maria White of Watertown in 1844 his father built them a cottage at the corner of Elmwood Avenue and Brattle Street that he called "Elmwood Junior" (*Letters*, 121).[29] Devastated by Maria's death in 1853, Lowell moved in with his brother-in-law, Estes Howe (whose wife, Lois, was Maria's sister), and took Longfellow's place as professor of modern languages at Harvard. He kept this position until 1886, though he was often absent. In 1857 Lowell married Frances Dunlap, his daughter's governess, and the small family moved back to Elmwood after his father's death in 1861. Strongly attached to Cambridge and to the old house, Lowell made them familiar to Americans through his writings and poetry. In 1871 he sold all the land he had inherited except for 2½ acres around the house. The proceeds gave him an income of $4,000 a year, which allowed him to take his family abroad. Thomas Bailey Aldrich leased the house while Lowell served as ambassador to Spain in 1877–80 and to Great Britain in 1880–85. After his death in 1891 Lowell's admirers wanted to create a memorial similar to Longfellow Park. Elmwood was held in trust for the poet's daughter, but the land behind it became Lowell Park (see chapter 5). In 1925 his heirs sold the house to fine arts professor Arthur Kingsley Porter, whose will provided that it go to Harvard when his widow, Lucy, died in 1962.

Lowell's 1871 property sale allowed the development of Channing Street, which Cambridge speculators Edward Hyde, Daniel Chamberlin, and James Sparrow laid out in 1872 on a 6½-acre parcel that Lowell had inherited from his first wife. Only one house (5 Channing, 1872) was built before the Panic of 1873. The next house, 4 Channing, was not begun until 1886, but by this time Chamberlin's son William had launched a distinguished career in architecture, and his father gave him the commission. Several other houses date from the 1890s, but the street was not built up until the 1920s. The twelve two-family houses that John J. Shine crowded onto Longfellow Road in 1923–25 occupy the former site of the Avon Home, which burned in 1918 (see chapter 7). Shine returned in 1935 to build three houses on the site of 5 Channing; one of these was replaced in 2014 with a new house by Anmahian Winton Architects.

Lowell's heirs laid out twelve lots in 1892 on the east side of Elmwood Avenue and on Traill Street, which they named after

an English ancestor (figure 4.78). The two streets were built up at first with spacious houses by well-known architects, including 8 Elmwood, designed in 1893 by Peabody & Stearns, 15 and 17 Traill (1898 and 1904, Lois Lilley Howe), 26 Elmwood (1899, Cram, Goodhue & Ferguson), and 15 Elmwood (1903, Allen W. Jackson). After World War I, when Mt. Auburn became a busy thoroughfare, the remaining lots were filled with two-family houses like those on the back pastures off Huron Avenue. The 1757 Daniel Watson house was moved from North Cambridge to the corner of Elmwood and Mt. Auburn Street in 1965 (see figure 6.27).

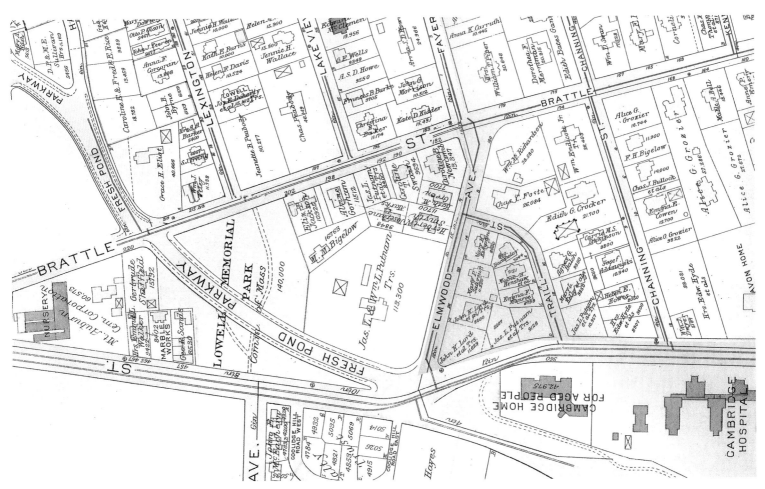

Figure 4.78 James Russell Lowell heirs' subdivisions on Elmwood Avenue and Brattle, Traill, and Channing streets, 1916.

The acreage that Joshua Coolidge purchased from Gerry's executors in 1816 stretched from Brattle Street to Fresh Pond. In 1832 he divided the property between his sons, Joshua Jr. and Josiah. Josiah already owned a significant part of Gerry's acreage south of Mt. Auburn Street, where he built a house in the 1820s that is now 24 Coolidge Hill Road. He acquired his brother's share in 1839 and in 1846–47 built a farmhouse, icehouse, and barn at what is now 12 Lake View Avenue (figure 4.79). Josiah harvested ice on Fresh Pond and cultivated his land until 1870 (see *Report Five: Northwest Cambridge,* figure 25).

A survey made in 1870, when Josiah sold the property to Person Davis, T. Alfred Taylor, and Reuben Demmon, depicted the agricultural landscape of West Cambridge (figure 4.80). The developers' subdivision a year later ignored natural topographic features and created thirty-five lots, mostly 100 feet wide, along two parallel streets that became Lake View and Lexington avenues. The northern part of the farm, beyond a cross street that

FIGURE 4.79   Josiah Coolidge house, 12 Lake View Avenue (1846–47). The round bay window and (probably) the gabled dormer were added in 1908. Photo 1967.

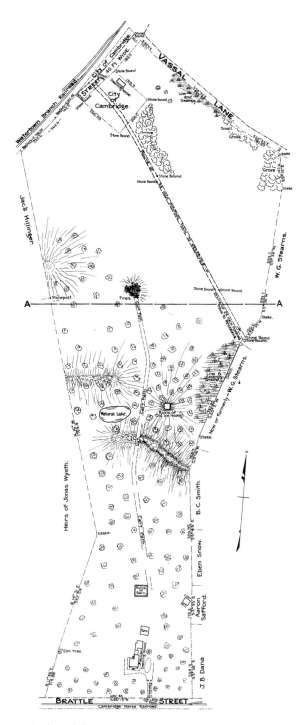

FIGURE 4.80   A plan of the Coolidge place in 1870 shows the house, barns, outbuildings, trees, and landscape features of a 19th century farm.

the city incorporated into Huron Avenue, was not initially platted. By 1873 developers Stephen Niles and Lewis Rice of Boston had laid out the west side of Lexington and enlarged the grid to Grozier Road (see below). Lake View developed first, as a tributary to the Brattle Street car line. William Smith, a housewright, built two conventional Mansard houses at 68 and 87 (1871–72) and a forward-looking Stick Style house at 88 (1874) on speculation, as well as a towered Mansard at 94 (1874) that he probably could not sell because of the recent panic and lived in himself (figure 4.81). The lots sold slowly, and by 1886 only eighteen houses stood on the lower end.

The opposite sides of Lexington Avenue from Brattle to Huron originated in different estates and had different histories. Davis and Taylor platted 15,000 square foot lots on the east side of Lexington in 1871 like those on Lake View. Most of the west side originated in the Jonas Wyeth farm and was laid out in a similar fashion by Niles and Rice, but their project stalled in the Panic of 1873 and turned out very differently. In 1884 Person Davis, the surviving partner of Davis & Taylor, declared bankruptcy, and his remaining land was assigned to creditors. The earliest houses were put up on lots bought from the bankrupt developer at 61 (1889) and 115–17 (by 1890). The city built the fire station at 167 Lexington in 1893; six years later, the fire chief, Thomas Casey, built a double house that the *Chronicle* described as "another in the group of houses now being erected for members of city departments in the vicinity of lower Huron Avenue" (Sept. 9, 1899; figure 4.82).

Construction boomed in the more remote fields north of Brattle Street after streetcar service began on Huron Avenue in 1894, in good time to attract the city's increasingly prosperous Irish-American households; in 1902 the area was described as "one of the most desirable residential neighborhoods which are at present attainable for persons without great wealth" (*Chronicle*, Sept. 20). The social demarcation between Tory Row and Huron Avenue can be traced quite clearly along the summit of Reservoir Hill; as the topography flattens west of Lake View the distinction is apparent in the crowded two-family houses built on speculation after 1895 (figure 4.83).

FIGURE 4.81 The development of Lake View Avenue spanned decades. William Smith put up a simple Italianate at number 97 (right) in 1877, but he built the elaborate Second Empire house at 107 (center) under more favorable conditions in 1881. The two-family house at 109–111 (background) went up in 1904. Photo ca. 1950.

FIGURE 4.82 Thomas J. Casey house, 168 Lexington Avenue (1899, John E. Muldoon, architect). Several stylish double houses designed to look like large singles went up on the developing fringes of Old Cambridge in the 1890s (see figure 4.170). Casey was chief of the Cambridge Fire Department from 1879 to 1905, and his new house was almost directly across the street from a fire house the city erected in 1893. Photo ca. 1900.

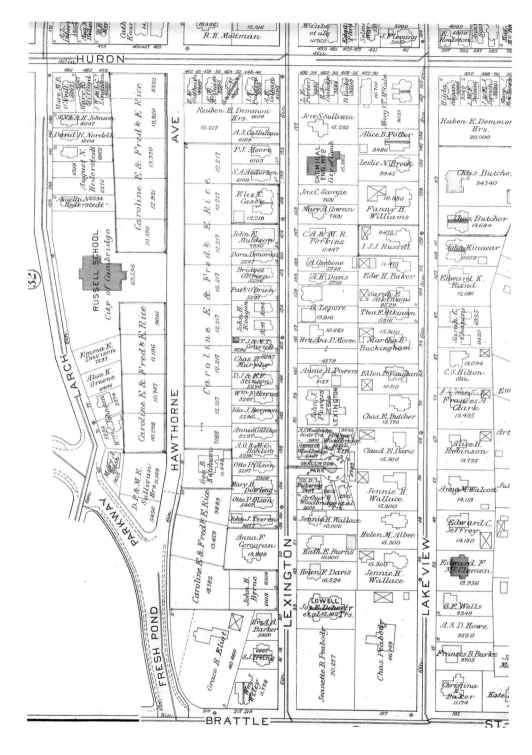

FIGURE 4.83 Lake View and Lexington avenues in 1916, with suburban development well under way. The titles of properties outlined in blue have been registered (confirmed) by the Massachusetts Land Court. Hawthorne Avenue was renamed Grozier Road in 1924.

Lexington Avenue's eclectic mixture of two-family houses, three-deckers, and apartment buildings was quite different from the neighborhood envisioned in the 1880s. The 15,000-square-foot lots were impractically large in the constrained economic environment of the 1890s. On the east side, most were resurveyed into smaller lots, but some attracted creative developers. James M. Hilton built the most highly decorated three-decker in the city, the Lowell, at 33 in 1900 (see figure 6.221). In 1911 John J. Powers put up a stucco apartment building, the Lexington, at 95–99, and in 1913 seven Mission style houses went up on Gracewood Park. On the west side, builder John L. Malcolm replatted the old Niles and Rice subdivision into narrow, 5,000-square-foot lots and populated them with sixteen two- and three-family gambrel-roofed houses (figure 4.84).

The Brattle Street frontage of Josiah Wyeth's house remained empty until 1954, when it was subdivided and an archeologically correct Georgian farmhouse and a prefabricated Techbuilt house went up side-by-side on Lexington Avenue. Ten years later, architect Hugh Stubbins built a house for himself on the Lake View corner, filling in one of the last open lots on Brattle Street (see figure 6.209).

FIGURE 4.84   The sixteen gambrel-roofed duplex houses at 58 through 140 Lexington Avenue designed by Elmer Buckley in 1912–13 demonstrated a uniformity of design not seen elsewhere in Cambridge. Photo 2009.

JOHN STRATTON FARM

West of the Tory estates a rural district stretched far into Watertown. In the 17th century, John Stratton's farm occupied almost all the land from Mt. Auburn Street to Fresh Pond between Lexington and Aberdeen avenues. A cartway known as Fresh Pond Lane (which only partially followed the current street of that name) ran up a gentle slope to a bluff above the pond. Most of this territory remained rural until the last quarter of the 19th century, and intensive development did not occur until after World War I (see figure 4.77).

Jonas Wyeth farm

In 1717 Stratton divided his property along what is now Larch Road, giving his son Samuel the eastern half and his son John the western. Samuel died in 1723, and in 1738 his heirs sold 40 acres with the family house and barn to John Hastings, a Watertown shoemaker. The land remained in his family until 1837, when his great-grandson sold it to Jonas Wyeth (a distant relation of Jonas Wyeth 2nd, the real estate dealer on Garden Street). The next year Wyeth sold 11 acres on Fresh Pond to his cousin Nathaniel, who was engaged in the ice-cutting industry. Jonas, who had leased the Fresh Pond Hotel from his uncle Jacob and "retired with a satisfactory fortune," built a new house facing Brattle Street about 1839 that survives at 17 Fresh Pond Parkway, though greatly remodeled (Paige, 705; figure 4.85; see also figure 4.89).

Wyeth's widow sold most of her land to Stephen Niles and Lewis Rice, who cooperated with Person Davis's partnership to lay out Lexington Avenue and Hawthorne Avenue (now Grozier Road) with 47 generous 15,000-square-foot lots (see figure 4.88).[30] Niles and Rice were soon caught up in the Panic of 1873, and their subdivision remained untouched for decades. Hawthorne originally extended to Brattle Street, but it had attracted no buildings except the Russell School (1896) when Fresh Pond Parkway eliminated the lower end in 1899 (see figure 5.57). A

FIGURE 4.85 Jonas Wyeth house, 17 Fresh Pond Parkway (1839). Photo ca. 1899–1909.

FIGURE 4.86 William L. Galvin's Brattle Circle development. Both 14 (foreground) and 11–12 were built in 1942. Photo 1945.

single house at 15 (1905) stood alone for almost twenty years. The street was renamed in 1924 for Edwin Grozier, the recently deceased publisher of the *Boston Post,* and began a period of rapid development by Frederick Rice and S.N. Niles, who were probably sons of the original developers. By 1929 Grozier was filled with closely spaced single and double houses, twenty-six of which were constructed in 1924 and 1925 alone. Neighborhood opposition to adaptive reuse for affordable housing led to the demolition of the Russell School in 1979 (see chapter 7). The following year, the city subdivided the site and sold the lots to the highest bidder, requiring that the six new houses on Grozier Road and the five on Larch Road be built of natural materials and with similar heights and setbacks to the older homes nearby.

The balance of the Wyeth farm, a triangle cut off by the 1812 extension of Brattle Street that contained John Hastings's 17th-century farmhouse, was largely acquired by Mount Auburn Cemetery in 1850. The Proprietors erected a house for the cemetery superintendent, a barn, and extensive greenhouses

that remained in place until 1938, when an investment group, organized by principals of the Cambridge Federal Savings & Loan Association and guided by Cambridge architect-developer William L. Galvin, acquired the 1.4-acre property and laid out Brattle Circle. Between 1939 and 1942 Galvin converted the old house and stable to apartments and designed ten Art Moderne houses on the property (figure 4.86). Robert Sands razed the old Hastings house in 1887 and established a monument works that served the cemetery trade until townhouses replaced it in 1980 (see figure 5.81).

Ebenezer Wyeth farm: William Gray Estate and Larchwood

John Stratton's 1717 division of his farm left the west portion in possession of his son John Stratton Jr. who in 1750 divided it along Fresh Pond Lane. Ebenezer Wyeth bought the eastern half in 1751 and built a farmhouse that survives at 36 Larch Road. His son Jacob, who graduated from Harvard in 1792, married

Elizabeth, a daughter of Nathaniel Jarvis, and established the Fresh Pond Hotel in 1796 on eight acres purchased from his father. Their son Nathaniel Jarvis Wyeth developed the ice harvesting business on Fresh Pond. After the water board acquired the surroundings of Fresh Pond, alderman John E. Parry bought the hotel at auction in 1892, moved it to 234 Lake View Avenue, and converted it to apartments (see *Report Five: Northwest Cambridge,* 135–36).

The Ebenezer Wyeth farm became the nucleus of the last estate assembled on Brattle Street. When Wyeth died in 1799, his 16-acre homestead contained a dwelling, a cider mill, and a barn. The buildings and 5¼ acres near the intersection of Brattle and Mt. Auburn streets passed to his son Ebenezer who sold the place to Jonathan Hastings (probably the postmaster of Boston) in 1801. In 1804–5 Hastings started building a large house that incorporated the Wyeth farmhouse as an ell, but in 1808 he sold the unfinished project to William Gray of Salem, who was reputed to be the richest man in America and its largest shipowner. Salem was in decline even before the embargoes of 1807–12, and Gray was one of many North Shore merchants who relocated to Boston about this time. His new summer place was conveniently close to that of Governor Gerry, who also hailed from Essex County and with whom he served as lieutenant governor. Gray called his Federal mansion "The Larches" after a stand of deciduous conifers nearby. Fresh Pond Lane, which was shaded by many fine trees and offered the most attractive approach to Fresh Pond, ran just west of the house (figure 4.87).

William Gray made several significant additions to the property, including a large piece of the John Stratton Jr. farm west of Fresh Pond Lane that he acquired in 1816 through foreclosure after Elbridge Gerry's death. In 1851 his son, John Chipman Gray, purchased 3½ acres behind the house that he filled with ornamental gardens and greenhouses. Professor John Chipman Gray, a law professor at Harvard and a founding partner of the Boston firm of Ropes & Gray, inherited the estate in 1881 on the death of his uncle of the same name. Gray also used the Larches as a summer retreat, but in 1882 he sold the greenhouses

and the land west of Fresh Pond Lane to Sarah Dee, whose son Thomas established a nursery there (see figure 5.77).[31]

In 1883 Frederick Fish laid out Larch Road along the fence separating Gray's land from the old Jonas Wyeth farm, and three suburban houses soon appeared on the east side of the street. Gray took steps to prevent encroachments and bought some nearby lots to protect his privacy. Three years later he changed his mind and planned a new street parallel to Brattle that he named after his son Roland. Gray sold some land to Fish in 1889, but nothing more was built until 71 and 77 Larch Road went up in 1895.

The street pattern changed dramatically with the construction of Fresh Pond Parkway from Mt. Auburn Street to Huron Avenue in 1900 and the creation of Larchwood in 1915. Charles Eliot and the Cambridge park commissioners envisioned the parkway as early as 1894. They hoped to incorporate Fresh Pond Lane as it then existed, but this would have meant following Mt. Auburn Street with its busy trolley tracks. Instead, the Metropolitan Park Commission constructed a new road that crossed

FIGURE 4.87 The grounds of the Larches, ca. 1885–95.

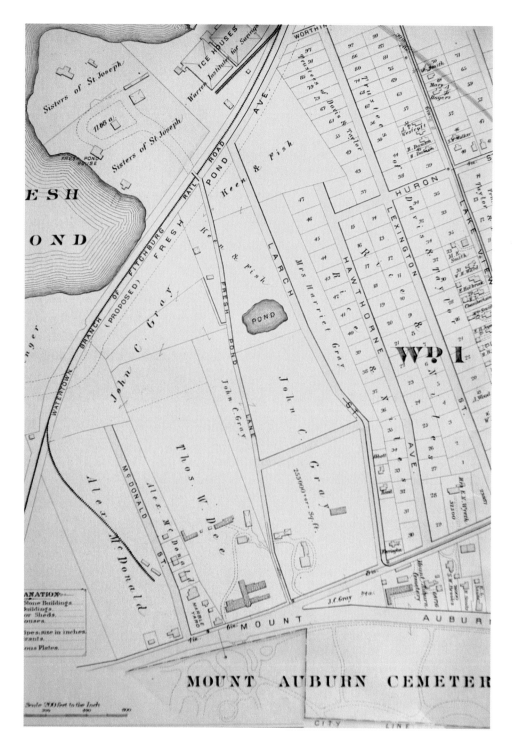

FIGURE 4.88 The John Chipman Gray estate in 1886, showing the Larches in its original location and Roland Street (not labeled) crossing the property behind the house. Thomas Dee's nursery is west of the house, and Alexander McDonald's stoneyard occupies Ebenezer Wyeth's 13-acre orchard. McDonald Street is now Aberdeen Avenue.

the Elmwood estate, the old Wyeth farm, and the Gray place to join Fresh Pond Lane at Huron Avenue (see figure 4.78). The parkway ended there until 1930, when the Metropolitan District Commission extended it to Concord Avenue and a connection with the Mystic Valley system via Alewife Brook Parkway. Route 2 was completed in 1934, but traffic did not really flood the parkway until the completion of Gerry's Landing Road, the Eliot Bridge, and Memorial Drive Extension in 1951.

The parkway crossed in front of the 1838 Wyeth farmhouse, which Harvard president Charles Eliot remodeled after he retired in 1909 (figure 4.89). Architect Charles Greco built his own house at number 36 a year later, but most construction took place after World War I (see figure 6.181). In 1924 Eliot successfully aroused public opposition to Roxbury contractor Jacob Sorkin's plan to build a 24-unit apartment house at the corner of Grozier Road; a single-family house appeared there instead.[32] Later houses were less substantial, as seen in the Dutch Colonial examples at 99, 101, and 103 built in 1926 by the Dix Lumber Company, which also put up many houses on Aberdeen Avenue during the same period. The last three houses on the parkway were built after World War II, when traffic must already have been significant (figure 4.90). In 1956 the constant din induced the owners of 17 Fresh Pond Parkway to erect a serpentine brick wall designed by landscape architect Grace Kirkwood.

Gray sold his lots east of Larch Road after Fresh Pond Parkway opened, but progress was very slow. August Hederstedt began replatting them about 1911 and built fifteen houses on Larch Road and four on the parkway, including one for himself at number 139.[33] In 1914 a new homeowner, Robert Fielding, put up a "toy theatre" across the street from the Russell School where his 14-year-old daughter Ruth, a dancer and child actress, "could produce such plays and entertainments as she desired" (*Chronicle,* Sept. 5, 1914). Miss Fielding later ran a drama school for children, but illness forced her to give up the venture, and in 1926 the "Parkway Bungalow" was remodeled into the house that still stands at 126 Larch Road (figure 4.91). The rest of the street was built up in the 1920s with uniform two-family dwellings.

FIGURE 4.89 The Jonas Wyeth house at 17 Fresh Pond Parkway after Charles Eliot remodeled it as his retirement home (1909, Hartley Dennett, architect). The house was further remodeled and expanded in 1927. Photo before 1927.

FIGURE 4.90 Fresh Pond Parkway, looking north from Larch Road. Houses like 61 and 63 Fresh Pond Parkway (both 1913, Charles Greco and William L. Mowll, architects) went up in a quieter era but retain their desirability despite relentless traffic. Photo 2015.

Gray's 23-acre estate was the last undeveloped tract on Brattle Street. After his death in 1915 its disposition was the subject of much conjecture; it had been in the same family since 1808 and had desirable frontage on Brattle Street, Fresh Pond Parkway, and Huron Avenue. In 1916 Roland Gray and Eleanor Gray Tudor sold the property to Boston realtor J. Murray Howe with the usual restrictions concerning use, setbacks from the street, and the value of future dwellings. Howe immediately resold it to Forris Norris, a Cambridge developer who had just purchased part of the Coolidge farm south of Mt. Auburn Street. The heirs moved the mansion from Brattle Street to Larch Road where it became a residence for Eleanor and her husband, Boston attorney Henry Tudor. The 1751 Wyeth farmhouse, which had been attached to the house as an ell, became a separate residence for Roland.

Forris W. Norris (1885–1965), a Quebec native who worked as an insurance agent in Central Square before entering the real estate business, hired Pray, Hubbard & White, a Boston firm of landscape architects, to prepare plans for both Larchwood and Coolidge Hill.[34] Norris wanted "to make [the Gray estate] one of the ideal residential sections" of Cambridge (*Chronicle,* May 22, 1915). He asked the landscape architects to design a garden

FIGURE 4.91 Larch Road looking north toward Huron Avenue, with the Parkway Bungalow (1914, H.A. Hansen, architect) in the center. Photo 2009.

suburb with winding streets and irregular lots that would preserve every possible tree and take advantage of the beautiful gardens and shrubbery. The *Chronicle* reported that:

> studies were made of development at Forest Hills, Long Island, the Country Club district of Columbus, Ohio, the Lawrence Park estates of Toronto and some of the most noted garden city developments in England, among them Letchworth and Hampstead. (Oct. 2, 1915)

The picturesque designs for Larchwood and Coolidge Hill contrast strongly with the ruler-straight streets of 19th century Cambridge (figure 4.92). Larchwood included one hundred house lots that varied in shape, size, and orientation, three gracefully curving streets with wide planting strips for trees, and several landscaped islands within the roadways.[35] The intricate plan did have some precursors in Cambridge. As early as 1868, Frederick Law Olmsted had proposed a subdivision with a curving parkway for the Shady Hill estate, where Charles Eliot laid out the present curved streets in 1888 (see figures 4.232–4.233). Similarly, Gardiner Hubbard's 1889 plan for his estate comprised a garden-like setting with narrow, winding streets. Larchwood was unusual because it was completed entirely according to the original design. It also established precedents that were reflected at Gray Gardens (1922) and the second part of Coolidge Hill (1925).

The promotional material for Larchwood emphasized the visual interest of its curving streets, which met the roads bordering the development in such a way as to discourage through traffic. Before selling any lots, Norris graded the streets and installed underground telephone and electric service. He refused to sell to speculative builders and made prospective homeowners "pass a rigid investigation as to their personal standing" (*Chronicle,* Oct. 8, 1921). Plans had to be submitted to the landscape architects "to insure the maintenance of a high-grade harmonious development throughout the whole" (Fresh Pond Parkway Realty Co., 7).

In November 1915 the *Chronicle* reported that four houses were under way; these were 71 Fresh Pond Lane, 72 and 78 Fresh Pond Parkway, and 17 Larchwood Drive, all commissioned by

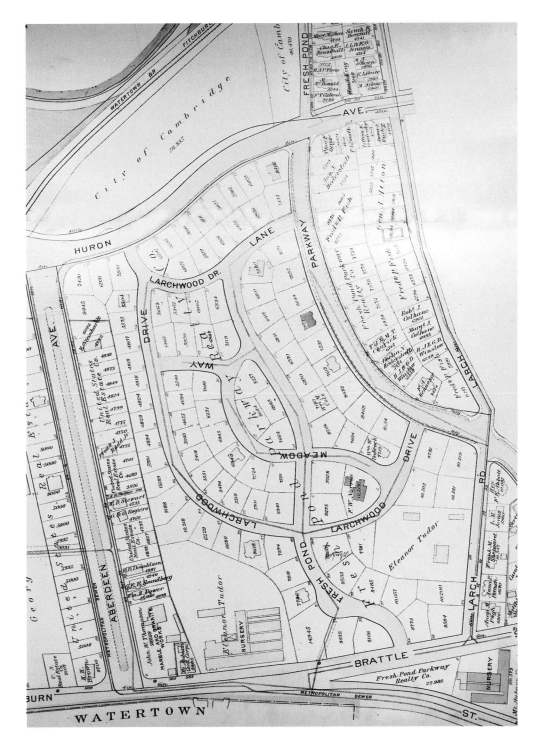

Norris and designed by Greco to show some encouraging activity and a high standard of architecture. The most impressive was Norris's own brick Georgian Revival on a corner lot (figure 4.93). Most houses went up in the 1920s; on the three interior streets only one house, 63 Fresh Pond Lane (1939), was built after 1930. Larchwood was highly successful as a garden suburb, and its winding lanes full of shade trees still provide the quiet oasis envisioned by the promoters. The strength of their vision is best demonstrated on Fresh Pond Parkway, where the houses are still desirable in spite of the constant high-speed traffic.

Gerry's Landing and Coolidge Hill

Sir Richard Saltonstall founded Watertown in 1630 at the head of a creek that entered the Charles River at about the site of the Cambridge Boat Club. The meetinghouse stood near the Cambridge Homes, while the parsonage was in the vicinity of Elmwood. In contrast to Newtowne, Watertown was a dispersed community; early settlers were allowed to live on their farms, so no village developed around the meetinghouse, which was

moved inland in 1635. Grants of land ranged from 3 to 12 acres, although Sir Richard received 16 acres on the north side of the landing, including a bluff (later known as Symonds' Hill) on the present site of Mount Auburn Hospital. A few families gathered the original allotments into larger farms that were annexed to Cambridge in 1754. Cambridge acquired more Watertown land for Cambridge Cemetery in 1855 and 1885 (see figure 5.74).

Questions arose about access to the wharf after Cambridge annexed the landing. In 1770 the selectmen drew lots, and Cambridge won the downstream side. Joshua Coolidge remembered that "in the deep snow of the winter of 1780 the farmers of Watertown drove their teams of wood and produce … on to the ice at this Landing and continued on to Boston" (*Cambridge Annual Documents,* 1884, 266). When the city established a bathing place at the landing in 1867, Joseph Coolidge, who owned the old Thatcher farm, insisted that "the road leading from [Thomas] Oliver's Wharf, so called, to Watertown" was not a public way and that his deeds gave him the right to erect fences and gates across it (ibid., 261). The city's examination of the ancient records found otherwise, and this remnant of the 17th century, variously known as Sir Richard's, Oliver's, and Gerry's Landing remained open to all. The city maintained the beach until 1949, when Gerry's Landing was obliterated by the extension of Memorial Drive (see figure 5.52).

The construction of Mt. Auburn Street from Gerry's Corner to the village shortened the route from Watertown to the West Boston Bridge and offered opportunities for development. In 1807 Gerry sold a lot between the new road and the landing to young John Gerry Orne, who built a store that soon failed. Two years later he sold the land back to Gerry and moved the building up the hill next to the old Thatcher farmhouse, which his mother, Sarah, had just purchased; she converted it into a dwelling at 10 Coolidge Hill Road that is now the oldest house in the neighborhood. Also remaining from the Orne homestead are the service wing (ca. 1840), which was detached in 1936 and made into a separate dwelling at 8 Coolidge Hill Road, and the stable (ca. 1819), which the architects Cram, Goodhue, & Ferguson converted in 1901 into the house at 6 Coolidge Hill Road. All were far enough up the hill that in 1936–37 the opportunistic Giles Taintor was able to build four small houses in front of them on Gerry's Landing Road.

In 1806 Gerry mortgaged 14 acres around the Thatcher house to Benjamin Lee (brother of "English Thomas"), who foreclosed after Gerry died in 1814 and sold the property to Boston merchant George Brimmer. Gerry mortgaged the remaining 33½ Thatcher acres to Thomas Melville, who also foreclosed and sold the property in 1821 to Josiah Coolidge (whose father had bought Gerry's land north of Brattle Street in 1816). Josiah's house (now 24 Coolidge Hill Road) appeared in the tax records in 1826 and was listed as "1 new house" until 1828, when it was presumably finished.

About this time, Brimmer began to consolidate the estate along the Watertown Road that he had been assembling since 1825 (see chapter 5). In 1830 he closed the old lane to the

FIGURE 4.94 Gerry's Landing and the Coolidge farm, ca. 1882–85.

Stone farm, which ran by the east side of the Thatcher house, laid out Coolidge Avenue along the boundary of the property he would convey to the Massachusetts Horticultural Society for Mount Auburn Cemetery in 1831, and sold the house and an acre of land on Mt. Auburn Street to Josiah Coolidge. In 1847 Josiah moved to a new house on Brattle Street (now 12 Lake View Avenue) and sold his 19-acre homestead to his eldest son, Joseph G. Coolidge, who built a house at 34 Coolidge Avenue in 1856 (figure 4.95). Like his father, Joseph followed the land; an account of produce he sold at Faneuil Hall between June and August 1862 shows a steady trade in lettuce, beet greens, squash, tomatoes, and apples (figure 4.96). In 1887, the last year of his life, he was listed in the Cambridge directory as "farmer, gardener, milkman, and florist."

The residential neighborhood of Coolidge Hill had several false starts. In 1890 the *Cambridge Tribune* reported that Joseph Coolidge's son Edward, who had built his own house at 16 Coolidge Avenue, planned to put a new street through the property and create a number of lots for "a good class of residences" (Feb. 1). Although Coolidge eventually remodeled his house for two families, nothing came of his subdivision and the property

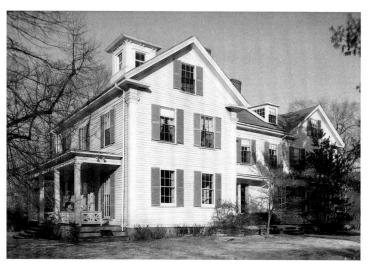

FIGURE 4.95 Joseph G. Coolidge farmhouse, 34 Coolidge Avenue (1856). Photo 1969.

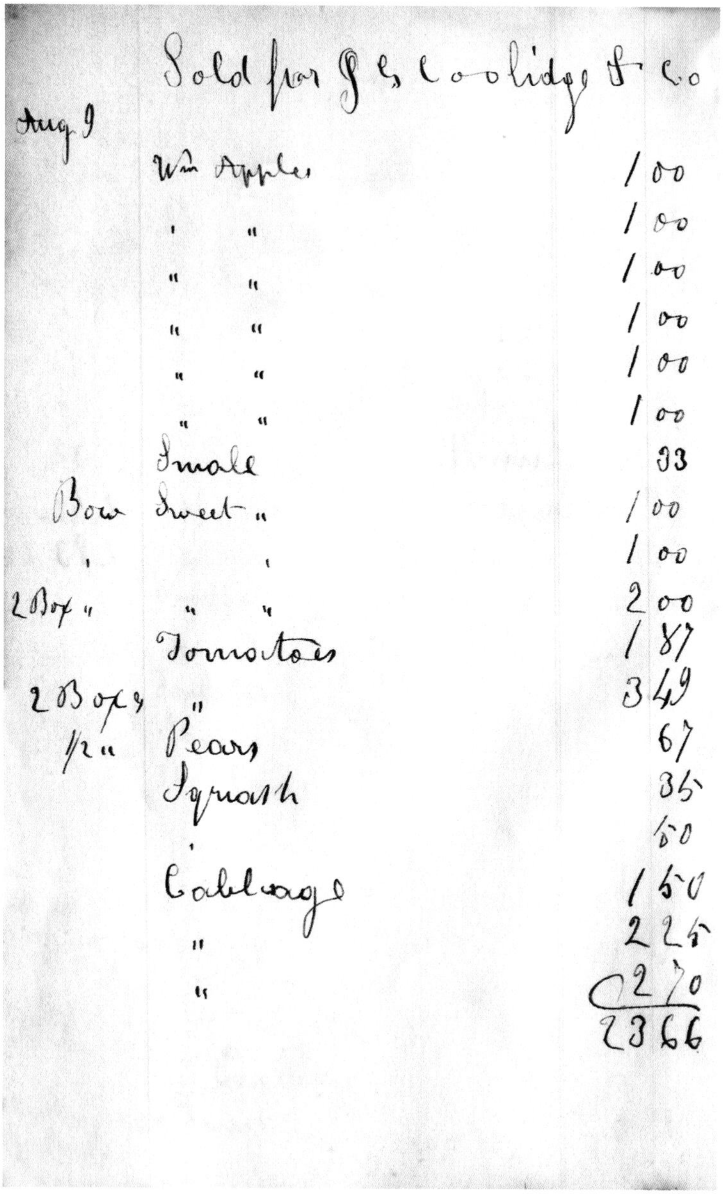

Sold for J. G. Coolidge & Co

Aug 9	Wm Apples	1 00
	" "	1 00
	" "	1 00
	" "	1 00
	" "	1 00
	" "	1 00
	Small	33
Bow	Sweet "	1 00
"	"	1 00
2 Box "	" "	2 00
	Tomatoes	1 87
2 Boxes	"	3 49
1/2 "	Pears	67
	Squash	35
	"	50
	Cabbage	1 50
	"	2 25
	"	2 70
		23 66

FIGURE 4.96 Joseph G. Coolidge's account book, documenting the sale of apples, cabbages, and berries at Quincy Market, August 9, 1862.

remained in agricultural use. For ten years the city tried to buy 35 acres to expand the cemetery. In 1904 the family agreed to sell it for $125,000, or eight cents a square foot, but taxpayers objected and the city withdrew its offer.

The farm continued undisturbed until 1911, when the Coolidges sold five acres of the meadow to the Browne & Nichols School, which leveled a small drumlin to create an athletic field (see chapter 7; figure 4.97). They also sold five acres on the hillside along the landing road to the Forbes family, with restrictions preventing its use as a cemetery and establishing standards for residential construction. Edward Waldo Forbes (later the director of the Fogg Museum) and his sister, Mrs. Kenneth Webster, built two substantial houses set well back from the future parkway below (see figure 4.101). A Coolidge descendant described the effect of this sale on the operations of the farm:

> When [the Forbes] houses were built it became immediately and painfully apparent that the days of pig raising on the Coolidge Farm were over. The pigpens were under the hill, exactly where the main building of Shady Hill School now stands, and the southwest wind which so frequently prevails blew gently and persistently right up to the houses of the new neighbors. (R. Coolidge, 99)

In 1915 the Coolidge heirs sold the last of their Gerry's Landing Road frontage to Forris Norris, the developer of Larchwood. Pray, Hubbard & White laid out Coolidge Hill Road "to conform to the natural contour of the land and to preserve the beautiful trees with which the property is covered" (City Realty Company, "Coolidge Hill," 3). Norris moved the Josiah Coolidge house closer to Coolidge Avenue and built two prototype houses at 20 and 44. As at Larchwood, purchasers had to have their plans approved by the landscape architects. Both single and semi-detached houses were allowed, and some of the earliest were triples. To encourage sales, Norris offered to finance and build "homes to suit the specifications desired by any purchaser of a lot at the smallest possible margin above the actual cost of materials and labor" (ibid., 7). By 1924 all but one of the twenty lots had been filled with modest Georgian and Colonial Revival houses.

FIGURE 4.97 The drumlin on the Coolidge farm, before the sale to Browne & Nichols School. Photo ca. 1890.

In its last decades the Coolidge farm became a year-round operation, with extensive greenhouses for flowers and vegetables. A labor shortage during World War I made it hard to manage:

> Farm workers became increasingly difficult to hire and a farm within a city became a luxury. It required skilled helpers to raise greenhouses full of violets, carnations, geraniums, and chrysanthemums. It was equally a tremendous job to raise fields and greenhouses of lettuce, cucumbers, tomatoes, corn, and down in the meadow wonderful celery, all to be sent to Faneuil Hall Market. (Coolidge, 100)

In 1924 the Coolidges sold the rest of the hill to Alva Morrison, a banker who had helped develop Gray Gardens East and West, and his Garden Terrace neighbor, Arthur Boylston Nichols, a broker. Their firm, Gerry's Landing Associates, cleared the site. "The big barn, stables, carriage house, the greenhouses, the two great chimneys and the boiler rooms were all taken down, and

FIGURE 4.98 Workers in a squash field on the Coolidge Farm, looking toward the Charles River with the chimney of the Boston Elevated Railway's power station on Kennedy Street in the distance. Photo 1898.

the last bit of rural Cambridge became residential" (ibid., 100). In 1925 and 1926, Shady Hill School (of which Morrison was chairman) bought the rest of the meadow and joined Browne & Nichols (see chapter 7). The developers hired Olmsted Brothers to lay out the new subdivision, which was also known as Coolidge Hill. The final plan of September 1925 included about thirty large lots along a winding road cut through the Coolidge's pear orchard, with a long, curving extension to Gerry's Landing (figure 4.99).[36]

Deed restrictions specified that each lot could contain a single-family residence at least two stories high with a garage for no more than two cars; setbacks controlled the siting, as they did at Larchwood. The project proved desirable, and by 1929 all but two lots were filled. Although designed by a variety of architects, most of the houses, such as 115 Coolidge Hill (1926, George C. Whiting) and 148 Coolidge Hill (1929, Duguid & Martin) were in the popular Georgian Revival style (figure 4.100).

Among these reproductions stands an 1801 Federal house which was moved from Appian Way to 144 Coolidge Hill in 1929.

The Forbes estate became the site of three distinguished Modern houses (figure 4.101). Edward Waldo Forbes built an enormous Georgian Revival mansion in 1911. An early convert to Modernism, he allowed his daughter Rosamund and her husband, William Bowers, to build Cambridge's first International Style house on the grounds in 1935. M.I.T. physicist Francis Bitter and his wife, the singer Ratan Devi, had Carl Koch design a house at the foot of the hill in 1946. In 1948 Forbes announced that he would raze his old place to save on taxes and hired Koch to design a new house at 42 Gerry's Landing Road. This became the Forbes residence, although the mansion still stands. Buckingham Browne & Nichols School demolished the Bitters house in 1997 and the Bowers house in 2006.

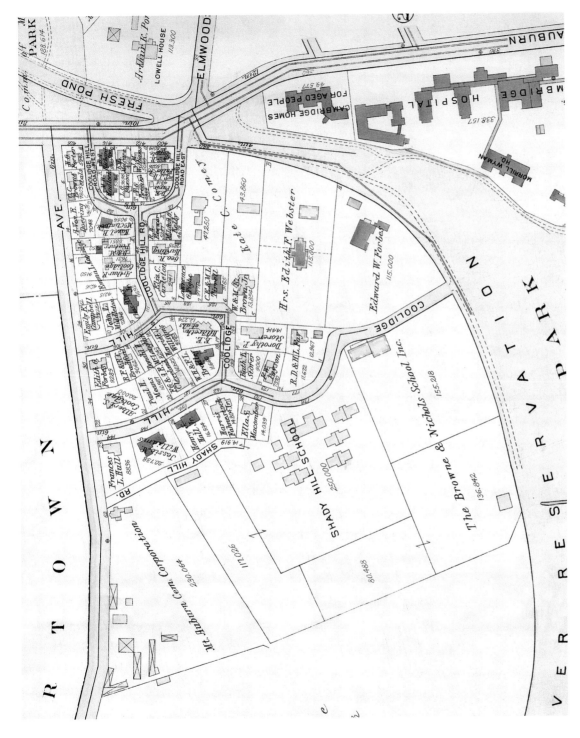

FIGURE 4.99 Coolidge Hill in 1930.

Residential Neighborhoods 249

FIGURE 4.100 The houses on Coolidge Hill showed a greater diversity of material and style than at Larchwood. Left to right, 115 Coolidge Hill (1926, George C. Whiting, architect), 123 Coolidge Hill (1926, Edward Sears Read), and 125 Coolidge Hill (1925, Andrews, Jones, Biscoe & Whitmore). Photo 1973.

FIGURE 4.101 The Forbes estate, ca. 1955. Clockwise from top left are the Forbes mansion at 30 Gerry's Landing Road (1911, J.E. Chandler, architect); Forbes's new house, 42 (1948, Carl Koch); Francis Bitter's, 44 (1946, Carl Koch; demolished 1997); and a partial view of the William Bowers house at 197 Coolidge Hill (1935, Howard T. Fisher; demolished 2006).

Simon Stone, an early Watertown settler, acquired a 50-acre homestead upstream from Coolidge Hill in the 1640s. Five generations later his descendants owned 150 acres approached by an "ancient private way to the mansion home of the late Moses Stone" (Middlesex Deeds, 369/357). George Brimmer bought most of the property in 1825. Moses Stone's widow retained 28 acres on the river, but the "mansion home" was destroyed by fire after her death in 1844. William P. Winchester of Boston acquired the southwest corner of the property in 1845 and built "a very magnificent mansion" in 1848–49 that was more elaborate than anything of its time in Cambridge (Bond, 952; figure 4.102; see also figure 6.78). Winchester, an East Cambridge soap and candle manufacturer for whom the town of Winchester is named, used the place as a country seat until he died in 1850 (see *East Cambridge*, 175). The city acquired 24 acres of the Stone farm for the Cambridge Cemetery in 1854. In 1885 the city bought Winchester's property, annexed the land from Watertown, and used the house as a funeral chapel before tearing it down in 1896.

FIGURE 4.102 William P. Winchester estate, "Fern Hill," Coolidge Avenue (1845, Arthur Gilman, architect; demolished 1896). Winchester's house stood on a bluff above the Charles River, where he had a boathouse with a Neoclassical portico. Photo ca. 1895.

WEST END HOMESTEADS ALONG GARDEN STREET

Garden Street and Concord Avenue both lead in a northwesterly direction, but Garden Street is older by almost two centuries (figure 4.103). It was the western boundary of the Lower Common as far as Linnaean Street, then climbed to the saddle between Avon and Observatory hills. Originally known as the Way to the Great Swamp and then as the road to the brickyards (after an early clay pit near Bond Street), parts of Garden Street were called Washington Street and Milk-Porridge Lane after the Revolution. The present name, given in 1848, recalls the Harvard Botanic Garden, which was established in 1805 at the corner of Linnaean Street. Concord Avenue was laid out in 1803 as the Cambridge & Concord Turnpike and went directly over Observatory Hill rather than follow the lower but longer path

FIGURE 4.103 The principal landmark of lower Garden Street is Christ Church, which stands between the Old Burying Ground and William Saunders's 1821 residence, now the rectory. This scene was painted between 1835, when Saunders built 2 Garden Street next door for Sarah Howe, and 1857, when the church was enlarged.

of Garden Street. Horsecar service was established on Garden Street, Concord Avenue, and Craigie Street in 1857; when a double-track electric line was extended to Huron Avenue in 1894 Concord Avenue was widened with a great loss of trees.

LOWER GARDEN AND BRATTLE STREETS BETWEEN HARVARD SQUARE AND MASON STREET

With the exception of the cemetery, the land between Harvard Square and Garden, Brattle, and Mason streets was granted to individuals in 1634 and 1635 as part of the West End allotments. Simon Bradstreet and John Haynes, who received the lion's share, were two of the most important men in the colony. Bradstreet, one of the founders of Newtowne, lived on the southeast corner of Harvard Square and was granted a parcel opposite his house that ran from the Burying Ground to about Palmer Street. The future governor of the Bay Colony soon left Cambridge and sold this land to Herbert Pelham in 1639 (figure 4.104).

John Haynes, who became governor in 1635, lived on Kennedy Street opposite Winthrop Square, and his six-acre lot beyond Bradford's ran past Appian Way. Haynes followed Hooker to Connecticut (where he was governor in 1639–54), and he sold the property to Elizabeth Glover, a widow who in 1641 married Harvard president Henry Dunster. In 1655 Dunster's "barn and plow land" was acquired by Richard Jackson, a selectman and representative (Middlesex Deeds 4/356). Jackson's executors divided his land in 1672. The greater part was acquired by Josiah Parker, an innkeeper, while a smaller tract, now traversed by Appian Way, was known as the "milne [miller's] field" (Middlesex Deeds 12/534). Jackson's will authorized his wife to sell two acres "to the owners of the windmill in case they desire to build to accommodate a miller" (Middlesex Probate 12450).[37]

Stephen Palmer, a tanner whose occupation determined the initial industrial character of Palmer Street and Brattle Square, acquired the east half of Josiah Parker's land in 1741. James Read, another tanner, acquired 3½ acres west of Palmer in 1726. In 1728 he left the land to his son, James Jr., who in 1760 sold a 100-foot-square next to the Burying Ground to the building committee of Christ Church. The Proprietors of Common Lands then transferred the town pound, a roughly equal adjoining parcel that was part of the common, to the committee and realigned the south side of Garden Street to run "strait from the north East Corner of the Burying place to prentices corner Near the widow Hills Dwelling House [at the corner of Mason Street]" (*Proprietors Records,* 358). The cemetery was thus enlarged, and several abutters, including Read, gained additional land along the new boundary (figure 4.105). Read died in 1770, and about 1771 his son James III, a self-styled "gentleman" who owned a store in the village, built an elegant Georgian house set well back from Brattle Street (figure 4.106). Levi Farwell bought the Read property in 1826, sold the house to Dr. John White Webster in 1827, and platted a subdivision on the remainder in 1834. The town acquired three lots for a school and half a century later renamed School Court as Farwell Place (see chapter 7).

The blacksmith Torrey Hancock laid out the first block of Church Street on land he acquired from Thomas Brattle's executors and built a house (now 53 Church Street) in 1827 (see figure 7.88). Painter and glazier Jacob Hill Bates had Oliver Hastings build one of his characteristic bow-fronted Federal houses facing Brattle Street in 1829, which he rented to Richard Henry Dana Sr. in 1832; Dana descendants lived there until 1872. The house was torn down when Church Street was widened in 1926, and the present stores at 47–49 Brattle Street were built in its place. The rest of Church Street developed as an adjunct of the Palmer Street light-industrial quarter, despite the presence of the First Parish Church after 1833 (figure 4.107; see also figure 3.16).

The miller's field passed through several hands until it came into the possession of Richard Hunnewell's executors, college steward Caleb Gannett, Dr. Aaron Hill, and Captain John Walton. In 1800 they laid out Appian Way, the earliest residential subdivision in Old Cambridge, and Joseph Holmes, a Cambridge housewright, built the first house in 1801 (figure 4.108). Five more soon followed, including a large Federal which was occupied by the Browne & Nichols School in 1883 (see figure

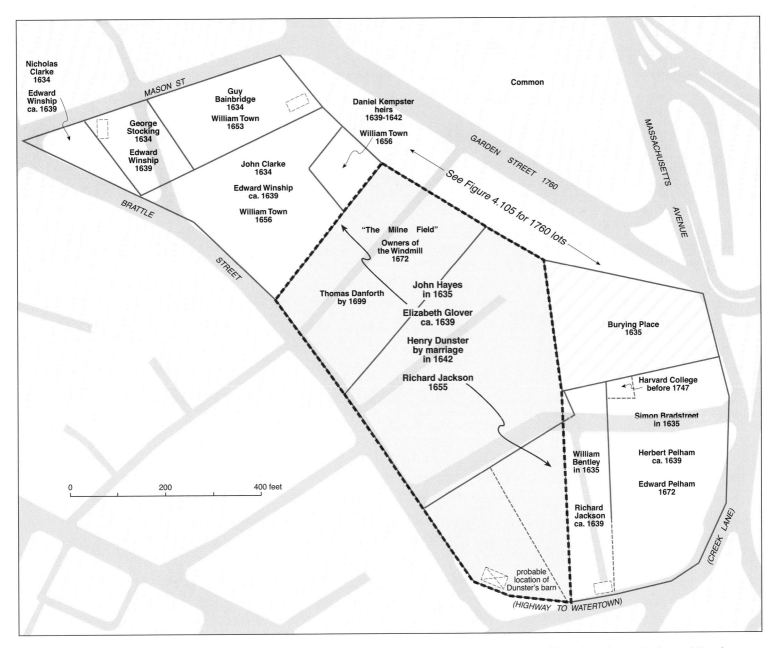

Nicholas
Clarke
1634

Edward
Winship
ca. 1639

MASON ST

Guy
Bainbridge
1634

William Town
1653

George
Stocking
1634

Edward
Winship
1639

BRATTLE

John Clarke
1634

Edward Winship
ca. 1639

William Town
1656

STREET

Daniel Kempster
heirs
1639-1642

William Town
1656

Common

GARDEN STREET 1760

MASSACHUSETTS AVENUE

See Figure 4.105 for 1760 lots

"The Milne Field"

Owners of
the Windmill
1672

Thomas Danforth
by 1699

John Hayes
in 1635

Elizabeth Glover
ca. 1639

Henry Dunster
by marriage
in 1642

Richard Jackson
1655

Burying Place
1635

Harvard College
before 1747

Simon Bradstreet
in 1635

William
Bentley
in 1635

Herbert Pelham
ca. 1639

Edward Pelham
1672

Richard
Jackson
ca. 1639

(CREEK LANE)

0   200   400 feet

probable
location of
Dunster's barn

(HIGHWAY TO WATERTOWN)

FIGURE 4.104 Distribution of lots along lower Garden and Brattle streets between Harvard Square and Mason Street, 1635–99.

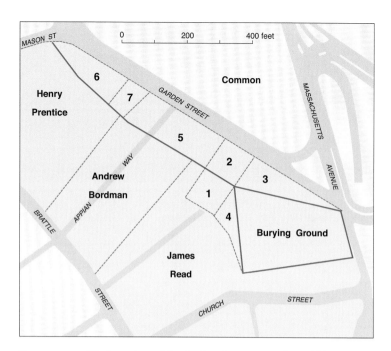

FIGURE 4.105 The boundary of Cambridge Common as adjusted following the Proprietors' sale of the town pound to Christ Church in 1760.

1. James Read to Christ Church, 1760
2. Town Pound: Proprietors to Christ Church, 1760
3. Proprietors to Burying Ground, 1760
4. James Read to Burying Ground, 1767
5, 6. Proprietors to adjoining owners, 1767
7. Schoolhouse lot

FIGURE 4.106 James Read house, 55 Brattle Street (ca. 1771–81), on the corner of Farwell Place. Harvard University moved the Read house further up Farwell Place to make room for Gutman Library in 1969. Photo ca. 1925.

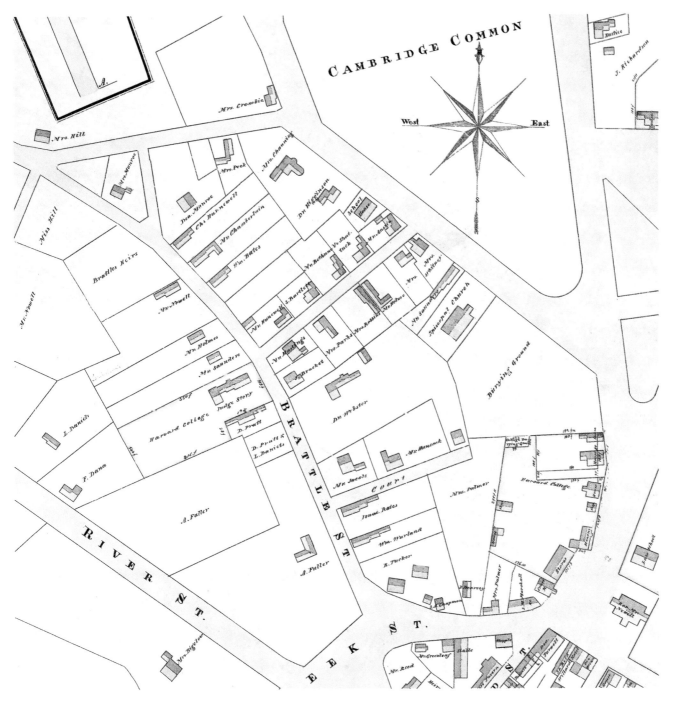

CAMBRIDGE COMMON

West   East

FIGURE 4.107 The western end of the Brattle-Garden block was largely built out by 1833, but the part nearest Harvard Square was only beginning to see the intense development that made it the commercial center of Old Cambridge later in the century.

7.58) The rest of the street filled up in the 1830s and '40s, producing a pleasant jumble of vernacular, mostly Federal style homes. The most notable was another bow-fronted house that Oliver Hastings put up in 1827 for his own use and later sold to John Nichols, a physician (figure 4.109). Radcliffe College displaced all the houses on the west side in the 1920s; only one was moved, to 144 Coolidge Hill in 1929. The east side remained intact until the 1960s, when Harvard began to expand the Graduate School of Education. In 1964 the Episcopal Theological School moved an 1821 house from the site of Larsen Hall to 13 St. John's Road. Harvard razed the rest but in 1969 moved the Read and Nichols houses to a courtyard off Farwell Place to make room for Gutman Library, leaving only carpenter Simeon Withey's 1856 Greek Revival at 10 Appian Way.

In 1821 Thomas Brattle's executors divided the field west of Appian Way into four lots with frontage on Brattle Street and sold them to some of the town's leading tradesmen. Chaisemaker Charles Hunnewell, housewright John Chamberlin, and mason William Bates built similar Federal houses, while John Warland, another mason, put up an early Greek Revival in 1838. The Bates house was moved to 38 Bradbury Road in 1875. The Chamberlin and Warland houses survive as Radcliffe's Buckingham and Putnam houses, but the site of Hunnewell's house became a parking lot in 1960.

After the creation of Appian Way several houses went up along Garden Street. Master housewright William Saunders built the present Christ Church rectory as his own residence in 1821. Sarah Howe, a widow from Northampton who had come to Cambridge to educate her children, bought the lot next door in 1836 and hired Saunders to build a wide-pedimented Greek Revival house with outside chimneys resembling those on Professors Row. Winslow Homer, the painter, grew up in a house west of Appian Way and probably lived there until he moved to New York in 1859 (figure 4.110).

The east corner of Garden and Mason streets passed down in the Prentice family until John Prentice inherited it in 1797. Despite his Harvard education (which his mother paid for

FIGURE 4.108 The north side of Brattle Street near Appian Way, as seen from the corner of Story Street in 1875. The ca. 1787 house at 59 Brattle Street that Thomas Brattle left to Lucy Windship, his housekeeper, in 1801, is across the street at right; the break in the fence beyond it is where Appian Way enters. The city took down the blacksmith's spreading chestnut tree (foreground) in 1876, after widening Brattle Street in 1870–71.

by sweeping the college buildings), Prentice was said to be a remarkably incompetent lawyer who was nonetheless attorney general of New Hampshire in 1787–92. In 1806 he sold the homestead to Nathaniel Ireland, the husband of Sally Prentice, his niece several times removed. Ireland built a magnificent brick house on the corner, but his business supplying iron to shipbuilders failed during the Embargo of 1807, and he lost the place through foreclosure. In 1814 it became the home of

FIGURE 4.109 Dr. John Nichols house, 63 Brattle Street (1827, Oliver Hastings, housewright) and the east side of Appian Way looking north from Brattle Street. Harvard razed most of these houses for Larsen Hall and Gutman Library in 1964–70. The Nichols house was moved to Farwell Place in 1969. Photo 1969.

FIGURE 4.110 Houses on Garden Street facing Cambridge Common. The houses at 1, 2, and 3 Garden survive; the rest were removed by Radcliffe College before 1930. Winslow Homer's childhood home was at 8 Garden Street, just left of Fay House. Photo 1875.

Boylston Professor Joseph McKean; after he died, his widow advertised it as "a lot … containing about one acre, with a new, large and convenient Dwelling House, a Barn, Out Buildings, and a Garden, containing a large number of the best kinds of young Fruit Trees … [being] one of the most pleasant and eligible situations in Cambridge, for a man of business, or a literary gentleman" (*Columbian Centinel,* Sept. 19, 1818). A number of distinguished occupants, including Edward Everett and William Ellery Channing, rented the house until it became the home of Judge Samuel P.P. Fay of the Middlesex County probate court in 1835 (figure 4.111). The Society for the Collegiate Instruction of Women acquired Fay House in 1885 and substantially enlarged it in 1890 and 1892 (see figure 7.76).

The triangular block at the intersection of Brattle and Mason streets exemplifies the architectural diversity of Old Cambridge. About 1718 Jacob Hill erected a house that was later owned by Deacon James Munroe, a blacksmith (figure 4.112). Munroe's

FIGURE 4.112 Jacob Hill-James Munroe house, 83 Brattle Street (1718–65). Moved to 8 Willard Street in 1908. Photo ca. 1908.

daughters Susan and Mary built Radcliffe's present Alumni House next door in 1836, and in 1846 his son James sold the lot west of the house to Michael Norton, a mason, who built the Gothic cottage at 85 Brattle Street (see figure 6.66). Cambridgeport grocer Theodore Seavey put up an incongruous brick row on Mason Street as an investment in 1869. Wadsworth Chambers, one of the few apartment houses to penetrate the defenses of the neighborhood, displaced the Hill-Munroe house to Willard Street in 1908.

HILL AND WYETH HOMESTEADS

West of Mason Street, two prolific families of Puritan descent, the Wyeths and the Hills, retained their homesteads when others were selling to Tories and remained to reap the benefits in the suburban era. Nicholas Wyeth, progenitor of the Wyeth family in America, settled near the corner of Garden and Berkeley streets in 1645, and his descendants remained in possession for more than two centuries. Four Hill brothers from Malden married into Cambridge families in the early 18th century and populated every corner of the village.

FIGURE 4.111 Fay House, the Washington Elm, and the Aaron Hill house on Garden Street opposite the Common, ca. 1873.

FIGURE 4.113 View west along Garden Street, ca. 1868. To the left of the Washington Elm is the ca. 1710 Solomon Prentice house at 14 Garden Street; at extreme right is the 1822 house of Rhoda Beal at 1 Waterhouse Street. The Massachusetts Arsenal stands in the distance, along with several more of the elms that once lined Garden Street.

The Hill homestead at the corner of Garden and Mason streets originated in a grant to Golden Moore about 1642. Captain Pyam Blowers, a shipmaster, purchased the property in 1672, and his son Thomas sold the house and four acres along Mason Street to Abraham Hill, a mason, in 1713. Five years later Hill married a shoemaker's daughter, Prudence Hancock, and built a house where he died in 1754. His son Aaron, also a mason, built another house on the homestead in 1755. In 1784 Aaron sold his father's house at Mason and Brattle streets with 1½ acres of land to Josiah Moore, a housewright, deacon, and selectman. After Moore's death in 1814 a dame school occupied the property until his heirs sold it in 1857. The Shepard Congregational Society acquired Hill's Corner from Samuel Batchelder in 1868 and built the present church a year later (see figures 7.20 and 7.56).

The Hills retained the rest of their property well into the 19th century. Abraham's grandson Aaron graduated from Harvard in 1776 and became a naval surgeon, merchant, and politician before ending his career as postmaster of Boston. When he died in 1830, he owned the three-acre homestead, 21 acres nearby, and about nine acres of marsh and meadow. Two of his daughters, Hannah and Harriet, successively married Willard Phillips, an attorney, who laid out Phillips Place after the property was partitioned among Hill's heirs in 1841. The trustees of the Episcopal Theological School bought the remainder and sold the Aaron Hill house to James Quigley, who moved it to 17 Brown Street in 1867 (figure 4.114; see also figure 4.40).

In 1645 Nicholas Wyeth, a mason, acquired a house on Garden Street west of the Hill place. He died in 1650, and by the end of the century his son John had greatly expanded the family's holdings. Jonas Wyeth, John's grandson, sold some fields to John Vassall in 1774 and to Andrew Craigie in 1797, and his son Major Jonas Wyeth was able to buy more land elsewhere. The major's second son, who called himself Jonas Wyeth 2nd, married Torrey Hancock's daughter Mary and became a merchant in Philadelphia. After his older brother, Augustus, died unmarried in 1831, Jonas returned and began to develop the family farm with stylish residences that he rented, always a good proposition in a college

FIGURE 4.114 Hill's Corner, looking north up Mason Street from the corner of Brattle, showing the Deanery (1879; demolished 1964; see figure 6.113), 2 Phillips Place (1852, moved to 170 Brattle Street, 1965), 11 Mason Street (1836), and the Shepard Congregational Church (1870). Photo ca. 1890.

FIGURE 4.115 Solomon Prentice house, 14 Garden Street (ca. 1710; demolished before 1886). Prentice was a husbandman and brickmaker whose house stood between the Hill and Wyeth properties. The house was extensively repaired about 1867, but in this view retains its early chimney.

town. In 1849 he was taxed for seven; three survive on Garden Street and Concord Avenue (figure 4.116). In 1859 Wyeth moved to a new house on Raymond Street, where he died in 1868.

The Greek Revival house at 22 Garden Street that Wyeth rebuilt from a much older dwelling about 1837 is associated with the notorious Parkman murder case. Wyeth rented the house to chemistry professor John White Webster, who had long struggled to support his family and was forced to give up previous residences on Ware and Brattle streets. Webster habitually borrowed small sums to cover expenses; among his lenders was George Parkman, a wealthy merchant who mysteriously disappeared on November 23, 1849. A few days later a custodian found human remains in a furnace at the Harvard Medical School. Webster was convicted on circumstantial evidence and executed in August 1850, and his wife and daughters left for an extended visit to Fayal in the Azores. George Browne, cofounder of the Browne & Nichols School, acquired the house in the 1890s, and in 1897 built a three-story classroom building on the side yard at the corner of Berkeley Street (see figure 7.59). The Wyeth-Webster house became a dormitory, and in 1897 Browne built a Shingle Style house for himself next door at 24 Garden Street (see chapter 7).

By the 1950s all four houses had been cut up into apartments, and their future seemed bleak. Cambridge developer Louis DiGiovanni obtained a variance for a fifty-room motel in 1974 but did not act on it. The owners of the Commander Hotel intended to replace them with a parking lot but were thwarted by Cambridge's rent control ordinance. When this was abolished in 1995, they moved to clear the site, but the historical commission brokered a compromise with adjoining property owners that restored the houses and allowed a small parking lot behind them.

In 1851 Jonas Wyeth 2nd and his neighbor, Joseph Worcester, laid out a new street parallel to Concord Avenue and offered house lots on terms that barred noxious trades and required generous setbacks. Berkeley Street's appeal was due in part to its proximity to the Harvard Branch station across the Common,

FIGURE 4.116 Jacob Wyeth's rental houses included the Wyeth-Webster house, 22 Garden Street (1837, left) and 26–28 Garden Street (1842, far right). The latter originally had a portico over two bow windows, a hallmark of houses built by Oliver Hastings, but Dr. Walter Wesselhoeft, Professor of Obstetrics at the Boston University Medical School, removed it in 1897. The Queen Anne style George H. Browne house, 24 Garden Street (1897, J.H. Wright, architect), stands between them. Another Wyeth rental at 10 Concord Avenue (1837) is out of sight at right. Photo 2009.

and it developed quickly as Boston lawyers and businessmen built houses of some distinction. Richard Henry Dana Jr., author of *Two Years Before the Mast,* described its appeal in 1851: "The situation is not beautiful, but it is central, yet retired, off the highway & free from dust. The beautiful situations are all too far off from coaches and stations, for a man who cannot keep a coach" (*Journal,* II, 437). Dana was the first resident of Berkeley Street in 1852 and named it for the English philosopher, Bishop George Berkeley (see figure 6.73). He moved back to Boston in 1869, but his family's renewed connection to Old Cambridge continued for another two generations.

Eleven of the eighteen houses now on Berkeley Street were completed by 1863, giving it the best concentration of Bracketed Italianates and Mansards in the city. That year schoolmaster Lyman Williston built Cambridge's sole remaining towered Italianate villa at number 15 (see figure 6.75). The house was set in a large garden with frontage on both Concord Avenue

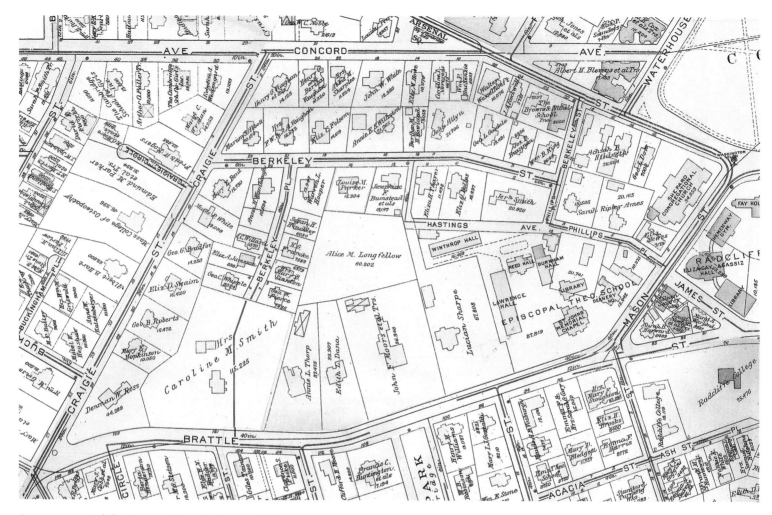

FIGURE 4.117 Berkeley Street and Berkeley Place in 1916.

and Berkeley Street; a one-story wing housed the Berkeley Street School. After Williston's death in 1899 the wing was detached, and in 1912 it was remodeled as a separate dwelling. The later Shingle Style and stucco houses were the work of well-known architects who maintained the street's high standards.

Berkeley Place underwent three waves of building activity. Reverend William Newell laid out four lots in his backyard at 20 Berkeley Street in 1890. Three houses were begun in 1892, ranging from a "cosy Colonial" at number 1 to a large shingled house at

3 for German literature professor Kuno Francke (*Chronicle,* Sept. 24, 1892). In 1900 the executors of Chauncey Smith, a patent attorney who had purchased the Joseph Worcester estate in 1870, extended the street "into the forbidden recesses of the old Longfellow estate" and laid out the first of eight house lots that they and the next owner, attorney Stoughton Bell, created gradually over the next forty years (*Tribune,* Aug. 11, 1900). The last two houses were built behind the Worcester house in 1941, about the same time that 121A, 123, and 125 Brattle Street went up in its side yard.

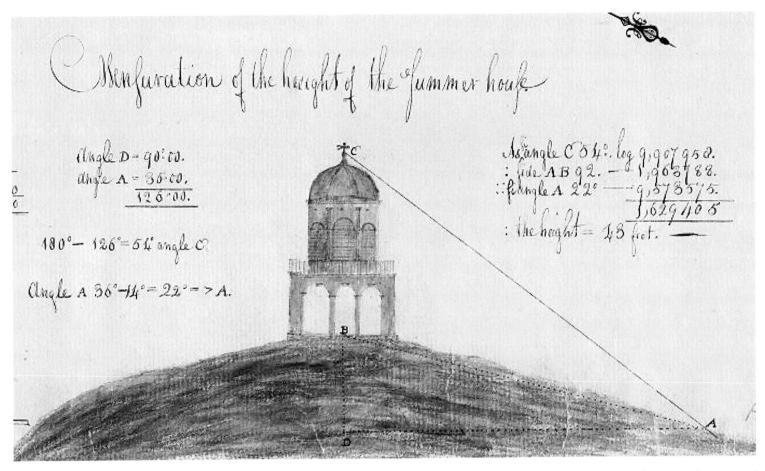

Mensuration of the height of the Summer house

Angle D = 90°:00.
Angle A = 36°:00.
126°:00.

180° − 126° = 54° angle C

Angle A 36° − 14° = 22° = > A.

As angle C 54°: log 9,907,958.
: side AB 92. — 1,963,88.
:: angle A 22° — 9,573,575.
1,629,405
: the height = 48 feet.

FIGURE 4.118 Nathaniel Tracy's ca. 1781–86 summerhouse near the summit of Observatory Hill, as seen in an undergraduate's mathematical thesis in 1802. As tall as a four-story building, it was still standing during Mrs. Craigie's ownership.

OBSERVATORY HILL

This part of the West End was laid out in 1634 with two- to eight-acre lots along the west side of Garden Street facing the Lower Common, and by 1635 it had about six homesteads. After the familiar process of consolidation, only three were left by 1750: John Wyeth's six-acre place opposite present Walker Street, Jacob Hill's 30 acres just beyond, and Thomas Prentice's 1½ acres now occupied by Garden Terrace. John Vassall

Jr. acquired Hill's farm in 1770 by writ of seizure for debt and thereby expanded his estate up the south-facing slope of the hill (see figure 4.22). The second rector of Christ Church, Winwood Serjeant, built a house on Garden Street opposite Linnaean "on land belonging to Col. John Vassall which he promised to give to the Church, and to pay Mr. Serjeant for the expense." This was evidently a four-room house that contained Reverend Serjeant's library of "near one thousand volumes worth in America £250," four feather beds, furniture, utensils, and sundry items, including "thirty gallons spirituous liquors." A Negro man valued at £50 presided over a two-acre garden enclosed by a board fence; all were confiscated or lost when the Serjeants fled Cambridge in 1775 (PRO, AO 13/48, 487–88).

The upper part of Vassall's land was known as "the summerhouse lot" after the Concord Turnpike severed it from the rest of the estate in 1803. The summerhouse, "a pretty piece of ornamental architecture," was said in 1792 to have been built by Nathaniel Tracy, which would date it to 1781–86 (figure 4.118). It was a 40-foot-high folly with a second-story belvedere that, "after Beacon Hill … presents the most beautiful, extensive, and variegated landscape in the world" (Cutting, 61). In 1792 Andrew Craigie acquired the Prentice homestead, removed the house, and laid a pipe from its spring to his mansion on Brattle Street; that property was subsequently known as "the aqueduct lot." Five years later he also bought the Wyeth homestead, which included an acre across Garden Street in the Lower Common.

Harvard acquired the summerhouse lot in 1841 as a site for its observatory, which was then on Quincy Street (see chapter 10). President Quincy had Alexander Wadsworth lay out Bond Street (named for astronomy professor George Phillips Bond) and divide the surplus land south of it into twenty-two lots (figures 4.119–4.120). In 1845 the university sold two lots at the south end to Thomas Stearns, who put up a stable for his New Line of omnibuses. Two years later, Epes Sargent Dixwell, master of the Boston Latin School, bought four lots at the corner of Bond and Garden streets and built a Classical Revival mansion at 58 Garden Street (figure 4.121). Dane Professor of Law Theophilus Parsons bought nine lots and built a large Greek Revival house facing Garden Street. When Professor Daniel Treadwell retired in 1847 he sold his 1838 Regency style house on Quincy Street to Professor Jared Sparks and had William Saunders build a near-duplicate on Concord Avenue (figure 4.122).

The south-facing lot at the intersection of Garden Street and the Concord Turnpike, a quarter of an acre "in the form of a heater," or triangular clothes iron, was severed from the Wyeth farm by the turnpike in 1803 and never belonged to Harvard.

John Richards of Newton sold the property in 1819 to Adam Lewis, "a man of culler" related to an extended family that settled nearby (Middlesex Deeds 231/98; see "Lewisville" below). Lewis sold his "black shingled little house with an outside staircase, in a plot full of dockweed" to Thomas Stearns, the omnibus proprietor, in 1846. Franklin Perrin, a Boston businessman, built the present Second Empire residence facing Arsenal Square on the site in 1870 (Bowen, "Follen Street," 94).

All three estates on the summerhouse lot were soon subdivided. William Dean Howells, then editor of *The Atlantic Monthly*, was the first buyer of Parson's land in 1872, when he and his wife were renting 3 Berkeley after leaving their first Cambridge home on Sacramento Street (figure 4.123; see also figure 4.207). Parsons died in 1882, and by 1886 there were five more houses on his Concord Avenue frontage. Van Brunt & Howe designed number 35 for George E. Carter, the son of a Cambridgeport businessman (see figure 6.124).

The car line that was built on Concord Avenue in 1894 made the neighborhood desirable for apartment houses in the 1920s. Hamilton Harlow designed the graceless forty-one-unit apartment building that his father's firm put up in 1924 at 52 Garden Street, next to the Parsons house (which was razed two years later). The Harlows built a thirty-three-unit building at 31 Concord Avenue in 1925, and in 1959 Continental Terrace, a seven-story apartment building designed by Hugh Stubbins & Associates, replaced the Treadwell house, although its carriage house survives next door (see figure 6.237). The Dixwell house was divided into condominiums, and the grounds were crowded with seven townhouses and a detached two-family house in 1977–79.

The south side of Concord Avenue evolved in a similarly dispiriting fashion. The Harlows built Bradlee Court, a thirty-two-unit building on Craigie Circle, in 1917, and by 1963 ten buildings containing 477 apartments had replaced eight single-family houses near the intersection of Craigie Street. Bainbridge Bunting, who witnessed much of this construction, described 20–22 (1929, Silverman & Brown) and 24–26 Concord Avenue

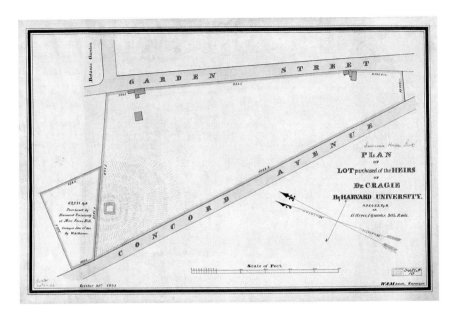

FIGURE 4.119 Craigie's executors described the summerhouse lot as "8 acres with 2 dwelling houses, separated from the homestead by [the] Concord turnpike" (Middlesex Probate 5303). The structure stood on the square mound near the northwest corner of the lot but had disappeared when this survey was made in 1841. The house in the upper right corner was Reverend Winwood Serjeant's rectory.

FIGURE 4.120 Harvard subdivided its land into house lots in 1842, at first reserving only the site of the summerhouse for the observatory. The lots north of Bond Street never materialized.

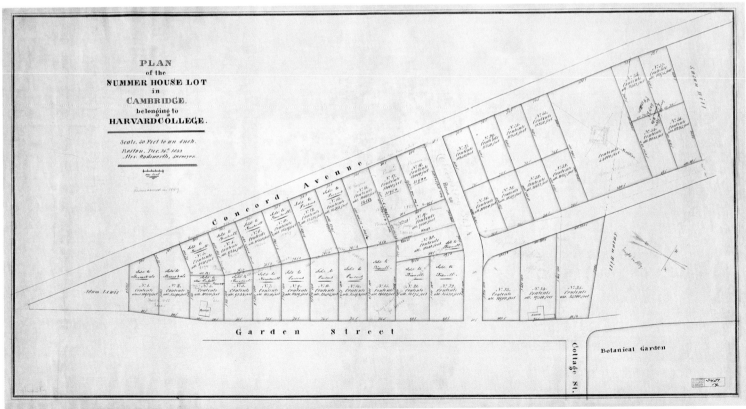

FIGURE 4.121 Epes Sargent Dixwell house, 58 Garden Street (1847–48, attributed to Henry Greenough, architect). See also figure 2.35. Photo ca. 1887.

FIGURE 4.123 William Dean Howells house, 37 Concord Avenue (1872–73, Elinor Mead Howells and William R. Mead, designers). Mrs. Howell's brother, William Rutherford Mead, was a principal of the New York architectural firm of McKim, Mead & White. Photo after 1894.

FIGURE 4.122 Professor Daniel Treadwell house, 29 Concord Avenue (1847, William A. Saunders, housewright; demolished 1959). Photo ca. 1938.

FIGURE 4.124 Franklin Perrin house, 1 Arsenal Square (1870), with 36–38 and 40–42 Garden Street (1993, CEA Group, architects). The new houses healed the scar left by demolition in the 1970s. Photo 2009.

(1970, Saul Moffie) as making "the grimmest blank, walled-in space in Cambridge. It shows what the city could easily become—a deadly mediocrity" (CHC inventory, ca. 1970).

The abrupt demolition of three houses on Concord Avenue and Garden Street in 1978 convinced the city council to adopt a demolition delay ordinance. Neighborhood protests blocked the project, and the site lay fallow for fifteen years until Cambridge developer Steven Cohen built four well-proportioned neo-Victorian two- and three-family houses. The visually important Perrin house on Arsenal Square was restored in 1992 (figure 4.124).

Beyond Craigie Street, Arthur Gilman's Cambridge School for Girls put up a classroom building at 34 Concord Avenue in 1898 and assembled a campus of older houses before relocating to Weston in 1934; this was occupied by the Lesley-Ellis Nursery School before it was acquired by Radcliffe College for the Bunting Institute in 1984 (see figure 7.65). Just uphill, Mansard and Queen Anne houses from the 1870s, '80s, and '90s perched on the slope above Healy Street. The Harlows displaced one of these in 1930. In 1975 the DiGiovanni brothers of Belmont took down 44 Concord Avenue, an artfully disguised six-family on the corner of Parker Street, and 54 Concord Avenue, a textbook late Mansard, and replaced them with two "pillbox" apartment buildings of the sort that threatened many neighborhoods at the time (figure 4.125).

Old Cambridge's earliest Irish immigrant settlement lay just outside the Vassall-Craigie estate. Dr. Aaron Hill acquired the summit of Observatory Hill in 1774, and it remained in agricultural use until his daughters, Susan Hill and Harriet Hill Phillips, inherited it in 1841. Asa Murdock, a Cambridgeport storekeeper, laid out five large lots on Concord Avenue and eleven small lots on an L-shaped alley originally called Sparks Street Court. Patrick Holly, a liquor dealer, bought two in 1847 and conveyed them to Bishop John Fitzpatrick for St. Peter's Church (see chapter 7). Murdock built a house on Concord Avenue and sold lots to the Irish laborers who flocked to the barren hilltop when entrepreneurs began to exploit the vast clay beds nearby (see *Report Five: Northwest Cambridge*). The expansion of the Deane estate at 80 Sparks Street in the 1860s displaced the houses on the south side of the alley, and in 1897 the diocese replaced Murdock's house with a parish hall (see figure 7.21). Sparks Street Court was renamed Manassas Avenue in 1908 for Reverend Manasses Dougherty, the parish's first priest, and in 1927 the Archdiocese razed four more houses for a school. Only the 1847 Patrick Cooney house at 21 recalls the workers' cottages that once characterized this area.

The balance of the Hill farm between Concord Avenue and Garden Street was also partitioned between the sisters. Susan sold half of her land to Harvard in 1842 and laid out the south end of Madison Street in 1846 with six lots on each side. Three were sold with the condition that the buyer erect at least one "good and convenient dwelling house, 2 stories high," but twenty-five years later there were only two houses on the street (Middlesex Deeds 500/399). Harriet extended Madison to Garden Street in 1847. Harvard owned most of the east side by 1873, but it never

FIGURE 4.125 Patrick Moriarty house, 44 Concord Avenue (1895, Eugene T. Harrington, architect; demolished 1974). Cambridge's 1962 zoning code encouraged the replacement of houses like this with large apartment blocks, to the detriment of neighborhood character. Photo 1967.

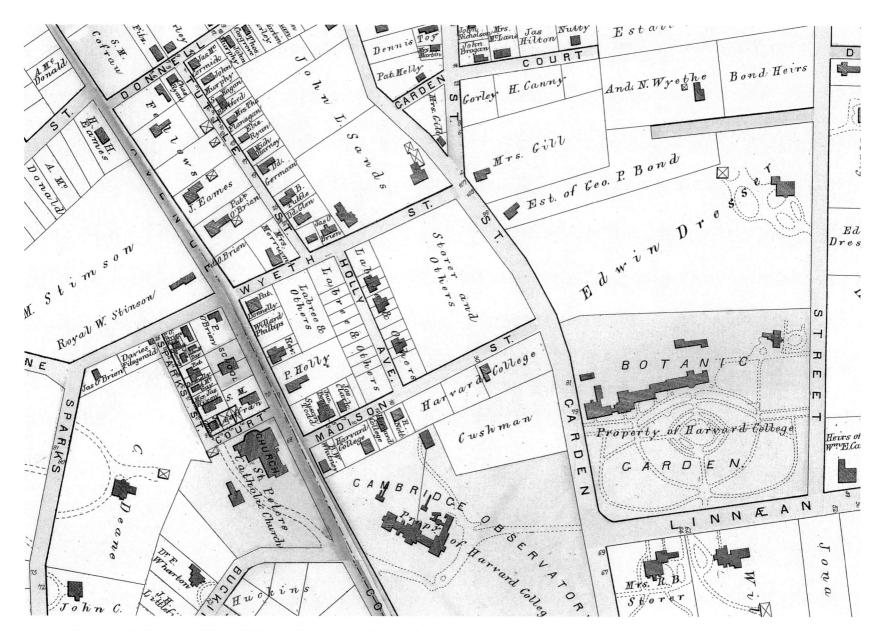

FIGURE 4.126 Observatory Hill in 1873. Garden Terrace was developed on the lot labeled "Cushman"; Gray Gardens West occupies the lot owned by "Storer and others."

FIGURE 4.127 The first house on Garden Terrace was number 6, designed by H. Langford Warren in 1904 as his own residence. Photo ca. 1906.

acquired Craigie's aqueduct lot and eventually sold the frontage for residential development (figure 4.126).

The Harvard Botanic Garden occupied a 7½-acre plot bounded by Raymond and Linnaean streets in the West End Field allotment of 1634 (see chapter 5). The garden was established in 1805 and laid out in 1808; in 1810 a house and conservatory were built for the resident professor (see figure 5.85). Harvard sold the house in 1910 to Allen Cox, an architect, who moved it to 88 Garden Street. The university closed the Botanic Garden after World War II and in 1949 hired DesGranges & Steffian to design the Botanic Garden Apartments for returning veterans (see figure 6.236). Two new streets were named for Benjamin Robinson and Merritt Fernald, past curators of the herbarium.

Until about 1900, the Botanic Garden's nearest neighbors were Noah Wyeth's ca. 1782 farmhouse at 107 Garden Street (altered in the mid-19th century and modernized in 1956 and 1962) and Mary Wyeth's 1841 cottage at 99 Garden Street. Boston lawyer Charles Cushman subdivided the aqueduct lot in 1904, and Garden Terrace became a pleasant (if crowded) cul-de-sac with six houses built between 1904 and 1930 (figure 4.127).

Gray Gardens was one of several early 20th century subdivisions influenced by the Garden City movement, where every aspect of the development was controlled to prevent the kind of overbuilding seen on Garden Terrace. In 1922 rumors that speculators (including future governor Charles F. Hurley) were threatening "an outbreak of 'two-deckers'" prompted some neighbors with no previous development experience—Garden Terrace residents Alva Morrison, a cotton broker, Arthur Nichols, a bond salesman, and Melville Eastham, a radio engineer—to take an option on an 8½-acre site bounded by Raymond and

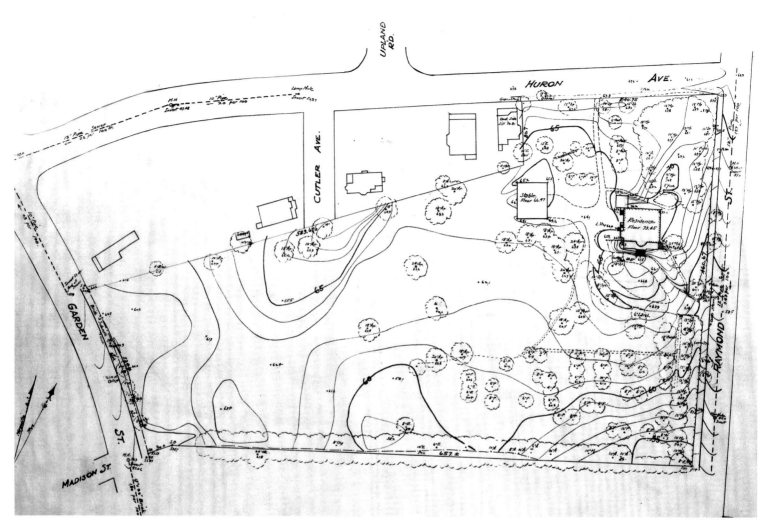

FIGURE 4.128 The Wyeth-Dresser house sat on an eminence overlooking the Botanic Garden; this topographical plan by the Olmsted Brothers in 1922 shows a gently sloping field that extended to Garden Street.

Garden streets known as the Dresser estate (*Chronicle,* July 14, 1923). This property had originated with Jonas Wyeth 2nd, who built a house at 60 Raymond Street in 1859 (figure 4.128). Edwin Dresser, a publisher of pocket diaries, purchased Wyeth's place in 1869 and later bought a field across Garden Street.

Gray Gardens was a remarkable citizen initiative of the pre-zoning era. Morrison, Nichols, and Eastham formed the Garden Street Trust with eighteen like-minded individuals. The Olmsted Brothers prepared a design for Gray Gardens East with

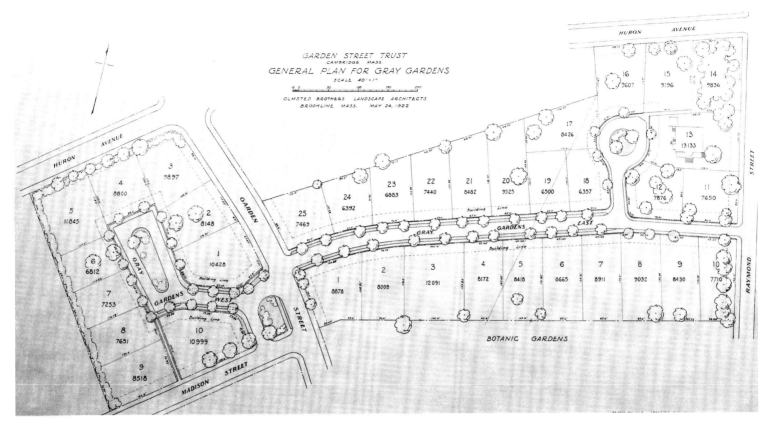

FIGURE 4.129   The Olmsted Brothers plan for Gray Gardens East and West, 1922.

twenty-five lots along a gently curving street between Garden and Raymond streets. For the 2.6 acres that became Gray Gardens West, they laid out ten irregularly shaped lots on a landscaped cul-de-sac that cut diagonally through the block (figure 4.129). The project was not meant to make a profit; investors paid only for the cost of land and improvements. Thirty-year deed restrictions controlled development, and speculators were excluded. Construction was limited to single-family dwellings, and a volunteer committee approved the design of each house.

Morrison and Nichols went on to develop Coolidge Hill in 1925, apparently on conventional for-profit principles.

Most of the homes on Gray Gardens East and West were Georgian Revival, and four architectural firms—Putnam & Cox (8), Duguid & Martin (4), Howe & Manning (3), and Frost & Raymond (2)—accounted for more than half. The most unusual are a small Arts & Crafts house at 16 Gray Gardens East that one of the original trustees, A. Graham Carey, designed for himself in 1922, and a 1798 house that was dismantled and moved from Hall's Corner in South Duxbury to 20 Gray Gardens West in 1930 (see figure 6.189). Gray Gardens remains surprisingly intact, although two houses that were constructed after the restrictions expired in 1952 prove the value of consistent design standards. Seventeen Gray Gardens East (1958) is a banal Ranch, while 22 (1962) is a remarkably insensitive three-story International Style box with minimal setbacks.

THE LOWER COMMON AND AVON HILL

The level plain behind the village was bounded on the north and west by the glacial moraine now known as Avon and Observatory hills and on the east by the Pine Swamp and Dana Hill. The road to Concord, which is now Massachusetts Avenue, ran due north, passing the foot of the moraine before turning northwest. Garden Street crossed the moraine at a low point and ended in the Fresh Pond marshes. In the first century of settlement, the public land between them extended to Linnaean Street at the base of Avon Hill; this was known as the Lower Common or Cow Common, to distinguish it from the communal Ox Pasture that ran from the north side of the hill to Alewife Brook (see figure 4.154). Today's Cambridge Common is a remnant of the Lower Common.

LOWER COMMON

The Proprietors of Common Lands divided the Lower Common in 1724. They had distributed most land in present-day Cambridge to the townsmen during the first decade of settlement but retained large tracts along Massachusetts Avenue as common pasture. The trend away from communal livestock herding eventually made these redundant, and the Proprietors' last large distribution consisted of 52 lots in present-day Arlington, 27 on Watson's Plain in North Cambridge, and 20 in the Lower Common.

Grants in the 63-acre Lower Common ranged from 1 to 5¾ acres. The Proprietors divided the land closest to the village into nine small parcels with valuable road frontage. At the north end, there were eleven fields 600 feet deep with 50 to 200 feet of frontage on Linnaean Street. No new roads were necessary, and only a gravel pit on Massachusetts Avenue and a watering hole on Garden Street were reserved for public use.

The distribution of lots followed ancient practice. In the 1648 division of Shawshine (Billerica), for example, the Proprietors awarded a few town leaders large tracts and then granted townsmen 10 to 400 acres in proportion to the land they already owned. Seventy-five years later, town clerk Andrew Bordman, who moderated the Proprietors' meetings, received the initial

FIGURE 4.130 Cambridge Common and Waterhouse Street in 1808–9, with Avon Hill and the Cooper-Frost-Austin farm in the distance. From left to right are the Frost-Waterhouse house (1753, now 7 Waterhouse Street), Walton brothers' carpentry shop, the Red Lion Tavern (1794), and the James Wyeth house (1724) on the Concord Road (Massachusetts Avenue at about Chauncy Street).

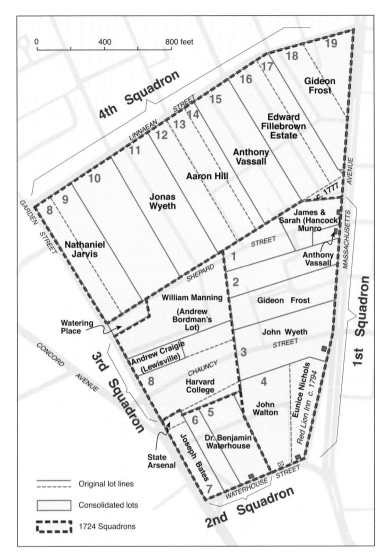

FIGURE 4.131 The Lower Common, showing the original divisions in 1724 (numbered lots and solid or dashed property lines) and ownership in 1800 (names).

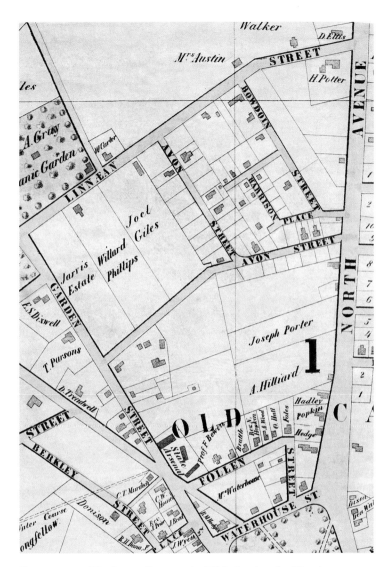

FIGURE 4.132 The Lower Common in 1854, showing the Waterhouse property, the Massachusetts Arsenal, and Lewisville (the cluster of houses above the state arsenal).

and largest distribution of the Lower Common, 5¾ acres next to the watering place. The remainder was divided into four "squadrons," from which eligible parties could literally draw lots according to their rank in the community.[38] The first squadron consisted of three lots on Massachusetts Avenue that were drawn

by future governor Jonathan Belcher, Captain Moses Bordman, a selectman, and the heirs of Nathaniel Fessenden, former register of probate and schoolteacher. Farmers Solomon Prentice and Ephraim Frost, Deacon Henry Prentice, and Harvard College drew the four lots facing the Common in the second squadron.

Jonathan Wyeth, a mason, won the only lot in the third squadron, but also the first lot in the fourth, on Linnaean Street. Most of the remaining lots were also drawn by high-ranking townsmen, including Judge Francis Foxcroft, Sheriff Samuel Gookin, and Lieutenant Amos Marrett. Rank was not an absolute prerogative, however; John Leverett, president of Harvard College and "ruler of the Town as well as [the] College" had to be satisfied with 4½ acres on Watson's Plain (Paige, 599).

The Lower Common was more suitable for pasture than cultivation, and most of the new owners soon sold out; fifty years later, only the Frosts, Bordmans, Wyeths, and Harvard College retained their grants. Some of the lots were consolidated into larger parcels, and some were divided again. Because the grantees all had homes elsewhere, the area remained unsettled for decades. In 1775 there were only three residents, all on the Concord Road. John Wyeth lived near the corner of Chauncy Street, while Benjamin Crackbone, a tanner, and Torrey Hancock (the blacksmith's father), a bricklayer, lived near Shepard Street. The land—probably worn out after nearly a century in common use—was affordable for African Americans. Anthony Vassall acquired Benjamin Crackbone's place, and Peter Lewis bought a field on Garden Street that became the nucleus of Lewisville, the only African American community in Old Cambridge.

The street layout of the Lower Common reflects the 1724 land divisions. Follen, Langdon, and Walker streets and Hudson Place are L-shaped or curved to maximize the frontage on parcels that were both deep and wide. Hurlbut, Bowdoin, Avon, Gray, and upper Walker streets run the length of the old fields off Linnaean Street, while Chauncy, Shepard, and Martin streets crossed lots and required coordination between owners (figure 4.132).

Waterhouse and Follen streets

Toward the end of the 18th century, the lots facing the Common were owned by the Walton brothers, who had a carpentry shop; Gideon Frost, a blacksmith, who rented out the house he built in 1753 (now 7 Waterhouse Street); Harvard College, which still owned the field it had been granted in 1724; and Joseph Bates, a housewright, who owned the corner of Garden Street. Captain John Walton erected the Red Lion Inn on the Massachusetts Avenue corner in 1794.

Harvard acquired Gideon Frost's house in 1793 for Dr. Benjamin Waterhouse (1754–1846), Hersey Professor of the Theory and Practice of Physic (see figure 6.32). Waterhouse was a Quaker from Rhode Island who had spent the war years studying in Edinburgh and Leyden, where he began a lifelong friendship with John Adams. On his return in 1782 he was one of the best-educated physicians in America, but Boston's home-grown doctors disliked his religion and questioned his loyalty; perhaps in consequence, he developed a reputation of being obstinate and contentious. The medical community also resented his introduction of Dr. Edward Jenner's improved smallpox vaccine (Waterhouse supplied Thomas Jefferson with enough to protect his family and two hundred slaves). James Russell Lowell alleged that Waterhouse had placed a boastful advertisement, "Lost, a gold snuff-box with the inscription, 'The Jenner of the Old World to the Jenner of the New'" (Lowell, *Fireside Travels,* 83). The actual inscription reads only "Edward Jenner to Bn Waterhouse."[39] President Madison appointed Waterhouse superintendent of military hospitals in New England after Harvard dismissed him in 1812. Such was the animosity toward him that two decades after his death Harvard librarian John Langdon Sibley had to hide his portrait to avoid the ire of such "old Fogies" as George Ticknor ("Private Journal," Jan. 12, 1864).

Waterhouse constantly badgered the college to improve his house, and in 1809 Harvard sold it to him along with an adjoining tract on Garden Street. In 1817, when the state approached him about selling some land for the arsenal, he argued that his 9 or 10 acres were "just enough to keep my creatures and amuse me in its cultivation." In 1835 he wrote that he had "raised every domestic vegetable underground and above it for my table, and grain for [my] horses and domestic animals" (A.M. Howe, 12, and Meyer, 18).

Joseph Bates's western lot had only a little frontage on Waterhouse Street, and when the Concord Turnpike was laid out across it in 1803 the remainder was a narrow triangle just big enough for two houses. About 1822 Rhoda Beal, a widow, built a house facing the Common, and Aaron Parker built another west of it facing Garden Street. Beal's house became the home of Reverend Richard Manning Hodges, a Unitarian minister noted for his arbor of black Hamburg grapes, while Parker's was for years occupied by two families of spinsters. Apartment buildings displaced both houses in the early 20th century (figure 4.133).

In 1861 Henry Glover, a Boston feather dealer, moved the Red Lion Inn to Wendell Street and replaced it with a large Mansard that now sits in perpetual shadow at 44 Follen Street, where it was moved in 1923 to make room for the Christian Science Church. Arthur Gilman, first regent of Radcliffe College and founder of the Cambridge School for Girls, put up a stylish Queen Anne at 5 Waterhouse about 1882, and Harold Whiting, a physics instructor, built an up-to-date Colonial Revival at 9 in 1887. Only the Waterhouse and Whiting houses remain, dominated by Mather Court (1916) and Concord Hall (1915) on the west and the Puritan Arms (1940) on the east.

Charles Follen, a German political refugee who arrived with a recommendation from the Marquis de Lafayette in 1824, was another prominent resident. Follen married Eliza Lee Cabot of Boston in 1828, and President Kirkland hired him as Harvard's first instructor in German after his father-in-law agreed to pay his salary for five years. The Follens were strong abolitionists, which alienated both family and school, and his appointment ended when Mr. Cabot declined to renew the arrangement. Follen became a Unitarian minister and designed the unique eight-sided church that still stands in East Lexington.[40]

Professor Follen built a house on the site of the Walton brothers' carpentry shop in 1831 and laid out four lots in the back yard after he lost his Harvard post (figure 4.134). A new street ran down his side yard and then turned to follow the 1632 "Pallysadoe," by then a ditch that carried an intermittent stream. The bow-fronted Federal-Greek Revival at 29 (1838), the only house built during Follen's lifetime, has had many distinguished occupants. Several young men set up housekeeping there in 1852.

FIGURE 4.133 Beal-Hodges house, 4 Concord Avenue (ca. 1823) with its greenhouse and grape arbor (all demolished 1916). The house at left is 7 Concord Avenue (1882), on its original site at number 5. Photo ca. 1890.

FIGURE 4.134 Charles Follen house, 11 Waterhouse Street (1831), demolished in 1940 and replaced by the apartment building at 50 Follen Street. Photo ca. 1938.

Geologist Josiah Whitney used it as a base between western expeditions; astronomers Joseph Winlock and Benjamin Gould mounted the fourth-largest telescope in the United States in the backyard; and Francis Child and George Lane taught English literature and Latin at Harvard. Mary Peabody Mann, one of the famous Peabody sisters of Salem and Boston and widow of educator Horace Mann, bought it in 1866 while their son was an undergraduate. Horace Mann Jr., a passionate botanist who had traveled to Minnesota with Thoreau in 1861 and to Hawaii in 1864, was Asa Gray's chosen successor at the Botanic Garden but died of tuberculosis in 1868.

The new street also gave access to the rear of the Waterhouse lot. Dr. and Mrs. Waterhouse put up a house at 11 Follen for their gardener in 1838 and in 1844 built a fine Greek Revival at 9 where they lived until the doctor's death in 1846 (see figure 6.54). In 1848 Louisa Waterhouse arranged an exchange with the Commonwealth so that Follen could be cut through to Concord Avenue. She sold 9 Follen to Francis Bowen, Alford Professor of Natural Religion, in 1853. Bowen's daughter Maria left the property to the Cambridge Historical Society in 1937, but the society had its eye on the Hooper-Lee-Nichols house at 159 Brattle Street and sold it in 1938. The house remained in near-original condition until 1988, when it was greatly expanded and divided into condominiums.

Follen Street has many houses by well-known architects; most were executed for people with Harvard connections. Peabody & Stearns designed the Stick Style house at number 10 (1875), and Longfellow, Alden & Harlow was responsible for both Edwin Abbot's Romanesque mansion (1888–89) and the early Colonial Revival house at 25 (1889). Guy Lowell's first residential commission after his return from the École des Beaux-Arts stands at number 13, next to H. Langford Warren's house for chemistry professor Theodore Richards at 15; both went up in 1900. The Mid-Century Modern houses of 1946–51 at 20, 22, and 34 (Arthur Brooks, Carleton Richmond, and A.A. Dirlam, respectively) are an uneasy fit on this predominantly 19th-century block (see figure 6.202).

The Massachusetts Arsenal

The Massachusetts Arsenal on Garden Street was one of two such facilities in the state before the Civil War. The first building, which was probably a Revolutionary barracks moved from the Common, stood on a small parcel purchased from Joseph Bates in 1796 (see figure 5.2). The Commonwealth bought additional land in 1813 and 1817 and the next year completed a fireproof brick warehouse "100 feet long by 40 feet wide and three stories high … to be used as a place of the more permanent deposit of tents, camp equipage, fixed ammunition, and other munitions of war" (A.M. Howe, 13). A keeper's house followed in 1848, a superintendent's office in 1852, and a machine shop in 1864. A visitor in 1856 found it stocked with 25 brass cannon and 7,000 muskets (figure 4.135–4.136).

The arsenal closed after the Civil War, and in 1876 the Cambridge Social Dramatic Club was allowed to convert the machine shop into "a charmingly cosy little theatre" for amateur performances (*Chronicle,* May 5, 1883). Edwin Dresser acquired the property in 1884 and cleared the site; the bricks and beams were used to build a factory on Franklin Street. Edwin Abbot, a Harvard alumnus who was president of the Wisconsin Central Railroad, bought the land in 1888 and built an elegant stone residence that was acquired by the Longy School of Music in 1937 (see figure 6.152). The Continental Hotel went up in Abbot's back yard in 1929. Today the only reminder of the facility is Arsenal Square, the triangular park between Concord Avenue and Garden Street that was given to the city in 1871.

Chauncy and Langdon streets

Chauncy Street has a simple layout because the adjoining land owners had only to bisect lots 3 and 8 of the 1724 subdivision. The first house was built in 1859 at number 12. By 1873 marketmen occupied several spacious houses near the avenue, while professors and Boston businessmen filled up the middle of the block in the 1880s and '90s (figure 4.138–4.139). Almost all

FIGURE 4.135 Massachusetts Arsenal, Garden Street at Concord Avenue, keeper's house and workshop (1848). The initial building at the arsenal, constructed in 1816–18, has been attributed to Asher Benjamin. The arsenal was an attractive nuisance to Harvard students, who harassed proctors by rolling stolen cannon balls down the stairs of their dormitories in the dead of night. Photo ca. 1865.

FIGURE 4.136 The cannon park at the Massachusetts Arsenal, looking east toward 12 Chauncy Street. Photo ca. 1865.

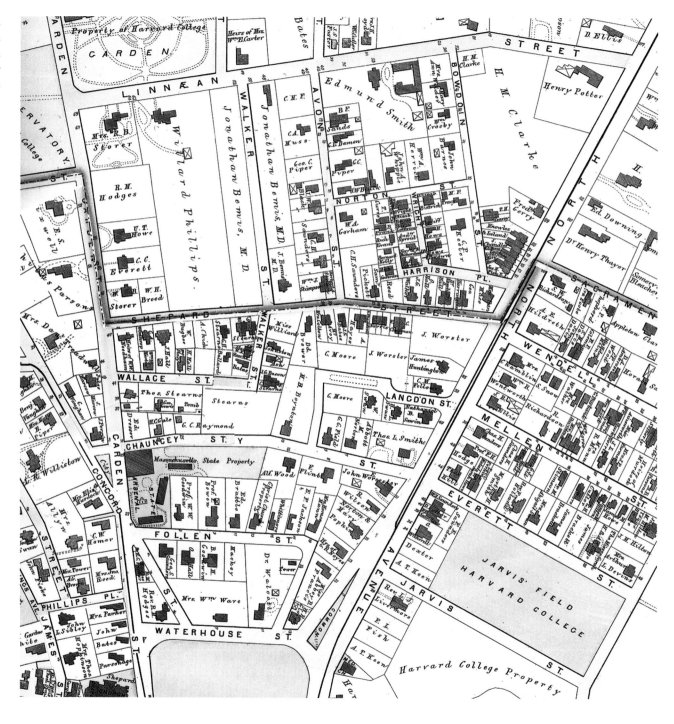

FIGURE 4.137 The southern part of the Lower Common in 1873. The tomb between Chauncy and Wallace (now Walker) streets was a distinguishing feature of Lewisville.

FIGURE 4.138 Civil War veterans paraded on Chauncy Street on April 17, 1886, in honor of Captain James P. Richardson. Richardson raised the first Massachusetts company of Union volunteers in 1861. After the war, he served as a judge in Texas, but he returned to Cambridge in 1886 to visit his daughter, Jennie Bunton, in her new house at number 16 (right). Architect Clarence Blackall bought the house in 1903 and designed the apartment building that replaced it in 1929.

FIGURE 4.139 Margaret Winthrop Hall, 21 Chauncy Street (1889, E.N. Boyden, architect). Arthur Gilman, founder of the Cambridge School for Girls, intended this dormitory to provide a refined domestic environment for boarding students. It was replaced by an apartment building in 1919.

their houses have been replaced by apartment buildings, the first of which the Harlow family put up at 10 Chauncy in 1917. Subsequent ventures (by the Harlows and others) included 1–3 Chauncy and 1610–1622 Massachusetts Avenue (80 units, 1925), 18–26 Chauncy (96 units, 1928), and the Hotel Continental at the corner of Garden Street (114 rooms, 1929).

By the end of the 1920s Clarence Blackall, an architect, was fed up.

Chauncy Street when we located there [in 1903] was all homes, quiet and suburban. No. 16 was in the middle of the block, and looked sideward to Concord Avenue across a wide open field where Mr. Abbott pastured his cows. … But by 1929 the apartments had begun to crowd out the single houses, and instead of being 35 families on the street, each owning their own homes, there were 350 families, mostly in apartments. When Mr. Abbott's land went for the Hotel Continental and a large apartment house, we felt our house had seen its best days. (Blackall, *Seed Time and Harvest*, 431–33, in Petrone, 31)

FIGURE 4.140 Chauncy Street looking east. The Elliott Apartments (Dow, Harlow & Kimball, architects) replaced Margaret Winthrop Hall in 1919. On the right, 18–26 Chauncy (Silverman & Brown) went up on the former arsenal cannon park in 1928. Photo 2009.

Blackall replaced his house with an apartment building, salvaging some fine interior finish for installation in his penthouse unit. Both the *Chronicle* and the *Boston Transcript* regretted the loss. "It seems a pity to tear this house down. … There is no reason why as a structure it should not last a century, … but simply the neighborhood has changed entirely" (*Chronicle*, Apr. 22, 1929). Chauncy Street is now a shadowy defile with almost 400 apartments in eight large buildings (figure 4.140). Fortunately, no other street in Old Cambridge has been as densely built up, although others share its desirable location and access to transportation.

Between Chauncy and Shepard streets the street pattern is more complicated because some of the original allotments were sold off piecemeal. Langdon Street was developed by real estate agent Horace Saunders, a son of housewright William Saunders who acquired part of lot 2 in 1868. Langdon Square, the small park in the center of the block, addressed the problem of laying out a generous but oddly shaped tract with limited frontage on Massachusetts Avenue. Saunders and his investors divided

the fourteen lots among themselves, but over the next five years only two houses went up at 20 and 30 Langdon Street. By 1873 the remaining lots were in the hands of three new owners, merchants and marketmen Morris Boynton, Charles Moore, and John Worster (or Worcester). In 1877 there were Mansards at 37, 50, 55, and 59; a few survive, as well as a very late example at 15 (1887). A wooden block containing six "tasteful and well-arranged" flats at 41–51 met "a ready rental by parties who appreciate a good quiet neighborhood and a handy location to the cars, churches, and stores" (*Chronicle*, May 7, 1892). The same advantages lured apartment developers in the 20th century. Sixty-five Langdon (1907), the Shepherd Apartments at 44 (1915), Langdon Court at 28–30 (1928), and 55 (1938) all replaced houses from the 1870s and 1880s and nearly overwhelmed the domestic scale of the square.

In 1885–86 Worster created Rutland Street, which zigzagged through two barely contiguous parcels on Shepard and Langdon

FIGURE 4.141 Benjamin F. Wyeth house, 9 Rutland Street (1892, C.H. Blackall, architect). Henry D. Wyeth, the last of the family known to reside in Cambridge, lived here until his death in 1975. Photo ca. 1904.

streets, avoiding an 1854 house at 10–12 Shepard. Charles Moore, a hardware dealer in Harvard Square, built the first house at number 2, a "comely semi-Queen Anne, with graceful curvatures and artistic fancy shingling" that attracted much favorable comment (*Tribune,* Jan. 1, 1887). The Rutland lots went on the market at a time of great prosperity, and by 1893 all were filled with stylish houses (figure 4.141).

Shepard Street

Shepard Street was laid out in two stages. The east end was originally part of Avon Street, which was opened between Massachusetts Avenue and Linnaean Street in 1845 (see figure 4.132). In 1847 Joseph Porter, a stable keeper who owned the frontage closest to the avenue, divided his land into twelve absurdly small lots. Thomas Stearns and others opened the connection to Garden Street five years later, and in 1853 the street was renamed for Reverend Thomas Shepard, the town's first permanent minister.

Five double houses stood on the east end of Shepard by the end of 1854. William A. Saunders, another son of the housewright, built the first, a transitional Greek Revival-Italianate at 27–29, as a rental property in 1852. By 1873 the street also

FIGURE 4.142 Thomas Stearns moved his 1845 omnibus stable to 38-44 Shepard Street in 1869 and converted it into a row house. Photo ca. 1947.

had two multifamily buildings, including the converted omnibus stable at 38–44 Shepard that Thomas Stearns moved here in 1869 (figure 4.142). The Panel Brick row at 15–17 and a double three-decker at 24 Shepard (1896) followed but did not establish a trend. Shepard has only three apartment buildings, and even the public scale and formality of the Radcliffe dormitories do not overwhelm its character (although two important houses were lost when Hilles Library went up in 1964).

Walker Street and Lewisville

Abel Willard and Thomas Stearns, former proprietors of the New Line of omnibuses, built up Walker Street and the west end of Shepard in the 1870s. Having sold his horses to the street railway company, Stearns took up real estate, and his relocation of the stable initiated an effort to redevelop the area. However, this part of the Lower Common had already been settled by an extended African American family whose properties Stearns had to acquire in order to proceed.

Lewisville consisted of several houses and a family burial ground owned by relatives and descendants of Peter Lewis of Cambridge and Minor Walker Lewis of Barre, an isolated hill town northwest of Worcester. Adam Lewis, a laborer, may have been the first family member to arrive in Cambridge.[41] He married Catherine Vassall about 1815 and thereby acquired the old Crackbone place on the west side of Massachusetts Avenue near Shepard Street that she had purchased from other heirs of her father, Anthony Vassall, in 1814. Adam and Catherine sold that house in 1816, and three years later they purchased the "heater lot" at the intersection of Garden Street and Concord Avenue. Enoch Lewis, Peter and Minor's oldest son, lived briefly in Professor Henry Ware's household in 1819 and rented Jonathan Ford's tenement on Massachusetts Avenue (now 35 Bowdoin Street) from at least 1823 to 1827. Peter and his third son, Walker, hired on with Dr. Thomas Foster in 1821, while sons Samuel and Joseph moved in with Adam and Catherine Lewis on Garden Street.

The nucleus of Lewisville was a one-acre field on Garden Street in the Lower Common that Peter Lewis acquired from Samuel Haven, a Craigie heir, in 1830. Walker Lewis, who lived in Boston, held the mortgage and conveyed two parcels to his brothers Enoch and Samuel and a rear lot to his brother-in-law William Bassett. He retained a third lot on the street and a large parcel in the rear. Samuel and Enoch built a double house and Peter Lewis a single on Garden Street in 1832; Adam Lewis and William Bassett were also taxed for new houses that year. In 1835 Walker conveyed to seven of his eight brothers and brothers-in-law a small lot, "now occupied by a Tomb just built together with a passageway eight feet wide from the street to the tomb, for the sole purpose of a family burying place for the grantor and grantees and their heirs" (Middlesex Deeds 348/138). Perhaps the death of Joseph Lewis, the only sibling missing from the deed, prompted the creation of this unique family burial plot,

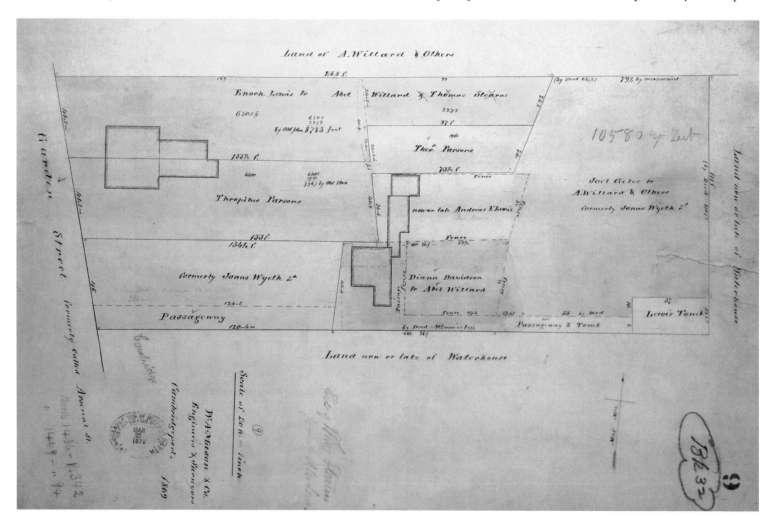

FIGURE 4.143   Part of Lewisville, showing Enoch and Samuel's house on Garden Street, William Bassett's house, and the Lewis family tomb (lower right corner), as surveyed in 1869.

FIGURE 4.144 Walker Street's vernacular tradesman's houses contrast with wealthier streets nearby. Number 30 (left) was built for Harvard Square grocer Orrin Hall in 1872; 34–36 is a four-unit double house built by George Stearns in 1885. Photo 2010.

although African Americans had always been buried with white Cantabrigians in the town cemeteries.

Death and emigration weakened the Lewisville community (see chapter 2). When Peter Lewis died intestate in 1844, the probate court appointed Richard Henry Dana Jr. administrator on behalf of his widow, Minor. Two white men bought Lewis's property at auction: George Rayne, an armorer at the Arsenal, purchased the house, and housewright Ebenezer Francis Jr. the back lot. Six black families containing nineteen individuals still occupied five houses in Lewisville at the time of the 1850 census, but only three remained in 1870.

The 1877 sale of the Lewis tomb to Thomas Stearns ended the brief era of Lewisville. The contents were transferred to the Cambridge Cemetery and placed in a plot that was later resold. The passageway, named Garden Street Place, remained until at least 1886, but by 1916 the Peter Lewis house had been demolished and the tomb lot had been incorporated into the backyard

of 33 Walker Street. Only one member of the family is known to have remained in the neighborhood: George Washington Lewis Jr. (1848–1929), a distinguished steward of the Porcellian Club, bought a house on Parker Street in 1890 where his descendants lived until the 1970s (see figure 4.34).

Stearns and Willard laid out Walker Street in 1868 and marketed its small lots to tradesmen and shopkeepers (figure 4.144). Stearns built 57–59 and 68–70 Walker in 1871 as rentals, while a pianoforte maker and a grocer built the modest houses at 26 and 30. Unconstrained by zoning, expressman Benjamin Hatch put up a stable behind his house at number 69.[42] Edwin Dresser put up four handsome doubles on the south side in 1874, but the most striking house on the street is the audacious little Queen Anne at 44 that Marshall Ney Stearns, a mason, built in 1880 to showcase his skill and good taste (see figure 6.115).

North of Shepard Street: the Fourth Squadron

Between Shepard and Linnaean are several streets parallel to the 1724 division lines that vary considerably because they were subdivided at different times. The long, narrow fields, which averaged 250 feet across, platted neatly into generous house lots, but some owners had to buy more land to bring their streets out to Massachusetts Avenue. The earliest was Bowdoin Street, in 1842; Wright, Hudson, and Avon streets followed in 1845. Hurlbut, Gray, the east part of Martin, and upper Walker streets came a generation later.

Wright and Hudson streets occupy the lower part of the 4½-acre lot 15 that Anthony (Tony) Vassall purchased in 1791 and 1793. Vassall's daughter Catherine inherited his house in 1811, and she and her husband, Adam Lewis, sold it to Israel Porter in 1816.[43] Beginning about 1837 Stillman Willis, a Boston jeweler, bought the old Vassall, Fillebrown, and Frost tracts in the northeast corner of the Lower Common and prepared them for development. Zephaniah Stetson moved the Edward Fillebrown house, which was built before 1772, from 1674 Massachusetts Avenue to 4–6 Hudson Place in 1843–44. In 1845

FIGURE 4.145 George Marston house, 52 Martin Street (1849, George W. Marston, housewright). Marston's small double house was more substantial than the "16-footer" workers' cottages that were prevalent in later neighborhoods. Photo 1969.

FIGURE 4.146 Henry Lamson house, 51 Martin Street (1851, Henry Lamson, mason). Photo 2009.

David Wright, a Cambridge builder, bought about an acre from Willis and put up two houses on Wright Street. A year later he began selling lots along Wright and part of Martin Street. The diminutive double house that George Marston built at the corner of Wright and Martin streets in 1849 was characteristic of the area (figure 4.145). By 1873 Wright owned a number of double houses built as rentals; the residents included a policeman, a gardener, and several laborers. Two- and three-family houses displaced several cottages between 1914 and 1930.

Wright laid out Martin Street from Bowdoin Street to Norton Place in 1846. After 1854 the street was put through to Avon and briefly named for Michael Norton, a masonry contractor who built some workers' cottages there. The house that Henry Lamson, a bricklayer, put up for his own use in 1851 illustrates the prosperity that some tradesmen achieved in this period (figure 4.146). The more elaborate houses east of Bowdoin were built after the street was extended to the avenue in 1882.

Stillman Willis built a house for himself on the northeast corner of the Lower Common in 1839 that is now at 1 Potter Park. He acquired lots 16 and 17 from the Fillebrown estate in 1842 and laid out Bowdoin Street from Hudson Street north to Linnaean. The first building was the simple Federal house at 35, which was built for Elizabeth Frost on Massachusetts Avenue between 1811 and 1819 and moved here in 1846 (figure 4.147). South of Martin, the west side of Bowdoin was a single property with a large two-story house that was built about 1855 for John Harmon, a Charlestown lumber dealer. After his death it was owned by C.P. Keeler, a well-known furniture manufacturer (see *East Cambridge,* 192–93). Cambridge developer Alfred Cohn demolished the Harmon-Keeler house in 1959 and replaced it with nine townhouses that are an early example of that form. The east side of Bowdoin north of Martin was acquired by Henry M. Clarke before it could be developed.

FIGURE 4.147 Elizabeth Frost's tenant house, 35 Bowdoin Street (ca. 1811–19; moved from 1702 Massachusetts Avenue, 1846; 2012 addition, Gerrit Zwartz, architect). The bay window was added about 1896 and the portico in the early 20th century. Photo 2015.

FIGURE 4.148 Queen Anne houses on Hurlbut Street. From left to right, the Emma and Abbie Blodgett house at number 9 (1885), the Gilbert A.A. Pevey house at 17 (1887, F. E. Kidder, architect) and the Horace Low house at 25 (1887, John C. Weld). The Blodgett sisters were the unmarried daughters of a Cambridgeport builder; Pevey, a Harvard graduate, was an attorney who later became city solicitor; and Low owned a dry goods store in Harvard Square. Photo 2013.

Reuben Demmon and William A. and Charles H. Saunders laid out Avon Street in an L-shape from Massachusetts Avenue to Linnaean Street in 1845. The earliest house, at 42–44 Avon, is a fine transitional Greek Revival/Italianate built in 1849 (see figure 6.71). The Saunders brothers also built 32 and 38 Avon in 1855–56. Some of the generous lots on Avon proved irresistible to apartment house developers; other houses were lost when the new Peabody School was built in 1960.

Hurlbut Street, the east side of Bowdoin, five lots on Linnaean Street, five more on Massachusetts Avenue, and the first block of Martin Street were laid out in 1882 on an empty tract acquired by Henry M. Clarke in 1867.[44] By 1887 the west side of Hurlbut, which was named for the owner's wife, Jane Hurlbut Clarke, contained seven Queen Anne houses; all are set back at least 10 feet from the sidewalk, as specified in the deeds, and comprised "one of the quietest and pleasantest neighborhoods in all the city" (*Chronicle,* Mar. 29, 1902; figure 4.148). Although Clarke's trustees closely controlled the development, the east side of Hurlbut remained mostly vacant until the fifteen-year setback restrictions expired, when Roxbury builder Patrick Lyons announced plans for three brick apartment buildings. As the Hurlbut at 28 was nearing completion, the *Chronicle* tried to assure readers that "the street has been improved rather than cheapened" (July 2, 1901). Lyons completed the Chester at 24–26 in 1902, but never built the third. That lot remained empty until a small Cape went up in 1936.

Houses on the east side of Bowdoin and the east end of Martin Street also showcase the high quality of Queen Anne architecture on the Clarke estate. James Fogerty designed 18 in 1887 and probably the very similar Queen Anne at 20 in 1888, and Boston architect Eugene Clark designed the double house at 31 Martin in 1890. Ten Martin (1886) was moved back from Massachusetts

Avenue in 1926 to make way for stores. (See "North Avenue" for the houses on Clarke's Massachusetts Avenue frontage.)

Linnaean Street, at the foot of Avon Hill, marks the northern edge of the Lower Common. While it dates from 1724, it was named for the Swedish botanist Carolus Linnaeus in 1850. The central part developed first. Edmund Smith of Brighton, a florist, bought the north end of Anthony Vassall's pasture and built the imposing Second Empire house at 32 Linnaean in 1863; a few years later he put up more Mansards at 36 and 38. When Gray Street was laid out in 1888 Smith's greenhouses were taken down and his stable was moved to 8–14 Gray and turned into a house. In 1889 Charles F. Goodridge moved the 1815 Elizabeth Frost house from 1705 Massachusetts Avenue to number 26. Several of the speculative Queen Annes on Gray Street are the work of Cambridge architect George Fogerty; the most elaborate is 31 (1893), with an octagonal tower and a major gable on each facade.

The creation of Gray Street and Potter Park spurred additional building on Linnaean; the *Tribune* reported in 1891 that "the houses are going in pretty thick" (Aug. 22). The eccentric house at 1 Potter Park originated on Massachusetts Avenue as a sober Greek Revival built by Stillman Willis in 1839. Henry Potter, a successful meat packer and North Cambridge landowner, purchased it in 1849 and lived there until his death in 1876. His heirs laid out Potter Park in 1883 and moved the house to its present site. Henry's son, H. Staples Potter, appears to have applied the idiosyncratic Queen Anne ornamentation in 1904 (figure 4.149).

The 1724 division and subsequent consolidation of holdings left three long, narrow 4½-acre lots running between Shepard and Linnaean streets in the northwest corner of the Lower Common (figure 4.150). In the early 19th century, the western lot was the property of Nathaniel Jarvis, a farmer on Massachusetts Avenue who died in 1812. His heirs began to sell house lots along Garden Street in 1854. The character of this frontage, which complemented the Dixwell and Parsons estates across the street, was exemplified by the sophisticated Second Empire house that Henry Greenough designed for Sabra Parsons at the corner of Garden

FIGURE 4.149 Willis-Potter house (1839), after it was moved from Massachusetts Avenue to 1 Potter Park and remodeled with Queen Anne ornamentation by H. Staples Potter in 1904. Photo 1904.

FIGURE 4.150 Linnaean Street looking toward Garden Street and the Harvard observatory in 1860, showing the Willard Phillips house (1841–42) on the left.

FIGURE 4.151 Benjamin Vaughan house, 57 Garden Street (1891, Longfellow, Alden & Harlow, architects). This was Radcliffe's Gilman House when it was demolished in 1965. Photo ca. 1960.

Radcliffe had been developing its campus around Fay House since 1885, but there was no room there for dormitories or playing fields. In 1900 the college acquired the Phillips and Bemis houses and converted the former into a dormitory. Radcliffe built the first of nine dormitories on Shepard Street in 1901 and completed its quadrangle in 1957. By this time the college owned all six houses along Garden Street and one near the corner of Shepard (figure 4.152). All were demolished in the 1960s: four in 1964 to build Hilles Library, one the next year to build Daniels House, and the last two in 1969 for Currier House (see chapter 10).

and Linnaean streets. The Georgian Revival designed by Longfellow, Alden & Harlow for Boston lawyer Benjamin Vaughan was equally accomplished (figure 4.151). By the 1890s six large houses faced Garden Street between Shepard and Linnaean.

Dr. Aaron Hill purchased the middle lot in 1823. In 1841 it passed to Willard Phillips, who married into the family in 1833. Phillips built an elaborate house facing the Botanic Garden and maintained the entire 4½ acres as an estate. The east lot belonged to Joel Giles, an 1829 Harvard graduate who built a modest house on Linnaean Street. Dr. Jonathan Bemis purchased it and by 1873 had a large house on Shepard Street. Bemis laid out an extension of Walker Street but kept it off the market for many years. By 1900, when Radcliffe College began to look for a place to expand, there were only two houses on the west side of Walker.

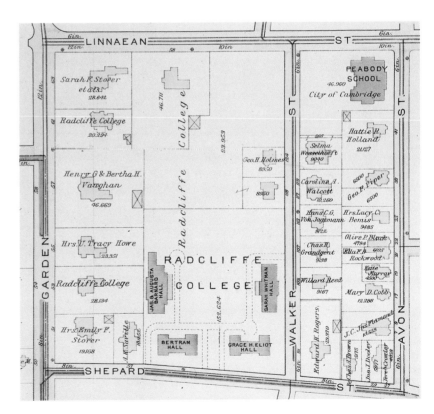

FIGURE 4.152 The future Radcliffe Quadrangle and surrounding properties in 1916.

The New West Field, which was divided in 1638, is distinguished by one of its early homesteads, the Cooper-Frost-Austin house of 1681–82 (figure 4.153; see also figure 6.1). William Jones, who arrived in 1635, was allotted six acres facing the Lower Common. When he sold his land to Edward Winship in 1638 or 1639, it was described as "Jones his hill," and this name survived into the 19th century (*Proprietors' Records*, 56). It was also known as Gallows Hill, for the gibbet that occupied a gravel pit on the east slope.[45] Real estate agents called it Cambridge Heights from the 1870s until the 1920s; "Avon Hill" began to be used in the 1890s. By the mid-18th century the Cooper, Frost, Prentice, and Jarvis families owned most of the hill, and their descendants sold it for development in the 19th.

FIGURE 4.153 Cooper-Frost-Austin house, 21 Linnaean Street (1681–82). One of the most distinctive features of the house is the north slope of its gable roof, which extends from the ridge almost to the ground.

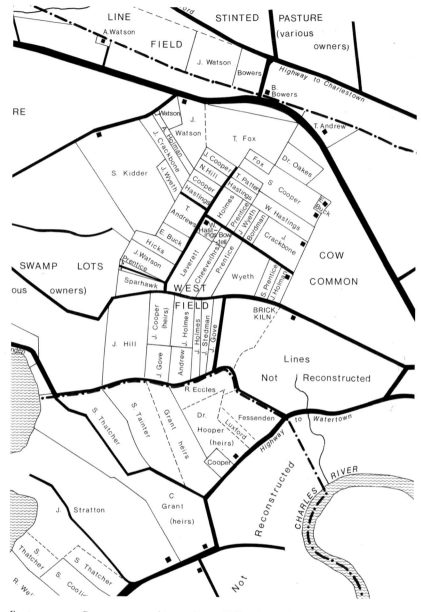

FIGURE 4.154 Property ownership on Jones Hill, 1681. The many small disconnected fields were gradually consolidated into four large farms.

The opening of passenger service at Porter Square in 1842 quite unexpectedly made land in the vicinity desirable for suburban development; White Street (1844) and Orchard Street (1845) were the first of several railroad-oriented subdivisions nearby. The station displaced the Davenport Tavern at the corner of Beech Street as the focus of a new business district (see figure 2.13 and *Report Five: Northwest Cambridge*). Avon Hill is still served by the North Cambridge post office, and the neighborhood was not considered part of Old Cambridge until the mid-20th century.

Although Avon Hill appears at first glance to have developed consistently as an upper-middle-class suburb with a neat grid of streets, its growth was marked by uncertainty and conflict. City water was not extended to the upper slopes until 1883, a quarter of a century after it was introduced elsewhere. The Cooper farm blocked access from the south until 1886. The situation was especially awkward on the north slope, where holdouts blocked Upland Road (then known as Lambert Avenue) for decades after it was laid out in 1847, denying landlocked owners a natural outlet to Massachusetts Avenue. Until 1882 Washington Avenue could be reached only from Arlington Street; Upland ended at Buena Vista Park, where two houses built in its path prevented it from crossing Mount Pleasant Street until it was put through to Raymond Street in 1887–88 (figure 4.156). In 1893 the city extended Huron Avenue to Massachusetts Avenue by making an awkward connection to Upland with two right-angle bends at Newell Street. When this became too confusing for visitors, the eastern part of the route was renamed Upland Road in 1898.

Avon Hill was largely spared the dense subdivisions and multifamily buildings that plagued other neighborhoods before the adoption of zoning in 1924. Longterm residents (many of whom were themselves developers) controlled the character of the area and fended off speculators. The long intervals at which parcels came on the market kept lots scarce and helped Avon Hill sustain its desirability. The area has been protected as a neighborhood conservation district since 1998.

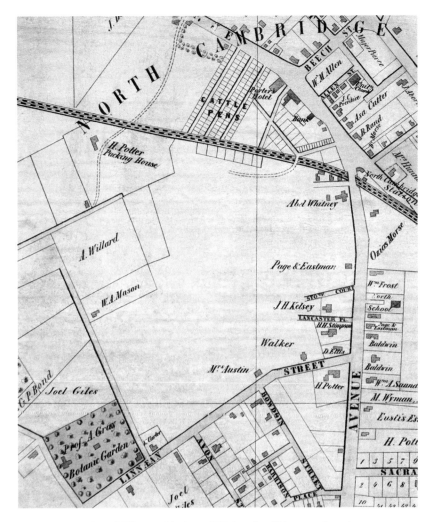

FIGURE 4.155 Avon Hill in 1854. Avon Hill (north of Linnaean Street) was almost entirely pastureland until after the Civil War; the mapmaker omitted most property lines but showed the few streets that penetrated the area, which was considered part of the North Cambridge neighborhood until the middle of the 20th century.

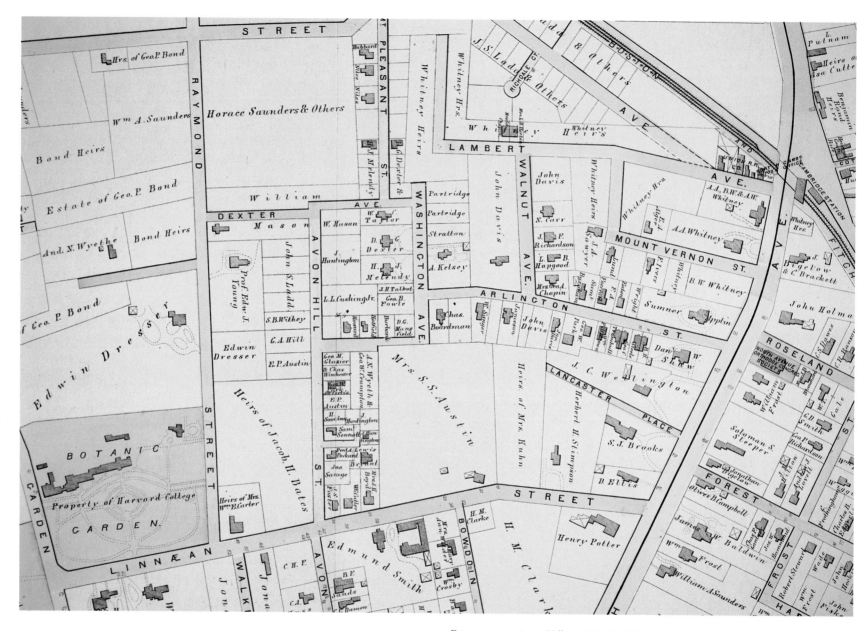

FIGURE 4.156 Avon Hill in 1873. D. Gilbert Dexter and Henry Melendy, who lived on top of the hill on Washington Avenue, built two houses on Mt. Pleasant Street to block the extension of Lambert Avenue (now Upland Road). Mt. Pleasant was projected to lead up the hill to an extension of Dexter (now Bellevue) Avenue, but this was never accomplished. When the city extended Lambert to Raymond Street in 1882 the two houses were relocated to 22 Mount Pleasant and 146 Upland Road.

Streets off Massachusetts Avenue: Upland, Mt. Vernon, Arlington, Lancaster

Abel Whitney, a cabinetmaker, acquired a ca. 1705 house on Massachusetts Avenue and part of the 18th century Prentice farm through his marriage to Susannah White in 1809 and so owned the hillside facing the station (see *Report Five: Northwest Cambridge,* figure 72). Whitney's heirs laid out Mt. Vernon Street and the first part of Upland Road in 1847, but there was little demand until after the Civil War, when Augustus Whitney, a furniture dealer in Brattle Square, built a house on the avenue, and four houses went in at the top of the street (figure 4.157). The rest of the tract, which extended far up the hill, was not successfully developed until the heirs replatted the lots along Upland Road in 1883 (figure 4.158).

William Gates, who had owned four acres of the Prentice farm since 1835, laid out the first section of Arlington Street in 1861.[46] Gates had better luck than Whitney, and by 1866 all but one of his twelve lots had dwellings on them. Three years later Arlington was extended to reach the landlocked fields at the top of the hill where Gideon Frost's granddaughter, Susan Austin, had recently sold a five acre parcel to Henry J. Melendy and D. Gilbert Dexter.

Melendy and Dexter were typical of the prosperous Boston businessmen who developed Cambridge Heights, buying large tracts, building houses for themselves, and selling off lots whose development they controlled. Melendy owned a shoe business in Boston; his partner Dexter went into real estate and founded the *Cambridge Tribune* in 1878. In 1871 they built twin Mansards on the crest of the hill. Dexter's mansion was destroyed by fire in 1939 and replaced by three modest houses, but Melendy's still stands at 81 Washington Avenue (see figure 6.93). William Taylor, a marble wholesaler, bought the lot next door to Dexter and put up 101 Washington Avenue in 1872 (figure 4.159). The elaborate Italianate house that Edward Jameson, a manufacturer of bonnets and woven straw goods, put up at 32 Arlington in 1871 was more advanced architecturally than anything else on the hill (figure 4.160).

FIGURE 4.157 Mt. Vernon Street looking west to the Jabez Sawyer house at 48 (1857; burned and rebuilt, 1865). Photo 1934.

FIGURE 4.158 Upland Road largely developed after the Panic of 1893 with substantial middle-class homes, many built by Eugene Niles to rent or sell. Houses at 73 Upland (1893, right) and 79 Upland (1895, both by E.K. & W.E. Blaikie, architects) illustrate the way this developer followed architectural trends. Photo 2013.

FIGURE 4.159 Houses on the west side of upper Washington Avenue were set very far back from the street, possibly to block the extension of Mt. Pleasant Street. Gilbert Dexter's house at 99 Washington (1871, left), William C. Taylor's house at 101 (1871), and the Governor John D. Long's cottage at 107 (1887, Samuel Thayer, architect) are shown on their original sites. Long's house was moved forward and remodeled with a Queen Anne turret in 1892. Photo ca. 1890.

FIGURE 4.160 Edwin Jameson house, 32 Arlington Street (1871).

Upper Arlington Street and Walnut Avenue were planned by another resident developer, John Davis, a Boston machinery dealer who bought five acres of the Jarvis farm in 1869. Davis gave Walnut Avenue an unusually wide 70-foot roadway with grass verges and setbacks of 30 to 50 feet. He built his own house at 26 Arlington in 1869 and three Mansards on Walnut in 1869–71. The street was completed two decades later by the Niles brothers, who grew up in North Jay, Maine, found success as pork dealers in the Faneuil Hall market, and established a slaughterhouse near Fresh Pond in what was then Belmont.[47] Sullivan Niles moved into Dexter's house on Washington Avenue about 1875, and in 1887 J. Harris Niles and Eugene M. Niles joined him in splendid Queen Anne houses at 6 and 9 Walnut Avenue, the former with a handsome shingled carriage house and the latter with an unusual lighthouse tower (see figures 6.135 and 6.136). Altogether they put up about twenty houses nearby, including nine on Upland Road and five on Whittier Street. The *Chronicle* credited them with having "done much to develop and protect the good character of the Heights" (Apr. 4, 1896). After the Niles brothers sold their slaughterhouse in 1896, their real estate office became one of the largest property managers in the Boston area.

The desirability of Avon Hill was reflected in the commitment that owners made to stay in the neighborhood. Some moved to new homes nearby, while others remodeled to keep up with the elegant Queen Anne and Colonial Revival houses that began going up in the 1880s. Albert Kelsey, a contractor who supervised the expansion of the Massachusetts State House, lived in an unpretentious double Mansard at 86–88 Washington Avenue before building a highly decorated cottage at 37 Arlington in 1874 (see figure 6.95). Examples of updating include the 1887 bay and tower added to 16 Arlington Street, the 1886 tower and gazebo added to 26, and the 1898 Colonial Revival remodeling of the Bracketed house at 24 (figure 4.161).

Without zoning, residents were on their own in 1896 when George Parke, a Boston attorney who had been forced by Davis to build his house at 24 Arlington Street 60 feet back from the

FIGURE 4.161 John Davis house, 26 Arlington Street (1869). The tower and corner gazebo were added by a later owner in 1886. Photo 1968.

street in 1870, decided to put up an apartment building in his front yard. The city council refused to enact a 20-foot setback to counter "a serious disfigurement to a very attractive locality," so the neighbors purchased Parke's property and sold it with restrictions to Wellington Fillmore, a respected commercial builder who remodeled the house for his own use (*Chronicle*, Feb. 29, 1896).

A four-acre field at the corner of Linnaean and Massachusetts Avenue had been owned by the Hastings, Cooper, and Frost families since the 17th century, ending up as part of the Cooper-Frost-Austin place. George Meacham bought the tract from Lucy Austin in 1835, subdivided it into four lots with avenue frontage, and laid out the first few feet of Lancaster Street in 1841. Houses soon filled each lot, but little else changed until Sumner J. Brooks arrived on the scene and proved that little experience was necessary for a successful career in real estate.

Brooks, a native of Petersham, sailed as supercargo on a trading voyage to Haiti in 1849. He stayed for eighteen years and amassed a "comfortable fortune" in the West Indies trade (*Chronicle*, Mar. 2, 1907). On a visit home in 1864 he put up a house at 1764 Massachusetts Avenue. After returning for good to become a commission merchant in Boston he acquired more land from his neighbors and laid out sixteen lots along Humboldt and Lancaster streets in 1882. By 1885 he had eleven single and double houses for rent. The designers are unknown, but all were built in less than a decade by the same North Cambridge carpenter, Nathaniel Bunker.[48] No two are exactly alike, but after a false start with some old-fashioned Italianate designs the rest were typical Queen Annes of the early 1880s (figure 4.163). The *Tribune* praised the project:

> It was mainly through Mr. Brooks's efforts that Lancaster, Agassiz and Humboldt streets were opened up. He did not … sell the land for others to build on, but with a wise foresight … went to work and literally covered the land with houses. Being attractive and substantially built residences, and in a first-class locality, they immediately attracted the attention of good tenants, and today every one of the twelve houses built by him is occupied and paying him a good and safe income. (Aug. 11, 1888)

FIGURE 4.162 By 1886 the streets on Avon Hill were approaching their present configuration. The way is open for Lambert Avenue (Upland Road) to be extended toward Raymond Street, and Arlington and Lancaster streets are almost fully built up. Only the fields around the Cooper-Frost-Austin house, owned by the "heirs of M.F. Kuhn," remain to be developed.

FIGURE 4.163 Sumner Brooks's Queen Anne rental houses on Lancaster Street (1885–89) compare well with contemporaneous work by professional architects on Washington Avenue. Photo 2009.

Sumner A. Brooks tore down his father's house in 1919 and planned to roof over the cellar for an eight-car garage. When neighbors objected he sold the entire property to a syndicate that put all the houses on the market in 1920. A row of stores went up on the avenue in 1921, and a 56-unit apartment building at 8–10 Lancaster Street replaced the mansion in 1924 (see figure 4.183).

Streets off Linnaean: Washington, Humboldt, and Agassiz

Gideon Frost (a grandson of Deacon Samuel Cooper) came into possession of the eight-acre Cooper place on Linnaean Street in 1788. Frost also owned two other farms on the hill, several farms east of Massachusetts Avenue, a house on Waterhouse Street, and the original Frost homestead on Kirkland Street. In 1886 Austin heirs William Kuhn and Martha Clark retained Mason & Son to lay out their remaining fields, reserving less than an acre around the house. The firm's task was not difficult, and they created a fairly dense subdivision of twenty-nine lots by extending Washington Avenue down to Linnaean Street, Lancaster over to Washington, and Agassiz parallel to Humboldt (figure 4.164).

Soap magnate James Mellen, molasses importer Stillman Kelley, wholesale grocer Henry Yerxa, and pipe manufacturer David Ritchie had a different vision for this south-facing slope, and each purchased multiple lots. The *Chronicle* described the splendid Queen Anne, Shingle Style, and Colonial Revival houses that Boston architects Hartwell & Richardson designed for them on Washington Avenue in 1886–89 as "among the best in the city" (June 25, 1887; figure 4.165, see also figures 6.137, 6.147, and 6.161). Their spacious setting could not be sustained, and an apartment building went up on Mellen's tennis court in 1912 (figure 4.166). A fine Colonial Revival house appeared on the other corner in 1901, but it was replaced by another apartment in 1929 (figure 4.167). The Kelley house at 49 Washington Avenue passed into institutional ownership when the Lincoln Field School acquired it in 1927, but the Cambridge School of Liberal Arts (later Cambridge Junior College), which owned it from 1936 until 1974, and Lesley College, which sold it to a private owner in 2001, did not fundamentally alter the property.

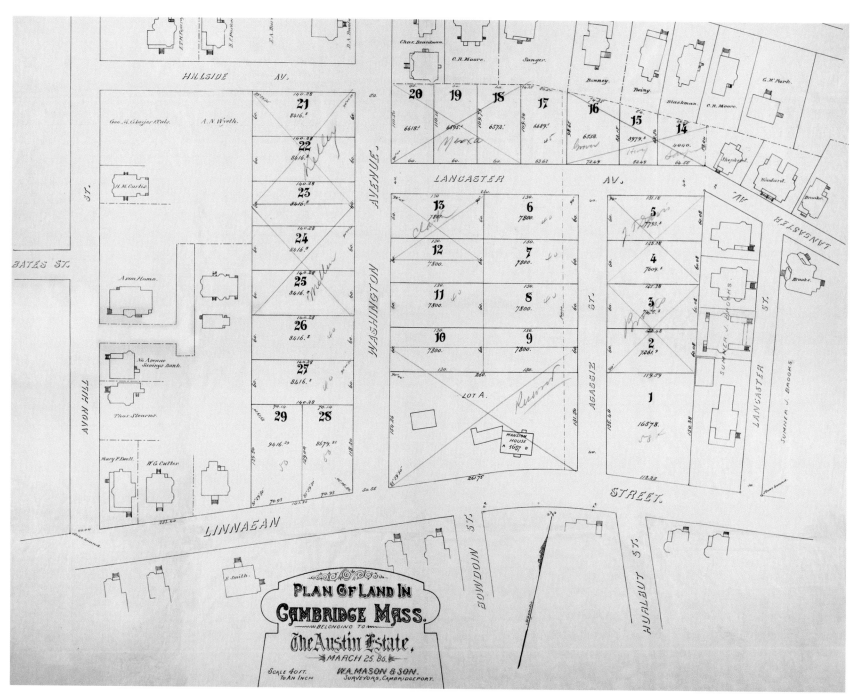

FIGURE 4.164 Subdivision plan of the Austin estate, 1886. Penciled annotations show lots that were combined by their purchasers.

FIGURE 4.165 A view up Washington Avenue in 1896, showing the James Mellen house at 33 and the Stillman Kelley house at 49 (1886–87, both Hartwell & Richardson, architects). The houses were surrounded by open lawns, and no fences, hedges, or foundation plantings screened them from the street. Photo 1896.

FIGURE 4.166 James Mellen's apple orchard and tennis court, on Washington Avenue at Linnaean Street, were replaced by an apartment building at 5–7 Washington Avenue in 1912. Photo ca. 1896.

Humboldt and Agassiz streets are modest in comparison to Washington Avenue. Brooks's rental houses on Humboldt are densely clustered throwbacks to the Bracketed houses of the 1850s, while Agassiz shows more individuality. Horace Blackman, a millwork foreman at the Mason & Hammond piano factory, built the unusual fieldstone and shingle design at 33 Agassiz (1890), and brick manufacturer Winslow Sands put up the brick and shingled Queen Anne facing it at 32 Agassiz (1891; see figure 6.141).

By 1900 the Cooper-Frost-Austin house was one of the few remaining First Period structures in the city. When the property came on the market in 1911, 150 Cambridge residents helped save it from destruction. Joseph Chandler, a Boston architect who specialized in the "restoration" of colonial buildings, carried out repairs for the Society for the Preservation of New England Antiquities; luckily, the money ran out before much work could be done. For a few years the house was occupied by a gift shop and tea room; later, it was rented as a residence before becoming a house museum.

FIGURE 4.167 The Austin heirs sold the corner of Linnaean Street and Washington Avenue in 1901. Boston marketman Benjamin Osgood's Colonial Revival house (1901, Warren B. Page, architect) was razed in 1929 for the apartment building at 25 Linnaean Street. Photo ca. 1915.

Raymond Street, at the western edge of Avon Hill, came into existence in the 1630s as "the other highway to the Great Swamp," but little building took place until the middle of the 19th century (Paige, 14). The chief gardener of the Botanic Garden, William Carter, lived in an old house on the premises until 1847, when he built the fine Greek Revival house at 49 Linnaean Street and retired there with his wife, Silence. At the top of the hill, brickmaker George Wyatt built 87 Raymond Street in 1846–47 but soon sold it and a prime piece of land to William A. Mason, the surveyor.

Boston distiller Henry Fuller and Jonas Wyeth 2nd built large Mansard houses on the hillside in 1857 and 1859, but the rest of Raymond Street saw no activity until after William Mason's son Charles, a civil engineer who carried on the firm of W.A. Mason & Son after his father's death, laid out West Bellevue Avenue in the 1880s. Wyeth's grand house and gardens were razed in 1922 during the development of Gray Gardens East. Only the Fuller mansion, with its extensive lawn and splendid beech trees, recalls the early estates, although an addition completed in 2013 is larger than the original house (figure 4.168).

Avon Hill Street separates Raymond Street and Washington Avenue but differs from both: the lots are smaller, and there is an unusual diversity of architecture. The lower part opened in 1858, but the first houses did not appear until 1872–73. In 1888, when Upland Road was graded west to Raymond Street, Avon Hill Street was to be extended to meet it. Four years later, it was still "undeveloped and ungraded … with the outlet shut off by a fence" (*Chronicle,* Sept. 17, 1892). Charles Mason finally gave up two lots on Bellevue Avenue to allow the street to be completed, and a number of double houses sprouted on the upper part. The California bungalow at number 71, designed for bakery executive Lester Hathaway by Boston architect Alfred L. Darrow in 1912, is the only one of its kind in Cambridge (see figure 6.183).

East Bellevue Avenue proved particularly attractive to journalists after C. Burnside Seagrave, editor of the *Cambridge*

FIGURE 4.168 Henry Fuller house, 79 Raymond Street (1857; remodeled by Eleanor Raymond in 1923 and 1930). Beginning in 2008, Raymond's balustrade was removed and the Mansard roof and cupola were restored as part of an extensive project designed by Washington, D.C., architect Alexander Zaras. Photo ca. 1938.

Tribune, built a Mansard cottage at 48 in 1886. Samuel Merrill, an editor at the *Boston Globe,* and his wife, Estelle, a journalist whose pen name was Jean Kincaid, put up a much more stylish Queen Anne two years later (figure 4.169). The *Tribune* proposed "Newspaper Row" as an appropriate name for the cul-de-sac that was "handy to everything, in a good neighborhood, with excellent views, and on the highest spot in the city" (Feb. 1, 1890).

Beyond Bellevue, the last piece of the puzzle was a 6.3-acre tract opened up by the extension of Upland Road to Raymond Street in 1888. Frederick Hastings Rindge laid out thirty-eight lots along Upland, Vincent, Whittier, Raymond, and Walden streets and offered them for sale in 1890. The large double houses put up by the Niles Brothers and others on these streets helped establish a new plan for this type, more gracious than the earlier side-by-sides that were standard in Cambridge. Some are located on corner lots, where they display two main facades and

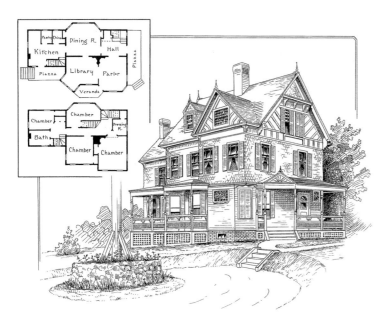

FIGURE 4.169 Samuel Merrill house, 45 Bellevue Avenue (1888, F.F. Gilman, architect). Merrill, who came from Haverhill, imported not only his architect but also the workmen; as the *Tribune* noted: "the stone and brick work, plastering, painting and teaming have also been in the hands of Haverhill parties" (Aug. 11, 1888). Rendering 1888.

separate entrances and porches, giving them the appearance of very large single-family residences (figure 4.170).

The last subdivision on Avon Hill was the work of Boston-born Charles W. Cook, a wealthy but mysterious character who built two houses in 1886 that were still empty at his death thirty years later. Cook, a merchant, settled in Calcutta after the Civil War, where his intended bride was fatally struck by a cobra while visiting him shortly before their wedding. Cook had already purchased 3.8 acres off Linnaean Street, laid out Bates Street, and had houses built for himself and his future wife and for his mother, who also died before she could move in. Cook sold only the lot at the corner of Raymond and Bates, where three attached dwellings in the Tudor style were built in 1905. He disappeared on a sea voyage in 1916. The rest of Bates Street finally filled up in 1924–25.

Double House, 169 Huron Avenue, corner Whittier Street,
✻ ✻ ✻ Sullivan Niles, Owner, ✻ ✻ ✻
BUILT BY

E. W. Boynton & Co.,
BUILDERS OF

FINE RESIDENCES AND

APARTMENT HOUSES.

The Best of References.

All Work Done on Honor.   Estimates Furnished.

RESIDENCE, 201 HARVARD STREET.

SHOP, 186 HARVARD STREET.✻✻✻

FIGURE 4.170 Sullivan Niles double house, 169 Upland Road/3 Whittier Street (1896, John A. Hasty, architect).

Avon Hill retains one significant anomaly from the prezoning era. In 1913 Mrs. William A. Parry of 140 Upland Road put up a cinderblock garage facing the abandoned stub end of Mt. Pleasant Street. The neighbors protested but only succeeded in blocking her plan to sell gasoline. Mrs. Parry said that she had been prevented from erecting an apartment house some years before and now wished to rent parking spaces to her friends. A trucking firm occupied the garage for many years, but in 1957 Paul Rudolph, the Modernist architect who studied with Walter Gropius at Harvard in 1947–49, remodeled it into a residence for his own use and screened it with a tall fence. This project by a master of 20th century architecture is comparable to the Philip Johnson house on Ash Street (see figure 6.206).

NORTH AVENUE

> Of the many beautiful avenues in our flourishing city, none bid fair to outstrip North Avenue. By the liberal foresight of our ancestors it was laid out six rods or one hundred feet wide … and runs about one mile on a straight line between the Common and the Railroad Bridge. Its sidewalks are laid out on each side one rod wide, and beautifully shaded with elm and maple trees. It is supplied throughout with gas and Fresh Pond water, and fire hydrants are located at the principal corners of cross streets. The rails of the horse railroad are laid on the centre of this wide thoroughfare, leaving a liberal driveway of thirty feet or more on each side of the track; thus combining all the advantages of railroad traveling, without interfering in the least with the pleasure travel. Already it has splendid residences, with ample grounds tastefully laid out, and gardens filled with trees and shrubs. (*Chronicle,* June 13, 1857)

Massachusetts Avenue above Cambridge Common was laid out in the early 17th century as the "Highway to Menotomy." The road went along the Lower Common, passed the gallows, swung westward around the foot of Avon Hill, and crossed Poverty Plain on its way to Concord, which was settled in 1635. In the 18th century it was known as the Great Road or the Concord Road and in the early 19th century as the West Cambridge Road. After

1841 it was called North Avenue. In 1894 when the Harvard Bridge was completed, all the old streets that made up the new cross-town thoroughfare were renamed Massachusetts Avenue.

The great width of the right-of-way, 33 yards (99 feet), had its roots in early English practice and allowed the traveler to pick the path of least resistance across the ungraded terrain. One old resident said that in the early days there were "no sidewalks to speak of, and going up North Avenue was like walking in the bed of a brook" (Bowen, "Follen Street," 91). For two centuries it was used mainly by residents of outlying towns to bring their produce to market or to reach the county seat, but when the Charlestown Branch Railroad opened a station at Porter Square in 1842 Boston was suddenly only twenty minutes away. North Avenue became the city's most desirable address for commuting businessmen, but in the 20th century apartments and stores displaced almost all their monumental Mansard, Queen Anne, and Colonial Revival houses (figure 4.171). The avenue now displays little of the character that made it desirable in earlier times.

In the 17th century there were several farmhouses on the east side of the highway, but the common land opposite was not settled for many years after it was distributed in 1724. The ca. 1670 house of Gilbert Crackbone, on the east side near Roseland Street, "faced south after the custom of its times; its gable toward the road and the roof sloping nearly to the ground on the north," in the manner of the Cooper-Frost-Austin house (DAR *Guide,* 144). By the 1840s there were only remnants of the agricultural period: ancient houses, barns in "tumble down condition," stone walls, old foundations, remnants of tanneries, and "ten-footers," the one-room shacks of the poorest families. One such place was Nathaniel Jarvis's 14-acre farm just above the Common. Jarvis died in 1812 and left the property to his spinster daughters, who sold milk from a small herd of cows until about 1860. "Everything in the house remained … as in their father's time," including the counters, bins, and scales in a room that had been used as a grocery, and an "immense kitchen, with a fireplace as large as a modern bedroom, its beams with

FIGURE 4.171 Massachusetts Avenue looking north from the Little Common about 1875. From the left are John Worcester's house at 1600 (1865; demolished 1979), the Michael Norton house (with a cupola) at 1610 (1860; demolished 1925), and the Nathaniel Sawin house at 1626 (1868). Henry James described a similar scene in the early 1880s: "The new paint on the square detached houses shone afar off in the transparent air; they had, on top, little cupolas and belvederes, in front a pillared piazza, made bare by the indoor life of winter, on either side a bow window or two, and everywhere an embellishment of scallops, brackets, cornices, wooden flourishes. They stood, for the most part, on small eminences, lifted above the impertinence of hedge or paling, well up before the world"(*The Bostonians,* 218).

strong hooks from which were suspended the hogs killed for Thanksgiving time" (Saunders, 4–6; figure 4.172).

There are no early houses left on the avenue. Edward Fillebrown's 1777 modest cottage was moved from the corner of Hudson Street to 46 Hudson Place in 1843, while a 1790 tenement belonging to Sarah Frost was taken down about 1897 (figure 4.173). Three Federal houses built by members of the Frost family survive in new locations. Walter Frost's 1807 house was moved from Massachusetts Avenue to 10 Frost Street in 1867 (see figure 4.215). Elizabeth Frost's house, built in 1815–16, remained at 1705 Massachusetts Avenue until 1889, when it was moved to 26 Gray Street. A smaller Frost residence, perhaps built for servants, was moved from 1702 Massachusetts Avenue (near Martin Street) to 35 Bowdoin Street in 1850 (see figure 4.147).[49]

The first significant development in the 19th century began on the west side of the avenue near the Common, where Oliver Hastings built three houses in 1831–33 for professors Convers Francis, Levi Hedge, and John Popkin. The Greek Revival was in vogue when railroad service began in 1842, and the first suburban houses near Porter's Station were in this style; one survives at 2A Forest Street (figure 4.174). William A. Saunders (1818–99), oldest son of housewright William Saunders, built a flashy Greek Revival opposite Linnaean Street in 1843. He married Mary Prentiss, a descendant of Jonathan Cooper, gave up carpentry, and became a hardware dealer in Boston. The Saunders house was moved to 6 Prentiss Street in 1925 and became a bed-and-breakfast, the Mary Prentiss Inn.[50]

When the horsecar line opened in 1856 there were still only about twenty-five houses along the avenue, clustered in the first block north of Waterhouse Street and at the north end near the station (figures 4.175–4.176). The middle stretch between Chauncy and Linnaean streets remained largely undeveloped until Joseph Smith of Somerville built seven attached brick houses at the corner of Hudson Street in 1866, an experiment in urbanism that was not repeated. The subdivision of Abraham Hilliard's Lower Common property in 1857 accommodated the east end of Chauncy Street and three lots on the avenue. Michael

FIGURE 4.172 Nathaniel Jarvis farmhouse (ca. 1750), about 1569 Massachusetts Avenue (opposite Waterhouse Street). The house was moved to Walker Street in 1871 and demolished about 1901. Photo ca. 1870.

Norton, a masonry contractor, built an elaborate Mansard in 1861 that established this as the preferred style for decades to come (see figure 6.89).

Nathaniel Sawin, a produce dealer in Boston, built a handsome Mansard on the south corner of Chauncy Street in 1865, replacing a gambrel built by John Wyeth about 1724. Three years later he sold it to marketman John E. Worcester and built a new house at 1626 Massachusetts Avenue that was designated a Cambridge landmark in 1981. James Huntington's 1867 Mansard at 1640 Massachusetts Avenue survives behind a block of stores erected in 1923 (figure 4.177). In 1862 Charles Hicks Saunders, a Boston hardware merchant and another son of the well-known housewright, began a spacious house on the corner of Mellen Street that exemplified the continuing fashion for ambitious Second Empire mansions (see figure 6.91). Mansards built in 1864 by Abijah Hildreth, president of the Cambridge Gas-Light Company, and in 1869 by William Wentworth, a marble manufacturer in Boston, disappeared in the mid-20th century.

FIGURE 4.173 Sarah Frost house, 1696 Massachusetts Avenue (1790; demolished ca. 1897). The house at right, 1702 Massachusetts Avenue (1886), was moved to 10 Martin Street in 1926. Photo ca. 1890.

FIGURE 4.174 Reuben Demmon house, 1771 Massachusetts Avenue at the corner of Forest Street (1843), demolished for a Cadillac showroom in 1926. A twin was moved off the avenue to 2A Forest Street in 1921. Photo ca. 1920.

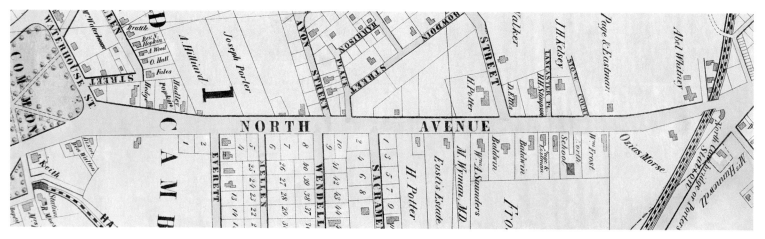

FIGURE 4.175 North Avenue in 1854.

FIGURE 4.176 North Avenue in 1861, looking north from Arlington Street with Roseland Street on the right. This promotional view for the Roseland Nursery development shows the Fitchburg Railroad station at left, with the steeple of the Allen Street Congregational Church behind it and Somerville's Spring Hill in the distance.

A defining moment on the upper avenue occurred in 1867, when the North Avenue Congregational Society moved the former Old Cambridge Baptist Church from Kirkland Street to the corner of Roseland Street. This had been the site of the 1856 Holmes Chapel, the society's first home, which they moved to the corner of Arlington Street in 1861 and then sold to a Methodist congregation that moved it down the avenue in 1868 to a site opposite Waterhouse Street. The church's presence confirmed the respectability of the avenue, and it was soon surrounded by new houses (figure 4.178).

FIGURE 4.177 James Huntington house, 1640 Massachusetts Avenue (1867), with 11 Shepard Street (1869) and 3–5 and 7–9 Shepard (both 1851) in the background. The Huntington house survives behind a store block constructed in 1923. The Montrose and the Dunvegan apartment houses now stand on the right. Photo ca. 1870.

FIGURE 4.178 The North Avenue Congregational Society moved the former Old Cambridge Baptist Church to the corner of Roseland Street in 1867. William Frost Jr. built the two Mansards next to the church as rentals in 1867; the society demolished the one shown in 1920. The steeple is a replacement installed after the original was struck by lightning in 1906. Photo ca. 1910.

FIGURE 4.179 Frank and Horace Partridge and Benjamin Hunt houses, 1718, 1722, and 1728 Massachusetts Avenue (1885). All were demolished by 1941. Photo ca. 1890.

The distinctive character of North Avenue attracted comment. In the early 1870s William Dean Howells mocked the pretensions of its homeowners:

The Avenue is [not only] our handsomest street … but probably the very dullest street in the world. It is magnificently long and broad, and is flanked nearly the whole way from the station to the colleges by pine palaces rising from spacious lawns. … On market days its superb breadth is taken up by flocks of bleating sheep, and a pastoral tone is thus given to its tranquility; anon a herd of beef-cattle appears under the elms; or a drove of pigs, many-pausing, inquisitive of the gutters. (*Suburban Sketches*, 87–88)[51]

The historian John Fiske described the social distance that separated Berkeley and Brattle streets from North Avenue:

When you pass beyond Garden St., you begin to approach the region of rich merchants and shoddy brokers, etc. North Avenue is their headquarters, as Brattle St. is the headquarters of the literary folk. We have no more to do with North Avenue folks than if we lived 1000 miles off. It is curious how sharply these regions are demarcated. (To Mary Fisk Stoughton, May 24, 1877)

The merchants and brokers were undeterred by Fiske's criticism and in the next period of prosperity introduced the Queen Anne style to the avenue. Horace and Frank Partridge and Benjamin Hunt, who operated an athletic goods store in Boston, built three exuberant Queen Annes just north of Martin Street, and Frederick Worcester, a Brattle Square furniture dealer, built another next door (figure 4.179).

The Colonial Revival style appeared in 1888–89, when James A. Wood, a Boston lumber dealer, had Hartwell & Richardson design a house on the corner of Sacramento Street that the *Chronicle* "classed with the handsome residences of Mr. Kelley, Mr. Mellen, and Mr. Yerxa on Washington Avenue" (Feb. 2, 1889).[52] So large that passersby thought the foundation was meant for a business block, Wood's house had exceptionally large rooms paneled in oak, mahogany, sycamore, and black walnut. Closer to Harvard Square, the Hartwell firm designed houses for former Cambridge mayor James M.W. Hall in 1888 and soap manufacturer Edwin D. Mellen in 1896 (figure 4.180).[53]

North Avenue reached its zenith just as it was renamed Massachusetts Avenue in 1894. Some of the finest homes in the city

FIGURE 4.180 Edwin D. Mellen house, 1590 Massachusetts Avenue (1896, Hartwell, Richardson & Driver, architects). Massachusetts Avenue reached its zenith as a residential street with the construction of the Greycroft, the grandest North Avenue mansion and the last of its era when it was demolished in 1980. Photo ca. 1899.

lined the broad sidewalks, but the great breadth of the street made it irresistible as a traffic artery. Harvard Square was a major transfer point for street railway passengers, and North Avenue was the most direct route to the emerging suburbs beyond Porter Square. Brattle Street residents were able to force the West End Street Railway to take up its tracks and build on other streets, but North Avenue people could not prevent the introduction of noisy electric streetcars in 1889 (figure 4.181). The completion of the Cambridge Subway in 1912 sparked a boom in apartment houses, which brought retail stores in their wake. Proliferating trucks and automobiles created traffic conditions incompatible with a residential neighborhood. Over the next two decades Massachusetts Avenue north of Shepard Street was transformed into a commercial strip.

The change began in 1898, when Canadian-born businessman William G. MacLeod built the city's first luxury apartment

houses, the Montrose and the Dunvegan, on an empty lot at the corner of Shepard Street (figure 4.182). Subsequent buildings invariably displaced single-family houses. The next to go up was Benlumay Court (1909), a Mission-style structure with 21 apartments near the corner of Everett Street. Across the street, the Georgian Revival Bay State (1915), a 38-unit building, resembled the private dormitories of the Gold Coast (see figure 6.228). Gradually the buildings became larger, as at Linnaean Hall (1914, 36 units), the Newport Apartments (1916, 80 units), the Lancaster (1924, 56 units), Chauncy Hall (1925, 80 units), and Oxford Court (1926, 101 units; see figure 6.233). In 1925 the *Chronicle* noted "the passing of many fine residences," and described ten that had recently disappeared (Aug. 8).

Stores first appeared on the avenue in 1910. Dr. George True, who gave up dentistry for real estate, planned to build some on the corner of Sacramento Street. The *Chronicle* anticipated the commotion: "These stores will be the first ones to be located between Porter's station and Harvard square and while there is an unquestionable demand for them, their presence will not be relished by those who desire to keep the neighborhood a residential one exclusively" (Apr. 2, 1910). Neighbors successfully appealed to the Supreme Judicial Court to enforce the 20-foot setback and residential restrictions in the subdivision deed of 1853, and Dr. True built the apartment houses at 1675–1679 Massachusetts Avenue instead.

While the court was upholding residential use on the east side of Massachusetts Avenue, Somerville druggist Adam McColgan was breaking ground for stores on the corner of Hudson Street, where there were no restrictions. Only one other retail block— 1607–1615 Massachusetts Avenue, at the corner of Everett Street—was erected before World War I, but commercial construction overwhelmed the avenue in the 1920s (figure 4.183). In 1926 the *Chronicle* counted 106 stores between Everett Street and the railroad bridge. An "optimistic and far-seeing" real estate man attributed this to the "great influx of families [that] will require many more trading places ... the stores now being built will in time be none too many" (May 29, 1926).

FIGURE 4.181 North Avenue at the beginning on the electric era, looking south from Upland Road. From right to left are the Prentice-Whitney house at 1858 Massachusetts Avenue (1705; demolished 1967) and the Augustus Whitney house at number 1840 (1870; demolished 1929). Photo 1891.

FIGURE 4.182 The Montrose and The Dunvegan, 1648 and 1654 Massachusetts Avenue (1898, J. St. Clair Harrold and Willard M. Bacon, architects, respectively). The developer, Canadian native William G. MacLeod, was a Boston businessman who retired in 1900 to pursue further opportunities in real estate.

FIGURE 4.183 Sumner A. Brooks razed his father's house at 1760–1770 Massachusetts Avenue in 1919. Samuel Flax of Roxbury put up a block of stores in 1921, and Jacob Sorkin built the fifty-six-unit Lancaster Apartments behind it in 1924. Photo ca. 1927.

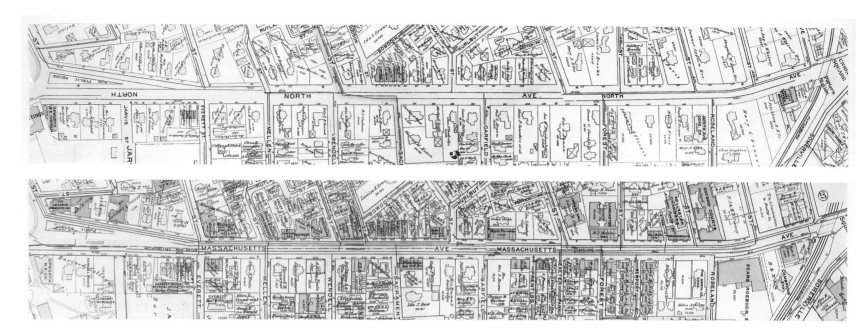

FIGURE 4.184 Massachusetts Avenue in 1894 and 1930. Wood frame residences are shown in yellow; masonry apartment buildings and stores are shown in red.

Almost all the stores were cheaply constructed single-story buildings. Some builders made gestures toward urbanity, but even architects could not improve on the mass-produced cast-stone swags, urns, and pilasters typical of these homely structures. Most of the damage was done before the Depression, but in 1940 an A&P market replaced a Queen Anne on the corner of Linnaean Street that the *Chronicle* once called the "handsomest house on the avenue," leaving the Frederick Worcester house stranded between two storefronts (Oct. 15, 1892; see figure 6.134).

The zoning map drawn by the planning board in 1922 placed the entire avenue in a residential district. When enacted two years later, the ordinance included a business district from Shepard and Wendell streets to Porter Square and allowed 100-foot-high buildings everywhere. The depth of this high-density corridor was quite narrow, however, and apart from the Sears, Roebuck

store built in 1928 only projects that could obtain variances to build in the adjoining 40-foot districts went up before the code was rewritten in 1962.

After 1958 the Massachusetts Department of Public Works began to rebuild the avenue from Harvard Square to the Arlington line. A concrete median replaced the streetcar tracks and safety islands, and every tree was removed as the sidewalks were narrowed from 17 feet to 11. Traffic flow improved at the expense of public transportation and pedestrian amenities (figure 4.185).

Developers returned in 1960, when a 137-room Holiday Inn replaced two Mansards between Mellen and Wendell streets. In 1968 Harvard took down two houses south of Jarvis Street to build Roscoe Pound Hall and put up a garage on the corner of Everett Street in place of buildings once occupied by the Sargent School of Physical Education (see chapter 7). Despite considerable opposition, the Greycroft and the John Worcester house

FIGURE 4.185 Massachusetts Avenue looking north from the corner of Roseland Street on August 30, 1958. Most of the Roseland Nursery's frontage was eventually developed for commercial purposes, including the Lovell Block (1882) and a Sears, Roebuck & Co. store (1928). After the streetcars stopped running, all the trees were removed and the roadway was widened by six feet on each side.

were replaced with condominiums in 1978–79 (figure 4.186). Two years later, the consequent enactment of preservation ordinances helped prevent the Park Street Church from razing the Sawin house on the corner of Langdon Street.

In 2007 the Harvard Law School began a long-anticipated redevelopment of the northwest corner of its campus. Wasserstein Hall might have swept away the last houses on this part of the avenue, but Harvard created a perfect site for them on the former Holiday Inn parking lot (figure 4.187). Meanwhile, Lesley University acquired the North Prospect Congregational Church property to accommodate its 1998 merger with the Art Institute of Boston. In 2011 the historical commssion approved plans to relocate the church and connect it to a new classroom building on the corner of Roseland Street.

Massachusetts Avenue seems awkwardly suspended between past and future. Several significant buildings are protected, and further removals are unlikely. Many stores were upgraded in the 1990s, when retailers displaced from Harvard Square reversed decades of tawdriness, but these one-story blocks are best seen as placeholders for future projects.

FIGURE 4.186 Two seven-story condominium buildings, 1580 Massachusetts Avenue (1978, Joseph T. Raduano, architect) and 1600 Massachusetts Avenue (1979, DiMeo Associates) replaced the Greycroft and the Joseph Worcester house in 1978–79. Photo 2013.

FIGURE 4.187 The Alden Keen (1876) and the D. Gilbert Dexter houses (1875) at their new location on the corner of Mellen Street. Photo 2009.

Kirkland Street and Massachusetts Avenue skirt an area of poorly drained historic wetlands. The "hither pyne swamp" at the bend of Oxford Street may have fed the brook that flowed through Harvard Yard and followed Brattle and Eliot streets to the Charles. The "further pyne swamp" northwest of Shady Hill drained into a swale with an almost imperceptible gradient leading to the Millers River near Union Square. Agricultural improvements transformed the swamps into pastures, and the aquifer was exploited by leather tanners who initially settled the area as well as by industry in the 19th century. The aquifer delayed the Red Line extension in the 1970s, and poor drainage required construction of an extensive system of storm-water holding tanks under Wendell Street, Museum Street, and Francis Avenue in 2000–2.

Settlement of the area began soon after founding. In 1635 the town granted four half-acre house lots inside the palisade, facing the village across the Common on what became Holmes Place. The next year, land outside the palisade in the New Ox Pasture was divided into six- and eight-acre tracts, and by the end of the century several homesteads lined the east side of Massachusetts Avenue, each facing south at the head of a long, narrow field running east to the Charlestown (now Somerville) line.[54] A homestead on a main road may have had commercial advantages, because early householders were usually tradesmen, not farmers, and their successors were blacksmiths, tanners, and curriers. By the Revolution most of the original smallholdings had been consolidated into farms belonging to the Jarvis, Hastings, and Frost families (figure 4.188). In the next century, the farms were subdivided in different circumstances, giving each a distinct residential character.

This part of Cambridge did not appeal to the West Indian planters looking for New England estates, which meant that the descendants of the original settlers continued to improve their holdings to the extent allowed by the Massachusetts laws of inheritance and dower. Heirs shared equally in an estate unless

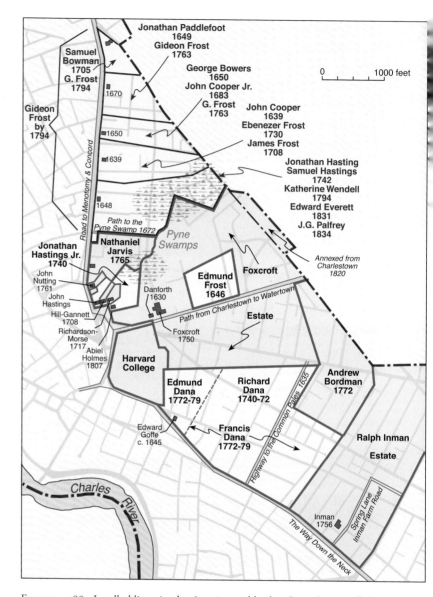

FIGURE 4.188 Landholdings in the Agassiz neighborhood on the eve of the Revolution.

they had been provided for during their father's lifetime, but the homestead was almost always left to the oldest son, who often bought out his siblings and tried to accumulate as much land as possible for the benefit of his own children. The mandatory protection of dower rights, which set aside one-third of a deceased husband's real property for his widow's support until her death or remarriage and then released it to her husband's heirs, helped keep land in family hands. The transition to a suburban economy created great pressure to sell ancestral fields, and a long-lived widow like Mary Teele Frost, who received her 18-acre dower in 1832 and died thirty years later, could impede orderly development and frustrate heirs for decades.

Nineteenth-century developers found this agricultural landscape challenging. The long, narrow fields were effectively landlocked even after 1805, when the Middlesex Turnpike—now Beacon Street in Somerville—was built just beyond the town line. The dilemma was solved about 1847 by James Hayward, a civil engineer and property owner who laid out Oxford Street in the course of developing a subdivision on the Wendell estate (figure 4.189). Successive promoters extended Oxford north until it reached Beacon Street about 1858. Development lagged until after the Civil War, despite the availability of public transportation on the Charlestown Branch Railroad beginning in 1842, on the Harvard Branch from 1849 to 1855, and on Massachusetts Avenue beginning in 1856. The blocks between the avenue and Oxford Street filled up first, while the back fields along the Somerville line developed only after horsecar service began on Beacon Street in 1882. In the 20th century the neighborhood adopted the name of the Agassiz elementary school on Sacramento Street.

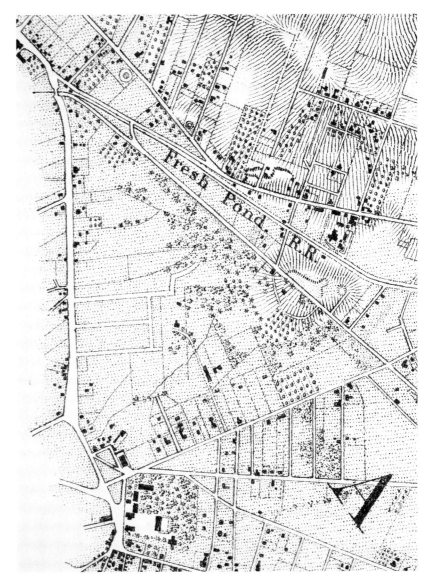

FIGURE 4.189 The Agassiz neighborhood and vicinity as surveyed in 1847, showing topography, streets, fence lines, open fields, and orchards. The doughnut-shaped feature northeast of Porter Square is the pond in the foreground of figure 2.13. Beacon Street (1805) approaches Porter Square on its original alignment south of the railroad.

HOLMES PLACE

Some of the earliest houses outside the village were located on the northeast side of the Common, facing the village on what became Holmes Place. Joseph Mygate received four acres "by the Pyne swamp," but soon left for Connecticut (Town Records, 9). In 1639 half-acre lots were awarded to John Meane, Percival Greene, and Richard Parke, who had arrived in 1635 with Reverend Thomas Shepard. John Hastings, a tanner, arrived from Braintree in 1654, married John Meane's widow, Ann, and settled on Brattle Street. Their son Walter married his stepsister and lived in the Meane house, which burned down along with Percival Greene's in February 1681/2.[55] Hastings rebuilt, but Greene's lot remained vacant until tanner Nathaniel Hill put up a house there in 1708. Reverend Caleb Gannett, a 1763 Harvard graduate who returned as mathematics tutor in 1773 and was steward from 1779 to 1818,

FIGURE 4.190 Holmes Place as seen from a third floor window of Hollis Hall about 1796. The Hastings-Holmes house is on the right and Nathaniel Hill's house (1708; demolished 1849) is beyond it.

bought the Hill place in 1781. Although described as "a man of slow powers, not gentle manners, and of forbidding person," he won Katherine Wendell, General William Brattle's granddaughter; after she died, Ruth, a daughter of Yale president Ezra Stiles, was said to have married him out of pity for his motherless daughters (Sibley, *Biographical Sketches*, XV, 394). A later owner sold the property to Harvard College, which allowed the Harvard Branch Railroad to raze the house and build a station in 1849.

Houses on Holmes Place had strong associations with the Revolution. Moses Richardson, a surveyor and housewright, lived in a 1717 house just east of Hill's. Called as a Minuteman just after midnight on the 19th of April, he was among six Cambridge casualties of the British raid on Concord and Lexington. From 1792 until 1872 it was the home of Royal Morse, a college goody's son who became a local office-holder, auctioneer, and public character. The university bought the house in 1881 and razed it to build Austin Hall.

Jonathan Hastings, Walter's grandson, was an ardent patriot who invited the Cambridge Committee of Safety to meet in his house on the old Mygate homestead.[56] General Artemas Ward, the first commander of the revolutionary army, was quartered there during the Siege of Boston. In 1792 Hancock Professor of Hebrew Eliphalet Pearson acquired the house and the 12-acre "low pasture," where he cut his own hay with a scythe until he resigned in 1806 after he was passed over for the presidency of the college.

Pearson founded the Andover Theological Seminary and in 1807 sold his house and five acres to Judge Oliver Wendell of Boston, who retired to Cambridge with his daughter, Sarah, and son-in-law, Abiel Holmes, the town's minister. Their son Oliver Wendell Holmes, the physician and author, immortalized it as "the old gambrel-roofed house" and wrote the poem "Old Ironsides" there in 1830 during the campaign to preserve the U.S.S. *Constitution*. Soon the house was mentioned reverentially in every guidebook. Brother John, as reclusive as Oliver was gregarious, lived at home until Harvard bought the property in 1871. He had little patience for the task of cleaning out the old house:

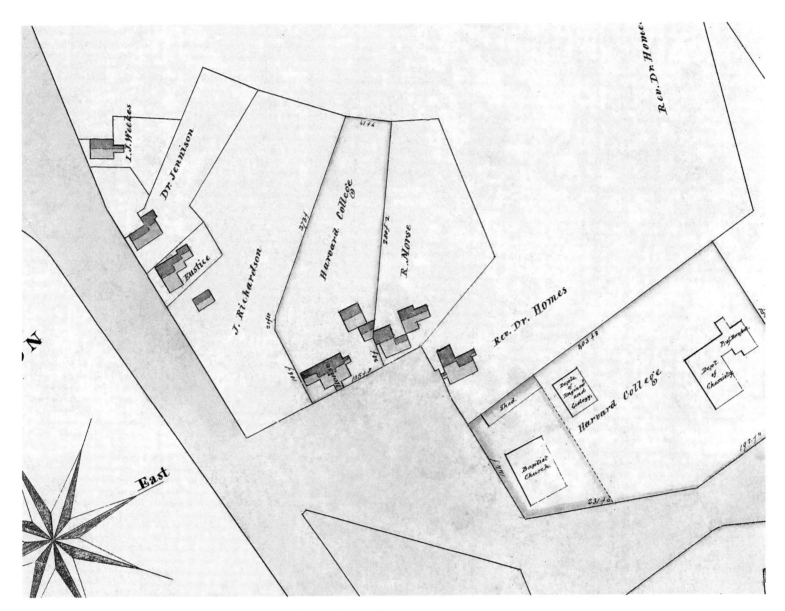

FIGURE 4.191 Holmes Place in 1833. J. Richardson's corner lot was the site of the house built by Walter Hastings in 1682 and razed in 1830. Harvard College owned the 1708 Hill-Gannett house, which would be displaced by the Harvard Branch Railroad station in 1849. Royal Morse lived in the 1717 Moses Richardson house, while Reverend Dr. Holmes had the 1737 Jonathan Hastings house. The Baptist Church and its carriage shed were added to the map after 1845.

FIGURE 4.192 The Hastings-Holmes house was commemorated as Oliver Wendell Holmes's birthplace by Minton's China Works of Stoke-on-Trent, England, four years after it was demolished in 1884.

I had to look over piles and piles of rubbish, some going back to the year 1715 or thereabout. The business papers and account books of my great-grandfather had been kept in the attic one hundred and fifty-six years. … I found commercial letters referring to Prince Charles Edward's invasion [of England in 1745], and such letters as contained any historical allusions I saved, and burned the residue, something under forty bushels. (Holmes, *Letters,* 81)

Dr. Holmes correctly predicted that "the stony foot of the great University will plant itself on this whole territory" (Stillman, 19). Although President Eliot called the Holmes house an "interesting relic," he did not hesitate to accept Edward Austin's condition that no structure could remain within 60 feet of the new lecture hall he was building for the law school (Harvard *Annual Report,* 1870–71; see chapter 10). Holmes could not resist describing this as "a case of justifiable domicide," but he mourned the loss in personal terms, noting that "the natural death of a house is very much like that of one of its human tenants."

What it is to see a human dwelling fall by the hand of violence! The ripping off of the shelter that has kept out a thousand storms, the tearing off of the once ornamental woodwork, the wrench of the inexorable crowbar, the murderous blows of the axe, the progressive ruin, which ends by rending all the joints asunder and flinging the tenoned and mortised timbers into heaps that will be sawed and split to warm some new habitation as firewood,—what a brutal act of destruction it seems! (Holmes, *A Mortal Antipathy,* 23, 29–30)

The suburban era arrived on Holmes Place in 1838, when Boston attorney Omen Keith built a temple-fronted Greek Revival on the corner of Massachusetts Avenue (figure 4.193). Harvard Branch Railroad service began ten years later (see chapter 2). The university purchased Keith's house in 1897 and somewhat ironically named it Gannett House. Harvard acquired Holmes Place and part of the Common from the city in 1929 in exchange for the site of the Central Fire Station and turned Gannett to face Mallinckrodt Hall in 1937 (see chapters 7 and 10).

FIGURE 4.193 Omen Keith house, Holmes Place (1838), shown in its original location facing Harvard Square. Photo ca. 1920.

FIGURE 4.194 John Nutting house, 1541 Massachusetts Avenue (1762; demolished 1888). Lois Lilley Howe sketched the view from Holmes Field in 1885, three years before it was razed for Hastings Hall. This is the house labeled "Dr. Jennison" in figure 4.191.

Around the corner from Holmes Place the houses facing the Common all disappeared in the 19th century. Harvard razed loyalist housewright John Nutting's house in 1888 for Hastings Hall (figure 4.194). William A. Saunders moved a modest Federal built in 1822 for Margaret Eustis, the widowed sister of Chief Justice Isaac Parker, from the present site of Hemenway Gymnasium to the corner of Oxford and Eustis streets in 1863 (see figure 4.218). The Harvard Epworth church displaced another, supposedly built of timber from the Revolutionary barracks, to Franklin Place in Cambridgeport in 1867. A "dilapidated 'ten footer' painted yellow" occupied by Marcus Reemie, the town barber, disappeared without a trace (Saunders, 3).

NATHANIEL JARVIS HOMESTEAD

The first large holding north of the Common originated as a quarter-acre grant to William Man, who expanded his property to an acre before he died about 1662. John Palfrey, a joiner, enlarged Man's house to accommodate his nine children and doubled the acreage. Several shoemakers, joiners, and blacksmiths owned the place before Nathaniel Jarvis, a tanner, bought it in 1765. Jarvis built a gambrel-roof addition to the old farmhouse and acquired six adjoining parcels between 1767 and 1788 (see figure 4.172). In 1861 his daughters' heirs subdivided the 14-acre farm into thirty-eight generous lots, but only five houses had appeared on the avenue when Harvard alumni acquired the back lots in 1867. They sold land east of Oxford Street to the trustees of the Museum of Comparative Zoology and set aside five acres for an athletic field to replace the Delta, the open triangle between Cambridge and Kirkland streets that was the intended site of Memorial Hall. Jarvis Field remained the center of college athletics until the development of Soldiers Field in the 1890s. The city closed Jarvis Street when the university built the Harvard Graduate Center in 1949.

KATHERINE WENDELL ESTATE

Robert Parker, a butcher, owned the east side of Massachusetts Avenue from Everett Street almost to Sacramento Street, and in the spring of 1648 was granted liberty "to fell some timber for … a dwelling house and some for a barn and fencing" (Town Records, 74). Walter Hastings, the tanner on Holmes Place, purchased the 20-acre Parker farm in 1687, as well as some contiguous parcels running back to the Charlestown line that included the "further pyne swamp." When Walter's son Jonathan died in 1742 he divided the property among his three children, who each received three-acre parcels on the highway; his widow Sarah's dower consisted of 12 remote acres with no frontage.

Jonathan Hastings's youngest son, Samuel, a glazier, bought out his siblings and lived in the old house until 1785, when he bequeathed it and his now-18½-acre farmstead to his unmarried daughter and only heir, Sarah Hastings. Sarah was carrying three mortgages when she sold the property to goldsmith James Hill just prior to their marriage in January 1791, when she was 42. She reserved the "use of the land and buildings for her life" but died two months later (Middlesex Deeds 105/82).

Katherine Brattle Wendell, the widowed daughter of Tory general William Brattle, acquired the Parker-Hastings place in 1794 and built "an aristocratic mansion … with liberal stables [and] coach houses" (Saunders, 6). Wendell's granddaughter Catherine Saltonstall Mellen Frisbie inherited a half interest, and when her husband, Professor Levi Frisbie, died in 1822 she also inherited their home on Kirkland Street. Catherine married James Hayward, a civil engineer and former professor of mathematics, in 1828. Hayward bought out the other Wendell heirs and in 1843 acquired two acres of Harvard's Divinity School tract, which enabled him to link his wife's properties.

Hayward and his neighbor William G. Stearns laid out the first few hundred feet of Oxford Street along their common property line, creating a framework for the successful development of the Agassiz neighborhood (figure 4.195). Early in 1847 Hayward removed Madam Wendell's house, laid out Wendell and Mellen streets, and extended Oxford Street across the Jarvis farm. He named the ancient lane to the pine swamp after Harvard's new president, Edward Everett, who had formerly owned the fields beyond Oxford Street. A few months later he sold the entire property to Boston promoters Gardiner Greene Hubbard, Peter Oliver, and George Derby, who recorded a subdivision plan with fifty-seven house lots.

Hubbard's related venture, the Harvard Branch Railroad, began passenger service in 1849, but only six houses had been completed when the line was abandoned in 1854 (figure 4.196). The pace picked up after the Civil War. In 1865 and 1868, Royal Richardson moved houses from Sacramento Street and Massachusetts Avenue to lots he owned at 11 and 13 Mellen Street. By 1873 some of the remaining lots on Mellen were occupied by new Mansards, but the slow pace of development allowed an interesting diversity of styles. Rebecca Hunt, a widow, built two notable examples of the Stick Style at 7 and 9 Mellen in 1882–83 (see figure 6.108). Charles H. McClare designed Queen Anne houses at 31 and 33 Mellen in 1892–93, and Edward T.P. Graham designed a dignified brick double at 35 in 1925.

One of the city's first apartment houses was built on Everett Street in 1890. The Jarvis, designed by Joseph and William Richards for Boston lawyer Frederick P. Fish, contained eight suites (see figure 6.218). The elaborate Queen Anne exterior conveyed the respectability of this new form of urban living, and the building attracted several widows and single women, as well as some Harvard instructors. At the beginning of the 20th century the Sargent School for Physical Education and the Lesley Normal School (now Lesley University) settled on the street. No trace of Sargent remains, but Lesley established a campus around Edith Lesley's home at 29 Everett Street and gradually acquired over thirty houses nearby. Lesley's post-WWII plans to substantially redevelop Everett, Mellen, and Wendell streets into a modern campus were thwarted by a downzoning petition in 1979, and many of the houses once slated for demolition have been restored (see chapter 7).

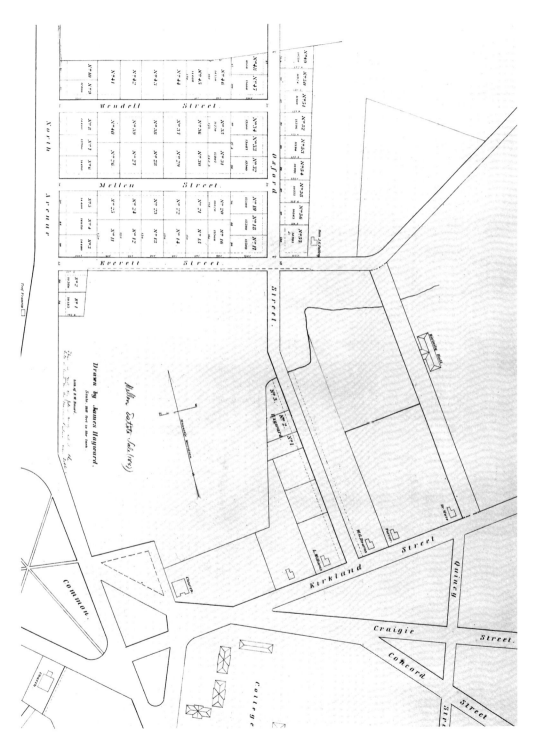

FIGURE 4.195 James Hayward's plan of Oxford Street and the house lots on the Wendell estate, ca. 1847.

Residential Neighborhoods   319

FIGURE 4.196 Josiah Sprague house, 19 Everett Street (1849, Isaac Melvin, architect; right) and the John Bubier house, 15 Everett Street (1849). Melvin designed this modest broad-pilastered Federal-Greek Revival house in 1849, but it was not erected until 1853. An apartment building replaced both houses in 1933. Photo ca. 1905.

FIGURE 4.197 Holmes Field, Jarvis Field, and the Wendell estate subdivision, with houses on lower Oxford Street in the foreground, as seen from the tower of Memorial Hall in 1875. Compare with figure 4.229, taken in 1923.

John Gorham Palfrey Estate

Walter Hastings left the "further pyne swamp" (which was described in later deeds as the "low pasture") and an adjoining four-acre field to his son Jonathan in 1705. The property stayed in the family until Jonathan Hastings III sold it and his father's house on Holmes Place to Eliphalet Pearson in 1792. Pearson retained the low pasture when he sold the house to Oliver Wendell but finally relinquished it to Professor Edward Everett in 1824.

Edward Everett (1794–1865) had been appointed to the Harvard faculty the day after his 21st birthday in 1815; a few days later he departed for Europe, where he drew a salary for four years while earning a doctorate at Göttingen. On his return, Professor Everett found Cambridge stultifying, even though he taught students like Ralph Waldo Emerson and his own successor as president of Harvard, Cornelius Felton. The Overseers refused his request to live in Boston, so he and his wife, Charlotte (a daughter of Peter Chardon Brooks, reputedly the richest man in Massachusetts), rented rooms from Madam Craigie. Everett's purchase of the low pasture in April 1824 might have been motivated by a recent conversation with Daniel Webster about a career in politics.[57] He was elected to the U.S. House of Representatives that November, and in 1825 he purchased a more dramatic site, six acres on Windmill Hill near the Charles River. Harvard dismissed him for nonresidence after he took office, and he sold both properties without ever building on them.

John Gorham Palfrey (1796–1881) seemingly modeled his life on Everett's. He was best known as a historian of New England, "but his curious career—minister, professor, politician, postmaster, editor, lecturer, writer, and historian—indicates a certain lack of purpose and aim" (Malone, 170). He succeeded Everett in the pulpit of Boston's Brattle Street Church and after serving as Dean of the Harvard Divinity School took his seat in Congress. Palfrey bought Everett's 12 acres of fields and meadows in 1831 and lived in Divinity Hall while his house, "Hazelwood," was under construction (see figure 6.45). He also built a summerhouse that incorporated elements of Medford's 1770

meetinghouse ("the great pulpit window, with its pilasters, was the back … and the sounding board the roof"), but an arsonist destroyed it (*Chronicle,* May 14, 1846). The only access was via the ancient lane that became Everett Street, so the university granted him a right-of-way through Divinity Avenue (figure 4.198).

No Cambridge landowner took a greater interest in developing his property or had less to show for it. Palfrey was bitterly disappointed when it could not be made to support him and his family. His interest was stimulated by talk of the proposed Harvard Branch Railroad and sharpened by his electoral defeat in 1849. The charter granted in April 1848 authorized the company to lay track from the Fitchburg Railroad in Somerville "to some convenient point near the Common, in Cambridge"

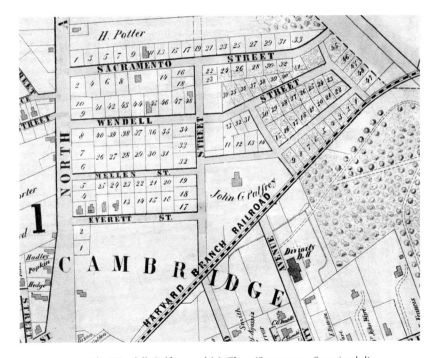

FIGURE 4.198 The Wendell, Palfrey, and McClure (Sacramento Street) subdivisions in 1854. After seven years there were only six houses on the forty-seven lots on the Wendell estate. The Harvard Branch Railroad was on the verge of abandonment at the time this map was made.

and "pass between the house of John G. Palfrey and Divinity Hall" (Mass. Laws 1848, ch. 107). Palfrey was so eager to see it completed that he returned from Washington in March 1849 to oppose the company's request for a three-month extension, because the delay might prevent him from selling lots he had laid out along the right-of-way. Construction began in October, and the first train passed Palfrey's house on December 23.

The next spring Palfrey promised "to renounce politics for the rest of 1850 & devote it to my book & the care of my property" (*Journal,* Mar. 15, 1850). Journal entries and letters document his enthusiasm for improvements: supervising workmen, negotiating exchanges of land with neighbors, and attending real estate auctions. Surveyors, woodcutters, ditch diggers, and road builders graded Gorham, Hammond, and Wendell streets, set out trees, put up fences, and built a platform for passengers at Carver Street. Palfrey also worked to rationalize his property lines, buying more than he sold; in 1847 he purchased four lots on Oxford Street that had been part of the Wendell estate, and in 1850 he acquired some Harvard land that had been cut off by the railroad. He and the Jarvis heirs exchanged parcels, and all the adjoining owners granted each other the right to pass and repass over their new streets. He was bitterly disappointed when an auction of fifty-one lots—subject to 20-foot setbacks and banning butchers, blacksmiths, tanneries, and "soaperies"—brought only one sale, to the contractor who had graded the streets. Charles Francis Adams, Palfrey's brother-in-law, agreed over dinner one night in 1850 to take two lots.[58] The house that Somerville carpenter Thomas Collins built on the corner of Carver and Sacramento streets in 1853 stood alone for nearly a decade.

When the railroad closed in 1854 Palfrey had sold just four lots. His subdivision was too remote to attract the Boston merchants who were the main engine of suburban growth in the 1850s. Without the railroad it was almost as distant from the stations at Porter Square and Park Street, Somerville, as it was from Harvard Square, and he was reduced to selling lots to tradesmen and speculators who built just nine more houses over the next twenty years (figure 4.199).

Mrs. Palfrey inherited Hazelwood and 4.6 acres around it in 1881, while sons Francis and John received the unsold lots in trust for the benefit of the Palfrey's five children. A year later the Charles River Street Railway began horsecar service from Porter Square via Beacon Street to Bowdoin Square in Boston, making the area accessible to mechanics and foremen in the factory district around Kendall Square. The nation had entered a long period of prosperity, and more convenient sites were finally filling up.

FIGURE 4.199 Thomas G. Collins house, 87 Wendell Street (1864, Thomas Collins, housewright). Collins built the first house in Palfrey's subdivision in 1853 and returned a decade later to put up three distinctive curly roofed gambrels that reflected the builder's Quebec heritage. Photo 1965.

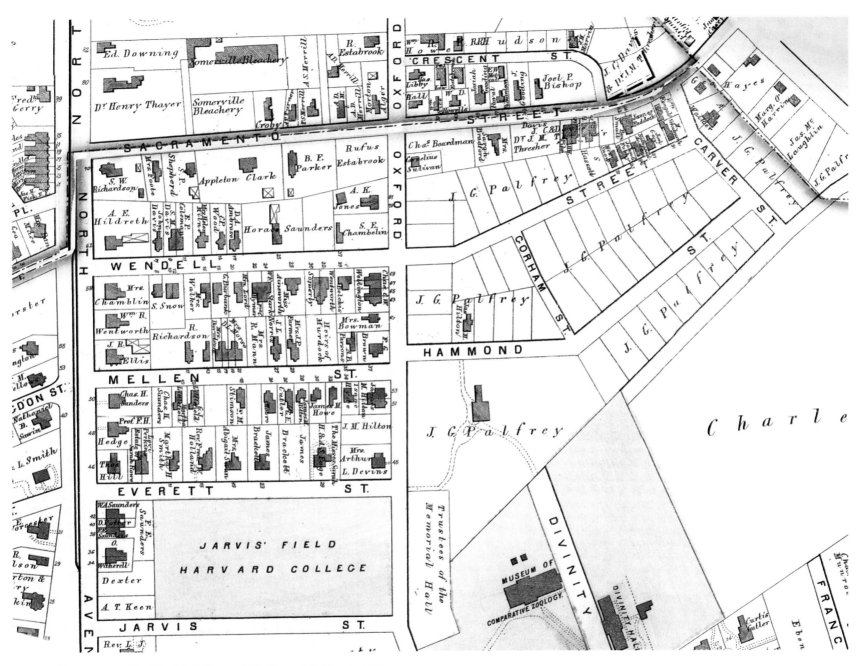

FIGURE 4.200 The Wendell, Palfrey, and McClure subdivisions in 1873.

FIGURE 4.201 Thomas F. Myles house, 55 Hammond Street (1892; architect unknown, George and Peter Dobson, builders). Houses built at the same time could vary widely in style. The Queen Anne Myles house was a decade out of date, while the adjoining Alonzo Hicks house at 65 (1892, Timothy F. Walsh, architect) was a forward-looking Colonial Revival. Myles was manager of the clothing department at the Harvard Cooperative Society; Hicks was a builder. Photo 2015.

John Palfrey, a West Point graduate, served in the Army Topographical Corps as a young lieutenant and understood land development far better than his father the minister and public intellectual. Between 1885 and 1889 he built Museum Street on the old railroad grade, opened Howland Street, replatted the subdivision, and lifted the setback requirements. Palfrey sold eighty lots over the next five years, so the neighborhood could at last be described as a "fast growing locality" (*Tribune,* Sept. 24, 1892). Many of the new houses were substantial two- or four-family residences. At 2–4 Gorham Street, for example, Howard F. Peak, a roofing contractor, put up an "old fashioned kind of double house with brick wall between. Each side has ten rooms and a bath and each side has a tower on the corner, an open fireplace in the sitting room, slated roof, electric gas fixtures and the usual modern appliances" (ibid., Apr. 6, 1895; figure 4.201).

Mary Ann Palfrey died at Hazelwood in 1897. She left the house to her sons, but stipulated that her daughters could live there rent-free as long as they remained single. When the last spinster died in 1917, her trustees leased the estate to the U.S. Navy, which ran a radio school at Harvard during World War I (figure 4.203). The navy immediately erected Radio Hall, a 28,000-square-foot drill hall on the corner of Oxford and Hammond streets. After the war, Radio Hall became the first Gordon McKay Laboratory and Palfrey House became a service building.[59] The Office of Naval Research built a cyclotron laboratory next to the house in 1946, and in 1957 work began on a massive electron accelerator along Hammond Street. The remaining land around the house was paved for parking, and its interior was destroyed during renovations in 1986.

The university and the Agassiz community began considering the future of Harvard's north precinct in 1997. The city adopted a transitional zoning district to mitigate the difference in scale between the neighborhood and the potentially dense academic area (see chapter 10). Harvard moved Palfrey House to Hammond Street and began construction of the Northwest Science Building in 2002.

Figure 4.202 The Palfrey subdivision in 1894.

Figure 4.203 The Palfrey house during World War I, when it served as a guard room for the U.S. Navy Radio School. Photo 1918.

Frost Family Holdings: Sacramento Street to Porter Square

In the 17th century members of the extended Cooper and Frost families gained control of four farms in the triangle formed by Massachusetts Avenue and the town boundary. When these were subdivided in the 19th century each retained a distinct identity that is discernible today.

John Cooper (1618–91) and Edmund Frost (d. 1672) arrived in 1634 or 1635. Cooper settled on Massachusetts Avenue opposite Linnaean Street in 1639, while Frost lived in the village before moving to Kirkland Street in 1646. Their descendants long remained members of the local yeomanry. Most of the men farmed, but some Coopers were also shoemakers and saddlers, while some Frosts were tanners and blacksmiths. Before the Revolution, one man in each line attended Harvard College but then moved away. The advancement of these families was measured in the land they accumulated rather than by their success in the larger world. With such a long history as neighbors, it is not surprising that they intermarried repeatedly, or that the more numerous Frosts gradually absorbed the Coopers and their holdings.

In the third generation, the oldest Frost son, Edmund (1680–1752) and his wife, Hannah Cooper Frost, inherited the family's Kirkland Street homestead, while his younger brother Ebenezer (1697–1768), a tanner, bought the original Cooper farm in 1730. Edmund's daughter Hannah married Samuel Bowman, whose farm faced Porter Square. Their son Gideon (1724–1803) acquired the Bowman and the Cooper farms and by the end of his life owned all the fields north of Wendell Street as well as much of Avon Hill and land in Charlestown. These holdings remained substantially intact until 1833.

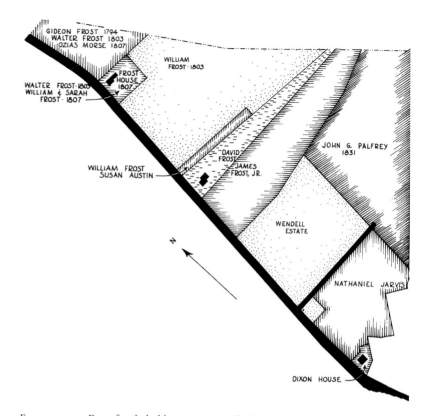

FIGURE 4.204 Frost family holdings in 1830. The land that Gideon and James Frost had accumulated before the Revolution was dispersed through inheritance and sale.

John Cooper-Ebenezer Frost Farm

In the initial division of the New Ox Pasture, Barnabas Lamson, a selectman, received a six-acre tract running back to the Charlestown line with about 150 feet on Massachusetts Avenue. John Cooper, who became a selectman, town clerk, and deacon of the First Parish, bought Lamson's house and farm about 1639. In 1652 he acquired the six-acre field north of his from its original grantee, Simon Crosby, and then the field south of him from Gregory Stone, his stepfather. When Cooper died in 1691, Samuel, his oldest son, inherited the house, the barn, and 13 acres adjoining the Parker-Hastings farm (later the Wendell estate). The second son, John Jr., who already owned the Bowers farm next door, inherited Crosby's field and some scattered properties elsewhere.

Samuel Cooper also inherited his father's seven-acre tract on Avon Hill, where he lived in the house he built on the occasion of his marriage to Hannah Hastings in 1682 (now the Cooper-Frost-Austin house at 21 Linnaean Street). Samuel rented out his father's place and left it to his oldest son, Samuel Cooper II, who sold the 17-acre property to his brother-in-law, Ebenezer Frost, in 1730. Frost, a tanner, lived there for almost forty years, and on his death in 1768 devised the back of the "mansion house" to his wife, Deborah, for her life. The rest of the estate went to his son James, provided that he build a kitchen for his mother, "12 feet wide, with chimney, fireplace and oven and with stairs into the cellar" (Middlesex Probate 8565). James Frost, a physician, died in 1770 and left his widow, Mary Prentice Frost, to share the house with her mother-in-law. Mary received for her dower the back eight acres, the front rooms of the house, and half the front garden, from the "middle of the foredoor to Sam'l Hastings fence" (Middlesex Probate 8588). The final partition of Frost's estate took place in 1788, following the death of his son David. The entire property, once again whole after Deborah's death and Mary's remarriage, was at that time divided between the oldest son, James Jr., and David's wife and children.

James Frost Jr.-Charles McClure place (Sacramento Street)

James Frost Jr., a tinplate worker, occupied his father's house on the southerly end of the homestead until his death in 1825; he was described near the end of his life as "terribly poor, old and filthy." Of the house, barn, currier's shop, and outbuildings he had inherited, all that was left was "a one-room building [that] looked like an office [with] a ladder only inside to a little [attic] above" (Saunders Ms.).[60] This was the first Frost property acquired by speculators, but neither the location nor the shape of the tract, 271 feet on the avenue and over a quarter of a mile deep, were advantageous for development.

Frost's executor recovered half an acre that Torrey Hancock had won in a judgment in 1823 and put the entire 8¾-acre property on the market in 1826. The purchaser was George Meacham, an associate of North Cambridge hotelier Zachariah Porter, who was described in 1852 as "tallow chandler, then stable-keeper, then real estate speculator, now broker" (Forbes, *Rich Men*, 106). Meacham sold the property to James Read, a stableman in the village, almost doubling his investment in two years. Read probably pastured his horses there before selling it in 1841 to Jonas Wyeth 2nd. Wyeth must have found the market for rental housing, his specialty, more attractive on Garden Street than on Massachusetts Avenue, because he sold the still-undeveloped property nine years later.

Charles F. McClure, who bought the property from Wyeth in 1850, was a returned forty-niner whose brother, David, had acquired the David Frost heirs' lot next door two years earlier. McClure recognized that the only feasible way to develop the property was to lay out a single street down its entire length, but he needed an outlet and at least one cross street to make it salable. He obtained a right-of-way to Beacon Street from James Friel of Somerville and exchanged land with Dr. Palfrey to gain access to Carver Street and the Harvard Branch platform. James Dana agreed to replat some of his lots in the Wendell estate to extend Oxford Street another block. McClure then laid out thirty-three generous parcels ranging from 7,300 to 15,500 square feet along

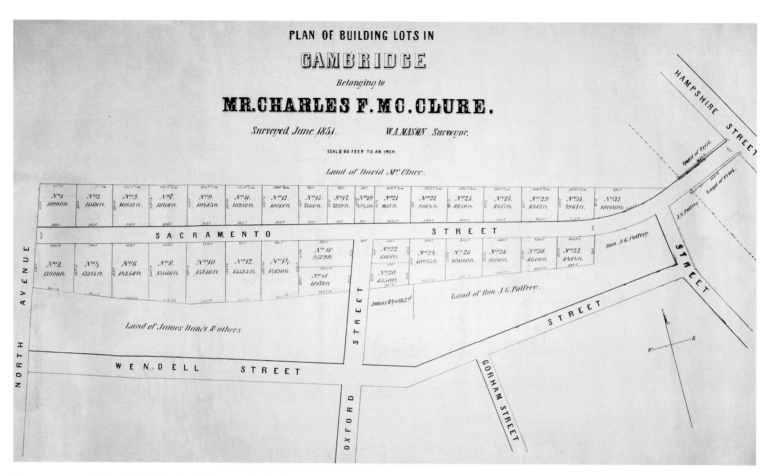

FIGURE 4.205 Charles F. McClure's subdivision plan for Sacramento Street, 1851. McClure soon realized that his 100-foot-wide lots were impractically large, and many of the parcels he sold disregarded this plan.

a narrow 40-foot-wide lane that he named Sacramento Street to commemorate his experience in the Gold Rush (figure 4.205).

McClure built the first house in his subdivision at 20 Sacramento Street in 1852 and quickly sold it to Almon Abbott, superintendent of a North Cambridge brickyard, along with 250 feet of frontage (figure 4.206). Henry Potter, a meat packer and North Cambridge landowner, bought both corners on the avenue, but McClure still owned seventeen lots a year later. East of Oxford, the earliest houses date from 1857, after he replatted the

street into affordable 60 feet lots. Thomas Pickhall, a sail maker, built a "cottage home" at 46 Sacramento, and McClure himself borrowed $1,500 from his infant daughter to put up a house at 41 that he sold to Eben Loomis, a "computer" (practical mathematician) (*Chronicle,* May 16, 1857; city directories, 1860–65).

William Dean Howells purchased 41 Sacramento in 1866, at the beginning of the postwar boom (figure 4.207). "Here and there in the vacant lots abandoned hoop-skirts defied decay; and near the half-finished wooden houses, empty mortar-beds,

FIGURE 4.206 Charles F. McClure-Almon Abbott house, 20 Sacramento Street (1852). McClure built this elaborate Italianate mansion to demonstrate his aspirations for the street. The house originally had a low hip roof, similar to 41 Sacramento; the Mansard was added in 1869. Photo 2013.

FIGURE 4.207 Charles F. McClure-William Dean Howells house, 41 Sacramento Street (1857). Howells described it as "a carpenter's box" on an embankment "lifting its base several feet above the common level" (*Suburban Sketches*, 11). The house, a Cambridge landmark, was stripped of disfiguring alterations and restored in 2013–15. Photo 2015.

and bits of lath and slate strewn over the scarred and mutilated ground, added their interest to the scene" (*Suburban Sketches*, 11). When he moved away in 1870 he reported that:

> Many of the vacant lots [had] flourished up, during the four years we knew it, into fresh-painted wooden houses. … The lessening pasturage also reduced the herds which formerly fed in the vicinity, and at last we caught the tinkle of cow-bells only as the cattle were driven past to remoter meadows. (Ibid., 242)

Sacramento Street attracted another author in 1870 when the legal commentator Joel Prentiss Bishop purchased six lots at the corner of Crescent Street. The last major construction on the street occurred in 1912–13, when Bishop's son, Cambridge real estate agent Charles S. Bishop, put up four Mission Revival three-deckers and an apartment building that he named "El Pueblo."

Sacramento Street has a more heterogeneous character than its neighbors because McClure neglected to adopt setback and use restrictions, but the city confirmed its desirability when it built the first Agassiz School in 1874. In 1879 Walter Hastings of Boston put up two anomalous brick rows on land sold by the Somerville Bleachery. That did not deter Adna Shaw, who built an elegant Shingle Style house in 1883 that was a showcase for his East Cambridge furniture business, Shaw, Applin & Co. (see figure 6.122). James Hazen, a manager at the New York Biscuit Co. in Cambridgeport, had George Fogerty design a Queen Anne house at 5 Sacramento Street—"first class in every particular"—that complemented James A. Wood's elaborate Colonial Revival on the corner of Massachusetts Avenue (now 3 Sacramento Street; *Chronicle*, Aug. 22, 1891).

Sacramento Street declined after World War II, and in 1962 most of the Agassiz neighborhood was rezoned for high-density residential buildings with no height limit. Harvard University acquired many houses for a planned student apartment complex similar to Peabody Terrace, a threat that was not extinguished until neighborhood protests forced the city to downzone the area in 1974.

Elizabeth Frost-David McClure Place (Sacramento Field and Crescent Street)   Sacramento Field and Crescent Street originated in the partition of James Frost Sr.'s 17-acre farm in 1788. David, the second son, inherited 9½ acres, but died just before the distribution. Because his estate was insolvent, the executors sold 4½ acres to John Foxcroft in 1790, leaving his widow, Elizabeth Allen Frost, a long, narrow strip extending to the Charlestown line with 165 feet of frontage on the avenue. One son became a carpenter and the other a painter and glazier, and with their help Elizabeth was able to build a new house in 1815–16. When she died in 1839, she bequeathed it and one across the street "used by a Negro family named Lewis" (now 35 Bowdoin Street) to her son-in-law, Jonathan Ford of Boston (Chronicle, July 26, 1891). Charles Goodridge, a grocer, acquired Elizabeth's house in 1877. He lived there twelve years and then had it moved to 26 Gray Street so he could build the present house at 1705 Massachusetts Avenue.

David McClure, a Cambridgeport varnish manufacturer, purchased Elizabeth Frost's homestead in 1848, shortly before his brother, Charles, returned from California and acquired the adjoining James Frost Jr. property. The principal feature was a spring-fed pond behind the house, which occupied a lot that was too narrow to accommodate a street with salable lots on both sides. Henry Potter bought part of the property in July 1851, subdivided the frontage, and auctioned the balance in 1853. The Somerville Dyeing & Bleaching Company (a commercial laundry) bought the spring lot, built a stone reservoir, drilled artesian wells to augment the natural supply, and installed a boiler house and pumps that supplied the plant on Somerville Avenue

with 100,000 gallons of water a day. "The bleachery owner … fenced in the property … planted trees, vines and flowers, and stocked the reservoir with many varieties of fish." The property was "bordered on three sides by arched arbors which in summer are weighted down with grapes … honeycombed with paths bordered with flower beds, and dotted with peach, pear and cherry trees" (*Chronicle,* Feb. 4, 1922; figure 4.208). The bleachery closed during the Depression, and the stagnant reservoir was filled in. The site became an informal park known as Sacramento Field, which Harvard held for future development until the city took it by eminent domain in 1980.

James Dana replatted the land between the reservoir and Oxford Street into thirteen unsalably small lots that were eventually reorganized around Sacramento Place, a dead-end street not fully built up until 1899. East of Oxford Street, Charles McClure combined his brother's land with his own and laid out Crescent Street in 1857 with nineteen 60-by-60-foot lots so small that

FIGURE 4.208 The Somerville Dyeing & Bleaching Company maintained the reservoir until Harvard University filled and graded it for a projected student housing project. Sacramento Field now occupies the site. Photo 1937.

FIGURE 4.209 Successive elementary schools on the corner of Sacramento and Oxford streets have lent their identity to the Agassiz neighborhood since 1874. The second Agassiz School was erected in 1915 and demolished in 1993 (see chapter 7). Photo ca. 1945.

several were still on the market almost fifty years later. Although they were offered with restrictions requiring that houses cost at least $1,000 and prohibiting accessory buildings, the ever-flexible McClure was quick to allow William Howe to build greenhouses near Oxford Street. After the Civil War densely packed two-family houses and three-deckers filled the street.

Wells-Eustis-Clarke Place (Garfield and Eustis streets) The three-way partition of James Frost Sr.'s 17-acre farm in 1788 left one more piece to be considered. David Frost's executors sold the northern 4½ acres with 155 feet on the avenue to John Foxcroft in 1790. Three years before his death in 1802 Foxcroft sold the property to Ebenezer Wells of Boston, a sail maker who put up a "large ... hip'd roof square house" at about 1715 Massachusetts Avenue (Saunders Ms.). Dr. William Eustis, who was

between appointments as President Madison's Secretary of War and Ambassador to the Netherlands, purchased Wells's mortgage in 1813, but after his return in 1818 acquired the Shirley-Eustis house in Roxbury and was living there when he was elected governor in 1823. Although Eustis died in 1825, his much younger widow allowed Wells's daughters to remain in the house for decades.

Henry M. Clarke, a wealthy paper manufacturer, acquired "the ancient dwelling house and the ancient barn" from Mrs. Eustis's executors in 1867, along with two acres that had originally been part of the adjoining William Frost place; this gave him almost six acres with 275 feet of frontage on the east side of the avenue (Middlesex Deeds 1010/11). He also purchased 4½ acres across the avenue from Stillman Willis. Clarke remodeled the Wells-Eustis house into an enormous Mansard and put up a

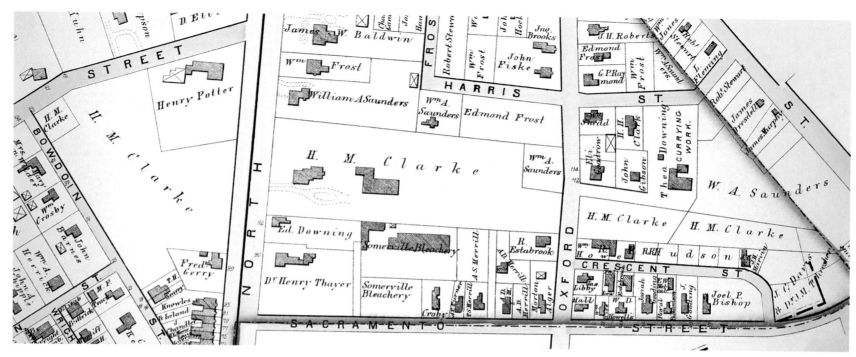

FIGURE 4.210 Henry M. Clarke holdings in 1873.

48-by-102-foot barn that was probably the largest ever built in Cambridge (figures 4.210–4.211).

Clarke's purchase of a 10-acre spread on a rapidly developing street near the village might be explained by his interest in breeding prize-winning cattle. The Jersey cows he raised on his gentleman's farm in Belmont routinely won awards at agricultural fairs, and in 1869 he imported the first Brown Swiss cattle to the United States. Cambridge assessed him for as many as eleven cows and twelve horses in the years between 1869 and 1876, and he may have thought of his Cambridge place as a demonstration stock farm.

Illness forced Clarke to retire in 1875, and he remained an invalid until his death in 1898. His brother-in-law and former partner, Boston paper mill owner Samuel D. Warren, became his trustee, along with attorneys Louis Brandeis and S.D. Warren Jr. In 1882 the *Chronicle* reported that they intended to move Clarke's house to the northwest corner of the lot and lay out a

street that would "open the whole estate, which has so long lain idle, and make the land … available for building lots" (Feb. 3). The trustees also laid out Hurlbut Street and an extension of Martin with a slightly less spacious plan more suited to that area.

Garfield Street, which at 50 feet wide is the most generous street in the neighborhood, is an agreeable contrast to Sacramento in part because the trustees adhered to their subdivision plan until all the lots were sold. John A. Rollins, a provision dealer at Quincy Market, made the first purchase in 1883 and built a Mansard facing the avenue. The trustees sold the rest of the lots in an orderly fashion, working eastward and leaving none vacant to annoy the new homeowners. By 1891 the street was complete, and every lot contained a new house. Most were in the Queen Anne style, although the only design control was a 10-foot setback (figure 4.212).

Garfield Street largely retained its value and character in the 20th century, even though Harvard landbanked many of the

FIGURE 4.211 Henry M. Clarke's house and cow barn, as seen from Memorial Hall in 1875. The tall structure left of the barn was the pump house of the Somerville Bleachery.

FIGURE 4.212 Queen Anne houses on Garfield Street. From left to right, the Edward A. Shepherd house at 39 (1886); the J.W. Estabrook house at 45 (1886, William E. Woodward, architect and builder); and the A.S. Bartlett house at 49 Garfield (E.L. Clark, architect). Photo 2009.

houses in the 1950s and '60s. In 1917 an apartment building replaced a community stable at 61 Garfield that had allowed residents to forgo individual carriage houses, and in 1930 a gas station and two small Capes replaced the Clarke mansion. The downzoning of Sacramento and Garfield streets in 1974 and the city's acquisition of Sacramento Field in 1980 stymied the university's plans for a student housing complex, and the houses it sold to faculty members in the 1990s were quickly restored. The MBTA razed the Rollins house in 1978, but it was replaced in 1995 by a sympathetically designed affordable housing project.

Clarke's trustees were not as careful with the less-valuable land east of Oxford Street. William A. Saunders laid out Eustis Street along Henry Clarke's fence soon after he moved the Margaret Eustis house from Holmes Place to the corner of Oxford in 1863. The trustees sold the southeast corner to Stearns Ellis, who built a livery stable there in 1876. Local builders put up three-deckers and gambrel-roof duplexes on the remaining lots in 1890–96. The north side of the street, part of Mary Frost's dower, developed separately between 1899 and 1904.

Gideon Frost Farm

The next large holding to the north originated as another six-acre grant in the New Ox Pasture, between Massachusetts Avenue and the Charlestown boundary. Probably meant for Reverend Thomas Shepard, the tract went instead to Gregory Stone, a farmer on Garden Street. Stone sold it to George Bowers, who in 1656 left a house to his son, Jerathmeel, with a life estate for his widow, Elizabeth. John Cooper Jr., who had grown up on his father's place next door, bought out Jerathmeel in 1683. Cooper was a shoemaker, but he accumulated a great deal of property, and by the time he died in 1735/6 his holdings included 11 acres of salt marsh, 4 acres of meadow near Fresh Pond, 4½ acres on Watson's Plain in North Cambridge, and 14 acres in the West Field, as well as tracts in Woburn, Charlestown, and Arlington.

Cooper left his widow, Sarah, in possession of half their house and the southerly eight acres of the homestead, but his 9-year-old

grandson John inherited most of the property. When he turned 21 in 1748 he was found to be "a person *non compos*," and the court allowed his guardian, next-door neighbor Ebenezer Frost, to be remunerated for some much-needed repairs: a thousand shingles in 1752, mending the casements in 1753, fixing the oven and clearing brush in 1754, and so on until John died in 1762. Frost asked special compensation "for his extraordinary trouble in taking care of his ward the three last years of his life which was exceeding troublesome" (Middlesex Probate 5166).

John's property reverted to his mother, Hannah, who had married Benjamin Crackbone in 1738. Having secured a clear title, Crackbone sold the entire 14-acre Cooper homestead, plus 2½ acres of salt marsh and 32 acres in Charlestown, to Gideon Frost in 1763. The Bowers-Cooper house at 1735 Massachusetts Avenue (just south of Prentiss Street) remained standing until about 1833. William A. Saunders described it as an "ancient lean-to roof house … with the small windows in diamond shape glass … [facing] south, end on road with long roof in rear" (Saunders Ms.). Traces of Crackbone's tanning vats were found near Forest Street when the area was developed in the 19th century.

Gideon Frost, a blacksmith, made an advantageous marriage to Sarah Ireland in 1753 and built the present Waterhouse house on the Common. After starting a family he moved to the Bowers-Cooper farm adjacent to his uncle Ebenezer's place. Here he "went into farming in earnest. [He] gave up his trade, but brought away his tools, and for himself or a neighbor occasionally did a job in his old line" (ibid.). In 1764 he purchased nine acres on Avon Hill surrounding the Gallows Lot. He received a 1½-acre piece of the family homestead on Kirkland Street from his brother Edmund's estate in 1782 and then bought out the other heirs. A year later he acquired six acres in Charlestown. He purchased the adjoining seven-acre Paddlefoot-Andrew-Bowman homestead from his widowed sister, Hannah Bowman, in 1786, the Cooper-Frost-Austin place on Linnaean Street in 1788, and the rest of the Bowman farm in 1794. In 1800 he was assessed for 95 acres in Cambridge, including two and a half houses, three barns, 26 acres of pasture, 35 acres of mowing,

16 acres of meadow, 10 acres of salt marsh, and eight acres of unimproved land, along with additional land in Charlestown and Uxbridge. His household included a former slave, Neptune Frost, who fought with the Cambridge militia in 1775.

Gideon Frost was the archetype of the respected Yankee farmer and town leader, whose death in 1803 foreshadowed Cambridge's transition to a suburban community. A selectman for six years and a deacon of the First Parish for twenty, his life differed only in degree from those of his forebears: prominent in town and deeply embedded in relations with other old families like the Coopers but distant from the college and from Boston affairs. His real estate activities, while more extensive than most, were typical for 18th-century men who accumulated land as a legacy for their descendants, rather than for its development potential. Frost's children were the first generation to capitalize on the social and economic opportunities that appeared during the turnpike era, and his male grandchildren either completed the transition from rural to mercantile pursuits or sought better farmland in the west.

Frost's will reversed the normal order of inheritance. His oldest son, Gideon, a doctor, had already established himself in Uxbridge and received nothing. The middle son, Walter, a tanner, was given the 16-acre Jackson-Bowman farm, plus a 12-rod (198 feet) square in the northwest corner of the Paddlefoot-Andrew-Bowman farm, with Crackbone's buildings, tan vats, and lime pits. The youngest son, William, received Gideon's residence (the Bowers-Cooper house on Massachusetts Avenue) and 28 acres comprising the John Cooper and Paddlefoot-Andrew-Bowman farms, plus the west half of the 10-acre Edmund Frost homestead on Kirkland Street. Daughter Martha received the other half of the homestead and was to divide the income from it with her sister, Sarah. Martha and Sarah were to share the Cooper-Frost-Austin house on Linnaean Street.

The assessors' records suggest that Gideon's children worked out different domestic arrangements. At first, William and his family lived in the Cooper-Frost-Austin house, while Martha and Sarah remained in the Bowers-Cooper house where they had been raised. In 1807 Martha married Reverend Thomas Austin and moved into the Cooper-Frost-Austin house, while William moved into one side of a new three-story house on the east side of Massachusetts Avenue bought from brother Walter on the eve of a foreclosure that drove him from Cambridge. In 1812 Sarah Frost sold her half of the Cooper-Frost-Austin house to Reverend Austin and rented the Bowers-Cooper house from William. She died in 1821 and left her half of Walter's 1807 house to William; it passed to his children when he died in 1832. William's son William Frost Jr. moved the house to 10 Frost Street in 1867, as described below.

Paddlefoot-Andrew-Bowman Farm (Prentiss, Forest, and Frost streets) The farm that Gideon Frost purchased from Samuel Bowman's estate in 1786 originated as an eight-acre grant to Samuel Shepard, a half-brother of Reverend Thomas Shepard. Both he and the next owner, Edward Winship, lived in the village. Jonathan Paddlefoot acquired the land from Winship in 1649 and was the first to build on it. Thomas Andrew, a mason, bought the two-room house in 1662 and in 1699 gave it to Rebecca, his only child, just before she married Samuel Bowman, a tanner from Cambridge Farms (Lexington). Rebecca retained ownership despite her marriage, and when she died in 1713 five of her seven children were alive to inherit it. (Samuel remarried and fathered seven more children who did not share in Rebecca's legacy.) Rebecca and Samuel's oldest son, Samuel Jr., married Hannah Frost and settled in Charlestown; he bought out his siblings, but since his stepmother stayed on the farm until they both died in 1783 he never had full use of it.

Gideon Frost, Samuel Bowman Jr.'s executor, purchased the farm through a straw in 1786. He combined the Bowman farm with his own and bequeathed both properties (minus Walter's 12-rod square) to his youngest son, William (1774–1832), the last of his line to follow the rural traditions of his ancestors. William worked on his father's place until he was 26 or 27, married late, and accumulated wood lots, fields, and marsh lots to pass on to his heirs. His children were the first Frosts to join the western migration; a daughter married and left for New York

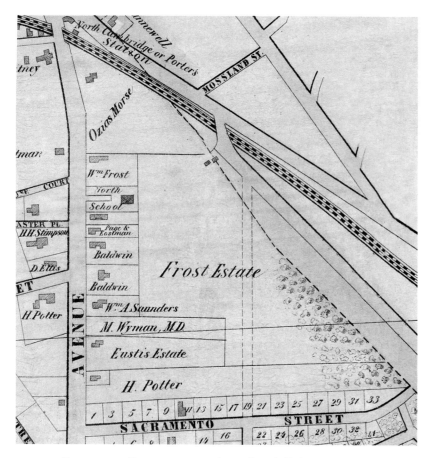

FIGURE 4.213 Frost properties in the northern half of the Agassiz neighborhood in 1854. William Frost's house is shown in its original location; the tract labeled "Frost Estate" is his widow's dower, and her house faces the Somerville line.

been left to his children by his sister Sarah in 1821), and about eight acres in Charlestown. His widow, Mary Teel Frost, was to have half the house and the entire farm for her dower, but the executor, Cambridge attorney William Whipple, needed cash to cover William's debts, so he capitalized on the value of the frontage by creating several lots along the avenue. Mary received the back 18 acres and a house facing Beacon Street for her lifetime (figure 4.213).

Whipple's method of dividing the property was grievously flawed. Mary Frost's dower land was accessible only by a narrow right-of-way. The avenue parcels averaged 135 feet wide, too narrow for a cross street with houses on both sides, and were 264 feet (16 rods) deep at a time when a very generous house lot might measure 100 by 100 feet. Buyers struggled with these ungainly proportions, acquiring adjacent land, subdividing, and setting off narrow strips for makeshift side streets, until in 1900 the two owners went to court over an overlooked six-inch-wide, 264-foot-long sliver along the south side of Prentiss Street. Development was haphazard compared to the lower avenue, where owners had larger parcels and a better understanding of the market.

James B. Read, a descendant of the village mercantile family, returned from his birthplace in Tobago, married Emily Wyeth in 1828, and acquired the Bowers-Cooper house and barn and 196 feet of frontage in 1833. He purchased another 109 feet of frontage in 1837 and in 1840 razed the old house and sold the southern 100 feet to William A. Saunders. A year later, having moved to Boston, James sold the remainder to his father-in-law, Jonas Wyeth 2nd. In 1841 the youngest Frost heir turned 21, and the executor divided the remaining frontage among William's three living sons, William Jr., Henry, and Frederick, and the heirs of a fourth, Thomas. William Frost Jr. (1801–87), the only grandson to achieve the prominence of his father and grandfather in Cambridge affairs, inherited half of the 1807 house and part of Lot 2 and purchased the remainder of these properties from his siblings. Lot 3 went to Frederick and Lot 4 to Henry, who sold it to bookkeeper Reuben Demmon in 1842.

State, while two sons moved to Illinois and then on to Iowa. He kept his father's farm intact except for a two-acre field along the southern boundary that he sold to his brother-in-law, Thomas Austin, in 1813. This passed through other hands to Henry M. Clarke in 1867.

When William Frost died intestate in 1832, his 22-acre farm had 710 feet on Massachusetts Avenue and 646 feet on Beacon Street and contained the Bowers-Cooper house, two barns, and various outbuildings. He also owned half of his brother Walter's 1807 house, half of the 12-rod square (the other half having

This put the entire frontage in play. The Charlestown Branch Railroad commenced passenger service from Porter's Station in January 1842, setting the stage for the first wave of construction along the avenue. Demmon put up a Greek Revival house just south of Forest Street in 1843 and sold it three years later to Boston merchant James W. Baldwin, who hired Calvin Ryder to design a high-style Bracketed Italianate house next door in 1852. Frederick Frost built two houses similar to Demmon's but sold them when he left Cambridge in 1847. William Frost Jr. relocated Walter Frost's 1807 house in 1867 and built two Mansards on the site (see figure 4.178).

The frontage maintained its early suburban character until the end of the 19th century. William A. Saunders's lot was broken up when Prentiss Street was put through in 1900. In 1904 ten houses on Exeter Park replaced the Baldwin house, and in 1916 the Newport Road apartments displaced two more. Several houses formerly on the avenue can now be found on the side streets that cross Mary Frost's dower (see figure 6.58).

Mary Frost's Dower

Mary Frost's 18-acre dower lay undeveloped long after her husband William's death in 1832. In 1851 William A. Saunders began to seek out her husband's heirs. He found Henry Frost in Illinois, and purchased his one-sixth share for $1,600. Edmund Frost had borrowed on his share, defaulted, and moved to Pennsylvania; Saunders retrieved the title from the mortgage holder in New Hampshire. Benjamin Frost, in Iowa, sold Saunders his share in 1867. William Frost Jr. retained his share, as did daughter Lucy, who had married a distant cousin, Gideon Frothingham, and was living in Pennsylvania. The sixth heir, her son Frederick, sold his share to Frothingham's brother-in-law, James Archibald.

When the dust settled, four partners—James Archibald, Gideon Frothingham, William Frost Jr., and William A. Saunders—held shares in Mary's dower land, but they could not take title during her lifetime. Looking ahead, they purchased

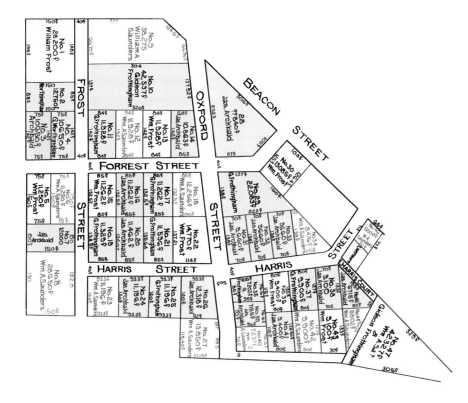

FIGURE 4.211 Mary Frost's dower as subdivided in 1858 (Harris is now Prentiss Street). William A. Saunders, Gideon Frothingham, and James Archibald each received between eleven and fifteen parcels, while William Frost Jr. was a minority holder with eight.

a lot in Charles McClure's subdivision and agreed to extend Oxford Street all the way to Beacon Street. In 1855 Saunders leased Mary's entire dower (except for three-quarters of an acre on Beacon Street, where she lived with Frederick) for $200 a year. Three years later the men filed a subdivision plan that laid out Frost, Forest, and Prentiss streets (figure 4.214). The parcels ranged from 5,000 to 42,000 square feet and must have been distributed by lot; few were contiguous, and the partners traded among themselves to rationalize the initial distribution. The owners were free to sell or subdivide as they wished, and the

FIGURE 4.215 William Frost Jr. moved his father's 1807 house from 1799 Massachusetts Avenue to 10 Frost Street in 1867. Photo 2009.

FIGURE 4.216 William Frost Jr. built 9 Forest Street in 1872 for James M. Hilton, who lived nearby and rented it to tenants.

original forty-seven parcels eventually became over one hundred building lots.

Mary Frost's long-anticipated demise in 1861 came at an inauspicious time, and sales were few until after the Civil War. William Frost Jr. was the most prolific builder in the neighborhood; in addition to moving his father's house to 10 Frost Street in 1867, he and his son, William E. Frost, built thirty Mansards between 1860 and 1877, exhausting the decorative possibilities of the style.[61] When William Dean Howells wrote of streets "upon which a flight of French-roof houses suddenly settled a year or two since, with families in them, and many outward signs of permanence" he must have been describing upper Oxford and Forest streets (*Suburban Sketches,* 61; figure 4.216).

The random pattern of ownership left plenty of empty lots at the end of the Mansard era, some of which were later filled with notable Stick Style and Queen Anne houses built for a middle-class clientele (figure 4.217). In the mid-20th century the neighborhood was plagued by owners who broke up large houses into single room occupancy and small apartments. The extension of the Red Line to Porter Square in 1986 made the area desirable once more, and many houses were restored to single-family occupancy after the abolition of rent control in 1995.

East of Oxford Street, brick manufacturer Lewis DeRosay built a large house with a four-story tower that occupied the triangle bounded by Beacon and Forest streets, while William A. Saunders moved the 1822 Eustis house to the corner of Eustis in 1863 (figure 4.218). The lots in between filled up with more Mansards that screened a low-lying one-acre tract between Eustis and Prentiss streets where Theodore Downing built a tannery that operated from about 1871 until shortly before his death in 1898. Investors led by Harvard Square builder R. Currie Grovestein razed the building in 1899 and built twelve double houses on Traymore Street.[62] Beginning in 1904, Grovestein packed ten three-deckers onto Arcadia, Eustis, and Harris streets, completing the last corner of Mary Frost's dower at roughly twice the density that would be allowed under the zoning code adopted in 1924.

Figure 4.217 Ward-Lovell house, 17 Frost Street (1886, Rand & Taylor, architects). Sylvester L. Ward, a Roxbury oil merchant, built this house for his daughter Mary when she married Frederick Lovell, a North Cambridge grocer. It was demolished for a parking lot in 1967. Photo 1966.

Figure 4.218 Margaret Eustis house, 114 Oxford Street (1822). William A. Saunders moved the Eustis house from Massachusetts Avenue near Holmes Place to its present location in 1863. Photo 2009.

Jackson-Samuel Bowman Farm (Roseland Street)

Richard Jackson, another early settler who served as selectman and representative, received the northernmost grant from the New Ox Pasture. Samuel Bowman Sr. acquired this six-acre field at the junction of Massachusetts Avenue and the town boundary in 1705 and left it to his son Noah in 1746 along with 10 contiguous acres in Charlestown. Noah's eldest son died in the Revolution, so he left the land to a grandson with a life estate for his wife, Hannah. Grandson Nathaniel Bowman graduated from Harvard College in 1786, became a doctor in Maine, and sold all 16 acres to Gideon Frost in 1794.

Walter Frost inherited the Bowman farm from Gideon in 1803 but lost it by foreclosure to Ozias Morse, a Charlestown farmer, in 1806.[63] The Middlesex Turnpike Corporation laid out Beacon Street across the fields in 1805; Somerville Avenue followed in 1806, and the Charlestown Branch arrived in 1840. Ozias Morse Jr. inherited the place in 1817 and developed the Roseland Nurseries on Massachusetts Avenue. In 1855 he removed the Bowman house and rented a lot to the North Avenue Congregational Society, which put up the chapel that it moved to the corner of Arlington Street when its lease expired in 1861 (see chapter 7). Morse then laid out Roseland Street with 25 small lots, along with 27 more on Mossland Street in Somerville (figure 4.219). John Lockey, a manufacturer from Leominster, purchased most of the Cambridge lots and sold one to the Congregationalists in 1866. He replatted his remaining land into 14 larger lots in 1868, and by 1873 there were eight houses on the street (figure 4.220). The remainder of the avenue frontage was eventually developed for commercial purposes (see figure 4.185 and *Report Five: Northwest Cambridge*).

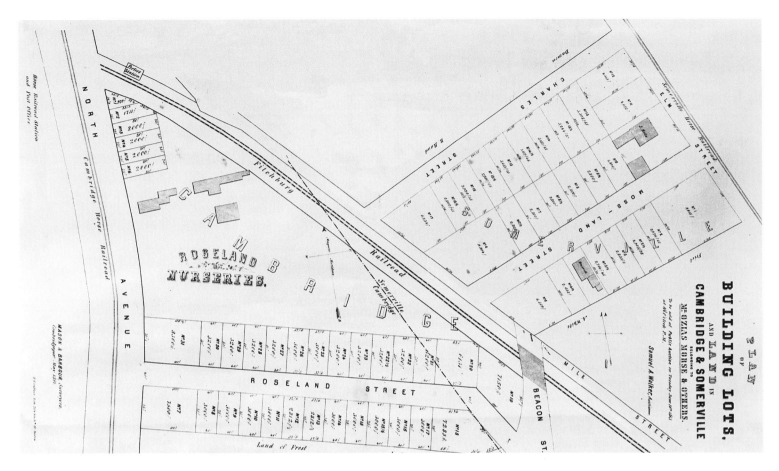

FIGURE 4.219 Ozias Morse Jr.'s subdivision plan for the Roseland Nursery, offered at public auction in 1863.

FIGURE 4.220 Roseland Street (right) in 1935, with 1 Frost Street (1885) in the foreground. All but three houses on the north side of Roseland Street were razed between 1928 and 1966 for the Sears, Roebuck store and parking lot.

FOXCROFT ESTATE: PROFESSORS ROW AND SHADY HILL

Kirkland Street was called the Charlestown Road until the 19th century. It traverses the level plain that extends from the village to Union Square, Somerville, at some point crossing an imperceptible divide between the Town Creek and Millers River watersheds. The Pine Swamp limited development to the north, but to the south Quincy Street was the first of many cross streets put through after 1804. Harvard created an academic suburb for senior professors along Kirkland Street in the 1820s. At the end of the century the Shady Hill neighborhood replaced Professors Row as the most desirable residence for faculty and became a landmark of American town planning and Colonial Revival architecture.

The first colonists called this tract the Ox Pasture. The Proprietors of Common Lands distributed 105 acres along both sides of Kirkland Street to eighteen townsmen in parcels of 1 to 13 acres each. One of the recipients, Thomas Danforth (1622–99), received a six-acre grant in 1638, the same year that he inherited the family homestead on Bow Street. In 1652 Danforth acquired a house on the north side of Kirkland built by Reverend John Phillips in 1640. By the end of the century he owned all but one of the early grants nearby and had consolidated the scattered fields into a 120-acre farm. During his forty-five years in public service, Danforth filled almost every office from selectman to deputy governor and acquired large tracts of land elsewhere, including 10,000 acres in Framingham.

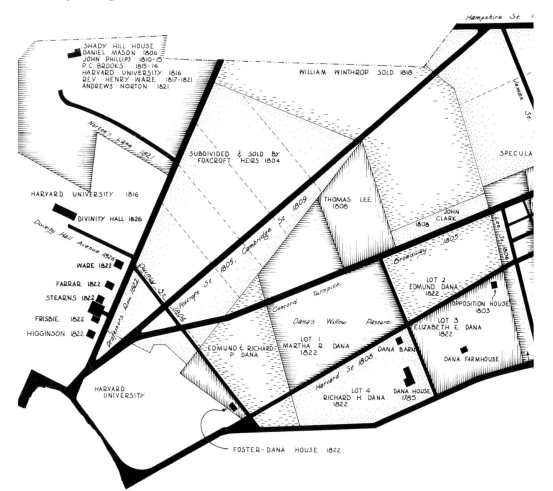

FIGURE 4.221 The Danforth-Foxcroft and Francis Dana estates in 1830. Dana's holdings south of Massachusetts Avenue are not shown.

All of Danforth's sons predeceased him. He was succeeded by English-born merchant Francis Foxcroft, the husband of his youngest daughter, Elizabeth. Foxcroft was one of Cambridge's earliest Tories, "a man of wealth and energy" who served as judge of common pleas and then of probate from 1707 to 1725. Although he had "worshipped and communed with the Congregational Church," he was buried as an Anglican, one of the few in Cambridge when he died in 1727 (Paige, 549).

Francis Foxcroft II (1694/5–1768) continued the family tradition of public service, serving as Middlesex County register of deeds for forty-five years and judge for twenty-seven. Between 1750 and 1760 Judge Foxcroft built a 17-room Georgian house on Kirkland Street that is known only through his probate inventory, which began with "the keeping room, the best room, the cloak room, the great entry" and ended with "the best kitchen, the kitchen, [and] the cellar." Another dwelling may have been the Phillips-Danforth house; there was also a barn, a stable, and even a "corn barn." Francis divided his estate between his two sons with the wish that it "be continued in the Posterity of that ancient and honored gentleman, Thomas Danforth, my grandfather" (Middlesex Probate 8408).

John Foxcroft (1740–1802), who had already succeeded his father as register of deeds, bought out his brother Francis, a physician in Brookfield. John was an outspoken loyalist but was not proscribed because he remained in residence. Three companies of militia were quartered at his house in May 1775. Two years later, when it was destroyed by fire, he said "that he would rather see his house burned than occupied by d—d rebels" (Sibley, XIV, 269). After this he may have lived in the house he obtained by foreclosing on the heirs of John Hicks, the Minuteman, who died in 1775.

Foxcroft's sister Phebe, whose husband, Samuel Phillips Jr., founded Phillips Academy in Andover, inherited the property in 1804. She sold the land south of Kirkland Street in twelve large parcels and in 1807 conveyed all 60 acres north of the road to John Phillips, a merchant and future mayor of Boston. John Phillips also bought a house on 4½ acres in Charlestown on the newly opened Middlesex Turnpike (now Beacon Street), but he

defaulted on the mortgage and lost it to Peter Chardon Brooks, the wealthy Medford merchant.

Foxcroft land surrounded the only grant that had escaped Thomas Danforth, a 10-acre farm established by Edmund Frost in 1646. Frost, the ruling elder of the Cambridge church, arrived with Thomas Hooker in 1634; his descendants, unlike Danforth's, remained in the Puritan camp and were prominent in town affairs well into the 19th century. The farmhouse disappeared by 1812, but the property stayed in the family until the 1830s. The Frost farm was eventually subsumed by Professors Row and Shady Hill, and its boundaries are no longer apparent.

PROFESSORS ROW

Professors Row originated with John Kirkland, who served as president of Harvard from 1810 to 1828 (figure 4.222). Kirkland and his successor, Josiah Quincy, hired cosmopolitan scholars who expected comfortable living conditions. Many raised their social standing by marrying into the Federalist mercantile aristocracy that now controlled the university. Bound by the "Laws of Residence" to endure the high cost of living in Cambridge, they were able to bargain with the Corporation for full professorships, higher salaries, and financial assistance to purchase land near the college.

Harvard bought the 64-acre Phillips property from Peter Chardon Brooks in 1816. The college sold 38 distant acres with the house in Charlestown to Professor Henry Ware Sr. and retained 26, including a right-of-way to the 20-acre field where Divinity Hall went up in 1825 and a lot near Holmes Place that was divided between the Old Cambridge Baptist Church and the Lawrence Scientific School twenty years later. Stephen Higginson, the college steward, laid out five residential lots along Kirkland Street, reserving the one closest to the Yard for himself (figure 4.223). Boston merchant Patrick Tracy Jackson paid for the lot and for Higginson's house, a simple but urbane Federal design as yet unseen in Cambridge that set the standard for faculty homes for the next fifteen years (see figure 6.43).[64] It passed

FIGURE 4.222 Kirkland Street looking east, with Stephen Higginson's house on the left and the Delta on the right. Photo ca. 1870.

FIGURE 4.223 Professors Row in 1833. By this time the original five houses were owned by Stephen Higginson, James Hayward, Asahel Stearns, John Farrar, and Reverend Henry Ware Sr. Henry Ware Jr.'s house and the lots east of Divinity Avenue are on the former Frost farm. The Baptist Church (1845) and the Scientific School (1847) are additions to the original map.

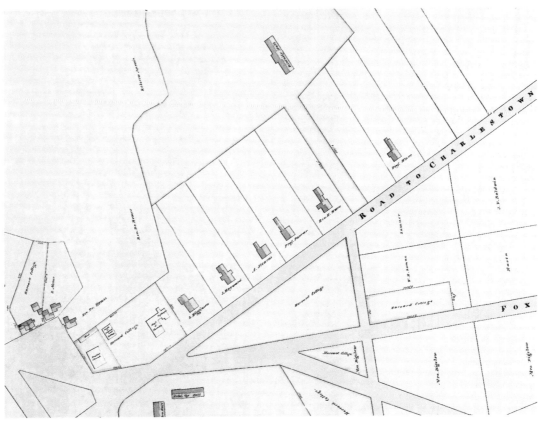

to Charles C. Foster, a brother of Bossenger and Joseph Foster, in 1836, and his descendants sold it to Harvard in 1955.

Next door, Professor of Moral Philosophy Levi Frisbie built a somewhat more elaborate residence on the site of the old Danforth mansion in 1822.[65] Law professor Asahel Stearns built on the third lot. Tired of paying rent in the village, he wrote the college treasurer "that it would be a safe and good calculation to erect a house sufficiently large to have five or six chambers to let." The rooms would net him $50 or $60 a year, and he asked the college to lend him $3,000, half the sum needed "to erect a three story dwelling house upon the lot of land marked out for me" (Harvard College Papers IX, 42; figure 4.224).

Harvard sold the fourth lot to mathematics professor John Farrar in 1828. John Palfrey recalled that Farrar had designed his house a decade earlier:

> As an occupation suited to his weak sight, he made a large wooden model of a house which he was intending to build, with every door, window, closet and staircase accurately finished. He had heard that gentlemen who undertook to be their own architects were apt to fall upon impracticable combinations; and he chose to put his own scheme to this test. (Palfrey, *Farrar*, 11–12)

Farrar's was a Federal design, much like Higginson's and Frisbie's, that he updated with a Greek Revival portico in the 1830s. It was demolished in 1968 so the Jared Sparks house could be relocated from Quincy Street.

Hollis Professor of Divinity Henry Ware Sr. (1764–1845) bought the easternmost lot in 1822, but in view of his purchase of the Phillips property he was not required to pay for it until 1827. In 1828 he built a house similar to the others and lived there until 1843, when he sold it to Ephraim Whitman, a Boston merchant. Ware moved into a cottage behind his old house that was relocated to Divinity Avenue in 1912 and to 41 Holden Street in 1929, where it remains (figure 4.225).

The 20-acre field behind the five faculty lots was initially "used between the neighbors as pasturing," but when the corporation planned to sell 9 or 10 acres to the Society for Promoting

FIGURE 4.224 Asahel Stearns house, 8 Oxford Street (1822). Although it gave the impression of an old-fashioned Georgian mansion, Stearns's house featured the innovative Federal detail of shallow bay windows under a portico that originally faced Kirkland Street. It was displaced from the corner by Lowell Lecture Hall in 1901 and demolished with 10 Oxford Street (1846) for Mallinckrodt Laboratory in 1926. Photo after 1902.

FIGURE 4.225 Henry Ware Sr. house, 25 Kirkland Street (1828, right) and cottage (1843). Photo before 1912.

Theological Education in Harvard College it "was let out for three years to be leveled, ditches filled, bushes removed, then planted, manured, and laid down to grass" (College Papers, Higginson to Davis, Dec. 5, 1825, and Oct. 27, 1827). The society erected Divinity Hall and a caretaker's house in 1825. Most of Harvard's remaining Foxcroft land lay vacant for over thirty years until it was allotted to the Museum of Comparative Zoology.

Harvard's intentions for Divinity Avenue are unclear; at 75 feet, the private way was as wide as Kirkland Street and much wider than the future Oxford Street. The east side bordered directly on the Frost farm, an arrangement that became troublesome as that area developed. In 1831 Walter Frost sold 3½ acres on the east corner of the avenue to Henry Ware Jr., Harvard's Professor of Pulpit Eloquence, who built a house aligned with its predecessors. Martha Frost Austin sold the lot next door to John Ware, Henry's brother, a medical doctor who became Hersey Professor of Physic. He built a Regency style country residence for his daughters in 1839 (now at 14 Kirkland Place).

Ebenezer Francis Jr. purchased the next lot from Martha Austin in 1836 and built a house for himself in 1838 (figure 4.226). Francis, a housewright, had served Harvard since 1831 as the first superintendent of buildings and grounds; he was in charge of "all repairs ... and the erection of any new buildings, doing such part of the work himself as may be consistent with the proper direction of others ... [and aiding] the steward in the general care and preservation of the college property" (Corporation Records, Sept. 15, 1831). He constructed another house behind his own in 1848. When he sold this to Reverend Charles Munroe in 1868 he laid out his driveway as Francis Avenue.

The south side of Kirkland also began to fill up in the 1840s, when Oliver Hastings, the Cambridge builder-architect, and his lumberyard partner, Luther Brooks, built three Greek Revival houses on land purchased from William Hyslop Sumner. The most elaborate of these speculative projects was a temple-fronted house that Hastings rented for several years before selling it to Joseph Lovering, Hollis Professor of Mathematics and Natural Philosophy (see figure 6.53). Apart from these and a few other

FIGURE 4.226 Ebenezer Francis Jr. house, 1 Francis Avenue (1838, Ebenezer Francis, housewright). The columned porch facing Kirkland Street was probably removed after a fire in 1935. Photo ca. 1890.

houses on Sumner Road, little else was built on the south side of Kirkland until the 1890s.

John Ware, who lived in Boston, caused some mischief for Harvard by selling outside the college community. In 1845 he acquired the last piece of the Frost farm, a lot on the east side of Divinity Avenue next to Divinity Hall, and sold it to Cyrus Rice, a trader, and stablekeepers Thomas Stearns and Daniel Pratt. Rice was soon arguing with Harvard about his right to use the avenue. The college already permitted passage to Dr. Palfrey, whose estate lay beyond Divinity Hall, and to Henry Ware Sr. "When Mr. Rice and his associates made their purchase and proposed to build upon it, they applied for a permanent right-of-way over Divinity Avenue, threatening to place the rear of the house on the avenue" if Harvard refused (Corporation Records, Aug. 14, 1847). Rice built his house facing the avenue anyway and began taking in boarders. He assured the president that the situation was only temporary, since he planned to build a new street off Kirkland on a 24-foot-wide strip immediately adjacent to Divinity Avenue that the Frosts had reserved for this purpose. Harvard finally bought the Rice house in 1900 and moved it behind Divinity Hall to make way for the Semitic Museum. It was moved again to 22 Divinity Avenue when the Biology Laboratories were built in 1930 and demolished in 1952 to make way for the Electron Accelerator.

Engineering professor Henry Eustis bought part of Rice, Stearns, and Price's land in 1850 and hired Hovey & Ryder to design a house at 29 Kirkland that was demolished for Randall Hall in 1898. Ephraim Buttrick, a wealthy East Cambridge attorney and Harvard graduate, built a house next door at 2 Divinity Avenue that became the residence of geology professor Josiah Dwight Whitney, for whom Mount Whitney is named. Harvard moved it to Frisbie Place in 1930 and again in 1978 to 6 Prescott Street, where it became the freshmen dean's office.

The western extremity of Harvard's land was still vacant when the Old Cambridge Baptist Society purchased part of it and built a church in 1845 (see figure 7.15). Two years later Harvard put up the Lawrence Scientific School between the church and the Higginson house. After the North Avenue Congregational Society removed the church the university repurchased the lot and put up the original Hemenway Gymnasium in 1876. Littauer Hall replaced Hemenway in 1938 (see figures 10.18, 10.33, and 10.76).

Oxford Street, Frisbie Place, and Kirkland Place also date from this period. James Hayward and William Stearns laid out the first section of Oxford Street along their common property line about 1847. Lower Oxford soon held houses built for law professor Seth Ames (15 Oxford Street, 1847) and McLean Professor of History Henry Torrey (20 Oxford Street, 1857). The street's best-known resident was Professor Louis Agassiz, the Swiss naturalist, who rented 12 Oxford in 1848. Twenty-two followers from Switzerland, a tame bear from Maine, and numerous other creatures shared the house, which was described as a "combination museum, aquarium, botanic garden, and breeding equipment station" (Lurie, 146).

Henry Ware Sr.'s executors laid out Frisbie Place in 1851. Charles Sanders of Salem, a wealthy graduate of the class of 1802, bought the back lots, sold Ware's cottage, and built a house there in 1852. A year before he died in 1863, Sanders deeded the property to Harvard and donated $50,000 that was used to construct Sanders Theater in 1874. The university demolished his house in 1978; Frisbie Place is now a footpath between the Sparks house and the former Busch-Reisinger Museum.

John Ware laid out Kirkland Place in September 1853. Housewright Isaac Cutler moved Ware's daughters' house to the back of the property, where it now sits at number 14, and erected four cross-gabled Italianates that he rented or sold to Boston businessmen. Edward G. Loring, a Suffolk County judge and lecturer at the law school, bought three lots and commissioned a house from his wife's brother-in-law, Henry Greenough, that originally faced Kirkland Street on ground that sloped down to a spring-fed pond (see figure 6.81). As commissioner of the federal circuit court in Boston, Loring was responsible for the rendition of escaped slaves Thomas Sims and Anthony Burns in 1851 and 1854. He became deeply unpopular and left Cambridge after President Buchanan appointed him to the U.S. Court of Claims

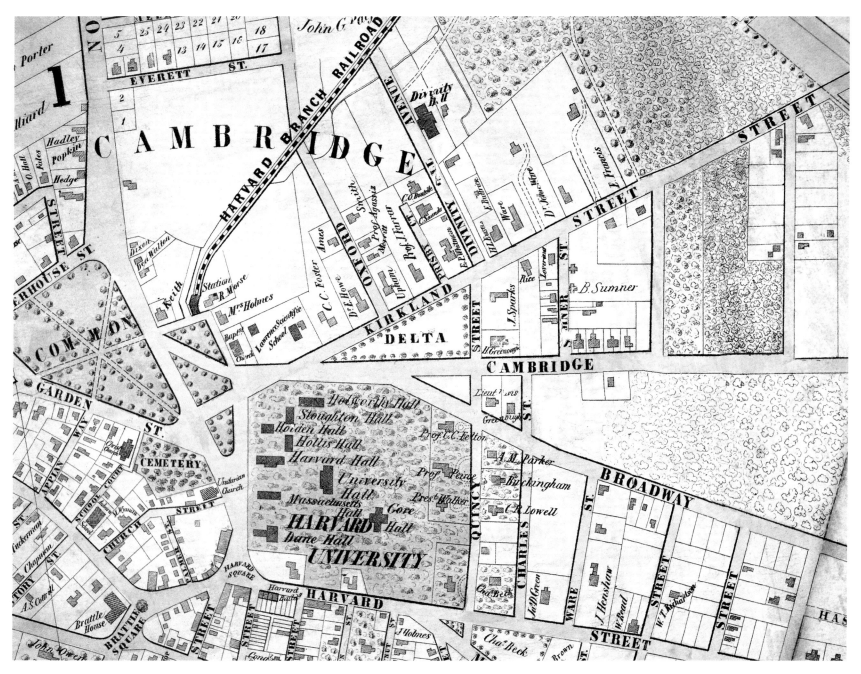

FIGURE 4.227 Professors Row and Quincy Street in 1854, at the beginning of
the suburban period.

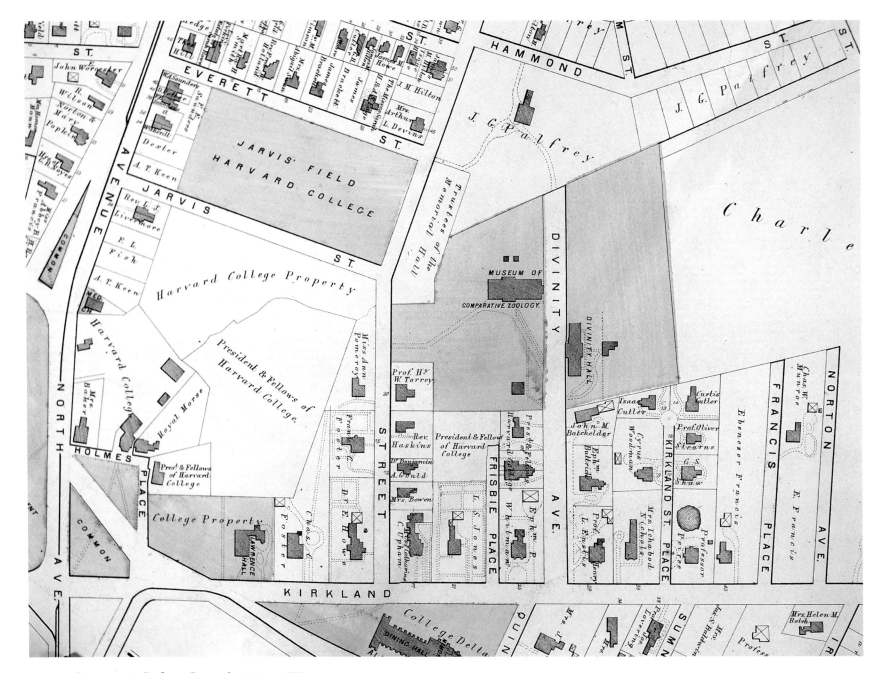

Figure 4.228 Professors Row and vicinity in 1873.

in Washington in 1858. In 1908 Samuel Fowler, a gas and electricity executive, moved it 40 feet north, freeing up the corner lot for the apartment building at 37 Kirkland Street.

Professors Row disappeared in the 20th century. Mallinckrodt Laboratory occupied the east side of Oxford Street in 1926, and Gordon McKay went up facing it in 1951. Some houses found a temporary refuge on Divinity Avenue but disappeared with the construction of the Biological Laboratory in 1930 and the Electron Accelerator in 1957. Harvard razed Henry Ware Jr.'s house in 1946 and built William James Hall in 1963. The Science Center replaced the Higginson house, the Lawrence Scientific School, and the Frisbie house in 1970. Only the Lovering house at 38 Kirkland Street and the Ebenezer Francis house at 1 Francis Avenue remain in their original locations.

Figure 4.229 Lower Oxford Street, as seen from the tower of Memorial Hall in 1923. The Frisbie-Hayward house at 13 Kirkland Street in the foreground was demolished for the Science Center in 1970. Beyond it is 15 Oxford Street, built for law professor Seth Ames in 1847, remodeled with a Mansard roof about 1870, and demolished for the Gordon McKay Laboratory in 1950. At far right, the Ann Pomeroy house at 19 Oxford Street (1855) was remodeled as a laboratory in 1942 and razed in 1971. In the background laboratory buildings, the first section of Langdell Hall, and Harvard's Carey athletic building surround Holmes Field.

Shady Hill

The Shady Hill neighborhood originated with the 34½ acres of the Foxcroft estate and the house in Charlestown that Professor Henry Ware Sr. bought from Harvard for $10,000 in 1817. In 1819 he asked the corporation either to let him live rent-free in his college-owned residence or forgive the interest he owed on his purchase, claiming that he was "unable to derive any benefit" from the property because he was required to live in Cambridge (College Papers, Ware letter, May 21, 1819). A year later the General Court obligingly adjusted the town boundary, directing that "so much of the real estate of Henry Ware … as lies within the town of Charlestown, be set off … and annexed to the town of Cambridge" (Ch. 24, Acts of 1820).

Catharine Eliot of Boston purchased Shady Hill from Ware in 1821 on the eve of her marriage to Andrews Norton, Dexter Professor of Sacred Literature (1786–1853). As required in Massachusetts until 1843, Catharine's property automatically passed to her husband, although she regained ownership through her husband's bequest in 1853. Mrs. Norton, who lived to be 91, became the matriarch of her extended family. She was particularly generous to her female relatives, many of whom did not marry. Her heirs carried on this tradition, generally leaving their share of Shady Hill to spinster daughters and nieces.

The Nortons immediately made improvements. Catharine's brother, Samuel Atkins Eliot, the future mayor of Boston, helped plan some changes before he left for Europe in 1821. Their architect was Solomon Willard, the future designer of Divinity Hall and the Bunker Hill Monument, and their builder was Cambridge housewright Oliver Hastings. Willard, who studied under Asher Benjamin, had opened his office in Boston just a year before. Shady Hill was Hastings's first documented building project, but he was already 30 years old and well-established in his long career. According to Catharine Norton, Willard designed the portico with its semicircular bow windows, a feature that Hastings copied repeatedly (see figure 6.48). Blinds and a balustrade completed the alterations, and Mrs. Norton wrote of Willard coming out "to view the beauty of his own proportions" (to Samuel Atkins Eliot, July 17 and 21, 1821).

Andrews Norton asked his brother-in-law to send plants from Paris and kept him informed of developments:

> There are admirable plans for draining the low lands (without a pond); accommodations for pigs and fowls, to say nothing of a cow, are contemplated. ... I shall let out the greater part of the land on shares ... to be planted with potatoes this year and laid down to grass the next. I set out 120 apple trees last fall in the field on the Charlestown Road. (To Samuel Eliot, Sept. 6, 1821, and Mar. 6, 1822)

A forbiddingly conservative theologian, Andrews Norton was known among transcendentalists as the "Unitarian Pope" (Morison, *Three Centuries,* 242). His intimates, however, appreciated "the beauty of his life in his domestic and social relations" (*Chronicle,* Sept. 24, 1853). His house was open to neighbors, friends, and extended family, which included the Danas, Lymans, Ticknors, Guilds, and Eliots. His son and daughters, "well educated, domestic, agreeable, good looking, well principled and with remarkably happy temperaments," attracted many admirers, and most of Old Cambridge society would turn out for their memorable parties (Dana, I, 218).

His son, Charles Eliot Norton (1827–1908), entered a counting house in Boston after graduating from Harvard in 1846, but after a single voyage to India as supercargo he decided to pursue a literary career. Traveling widely, he became an intimate of John Ruskin and was on close terms with the Pre-Raphaelites, Thomas Carlyle, and the Brownings. His American friends included Emerson, Lowell, Longfellow, and Holmes; he helped young William Dean Howells secure a house on Sacramento Street. Frederick Law Olmsted reinforced his interest in preserving rural landscapes and alleviating living conditions among the poor and sharpened his focus as a social critic. He organized the first night school in Cambridge, although he later deplored the growing presence of immigrants. President Eliot recruited him in 1873 to begin "the first continuous university instruction in the history of the fine arts" (Malone, 570). Norton was influential in

FIGURE 4.230 Charles Eliot Norton at Shady Hill. Photo ca. 1900.

the fields of art history, architecture, and city planning, but his vigorous denunciation of Harvard's new buildings made him a special burden to the administration (see chapter 10).[66]

Three generations of Nortons understood the development potential of Shady Hill. As early as 1821, Catharine praised her husband's never-fulfilled plan to subdivide the place into about fifty lots. "And when this is done, I shall advise him to take another estate upon the same terms and lay it out in the same manner" (to Samuel Eliot, July 21, 1821). The Nortons began to sell lots on Kirkland Street to family members in 1858. When Catherine's brother Samuel Eliot went bankrupt, she sold 40,000 square feet to his wife, Mary, for $1. Their son Charles, the future Harvard president, gave his mother $12,000 and invested another $18,000 in a double house that he designed himself (figure 4.231). "Mr. Edward Cabot's architectural firm lent him the facilities of his office, and there he drew up plans for the new house. He oversaw its erection and lodged his parents and three unmarried sisters in the westerly half" (James, *Eliot,* I, 75).

FIGURE 4.231 Charles W. Eliot house, 61 Kirkland Street (1858). The west (rear) half was demolished in 1927. Photo ca. 1938.

Members of the Norton circle built two other houses on Kirkland Street. When Charles Eliot Norton married Susan Ridley Sedgwick of New York in 1862 they moved in with his mother. Catharine sold Susan's sister Elizabeth a lot in 1863, where she and her husband, Professor Francis Child, built the Mansard cottage at 67 Kirkland Street. Norton built a house for Anne and Grace Ashburner, who had taken in the orphaned Sedgwick children in 1859 and wanted to live in Cambridge while Arthur Sedgwick attended Harvard.

Norton considered putting his social ideals in practice by developing Shady Hill as a garden suburb with a public "pleasure ground." He had met Olmsted in 1863 and became associated with him at *The Nation*, a new general interest magazine, in 1865. Olmsted proposed that 5 to 12 acres should be set aside to preserve the woods and make the house lots more appealing. "The community from which your purchasers are to come is an uncommonly well educated one (morally and artistically I mean) but perhaps I am in danger of overestimating the degree

in which it would be influenced by sylvan attractions" (Norton papers, Olmsted to Norton, Jan. 11, 1867).[67]

Olmsted projected a Y-shaped parkway connecting Beacon, Kirkland, Oxford, and Museum streets that would divide the estate into three parts (figure 4.232). A "secluded, sheltered, and sylvan" footpath from Cambridge Common would approach a public green, around which "the more agreeable rural character of a New England village may be perpetuated." The design would "open convenient communications across the property … with a view toward future wants, not merely of the neighborhood, but to the districts on each side of it, even when the latter shall be much more densely occupied than at present" (Norton Papers, Olmsted, Vaux & Co. memo, Feb. 7, 1868).

Norton put these plans aside when he sailed for Europe with his family in 1868. During the trip his wife died, and he returned to Cambridge with their six children.

> The place has grown even more beautiful during our stay abroad, and you would not find many prettier narrow views in New England than that from our piazza down the fields on either side of the avenue, belted as they are with old pine trees and oaks. We seem to be far in the country, for not another house is in sight, and the woods apparently extend far away; but we are on the edge of a busy town and surrounded by all that is suburban and ugly. (Norton to Constance Hilliard, Oct. 15, 1873, in Norton and Howe, 17)

Norton's mother, Catharine, died in 1879 and left the house and an acre of land in trust to him and his sister Grace; the remainder went to Charles, Grace, and Louisa Bullard (her third surviving child) as tenants in common. Twelve years later, Grace gave lifetime use of the house to Charles and his three daughters, who, like her, chose not to marry.

When Norton finally undertook the development of Shady Hill in 1886, he asked his nephew, Charles Eliot, son of the Harvard president, to lay it out. Eliot was just beginning to practice as a landscape architect after an apprenticeship with Olmsted. He had inherited an interest in the preservation of early New England estates from relatives such as the Lymans

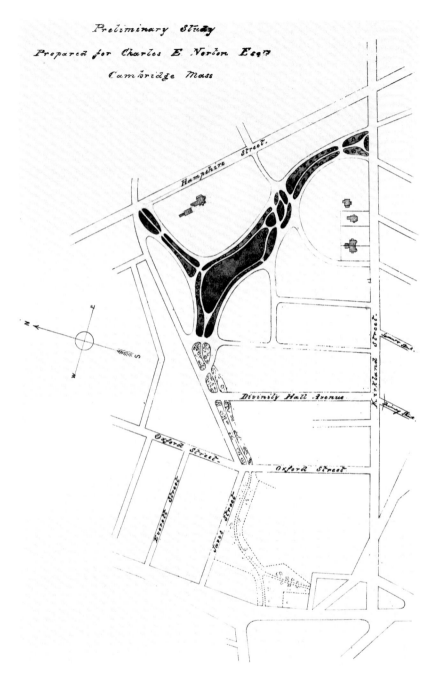

FIGURE 4.232   Frederick Law Olmsted's study for the development of Shady Hill, 1868.

and Derbys, so he was working in a familiar milieu (see chapter 5). He must have seen Olmsted's 1868 design, but he adopted a more conventional layout. Three principal streets, Irving, Scott, and Everett, were given gentle curves, providing equal access to Massachusetts Avenue, Kirkland Street, and Park Street. North of Everett, Eliot laid out "one hundred generous house lots" that would have obliterated the mansion (*Chronicle,* Mar. 10, 1888). This part of the plan may have been a response to the recent success of the Palfrey estate, which had just been replatted with small lots to attract workingmen; luckily, it was never executed (figure 4.233).[68] He also deleted Olmsted's pleasure grounds. Andrews Norton himself had made a path across the fields and through Stephen Higginson's yard but complained about pedestrians traveling between the village and the railroad station at Park Street. Although Somerville was filling up with immigrants and their unruly children, the Nortons allowed the public free run of the property "until the abuse of the privilege obliged them" to build a perimeter fence (*Tribune,* Feb. 2, 1889).

The development of Shady Hill entailed an early collaboration among proponents of the Colonial Revival movement, which combined a contemporary approach to architecture and planning with a nostalgic perspective on American life before mass immigration and urbanization. It was the first comprehensive application of the style in Cambridge, a city which had seen its earliest stirrings in Arthur Astor Carey's house at 28 Fayerweather Street in 1882. Among its leading practitioners, William Ralph Emerson explored the possibilities of the style in houses for Professor of Philosophy William James at 95 Irving Street (1889), Mrs. Julia Davis at 110 Irving Street (1889), and Professor of Botany Roland Thaxter at 7 Scott Street (1891), while Alexander Wadsworth Longfellow designed a center-entrance Colonial for M.I.T. professor Alphonse Van Daell at 105 Irving Street (1890). Norton imposed strict controls on buyers. Professor James, for example, agreed to construct "no building other than a private dwelling house costing not less than Forty-five Hundred Dollars above the foundation, and adapted for the use of one family only, and one private stable" (Middlesex Deeds

352   Chapter 4

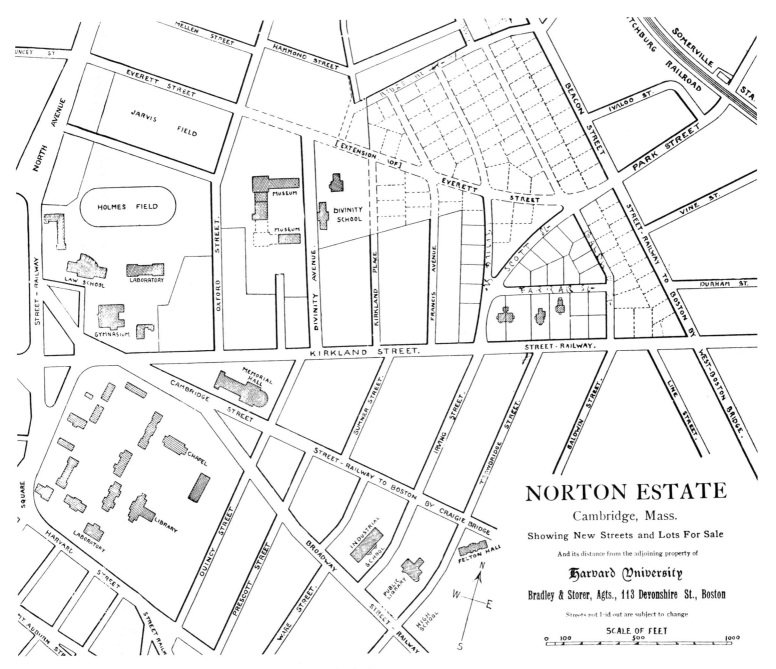

FIGURE 4.233 Charles Eliot's 1888 plan for the Norton estate. Initially, development focused on Irving and Scott streets; the lots shown with dotted lines represented a density similar to that of the replatted Palfrey estate but were never realized.

1896/7). Setbacks were precisely defined, contributing to the somewhat mechanical arrangement of the houses (figure 4.235).

Families with Harvard connections occupied every house put up between 1889 and 1894. Among these were professors Josiah Royce (Philosophy), Charles Lanman (Sanskrit), Frank Taussig (Economics), and Edward Cummings (English, Political Economy, and Sociology, and father of the poet). A few parents bought houses while their sons attended Harvard, but for many years "houses were handed on from one academic to another; even the real estate agents, with unusual sensitivity to intellectual atmosphere, seemed to conspire to maintain a high level of academic occupancy and few ringers were allowed in" (Schlesinger, 119).

Norton lived at Shady Hill without gas or electricity until his death in 1908. Edward Waldo Forbes, director of the Fogg Museum, rented the house from 1909 to 1912, when the heirs sold it with six acres of land to art collectors Walter and Louise Arensberg. They in turn sold the place to Professor Paul Sachs, Associate Director of the Fogg, in 1916. With Norton gone and no family in residence, there was little incentive to keep the property intact. The heirs sold 4.8 acres west of Francis Avenue to

FIGURE 4.234 A path in Norton's Woods, ca. 1890–91. A journalist reported: "oaks and chestnuts of a size and beauty not surpassed in Massachusetts, and beyond these ... the straight stems of the pines rise as if they had still a right to live in New England. ... It is difficult to realize that two or three years will see the ground cleared and houses built in all directions" (*Cambridge Tribune,* Feb. 2, 1889).

FIGURE 4.235 Houses on Irving Street were carefully sited with uniform setbacks. From left to right, these were the residences of Judge Jabez Fox and Professors Josiah Royce, Alphonse Van Dael, and Edward Cummings. Photo ca. 1890–91.

NORTON'S WOOD
A PORTION OF THE
NORTON ESTATE
CAMBRIDGE

the Andover Theological School in 1909 and engaged George Howland Cox, a former member of the Cambridge Park Commission, to develop the remainder. He had Brookline engineer Henry Bryant lay out sweeping extensions of Francis Avenue and Irving Street (figure 4.236). Cox decreed that the architecture should be "the New England colonial type of townhouse" and

personally approved each design. By World War I the neighborhood already had a "comfortable air of long residence," which was attributed to "the architecture of the new houses, each of which is in some form a modern expression of the colonial." *The House Beautiful* praised it as having a "pleasant freedom from the sense of having been 'planned'" (Bergengren, 168).

Meanwhile, Ebenezer Francis III continued the subdivision of the old Frost farm. Although Francis limited construction to "dwelling houses, for private occupancy, costing not less than $5,000 each" (excluding "any private stable for more than four horses, with a proportionate number of carriages"), he did not exercise the rigid control that Norton and Cox did at Shady Hill (Middlesex Deeds, 1907/563). For all practical purposes, the boundary between the two ancient farms disappeared when Cox extended Francis Avenue to Bryant Street in 1910 (figure 4.237).

Harvard faculty accounted for six of the eight new houses along upper Francis Avenue. Boston architect Allen Jackson designed substantial Georgian Revivals for professors Herbert Langfeld (1 Bryant Street, 1911) and Ralph Perry (138 Irving Street, 1913), and renovated Norton's barn for medical school professor Elmer Southard. Professor of Arabic James Jewett, whose wife, Margaret, was an heir to the Weyerhaeuser fortune, built by far the most substantial house at 44 Francis Avenue in 1913. The lone exceptions to the prevailing Revivalist orthodoxy were an Arts and Crafts house designed by Gustav Stickley for E.F. Scheibe, a businessman, in 1911, and the strangely Teutonic house built for Dr. Walter Wesselhoeft at 24 Bryant Street in 1916 (see figure 6.182).

In 1915 the Community Trust, a for-profit venture organized by engineers John Chatman and Charles Nutter of Boston, hoping to meet the demand created by "the presence of many [student and faculty] families of refinement and comparatively small income," bought two acres of land on Holden Street (Bergengren, 167). Architect J.W. Ames designed Shady Hill Square, a community of five double houses and two singles that shows the influence of the Garden City movement (figure 4.238). A year later the Norton heirs sold a lot on the opposite corner of Holden Street to the Cooperative Open Air School, which put up an assembly hall and five buildings before it relocated to Coolidge Hill in 1926 (see chapter 7).

Charles Eliot Norton's vision for the careful development of Shady Hill was abandoned in 1922 when Grace Norton (Catharine's last surviving heir) and her trustees sold the remaining

FIGURE 4.237 Jennie Rand house, 49 Kirkland Street/4 Francis Avenue (1886, James T. Kelley, architect). Rand, a widow who had moved to Cambridge in 1877 while her son attended Harvard, built a well-proportioned Colonial Revival that preceded similar houses on the Shady Hill estate. Photo 1890–91.

land on Kirkland and Beacon streets (partly in Somerville) to Roxbury developer Louis Levy, who laid out a new street and twenty-three lots around an apartment house that Grace had put up in 1911. When three double houses appeared on the corner of Holden, nearby homeowners quickly organized a "two-fold project of offering assistance to the school and protecting values of the neighborhood. … This enterprise," they wrote, "seems to be the one thing remaining to protect the Norton's Woods district" (Shady Hill-Norton's Woods Enterprise subscription letter, June 19, 1922). The neighbors acquired Levy's remaining land in 1923, except for the lots on Holden Street where Somerville businessman Thomas DeWire built two double houses in 1926. In 1927 they sold most of it to the Harvard Housing Trust, the

for-profit corporation that had created Shaler Lane a year before. Holden Green was a much more elaborate scheme, consisting of ten Georgian Revival buildings with apartments for 134 married graduate students. Architect-developer William M. Duguid acquired the remaining lots and built three small houses on the corner of Farrar Street in 1928.

In 1926 Grace Norton bequeathed her aunt's half of the Eliot residence at 59–61 Kirkland Street to the South End House Association of Boston, which sold it at the first opportunity. Daniel Cronin, a real estate agent, demolished the house, subdivided the parcel "in spite of zoning ordinances somehow circumvented during the summer months when neighbors were away," and erected five new houses on the corner of Irving Street

(Cushman, 15). The last significant residential development occurred when William Duguid built four houses on the site of the Sedgwick-Ashburner place in 1931 (figure 4.239).

Harvard purchased the last five acres of Shady Hill from Paul Sachs in 1948 and razed the house without warning in 1955. Although the zoning allowed only twenty-eight single-family houses, the university announced plans in 1969 to build two towers of eighteen and twenty stories containing 288 apartments, as well as nine townhouses and a 400-car parking garage (figure 4.240). Professor Arthur Schlesinger led infuriated neighbors to block the project, and the grounds grew wild until the university transferred the land to the American Academy of Arts & Sciences in 1978 (see chapter 7).

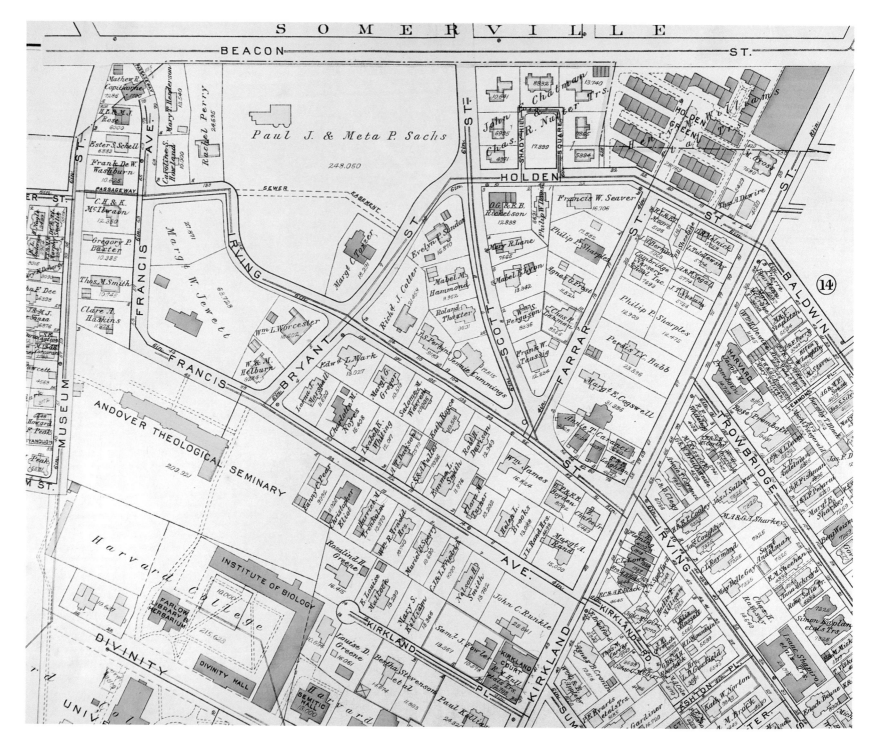

Figure 4.239 Shady Hill in 1930.

FIGURE 4.240 Housing proposal for the Sachs Estate (1969, John Harkness for The Architects Collaborative). Harvard's planned development generated intense mistrust that lasted for decades.

QUINCY STREET AND THE FRANCIS DANA ESTATE

In the decade and a half after the opening of the West Boston Bridge in 1793, four new highways—Cambridge Street, Broadway, Harvard Street, and Massachusetts Avenue—reached Old Cambridge from Boston. The Foxcroft heirs allowed Andrew Craigie and William Winthrop to lay out Cambridge Street to Lechmere's Point in 1804 (see *East Cambridge,* 21). A year later, the legislature authorized the Cambridge & Concord Turnpike Corporation to extend its road from Garden Street to the West Boston Bridge. South of Broadway, Francis Dana allowed a stretch of present Massachusetts Avenue to be built between Bow and Arrow streets as a short cut to the West Boston Bridge, but he opposed a plan to lay out Harvard Street because it bypassed land he was trying to develop in Cambridgeport.

The Foxcrofts laid out Quincy Street between Cambridge Street and Broadway in 1804 and divided 60 acres south of Kirkland Street into twelve parcels. Abraham Biglow, clerk of the Middlesex Superior Court, acquired several of these, including what is now the northeast corner of Harvard Yard, but most of his property was still undeveloped four decades after his death in 1832. John Phillips, who purchased all 60 acres north of Kirkland, also bought a parcel on Quincy Street that he sold to Harvard in 1816, allowing the university to complete the Delta. William Hyslop Sumner of Roxbury, a recent Harvard graduate, left another parcel untouched for thirty years while he developed East Boston (where the tunnel was named for him in 1934).

Professor Daniel Treadwell bought Sumner's Quincy Street frontage in 1837, and housewrights Oliver Hastings and Luther Brooks acquired the rest. Treadwell put up a house in the locally popular Regency style, while Hastings and Brooks built two houses opposite Professors Row and a few cottages on the west side of Sumner Road. Royal Richardson, a Boston soap dealer, put up "Richardson's Row," four double Greek Revival houses on Cambridge Street that remained on the fringes of Old Cambridge until they were overtaken by suburban development in the 1880s (see figure 6.56).

FIGURE 4.241 Quincy Street looking north from Harvard Street in 1885. The Edward Tyrrel Channing house, 16 Quincy Street (1832, attributed to Oliver Hastings, builder) is on the right.

South of the Foxcroft estate lay Chief Justice Francis Dana's great landholdings, which by the time of his death in 1811 extended from Harvard Yard to Hancock Street on the north side of Massachusetts Avenue and from Putnam Avenue to Fort Washington on the south. The western part of Dana's property was once the homestead of Edward Goffe, who sold his house near the village to Harvard College and settled on the hillside near Quincy Square about 1645.[69] Goffe, a member of Shepard's company, assembled a 32-acre farm from lots that originated in the 1635 division of Small-Lot Hill and the Old Field. His land ran from the parsonage to about Ellery Street, and his house stood until about 1774 (see *Report Two: Mid Cambridge,* 10–13). Boston attorney Richard Dana acquired a share of the

FIGURE 4.242 Francis Dana mansion, Massachusetts Avenue between Ellery and Dana streets (1785). Dana's house mimicked the Tory mansions of the 1760s, but in the more restrained style of the Federal period. Shown here in 1806, it burned in 1839.

Goffe farm from his brother-in-law, Edmund Trowbridge, in the settlement of Edmund Goffe's estate in 1740. Dana died in 1772 and left the farm to his children, Edmund, Lydia, and Francis, and to Edmund Trowbridge Jr. Edmund Dana retained his share, while Francis bought out the others.

The Danas' relations were nearly as complex as those described by Baroness Riedesel among the loyalists. The earliest Richard Dana settled on the south side of the Charles. His grandson Richard, the first in his line to graduate from Harvard, in 1718, married Lydia Trowbridge, whose mother was a Goffe. Lydia's brother Edmund graduated from Harvard in 1728 and married Martha, the daughter of Judge Jonathan Remington. He was attorney general of the province and a member of the Governor's Council, but he resigned in 1770 and was not molested during the Siege. Among the law students who studied in his office and lived in his home on Mt. Auburn Street were William Ellery, Christopher Gore, Theophilus Parsons, Harrison Gray Otis, and his own nephew, Francis Dana.

Francis Dana graduated from Harvard in 1762 and married Elizabeth Ellery of Newport in 1773. He was in England during the Siege of Boston, but on his return he joined the Governor's Council and represented privateers in admiralty court until he was elected to the Continental Congress in 1777. In 1779 he accompanied John Adams on a mission to Paris, and in 1781 he was sent as ambassador to St. Petersburg (although Catherine the Great refused to accept his credentials). A year after his return he built a great mansion on Dana Hill (figure 4.242). After the war he promoted the construction of the West Boston Bridge and aggressively purchased land in present-day Cambridgeport, the development of which occupied his descendants for decades (see chapter 2 and *Report Three: Cambridgeport,* 17–19). Dana was appointed to the Supreme Judicial Court in 1785 and served as Chief Justice from 1792 until 1806.

When Justice Dana's will was probated in 1819, his brother Edmund, the elderly rector of Wroxeter in Shropshire, received an 11-acre parcel now traversed by Quincy, Prescott, and Ware streets. In 1823 Reverend Dana sold about two acres along

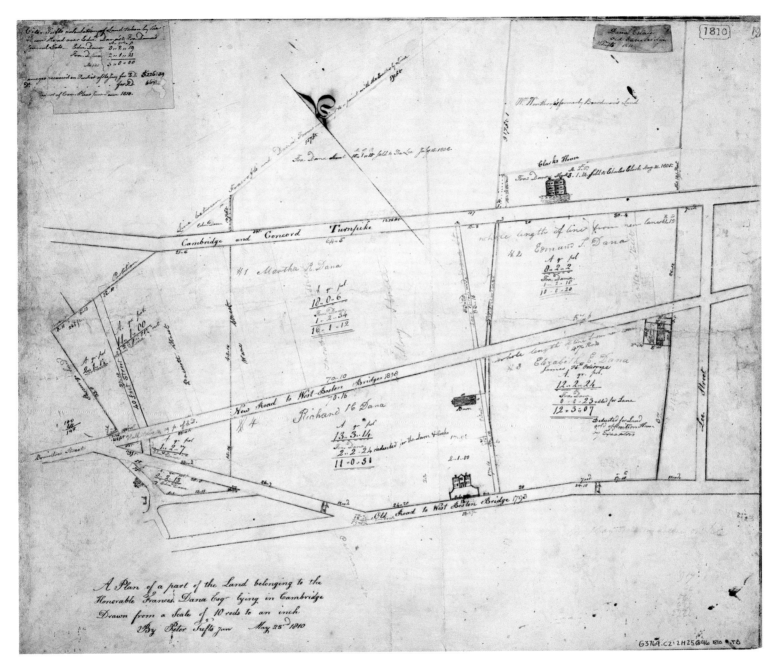

FIGURE 4.243 Francis Dana estate, 1810, as surveyed by Peter Tufts. Dana's land ran from west of Quincy Street nearly to Lee Street, and from Massachusetts Avenue and Arrow Street to the Foxcroft estate beyond Broadway. The mansion and barn are at the bottom of the plan. The 1807 Opposition House, so called because Dana built it in a failed attempt to block the construction of Harvard Street, is at right; it was moved in 1860 to 2 Hancock Place.

the west side of Quincy Street to Thomas Foster, a nephew of Andrew Craigie, who built a house for two of Justice Dana's daughters who were engaged to his brothers (figure 4.244). The young men died just before the wedding, and Elizabeth and Sarah Dana lived in mourning in their new house with their brother, Richard Henry Dana Sr., his children, and another sister, Martha. The Danas moved to Brattle Street after Martha married the artist Washington Allston in 1830, and in 1835 President Quincy bought the Foster property and Abraham Biglow's two acres north of it to complete the acquisition of Harvard Yard (see figure 10.14).

Reverend Dana's son William began developing his remaining land in 1831. James Hayward's subdivision plan laid out Prescott Street so close to Quincy that many of the lots were merged to run from one street to the other. In 1832 Joseph Buckingham, editor of *The Boston Courier*, hired Asher Benjamin to design a five-bay house similar to those on Professors Row (see figure

FIGURE 4.244 Foster-Dana (now Dana-Palmer) house (1823), with the observatory still in place. This austere Federal house, the first on Quincy Street, was old-fashioned compared to its contemporaries on Professors Row; the Greek Revival porch was added later. It was moved across Quincy Street in 1947 to make way for Lamont Library. Photo ca. 1871.

6.46). Charles Beck, a republican exile from Germany who was appointed Professor of Latin in 1831, bought five lots and built a house similar to Buckingham's (see figure 6.47). Beck was an ardent abolitionist, and a surviving trap door in the front hall may be evidence that he participated in the Underground Railroad. In 1876–77 his daughter, Anna Moëring, built Beck Hall on a 1¼-acre garden across Harvard Street known as Beck's Park (see figure 7.18). Henry Warren, a professor of Sanskrit, purchased Beck's house in 1891 and added an Ottoman loggia of brick and colored tile designed by H. Langford Warren. Harvard received the property after Warren's death, and in 1900 moved the house to the edge of Prescott Street to make way for the Harvard Union (see chapters 6 and 10).

Edward Tyrrel Channing, Boylston Professor of Rhetoric and Oratory, lived next to Beck in a house built about 1832. Typical of residences put up by Oliver Hastings in this period, it had "a piazza with broad flight of stone steps leading up to a central door flanked by two 'swell-front' bay windows" (Farlow, 40; see figures 6.49 and 7.66). Van Wyck Brooks credited the New England literary renaissance to Channing's students, Emerson, Holmes, Dana, Thoreau, Motley, and Parkman, and quoted Holmes on the professor's rigorous manner in the classroom (Brooks, *Flowering*, 43):

Channing, with his bland, superior look,
Cold as a moonbeam on a frozen brook,
While the pale student, shivering in his shoes,
Sees from his theme the turgid rhetoric ooze.

When Channing's house was taken down in 1947 to make room for the Dana-Palmer house, some contended that Harvard had destroyed the wrong building.

William Dana's Quincy Street lots sold well, but the more remote ones on Prescott and Ware streets had to be auctioned off in 1838 (figure 4.245). Martha Dana Allston sold a tract on the east side of Ware Street to Professor John White Webster, who could not afford the expensive house he built there and moved to rented quarters on Garden Street in 1837.[70] Cornelius Felton, "the great professor of Greek, Longfellow's closest friend and the

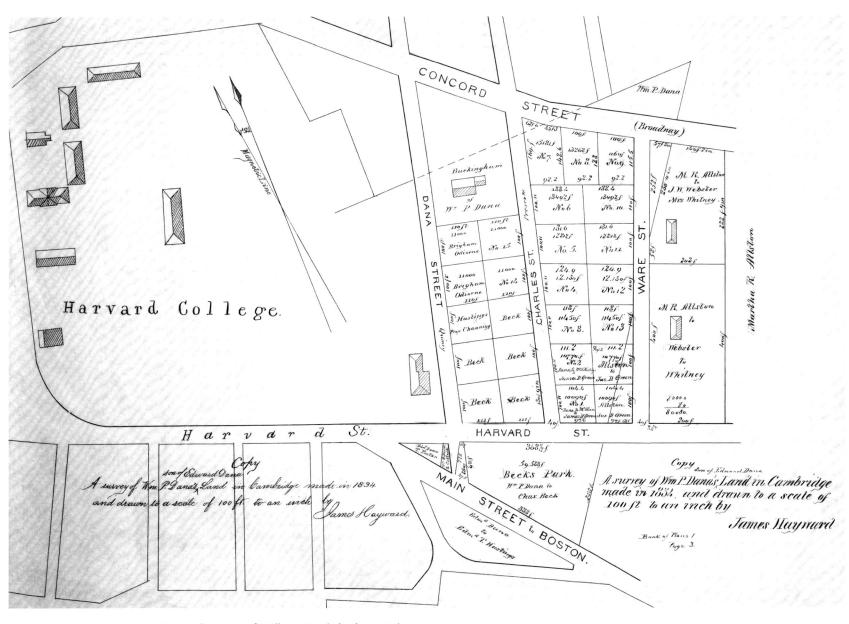

FIGURE 4.245 James Hayward's survey of William Dana's land in 1834. Dana Street is now Quincy, and Charles Street is now Prescott.

friend of Dickens," lived next to Webster in "a pretty, new-built house, about as large as a fly-cage, which the students call Mr. Felton's Box" (ibid., 447; Longfellow to G.W. Greene, Aug. 6, 1838, in Hilen, 93).

Harvard began to focus on Quincy Street in 1839. Professor Felton reported that:

> President [Quincy] and I began to explore the neighboring country for a good place and the neighboring purses for the means to erect an observatory. The farmers, thinking the college to be infinitely rich, refused to sell the hill tops for less than about six times the value of the best lands, so [we] were compelled to come nearer home. The west side of the Dana house was finally hit upon, ...[and] old Mr. Bond takes [it], the rent being given him for keeping watch upon the stars. (Felton to Francis Bowen, Dec. 27, 1839)

William Cranch Bond, the astronomer, mounted a revolving turret on the roof that Felton described as "a caboose ... with a telescope that commands an unobstructed view of all the chambers in the neighborhood" (ibid.). Bond complained of buildings "interrupting the horizon in every direction " (W. Bond, vi). In 1842 a new barn on Massachusetts Avenue obscured a crucial reference point on Blue Hill; for $200, Harvard purchased "a free and open and unobstructed air-line not exceeding twenty inches by sixteen inches" over Thomas Russell's land, "the same width and height as the opening now made through the roof of the barn" (Middlesex Deeds 417/363). After Bond moved to the observatory in 1844 Harvard rented the house. The philosopher George Herbert Palmer arrived in 1894 with his wife, Alice Freeman Palmer, the former president of Wellesley College, and stayed nearly forty years. Harvard moved it across Quincy Street in 1947 to make room for Lamont Library and called it Dana-Palmer House.

Harvard's purchases allowed it to address continuing faculty complaints about the expense of living in Cambridge. The college began renting houses to faculty in the 1790s and started offering lots and financing in 1818. With few exceptions it did not construct faculty residences itself until 1843, when the Corporation decided to build houses for the president and three professors on Quincy Street.[71] Alexander Wadsworth's site plan located the president's house next to the Danas and the faculty residences down the hill toward Broadway (figure 4.246). Housewrights Benjamin Babbitt and Isaac Melvin built houses that were rented to Professors James Walker and Benjamin Peirce (figure 4.247). A third, probably by housewright Isaac Cutler, was put up in 1849 for Professor Felton. Cambridge assessors precipitated the first of many conflicts with the university when they claimed that the houses were taxable because the faculty paid rent to live in them (see chapter 10).

The site reserved for the president's house stayed empty for decades. Isaiah Rogers, an architect practicing in Boston and New York, designed a formal Neoclassical residence, but President Quincy, nearing retirement, remained in Wadsworth House. President Edward Everett may have disliked an Italianate design that Rogers drew in 1846, because George Dexter soon prepared a Gothic version. Everett's father-in-law contributed $10,000 toward the project, but Everett was ambivalent about remaining in office, and the money was allowed to accumulate "until the need for a new dwelling house became more urgent" (Treasurer's Report, 1846). Jared Sparks, who succeeded Everett in 1849, became the first president since 1726 to live in his own home. The father of his second wife, Mary Crowninshield Silsbee of Salem, purchased Professor Treadwell's house on Quincy Street for them.[72] James Walker, Sparks's successor, also remained at home on Quincy Street.

By 1860 the building fund had more than doubled. President Felton commissioned plans for an official residence from Boston architect Edward Clark Cabot, who had designed the Boston Athenaeum in 1847. According to one observer, "the architect wished to build a large and rather imposing house," but President Felton's mother-in-law "told him that the proper thing for Cambridge was a cottage mansion" (Farlow, 42–43; figure 4.248). Many thought the house was mean and inadequate. President Eliot was stoic about its inadequacies, but President Lowell found it intolerable. In 1911 he commissioned his cousin, Boston architect Guy Lowell, to design a new residence

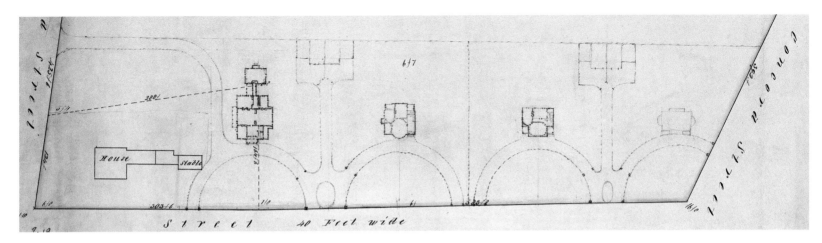

FIGURE 4.246 Alexander Wadsworth's 1843 plan for the west side of Quincy Street, showing the linked semicircular drives and the footprint of Isaiah Rogers's design for the new president's house (next to the Foster-Dana house). The formality of this scheme contrasts with ordinary subdivisions of the period, the best of which were controlled only by uniform setbacks and use restrictions.

FIGURE 4.247 Benjamin Peirce house, 31 Quincy Street (1844, Isaac Melvin, architect). The Peirce house was moved in 1878 to Frisbie Place to make way for Sever Hall, moved again about 1927 to 9 Oxford Street, and demolished for the McKay Laboratory in 1950. Photo before 1878.

FIGURE 4.248 Harvard President's house, 17 Quincy Street (1860, Edward Clark Cabot, architect). Photo ca. 1880.

that remained in use until 1971, when student unrest made it advisable for the president to retreat to Elmwood.

In the 1840s and '50s Quincy Street became notable for houses designed by Henry Greenough, an early proponent of the Second Empire style and a brother of sculptor Horatio Greenough (see chapter 6). In 1844 Greenough built a house on the northeast corner of Cambridge Street for his mother before embarking on an extended tour of Europe (see figure 6.79). The following year, Lieutenant Charles Davis, a distinguished hydrographer who had left Harvard before graduation to enter the navy, returned to study with mathematician Benjamin Peirce and commissioned his classmate to design a house at 38 Quincy Street (figure 4.249). On his return from abroad, Greenough built a three-story Neoclassical mansion at 1737 Cambridge Street for his own use and a house at the corner of Broadway for Louis Agassiz. None of these survive. Agassiz's house was destroyed by fire in January 1917. In 1921, "exceedingly attractive and in perfect condition," and recently renovated under the direction of heraldic artist Pierre LaRose, Greenough's house with all its furnishings was offered for sale as "an excellent house for a rich professor." Ominously, the agent admitted that the location was "not in the fashionable quarter," and John J. Shine razed it for the Ambassador Hotel in 1926 (William C. Codman to Benjamin S. Ellis, Ellis & Andrews Papers, Apr. 4, 1921).[73] Harvard took down the Davis house in 1950, and Mrs. Greenough's house burned in 1968; Gund Hall now occupies its site.

In 1866, after traveling with his family for years between New York, Newport, and the Continent, Henry James Sr. settled on Quincy Street while his son William attended Harvard Medical School. James acquired a Second Empire house that had been put up in 1856 by Louis Theis, curator of the Gray collection of engravings (figure 4.250). Henry James, the author, lived there on and off until he left for Europe in 1875. After Mrs. James died in 1882, Alice James and her father gave up the house and moved to Boston. William commissioned sketches from both H.H. Richardson and Peabody & Stearns for a new house on an adjoining lot, but he and his wife built 95 Irving Street instead

FIGURE 4.249 Lieutenant Charles Davis house, 38 Quincy Street (1846, Henry Greenough, architect). The Davis house and the Cornelius Felton house (rear) at 40 Quincy Street were razed in 1950 for Allston Burr Hall, which was in turn replaced by the Sackler building of the Harvard Art Museums in 1982. Photo ca. 1948.

FIGURE 4.250 Henry James Sr. house, 20 Quincy Street (1856). The father of Professor William James and author Henry James occupied this house with his family until 1882. The Colonial Club purchased it in 1889 and completely remodeled it in 1890–92; the Harvard Faculty Club replaced it in 1930.

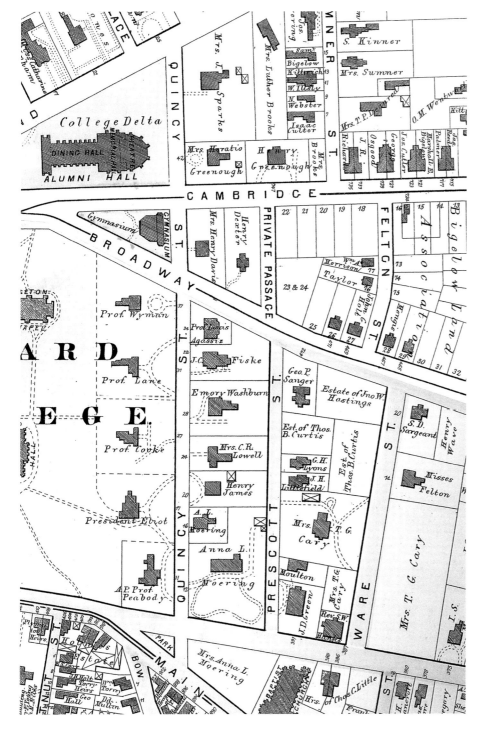

FIGURE 4.251 Quincy Street in 1873.

FIGURE 4.252 After the Civil War the streets east of Memorial Hall filled with Mansards, many of which were built as boarding houses for students. This view looking east on Cambridge Street shows the Henry Greenough house in the left foreground. The large porticoed building is the city's Washington School (1901, George Fogerty, architect); next to it is the Rindge Technical School (1888); beyond are the Cambridge Latin (1896) and English (1889) high schools. Photo 1923.

in 1889. The house became the Colonial Club, and the site is now occupied by the Harvard Faculty Club (see chapter 7).

As early as 1858 the college recognized that its Quincy Street frontage would "without doubt, be at some future time wanted for public buildings, and … the dwelling houses may be moved or taken down before they are worn out" (College Papers, 2nd series, vol. 25, p. 325). Sever (1878), the Harvard Union (1900), Robinson (1901–4), and Emerson (1904) halls all displaced houses to less prominent sites.[74] In 1898 President Eliot built a house for Mary Pitkin Eliot, the recent widow of Charles Eliot, the landscape architect, but this was razed with three others in 1925 for the Fogg Museum. The last house on the block, a Gothic Revival built for Boston wholesale druggist Hammond Whitney in 1847, was taken down in 1960 to make way for the Carpenter Center. Most houses on Prescott and Ware streets fared no better and fell to apartment buildings at an alarming rate. The most significant loss was the house of Professor Josiah Parsons Cooke, who succeeded John White Webster as Erving Professor of Chemistry in 1851 and bought his two-acre house lot in 1884. The architect of Cooke's house cannot be identified, but the exterior was thought to have been "suggested … by English homes which he had visited" (*Tribune,* Sept. 20, 1902; figure 4.253). The New England Telephone Co. replaced it with a telephone exchange in 1932 (see figure 8.32).

FIGURE 4.253 Professor Josiah Parsons Cooke house, 12 Ware Street (1884; altered 1900, Clarence Blackall, architect). William A. Bancroft, who served as mayor in 1893–97 and as first president of the Boston Elevated Railway in 1897–1916, called the place Arborcroft. The company photographer made several 11" × 17" glass plate negatives to document the house.

SPENCER PHIPS ESTATE

The 44-acre Spencer Phips-William Winthrop estate abutted the southern edge of the Goffe-Dana farm on Arrow Street and ran from the foot of Holyoke Street down Little Neck almost to Western Avenue.[75] Although it was immediately adjacent to the village, the property remained intact until 1857, when it became one of Cambridge's first Irish-American neighborhoods.

Phips-Winthrop Estate

The Spencer Phips estate originated in a welter of early quarter- and half-acre grants on the sunny slope south of Arrow Street. Roger Shaw, a selectman, consolidated these into a two-acre homestead but moved to Hampton, New Hampshire, about 1650. About 1670 his daughter sold the "mansion house" and a farmhouse to Daniel Gookin, who had settled in Virginia in 1621 and relocated to Massachusetts about 1644 (Middlesex Deeds, 4/214). Gookin arrived in Cambridge in 1647 and served as licenser of the printing press, selectman, representative, assistant, and commander of the colony's military forces before his death in 1686/7. An ally of Oliver Cromwell, he was a strong defender of Massachusetts liberties after the Restoration.

Spencer Phips (1685–1757), an immensely wealthy member of the leisured gentry that settled in Cambridge in the 18th century, was born Spencer Bennett to middle-class parents in Rowley. Governor Sir William Phips adopted him and left him the bulk of his property in 1695.[76] In 1704, a year after graduating from Harvard, Spencer purchased the 300-acre Atherton Haugh farm in East Cambridge for a country place. He married Elizabeth Hutchinson in 1707 and acquired the Gookin farm, "with the barns, stables, orchards, [and] gardens" in 1714 (Middlesex Deeds 13/524). Phips was elected to the General Court in 1721 and in 1732 was appointed lieutenant governor, an office he held until his death in 1757. By 1737 he owned 46 acres southeast of the village.

Spencer and Elizabeth's wealth and family connections placed them at the center of the loyalist establishment in Cambridge. Of their eleven children, Rebecca married Joseph Lee, Elizabeth wed Colonel John Vassall, and Mary married Richard Lechmere, all of whom built estates on Tory Row. Phips furnished his estate "with every procurable elegance":

> Life-sized wooden figures of Indians gay in paint and feathers and armed with bows and arrows sentineled the principal entrance to the grounds, startling the casual observer and frightening children. They held their place for many years, while owners came and passed on, and the remembrance of their fierce and life-like appearance endured to a late generation. (DAR *Guide,* 82)

David Phips, Spencer's only surviving son, inherited the estate, Elizabeth Island in Spy Pond, and three African slaves. The farm in East Cambridge was divided among four children (see *East Cambridge,* 7–11). As high sheriff of Middlesex County, Phips led a British raid on a Provincial powder magazine at Medford in September 1774. This made it impossible for him to remain in Cambridge, and a few days later he fled to Boston. He entered the Royal Navy but was captured by the French in 1782 and interned for seven months in Cambridge as a prisoner of war. Having been proscribed in 1778, he never recovered his property and died in England in 1811.

Phips's place was comparable to the estates on Brattle Street. According to his claim for compensation, it contained an eleven-room mansion fully furnished and newly repaired, with a farm that rented for £80 a year "completely fenced and enclosed containing about forty six acres of choice highly cultivated land" valued at £25 per acre, "a very large new built barn," and "a Negro man servant left on the farm" valued at £20 (PRO, AO 13/48, 258). The Commonwealth auctioned the furniture, paintings, and silver in 1780, and in 1781 Isaiah Doane, a Boston merchant who also bought John Vassall's confiscated Boston town house, bought the house and 50 acres.

William Winthrop (1753–1825), who purchased the Phips place from Doane in 1784, was the youngest son of Professor

FIGURE 4.254 The view south from Memorial Hall in 1875. The Felton, Peirce, Walker, and President's houses in the left foreground face Quincy Street; Gore Hall is at right. William Winthrop's house is visible above the cupola of the Foster-Dana house; all the buildings beyond it and as far south as the Western Avenue Bridge were built on the Phips-Winthrop estate. None of the buildings across from the Yard except the Apthorp house survived the 20th century.

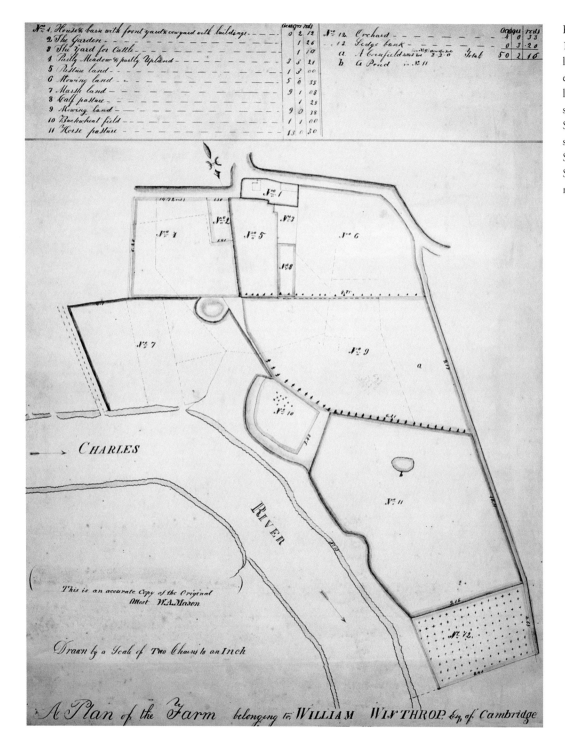

No. 1. House & barn with front yard & cowyard with buildings ----- 0 2 12
    2. The Garden ----- 1 26
    3. The Yard for Cattle ----- 1 10
    4. Partly Meadow & partly Upland ----- 3 8 21
    5. Pasture land ----- 1 3 00
    6. Mowing land ----- 5 6 33
    7. Marsh land ----- 9 1 08
    8. Calf pasture ----- 1 21
    9. Mowing land ----- 9 0 38
    10. Buckwheat field ----- 1 1 00
    11. Horse pasture ----- 13 0 30

No. 12. Orchard ----- 4 0 33
    13. Sedge bank ----- 0 3 20
    a. A Cornfield was in 2 2 0
    b. A Pond in No. 11

Total 50 2 16

CHARLES

RIVER

This is an accurate Copy of the Original
Attest W.A. Mason

Drawn by a Scale of Two Chains to an Inch

A Plan of the Farm belonging to WILLIAM WINTHROP Esq. of Cambridge

FIGURE 4.255 William Winthrop's farm about 1800. Arrow Street is at the top, with the house lot outlined in red; Putnam Avenue follows the esker down the right side of the map. Fields are labeled according to their use; there are two small ponds, a clay pit now crossed by Flagg Street, and a low hill where Mather House now stands. When the town laid out Mt. Auburn Street in front of the house in 1808, Arrow Street, bypassed on both sides, became little more than an alley.

John Winthrop (1714–79), the great mathematician. At the end of his senior year at Harvard, William was placed in John Hancock's Boston counting house, where he served as supercargo on at least one voyage. He returned to Cambridge after the Revolution and became one of the few men of business in the town. When he purchased the Phips estate it included a clay pit that had been active since the first decade of settlement. There were about 8½ acres of salt marsh between Holyoke and DeWolfe streets, and below that the river bank was relatively firm. The 35 acres of upland included 20 acres of "English mowing" (hayfields) and four acres in cultivation. The rest was pasture, which supported six cows Winthrop kept to supply milk to the college (figure 4.255). The Phips mansion may not have been habitable, because he maintained his residence in the old Cooke place. In 1818 Winthrop built a new house on the old foundation that was similar to Thomas Lee's on Brattle Street. It overlooked the wharf where his schooners landed cargos of wood and building materials; a weathervane on the roof operated a dial that showed him the direction of the wind when a ship was ready to sail (figure 4.256).

Winthrop died childless in 1825, leaving his estate in trust for the five children of his brother, John; the property was to be divided among them after twenty-one years. The trustees kept the place intact at first but sold the house in 1839. The new owner, Samuel Newell, defaulted on three mortgages; his wife, Elizabeth, bought him out with her own money, securing the property "for her sole use and control … as absolutely in all respects as if she were not married and in no degree subject to [his] interference" (Middlesex Deeds, 392/434). Ten years later she sold the place to James Brown, the bookseller and publisher who had established a printing plant on Remington Street in 1848 (see chapter 9). Brown leased the house in 1854 for ten years to Nathaniel Read, a Boston innkeeper, and Levi Lincoln Gould on the condition that it be operated as a "quiet, orderly and respectable" boarding house or hotel (ibid., 680/433). Just before the lease expired, Brown's widow subdivided the property in a way that would have crowded the lawn with eight small

FIGURE 4.256   William Winthrop house, 43 Mt. Auburn Street (1818). The Winthrop house faced Mt. Auburn Street; in this view DeWolfe Street is at left. The house was razed in 1915 for St. Paul's Church. Photo before 1907.

houses. Instead, it passed intact to Joseph Ames, an artist and portrait painter, and then in 1866 to Gordon McKay (1821–1903), one of the richest men in Massachusetts.

McKay purchased the Winthrop house and lived there for twenty years despite the presence of the Reversible Collar Company next door and the densely settled working-class neighborhood that was developing across Mt. Auburn Street. McKay, a son of a Pittsfield cotton manufacturer, never attended college but studied engineering while working on the Boston & Albany Railroad and the Erie Canal. He operated machine shops in Pittsfield and Lawrence until 1859, when he became interested in a device that stitched shoe soles to uppers. He acquired the patent and perfected the mechanism in 1861, just as demand surged for army boots. MacKay's masterstroke was to lease the machines and demand payments based on the volume of production; by 1876, he had already collected royalties on 177 million pairs of shoes and was earning $500,000 a year. McKay divorced his first wife and married Marian Treat, the daughter of his housekeeper, in 1878. They moved to Newport in 1889 and sold the Winthrop house to the Archdiocese of Boston. The Sisters of St. Joseph lived there until it was razed in 1915 for St. Paul's Church. McKay left most of his wealth to Harvard (see chapter 10).

Kerry Corner

Winthrop's farm remained intact until 1843, when the trustee of his estate, Cambridge attorney Abraham Hilliard, sold off the extremities of the long, narrow block between Mt. Auburn and Arrow streets. Housepainters and glaziers Joshua and James Thayer bought a lot near the corner of Massachusetts Avenue and Mt. Auburn Street; their house at 11 Mt. Auburn is the oldest still standing on the farm. East Cambridge brickmaker Ivory Sands leased the clay pit and bought the corner lot. His brothers John and Hiram built 22 Putnam Avenue in 1848 to advertise their products (figure 4.257).

Attorney Hilliard had Joseph Bennett of Boston prepare a subdivision plan for the fields south of Mt. Auburn Street in

FIGURE 4.257 John and Hiram Sands house, 22 Putnam Avenue (1848). Cambridge brickmakers advertised their products in building their own homes. Other brickmakers' houses stand at 145 Elm Street (1839), 336 Rindge Avenue (1848), and 140 Upland Road (1887). Photo 2015.

1844 but sold no other land before the trust dissolved in 1846 (figure 4.258). By this time all three of John Winthrop's sons had died, leaving his daughters, Sarah Andrews of Boston and Harriet Winthrop of Providence, and his son John's three adult children, who lived in Rhode Island and Louisiana, to share the estate. In 1847 the Court of Common Pleas confirmed a distribution that gave John Jr.'s children, led by Providence physician John J. DeWolf, 10½ acres along Mt. Auburn Street as tenants in common, while Harriet and Sarah shared alternating blocks between Putnam Avenue and the river.[77] Poorly advised, the heirs found themselves competing with one another in an uncertain market caused by the Mexican War and the California Gold Rush.

When their land finally began to sell, the principal purchasers were James Brown, George Meacham, Thomas Stearns, and Solomon Sargent. Brown bought the Winthrop mansion from

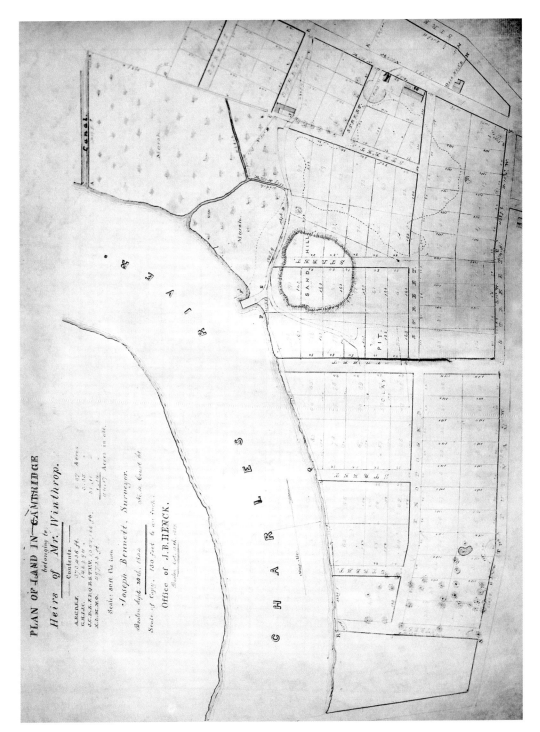

FIGURE 4.258 The Winthrop heirs' 1844 subdivision plan shows barns, a farm pond, and a wharf, as well as the new Thayer house on Mt. Auburn Street.

Elizabeth Newell in 1850. In 1851 Harriet sold about 10 acres and the wharf to Stearns and Sargent, and a year later Sarah sold two abutting tracts to Brown. Stearns and Sargent then sold their holdings to Brown too. All the parties agreed to abandon the "ancient way … near the line of a row of buttonwoods" that led to Winthrop's Wharf and build the streets projected in the Bennett plan (Middlesex Deeds 660/28).

James Brown and Charles Little gave up their Remington Street plant and founded The Riverside Press in the former Cambridge Almshouse in 1852 (see chapter 9). By 1854 they owned all the river frontage as far as River Street. Brown put up only one house before his untimely death in 1855, when his executors divided his holdings into nineteen parcels and distributed them among his widow and five children.[78] Although the partition was intended to be "just and equal, preferring males to females among the children of the deceased and elder to younger sons in the assignment of … the premises," the small, discontiguous parcels and the unsuitability of the plan discouraged development (Middlesex Deeds, Executions, Depositions, and Partitions, 23/238).

Brown's partition was based on the 1844 plan developed for Winthrop's trustee. The 111 parcels were large and awkwardly arranged; most had 80 feet of frontage and were 140 feet deep, containing over 11,000 square feet. By contrast, typical lots in Cambridgeport and East Cambridge were 40 or 50 feet wide and 100 feet deep. To make matters worse, riverfront land was not desirable for residential purposes because of poor drainage, flooding from spring tides, and, somewhat later, the presence of malaria-carrying mosquitoes.[79] Much of the land was salable only for workers' housing or industry, and even the better lots on Putnam Avenue saw little activity until the 1870s. George Meacham, who lived nearby on Bow Street, initiated the earliest development in 1854 by laying out courtyards off Plympton Street to compensate for the lack of street frontage in the unwieldy Bennett plan. He built nothing himself but sold lots to tradesmen and investors who put up row houses and tenements.

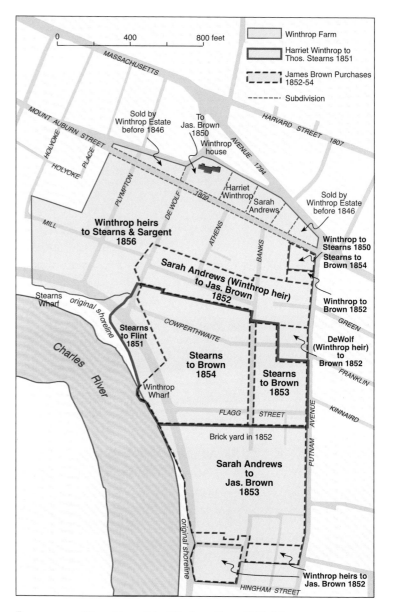

FIGURE 4.259 Disposition of the Winthrop farm, 1846–54.

Stearns and Sargent returned to the field in 1856, when they purchased five acres of marsh east of the College Wharf. Thomas Stearns had come from Maine about 1830, established himself in the livery business in Harvard Square, and started a successful omnibus line. He and Solomon Sargent turned to real estate after they sold their business to the Cambridge Railroad. They erected a dike and a wharf along the river between Holyoke Street and DeWolfe Street, put up lumber sheds and a planing mill, and filled in the marsh. Their 1867 plan shows thirty-one lots of about 4,000 square feet each on Mill and Dyke streets (now Riverview Avenue). Those near the river did not sell easily; the high basement of the surviving early house at 101 Plympton Street testifies to the threat of flooding from spring tides, which continued until the Charles River Dam was completed in 1909.

The Winthrop heirs began their first venture on their remaining land by removing a barn and filling in the farm pond. The thirty small lots on well-drained ground that William A. Mason laid out with 40 feet of frontage on Mt. Auburn Street brought 18¢ a square foot when they were put up for auction in 1858 (figure 4.260). These were more marketable than the eleven large parcels on the 1844 plan, and the street rapidly filled with single and double houses occupied by skilled tradesmen and shopkeepers.

The Brown heirs began the long process of selling their land in 1859. Mary, the eldest child, owned 10 acres between Banks Street and the river. Soon after her father's death she married Joseph Cowperthwaite, a Philadelphia bookseller, and they retained Frederick Parker, a Boston attorney, to sell the property. Boston surveyors Shedd & Edson laid out lots that ranged from 8,000 to 11,400 square feet. Although smaller than Bennett's, they were still too large. Parker finally had the surveyors lay out Crane, Cowperthwaite, Otter, and Beaver Streets with sixty-six lots, most with 40 feet of frontage. Here, at last, was a marketable plan (figure 4.261). The land was low and not very desirable, but the lots were priced to move. Between 1859 and 1873 all were sold at a uniform price of 8¢ a square foot, or $320 for a typical 4,000-square-foot lot. Almost all the buyers were Irish laborers or building tradesmen, and most lived elsewhere in Old Cambridge,

IMPORTANT AND PEREMPTORY LAND SALE.

30 BEAUTIFUL BUILDING LOTS, formerly owned by Hon William Winthrop on Mt Auburn street, Old Cambridge, situated opposite the Winthrop Mansion House in the immediate vicinity of the Colleges, and but a few rods from the Horse Railroad, located in the compact part of the city, and in a most unexceptionable neighborhood. THE BRIDGES CONNECTING BOSTON WITH CAMBRIDGE ARE NOW FREE FOREVER. These lots will be sold on the premises, without reserve, to the highest bidder. MONDAY, April 12, at 3 o'clock, P. M. From 40 to 45 feet front on the street, by 120 to 130 feet deep, and containing from 5000 to 6000 feet of land in each. An uncommon inducement is offered to purchase, not only by the exceeding liberality of the terms of payment, but from the fact that real estate in this locality has advanced, and will continue to advance still more rapidly in value, from the impetus given it by the freedom of the Bridges and the Horse Railroad. Gentlemen may by assured that this is one of the most safe and profitable forms of investment that ever has been offered to the public. For further particulars apply to the auctioneer. 12—4w

FIGURE 4.260 The Winthrop's auction notice showed that tolls had recently been lifted from the Charles River bridges, as well as the proximity of the horsecar line. Few gentlemen saw these lots as a good investment; most buyers were tradesmen who responded to the "exceeding liberality of the terms," and the sellers took back a mortgage on almost every sale.

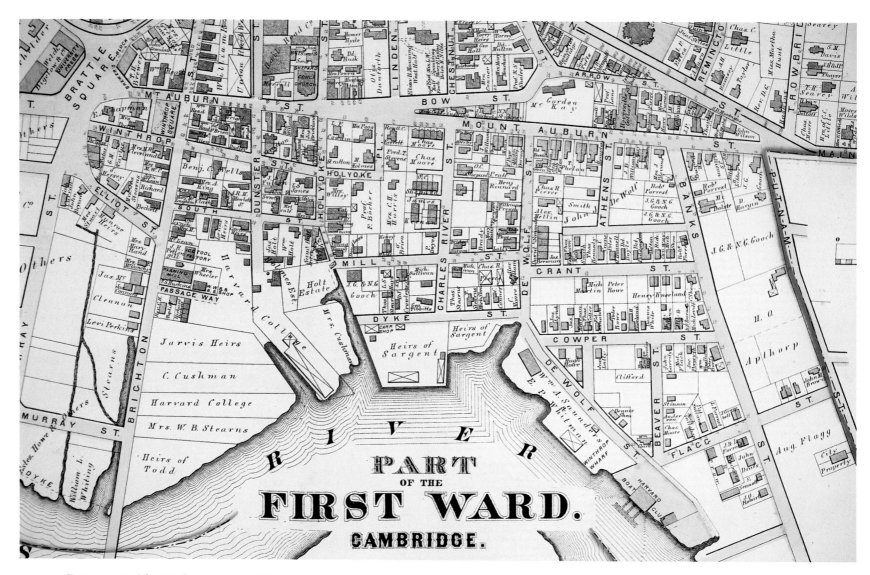

FIGURE 4.261 The Winthrop estate in 1873. Almost all the property owners had Irish surnames.

usually in the 18th-century streets of the village. After one early sale to Edward Connerton, a painter who was listed in the 1863–64 directory as living "on [the] marsh," Parker made all further transactions subject to an unusual restriction designed to prohibit shanties and the pursuit of home occupations:

> Said land shall not be used for any other purpose than a dwelling house of not less than sixteen feet by thirty feet on the ground, and … no building and no fence over six feet high shall be placed within eight feet of [the] street; but the erection or use of any other building, or the occupation of the land contrary to these provisos … shall be conclusively deemed a nuisance for which the releaser … may have remedy by due process of law; or may, at their option, enter or send agents on said land, and remove and abate such nuisances at the expense of the releasee. (Middlesex Deeds, 873/177)

The houses "sixteen feet by thirty feet on the ground" that were initially built on the marsh were similar to the three-bay, center-entrance, high-basement workers' cottages found in East Cambridge and on the clay lands of North Cambridge. They had two rooms per floor, with the kitchen typically in the basement or, later, in an ell; the earliest had neither running water nor indoor toilets. Only a handful remain in their original locations. Many, including 15R Cowperthwaite, 25½–25⅓ Grant, and 112 Banks streets, were moved back on their lots in the 1890s to make way for three-deckers, the next generation's housing of choice in working-class neighborhoods (figures 4.262–4.263).

Workers' cottages were often built from recycled materials. One family dismantled Dexter Pratt's "village smithy" in 1854 and reerected it as a cottage at 155 Banks Street. Parker's restrictions did not prevent the erection of tenements, although these were rare (figure 4.264). Some owners found it expedient to bring in houses that were no longer needed in their current locations. In 1857 Stearns and Sargent moved the 1765 house of Professor Stephen Sewall from Harvard Yard to 15 DeWolfe Street, where it lasted until 1946 (figure 4.265). In 1865 Irishman Thomas Eagleson, a cook, acquired a shed or similar structure and moved it from Linnaean Street to 27 Grant Street, where he converted it to a house that was restored in 2015.

FIGURE 4.262 John "the Orangeman" Lovett house, 8 Beaver Street (1871). The Lovett house, a two-family, was somewhat larger than most high-basement workers' cottages. It was demolished in 1968, and the site is now occupied by Mather House. Photo ca. 1900.

FIGURE 4.263 John Blevins house, 48 Banks Street (1866). The patterned slate roof reflects the trade of the original owner, a roofer. The house was moved from 12 Mount Auburn Street in 1891. Photo 2015.

FIGURE 4.264 Lawrence Forrest house, 35–37 Flagg Street (1870). Forrest, a house painter, was born in Ireland in 1842 and arrived in America in 1860; in 1880 he and his wife had seven children living at home. The oddly shaped projection, termed a "bay window" on the building permit, was added when the house was converted into a tenement in 1909. The building was demolished in 1967. Photo ca. 1925.

FIGURE 4.265 Professor Stephen Sewall house, 15 DeWolfe Street (1765). The Sewall house was relocated from the site of Boylston Hall in 1857 and converted to a tenement. It was demolished in 1946 and replaced by Quincy House in 1958. Photo ca. 1945.

The Brown heirs' last big sale took place in 1865, when forty-eight lots south of Flagg Street went to auction. The large parcels on the river, optimistically characterized as wharf lots, were not developed until after the Cambridge Park Commission took the frontage in 1894. The Sterling Knit Goods Co. and the Hingham Knitting Co. built small factories there in 1912 and 1914 to tap the local labor force (see chapter 9). Downriver, some large tracts were purchased by investors like Charles Porter, who in 1873 laid out Elmer Street to create a dense new subdivision between Putnam Avenue and Banks Street. Porter's meager 2,550-square-foot lots were among the smallest attempted in Cambridge; by 1903 most were packed with three-deckers.

The Brown parcels on Putnam Avenue began to sell in the 1870s. John M. Brown sold his house at number 37 to Harrison

O. Apthorp, an elocution teacher, in 1871, and in 1878 divided his remaining land into eleven small lots on Fallon Place. Apthorp, in turn, laid out Surrey Street with ten lots in 1881. Augustus Flagg, a partner in Little, Brown & Co., owned some Brown land just long enough to lay out the street that bears his name. A few substantial houses were built on Putnam in the 1880s, the most notable of which belonged to William A. Bancroft, the newly appointed president of the Cambridge Railroad (figure 4.266). Edward Brown and Mary Brown Cowperthwaite retained some acreage on the street but not long enough to profit from its acquisition by the Reversible Collar Co. about 1895.

The low-lying meadows of the Winthrop farm became one of Cambridge's earliest Irish neighborhoods, at first called the "Lower Marsh" to distinguish it from the "Upper Marsh"

FIGURE 4.266 William A. Bancroft house, 5 Putnam Avenue (1886, James Fogerty, architect). The Bancroft house was moved to 460 Franklin Street in 1965. Photo 1900.

settlement near Sparks Street and later known as "Kerry Corner" for its many families from that part of Ireland. By 1860 Irish immigrants comprised nearly a quarter of the population of Ward 1 (west of Dana Street and south of Shepard Street). Their original focus was St. Peter Parish on Observatory Hill, but in 1873 Father Manasses Dougherty purchased the disused Shepard Congregational Church at the corner of Mt. Auburn and Holyoke streets as a "chapel of ease" for the 1,200 Catholics already living in the vicinity (Wills, 4). Two years later St. Paul's became a separate parish, and Father William Orr, the first pastor, occupied the old parsonage as his rectory (see figures 4.275 and 7.22).

Kerry Corner was a community of contrasts. John "the Orangeman" Lovett (1833–1906), a shambling, unkempt, often inebriated peddler with a deep brogue who sold snacks from a donkey cart in Harvard Yard, embodied every popular caricature of Irish immigrant behavior and became a popular undergraduate mascot. Michael O'Sullivan (ca. 1833–1923) was a successful contractor who built Hemenway Gymnasium, Phillips Brooks House, the A.D. Club, and Randolph Hall; his residences on Plympton Street—a high-basement workers' cottage of 1870 and an elegant 1899 Colonial Revival at 11 Riverview Avenue— symbolize the arc of his career (see chapter 10). Kerry Corner was also the earliest home of many Irish politicians, including Mayors John H.H. McNamee (1902–4), Augustine Daly (1904–5), and Timothy Good (1914–16), although they all moved to more comfortable parts of Cambridge as they achieved success. In contrast, the political dynasty founded by Michael A. Sullivan in 1936 remained in the area for many decades (see chapter 2).

St. Paul's Parish and the Kerry Corner neighborhood were greatly affected by the city's reclamation of the riverfront and Harvard's subsequent expansion toward the Charles. Plans to build Memorial Drive were announced in 1893 (see chapter 5). Until that time Harvard had expanded north, away from the settled areas of Old Cambridge, but the reclaimed riverfront, made healthful by an interceptor sewer, proved irresistible to imaginative alumni. In 1897 some of them retained Frederick Law Olmsted Jr. to design a new approach to the university from the river parkway. Olmsted's plan to make DeWolfe Street a boulevard 80 feet wide would have taken Quincy Hall, a private dormitory owned by John McNamee, and several houses belonging to St. Paul's (figure 4.267). Community opposition was intense. Father John J. Ryan charged that "President Eliot wishes to sacrifice the DeWolf Street population to his lofty notion of art and taste" (*Chronicle,* Jan. 11, 1902). Proponents claimed the city would recover the cost from higher assessments, but to no avail. Although the plan was revived in 1907, its failure was foretold by Father Orr's refusal to sell. When asked how much land he wanted to keep, he replied, "I want it all. I will not give one inch" (*Chronicle,* Feb. 22, 1902).

Alumni began to buy land as early as 1901 and formed the Harvard Riverside Associates in 1903 to acquire property for eventual transfer to the university (see chapter 10). The Associates made good progress until the *Chronicle* publicized their activities and reported that "the inhabitants of 'the marsh' expect to retire in ease and affluence from what they will realize from the sale of their land" (Mar. 21, 1903). One significant holdout was Michael O'Sullivan, who declined an offer of $25,000 to move his houses to DeWolfe Street. Gore Hall (now part of Harvard's Winthrop House) had to share the riverfront with O'Sullivan, and when he died in 1926 President Lowell refused to deal with his heirs. Harvard acquired the houses in 1932 for about $23,000 and rented them to graduate students until it incorporated them into Winthrop House in 2016 (figure 4.268).

Kerry Corner began to shrink with the construction of three freshman dormitories in 1913. Standish and Smith halls replaced a planing mill and the remnants of the College Wharf, but Gore displaced twenty-seven families in ten houses on Mill Street and Riverview Avenue. The associates razed a row house on Mill Street, described as "a poor class of property," before the students moved in, plus eight more houses on South Street for aesthetic reasons before disbanding in 1918 (Cooney, "Harvard Riverside Associates"). Some houses were relocated and demolished later; 31 Athens Street, which was moved from 48 Holyoke Street (the future site of Lowell House) in 1916, is a rare survivor. In 1924, Father Ryan noted that already "more than half a dozen streets with the dwellings of a Catholic population estimated at 1,200–1,500 souls were taken over [and] these people were compelled to seek homes elsewhere" (Ryan, 46).

Harvard began acquiring property on its own account with the block east of Plympton Street, where McKinlock Hall was built in 1925–26. By 1930, the university owned the entire parkway frontage between Kennedy Street and Western Avenue except for Cpl. Burns Park. Construction resumed in 1929 with Lowell House, which displaced 27 houses, Malkin Athletic Center (9), Mather Hall (14), and Dunster House (23). Between 1958 and 1967, Harvard razed 104 more buildings containing 138 units to make room for Leverett, Quincy, and Mather houses and Peabody Terrace. Banks, Grant, and Cowperthwaite streets also lost houses.

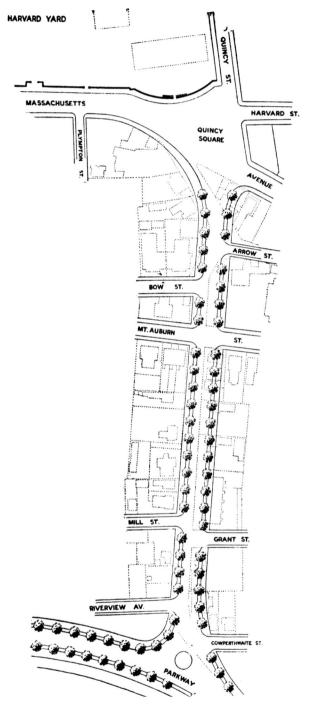

Figure 4.267 The proposed widening of DeWolfe Street in 1902 would have affected Mayor McNamee's Quincy Hall on Massachusetts Avenue and the future site of St. Paul's Church.

FIGURE 4.268 Michael O'Sullivan's successive houses exemplify the upward mobility of Cambridge's Irish immigrants and their resistance to Harvard expansion in the 20th century. O'Sullivan's first residence, 101 Plympton Street (1870, the small yellow house in the middle of the photo), was a typical high-basement workers' cottage; his later house, 11 Riverview Avenue (1899, E.T. Harrington, architect), was the finest private residence in the neighborhood. Harvard's Gore Hall (1913) is at left; McKinlock Hall (1925) is at right. Photo 2010.

FIGURE 4.269 Riverside and Kerry Corner from the southeast in 1958, with Western Avenue at the bottom and Putnam Avenue on the right. The Reversible Collar factory, the Sterling knitting mill, and many of the houses around them were razed in 1960–62 for Peabody Terrace. The Hingham knitting mill was taken down in 1971 after it was occupied by radical feminists and antiwar protesters, while the Treeland (Mahoney's Nursery) site at the corner of Memorial Drive and Western Avenue is now occupied by a park and university housing constructed in 2010–11. Photo 1958.

In all, Harvard demolished about 225 dwellings and displaced over 300 families to create the River Houses and Peabody Terrace.

Riverside and Kerry Corner residents forcibly occupied commencement in 1970 in response to Harvard's plans for more construction. Old grievances were renewed three decades later, when Harvard announced plans to build a museum at the corner of Western Avenue (see chapter 10). When this was rejected, the University put up housing and a park instead. A 2007 project included a five-story building on Cowperthwaite Street and eight two- and three-story houses for Harvard affiliates on Grant and Banks streets, filling in vacant lots created for expansion in the 1960s. The bitterness created by a century of Harvard expansion was evident throughout this period.

APTHORP-BORLAND ESTATE AND THE JOSEPH COOKE PLACE

In the 18th century the village thinned out east of Dunster Street. There was a pond where Holyoke Center now stands, and beyond that Crooked (now Holyoke) Street was only a narrow lane. Braintree Street and the road to the Oyster Banks (now Massachusetts Avenue) ran along the south-facing slope at the edge of the college yard, while Back Lane ran east from Holyoke Street partially on the alignment of present-day Arrow Street (see figure 1.15). The six-acre Apthorp-Borland estate came into play after the West Boston Bridge was completed in 1793, and by 1800 its owner had added three new streets—Linden, Plympton, and part of Bow—that seem indistinguishable from the town's 17th-century grid. The two-acre Joseph Cooke property now traversed by Holyoke Place was subdivided in 1836.

EAST APTHORP ESTATE

The south-facing hillside east of the village was divided about 1635 into six parcels containing an eighth to three-quarters of an acre that were soon consolidated into four homesteads along Back Lane. Thomas Danforth sold his father's place in 1652, and the homestead soon passed to Edmund Angier, a woolen-draper. The Danforth-Angier house disappeared by 1722, but a two-acre tract called "Angier's orchard" stayed in the family until 1759 (Middlesex Probate 445). Another early homestead belonged to Samuel Gookin (1652–1730), high sheriff of both Middlesex and Suffolk counties, who made his son a deputy when he was 19 years old. Samuel II held this office for sixty-four years, but financial setbacks forced him to sell the homestead to Reverend East Apthorp in 1759. By this time the Gookin place included another eighth-acre homestead that was used as a house of correction until Middlesex County built a jail on Winthrop Street in 1660.

The Massachusetts Avenue frontage from Holyoke to Bow Street belonged to Samuel Shepard, who built a house at the corner of Holyoke Street facing the parsonage of his half-brother Thomas. Shepard was a selectman, representative, and deputy until he returned to England in 1645 to serve in the Parliamentary forces during the Civil War. In 1650 he sold the house to Edward Mitchelson, marshall-general of the General Court. Half a century later, Joseph Coolidge of Watertown, a tailor, purchased the 1½-acre homestead, with "mansion house and barn, outhouses [and] orchard," and left it to his son, Dr. Stephen Coolidge, in 1737 (Middlesex Deeds 17/311). When Dr. Coolidge died in 1758 his executor sold the house to widow Martha Champney, "a distinguished school-dame" (Paige, 508).

The formation of the Apthorp estate was associated with the founding of Christ Church (see chapter 7). In 1759 David Phips, a member of the building committee, bought Angier's orchard on behalf of East Apthorp, the first rector. The son of a wealthy Boston merchant, Apthorp graduated from Cambridge University in 1755 and returned to America when his father died in 1758. The grandeur of the rector's residence and its placement so close to the college raised suspicions about the intentions of his London sponsor, the Society for the Propagation of the Gospel in Foreign Parts. Almost immediately a rumor arose that Apthorp was a spy and that his house was intended to become the seat of an Anglican bishop. He returned to England in 1764, and his house has been known as "the bishop's palace" ever since.

Apthorp sold his house to John Borland, who moved from Quincy so that his wife, Anna, could be close to her Vassall relatives. The Borlands added a third story to accommodate their twelve children and also bought the remaining Shepard-Coolidge frontage on Massachusetts Avenue. The Committee of Correspondence seized the property when the Borlands fled to Boston in 1775. During the Siege of Boston it was occupied by several companies of Minutemen, and in 1777–78 the captured British general Burgoyne was interned there. Perhaps because Borland had died in Boston before the evacuation and taken no active part in the hostilities, his widow was able to regain the property in 1783 on behalf of their sons, John and Leonard. This was unusual because John was a career British Army officer, and the family remained loyal to the Crown.

FIGURE 4.270 Reverend East Apthorp house (1760, attributed to Peter Harrison, architect; third floor added by John Borland between 1765 and 1775). Randolph Hall (1897) now surrounds the house. Photo ca. 1880.

Jonathan Simpson Jr., Borland's brother-in-law, bought the estate in 1784. A loyalist merchant, he had spent most of the war in British-occupied Charleston, South Carolina, but had escaped proscription by the Massachusetts authorities. By this time the property ran from Holyoke Street to Bow Street and lacked only the Coolidge-Champney lot to complete the block. In 1786 he bought land south of Back Lane and three years later convinced the town to relocate the road to the bottom of the slope. He gave the town a 45-foot right-of-way that is now occupied by the lower part of Bow Street and received in turn the old 20-foot-wide "road or street from the Market-Place to the Neck" where it passed through his land (Middlesex Deeds 100/318).

Simpson turned to Francis Dana (the new owner of Edmund Trowbridge's property on Mt. Auburn Street) and Harvard College to straighten Crooked Street and prepare it for development. The new street, 31 feet wide, was located slightly west of the old one and required the abutters to engage in a complicated series of transactions involving many oddly shaped parcels. The town accepted it in 1798 but maintained the old name until it became Holyoke Street about 1850. The relocation westward created two 200-foot-long blocks between Dunster and Linden streets and enabled the development of the Apthorp estate to blend imperceptibly into the original village grid.

Simpson laid out an alley up the middle of the block (between Ridgely and Claverly halls) and began selling lots. Samuel Flagg Sawyer, a bricklayer from Sterling, Massachusetts, bought the Bow Street corner in 1797 and put up a two-story house with brick gable ends; it was given a third story and converted to a student dormitory before it was demolished in 1927 (see figure 10.36). Sawyer's barn was remodeled as a house about 1846 and survives at 20 Holyoke Street. William Wesson, a coachmaker, and James Fillebrown, a housewright, built houses that were moved or demolished for the Hasty Pudding Club (1887) and Apley Court (1897).

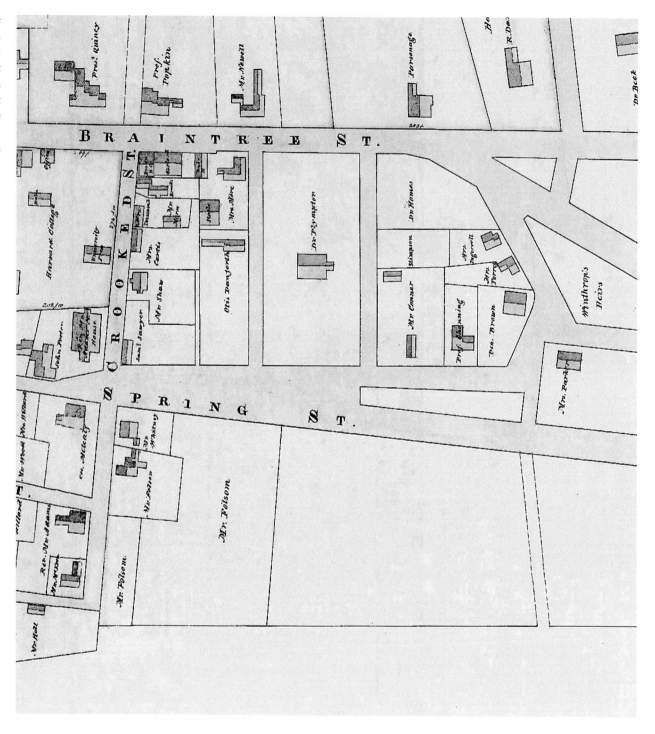

FIGURE 4.271 The Apthorp estate and the east end of the village in 1833. Crooked (now Holyoke) Street has been substantially built up. Although the town accepted Chestnut (now Plympton) Street in 1803, thirty years later there were still only six houses east of it. The Cooke property (lots labeled "Mr. Folsom") is undeveloped.

In 1801 Simpson defaulted on a loan from Boston merchants Jonathan Amory Jr. and James Cutter and lost the Apthorp house and all his land except the remaining frontage along Holyoke Street—about five acres in all. Simpson or Amory laid out thirty-five house lots on Linden and Plympton (originally Chestnut) streets east and west of the mansion. Amory sold Francis Dana five lots "on a way twenty-five feet wide [Linden Street] running from the great north road [Massachusetts Avenue] to the great south road [Mt. Auburn Street]" (Middlesex Deeds 140/489). Simpson moved to Boston, where he survived by selling smaller and smaller shares of his wife's inherited properties until he died practically destitute in 1834.

Dr. Timothy Lindall Jennison and Thomas Warland, a tailor, acquired Simpson's remaining interest in the Apthorp house in 1802, but in 1803 Jennison leased Warland the easterly half for 1,000 years "at the rate of one cent per year if the house shall so long stand and endure" (DAR *Guide,* 79). Warland's daughters and their heirs occupied it for the rest of the century. Mary Warland married Dr. Sylvanus Plympton; the street is named for one of their sons who died in the Civil War. Elizabeth Warland married Dr. Samuel Manning in 1822, but he died almost immediately. One of her boarders, W. Harmon Niles, was a student of Louis Agassiz who held simultaneous appointments at M.I.T., Boston University, and Wellesley College. He married Dr. Plympton's youngest daughter, Helen, in 1868 and helped the family develop their Massachusetts Avenue frontage. They built a two-story building with stores and a studio for the Notman Photographic Company in 1885 and a private dormitory, the Warland, in 1889; these buildings at 1282–90 and 1274–80 Massachusetts Avenue were razed in 1984 (see figure 8.44). The Coolidge brothers acquired the lower part of the garden in 1897 for Randolph Hall and then bought the Apthorp house itself in 1901 and converted it to student lodgings. It became the Master's Residence of Adams House in 1931.

Figure 4.272 Plympton Street looking north toward Mt. Auburn and Bow streets in 1902. From left to right are Randolph Hall (1897), Russell Hall (1899; demolished 1931), and a four-story tenement erected by Hycent Purcell in 1889. In this period the Gold Coast coexisted with the Irish neighborhood south of Mt. Auburn Street, and there were plenty of children to mob the photographer.

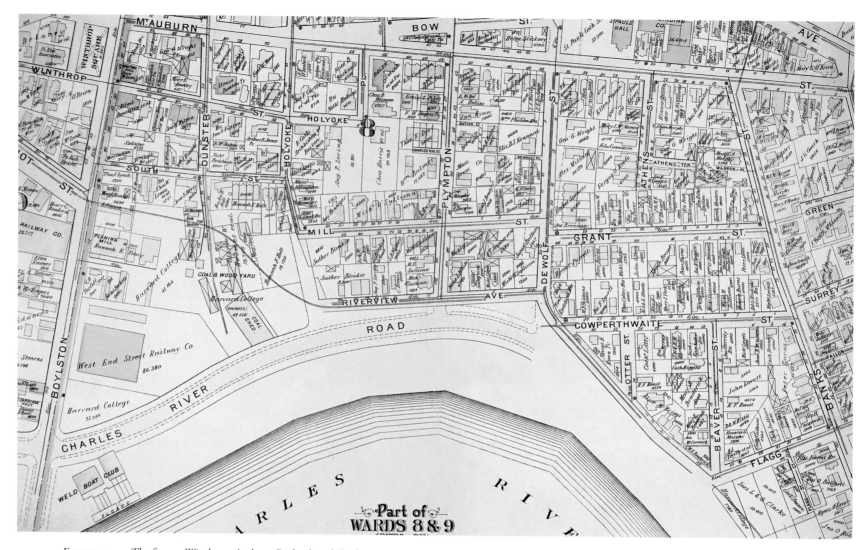

FIGURE 4.273 The former Winthrop, Apthorp-Borland, and Cooke estates in 1903.

Joseph Cooke Place

One other important homestead bounded the village on the southeast. George and Joseph Cooke arrived from England in 1635 with Reverend Shepard and bought several lots southeast of the village from settlers who were leaving for Connecticut. George served as speaker of the General Court and captain of Cambridge's first militia company, but he returned to England in 1645 and became a colonel in Cromwell's army. Joseph held local offices and raised a family in America before he went back in 1658. Their homestead—bounded today by Mt. Auburn, Plympton, Mill, and Holyoke streets—included "the hill by his house which have been hitherto reserved for a place to build a fort upon for defense with all the lane leading thereto provided that if the town shall ever make use of it for that end he shall yield it again" (Town Records, Jan. 2, 1636, 25).

In 1665 Joseph Cooke Jr. received the five-acre homestead from his father as a wedding gift, and the next year the town granted him "liberty for timber on the Common to build him a dwelling house" (ibid. 162). Three generations of Cookes made little further impression on the town, and in 1761 President Edward Holyoke, anticipating retirement, purchased the property. It passed through Holyoke's estate in 1769 and was acquired by William Winthrop in 1803.

Winthrop remodeled the Cooke house and lived there until 1811. In 1832 Sidney Willard, Professor of Hebrew and Oriental Languages, sold it to Charles Folsom, the former Harvard librarian, who purchased the University Press from Eliab Metcalf a year later (see chapter 9). In 1836 Folsom laid out Holyoke Place and subdivided the two-acre property into eight lots. The house passed through many hands until the heirs of the last owner-occupant sold it to the trustees of the Phi Delta Psi Club in 1901. It was probably Cambridge's oldest house when the club demolished it in 1905 (figure 4.274).

Folsom's subdivision appealed to local businessmen and Harvard people who did not qualify for a place on Professors Row. The Shepard Congregational Society built a parsonage for its minister, Reverend John Albro, in 1837 (figure 4.275).

FIGURE 4.274 Cooke-Winthrop house, 30 Holyoke Street (1666; demolished 1905). In 1803 William Winthrop "removed the old cills and roof … raised the house and put in new cills; added the third story and put on the present roof instead of the old gambril roof" (William T. Harris, DAR *Guide,* 74).

FIGURE 4.275 Shepard Congregational Church parsonage, 34 Holyoke Street (1837; demolished by 1929). The parsonage became the first rectory of St. Paul's Church. Photo ca. 1929.

Residential Neighborhoods   389

FIGURE 4.276 The Cooke estate and its environs in 1897, as seen from the chimney of the Boston Elevated Railway power station at the corner of Kennedy Street and Memorial Drive. Mill Street is in the lower right corner; Holyoke Street runs from lower right to upper left, toward Harvard Square. Although some of these houses were moved, most were razed between 1900 and 1935.

Thaddeus Harris, one of Folsom's successors as university librarian, built a house about 1844; Professor Ferdinand Boucher, who taught modern languages from 1861 to 1902, occupied another. Many houses remained in family ownership until the Riverside Associates acquired them for university expansion in the early 20th century; none survive (figure 4.276).

In 1929 a *Crimson* headline read "Historic Site Fast Becoming Wiped Out By Steam Shovels in Construction of New Gym."

> Now that we see truck load after truck load of precious earth rumbling off, some to the Law School, some to the site of the Dean's House at the Business School, and some to Soldiers Field, we are witnessing a great ending. The bones of our old town soon will be scattered to the four winds. (Apr. 2)

Lowell House went up on the hill reserved for a fort in 1929, and the boundaries of the Cooke place, like those of the Apthorp estate, disappeared into the urban fabric of Old Cambridge.

FIGURE 4.277 Winthrop Street in 1930. From left to right are the Charles Stratton house at 45 (1869; demolished 1953), the John Read house at 43 (ca. 1845), Lowell House (1929), and the Indoor Athletic Building (now the Malkin Athletic Center, 1928). Malkin displaced nine houses on the block bounded by Dunster, Holyoke, Winthrop, and South streets. Theodore Roosevelt's college boarding house is memorialized by a plaque near the entrance.

FIGURE 5.1 Cambridge in the 1770s. The layout of the village is somewhat conjectural, but this map by British Army mapmaker John Hills accurately depicts the buildings surrounding the Common and the college. The wide spot in the road leading from the Meetinghouse to the Great Bridge is the Market-place, later Winthrop Square.

5 PARKS, CEMETERIES, AND GARDENS

Public open spaces in Cambridge were entirely utilitarian until the 1830s, and the idea that municipalities should acquire and maintain parks for general enjoyment was not fully realized for another six or seven decades. Private citizens enclosed and beautified Cambridge Common and Winthrop Square. Members of the Massachusetts Horticultural Society pioneered the concept of the garden cemetery and made Mount Auburn the most popular pleasure ground in New England. Neighboring landowners donated Fort Washington and Hastings Square to the city, and followers of Longfellow and Lowell established parks in their memory. Mayor James D. Green voiced the prevailing attitude when he told the city council that there was no allowance in law for spending public money on the "purchase or embellishment of public squares, the rebuilding of forts, or erection of flagstaffs … these should be done by private subscription" (*Cambridge Chronicle,* Jan. 2, 1860). When Harvard's President Eliot and the chairman of the Water Board, Chester Kingsley, debated "the public park system of Cambridge" in 1891, the *Cambridge Tribune* observed that the topic was poorly chosen, since "Cambridge has no park system" (Oct. 21). Once a new mayor secured legislation and appointed a park commission, the city rapidly put the innovative ideas of landscape architect Charles Eliot into effect and began in 1894 to develop the banks of the Charles and several inland parcels for public recreation (see chapter 2 for a description of the parks movement in Cambridge).

PARKS AND PARKWAYS

Until the late 19th century, the only public open spaces in Old Cambridge were Cambridge Common, Winthrop Square, and the Old Burying Ground. Although the Common was nationally known as one of the landmarks of the American Revolution, it was indifferently maintained; those wishing a civilized outdoor experience went instead to private places such as Mount Auburn Cemetery, the Harvard Botanic Garden, and Waverly Oaks in Belmont. Cambridge was not yet fully developed, and for many people the open countryside still lay close at hand.

CAMBRIDGE COMMON

Cambridge Common is a remnant of the original Massachusetts Bay lands allotted to Newtowne in 1630 (see chapter 1). By the 1660s the remaining commons in present Cambridge were the Ox Pasture (100 acres between Rindge Avenue and Alewife Brook) and the Cow Common (86 acres between Garden and Linnaean streets and Massachusetts Avenue, known by this time as the Lower Common). The Proprietors of Common Lands divided the Ox Pasture in 1703 (see *Report Five: Northwest Cambridge*). In 1724 they distributed 63 acres of the Lower Common, leaving approximately 16 acres from which today's Cambridge Common was formed in 1830.

In November 1769 the Proprietors ensured the continued existence of the Common as a public open space when they voted that:

all the common Lands belonging to the Proprietors, Frunting the Colledge, (commonly called the Town Commons) not heretofore granted or allotted to any particular person or persons or for any Special or particular Use, be … granted to the Town of cambridge, to be used as a Traineing Field to lye undivided, and to Remain for that use for Ever. (*Proprietors' Records,* 362)

The Common served as a militia training ground from a very early date. Captain Daniel Patrick, who commanded the Massachusetts Bay militia from 1632 to 1637, lived in the village, and the senior officers of the Middlesex Regiment were generally Cambridge men.[1] There were no military facilities on the Common, but because of its central location militiamen from several towns assembled there for duty on the frontier or in the wars against the French. After the British retreat from Lexington and Concord on April 19, 1775, Minutemen from all over New England mustered on the Common, and more than a thousand men gathered there before the Battle of Bunker Hill. During the Siege of Boston, which lasted through the winter of 1775–76, Cambridge became the principal military center of the colonies. Almost 10,000 men were encamped in and around the town, including 640 in barracks on Cambridge Common (figure 5.2).

The Common at this time was an unfenced, undifferentiated open space crisscrossed by footpaths and rough tracks that expressed travelers' desire lines. The only fences were those erected by abutters to keep out the cattle, pigs, sheep, geese, and even turkeys that were driven over the roads to market. After the completion of the West Boston Bridge in 1793, the Concord Turnpike in 1803, and Craigie's Bridge in 1809, the Common became a busy intersection of major routes between Boston and upcountry towns. To the dismay of many villagers, drovers adopted the custom of resting their herds overnight on the Common before proceeding to markets in Boston or to the stockyards that had been established in Brighton during the war.

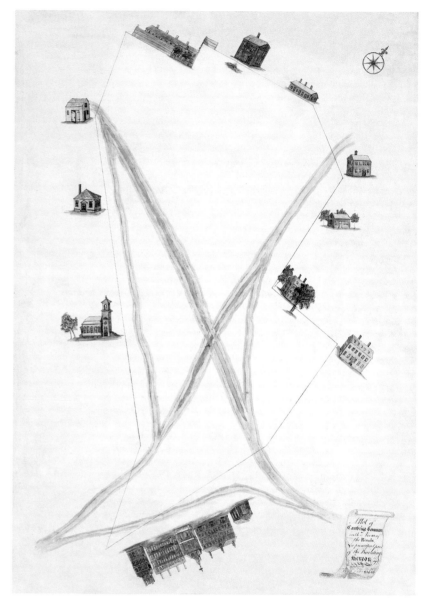

FIGURE 5.2 Cambridge Common ca. 1781, showing the cart tracks and paths that traversed it before the enclosure. Clockwise from the bottom are Harvard College, Christ Church, the schoolhouse, a barn on the Prentice estate, the Massachusetts Arsenal (housed in a former Revolutionary War barracks), the Gideon Frost (later Benjamin Waterhouse) house, a blacksmith's shop, John Nutting's house, John Hasting's barn and house, and the Hastings-Holmes house.

FIGURE 5.3 Cambridge Common in 1809, looking south from Holmes Place. Kirkland Street enters from the left and Massachusetts Avenue from the right. The steeple of the Fourth Meetinghouse rises in the center.

FIGURE 5.4 Cambridge Common in 1809, looking north from Christ Church. Garden Street occupies the foreground, while Massachusetts Avenue recedes in the distance. Avon Hill rises behind the houses on Waterhouse Street; Holmes Place is on the right.

The Common was also used for revivals, elections, and celebrations. Until the early 19th century it was the site of weeklong festivities during Harvard commencements, which were the only sanctioned public events in Puritan Massachusetts (see chapter 10). The crude revelries attended by thousands from across New England caused Harvard and nearby neighbors to support an enclosure movement. In 1823 William Hilliard, a former selectman, town clerk, and state representative, presented a petition at town meeting "to make certain improvements on the Common … by setting out trees … and fencing in certain parts … not incompatible with the original grant to the town," at the petitioners' own expense (Paige, 236). They were no doubt inspired by a recent movement to landscape Boston Common and by similar plans in nearby Lexington and Medford, but voters rejected the proposal. Seven years later, another set of proponents, including Stephen Higginson, the recently retired steward of Harvard College who had worked with President Kirkland to enclose and landscape Harvard Yard, law professor Asahel Stearns, innkeeper Israel Porter, and Francis Dana Jr. went directly to the General Court. The legislature authorized the enclosure in 1830 and empowered the committee to "level the surface of the ground, to plant trees, and to lay out and make walks within said enclosure … leaving suitable and convenient avenues for the accommodation of persons who may have occasion to enter or pass over any part of said enclosure on foot" (*Mass. Special Laws,* vii, 7, in Paige, 236; figure 5.5). President Quincy contributed $500, and the Common soon resembled the Yard, with a granite post and rail fence and widely spaced elms, although the grass was not regularly mown to make a lawn until the 1870s (figure 5.6). All the roads except Massachusetts Avenue and Cambridge and Kirkland streets were eliminated, leaving an 8½-acre park and three triangular parcels of about a half-acre each.[2]

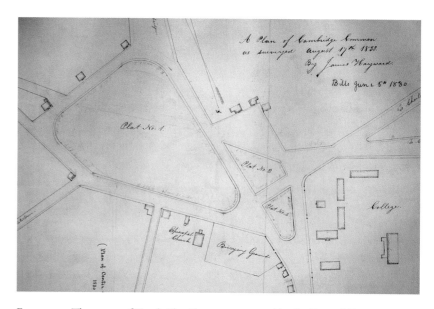

FIGURE 5.5 The survey of Cambridge Common approved by the General Court in 1830.

FIGURE 5.6 Cambridge Common in 1862, thirty years after enclosure, with straight graveled paths, a granite post and rail fence, and widely spaced elms.

A legislative committee trying to sort out the controversy observed that:

> Both parties admire the grounds as now laid out, the tasteful arrangement of the walks, and the promising growth of trees that line the margin, and are disposed in the centre of the Common. The entire consecration of this spot to such purposes of public ornament as should be a permanent monument of the refinement and taste of the citizens of that part of Middlesex, and still further distinguish a village already widely and highly distinguished … was a common sentiment. (Mass. Senate No. 23 [1832], 11)

In the early 19th century the Common became firmly associated in the public mind with a compelling patriotic legend. General George Washington arrived in Cambridge on July 2, 1775, to take command of the American army; the next day a soldier reported in his diary that the troops "turned out Early In the Morning [and] Got in Rediness to Receive the General" (Sleeper, July 3, 1775). Somehow this event became associated with a particular tree near the northwest corner of the Common, one of a dozen elms that were planted along Garden and Linnaean streets about 1700.[3] Edward Everett made the earliest known public reference to the Washington Elm in an Independence Day speech in 1826, but an 1837 article by Harvard librarian John Langdon Sibley in the *American Magazine for Useful Knowledge*, in which he repeated the oral tradition, probably had a greater impact. Sibley wrote that Washington "drew his sword as commander-in-chief of the army, for the first time, beneath its boughs" (vol. III, 432). Guidebooks and popular literature embellished the story, and in 1864 the city placed a commemorative tablet at the base of the tree (figures 5.7–5.8). The actual source of the frequently repeated description of "the majestic figure of the General, mounted on his horse beneath the widespreading branches of the patriarch tree" was the fictional "Diary of Dorothy Dudley." Arthur Gilman had commissioned this purported eyewitness account from a young Centre Street resident, Mary Williams Greely, for *The Cambridge of 1776*, a commemorative volume of essays, poems, and reminiscences published in 1876.

FIGURE 5.7 This imagined scene of Washington taking command appeared in *Ballou's Pictorial,* a magazine with a national circulation, on July 7, 1855.

FIGURE 5.8 The Washington Elm was documented by countless photographers, and wood from it was used to make many commemorative artifacts. This realistic book was made at the direction of the city council by Cambridgeport craftsman Henry A. Scranton for exhibit at the Centennial Exposition in Philadelphia in 1875.

As early as 1869, Sibley wrote in his diary that the elm was "dying from age and want of nourishment" (Apr. 13). By the late 1870s Garden Street had been widened at the expense of the Common, and the elm stood in the middle of the intersection with Mason Street (see figure 4.113). When it finally toppled on October 26, 1923, the police had to repel souvenir hunters (figure 5.9). The mayor ordered the trunk sawn into hundreds of fragments that were distributed nationwide; the site of the elm was marked with a large brass plate in the middle of the intersection. The hysteria offended historian Samuel F. Batchelder, who analyzed contemporary accounts (which describe Washington as hurried and anxious about a threatened attack), the disposition of forces (scattered), and the weather (rainy). His carefully considered paper, published in 1925, concluded that a formal ceremony could not have taken place.

The legend continued to be an article of faith for many, and in 1945 Frank A.K. Boland, manager of the Commander Hotel (named after Washington and bearing a miniature replica of Mount Vernon on its facade), proposed that the city install a

HISTORIC TREE TOPPLES OVER

Famous Washington Elm Crashes to Ground—Knocks Down Wires, Wrecks Fence and Nearly Strikes Pedestrians— Long a Shrine for Tourists—Was Soon to Be Felled

FIGURE 5.9 The demise of the Washington Elm made headlines across the country. Some commentators accused the city of negligence, and one said that it could have been preserved by pouring concrete around its trunk.

bronze bas-relief depicting the occasion. The project went ahead even though Professor Samuel Eliot Morison advised the city manager that the tradition "had best be allowed to die" (to John B. Atkinson, Oct. 27, 1949).

Monuments began to accumulate on the Common in 1870. A civic debate over an appropriate memorial to the 346 Cambridge men who died in the Civil War began soon after Appomattox. Some advocated a new municipal building with a memorial hall; others preferred a monument in Cambridge Cemetery. The Common was chosen because of its size, central location, and historical associations.[4] Planning began in January 1869 when Mayor Charles Hicks Saunders charged the common council and the board of aldermen with the task of erecting a monument on the "flagstaff-common" (now Flagstaff Park). A committee instead chose the "large common" and resolved to "build an edifice, that, while it would suitably commemorate those whose names and services we desired to cherish and perpetuate, should be creditable to us as a work of art, and worthy of the historical character of Cambridge" (City of Cambridge, *Soldier's Monument*, 57).

A competition attracted thirty-four designs from twenty-two artists. Advised by Boston architect Nathaniel Bradlee, the committee selected a proposal from Cyrus and Darius Cobb, Malden twins who had served in the 44th Massachusetts Regiment. Cyrus was a sculptor who also practiced law; Darius was a portrait painter (figure 5.10). Second place went to Joseph R. Richards, a Cambridge architect who had designed several schools for the city. Only one other design has survived, that of William Pitt Preble Longfellow, the poet's nephew (figure 5.11). Meanwhile, dissidents sought an injunction against the project on the grounds that the Proprietors of Common Lands had granted the Common to the town solely for use as a training field. Some of the plaintiffs, who were represented by Richard Henry Dana Jr., preferred a monument in East Cambridge or Cambridgeport, while others opposed any commemoration of the war.

Cambridge stonecutters Alexander McDonald and Jonathan Mann constructed the Soldiers Monument from exceptionally

FIGURE 5.10 The newly completed Soldiers Monument as designed by Cyrus and Darius Cobb, ca. 1876.

FIGURE 5.11 William P.P. Longfellow's unsuccessful design for the Soldiers Monument, 1869. Longfellow executed very few buildings and was better known as an academic architect and author; he later taught architecture at M.I.T.

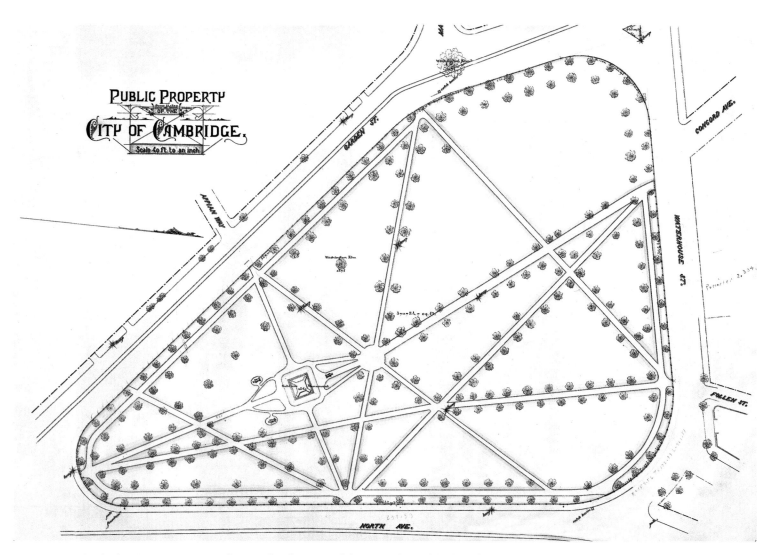

FIGURE 5.12 Cambridge Common in 1877, showing the placement of three British cannon around the Soldiers Monument. This layout of paths survived until 1976.

large blocks of New Hampshire granite. Buttresses bear plaques listing the names and units of deceased soldiers. The cupola is surmounted by a statue of a soldier with his head bowed in mourning, but for many years the plinth stood empty. The original proposal for an angel holding a dying soldier was considered too graphic; in 1888 Cyrus Cobb suggested an allegorical figure of America. In 1936 Francis J. O'Reilly, last Cambridge veteran of the war, began a campaign to raise pennies from schoolchildren for a statue of Abraham Lincoln. A copy of an 1887 bronze by Augustus Saint-Gaudens was installed in 1937.[5]

The centennial celebrations of 1875–76 generated enthusiasm for commemorating American history. Three 18th-century cannon—two 32-pounders and a 12-pounder—were installed near the Soldiers Monument. Contrary to legend, these had not been brought from Fort Ticonderoga by General Knox but were abandoned by the British during the evacuation of Castle William (Fort Independence) in 1776. Stored at the State Arsenal on Garden Street, they had been spared when thirty-four obsolete cannon were sold to the South Boston Iron Works in 1848. In 1880 the city council voted to install granite markers at Revolutionary sites throughout the city. Samuel Bridge, a sixth-generation descendent of early settler John Bridge, engaged Thomas Ridgeway Gould, an American sculptor living in Florence, to create a statue of his ancestor and arranged to have it placed on the northeast corner of the Common in 1882.[6]

In 1904 the Boston chapter of the Daughters of the Revolution proposed a triumphal arch opposite the Washington Elm. The Municipal Art Society protested the structure's size and location, and it was erected in 1906 on a smaller scale at the end of the Common facing Harvard Square (figure 5.13). Perhaps in response, the Hannah Winthrop Chapter of the Daughters of the *American* Revolution replaced a flagstaff that had stood nearby since 1857 with a new one designed by Peabody & Stearns to commemorate "the suffering and fortitude of the men and women of Cambridge during the Revolution" (figure 5.14).[7]

The Cambridge Park Commission (CPC) took charge of the Common in 1892 and soon complained about the difficulty of preventing its use "as a playground for the rough sports of men and boys … many complaints have been made as to the danger to life and limb to those passing through the Common, and for this reason it is shunned by some of our people who would otherwise gladly use it" (*Annual Report,* 1894, 15). In 1898 the commissioners asked their landscape consultants, Olmsted, Olmsted & Eliot, to plan improvements, but no work was carried out under their direction, and the Common retained its traditional character of straight diagonal paths and deciduous trees.

Cambridge, Mass. Entrance to Cambridge Common.

FIGURE 5.13 George Washington Memorial Gate (1905, F.J. Untersee, architect). The Daughters of the Revolution commissioned the design from a Swiss-born Boston architect, Franz Joseph Untersee, and paid for the project. The cast iron bollards protected the Common from cattle, which were driven through nearby streets until the 1920s. Photo ca. 1910.

FIGURE 5.14 Memorial Flagstaff on Flagstaff Park (1913, Peabody & Stearns, architects). The Daughters of the American Revolution raised about a third of the cost through popular subscription; the city contributed the rest. The original Oregon pine flagpole rotted at the top of the concrete base and fell during a storm in 1929. During construction of the Red Line extension in 1984, the replacement pole was cut off above the base and then reinstalled; this left it about 60 feet high, only half the height of the original 1857 flagstaff. Photo 1929.

The three isolated sections of the Common east of Massachusetts Avenue received relatively little attention until 1902, when a statue of Charles Sumner by Anne Whitney was placed north of Kirkland Street (figure 5.15). A native of Watertown who grew up in East Cambridge, Whitney went to Rome after the Civil War to study sculpture and in 1875 entered a competition for a statue of Sumner to be placed in Boston's Public Garden. When the judges learned that the winning artist was a woman, they rejected her entry in favor of a design by Thomas Ball. In 1900 Whitney had the statue cast at her own expense, and in 1902, "on behalf of a certain unknown donor," Professor Edward Cummings offered it to Cambridge (*Annual Report,* 1902, 6). Sumner

(1811–74), a radical abolitionist and U.S. Senator from 1851 to 1874, had enjoyed strong support in Old Cambridge.

In 1909–12, the two small commons between Massachusetts Avenue and Peabody Street were combined to accommodate a ramp for streetcars to enter the new Harvard Station. The Boston Elevated Railway faced the walls of the incline with brick to complement the buildings in the Yard and created a plaza for the Sumner statue (see figure 10.76). During the construction of the subway from Harvard Square to Alewife in 1978–86 the walls were eliminated to reunite the Yard and the Common, and the statue was moved to a new park opposite Johnston Gate. The city traded the third triangle, along with Holmes Place, to Harvard

FIGURE 5.15 Cambridge Common from Austin Hall with the Charles Sumner statue in its original location, before the smaller commons were consolidated into Flagstaff Park. Photo ca. 1905.

in 1932 for a parcel on Broadway that was needed for a new fire station; Littauer Hall now stands on this site (see chapter 4).

The Common underwent an astonishing transformation during World War I. On May 3, 1917, less than a month after Congress declared war on Germany, the city council voted to allow the U.S. Navy to occupy the park for a radio school to be run in conjunction with a training program at Harvard. In July the navy enclosed the Common with a high board fence topped with barbed wire and erected thirteen barracks and classroom buildings (figures 5.16–5.17). After these were dismantled in August 1919, the city plowed and harrowed the entire surface and set out seventy-six Norway maples among the remaining elms, giving the Common a more forested appearance.

Toward the end of World War II, a committee of Cambridge veterans advised by architecture deans Joseph Hudnut of Harvard and William W. Wurster of M.I.T. asked Modernist architects Marcel Breuer and Lawrence Anderson to design a roll of honor. Their proposal featured eight upright slabs of translucent glass on a flagstone plaza with the names of 15,000 Cambridge servicemen and women (figure 5.18). Most veterans preferred a "living memorial," and Cambridge instead built the War Memorial pool on Cambridge Street (*Chronicle,* Oct. 24, 1946).

The growing popularity of the automobile threatened the integrity of the Common. In 1925 the perimeter sidewalks were placed inside the fence so cars could park along Massachusetts Avenue, Garden Street, and Waterhouse Street. After World War II pressure mounted to provide parking for nearby hotels and merchants. Half of Flagstaff Park was paved for parking in 1950, and in 1951 the chairman of the traffic board suggested that the Common itself should be paved over. The city studied the feasibility of an underground garage in 1958, and in 1964–65 the Massachusetts Parking Authority, which had recently completed a 1,400-car garage under Boston Common, offered to build a facility for 1,000 cars. This project was finally defeated in 1972 (figure 5.20). Governor John Volpe vetoed Cambridge developer John Briston Sullivan's proposal for a bus station and a fifteen-story office building for Flagstaff Park in 1961 (see figure 2.63).

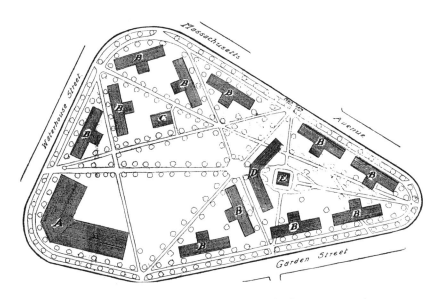

FIGURE 5.16 Plan of the Radio School barracks on Cambridge Common published in the *Cambridge Chronicle* on May 18, 1918.

FIGURE 5.17 During the summer of 1918, 5,000 sailors attended the U.S. Navy Radio School; 1,800 lived in barracks on the Common.

PLOT PLAN SHOWING LOCATION ON COMMON

FIGURE 5.18 The war memorial designed by Marcel Breuer and Lawrence Anderson for the southern end of Cambridge Common in 1944 was decades ahead of its time.

FIGURE 5.19 Flagstaff Park (foreground) and Cambridge Common in 1958, showing the plaza and ramp constructed by the Boston Elevated Railway in 1909–12, the flagstaff installed by the Daughters of the American Revolution in 1913, and the parking lot built by the city in 1950.

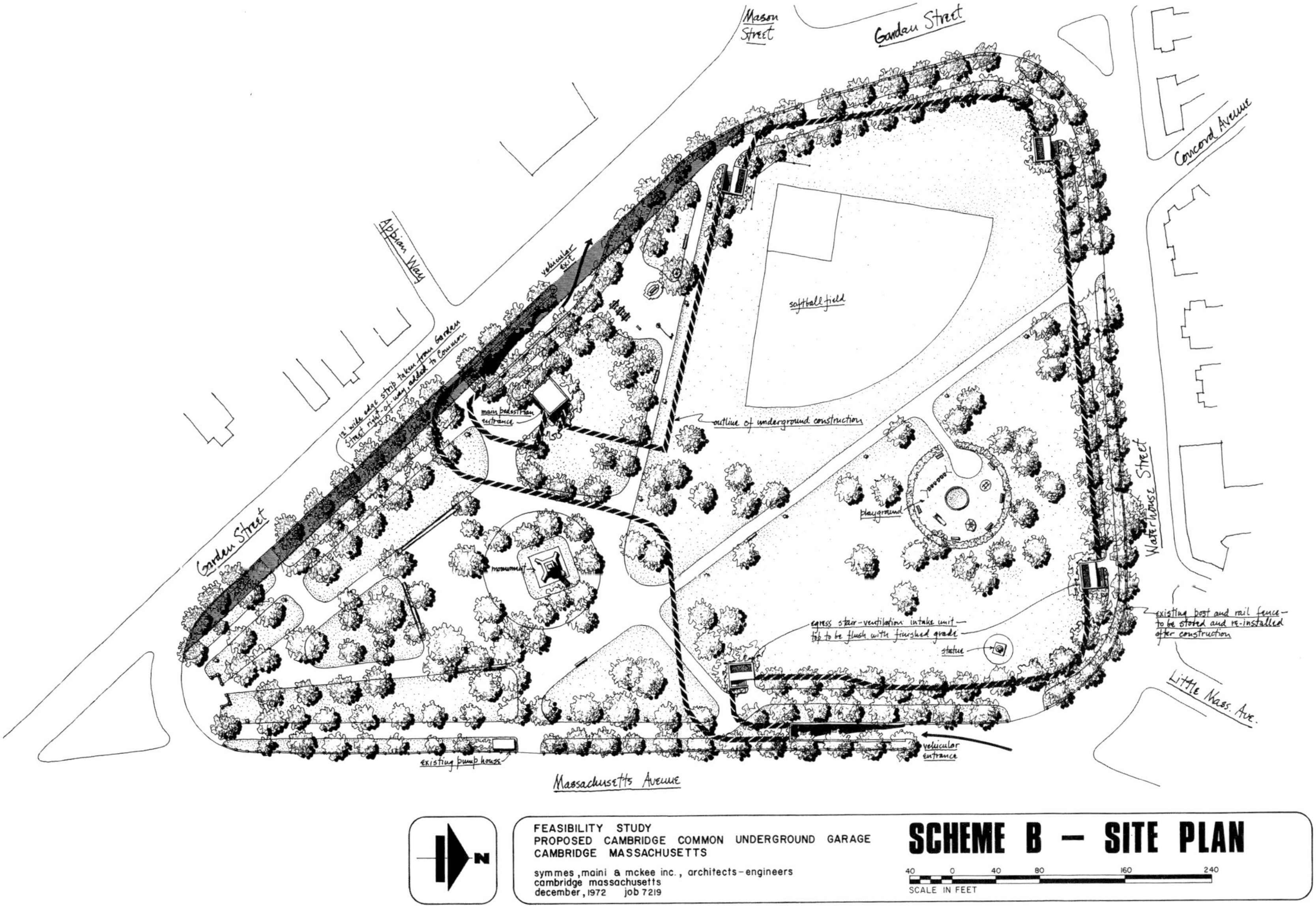

Mason Street
Garden Street
Concord Avenue
Appian Way
vehicular exit
12' wide edge strip taken from Garden Street right-of-way added to Common
softball field
main pedestrian entrance
outline of underground construction
Garden Street
Waterhouse Street
playground
monument
egress stair-ventilation intake unit—top to be flush with finished grade
statue
existing post and rail fence—to be stored and re-installed after construction
Little Mass. Ave.
vehicular entrance
existing pump house
Massachusetts Avenue
N
FEASIBILITY STUDY
PROPOSED CAMBRIDGE COMMON UNDERGROUND GARAGE
CAMBRIDGE MASSACHUSETTS
symmes, maini & mckee inc., architects-engineers
cambridge massachusetts
december, 1972 job 7219
SCHEME B — SITE PLAN
40 0 40 80 160 240
SCALE IN FEET

Figure 5.20 Site plan for the proposed Cambridge Common underground garage with an entrance on Massachusetts Avenue and an exit on Garden Street (1972, Symmes. Maini & McKee, Inc.)

In the late 1960s, the Common became a destination for disaffected youth from around the country. "Vandalism, panhandling, assaults, bag snatching, and the outdoor sale and use of marijuana" were frequent, as were concerts that drew thousands of young people (*Chronicle,* July 23, 1970; figure 5.21). Riots on April 15 and July 25, 1970, brought proposals to ban the concerts, but instead the city refurbished the Common to accommodate them. A design by the Cambridge firm of Mason & Frey paved a broad area around the Soldiers Monument, closed several entrances, and relocated many of the paths. The original granite setting of the Washington Elm bas-relief was discarded, and most of the monuments were grouped around the cannon in a kind of historical theme park near Garden Street (figure 5.22).

In 1975 descendants of William Dawes asked the city to recognize their ancestor, who had ridden through Cambridge on the night of April 18, 1775, with news of the British march on Concord and Lexington. The historical commission, not wishing to see a representational monument, proposed that a traffic island at the corner of Massachusetts Avenue and Garden Street be redesigned as a commemorative park. An 18th-century-style horseshoe forged at Old Sturbridge Village provided the pattern for the bronze hoof prints of Dawes's mount; explanatory markers were erected nearby. The most recent monuments on the Common commemorate the Irish famine of 1845–50 (1996) and the African American Mason and patriot, Prince Hall (2013).

By the beginning of the 21st century the Common was overdue for renovation. Many of the Norway maples planted in 1920 were in decline. The large paved area was superfluous, as the popularity of outdoor concerts had decreased. A plan by the Halvorson Design Partnership adopted in 2013 incorporated diverse plantings of deciduous trees and maintained the traditional character of a New England common with straight diagonal paths and a minimum of ornamental planting. Green space and a bicycle path were added to Flagstaff Park by eliminating a traffic lane from Massachusetts Avenue.

FIGURE 5.21 Vandalism created a threatening atmosphere in 1970. The Washington memorial was demolished in 1976, and the bronze reliefs were remounted in a less monumental setting.

FIGURE 5.22 Cambridge Common renovation plan (1973, Mason & Frey, landscape architects). The large paved area around the monument responded to the popularity of free concerts in the early 1970s, but by the time the project was implemented in 1976 interest in these events had passed. The designers also relocated many of the paths, disregarding the old allées of trees.

WINTHROP SQUARE

Winthrop Square began as a house lot assigned to Sir Richard Saltonstall in the first division of Newtowne in 1631. Although other officials built houses as agreed, Saltonstall returned to England after spending the harsh winter of 1630–31 in Watertown. When it became clear that he would not return, his lot reverted to the Proprietors and was designated as the town marketplace. For the next two centuries the market functioned in obscurity; no stalls were built, but town records indicate that wood, hay, and produce were traded there (see figure 1.4). The site was probably named for Professor John Winthrop (1714–79), an eminent mathematician and astronomer whose house faced the marketplace across Mt. Auburn Street.

The beautification movement that brought elms to Harvard Yard and enclosed Cambridge Common reached the old marketplace in 1834. The selectmen authorized some of the same activists to enclose "the Market Place, so called … for the ornament and benefit of the town and the petitioners; provided that the enclosure shall be of a permanent nature and without expense to the town" (Paige, 230). The petitioners laid out diagonal paths, planted elm trees, and enclosed the park with a granite post and rail fence (figure 5.23; see also figure 3.7).

In 1896 the Cambridge Park Commission directed Olmsted, Olmsted & Eliot to redesign the park to accommodate their plan—never completely implemented—for widening John F. Kennedy Street into a boulevard 60 feet wide. The initial proposals were formal compositions featuring benches with

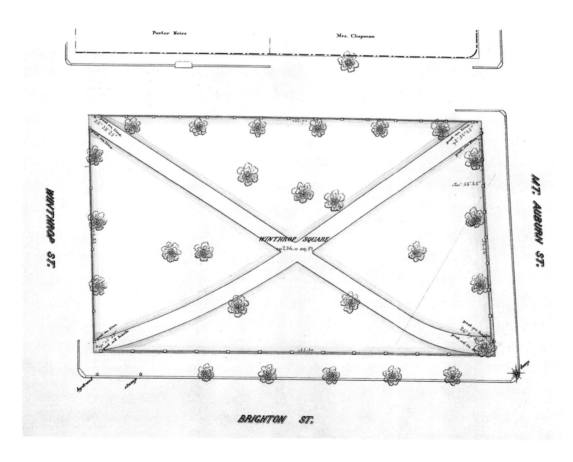

FIGURE 5.23 Winthrop Square in 1879. The city maintained the park's layout after Kennedy Street was widened to 40 feet about 1850 and to 50 feet in 1874, although the paths had to be curved as they approached the street. In 1897 the park commission took another 10 feet from the park in anticipation of a plan to widen Kennedy Street still further, but this was recovered when the park was restored in 1985.

408   Chapter 5

built-in electric lights; one alternative had an ornamental pool. The design accepted in 1897 included a semicircular path with a small lawn and an intensively landscaped garden tended by a full-time gardener during the warm months (figure 5.24). This level of maintenance could not be sustained, and in 1916 the Commissioners reported that: "The boys insist on playing ball, breaking down fences, trampling down the shrubs, and while we are doing everything in our power to keep this as attractive as possible, our work will be fruitless unless we receive the cooperation of the Police Department" (*CPC Annual Report,* 17).

By the 1970s the elaborate plantings had long since disappeared, and the park suffered from years of neglect and a design that discouraged active users. The redevelopment of the MBTA yards drew more attention to the southwest sector, and in 1985 the city, in partnership with Harvard Square business owners and the Cambridge Plant and Garden Club, restored the earlier layout. *Quiet Stone,* commissioned by the Cambridge Arts Council from Carlos Dorrien, recalls a broken cornice from a market house that never actually existed (figure 5.25).

FIGURE 5.25   Winthrop Square Park after the 1985 renovation (Brown & Rowe, landscape architects). A superfluous traffic lane was removed from Kennedy Street to restore the park's 1896 dimensions. Photo ca. 2010.

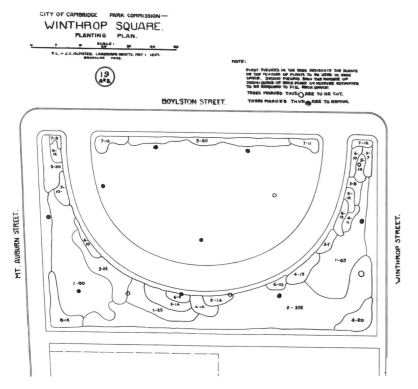

FIGURE 5.24   Olmsted, Olmsted & Eliot's 1896 planting plan for Winthrop Square Park included thirty beds containing more than 900 plants.

Longfellow Park was created by the heirs of Henry Wadsworth Longfellow to preserve the setting of the 18th-century Vassall-Craigie-Longfellow house and the view of the river that the poet commemorated in his verse (see chapter 4):

River! that in silence windest
Through the meadows, bright and free
Till at length thy rest thou findest
In the bosom of the sea!

("To the River Charles," in Stillman, 31)

Longfellow's view encompassed land across Brattle Street that his father-in-law had purchased with the house and deeded to his daughter after her marriage in 1843 (figure 5.26). A steep bank about 400 feet from Brattle Street separated the upland from the low-lying former salt marsh that had been cut off from the river by the construction of Mt. Auburn Street in 1808. Several ancient willows were thought to be survivors of those planted along the Common Pales in 1632.

A few days after the poet's death in 1882, eighteen men met at Arthur Gilman's home on Waterhouse Street to organize the Longfellow Memorial Association. They elected Longfellow's former student James Russell Lowell as president and Charles W. Eliot, Oliver Wendell Holmes, William Dean Howells, and John Greenleaf Whittier as vice presidents. The association's purpose was "the erection … of a monument upon the lot of land opposite the late residence of Mr. Longfellow, including a portrait statue protected by an architectural canopy or other protection, and the laying out of the lot as a public park, to be surrendered to the City of Cambridge to be kept open forever, when the city is ready to accept the trust" (Scudder, 8). For a donation of 10¢, schoolchildren received a poem and a picture of Longfellow's house; for a dollar, adults became honorary members and received a certificate. Additional funds were raised through public readings. Participants at the first benefit, held

FIGURE 5.26 A view across Hawthorn Street toward Mt. Auburn Street and the Charles River. The sunken meadow behind the embankment at far right was filled in to create the lower part of Longfellow Park. Photo ca. 1875–94.

in Boston in 1887, included Edward Everett Hale, Julia Ward Howe, Thomas Bailey Aldrich, Thomas Wentworth Higginson, and Samuel Clemens.

Longfellow's children gave the association a 2.1-acre strip of land opposite the house in 1883. In order to protect the vista from the house to the river, the association agreed that "no tree whatsoever shall ever be planted or suffered to exist" in the park without the heirs' consent and pledged to keep shrubs in the upper park trimmed (Middlesex Deeds, 1629/459). Four years later they added a parcel between Mt. Auburn Street and the river that linked the park to 70 acres of marsh in Brighton that Longfellow and several of his Brattle Street neighbors had given Harvard in 1870.[8]

In 1887 the association commissioned Charles Eliot to lay out the grounds. At 27, Eliot had just completed a European tour, and Longfellow Park was one of his first commissions. He emphasized the separate character of the upland and the marsh with an exedra overlooking the river and the view upstream to

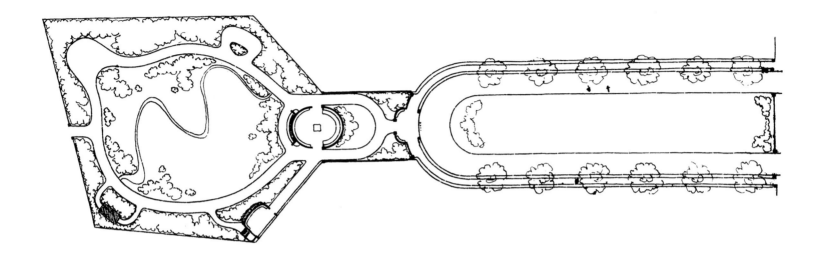

Mount Auburn; below it would be a garden adapted "to the use and enjoyment of all orderly citizens, and women and children in particular" (Eliot, *Charles Eliot,* 211; figure 5.27). Boston architects C. Howard Walker and Herbert Best executed Eliot's plan in 1889 with a monumental staircase in pink Milford granite and a wall along Mt. Auburn Street; the latter was supported by piles driven 48 feet into the marsh (figure 5.29).

The Memorial Association reserved the right to erect a monument when it deeded the park to the city in 1907. Five years later, the trustees commissioned Daniel Chester French to create a bust and sculptural panels.[9] Siting the monument was difficult because of the topography and the constricted view from the house. Longfellow's children wanted it in the upper park. French, who favored the lower park, said the family believed "that the lower lot is wet and is not frequented by the same class of people as the upper lot" (Olmsted Associates Records, French to F.L. Olmsted Jr., Apr. 3, 1912).

FIGURE 5.27 Charles Eliot's "Preliminary Study for Grounds of Longfellow Memorial Association," June 23, 1887. Eliot intended to solve the drainage problem of the lower section by directing a brook, perhaps the outlet of Worcester's Pond, on a winding course across a "quiet and restful little scene" comprising wild plants, lawn, and scattered shrubs. Saltwater intrusion from the Charles would have to be addressed by a tide-gate.

FIGURE 5.28 The view from the Longfellow house after the completion of Longfellow Park, unobstructed by trees or structures. Photo ca. 1899.

FIGURE 5.29 The granite steps between the upper and lower park were conceived by Charles Eliot and designed by Walker & Best. The final design for the lower garden eliminated the brook but included elaborate plantings and extensive gravel paths. Photo ca. 1910.

Frederick Law Olmsted Jr. disliked Walker's steps and terrace, "the architectural expression of which is wholly foreign to that of the building with which they are associated and of the period in which Longfellow lived" (Olmsted to French, Apr. 11, 1912). When he realized that Walker had only enlarged upon Eliot's sketches, he corrected himself and asked French not to repeat his opinion. Later he talked with John Nolen, the city planner, and Arthur Shurcliff, the landscape architect. Shurcliff agreed that "if the present steps were to be reconstructed and the memorial and steps incorporated in a single design," the monument would be "more nearly in accord with Charles Eliot's original conception" (ibid.). French "felt some hesitation about taking away Howard Walker's steps, which might seem to be a reflection on his good taste," but soon acquiesced (French to Olmsted, Apr. 15, 1912).

Longfellow's family finally relented. French retained Henry Bacon, a New York architect with whom he later designed the Lincoln Memorial in Washington, to draw up plans for the new steps and retaining wall, and the association retained landscape architect Paul Frost to assist him. French's design included a bronze portrait bust of the poet on a plinth in front of a bas-relief of pink Tennessee marble containing figures of six characters from Longfellow's best-known poems (figure 5.30). Dedicated in October 1914, it was immediately criticized for intruding on the view of the house from Mt. Auburn Street. Frost himself sided with many later critics:

It was unfortunate too that the monument was not designed with a keener conception of the fundamental landscape conditions. … It seems to me [that] here is an illustration of how the best of us in this country still sometimes fail to appreciate the importance of landscape setting in designing a monument or placing a building, and how a monument of supreme excellence in itself may contribute little to the larger landscape scheme of which it is an essential element. (Frost to Olmsted, Aug. 29, 1922)

Longfellow Park declined under the city's care. The peastone paths were replaced with concrete in 1937, and the macadam roadway was asphalted in 1938. The limitation on planting was forgotten, and elms were placed in front of the monument in the 1940s. In 1990 the Cambridge Historical Commission and Carol R. Johnson & Associates developed a plan to recapture the view. Over sixty volunteer trees were removed from the lower park, and the lawn was extended out to the fences as originally intended. New plantings included a scion of one of the ancient willows, perpetuating the tradition of their descent from the 17th-century pallysadoe.[10]

FIGURE 5.30 The view from lower level of Longfellow Park looking north toward the poet's house, ca. 1915. The monument stands in a sunken garden with marble benches on either side, flanked by rubble-stone walls and steps of smooth bluestone. The simplified landscape by Paul Frost made the circumferential path a perfect oval. The only remnants of the original design are the "dwarf walls" in the upper park and the fence and gate on Mt. Auburn Street (not shown).

FIGURE 5.31 The Charles River in the early 1870s, as seen from Gerry's Landing. Alexander McDonald's Monument Wharf at the foot of Sparks Street is at left; behind it are the tenements that still stand at 185–199 Mt. Auburn Street, at the corner of Willard. A schooner is moored at the Cambridge Gas-Light Company's Brick Wharf, and men are harvesting salt hay on the Brighton marshes.

THE CHARLES RIVER RESERVATION

> Nature has given to the city a golden opportunity in its river, which borders nearly all its eastern and southern boundaries, a river that, if properly treated, will furnish to Cambridge one of the finest water parks in the world. … Shall the city control [the banks] and embody them into a park system, or shall they be neglected and be built upon by factories and cheaply constructed sheds? (*CPC Annual Report*, 1894, 4)

The concept of riverfront parks in Cambridge and Boston surfaced early in the 19th century but was not seriously discussed until the 1870s. Cambridgeport industrialist Charles Davenport proposed a parkway between the Craigie Bridge (now the Charles River Dam) and Dunster Street as part of a private scheme to develop the flats opposite Boston's Back Bay, which he implemented through the Charles River Embankment Company beginning in 1883 (see *Report Three: Cambridgeport* and figures 5.32–5.33). The Cambridge and Metropolitan Park Commissions continued his work on a larger scale.

The development of the riverfront into a public park presented particular challenges. The river was still an artery of commerce, although its importance was declining. The shore was

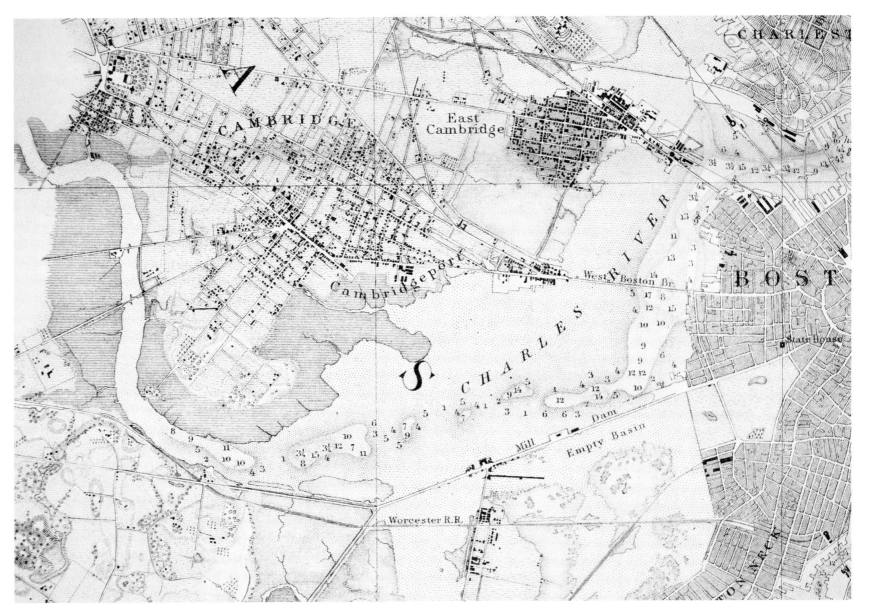

FIGURE 5.32 The Charles River as surveyed in 1847, bordered by marshes and mudflats. See figure 9.5 for a chart of the navigation channel.

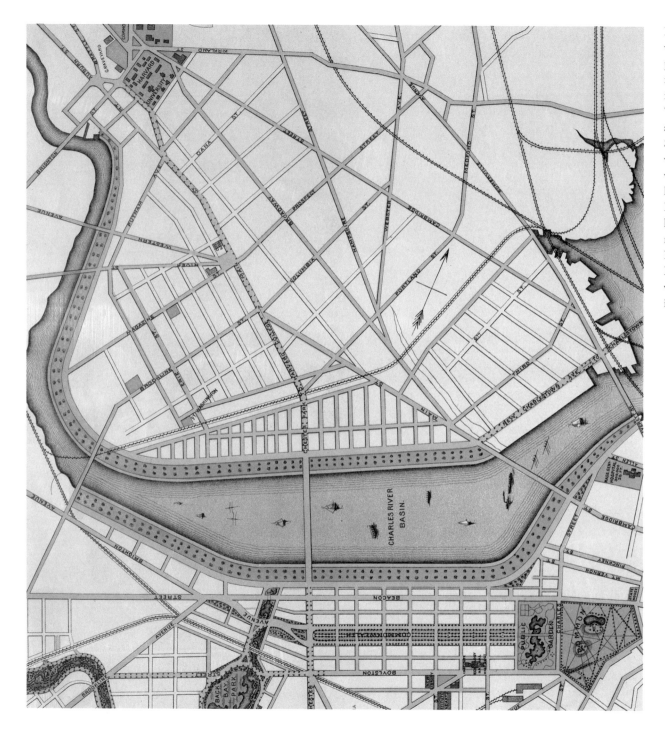

FIGURE 5.33 Charles Davenport's vision of the Charles River Basin, published in 1875 as a prospectus for the development of the tidal flats he owned in Cambridgeport. "Boulevard Harvard" (Massachusetts Avenue) would link Harvard Square and Boston's Back Bay with a new bridge, while a parkway on the Cambridge side ("Boulevard Metropolis") would end at Dunster Street, avoiding the College Wharf. The legislature authorized construction of the Harvard Bridge in 1882, and Charles Eliot's plan for a riverfront parkway in Cambridge was published in 1894 (see figure 5.36).

held by a multitude of private owners. The banks were low and subject to flooding, and the degraded salt marshes harbored malarial mosquitoes. Worst of all, the effluent of the Back Bay, Roxbury, Cambridge, and upriver towns drained untreated into the river and at low tide baked in the summer sun on hundreds of acres of odiferous flats. The once-pristine river had become an open sewer (figures 5.34–5.35). In the summer of 1892, hundreds of Cambridge residents petitioned the Massachusetts Board of Health for relief.

> Along the bottom and banks of the Charles River is deposited a bed of apparently putrescible sludge, consisting of decomposed animal and vegetable matter from the shores, and noxious filth from the sewers, long held in suspension on the flowing and ebbing current and finally precipitated to the bottom, where to the depth of several feet it is commingled with the detritus washed down the stream, and can be effectually removed only by dredging. (City of Cambridge, *Report of the Committee on Public Parks,* 7)

FIGURE 5.35 Privies on the riverbank at the foot of Murray Street, ca. 1890.

FIGURE 5.34 Looking upstream from the Riverside Press, past the Western Avenue Bridge toward the waterfront below Harvard Square, ca. 1875.

Successful development of the riverfront depended not only on completion of the north and south metropolitan interceptor sewers, which were begun in 1889 and completed in 1897, but also on changes in the attitudes of taxpayers and decision makers, both locally and in the state house. In large part success can be attributed to the vision of Charles Eliot, the landscape architect.[11] Today, the river is an entirely man-made landscape:

> As you glance up and down and across the river not one of the old landmarks presents itself. Gone are the mudflats, the salt marshes, the wooden pile bridges, the coal wharf above. … Instead are driveways on both sides and arches of brick and concrete crossing the river at four or five points nearby … even the curves of the river seem to be in the wrong places. But turn the back to the river and glance the other way, and certain familiar old wood houses can be vaguely remembered as the same. (Updike, *Harvard Boathouse Memorial,* 9)

Charles River Road

In 1894 Charles Eliot proposed that the riverfront should be developed into distinctly different sections linked by a continuous parkway: The Front, in East Cambridge, with seawalls and a beach; the Esplanade, along the partially completed seawall of the Charles River Embankment Company; Captain's Island, a recreational area, now Magazine Beach; the River Road, from Captain's Island to Mount Auburn Hospital; and Elmwood Way (Gerry's Landing Road and Fresh Pond Parkway) connecting the river with Fresh Pond, which the Cambridge Water Board was developing as a park (figure 5.36)

The approaches of Cambridge, via the Harvard, Brookline, and Boylston [Kennedy] street bridges, thus improved and made beautiful, it only remains to connect them with a shore drive. This driveway … will follow the embankment from the Harvard Bridge … to a point on Boylston Street, just back of the Weld boat house. … From Boylston Street, the choice of two drives is offered—one by continuing along the shore to Mt. Auburn Street, which should be widened into a handsome boulevard; the other via Eliot Street, Brattle Square, and Brattle Street—both routes leading to Fresh Pond Lane. This beautiful lane, shaded by many fine trees, offers one of the most attractive approaches to Fresh Pond, and should be included in the park system. (*CPC Annual Report*, 1894, 5)

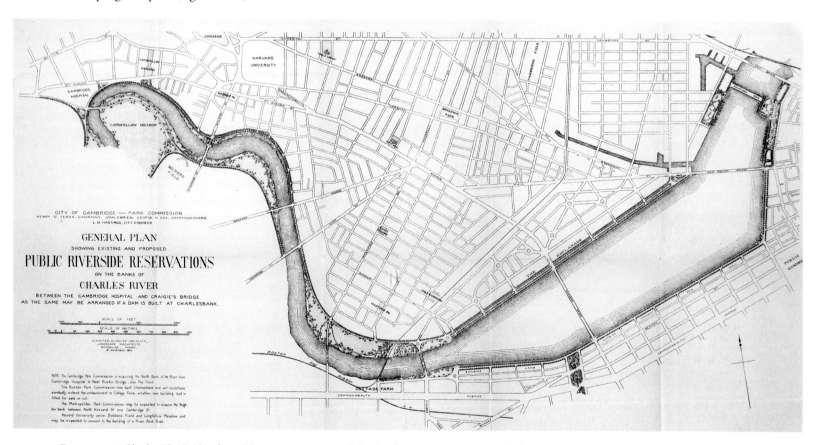

FIGURE 5.36 Charles Eliot's plan for public reservations on both banks of the Charles River, 1894. Eliot's work with the Cambridge Park Commission and the Joint Board on the Improvement of the Charles River enabled him to prepare a unified plan for a dam and parkways on both sides of the river linked by a bridge at Gerry's Landing that would not be completed until 1951.

The treatment of the riverbank was critical to the success of the project. The Charles River Dam was still an uncertain prospect; the tidal range of the river averaged 9.5 feet, while spring tides of 12 feet or more flooded many basements in low-lying areas. Eliot opposed extending the seawall beyond the lower basin; he favored a naturalistic gravel beach with stone riprap to eliminate the muddy banks at low tide, even though this would require extensive dredging and filling (figures 5.37–5.38).

Henry Yerxa, chairman of the Cambridge Park Commission, was an early supporter of a dam, having toured Europe in 1894 to inspect the Alster Basin, a water park in Hamburg that Eliot advocated as a prototype. The Joint Board on the Improvement of the Charles River (with Eliot as a consultant) recommended building a dam 600 feet upstream from Craigie's Bridge. Back Bay property owners objected, while Harvard rowers opposed an 1898 act authorizing a dam near the Cottage Farm (Boston

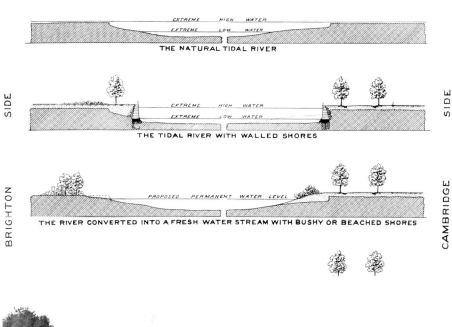

FIGURE 5.37 Proposed alternative treatments of the Charles River shore, 1896. Eliot strongly opposed extending the seawalls upstream and had to convince the Cambridge Park Commission that a naturalistic treatment was more desirable.

FIGURE 5.38 Gerry's Landing at high tide, ca. 1897. This view downstream shows the fenced-in Leif Ericsson monument and the city's bathing beach, with a life ring and ladder for ice rescues.

University) Bridge. The controversy dragged on until the present dam was approved in 1903.

Eliot finished his plans for the Cambridge riverfront by the end of 1895 (figure 5.39). The commissioners began with a demonstration project west of Kennedy Street, where they identified conditions that required immediate attention. "The marsh lands are of the poorest description, filthy and obnoxious, and the few buildings now upon them are totally unfit for human habitation" (*CPC Report,* 1894, 5). This section provided a useful laboratory for testing Eliot's treatment of the riverbanks, as it included both the relatively stable Ox Marsh near Kennedy Street and a much more difficult stretch of peat and quicksand near Longfellow Park. The Brick and Monument wharves were removed in the spring of 1895 (figure 5.40). Over 25,000

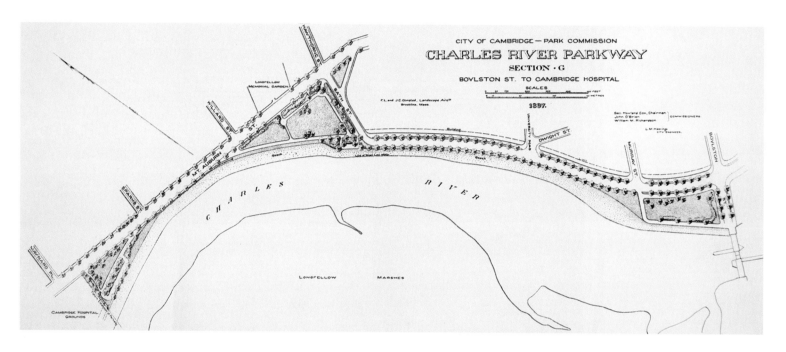

FIGURE 5.39 The riverfront between Kennedy Street and Mount Auburn Hospital encompassed some of the most difficult conditions on the river. By turning the parkway inland along Bath Street, the landscape architects avoided the expense of narrowing the channel and building across a treacherous marsh with no firm bottom. Their 1897 design served as a prototype for the other sections of the parkway.

FIGURE 5.40 The landscape architects put their theories into practice on the section upstream from Kennedy Street, as seen here in a photo taken from the chimney of the Boston Elevated power plant in 1895. The river has been dredged and the banks reshaped. Workmen on lighters are dismantling the Brick Wharf.

cartloads of ashes and gravel were dumped along the river, and the flats were reshaped into a sloping gravel beach. The new road was given a macadam surface, and the first of many London plane trees (popularly called sycamores) was planted on April 22, 1897.[12] Opposite Willard Street the fill slumped as much as 10 feet, displacing thousands of cubic yards of mud into the channel. The park commission built a bulkhead 300 feet long to retain the fill and dredged the river to maintain navigation.

The westbound parkway terminated at the foot of Hawthorn Street because the bank upstream was too narrow to accommodate it. Eliot thought the tract opposite Longfellow Park was an opportunity to create a substantial open space, in contrast to the linear park elsewhere. "The afternoon prospect from the great willows across the Longfellow marshes to the tower of Mount Auburn is doubtless the most peacefully beautiful landscape Cambridge is ever likely to possess" (*CPC Annual Report,* 1896, 43).

For several years the College Wharf blocked construction downstream from Kennedy Street. Completion of the Newell Boathouse in 1899 allowed the university to abandon its facilities at the foot of DeWolfe Street, and the commission razed most of Richardson & Bacon's 330-foot-long coal shed in 1901. The granite blocks and wooden piles of Stickney's and Sargent's wharves were salvaged for reuse. With the report that "the canal west of Richardson & Bacon's has been partially filled with city ashes," the last vestige of the Town Creek disappeared, and commercial use of the waterfront ended (ibid., 1901, 20; figure 5.41).

The election of a Democratic mayor in 1902 imposed different priorities on the park commissioners (see chapter 2). The parkway had been so neglected that when a new administration took office in 1906 the grass had to be cut with scythes, and it took four men three weeks to weed and prune the shrubbery; what little construction had been accomplished needed to be redone. The parkway between Kennedy Street and Western Avenue was completed in 1908. The last stretch between there and River Street involved razing the Cambridge Electric Light Company's coal wharf and some buildings of the Riverside Press and was opened to traffic for Harvard commencement in 1914.[13]

FIGURE 5.41 Parkway construction, looking upstream from the chimney of the Cambridge Electric Light Co.'s plant on Western Avenue in 1901. Soldiers Field Road and Memorial Drive have been completed west of the Great Bridge, but work on the Cambridge side has halted while the College Wharf is dismantled.

The benefits of the parkway were immediately apparent. In 1897 the assessed value of land abutting the first completed section increased by 85 percent. The city imposed restrictions on properties that had once been taken by the commission or whose owners sought access to the parkway. New buildings could not be used as stables "or for any mechanical, mercantile, and manufacturing purposes," could not exceed five stories, or 60 feet in height, and had to be set back 20 feet (*CPC Annual Report,* 1896, 12). The commission's vision is reflected in the apartment houses built near Ash Street in 1914–16 (see chapters 4 and 6). The effect of the parkway on other adjacent properties was mixed. Michael O'Sullivan's 1899 Colonial Revival house at 11 Riverview Avenue (on the corner of Plympton Street) might have been the prototype for others, but Harvard's acquisition of land for the River Houses precluded further residential development (see figure 4.268). The Sterling and Hingham knitting mills just off Memorial Drive escaped the commission's restrictions on inappropriate uses in 1912 and 1914 (see figure 4.269). Some properties on the parkway remained vacant or underutilized until 2005, when the last phase of Harvard's riverfront development finally began to be realized.

Cambridge's fear of metropolitan entanglements was overcome by the fiscal reality of maintaining the parkway for regional automobile traffic. As early as 1909 the park commissioners, fearing that the city would not complete the project as originally planned, favored transferring it to the Commonwealth. The General Court authorized the Metropolitan District Commission (MDC) to take over the parkway in 1920 but allowed the city to retain The Front (between the Longfellow Bridge and the Charles River Dam) for industrial development. Cambridge voters approved the transfer by a 3-to-1 majority, and the riverfront park passed to the MDC in 1921. Two years later, Charles River Road was renamed Memorial Drive in honor of Cambridge's casualties in the recent war.[14]

Memorial Drive Extension, Gerry's Landing Road, and Greenough Boulevard

Charles Eliot's concept for the metropolitan park system included roads on both banks of the Charles as far as Watertown Square and a new bridge at Gerry's Landing. On the Brighton shore, the Metropolitan Park Commission (MPC) opened the Speedway, a one-mile course for pleasure driving, along the west side of Soldiers Field from Western Avenue to a loop opposite Gerry's Landing in 1899. The commission built Soldiers Field Road from the end of the Speedway to North Harvard Street before 1901, extended it to Cambridge Street (Brighton) in 1926, and reached a connection with Bay State Road in 1929. Storrow Drive completed the parkway on the Boston side in 1951.

In Cambridge, Memorial Drive incorporated Bath Lane and terminated at Hawthorn Street. Motorists then used Mt. Auburn Street to reach Fresh Pond Parkway, which was extended

to Concord Avenue in 1930, completing a through road to the Middlesex Fells via Alewife Brook Parkway. The legislature approved a plan to complete the river parkways and construct a direct connection between them in 1929 but soon rescinded authorization for a bridge at Gerry's Landing. The MDC proceeded to widen the riverbank west of Hawthorn Street, but it deferred road construction in the face of protests by influential members of the Cambridge Boat Club whose building lay in its path. Residents continued to oppose the extension, and the MDC did not authorize construction until 1946 (figure 5.42). Memorial Drive was extended via Gerry's Landing Road to a connection with Fresh Pond Parkway in 1949. The Eliot Bridge was completed in 1951, linking the river parkways as envisioned in the 1890s (figure 5.43).

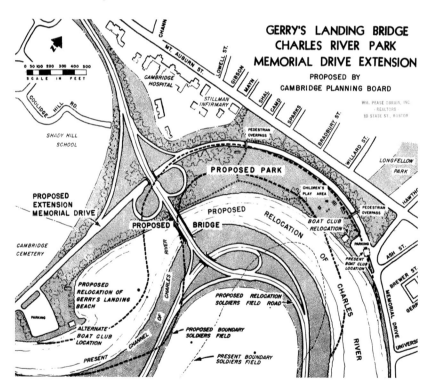

FIGURE 5.42 In 1933 the Cambridge Planning Board endorsed a plan to create a large new park by shifting the course of the Charles River at Boston's expense. The cost of the bridge at Gerry's Landing could be reduced by building it on dry land.

FIGURE 5.43 The widened riverfront park east of Hawthorn Street before construction of Memorial Drive Extension, 1949.

Gerry's Landing Road was the missing link in the metropolitan parkway system for about half a century. The road originated in the 17th century as a cartway between the river landing and the first Watertown meetinghouse (see chapter 4). At the beginning of the 20th century it occupied one of the most beautiful public landscapes in Cambridge, but the swale it traversed was doomed by its location on an irresistible desire line between the river parkways and the western suburbs. The extension of Memorial Drive and the completion of the Eliot Bridge flooded West Cambridge with high-speed traffic, and Gerry's Landing Road became "a terrifying stretch of asphalt onto which no pedestrian should ever venture" (*Report Four: Old Cambridge*, 68; figures 5.44–5.45).

The state's emphasis on developing highways at the expense of parkland met resistance after World War II. The extension of Memorial Drive past Gerry's Landing to North Beacon Street in Watertown attracted national attention. This was the only remaining natural area on the lower river, although it had been disfigured by dumping and neglect. In the late 1950s Cambridge Plant Club activists joined historian and conservationist Bernard DeVoto to preserve "Hell's Half Acre," as the tract was known. In spite of their campaign, Greenough Boulevard was completed in 1966 (DeVoto, 10).

In 1962 the MDC announced plans to widen Memorial Drive from 40 to 52 feet and build underpasses at River Street, Western Avenue, and Kennedy Street, converting it to a limited access highway similar to Soldiers Field Road and destroying dozens of the plane trees planted in 1897. Lowell Street resident Edward L. Bernays, the retired "father of public relations," and Cambridge activist John Moot formed the Citizen's Emergency

FIGURE 5.44 A view of the swale now traversed by Gerry's Landing Road, looking from the river toward Mt. Auburn Street and the Cambridge Homes (behind the trees at right). The Metropolitan Park Commission graded and seeded the land in 1899 but did not build the highway linking Memorial Drive to Fresh Pond Parkway until 1950. Photo ca. 1910.

Committee to Save Memorial Drive and coined the group's alliterative (but inaccurate) rallying cry, "Save the sycamores!" (*Crimson,* June 9, 1964). This campaign also attracted national attention, and Jacqueline Kennedy and Secretary of the Interior Stuart Udall joined the cause. Five hundred Cambridge residents demonstrated peacefully at the State House, but MDC police used dogs to break up a student protest in Cambridge. An MDC offer to transplant thirty-five trees, build a pedestrian overpass at the Weeks Bridge, and fill in the river to replace lost parkland was viewed as poor compensation, and Governor Volpe killed the project in 1965 (figure 5.46). Activists who cut their teeth on this campaign went on to contest the Kennedy Library and innumerable institutional and commercial projects in the neighborhood. Fifty years later, the Massachusetts Department of Conservation and Recreation acknowledged the end of the roadbuilding era when it announced that Greenough Boulevard would be reduced in width, calming traffic and returning land to park use.

FIGURE 5.45 The junction of Gerry's Landing Road and Mt. Auburn Street included a rotary that was removed after streetcar service ended in 1958. Photo 1958.

FIGURE 5.46 Sketches illustrating the effect of the proposed widening prepared by the Citizens Emergency Committee to Save Memorial Drive received national attention when they were published in *Time* magazine in February 1964.

Once the Charles River Road was under construction, the park commission began to promote a new bridge at the foot of Kennedy Street. The old span, a narrow timber structure with a 30-foot draw, was descended from the Great Bridge of 1660. It had been rebuilt in 1685, 1733, and 1862 and was once again in disrepair. Boston and Cambridge were indifferent to the problem until the Harvard Stadium opened in 1904. By this time the university had begun to realize the development potential of the riverfront, and President Eliot pressed for a bridge that would be aesthetically pleasing (figures. 5.47–5.48).

In 1904 the legislature authorized the Cambridge Bridge Commission (which was then engaged in building the Longfellow Bridge) to replace the bridges at Brookline and Kennedy streets. The new Cottage Farm Bridge was an unadorned wooden structure, and Boston refused to pay for anything better at Kennedy Street, where mainly Cambridge interests would be served. In 1907 the bridge commissioners proposed a new wood pile structure next to the Great Bridge, retaining the dangerous draw. Another difficulty lay with the federal government. Congress and the War Department had to approve any bridge in the path of waterborne commerce. Although sailing vessels had been excluded from the upper river since 1904 by the fixed-span Longfellow Bridge, the Watertown Arsenal maintained a wharf, and in Brighton the abattoir and a fuel dealer still received coal by barge. As long as there was any potential for commercial use the War Department would require the span to have either a draw or a 27-foot vertical clearance, which would make the approaches impossibly lengthy and expensive.

The campaign for an appropriate new bridge was long and arduous. President Eliot lobbied President Theodore Roosevelt, an alumnus, predicting that "we shall never be in a better position … to get a favorable consideration at Washington" (*Chronicle,* July 6, 1907). He attended a bridge commission hearing in Boston with a delegation that included Henry Lee Higginson, architect Clarence Blackall, Professor H. Langford Warren, and

FIGURE 5.47 The Great Bridge about 1900, after the completion of the park improvements upstream; a tugboat waits to pass through the draw.

several Cambridge aldermen. In 1908 the Municipal Art Society held a design competition; the judges, Eliot, Warren, and Blackall, selected three sketches for further consideration. In 1910 Cambridge attorney Richard Henry Dana III, who had been chairman of the Charles River Dam Commission, extracted a promise from the War Department that a bridge with a clearance of 16 feet would be acceptable if the entire riverfront were in public hands. Eliot and Blackall then successfully petitioned the General Court to direct the Metropolitan Park Commission to take the abattoir wharf, eliminating the last shipper on the upper river. Congress resisted until Dana countered the abattoir's lobbyists with another delegation from Cambridge. The executive

branch finally concurred after Cambridge police refused to take responsibility for President Taft's safety when he wished to cross the old bridge to visit the stadium on July 4, 1910.

Larz Anderson of Brookline, a Harvard graduate, Spanish-American War veteran, and diplomat, resolved the dispute with Boston by donating the entire cost of the new bridge to memorialize his father, Civil War general Nicholas Longworth Anderson (figure 5.49). Downstream, the university constructed the Weeks Bridge in 1926 to provide pedestrian access and steam heat to the new Business School campus. Business associates of John Wingate Weeks, a former mayor of Newton, congressman, and Secretary of War under Presidents Harding and Coolidge, raised the funds (figure 5.50).

FIGURE 5.49 The Anderson Bridge (1912, Wheelwright, Haven & Hoyt, architects) and Harvard Stadium (1902, Ira Hollis, C.E. and L.J. Johnson, M.E, with McKim, Mead & White). Photo ca. 1913.

FIGURE 5.50 The Weeks Bridge (1926, McKim, Mead & White, architects) at its dedication in 1927.

Organized recreational use of the river began in 1800, when Thomas Brattle joined with Harvard College to build a bathhouse near the Brick Wharf. Deaths by drowning were not infrequent, and both the college and the town prohibited swimming off the Great Bridge. The new bath was probably a float with a caged well to secure bathers from the current. In 1830 the Cambridge Humane Society subsidized a bathhouse near the Great Bridge; donors received free tickets for their families. The Cambridge Park Commission maintained beaches for swimming at Gerry's Landing and Captain's Island until 1949 (figures 5.51–5.52).

The college once tried to keep students off the river entirely. When one member of the class of 1839 claimed that no rule prohibited his having a boat, the faculty responded that no student was allowed to keep a domestic animal, and that "a boat was a domestic animal within the meaning of the statute" (Vaille, 2:188). Students formed the first rowing club in 1844 with an eight-oared, 37-foot longboat, *Oneida,* which was sometimes raced but more often used for excursions. Boats were kept in a shed in Brighton until 1846, when students built a boathouse near the College Wharf. A new type of racing shell introduced in 1857 weighed only 150 pounds and could be launched from a float (figure 5.53).

Private clubs began to use the river after the Civil War. Ernest Longfellow and his friends organized the Cambridge Casino in 1882 and built tennis courts, a bowling alley, and a boathouse at the foot of Hawthorn Street (see figure 2.20). Alumnus George Weld retained Robert S. Peabody, who had been captain of the varsity crew in 1866, to design the first Weld Boathouse and opened the Harvard Rowing Club to all undergraduates in 1890 (figure 5.54). The Irish-American workmen at the Riverside Press, who founded the Riverside Boat Club in 1869, kept their craft in the factory; twenty years later, the club built a boathouse at the foot of Albro Street, near Western Avenue (figure 5.55).

The park commission acquired all of these buildings in 1894 but leased some back to their previous owners. The casino closed,

FIGURE 5.51 The Cambridge Park Commission continued to operate the bathing beach at Gerry's Landing after the state took over the reservation in 1924. Photo 1924.

FIGURE 5.52 Gerry's Landing Beach was nearly destroyed by the Metropolitan District Commission in 1930 in anticipation of extending Memorial Drive, but remained open until 1949. This view shows the beach in the center, the advancing fill, the changing house operated by the Cambridge Park Commission, and Mount Auburn Hospital's isolation building. Photo 1930.

FIGURE 5.53 Boathouses at the foot of Flagg Street (1869), ca. 1890. From right to left are John Blakey's boat-building shop; the University's boathouse (the new viewing platform shows the growing popularity of competitive rowing as a spectator sport); and a rowing club boathouse. Photo ca. 1890.

FIGURE 5.54 The first Weld Boathouse (1889, Robert S. Peabody, architect), photographed at high tide on an icy winter day with Richardson & Bacon's 300-foot-long coal wharf in the background. Photo ca. 1895.

FIGURE 5.55 The Riverside Boat Club (1889, John A. Hasty, architect) at its original location, between the Cambridge Electric Light Company wharf (left) and the Riverside Press. After the building burned in 1911, the club leased a new site near the foot of Pleasant Street. Photo ca. 1900.

and the commission floated the building downriver to a temporary site opposite DeWolfe Street in 1897; its ultimate disposition is unknown (see figure 9.11). The commission placed the Weld Boathouse on a new bulkhead in 1897 and demolished the varsity's 1869 boathouse in 1901, after the crews moved to the Newell Boathouse across the river. Peabody & Stearns designed the present Weld Boathouse in 1906, and in 1908 the commission sold the old one to St. Joseph's Mission in Brighton, which moved it to a site across the river near the Cottage Farm Bridge. The commission also razed a boat-builder's shop where John Blakey and William H. Davy had built shells for Harvard since 1870, but Davy and his son continued in the trade for many more years in a two-story shop on Hayes Street. In 1909 the Cambridge Boat Club leased a site near the old casino and built a boathouse that was moved in 1947 when the MDC extended Memorial Drive (figure 5.56). The Riverside Boat Club lost its building to a fire in 1911 and built a new one downriver in 1912.

The Charles River Dam excluded the tides in 1909, and the basin began to fill with fresh water. Iceboats appeared on the river during the exceptionally cold winter of 1910, and members of the Cambridge Boat Club found a new method of reaching Boston:

> During the years when the Boston Elevated Railway was constructing its tunnel from Park Street to Harvard Square, and travel by surface car usually consumed forty minutes from Harvard Square to Scollay Square, it was found during a considerable part of the winter … that one could skate to the Union Boat Club comfortably in thirty minutes and walk over Beacon Hill in another ten minutes. (Judge Robert Walcott, in Ralph May, 133)

The concrete bridges built at Western Avenue and River Street in 1926 retained too much warmth to allow reliable ice to form around them, ending the opportunity for long-distance skating.

FIGURE 5.56 The Cambridge Boat Club, 994 Memorial Drive (1909, J.W. Ames, architect). The clubhouse is being prepared for relocation to Gerry's Landing Road to make way for the extension of Memorial Drive. Photo 1947.

LOWELL MEMORIAL PARK AND FRESH POND PARKWAY

Lowell Memorial Park was the result of a movement to preserve Elmwood, the estate of James Russell Lowell. In the late 19th century, Lowell, Longfellow, and Oliver Wendell Holmes were nationally popular figures who were associated with landmarks of the American Revolution. Longfellow's heirs preserved Washington's headquarters in 1882, but Harvard demolished the Hastings-Holmes house in 1883 (see chapter 4). When Lowell's executor put the estate on the market in 1896, a group of "public spirited ladies" began to raise $35,000 to preserve it as a memorial. The house turned out to be held in trust for the poet's daughter and her children, so the group turned its attention to preserving some of its landscape, more than three acres of land "picturesquely diversified in surface and covered in part by a grove of beautiful pines, often the poet's theme" (*Chronicle*, Dec. 4, 1897). The *Boston Herald* called Elmwood one of the "notable antiquities of Cambridge."

> It belongs to that class of objects which have given Massachusetts a unique hold upon the enthusiasm of the American people. More and more persons are every year coming to Boston to see the antiquities of America, and it is for them quite as much as for Cambridge that these historical localities should be preserved. (*Chronicle*, Feb. 29, 1896)

Cambridge's park commissioners already had a full slate of projects and declined to take on another one that would remove a desirable residential tract from the tax rolls. President Eliot instead convinced the Metropolitan Park Commission to pledge a third of the cost and enlisted President Grover Cleveland, Senator Henry Cabot Lodge, Theodore Roosevelt, Thomas Wentworth Higginson, William Dean Howells, and John Fiske to sign a public appeal that secured the remaining funds by June 1898. In addition to the parkway, the design featured winding paths among the mature pine trees (although many were visibly decayed and soon had to be removed). In 1905 the Olmsteds prepared a more formal layout, and the Boston firm of Stickney & Austin designed brick walls and piers at the parkway entrances that bore

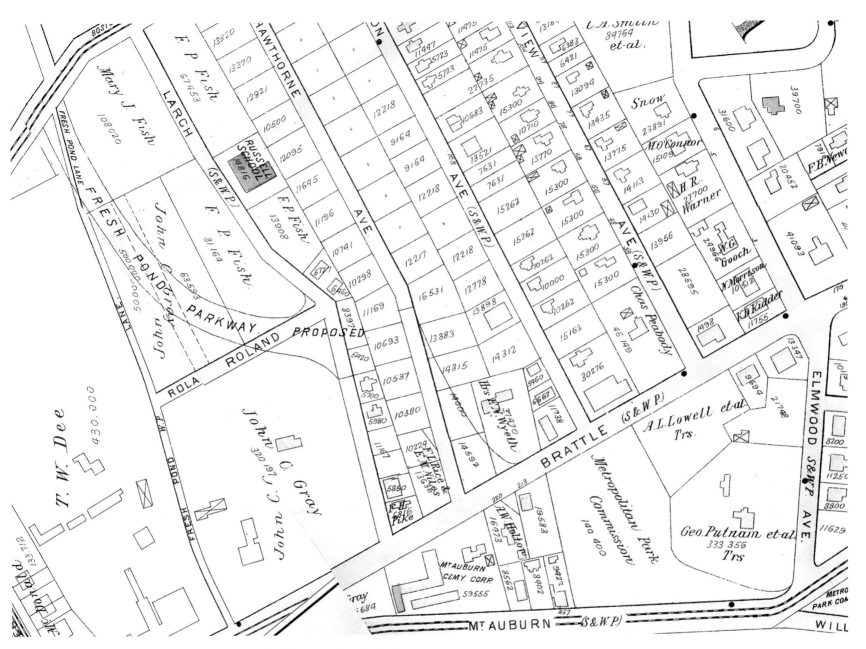

FIGURE 5.57 Fresh Pond Parkway as proposed by the Metropolitan Parks Commission about 1899. The route began on Mt. Auburn Street at Lowell Park, followed Grozier Road (Hawthorne Avenue) for a few hundred feet and then veered west to pick up Fresh Pond Lane before ending at Huron Avenue.

FIGURE 5.58 Lowell Park looking north from Mt. Auburn Street, ca. 1910.

ARSENAL SQUARE, WASHTUB SQUARE, BRATTLE BEACH, AND JOHN F. KENNEDY PARK

The intersection of Concord Avenue and Garden Street is named for the Massachusetts Arsenal, which stood nearby until 1887 (see chapter 4). The park was created in 1871, when Chauncy Street was extended to Concord Avenue. The Spanish-American War statue, known as "The Hiker," was installed in 1947. Theo Ruggles Kitson, the first American woman sculptor to receive an award at the Paris Salon, made the original in 1906; copies appear in about fifty other communities.

The intersection of Brattle Street with Craigie and Sparks streets became known as Washtub Square after Brattle Street resident Mary Blatchford placed a stone watering trough there in 1889 as a memorial to Abigail Williams May, a daughter of abolitionist Samuel May and the first woman elected to the Boston School Committee (figure 5.59). The present fountain was given to the city in 1971 by the grand-niece and grand-nephew of John Ross, a Boston merchant who purchased 24 Craigie Street in 1871. Patricia Ross Pratt, a landscape designer, relocated the coping of an old fountain to the present site and had a Vermont quarry fabricate the cone-shaped granite disk that nearly fills the basin. The Cambridge Historical Commission restored Albion Welch's 1870 "stone fence" in 2006–7 and with the Cambridge Plant and Garden Club refurbished the fountain and plantings. Neighborhood children know the site as "Brattle Beach" (figure 5.60).

The compromise that placed the John F. Kennedy Library and Museum at Columbia Point and divided the subway yards among academic and commercial uses reserved five acres for a memorial park (see chapter 3). The commonwealth recovered the yards from the Kennedy Library Corporation in 1976 and transferred one-third of the property to the Metropolitan District Commission. The cost of creating the park was to be defrayed by selling part of the yards as commercial property. The MDC proposed that the park be "simple, open, dignified, largely natural … standing as a special place in its own right but closely

memorial inscriptions by President Eliot. Some of these walls were relocated when the parkway was widened in 1966.

Charles Eliot envisioned Fresh Pond Parkway as a link in a chain of pleasure roads connecting the Blue Hills with the Middlesex Fells. He had hoped the road would follow Fresh Pond Lane, an ancient cart path, but after his death John Chipman Gray donated most of the land for the present route, and the Olmsted firm laid out a gently curving road that cut across Lowell Park (see figure 4.78). The MPC opened Fresh Pond Parkway from Mt. Auburn Street to Huron Avenue in 1900; the MDC extended it to Concord Avenue and a connection with Alewife Brook Parkway in 1930. After completion of the Concord Turnpike (Route 2) in 1934, the parkway became a major artery connecting Boston with its northwestern suburbs. The opening of the Eliot Bridge in 1951 brought a torrent of traffic through West Cambridge. Lowell Park is now only an adjunct to Fresh Pond Parkway; the pine grove and its associations with the poet have long since passed from public memory.

FIGURE 5.59 The Abigail May memorial fountain (also known as "Abby May's bathtub") at the intersection of Brattle, Craigie, and Sparks streets. It was removed about 1930 as an obstruction to traffic. Photo before 1894.

FIGURE 5.60 The fountain installed by descendants of John Ross in 1971. The 1870 cast stone wall was replicated by the Cambridge Historical Commission in 2006–7. Photo 2015.

related to the Charles River Reservation" (MDC, "Request for Proposal," Mar. 8, 1984, 3). The Cambridge firm of Carol R. Johnson & Associates won the commission, and the park was dedicated on what would have been President Kennedy's 70th birthday, May 29, 1987. Granite pillars at each gateway bear quotations from the late president, and trees that bloom in late May surround a pool placed on axis with a shaded path that leads to Eliot Square.

The cemeteries of Old Cambridge illustrate the history of burial practices in New England. The Old Burying Ground, a Puritan cemetery that remained active until the beginning of the 19th century, stands in stark contrast to Mount Auburn Cemetery, the prototype for the garden cemetery movement, and to Cambridge Cemetery, its municipal successor. The cemeteries gave rise to an important stone-fabricating and monument industry.

OLD BURYING GROUND

The first burying ground in Newtowne was on the south side of Brattle Street between Ash Street and Longfellow Park, outside the Common Pales. The site had no protection from wild animals and was discontinued before the West End fields were opened for settlement in 1634. No trace of this cemetery has been found.

The Old Burying Ground was set aside before 1635. Initially it covered only about an acre, but its size doubled as more common land was enclosed. The construction of Christ Church in 1760 established both the line of Garden Street and the western boundary of the cemetery; the First Parish Church on the other side was built in 1833 (figure 5.61).[15] As the only cemetery in Cambridge for nearly 200 years, the Old Burying Ground received a cross section of the population, from paupers to Harvard presidents, and contains many more remains than the 1,218 marked burials indicate; graves were routinely dug up and reused after a few years (figure 5.62).

Most of the monuments are slate headstones with scalloped shoulders. The earliest stones have death's heads of medieval origin. This motif changed to winged cherubs under the influence of the Renaissance and finally to graceful urn-and-willow patterns in the Neoclassic period. The oldest, dated 1653, belongs to Anne Erinton, but the stone may have been placed later, as headstones did not come into general use until the 1670s. The finest are six works by the Lamson family of stone carvers, whose straightforward naturalism and inventive use of detail are seen

FIGURE 5.61 The Old Burying Ground in 1899, with the John Vassall tomb in the foreground.

in the ca. 1713 stone of Samuel Sparhawk (figure 5.63). Interspersed among the traditional markers are late 18th century altar stones denoting the wealth and social standing of their largely Anglican owners. As in Britain, upper-class families wished to be interred in burial vaults rather than in caskets placed directly in the ground. The John Vassall tomb stands over an extensive subterranean vault; when last opened in 1862, it contained twenty-five caskets, including that of Andrew Craigie, who had acquired the family's Christ Church pew and burial plot when he bought the Vassall estate in 1792.

Eight Harvard presidents lie in the Old Burying Ground. Three of the first four—Henry Dunster, Charles Chauncy, and Urian Oakes—were buried there before Harvard obtained its own adjoining plot at some point between 1711 and 1747. In 1846 the university decided to restore the monuments of its early presidents and undertook a search for the resting place of

FIGURE 5.62 The disposition of graves in the Old Burying Ground, as recorded in 1923. The cemetery commissioners resisted the temptation to reorganize the stones in orderly rows, as had been done in most of Boston's old cemeteries. Harvard University's own burying ground behind the First Parish Church contains eight marked graves.

Henry Dunster, who died in 1654. Several likely graves were opened and found to contain brick vaults covered with slabs of stone, enclosing coffins and remains in various states of preservation. None could be identified positively, but the authorities decided that one skeleton wrapped in a tarpaulin in a coffin stuffed with tansy (an aromatic native plant used to conceal the smell of decomposition) was Dunster's and ordered a monument for him. John Langdon Sibley, who recorded the exhumations in his *Private Journal,* was skeptical. Historian Robert Nylander thought it was more likely to be the body of the town's second minister, Reverend Jonathan Mitchell, who died in July 1668.

The cemetery contains the graves of at least nineteen soldiers killed during the Revolution, including John Hicks, William Marcy, and Moses Richardson, who were hastily buried after the hostilities of April 19, 1775, and the slaves Neptune Frost and Cato Stedman. After the Battle of Bunker Hill many wounded soldiers were also buried in a field across the road from Thomas Oliver's mansion, which had served as a hospital (see chapter 4).[16] The dedication of the Soldiers Monument on Cambridge Common in July 1870 reminded the city that there was no monument for casualties of the Revolution. Professor Eben Horsford claimed to have found the soldiers' common grave after examining a scrap of bloody cloth excavated from the Old Burying Ground, and a granite shaft was erected in their memory before the end of the year (figure 5.64).

In 1811 the town opened a new cemetery in Cambridgeport. Regular interments in the Old Burying Ground ceased, although owners of family tombs continued to use them; one of the last interments was that of Richard Henry Dana, the poet, in 1879. When Mrs. Elizabeth Pickett's remains were placed in her family's tomb in 1900, the *Tribune* noted that it had been a long time since a burial had taken place there; "occasionally one of the old tombs is opened for a burial or to remove a body, but it has been many years since a grave was dug" (Oct. 13). Except for the ashes of Christ Church's minister, Dr. Gardiner Day, which were placed under a path in 1981, the last known burial was that of the Reverend Samuel McChord Crothers, a minister of the First Parish, Unitarian, in 1927.

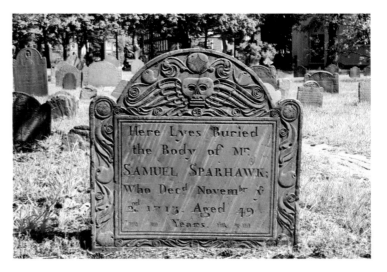

FIGURE 5.63 A headstone made for Samuel Sparhawk (1664–1713), probably by James or Nathaniel Lamson of Charlestown. Sparhawk was a third-generation settler who owned large tracts of land in the Second Parish, now Brighton. Lamson family members were among the best documented New England stone-cutters, known to scholars for enlarging on conventional motifs with new themes expressed in deeply carved, well-integrated compositions. Photo 2015.

The old cemetery rarely received more than minimal maintenance. In 1701–2, Aaron Bordman, "requesting that he might have the improvement of the Burying-yard (to keep sheep in)," agreed to repair the gate and pay the selectmen six shillings a year for the privilege (Town Records, 337). There are no records of repairs made at public expense until 1735, when the college built a stone wall on the side facing the Yard. This was in ruins by the 1840s, when an observer noted that:

It is rather surprising that, in this age of improvement, Cambridge should fall behind her neighbours, and suffer her ancient grave-yard to lie neglected. … Many of the tombs are without the names of the owners; many of the grave-stones have been broken, and more are broken every year; brambles abound instead of shrubbery; and what might be a beautiful cemetery is converted into a common passage-way. Unfitting is it, indeed, that the sod beneath which rests the ashes of a Shepard, a Dunster, and a Mitchell, should be rioted over by every vagrant schoolboy. (Harris, v)

FIGURE 5.64 The Revolutionary War monument decorated for the celebration of the Centennial in 1875.

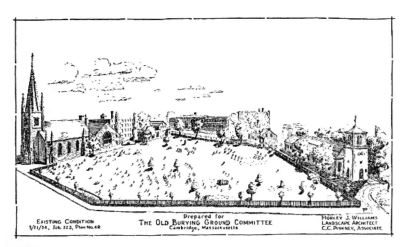

FIGURE 5.65 During the Depression, workers partly paid with federal relief funds laid out brick paths and planted trees in the Old Burying Ground according to plans drawn in 1934 by Morley Williams of Harvard's School of Landscape Architecture, who had previously consulted on the landscape of Mount Vernon.

It was 1860 before the city replaced the ruined wall with a picket fence. Conditions improved after the Centennial, and the present iron fence was installed in 1891. In 1900 the cemetery commissioners, "after twenty years of effort to save money," rebuilt twenty brick tombs, reset innumerable headstones, and (apparently for the first time) planted trees and landscaped the grounds (*Chronicle,* Nov. 10, 1900). The present layout of paths dates to 1934–38, when a committee that included Mayor Richard Russell, President Conant, Professor Samuel Eliot Morison, and preservationist William Sumner Appleton raised funds to match grants from the Emergency Relief and Public Works administrations (figure 5.65). A burst of enthusiasm during the Bicentennial enabled the Cambridge Historical Commission to restore many grave markers, and this work continues on a regular basis.

All around us there breathes a solemn calm, as if we were in the bosom of a wilderness, broken only by the breeze as it murmurs through the tops of the forest. … Ascend but a few steps, and what a change of scenery to surprise and delight us. … Below us flows the winding Charles with its rippling current, like the stream of time hastening to the ocean of eternity. In the distance, the City … rears its proud eminences, its glittering spires, its lofty towers, its graceful mansions, its curling smoke, its crowded haunts of business and pleasure, which speak to the eye, yet leave a noiseless loneliness on the ear. Again we turn, and the walls of our venerable University … the cultivated farm, the neat cottage, the village church, the sparkling lake, the rich valley, and the distant hills are before us, through opening vistas; and we breath amid the fresh and varied labors of man. … We stand, as it were, upon the borders of two worlds. (Joseph Story, *An Address Delivered on the Dedication of the Cemetery at Mount Auburn,* Sept. 24, 1831)

Mount Auburn is usually considered a Cambridge institution, although it was conceived by Bostonians and lies mainly in Watertown. Its fame is widespread, both as the burial place of eminent people and as the first garden cemetery in America. It became one of the area's outstanding sights and served as the prototype for such well-known cemeteries as Laurel Hill in Philadelphia (1836) and Green-Wood in Brooklyn (1838).[17]

In the early 19th century, burying grounds in Boston were dank, overcrowded, poorly maintained, and widely considered a threat to public health. Changing attitudes toward death and the awakening Romantic Movement cast these urban cemeteries in an unfavorable light. The founding fathers and mothers were dying, and some thought it was important to memorialize the heroes of the new republic. Since burying grounds in Puritan New England had never been associated with churches as consecrated ground, only custom prevented the establishment of burial sites in remote areas.

FIGURE 5.66 Mount Auburn Cemetery with Fresh Pond in the distance, 1847.

The moving spirit behind Mount Auburn Cemetery was Jacob Bigelow, a Boston physician and a professor at the Harvard Medical School, who was knowledgeable in architecture, botany, and landscape design. An interest in burial reform led him to advocate the establishment of spacious rural cemeteries, "in which the beauties of nature should … relieve from their repulsive features the tenements of the deceased" (Bigelow, 1). In 1825 he convened a group that included Supreme Court justice Joseph Story, General Henry A.S. Dearborn, the first president of the Massachusetts Horticultural Society, and Professor Edward Everett, the future Harvard president. A suitable site eluded them for almost five years; properties such as the Aspinwall estate in Brookline were too expensive, and some landowners were reluctant to sell for the intended purpose.

The committee finally acquired part of the Simon Stone farm, which had been established on the Charles River above Gerry's Landing in Watertown in 1635. The terrain was very irregular; there were several ponds, and a glacial esker formed a sinuous ridge with a level summit running from southeast to northwest. A hilltop 125 feet above the Charles River gave a panoramic view of Boston and the surrounding countryside. Among the Harvard students who appreciated its picturesque beauty, this district became known as "Sweet Auburn" from Oliver Goldsmith's poem, "The Deserted Village," which was published in Boston in 1790:

> Sweet Auburn! loveliest village of the plain
> Where health and plenty cheered the lab'ring swain
> Where smiling spring its earliest visit paid
> And parting summer's ling'ring blooms delay'd.

George Brimmer, a Boston merchant, began to acquire parts of the Stone farm in 1825, and after five years he owned a large contiguous tract south of Mt. Auburn Street and west of present Coolidge Avenue. In 1831 the Massachusetts Horticultural Society, with Bigelow as secretary, agreed to purchase Brimmer's 72 acres for a cemetery and experimental garden as soon as a hundred burial plots had been sold.[18] General Dearborn, an enthusiastic

horticulturist with some experience in civil engineering, ordered prints of Paris's Père Lachaise Cemetery and Sir Humphrey Repton's works on landscape architecture and took charge of laying out the grounds. The picturesque landscape he created combined Repton's naturalism with classical forms (figure 5.67).

> The chief object was to follow the natural features of the land in the … avenues and paths, and to run them as nearly level as possible by winding gradually and gracefully through the vales and obliquely over the hills. … To accomplish this, elliptical curves were invariably used … instead of these stiff circular lines which are incompatible with elegance of form and a pleasing effect. (Dearborn, in Linden-Ward, "Putting the Past in Place," 183)

Dearborn, "hoe in hand, day after day, at the head of his laborers," laid out the roads and paths himself (Putnam, in Linden-Ward, ibid., 182). Later superintendents altered the topography somewhat; the highest hill, Mount Auburn, remains, but others were cut down to fill the smaller ponds and bogs. Despite these changes, the initial design survives substantially intact along Central and Mountain avenues and around the Dell.

Dearborn set aside 32 acres along the Watertown Road for an experimental garden, but the lot owners, supported by Story and Bigelow, were unwilling to commit sufficient resources to the endeavor. In 1835 the legislature created the Proprietors of the Cemetery of Mount Auburn; the Horticultural Society abandoned the garden and transferred the property to the cemetery in return for a share of the proceeds from lot sales. Story served as president until 1845 and Bigelow until 1871.

Bigelow and Dearborn were both interested in architecture, but their preferences differed. Dearborn, the older man, had completed a two-volume *Treatise on Grecian Architecture* in 1828. Bigelow, who had lectured on architecture as Harvard's Rumford Professor, chose the Egyptian style for the main gate because of its associations with the burial practices and mythology of that ancient civilization, which had been rediscovered by Europeans during Napoleon's conquest of the Nile (figure 5.68). This was first executed in 1832 in wood sand-painted to

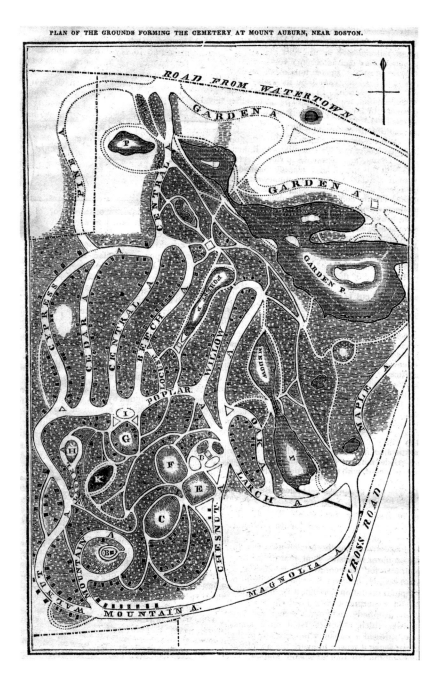

FIGURE 5.67 Jacob Bigelow's landscape design for Mount Auburn was formalized by the Cambridge surveyor Alexander Wadsworth in 1831. This version appeared in 1833.

resemble masonry, but in 1842 it was rebuilt in granite by Octavius Rogers of Quincy, the only contractor able to fabricate the 22-foot monolithic cornice. Bigelow also designed the iron fence that was erected along Mt. Auburn Street in 1844 and extended along Coolidge Avenue in 1849–51.

Bigelow initially agreed with Dearborn that the chapel should resemble a Greek temple and prepared such a design in 1834. By this time the Gothic Revival style was gaining popularity, and the trustees decided to hold an architectural competition in 1844. Well-known architects Gridley Bryant, Richard Bond, and Ammi Young all submitted plans, but the trustees once again chose Dr. Bigelow as their architect, and his chapel, a somewhat gauche interpretation of Harvard's Gore Hall, was completed in 1846 (see figure 10.13). It was soon discovered that iron deposits were causing the granite blocks to disintegrate, and the masonry was rebuilt with slightly more exterior embellishment in 1855 (figure 5.69). Poor acoustics made the chapel undesirable for services, so it served primarily as a sculpture gallery until 1899, when it was remodeled to incorporate a crematorium.[19] The interior was remodeled again in the 1920s for renewed use as a chapel; the spectacular stained glass window in the chancel that Bigelow commissioned from the Edinburgh firm of Ballantine & Allan in 1845 was restored in 2006. Bigelow also had a hand in designing Mount Auburn's 62-foot granite lookout tower commemorating George Washington, although the drawings came from Bryant's office in 1852.

Mount Auburn soon became a popular destination for daytrippers. By 1845 an hourly omnibus ran directly to the gate from Boston, providing an inexpensive summer excursion. The Fitchburg Railroad opened a station on the Watertown Branch in 1847, and in 1856 the cemetery was a principal destination of the Cambridge Railroad, New England's first street railway (see chapter 2 and *Report Five: Northwest Cambridge,* figure 269). In 1870 Boston architect Nathaniel Bradlee designed a reception house for visitors on Mt. Auburn Street (figure 5.70). Visitation declined after the Civil War, when death could no longer be romanticized, and municipal park systems began to provide other venues for public enjoyment.

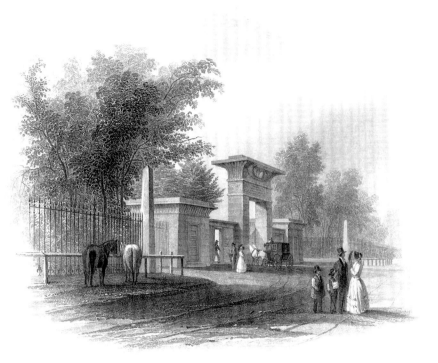

FIGURE 5.68 The Egyptian Revival gate (1832, Jacob Bigelow, designer) as rebuilt in granite in 1842. The style perplexed some New Englanders and offended others, including one writer on American architecture who in 1836 called it "the architecture of embalmed cats and deified crocodiles" (Henry Russell Cleveland, in Linden-Ward, *Silent City,* 265). This gate established the precedent for Egyptian Revival cemetery gateways in America, including those at the Old Granary Burial Ground in Boston (ca. 1837) and Grove Street Cemetery in New Haven (1848).

FIGURE 5.69 Bigelow Chapel (1846, Jacob Bigelow, designer). Photo ca. 1902.

In the 20th century, questions of liability and ownership meant that some important monuments were allowed to decay. In 1980 the cemetery decided to replace Bigelow's cast-iron Egyptian fence with vinyl-covered chain link (figure 5.71). The uproar that played out in the local press awakened the proprietors—some of them descendants of the founding families—to the public's interest in preserving the cemetery, and they agreed in 1982 to restore 140 feet of the fence around the main gate. Under the leadership of president William Clendaniel, who took office in 1988, Mount Auburn hired archivists and preservation specialists and began to restore its landscape and selected monuments. Landscape architect Craig Halvorson prepared the cemetery's first master plan in 1990, and the cemetery was designated a National Historic Landmark in 2003.

FIGURE 5.70 Mount Auburn Cemetery gate and reception house, 583 Mt. Auburn Street (1870, N.J. Bradlee, architect). The reception house served as the cemetery office until 1898; it was sold to a monument dealer in 1928. Photo ca. 1885.

FIGURE 5.71 Mount Auburn Cemetery's Egyptian Revival perimeter fence, erected in 1844, originally extended for over half a mile along Mt. Auburn Street and Coolidge Avenue. All but a few panels on either side of the main gate were replaced with chain link in 1980–81. The stone marks the boundary between Cambridge and Watertown. Photo September 1980.

CAMBRIDGE CEMETERY

Cambridge Cemetery was a necessary replacement for the town's 2.4-acre Cambridgeport burial ground. The city was reluctant to follow Mount Auburn into the countryside, but by 1848, when Henry Dearborn established Forest Hills as a municipal cemetery in Roxbury, there were already garden cemeteries in Worcester, New Bedford, Springfield, Newburyport, and Salem. Many Cambridge families had purchased lots at Mount Auburn

FIGURE 5.72 Cambridge Cemetery's topography is not as dramatic as Mount Auburn's, but the early sections were laid out in a naturalistic manner. The Brighton abattoir is visible in the background. Photo ca. 1895.

before the city finally established a new burying ground on 24 acres of the Stone farm in 1854. The Cambridgeport cemetery was discontinued in 1865 and became Broadway Common (now Sennott Park).

Cambridge made a garden cemetery burial accessible to all. Mount Auburn appealed to Boston's upper class, and the price of its lots rose from $60 in 1832 to $150 in 1854. The city council restricted Cambridge Cemetery to residents and priced its lots at 10¢ a square foot, one-fifth the cost across Coolidge Avenue. Among the prominent Cantabrigians buried there are Henry James Sr. and his children, William, Henry, and Alice; authors William Dean Howells and Thomas Wentworth Higginson; architect Henry Van Brunt; publisher Henry Houghton; and Elias Howe, the inventor of the sewing machine. Sibley thought that "if the Cemetery were not so near Mount Auburn, but belonged to some country town, it would be considered very beautiful" (*Private Journal*, Sept. 25, 1864; figure 5.72).

Architects William Hovey Jr. and Calvin Ryder laid out Cambridge Cemetery in imitation of Mount Auburn's naturalistic design, with miniature avenues squeezed tightly between low hills and a small pond (figure 5.73). In the lower, less desirable parts near the river, a simple grid was platted for the public lots; a planned approach along the river from Mt. Auburn Street was never realized. In 1865 the city purchased 11 acres from the Coolidge farm, and Josiah Chase (who became Cambridge's first city engineer two years later) laid out the addition on a somewhat less picturesque plan (figures 5.74–5.75). Another purchase in 1885 added the 26-acre Winchester estate (see figure 4.102). Boston landscape architects Gray & Blaisdell platted this area on the "lawn" principle, using the former carriageway (now Winchester Avenue) as a central boulevard. The city razed the mansion in 1896 to provide more land for burials. A final five acres along Coolidge Avenue were acquired from Mount Auburn Cemetery in 1942; this parcel is devoted to veterans and features a World War I memorial by Karl Skoog.

The support structures at Cambridge Cemetery have always been modest. Hovey & Ryder designed a lodge, fence, and gate in

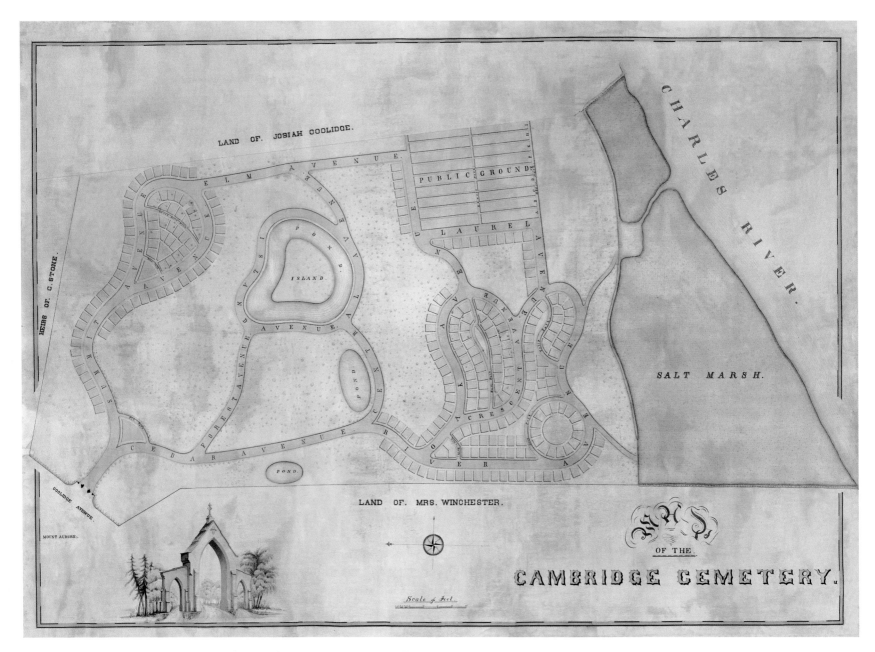

FIGURE 5.73 The original design of Cambridge Cemetery (ca. 1855, William T. Hovey Jr. and Calvin Ryder, architects). The architects worked with the natural features of the site, which included three ponds and a brook, to create a scenic cemetery like Mount Auburn while accommodating inexpensive public lots. The vignette in the lower left corner depicts the original Gothic gate.

FIGURE 5.74 Cambridge Cemetery ca. 1882–85, showing the additional tract purchased in 1865. The city acquired the 26-acre Winchester estate (labeled "Brown Heirs") in 1885 and five acres from the Mount Auburn Cemetery Corporation in 1942.

FIGURE 5.75 The bluff near the river that the city acquired in 1865 became a memorial ground for Cambridge's Civil War dead. The marble headstones were removed in 1972. Photo ca. 1901–7.

the fashionable Gothic style in 1854. The lodge burned in 1867 and was replaced by a diminutive stone building that served as a chapel, superintendent's office, and equipment storeroom (figure 5.76). After the present iron gate and rusticated granite piers were installed in 1893, the *Chronicle* noted approvingly that the overgrown larches and cedars, once considered symbols of eternity, had been removed and the "forbidding appearance" of the old entrance had been dispelled (*Chronicle,* May 23, 1896). The current office building went up in 1923.

FIGURE 5.76 The lodge that replaced Hovey & Ryder's original building in 1868 was designed by an unknown architect in a modified Gothic Revival style of ledgestone with dressed granite trim similar to the Old Cambridge Baptist Church. It originally contained the superintendent's office and a public waiting room. Altered in 1897 and converted to a chapel in 1923, it became a maintenance shop and then a staff lunch room. The exterior was restored in 2006. Photo 2008.

Monument Makers and Nurseries

The cemeteries attracted monument firms and florists, which were conspicuous features of the neighborhood until the mid-20th century (figure 5.77). Monument makers initially specialized in marble or granite but after the Civil War worked in both mediums. Marble, a relatively light, soft stone that was easy to transport and work, came from Vermont or New York. Granite, heavy and dense, reached Cambridge by canal boat or barge from Chelmsford and Quincy, by sail from Cape Ann and Maine, and later by rail from inland quarries.

Cambridge's best-known stone dealer was Alexander McDonald, a native of Scotland who came to America in 1852. He arrived in Cambridge in 1856 and succeeded to the marble business of another Alexander McDonald, an older native of Nova Scotia. McDonald built the Monument Wharf and a stone yard on Mt. Auburn Street opposite Shaler Lane in 1862, but after 1867 transferred most of his stone-cutting operations to a 12-acre field on Mt. Auburn Street that he acquired from the estate of Jonas Wyeth (figures 5.78–5.79). This site was accessible by rail, which proved useful when he purchased a granite quarry in

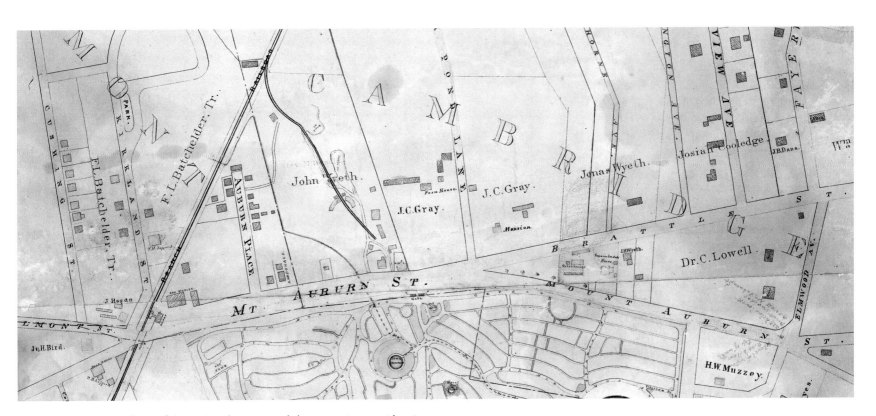

FIGURE 5.77 Some of the services that supported the cemeteries are evident in this 1867 plan. From left to right, the Mount Auburn Station of the Fitchburg Railroad; the carbarns of the Union Railway; Alexander McDonald's marble works (at the end of the railroad siding); John Chipman Gray's farmhouse, later to be Thomas Dee's nursery; and the Mount Auburn Cemetery Corporation's own greenhouses and superintendent's house between Brattle and Mt. Auburn streets.

FIGURE 5.78 Alexander McDonald supplied architectural stone as well as monuments. Cambridge Directory, 1869.

Mason, New Hampshire, and established branch offices in other cities. McDonald and a partner constructed the Soldiers Monument on Cambridge Common in 1869. He laid out McDonald Street with some house lots by 1886; before his death in 1906 this became Aberdeen Avenue, a boulevard with a central reservation for streetcar tracks.

John McNamee, an Irish marble worker (no known relation to Mayor John H.H. McNamee), leased the site of the John Gerry Orne store on Mt. Auburn Street from Reverend Charles Lowell's heirs and established a stoneyard in 1866 (figure 5.80). Robert Sands, McNamee's foreman, established his own firm on Coolidge Avenue in 1873. Six years later he moved to Mt. Auburn Street, where his son and grandson remained in business until 1980 (figure 5.81).

FIGURE 5.79 Large blocks of granite fabricated by Alexander McDonald for monuments were hauled by teams of oxen to nearby towns. Photo ca. 1890.

FIGURE 5.80 John McNamee's Union Marble & Granite Works, 380 Mt. Auburn Street, was established in 1869. The property was taken by the Metropolitan Park Commission in 1899 and eventually occupied by Gerry's Landing Road. Photo 1869.

Nurseries and greenhouses also served the cemetery trade. The largest grower originated on William Gray's estate, the Larches (see chapter 4). In 1882 John Chipman Gray sold his uncle's three greenhouses and 9½ acres west of Fresh Pond Lane to Sarah Dee and her son Thomas, a florist. They built a house at 36 Larchwood Drive (1882) and established a nursery that soon included six greenhouses, four hothouses, an office, a farmhouse, and a stable. The Dees sold the property to Sidney Hoffman of Roxbury about 1904. Harold A. Ryan, who took over about 1915, added a shop and greenhouse that ran 230 feet along Mt. Auburn Street (figure 5.82). Ryan developed Old Dee Road in 1937, and the greenhouses operated under his name until 1974 (figure 5.83).

FIGURE 5.81 George R. Sands & Sons monument company, 457 Mt. Auburn Street (1915, Edgar T.P. Walker, architect). This building was replaced by townhouses in 1980. Photo 1979.

FIGURE 5.82 Harold A. Ryan greenhouses, 575–581 Mt. Auburn Street, ca. 1920.

FIGURE 5.83 Greenhouses and monument dealers clustered near the gates of Mount Auburn Cemetery. The field behind the greenhouses is now occupied by the houses on Old Dee Road. Photo 1937.

HARVARD BOTANIC GARDEN

The Harvard Botanic Garden, a semipublic study collection of live plants, occupied a seven-acre hillside site bounded by Garden, Raymond, and Linnaean streets. The Massachusetts Constitution of 1779 directed the legislature to encourage the study of science and natural history. Four years later the Consul General of France wrote the president of the Massachusetts Medical Society that if the commonwealth established a botanic garden, the king would send "at his Majesty's expense, from his Royal Garden, every species of seeds and plants that the Director of the Botanical Garden in Massachusetts Bay may wish to have." Responding to a query from the General Court, a Harvard committee concurred that a botanical garden "for the cultivation of the useful and curious productions of America, would not only be highly honorary to the Commonwealth of Massachusetts, but greatly beneficial to this and the other states in the Union, as well as to this university" (Corporation Records, 3, 1784, 187–88). Nothing came of these efforts, however, and the French Revolution soon extinguished any possibility of assistance from the king.

In 1792 Samuel Adams and twenty-seven wealthy merchants, lawyers, and statesmen incorporated one of the earliest agricultural societies in the United States, the Massachusetts Society for Promoting Agriculture (MSPA). Two years later the society's trustees appointed a committee "to consider the expediency of procuring a piece of ground for the purpose of agricultural experiments" (MSPA *Trustee Records*, Feb. 1794). In 1802 the society appropriated $500 "for the establishment of a professorship of natural history" and embarked on a private subscription campaign to raise additional funds (ibid., July 3, 1802). In 1805 the position was finally created at Harvard with the understanding that one of the professor's duties would be to form a botanic garden on grounds provided, and the society pledged "to purchase a suitable place for a Botanic garden and for the habitation of the professor as near the scite of the College in Cambridge as conveniently may be" (ibid., Feb. 21, 1805). The

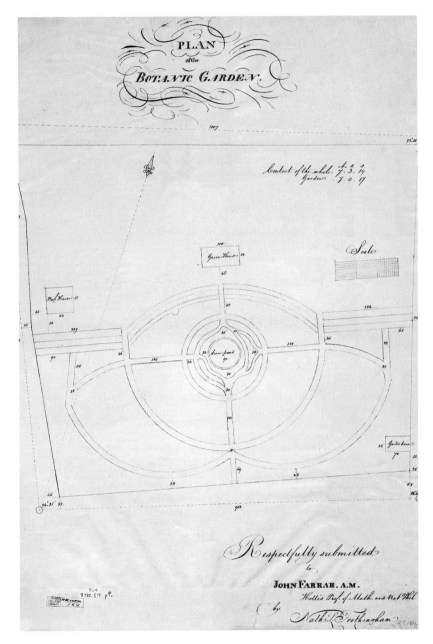

FIGURE 5.84 The Botanic Garden as constructed, ca. 1811.

MSPA purchased five acres of Daniel Prentice's farm on Raymond Street in 1806, and Andrew Craigie donated an adjoining two-acre orchard. The land included a spring along Linnaean Street that could be adapted for aquatic plants and a small house that could be used by the gardener. The garden was to be deeded to Harvard as soon as possible, although a charter limitation on the value of college landholdings prevented it from accepting the gift until 1818. The legislature provided no direct funding but granted the society land in Maine that it could sell to help finance the project.

The board of visitors that oversaw the professorship comprised the trustees of the agricultural society and the presidents of Harvard, the American Academy of Arts and Sciences, and the Massachusetts Medical Society. William Dandridge Peck, a self-taught naturalist who had graduated from Harvard in 1782 and won several agricultural society prizes, was appointed the first Massachusetts Professor of Natural History, much to the distress of Dr. Benjamin Waterhouse, who had been teaching natural history there since 1788. Peck soon departed for Europe to study botanic gardens, obtain a garden plan and specimens, and consult with eminent naturalists. He hired an English gardener, William Carter, as it was generally felt that a qualified man could not be found in America. Peck's studies kept him away almost three years in England, Holland, Belgium, Sweden, and France, but a suitable plan for the Cambridge garden proved difficult to come by. He had hoped to find plans of the major European botanic gardens in Linnaeus's study in Uppsala, Sweden. When he discovered that these were no longer extant, Peck went to Paris, where he prevailed upon Gabriel Thouin, "a gentleman of eminence in the profession of ornamental gardening" connected to the national Jardin des Plantes, to draw a plan for the Cambridge site (ibid., June 24, 1808). Thouin's schematic design included a central pond with curving outlets and footpaths. Planting beds in fourteen concentric circles formed the instructional part of the garden, while intertwining paths led visitors through plots of trees and flowering shrubs.

Peck had seen the site only once before he left for Europe. When he returned he found the terrain was more irregular than he remembered. He simplified Thouin's plan to conform to the sloping site but retained the central pond and some of the curving paths and concentric beds (figure 5.84). Building the garden was fraught with difficulty and unforeseen expense; the soil was found in 1808 to be "stiff and difficult to cultivate," and in 1809 it took seven men to repair the mistakes of the previous season and to lay a "very expensive but necessary drain at the foot of the hill" (ibid., Aug. 27, 1808, and July 29, 1809).

By 1810 a considerable number of species had been planted, and the committee superintending the garden hired 26-year-old Ithiel Town (1784–1844), "an artist well recommended," to design and build a residence and greenhouse for Peck and his bride, Harriet Hilliard (ibid., June 30, 1810). A Connecticut native, Town had grown up in Cambridge and trained with Asher Benjamin. He was later known as an architect and designed many fine Greek Revival buildings, primarily in Connecticut (some in partnership with architect Alexander Jackson Davis in 1829–35); he also patented a lattice bridge truss that made him wealthy. The botanic garden house was his first architectural commission, and he was paid $4,030 for the house and greenhouse (see figure 6.37).

Although an official opening date has not been found, the committee reported in April 1811 that the garden was sufficiently advanced to draw up rules for visitors. Tickets sold for 25¢, a prohibitive amount for working people, although subscribers, public officials, important foreign visitors, and clergy were admitted free. As a popular horticultural destination, the Botanic Garden prefigured Mount Auburn Cemetery by twenty years. By 1812 William Carter was working full time as gardener and living in the old house on the southeast corner of the property.

After Peck died in 1822 Harvard discontinued the professorship because the endowment could no longer support it. In 1825 the university hired Thomas Nuttall, an English botanist, as curator of the garden and paid him $100 for each natural history course he taught. He lived in two rooms of the professor's residence, while boarders occupied the rest. When he resigned in 1834 to accompany Nathaniel Wyeth on an expedition to Oregon, responsibility for the garden fell to Carter. In 1835 he asked Harvard to examine the house where he had lived for more than twenty years; it was found to be "utterly untenable and incapable of repair" and a new one was authorized (College Papers, 2nd Series, vol. VII, p. 78, May 6, 1835).

By 1847 there were insufficient funds to maintain the garden, and Carter wrote to President Everett to resign his position. He stressed the original importance of the garden as the first of its kind in the country but stated that many well-financed public gardens had since been established, while Harvard's had fallen into "decay and insignificance ... without the means of renovating its exhausted soil." Although the exchange of plants with botanical establishments in America and abroad had grown considerably, the greenhouse could not be heated during the winter of 1846–47, and "our plants, one of the most valuable collections in the country, have been sold and scattered" (Carter to President Everett, Feb. 23, 1847). Harvard discontinued the gardener's position at the end of the academic year but granted Carter half a year's salary "in consideration of his long and faithful services" (Corporation Records, vol. 8, 367, June 12, 1847). Carter then built himself a fine Greek Revival house at 49 Linnaean Street, where he lived with his wife, Silence, within sight of the garden.

In spite of these difficulties, Asa Gray (1810–88) was appointed Fisher Professor of Natural History in 1842, lived in the garden house, and trained young botanists for forty-five years. An early supporter of Charles Darwin (and therefore an opponent of Louis Agassiz), Gray was America's greatest botanist, and Harvard did everything possible to accommodate him. The garden house was enlarged several times as Gray's collections and the popularity of his courses increased. In 1848 a two-story addition afforded him a large ground floor study and bedrooms upstairs that he could rent to students. Harvard built a new conservatory in 1858, and in 1864, when Gray offered to give all his

FIGURE 5.85 Botanic Garden (later Asa Gray) house (1810, Ithiel Town, housewright), with the two-story addition of 1848 and the Thayer Herbarium (1864, Ryder & Harris, architects). Photo 1867.

FIGURE 5.86 The Harvard Botanic Garden in the late 19th century, looking southeast from the Gray Herbarium toward William Carter's house at 49 Linnaean Street, on the corner of Raymond Street.

specimens and his library to the college if they were housed in a fireproof building, Nathaniel Thayer paid to build a brick herbarium connected to the house (figure 5.85). After Mrs. Gray's death in 1909, Harvard sold the house to architect Allen H. Cox, who moved it across Garden Street and remodeled it as his own residence (see chapter 6). The ancillary buildings were replaced by a new library and herbarium (1911, 1914, William Mowll, architect), now called Kittredge Hall and occupied by the Harvard University Press.

The Botanic Garden declined in the 1920s as academic studies shifted to the Arnold Arboretum and the Harvard Forest in Petersham. Skilled gardeners retired, the soil was not renewed, and ice storms took their toll on mature plantings. The Herb Society of America took charge of 1,400 square feet in the upper garden in 1937 and some research continued on hardy herbaceous plants, but by World War II only one gardener remained. In 1948 the *Boston Globe* reported that "the whitest birches in America" were doomed by the construction of the Botanic Garden Apartments for returning veterans (May 2; see figure 6.236). Today, only a few specimen trees recall the history of the site.

Arthur Astor Carey house, 28 Fayerweather Street (1882). See figure 6.154.

6 RESIDENTIAL ARCHITECTURE

Cambridge provides a rich field for the study of residential architecture because of its diverse social history and the survival of a wide range of high-style and vernacular houses from all periods of its history. The colonial aristocracy that settled in Cambridge in the mid-18th century introduced notions of architectural refinement that were foreign to the descendants of the Puritans. In the 19th century, the continuing presence of a moneyed, literate elite kept Old Cambridge current with the latest architectural trends. As Old Cambridge became a suburb of Boston, local builders increasingly adopted elements of high-style buildings, attempting to make even the most modest cottages at least somewhat up-to-date. In the 20th century, the growth of architecture as an academic discipline at Harvard and M.I.T. exposed the city to international developments in residential design.

THE COLONIAL PERIOD

The majority of colonists who settled in Massachusetts Bay in the 17th century came from rural England, primarily East Anglia and the southwestern counties. They brought with them English post-Medieval building traditions. Abbott Cummings in *The Framed Houses of Massachusetts Bay 1625–1725* stated that "the characteristic smaller farmhouse from which most of the first emigrants to Massachusetts Bay set forth in the 1630s … was the house of two rooms on the ground floor, both chambered over,

the chambers reached by a winding stair alongside the central chimney and often situated between the stack and the entrance" (9–10). Some First Period (from European settlement to 1725) houses in Massachusetts Bay followed this plan from the beginning; others began as single-room, end-chimney dwellings that were later expanded into two-room, center-chimney houses. The only two surviving First Period houses in Cambridge followed this pattern of expansion.

The town records include some clues to 17th-century building practices. As discussed in chapter 1, buildings were wood, and the town fathers in 1633 ordered that all houses be roofed with "slate or board but not with thatch" for fear of fire (Town Records, 4). The need to erect a great number of houses in a short period, coupled with the settlers' wish to avoid the deforestation they had witnessed in England, led Massachusetts Bay towns to regulate the trade in timber. As early as 1634–35 Newtowne established penalties for cutting trees without permission and for selling trees for "Boards, Clapboards or frames of houses" out of town (ibid., 8).

Little is known about the appearance of the earliest Newtowne buildings, but some, such as the Hooker-Shepard-Wigglesworth house, lasted long enough to be recorded (see figure 1.6). The oldest houses still standing in Cambridge are the Cooper-Frost-Austin house at 21 Linnaean Street and the Hooper-Lee-Nichols house at 159 Brattle Street. Although enlarged and updated in the 18th and 19th centuries, both retain evidence of their late 17th century origins.

Dendrochronology, the comparative analysis of tree ring and climate data, has established a firm construction date for the Cooper-Frost-Austin house (figure 6.1). In 1681–82 Samuel Cooper built a two-bay structure (the east half of the present house) with a sharply pitched roof, an integral lean-to, and a chimney on the west end; framing details and evidence exposed during reroofing in 2012 indicated an original front gable and possibly triple casement windows (figure 6.2). Integral lean-tos began to appear in the late 17th century and generally had continuous rafters that ran the entire length of the rear roof slope. Framing details of Cooper's original house are consistent with other late 17th century Middlesex County houses, but the lean-to is unusual as the rafters are in two pieces, one supporting the main part of the roof and one the lean-to. The interior contained a main east room or hall, a chamber above, and two small rooms in the lean-to. Many New Englanders moved cooking functions out of the main room in the mid- to late 18th century, but according to Cooper's 1718 inventory his kitchen was already in the lean-to.

Samuel's son Walter married in 1722 and added the west half of the house between 1720 and 1725. This produced a typical center-chimney plan with two main downstairs rooms, a narrow winding staircase in front of the chimney, and a lean-to kitchen extending the width of the house (figure 6.3). The west end probably had sash windows instead of casements, but the earliest windows now on the west side date from the mid-18th century. A comparison of the east and west ground floor rooms shows the differences between 17th and early 18th century taste and building practices (figure 6.4). In the 1680s hall, called the Low Room in the 1718 inventory, the ceiling was originally unplastered, the framing exposed, and the chimney girt and massive summer beam ornamented with chamfers. The plaster chimneybreast was coved to support the second floor hearth, and the fireplace wall had molded wood sheathing typical of the 1690s. In the 1720s parlor on the west side, the ceiling was plastered

FIGURE 6.1 Cooper-Frost-Austin house, 21 Linnaean Street (1681–82). The original house included the entry and the east (right) end. The west two bays were added in 1720–25 and the vestibule in the 1830s. Photo 1913–14.

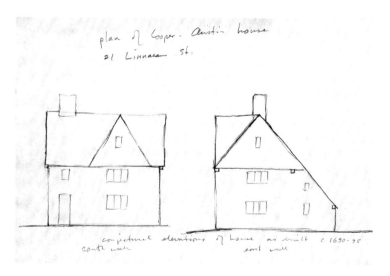

FIGURE 6.2 Conjectural south and east elevations, Cooper-Frost-Austin house as built in 1681–82, showing the front gable, integral lean-to, and east gable overhang.

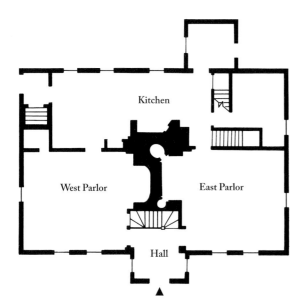

FIGURE 6.3 First floor plan, Cooper-Frost-Austin house after restoration in 1912.

FIGURE 6.4 East room (1681–82), Cooper-Frost-Austin house as restored by Joseph Chandler in 1912. Photo 1973.

to hide the joists and present a more finished appearance; the hewn girts and summer beam that project below the plaster were ornamented with bead moldings instead of chamfers. The large west fireplace was old-fashioned for the 1720s, but its size may indicate earlier construction. Cummings surmises that when the house was originally built, an addition was anticipated and fireplaces were built on the west end and walled over. When the west wall was removed in preparation for the addition, the early fireplaces were uncovered and trimmed in the 1720s manner.

The house remained in the Cooper family until 1788. In 1807 it passed by inheritance and purchase to Susan and Thomas Austin, who added the side porch with arches about 1810 and the present entry vestibule in the 1830s. The Austins reconfigured the fireplaces for greater efficiency and reversed the direction of the interior stairway, adding a turned newel and thin rectangular balusters that are typical of early 19th century houses in Cambridge. In 1912 the Society for the Preservation of New England Antiquities purchased the property from the Austin heirs and hired Joseph E. Chandler, an architect who had worked on restoring the Paul Revere House in Boston and the House of Seven Gables in Salem. Chandler made structural repairs and opened the two first-floor fireplaces to their original size. The upstairs fireplaces were opened in 1962.

The second house with known 17th-century origins is the Hooper-Lee-Nichols house at 159 Brattle Street, home of the Cambridge Historical Society since 1957 (see figure 6.11).[1] Dr. Richard Hooper began the house between 1684 or 85, when he bought the land (which was then in Watertown), and 1689, when he was listed as a Watertown resident. The west end is older, but it is difficult to determine its exact extent. The house may have started with only one first floor room and a chamber above, although the chimney bay is so wide that it could have accommodated fireplaces on both sides; if there were east rooms in this period, they did not survive. While the house appears to have been modest and unpainted on the exterior, the ceilings in the west end were plastered between the joists from the beginning, a practice associated with finer houses in the late 17th century.

The subsequent history of the house left little 17th-century work intact. Hooper died in 1691 and his wife in 1701, at which time probate records described the house as "much out of repair." Later records refer to "damage by ye worms" and indicate that it had become uninhabitable. In 1717 Hooper's son, Dr. Henry Hooper, added the present east portion of the house (perhaps replacing earlier east rooms) and built a massive 12-foot-square center chimney. Hooper's east end may have been an existing one-room house that he moved and grafted onto the west end, as the floor heights, dimensions, and orientation of the summer beams in the two ends are different.

Cornelius Waldo, a wealthy Boston merchant, purchased the house in 1733 and by 1742 had reworked it in the fashionable Georgian style. He built the third story in place of the original steep roof, substituted larger windows and window caps, and added chamfered wooden corner blocks to resemble stone quoins. The next owner, Judge Joseph Lee, added roughcast (a type of 18th-century stucco) to the west elevation about 1760 and had it scored to resemble ashlar; he probably also added the unusually wide projecting vestibule, although the door is later. The louvered shutters added at the end of the 18th century were somewhat innovative at the time. After Lee's death in 1802, the house was largely rented until 1861, when George Nichols bought it and added a roof balustrade made from parts of the chancel of St. Paul's Cathedral in Boston.

In 1916 Joseph Chandler uncovered some original fireplaces and early paneling and expanded the rear of the house to three stories. He also added a roughly finished chamfered beam to the present library and fireplace tiles in the second floor west room, reflecting his romantic ideas about early building practices. The house now displays several centuries of work and has been described as "a First Period structure that was remodeled in the Georgian style in the 18th century, decorated with scenic wallpaper in the 19th century, and then given a Colonial Revival addition in the 20th century" (CHS, *Rediscovering,* 11).

Traces of 17th-century construction may also survive in the Henry Vassall house at 94 Brattle Street, but extensive rebuilding in the 18th and 19th centuries has obscured most early evidence (see figure 6.12). Deeds indicate a dwelling owned by William Adams in 1637–38, and some framing members in the southwest corner may be that early. The rest of the western end was added later in the 17th century, possibly by Jonathan Remington, a carpenter who bought the place in 1665 and was granted the right in 1669 to cut timber "for an ende to his house" (Town Records, 185).

The typical two-room 17th-century house plan with a central chimney and tight winding stairs persisted in vernacular dwellings into the Georgian era. The continued use of earlier architectural details and forms in modest structures or less important rooms reflected the conservatism of Cambridge and the time it took for new features to spread from an urban center; despite the proximity to Boston, many Cambridge buildings exhibited a lag well into the 19th century.

THREE PHASES OF GEORGIAN BUILDING

In the early 18th century builders began to abandon the English post-Medieval traditions of the First Period and adopt the more formal Georgian style that corresponded roughly with the reigns of Kings George I through George IV (1714 to 1830). Georgian features first appeared in seaports such as Boston and Salem, which were in close communication with England, before spreading inland.

The early phase of the Georgian style in Massachusetts relied on classically based details and proportions derived primarily from modest detached houses that proliferated in English provincial towns and were themselves based on the work of classically inclined architects such as Inigo Jones and Christopher Wren. Seventeenth century verticality gave way to Georgian horizontality, facades became symmetrical, gambrel roofs became common, fenestration changed from small leaded casements to larger, double-hung windows, and eaves recalled Classical cornices. While the English precedents were masonry, almost all New England examples were wood.

The High Georgian period extended from approximately 1740 to 1790 and produced the great pre-Revolutionary mansions of New England, including many of Cambridge's Tory Row houses. Housewrights applied elaborate Renaissance detail derived from Roman antiquity at doorways, windows, and building corners. The Late Georgian or Federal period extended from about 1790 to 1820 and included the work of Boston architect Charles Bulfinch (1763–1844). Houses from this period emphasized proportion rather than applied detail, and ornament was elegant and restrained. This style persisted in Cambridge vernacular buildings as late as 1840.

EARLY GEORGIAN

The best surviving Early Georgian houses in Cambridge were built in the village in 1726–27. The General Court appropriated £1000 "for the Building and Finishing a handsome Wooden Dwelling House, Barn, Out-House … for the Reception and Accommodation of the Reverend the President of Harvard College" (Harvard College Records I, cxvii—cxviii). At least thirty-one artisans were involved in its construction; the most important were housewrights Samuel Chandler and John Hunt of Concord who began the framing in 1726 and the Coolidges of Watertown who were paid for 87 days of carpentry work. Benjamin Wadsworth, the college's ninth president, recorded in his diary that he moved into the house in November 1726, although the interior was far from finished; it was completed the following year and used by Harvard presidents until 1849.

The town's finest house when it was built and the only surviving pre-Revolutionary mansion not constructed by a Tory sympathizer, Wadsworth house clearly shows the change in architectural style from the earlier period (figure 6.5). The symmetrical five-bay facade, gambrel roof with hip dormers, placement of windows close to the eaves, and projection of window frames more than two inches from the wall are all characteristic of Early Georgian work. The eaves are boxed to form a cornice supported by small brackets, a detail repeated in William

FIGURE 6.5 Benjamin Wadsworth house, 1341 Massachusetts Avenue (1726). Photo ca. 1895.

Brattle's house the next year. The twelve-over-twelve sash are substantially larger than First Period windows, but each pane is quite small. The front clapboards are narrow and planed to a beaded edge; their curious lapping at the corner is awkward but not unique in 18th-century Middlesex County.

Like all of Cambridge's early houses, Wadsworth house has undergone many changes. The interior retains its original Georgian center-hall plan with wide stairs placed far back from the entrance, a major improvement on the cramped stairways of First Period houses (figure 6.6). Bills for repairs and carpentry in 1781 and modern paint analysis date the one-story wings and probably the entrance porch. An 1804 bill for repairing the porch may account for its thin dentil cornice, which is characteristic of the Federal period and differs from the heavy Early Georgian cornice of the original house. Shutters also date from the early 19th century, and an 1810 fireproof brick addition held the college archives.

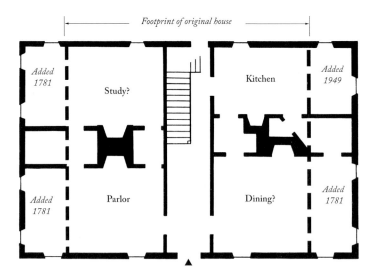

FIGURE 6.6 First floor plan, Wadsworth house. The one-story additions were made to the east and west elevations in 1781 to enlarge the public rooms.

FIGURE 6.7 William Brattle house, 42 Brattle Street (1727; vestibule ca. 1899–1905). Photo 1937.

William Brattle's 1727 house at 42 Brattle Street follows the same Early Georgian form (figure 6.7). It has a similar five-bay facade, bracketed cornice, and second floor windows tucked under the eaves, but since it is only one room deep on either side of the central stair, the gambrel roof is narrower and has a steeper pitch. The three pedimented dormers are in their original locations but may have been altered. The right parlor has original paneling, with pilasters on pedestals and ornate moldings over the mantel; these elements were intended to reproduce the rich surfaces fashionable in England and were elaborate for Cambridge in this period (figure 6.8). Only the newel and balusters of the original stair remain; the rest was rebuilt after a 1955 fire. The Cambridge Social Union acquired the building in 1889 and had Alexander Wadsworth Longfellow add the entrance vestibule. The Cambridge Center for Adult Education took over the building in 1938 and in 1962 erected a brick classroom wing, replacing parts of an earlier ell.

FIGURE 6.8 Right parlor paneling, William Brattle house. Photo 1937.

Many of Cambridge's Early Georgian houses with similar five-bay center-entrance plans and gambrel roofs are now known only through photographs. The most basic examples of this type, such as the Joseph Hicks house on South Street, were only one story high (see figure 1.25). Others varied in size from the narrow gambrels of the Abraham Hill house (ca. 1718) at 11 Garden Street and the modest Dr. William Kneeland house (ca. 1748) on Winthrop Square to the unusually wide gambrel roofs of the Hastings-Holmes house (ca. 1737) and the Prentice-Webber house (1750) in Harvard Square (figures 6.9–6.10; see also figure 1.17). The gambrel remained popular for modest houses until the 1760s, although by this date Georgian houses with hip roofs were more common, particularly along Brattle Street. The John Hicks house (1762) now at 64 John F. Kennedy Street is an unusual survivor in Harvard Square; the similar 1760 Edward Marrett house at 77 Mt. Auburn Street was moved out of Cambridge in 1926 to preserve it (see figures 6.29 and 6.31).

The best Early Georgian interiors in Old Cambridge survive at 159 and 94 Brattle Street, both begun in the 17th century. The Hooper-Lee-Nichols house was remodeled in 1716–17, 1733–42, and 1760, but the paneling seems to date primarily from the 1740s (figure 6.11). Characteristic Early Georgian features include a simple horizontal overmantel, the absence of a mantel shelf, and heavy bolection moldings (moldings that project beyond the face of a panel). Cornelius Waldo's carpenters cased the exposed 17th-century girts and summer beams, plastered the ceilings, and reduced the size of the fireplaces. The present three-run stair was probably installed in the 1740s when the house was raised to three stories, although the paneled square newel is simpler than the turned newels of the 1720s and '30s. A 2010 paint analysis indicated that the final Georgian-style changes included furring out the exterior walls in the west parlor and adding interior shutters and window seats; these occurred after Judge Lee purchased the house in 1758.

The complicated history of the Henry Vassall house at 94 Brattle Street includes 17th-century beginnings and a role in the Revolutionary War, but its chief importance for Cambridge

FIGURE 6.9 Hastings-Holmes house, Holmes Place (ca. 1737; demolished 1884). Photo ca. 1884.

FIGURE 6.10 Stairway, Hastings-Holmes house. Drawing by Lois Lilley Howe, 1884.

FIGURE 6.11 Hooper-Lee-Nichols house, 159 Brattle Street (begun 1684–89). The ca. 1890 photo shows the 18th- and 19th-century additions, original ell, and carriage barn (left).

FIGURE 6.12 Henry Vassall house, 94 Brattle Street. Partly constructed in the 17th century with 1746 and 1841 additions, the Vassall house may contain some of the oldest building fabric in the city. The west side (shown) is the oldest section and that elevation appears much as it did during the colonial period. Only three bays of the kitchen wing on the right survived the 19th century. Photo ca. 1874.

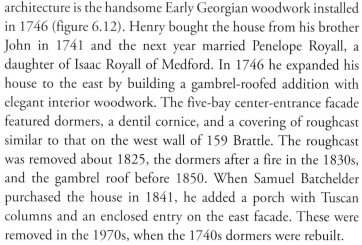

architecture is the handsome Early Georgian woodwork installed in 1746 (figure 6.12). Henry bought the house from his brother John in 1741 and the next year married Penelope Royall, a daughter of Isaac Royall of Medford. In 1746 he expanded his house to the east by building a gambrel-roofed addition with elegant interior woodwork. The five-bay center-entrance facade featured dormers, a dentil cornice, and a covering of roughcast similar to that on the west wall of 159 Brattle. The roughcast was removed about 1825, the dormers after a fire in the 1830s, and the gambrel roof before 1850. When Samuel Batchelder purchased the house in 1841, he added a porch with Tuscan columns and an enclosed entry on the east facade. These were removed in the 1970s, when the 1740s dormers were rebuilt.

Vassall and his wife moved in the most fashionable circles of the province, so it is not surprising that their 1746 interior

reflected the latest mode. Even the carpenter is known, a rare attribution for 18th-century Cambridge. The *Boston Gazette* of November 11, 1746, reported that Joseph Eayres of Boston "was just finishing Mr. Vassel's House." Much of Eayres's interior woodwork remains, although many of his window frames and sash were changed in 1825. The stair hall is spanned by an elegant paneled elliptical arch similar to one in the Royall house in Medford, and the stairs seem to be an early version of John Vassall's 1759 stairway at 105 Brattle. A second floor chamber contains the most elaborate Early Georgian woodwork in Cambridge: pilasters on paneled pedestals divide the wall into bays filled with bolection moldings and eight-panel doors (figures 6.13–6.14).

FIGURE 6.13 Stairhall, Henry Vassall house (1746, Joseph Eayres, carpenter/joiner). Photo ca. 1935.

FIGURE 6.14 Paneling in the second floor chamber, Henry Vassall house (1746, Joseph Eayres, carpenter/joiner). Photo ca. 1935.

HIGH GEORGIAN

The High Georgian period in the American colonies reflected the Palladian movement that began in England following the publication of Colen Campbell's three-volume *Vitruvius Britannicus* in 1715–25 and Andrea Palladio's *Four Books of Architecture* in 1738. Campbell was a pioneering Scottish architect whose book was a compilation of classically inspired buildings of his own design and others by Inigo Jones and Christopher Wren. Palladio was a 16th-century Italian architect who was noted for his strict use of the Classical orders and the bold scale of his austere designs. Promoted by the aristocracy after 1720, the new style found ready acceptance among architects of monumental houses in England. It was transmitted to the colonies in diluted form through architectural pattern books published in London. Some of these, such as James Gibbs's *A Book of Architecture* (1728), featured smaller buildings with monumental facades that became popular with housewrights and enlightened patrons in the colonies.

In Cambridge, as in other colonial centers during the mid-18th century, there were no professional architects and no original American architectural pattern books until Asher Benjamin's *The Country Builders Assistant* was published in Greenfield, Massachusetts, in 1797. Well-educated amateurs such as British colonial governor Francis Bernard (1712–79) and the talented English-born Peter Harrison (1716–75) brought architectural knowledge from England and provided designs for such substantial undertakings as Harvard Hall (1764) and Christ Church (1760). Such men generally drew only the elevations and were not involved in construction. That field belonged to builders who followed the plans provided or relied on pattern books and past experience, borrowing details for doorways, pilasters, etc., and grafting them onto the basic block of the Georgian house.

The most sophisticated builders at this period adopted the projecting pedimented central pavilion and monumental pilasters featured in English architectural books. Others incorporated only a single item, such as a doorway, from pattern books like Batty Langley's *The City and Country Builder's and Workman's*

Treasury of Designs, which was published in London in 1740 and 1756.[2] Aristocratic builders and clients relied on the designs of Isaac Ware or Colen Campbell, published in more expensive editions. Colonial builders often thought in terms of isolated details rather than overall composition, and pattern books provided a wealth of details and guidance on how to execute them. Many High Georgian houses in New England continued the Early Georgian symmetrical center-hall plan one or two rooms deep, with service quarters fitted into a basement or wing. A hip or gable roof replaced the earlier gambrel, and its slope became lower as the century progressed. The style and quantity of applied ornamentation became more classical and more profuse.

The most ambitious High Georgian houses in Cambridge were erected between 1759 and 1767 for a small group of wealthy Tories with strong ties to England and the West Indies. Located mostly on the north side of the Watertown road (now Brattle Street), these mansions adorned large country estates and provided an appropriate setting for the lavish aristocratic lifestyle of their owners. Five of these High Georgian houses survive and demonstrate upper-class architectural taste just before the Revolution.

The Vassall-Craigie-Longfellow house at 105 Brattle Street, now the Longfellow House-Washington's Headquarters National Historic Site, was built in 1759 by 21-year-old John Vassall, a recent Harvard graduate who had inherited his father's Cambridge properties and Jamaican sugar plantations, as well as part of his grandfather Spencer Phips's vast estate (figure 6.15; see chapter 4). Washington made it his headquarters during the Siege of Boston. Speculator Andrew Craigie bought the house in 1791 and altered it to accommodate his own extravagant lifestyle, while preserving its essential character. In 1844 Fanny Longfellow, wife of the poet Henry Wadsworth Longfellow, received the house from her father as a wedding present. Because of the couple's great respect for Washington, they made few changes, and Longfellow publicized the house through his poetry. Its twin associations with the father of the country and its most beloved poet made it an icon of 18th-century architecture that was frequently reproduced in diluted form. The Longfellows' daughter

FIGURE 6.15 Vassall-Craigie-Longfellow house, 105 Brattle Street (1759). Photo 1908.

Alice commissioned her uncle Alexander Wadsworth Longfellow to make some alterations in the Colonial Revival style. She lived in the house until her death in 1928. Careful research has guided the National Park Service in restoring the interior to the end of family occupancy in 1928 and continuing the exterior paint scheme of yellow ochre clapboards and off-white trim.

John Vassall's two-story house has a symmetrical five-bay center entrance facade with decorative detail characteristic of the High Georgian period. A shallow projecting central pavilion surmounted by a classical pediment and flanked by tall pilasters enlivens the facade and provides a dignified focus to an otherwise straightforward building. The same feature appears on East Apthorp's house at 10 Linden Street (1760) and on the college's Hollis (1762) and Harvard (1764) halls on a larger scale (see figure 10.6). In all these buildings the entrance pavilion is an applied decorative element, rather than a structural feature, since it projects only a few inches and makes no appreciable impact on the interior plan.

The entry derives from plate 32 of Batty Langley's pattern book *The City and Country Builder's and Workman's Treasury of Designs* (figures 6.16–6.17). The glass upper panels of the door provide the only light for the entrance hall; sidelights and transoms did not appear in Cambridge until after the Revolution. With most of the detail concentrated on the facade, the rest of the building was originally quite plain. Pilasters near the front corners echo those on the entrance pavilion but are not present on the side elevations. As in other contemporary Georgian houses with colossal pilasters, such as the Royall house in Medford and the Shirley-Eustis house in Roxbury, a complete entablature occurs only over the capitals; above the windows there is only a narrow frieze and modillion cornice.

Some exterior features of the Vassall house date from the 1790s, when Andrew Craigie added two wide one-story porches

FIGURE 6.17 The entrance of the Vassall-Craigie-Longfellow house differs from Langley's design only in the details of the carvings. Photo 2014.

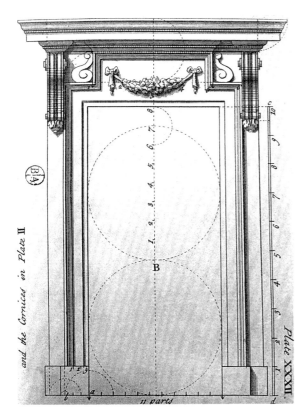

FIGURE 6.16 Doorway design by Batty Langley, 1740.

(called piazzas in the 18th century) on either side of the facade; he also added an ell, created a new entrance on the west side, and extended the first floor to make a ballroom. The windows and shutters on the main facade also probably date from Craigie's remodeling. The windows on his ell, however, have projecting frames and heavy muntins typical of the 1760s, suggesting that he may have had his carpenters move the house's original windows to the ell and install fashionable new ones on the front.

The center hall extends the depth of the house but is divided by a transverse wall to create a front and back hall, with two landings and two flights of stairs that almost mirror each other (figure 6.18). The front three-run staircase is quite elaborate, with a complicated newel consisting of opposing spirals, one inside the other, and balusters that alternate three spiral designs (figure 6.19). This High Georgian stair is considerably more graceful and finely detailed than earlier designs, such as at Wadsworth House, but it was not unlike that of John Hancock's 1737 house in Boston. The back staircase is much simpler; the balusters are all the same pattern, and the angular rise of the stair more closely resembles earlier examples, as is often true of woodwork in less prominent locations. The unusual arrangement of mirrored stairs also occurred in the Hastings-Holmes house (1737, demolished), Elmwood (1767), the Thomas Lee house (1803) and possibly the Apthorp house (1760).

The first-floor rooms have elaborate paneling on the fireplace walls. Three have overmantels composed of a single panel framed by moldings with crossettes (projections at the corners), a motif that replaced the Early Georgian raised panels and bolection moldings. The parlor paneling is particularly ornate, with elliptical arches and an overmantel flanked by broad pilasters and crowned by a broken pediment (figure 6.20). The parlor's fine marble mantelpiece may be original; marble mantelpieces were unusual but some 18th-century mansions, such as the Royall house in Medford and the Hancock house in Boston, had them. In the 1840s the Longfellows replaced three early wooden mantelpieces with marble mantels and iron grates.

East Apthorp, son of a wealthy Boston merchant, became the first minister of Christ Church in 1759, and in 1760 built a house surprisingly similar to John Vassall's that may be the work of the same designer or builder (figure 6.21; see also figure 4.270). Both share the same symmetrical five-bay composition with a projecting central pavilion and main entrance derived from Batty Langley. The interiors were equally ornate, and the newel post, balusters, and configuration of the main stair were quite similar (figures 6.22–6.23). Some have suggested that these

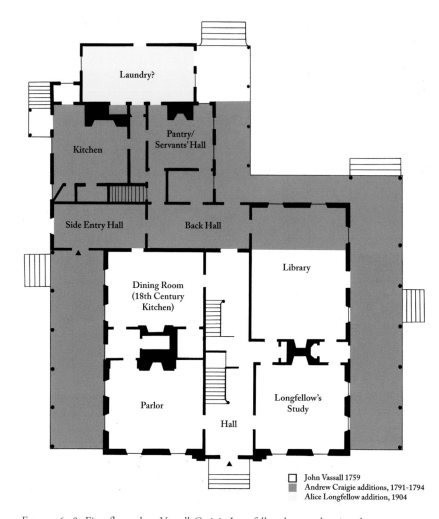

FIGURE 6.18 First floor plan, Vassall-Craigie-Longfellow house, showing dates of additions. Andrew Craigie added the side porches, back hall, and kitchen wing in 1791–94; Alice Longfellow added the laundry in 1904.

FIGURE 6.19 Entrance hall and staircase, Vassall-Craigie-Longfellow house. Photo 2011.

FIGURE 6.20 Parlor, Vassall-Craigie-Longfellow house. Photo 1972.

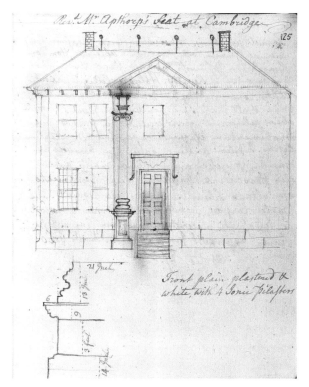

FIGURE 6.21 East Apthorp house, 10 Linden Street (1760). This sketch made by Yale president Ezra Stiles in 1761 shows the similarities with the 1759 Vassall-Craigie-Longfellow house.

FIGURE 6.22 Staircase, East Apthorp house. Photo 1885–95.

FIGURE 6.23 Parlor fireplace, East Apthorp house. Photo 1885–95.

sophisticated houses were designed by Peter Harrison (1716–75), often called America's first architect. Little is known about Harrison's training. Born and raised in England, he came to Rhode Island in 1739 on a ship commanded by his brother and made several subsequent voyages as a captain himself. After living in England from 1743 to 1745, he returned to Newport with a knowledge of shipbuilding, navigation, surveying, drawing, and architecture. Harrison practiced architecture as an avocation and in 1749 designed King's Chapel in Boston, where John Vassall worshipped. Vassall also served on the committee that retained Harrison to design Christ Church in 1759–60. A revolutionary mob sacked Harrison's home in New Haven in 1775 and burned all his drawings and records, so any connection between Harrison and the Vassall and Apthorp houses remains conjectural.

Other examples of the High Georgian include 175 Brattle Street (ca. 1764), built for Jamaican planter George Ruggles, and 33 Elmwood Avenue (1767), built for Thomas Oliver (figures 6.24–6.25). Both follow the same five-bay, four-room plan as the Vassall and Apthorp houses, but they rise a full three stories with low hip roofs and no dormers or entrance pavilions. The third floor windows are small and sit directly under the eaves, indicating the lesser importance of the attic rooms. The exterior of Elmwood in particular gives a clear idea of the goals of the Georgian builder. The central bay is articulated with columns and a second-story pediment that focuses attention on the main entrance (figure 6.26). No designer is known, but Oliver paid £140 to local housewright John Nutting for at least part of the construction. Elmwood's three-story form was popular in

FIGURE 6.24 Ruggles-Fayerweather house, 175 Brattle Street (ca. 1764). Photo ca. 1890–1910.

FIGURE 6.25 Elmwood, 33 Elmwood Avenue (1767). Photo ca. 1895–1900, showing the gardener's cottage that was attached to main house.

PLATE IV

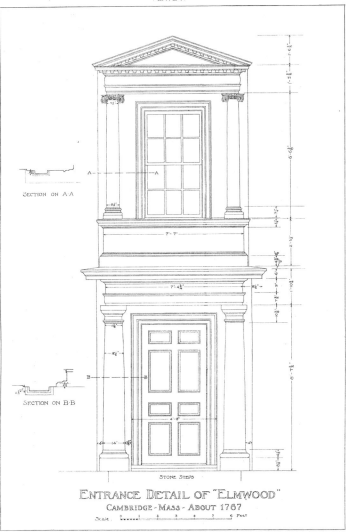

SECTION ON A·A

SECTION ON B·B

ENTRANCE DETAIL OF "ELMWOOD"
CAMBRIDGE · MASS · ABOUT 1767
Scale

FIGURE 6.26 Frontispiece, Elmwood. Measured drawing by Lois Lilley Howe, 1913.

coastal towns and had appeared in Boston as early as the 1680s; it seems to have been introduced in Cambridge in the 1740s, when the Hooper-Lee-Nichols house was raised to three stories, and it became particularly fashionable in the 1760s and early 1770s. Housewright William Saunders's house at 1 Garden Street (1820) demonstrated its continued popularity in the Federal period (see figure 6.39).

James Russell Lowell, the poet and diplomat, was born at Elmwood in 1819 and inherited the property in 1861. In 1875 Lowell described "our new veranda, which we built last fall on the north side of the house," but he seems to have made few other changes (*Letters*, II, 359). After his death in 1891, his daughter, Mabel Burnett, commissioned her cousin Lois Lilley Howe to design the stable in 1895 and an addition in 1898. In 1895 Howe was also involved in moving and attaching to the back of Elmwood a gardener's cottage which was in the path of Fresh Pond Parkway.

Cambridge's last High Georgian mansion shows how traditions lingered after the aesthetically progressive Tories decamped. Instead of keeping up with the architectural innovations of Charles Bulfinch and others in Boston, North Shore merchant Thomas Lee Jr.'s 1803 house at 153 Brattle Street was decidedly old-fashioned. The exterior has a projecting vestibule similar to the Hooper-Lee-Nichols house and a cornice similar to the simpler Read house (ca. 1771–81), discussed below; only the lighter scale of the door and window trim shows some awareness of Federal taste.

Table 6.1 includes the eight modest vernacular Georgian dwellings (1750–75) that survive in Old Cambridge. Stylistically, all were squarely aligned with the conservative building traditions of Massachusetts Bay, especially compared to the stylish Georgian mansions erected during the same period. Four have old-fashioned gambrel roofs, a feature that was still a practical solution for small lots, as it provided more usable attic space within a small footprint.

The two-story, five bay gambrel house at 30 Elmwood Avenue (ca. 1757) was built on Russell Street in North Cambridge for Daniel Watson, a prosperous farmer who served in

TABLE 6.1 PRE-1800 HOUSES

Original owner/builder/current location	Date	Original location/date moved
1. William Adams, 94 Brattle Street	1637–38	
2. Samuel Cooper, 21 Linnaean Street	1681–82	
3. Richard Hooper, 159 Brattle Street	1684–89	
4. Jacob Hill-James Munroe, 8 Hilliard Street	1718, 1765	83 Brattle Street, 1908
5. Harvard College (Wadsworth house), 1341 Massachusetts Ave.	1726	
6. William Brattle, 42 Brattle Street	1727	
7. Ebenezer Wyeth, 36 Larch Road	ca. 1751	245 Brattle Street, 1915
8. Gideon Frost, 7 Waterhouse Street	ca. 1753	
9. Aaron Hill, 17 Brown Street	ca. 1754	99 Brattle Street, 1867
10. Daniel Watson, 30 Elmwood Avenue	ca. 1757	5 Russell Street, 1965
11. John Vassall, 105 Brattle Street	1759	
12. East Apthorp, 10 Linden Street	1760	
13. Edward Marrett, Manchester, Mass.	ca. 1760	30 Dunster Street, ca. 1870; 77 Mt. Auburn Street, 1926
14. Richard Lechmere, 149 Brattle Street	1761	145 Brattle Street, 1869
15. John Hicks, 64 Kennedy Street	1762	64 Dunster Street, 1928
16. George Ruggles, 175 Brattle Street	ca. 1764	
17. Thomas Oliver, 33 Elmwood Avenue	1767	
18. James Read, Farwell Place	ca. 1771–81	55 Brattle Street, 1969
19. Noah Wyeth, 107 Garden Street	ca. 1782	
20. Joseph S. Read, 1380 Massachusetts Ave.	ca. 1782	
21. "Hall Tavern," 20 Gray Gardens West	1798	South Duxbury, Mass., 1930

the Revolution; it was moved to this location in 1965 and very accurately restored (figure 6.27). It has a typical mid-century center-entrance plan with one room on either side of a center hall. Most of the window casings are original, and a few have original six-over-nine sash; the cornice breaking over the second-story windows seems original, but the front door and transom probably date from about 1800. The old-fashioned Early Georgian paneling is the best that has survived in an 18th-century farmhouse in Cambridge and shows how conservative architectural taste was at this level of building (figure 6.28). The second floor chambers have similar but somewhat simpler paneling on the fireplace walls. The turned newels and balusters of the stairway resemble those of the Wadsworth house thirty years earlier, although the placement of the stairs at the back of the hall is consistent with the 1757 date. The 1965 reconstruction exposed valuable information about 18th-century construction methods. The house had the same braced framing system observed in the 17th-century Cooper-Frost-Austin house, but all the members that projected into the rooms were decoratively cased, and the summer beam was concealed within the ceiling, which by this period was always plastered. Other modest Georgian houses in Cambridge may have shared framing details with the Watson house, but none have been examined so thoroughly.

The Edward Marrett house, begun about 1760 as a combination residence and tailor shop at 30 Dunster Street, was moved to 77 Mt. Auburn Street in the 1870s and then to Manchester, Massachusetts, in 1926 (figure 6.29; see figure 1.26). The paneling and stair-hall details were transitional in style but surprisingly elaborate for an artisan's house; the raised panels and bolection moldings in a parlor were Early Georgian, and the crossetted overmantel and dentil cornice in the southwest chamber were later Georgian in style (figure 6.30). The John Hicks house was built in 1762 on a Dunster Street lot little wider than the house itself (figure 6.31; see figure 3.10). Hicks, a carpenter, was one of three Cambridge minutemen killed by the British in North Cambridge during their retreat from Lexington and Concord on April 19, 1775. Erected three years after the Longfellow house, it had

FIGURE 6.27 Daniel Watson house, 30 Elmwood Avenue (ca. 1757), after it was moved from 5 Russell Street in 1965 and restored. Photo ca. 1967.

FIGURE 6.28 East parlor paneling, Daniel Watson house, before restoration. The paneling and shell cupboard are Early Georgian in design; the use of bolection moldings was old-fashioned in 1757. Photo 1964.

FIGURE 6.29 Edward Marrett house, 77 Mt. Auburn Street (ca. 1760). The house was moved from 30 Dunster Street to this location in 1870. In 1926 it was dismantled and moved to Manchester, Massachusetts. Photo 1926.

FIGURE 6.31 John Hicks house, 64 Dunster Street (1762). Harvard University moved the house from the corner of Winthrop and Dunster streets to 64 Kennedy Street in 1928 to become the library of Harvard's Kirkland House. Photo before 1928.

FIGURE 6.30 Southwest chamber paneling, Edward Marrett house, with crossetted overmantel and dentil cornice. Photo 1926.

an old-fashioned center-chimney plan and a cramped, three-run staircase. Some details were more up-to-date, such as a paneled fireplace wall in an upper chamber and first floor fireplace walls that were framed for lath and plaster, which was becoming fashionable by 1760. An 1802 inventory indicated that the kitchen was in the main block of the house; the ell with its large kitchen fireplace was an addition. Preserved because of its Revolutionary War connection and moved to 64 Kennedy Street in 1928, it now serves as the library for Harvard's Kirkland House.

Gable-roofed houses of this period shared some features with the gambrels. The facade of 7 Waterhouse Street had the same low eave line, causing the lower moldings of the cornice to break over the projecting window frames (figure 6.32). Begun about 1753 by blacksmith Gideon Frost, the original dwelling consisted of the left three bays of the present house, as seen in a ca. 1781 view (see figure 5.2). The right half was probably added about 1793 when Harvard College acquired it for Dr. Benjamin Waterhouse, who taught at the medical school and is best known for introducing smallpox vaccination to the United

FIGURE 6.32   Frost-Waterhouse house, 7 Waterhouse Street. Blacksmith Gideon Frost built the west (left) side ca. 1753; Harvard College added the east side ca. 1793. Dr. Benjamin Waterhouse installed the shutters in 1801, and his widow probably added the two-story entrance porch about 1848. Photo 1916.

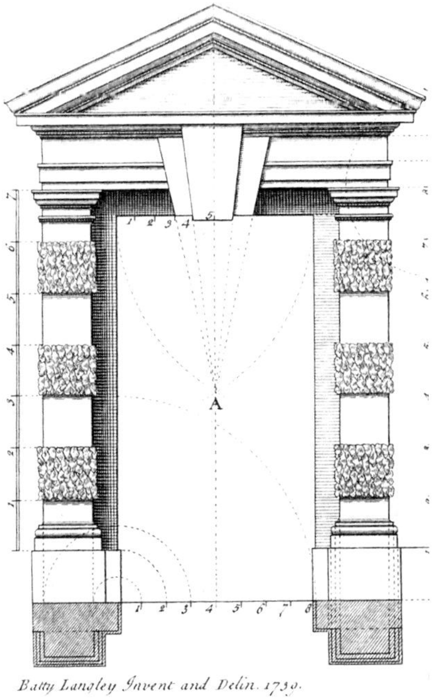

States. Waterhouse added a full set of shutters in 1801, one of the few documented dates for the introduction of this feature.[3] He purchased the house from Harvard in 1809 and occupied it until 1844. His widow, Louisa, probably added the two-story entrance porch and Greek Revival interior details about 1848.

Cambridge storekeeper James Read's house, built between 1771 and 1781 at 55 Brattle Street and moved to 15 Farwell Place in 1969, had a modest center-entrance plan with projecting window frames and an elaborate doorway. The original cornice was retained when a gable roof replaced the original hip roof in the mid-19th century, creating a pedimented effect on the gable ends. The excellent Georgian doorway with its rusticated pilasters, massive keystone, and heavy pediment was inspired by Plate 33 in Batty Langley's 1740 pattern book, demonstrating the persistence of imported English designs among colonial builders (figures 6.33–6.34).

FIGURE 6.33   Doorway design by Batty Langley, published in *The City and Country Builder's and Workman's Treasury of Designs* in 1740.

FIGURE 6.34   Doorway, James Read house (ca. 1771–81), now at 15 Farwell Place. In the early 1960s the house was occupied by the Modernist architect Carl Koch. See figure 4.106 for the house in its original location at 55 Brattle Street. Photo 1964.

FEDERAL

After the Revolutionary War, American domestic architecture was increasingly influenced by the Neoclassical movements fashionable in England and France that had been inspired by archeological discoveries at Greek and Roman sites in the late 18th century. Architect Charles Bulfinch was largely responsible for introducing the new classically based Federal style to Boston after he returned from a trip abroad in 1785–87. Bulfinch admired in particular the work of English architects and furniture designers Robert and James Adam, and their use of Neoclassical decoration and varied room plans inspired many of his subsequent projects.

The Federal style in the United States constituted a refinement and lightening of the Georgian vocabulary that had dominated pre-Revolutionary architecture. Federal exteriors had less ornamentation than their predecessors and showed more concern with geometric form and proportion. Although facades were symmetrical, interiors often deviated from the traditional Georgian center-hall plan. Decorative details were increasingly classical in derivation and delicate in scale. Reflecting advances in glass manufacture, windows and window panes in Federal buildings were generally larger than in earlier periods. Doorways had sidelights, fanlights, and projecting porches supported by classical columns, and windows were sometimes set in recessed blind arches. Hip roofs were lower, less prominent, and usually without dormers. Wood remained the material of choice in Cambridge; brick, the most common material for Federal houses in Boston and Salem, was rarely used.

The new style was slow to reach Cambridge, since many of the town's educated patrons of architecture were Tories who had departed before the war. The Embargo of 1807, the War of 1812, and the resulting economic depression further slowed building activity. The few who did erect up-to-date houses during this period were primarily wealthy merchants relocating from North Shore port towns, or gentlemen who had Boston connections and were familiar with the recent buildings of Bulfinch and Asher Benjamin. Nathaniel Ireland's house at 10 Garden Street (1806–7, now Radcliffe's Fay House), and the Larches at 22 Larch Road (1808) are among the most important survivors. The original appearance of John Phillip's 1806 house (later Shady Hill) on Beacon Street is unknown, while William Winthrop's 1818 mansion on Bow Street is known only through photographs (see figure 4.256).

Nathaniel Ireland's was the finest Federal house in Cambridge at the time of its construction and the only brick example in Old Cambridge (see figure 4.111). Built for this Boston merchant who supplied iron for ships, the house originally rose two stories with a flat roof and handsome half-round bays facing the Common and his garden. Such bays and the resulting interior oval rooms were characteristic of Federal houses in Boston, particularly those of Charles Bulfinch beginning in the 1790s, but were perhaps too advanced (or expensive) for Cambridge. No others appeared until 1844, when Oliver Hastings built his showplace at 101 Brattle Street (see figure 6.62).

No early images of Ireland's mansion survive, and the house has been changed almost beyond recognition. The main entrance faced Mason Street, but in the 1830s a subsequent owner moved the staircase and changed the entrance to the bay facing Garden Street. In 1870 a Mansard replaced the original low hip roof. Further changes took place after 1885, when Judge Samuel Fay's daughter sold it to the Society for the Collegiate Instruction of Women (see figure 7.76). In 1890 and 1892 Alice Longfellow provided funds and her cousin A.W. Longfellow Jr. drew plans to replace the Mansard with a full third story containing a skylit library; they also added a large three-story wing on the garden side and an auditorium and classroom wing toward Mason Street, bringing the house to its present configuration.

The best example of Federal design in Old Cambridge is the Larches, now at 22 Larch Road. Jonathan Hastings bought 5¼ acres of land at the west end of Brattle Street from Ebenezer Wyeth in 1801 and began to build a High Georgian house in front of the existing Wyeth farmhouse, which then became an ell. When Hastings ran into financial difficulties in 1808 he turned his unfinished house over to his creditor, wealthy Salem shipowner William Gray, who finished it as a country estate. The Federal qualities of the Larches are most apparent in a drawing made before it was moved from its original location at 245 Brattle Street in 1915 (figure 6.35). The delicate cornice resembles designs published by Asher Benjamin and Daniel Raynerd in *The American Builder's Companion* in 1806. The sidelights, graceful elliptical fanlight, and porch with fluted columns and papyrus-leaf capitals are similar to those at 15 Appian Way, built in 1801 by housewright Joseph Holmes and moved to 144 Coolidge Hill Road in 1929. The side porches were an important part of the original scheme but were removed in 1915.

In spite of the exterior changes, the first floor of the Larches remains the best Federal interior in Cambridge (figure 6.36). The great length of the entrance hall directs attention toward the graceful flight of stairs at the far end. The simplicity of this staircase and its scrolled newel contrasts with the intricate turned newels and balusters of the previous period. Door surrounds in the hall have delicate friezes of molded composition glued to the wood which, when painted, resembled intricately carved relief. The level of sophistication here compared to the second floor raises the question of how much of the house was finished when Gray acquired it. His great-granddaughter believed that Hastings had not progressed beyond the cellar hole, while her brother thought that the house had been framed. Stylistic variations suggest that Hastings may have completed the exterior and the second floor, leaving the first floor to be finished by Gray, who as a prosperous merchant probably would have wanted the most current Federal embellishments. The house Gray built in Salem a few years earlier (176½ Essex Street, demolished) and the Larches shared similar floor plans and elegant finishes, much of which seem derived directly from *The American Builder's Companion*. Many details at the Larches were part of a standard decorative vocabulary in the Federal period, but the competence with which they are carried out indicates the work of a skilled designer and craftsman.

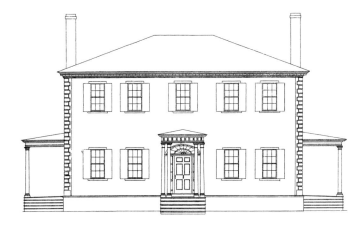

FIGURE 6.35 The Larches, 22 Larch Road (1808, formerly 245 Brattle Street). Cambridge architects Lois Lilley Howe and Constance Fuller made this measured drawing before the house was moved in 1915.

FIGURE 6.36 Stair hall, the Larches. Photo 1969.

The 1810 Federal house now at 88 Garden Street was originally built by Harvard University in its newly established botanic garden (figure 6.37; see also figure 5.85). Built for William Peck, the first head of the garden, and later the home of the distinguished botanist Asa Gray, it is the earliest known work of Ithiel Town, an architect and engineer who studied under Asher Benjamin and later achieved prominence for his Greek Revival designs. Original Federal features include the low hip roof, crisp dentil cornice, flush siding, and entrance with a fanlight and sidelights. Most of the details and molding profiles are similar to those in pattern books of the period, but the proportions are not as light as in other Federal buildings, and the corner pilasters are reminiscent of several High Georgian houses in Cambridge. Town, who later patented a wooden bridge truss that brought him a considerable fortune, practiced chiefly in New York City and New Haven, and his buildings often demonstrated his interest in engineering. The attic of his 1810 house displays an unusual method of supporting the hip roof: from a massive central "roof tree" six braces branch out to support the rafters (figure 6.38).

Most of the Federal style houses remaining in Old Cambridge are modest vernacular designs that follow a symmetrical center-entrance plan and range from one to three stories. Elizabeth Frost's two-story Federal at 26 Gray Street (1815) has a four-room plan, hip roof, and simple fanlight. More common was a narrower two-room plan seen in the three-story houses at 10 Frost Street (1807) and 1 Garden Street (1820) and the one-story cottage at 17 South Street (1826). Because this type was only one room deep, it could be adapted to a narrow lot by turning the main entrance toward the side yard, as housewright William Saunders did for his own house at 1 Garden Street (figure 6.39).

The William Frost house at 10 Frost Street has been attributed to William Saunders because of its similarities to his known houses (see figure 4.215). Built originally on Massachusetts Avenue in 1807 and moved to Frost Street in 1867, it has the characteristic Federal five-bay facade, center entrance with six-panel door and semicircular fanlight, shorter third floor

FIGURE 6.37 Botanic Garden (later Asa Gray) house (1810, Ithiel Town, architect) on its original site in the Harvard Botanic Garden. The wing on the right was added in 1848 for Gray's study. The house was moved to 88 Garden Street in 1910 to allow construction of Kittredge Hall. Photo before 1910.

FIGURE 6.38 Attic, Botanic Garden (Asa Gray) house, showing the central post and braces that support the hip roof. Photo 1973.

FIGURE 6.39 William Saunders house, 1 Garden Street (1820, William Saunders, builder). The Greek Revival entrance porch was probably added in the 1840s. Photo 2015.

FIGURE 6.40 Jacob Hill Bates house (1813, Oliver Hastings, builder) at its original location, 45 Brattle Street, on the east corner of Church Street. It was moved to 11 Hawthorn Street in 1926 to allow construction of Sage's Market. Photo 1926.

windows, and rear wall chimneys. Fixed-louver shutters and narrow clapboards with skived joints appear to be largely original.[4] The one-story porch with Doric columns was added about 1840 when the owner updated it in the popular Greek Revival style. Houses of this period were sited with the entrance facing east or south, if possible. Other examples of this orientation include 54 Brattle Street (1808), 77 Brattle Street (1821, John Chamberlin, carpenter), and 45 Brattle Street (1813) and 69 Dunster Street (1829; both Oliver Hastings, builder). The main Federal details in many of these houses are a simple elliptical fanlight and entrance surround (figure 6.40).

Late in the Federal period a side-hall plan was occasionally used, although it seems to have been rare in Old Cambridge, and no examples survive. The William Warland house at 22 Appian Way (ca. 1825), with its gable end facing the street, thin cornice moldings, and a recessed side entrance opening onto the stair hall was similar to Federal houses in East Cambridge, such as 96 Thorndike Street (1826–27; figure 6.41). Side-hall plans became ubiquitous over the next few decades in Greek Revival and Italianate houses. One built by William Saunders

at 62 Brattle Street (1834) provides an example of that transition. The narrow corner boards, absence of pilaster capitals, and outside chimneys come from the Federal period, while the flush-boarded gable treated as a pediment and the finely detailed entrance with paneled pilasters, transom, and sidelights are typical Greek Revival elements (figure 6.42).

Two distinct stylistic variations of the Federal tradition emerged in Old Cambridge in the early 1820s. In 1821 Harvard officials and faculty began building austere, broad-gabled houses on a part of Kirkland Street that became known as Professors Row. These were similar in plan to the center-entrance, hip-roofed Federal houses of the preceding period, but had broad gable fronts treated as pediments and other features typical of both Classical Revival and Greek Revival styles. In the same year Boston architect Solomon Willard introduced a more expressive bow-fronted plan with a full portico that echoed Federal practice in Boston and became the specialty of Old Cambridge builder Oliver Hastings in the 1820s and 1830s. Both variants emerged from the developing tastes of Boston's Federalist merchant class, which was then enlarging its influence on the university.

FIGURE 6.41 William Warland house, 22 Appian Way (ca. 1825; demolished 1963). Photo 1963.

FIGURE 6.42 William Saunders house, 62 Brattle Street (1834, William Saunders, builder). The Episcopal Theological School moved the Saunders house to 11 St. John's Road in 1959 to allow construction of the Loeb Drama Center. Photo 1958.

Patrick Tracy Jackson, a wealthy Boston merchant and industrialist, built the first house on Professors Row in 1820–21 for a former business associate, Stephen Higginson. Higginson was evidently a man of sophisticated tastes, as he had commissioned Charles Bulfinch to design his previous house at 87 Mount Vernon Street on Beacon Hill. He had gone bankrupt, however, during the Embargo of 1807 and through the influence of his friends had been appointed steward (chief administrative officer) of the college in 1818. His house at 7 Kirkland Street had a side entrance and broad gables with only short cornice returns, rather than a full pediment, and narrow moldings that were typical of other late Federal houses in Old Cambridge (figure 6.43). There is no evidence that Bulfinch had a hand in the design, but its form set a precedent for others on Professors Row. In 1821 Professor Levi Frisbie began a similar house next door, but faced the broad gable end toward the street (figure 6.44). Frisbie's facade featured shallow Federal blind arches in the flush-boarded gable end, a characteristic feature seen in several Bulfinch-designed brick houses on Beacon Hill.

Mathematics professor John Farrar designed a broad-gabled, center-entrance house at 21 Kirkland Street in 1828 and later updated it by adding a Greek Revival portico. John Gorham Palfrey built a similar house at the end of Divinity Avenue in 1831 when he was appointed Dexter Professor of Sacred Literature at Harvard. Here the broad front gable was treated as a pediment, evidence of the advancing influence of the Greek Revival (figure 6.45). The wide gable form persisted as late as 1849, when Professor Theophilus Parsons built a version with Italianate details at 54 Garden Street

Only one of these broad-gabled, transitional Federal/Greek Revival houses can be attributed to an architect. Joseph T. Buckingham, an influential newspaper editor in Boston, retained Asher Benjamin in 1832 to design a house at 28 Quincy Street (figure 6.46). The conservative five-bay facade with a low broad gable looked back to Frisbie's and Palfrey's houses nearby. Perhaps Buckingham wished to associate himself with the Cambridge intelligentsia, because it was a strikingly restrained design to come from Benjamin's pen. Two decades later, when "to occupy

FIGURE 6.43 Stephen Higginson house, 7 Kirkland Street (1820–21; demolished 1963). The one-story porch with four widely spaced Doric columns was probably added after 1836. Photo 1914.

FIGURE 6.44 Levi Frisbie house, 13 Kirkland Street (1822; demolished 1970). Architect Robert S. Peabody designed the curved bay at the right for his brother Reverend Francis Peabody in 1887. The Undergraduate Science Center now occupies the site. Photo 1969.

FIGURE 6.45 John Gorham Palfrey house, 50 Oxford Street (1831; moved to Hammond Street, 2002). The character of the original porch is unknown, as no drawings or photographs predate the Italianate porch and other changes Palfrey made about 1860. Photo ca. 1895.

a Greek Revival house … was to be visibly out of touch with the world of fashion and ideas," Buckingham commissioned Joseph R. Richards to modernize the residence in the popular Second Empire style (Quinan, 291; see figure 6.85).

The house erected in 1833 for Professor Charles Beck (now Harvard's Warren House) is related to the Professors Row houses but more elaborate in form (figure 6.47). The two and a half-story, broad-gabled main block of the house is flanked by lower side wings, a form derived from Palladio's 16th-century Italian country villas. This three-part plan was both more complex and more sophisticated than other Cambridge houses of the period, but suited its original commanding location on a lot that stretched from Quincy to Prescott streets. Like the Palfrey house built two years earlier, it includes both Classical Revival and Greek Revival elements. The gable on the five-bay facade is treated as a pediment, but it contains a half-round window, only a simple cornice, and no entablature. The three-bay Doric porch, the most archeologically correct part of the composition, has a full entablature with triglyphs and metopes (see figure 6.51). Sanskrit scholar Henry Warren purchased the house in 1891 but made only a few exterior alterations, including the Colonial Revival leaded fanlight and sidelights at the main entrance and quoins on the wings. His most interesting addition was the exceptional two-story enclosed buff brick porch with oriental-design Grueby tiles that H. Langford Warren, founder of the School of Architecture at Harvard, designed in 1897.

A less austere Federal variation with a double bow-fronted facade developed simultaneously with the Professors Row houses and became popular in Old Cambridge in the 1820s and 1830s. Boston architect Solomon Willard, best known as the designer of the Bunker Hill monument, created the first example in 1821, when he remodeled John Phillips's house for Professor Andrews Norton, who named it Shady Hill. Willard and his builder, Oliver Hastings, changed the principal facade to the Cambridge side and added two shallow rounded bays under a columned one-story porch. This feature may have originated with Asher Benjamin's 1808 design of 55 Beacon Street in Boston, which

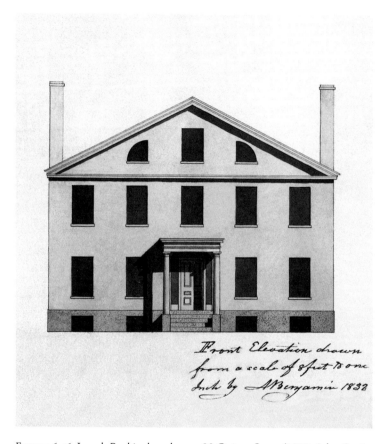

FIGURE 6.46 Joseph Buckingham house, 28 Quincy Street (1832, Asher Benjamin, architect). The house was remodeled in 1856 and demolished for the Fogg Museum in 1925 (see figure 6.85).

introduced the swell fronts that became ubiquitous on brick row houses on Beacon Hill after 1835. Willard had studied with Benjamin, and the bow-fronted form that he devised for Shady Hill became a distinctive new Federal/Greek Revival type of two-story frame house in Cambridge (figure 6.48; see figure 4.230).

Willard's only other local project was Divinity Hall, but Hastings went on to a long career as one of Cambridge's most creative housewright-designers of this period. He adopted the bow-fronted form for many of his houses. Three are still standing, and several others are known from photographs. In 1827 he built a house for himself at 63 Brattle Street (later occupied by

FIGURE 6.47 Beck-Warren house, 12 Quincy Street (1833). Professor Beck's house was moved to 1 Prescott Street in 1900 to make way for the Harvard Union (now the Barker Center).

Dr. John Nichols; now at 11 Farwell Place) with the same wide shallow bays and full portico as Shady Hill (see figure 4.109). Two years later his contract with Jacob Hill Bates for a house at 47 Brattle Street described it as similar to his own, with a "Piazza on the front 6 ft. 6 in. wide, 4 columns, swelled front to

both front rooms under piazza" (CHS, Jacob Hill Bates Papers, "Agreement to Erect a Dwelling House"). Similarly, Hastings's 1830 contract for William Hilliard's house on Holyoke Street stated that it was "to be finished on the outside as well as the one built by Mr. Hastings for Mr. Jacob H. Bates" and was to have a

FIGURE 6.48 Shady Hill, 136 Irving Street (ca. 1806; remodeled 1821, Solomon Willard, architect). This double bow-fronted facade with a one-story por-tico was the precedent for several houses by Cambridge builder Oliver Hastings. Harvard University demolished the house in 1955. Photo undated.

portico and piazza (Middlesex Deeds 300/208). His 1834 house for Professor Edward Tyrrel Channing at 16 Quincy Street had a unique arrangement of bow fronts on two elevations. The 1838 Mary Ann Fales house at 29 Follen Street belongs to the same type but has no attributed builder. None of these houses are known to have had sophisticated interior spaces such as the oval rooms in Fay House. Only the outer walls of the front parlors were bowed; measured drawings of demolished examples, such

as 8–10 Nutting Road, 16 Quincy Street, and 89 Winthrop Street, show that the bows, while quite wide, were only three or at most four feet deep (figures 6.49–6.50).

Hastings also built the First Parish Unitarian Church (designed by Isaiah Rogers) in 1832, a number of important transitional and Greek Revival houses such as 38 Kirkland Street (1839–40) in the 1830s and 1840s, and his own sophisticated Regency-style house at 101 Brattle Street (1844). In 1831 he

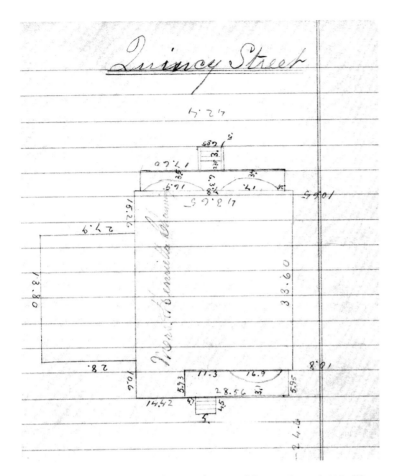

FIGURE 6.49 Edward Tyrrel Channing house, 16 Quincy Street (1832, Oliver Hastings, builder; demolished 1945). The city engineer measured the footprint of every Cambridge house beginning about 1870; dimensions are in tenths of a foot. Cambridge Engineering House Book, ca. 1870. See also figure 7.66.

FIGURE 6.50 First floor bow fronts and porch, Mary Ann Fales house, 29 Follen Street (1838). Photo 1970.

and a partner, Luther Brooks, purchased a lumber wharf in East Cambridge that became a chief source of his wealth. In the 1850s and 1860s, Hastings worked chiefly at his lumber business and limited his commissions to houses for relatives, including homes for his daughters at 23 Craigie Street (1855) and 8 Berkeley Street (1860). After his death he was remembered in the *Cambridge Chronicle* as one of the "oldest, wealthiest and most esteemed citizens" of the city (Feb. 22, 1879).

By the end of the 1830s all variations of the Federal style had run their course, and American architecture experienced a major change in perspective as the delicate ornament of the Federal period gave way to the heavier classical details of the Greek Revival. The discovery of the ancient Roman cities of Pompeii and Herculaneum had spurred interest in Roman classical architecture. New finds in Greece and illustrated books such as Stuart and Revett's *Antiquities of Athens,* a four-volume collection of their measured drawings of ancient temples published between 1762 and 1818, inspired architects and designers to adopt Greek forms for their buildings, furniture, and decoration (figure 6.51). In addition, the Greek war of independence from Turkey (1821–30) recalled for Americans their own recent struggle for freedom and found support among intellectuals in the Boston area. Coinciding with a period of tremendous growth in population in Massachusetts, the Greek Revival and its local variants dominated residential architecture in the 1830s and 1840s and seemed to resolve the country's desire for a democratic, national style.

FIGURE 6.51 Elevation of the Temple of Theseus at Athens, as published by Stuart and Revett in *The Antiquities of Athens* in 1762.

The new Greek Revival style enjoyed great popularity, although some critics disliked the indiscriminate use of Greek forms. Instructions for building in the new style filled American builders' guides and pattern books, beginning with the 1827 edition of Asher Benjamin's *The American Builder's Companion* and continuing with multiple editions of *The Practical House Carpenter* (1830), *The Practice of Architecture* (1833), and *The Builder's Guide* (1839), as well as Minard Lafever's *Modern Builder's Guide* (1833) and Edward Shaw's *Rural Architecture* (1843). Benjamin derived his information from authors like Stuart and Revett, who presented archeologically accurate images of ancient architecture, but many other pattern books appealed to popular taste and included interior and exterior details that builders combined in a variety of ways. Those without access to pattern books could copy existing houses, as surviving building contracts illustrate.

The Greek Revival style first took root in the southern and Middle Atlantic states, where William Strickland's 1818 Bank of the United States in Philadelphia provided a complete example of a temple-front building modeled on the Parthenon. The style was also particularly popular in upstate New York and Ohio. By contrast, eastern Massachusetts maintained cultural ties with England, and many of its early 19th century buildings, especially those by Charles Bulfinch, continued in the delicate Adams tradition. The new style first appeared locally in nonresidential buildings in Boston at Alexander Parris's Quincy Market (1824) and Ammi B. Young's Custom House (1837), and in Cambridge at Solomon Willard's Divinity Hall (1825) and Harvard's Dane Hall (1832, architect unknown). The specifications for Benjamin's Cambridge town hall on Norfolk Street (1832, burned 1853) called for a portico with six fluted Doric columns, entablature, and pediment on each end.

Divinity Hall was predominantly Federal but had Doric porticoes at the entrances. The first fully Greek Revival building in Old Cambridge was Dane Hall, which had a temple front and four two-story Ionic columns (see figure 10.12). This striking building seems to have had little immediate effect on residential builders, and many continued to employ Federal forms until the late 1830s. The Greek Revival became well-established in the 1840s, largely through the work of housewrights and master carpenters like Oliver Hastings and William Saunders, whose buildings set the standard for vernacular builders. Old Cambridge examples ranged from elegant temple-front houses to the simplest side-hall homes with no columns or porch. As the style gained in popularity, builders updated earlier houses by adding Greek Revival porches or columned entrance porticoes. Greek features appeared on some vernacular buildings until the Civil War.

The most ostentatious Greek Revival buildings had temple fronts like Dane Hall, with monumental two-story columns supporting pediments with full entablatures that projected beyond the body of the building and formed a deep porch. Three prominent examples were built in Old Cambridge in 1838–39, but the form does not seem to have enjoyed much popularity locally; a surviving example at 135 Western Avenue was old-fashioned when it was built in 1846.

The broad gable of Gannett House (1838), built for Boston lawyer Omen Keith, resembles that of Dane Hall (see figure 4.193). Atypically correct in its broad proportions and austere Doric capitals, its unusual width in proportion to its height recalled its antecedents on Professors Row and allowed the rooms to be generously proportioned. The Edmund Chapman house at 104 Mt. Auburn Street (1838, demolished) and the Joseph Lovering house at 38 Kirkland Street (1839) were taller in proportion and much more elaborate, with fluted Ionic columns and a wealth of ornamental detail concentrated on the flush-boarded facades (figures 6.52–6.53). All three featured the long triple-hung windows and broad entrances with pilasters and sidelights that were characteristic features of even modest Greek Revival houses. Socially, they occupied very different spaces. Chapman was a carriage builder, and his house on Eliot Square faced his workshop, while the Lovering house, built as a speculation by Oliver Hastings and Luther Brooks, faced the settled precinct of Professors Row.

FIGURE 6.52 Edmund Chapman house, 104 Mt. Auburn Street (1838; demolished 1930). Photo June 1909.

FIGURE 6.53 Joseph Lovering house, 38 Kirkland Street (1839, Oliver Hastings and Luther Brooks, builders). The second floor iron balcony is unusual for Cambridge. The exterior chimneys are not original. Photo 2009.

Between 1830 and 1845 the population of Cambridge doubled, and the demand for housing brought construction of countless vernacular Greek Revivals. Much simpler than the temple-front showplaces, these followed several standard plans. Some continued the Georgian and Federal center-entrance layout, but most adopted the side-hall plan with the gable end facing the street, a more practical arrangement dictated by the city's typically long and narrow lots. Of those with porches, most have Doric columns, some have Ionic, and less than a handful survive with variations of the Corinthian. Columns in varying lengths were standard manufactured products that began at about $3.00 each. Yankee carpenters who assembled the stock columns and capitals needed only a few moldings and some wide boards for pilasters to create "correct" Classical details without further reference to Benjamin's handbooks.

The house at 9 Follen Street that Charles Saunders (son of master carpenter William) built for Mrs. Benjamin Waterhouse in 1844 is a good example of the broadside type, with fully articulated gable pediments, corner pilasters, and a one-story porch with Doric columns (figure 6.54). The juncture of roof and facade is emphasized by a full entablature and the windows are surrounded by crossetted casings, quite different from the low cornice and crisp moldings of Federal houses. The absence of pilaster capitals is consistent with the restrained expression of the Greek Revival style in many Old Cambridge houses.

Slight modifications in the plan of 9 Follen Street break the symmetry of the four room, center-hall, Georgian plan (figure 6.55). The left parlors were divided unequally to create a smaller front reception room and a large rear parlor with a fireplace, connected by pocket doors. The interior woodwork was robust in scale, with bold moldings and shallow pedimented lintels over doors and windows. Typical of the period, the main rooms were furnished with marble mantelpieces, ranging from a beautiful black veined example in the parlor to a simpler one in the main bedroom. Less important bedrooms had wooden mantels, while third-floor rooms had only a shelf above a stove outlet. Marble mantelpieces were turned out by local stone-yards and, though

FIGURE 6.54 Louisa Waterhouse house, 9 Follen Street (1844, Charles Saunders, builder). Photo 2015.

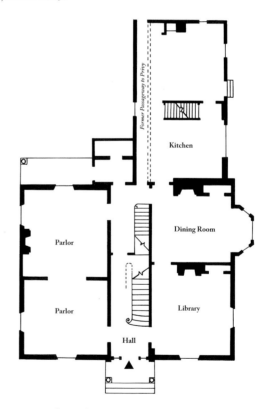

FIGURE 6.55 First floor plan, Louisa Waterhouse house.

monumental-looking, were assembled from thin slabs of pre-cut stone (see figure 5.78). The building contracts for the Greek Revival houses at 1697–1699 Cambridge Street (1844, demolished) and 1715–1717 Cambridge Street (1845) specify similar mantelpieces costing $25 each, about $800 in 2013 dollars.

As late as 1973, 9 Follen Street retained traces of a narrow interior passageway leading to a double privy at the rear of the kitchen wing. Water closets were introduced along with city water in the mid-1850s, but they were long confined to the rear of the ell, or sometimes a half-level below the kitchen in a backhouse. This location probably derived from the need to drain them into the backyard cesspool that was a feature of many Cambridge houses until the introduction of sewers in the 1890s.

Some Greek Revivals built broadside to the street featured a one-story columned porch or piazza across the facade, such as Professor Joel Parker's house at 5 Phillips Place (1847). The most striking examples of this type were four double houses known as "Richardson's Row" that Royal Richardson built at 1689–1717 Cambridge Street in 1840–45 (figure 6.56). His 1840 contract with carpenters Moses and Jedediah Ricker stated that the house at 1689–1691 Cambridge Street would be "of a like description as the house in which said Richardson now lives" except for a few variations, such as a piazza with four columns (Middlesex Deeds 392/509).[5] The contract for each subsequent double house used its neighbor as a model but also added several individual features such as marble mantelpieces and a different number of porch columns. Characteristic Greek Revival features in all the houses included one-story Doric porches with full entablatures, triple-hung windows, wide pilasters with moldings to resemble capitals, and pedimented gable ends and dormers. Only 1707–1709 and 1715–1717 Cambridge Street (1845) remain; the others were razed in 1927 and 1971.

Houses with the gable end facing the street were much more common and spanned a succession of later styles. Greek Revival examples typically had two or three bays and the main entrance at one side of the facade; a few, such as 34 Kirkland (1839) and 41 Winthrop Street (1845), had a center entrance on the broad

FIGURE 6.56 One of four double houses that comprised Richardson's Row, 1715–1717 Cambridge Street (1845, John A. Pickering and Zenas Crowell, housewrights). The paired doorways have Greek Revival transoms and sidelights, but the doors have unusual Gothic arches. Photo 2009.

FIGURE 6.57 West elevation, John Merrill house, 112 Brattle Street (1846, S.D. Brown, housewright). Photo 2009.

FIGURE 6.58 William A. Saunders house, 6 Prentiss Street, (1843–44, William A. Saunders, builder). Moved from 1735 Massachusetts Avenue in 1925. Photo 1947.

like the anthemion at the peak of the entrance pediment were often manufactured from mastic or cast iron that when painted resembled carved wooden ornament. Similar molded details were also used in some interiors; the contract for 1715–1717 Cambridge Street specified "suitable composition ornaments for the parlor" (Middlesex Deeds 463/481).

Greek Revival houses in Cambridge often had a one-story porch across the gable end. William A. Saunders built an unusual example at 6 Prentiss Street in 1843–44 on the eve of his marriage to Mary Prentiss (figure 6.58). Marking the end of his apprenticeship to his housewright father and the beginning of his independent career as a merchant, Saunders's house follows the broad-gable, center-entrance form of the Professors Row houses, but with two-story pilasters across the facade and an Ionic porch; applied mastic wreaths occur on the porch frieze, bays, and interior doorways. The only other surviving local example of a Greek Revival porch with wreaths is 125 Antrim Street, built at the same time.

side of the house that faced a side yard. The street-facing gable was treated as a Classical pediment with a heavy raking cornice and a broad horizontal shelf forming an entablature. A one-story porch supported by Doric or Ionic columns typically ran across the facade, or alternatively, along a side elevation. At 41 Winthrop, the contract called for "an Entablature on three sides and pilasters at least 18 inches with Doric caps in good style" (Middlesex Deeds 409/419).

The most ornate Greek Revival side-hall house remaining in Old Cambridge is 112 Brattle Street, which housewright Stephen D. Brown built in 1846 (figure 6.57). The gable facing Willard Street was treated as a classical pediment, and the main entrance was unusually elaborate for Old Cambridge. The corner location created a second principal facade along Brattle Street that has floor-length, triple-hung windows and a shallow one-story porch with a full entablature and Doric columns. Ornaments

FIGURE 6.59 John Warland house, 69 Brattle Street (1838), now the Radcliffe Institute's Putnam House. Photo ca. 1938.

The Lucy Willard house at 78 Mt. Auburn Street (1839–40), a more typical gable end example, is also attributed to William Saunders, who cited it in later building contracts. The house has all the standard elements: three-bay side-hall facade with side lights, transom, and pilasters around the entrance, a pedimented gable, corner pilasters with capitals, and a full entablature. The one-story porch originally had four fluted Doric columns similar to those on the side-hall Greek Revival at 69 Brattle Street built in the same year (figure 6.59). Another side-hall house at 130 Mt. Auburn Street is a 1984 replica of 8 Ellery Street (1841).

The simplest form of side-hall Greek Revival house in Old Cambridge had no porch; the pedimented gable end and pilastered entrance surround were the only Greek Revival references. William Saunders built an early version at 62 Brattle Street in 1834 (see figure 6.42). The carpenter Charles Hunnewell built a similar one for himself at 134 Mt. Auburn Street (1841). The back-to-back double house at 9–11 Mt. Auburn Street, built in 1843 for painters James and Joshua Thayer, was a variant.

Columned porches became an important symbol of modernity as the Greek Revival became universally popular in the 1840s. Many owners of older houses updated them by adding porches with Greek columns, as at 1 Garden Street and 10 Frost Street, even if they left other features alone. Samuel Batchelder added a full portico with Tuscan columns to the Georgian style Henry Vassall house at 94 Brattle Street, and Cornelius Felton added a handsome Doric porch to the Federal style Dana-Palmer house (1822), now on Quincy Street (see figures 4.18 and 4.244). Even the simplest Federal workers' cottages were sometimes modernized with a Greek Revival entrance.

REGENCY

A few houses built in Old Cambridge during the 1830s and '40s followed a form of the Classical Revival style that was related to the English Regency period of the early 1800s. These flush-boarded houses had cube-like massing, low hip roofs, and broad pilasters without capitals repeated across the facade.

FIGURE 6.60 Treadwell-Sparks house, 48 Quincy Street (1838, William Saunders, builder). Harvard moved the house to 21 Kirkland Street in 1968 to build Gund Hall. Photo ca. 1890.

This conservative, academic style was found primarily in the Boston area but also occasionally along the Maine coast. James O'Gorman speculates that Isaiah Rogers may have initiated this house type in 1833 with his design for Captain Robert Forbes's house in Milton. The earliest Cambridge example is the house that William Saunders built for Daniel Treadwell in 1838, now Harvard's Sparks House (figure 6.60). Treadwell, an engineer whose inventions equipped the ropewalk at the Charlestown Navy Yard, was appointed Rumford Professor at Harvard in 1834 and supervised construction of Gore Hall in 1837. A trip to England in 1835 to gather material for his lectures may have influenced his choice of the Regency style for his new house. The wide pilasters form a subtle rhythm with the flush boarding of the walls but were not intended to be perceived as Greek columns. A deeply recessed entrance and a low hip roof with four tall chimneys completed the composition, which was originally painted tan to resemble stone. While fewer than a dozen of these broad-pilastered houses were built in Cambridge, Treadwell was responsible for two of them. Treadwell sold his house in 1847 to

FIGURE 6.61 Joseph Worcester house, 121 Brattle Street (1843). Photo 2014.

FIGURE 6.62 Oliver Hastings house, 101 Brattle Street (1844, Oliver Hastings, builder-designer). Photo 2015.

Nathaniel Silsbee whose daughter, Mary, was married to Jared Sparks. When Sparks became president of Harvard in 1849, Silsbee passed it to them, and Treadwell hired Saunders to build a similar house at 29 Concord Avenue (see figure 4.122).

Lexicographer Joseph Worcester's Regency house at 121 Brattle Street (1843) included some Greek Revival features but also anticipated the emerging Italianate style (figure 6.61). The broad-pilastered house with flush boarding on the facade has columned side porches and a gable roof instead of the usual hip. The projecting roof without a strong cornice on the gable end precludes any suggestion of a Greek pediment above the pilasters. The innovative T-shaped plan resembles that of Isaac Melvin's 1842 house at 19 Centre Street, but that building's deep pediments and profusion of Greek Revival detail create a very different effect. Like the Treadwell-Sparks house, 121 Brattle was originally painted a monochromatic tan to resemble stone.

Oliver Hastings's own house at 101 Brattle Street (1844) challenged the austere principles of the Regency style (figure 6.62). Set monumentally on a terraced rise, his stately composition maintained the geometric clarity of the standard symmetrical broad-pilastered square facade but added a projecting elliptical bay supported by finely detailed fluted columns that became the focal point of the design.[6] The Corinthian capitals are patterned after those of the Tower of the Winds, which had been illustrated in *Antiquities of Athens* and became a popular choice for elegant houses in the 1830s and '40s. Horizontal flush boarding of the walls and vertical flush boarding of the pilasters create the appearance of smooth stone rather than wood. Reverend (later Bishop) William Lawrence purchased the house in 1887 and the next year hired Peabody & Stearns to make additions and build a stable. Side wings were added in 1892, when the entrance was moved from the bay to the east side. The interior was extensively altered in 1964 to create apartments for the Episcopal Divinity School, but the exterior, restored by Lesley University in 2011 and painted the original stone color in 2011, remains an unusually fine example of the Regency style.

Many of the same features, including cast-iron balconies, elaborate capitals, and fluted columns, once ornamented another high-style example at 127 Mt. Auburn on the west corner of

FIGURE 6.63 James Munroe Jr. house, 127 Mt. Auburn Street (1845, William Hovey, architect). The Mansard roof and brackets were added ca. 1868. The entrance columns with acanthus capitals were removed in the 1960s. Photo ca. 1950.

FIGURE 6.64 Adam Cottrell house, 18 Story Street (1851; demolished 1953). Photo 1947.

Story Street (figure 6.63). Designed in 1845 by architect William Hovey for James Munroe Jr., a Harvard Square bookseller, the three-bay, broad-pilastered house resembled the 1838 Treadwell-Sparks house until a Mansard roof and brackets were added in 1868. The elegant recessed entrance had two fluted columns *in antis* and Temple of the Winds capitals surmounted by wreaths. Inside, the trim was solidly Greek Revival with heavy woodwork and acanthus designs; a black marble mantel in the right drawing room resembled one in the Sparks house.

A more modest 1851 Regency house on the other side of Story Street also faced Mt. Auburn; it had a pedimented gable, deep projecting cornices, and wide pilasters on the flush-boarded facade, but an Italianate bracketed hood over the main entrance (figure 6.64). While several later Regency houses, such as 17 Hilliard Street (1855), also display transitional features, 170 Brattle Street, built in 1852 by Oliver Hastings and moved from 2 Phillips Place in 1965, maintained the broad pilasters, flush boarding, minimal window trim, and low hip roof of the earliest examples.

MID-CENTURY ROMANTICISM

During the middle decades of the 19th century far-reaching changes took place in American residential design as a restless eclecticism replaced the unity of style that had dominated the preceding Georgian, Federal, and Greek Revival periods. Influenced by the Picturesque movement in England, which advocated naturalism in relating buildings to their landscapes, builders embraced a variety of romantic revival styles in reaction to the classical ideals of the Greek Revival. New American pattern books appealed directly to homeowners with discussions of the theory of Romanticism and the philosophy of styles. These books featured plans, elevations, and perspective sketches of houses in naturalistic landscape settings, rather than the technical content and precise drawings of classical orders found in earlier books intended for builders. Alexander Jackson Davis, a successful architect and dedicated romantic, published the earliest, *Rural Residences,* in 1837 "with a view to the improvement of American country architecture" (frontispiece). Landscape architect Andrew Jackson Downing's *Cottage Residences* (1842) and *The Architecture of Country Houses* (1850) were among the most popular, setting the standard for picturesque, asymmetrical design and introducing a variety of styles meant to harmonize with the landscape. Downing wrote in *Cottage Residences* that "the pure Grecian style was not intended, and is not suitable for domestic purposes," but that "the Rural Gothic style, characterized mainly by pointed gables, and the Italian, by projecting roofs, balconies, and terraces, are much the most beautiful modes for our country residences [and the most] harmonious with nature" (21, 23). Downing's books were reprinted for decades, and his influence as an arbiter of taste continued long after his untimely death in 1852.

Picturesque in appearance, irregular in outline, and asymmetrical in plan, Gothic and Italianate designs appealed to owners and builders in suburban Cambridge at the same time that a continual rise in the city's population created increased demand for housing. By 1860 the population of Cambridge reached 26,060, and the breakup of former estates created new streets ready to be filled with houses.

GOTHIC REVIVAL

The most romantic of the picturesque styles and the one that first attracted American architects and builders was the Gothic Revival. Although Gothic motifs had been incorporated in English residences since Horace Walpole's Strawberry Hill (1749–76), the style first appeared in the United States in churches and was not widely adopted for houses until well into the 19th century.

Interest in Gothic was inspired by Sir Walter Scott's Waverly novels, which captured the American imagination in the 1820s, and then by the pattern books that gave these ideas form. Davis's *Rural Residences* (1837) was the first to present plans of Gothic Revival houses for American builders. Espousing a picturesque aesthetic, Davis thought that the irregularity and variety of decoration of Gothic architecture were particularly well suited to the rugged American landscape. Andrew Jackson Downing's books elaborated on Davis's philosophies and continued to promote the Gothic Revival among American homeowners.

Based on the English aesthetic ideal of the picturesque rather than a real understanding of the prototypes, the first attempts at Gothic in this country were not much more than facades decorated with fanciful medieval forms and pointed arches. The irregular silhouettes, steep roofs, multiple dormers, pointed windows, and profusion of decorative bargeboards of these early examples reflected a growing taste for ornamentation but with little regard for archeological or structural correctness. Later in the century, the works of British architects and designers such as Pugin, Ruskin, and Butterfield helped American builders produce more correct interpretations; Old Cambridge examples that postdate the Civil War are described in a following section.

The earliest Gothic Revival buildings in Cambridge were the First Parish Church (1833; see figure 7.5) and Harvard's Gore Hall (1838; see figure 10.13). Gothic Revival houses began to

FIGURE 6.65 James Hunnewell house, 6 Ash Street Place (1846, Peter Nye and George W. Marston, builders). The finials and jig-sawn bargeboards shown in this ca. 1860 photo have been removed, leaving only the open brackets at the entrance.

appear in the 1840s, after the publication of *Cottage Residences,* but the style never enjoyed widespread popularity here. Only a few have been identified, and most of those have been razed or, like James Hunnewell's 1846 cottage at 6 Ash Street Place, have lost most of their Gothic trim (figure 6.65). The best surviving example is the wooden cottage at 85 Brattle Street put up in 1847 by Michael Norton, a mason and builder (figure 6.66). The design is far more sophisticated than other Cambridge examples and can be traced to New Haven architect Henry Austin's "Villa in the Cottage Style" published in the 1847 edition of Chester Hills's *The Builder's Guide* (figure 6.67). Few Cambridge examples illustrate the use of pattern books as clearly as this house.

Norton's interpretation of Austin's design has a slightly asymmetrical cross-gable plan with a prominent center gable and a tall bay window projecting from the main facade. Heavy projecting L-shaped moldings over the windows and doors follow

FIGURE 6.66 Michael Norton house, 85 Brattle Street (1847, Michael Norton, mason-builder). Photo 1968.

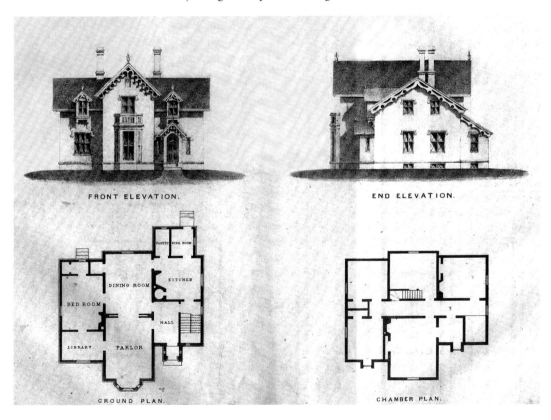

FIGURE 6.67 "Villa in the Cottage Style," (1847, Henry Austin, architect). Austin's design clearly guided Norton when he built 85 Brattle Street.

Gothic stone profiles, and a characteristic trefoil motif appears in the gable window and the balustrade of the bay window. More restrained than many New Haven buildings of the period, the composition lacks pointed arches, pinnacles, and decorative bargeboards (or none survive). Although built entirely of wood, the flush siding is scored to resemble ashlar masonry, and the details are derived from masonry precedents. The original monochromatic paint was probably dusted with sand to simulate the texture of stone, as had been done at the First Parish Church.

While the exterior of 85 Brattle is consistently Gothic, the interior trim and moldings are Greek Revival. The parlors contain stock marble mantels, and the spiral stair employs the familiar scroll newel and simple balusters of that period (figure 6.68). This discrepancy reflects the growing eclecticism of American taste at mid-century and the conservatism of Cambridge builders. Comparable mantles, a spiral stairway, and Greek Revival moldings also define the interior of the cottage at 7 Dana Street

FIGURE 6.69 James Walker house, 25 Quincy Street (1844, Benjamin C. Babbitt, builder). Harvard moved the house twice, to Divinity Avenue in 1911 to clear the site for Emerson Hall and again in 1929 for the Biological Laboratories. It was razed in 1952 for the biology department greenhouses. Photo ca. 1938.

(1841) in Mid Cambridge, whose unusual exterior combines both Greek and Gothic Revival features.

Cambridge's largest and most inventive Gothic Revival houses have all been lost. Harvard moved President James Walker's 1844 house from 25 Quincy Street to Divinity Avenue in 1911 and demolished it in 1952 (figure 6.69). A T-shaped cottage erected for Samuel Batchelder in 1847 on the site of Mifflin Place had a pastiche of applied detail, including corner porches with battlements and pointed gable posts, trefoil and lancet windows, tall finials, and curving bargeboards; it was razed in 1971 (figure 6.70). The house that Charles C. Little built at 64 Highland Street (1860) was one of the last in this style and came down in 1963 (see figure 4.64).

FIGURE 6.68 Spiral staircase, Michael Norton house. Photo 1973.

FIGURE 6.70 Samuel Batchelder cottage, 117 Mt. Auburn Street (1847). Converted to a tenement in 1889, the house was demolished in 1971. Photo ca. 1870.

BRACKETED-ITALIANATE

The Italianate style enjoyed wide currency from the late 1840s until the early 1870s. Irregular in massing and replete with porches, bay windows, and a wide range of architectural decoration, Italianate houses were championed by Downing and others for their picturesque naturalism. The most complete expression, the asymmetrical Tuscan villa, was based on early 19th century English country houses inspired by Italian prototypes, but full-blown examples were rare in Cambridge. Local builders more commonly applied Italianate elements to the familiar gable-roofed, three-bay, side-hall plan house carried over from the preceding period. These modest Italianate houses featured deep overhanging eaves and door hoods supported by ornamental brackets, one or more arched windows, paneled pilasters, and bracketed porches. Some Italianates in Cambridge followed an L- or T-shaped plan with a gable roof, a square plan with a low hip roof, or a rectangular plan with a projecting center gable; a few of these less common examples can be traced to builders from other parts of the country.

Italianate houses tended to have more varied silhouettes and steeper roofs than Greek Revivals. Quoins, corner boards with stout three-quarter-round moldings, and one-story porches with bevel-edged square posts replaced the pilasters, capitals, and columned porches of the Greek Revival. In place of the three-part Greek entablature, Italianate designers used heavy projecting cornices, usually supported by brackets and with only short returns at the eaves. Fenestration was more varied, and arched or round-headed windows were often grouped in pairs or triplets, particularly on gable ends. Technological advances allowed production of larger sizes of glass, so two-over-two sash typically replaced the six-over-six windows of earlier periods.

The most characteristic element of the Italianate was the ubiquitous wooden bracket, made possible by the 19th-century development of jigsaws and lathes that allowed inexpensive production in almost unlimited quantity and variation. While the most common placement was along the main cornice, singly

or in pairs, larger brackets supported hoods over doorways and balconies, and smaller ones appeared under window caps and sills. Their adaptability and low cost appealed to American housewrights, who sometimes embellished their designs with extraordinary numbers of them. Some of Cambridge's most sophisticated Italianate houses omitted brackets entirely, but in simple vernacular buildings the bracket was often the design's most distinctive feature; these houses are termed Bracketed-Italianate or just Bracketed.

Downing considered appropriate paint colors a subject "of very great importance in domestic architecture." He abhorred white and advocated painting picturesque houses in mellow stone or earth tones to harmonize with their natural settings, with the trim several shades lighter or darker than the body. His *Cottage Residences* included a color card with shades of gray and "drab" or "fawn" (warm yellow ochre) that he considered "highly suitable for the exterior of cottages and villas"(15). This marked the first time that an American pattern book presented actual color samples instead of just descriptions.

The earliest Italianate houses in Old Cambridge date from the late 1840s and early 1850s, but the transition occurred gradually and unevenly. Some houses were predominantly Greek Revival with a few Italianate features, while others retained only a few elements of the older style. An unusual example at 15 Everett Street (1849) had an Italianate cross-shaped plan and octagonal cupola, with narrow porches and gable ends dripping with Gothic ornaments. The double house at 42–44 Avon Street, also built in 1849, was predominately Italianate with heavy paired brackets and an unusual bracketed porch, but the entrance surrounds were Greek Revival (figure 6.71). The proportions of 11 Fayerweather Street (1850–51), with a one-story porch, wide corner boards, and floor-length windows facing south toward the river, were Greek Revival, but the deep overhanging eaves, bracketed window caps, arched gable windows, and square porch posts all belonged to the Italianate (figure 6.72). At 27–29 Shepard Street (1852–53) the wide porch with heavy Doric columns sheltered a double Greek Revival doorway, but the broad pilasters

FIGURE 6.71 Ezra Braybrook house, 42–44 Avon Street (1849). Photo 1947.

FIGURE 6.72 John B. Dana house, 11 Fayerweather Street (1850–51). Photo 1900, before a remodeling by Lois Lilley Howe eliminated many original features, including the porch.

supporting a broken entablature, the cross gable, and the arched and oculus windows were Italianate. Even in the mid-1850s a double house like 156–158 Mt. Auburn Street (1856) could have an Italianate projecting center entrance pavilion and arched windows but retain Greek Revival entrances and entablature. Vernacular architecture in this period was becoming a free-for-all, and the wide availability of disparate styles and components freed housewrights to test the market by exercising their imaginations.

Italianate and Bracketed houses are located throughout Old Cambridge, but Berkeley Street boasts a particularly fine collection, including the city's only example of an "Italian Villa." Berkeley was laid out in 1851 and 1852, and by 1857 had eight Italianate houses with four more nearby on Craigie Street. Three of the earliest were by known architects and builders and showed the versatility of the style; all employed complex plans with multiple gables to create picturesque silhouettes enlivened by brackets, porches, and bay windows.

The first two houses on Berkeley Street both went up in 1851. Boston architect Hammatt Billlings designed 4 Berkeley for Richard Henry Dana Jr., author of *Two Years Before the Mast*. Set on a corner lot, Dana's house had tall six-over-nine windows overlooking a spacious lawn (figure 6.73). Although entered from Berkeley Street through an unusual porch with chamfered posts and circular struts, the house was also meant to be seen from Phillips Place, and the floor-length window on that facade was roofed and trimmed like an entrance porch. An 1880s side porch with turned columns and a 1900 ell reduced the original focus on that facade. Across the street, Calvin Ryder designed 5 Berkeley for land developer Jonas Wyeth 2nd (figure 6.74). This early work by Ryder, who practiced extensively in Maine as well as in the Boston area, had an asymmetrical T-shaped plan with paired corner porches and a profusion of brackets, window shapes, and porch trim that varied the facade; the east porch held the original entrance.

Despite differences in external detail and massing, the interiors of these 1850s Italianates resembled those of their Greek Revival predecessors. Door frames in the formal downstairs rooms at 6

FIGURE 6.73 Richard Henry Dana Jr. house, 4 Berkeley Street (1851, Hammatt Billings, architect). Although not the first Italianate example in Cambridge, it was perhaps the most influential because of Dana's status. Photo ca. 1880.

Berkeley (1853, Moses and Jedediah Ricker, builders) employed familiar crossettes, while the newel post of the main stairway had the potbellied profile found in late Greek Revival residences. Fireplaces had stock marble mantels, although with arched openings fitted with coal grates that came into use about 1850. Rooms became loftier in proportion once furnaces became common in the 1850s, and the plaster cornices and ceiling medallions in principal rooms were heavy and richly detailed. Hardwood floors were often patterned and polychromatic, as in 6 Berkeley Street.

The city's only known towered Tuscan villa was erected at 15 Berkeley Street in 1863, a decade after its Italianate neighbors (figure 6.75; see also figure 7.57). Built for Lyman Williston, who ran a girls' school there, the house had a generous lot that originally stretched from Berkeley Street to Concord Avenue and created a picturesque setting now hard to imagine in this neighborhood. It stood on a raised mound and was approached

FIGURE 6.74 Wyeth-Allen house, 5 Berkeley Street (1851, Calvin Ryder, architect). Wyeth's house, constructed at the same time as Dana's across the street, shows how two skilled architects adapted a common architectural vocabulary. Photo 2014.

FIGURE 6.75 Lyman Williston house, 15 Berkeley Street (1863). Photo 2014.

by curving drives from both streets, increasing its grandeur and protecting it from periodic flooding from an old watercourse nearby. The asymmetrical composition with wide overhanging bracketed eaves, tall arched windows, elaborate door and window surrounds, and prominent square tower made it a textbook example of the form advocated by Downing. The flush board siding was intended to resemble smooth masonry. The richly appointed interior featured high ceilings, stenciled walls, glass-fronted walnut bookcases, and a variety of marble fireplaces. The main staircase rose three stories from a paneled, six-sided newel post on the ground floor to an unusual circular etched glass laylight in the attic floor. A meticulous restoration earned the owners a Grand Prize from the National Trust for Historic Preservation in 1993.

Few of the city's Italianate houses were this elaborate. One variant was the three-bay center-entrance house with projecting center gable, deep bracketed eaves, and applied ornament that recalled the "Cottage Villa in the Bracketed Mode" in Downing's *Cottage Residences,* first published in 1842. Architects Isaac Melvin and Isaiah Young designed 146 Brattle Street in 1850 for Gardiner Greene Hubbard on the extensive estate he had purchased the year before. His two-and-a-half-story house had a characteristic bracketed center gable, as well as bracketed side gables, oculus and arched windows, and a porch with chamfered posts and lavish decoration across the front (figure 6.76). Surviving examples from the 1850s include 21 Berkeley Street (1855), 25 Craigie Street, and 156–158 Mt. Auburn Street (both 1856). At 25 Craigie Street, built for hardware merchant Isaac Danforth in 1856, builder K.W. Baker of Winchester created an elaborately detailed central bay set off by bracketed pilasters and a profusion of round-arched Italianate motifs in the porch (figure 6.77). In 1901 architect Lois Lilley Howe removed most of the trim and substituted flush siding, broad pilasters, and a classical porch that recall an earlier period. Only a few surviving windows on the Buckingham Street side show the robustness of the original Italianate design.

FIGURE 6.76 Gardiner Greene Hubbard house, 146 Brattle Street (1850, Melvin & Young, architects; demolished 1939). Photo ca. 1860.

FIGURE 6.77 Isaac Danforth house, 25 Craigie Street (1856, K.W. Baker, builder). Photo 1901, before alterations by Lois Lilley Howe.

Related in form but far more sophisticated was William P. Winchester's monumental 1848–49 brick and stone house on Coolidge Avenue (then in Watertown) that Longfellow termed "Palazzo Winchester" for its references to the Italian Renaissance (Paterson I, 437; figure 6.78; see also figure 4.102). The earliest known residential design by Boston architect Arthur Gilman (1821–82), it featured a projecting central bay with a pediment and a columned entrance porch, bracketed and pedimented window moldings, heavy quoins and a belt course; an elaborate cornice, frieze, and balustrade crowned the composition. Although patterned on an urban palazzo, it was used only as a summer residence or country retreat, as Winchester continued to live in Boston. Gilman's training is unknown, but he was listed in the Boston Directory as an architect from 1843 until he moved to New York in 1867. Known in the 1840s for a series of articles on the state of American architecture in the *North American Review* (1843–44) and twelve lectures on architecture at the Lowell Institute (1844–45), he went on to design the street layout for Boston's Back Bay (1856), the Arlington Street Church (1860), and Boston City Hall (1862–65) with his associate, Gridley Bryant. He did no other known buildings in Cambridge. Winchester died in 1850, and his estate later became part of Cambridge Cemetery, which demolished the house in 1896.

Bangor housewrights Ivory Estes and Joseph Littlefield offered a different Italianate model in 1855–57. Their three-bay, center-entrance houses at 27 and 37 Cogswell Avenue, 46 and 48 Trowbridge Street, and 41 Sacramento Street had low hip roofs, very deep eaves, a wide dentil frieze, and heavy paired brackets with turned drops (see figure 4.207). The two-bay houses with wide overhanging eaves and complicated brackets at 18 and 20 Wendell Street were a plainer variation built in 1856 by real estate dealer James Tamplin.

Many Old Cambridge Italianates were considerably simpler and are better characterized as simply Bracketed in style. These standardized, side-hall plan, gable-end houses, such as 32 and 38 Avon Street (1854–55), both with flush-boarded facades, had bracketed cornices and door hoods but few other period details.

Figure 6.78 William P. Winchester house, Coolidge Avenue overlooking the Charles River (1848–49, Arthur Gilman, architect). The City of Cambridge demolished the house in 1896, and the site is now part of Cambridge Cemetery. Photo ca. 1890.

So persistent was the style that it was used in Old Cambridge as long as two decades after the height of its popularity. Late examples include 153 Mt. Auburn Street (1874), with a center gable, corner quoins, and flush boarding scored to resemble ashlar and the 1871 L-shaped houses at 24 and 32 Avon Hill Street. Amos Frothingham, a Boston bank executive who lived at 338 Harvard Street, seems to have patterned his 1877 rental house at 4 Walnut Avenue after an Italianate that fellow banker Caleb Warner had put up at 336 Harvard Street almost twenty years earlier. Among the last examples were three bracketed houses at 9–11, 10, and 15 Humboldt Street that Sumner Brooks built as rentals in 1882 and 1883.

ACADEMIC STYLE

The emergence of architecture as a distinct profession and its practitioners' increasing concern for historical correctness were reflected in several formal houses constructed in Old Cambridge in the 1840s and 1850s. Architectural historian Bainbridge Bunting characterized the Academic style as symmetrical and rational, drawing ornament from historical sources and using it in a disciplined way to accent areas of critical architectural importance. This approach was not new, but rather a continuous current in English architecture since Inigo Jones and Christopher Wren. It was an integral element in many Georgian and Federal buildings and was evident in Old Cambridge in the 1820s and '30s houses at Professors Row, the Treadwell-Sparks house of 1838, and William Winchester's mansion of 1848–49. The Academic movement was generally overshadowed by romantic revivals during the 1830s and 1840s, but it enjoyed a resurgence in Boston and Cambridge in the 1850s.

The leading Academic designer in Cambridge was Henry Greenough (1807–83), a gentleman architect who grew up in Jamaica Plain in an artistic family; his brothers included the sculptors Horatio and Richard Greenough. After withdrawing from Harvard in 1826, Henry worked in his father's real estate business and supplied designs for his buildings. Nothing is known of his training, but his background was quite different from the experiences of builder-designers, such as Oliver Hastings, William Saunders, Isaac Cutler, and Isaac Melvin who had been brought up in the building trades since boyhood.

Apparently working with artist Washington Allston, Greenough designed his first known building in Cambridge, the Shepard Congregational Society church at Mt. Auburn and Holyoke streets, at age 22 (see figure 7.14). After construction began in 1830, he joined Horatio in Florence, where he studied painting until 1833. On his return he managed the family business until his father's death in 1836. A talented dilettante, Greenough designed seven houses in Cambridge between 1844 and 1856 while also spending long periods in Europe; he was

fortunate to have eleven siblings to provide him with commissions. He also designed the Cambridge Athenaeum in Cambridgeport in 1851 and Harvard's Museum of Comparative Zoology in collaboration with George Snell in 1859. Greenough was one of the first architects in the Boston area to work in the fashionable Second Empire or Mansard style, and the houses he designed in the 1850s were the first of this type in Cambridge.

The dignified, hip-roofed house that Greenough designed for his mother at 42 Quincy Street in 1844 was a square, three-bay block with flush-boarding and quoins at all four corners (figure 6.79). It had balustraded balconies, deep pedimented window hoods, and elaborate Italianate canopies with round arches and pendants ornamenting the front entrance and long side windows. A contemporary described the Greek Revival interior as spacious and lofty, with parlors "well suited to the fine copies of large Italian pictures which hung on the walls" (Farlow, CHS Proc. 18, 33). Greenough's 1847 house for Charles H. Davis at

FIGURE 6.79 Mrs. David Greenough house, 42 Quincy Street (1844, Henry Greenough, architect; demolished 1968). Photo ca. 1910.

38 Quincy Street had unusual bargeboards, window trim, and a porch with clustered colonnettes (see figure 4.249). He may also have designed the 1848 house at 58 Garden Street for his Harvard classmate, Epes Dixwell (see figure 4.121).

Most of Greenough's buildings have been demolished, including all of those on Quincy Street and his own 1855 house at 1737 Cambridge Street (see figure 4.252). The most important survivor is 27 Craigie Street, built in 1854 for Professor Arnold Guyot (figure 6.80). Here Greenough adopted a symmetrical Palladian scheme with a projecting center pavilion and a porch with unusual circular wooden tracery. The facade is severe, faced with flush boards scored to resemble ashlar and bounded by a simple string course between floors. As in much of Greenough's work, the volumes and cubic mass of the house seem more important than the details. Local housewrights working in this mode produced much less sophisticated buildings, such as 3 Craigie Street (Isaac Cutler, 1854), a simple blocky design with a low monitor roof and flush siding scored to resemble stone.

FIGURE 6.80 Arnold Guyot house, 27 Craigie Street (1854, Henry Greenough, architect). Photo ca. 1900.

MANSARD/SECOND EMPIRE

An architectural style characterized by its principal feature, the Mansard roof, flourished in Cambridge for over three decades. The form originated with the 17th-century French architect François Mansart and reappeared with Neoclassical ornamentation in Paris during the reign of Napoleon III (1852–70), a period known as the Second Empire. This more elaborate variant was considered appropriate for monumental civic buildings, such as Boston's City Hall, but most of the wooden houses built in Cambridge during this period are too vernacular to be termed Second Empire and are often described simply as Mansards.

The 19th-century Mansard roof had practical as well as stylistic considerations, as it provided a full story of usable space in what would have been merely an attic under a traditional gable roof. Described in the *Boston Transcript* as the "new French roof," it soon became the dominant feature in American architecture (Mar. 12, 1866). Buildings with French roofs were generally more vertical, formal, and symmetrical than Italianate structures, although many used Italianate ornament, particularly window hoods and cornices with elaborate brackets. Derived from a masonry tradition in France, wooden Second Empire or Mansard houses in the United States often have facades covered with flush boarding scored to resemble masonry and corners delineated with quoins rather than corner boards. Virginia and Lee McAlester point out in their *Field Guide to American Houses* that, unlike the Gothic Revival and Italianate styles, which looked to a romanticized past for inspiration, this style was modern, imitating the latest French fashion.

The style appeared in Cambridge as early as 1854 with houses designed by Henry Greenough, became increasingly widespread by 1860, and enjoyed enormous popularity during the postwar building boom. Over the next decade, Mansards became increasingly varied in design, with patterned roofs, towers, a profusion of wooden detail, and irregular silhouettes. The last Mansards that appeared in the 1880s exhibited elements of the Stick Style and Queen Anne rather than the classical and Italianate details of the 1860s.

Apart from Henry Greenough, who would have seen Mansard buildings on his visits to the Continent, most practitioners relied on pattern books such as Calvert Vaux's *Villas and Cottages* (1857) and George Woodward's *Architecture and Rural Art* (1868). Woodward's *National Architect* (1869) presented "1000 original designs, plans and details" showing construction details for both the Mansard and the Stick styles, with written specifications to guide the builder.

Old Cambridge Mansards were almost all freestanding single-family or double houses with center-entrance or side-hall plans. Although Mansard roofs were naturally suited to row houses, as in Boston's Back Bay, most of Cambridge was laid out with lots suitable for detached houses. The few Mansard rows here were mostly built of brick and isolated from one another, giving them the air of experimental ventures intended to test the market for this type of urban living. Examples in Old Cambridge include a row of four built in 1866 at 1676–1686 Massachusetts Avenue (of which only two remain) and four houses at 6–12 Mason Street (1869) put up as an investment by Theodore H. Seavey, a Boston merchant who lived on Trowbridge Street. Later row houses with Panel Brick detail at 61–67 Sparks (1875) and 9–13 and 15–19 Sacramento Street (1879) stand out for their rarity (see figure 6.111).

Greenough's Mansards for Professor Louis Agassiz at 36 Quincy Street (1854), Sabra Parsons at 63 Garden Street (1855), and Judge Edward Loring at 4 Kirkland Place (1856) were the first in Cambridge and among the earliest in the Boston area. All were three-bay center-entrance compositions with low roofs and narrow pedimented dormers on each facade. The Agassiz and Loring houses had high basements and restrained facades with columned entrance porticos and balustrades, while the Parsons house retained some Italianate features (figure 6.81). The roofs of 36 Quincy and 63 Garden had low, straight profiles; 4 Kirkland had a flaring concave roof, similar to that on Greenough's own severely Neoclassical house at 1737 Cambridge Street, planned in 1846 but constructed in 1855 after his return from Europe.

FIGURE 6.81 Judge Edward Loring house, 4 Kirkland Place (1856, Henry Greenough, architect). Greenough's only surviving Mansard originally faced Kirkland Street but was moved back, turned, and set on a lower foundation in 1908. Photo ca. 1914.

Other early three-bay, center-entrance Mansards, such as the Joel Parker house at 5 Craigie Street (1855), the William Newell house at 20 Berkeley Street (1857), and the James and Mary Longfellow Greenleaf house at 76 Brattle Street (1859), also have roofs with low, flaring concave profiles, triple-arched entrance porches, and bracketed cornices. Judge Parker's house had round arches and slender colonnettes on the side porches, bulbous turnings on the balustrades, and a triple-arched window on the side bay, all characteristic Italianate features. The heavy corner quoins and bracketed window hoods were common to both styles. The flaring roof was decidedly modern, but the clapboard siding made no attempt to resemble masonry (figure 6.82). By contrast, the Greenleaf house clearly invoked the style's masonry antecedents. Constructed of brick covered with stucco that may originally have been scored to resemble ashlar, the house had a simple modillion cornice and unornamented arched windows instead of the elaborate hooded windows of the Italianate period. The porch railings and balconies above the first floor windows employed Gothic motifs (figure 6.83). Three-bay Mansards with projecting center bays appeared in the late 1850s at 80 Sparks Street (ca. 1858–59) and 23 Craigie Street, which Oliver Hastings built for his daughter Caroline in 1855 (figure 6.84). This variation became particularly wide-spread in the 1860s and 1870s.

The popularity of the Mansard style reached its peak in the 1860s and 1870s. Builders continued to put up three-bay, center entrance, symmetrical houses, with or without projecting central pavilions or gables, but side-hall plan houses with two full stories plus a Mansard roof were much more common; in the 1860s these were particularly abundant along Massachusetts Avenue and throughout the Agassiz neighborhood. One-story examples date primarily from the 1870s, with a heavy concentration on Walker (1871–74) and Sacramento streets (1872–75). So popular was the style that a number of older houses were updated with Mansard roofs; for example, in 1856 Joseph Buckingham hired Joseph R. Richards to update his 1832 Asher Benjamin house on Quincy Street (figure 6.85).

FIGURE 6.82 Judge Joel Parker house, 5 Craigie Street (1855; demolished 1920). Photo 1858.

FIGURE 6.83 James and Mary Greenleaf house, 76 Brattle Street (1859). Radcliffe College acquired the house in 1905 and subsequently removed the stucco and some of the trim; it became the official residence of Radcliffe presidents in 1913. Photo ca. 1912.

FIGURE 6.85 Joseph Buckingham house, 28 Quincy Street. In 1856 Boston architect Joseph R. Richards proposed this Second Empire update of Asher Benjamin's 1832 design.

FIGURE 6.84 Caroline Hastings Henshaw house, 23 Craigie Street (1855, Oliver Hastings, builder). Elaborate oversized brackets support a balcony on the projecting central pavilion where a concave Mansard continues the profile of the main roof. Photo ca. 1938.

Changes in roof profiles and decorative details occurred throughout the period. In the 1850s, roofs were generally low in height with either straight or slightly concave sides, while between 1855 and 1865 they often had dramatically flared concave slopes. Roofs with steeper straight sides and a low-pitched upper section, as at 9 Forest Street (1872), generally date from 1860 to 1875; bands of contrasting slates appeared in the late 1860s and 1870s. As in the Italianate style, brackets almost always supported the cornice, but Mansard brackets were often more elaborate and paired, particularly at corners.

Dormers were essential for lighting the living spaces within the roof. In the 1850s and early 1860s they often projected significantly and had pediments or arched openings reflecting the window openings in the house below. Located halfway up the slope of the roof, these dormers often had decorative scrollwork at the base, as at 23 Craigie Street (1855), 44 Follen Street (1862), and 1627 Massachusetts Avenue (1862). Dormers in the 1860s were located higher so that the slope of the upper part of the Mansard formed a shed roof for the dormer, as at 1626 Massachusetts Avenue (1868). Some were partially recessed, as at

24 Craigie Street (1868). This configuration often leaked badly, and builders soon returned to projecting dormers, although steep roof slopes in the 1870s meant that the projection was slight, as at 57–59 Walker Street (1871). Gable or pedimented dormers with scrollwork as at 1581–1583 Massachusetts Avenue (1876) were typical of the 1870s.

Several window shapes and details were common and sometimes varied by floor. Segmental arched windows with simple moldings appeared throughout the 1860s, as at 154 Brattle Street (1861). Projecting flat or pedimented window hoods with side brackets, as at 5 Craigie Street (1855) and 24 Craigie Street (1868), were characteristic of the 1850s and 1860s. Lintels in the 1870s were often more fanciful in design, as at 135–137 Oxford Street (1872) and 94 Lake View Avenue (1874). The design of bay windows also increased in complexity. Early bays seldom exceeded one story and were usually confined to side elevations. As houses became more asymmetrical in the 1860s and '70s, bay windows appeared on facades and sometimes rose two stories or extended above the main cornice. After 1873 some rose high enough to resemble towers.

The finest example of an academic Mansard house in Old Cambridge is 24 Craigie Street, designed in 1868 by Boston architect Joseph R. Richards for Albion K.P. Welch, an owner of the prestigious University Press in Brattle Square. Of the ten Mansards built on Craigie Street between 1854 and 1873, only 24 Craigie can be accurately termed Second Empire in style. Splendidly sited on a large triangular lot at the intersection of Brattle and Craigie streets, it was designed with three public facades, each rigidly symmetrical and academically correct but slightly different from one another. The north elevation has a recessed central bay, while the south has a projecting central bay with an entrance toward Brattle. The third facade, facing the intersection, has no change in plane, but a change in window trim highlights the center bay. The Welch house has flush boarding and restrained academic decoration, including modillions, rather than brackets, at the cornice. Segmental and pedimented windows alternate on the first floor and in reverse order in the

dormers. The second floor windows, supported on brackets and with crossetted corners, are uniform throughout. By following established rules of academic design, the architect produced an unusually dignified composition (figure 6.86).

Born in Boston, Joseph R. Richards (1828–1900) trained in the office of Gridley J.F. Bryant before establishing his own architectural practice in Boston in 1851. He lived in Richardson's Row on Cambridge Street, and his first known Cambridge commission was remodeling Joseph Buckingham's Quincy Street house in 1856 (see figure 6.85). At times during the 1860s and '70s he practiced with his brother Samuel and his brother-in-law, William Park. He worked alone from 1872 until 1880, when his son, William P. Richards, who had graduated from Harvard in 1875 and worked in the office of Peabody & Stearns, joined him. They began to specialize in the Queen Anne style in the 1880s, and together designed dozens of houses, two of Old Cambridge's earliest apartment buildings, and many commercial buildings in Boston and surrounding towns.

FIGURE 6.86 Welch-Ross house, 24 Craigie Street (1868, Joseph R. Richards, architect). The wing at left was expanded by Denman Ross in 1893 and remodeled in 1971. Photo ca. 1968.

At 24 Craigie, Richards placed the staircase between the dining room and the library to provide an unobstructed hall with a view from the main entrance on Craigie Street to the carriage entrance on Brattle (figure 6.87). The first floor had lofty 13-foot ceilings with elaborate plaster cornices and ceiling medallions for gas chandeliers. Several soapstone hot-air registers and the original hot-air furnace survived into the late 20th century, but by that time only the white marble mantel in the library was original; mantels in the other principal rooms dated from 1893.

The dark, varnished interior woodwork was unlike the painted woodwork of earlier periods, and the molding profiles were more complex and three-dimensional. Wood paneling was used as a dado on the stairway and in the halls. The design of the staircase was fairly complicated, but all the components were produced by machine, and the straight handrail between the posts was considerably easier to construct than the curving rails of Federal and Greek Revival designs. Rather than the pot-bellied newel post popular in the 1840s and 1850s, the newel was a monumental octagonal composition that was probably topped by a gas lamp on a metal standard. The silvered doorknobs and the etched glass panels in the main vestibule may be the work of the New England Glass Company in East Cambridge, which produced such designs in the 1850s and 1860s. The door panels representing the Brewer fountain on Boston Common and the Hartford Stag were characteristic of fine entrances in this period.

After Welch and his wife died in 1870–71 the house was valued at $30,000, almost twice as much as the Arnold Guyot house across the street. It was purchased in 1871 by Boston businessman John Ludlow Ross, whose son became its most notable resident. Denman Ross graduated from Harvard in 1875, received a PhD in history in 1880, and joined the faculty as a lecturer on the theory of design in 1899. Well-known as a collector of oriental art, he donated 11,000 objects to the Boston Museum of Fine Arts and another 1,500 to the Fogg Museum. In 1893 he hired Frank Warren Smith to enlarge the original ell and add a second floor studio (figure 6.88). After his death in 1935, his heirs converted the Brattle Street entrance into a conservatory

FIGURE 6.87 Stair hall, Welch-Ross house. The placement of the main stair perpendicular to the entrance left the hall open from Craigie to Brattle streets. Photo ca. 1968.

FIGURE 6.88 Denman Ross studio, Welch-Ross house. The artist's studio occupied the second floor of the wing that architect Frank Warren Smith designed for Ross in 1893. Photo ca. 1968.

and removed the first floor window balustrades. Few other exterior changes occurred until 1971, when the house passed out of the Ross family, and the ell became a separate dwelling. Before the sale, the heirs placed the property under the jurisdiction of the Cambridge Historical Commission and donated a fountain at the intersection to the city.

Most Mansards in the 1860s owed their designs to carpenters or master builders rather than architects. One of the most popular models remained the three-bay center-entrance plan, such as Boston merchant Henry Glover's 1862 house on Waterhouse Street at the corner of North Avenue (now at 44 Follen Street). Glover's house had a low, flaring Mansard with round-headed dormers, a wide cornice with decorative frieze and paired brackets, and a balustraded porch. Other examples of this type included 154 Brattle (1861), 21 Craigie Street (1866), and the double house at 56–58 Shepard Street (1867). A popular variation of the three-bay Mansard had a projecting center entrance pavilion with its own fully articulated roof. Michael Norton (builder of 85 Brattle Street and 17 Farwell Place) gave his own house at 1 Chauncy Street an unusually elaborate Mansard in 1860. By also angling his house to face down Massachusetts Avenue and crowning it with an octagonal cupola encircled with pairs of round-headed windows, Norton clearly intended to make a display of style and wealth among his less flamboyant neighbors (figure 6.89; see also figure 4.171). In some examples the entrance pavilion barely projected, as at 20 Craigie, or a square bay over the porch took the place of a fully projecting bay, as at 5 Walnut Avenue (both 1869).

Other three-bay houses such as 32 Linnaean Street (1863) and 33 Fayerweather Street (1864) had only a Mansard center gable with the characteristic concave profile (figure 6.90). One of the finest surviving examples of this type is 1627 Massachusetts Avenue, now owned by Lesley University. Built for Charles Hicks Saunders, a Boston hardware merchant elected mayor of Cambridge in 1868, this house set a new standard for ambitious Mansard mansions on the avenue (figure 6.91). One of the builders penciled an unusual record of its history on a shingle found inside a door jamb:

FIGURE 6.89 Michael Norton house and carriage house, corner Chauncy Street and Massachusetts Avenue (1 Chauncy Street, 1861). The house was demolished for an apartment building in 1925. Photo 1909.

This House is now being finished by J.H. Littlefield for Charles H. Saunders. It was commenced July 1862 and is to be completed April 1 1863. The cost of the House exclusive of the land will be $6500.00, Land value $3500.00, Total $10,000. Our country is now engaged in Civil War and has 700,000 men in the military service. … Cambridge has thus far sent 1950 men to the war. Jan. 20, 1863.

Joseph H. Littlefield (1830–1904), a Maine native, was listed as a builder in Cambridge directories from 1850 to 1864 and as an architect in Boston from 1872 to 1876. His most important commission in Cambridge was the 1874 City Building in Brattle Square. The house he built for Saunders followed the familiar three-bay center entrance plan with an unusual level of decorative detail for the early 1860s, including at least five patterns of complex brackets and dentils. A three-bay porch with chamfered

FIGURE 6.90 Eben Snow house, 33 Fayerweather Street (1864). The Mansard roof and much of the trim were removed in 1955 by architect Eleanor Raymond. Photo ca. 1875.

FIGURE 6.91 Charles Hicks Saunders house, 1627 Massachusetts Avenue (1862, Joseph H. Littlefield, builder). Photo 2015.

posts and segmental arched struts led to double entrance doors with decorative cut and etched glass panels. Because of the prominent corner site, ornament continued on the side elevations with bay windows and dormers with elaborate scrollwork. The interior was richly appointed with a gracefully curving staircase and eight-sided newel, wide plaster cornices and ceiling medallions, white marble parlor mantels, and a parquet floor (figure 6.92). The excellent 19th-century cast iron fence with granite posts and base is a rare survivor.

As the 1860s progressed, the strict symmetry of the earlier buildings relaxed into more complex L- or T-shaped plans with off-center entrances and extensive porches on more than one facade. Examples of the former include Samuel Scudder's house at 156 Brattle Street (1857) and produce dealer Nathaniel Sawin's

house at 1626 Massachusetts Avenue (1868). Unlike the center-entrance houses, the south-facing entrance to Sawin's house was tucked inconspicuously under a porch at the angle where the main block joined the ell. A two-story bay with a bell-shaped roof prefigured the Mansard towers of the 1870s. Orrin Hall, a Harvard Square grocer, had builder Matthew Anderson design and construct a similar L-shaped house at 6 Follen Street in 1868; its one-story Mansard stable is one of few surviving from this period.

After 1868 exterior walls were sometimes articulated with stickwork, a system of projecting boards that suggested structural framing and was commonly seen in Stick Style houses of the same period. The earliest examples had only a simple flat belt course circling the house between the first and second floors, as at 1626 Massachusetts Avenue, 6 Follen Street, and 164 Brattle

FIGURE 6.92 Stairhall, Charles Hicks Saunders house. Photo 1964.

Street. A later example at 165 Brattle Street (1872), built for John Bartlett of *Bartlett's Quotations*, had extensive stickwork and a splendid Mansard barn (ca. 1875) with similar details. Stick Style bands and an asymmetrical plan also characterized 37 Concord Avenue, which Elinor Mead Howells, sister of William

R. Mead of McKim, Mead and White, designed for herself and her husband, William Dean Howells, in 1872 (see figure 4.123).

The 1870s produced the most flamboyant Mansards in Old Cambridge, with great flexibility of plan and silhouette, a profusion of architectural ornament, and bay windows soaring into Mansard-roofed towers. Much of the greater freedom in architectural detail may be attributed to the widespread use of woodworking machinery. High wages for craftsmen after the Civil War impelled builders to use cheaper machine-made instead of hand-carved architectural decoration in all but the most opulent commissions. Forms were often reduced to geometric shapes that machines could reproduce. Many of the new decorative elements were turned on a lathe or cut with a jigsaw and then nailed together, because ornamentation composed of separate parts could be more elaborate than if carved from a single piece of wood. Machines also facilitated popular details, such as chamfered edges and incised linear designs on exterior ornament and interior marble mantels. The variety of trim on 36 and 28 Arlington Street (1872 and 1876) and 92 Washington Avenue (1876) provide good examples of the machine-made rope moldings, incised brackets, applied bosses, and intricate pilaster caps that characterized 1870s work.

On one of the highest spots in the city, a profusion of detail enhanced opulent twin mansions built side by side in 1871 for Henry J. Melendy and D. Gilbert Dexter, partners in a boot and shoe business in Boston. Dexter's house burned in 1939, but Melendy's at 81 Washington Avenue remains in remarkably original condition. The projecting entrance pavilion displayed a great freedom of design in the elaborate jigsawn and routed scrollwork, bargeboard, brackets, pilasters, and recessed dormers (figure 6.93). A dramatic concave-roof cupola crowned the patterned slate roof and offered a spectacular view of Boston. The attention to detail continued on the interior with high ceilings, ornate woodwork, and patterned wood floors.

Some 1870s entrance bays took the form of towers, particularly on one-story houses such as 77 Lake View Avenue (1871) and 78 Washington Avenue (1874). Housewright William

The most widespread Mansard house type built in Old Cambridge in the 1870s followed the traditional side-hall plan. Although occasionally three bays wide, as at 12 Sacramento Street (1861), built for lumber dealer Sumner Shepard, this type was more often only two bays wide with a bay window next to the entrance; these ranged from a simple example at 101 Washington Avenue (1872) to the elaborate 37 Arlington Street (1874). The side-hall Mansards that Somerville builder Thomas Elston erected in 1875–76 differed from each other only in detail. The scroll brackets with incised decoration, porches with chamfered posts and corner brackets, and elaborate dormers and window hoods of his houses at 92 Washington Avenue, 24 and 26 Linnaean Street, 121 Oxford Street, 81 Garfield Street, and 42 Prentiss Street are good examples of machine-made ornament of the period.

FIGURE 6.93 Henry J. Melendy house, 81 Washington Avenue (1871). Photo 1968

Smith of Roxbury built himself a diminutive one-story cottage at 94 Lake View Avenue (1874) in which the tower had a convex Mansard that contrasted with the concave roof of the main house.[7] Other 1870s Mansards carried a bay window through the main cornice. The double house at 1581–1583 Massachusetts Avenue (1876) displayed multiple bays and a profusion of 1870s details, including complicated brackets, elaborate window hoods, and applied diamond accents (figure 6.94). The house at 68–70 Walker Street (1871) also has applied ornament, patterned slate, and bays extending into the roof, but the overall appearance is much simpler.

FIGURE 6.94 Front elevation, Alden Keen house, 1581–1583 Massachusetts Avenue (1876). Harvard University relocated the Keen house to 1637 Massachusetts Avenue in 2008.

Other side-hall examples with a rich profusion of vernacular detail, such as 37 Arlington Street (1874) and 1587 Massachusetts Avenue, further illustrate the devolution of the Mansard style. D. Gilbert Dexter, who lived in the elaborate 1871 Mansard at the summit of Washington Avenue, built 1587 Massachusetts Avenue in 1875. This stretch of the avenue was one of the most prestigious addresses in Cambridge, and Dexter's house shows both the continuing popularity of the style and its flexibility in accommodating vast amounts of detail. In 2007 Harvard moved both 1581–1583 and 1587 Massachusetts Avenue and the latter's carriage house to the corner of Mellen Street and restored them for Law School housing (see figure 4.187).

The facade of 37 Arlington Street (1874) provides the most lavish display of ornament on the smallest surface of any Mansard in Cambridge (figure 6.95). Builder Albert H. Kelsey's diminutive one-story house shattered the formal symmetry and contained silhouette admired in early Mansard compositions, and the design bursts with the energy and inventiveness that would become a hallmark of the Queen Anne style in the 1880s. The dominant bay window is practically an independent tower, accentuated by unconventional diamond-shaped dormers and iron cresting. Other details are equally idiosyncratic; wooden finials sprout from the corners of the cornice and dripping brackets slide down the bay and corner boards, leaving little room for clapboards.

By contrast, 22 Berkeley Street, designed by New York architect Griffith Thomas for historian John Fiske in 1877, is surprisingly restrained for its late date (figure 6.96). Fiske's stepfather, who lived in New York City, financed the house and chose the architect. Fiske himself specified many key features, including a "Mansard roof, like [William Dean] Howells', 8 feet high, with inclination of not more than 8 inches" because "there is no way so cheap for getting abundance of room" (John Fiske Papers, Fiske to Mrs. Stoughton, May 24, 1877). Fiske had been impressed with the layout and construction of Howells's house at 37 Concord Avenue, which he had seriously considered buying. He hoped to use Howells's builder, William Bugbee, who was considered by some "the most thorough builder in

FIGURE 6.95 Albert H. Kelsey house, 37 Arlington Street (1874, Albert H. Kelsey, builder). The photo was taken about 1938, before later owners removed some of the original details.

Cambridge," but in the end one of the Chesley brothers of Boston constructed the house (Fiske, *The Letters of John Fiske*, 362). Much of Fiske's correspondence expressed concern for keeping the exterior simple and the costs down. The flat three-bay facade, flush boarding, corner quoins, and simple pedimented lintels reflected the directness of masonry-based Mansard buildings from the 1860s, an impression reinforced by the original monochromatic gray paint scheme. Fiske even wanted to eliminate the quoins and substitute clapboards for the flush boarding, observing that "in a wooden house for the country the simpler

FIGURE 6.96 John Fiske house, 22 Berkeley Street (1877, Griffith Thomas, architect). Photo ca. 1938.

FIGURE 6.97 Library, John Fiske house. Photo 1967.

the finish the better" (Fiske to Thomas, July 29, 1877). Inside, however, he spared no expense, and his private spaces were richly appointed with hardwood trim, highly decorated ceilings, and extensive built-in bookcases (figure 6.97). Although Fiske's exterior was extremely conservative for 1877, only five years later he convinced his mother to hire H.H. Richardson to design a trend-setting Shingle Style house at 90 Brattle Street.

Mansard houses of the late 1880s often incorporated Queen Anne details and technology. The change was particularly noticeable on porches, where the brackets and beveled square posts of the 1860s and '70s gave way to lathe-turned posts and Queen Anne balustrades. Compound brackets with jigsawn scrollwork, Queen Anne sunburst motifs, and high hip roofs above the Mansard also distinguished these later houses. The meshing of styles is evident at 48 Bellevue Avenue, which Nova Scotia-born Cambridge carpenter Miner W. Himeon built in 1886 for journalist Charles Seagrave. The building permit for this asymmetrical one-story house notes its "French roof," but the turned posts and decorative balustrade of the porch looked forward to the popular Queen Anne style (figure 6.98).

Some of the best late Mansards were the work of local carpenter-turned-architect James Fogerty, who designed over one hundred Cambridge houses, as well as eight city schools and three fire stations. The side-hall house at 1746 Cambridge Street that he designed in 1887 for Timothy D. Sullivan, a skilled type finisher with the University Press, exemplified his integration of styles. The front and side bays rose with Queen Anne exuberance, and the cornice brackets combined Queen Anne sunburst motifs with geometric carving and delicate filigree. Fogerty also used sunburst brackets at 15 Langdon Street (1887), but 1746 Cambridge Street was his only Mansard to use the Queen Anne motif as a unifying element throughout, from the peaks of the gabled dormers to the decorative band on the bay windows (figure 6.99).

FIGURE 6.98 Charles Seagrave house, 48 Bellevue Avenue (1886, Miner W. Himeon, builder). A tower facing east is no longer visible from any street. Photo 1968.

FIGURE 6.99 Timothy D. Sullivan house, 1746 Cambridge Street (1887, James Fogerty, architect). Photo 2013.

DEVELOPMENT OF THE QUEEN ANNE

The exuberance of form and detail in many of Old Cambridge's late Mansard houses found fuller expression in the Queen Anne style of the 1880s, but first two new styles made brief appearances. The steep-gabled wooden houses with distinctive applied flat trim that architectural historian Vincent Scully described as Stick Style were a transitional link between the Gothic Revival cottages of the mid-century pattern books and the English-derived Queen Anne houses of the late 19th century. This distinctly American form flourished in the Northeast in the 1860s and 1870s but enjoyed only brief popularity in Cambridge. The Ruskinian Gothic that emerged as a residential style with the completion of Harvard's Memorial Hall in the mid-1870s had direct English antecedents and was popular among the educated class of well-traveled Anglophile Americans.

The Stick Style

The Stick Style was named for the flat wooden boards or stickwork that projected slightly in front of the siding. The style's approach to ornament changed the wall from a neutral surface supporting applied decoration to a dynamic design component. Stickwork details first appeared on a few late Mansards, such as 1626 Massachusetts Avenue (1868), but the earliest known Stick Style houses, 45 and 51 Highland Street and 25 Reservoir Street, date from 1872. The financial panic of 1873 brought a substantial slowdown in building activity in Cambridge, and by the time the economy rebounded in the 1880s, the style's popularity had waned.

Stick Style examples in Old Cambridge often had complex irregular silhouettes with a variety of bays (some with overhanging second stories), square towers, gables with trusswork or protruding peaks, and open strut porches, as well as the characteristic stickwork. The stickwork, in horizontal, vertical, and diagonal patterns, generally reflected the underlying structural members of the building but was strictly decorative. Steep roofs often had a front-facing gable and several flared cross gables, as at 23 Buckingham Street (1877). Also common were high hip roofs with steeply gabled dormers and bays, as at 45 Highland Street (1872) and 10 Follen Street (1875), a combination of hip and gable roofs and shed dormers, as at 57 Shepard Street (1874), and multiple hip roofs, as at 35 Prentiss Street (1877).

In 1872 Boston architects Sturgis & Brigham designed a house with Stick Style features at 25 Reservoir Street for Edward W. Hooper, treasurer of Harvard College (figure 6.100). Distinctive details included the band of recessed vertical and diagonal boarding between the first and second floors and a paneled balustrade. The street facade featured a bracketed three-story center bay with an unusual patterned-slate gambrel roof, but the main entrance and porch faced the garden, away from public view. In 1902 Lois Lilley Howe added a Georgian Revival doorway to the street facade, reinforcing the colonial feel of the house's gambrel roof and symmetrical facade. Twentieth century remodelings removed other original elements.

FIGURE 6.100 South elevation, Edward W. Hooper house, 25 Reservoir Street (1872, Sturgis & Brigham, architects). Architects' drawing, , 1872.

FIGURE 6.101 William B. Storer house, 57 Shepard Street (1874; demolished 1964). Photo ca. 1938.

FIGURE 6.102 Frederick and Evelyn Wood house, 35 Prentiss Street (1877, F.W. Channing Wood, architect). Photo ca. 1965.

The William B. Storer house at 57 Shepard Street (1874) showed how quickly the new vocabulary was adopted for middle-class homes (figure 6.101). Storer (1838–84) was a Boston merchant specializing in trade with Russia. The Frederick and Eveline Wood house at 35 Prentiss (1877) was an early design by their son F.W. Channing Wood and featured a dramatic corner bay and entrance porch supported by a single chamfered post with splayed struts, as well as characteristic stickwork (figure 6.102). Wood went on to have a long career as a draftsman and architect in the office of the Shingle Style master, William Ralph Emerson.

The Stick Style house at 10 Follen Street that Peabody & Stearns designed for Barnard and Frances MacKay in 1875 was published two years later in *The Architectural Sketchbook*, a leading American journal of the period (figure 6.103). The unusually symmetrical design featured a carefully orchestrated juxtaposition of shapes and a profusion of well-articulated detail. Horizontal stickwork and an unusual cornice between floors encircled the house, while deep eaves cast the walls and

FIGURE 6.103 Barnard and Frances MacKay house, 10 Follen Street (1875, Peabody & Stearns, architects). Photo 2014.

windows into shadow. Soaring finials, an intricate porch, a steep projecting center gable with flared ends, open trusswork, and characteristic wall treatment completed the composition.

Cambridge's best example of an asymmetrical Stick Style house is 23 Buckingham Street (1878), which projects restless energy with unexpected juxtapositions of gables and a profusion of applied ornament (figure 6.104). James Laughlin, a recent graduate who became a distinguished economist at Harvard and the University of Chicago, purchased the lot in 1877 from carpenter-architect Joseph Littlefield and was taxed in 1878 for a moderately expensive new house assessed at $6,500.[8] The plan anticipated the freedom and inventiveness of Queen Anne interiors in the next decade (figure 6.105). The arrangement of the stair hall with angled doors into adjoining rooms was an early example of the transformation of the typical narrow front hallway into living space, a concept that became fully developed in the 1880s and 1890s. The irregular shapes of the rooms imparted a feeling of anticipation, since the plan could not be deduced from the exterior.

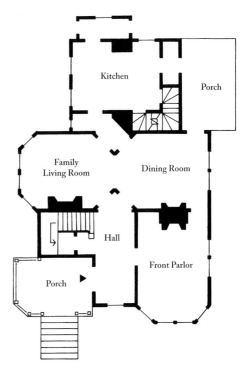

FIGURE 6.105 First floor plan, James Laughlin house, 1878.

FIGURE 6.104 James Laughlin house, 23 Buckingham Street (1878, Joseph Littlefield, architect). Most of the Stick Style detail was removed in 1946, but in 1985 a new owner recreated the projecting stickwork, gable trusses, picket-fence siding, and porch openwork based on early photographs and original fragments found under the porch. Photo ca. 1938.

Stickwork elements continued to be incorporated into Queen Anne and vernacular designs in the 1880s. The most notable example is the Sarah and Emma Cary house at 92 Brattle Street (1881–82), where shingles instead of vertical siding fill the horizontal bands and gable peaks (figure 6.106). Side-hall plan, gable-end houses at 52 Shepard Street (1883) and 7 and 9 Mellen Street (1883–85) feature both applied stickwork and Queen Anne details, such as sunbursts in the porch gables and small round brightly painted wooden bosses at key junctures (figure 6.107–6.108). The similarity of these details leads to the supposition that all were designed by the same unknown hand. In the early 20th century, owners of flamboyant Stick Style houses at 106 Brattle Street (1871, Peabody & Stearns), 51 Highland Street (1873), and 88 Lake View Avenue (1875, William Smith) obliterated their stylistic features with stucco, leaving only the original complex silhouettes.

FIGURE 6.106 Sarah and Emma Cary house, 92 Brattle Street (1881–82, architect unknown). Photo ca. 1938.

FIGURE 6.107 Thomas Stearns house, 52 Shepard Street (1883). Photo 1969.

FIGURE 6.108 Rebecca Hunt and James Hilton houses, 7 and 9 Mellen Street (both 1883). Photo 2009.

RUSKINIAN GOTHIC

A few high-style brick and stone houses in Cambridge combined the decorative concepts of the Stick Style with medieval influences suggested by John Ruskin's writings. Designed in the 1870s by well-known Boston architects and widely illustrated in American architectural journals, these houses followed the stylistic lead of the Episcopal Theological School campus and Harvard's Memorial Hall, both designed by Ware & Van Brunt, the leading Ruskinian practitioners of the day. They combined diagonal, rectangular, and polychromatic brick patterns, wooden elements from the Stick Style and the developing Queen Anne, and features of what Bainbridge Bunting termed the Panel Brick Style that had been introduced in Boston's Back Bay in 1869.

The first Ruskinian residence in Cambridge was 71 Appleton Street, which was designed in 1875 by William Pitt Preble Longfellow, a nephew of the poet, and published in *The Architectural Sketch-Book* in September 1875 (figure 6.109). Longfellow was a gifted designer, but his output was small, and he is better known as a writer and editor of the first major American architectural periodical, the *American Architect and Building News (AABN)*. He began teaching architectural design at M.I.T. in 1881. His only other known Cambridge house is 70 Sparks Street (1878), built for his cousin, Boston lawyer Edward S. Dodge (see figure 6.114).

Longfellow's client, William Cook, had been hired to teach German and rhetoric at Harvard in 1873. A Civil War veteran with a growing family, he may have been attracted by the Ruskinian Gothic style of Memorial Hall, which was then under construction. Longfellow's two-story asymmetrical design has polychrome wall surfaces, decorative Panel Brick chimneys, and multiple gables with flared overhangs, as well as wooden Stick Style dormers and porches with open struts. Bands of brownstone and black bricks (made by immersing the bricks in hot tar), a narrow patterned string course between the first and second stories, and pointed-arch windows trimmed in brownstone all contribute to the Ruskinian Gothic feeling.

FIGURE 6.109 William Cook house, 71 Appleton Street (1875, W.P.P. Longfellow, architect). Photo 2016.

The Cook house illustrated the freedom of plan that began to appear in some Stick Style houses and would become fully developed in Queen Anne interiors in the 1880s. Longfellow discarded all vestiges of center-hall symmetry and adjusted the location and size of rooms according to their use. Some were large and accessible, others cozy and secluded, but their arrangement could not be discerned from the exterior. From an octagonal vestibule with pointed arches and Minton tile floor, doorways opened into the parlor, the dining room, and a splendid 20-by-15-foot, two-story stair hall that formed the core of the house. Lit by a skylight, the hall featured a slate fireplace, walnut wainscoting, and stairs with elaborately turned balusters that continued around a second floor balcony; an elongated decorative post visually united the first and second stories. (figure 6.110). The formal rooms on the first floor had elegant walnut, cherry, or chestnut trim and fireplaces, some with Minton tile hearths. The large front parlor had an unusual Eastlake fireplace with

FIGURE 6.110 Stairhall, William Cook house. Photo 1973.

FIGURE 6.111 John Brewster row houses, 61–67 Sparks Street (1875). Photo 2009.

double flues flanking a stained glass window; when opened to the intimate sitting room behind, it created a 40-foot-long room for entertaining. A renovation in 2015 restored the exterior and rearranged some interior spaces.

Brattle Street property owner John Brewster built a row of four elaborate Panel Brick houses at 61–67 Sparks in 1875 (figure 6.111). The combination of Nova Scotia sandstone string courses and door surrounds, corbelled chimneys, and indented geometric patterns shows how ornamentation in this style was not applied, but emerged from the masonry itself. A

later Panel Brick row at 55–61 Frost (1882), distinguished by a wide corbelled brick cornice and delicately incised sandstone lintels, followed a form more common in Mid Cambridge and Cambridgeport.

Ware & Van Brunt designed two Panel Brick/Ruskinian Gothic houses in Old Cambridge. Both were published in *AABN*, but do not seem to have inspired other buildings here. Twelve Reservoir Street, designed in 1877 for Boylston Professor of Rhetoric and Oratory Adams S. Hill, was more regular in plan and massing than 71 Appleton, but made similar use of contrasting black brick to vary the wall surfaces (figure 6.112). The steep wood gables with decorative bargeboards and board-and-batten siding recalled the Stick Style, while the turned porch posts were purely Queen Anne. The interior plan was quite regular, with a wide center hall and rooms aligned symmetrically, unlike the dramatic spaces and vistas of 71 Appleton Street.

FIGURE 6.112 Adam S. Hill house, 12 Reservoir Street (1877, Ware & Van Brunt, architects). Architects' drawing, published 1877.

Ware & Van Brunt's Deanery at the Episcopal Theological School (1879) was a particularly exuberant composition constructed of random-laid Roxbury puddingstone with contrasting red brick trim, massive ribbed chimneys, patterned shingles, clapboards, stickwork, and a steep polychromatic slate roof (figure 6.113). The domestic use of stone was unusual for Cambridge, but recalls the firm's other commissions at ETS. Described in the *Cambridge Tribune* as a "picturesque mansion admired by every beholder," the Deanery had some of the most varied facades, materials, and roof silhouettes of any house in Cambridge (Apr. 9, 1880). The stone first floor featured a Queen Anne piazza with turned posts and balusters, the clapboard second floor had wooden stickwork, and the third floor had patterned shingles and a spindle screen in the gable. The interior was sumptuously detailed and reflected the developing interest in open planning. Major rooms opened asymmetrically

FIGURE 6.113 The Deanery, Episcopal Theological School, 3 Mason Street (1879, Ware & Van Brunt, architects; demolished 1965). Photo ca. 1890.

off a monumental living hall, patterned after the great halls of medieval buildings. A decorative three-run staircase rose near the middle of the hall that had a Queen Anne tiled fireplace, beamed ceiling, and variegated wooden wainscoting and floor. One of the most sophisticated domestic designs of the 1870s, the Deanery was an excellent example of the short-lived High Victorian Gothic, and its demolition in 1965 was a great loss to the city's architectural heritage.[9]

QUEEN ANNE

The inventiveness and asymmetry of Old Cambridge's Stick Style and Ruskin-inspired houses were developed more fully by other practitioners in the 1880s. Their picturesque domestic architecture was referred to rather imprecisely as "Queen Anne" in style, although it related more to earlier Elizabethan, Jacobean, and late-medieval periods than to the architecture of Queen Anne's reign (1702–14). Half-timbering, tile-hung walls, patterned surfaces, multiple gables, ribbed and paneled chimneys, and asymmetrical elevations characterized the London houses and large country homes that were the sources for this style in North America. Interiors featured large two-story stair halls with monumental fireplaces and built-in seating, patterned after medieval great halls.

The British government's exhibit at the 1876 Centennial International Exhibition in Philadelphia included two half-timbered Old English buildings that introduced some of these ideas to the American public. Similarly, Japan's exhibit of a traditional house introduced motifs and planning that became important components of the Queen Anne style in the United States. As in England, American Queen Anne drew inspiration from a variety of styles and placed a premium on individual invention, good craftsmanship, picturesque massing, and the play of light and shadow, while striving for openness and functionalism in plan.

The Centennial Exhibition coincided with the inauguration of W.P.P. Longfellow's periodical, the *American Architect and Building News*, which featured discussions of architectural theory and illustrations of contemporary buildings. Robert Peabody's 1877 articles, "A Talk About 'Queen Anne'" and "Georgian Homes of New England," illustrated the parallel currents of architectural taste at the time. *AABN* was based in Boston, where the country's first architectural school was founded in 1866 at M.I.T., and it regularly published the work of Boston area architects.

English architect Richard Norman Shaw also had a significant influence on the development of American Queen Anne architecture. His buildings were exhibited regularly at the Royal Academy in the 1870s, and plans and perspectives of his country houses were widely published. H.H. Richardson translated some of Shaw's characteristic features into American materials, in particular substituting patterned wooden shingles for hanging tiles and half-timbering. The use of shingles in various patterns subsequently became a central feature of American Queen Anne houses and developed into a distinctly American variant known as the Shingle Style. The fluid, horizontal compositions of Shingle Style houses contrasted with the multiplicity of materials and lathe-turned details that characterize the American Queen Anne style. The stone and shingle house that Richardson built in Newport, Rhode Island, in 1874 for William Watts Sherman reflected Shaw's work and set a high standard, although few American architects hewed as closely to English precedents. In Old Cambridge only the brick and shingle house at 70 Sparks Street that W.P.P. Longfellow and Theodore Clark designed for John C. Dodge in 1878 directly recalled the Watts Sherman house (figure 6.114).

Paralleling the American public's enthusiasm for foreign architecture at the 1876 exhibition was a nationwide surge of pride in its own history. American architects associated 17th-century English architecture with that of the British colonies in North America, and the British Revivalists' enthusiasm for vernacular architecture fostered a similar American interest. In an influential article, architect Robert Swain Peabody wrote: "With our centennial year have we not discovered that we too have a past worthy of study? … In studying this colonial work, we find

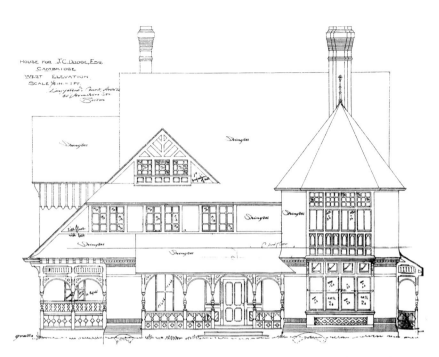

FIGURE 6.114 West elevation, John C. Dodge house, 70 Sparks Street (1878, W.P.P. Longfellow and Theodore Clark, architects). Dodge evidently commissioned this design and built the house at the rear of his property for his son Edward S. Dodge, to whom it is usually attributed. Architects' drawing.

all the delicacy, grace and picturesqueness that any model can suggest to us" (*AABN,* Oct. 20, 1877).

Colonial elements such as gambrel roofs, lean-tos, classical columns, Palladian windows, and dentil cornices were incorporated into Queen Anne designs and then became standard features of Colonial Revival houses in the 1880s and 1890s. Before the 1890s, when articles on American colonial architecture in the *American Architect* and *Architectural Record* (founded in Boston in 1891) established a clearer distinction between 17th- and 18th-century designs, architects used colonial elements with considerable freedom. Bainbridge Bunting termed these Queen Annes "Free Classic" for their nonacademic use of classical elements. In Cambridge, reverence for the area's colonial heritage was always strong. Many Queen Annes, such as 49 Washington Avenue (1887–88), incorporated colonial details, while early Colonial Revival designs, such as 28 Fayerweather Street (1882), exhibited Queen Anne asymmetry.

Several Cambridge houses illustrate the transition from the Stick Style toward the first stirrings of the Queen Anne. One of the most charming is the narrow brick and frame house at 44 Walker Street designed in 1880 by James Fogerty for masonry contractor and builder Marshall Ney Stearns. This exuberant combination of Panel Brick, Stick, and Queen Anne styles has brick on the first floor, and clapboards, crossed and diagonal stickwork, and picket siding on the upper floors. Born in Nova Scotia in 1830 and trained as a carpenter, Fogerty began practicing as an architect in 1872. His design for Stearns presents a virtual catalog of ornament, as well as complex intersecting rooflines, dormers and gables, exposed decorative chimneys, and a variety of windows placed at odd angles. No other Queen Anne house in Old Cambridge packed so much into so tight a space (figures 6.115–6.116).

The house at 128 Lake View Avenue that carpenter William Smith built for himself in 1882 also exhibits elements of both styles. Smith had put up at least eleven Mansard and Stick Style houses on Lake View since 1871, including his own Mansard home at 94 (1875). His new house had many Queen Anne

FIGURE 6.115 Marshall Ney Stearns house, 44 Walker Street (1880, James Fogerty, architect). Photo 2009.

FIGURE 6.116 Side elevation, Marshall Ney Stearns house. Architect's drawing showing the main entrance and details omitted during construction or later removed.

features, including clipped gable ends with projecting pent roofs and the shingled diamond motifs often used by Boston-area architects in this period. The chamfered porch struts and the inverted picket fence detail, however, recall Stick Style houses such as 35 Prentiss Street (1877). The interior had old-fashioned moldings and marble fireplace surrounds similar to early Mansards, while the stair hall featured an unusual twisted newel post and a figured cranberry-glass window in a wall between the entry and the stair (figures 6.117–6.118).

The city was still suffering from a lingering real estate slowdown caused by the financial crisis in 1873 when these transitional houses were built. The *Chronicle* reflected that from "the panic of 1873, down to 1883, real estate transactions were very dull, not only in Cambridge, but in Boston itself and all the surrounding suburbs" (Jan. 1, 1886). Demand for residential lots began to rebound in 1883, and the first substantial Queen Anne and Shingle Style houses were soon under construction. The next year brought an explosion of building; the *Chronicle* estimated that close to 400 new houses were added to the city.

FIGURE 6.117 William Smith house, 128 Lake View Avenue (1882, William Smith, carpenter). Photo 2009.

FIGURE 6.118 Stair hall and newel post, William Smith house. Photo 2009.

The boom left Old Cambridge with an impressive variety of Queen Anne houses, ranging from architect-designed examples such as Henry Van Brunt's own house at 167 Brattle Street (1883) to Sumner Brooks's rental properties on Agassiz, Humboldt, and Lancaster streets (1882–88) and the Clarke trustees' subdivisions on Garfield and Hurlbut streets (1883–91). Most displayed a profusion of lathe-turned and applied decoration and a combination of clapboard first floors and shingled upper floors, although some had only shingles; a few later examples combined brick or stone first floors with shingles above. Steeply pitched roofs, dormers, towers, bay windows, decorative exposed chimneys, overhangs, and porches characterized these asymmetrical compositions. Shingles in multiple patterns—fish scale, diamond, and chisel—appeared in alternating bands in gables and in wide bands between floors. Window sash with small panes of glass surrounding a large pane became common, and banks of tall stained glass windows embellished stair halls. Lathe-turned spindle friezes, brackets, and elaborately turned posts and balustrades often ornamented porches that extended around more than one side of a house. All these features demonstrated the ease and economy with which wood could then be transformed by machine. Most of Old Cambridge's Queen Annes were fairly restrained, however, especially when compared to those in nearby towns such as Newton and Brookline where residents were building larger homes in less urban settings than were available in Cambridge.

Queen Anne floor plans were irregular and often focused on a central living hall that served as an entrance, stair hall, and sitting room. In large houses, the living hall featured a substantial fireplace and seating area. In modest homes, where the client was reluctant to omit any rooms customarily found in elegant houses, making space for a Queen Anne living hall often meant decreasing the size of other rooms or creating a strangely cut-up plan, as at 18 Lancaster Street (figure 6.119).

The Queen Anne appealed as much to the public as to architects during the 1880s, and the press regularly reported on the style. The 1880 clapboard and shingle house at 29 Buckingham Street that William Bigelow designed for Thomas Wentworth Higginson was described by the *Chronicle* as the "Queen Anne-est home of them all" with "dark and sober hues" (Dec. 16, 1882; figure 6.120). Bigelow was an early partner of Charles F. McKim and William R. Mead in New York and later became design director of Herter Brothers. The house had an elaborate porch with intricately carved pediment and deeply recessed entrance. A rustic fence of diagonal bark-covered cedar pickets completed the picturesque setting. The pediment remains, but alterations in the 1930s modified the windows and porch, and a 1998 renovation expanded the house and replaced the original siding and much of the trim.

Henry Van Brunt's own house at 167 Brattle Street (1883) and his firm's designs at 35 Concord Avenue (1884) and possibly 16 Sacramento Street (1883) are excellent examples of sophisticated, architect-designed Queen Anne houses of the early 1880s. For his own house, Van Brunt combined a series of subtly intersecting masses, gables, and sloping rooflines to create a complex composition with little applied ornament beyond the turned posts and balusters and splayed brackets of the corner porch (figure 6.121). The juxtaposition of shapes creates a play of light and shadow across the facade, while patterned shingling and half-timbering provide textural changes in the wall surfaces. The irregular massing makes it impossible to read the interior floor plan from the exterior and adds to the picturesque quality so desired in the 1880s. Van Brunt moved his practice to Kansas

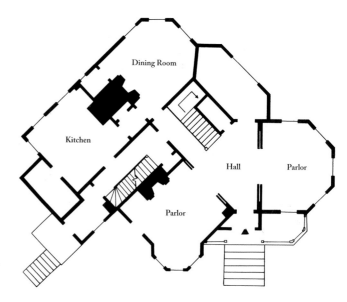

FIGURE 6.119 First floor plan, 18 Lancaster Street (1885).

FIGURE 6.120 Thomas Wentworth Higginson house, 29 Buckingham Street (1880, William Bigelow, architect). Photo ca. 1938.

FIGURE 6.121 Henry Van Brunt house, 167 Brattle Street (1883, Henry Van Brunt, architect). Photo ca. 1938.

City in 1887 and sold the house to Sarah Swan, whose daughter and son-in-law, Mayor William E. Russell, lived across the street at 174 Brattle in a house that she had built for them in 1885, possibly by Van Brunt & Howe. Mrs. Swan added to 167 Brattle in 1888, 1892, and 1902, and after her death in 1910 it was remodeled for two families. A restoration in 2004 reversed some of these changes and recreated Van Brunt's original multicolor paint scheme.

The unusual clapboard and shingle house at 16 Sacramento Street (1883) is attributed to Van Brunt & Howe. It was built by Adna Shaw, son of a founder of the Braman, Shaw & Co. furniture company (later Shaw, Applin & Co.) in East Cambridge, whose employees must have been responsible for the elaborately carved interior. The exterior features a variety of projecting forms, recesses, and textures: a wide band of vertical boards separates the clapboard first floor from the patterned shingle upper floors, and an unusual corner oriel with a curved dome seems suspended over a deeply recessed entrance porch (figures 6.122–6.123).

A year later, Van Brunt & Howe designed 35 Concord Avenue for George E. Carter, son of a prominent Cambridge office-holder, George Putnam Carter (figure 6.124). Here the architects applied a compendium of features to the most common form of early Queen Anne house: a high hip roof, lower cross gables, and materials that changed from floor to floor. The profusion of detail constitutes the opposite approach to ornamentation from Van Brunt's own house, where visual interest was created through forms and shapes rather than applied decoration. Both methods were current in the 1880s, depending on the taste of the owner and/or designer. The same architects were probably responsible for Carter's father's house at 50 Buckingham Street (1883), a more compact, integrated design in which the slope of the front gable sweeps down to form the roof of a diminutive porch, rather like the one Van Brunt designed for himself (figure 6.125).

FIGURE 6.123 Stair hall, Adna Shaw house. Photo 1966.

FIGURE 6.122 Adna Shaw house, 16 Sacramento Street (1883, attributed to Van Brunt & Howe, architects). Photo 1966.

FIGURE 6.124 George E. Carter house, 35 Concord Avenue (1884, Van Brunt & Howe, architects). The elaborate pedimented porch was removed and the exterior covered with aluminum siding in 1953, but the house survives. Photo ca. 1890.

FIGURE 6.125 George Putnam Carter house, 50 Buckingham Street (1883). Photo 2014.

As the 1880s progressed, building activity accelerated at all levels. When the *Tribune* asked a real estate agent on January 1, 1886, "What sections of the city have grown most during the past year, and what kinds of buildings have been built," he singled out Old Cambridge as having "developed wonderfully … principally with fine, handsome houses of the Queen Anne style, costing anywhere from $6,000 to $10,000." Some new streets reflected the vision of a single owner who hired the architects, built the houses, and initially rented rather than sold them. These included Gardiner Hubbard on Mercer Circle, John Brewster on Riedesel Avenue, and Sumner Brooks on Lancaster and Humboldt streets. Other streets, such as Garfield, Hurlbut, and Martin, had no deed restrictions except 15-foot setbacks. Homeowners could choose their own architects, builders, and style, but the streets were developed within such a short period that all the houses were Queen Anne.

The first phase of Gardiner Hubbard's development involved laying out Mercer Circle in 1884 and commissioning Francis R. Allen of Allen & Kenway to design four houses in the Queen Anne style (see chapter 4). The most picturesque was the clapboard and shingle house at 3 Mercer Circle, where the characteristically Queen Anne asymmetrical massing and irregular window placement were united by a handsome porch with shingle and sunburst trim. Allen's other Queen Anne houses at 1, 4, 6, and 8 Mercer Circle (1884–85) were simpler, but together they formed a stylistically up-to-date and consistent neighborhood near Hubbard's residence at 146 Brattle. Hubbard wanted all his houses to be "unique in architecture, handsome and convenient in design." While he rented them at first, he always intended to sell "when the right sort of people occupy them" (*Tribune*, Aug. 14, 1886).

John Brewster erected six Queen Anne houses on his estate in 1883–85: a row of four houses at 29–35 Brewster Street, two exuberant doubles at 17–19 and 23–25 Brewster, and three comfortable singles at 5, 7, and 9 Riedesel Avenue (see figure 4.53). Assessed for $6,500 to $7,000 each, the single houses display the usual Queen Anne high hip roof and combination of textures and shapes, but with differing details: the porch at 5 Riedesel has deep arches and an unusual curved roof, while 7 and 9 each have an elliptical bay window, large shingled brackets, and a panel of molded floral ornament. The double houses incorporate a wealth of ornament and surface textures (figure 6.126). Their overall form is surprisingly symmetrical, with paired center entrances. Some elements are echoed in the Riedesel houses, but the doubles are bolder and vibrate with textural variation. In these the wide central dormer, sunburst arch, and curvaceous center porch with basket-weave spandrels unite the facade, while an unusual center post cuts it in half. Architect John Besarick designed 29–35 Brewster Street and may have been responsible for the others. Best known for his buildings in Dorchester, Besarick was born in Canada and trained in the offices of S.J.F. Thayer in Boston and Richard Morris Hunt and McKim, Mead & White in New York before opening a Boston practice in 1869.

A year after John Brewster's death in 1886, his son William hired Andrews & Jaques to design three more shingled houses with Colonial Revival overtones at 2, 4, and 6 Riedesel Avenue, as well as a Colonial Revival house for himself at 145 Brattle Street. The contrast between the elder Brewster's Queen Annes, these shingled transitional designs, and William's own house shows the wide range of styles that were current within a two-year period. In 1887 the firm designed a 17th-century inspired house at 113 Brattle Street for Longfellow's middle daughter, Edith, and her husband, Richard Henry Dana III, son of the author of *Two Years Before the Mast* (figure 6.127). Described in the *Chronicle* as "picturesque and peculiarly attractive with its gables and latticed windows," the house was simple in form and detail, but striking with its steep paired gables and bold color scheme (Dec. 3, 1887). The clapboards and shingles were stained deep red. The clear cypress trim was originally finished with shellac, but that did not weather well, and it was soon painted a grayish tan. The Lincoln Institute of Land Policy recreated these early colors during a restoration in 1990.

Sumner Brooks, a commission merchant, laid out sixteen small lots on Lancaster and Humboldt streets behind his

FIGURE 6.126 John Brewster double house, 23–25 Brewster Street (1884, John Besarick, architect). Photo ca. 1938.

FIGURE 6.127 Edith Longfellow Dana house, 113 Brattle Street (1887, Andrews & Jaques, architects). Photo ca. 1890.

Massachusetts Avenue house in 1882 and started building rental houses for middle-class tenants. His builder, North Cambridge carpenter Nathaniel Bunker, put up three surprisingly old-fashioned Italianate houses at 9–11, 10, and 15 Humboldt in 1882–83. Soon, however, Brooks changed styles, perhaps influenced by boot and shoe dealer Cyrus D. Wilder's up-to-date Queen Anne at 13 Lancaster designed by Boston architect J. Merrill Brown in 1885. In 1884 and 1885 Brooks built restrained Queen Anne houses on his narrowest lots at 15, 17, and 19 Lancaster and more expansive irregular compositions on his larger lots at 9 and 18 Lancaster and 12 Humboldt streets (figure 6.128). Nine Lancaster shows the lively surface variation and asymmetry that was produced by multiple shingle patterns, bands of vertical siding, and irregular window placement, while 18 Lancaster (1885) boasted a diagonal porch and two-story octagonal bays to take advantage of its corner location (see figure 6.119).

FIGURE 6.128 Sumner Brooks tenant house, 9 Lancaster Street (1885). The unknown designer relied on ornament and texture to establish asymmetry, unlike Henry Van Brunt's subtle juxtaposition of shapes at 167 Brattle Street. Photo ca. 1938.

Unlike these single-owner ventures, other new streets developed in the 1880s with houses built by individuals. Henry M. Clarke's trustees laid out Hurlbut Street in 1882 and sold the empty lots. All but one of the ten single-family houses are Queen Anne in style, and most date from 1885 to 1887. The earliest, 3 Hurlbut (ca. 1882), belonged to Michael Tracey, a builder living on nearby Bowdoin Street, who used Queen Anne elements to accent its corner location. Others were set on fairly narrow lots and organized around large front-facing gables with decorative shingles, such as 33 Hurlbut (ca. 1885), built for real estate broker Enos Reed, 25 Hurlbut (1887, John C. Weld), built for Harvard Square dry goods dealer Horace Low, and builder Zebah Hayden's house at 39 Hurlbut (1886). A house at 9 Hurlbut, built in 1885 for Emma and Abbie Blodgett, unmarried sisters whose father had been a builder in Cambridgeport, shows how inventively Queen Anne picturesqueness could be achieved in a simple overall form (see figure 4.148).

When the Clarke trustees began to develop Garfield Street in 1883, the first houses near Massachusetts Avenue were fairly conservative late Mansards and side-hall Queen Annes, but as construction proceeded the street acquired a compendium of elaborate Queen Anne designs. Built primarily by local architects and builders between 1885 and 1891, these houses are notable for their decorative porches, applied details, and inventive turrets and towers, the opulence of which increased as the decade progressed. Two of the earliest examples, 31–33 and 39 Garfield (both 1886), have elaborate porches wrapping around the front and one side and containing pediments with carved or mastic ornaments leading to the main entrance (see figure 6.129). These seem to have set a standard for the street, as pedimented porches occur on nine of the Queen Anne houses built in the 1880s (figure 6.130). Porches became so important that Robert Farquhar, a Boston seedsman displeased with the plainness of his 1891 house at 34 Garfield, soon hired builder C.F. Willard to add an extensive wrap-around porch with "a very ornamental balustrade and cornice" (*Chronicle,* Sept. 30, 1893).

FIGURE 6.129 Herbert M. Shepherd house, 31-33 Garfield Street (1886). The projecting female head in the porch gable was probably a stock item; a similar figure appears at 2343 Massachusetts Avenue, which carpenter John Sewell built a few months later for brickmaker John E. Parry. Photo 2009.

FIGURE 6.130 Edward E. Wood house, 28 Garfield Street (1886, John A. Steadman, architect and builder). The double pedimented porch, shingled bands, and a lively color scheme were perhaps intended to showcase Woods's paint business and up-to-date taste. Photo 2014.

Towers and turrets were also important features on Garfield Street. Boston architect and builder William Woodward's only Cambridge commission included a second floor corner turret perched dramatically on a single curved bracket at 45 Garfield (1886), the home of produce dealer Joseph Estabrook. James Fogerty's design for Sarah B. Coon at 36 Garfield, described by the *Tribune* on September 17, 1887, as "slightly Queen Anne," featured a prominent three-story square corner tower rising through a decorative pedimented porch (figure 6.131). Boston architect Eugene L. Clarke designed a tall three-story cylindrical tower that emerges from the side of 49 Garfield, follows the curve of the porch, and dominates the composition (figure 6.132).

Enthusiasm for the "new Queen Anne houses" going up on Massachusetts Avenue and Avon Hill in the mid-1880s was nearly unbounded. The *Chronicle* and the *Tribune* described them as "splendid," "decidedly handsome," and "among the

best in the city," on "sites unsurpassed" (*Tribune,* Jan. 1, 1886; *Chronicle,* Jan. 9, 1886, June 25, 1887). The towered houses at 1718, 1722, and 1728 Massachusetts Avenue, built in 1885 for Frank and Horace Partridge, athletic goods manufacturers and importers, and B.F. Hunt, a Boston ladies' accessories merchant, were the most flamboyant on the avenue (see figure 4.179). At the corner of Lancaster Street, Edward Wardwell, a Boston dealer in fancy goods, built a many-gabled Queen Anne in 1884–85 (figure 6.133). Although Wardwell's lot had only 60 feet of frontage on the avenue, the unknown designer took full advantage of its location by adding gables, dormers, and bays to the high hip roof and accenting the wraparound porch with a fanciful gazebo. The house is gone, but remnants of Wardwell's unusual granite fence and his handsome shingled stable, designed two years later by the Boston firm of Rand & Taylor, survive on Lancaster Street.

Figure 6.132 A.S. Bartlett house, 49 Garfield Street (1888, Eugene L. Clarke, architect). Photo 2009.

Figure 6.131 Sarah B. Coon house, 36 Garfield Street (1887, James Fogerty, architect). Photo 2014.

FIGURE 6.133 Edward Wardwell house, 1776 Massachusetts Avenue (1884–85; demolished 1979). Photo ca. 1938.

FIGURE 6.134 East elevation, Frederick and Mary Worcester house, 1734 Massachusetts Avenue (1885-86, J. Merrill Brown, architect). Architect's drawing.

The Frederick and Mary Worcester house at 1734 Massachusetts Avenue (1885-86), just north of the Partridge houses, is the sole Queen Anne survivor on the street (figure 6.134). Mary Gass, daughter of a marketman, purchased the lot in March 1885 and married Worcester, the owner of a retail furniture business in Harvard Square, in December; by the following March they were "at home" on Fridays (*Chronicle,* Mar. 6, 1886). Worcester was one of a new class of Cambridge entrepreneurs who announced their prosperity by settling near the Boston marketmen who had pioneered the suburban development of the avenue in the 1850s. J. Merrill Brown designed the clapboard and shingle house with a high hip roof and center-entrance plan reinforced by the center gable of the porch. He introduced a

subtle asymmetry on the second floor by pulling the left side of the facade forward under a large off-center multitextured gable, but he maintained the decorative focus on the porch with its elaborate turnings and wide center gable with applied scrollwork and rosettes. Lavish interior finishes included an elegant paneled stair hall and a stained glass window at the landing. The Worcester house was converted to office use and restored in 1996.

Avon Hill contains many excellent Queen Annes, including two J. Merrill Brown designs on prominent hilltop locations. Built for J. Harris Niles and Eugene M. Niles, meat packers and marketmen who grew up on a farm in North Jay, Maine, 6 and 9 Walnut Avenue typify the period's passion for the picturesque. The Niles brothers owned a slaughterhouse on Concord Avenue and a store in Boston but were also involved in real estate with another brother, Sullivan Niles (see chapter 4). By 1896 each had built three or four houses, including their own homes. The Niles brothers were typical clients for Brown, a prominent but not top-flight Boston designer, but they generally hired less well-known architects or builders for their speculative projects.

Harris Niles's house at 6 Walnut Avenue (1885) features subtle bands of patterned shingles, a three-story octagonal corner tower, and a prominent overhanging center gable supported by a graceful curved shingled bracket (figure 6.135). The handsome Queen Anne interior included a paneled stair hall with double-spindle screen and a red marble fireplace in the parlor. The diminutive corner tower and ogee-profile dome of the fine shingled carriage house echo those of the house. Eugene's house at 9 Walnut (1887) has a dramatic tower with unusual cone-shaped shingled corbels that support a large circular balcony and glassed-in observatory (figure 6.136). The elevation of the lot and the spectacular views it affords may explain the tower's height, but the lighthouse design is pure fantasy.[10] The porch,

FIGURE 6.135 J. Harris Niles house, 6 Walnut Avenue (1885, J. Merrill Brown, architect). The gazebo porch was added after 1896; a later owner rebuilt both porches with Queen Anne turned posts instead of the smooth columns in this image. Photo ca. 1938.

FIGURE 6.136 Eugene M. Niles house, 9 Walnut Avenue (1887, J. Merrill Brown, architect). The lighthouse tower has an unusual circular balcony. Architect's drawing, published 1890.

with its irregular shape, curving balusters, and bulbous clustered columns, accents the asymmetry of the facade and is almost as compelling as the tower, but the rich array of Queen Anne details on the rest of the house are not well integrated, and the overall design is a composite, much like other Brown designs. The house eschewed the dark, rich colors usually associated with Queen Anne for a lighter Free-Classic palette with warm gray shingles and cream-colored first-floor clapboards and trim that was recreated during a 2009 restoration.

The *Tribune* reported that the frame of 9 Walnut Avenue was made by the Kennebec Framing Co. in Fairfield, Maine, and was "entirely put together before a board was nailed on" (Aug. 6, 1887). The idea of using machinery to manufacture house frames was the brainchild of Waterville inventor O.H. Smith; the prefabricated frames could be "shipped hundreds of miles and put together with the absolute certainty that the pieces will join as perfectly together as though shaped slowly and laboriously on the spot by the most skilled mechanics" (*Leading Business Men of Lewiston and Vicinity,* 231). The Niles brothers are not known to have used Kennebec frames in their other houses, but the practice was unusual enough to warrant comment at the time.

Between 1887 and 1889 the Boston partnership of Henry Hartwell and William C. Richardson designed four houses for newly prosperous merchants and manufacturers on Washington Avenue: a Queen Anne with Colonial Revival overtones at 49 Washington, Shingle Style houses at 33 Washington and 37 Lancaster, and a Colonial Revival at 26 Washington. Three of the houses were permitted on the same day, June 16, 1887, and all employed the same builder, Leander Greeley, who also obtained a permit for his own Hartwell & Richardson house at 284 Harvard Street (1887; demolished 1970).

The firm designed a rather formal house at 49 Washington Avenue for Stillman Kelley, a Boston molasses merchant. Kelley was typical of the firm's clients at this period: newly successful businessmen and merchants looking for houses that were architect-designed, finely appointed, and comfortably up-to-date without being too innovative stylistically. The Kelley house incorporates a number of Colonial Revival details but is clearly Queen Anne in its variety of projecting bays, irregular fenestration, textures, and ornament (figure 6.137). Its basic massing, however, is restrained, and the asymmetry of its main facade is subtle, with two almost balanced gables interrupted by a decorative exterior chimney and a truncated corner turret. Using the corner location to advantage, the architects accented the long Hillside Avenue elevation with a wide overhanging gable and a conical tower. The drawings did not originally include the eyebrow window, but it was a popular motif in the 1880s and may have been added to be more up-to-date. Kelley purchased several lots to ensure that his house would have a dramatic setting. The landscape plan, drawn by Olmsted, Olmsted & Eliot in 1895, placed elaborate flower beds around the house but at Mrs. Kelley's request left the rest of the site open to create an impressive view up Washington Avenue (see figure 4.165). The carriage house at 14 Hillside Avenue was originally built by James Mellen to go with 33 Washington Avenue; Mr. Kelley purchased it

FIGURE 6.137 Stillman Kelley house, 49 Washington Avenue (1887, Hartwell & Richardson, architects). Photo 2015.

from a later owner in 1907. In 2014 it was sold separately from 49 and converted to a residence.

The plan of the Kelley house is basically square, with an oak-paneled center hall that the *Tribune* described as "a spacious room" but which was actually too narrow to function successfully (Aug. 6, 1887; figure 6.138). Instead this constrained space created an impressive vista through a lattice screen into the contrasting openness of the multirun stairway. As in other Hartwell & Richardson designs, the stairway, brilliantly lit by long stained glass windows, was the most successful space in the house. The elaborate turnings and arched screens, the careful juxtaposition of shapes and openings in the paneled walls and ceiling, and the elegantly carved newel posts attested to the firm's talent in interior design (figure 6.139). Major first floor rooms showcased a variety of marble and onyx fireplaces, oak, cherry, and mahogany paneling and mantels, and intricately carved built-in furniture, all typical of the firm's careful attention to detail. The third floor contained an elegant billiard room, and all floors had the latest in electric and gas lighting, steam heat, and speaking tubes. Completed in 1888, the house was reported to have cost close to $50,000, a vast sum when other fine houses nearby cost $6,000 to $10,000. Subsequent owners restored Kelley's original color scheme of yellow ochre with cream trim and in 2015 removed multiple layers of paint to reveal the intricate carvings and joinery of the exterior.

Queen Anne houses with brick or stone lower stories and shingles above were far less common in Old Cambridge than in Newton and Brookline, but several good examples exist on Avon Hill. The most successful is 140 Upland Road (1887), home of William Parry, whose Parry Bros. & Co. brickyard was at the foot of Raymond Street (figure 6.140). Built to accommodate two families but resembling a large single, the house displayed the highest quality pressed brick laid with black mortar on the first and second floors, "tasty trimming" of sandstone at the windows, and a new way of applying terra-cotta decoration invented by the builder, R.A. Hines & Son of Somerville. An elaborate porch with carved brick or terra-cotta in the gable, decorative

FIGURE 6.138 Entrance hall, Stillman Kelley house. Photo 1967.

FIGURE 6.139 Upper stair hall, Stillman Kelley house. Photo 1967.

FIGURE 6.140 William Parry house, 140 Upland Road (1887, William Parry, probable designer). Photo ca. 1938.

FIGURE 6.141 Horace P. Blackman house, 33 Agassiz Street (1890, Eugene Clarke, architect). Photo 2015.

bargeboards, patterned shingles, and "a generous sprinkling of bay windows" contrasted with the formality of the brick facade (*Tribune*, May 28, 1887). The clumsiness of the composition suggests that Parry may have been his own designer, as he was for a two-story addition in 1904.

Boston architect Eugene Clarke, who built several Queen Anne houses on Garfield Street, designed 33 Agassiz Street in 1890 for Horace Blackman, millwork foreman at the Mason & Hamlin Organ & Piano Company in Cambridgeport (figure 6.141). This was the only house in Old Cambridge to use fieldstone for the first story, although H.H. Richardson and others had used stone this way in nearby towns. The patterned shingles were originally treated in an unusual way: each was dipped in either light or dark stain and then laid randomly to reflect the mottled appearance of the stone below. Directly across the street, William Mooney of Rand & Taylor designed the brick and shingle house at 32 Agassiz in 1891 for brick manufacturer

Martin Winslow Sands, who had inherited his father's brickyard at Walden and Garden streets.[11] Both 32 and 33 have towers anchoring the corner and major gables facing each street, but the bold fieldstone arches trimmed with smooth Milford granite at 33 made a more elegant entrance.

In the late 1880s and early 1890s, many builders constructed modest Queen Anne houses that continued the side-hall, gable-end to the street form that had prevailed since the 1840s. A typical client for this type of house was Samuel Holden of 109 Avon Hill Street, a conductor on the Fitchburg Railroad. Other side-hall houses such as 23 Bellevue Avenue (1887), built by carpenter W.T. Smith of Somerville, and 20 Martin Street (1888), by Zebah Hayden, added bracketed porches, angled bay windows, and patterned shingling in the gable (figure 6.142). Hayden was a prolific speculative builder who put up over a hundred houses in Old Cambridge and North Cambridge between 1873 and 1923. Although he often worked with James Fogerty, who had

FIGURE 6.142 Zebah Hayden houses, 18 Martin Street (1887, James Fogerty, architect, left) and 20 Martin Street (1888, Zebah Hayden, designer and builder). Photo 2009.

FIGURE 6.143 Mrs. Elizabeth Anthony house, 28 Linnaean Street (1890, C.H. Blackall, architect). The broken-scroll pediment was recreated in 1994 following the architect's original plans. Photo 2009.

designed a similar side-hall Queen Anne at 18 Martin for him the year before, Hayden apparently drew the plans for 20 himself, borrowing heavily from Fogerty's earlier design. Other examples include 42 Sacramento Street, which Fogerty designed in 1886, and 32 Bowdoin Street, which J.R. & W.P. Richards designed in 1891. By this time the style was on the wane, but Queen Anne details continued to appear on some modest houses.

Elements of the Shingle Style and Colonial Revival movements that emerged in the 1880s became important features of some Queen Anne designs. Many large houses, such as 33 Hurlbut Street (ca. 1885) and 49 Washington Avenue (1887–88), incorporated Palladian windows, dentil cornices, and other classical details. Others, such as 75 Garfield Street (1889–90, Charles H. McClare) and 50 Garden Street (1890, Clarence H. Blackall), used classical columns rather than turned porch posts. One of the most original combinations of Queen Anne and Colonial Revival elements occurs at 28 Linnaean Street (1890), which was

designed for a widow, Elizabeth Anthony, by Clarence Blackall for $6,000 (figure 6.143). The dramatic, oversize broken-scroll pediment above the entrance was unusual, but the large overhanging gable with deep, shingled eaves and a central Palladian window appeared in other Blackall houses, notably 50 Garden Street (1890) and 9 Rutland Street (1892). By the 1890s the quirky exuberance of the Queen Anne period was being replaced by Colonial Revival symmetry and classical forms.

THE SHINGLE STYLE

One of the most interesting variants of the Queen Anne movement was what Vincent Scully termed the "Shingle Style" and James O'Gorman described as "the American version of the English Shavian or Queen Anne" (O'Gorman, *Richardson*, 47). This distinctly American style, which flourished in the 1880s in New England coastal locations, produced long, low, often

L-shaped, houses, with walls, roofs, and almost all ornamental accents sheathed entirely in shingles. Functioning as a flexible membrane, the shingles stretched over a structural framework and could be distended, curved, or punctured. Since shingles formed most of the accents, texture, and ornamentation of these houses, decoration seemed to be an organic part of the structure.

Seventeenth-century New England buildings were commonly shingled, and some 1880s designers used steep overhanging gables to evoke nostalgia for that era; others used large gambrel roofs as a central organizing feature. The use of shingles for walls was certainly not new, but the way Shingle Style architects used the shingles to envelop a building in an unbroken and often undulating skin was unlike earlier practice. The Shingle Style shared major organizing elements with the contemporary but more ubiquitous Queen Anne. Both styles employed asymmetrical facades, varied window treatments reflecting open and often irregular floor plans, extensive porches and verandas, and a penchant for towers (although often only partially articulated and barely emerging from the shingled skin of the building).

The Shingle Style was largely an architect's rather than a builder's style. The earliest and most notable example is the house that H.H. Richardson designed for Mary Fisk Stoughton at 90 Brattle Street in 1882 (figure 6.144). This was the only residence that Richardson designed in Cambridge, his other buildings being Sever (1878) and Austin (1881) halls at Harvard. Richardson was not the first practitioner of the Shingle Style, and the Stoughton House was not his first use of shingles, but it was his earliest shingled country house in the Boston area, setting a high standard for those that followed.

The Stoughton house was praised in the architectural press, but its design and construction did not run smoothly, and the client was far from happy with the results. After the death of her husband, Mrs. Stoughton wanted to move to Cambridge to be near her son, the popular historian John Fiske, who lived at 22 Berkeley Street. On his recommendation she bought a lot on the corner of Brattle and Ash streets in May 1882. Mrs. Stoughton was accustomed to a very formal urban life on Fifth

FIGURE 6.144 Mary Fisk Stoughton house, 90 Brattle Street (1882, H.H. Richardson, architect). This early photo shows the original configuration of the house, before the loggia was enclosed in 1900. Photo ca. 1890.

Avenue in New York City, and Richardson seems to have been her son's choice rather than hers. The architect received the commission in June 1882, just before he left for a three-month tour of Europe; Mrs. Stoughton also left to travel abroad, leaving Fiske to handle all architectural decisions. The plans were most likely prepared after Richardson's return in the fall. Although Fiske wrote to his mother in October 1882: "I think building a house will be good for you," she was not particularly pleased with this shingled country residence (Fiske letters, 475–76). Her complaints during construction were so numerous that Richardson withdrew from all but the exterior work, writing to her on August 1, 1883, that "you certainly must prefer to consult some architect in whom you have more confidence" (Floyd, *Henry Hobson Richardson*, 256). Much of the interior remained unfinished when she moved in on December 17, 1883, and it is not known who completed the formal rooms. Only the stair hall and

dining room are assumed to be Richardson's work, and there is a curious disjunction between the interior and exterior of the house (figure 6.145).

Unlike the assemblage of disparate parts that characterized many Queen Annes, the exterior of the Stoughton house as originally designed exemplified the organic qualities that were distinguishing features of the Shingle Style. Sheathed in large cypress shingles stained deep green-brown and trimmed in dark olive, the L-shaped house spread horizontally along Brattle Street and depended on projecting volumes, voids, and shadows instead of applied ornament. From the gable on the corner of Ash Street the shingles bent around a partial tower nestled in the angle of the L and across an open loggia to an end bay that in early sketches had a gable. The flow of the composition was not interrupted even by the main entrance, which Richardson tucked into the shadows under the porch.

By 1889 Fiske could write that his mother had "grown to love 90 Brattle" and wanted him to move in with her (ibid., 569). In 1900 he hired Richardson's successor firm, Shepley, Rutan & Coolidge, to enlarge the house with a music room and entrance on Ash Street, a conservatory off the dining room, and a 47-foot-long Edwardian library that he described as "a miracle of beauty and coziness" (Fiske papers, Dec. 30, 1900). The loggia, which had originally been filled with vines and flowers, became an enclosed hall and gallery leading to the new library, thus altering one of the most picturesque elements of Richardson's design. Fiske never moved in. He died suddenly in 1901 while his library was being relocated; his mother died in 1904. The house remained in Mrs. Stoughton's estate until 1925 and survived substantially unchanged until 1988, when a new owner installed an elevator (disguised as a massive brick chimney) and converted the kitchen in Fiske's library wing into a garage.

Between 1885 and 1895, contemporaries and followers of Richardson built some fine examples of the Shingle Style. William Ralph Emerson (1833–1917), an Illinois native who grew up in Boston and apprenticed with builder-architect Jonathan Preston, had shown a strong interest in vernacular colonial architecture as early as 1869. Emerson had no academic training beyond a public school education, but he lectured on the subject and worked on the restoration of the Old Ship Meetinghouse in Hingham. His designs for homes in Milton and summer houses on the New England coast advanced the development of shingled architecture in the 1880s.[12] He integrated Colonial Revival elements, particularly large gambrel roofs, into his designs, and experimented with the decorative possibilities of shingles well into the 1890s.

The ten houses that Emerson designed in Old Cambridge between 1884 and 1901 show the range of his work. His first, 158 Brattle Street (1884), was an early Colonial Revival with picturesque Queen Anne features; the dramatic sweep of clapboards over the finely detailed colonial doorway anticipated his later use of undulating shingle forms (see figure 6.157). Houses at 45 Garden Street (1885–86), 11 Berkeley Street (1886), and 182 Brattle Street (1895) display his fluid use of shingles (figure 6.146). Others at 76 Sparks Street (1886) and 110 Irving Street (1889), although shingled, have pitched roofs, gabled dormers, and overhanging gables that recall vernacular colonial precedents. His house for William James at 95 Irving Street (1895), with its massive gambrel roof and formal composition, anticipates the impending triumph of the Colonial Revival.

Emerson's use of an undulating shingled skin is well illustrated at 11 Berkeley Street, which he designed in 1886 for John Allyn, a Shakespeare scholar and founder of the Boston publishing firm Allyn & Bacon. Built on a deep half-acre lot carved out of Allyn's mother's adjoining property, 11 Berkeley was able to follow the long, horizontal form characteristic of Shingle Style houses by setting the narrow gable end toward the street. Rounded second floor corners are echoed in the graceful curves of the porch, while sawtooth shingles, canted windows in the gable end, and

FIGURE 6.146 Helen Allyn Upton house, 45 Garden Street (1885–86, William R. Emerson, architect). Photo 1968.

an exposed chimney create a play of light and shadow. The juxtaposition of projections and recesses continues on the informal garden facade. The house has undergone a number of changes, including the loss of Emerson's original interior trim, but the unusual twisted porch columns have been restored.[13] His much smaller shingled house at 45 Garden Street (1886-86) designed for John's sister, Helen Allyn Upton, was also organized around a large gambrel roof. The undulating window hoods, sweeping front gambrel, and merging of shingled wall and roof were characteristic of his work.

The 1887 Shingle Style house and stable complex at 37 Lancaster Street built for Henry Yerxa, head of a retail grocery company, was Hartwell & Richardson's masterpiece (figure 6.147). Set on a prominent corner near the top of Avon Hill, the basic geometry of the house is deceptively simple: a rectangular box capped by a hip roof and varied by unequal corner towers. A gracefully curved and angled porch, partly open and partly enclosed, unifies the facade. The porch, balanced dormers, and

FIGURE 6.147 Henry Yerxa house, 37 Lancaster Street (1887, Hartwell & Richardson, architects). Photo 2009.

easy flow of design elements impart a sense of equilibrium to the asymmetrical composition. The irregular size and placement of windows was determined by interior considerations rather than by exterior balance. The shingles themselves provide the ornament, curving out over the windows, creating a recessed balcony on the west end, and rounding the corners of the dormers and entrance porch so that the entire house seems enveloped in a continuous shingle skin. The house had only two owners before 2011 and remained in almost original condition, although the wood shingle roof, an important component in establishing the visual continuity between roof and wall planes in Shingle Style houses, was replaced with asphalt in 2003.

The floor plan of the Yerxa house was Hartwell & Richardson's most effective attempt to open up interior residential space in the manner that was so characteristic of the 1880s (figure 6.148). The front rooms flowed together through wide openings, while

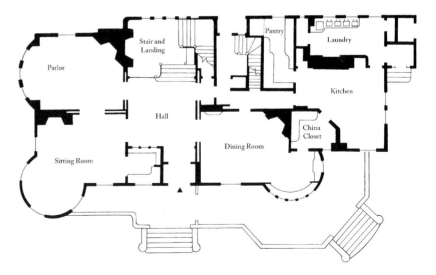

FIGURE 6.148 First floor plan, Henry Yerxa house.

the central hall was a true living space that extended through two floors, a favorite device of this firm. A narrow vestibule provided a dramatic entrance into the large open hall and focused attention on the elaborate oak stairway and the monumental carved-brick fireplace and sitting area at the landing (figure 6.149). The heavy beamed ceiling of the lower hall contrasted with the soaring two-story paneled stairway, which was lit by brilliant stained-glass windows (figure 6.150). Other interior finishes included elaborate carved niches, turnings, and woven wood spandrels, intricately detailed fireplaces, and patterned Lincrusta friezes, as well as a panoply of built-in chests, seats, and inglenooks. In the dining room a massive stone fireplace contrasted with the golden oak woodwork, grisaille and yellow glass, and finely carved china cupboard and window seat built into a corner tower. The carriage house also showcased the flexibility and picturesqueness of shingle construction, with rounded corners, recessed windows, and a great sweeping gable roof with a recessed arch supported on shingled brackets.

Hartwell & Richardson's Shingle Style design at 33 Washington Avenue shares elements with the Yerxa and Kelley houses, which were all permitted on the same day in 1887. Built for James Mellen, head of Curtis Davis & Co., a Cambridgeport soap manufacturer that later became part of Lever Brothers, 33 is shingled but similar in massing to 49 Washington and to Colonial Revival houses that the firm designed in Arlington and North Andover. The street facade balances a gable and a corner tower around a high hip roof, and a shingled porch pulls the facade together, as in the Yerxa house. The interior showed the elegant paneling, stairway, stained glass windows, and attention to detail that characterized the architects' best work.

While the Yerxa house and stable marked the height of the Shingle Style in Old Cambridge, it was considerably later in date than H.H. Richardson's trend-setting Stoughton house and Emerson's pioneering shingled work. Hartwell & Richardson were not in the forefront of architectural innovation. They relied principally on precedents established by others, but they were skillful designers and much in demand among a certain

FIGURE 6.149 Carved brick fireplace on stair landing, Henry Yerxa house. The andirons and chandelier are original. Photo 1967.

FIGURE 6.150 Stair hall, Henry Yerxa house. Intricate carved oak woodwork and original tooled wallpaper showed the firm's expertise in interior design. Photo 1967.

clientele. In the large shingled houses they built for successful businessmen they created well-designed, well-constructed, and beautifully appointed examples of this style.

Other Boston architects building Shingle Style houses in Old Cambridge included Longfellow, Alden, & Harlow and Andrews & Jaques. All five principals in these firms received their architectural education at M.I.T., and at least three (Alexander Wadsworth Longfellow, Frank Alden, and Robert Andrews) worked as draftsmen in H.H. Richardson's office in the 1880s before establishing their own practices. Both firms were strongly influenced by colonial architecture. Their Shingle Style houses combined the multiple gables, overhangs, and diamond paned windows of the 17th century with the open planning and irregularity of the Queen Anne, while their interiors often incorporated more formal 18th-century elements. Both firms also designed traditional Colonial Revival buildings during the same period. The styles coexisted comfortably, as shown in the adjacent houses built in 1887 for Longfellow's daughters: the 17th-century-inspired design at 113 Brattle Street by Andrews & Jaques, and the Colonial Revival at 115 Brattle by Longfellow & Harlow (see figures 6.127 and 6.158).

The shingled houses that Andrews & Jaques (Andrews, Jaques & Rantoul after 1889) designed in Old Cambridge tended to take their inspiration from the 17th century, with steep overhanging gables, diamond-paned windows, and shingled string courses between floors. In addition to 113 Brattle Street, examples include 9 Mercer Circle/132 Brattle Street, designed in 1886 as part of Gardiner Hubbard's development; 147 Brattle Street, designed in 1887 for Judge Charles Almy; and 11 Highland Street, designed in 1891 for Boston lawyer Moses P. White with very deep overhangs supported by curved and shingled consoles.

The firm of Longfellow, Alden & Harlow (Longfellow & Harlow before 1887) is best known for the Richardsonian Romanesque Cambridge City Hall (1888), but they also designed twenty houses in Cambridge between 1886 and 1894. While most of these are formal Colonial Revival designs, 155 Brattle Street (1889), 9 Buckingham Street (1892), and 6 Channing Place (1894) are excellent examples of the 17th-century-inspired Shingle Style. As Margaret Floyd pointed out, many of the firm's commissions came through Longfellow's Harvard and yachting connections. For his sailing friend Arthur Lithgow Devens (Harvard 1874), Longfellow designed 155 Brattle in 1889 with characteristic dark shingles, overhanging steep gables and floors, and a shingled Gothic arch in the principal dormer, a motif that recurs in a number of the firm's buildings. Nine Buckingham Street (1892), built as rental property for fellow Maine sailor and Harvard friend William Griswold, is simpler but has a typical Shingle Style dark undulating skin, oriel window, and hollowed-out corner porch.

The firm's most picturesque Cambridge house, 6 Channing Place, was designed in 1894 for Olive Swan and her husband, J. Bertram Williams, who graduated from Harvard a year after the architect. Floyd described it as the firm's "masterpiece of these medievalizing, wooden domestic designs" that "evoked the buildings of 17th century New England" (*Architecture After Richardson*, 93; figure 6.151). Steep decorative gables project from each facade, overhangs at every floor organize the composition horizontally, and a characteristic pointed arch marks the front gable. The flexible shingled skin controls the design, projecting and receding to incorporate a variety of recessed and open porches and changes in floor levels. The regrettable two-story addition on the west side that Longfellow designed for Mrs. Williams in 1911 upset the original subtle balance of gables and dormers.

The firm's unusual stone house at 1 Follen Street was designed in 1888 for Edwin H. Abbot, a prominent attorney and president of the Wisconsin Central Railroad. Constructed of tawny ochre granite with red sandstone trim and an orange tile roof, the house has roots in the Shingle Style and is sometimes compared to H.H. Richardson's Glessner house in Chicago, which was completed in 1887 (figure 6.152). Much has been made of Abbot's being a Midwesterner, but he was born in Beverly, Massachusetts, and graduated from Harvard College in 1855 and the Law School in 1862. After practicing law in Boston, he went west in 1876 to begin what the *Boston Transcript* called "his great railroad career" (May 31, 1927). His choice of building

FIGURE 6.151 Olive and J. Bertram Williams house, 6 Channing Place (1894, Longfellow, Alden & Harlow, architects). Photo ca. 1900.

FIGURE 6.152 Edwin H. Abbot house, 1 Follen Street (1888, Longfellow, Alden & Harlow, architects). Photo 2015.

material may have been influenced by his concern about fire, rather than his familiarity with Midwestern building practices.[14] Abbot used not only the architects of Cambridge City Hall, but also H.H. Richardson's masters of masonry construction, Norcross Bros., to erect "the first stone house in the city" and "one of the most costly" (*Tribune*, July 27, 1889). Ten years after his death in 1927, his son sold the house to the Longy School of Music, which added a concert hall and library in 1968.

The Abbot house follows an L-shaped plan with three low, partially emerging towers that vary the otherwise flat facades in a manner characteristic of Richardson's Sever Hall, Crane Memorial Library, and Stoughton House. The quarry-faced stone is set in regular courses, while the brownstone bands and the spaces between them vary in width to produce a lively exterior. An eyebrow window adds another Richardsonian touch. The heavy medieval-inspired door with large iron strap hinges is recessed behind a low sandstone arch. The interior was sumptuously paneled and carved, with heavy beamed ceilings but also classical moldings and pilasters, indicative of the designer's increasing use of colonial motifs in the late 1880s.

Old Cambridge also has several Shingle Style houses by less well-known architects. The house that Boston architect Henry Burdett designed in 1886 for young Boston lawyer Warren K. Blodgett at 7 Acacia Street nearly abutted the Stoughton house and was clearly influenced by it (figure 6.153). The characteristic flowing composition with an integral turret was disrupted when Blodgett retained Dwight & Chandler in 1896 to add a nearly freestanding turret at the opposite front corner. In 1887 Hingham resident John D. Long, a former governor of Massachusetts, commissioned Boston architect S.J.F. Thayer to design 107 Washington Avenue as an investment (see figure 4.159). Set well back on the lot, this modest shingled cottage had a steep sloping roof that incorporated a wide gabled dormer and a simple porch with shingles that flared out at the ground level, similar to the battered lower courses of larger houses. Five years later a new owner moved the cottage closer to the street and greatly extended it, diluting its Shingle Style character with Colonial

FIGURE 6.153 Warren K. Blodgett house, 7 Acacia Street (1886, H.C. Burdett, architect). Sketch published 1889.

Revival forms and detail. Other modest examples include 11 Hillside Avenue (1887, J.R. & W.P. Richards) and 46 Brewster Street (1890, Chamberlin & Austin).

A popular Shingle Style variation featured an encompassing gambrel roof that occupied more than half of the total height of the house and blurred the division between roof and wall, as at 45 Garden Street (1885–86, William R. Emerson) and 6 Appleton Street (1887, Cabot & Chandler). Shed dormers were often fused into the slope of the gambrel roof. As in other Shingle Style houses, there was no extraneous ornament, and the shingles themselves provided the decorative interest. The construction of 6 Appleton for the recently widowed Mrs. Estes Howe inspired her 23-year-old daughter, Lois Lilley Howe, to study architecture at M.I.T.

Cambridge lacked the large open spaces, picturesque views, and irregular natural sites that made the Shingle Style so appropriate for coastal and country locations. By 1895 the best shingled work in Old Cambridge had been done, and architects turned toward more formal compositions and Colonial Revival ornamentation, as at 5 Fayerweather Street (1894, C.H. McClare) and 107 Walker Street (1894, John Bemis). Fenestration became less varied, and large arched windows accented third floor gables, as at 15 Channing Street (1899, Clark & Russell) and 12 Concord Avenue (1890, Cabot, Everett, & Mead). The use of shingles by no means ended after 1900, but by then practitioners had conclusively moved away from Queen Anne principles, and houses were increasingly Colonial Revival in style.

EARLY GEORGIAN REVIVAL

The 1876 Centennial Exposition in Philadelphia not only introduced contemporary English Queen Anne buildings and architectural trends, but also sparked interest among Americans in their own colonial heritage. Healing the scars of Reconstruction and the lingering effects of the financial panic of 1873, the centennial celebration fostered nationalism and a nostalgia for the past that had a profound effect on the development of American architecture. The exhibition's New England log house and Connecticut saltbox focused attention on the vernacular buildings of the American colonies and increased interest in colonial forms, particularly among architects. In 1877 New York architects Charles McKim, William Mead, and Stanford White, who became the country's leading practitioners of the Neoclassical style, traveled to New England to make "sketches and measured drawings of many of the important Colonial houses" (Scully, 30). Other architects followed their lead.

The term "Colonial" in the 19th century encompassed many forms. New houses that drew inspiration and motifs from 17th-century prototypes were often grouped with the Shingle Style, while designs that reflected Georgian ideals and displayed classical details from 18th-century buildings were labeled Colonial Revival. Equally rooted in the colonial past, these trends developed contemporaneously in the 1880s and were often combined: Queen Anne and Shingle Style compositions often incorporated Georgian and other classical motifs, while Colonial Revival houses with symmetrical, Georgian plans sometimes showed a Queen Anne freedom of detail. The two very different houses that Longfellow's daughters built next to their father's 1759 Georgian mansion demonstrated the popularity of both trends. Edith Longfellow Dana's dark-shingled, 17th-century-inspired house at 113 Brattle was described as "picturesque and peculiarly attractive with its gables and latticed windows," while Anne Longfellow Thorp's serenely classical house at 115 based on 18th-century forms was called "an admirable specimen of the best Colonial style" (*Chronicle*, Dec. 3, 1887).

Georgian Revival buildings became increasingly popular as the Shingle Style waned. Cambridge's surviving 18th-century buildings were recognized as national landmarks and set the tone for much of the city's new residential construction. A booming real estate market in the 1880s provided many opportunities for architects to complement Brattle Street's Georgian mansions, and some of the most prominent architects of the time worked in Old Cambridge in the new style. The earliest examples used colonial models quite inventively. By the 1890s designs were generally more formal and showed greater understanding of the sources; some were even copies of specific 18th-century houses.

In addition to being a virtual warehouse of Georgian prototypes, Old Cambridge was becoming the residence of choice for affluent families with Harvard connections, architects with deep New England roots, and recent graduates of two of the oldest American architectural schools, M.I.T. (1866) and Harvard (1893). Memories of ancestral homes and college haunts combined with postcentennial nostalgia to spur the development of the Colonial Revival style. At the same time, the growing number of architects who had studied at the École des Beaux-Arts in Paris reinforced the general trend toward the Neoclassical. The overwhelming classicism of the World's Columbian Exposition in Chicago in 1893 showed how far the country's architecture had shifted since 1876, and an increasingly formal, symmetrical, and often archeologically correct Georgian Revival became the most prevalent residential style.

This growing awareness of the country's early heritage also stimulated a movement toward historic preservation. Boston architects pioneered the direct study of surviving buildings and promoted interest in early American architecture through lectures and articles. John Hubbard Sturgis (1834–88) was particularly active in one of the country's earliest historic preservation struggles, the unsuccessful fight to save the 1737 John Hancock house on Beacon Hill. His measured drawings of the house made just prior to its demolition in 1863 were the first of their kind in this country and enabled many subsequent renditions of Georgian features. By incorporating Hancock's staircase in a new house in Manchester, Massachusetts, Sturgis also established a precedent for the reuse of original fabric, which gained a wide following.

In the 1870s and 1880s scholarship on American colonial architecture was still in its infancy, and many designers were later criticized for their painstaking copies of original elements on the one hand and their lack of comprehensive understanding of the period on the other. Like many architects, Lois Lilley Howe collected photographs and made measured drawings of colonial houses and details to use in her projects; now preserved in the M.I.T. archives, these provide a valuable record of architectural practice in this period. New developments in photography opened the medium to amateurs and allowed images to be mass-produced, creating a vast library of architectural imagery available to the public, although often with little discussion of period context.

Sturgis and his partner, Charles Brigham, based two Cambridge houses on the Hancock house. The Edward W. Hooper house at 25 Reservoir Street (1872) and the Arthur Astor Carey house at 28 Fayerweather Street (1882) had gambrel roofs, center-hall plans, and interior elements that recalled the Hancock house, although the overall massing and detailing were influenced by the prevailing taste for the picturesque. The Hooper house, which was a decade before its time stylistically, had Stick Style features that lessened the Colonial Revival feeling of the exterior (see figure 6.100). Widely published, the Carey house was a pioneering effort in the development of the Colonial Revival in New England. The rear lean-to recalled the 17th-century

FIGURE 6.154 Arthur Astor Carey house, 28 Fayerweather Street (1882, Sturgis & Brigham, architects). Photo ca. 1886.

FIGURE 6.155 This romantic sketch done in 1888 by Sturgis & Brigham shows the north and east facades of the Arthur Astor Carey house as seen from Reservoir Street; a later owner incorporated the saltbox roof into a gambrel ell.

Cooper-Frost-Austin house (figures 6.154–6.155). Other features, including the gambrel roof, dormers with alternating triangular and segmental pediments, a balcony projecting over the entrance on scrolled consoles, and an elaborate broken-scroll pediment were derived directly from the Hancock house. By contrast, the asymmetrical plan, massing, and irregular fenestration showed the architects' desire to create a picturesque exterior and more open interior plan. Architectural historian Margaret Floyd considered Sturgis & Brigham's design as important to the formulation of the Colonial Revival movement as the better-publicized early work of Charles McKim. With this house Sturgis can be credited with re-introducing Georgian details to Cambridge architecture.

The lavishly appointed interior of 28 Fayerweather Street reveals how closely intertwined the Queen Anne and Colonial Revival styles were in the early 1880s. The large entrance hall, with its massive fireplace, picturesque staircase, and quaint corner writing nook, was essentially a Queen Anne feature, but the stair balusters and newel posts referenced the 1737 Hancock stairway (figure 6.156). Carey, a grandson of John Jacob Astor of New York and a recent Harvard graduate, was a sophisticated client who played an important role in the Boston arts community and helped to found the Society of Arts and Crafts in 1897.

William Ralph Emerson designed the city's first symmetrical Colonial Revival house at 158 Brattle Street in 1884 for publisher Charles E. Wentworth (figure 6.157). Emerson was an early spokesman against the destruction of colonial houses, which he characterized in 1869 as "the only true American architecture" (in Zaitzevsky, *Emerson,* 3). His Shingle Style designs often included wide gambrel roofs and Colonial Revival ornament. The Wentworth house is an unusually early example of the formal Georgian center-hall type that became so popular in the early 20th century. The symmetrical three-bay facade, topped by three pedimented dormers connected by a balustrade, has a formal center entrance with leaded fan, sidelights, and classical details, but the gracefully undulating clapboards of the oriel

FIGURE 6.156 Entrance hall and staircase, Arthur Astor Carey house. Photo ca. 1886

FIGURE 6.157 Charles Wentworth house, 158 Brattle Street (1884, William R. Emerson, architect). Photo 1968.

projecting over the entrance show a Queen Anne–like freedom characteristic of Emerson's work.

The Colonial Revival buildings of Alexander Wadsworth Longfellow, a nephew of the poet who had been educated at Harvard, M.I.T., and the École des Beaux-Arts, were less picturesque but more correct than those by Sturgis and Emerson. His first Cambridge commissions were both on the drawing boards at the end of 1886. John Brooks, a brother-in-law of John Fiske whose mother had commissioned H.H. Richardson's landmark Shingle Style house, hired Longfellow to design a Colonial hip-roofed house next door at 5 Ash Street; at the same time he was designing a house nearby for his cousin, Anne Longfellow Thorp.

Joseph and Anne Thorp's house at 115 Brattle Street was Longfellow's most influential early work. The gambrel-roofed, center-entrance house was one of the earliest "correct" Colonial Revival houses in Cambridge, and its advanced design, prominent location, and distinguished client attracted considerable attention (figure 6.158). The overall proportions of 115 Brattle are robust, and the steep gambrel roof projects on a modillion cornice well beyond the facade. These features contrast with the proportions of a Bulfinch-inspired central bay with attenuated Corinthian and Ionic columns, swag-and-garland decorative frieze, and delicate balustrade. The grouping of the first floor windows in triplets, the use of undivided sash, and the elaborate side porch and porte-cochère were contemporary touches. The house was originally "painted a delicate cream with white trimmings" to echo the appearance of the Vassall-Craigie-Longfellow house at that time; these colors were published nationally in the 1890s as a model for Colonial Revival houses, and soon became the most popular colonial paint scheme in Old Cambridge (*Tribune,* Jan. 28, 1888).

The interior plan and variety of finishes demonstrate the relationship between the Queen Anne and early Colonial Revival movements. Although ornamental details came from 18th-century sources, unusually wide openings between rooms and hallways produced a spaciousness very different from Georgian compartmentalized rooms. The large open hall had dark

FIGURE 6.158 Anne Longfellow Thorp house, 115 Brattle Street (1887, Alexander W. Longfellow, architect). Photo 1887.

FIGURE 6.159 Hallway with dark Queen Anne woodwork, Anne Longfellow Thorp house. Photo 1887.

woodwork more characteristic of Queen Anne interiors, while the parlor had light woodwork with Adamesque swags, columns, and delicate oval fireplace motifs (figure 6.159).

Peabody & Stearns, Andrews & Jaques, Arthur Little, Hartwell & Richardson, and Chamberlin & Whidden all designed Colonial Revival houses in the area. Andrews & Jaques's 1887 design for William Brewster at 145 Brattle Street has a Colonial Revival cornice, porch, and gambrel roof. The combination of clapboard facade and brick end walls was common in the 18th century, although not in Cambridge.

Chamberlin & Whidden's 1886 house at 54 Highland Street for wealthy lawyer and amateur historian Robert Noxon Toppan was the first all-brick Colonial Revival residence in Old Cambridge (figure 6.160). Common brick walls laid in white mortar were accented by pressed brick quoins laid in red mortar and a wide wooden cornice, a striking combination at this period. The asymmetrical arrangement and variety of windows and the exaggerated Palladian window lighting the stairs show a lingering Queen Anne influence. William E. Chamberlin, son of a Cambridge hardware dealer and builder, graduated in 1877 from M.I.T.'s architecture program, where he overlapped one year with A.W. Longfellow. After gaining experience in the Boston office of Sturgis & Brigham and the New York office of McKim, Mead & White, he launched his own practice in Boston in 1884. William M. Whidden, a classmate, joined McKim, Mead & White after spending four postgraduate years at the École des Beaux-Arts. The firm sent him to Portland, Oregon, in 1882 to superintend construction of a hotel there, but he returned to Boston after two years to join Chamberlin's practice. The *AABN* illustrated the Toppan house in 1887, complementing an influential series of measured drawings of Georgian and Federal houses that it had been publishing since February 1886. Chamberlin & Whidden's design for 9 Waterhouse Street, built for Harvard physics professor Harold Whiting in 1887, featured an elaborate overhanging cornice and a double bow front facing the Common. In the same year the *Tribune* described their shingled gambrel design for 29 Lancaster Street as "intensely

FIGURE 6.160 Anne and Robert Noxon Toppan house, 54 Highland Street (1886, Chamberlin & Whidden, architects). Photo 1968.

colonial" (Aug. 6, 1887).[15] The restrained Classicism of the partners' houses perhaps reflected their experience with the McKim firm.

The house that Hartwell & Richardson designed in 1889 at 26 Washington Avenue is an outstanding example of the early Colonial Revival and makes an interesting comparison with their Queen Anne and Shingle Style houses nearby (figure 6.161). Built for David A. Ritchie of Lamb & Ritchie, a pioneering Cambridgeport manufacturer of galvanized pipe and gutters, the high hip-roofed, center-entrance house exhibits the firm's characteristic controlled asymmetry. Although many decorative elements, such as the entrance porch and roof balustrade, are Georgian-inspired, the way these are used contributes a lingering Queen Anne feeling. Curved oriels are tucked under a second story overhang and supported on carved consoles, a brick chimney appears and recedes on the end wall, and a variety of small-paned sash enlivens the window treatment. A spacious stable with cross-gabled roof and diamond-paned sash takes

FIGURE 6.161 David A. Ritchie house, 26 Washington Avenue (1889, Hartwell & Richardson, architects). Photo ca. 1890.

FIGURE 6.162 Edwin D. Mellen house, the Greycroft, 1590 Massachusetts Avenue (1896, Hartwell, Richardson & Driver, architects; demolished 1980).

advantage of the sloping site to shield this mini-estate from surrounding properties.

Hartwell & Richardson designed two other Colonial Revival houses that shared similar features and were among the largest and most costly residences on Massachusetts Avenue. On the corner of Sacramento Street, Boston lumber dealer James A. Wood's 1888 house had a Palladian window, pedimented dormers, and a second floor overhang supported on scrolled brackets that recalled 26 Washington Avenue. A few blocks away, soap manufacturer Edwin D. Mellen, whose father had commissioned Hartwell & Richardson to build 33 Washington Avenue in 1887, hired Hartwell, Richardson & Driver in 1896 to design an even more elaborate mansion at 1590 Massachusetts Avenue. The *Chronicle* described the Greycroft as a superb residence in a style that was "quite purely that of the old Colonial" (May 22, 1897). A circular columned porch and balustrade faced the avenue, while decorative pilasters accented the corners of the house and the central section of the equally opulent

garden facade (figure 6.162; see also figure 4.180). Arched and pedimented dormers and a wide modillion cornice ornamented the high hip roof, and oriel and decorative windows faced the garden. The interior contained the richly carved quartered oak woodwork, built-in cabinetry, and elaborate fireplace on the stair landing that were characteristic of these architects' work. It also had the most up-to-date technology, including centrally controlled electric clocks in every room, fourteen telephones, a lift, and an incinerator for kitchen waste. While James Wood's house was moved around the corner to 3 Sacramento Street in 1925 and now serves as a Harvard dormitory, the Greycroft was demolished in 1980 for an eight-story apartment building. As a consequence of its loss the city council enacted a landmark designation ordinance in 1983.

The house at 168 Brattle Street that Joseph G. Thorp, a wealthy Wisconsin lumberman, commissioned from Boston architect Arthur Little in 1888 is one of the city's most creative and unusual Colonial Revivals. Thorp built the house to live in

FIGURE 6.163 Joseph G. Thorp house, 168 Brattle Street (1888, Arthur Little, architect). The main entrance faced south to the garden rather than north to Brattle Street. Photo ca. 1890.

with his daughter Sara, the young widow of noted Norwegian violinist Ole Bull; she was quite involved in its planning and inherited it in 1895. Arthur Little studied at M.I.T. in the 1870s and started as a draftsman in the office of Peabody & Stearns. He and Robert S. Peabody shared an early interest in New England's 18th-century houses; in 1877 Peabody published an article, "Georgian Houses of New England," in *AABN,* and Little published a sketchbook, *Early New England Interiors.* As England had revived its so-called classical style, Little stated, so the United States "should revive our Colonial style, which is everywhere marked with peculiar dignity, simplicity, and refinement" (Sturges, "Arthur Little and the Colonial Revival," 150). Despite his qualifications, it is surprising that Thorp commissioned Little and not A.W. Longfellow, who had recently completed 115 Brattle for Sara's brother, Joseph Thorp Jr., and his wife, Anne.

Little was an authority on revivalist architecture, but his early buildings often exhibited a picturesque expression of the Colonial Revival, using Georgian elements quite freely and imaginatively. He faced the Thorp house south toward the river, although to do so he had to turn it away from fashionable Brattle Street. The 450-foot-deep lot offered a view of the Charles from the upper stories and inspired the owners to name the house "Riverview." In addition to its unconventional orientation, the plan was irregular, the window sizes and shapes unpredictable, and the details unorthodox. The most prominent Brattle Street element, a portico with monumental two-story columns and high oval windows, marks only the service wing (see figure 4.49). The main entrance, with an oversized portico supported by columns, arches, and long scrolled brackets, is on the back of the house (figure 6.163). Although many features stem from

FIGURE 6.164 Parlor and music room, Joseph G. Thorp house. Photo 1990.

traditional Georgian sources, the architect treated these elements with surprising individuality. Little had designed similar over-sized elements in an 1885 addition to the Federal James Emerton house in Salem; that porte-cochère supported by arches and long scrolled brackets, a portico with two story columns, and a curious polygonal corner bay are all echoed at 168 Brattle.

The unusual interior followed neither a typical 1880s open plan around a large living hall nor a traditional center-hall plan. Instead, the main entrance is below the first floor and opens into a multirun stair with spacious landings at intermediate levels. The magnificent parlor and music room, which could hold up to 200 people at Mrs. Bull's frequent salons, had carved teak paneling that New York decorator Lockwood De Forest imported from India (figure 6.164). An octagonal reading nook painted white provided an intimate cozy retreat, and a "Norwegian room" with

a beamed ceiling, traditional corner fireplace, and carved Norse inscription recalled Mrs. Bull's late husband. The stable, which had been converted into a studio house for visiting artists in 1897, was demolished in 1972.

About this time whole "Colonial" neighborhoods began to appear in Old Cambridge. In 1887–88, landscape architect Charles Eliot laid out Irving, Scott, and Farrar streets on Charles Eliot Norton's estate, Shady Hill. Professor Norton sold the lots with stipulations governing the type and quality of houses. Although style was not restricted, the first houses erected on these streets in 1889 showed the overwhelming popularity of the Colonial Revival. The style continued to dominate into the 1920s, making this one of the first Colonial Revival neighborhoods in the city. Some of the same architects responsible for Colonial Revival houses in the Brattle Street area just a few years earlier also designed houses in Shady Hill: William Ralph Emerson at 95 and 110 Irving (1889) and 7 Scott (1891), Chamberlin & Whidden at 99 Irving (1889), and Longfellow, Alden & Harlow at 105 Irving (1890).

Emerson designed 95 Irving for philosopher and psychologist William James, who was one of the "pioneer builders on the Norton estate" (*Tribune*, July 27, 1889). The two-and-a-half-story, rigidly symmetrical, shingled facade was capped by the type of broad gambrel roof that Emerson favored (see figure 4.235). James himself is said to have been involved in the design, which may account for the curious eyebrow window, awkward vestibule and hall, and generous library with floor-to-ceiling bookcases. His descendants occupied the house until 1968. At 103 Irving (1889), Andrews & Jaques designed a Colonial Revival that combined Georgian and 17th-century elements and shared some features with 113 Brattle. Built for philosopher Josiah Royce, who taught at Harvard from 1882 to 1916, the house was pictured in *Harper's Weekly* in 1889. From 1958 to 2001 it was the home of chef and author Julia Child; after her death, her kitchen was removed and installed in the Smithsonian Institution.

The Shady Hill neighborhood also offered opportunities for local architects such as C. Herbert McClare, who by 1889 was beginning to experiment with Georgian Revival idioms. Originally a carpenter from Nova Scotia, McClare moved to Cambridge in 1887, and by 1889 was advertising his specialties as "Queen Anne and Colonial villas and Cottages" (*Cambridge Directory*, 648). His house for Professor Alpheus Hyatt at 19 Francis Avenue (1889) used Colonial Revival detail in a picturesque Queen Anne way and was illustrated in *Harper's Weekly*. McClare was responsible for about sixty buildings in Cambridge, including the houses at 10 and 17 Francis Avenue (1894 and 1896).

The proliferation of articles and measured drawings of colonial houses in the 1890s sparked an interest in creating more historically correct Georgian designs. Details were generally more accurate than in the previous decade, although some freer elements persisted, such as steeply pitched gambrel roofs, elaborate entrance compositions, and overly complicated fanlights. H. Langford Warren began teaching architecture at Harvard in 1893 and introduced a broad historical curriculum to complement the prevailing classicism and Beaux-Arts approach to design education. As American colonial architecture shifted from being a source for invention to a subject of detailed study, the term "Georgian" was increasingly used to designate the new buildings, and the 1880s freedom of design gradually gave way to the symmetry and formality that became ubiquitous by the turn of the century.

The new focus on scholarly correctness led lawyer Robert Weston-Smith to commission Boston architect Herbert D. Hale to design a near replica of Elmwood at 22 Fayerweather Street in 1898. Reconstructions of specific historic structures had been a popular choice for state buildings at the 1893 World's Columbian Exposition in Chicago, although Peabody & Stearns's Massachusetts Building, modeled after the John Hancock house, still showed a free interpretation of the original. Two Colonial Revival houses that Gardiner Greene Hubbard commissioned from Longfellow, Alden & Harlow in 1892 followed this trend (figure 6.165). Both 14 and 20 Hubbard Park share the blocky, hip-roofed forms and columned balustraded entrances of the

FIGURE 6.165 Hubbard-Woodman house, 14 Hubbard Park (1892, Longfellow, Alden & Harlow, architects). Photo before 1933.

firm's 1886 house at 5 Ash Street but have more regular facades and symmetrical fenestration. The projecting central pavilion and two-story pilasters at 14 Hubbard Park recall the 1759 Vassall-Craigie-Longfellow house, and the curved balustraded side porch recalls the porte-cochère of the Thorp house at 115 Brattle Street and the Cambridge Social Union at 40 Brattle Street. Both houses have large single-pane sash and interior woodwork painted in light colors, reflecting a new appreciation for well-lighted interiors.

Other 1890s examples by Longfellow, Alden & Harlow include an impressive mansion for Benjamin Vaughan at 57 Garden Street (1891), demolished in 1965 for Hilles Library, and houses at 21 Fayerweather Street (1893) and 1 Highland Street (1894). Although some elements of 1 Highland follow Georgian precedent, the heavy consoles supporting the second-floor overhang, the asymmetrical bay window, and Federal

FIGURE 6.166 James A. Noyes house, 1 Highland Street (1894, Longfellow, Alden & Harlow, architects). Photo 1895.

Lowell's daughter, hired her to design a stable in 1895 and an addition in 1898. She included measured drawings of Elmwood in her 1913 book, *Details of Old New England Houses* (see figure 6.26). Howe's first new house in Old Cambridge was a three-bay center-entrance design at 1 Kennedy Road (1894) for Harvard librarian Alfred C. Potter (figure 6.167). Given her historical interests, it is not surprising that the majority of Howe's residential commissions were based on Georgian and Federal precedents, but her approach was by no means archeological. At 49 Hawthorn Street (1900), the height of the third story, the detailing of the second-story pediment, and the irregular placement of the chimneys mark this as an especially well-designed revival rather than a historic building.

motifs at the main entrance show the architects' independent approach (figure 6.166). Designed for James A. Noyes of the Harvard library, this is the firm's most fully documented work, with extensive photographs and portfolios of original interior finishes that provide important information on period taste. In addition, the Olmsted National Historic Site has Olmsted's landscape plans and images of the grounds.

Cambridge native Lois Lilley Howe (1864–1964), one of the first women to graduate from M.I.T.'s school of architecture and the only woman in the class of 1890, specialized in Colonial Revival designs. In spite of her training, contemporaries focused on what they considered her natural ability to design comfortable homes. The *Chronicle* noted that "her houses are well known for their home-like and convenient attributes, for with a woman's eye, she can detect the cozy, and with a woman's mind, she arranges the convenient" (Dec. 14, 1901). Her first commissions were remodeling jobs for family and friends, and her interest in 18th-century details brought her work on a number of early houses. At Elmwood, Howe's cousin Mabel, James Russell

FIGURE 6.167 Alfred C. Potter house, 1 Kennedy Road (1894, Lois Lilley Howe, architect). Howe's first residential commission featured a prominent gambrel roof and balustraded porch similar to houses by A.W. Longfellow. Photo ca. 1896.

In 1893 Shaw & Hunnewell designed an outstanding example of a symmetrical center-entrance Georgian Revival at 3–5 Channing Place for Thomas B. Gannett, superintendent of the Revere Sugar Refinery in East Cambridge (figure 6.168). The use of two-story bow-front windows to organize the facade recalls Chamberlin & Whidden's house at 9 Waterhouse Street (1887), but the classical details are considerably more elaborate, particularly the fluted corner pilasters with composite capitals and carved shell blocks, the recessed arched entrance with rusticated voussoirs, and the wide-paneled entablature and modillion cornice. A long service wing with a large Palladian window was converted into a separate dwelling in 1927 and was once the home of poet May Sarton.

Formal center-entrance Georgian Revival houses by other Boston architects appeared throughout Old Cambridge in the 1890s. Almost all emphasized the center bay of the composition, some with a projecting porch surmounted by a Palladian window as at 26 Elmwood Avenue (1899, Cram, Goodhue, & Ferguson) built for Mrs. Ruth Benson. Others had a projecting entrance bay capped by a pediment, as at 183 Brattle Street (1893) which William Y. Peters built for retired mining executive Alfred Kidder.[16] Samuel J. Brown designed several high hip-roofed, center-entrance houses for successful Boston merchants, including 25 Arlington Street (1895) and 30 Hillside Avenue (1898). Grocer Isaac Jouett's house at 25 Arlington varied the usual scheme with a broad circular entrance porch and shallow bay windows tucked under the overhang; it was described in the *Chronicle* as showing "the free treatment of the old colonial style" (Apr. 27, 1895).

The five-bay center-entrance Georgian Revival house at 90 Raymond Street, designed in 1896 by Charles F. Willard for Edward Sherburne, a dealer in plate glass, is a textbook example of the type (figure 6.169). The high hip roof, modillion-and-dentil cornice, central Palladian window at the stair landing, and pedimented entrance porch are all hallmarks of this period. Willard began as a cabinetmaker in his grandfather's shop in Sterling, Massachusetts, but soon turned to carpentry. In 1880 at

FIGURE 6.168 Thomas B. Gannett house, 3–5 Channing Place (1893, Shaw & Hunnewell, architects). Photo 2009.

age 22 he went west, but returned three years later and pursued a successful career as a contractor in Cambridge, designing and building at least nine houses in Old Cambridge in the 1890s. Good examples of his work are his own house at 43 Martin Street (1895), with a prominent balustraded porch, and 150–152 Upland Road (1895) a large double house with paired bow front windows.

Other local builder/architects, such as Charles H. McClare, Timothy F. Walsh, Joseph R. and William P. Richards, James A. Hasty, and Edwin K. and William E. Blaikie, had all put up Queen Anne houses in the 1880s and began to build less expensive single and double houses with Georgian Revival details in the 1890s. Their designs sometimes borrowed elements or entire schemes from revival houses rather than from colonial models. McClare's 10 Francis Avenue (1894), for example, is quite similar to Longfellow & Harlow's 1887 house at 5 Ash Street.

FIGURE 6.169 Edward C. Sherburne house, 90 Raymond Street (1896, Charles F. Willard, builder). Photo 1970.

Many of these houses were built on speculation after the economy recovered from the financial panic of 1893 and the Huron Avenue car line opened new land for development.

The Niles brothers, who had built large Queen Anne homes on Avon Hill in the 1880s, went into real estate in the 1890s and were praised in the *Chronicle* for protecting the character of the neighborhood by erecting only first-class houses. At least ten of these, including 182 Upland Road (1896, J.A. Hasty) and 103–105 Raymond/196 Upland (1898, E.K. and W.E. Blaikie) are good examples of the popular Colonial Revival style in careful hands. The Blaikies, whose portfolio included several apartment buildings in Boston's Back Bay, designed 103–105 Raymond for J. Harris Niles as an experimental three-family house, but the three separate entrances made it visually chaotic. The double houses that they and others designed for the Niles, such as 94–96 Avon Hill Street (1894) and 169 and 186–188

Upland Road (1896 and 1897), were more successful and gave the appearance of large singles (see figure 4.170).

A variant of the Queen Anne style at this period was characterized by half-timbering, informal massing, and stucco exteriors and often displayed medieval details such as carved bargeboards and leaded window sash. These houses had complex profiles reminiscent of the Queen Anne mode but were considerably more disciplined. The prominent display of craftsmanship was intended to demonstrate the limitations of machine-made ornament. Two of the earliest and most prominent designers in this style, Ralph Adams Cram and H. Langford Warren, were also influential scholars and educators.

Ralph Adams Cram (1863–1942) was the foremost practitioner of the institutional Gothic Revival style in the United States. After attending Exeter Academy and spending five years in the office of Rotch & Tilden, he traveled abroad in 1886–87

FIGURE 6.170 Ruth E. Parker house, 128 Brattle Street (1892, Ralph Adams Cram, architect). Photo before 1916.

and became inspired by the 15th-century Perpendicular Style churches he observed in England. He experienced a religious conversion while in Rome and thereafter identified with the Anglo-Catholic wing of the Episcopal Church. Known primarily for his ecclesiastical and collegiate buildings, Cram taught the philosophy of architecture at M.I.T. and headed the program there from 1914 to 1919. He and his partner from 1891 to 1910, Bertram Grosvenor Goodhue, were among the founders of the Society of Arts and Crafts, Boston. A Ruskinian purist who idealized the medieval world, Cram represented the conservative side of early arts and crafts advocates.

Cram's houses in Cambridge were some of his earliest residential works. For his domestic projects, Cram preferred 16th-century models from what he considered "the best period of English domestic architecture" (Cram, 130). The houses he designed at 126 and 128 Brattle Street in 1890–92 for Ruth Parker, a young single woman, featured overhanging second and third stories, projecting stuccoed gables with half timbering, banks of leaded casement windows, and large paneled chimneys (figure 6.170). The *Chronicle* described 128 Brattle as an "English Surrey cottage" (Sept. 24, 1892), but the *Tribune* declared it "of no particular style," perhaps because it differed from other houses being built at the time (Sept. 24, 1892). When Lois Lilley Howe designed a rear addition in 1916, she agreed with the owners that the facade, with its "charm of an old English cottage," should not to be changed, although she did add a two-story bay window ("A Problem in Remodeling," 56). Howe also suggested that a stucco exterior would work better with the half timbering, but the cost was too high and the house remained covered in dark stained shingles.

The other prominent medievalist in Cambridge was H. Langford Warren, of whom it was said that "he was one of a few among his contemporaries who understood Gothic, and one of a handful who could teach it" (Boyd, 590). Trained in architecture at M.I.T. in 1877–79 and in fine arts at Harvard under Charles Eliot Norton in the 1880s, Warren worked in H.H. Richardson's office in 1879–84 and established his own practice in 1885.

In 1893 he began teaching architecture at Harvard, where his openness to other architectural traditions besides the Beaux-Arts earned him the enmity of classically trained architects: "in some quarters he was chided not only for appreciating Colonial architecture, but for teaching it in design problems" (ibid. 589). Warren remained at Harvard throughout his career and served as the first dean of the newly organized School of Architecture from 1914 until his death in 1917. Among his few residential commissions in Cambridge were 195 Brattle Street (1896), a shingle and stucco house with medieval overtones for Harvard English professor George Pierce Baker (figure 6.171).[17]

William Gibbons Rantoul designed a house with a similar combination of medieval, Queen Anne, and Shingle Style details at 157 Brattle Street for Boston leather dealer Coolidge Roberts

FIGURE 6.171 George Pierce Baker house, 195 Brattle Street (1896, H. Langford Warren, architect). Photo ca. 1900.

in 1895 (figure 6.172). He completed this independent commission just before he left the firm of Andrews, Jaques & Rantoul, where he had worked on several Shingle Style and Colonial Revival houses in Cambridge. Prominent Tudor features include the carved bargeboards, ogee-arched doorway, and diamond-paned windows, while other details seem more akin to English Queen Anne work. The interior also combined styles. Described in *AABN* as "somewhat in the style of the old English half-timber houses," the hall, dining room, and library had quartered oak and dark cherry wainscoting and deep recessed fireplaces with settles, while the Georgian-style drawing room was painted ivory (Dec. 5, 1896). None of this survived a 1948 modernization by Saltonstall & Morton that resulted in an elegant Moderne interior, which was in turn destroyed in a 2009 remodeling.

FIGURE 6.172 Coolidge S. Roberts house, 157 Brattle Street (1895, William Gibbons Rantoul, architect). Photo 1968.

GEORGIAN REVIVAL AND THE ARTS AND CRAFTS MOVEMENT

In the early 20th century, the architecture of the late Victorian period was criticized for its ornateness, its inefficient use of space, and the obsolete lifestyles it represented. Popular periodicals such as *The Craftsman, House & Garden, House Beautiful,* and *Ladies Home Journal* helped establish new family ideals for middle-class America. These publications embraced simplicity and influenced public tastes by discussing such issues as the changing role of women, the elimination of servants in middle-class households, developments in medicine that created widespread concern about hygiene, and modern conveniences such as indoor plumbing, electric lighting, and the automobile. In response, architects and builders simplified interior plans and introduced new features. The number of rooms in the average middle-class house decreased, as did the provision of separate maid's quarters, while the number of bathrooms and the prominence of garages grew. The Georgian center-hall layout provided efficient circulation and became the most common floor plan. A single living room replaced the front and rear parlors of earlier periods, usually occupying the whole width of the house along one side of a center hall. The 19th-century living hall gave way to a smaller entrance hall that seemed to become narrower with each decade. Larger closets, baths, lavatories, and garages reflected new life styles. Between 1905 and 1930 breakfast rooms, sunrooms, and sleeping porches became popular, but these dropped out of fashion as houses grew smaller.

Of the approximately 350 single-family houses built in Old Cambridge between 1904 and 1930, many (if not most) were Georgian Revival or Federal Revival, the style of choice for the majority of Americans. Acceptance of colonial imagery reflected both innate national pride and goals of assimilation into American society, as the broad prosperity of the 1920s lifted many families into the middle class. These houses, unlike their 19th-century predecessors, were quite simple in form and plan, usually consisting of a rectangular block with a center entrance and symmetrically placed windows. Minor facades and projecting ells might show some variation, but the main facade was generally quite symmetrical. All phases of the Georgian and Federal periods served as models for these houses, and many showed more historical accuracy than in previous decades.

Four houses built between 1902 and 1915 on Brattle Street between Brown and Willard streets are good examples of the five-bay, center-hall form, painted in the light colors that were popular for Georgian Revival residential architecture. The architect, John Worthington Ames (1871–1954), was a widely traveled Concord native who had studied at Harvard and the École des Beaux-Arts and worked as a draftsman for McKim, Mead & White. Practicing on his own or with William Chase, Ames designed at least 20 houses in Old Cambridge between 1898 and 1922. In this instance, he worked for both a private client and a corner-cutting developer, Giles Taintor, on a one-acre lot that had previously held only one double house. Taintor purchased the property in 1902 and hired Ames to design 120 Brattle for his own use at the back of the lot. He sold the Willard Street corner in 1903 to Clarence S. Fisher, an architect-turned-archeologist, who had Ames design 114 Brattle Street, a more elaborate house with brick ends and an elaborate elliptical entrance porch with Ionic columns. Taintor and Ames completed the ensemble with two rental houses in 1908 and 1915. Ames seems to have conceived the four houses as a group, varying the roof forms and using stock parts to create individual entrance designs for each. The modest proportions and details of the houses Ames designed for Taintor were typical of the new century and were repeated with variations elsewhere (figure 6.173). On the higher end and more comparable to Fisher's house are the fine three-story Federal Revival houses at 49 Hawthorn Street (1900) by Lois Lilley Howe and at 4 Willard Street (1904) designed for Winthrop Saltonstall Scudder, longtime art editor at Houghton Mifflin, by Ernesto M.W. Machado, an M.I.T.-trained architect of Cuban decent (figure 6.174).

Variations of the Colonial Revival style continued to be a fashionable, though conservative, choice for all levels of residential design through the 1920s. At the high end, Harvard president A.

FIGURE 6.173 Clarence S. Fisher house, 114 Brattle Street (1903) and Giles Taintor rental house, 124 Brattle Street (1915, both John W. Ames, architect). Photo 2015.

FIGURE 6.174 Winthrop Saltonstall Scudder house, 4 Willard Street (1904, E.M.W. Machado, architect). Photo 2015.

Lawrence Lowell commissioned his Beaux-Arts-trained cousin Guy Lowell in 1911 to design a handsome brick Federal Revival residence at 17 Quincy Street that recalled Bulfinch's Beacon Hill houses. In the same year, Joseph Everett Chandler, who had worked on the historic Hooper-Lee-Nichols house, designed a Georgian Revival residence of monumental proportions at 30 Gerry's Landing for Edward Waldo Forbes, director of Harvard's Fogg Art Museum (figure 6.175; see also figure 4.101). The abbreviated U-shaped plan accommodated large formal rooms with fireplaces and a variety of modern amenities—a gymnasium, a garden room, a studio, sleeping porches, and glazed piazzas. Chandler was known for his free adaptations of colonial sources, and the romantic nature of some of his early 20th century restorations, such as 159 Brattle Street (1916), helps put his revival designs into perspective.

Harvard librarian Alfred Potter's second house in Cambridge, at 55 Fayerweather on the corner of Gurney Street (1905), illustrates the high level of detail and craftsmanship that could still be achieved before labor and materials came into short supply during World War I (figure 6.176). The architect, Richard Arnold Fisher (1868–1932), trained at the Boston Museum of Fine Arts and designed furniture for A.H. Davenport in East Cambridge before turning to architecture; he later published a monograph on Federal period houses in Newburyport (1910). The site planning and landscaping made maximum use of the deep, sloping corner lot, achieving the integration of homes with nature advocated in popular periodicals of the period. The center entrance with Doric columns faces the privacy of the garden; the orientation of this principal facade away from both streets suggests the increased impact of the automobile on domestic design. In contrast, the Gurney Street elevation drops a full story and incorporated modern precepts with bold lines, an exposed concrete foundation, and basement garage.

Other Cambridge architects were attracted to the work of contemporary British designers such as C.F.A. Voysey and C.R. Ashbee. The pre–World War I years were the heyday of the Arts and Crafts movement, which originated in England under the influence of John Ruskin and William Morris. Named for the Arts

FIGURE 6.175 Edward Waldo Forbes house, 30 Gerry's Landing Road (1911, Joseph E. Chandler, architect). The house was designed with two major facades to take advantage of its location high above Gerry's Landing. The garden elevation, shown here, had a broad view of Cambridge and Boston from its perch above Gerry's Landing. Photo 2016.

FIGURE 6.176 Garden facade, Alfred Potter house, 55 Fayerweather Street (1905, Richard Arnold Fisher, architect). Photo ca. 1915.

& Crafts Exhibition Society in London, which was established in 1887, its advocates deplored the effects of industrialization on art, architecture, and society. Morris and other social theorists believed that mechanization had severed the traditional relationship between craftsman and designer, and they found an appealing precedent in the guild practices of the Middle Ages. They advocated reforming the means of production so that skilled craftsmen could use traditional techniques and materials to produce handcrafted objects in place of the mass-produced, poor-quality goods that dominated the marketplace in the Victorian era.

The first allied American organization, the Society of Arts and Crafts, was founded in Boston in 1897 "for the purpose of promoting artistic work in all branches of handicraft"; it soon became a prototype for groups throughout the country (Meyer, 33). The movement appealed to many members of New England's intellectual elite, who embraced its high standards for materials, design, and craftsmanship. The society encouraged membership among craftsmen, but the most active participants were architects and academics who collaborated with them. Among the early members were a number of architects known for their Georgian Revival and restoration work in Cambridge, including Lois Lilley Howe, Alexander Wadsworth Longfellow, Richard Arnold Fisher, Guy Lowell, and Robert D. Andrews. English architect C.F.A. Voysey's philosophy of simplicity and directness resonated with a number of Boston Society members, and his work reached area architects through publication in British and American periodicals and one-man shows in Boston. The first three presidents of the society, Harvard fine arts professor Charles Eliot Norton, arts patron Arthur Astor Carey, and architect H. Langford Warren, were all Cambridge residents. Norton was a personal friend and promoter of Ruskin and other early English Arts and Crafts practitioners. British-born and raised Warren maintained a long relationship with English architect Charles Robert Ashbee, with whom he shared the goal of architects collaborating with craftsmen; he visited Ashbee's workshops in England in 1903 and promoted his U.S. lecture tours in 1900 and 1909.

Warren directed Harvard's architecture program from 1893 to 1917 and disseminated contemporary English ideas through his writings and architectural designs. His article in the *Architectural Review* in January 1904 extolled the modern English country house, derived from early manor houses and yeoman's cottages, as the expression of all that was best in English domestic life. The plain stucco exterior, varied window placement, and steeply pitched roof and gables of his own house at 6 Garden Terrace (1904) recall some contemporary English work, but he made few allusions to early styles beyond the Renaissance ornament at the entrance (figure 6.177; see also figure 4.127). The house was built into a hillside so that the main entrance fronted the street at the lower level, while the living and dining rooms faced the garden a story above.

A small group of rather austere stucco houses in Old Cambridge were inspired by turn-of the-century work in England. Almost all came from well-known architects, including Allen W. Jackson at 33 Reservoir Street (1909), Hartley Dennett at 16 Berkeley Street (1905) and 43 Reservoir Street (1913), and Newhall & Blevins at 15 Hubbard Park (1914). Other than these high-end projects, stucco was never very popular in Cambridge except for a time in the 1920s when the city's building code required it on some three-family houses.

Allen Jackson was a specialist in English Tudor architecture and the most prolific Arts and Crafts practitioner in Cambridge, designing over thirty houses between 1903 and 1939. An 1897 M.I.T. graduate, Jackson traveled abroad before beginning practice in Boston. His 1912 book, *Building the Half-Timber House*, railed "against the stereotyped use of certain historical styles for contemporary use," particularly the "tyrannical symmetry" of the Georgian style, and he promoted instead the flexibility of "rambling timbered or plastered houses" of the English Tudor period for their adaptability to the needs of modern living (xi, 20–21). Jackson's first design in Cambridge was his own half-timbered residence at 202 Brattle Street, where he combined stucco, half-timbering, and brick with steep projecting gables, flared roofs, heavy rough-sawn and carved wood trim, and leaded casements

FIGURE 6.177 H. Langford Warren house, 6 Garden Terrace (1904, Warren, Smith & Biscoe, architects). Photo 1968.

to create what he termed a modern American adaptation of an English tradition that expressed interior arrangements on the exterior (figure 6.178). Free from the restrictions of the symmetrical Georgian style, his design was malleable enough to incorporate "the most incongruous matters under one roof," including the city's first private garage within the body of a house (ibid., 22). While much of Jackson's work incorporated half-timbering and other elements of medieval English architecture, his stucco houses at 15 Elmwood Avenue (1903) and 229 Brattle Street (1910) followed the more progressive aspects of contemporary British practice. Physics instructor George W. Pierce's L-plan house at 7 Berkeley Place (1913) is geometric and severe, with little ornamentation beyond the deep overhanging gables and eaves, dramatically placed banks of casement windows, and broad bargeboards on the gabled porch.

Hartley Dennett (1870–1936) was influenced by traditional New England forms as well as by the English Arts and Crafts movement, having grown up in a colonial-era house in Saco, Maine, and studied architecture at Harvard and M.I.T. He was a founding member of Boston's Society of Arts and Crafts, and his wife, the designer, educator, and social reformer Mary Ware Dennett, served on the board. When their fellow member Arthur Astor Carey (who had sold his trend-setting Colonial Revival at 28 Fayerweather Street in 1892) returned to Cambridge in 1904 he asked Dennett to design a Federal Revival house at 48 Fayerweather. Carey's new house showed none of the features of progressive English Arts and Crafts architecture that characterize some of the architect's other designs. It captures some of the severity of high-style Federal architecture, but has an Edwardian heftiness compared to its possible prototype, 175 Brattle Street, and other revival houses such as 49 Hawthorne Street and 4 Willard Street.

Dennett's stucco houses at 16 Berkeley Street (1905) and 43 Reservoir Street (1909) were clearly influenced by the Arts and Crafts movement. Their long, low proportions and plain

FIGURE 6.178 Allen W. Jackson house, 202 Brattle Street (1903, Allen W. Jackson, architect). Photo before 1912.

surfaces recall Voysey's abstract versions of rural vernacular English cottages. In particular, 16 Berkeley has a characteristic asymmetrical facade, deep overhanging roof, and banks of irregularly placed casement windows, while the recessed vestibule and stucco chimney reflect Voysey's work. The irregular floor plan with rooms and halls flowing into each other presages modern open interiors. Designed for Harvard professor of zoology George Parker, this ranks as Dennett's finest design in Cambridge (figure 6.179).

Several large hip-roofed stucco houses demonstrate the range of Arts and Crafts influence. At 7 Garden Terrace (1914, Harold Field Kellogg), built for Roger Noble Burnham, a sculptor, lithographer, and instructor at Harvard School of Architecture (1912–17), the architect produced a spare geometric house with characteristic deep overhanging eaves but no applied ornamentation or allusions to historical styles. Wax manufacturer Charles Butcher's house at 117 Lake View Avenue (1910, Charles H. Bartlett) seems heavier and more conventional, with exposed rafter ends on the bay windows, dormers, and deep eaves of the

main roof, as well as a dark-paneled interior suitable for polishing to a high gloss (figure 6.180). Other stucco houses of the period, such as 3 Clement Circle (1903, Charles Cummings), used steeply pitched gable roofs for complicated silhouettes that recalled Voysey's houses in England.

Architect Charles R. Greco's own 1910 house at 36 Fresh Pond Parkway in the new Larchwood subdivision displays a loose asymmetry and a variety of stylistic influences. Decorative bargeboards, clipped gables, deep eaves with exposed rafter ends, and inset red and green tiles vary the stucco exterior, while windows range from small leaded casements to large doublehungs. The living room reflects Arts and Crafts architecture in both England and the western United States, with dark wood paneling and built-in settles and bookcases flanking the chimney. Greco grew up in Cambridgeport, studied at Harvard's Lawrence Scientific School, and began his prolific architectural career in 1894, practicing alone and in a variety of styles until 1960. He lived in this house only ten years, but it remained in remarkably fine original condition until 1991, when the owner

FIGURE 6.179 George Parker house, 16 Berkeley Street (1905, Hartley Dennett, architect). Photo 2014.

FIGURE 6.180 Charles Butcher house, 117 Lake View Avenue (1910, Charles H. Bartlett, architect). Photo 2014.

removed and stored all of the paneling, moldings, and fixtures to prevent their destruction by a prospective buyer (figure 6.181).

The related Craftsman style originated in southern California with the work of Greene & Greene and was popularized through plans, elevations, and illustrations that appeared regularly in *The Craftsman*, published by New York furniture manufacturer Gustav Stickley (1858–1942), another pioneer of the Arts and Crafts movement. Although Craftsman houses and bungalows with sweeping low-pitched gable roofs, wide eaves, exposed rafter ends and roof braces, and porches supported by tapered square columns enjoyed immense popularity in other parts of the country between 1905 and the 1920s, only a few examples appeared in Cambridge. The building permit for 114 Irving Street (1911) listed "The Craftsman" as the architect; a subsequent article in the magazine described it as "extremely plain," but added that "the dormers, hooded doors, balcony and chimney form a satisfying whole" (vol. 24, 1913; figure 6.182). The client, glass manufacturer Edgar F. Scheibe, was involved in the industrial arts; he had a workshop next to the basement garage and a parlor organ on

Gustav Stickley, Architect.

TWO VIEWS OF THE CRAFTSMAN HOUSE BUILT FOR MR. E. F. SCHEIBE AT CAMBRIDGE, MASS. (FROM SPECIAL PLANS), STUCCO AND STONE ARE USED AND THOUGH THE CONSTRUCTION IS EXTREMELY PLAIN, THE DORMERS, HOODED DOORS, BALCONY AND CHIMNEY FORM A SATISFYING WHOLE.

FIGURE 6.182 Edgar F. Scheibe house, 114 Irving Street (1911, The Craftsman, architect). Illustrated in *The Craftsman,* 1913.

FIGURE 6.181 Charles R. Greco house, 36 Fresh Pond Parkway (1910, Charles R. Greco, architect). Photo 2015.

FIGURE 6.183 Lester Hathaway house, 71 Avon Hill Street (1912, Alfred L. Darrow, architect). Photo 1969.

the second floor that was so large that its pipes extended into the attic. Cambridge's lone bungalow at 71 Avon Hill Street (1912) was designed by local architect Alfred L. Darrow for Lester Hathaway, a partner in his father's Richdale Avenue bakery since 1899 (figure 6.183). Low sweeping roofs and large airy porches were well suited to California living, but less appealing in the New England climate. The style did not appear again in Cambridge, nor did any examples of the Prairie style that Frank Lloyd Wright was developing at the same time in the Midwest.

THE INTERWAR PERIOD

More than twice as many houses were constructed during the 1920s in Cambridge than in the previous decade. As in the rest of the country, most were the work of builders who relied on stock plans and millwork. Even the *Cambridge Chronicle* advertised plans for small, economical residences that readers could buy for as little as $1.00. The crash in 1929 coincided with the depletion of undeveloped land in Cambridge and the beginning of a thirty-year hiatus in residential construction caused by depression, war, and loss of population. During the thirties few could afford to build a single-family house, and the architects who found such work often created smaller and cheaper versions of their past designs. With a handful of significant exceptions, when residential development resumed in Cambridge in the 1960s the prevailing form was the three-story boxy "pillbox" apartment building and, in the 1970s, the townhouse.

THE PERIOD HOUSE, 1915–30

The most striking feature of interwar residential architecture was the disappearance of regional differences and the rise of mass-produced housing for the middle class. John D. Rockefeller's vast project at Colonial Williamsburg, begun in 1926, reinforced the public's interest in early American design. Historians and design professionals recognized regional styles beyond those of New England and Virginia, but in the popular literature differences were simplified and categorized as colonial types rather than styles. A 1925 article in *Country Life* titled "What Type of House Should I Build" suggested that period houses could be divided into six categories, all of which could be easily produced by builders without the expense of an architect: the New England Colonial, the Dutch Colonial, the Philadelphia Colonial, the Southern Colonial, the Georgian, and "a free rendering of the Colonial style" (Gebhard, 120). Vernacular examples of all colonial types were built throughout the country with little regard to regional context. Sears, Roebuck & Co. and several other national retailers offered catalogs of kit houses, while North Cambridge's Dix Lumber Company built houses according to stock plans that customers selected at their retail outlet on Massachusetts Avenue.

The Georgian Revival continued to be the most popular style for middle-class homes in Old Cambridge, although Dutch Colonial and English modes also enjoyed some currency. The iconic Vassall-Craigie-Longfellow house inspired replicas all over the country, particularly after it was featured on the cover of Sears, Roebuck's *Honor Bilt Modern Homes* catalog in 1918.

After World War I, designers were asked to produce smaller houses and simpler designs with fewer specialized features. The result was whole streets of similar houses, such as Larchwood Drive, that illustrated the most popular trends of the period. Clapboards and shingles, so long preferred in Cambridge, continued to predominate, but brick veneer over wood framing also gained in popularity. Decorative shutters with cut-out designs and clinker or tapestry brick were also characteristic of this period; the exterior of the New England Brick Company's office building in North Cambridge demonstrated some of the textures and products available (figure 6.184). Stucco was less popular in the 1920s, despite the introduction of a spray-on process that Napoleon Bernier, a West Cambridge contractor, developed for his new firm, the California Products Company (later known for its California Paint brand).

In the postwar period, lumberyards everywhere began to stock the same mass-produced components. Several types of entrance compositions could be ordered from millwork catalogs. One of the most popular included a door surrounded by sidelights and a fanlight, to which a shallow porch with freestanding columns could be added (figure 6.185). Millwork manufacturers adopted uniform moldings that were pale imitations of colonial profiles. The growing shortage of old-growth lumber necessitated the use of veneers and the development of synthetic products. Boston Pattern window sash, made to dimensions that had been standardized in the 18th century, remained one of the few regionally distinct building products.

Dutch Colonial houses were most popular in their birthplace, New York and New Jersey, but gained acceptance nationwide after 1923 when the Standard Homes Co. of Washington, D.C.,

FIGURE 6.184 Brick demonstration wall, installed after 1934, New England Brick Company, 324 Rindge Avenue. Photo 2015.

FIGURE 6.185 The Wm. C. McConnell Co. of Waverly Street in Cambridgeport published a millwork catalogue in the 1920s featuring standard designs for "true Colonial" architectural details.

published examples in *Better Homes at Lower Cost* (Rhoads, 120). The hallmark of the style was a gambrel roof with flared eaves that encompassed the second floor. The earliest examples in Old Cambridge were designed by Cambridge architect Charles Greco in 1915 at 72 and 78 Fresh Pond Parkway for Larchwood developer Forris Norris. Others were the work of builders rather than architects. Between 1917 and 1919, the Massachusetts Engineering Company built several variations, including 42 Fresh Pond Lane, 7 Meadow Way, and 20 and 54 Larchwood Drive. The Dix Lumber Company erected a group of Dutch Colonials in 1926 for developer James H. Murray at 99, 101, and 103 Fresh Pond Parkway, all with sun porches and shutters with cut-out patterns. (figure 6.186).

Not all houses in the 1920s used standard components; fine workmanship and innovative designs were still achievable at the high end. The developers of Larchwood, Coolidge Hill, and Gray Gardens required purchasers to submit their plans for approval. Most of the twenty-four houses at Gray Gardens were Georgian Revival in style and fairly accurate in detail, and all were architect-designed. Howe & Manning designed 4 Gray Gardens West in 1922 for bank president Francis Frothingham, with fences and landscaping by Fletcher Steele (figure 6.187). Published in 1927 in Ethel Power's *The Smaller American House*, it was praised for its proportions, simplicity, and excellent colonial porch. At Coolidge Hill, accurate reproductions of early houses of New England and the Middle Atlantic states stand next to picturesque cottages. One of the earliest, the five-bay center-entrance house at 125 Coolidge Hill (1925, Andrews, Jones, Biscoe & Whitmore), has a fine entrance and circular fan light reflecting the 1780s. Other houses recalled specific buildings. For example, Perry, Shaw, & Hepburn adapted elements of the 1722 Virginia Governor's Palace for the main block of 134 Coolidge Hill (1928), which they designed for cotton mill executive Walter H. Bradley at the same time they were overseeing the restoration of Colonial Williamsburg.

Symmetrical service ells projecting from both sides of a central block were characteristic of early architecture in southern

FIGURE 6.186 James H. Murray rental house, 99 Fresh Pond Parkway (1926, Dix Lumber Company). Photo 1969.

and mid-Atlantic states. For revivalists in Cambridge who were simply trying to incorporate a garage into the design, a single ell as at 134 or 111 Coolidge Hill (1926, Howe, Manning & Almy) was sufficient. The brick exterior, end chimneys, and projecting service ells of 148 Coolidge Hill, designed by William and Mary Duguid in 1929 for Harvard economics professor John H. Williams, recall early Georgian homes in the mid-Atlantic states, and its entrance is a near replica of the 1774 Hammond-Harwood House in Annapolis. The Duguids specialized in modest middle-class homes on small urban lots, and the Williams house is unusually elaborate compared to their other work in Cambridge.

Some 17th-century-inspired houses built in the 1920s tended to be more picturesque than the originals. Extra dormers and gables enhance the silhouettes of 116 and 110 Coolidge Hill (1926 and 1927, T.B. Epps), and of 84 Garden Street (1922, Putnam & Chandler), where a steeply pitched roof and long banks of casement windows complete the composition. English medieval leaded windows, steeply pitched roofs, half-timbering,

The House of Francis E. Frothingham, Esq.

Howe, Manning & Almy, Architects

OF WOOD-FRAME CONSTRUCTION WITH A VENEER OF WATERSTRUCK BRICK, THIS HOUSE FACES NORTH ON A LOT IN CAMBRIDGE, MASSACHUSETTS. THE EXTERIOR TRIM, FENCE, AND PORCH ARE PAINTED A CREAM COLOR AND THE ROOF IS OF UNFADING GREEN SLATE. THE HOUSE HAS SATISFYING PROPORTIONS, SIMPLICITY, AND DIGNITY. THE COLONIAL PORCH SHOWS EXCELLENT DETAIL

FIGURE 6.187 Francis E. Frothingham house, 4 Gray Gardens West (1922, Howe & Manning, architects). Photo ca. 1927.

and Tudor arches also contribute to the picturesqueness of houses such as 123 Coolidge Hill (1926, Edward Sears Read). Allen Jackson's complex multigabled, half-timbered house for Harvard mathematics professor Edward V. Huntington at 48 Highland Street (1927) showed the architect's continued high standards twenty-five years after his own half-timbered house at 202 Brattle Street (figure 6.188). William Duguid's medieval English house for banker C. Wesley Purdy at 11 Garden Terrace (1930), with textured brick walls, dark carved wood trim, and a steep roof of rough split slate, was similarly well-designed.

Arthur Graham Carey (1892–1984) used some of the same elements—coarse brick, heavy split slate, half-timbering, steep gables, dark stained carved bargeboards—in the house he designed for his family in 1922 at 16 Gray Gardens East, the best English Tudor-inspired house in Old Cambridge (figures 6.189–6.190). A son of Arthur Astor Carey, second president of Boston's Society of Arts and Crafts, Graham Carey studied fine arts and European history at Harvard. After the war he studied architecture for two years and worked as a draftsman for Bigelow & Wadsworth in Boston, but left in 1927 to work as a craftsman in stained glass and precious metals.

FIGURE 6.188 Edward V. Huntington house, 48 Highland Street (1927, Allen Jackson, architect). Photo 2014.

FIGURE 6.189 A. Graham Carey house, 16 Gray Gardens East
(1922, A. Graham Carey, architect). Photo 2015.

FIGURE 6.190 Detail of bargeboard, carved by Carey, A. Graham Carey house. Photo 2015.

Carey grew up under the influence of the Arts and Crafts movement, and described himself as a "Ruskinian Romantic" (Harvard College *Class Report,* 1969). His house provides a perfect example of the kind of collaboration between designer and craftsman that the movement celebrated. Carey salvaged the exterior brick from the recently demolished 1859 Wyeth-Dresser house at 60 Raymond Street. He carved the elaborate bargeboards himself, incorporating motifs from his and his wife's family coats of arms. On the interior he worked with craftsmen to produce an exceptional carved soapstone fireplace in the living room, wood carvings in the dining room (including the Latin inscription "Honor Nourishes the Arts"), and hand-forged iron sconces, chandeliers, and decorative radiator covers throughout. Carey always intended to enlarge the house, and 1933 drawings by Wadsworth, Hubbard & Smith show an elaborate half-timbered gabled addition with leaded glass and ornament to be carved by the owner. While he never carried out these plans, he did extend the living room and created an interior connection to his workshop. A subsequent owner made some changes in the 1970s, but the exterior and principal rooms remained largely as Carey designed them.

During the 1930s books on colonial styles proliferated, while British Georgian and medieval models received less attention. Shifts in terminology linked the term Georgian with the formal architecture of Maryland and Virginia, particularly Williamsburg. At the same time, the more informal Cape Cod cottage and New England Colonial house gained in popularity. Melrose architect Royal Barry Wills (1895–1962) did more than any other individual to popularize and improve the quality of traditional small house design nationwide. His award-winning designs for *Life* and *Better Homes and Gardens* and for Herbert Hoover's "Better Homes in America" program made him one of the country's most well-known and popular practitioners. He based his design for 19 Old Dee Road (1940) on the 17th-century Parson Capen House in Topsfield, and gave it an overhanging second story with pendant drops, a steep roof, and windows tucked under the eaves. To make the house more livable, he substituted modern windows and stairs for the tiny casements and cramped interior staircase of the original and skillfully adapted the lean-to as a garage. Wills only designed one other house in Cambridge, a one-story colonial at 20 Coolidge Avenue (1958).

From their home office at 12 Dunstable Road, Scottish civil engineer William Duguid (1880–1967) and his Philadelphia-born wife, Mary (1888–1975), produced more small, high-quality period houses in Cambridge from 1922 through 1939 than any other firm. After building housing for war victims in France with the American Friends Service Committee during World War I, they moved to Cambridge in 1920 and began to practice together in 1925, specializing in colonial homes. Mary Elkinton Duguid studied history at Wellesley College and interior design at the Cambridge School of Architecture. With her sense of history and design, his technical knowledge, and their combined social conscience, the firm Duguid & Martin was well suited to address the small-house market of the 1930s.[18] Their design for 7 Old Dee Road (1937) reflects the simpler houses of the Early Georgian period, a period that generally appealed less to revivalists than the High Georgian. At 10 Fayerweather Street (1936), William Duguid designed a brick house with small-paned 12-over-12 sash and a finely detailed entrance that recalls houses along the Connecticut River. For his last major commission, 146 Brattle Street in 1939, he designed a two-story replica of the 18th-century Hooper-Lee-Nichols house for Russian émigré Victor de Gérard and his American wife, Alexandra. Duguid convincingly recreated the form and details of the original, and the setting behind two beech trees from the former Gardiner Hubbard estate added to its historic feeling (figure 6.191). More often the firm used colonial precedents only as historical

FIGURE 6.191   Victor de Gerard house, 146 Brattle Street (1939, William Duguid, architect). Photo 1968.

reference points for designs that were otherwise quite modern, as in the 1937 Friends Meeting House on Longfellow Park.

THE TRANSITION TO MODERNISM, 1930–41

The arrival of European Modernism during the 1930s created a rupture in American domestic design. While the small period house was promoted in the media as ideal for the majority of Americans, the Modern movement attracted progressive architects and clients. Criticism of the period house had been building since publication in 1924 of Lewis Mumford's influential *Sticks and Stones,* in which he questioned the appropriateness of the Colonial Revival for the modern world. The majority of American homebuyers, however, continued to prefer period homes. Some American architects, such as Eleanor Raymond and William L. Galvin in Cambridge, began to work out their own approach to Modernism, creating Art Moderne designs that were notable for their clean lines and absence of traditional details. These ventures, reminiscent of the emergence of an American architectural language in the 1880s, were overtaken by the rigid orthodoxy of European Modernism. Frank Lloyd Wright alone among major U.S. architects was able to maintain a distinctly American approach to modern design, although critics thought his work too idiosyncratic to be taken seriously.

Modernism began to attract younger members of the academic community during the 1920s and 1930s. A 1932 exhibition at the Museum of Modern Art in New York organized by Henry-Russell Hitchcock and Philip Johnson (and cosponsored by Harvard's School of Architecture and the Fogg Museum) introduced the International Style to the American public, well after it flowered in Europe in the 1910s and 1920s. The exhibit defined the style in formal and aesthetic terms through the work of its pioneers, while omitting the social and political influences crucial to its development in Europe. The impact on American architecture was immediate, particularly among students dissatisfied with the classically based Beaux-Arts approach then current in the United States.

The world's fairs in Chicago in 1933 and New York in 1939 exposed millions to European Modernism. When the masters of Modern architecture, Walter Gropius and Mies van der Rohe, left Germany in 1937 and settled at Harvard and the Illinois Institute of Technology (Chicago) respectively, they brought with them mature philosophies and design vocabularies that had a profound effect on American life. Gropius introduced an aesthetic based on the teachings of French architect Le Corbusier that rejected all traditional approaches to architectural design and urbanism. In 1938–39, the Swiss scholar Sigfried Giedion delivered a series of lectures at Harvard explaining the historical roots of the "new architecture" that became the basis for his influential book, *Space, Time, and Architecture*. Alvar Aalto served as a visiting professor at M.I.T. in 1940, following the success of his design for the Finnish Pavilion at the 1939 New York World's Fair. He returned after the war to teach what some writers have called the humanistic side of European Modernism, in contrast to the stark geometry of the International Style. The opportunity to study with these men attracted a new generation of young architects to Cambridge.

The first Modern houses appeared in Cambridge in 1935, just as Joseph Hudnut arrived to begin the Modernist revolution at Harvard's School of Architecture (see chapter 10). Fogg Museum director Edward Forbes, a strong supporter of the movement, purchased a prefabricated house from General Houses, Inc. and had it erected on a corner of his Coolidge Hill estate as a wedding present for his daughter, Rosamund, and her husband, William Bowers. Chicago architect Howard T. Fisher, who graduated from Harvard in 1926, founded General Houses, Inc., in 1932 and showed a model prefabricated home at the 1933 Century of Progress International Exposition in Chicago. Fisher conceived of his houses as an experiment in modern technology and a model for mass-produced housing, since costs could be kept to a minimum. The International Style steel-framed house at 197 Coolidge Hill included many of the stylistic features that Americans had seen only in Chicago or in photographs of Bauhaus projects: flat roofs, banks of windows meeting at corners, metal string courses and deck railings, and a complete absence of conventional ornamentation (figure 6.192). The Bowers house was torn down in 2006 after an unsuccessful search for a new owner to relocate it.

Eleanor Raymond's design for banker Horace Frost at 16 Longfellow Park (1935) was innovative in appearance but lacked the technical and theoretical innovations of the Bowers house; American architects in this period were experimenting with forms adapted from European prototypes, but (with some exceptions) were reluctant to surrender traditional building techniques (figure 6.193). Raymond (1887–1989) grew up in Cambridge, graduated from Wellesley College in 1909, and volunteered in Fletcher Steele's office in 1915–16 before becoming a student of Henry Atherton Frost at his recently established

FIGURE 6.192 William and Rosamund Forbes Bowers house, 197 Coolidge Hill (1935, Howard T. Fisher, architect, for General Homes, Inc.; demolished 2006). Photo 1981.

Cambridge School of Architecture (see chapter 7). After graduating in 1919 she became his architectural partner; the firm of Frost & Raymond continued until 1935, when she went into practice by herself. Raymond designed both traditional Colonial Revival and European-influenced Modern houses and experimented with solar heating.

Raymond first encountered European Modernism in France in 1928. After a 1930 trip to Scandinavia and Germany (which included a visit to the Bauhaus in Dessau), she designed an International Style house in Belmont for her sister in 1931. In a 1981 interview she recalled: "What we did was to keep the style but to do it in local New England materials. Over there it was all concrete and stucco, never wood. … I used rough-sawn matched wood boards for the outside finish of the walls" (Gruskin, 105–6). Raymond's 1935 design for 16 Longfellow Park combined a traditional two-story hip-roofed, center-entrance main block with modern flat roofed one-story wings flush with the facade. Like her Belmont house and Gropius's own house in Lincoln

(1939), it was sheathed in wood, in this case fir tongue-and-groove siding that created a smooth surface over which Raymond applied a rectangular grid of wooden lattice-work on the first floor. Used previously on a 1921 Frost & Raymond house in Winchester, Massachusetts, the lattice was intended to support vines and roses, but it also reinforced the streamlined character of the design.

Carl Koch's International Style residence at 4 Buckingham eclipsed other local experiments in Modernism (figures 6.194–6.195). Koch (1912–98) graduated from Harvard in 1934 and from the Graduate School of Design (GSD) in 1937, one semester after Gropius began teaching there. Dissatisfied with the Beaux-Arts system of instruction he had experienced, he traveled to Sweden to study under Sven Markelius, designer of the Swedish pavilion at the 1939 New York World's Fair. When he designed the Buckingham Street house for his parents in 1937 he had to enlist Edward Durrell Stone (1902–78) to sign the drawings, as he was not yet licensed. Stone recalled that "though there were few practicing architects who were designing modern houses in those days, the students were becoming enthusiastic modernists" (Stone, 35).

International Style features of 4 Buckingham Street included a flat roof and block-like massing, strip windows, emphatic contrasts of textures, an absence of applied ornamentation, and a close relation between interior and exterior space. Smooth-faced concrete block, which was relatively new in Cambridge, was used as the equivalent of European brick-and-slab construction. The house won prizes from both *Architectural Forum* and *House & Garden* in 1939. Contemporaries admired its creative use of glass and an innovative plan that maximized available space by using a high perimeter wall to incorporate the garden into the house. In 1992 Koch returned to Cambridge and added an incongruous Mansard roof to give himself a third floor studio. Followers of Modernism were appalled, but he seemed amused by the controversy.

Bainbridge Bunting believed that the Koch house played an important role in converting a generation of architectural students at Harvard and M.I.T. to the cause of Modernism. Its

Figure 6.193 Horace W. Frost house, 16 Longfellow Park (1935, Eleanor Raymond, architect). Photo ca. 1940.

Figure 6.195 View from the covered terrace into the garden. Albert C. Koch house. Photo ca. 1939.

Figure 6.194 Albert C. Koch house, 4 Buckingham Street (1937, Carl Koch, architect). Photo 1982.

contemporary furniture and fabrics, many of them imported from Sweden, created a warm and inviting interior, and the house showed that Modern architecture need not be cold and impersonal. Koch became an important advocate for low-cost housing and designed the immensely popular and flexible Techbuilt system, earning him a perhaps inaccurate title, "The Grandfather of Prefab" (*Progressive Architecture,* Feb. 1994, 62).

The Professor Edward B. Hill house at 11 Berkeley Place had a similar origin. George E.B. Hill graduated from M.I.T. in 1940, and designed the house for his parents in 1941. As in most early Modern houses, the roof is flat, and strip windows combine fixed glass panels and undivided steel casements (figure 6.196). Hill's admiration for the work of Alvar Aalto prompted him to choose tongue-and-groove fir siding with a clear finish. In 1971 he recalled collaborating with his classmate I.M. Pei on the design, but Pei responded that the collaboration was actually on an unexecuted design that was considered "too modern" to secure a mortgage.

The use of red brick salvaged from a demolished Back Bay house kept 45 Fayerweather Street from being a textbook example of International Style design, but the texture of the masonry enlivens the strong geometry of the composition. The house sits near the sidewalk on a large wooded lot; the somewhat forbidding exterior conceals a verdant garden created in the foundation of the previous house on the site (figure 6.197). Harvard architecture professor Walter Bogner (1899–1993) designed it in 1940 for mathematician Garrett Birkhoff and his wife, Ruth, a talented gardener. Although Bogner trained in the Beaux-Arts tradition and had served on the faculty since 1927, he was sympathetic to the Modernist cause. In 1939 he built his own Modern house near Walter Gropius's in Lincoln, both of which were featured in *The Modern House in America* in 1940. He was one of the few faculty members who kept his position during the reorganization of the school under Dean Hudnut and remained on the faculty until 1966; this was his only house in Cambridge. The city council designated the house a landmark in 2012.

Local architect William L. Galvin (1902–83) designed ten small houses on Brattle Circle, a cul-de-sac that he developed

FIGURE 6.196 Professor Edward Burlingame Hill house, 11 Berkeley Place (1941, George E.B. Hill, architect). Photo 2009.

FIGURE 6.197 Garrett and Ruth Birkhoff house, 45 Fayerweather Street (1940, Walter Bogner, architect). South elevation, facing garden. Photo 2012.

from 1939 to 1942 on property purchased from Mount Auburn Cemetery. Galvin maintained an active real estate practice while studying at the School of Architecture and after graduation combined the two careers to become what he termed a "promoting architect" (see chapter 2). Galvin designed sleek Art Moderne style commercial buildings in Harvard Square at 23–25 Church Street (1936) and the Cambridge Federal Savings and Loan at 38A Brattle Street (1937); apartment buildings at 10 Forest Street (1937) and 36 Highland Avenue (1940); and a dental office at 2161 Massachusetts Avenue (1939). His Brattle Circle houses featured ribbon windows, flat surfaces, and flush vertical board siding; some had hip roofs that placed them within the Moderne rather than International Style (see figure 4.86).

Of all the Modern houses built in Cambridge just before World War II, the small enclosed International Style house that Philip Johnson designed at 9 Ash Street in 1941 attracted by far the most attention (figure 6.198). A book he coauthored in 1932 with Henry-Russell Hitchcock, *The International Style: Modern Architecture since 1922*, and the concurrent exhibit at the Museum of Modern Art in New York (where he was director of the Department of Architecture in 1931–34) had introduced the style to the United States. In 1940, at age 34, Johnson left New York to study architecture at Harvard and rented a small house at 995 Memorial Drive. Architecture students at that time were required to have three months of practical construction experience, and Johnson satisfied the requirement by designing and building a house for himself. He received a building permit in September 1941, moved into the house in August 1942, and successfully petitioned in 1943 to have it accepted as his thesis project.

Johnson's house is a simple 20 × 61 foot rectangle on a 60 × 80 foot lot on the corner of Ash and Acacia streets. All that is visible from either street is a 9-foot wall of stressed-skin plywood panels with vertical striations, known as "Weldtex," that encloses the courtyard and forms the exterior walls. The entrance is a door in the wall facing Ash Street. Behind the plywood enclosure, the glass facade faces a secluded bluestone courtyard, providing a perfect integration of interior and exterior space. Three

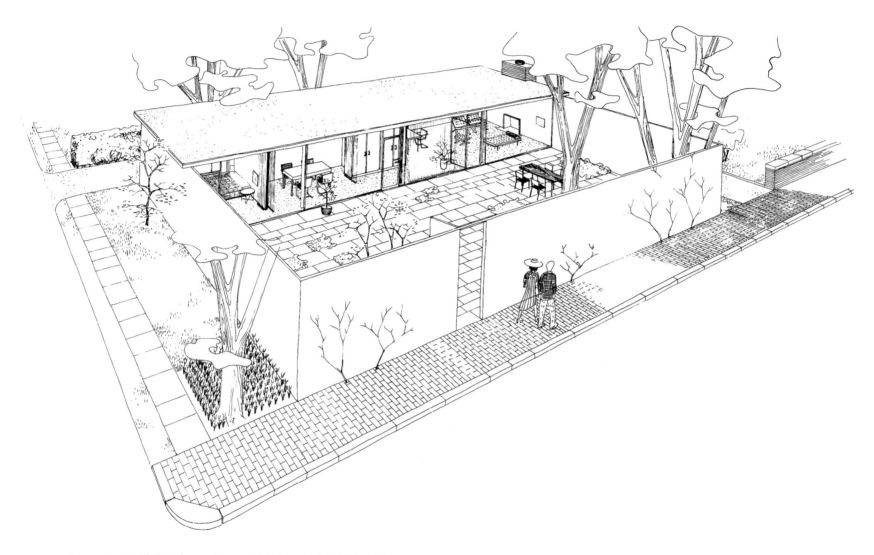

Figure 6.198   Philip Johnson house, 9 Ash Street (1941, Philip Johnson, architect). Axonometric plan, 1942.

laminated maple columns along the front wall support the flat roof and offer great freedom in the arrangement of the interior. Johnson worked on the project with architect S. Clement Horsley, whose Horsley Company of New York was involved in prefabrication.[19] All of the materials, including wall and roof panels, window frames, and insulation were delivered to the site and assembled without nails. Custance Brothers, a Lexington contractor that had built houses for Eleanor Raymond and Walter Bogner, bolted and glued them together to make what the *Cambridge Chronicle-Sun* described as "a four-room house, the like of which Cambridge has never seen before" (Apr. 23, 1942).

Johnson's early projects were often compared to those of Mies van der Rohe, and the *Architectural Forum* considered the Cambridge house as "probably the best example in America of the same attitude towards design" (Dec. 1943, 91). According to one source, Johnson based it on what he called Mies's "earth-hugging court-houses," designed in 1931–38 with glassed living spaces facing a walled courtyard, although only one of these was ever built (Jacobus, 25).[20] The house was intended to provide modest living quarters and privacy for its bachelor architect, who arranged his modern furniture as precisely as if it were a museum gallery (figure 6.199). There was no thought of its usability for mass production or its impact on the streetscape. The solid nine-foot wall created a visual barrier, and the *Architects Journal* criticized Johnson's disregard for "the traditional American neighbourhood pattern" (Mar. 16, 1944). The local architectural community, however, was intrigued; M.I.T. and Harvard faculty and students were frequent visitors, and the Society of Architectural Historians, founded in 1940 by Johnson's cousin, Professor Kenneth Conant, held at least one early meeting there. Johnson left Cambridge to serve in the army during the war and sold the house in 1945. Harvard's Graduate School of Design purchased it in 2010 and has rebuilt it as a residence for visiting scholars.

In the decade after the 1932 MOMA exhibit, the International Style went through a process of Americanization that was recognized in a new show, "Built in USA, 1932–1944." In the catalog, Elizabeth Mock wrote: "Rereading the catalog [of the

FIGURE 6.199 Interior, Philip Johnson house. Photo 1942.

first exhibit] after twelve years is a nostalgic experience, as it brings back the European scene of the late 'twenties and early 'thirties, with its magnificent work in progress and its tragically unrealized promise of new and better possibilities in architecture and society" (*Built in USA*, 10). While the first exhibition presented the masters of European Modernism and relegated Frank Lloyd Wright to the status of "half-modern," the second dealt exclusively with American architecture, which in the years since 1932 had developed a renewed interest in Wright's organic approach to design, an appreciation for wood and other natural materials, and a relaxation from the rigid geometry of the 1920s. The American Modern house tended to relate more intimately to its site and the surrounding landscape than the European equivalent, which was meant to stand apart from the natural world. This distinction continued after World War II, although there continued to be sharp disagreements among practitioners.

Residential construction in Cambridge ceased during World War II, but architects working on housing projects for the military made advances in building materials and construction that passed quickly into the private sector after 1945. Under Dean William Wurster the architecture school at M.I.T. became known worldwide for its pioneering research in prefabrication and modular housing components, while Harvard's Graduate School of Design emphasized advances in architectural theory and practice (see chapter 10). Harvard-educated architects were responsible for the majority of postwar houses in Old Cambridge, although many used techniques and components developed by colleagues at M.I.T.

The earliest postwar houses in Old Cambridge reflected both traditional and International Style designs of the interwar years. One of the first was the Modern residence that Carl Koch and an associate, Frederic L. Day, designed in 1946 for a sloping site on the Edward Waldo Forbes estate, near Howard Fisher's 1935 Bowers house. Unlike some of Koch's later work with prefabricated housing components, 46 Gerry's Landing Road was custom-made to meet the needs of the owners, Francis Bitter, a physicist at M.I.T., and his wife, Alice Richardson Coomaraswamy, a singer who performed as Ratan Devi. The unusual plan created two distinct living areas separated by a glass-roofed garden room that served as an entrance hall. The bedroom wing was constructed of economical concrete block, while the main house, which required good acoustics for Ms. Devi's concerts, was sheathed in vertical tongue-and-groove fir boards and heated with copper pipes built into the ceiling. A dramatic hooded fireplace separated the living and dining areas. On the lower level Koch took advantage of the sloping site to provide abundant natural light for Professor Bitter's study. The glass walls, terraces, and close interrelation of indoor and outdoor space recalled Koch's early planning experiments and his well-known houses at Snake Hill in Belmont. Like those and his later Techbuilt designs, the Bitter house exhibited modular features, a low horizontality, and shed-roofed elements. *Architectural Record* praised its "straightforward, thoughtful planning that reflects and serves the owners' individual needs and desires-convenient, cheerful, efficient, informal" (Jan. 1949, 105: 76). Buckingham, Browne & Nichols School razed the Bitter house in 1997 to make room for a new athletic center.

Two years later, Koch designed a second Modern house on the Forbes estate at 42 Gerry's Landing Road. At one time Mr. and Mrs. Forbes intended to replace their elaborate 1911 Georgian Revival house with a smaller Modern residence, but they ultimately decided to leave the old house and build next door. Above a concrete base containing the main entrance and garage, the house was sheathed in vertical board siding and punctuated by vast expanses of glass. A feeling of openness and spatial flexibility suffused the interior, and the design took advantage of the southeastern exposure to create a two-story, all-glass conservatory for their camellias (figure 6.200).

The first Cambridge project by The Architects Collaborative was a house at 18 Old Dee Road (figure 6.201). Designed in 1947 for florist Harold A. Ryan, who had subdivided the Dee nursery in 1937, this small, flat-roofed International Style house was important as the work of one of America's most influential postwar firms. TAC was formed in December 1945 with Walter Gropius as the senior member. Most of the partners were graduates of the School of Architecture at Yale, not Harvard, and they brought the studio team method of their training into the professional sphere. Some of the original partners, including Norman and Jean Fletcher and John and Sarah Harkness, built houses for themselves at Six Moon Hill in Lexington beginning in 1948. The firm's only other house in Cambridge is 15 Hemlock Road (1952). Like many Modern houses 18 Old Dee was not built to last, and a new owner replaced it with a neo-Greek Revival house in 2005.

The firm soon turned to commercial and institutional work. Gropius and TAC designed Harkness Commons and the Harvard Graduate Center in 1947–49 and were later responsible for numerous buildings in the United States and abroad, including

FIGURE 6.200 Edward Waldo Forbes house, 42 Gerry's Landing Road (1948, Carl Koch, architect). Photo 1969.

FIGURE 6.201 Harold A. Ryan house, 18 Old Dee Road (1947, The Architects Collaborative). West (rear) elevation. Photo 2005.

the Pan American World Airways Building in New York (1958), the firm's headquarters at 46 Story Street (1966), and the Bauhaus Archive/Museum of Design in Berlin (1976). One of the original partners, Benjamin Thompson, exercised a profound influence on American residential design through Design Research, a modern furnishings store he founded in Cambridge in 1953 (see figure 8.40). Thompson left TAC in 1966 to start his own practice, specializing in urban revitalization projects like Boston's Quincy Market (1971–76). He never designed a house in Cambridge, but he remodeled the interior of his residence at 27 Willard Street in the D/R style.

In the 1950s domestic designs again expressed the pitch of the roof and highlighted differences in materials. Whereas the first International Style designers in this country installed wood siding as flat as possible and painted it white to imitate the stuccoed masonry used in Europe, architects in the 1950s began to emphasize textures, using natural stains and applying siding in

different ways, as at 5 Hemlock Road (1956, James C. Hopkins). Ranch houses were popular in the 1940s and '50s in suburbs throughout America, but few were built in Cambridge, and most of those are clustered on Blanchard Road and Grove Street west of Fresh Pond. The ranch that Cambridge architect Arthur H. Brooks Jr. (1916–2001) designed for his wife's parents in 1949 at 20 Follen Street has a low-pitched roof, stained redwood clapboard sheathing, and white-painted plywood panels that show a remarkable disregard for context. Brooks had impeccable credentials: he grew up in the house that Alexander Wadsworth Longfellow designed for his grandfather, John Brooks, at 5 Ash Street, and lived in Anne Longfellow Thorp's house at 115 Brattle Street. He graduated from Harvard's School of Design in 1942, a year before Philip Johnson, worked as a draftsman for Walter Bogner in 1944–45, and established his own practice in Cambridge in 1947. He designed houses at 11 Old Dee Road (1950) and 93 Fresh Pond Parkway (1956), the modernization of the First Parish Church (1956), and a 1965 addition to H. Langford Warren's Swedenborgian Church. Brooks remained a committed Modernist throughout his career but wholly in the postwar American vernacular.

The boxy, flat-roofed house with ribbon windows that architect Carleton Richmond Jr. (1915–99) built for himself in 1951 at 22 Follen Street recalls the early International Style, but seems better suited to the site than Brooks's project next door (figure 6.202). Textured glass, dark stained vertical siding, and a variety of panels and windows sharply delineated by white trim add textural variety to the exterior, while the interior plan with varied ceiling heights and floor levels and movable partitions was praised in *Architectural Record* in 1954 for its openness and flexibility. Trained at the GSD, Richmond worked in Walter Bogner's office in 1941 and 1946–47 and became a partner before opening his own office in 1952. Richmond later partnered with Ronald Gourley, with whom he designed faculty housing for Radcliffe College at 48–54 Linnaean Street in 1970.

Carl Koch & Associates introduced a revolutionary two-story prefabricated house in 1953 that seemed especially suited to urban lots. Techbuilt, Inc. of Cambridge initially marketed seven different models; twenty-five went up in the Boston area within a year. In December 1954 Edward Diehl, the general manager, put one up for himself at 23 Lexington Avenue (figure 6.203). The glassed end walls and low-pitched roof of this first Techbuilt structure in Cambridge were not unusual elements in the early 1950s, but the complete flexibility of plan was. The house was designed on a 4-foot-square module around a core that contained utilities, stairs, chimney, and bathroom; this left the rest of the space free to be divided with prefabricated partitions that could be adjusted to meet evolving needs. The prefabricated panels were provided by Acorn, a company founded by Koch that relied on studies of modular buildings conducted by the Bemis Foundation at M.I.T. Interior finishes included stained clapboards, brick walls, and other materials valued for their ease of maintenance but traditionally reserved for exterior use.

FIGURE 6.202 Carleton Richmond house, 22 Follen Street (1951, Carleton Richmond, architect). The panel on the right side of the facade was originally a garage door. Photo 2014.

FIGURE 6.203 Edward Diehl house, 23 Lexington Avenue (1954, Techbuilt). Photo before 1967.

House & Home reported in February 1954 that prefabrication enabled a Techbuilt house like 23 Lexington to be assembled in less than a week:

> First day: site prepared, excavated with bulldozer-shovel tractor. Second day: portable forms placed and foundations poured. Third and fourth days: foundations allowed to cure. Fifth day: sections trucked to site; walls and gable ends tilted up; posts and beams put in and floor panels slid into place. Sixth day: roof panels placed; roofing, glazing and exterior wall finish applied. House tight to weather, ready for interior finish. (108)

Although the company stated that the interior was flexible enough to meet a family's needs for a lifetime, Diehl used Techbuilt vacation cottage plans to add a garage (1955) and split-level office (1960). Other Techbuilt houses stand at 12 Blanchard Road (1958) and 60 Francis Avenue (1961)

In 1954 Hugh Stubbins & Associates designed two houses on St. John's Road for Episcopal Theological School faculty that turned out to be quite compatible with the 19th-century houses E.T.S. moved to the street a few years later. In October 1955, *Progressive Architecture* described them as compact homes with the kind of low pitched roof and deep eaves that Stubbins had found practical and economical in earlier work. The projecting sunshades made of vertical boards became a common feature in this period. These may have been prototypes for an affordable house that Stubbins designed for mass production in 1955 and that *Better Homes & Gardens* designated their "Idea Home" of the year; while this was never built in Cambridge, builders were said to have erected them in a hundred U.S. cities.

Born in Birmingham, Alabama, and educated at Georgia Tech, Stubbins (1912–2006) studied at Harvard's School of Architecture during its Beaux-Arts period (1933–35). He taught there from the 1940s until 1972 and established his own firm in 1949. Like Koch, Stubbins stressed the importance of designing buildings that were workable for the original clients and adaptable for future users. The Stubbins firm, like TAC, soon moved away from residential design and found its niche in institutional and commercial work, designing Congress Hall in Berlin (1957), the Loeb Drama Center in Cambridge (1960), Citicorp Center in New York City (1978), and the Federal Reserve Bank in Boston (1978), as well as innumerable dormitories, libraries, hospitals, laboratories, and U.S. embassies.

Another internationally renowned figure practicing in Cambridge during this period was the Catalan architect Josep Lluis Sert (1902–83), who succeeded Joseph Hudnut in 1953 as dean of the GSD. At first Sert commuted from New York City, but in 1957 he established Sert, Jackson & Gourley in Cambridge and began construction of his own residence at 64 Francis Avenue on a lot that he leased from the university.[21] Sert designed his inward-looking house around a traditional Mediterranean courtyard using the most common local materials, wood and brick (figures 6.204–6.205). The street facades are solid board panels or plain brick walls with a few narrow slit windows, while the all-white interior was open and airy and incorporated artwork by Costantino Nivola, Miró, Leger, and Picasso. The glass walls of the living areas face inward and outward onto enclosed courtyards, creating an intimate exchange between interior and exterior spaces. To adapt this traditional plan to Cambridge's northern climate, Sert oriented the house to maximize sunlight in the courtyards in winter. He described its appeal in *House & Home*: "Both indoor and outdoor living space is private and serene. Every room can have pleasant views regardless of what is beyond the walls" (Oct. 1958).

Some nonresidential structures were converted to housing in the 1950s before the practice of adaptive reuse became widespread. In 1957 New Haven architect Paul Rudolph, later dean of Yale School of Architecture, replaced the front wall of a cement block garage at 144 Upland Road with glass to create a light-filled house for his own use. Because the roof was supported by steel trusses, the 3,000 square foot building offered unlimited interior possibilities (figures 6.206–6.207). Ten years later Sheldon and Annabel Dietz, a businessman and an artist, carried out an innovative residential reuse on Sparks Place, where they converted a warren of 1923 garages too small for modern automobiles into two residences.

FIGURE 6.204 Josep Lluis Sert house, 64 Francis Avenue (1957, Josep Lluis Sert, architect). Photo 1968.

FIGURE 6.205 Courtyard, Josep Lluis Sert house. Photo ca. 1960.

FIGURE 6.206 Paul Rudolph house, 144 Upland Road (1913, Alden Parry, architect; remodeled for residential use, 1957, Paul Rudolph, architect). Photo 2014.

FIGURE 6.207 Interior view, Paul Rudolph house. Photo 2014.

Fewer than a dozen new houses were built in Old Cambridge in the 1960s, but they were surprisingly diverse and demonstrated a renewed search for an architectural style related to its time and place. No longer was just one idiom considered "modern." Two adjoining houses on Kennedy Road demonstrate this new freedom. In 1963 Emerson College president Richard Chapin hired James Freeman (designer of the 1962 Riverview apartments at 221 Mt. Auburn Street) to design 13 Kennedy Road as "a one-story house with three zones: one for adults and peace; one for children and activity; one where we all get together" (*House Beautiful*, Aug. 1968). The dark finishes and low-pitched roofs of the three freestanding pavilions are reminiscent of 1950s designs, but the house has an oriental quality that sets it apart from European Internationalism (figure 6.208). On an adjoining lot at 4 Kennedy Road, Sargent Kennedy, secretary to the Corporation at Harvard, commissioned a house from Deck Associates (later Deck House, Inc.) in 1966. Architectural designer William J. Berkes had founded Deck in 1959 to manufacture house components that could be delivered to a building site ready for assembly. In contrast to Freeman's house, 4 Kennedy Road featured the light smooth surfaces, vertical siding, and clear geometry of traditional Modernism while accommodating a sloping site.

In 1973 Bainbridge Bunting described the house at 199 Brattle Street that Hugh Stubbins designed for himself in 1965 as "perhaps the city's most successful recent dwelling" (*Report Four: Old Cambridge*, 132). Stubbins developed a regional style for his modern domestic architecture, often looking to traditional New England barns for inspiration. Siting his new house on a corner lot on historic Brattle Street, he stated: "I wanted my addition to this street to be compatible, but also a reminder of its own era. … The idea of the house is … like a barn with open lofts." (*Architectural Record Houses of 1967*, 89) A high wall of waterstruck brick screens the large windows and glass sliding doors from the street and creates a private garden space, while the rough-sawn weathered redwood siding blends in with the painted houses nearby (figure 6.209). Inside, the exposed post-and-beam construction of the main living area rises 26 feet to

FIGURE 6.208 Richard and Maryan Chapin house, 13 Kennedy Road (1963, James Freeman, architect). Photo 2011.

FIGURE 6.209 Hugh Stubbins house, 199 Brattle Street (1965, Hugh Stubbins, architect). Photo 2015.

the ridge. Widely praised in the architectural press at the time of its construction, it remains a fine example of 1960s design.

Kenneth Redmond (1931–2000) earned a master of architecture degree at Harvard in 1964 and soon built a Mid-century Modern house for his family at 11 Reservoir Street. Although he used traditional New England materials such as weathered clapboards and white trim, the strong geometric forms, large glazed and solid vertical panels, and prominent projecting and receding square bays place it firmly in the 1960s (figure 6.210). In 1971 he designed a more severe but equally geometric house for himself at 16 Gurney Street with similar projecting square bays. Redmond continued to practice architecture, briefly in partnership but mostly on his own; he designed no other houses in Cambridge. A different vocabulary of projecting bays and dramatic slanting roofs characterized attorney Peter Hiam's house at 46 Fayerweather Street designed by Geometrics, Inc., a firm that William Ahearn and William Wainwright founded in 1954 in association with Buckminster Fuller (figure 6.211).

One of the most striking Modern houses in Old Cambridge is 133 Brattle Street, designed in 1970 for an unusual triangular lot that was created during the subdivision of the Denman Ross property at 24 Craigie Street. A preservation restriction required Cambridge Historical Commission approval of the design. The owners, Madelon and Dr. Martin Falxa, a young materials scientist, desired a contemporary house to display their art collection. Following extensive public hearings and several design modifications, plans by Fenton Hollander of Hill, Miller, Friedlander, Hollander (now HMFH Architects, Inc.) were approved in January 1971. Although the design was representative of the period, the low profile and vertical redwood siding stained gray deferred to the height and stony hues of the Ross House (figure 6.212). Hollander wrote that it represented "an effort to accommodate an ambitious program on a curious site, live within historical and community requirements, respond to the needs of an adventurous client, and provide for this street a residence worthy of its time and place" (*Boston Herald-American*, July 1, 1973). The Historical Commission's approval established

FIGURE 6.210 Kenneth Redmond house, 11 Reservoir Street (1964, Kenneth Redmond, architect). Photo 2015.

FIGURE 6.211 Peter Hiam house, 46 Fayerweather Street (1968, Geometrics Inc., architects; demolished 2007). Photo during construction, 1968–69.

FIGURE 6.212 Dr. Martin and Madelon Falxa house, 133 Brattle Street (1970, Fenton Hollander of Hill Miller Friedlander Hollander, architect). Photo ca. 1972.

the principle that contemporary design can be appropriate in a historic district.

The largest group of new homes erected in Old Cambridge in the last quarter of the 20th century occurred on Grozier and Larch roads, where demolition of the Russell School in 1979 allowed the city to offer eleven lots for construction of one and two-family houses. Rudimentary design criteria included the use of natural materials, restrictions against aluminum siding, and compatibility with existing structures. The ten double houses at 46 to 64 Grozier Road and 93 to 107 Larch Road (1980–82) combined traditional and contemporary features, but few were particularly successful. The only notable house was a single-family at 44 Grozier Road designed by the Argentine-American architect Eduardo Catalano (1917–2010) for his own use. It features dramatic sloping roofs, vertical flush boarding, and a massive solar greenhouse with sloped roof at the rear, but it is not as daring as the building that made his reputation in 1954, a house in Raleigh, North Carolina, with an unusual hyperbolic paraboloid roof.

The most significant late Modernist house in Old Cambridge is 5 Lowell Street, a 9,800-square foot home that Cambridge architect Graham Gund built for his family in 1999–2001 in the center of the block between Lowell and Channing streets. An earlier project to build twenty-two row houses on this wooded 1½-acre lot had fortunately never been carried out. Set deep within the site and not visible from the street, the house consists of three pavilions clad in ship-lapped redwood clapboards and connected by one-story passageways covered in zinc. The pavilions are organized asymmetrically around a courtyard, and their extensive use of glass allows private vistas into the seemingly vast and imaginatively landscaped grounds (figures 6.213–6.214).

The treatment of older houses varied during this period. In the 1960s and '70s, Modernist architects like Frederick Bruck specialized in renovations that stripped out decorative woodwork and plaster in favor of white-painted gypsum board. By the 1980s Victorian-era houses were once again considered appealing and were still affordable for young families. Among the noteworthy preservation projects carried out by individual

FIGURE 6.213 Graham Gund house, 5 Lowell Street (1999–2001, Graham Gund, architect). Photo 2009.

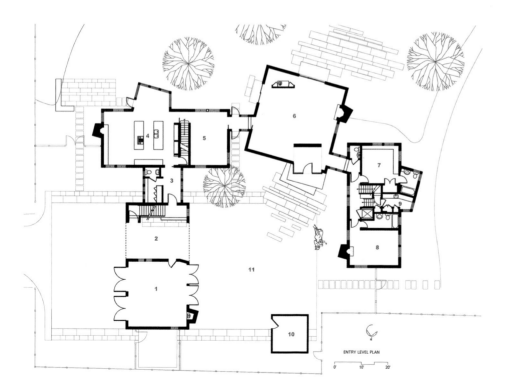

ENTRY LEVEL PLAN

0'   10'   20'

FIGURE 6.214 Site plan, Graham Gund house.

1. Garage
2. Porte cochère
3. Mud room
4. Kitchen
5. Dining room
6. Living room
7. Bedroom
8. Guest bedroom
9. Laundry
10. Shed
11. Paved courtyard

homeowners were the Henry Vassall House, restored and converted to two-family use in 1974; 23 Buckingham Street, restored and its original stickwork recreated in 1985; H.H. Richardson's Stoughton House, restored with sympathetic alterations in 1989; Cambridge's only Italianate villa at 15 Berkeley Street, awarded a national prize for restoration in 1992; and 71 Appleton Street, restored with careful replication of the original porch in 1999. The owners of these houses evidenced a marked concern for preserving original fabric and a notable willingness to tolerate the idiosyncrasies of old-house living.

The end of rent control in 1995 and a strengthening economy at the close of the decade attracted new residents and developers who invested heavily in Cambridge. At the same time, institutions curtailed their practice of landbanking residential properties. However, a notable change in expectations and purchasing power also became apparent in the late 1990s. Unlike the urban homesteaders that preceded them, many buyers entering the Old Cambridge market after about 1995 did not want to put up with the imperfections of an old house. Cambridge's strict zoning laws prevented nonconforming buildings from being demolished and rebuilt to the same dimensions, so developers and wealthy individuals began to buy older houses, strip them down to the bare frames, and rebuild with all new finishes inside and out. In some cases these projects involved a heroic restoration of lost details known from early photographs, as at 167 Brattle Street in 2006, but others resulted in a complete change of character as they replaced original fabric and features with undefined eclecticism, as at 47 Raymond Street in 1997, or with faux historicism, as at 40 Huron Avenue in 2006–12. Enormous additions also became common. Some of these completely overshadowed the original structure, as at 79 Raymond Street (2007–12), but others, such as at 88 Appleton Street (2008), had architectural merit in their own right (figure 6.215).

Most single family houses constructed in Old Cambridge from the 1990s on were modest and fairly traditional, but all entailed demolition of existing houses. On Old Dee Road, an Acorn Structures house at number 6 (1994) and a two-story

FIGURE 6.215 William Read house, 88 Appleton Street (1859; 2008 addition, Ann Beha Associates, architects). Originally a Mansard, the house was remodeled as a Colonial Revival by Allen W. Jackson in 1922 and given a major modern addition in 2008. Photo 2008.

neo-Craftsman design at 12 (2000) replaced two 1948 colonials that were part of the original 1937 subdivision. A house at 5 Kenway Street was built in 1990 on the foundations of a small house that Mary and William Duguid had designed in 1927. In 1999 a traditional center-entrance house with a high hip roof replaced a singular 1927 Spanish Eclectic style stucco house at 40 Larch Road designed by Boston architect Harold Smilie. Mid-century Modern houses were particularly vulnerable to this trend, as popular taste once again embraced traditional forms. The striking 1968 house by Geometrics, Inc. at 46 Fayerweather Street had only a single owner before it was replaced in 2007 by a residence intended to recall a traditional New England farmhouse. Nearby, a 2014 neo-Craftsman house replaced 26 Reservoir, designed by California architect Frederic S. Coolidge for his parents in 1955. These and other vanished Modern houses such as 14 and 18 Reservoir were among several that populated the top of Reservoir hill after 1949. The most significant loss was William Wainwright's own house at 61 Highland Street (1958), which was razed in 2003 to enlarge a neighboring property (see figure 4.70).

New houses in the 21st century could be designed in almost any style. The Cambridge Historical Commission offered to consider a contemporary design when the 1810 John Appleton house at 163 Brattle Street burned to the ground in 2005, as it had at 133 Brattle in 1972, but the owners preferred a traditional look and retained Peter Pennoyer of New York to design a neo-Federal replacement. A few years later Nick Winton of Anmahian Winton designed up-to-date houses at 2 Hemlock Road (2013) and 7 Channing Street (2014). Clad in zinc panels and hardwood rainscreens punctuated by widely spaced windows, these houses created a contemporary presence in their long-settled neighborhoods (figure 6.216).

FIGURE 6.216 2 Hemlock Road (2013, Anmahian Winton Architects). Photo 2014.

APARTMENT HOUSES

Apartment buildings made a relatively late appearance in Cambridge and never became as ubiquitous as they were in Brookline, a more convenient streetcar suburb of Boston. Throughout the 19th century privacy was an important concern of upper- and middle-class families; most considered the single-family house ideal, even if they had to take in roomers to afford one, while multifamily housing was generally associated with transience and unhealthy conditions. The Pelham House (1857, Arthur Gilman) at the corner of Boylston and Tremont streets in Boston has been described as "the first apartment building for the middle class in the United States" (Cromley, 18). The development of public transportation in the second half of the century made it feasible to work in Boston but live in the suburbs and thus avoid the loss of privacy entailed in urban living, but it was decades before apartment houses appeared in Cambridge. Even in large urban centers like New York residential hotels or "French Flat" buildings were not generally accepted as family housing until well after the Civil War.

Beck Hall (1876), the first top-tier private dormitory, showed that apartment buildings could be socially acceptable for bachelors and students but offered no usable precedent for families (see chapter 10). The earliest Old Cambridge apartment houses, the Stanstead (1887) at 19–21 Ware Street and the Jarvis (1890) at 27 Everett Street, were relatively small, three-story buildings with only two apartments per floor and were generally considered experimental. By this time, many well-to-do residents in New York and Boston had recognized the advantages of apartments that provided living spaces comparable to single-family houses but laid out on a single floor and offering amenities such as first-class restaurants, elevators, telephones, and electricity. Old Cambridge, however, remained skeptical, and many residents probably agreed with entrepreneur Gardiner Hubbard when he told the *Tribune*: "I am a firm believer in single houses with light and air on every side" (Aug. 14, 1886). The Cambridge directory for 1890 listed thirty-five apartment hotels in the city but mostly in Cambridgeport and only one, the Stanstead, in Old Cambridge.

The first large apartment houses in Old Cambridge targeted an upscale market by offering luxury accommodations and services similar to those in private dormitories. Such amenities aimed to establish a clear distinction between the apartment and the tenement, but negative associations were difficult to overcome. Apartment buildings were slow to gain acceptance until the completion of the subway in 1912 opened the area to white-collar commuters and triggered a boom in apartment construction along the trolley lines leading away from Harvard Square. By this time apartments were accepted as an economical yet comfortable housing option for singles, widows, and young married couples, and they were becoming an acceptable alternative for families. Between 1912 and 1930 at least sixty-six apartment buildings went up in Old Cambridge, but the Depression and the middle-class flight to the suburbs after World War II greatly diminished demand. The market finally rebounded in the 1980s, bringing the first luxury condominiums at University Green and Charles Square.

When the Stanstead at 19–21 Ware was under construction in 1887, a journalist referring to recent construction activity in Cambridgeport noted that the new building would be "a higher grade apartment house than has thus far been erected," as well as the first heated by steam (*Tribune,* July 23, 1887). Built for John H. Hubbard, a Harvard Square apothecary who had recently erected a traditional row of four attached houses next door, the Stanstead clearly announced its multifamily use with a single entrance marked by an imposing Richardsonian Romanesque arch and the name of the building carved in stone (figure 6.217). It was basically a double three-decker in plan but more sophisticated in material and style and directed at a higher-class clientele. It now seems small compared to the apartment houses nearby, but in 1887 its scale, large entrance, and lobby resembling that of a public building made it stand out on what was then a street of single-family houses.

The Stanstead was divided horizontally, with all the rooms in each flat on the same floor, an arrangement referred to as "French flats" after a system of apartment design common in Paris; this arrangement was also standard for the three-deckers that became

FIGURE 6.217 The Stanstead, 19–21 Ware Street (1887, Joseph R. & William P. Richards, architects). Photo 2015.

ubiquitous in many neighborhoods after 1890. Most upper- and middle-class American families, however, were used to a vertical division of living space, with public and private rooms on separate floors, and this difference proved to be a stumbling block in their acceptance of apartment living. In a novel about Boston and Cambridge that was published while the Stanstead was under construction, William Dean Howells wrote:

For the most part [flats] were plainly regarded as makeshifts, the resorts of people of small means, or the defiances or errors of people who had lived too much abroad. They stamped their occupants as of transitory and fluctuant character; good people might live in them, and did, as good people sometimes boarded; but they could not be regarded as forming a social base, except in rare instances. They presented peculiar difficulties in calling, and for any sort of entertainment they were too—not public, perhaps, but—evident. (*April Hopes,* 68)

The six-unit Jarvis (1890) at 27 Everett, also by J.R. & W.P. Richards, was more advanced in design with a polychrome exterior executed in Perth Amboy brick and terra-cotta trim (figure 6.218). Each apartment had a large parlor, sitting room, dining room, bathroom, kitchen, and two or three bedrooms; servants had rooms on the top floor. There were separate back stairs for each side of the building, a lift for coal and ice, and a boiler that furnished hot water throughout, new features that became standard in the 1890s. Light was a primary consideration, and the U-shaped plan and variety of gables and projecting bays created well-lit and airy rooms. Like the Stanstead, the Jarvis was set 25 feet back from the street, in line with nearby houses; later apartment houses often had no setbacks and disrupted the domestic scale of residential streets.

Fears of tenement construction drove the vehement opposition to a developer's plan to construct a large apartment house at 24 Arlington Street on fashionable Avon Hill in 1896. Nearby residents felt "obliged to buy him out in order to avert the impending unsightliness and disgrace to the neighborhood" (*Chronicle,* Apr. 18, 1896). Only three years later, the *Chronicle* noted that while "these buildings are to change in a very marked way the appearance of our main avenue and other streets," this would not be a bad thing, because "they will bring to Cambridge a class of residents greatly to be desired, socially and in every other way, especially as tax payers" (Apr. 29, 1899). This did not represent the prevailing opinion in Old Cambridge, and apartment houses were frequently resisted until the introduction of zoning in 1924.

In 1898 construction began on four "mammoth apartment hotels which will probably be the largest and most expensive of

FIGURE 6.218   The Jarvis, 27 Everett Street (1890, Joseph R. & William P. Richards, architects). Photo 2014.

any buildings of this character in Cambridge" (*Chronicle,* Apr. 2, 1898). Two of these, the Majestic and the Regent at 884–888 Massachusetts Avenue, were in Cambridgeport, while the other two stood side by side at the corner of Massachusetts Avenue and Shepard Street. The Montrose and the Dunvegan were built for real estate magnate W.G. MacLeod with "every possible device for convenience and comfort in living" (*Chronicle,* Oct. 1, 1898; figure 6.219; see figure 4.182). Designed by Boston architects J. St. Clair Harrold and Willard M. Bacon, the imposing six-story yellow brick structures filled their lots and were more symmetrical and uniform in detail than the Jarvis, which had attempted to give each unit a separate identity on the exterior. The interior layout was spacious, with most floors having only two ten-room apartments (figure 6.220). Each building had twelve large family suites, and the Dunvegan also offered a dozen two-room bachelor suites. Promotional materials stated that the aim was "to present an appearance of richness and refinement such as a man

FIGURE 6.219 The Montrose and the Dunvegan, 1648 and 1654 Massachusetts Avenue (both 1898, J. St Clair Harrold and Willard M. Bacon, architects, respectively). Photo 2015.

FIGURE 6.220 Floor plan, the Dunvegan.

of wealth and culture would desire to have in his private house but which is not ordinarily seen in a building of this nature," (MacLeod, 31). MacLeod may have misjudged the market for large apartments, because only a few more buildings of the size and opulence of the Montrose and the Dunvegan were built in Cambridge. MacLeod's heirs soon subdivided the apartments, and by the time they sold the buildings in 1924 the Montrose had thirty units instead of the original twelve. By 1962 the Dunvegan's flats had become forty-eight small apartments.

Through the first decade of the 20th century, most multifamily buildings in Old Cambridge were relatively small. Of the fifteen or so erected between 1900 and 1910, twelve were three stories high, and only four contained more than fifteen units. Many resembled expanded three-deckers. The Lowell at 33 Lexington Avenue (1900, John A. Hasty) was the most flamboyant of these, with Ionic columns and pilasters and a wide entablature capped by a monumental broken-scroll pediment; its location in an upscale suburban neighborhood may have influenced its bold design (figure 6.221). Owner James M. Hilton was a Cambridge businessman and real estate developer who put up thirty-eight buildings in Old Cambridge between 1860 and 1903, including several private dormitories in Harvard Square. Hasty, who had designed a number of three-deckers and apartment houses in the 1890s, is best known for the Cambridge Mutual Fire Insurance Building (1888) in Central Square.

Larger than the Lowell but less interesting architecturally is the Greenacre, a nine- family frame building of five- and six-room units at 124 Oxford Street (1901, Edwin Earp Jr.), with a Colonial Revival entrance and semicircular porch facing the corner. The Greenacre contained rooms for servants, but as in earlier, more modest apartments, they were located in the basement. Patrick J. Lyons, a Roxbury builder, erected two brick apartment houses, the Chester and the Hurlbut at 24–26 and 28 Hurlbut Street in 1902. Designed by Charles A. Russell, also of Roxbury, the bow-fronted three-story brick and limestone buildings hugged the sidewalk; each contained six seven-room suites. While these were typical of buildings along Warren Street

FIGURE 6.221 The Lowell, 33 Lexington Avenue (1900, James A. Hasty, architect). Photo 2015.

in Roxbury and in the Mission Hill area of Boston, they contrasted sharply with the setbacks and handsome Queen Anne single family houses across the street.

The two largest apartment buildings in this decade led the transition from the French flat in favor of smaller apartments accessed off common hallways. Both stood on Brattle Street near Harvard Square and were designed with Jacobean details by Newhall & Blevins, one of Cambridge's most prolific firms. Washington Court at 51 Brattle Street contained forty-two suites in an L-shaped, six-story brick and terra-cotta building. Lavish details included heraldic shields and a crenellated roofline, as well as handsome interior oak wainscoting and beamed ceilings (figure 6.222). Built in 1905 for Dr. Albert August, a Cambridge physician, the building offered a variety of modern services such as continuous hot water and a telephone in each suite. Half the suites were bachelor flats with no kitchens, and the rest were

FIGURE 6.222 Washington Court, 51 Brattle Street (1905, Newhall & Blevins, architects). Photo 1909.

arranged for "light housekeeping," making them suitable for a greater variety of tenants than the Montrose or Dunvegan. The ground floor featured a café; Dr. August's office and apartment were accessed through a separate entrance. Washington Court was one of the city's earliest courtyard apartment buildings. This arrangement, used in the 1890s in Boston apartments and Cambridge private dormitories, became the favored form for apartment houses after 1900. Compared to a simple block form, the courtyard plan maintained some of the site as open space and allowed more exposure to light and air. Newhall & Blevins designed one of the city's most elaborate courtyard buildings, Burton Hall, at 10 Dana Street in 1909.

In 1908 Newhall & Blevins undertook the first of several apartment projects, serving as both designers and developers. At 83 Brattle Street, the six-story Wadsworth Chambers repeated many of the successful features of Washington Court, including

its Jacobean details and elegant finishes. Tiers of bay windows facing a cramped courtyard gave rooms additional light. The building contained thirty apartments and was designed for those "who desire small suites for light housekeeping," including Blevins himself, who was a bachelor (*Chronicle,* Oct. 3, 1908). Citing the success of recent buildings with smaller suites, the *Chronicle* commented: "to judge of the rate at which they have been rented, their owners would seem to have correctly gauged the trend of the times" (Oct. 23, 1909).

Between 1911 and 1920, Old Cambridge gained twenty-seven new apartment buildings, several of which filled entire new streets. The number of units in each building ranged from sixteen to forty-eight, but most had fewer than thirty. World War I caused a temporary halt in construction, but in the 1920s developers concentrated on several areas: Massachusetts Avenue and the side streets running west off the avenue (fourteen buildings); the Agassiz neighborhood (seven); and Memorial Drive west of Harvard Square (five). Apartment buildings were not limited to these areas, however, and until the enactment of zoning in 1924 they continued to appear wherever an available site could be found.

The formulaic approach that characterized later apartment design did not yet dominate the field, and until the World War I architects were still experimenting with various floor plans, styles, and materials, but the double-loaded corridor was now ubiquitous. Variants of the courtyard plan included a U-shaped plan around a center courtyard, such as Linnaean Hall at 3–5 Linnaean Street (1914) and Mather Court at 1 Waterhouse Street (1916, both Newhall & Blevins); an L-shaped plan with a corner entrance and garden space along one side, such as 34–36 Ash Street (1915, William L. Mowll); and an H-shaped plan with two rectangular blocks connected by a narrow middle section (figures 6.223–6.225). Sometimes two L-plans were set back-to-back, forming a T-shaped structure that allowed the bulk of the building to be at the back of the lot, as at 19 Agassiz Street (1912, Newhall & Blevins) and 46 Shepard Street (1919, Hamilton Harlow). The H-plan was used infrequently

LINNAEAN HALL
CAMBRIDGE
NEWHALL & BLEVINS · ARCHTS

TYPICAL FLOOR PLAN

FIGURE 6.223 U-shaped plan, Linnaean Hall, 3–5 Linnaean Street (1914, Newhall & Blevins, architects).

FIGURE 6.224 L-shaped plan, 34–36 Ash Street (1915, William L. Mowll, architect).

before 1920 but became quite common in the 1920s and '30s with such buildings as 41–43 Linnaean Street (1922, Hamilton Harlow) and 20 Concord Avenue (1929, Silverman & Brown). Simple rectangular blocks of apartments were also constructed, but in Old Cambridge courtyard plans initially outnumbered this monolithic urban form.

Stylistically, apartment buildings in the 1910s followed the Craftsman and Jacobean styles, as well as the always-popular Georgian Revival, which was recommended for general adoption in 1913 by a group considering the future development of Harvard Square. Both stucco and a variety of brick patterns were common, including a rough-surfaced combed brick known as tapestry brick; an overfired, deformed clinker brick; and the New England Brick Company's popular Harvard Brick with glazed headers (figure 6.184; see also figure 10.28). Limestone trim, leaded windows, and slate or tile roofs were popular details; some designers ornamented their work with decorative tiles and wrought iron gates and light standards.

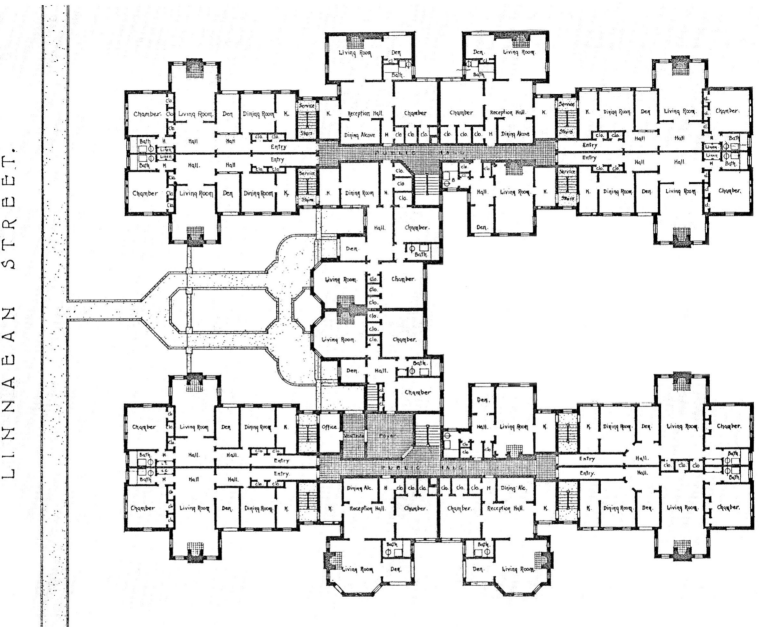

FIGURE 6.225 H-shaped plan, 41–43 Linnaean Street (1922, Hamilton Harlow, architect).

Newhall & Blevins designed the earliest Craftsman-style apartment buildings at 10–14 Remington Street (1910) and 41 Hawthorn Street (1911), where stucco cladding over a wood frame was a low-cost alternative to masonry. This type of construction was considered to violate city building codes, and later structures such as 19 Agassiz Street (1912) were built of stucco-covered terra-cotta blocks (figure 6.226). Some of these provided sleeping porches, a popular feature in single-family houses of the period. The firm's influence was most evident in the four large brick apartment houses they built near Cambridge Common between 1915 and 1925. Concord Hall (1915) at 3 Concord Avenue is a six-story triangular brick building squeezed onto an irregular lot and organized around a multitude of square bays (figure 6.227). Although nominally Georgian Revival, Concord Hall's only stylistic features are a strong classical cornice, small-paned window sash, and Flemish bond masonry. The cramped courtyard, multiple square bays, flat roof, six-story height, and brick construction set the tone for Mather Court (1916) at 1 Waterhouse Street, Lexington Hall (1917) at 5 Concord Avenue, and Whitfield Hall (1925) at 17 Garden Street. This four-building cluster contained 168 apartments; Newhall & Blevins owned 91, and other investors rented out the remainder.

Newhall & Blevins's success demonstrated the business opportunities in apartment house design and development, and the Harlow family soon followed their lead. In 1914 Boston lawyer Frank S. Harlow and his architect son, Hamilton, built their first apartment block, the Humboldt, at 7 Linnaean Street next to Newhall & Blevins's Linnaean Hall (also 1914). Frank Harlow already owned a Newhall & Blevins-designed building at 2–4 Avon Street (1909), but with his son's participation as designer the family's holdings increased dramatically. The Humboldt was the first of seventeen buildings that Harlow Realty constructed in Old Cambridge; all were designed by Hamilton Harlow, his nephew Frank E. Harlow, or Hamilton's firm, Dow, Harlow & Kimball. These included 11 Story Street (1916), 10–10A Chauncy Street, 61 Garfield Street, and 6–8 Craigie Circle (all 1917), 46 Shepard Street and 21 Chauncy Street

FIGURE 6.226 Agassiz Hall apartments, 19 Agassiz Street (1912, Newhall & Blevins, architects). Photo 2015.

FIGURE 6.227 Concord Hall (1914) and Lexington Hall (1917), 3 and 5 Concord Avenue (both Newhall & Blevins, architects). Photo ca. 1920.

(both 1919), and 5–7 Craigie Circle (1920) (see figure 4.140). Harlow's projects anticipated the utilitarian apartment blocks of the 1920s. With the exception of the Craftsman-style building on Story Street, all incorporated the minimal Georgian Revival motifs that became ubiquitous in apartment design. Standard features included textured brick in Flemish or English bond, staggered quoins to accent corners, and cast-stone window sills, keystones, and roofline entablatures as a lower-cost alternative to the limestone trim used on the earliest apartments. A number of Harlow designs, as well as other pre-1920 apartment buildings, had sun porches, a feature borrowed from house and three-decker designs. Porches that were next to kitchens were often later glassed in and converted to dinettes.

Three new luxury buildings with much larger suites and accommodations for servants served the upper end of the market in this decade. The five-story Georgian Revival Bay State at 1572 Massachusetts Avenue (1915) is one of Old Cambridge's most elaborately detailed apartment houses. The *Chronicle* reported that the architect, former Cambridge resident Henry Mears, had "made a special study of apartments during his ten years in New York City" (Aug. 7, 1915). The entrance and landscaped courtyard of the 40-unit, U-shaped building face south toward the Common, while the Massachusetts Avenue facade is accented with three large bays and an ornate recessed arch with colorful Grueby tiles depicting a ship at sea and the owner's crest (figure 6.228). The entrance, vestibule, and inner stair hall have similar tile work. The Bay State was built for affluent tenants, and accommodations ranged from two rooms with bath to seven rooms with bath and a maid's room renting for $420 to $1,080 a year. Owner David Lonergan, a "confidential business agent of the Boston Elevated Railway," occupied a sumptuously paneled suite that took up half the first floor (*Chronicle,* Mar. 24, 1924).

In 1913 Forris W. Norris, one of the most successful developers of the period, acquired a two-acre site formerly occupied by the Cambridge Gas Light Company and announced plans to build three apartment blocks and a hotel at the foot of Ash Street. The first, Strathcona-on-the-Charles at 992–993 Memorial Drive (1914, William L. Mowll) had thirty-six apartments; the living rooms all faced the river and had "old fashioned" fireplaces (*Tribune,* Oct. 3, 1914). Radnor and Hampstead halls (1916, Charles R. Greco) at 983–984 and 985–986 Memorial Drive, were even more elaborate. Greco's monumental six-story Georgian Revival brick and cast-stone buildings feature ingenious floor plans, lavish appointments, and spacious courtyards facing

FIGURE 6.228 Arched window with Grueby tiles, Bay State apartments, 1572 Massachusetts Avenue (1915, Henry A. Mears, architect). The Grueby Faience Company was founded in Revere, Massachusetts, in 1894 and won international awards for its pottery and glazed terra-cotta architectural tiles. Photo 2007.

the river. The most difficult issue confronting the designer of luxury apartments was how to accommodate the conflicting demands of public living spaces, private sleeping quarters, and service and utility areas on a single level. Greco achieved this by designing a unique plan for each suite and creating unusual spaces, oddly angled rooms, and an abundance of bays and banks of windows. These were the first buildings in Old Cambridge that successfully resolved the ideal of luxury living with the spatial constraints of an apartment layout (figures 6.229–6.230).

The Radnor and the Hampstead were constructed separately but are connected: the Radnor, with a V-shaped plan containing only four suites per floor, was begun first and occupies the eastern half of the lot, while the Hampstead, containing five suites per floor, forms a U on the other side. Suites generally contained seven or eight rooms, including a maid's room, and the irregular floor plans allowed the bedchambers and service areas to be separated from the principal rooms. All the rooms were quite large (living rooms averaged 14 × 20 feet), and many had special features, such as semicircular bays and fireplaces. Careful planning, augmented by a stylish exterior, generous landscaping, and a prime riverside location placed these buildings at the apex of apartment house design in Cambridge. W.L. Mowll had plans ready for a fourth apartment building in 1917, but the war intervened. In 1924 Norris headed another investment group that retained Roscoe Whitten to design Barrington Court, a handsome Tudor Revival courtyard building next door at 987–988 Memorial Drive. Although considerably less elaborate than Radnor and Hampstead halls, it completed the line

FIGURE 6.229 Radnor Hall and Hampstead Hall, 983–984 and 985–986 Memorial Drive (both 1916, Charles R. Greco, architect). Photo 1918.

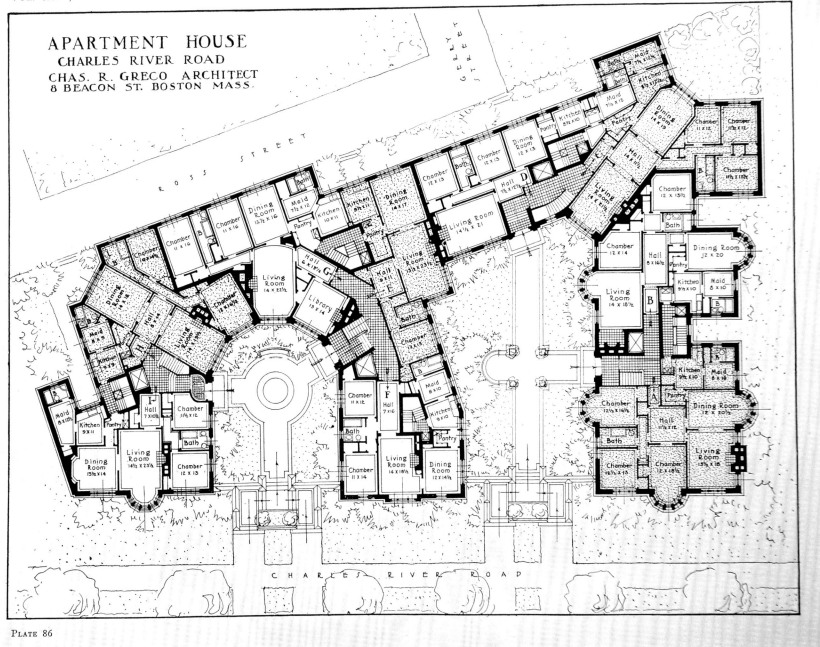

VOL. CXIII, NO. 2203

MARCH 13, 1918

APARTMENT HOUSE
CHARLES RIVER ROAD
CHAS. R. GRECO ARCHITECT
8 BEACON ST. BOSTON MASS.

PLATE 86

FIGURE 6.230 Typical floor plan, Radnor and Hampstead halls.

of apartments along this stretch of riverfront and maintained the grand scale and formal presentation of the earlier buildings. Both Greco and Whitten also designed houses for Norris in his nearby Coolidge Hill and Larchwood subdivisions.

The development of two streets completely lined with apartment buildings, Newport Road in 1916 and Craigie Circle in 1917–20, was a clear indication of the acceptance of apartment living in Old Cambridge among owners and tenants, if not neighbors. John A. Hasty designed two rows of attached four-story yellow brick and limestone apartment buildings on Newport Road and two similar buildings with rounded corners on Massachusetts Avenue for real estate agent Edward A. Barnard (figure 6.231). Barnard had already commissioned an apartment complex from Hasty at 27–31 Linnaean Street in 1912 with similar corner bays. For Newport Road, Barnard demolished two houses on deep lots to create the new street, but he kept an 1897 dwelling, now 12 Newport Road, that relieves the monotony of the identical apartment buildings.

Apartment construction peaked in Old Cambridge in the 1920s, when 39 buildings with a total of 1,758 units went up. The years 1924–26 saw the heaviest activity (17 buildings), with more than 250 units added each year. As the number of buildings increased, so did the number of units in each building; almost half of those constructed in the 1920s contained over 40 units, and one had 101. Designs and materials became increasingly uniform and less interesting. Brick was almost universal, but costly trimmings made of limestone, terra-cotta, and wrought iron were eliminated or replaced with cast stone. The Georgian Revival style, or some gesture toward it, was now standard.

Three firms typified the minimalist approach to apartment house construction. Hamilton Harlow continued to work on his family's developments in the 1920s. David R. Silverman, Parker J. Brown, and Edward F. Heenan formed Silverman, Brown & Heenan in 1922, and together or separately designed ten apartment buildings in Old Cambridge between 1924 and 1930, as well as the Commander Hotel (1926). These were typically four-story structures built out to the property lines, such as 1–3

FIGURE 6.231 The Newport Apartments, 1–7 (left) and 2–8 Newport Road (1916, John A. Hasty, architect). The view looks west toward Massachusetts Avenue. Photo ca. 1935.

Chauncy Street (1925) and 64 Oxford Street (1926). Many contained more than fifty units, and all were monolithic in appearance, unrelieved by variations in fenestration or massing. A young Boston architect, Saul Moffie, began practicing in 1923 and designed twelve similarly generic apartment buildings, including 37–41 Wendell (1924), 16–18 and 17–19 Forest (1926 and 1928), 50 Follen (1940), and 60 Brattle streets (1946).

Some firms executed higher-quality work. The Larches at 240–244 and the Birches at 246–260 Brattle Street were designed in 1924 by Whitten & Gore with only sixteen units each and were carefully detailed with well-executed Georgian Revival entrances, with leaded fanlights and porches with slender Doric and Ionic columns (figure 6.232). Sited on a narrow triangular lot, they provided an attractive buffer between the traffic on Mt. Auburn Street and the single-family houses in Larchwood.

In 1926 the Boston firm of Blackall, Clapp & Whittemore designed Oxford Court, a high-end building at 1804–1818 Massachusetts Avenue/1–9 Arlington Street (figure 6.233). The 101 units made it the largest apartment building in Cambridge, but its handsome exterior and ingenious planning were an asset to the neighborhood. Using the sloping site to provide store-fronts along Massachusetts Avenue, the architects extended the building along Arlington Street in an E-shaped plan around two generously scaled terraced courtyards with stately wrought-iron entrances that diminish the bulkiness of the structure. Three years later, the architects reproduced the design on a smaller scale for Stratford Manor at 4–6 Washington Avenue.

The 1920s saw some innovative solutions to apartment living. The Harvard Housing Trust, an independent investment group, built three projects for Harvard's growing number of married graduate students, Shaler Lane (1926), Gibson Terrace (1927), and Holden Green (1927). By commissioning Kilham, Hopkins & Greeley, the most experienced designer of planned housing developments in New England, the Trust endorsed the model housing movement's goal of providing modest but attractive accommodations in a traditional village setting. Both Walter Kilham and his younger partner, Roger Greeley, were active in the emerging field of city planning and designed houses, schools, and libraries. They were also enthusiastic proponents of the popular revival styles, as seen in the firm's first planned housing development, Woodbourne (1912), a model community at Forest Hills in Boston. Similar projects in Salem, Massachusetts (Salem Rebuilding Trust, 1915), and Portsmouth, New Hampshire (Atlantic Heights, 1918) established the firm's reputation in low-cost housing. Although originally intended for working families, the model community idea also suited the needs of graduate students. The firm noted that while the Shaler Lane apartments were "designed to meet a peculiar need, they may become of importance as one solution of the general housing problem" (*American Architect,* Jan. 5, 1927).

At Shaler Lane, two-story brick rows with minimal Colonial Revival detailing contain forty-three apartments and face each other across a narrow alley "after the fashion of many a picturesque village in old England" (ibid.; figure 6.234). The architects explained that "owing to building law, fire, and convenience requirements, it had become no longer economical to

FIGURE 6.232 The Birches, 246–260 Brattle Street (1924, Whitten & Gore, architects). Photo 2013.

FIGURE 6.233 Oxford Court, 1804–1818 Massachusetts Avenue/1–9 Arlington Street and (1926, Blackall, Clapp & Whittemore, architects). Photo 2009.

build many-storied apartment houses for the kind of use required by the graduate students" (ibid.). The apartments were quickly oversubscribed, and in 1927 the Trust put up two more four-unit buildings on Mt. Auburn Street and began Gibson Terrace, a two-story, U-shaped eighteen-unit building. The Trust also began Holden Green, a complex of ten Georgian buildings for married graduate students at Shady Hill designed by the same architects. The Trust remained independent but eventually sold Shaler Lane and Holden Green to the university; Gibson Terrace remained in private hands.

New construction slowed dramatically with the onset of the Depression. Of the six buildings constructed between 1931 and 1940, the seventeen-unit Lochiel Apartments at 10 Forest Street that William l. Galvin designed in 1937 is noteworthy as Old Cambridge's first multifamily building to incorporate Modern design elements. Built for Robert Cameron, a Scottish horti-culturalist who spent thirty years at Harvard's Botanic Garden, the blocky, four-story yellow brick building had banks of metal casement windows and horizontal brick bands that gave it a streamlined quality. The corner windows and the glass block and stainless steel entrance tucked in a corner back from the street were classic features of the Art Moderne style (figure 6.235).

The crush of returning veterans after World War II created an intense demand for housing. Cambridge responded by building temporary barracks for ex-servicemen and their families on parks and waste grounds throughout the city, but federal law required them all to be removed by 1952. The city threatened to take the abandoned Botanic Garden for veterans' housing, but Harvard built its own Botanic Garden Apartments there. Like the Har-vard Housing Trust projects in the 1920s, this was a planned community with 117 single-family, duplex, and apartment units for faculty and married students. Robinson Street and Fernald Drive followed the old garden paths, and Desgranges & Stef-fian, the architects, tried to respect the terrain and preserve some specimen trees. Along the northern boundary single-family and semidetached houses adjoined Gray Gardens East, while two-story buildings along Linnaean and Garden streets created a

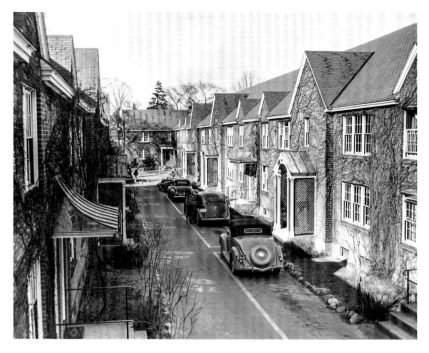

FIGURE 6.234   Shaler Lane (1926, Kilham, Hopkins & Greeley, architects). Photo 1941.

transition to the higher-density three-story apartment blocks that occupied the center of the complex (figure 6.236).

The flight of the middle class to the suburbs and the satu-ration of Old Cambridge with apartment houses diminished the market for new buildings, and only three were constructed between 1945 and 1960. Brattle Arms at 60 Brattle Street (1946, Saul Moffie) perpetuated the design pattern set before the war, but the others reflected newer trends in multiple-family dwellings. Samuel Glaser designed the three-story International Style Raymond Apartments at 45 Linnaean Street (1952) with its narrow brick and glass end facing the street. Although the building contained twenty-five studios accessed by seven sepa-rate entries along its length, the orientation diminished its size visually from Linnaean Street. The Cambridge Housing Author-ity and Monacelli Associates converted the building to senior housing in 1980.

FIGURE 6.235 Lochiel Apartments, 10 Forest Street (1937, William L. Galvin, architect). Photo 1938.

FIGURE 6.236 Botanic Garden Apartments (1949, Desgranges & Steffian, architects). Two-story perimeter units along Garden and Linnaean streets face an interior complex of three-story buildings. Photo ca. 1950.

The high-rise apartment made its debut in Old Cambridge in 1959 with Hugh Stubbins & Associates' Continental Terrace, an eight-story brick cube at 29 Concord Avenue built for Chauncey Depew Steele Jr., owner of the nearby Continental Hotel (figure 6.237). To conform to a 65-foot height limit, the building's first level sits a half-story below grade and contains the entrance, parking, six small apartments, and a walled garden. Continental Terrace's predominantly studio apartments, some with only kitchen alcoves, represented a considerable scaling-back in apartment living from prewar standards. A lightwell with skylights and large expanses of glass opening onto concrete balconies were intended to provide some outdoor access to compensate for the small size of the units.[22] Steele then put up Continental Gardens (originally Continental Motor Gardens) at 14–16 Concord Avenue, a luxury apartment building designed by Arthur Brooks. While it is much taller than would be permitted today,

Figure 6.237 Continental Terrace, 29 Concord Avenue (1959, Hugh Stubbins & Associates, architects). Photo 1961.

the complex profile compares favorably to Stubbins's rather forbidding Continental Terrace, and may be Brooks's best work (figure 6.238).

The seven apartment buildings built in Old Cambridge in the 1960s included three mid-rise buildings with balconies, three townhouse complexes, and a high-rise tower at 1010 Memorial Drive. The eight-story Riverview at 221 Mt. Auburn (1962, Harris & Freeman, Inc.) took advantage of its location overlooking the Charles with extensive glazing behind a grid of balconies (figure 6.239). In 1963, 1010 Memorial Drive (Cohen Haft & Associates) rose twenty stories on the site of Harvard's Stillman

Infirmary (figure 6.240). It contained eighty-six apartments and a penthouse, most with commanding views; a garage was concealed below a raised terrace. Like the towers of Mather House and Peabody Terrace, 1010 Memorial Drive is a strong vertical presence along the Charles, but the greater openness of the site on a broad curve in the river softens its impact.

The brick Brutalist style complex at 1–10 Chauncy Lane (1966, F.A. Stahl Associates) was the first of the townhouse projects that in the 1970s began to displace older houses and fill in side yards (figure 6.241). Allowed by an amendment to the Cambridge zoning code that encouraged townhouses as an alternative to the characterless "pillbox" style apartment houses invading many neighborhoods, the two rows face each other across a narrow lane. The structure of the units is expressed by the party walls projecting above the roofline, deep balconies, and shallow recessed windows. Their geometry and strong play of projecting and receding elements make them a modest example of a building type considered progressive in the 1960s.

The increase in density and height allowed by the 1962 zoning code promised to wreak havoc on neighborhoods in the vicinity of Harvard Square. As part of an affordable housing initiative, Harvard University erected an eleven-story concrete tower designed by Donald Stull at 2 Mt. Auburn Street in 1970. Around the corner at 1105 Massachusetts Avenue, private investors put up a fourteen-story tower containing 100 units designed by Hugh Stubbins & Associates in 1972 (see figure 2.65). None of the dozen or so apartment buildings that were erected in Old Cambridge between 1970 and 1990 were particularly distinguished, and all went up on lots created by demolishing single-family houses. The most significant loss was the Greycroft, which was replaced in 1979 by a bland sixty-eight-unit building at 1600 Massachusetts Avenue designed by DiMeo Associates (see figure 4.186).

Beginning in the 1980s, a booming real estate market elevated property values and created new opportunities at the top of the market. Old Cambridge's first luxury condominiums were designed by Bruce Graham of Skidmore, Owings & Merrill's

FIGURE 6.238 Continental Gardens, 14-16 Concord Avenue (1963, Arthur H. Brooks, architect). Photo 2009.

FIGURE 6.240 1010 Memorial Drive (1963, Cohen Haft & Associates, architects). Photo 2015.

FIGURE 6.239 Riverview, 221 Mt. Auburn Street (1962, Harris & Freeman, Inc., architects). Photo 2009.

FIGURE 6.241 Chauncy Lane townhouses, 1–10 Chauncy Lane (1966, F.A. Stahl Associates, architects). Photo 1967.

Chicago office in 1984 (see figure 3.85). University Green's fifty-two units had twenty-seven different layouts ranging in size from studios to three-bedroom duplexes. The red-brick complex included an office building (University Place) and a private park on Mt. Auburn Street. The low-rise character of the units provided a transition from commercial Harvard Square to the residential Half Crown neighborhood. A year later, eighty-six condominium units opened at Charles Square behind the Charles Hotel. These two- and three-bedroom flats and duplexes occupied a multilevel building fronting Kennedy Park. Designed by Cambridge Seven Associates, the building has a fractured, geometric quality, and its complex, clustered plan allows views of the river from each unit (see figure 3.81).

In 1996 the Winthrop Park condominiums entered the high end of the market (figure 6.242). Designed for Intercontinental Developers by Tsoi Kobus & Associates, the brick and limestone building successfully bridged the 1983 Brutalist Coolidge Bank building and Winthrop Square's restored Pi Eta Club and Chapman heirs' house (see figure 3.89). In 2011 the Sundance Residences at 1075 Massachusetts Avenue presented a blue glass and

FIGURE 6.242 Winthrop Park condominiums (1996, Tsoi Kobus & Associates, architects). Photo 2015.

brushed-aluminum facade that broke developers' long-ingrained habit of employing red brick to gain community acceptance (figure 6.243).

The built-up nature of Old Cambridge, the gentrification of former working-class neighborhoods, and the enactment of ordinances to discourage demolition of significant older buildings have reduced opportunities for large-scale apartment and condominium development. Only Massachusetts Avenue between Quincy Square and Porter Square retain the possibility of advancing this urban form in the 21st century.

FIGURE 6.243 Sundance Residences, 1075 Massachusetts Avenue
(2011, Peter Quinn, architect). Photo 2015.

Cambridge Skating Club, 183 Mt. Auburn Street (1930, Allen W. Jackson, architect). See pp. 642-643.

7 Civic and Religious Architecture

For two hundred years, all the civic and religious buildings of the First Parish stood in the village. Their history chronicles the evolution of Cambridge from a closely knit community that governed and worshiped in the same meetinghouse to a secular municipality with a diverse population. Old Cambridge now has few municipal buildings, but the architecture of its churches, public and private schools, colleges, and professional schools expresses many different traditions.

MEETINGHOUSES AND THEIR SUCCESSORS

Early meetinghouses played a central role in the life of a community. The Puritans of Massachusetts Bay formed their towns and churches by covenants: a civil covenant united the inhabitants into a political body, and a church covenant gathered them into a Christian body. This Standing Order bound together religion and government and required each town to support the established Congregational church. Public funds built the meetinghouses that were used for both worship and civic meetings and in Cambridge also for college ceremonies such as commencement. The governing body of each town consisted of church members voting on secular concerns. Over time, the population included growing numbers of people who were not church members but who were nevertheless required to pay taxes to support the church and its ministers. This arrangement lasted in

Massachusetts until 1833, when the Standing Order was overturned, and church and state were legally separated.

The First Meetinghouse in Cambridge was erected by December 1632 on the southwest corner of Dunster and Mt. Auburn streets, the highest point of land in the village. Seventeenth-century sources indicate that it probably had a square plan and a gable roof. References to building repairs in 1639 and a pulley for the bell rope in 1640 suggest that the belfry was added around that date, although the congregation had owned a bell since 1632. The building was small and must have been roughly constructed, because in February 1650 the town voted that "the meeting house shall be repaired with a 4:square [hip] roof and covered with shingle." Within a month, the Proprietors instructed the workmen to cease making repairs and begin building "a new house, about forty foot square and covered as was formerly agreed for the other" (Town Records, 85). By February 1652 the old building was gone, and the empty lot was for sale.

The Second Meetinghouse, in use by 1651, stood on Watch House Hill near today's Lehman Hall. This was a more convenient location for the college, which contributed to the cost of all later meetinghouses and held a partial right of ownership. Known only through town records (but possibly shown in a 1693 vignette), the new building was similar to other square New England meetinghouses of the period, with a truncated hip roof and a central belfry (figure 7.1). Harvard students sat

FIGURE 7.1 First or Second Cambridge Meetinghouse. This 17th-century view appears as a vignette on a map of Boston published by the French cartographer Jean-Baptiste Franquelin in 1693 (see figure 1.13). It corresponds to descriptions of the First Meetinghouse that was razed in 1650 or 1651 but may have been based on information gathered decades before the map was published.

in a gallery along the east wall. A south gallery was added in 1660–61, and a 1673 order to build a north gallery specified that it be like the east gallery in workmanship and extend "soe far as the Roofe does not hinder," indicating that the meetinghouse was not quite two full stories (Town Records, 212). Until the 1690s, when well-to-do families began to install box pews, congregants sat on long, narrow benches, men separated from women and adults from children, in places assigned to them by the elders, deacons, and selectmen according to their rank in the community.

In 1670 the town acquired a four-acre lot on Massachusetts Avenue near Widener Library and for £236 built a two-story center-chimney parsonage that remained in use until 1843 (see figure 3.2). This was the earliest parsonage; the first permanent minister, Thomas Shepard, had lived in his own house.

In 1703 the town voted to build a new meetinghouse on the same site as the second, financed by a £280 levy on the inhabitants and a £60 contribution from the college (figure 7.2). In 1718 Harvard paid one-seventh the cost of adding an upper gallery, with the stipulation that part of the lower gallery be reserved for students. The Third Meetinghouse was the last religious building used routinely for town meetings. After 1708 these were held in the county courthouse in Harvard Square, although unusually large gatherings took place in the meetinghouse until Cambridge built its first town hall in Cambridgeport in 1832.

The town decided to build a fourth meetinghouse in 1753 directly north of its predecessor; construction began in 1756 and was completed a year later (figure 7.3; see also figure 3.1). The Puritan "plain style" tradition in church architecture was still dominant, and the new building followed the same rectangular plan (71 by 51 feet), with the main entrance on the long south side behind a one-story porch. Instead of the ritualistic axis favored by the Church of England that emphasized the altar, the interior focused on a high pulpit placed against the long north wall, opposite the entrance; decorative carving, religious imagery, and stained glass were conspicuously absent. A large, round-headed window between the first and second levels rose behind the pulpit, and a gallery ran around the other three sides. A two-story porch on the east end contained the stairs to the students' gallery. The tower on the west end was capped with a handsome two-story octagonal spire closely resembling that of the 1729 Old South Meeting House in Boston.

A seating diagram of the Fourth Meetinghouse demonstrates the social and financial organization of an 18th-century congregation (figure 7.4). The most desirable seats were along the outside walls under the gallery and not, as one might assume, in the center of the main floor. Pews sold for £6 to £40 and netted £836, somewhat more than half the £1,493 cost of construction. Harvard again contributed one-seventh of the cost.

Both the first and last periods in the life of the Fourth Meetinghouse were fraught with divisions within the congregation. Several prosperous members broke away to establish Christ Church in 1759, and its last years witnessed the agonizing Trinitarian-Unitarian controversy that resulted in a permanent division of the parish in 1829 (see chapter 2). The Unitarian faction, which comprised a minority of the active members of the parish, retained the meetinghouse and the rectory but traded them to Harvard for a new site next to the Old Burying Ground. The college demolished the old building in 1833 and incorporated the site into Harvard Yard, but it remained vacant until Lehman Hall was constructed in 1927.

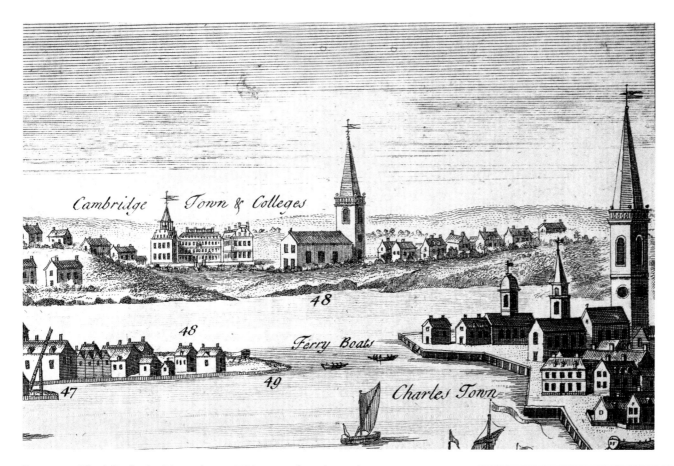

FIGURE 7.2 Third Cambridge Meetinghouse, 1703, as seen from the northeast in 1743. The entrance was in the middle of the opposite side, as in the Fourth Meetinghouse. The steeple may have dated from 1706 or from a 1717 remodeling and was an early example of this feature in New England. (The first known instance was the 1699 Brattle Street meetinghouse in Boston.)

FIGURE 7.3 Fourth Cambridge Meetinghouse, 1756–57, as seen from the south in 1803.

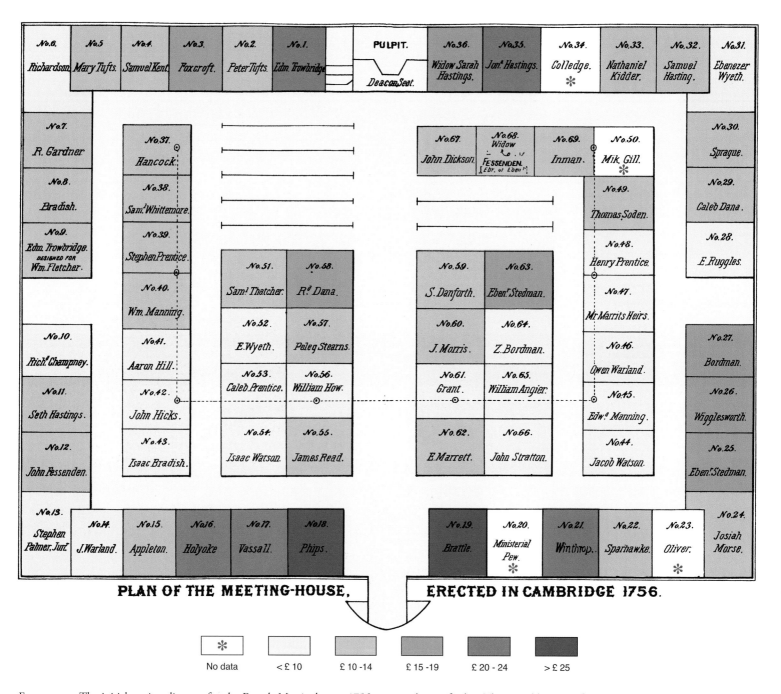

| No.6. Richardson | No.5. Mary Tufts. | No.4. Samuel Kent. | No.3. Foxcroft. | No.2. Peter Tufts. | No.1. Edm. Trowbridge | PULPIT. Deacon Seat. | No.36. Widow Sarah Hastings. | No.35. Jonᵃ. Hastings. | No.34. Colledge. ✳ | No.33. Nathaniel Kidder. | No.32. Samuel Hasting. | No.31. Ebenezer Wyeth. |

PLAN OF THE MEETING-HOUSE, ERECTED IN CAMBRIDGE 1756.

✳ No data | < £ 10 | £ 10 -14 | £ 15 -19 | £ 20 - 24 | > £ 25

FIGURE 7.4 The initial seating diagram for the Fourth Meetinghouse, 1756. Spencer Phips demonstrated his place at the head of Cambridge society by paying £40 for the first pew on the left of the entrance, while John Vassall paid only £20 for his. Those unable to pay for a pew sat on benches upstairs in the gallery, which extended to the dotted line.

The Unitarians procured plans for a new meetinghouse from Asher Benjamin in 1831, but at President Quincy's request they obtained a more commodious design from Isaiah Rogers.[1] Harvard again contributed to the cost of construction in return for use of the building at commencement, a practice that continued until 1873.[2] The fifth meetinghouse, known then as the First Parish Church and now as the First Church in Cambridge, Unitarian Universalist, was dedicated in December 1833. Built of wood sand-painted to resemble stone, its decorative veneer of flush-boarded siding, pointed arches, crocketed finials, and wooden buttresses made it an early example of Gothic Revival architecture (figure 7.5).

By the end of the century the building had begun to deteriorate, and about 1894 the congregation received a bequest toward a new one. President Eliot, a member of the congregation, took charge of fundraising, and in March 1899 a committee was chosen to procure plans and estimates. After three months the group reached a stalemate. Six members favored a brick church "in the so-called Colonial style" then becoming popular at Harvard, while three insisted on a stone church "in the Gothic style, suggestive of the old church" (First Parish in Cambridge, *In the Matter of a New Meetinghouse*, 35). Designs by architects Cabot, Everett & Mead and Cram, Goodhue & Ferguson were displayed in the vestry along with a Georgian brick and limestone church by Boston architects Chase & Ames, and the parish met repeatedly until a unanimous vote in October rejected brick and called for the new church to be built of stone (figures 7.6–7.7).

When the question of style was put to a vote in December 1899, 70 percent favored a Gothic church. The Colonial party, undaunted, asked for a delay while President Eliot obtained a design for a granite church in "the Colonial and classic style" from McKim, Mead & White (figure 7.8). Both Cram and McKim published statements in the newspapers justifying the appropriateness of their designs. The controversy between "the Colonials" and "the Goths" raged on for another year without resolution (*Cambridge Tribune*, May 19, 1900).

FIGURE 7.5 First Parish Church, 1450 Massachusetts Avenue (1833, Isaiah Rogers, architect). The cupola of the 1757 courthouse, which was moved to Palmer Street in 1841, is visible at left. Photo before 1860.

All the participants in this extraordinary conflict had complex motives; theology, economy, aesthetics, civic pride, and town-gown relations influenced the debate. President Eliot, who had adopted the Georgian Revival as the unofficial style of the university, contended that a Gothic building would not be compatible with the principles of Unitarian belief or New England traditions (notwithstanding the choice of this style in

FIGURE 7.6 Proposed First Parish Church (1899, Cram, Goodhue & Ferguson, architects). Ralph Adams Cram was a prominent advocate of the Gothic Revival style; this is one of four schemes his firm prepared for the First Parish in 1899–1900.

FIGURE 7.8 Proposed First Parish Church (1900, McKim, Mead & White, architects). McKim's design for a granite First Parish Church in the Colonial style was solicited by President Eliot at the same time the firm was preparing plans for the Harvard Union and the fence around Harvard Yard.

FIGURE 7.7 Proposed First Parish Church (1899, Chase & Ames, architects).

1831–33); he attacked the Cram firm as "not safe to deal with" and said their building would be too expensive (*Chronicle,* Nov. 24, 1900). William Read, the leading advocate of the Gothic style, was a local businessman with deep roots in Cambridge and broad support in the parish. Many parishioners (including architect Henry Van Brunt) favored Gothic because it would preserve the tradition of the existing building; a colonial structure seemed too secular to them. The matter was resolved in March 1901, when the parish voted to restore the church to its original appearance, "so thoroughly as to put the question of a new church at rest for some time," and to build a new stone vestry and parish hall, using the seam-faced Weymouth granite Cram had proposed for his Gothic church; both projects were designed by William P. Richards (*Boston Globe,* Mar. 19, 1901).[3]

In 1914 the Colonial faction succeeded in having Allen W. Jackson remodel the sanctuary in a bland Georgian manner. He backdated the Gothic Revival interior "to the style of the earlier parish meetinghouses ... taking again [sic] the appropriate historical place to which it was entitled among its ancient neighbors" (Jackson, "Alterations," 113). The pointed arch behind the altar was transformed "with a sort of Palladian motif," and new doors to the parish house were given elaborate broken pediments. The Gothic capitals and quatrefoil panels in the balcony were removed, and colonial-era box pews replaced the original curved black walnut benches. On the exterior, the Gothic balustrades were removed from the gable end, and the parapet lost its battlements. The spire survived the hurricane of 1938 and was reinforced with steel in 1949, but back-to-back hurricanes caused severe damage in 1954. Cambridge architect Arthur Brooks subsequently eliminated most of the remaining Gothic embellishments, making the exterior barren of detail in the Modern manner (figures 7.9–7.10).

FIGURE 7.10 First Parish Church, after renovations by Cambridge architect Arthur Brooks in 1956. Only the tall pointed-arch windows, trefoil panels, and wooden buttresses recall its original Gothic Revival style. Photo 2015.

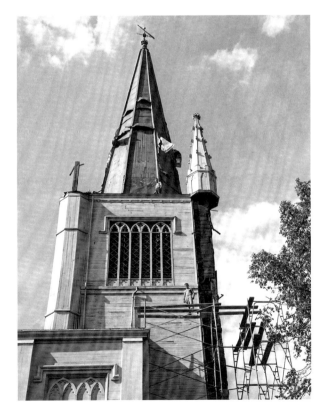

FIGURE 7.9 First Parish Church during removal of decorative elements weakened by hurricanes in 1954.

Christ Church, the town's first religious building that was not a meetinghouse, is one of Cambridge's best-known pre-Revolutionary structures. In 1759 eight prominent townsmen who were sympathetic to the Church of England petitioned the Society for the Propagation of the Gospel in Foreign Parts (SPG) in London to establish a mission in Cambridge and to appoint as rector East Apthorp, son of a Boston merchant and a recent Oxford graduate. A building committee that included John and Henry Vassall, Joseph Lee, Ralph Inman, Thomas Oliver, and David Phips secured a site and chose Peter Harrison of Newport, Rhode Island, as their architect. The committee wrote to Harrison on September 28, 1759, requesting

FIGURE 7.11 Christ Church before 1820. On the right is a house built for Sarah Brewer, a widow, in 1781; it was razed or moved when William Saunders built the present rectory in 1820. The Middlesex County Courthouse is just visible on the left, across the Old Burying Ground.

a Plan and Elevation of the Outside and Inside and of the Pulpit and Vestry of the Church; and that, if Mr. Harrison approves of it, there be no steeple, only a Tower with a Belfry … that the extreme dimensions of the Church, including the thickness of the Wall, but exclusive of the Chancel and Tower, be Sixty Feet in Length and Forty-five Feet in Breadth … that the building be of wood, and covered on the outside with Rough-cast; that there be only one tier of windows, and no Galleries, except an organ loft. (Day, 5)

Christ Church turned out to be a diminutive version of Harrison's King's Chapel in Boston (1749), where several members of the building committee worshipped. Unlike the Puritan meetinghouses, the main axis ran the length of the building and centered on a freestanding pulpit and an altar in a shallow apse. Although the original building was wide for its length, the coved ceiling of the nave and the two rows of columns directed attention to the pulpit and altar. The exterior walls were undecorated except for the heavy Doric frieze and cornice and the sequence of stately, round-headed windows. The tower terminated in a simple hip roof and cross; the present belfry was added in 1766. Roughcast was a form of stucco used on the homes of building committee members Henry Vassall and Joseph Lee (where it is still visible at 159 Brattle Street). However, the final cost of the building greatly exceeded the £500 budget, and the exterior was faced instead with flush boards whose freshly painted surfaces were probably dusted with sand to simulate stone. Watercolors made in 1783, 1793, 1803, and about 1830 show the exterior in stone-like colors of gray or tan; in the 1793 view the trim is white and the doors red.

Architecturally, Christ Church shows a confidence and authoritative unity that many colonial buildings lack. A gentleman-architect, Peter Harrison had traveled in England and possessed a theoretical understanding of architectural design. His work presents a marked contrast to the town's 18th-century houses, whose designs tended to be a compilation of separate elements. When Christ Church was built, timbers of great size could still be found in the area; logs for the eight interior columns were cut at the headwaters of the Charles River and floated down to Cambridge, where they were turned on a lathe set up on the Common and their centers were bored out to prevent checking. For economy, the columns were installed unfinished; Isaiah Rogers carved the Ionic capitals in 1826.

Christ Church was consecrated in 1761, its very existence a provocation to the Congregationalist townspeople who dubbed Reverend Apthorp's mansion the "Bishop's Palace" (see chapter 4). Closed during the Siege of Boston, the church was opened for a New Year's Eve service in 1775 at Martha Washington's request. In June 1778 a mob broke up a British officer's funeral and took the opportunity "to plunder, ransack, and deface everything they could get their hands on," leaving the church open to the weather, "the windows … totally destroyed, the Pews, Altar and Pulpit exceedingly injured, and the Organ wholly torn to pieces" (*DAR Guide*, 133, and Batchelder, *Christ Church*, 48–49). The building was repaired in 1790 with donations from members of Trinity Church in Boston.

In the mid-1850s the parish discussed whether to expand the church or erect a new one nearby. A proposal by Boston architect Arthur Gilman to build in New Jersey freestone "a precise and exact copy … one-third larger in scale" failed by only one vote (*Boston Daily Evening Transcript*, Aug. 27, 1857). Someone recalled Apthorp's report to the SPG that "in case of future accessions to the congregation it may easily be enlarged," and the congregation instead voted to move one bay and the apse back 23 feet and insert two new bays in the old frame (Batchelder, 62). The workmen found that the original builders had anticipated an extension, as the timbers were spliced in such a way that the frame could be separated by removing some pegs.

The *Transcript* praised the architectural qualities of the old church. Remarkably for the time, the architect, George Snell, did not attempt to adapt it to Victorian tastes. The new sections repeated the old in almost every detail; in this respect, the work represents an early milestone in the 19th-century rediscovery of the aesthetic value of Georgian architecture (figure 7.12). A generation later the congregation could not resist the temptation to modernize the interior, and under the direction of Henry Van

FIGURE 7.12 Christ Church after the sanctuary was expanded by inserting two bays between the fourth and fifth bays of the original building. In the Victorian period the church was painted dark brown with black sash. Photo ca. 1890.

FIGURE 7.13 Christ Church's sanctuary after it was redecorated in 1883 by Henry Van Brunt and Frank Hill Smith. The stained glass windows in the apse were preserved behind shutters when the sanctuary was returned to its earlier appearance in 1920. Photo ca. 1893.

Brunt and Frank Hill Smith, a Boston artist and fresco painter, the walls, ceilings, and pillars were decorated in a somber scheme enlivened with stenciled patterns (figure 7.13). In 1920 the congregation had Boston architect R. Clipston Sturgis redecorate the church in a more colonial manner with a gray and white color scheme inside and out. Sturgis's sources are not known, but he was an Anglophile designer who restored the Old North Church in 1913 and published an article on Christopher Wren in the *Journal of the American Institute of Architects* in 1923. The interior remained intact until 2013, when in response to changes in the Episcopal liturgy the altar and pulpit were moved forward into the sanctuary, displacing several rows of pews.

Christ Church built a parish hall in 1868 but replaced it in 1897 with the present porticoed structure designed by George Moore. A study and reception room added behind the church in 1910 partially covered the apse. When larger Sunday school quarters were required in 1948, Charles Collens designed a brick wing facing Farwell Place, replacing a Greek Revival house that had served the same purpose. The rectory at 1 Garden Street dates from 1820 but was not acquired by the church until 1916 (see figures 4.110 and 6.39).

The congregation of Christ Church underwent many changes. Reverend Winthrop Serjeant, the second rector, observed that originally there had been "fifteen or twenty families … 'six of them possessed of ample fortunes, the rest in very easy circumstances'" (Day, 18–19). For decades after the Revolution the parish was too poor to support a full-time minister, even though Harvard contributed to the building fund in 1825 to accommodate the one-seventh (about thirty) of its students who were Episcopalians. Reverend Nicholas Hoppin arrived in 1839 and saw the number of communicants grow from 29 to 209 by 1861. However, the opening of St. John's Chapel at the Episcopal Theological School in 1867 robbed the congregation of "the rich, the attractive, [and] the socially gifted" residents of Brattle Street, and the end of compulsory church attendance for Harvard students a few years later reduced attendance by one-fifth (Day, 73). The competition with St. John's lasted until 1931, when its 270 communicants rejoined the older parish.

After the division of the First Parish in 1829, the conservative Trinitarian party, which consisted of the Reverend Abiel Holmes and two-thirds of the communicants, organized the Shepard Congregational Society and broke ground in 1830 for a new church at the corner of Mt. Auburn and Holyoke streets. The Orthodox Meetinghouse (as it was called) has been attributed to Washington Allston, the painter, and Henry Greenough, the architect. Allston was a family friend and something of a mentor to Greenough, who was only 22 at the time (figures 7.14). The exterior forecasts the restrained style of Greenough's Quincy Street houses and his much later 1851 Cambridgeport Athenaeum (see figure 6.79 and *Report Three: Cambridgeport,* figure 233).

After the repeal of the Standing Order in 1833, other denominations settled in the village. In 1844 Levi Farwell and about eighty members of the First Baptist Church in Cambridgeport gathered as the Old Cambridge Baptist congregation, secured a lot from Harvard University, and erected a church on Kirkland Street facing Harvard Square (figure 7.15).[4] Essentially late Georgian in form, Isaac Melvin's design had a 125-foot, three-stage tower and spire that closely recalled the New South Church in Boston. Corner piers and two heavy columns with Egyptian capitals anchored a pedimented portico topped by wooden acroteria. Inset panels with carved ornament above the three pedimented entrances probably followed Asher Benjamin.

FIGURE 7.14 Shepard Congregational Church, 75 Mt. Auburn Street (1830, attributed to Washington Allston and Henry Greenough, designers). The church was lengthened 16 feet in 1844 and enlarged again in 1852 under the direction of Alexander R. Esty. Photo before 1872.

FIGURE 7.15 Old Cambridge Baptist Church, 1 Kirkland Street (1845, Isaac Melvin, architect). This view looking north along Peabody Street shows the church on its original site; Harvard Yard is at right and Flagstaff Park is on the left. Littauer Hall now occupies this site. Photo before 1867.

In 1867 the North Avenue Congregational Society, which had sold its 1857 chapel to the North Avenue Methodist Episcopal Society, bought the Baptist church and moved it to the corner of Massachusetts Avenue and Roseland Street. The society added transepts and a chancel about 1872 to increase the building's capacity from 550 to 1,000. The spire and the upper stages of the tower were replaced in 1906 with a square belfry and a copper dome that was destroyed by lightning in 1964 (figure 7.16). Lesley University acquired the church in 2007, and in 2014 restored the exterior with a replica of the 1906 belfry, replaced the missing acroteria and capitals, and repurposed the building as a library.

Harvard's Appleton Chapel of 1856 was an influential building in its day, fully visible from Broadway before the Yard was hemmed in with buildings and a perimeter fence in the early 20th century. Funds for erecting a "granite, freestone, or marble" chapel came from the estate of Samuel Appleton, a wealthy industrialist. Boston architect Arthur Gilman proposed a "Perpendicular Gothic" design based on the 15th-century Merton College Chapel at Oxford, but Harvard chose the plans of a German immigrant, Paul Schulze (College Papers xxl, 375, 387).[5] The chapel's Nova Scotia sandstone contrasted with Harvard's usual brick, while its ungainly style—to American eyes, somewhat Italianate but actually derived from the German Rundbogenstil (literally, "round arch style") popular in Munich in the 1840s—made it an odd neighbor (figure 7.17). Although Appleton suffered from terrible acoustics, it survived until Memorial Church replaced it in 1931.

Appleton established a precedent for stone churches in Cambridge. Having outgrown its original home, the Old Cambridge Baptist Church purchased a lot near the junction of Harvard Street and Massachusetts Avenue and in 1867 commissioned a new building from Framingham architect Alexander Esty (figure 7.18). Although his cruciform Gothic Revival church closely resembles the Church of the Unity in Springfield, Massachusetts, designed by H.H. Richardson in 1866, Esty was experienced with the style. He had designed both Emmanuel Episcopal

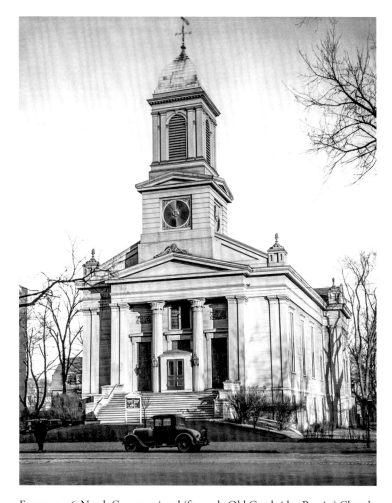

FIGURE 7.16 North Congregational (formerly Old Cambridge Baptist) Church, 1803 Massachusetts Avenue. This 1931 photograph shows the cupola that replaced the original steeple in 1906, which was itself replaced with an inappropriate fiberglass steeple after a lightning strike in 1962. After a merger in 1985 it was known as the North Prospect Congregational Church.

FIGURE 7.17 Appleton Chapel (1856, Paul Schulze, architect). Appleton occupied the present site of Memorial Church until 1931. Photo ca. 1870.

FIGURE 7.18 Second Old Cambridge Baptist Church, 398 Harvard Street (1867–70, Alexander R. Esty, architect). The fenced area in the right foreground was popularly known as Beck's Park until Beck Hall was constructed there in 1876. Photo ca. 1866–77.

Church at 15 Newbury Street in Boston in 1861 and St. Mark's Episcopal in Southborough in 1863 in the English Gothic manner. As in the Springfield church, the traditional plan suggested by the exterior does not exist, because the nave in the north end and chancel in the south are separated by an interior wall. The ceiling was "painted blue and besprinkled with stars," a popular treatment in this period (*Chronicle*, Oct. 1, 1870). After an 1889 fire the chancel was remodeled as a parish hall with brilliant stained glass windows by the Tiffany Studio in New York.

The relatively weak lime mortar in use at the time was insufficient to hold the irregular blocks of dark blue ledgestone (argillite) that Esty chose for the exterior, and the prospect of rebuilding the steeple in 1908 led the church to consider selling the property to St. Paul's Roman Catholic parish. In the 1960s the small, socially responsible congregation began renting the basement to a multitude of progressive organizations, which helped sustain the building. In 1990 Harvard University reinforced the steeple, nave, and south wall to withstand construction of The Inn at Harvard, and the congregation began a decades-long restoration of the roof, masonry, and windows. In 2001 the José Mateo Ballet Theater leased the sanctuary for ninety-nine years, providing the church with an essential source of income to maintain the building and support its mission.

St. John's Chapel, a striking example of Victorian Gothic architecture, was built in 1868 for the Episcopal Theological School with a gift from a wealthy donor seeking to expand the influence of his denomination in the academic community. St. John's was designed by Ware & Van Brunt in the spirit of a 14th-century English parish church, reflecting an ongoing controversy between the Anglo-Catholic ("High Church") and

Evangelical ("Low Church") factions of the Anglican Church in America and England. The design appealed to St. John's wealthy and influential neighbors and in some respects surpassed contemporary churches by H.H. Richardson (figure 7.19). As in Ware & Van Brunt's 1867 First and Second Church in Boston, the square stone tower with its slender octagonal spire stands somewhat apart from the central mass of the church. The voussoirs of alternating brown- and cream-colored stone indicate an awareness of contemporary Ruskinian theories in England, yet the polychromy does not compete with the tawny Roxbury puddingstone of the walls. The public entrance was originally halfway down the nave, making the side facing Brattle Street the principal facade.[6] The vestry on the north side was designed by Henry Vaughn in 1901. The chancel was remodeled in 1930 and 1967 and the exterior restored in 2001.

The Shepard congregation's ledgestone and granite church on Garden Street was the most expensive religious building in the city when it was dedicated in 1872 during the pastorate of one of the most prominent Congregational ministers in New England, Reverend Alexander McKenzie. Designed in 1870 by Abel C. Martin, an 1856 graduate of the Lawrence Scientific School who trained under Boston architect Arthur Gilman, it cost $135,000. The beautifully proportioned spire, completed in 1873, originally rose 170 feet to dominate a conspicuous corner facing the Common (figure 7.20). The splendid rooster weathervane made by Shem Drowne in 1721 came from the New Brick or "Cockerel" Church on Hanover Street in Boston in 1873.

Two Roman Catholic parishes—St. Peter's and St. Paul's—were organized in Old Cambridge in the 19th century. St. Peter's, the second Catholic parish in Cambridge, was established in 1848 by Father Manasses Dougherty as an offshoot of St. John's in East Cambridge (1842). From its site on the summit of Observatory Hill, the parish served not only the Irish brickyard workers of North Cambridge but also Catholics from nineteen towns in outlying Middlesex County (see figure 2.30).[7] The cornerstone was laid in 1848, but only the broad brick

FIGURE 7.19 St. John's Chapel, Episcopal Theological School, 99 Brattle Street (1868, Ware & Van Brunt, architects). The public entered the sanctuary through the door at the base of the steeple until 1967, when a new entrance was made in the narthex at the west end of the building. Photo before 1872.

pilasters and strongly projecting bracketed cornice remain from the original Italianate design. The interior was altered in 1889 by Patrick W. Ford, an Irish-American architect responsible for many Catholic churches in the late 19th century. The present Georgian Revival exterior derives from a drastic remodeling in 1914 and a replacement steeple installed in 1955, both designed by Maginnis & Walsh. The parish complex grew to include an imposing rectory and a parish hall with stores on the first floor (figure 7.21). The elementary school and high school that the diocese built in 1927 and 1959 were similar in most respects to public schools of the period.

FIGURE 7.20 First Church, Congregational, 11 Garden Street (1870, Abel C. Martin, architect). The parish house (left) was rebuilt in its present form in 1926, and the original spire was taken down and rebuilt with a patterned slate cap just before the 1938 hurricane. Photo ca. 1875.

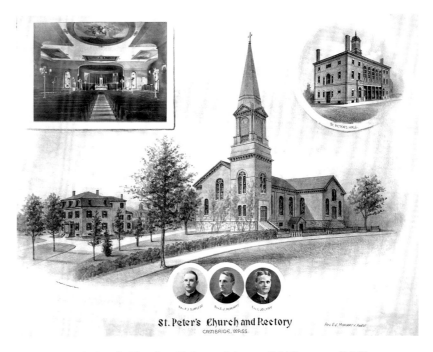

FIGURE 7.21 St. Peter's Church, 146 Concord Avenue (1848), rectory (1868), and parish hall (1897, Edward T.P. Graham, architect) as seen ca. 1900. The inset at left shows the interior as remodeled by Patrick W. Ford in 1889.

Father Dougherty also organized the parish of St. Paul, the fourth in Cambridge after St. Mary's in Cambridgeport (1864). In 1873 Bishop John J. Williams purchased the former Shepard Church on Mt. Auburn Street and its parsonage on Holyoke Street (see figure 4.275). P.W. Ford remodeled the church in 1890–91 to meet the needs of the growing congregation (figure 7.22). In 1889 Bishop Williams acquired the Gordon McKay estate, which included a large sloping lot between Mt. Auburn and Arrow streets and an 1818 house built by William Winthrop (see figure 4.256). The house was converted to classrooms and a convent, and Ford was engaged to draw plans for a school that was completed in 1891.

FIGURE 7.22 St. Paul's Church, 75 Mt. Auburn Street (formerly Shepard Congregational Church), after architect Patrick W. Ford added two bays to the facade and rebuilt the tower in 1890–91. Harvard University bought the building from the Archdiocese and razed it in 1924. Photo 1895.

In 1904 St. Paul's Parish obtained a building permit for a large stone church designed by F.A. Norcross (a cousin of H.H. Richardson's principal contractors, the Norcross brothers). About this time there were plans to turn DeWolfe and Bow streets into a boulevard, which would have cut 30 feet off the western edge of the property. The parish vigorously opposed this idea but hesitated to put up a building that might have to be torn down (see chapters 4 and 10). In 1906 the diocese bought a house on the corner of Massachusetts Avenue and Ellery Street with the idea of building a church, school, and parochial residence; Bishop Williams also considered buying the Old Cambridge Baptist Church. Once the boulevard plan was defeated, the parish razed Winthrop's house and began the present church in 1915.

St. Paul's Church is a particularly striking building that gives the intersection of Bow and Arrow streets the feeling of an Italian piazza (figure 7.23). Modeled after the Church of San Zeno Maggiore in Verona, Italy, with a tower based on the campanile of Verona's Scaglieri Palace, it was designed by Edward T.P. Graham, a Cambridge native who graduated from Harvard in 1900. After working briefly at Shepley, Rutan & Coolidge and Peabody & Stearns, Graham traveled in Europe for two years and opened his own practice in Boston in 1903. He was a prolific ecclesiastical architect, completing dozens of Catholic churches, schools, rectories, and hospitals before his death in 1964. St. Paul's is his finest work.

St. Paul's performs a dual role as a parish church for Kerry Corner and a mission to Catholics at Harvard, who became more numerous in the 20th century. Graham designed the rectory on Mt. Auburn Street in 1924. Ford's handsome brick school (occupied by the Boston Archdiocesan Choir School after 1969) formed an intriguing urban landscape with the church but was demolished in 1989 (figure 7.24). The architects of the new school matched the extraordinarily rich masonry of the church and retained the publicly accessible courtyard while creating a more complex massing of forms and materials (figure 7.25).

FIGURE 7.23 St. Paul's Church, 24 Arrow Street (1915, Edward T.P. Graham, architect). Photo 2014.

FIGURE 7.24   St. Paul's Choir School, 29 Mt. Auburn Street (1889, Patrick W. Ford, architect; demolished 1989). Photo ca. 1965.

FIGURE 7.25   St. Paul's student center and Boston Archdiocesan Choir School, 29 Mt. Auburn Street (1989, Koetter Kim & Associates, architects). Photo 2014.

Protestant churches also built in stone. In 1868 the North Avenue Methodist Episcopal Society purchased a lot on Massachusetts Avenue facing Cambridge Common and moved the Holmes Congregational Society's chapel there from the corner of Arlington Street (see figure 10.34). The present Harvard-Epworth United Methodist Church, completed in 1893, was designed by Amos P. Cutting, a noted ecclesiastical architect from Worcester (figure 7.26).[8] Frederick Hastings Rindge was the principal benefactor and chose the same Richardsonian Romanesque style as his other donations—Cambridge's City Hall, Main Library, and Manual Training School. Set on a narrow lot, the church presents an active silhouette to the Common, with a 110-foot tower and belfry flanked by two projecting bays on the front and multiple gables on the north facade. The rough red Southville granite trimmed with darker East Longmeadow brownstone emphasizes the building's weight and mass. In 1941 the sanctuary was modernized with a dropped ceiling, the altar was relocated to the east side, and the semicircular pews were removed. Fifty years later the ceiling was taken down, exposing the original stained glass windows and roof trusses.

The Cambridge Society of the New Jerusalem (Swedenborgian) established a theological school in the Jared Sparks house on Quincy Street in 1891 (see figure 6.60). Nine years later it enlisted H. Langford Warren, a son of Swedenborgian missionaries, a charter member of the Boston Society of Arts and Crafts, and first head of the Harvard School of Architecture, to design a church at the corner of Kirkland Street (figure 7.27). His fine interpretation of an English Gothic chapel, built of Brighton ledgestone with Indiana limestone tracery and trimmings, was completed in 1901. The chancel and nave beneath an open timber roof display many Arts and Crafts details illuminated by stained glass windows that Warren also designed. The building's diminutive scale and careful workmanship add to its charm, although it suffers from an insensitive 1965 addition by Arthur Brooks. In the 1990s the church became entangled in a controversy between the congregation and the owner, the land-rich and cash-poor New Church Theological School of Newton. A developer intended to make the sanctuary

FIGURE 7.26 Harvard-Epworth United Methodist Church, 1555 Massachusetts Avenue (1891, Amos P. Cutting, architect). Photo 2013.

the lobby of a high-rise condominium, but the congregation purchased the building and it remains a place of worship.

In 1919 a Christian Science congregation meeting at Brattle Hall hired the Boston firm of Bigelow, Wadsworth, Hubbard & Smith to design a church at 13 Waterhouse Street facing the Common. Begun in 1923 but not completed until 1936, the building displaced an 1862 North Avenue mansion that was moved to 44 Follen Street. Its central plan and Pantheon-like dome and portico distinguish it as a Christian Science church, but the red brick and Georgian Revival detail give it an uncanny resemblance to Thomas Jefferson's 1822–26 Rotunda at the University of Virginia. The serene exterior belies the complex

FIGURE 7.27 Cambridge Society of the New Jerusalem/Swedenborg Chapel, 50 Quincy Street (1901, Warren Smith & Biscoe, architects). Photo 2015.

FIGURE 7.28 First Church of Christ, Scientist, 13 Waterhouse Street (1923, Bigelow, Wadsworth, Hubbard & Smith, architects). Photo 1930.

organization of the interior space, with a two-story Sunday school in the basement and an extraordinary sanctuary with Guastavino tile vaulting (figure 7.28).

The Conventual Church of St. Mary and St. John at 980 Memorial Drive is perhaps the most exquisite small church in Cambridge. The Society of St. John the Evangelist, an Anglican monastic order, was founded at Cowley in Oxfordshire in 1866, established a branch in Boston in 1870, and built the Church of the Advent on Brimmer Street in 1879. In 1924 the Cowley Fathers, as they are still called, purchased land from the University Press and put up a small wooden chapel and a monastery, supported in part by gifts and a bequest from Isabella Stewart Gardner. The church, constructed in 1936 of granite with buff limestone trim to designs of Cram & Ferguson, illustrates the sympathy and accuracy with which medieval forms—in this case, 12th-century Burgundian—were sometimes reproduced. The landscape of the still-incomplete cloister was designed by Fletcher Steele (figure 7.29).

FIGURE 7.29 Conventual Church of St. Mary and St. John (left, with tower) and the unfinished cloister of the Monastery of the Society of St. John the Evangelist, 980 Memorial Drive (1924–36, Cram & Ferguson, architects). Photo 2015.

The Friends Center on Longfellow Park began as a residence for the poet's granddaughter Amelia Thorp Knowles and was acquired by the Society of Friends in 1936. The meetinghouse was designed by meeting members William and Mary Duguid, exponents of the Georgian Revival style who were better known for their residential commissions; it adheres to the material, style, and domestic scale of the house and supports the placid environment of Longfellow Park.

The University Lutheran Church on Winthrop Street is the only example of Modern church architecture in Old Cambridge. The congregation had contemplated a traditional colonial building as early as 1928, but by the time construction began in 1949 plans had changed several times.[9] A 1936 proposal with a distinctly North German appearance was discarded after the war in favor of a design by Boston architect Arland Dirlam (figures 7.30–7.31). With simple fenestration and broad, unadorned surfaces, University Lutheran recalls the leading role the denomination played after World War II in the adoption of contemporary architecture. A ramp constructed in 1999 supported the congregation's mission to serve the homeless but displaced the lawn that softened the church's presence in this still domestically scaled part of Harvard Square.

Two religious buildings that appeared on Brattle Street in 1955–60 stimulated interest in protecting the neighborhood from further institutional construction. The Church of Jesus Christ of Latter-Day Saints acquired the 1896 Henry M. Williams house at 100 Brattle Street in 1941, the 1881 Isabella Gozzaldi house at 98 Brattle in 1943, and the 1881 William Stone house at 15 Hawthorn Street in the early 1950s (see figure 4.20). In 1954 the church razed the latter two and moved the Williams house to 15 Hawthorn Street. William F. Thomas of Salt Lake City and Ellsworth Tidd of Massachusetts designed a Georgian Revival meetinghouse that contemporary critics thought exhibited an uneasy contradiction in scale between its oversize fenestration and the attenuated proportions of the spire, but after it suffered a catastrophic fire in 2009 there was little debate about allowing it to be rebuilt in identical form (figure 7.32).

FIGURE 7.30 Proposed University Lutheran Church, corner of Winthrop and Dunster streets (1936, Frohman, Robb & Little, architects).

FIGURE 7.31 University Lutheran Church, 66 Winthrop Street (1950, Arland Dirlam, architect). In 1952 the Boston Society of Architects awarded Dirlam the Harleston Parker Award for this building. Photo 2015.

The Holy Trinity Armenian Church on the corner of Brattle and Sparks streets was designed in 1960 by John Bilzerian as a close copy of the Church of St. Hripsime in south-central Armenia (figure 7.33). The church occupies the side yard of William Brewster's Colonial Revival house at 145 Brattle Street, which the congregation preserved along with Brewster's private ornithological museum. While a design based on 7th-century Armenian architecture is no more inappropriate in a 19th-century New England neighborhood than a Gothic Revival church, the size of the complex and its sudden appearance in a purely residential area were quite controversial (see chapter 4).

FIGURE 7.32 Church of Jesus Christ of Latter-Day Saints, 4 Longfellow Park (1955, William Thomas & Ellsworth Tidd, architects; rebuilt 2010–11). Photo 2015.

FIGURE 7.33 Architectural model of the proposed Holy Trinity Armenian Church, 145 Brattle Street (1960, John Bilzerian, architect). The portico, which was added to the prototype Church of St. Hripsme in 1651–53, was omitted from the final design. Photo 1958.

Early Cambridge had a succession of county buildings in addition to the meetinghouses that were used for municipal purposes. These symbols of community leadership were lost to East Cambridge and Cambridgeport in the early 19th century, leaving fire stations, police stations, and schools as the principal civic buildings in Old Cambridge (see chapter 1 and *East Cambridge*).

COURTHOUSES AND JAILS

Civil and criminal courts were held in Newtowne beginning in 1636, and Cambridge was designated a shire town when Middlesex County was created in 1643.[10] The exact date of the first courthouse is unknown. Before 1643 the meetinghouse may have served this purpose, and it continued to be used for particularly well-attended hearings or trials. An early courthouse burned in 1671, and no record exists of another until 1707 or 1708. This stood until about 1757 in the middle of what is now Harvard Square (see figure 1.15). The small frame building, measuring 30 by 24 feet, was erected jointly by the county and the town and contained a single courtroom on the second floor; merchants occupied ground-floor shops and a cellar, recalling the organization of late-medieval town halls in England. The shops were separated by a six-foot-wide central passageway that contained stairs to the courtroom above. In 1756 the town voted to erect a new courthouse with materials from the about-to-be-demolished Third Meetinghouse and secured land on the present site of the Harvard Cooperative Society. The old site was still vacant in 1784, when the town offered it to Middlesex County for a new probate court; a market house was later built there.

The 1758 courthouse was only slightly larger than its predecessor, a 26-by-30-foot frame structure with an open cupola (figure 7.34; see figure 1.17). Its resemblance to early meetinghouses and schools indicates the colonial builder's limited repertoire of architectural forms. Town and county shared the building until the court moved to East Cambridge in 1816, and town meetings

FIGURE 7.34 Middlesex County Courthouse, Harvard Square (1758). The town's third courthouse stood on the site later occupied by the Harvard Cooperative Society. The last courthouse built in Old Cambridge, it was moved to Palmer Street in 1841 and incorporated into a store that was razed in 1930. Watercolor 1800.

were held there until 1832, when a town hall was built in Cambridgeport. In 1841 the Cambridge Lyceum acquired the site, and a new owner moved it to Palmer Street near the corner of Brattle, where it served as a billiard parlor and bowling alley, a gymnasium for Radcliffe College, and finally as a storeroom (see figure 9.11). The Cambridge Historical Society asked Lois Lilley Howe to evaluate the building in 1922, but little of the original remained and it was razed in 1930.

In 1655 the town purchased a dwelling on Holyoke Street to serve as a house of correction; after 1660 it also served as a county lockup. A new jail on the north side of Winthrop Street next to Winthrop Square was in use before 1681. Eleven years later, the General Court ordered that "their majesties Gaol at Cambridge be repaired" during the witchcraft panic, when facilities in several counties were requisitioned to hold the accused (Paige, 216). In 1715 the county replaced the older part with a two-story building with accommodations for the keeper. Roger Buck of the New West Field was the public executioner in the 17th century, meting out lashes and hanging the condemned at the Gallows Lot, a sand pit on the side of Avon Hill. This facility and the jail served until 1816, when their functions were transferred to East Cambridge. The jail was demolished before 1820, and the Gallows Lot was sold to William Frost in 1826 (see chapter 4).

Fire and Police Stations

The threat of fire was always present in early Cambridge. In March 1631, Thomas Dudley decreed that "in our new town … no man there shall build his chimney with wood, nor cover his roof with thatch," and this early code was adopted by a town meeting in 1633. In 1650, in view of "dreadful experience," the town required that chimneys be swept monthly and that every household have a ladder to reach the top of the house (Paige, 18, 56).

Although Boston had a hand-powered pumping engine before 1679, the first recorded fire apparatus in Cambridge belonged to Henry Vassall; in 1755 the town declined to appropriate funds to improve his pumper for public use. After Harvard Hall burned in 1764 the legislature appropriated £100 for the college to acquire a pumper. The president appointed the captain of the fire company, but students operating the engine delighted in turning out on any pretext until 1822, when they flooded the office of a college official through an open window. President Kirkland then disbanded the company and sold the engine to the town.

Until 1832, when the General Court established the Cambridge Fire Department, firefighting was conducted by private societies organized to protect the property of members and subscribers. Sixteen householders including Aaron Hill, Samuel Manning, Israel Porter, Joseph Read, and James Winthrop organized the Friendly Fire Society in 1797. Each member was required to have two leather buckets and a four-bushel sack for removing household goods; the first town company, Cambridge 1, may have been a descendant of this group. The origins of the Hunneman Company, named after the manufacturer of its hand pumper, have not been determined, but its volunteers responded to fires in Old Cambridge long after the establishment of the municipal department, and the town paid an hourly rate for its services until it disbanded in 1869 (figure 7.35).[11] The town built a brick firehouse, known as Cambridge 1, across the street from the volunteer company in 1834 and enlarged it for a steam pumper in 1864 (figure 7.36; see also figure 3.16).

Although the General Court appointed a constable in Cambridge as early as 1632, the city's modern police force can be traced to the anti-Catholic riots of 1834, when the selectmen, concerned that Nativist mobs from Boston and Charlestown might attack Harvard, stationed a watchman in East Cambridge. In 1846 Mayor James D. Green noted that a town "situated like Cambridge, in immediate proximity to a large and overflowing commercial metropolis, crowding out into the suburbs, from year to year, its surplus population," was ill equipped to prevent "riotous noises … furious driving, [and] depredations upon [private] or public property" (Green, 1846, 5). He appointed a city marshal, but the three villages already had constables who contested his authority, and the department was not reorganized under a full-time chief until 1857.

The two Old Cambridge policemen were based on Kennedy Street until 1854, when the city moved their watch-house to Church Street. When the city rebuilt the Cambridge 1 firehouse in 1864, it put up Station 1 next door in a similar Italianate style. Ten years later, James White's carriage factory took over both buildings when the police and firemen relocated to the new City Building (see figure 9.14). The granite lintel inscribed "Cambridge, 1." was incorporated into the facade of a garage

FIGURE 7.35 Hunneman Engine Company #7, opposite 27 Church Street. The volunteer company's hand pumper was no longer useful after the city acquired a steam fire engine for Old Cambridge in 1864; the members disbanded in 1869. Photo ca. 1863.

FIGURE 7.36 Cambridge 1 Firehouse, 27 Church Street (1834, enlarged 1864). This photo was probably taken soon after the delivery of the company's new steam pumper in 1864.

that replaced the firehouse in 1922 (see figure 9.18). Stuccoed over when the building became a restaurant in 1947, the lintel was uncovered in 2001. Next door, Station 1 survives with an unaltered upper story and gradually weathering signs from its days as a carriage factory.

Old Cambridge's municipal facilities were consolidated at the new City Building on Eliot Square in 1875. Local carpenter-turned-architect Joseph H. Littlefield designed a four-story, elaborately detailed brick edifice with many of the features that

made Ruskinian architecture so unpopular in the first half of the 20th century, including an ostentatious Mansard roof with a clock tower and ornate turrets with iron cresting (figure 7.37). The City Building contained a courtroom, police station, firehouse, twenty-eight jail cells, schoolrooms, and a fire-alarm telegraph.[12] An armory and a wardroom provided meeting spaces for civic and private groups. This was a period of tight money, and many citizens protested the $75,000 appropriated for its construction. The building was mostly taken down in 1935 after the fire company moved to its present headquarters on Broadway, but one corner was roofed over and remained in use until neighborhood police stations were abolished in 1942.

Three firehouses serve Old Cambridge. In 1893 the burgeoning Huron Avenue district was given a conservatively designed brick station at 167 Lexington Avenue that housed Chemical

FIGURE 7.37 City Building, Eliot Square, 110 Mt. Auburn Street (1874, Joseph H. Littlefield, architect; demolished 1935–42). Photo 1907.

FIGURE 7.38 Chemical Engine No. 2, 167 Lexington Avenue (1893, Wilfred A. Norris, architect) during a flag-raising exercise in 1917.

Engine No. 2 (figure 7.38). The Taylor Square Fire Station (1904), the last house built for horse-drawn equipment, provides an impressive focus for the intersection of Garden Street with Huron Avenue (see *Report Five: Northwest Cambridge*, 130). The city built the Central Fire Station at Broadway and Cambridge Street after Mayor Edward Quinn and President Lowell agreed in 1929 to exchange a part of the Common enclosed by Holmes Place for the triangle bounded by Broadway and Cambridge and Quincy streets. The city retained R. Clipston Sturgis and William Stanley Parker to design a Georgian Revival building that would complement the Harvard structures nearby (figure 7.39).

In 1931 William L. Galvin's thesis project at the School of Architecture for a municipal auditorium at Flagstaff Park (a project suggested by the city's veterans' organizations in 1928) attracted the attention of Mayor Richard M. Russell. At his

FIGURE 7.39 Central Fire Station, 489–491 Broadway (1933, Sturgis Associates, architects). Photo 2015.

FIGURE 7.40 Proposed Cambridge Municipal Auditorium, Flagstaff Park (ca. 1932, William L. Galvin, architect). The auditorium would have bridged the streetcar ramp into Harvard Square Station and covered the entirety of Flagstaff Park. The Moderne design foretold some of Galvin's commercial buildings of the 1930s and '40s (see chapter 8).

request Galvin refined his design into a sleek Moderne building with a capacity of 3,800 (figure 7.40). Economic conditions and the difficulty of building on such a constrained site doomed the idea, but a 1939 high school addition on Broadway at the corner of Ellery Street included a similar auditorium.

HALLS AND CLUBHOUSES

Fraternal lodges, veterans' groups, temperance societies, and ethnic associations were an important part of late 19th century urban life, and many erected halls in Central Square and East Cambridge. Old Cambridge residents favored clubs and specialized voluntary organizations that generally met in private homes, restaurants, public halls on the upper floors of commercial buildings (such as Whitney and Estes's building at 13–25 Brattle Street), or, after 1874, in the wardroom of the City Building. Despite the prosperity of the community, only a few erected their own buildings.

The Cambridge Lyceum was organized in 1829 to offer public lectures and discussions. The early years of the Lyceum are obscure, but it was successful enough to have Richard Bond, architect of Harvard's Gore Hall, design a building on the site of the old courthouse (figures 7.41). The proprietors must have found Bond's design impractical, because they erected a quite different building in 1841 (figure 7.42). The Lyceum's broad stairs, oversized windows, and Doric portico conveyed its cultural role, while a market hall on the ground floor generated income. Ralph Waldo Emerson lectured there in 1849, but Cantabrigians mainly remembered it as the site of Lorenzo Papanti's dancing academy. New venues eventually supplanted the Lyceum, and the proprietors sold the property in 1895. The Harvard Cooperative Society bought it in 1903 and put up the present building on the site in 1924 (see chapter 8).

Boston merchant William W. Vaughan, a Craigie Street resident, and a group of like-minded citizens that included Reverend McKenzie and Samuel Batchelder Jr. founded the Cambridge Social Union in 1871 to provide entertainment and foster self-improvement for young men and women. In addition to lectures, concerts, dramatic performances, and social affairs, the Union organized a boys' club, a reading room, a library, and inexpensive night classes taught by Harvard students. Meetings took place initially in Lyceum Hall, but in 1889 the trustees purchased the William Brattle house at 42 Brattle Street and built Brattle Hall next door (figure 7.43). The hall was enlarged in 1899 and remodeled with a Georgian Revival facade by architect Charles N. Cogswell in 1907. In 1938 the Cambridge Social Union collaborated with the Boston Center for Adult Education to found the Cambridge Center for Adult Education, which became independent in 1941. The Center almost closed when enrollment dropped in 1942 but was quite successful during World War II. In 1972 it acquired the Dexter Pratt house at 54 Brattle Street from The Window Shop, an organization founded in 1939 to assist European refugees of World War II.

Brattle Hall was an enormously popular community venue; among other groups, the Cambridge Social Dramatic Club held

FIGURE 7.41 Proposed Lyceum Hall (ca. 1841, Richard Bond, architect). Bond's austere three-bay facade recalled the broad-pilastered Regency houses then being erected by Cambridge's elite.

FIGURE 7.42 Lyceum Hall, 1400 Massachusetts Avenue (1841, architect unknown; demolished 1924). This image shows the building after it was expanded 30 feet to the rear in 1855. Photo 1868.

FIGURE 7.43 Brattle Hall, 40 Brattle Street (1889, Longfellow, Alden & Harlow, architects). Brattle Hall's broad gambrel roof, Colonial Revival porte-cochère, and Palladian window were designed to complement the 1727 Brattle house. The building was extended to the rear in 1899, and in 1907 it was remodeled with a Georgian Revival facade designed by architect Charles N. Cogswell (see figure 3.59). Architect's rendering, 1889.

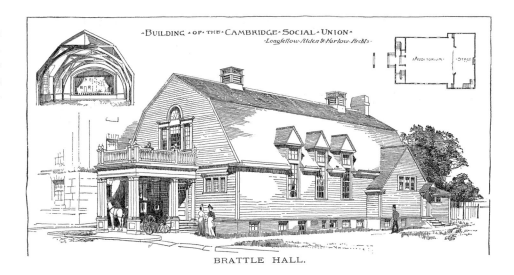

BUILDING · OF · THE · CAMBRIDGE · SOCIAL · UNION ·
Longfellow · Alden & Harlow Archts.

BRATTLE HALL.

regular performances there from 1891 until 1950. In 1948 the Cambridge Center sold the building to the Brattle Theater Company, a community players group that disbanded four years later. Bryant Haliday, an actor, and Cyrus Harvey, a Harvard student, opened one of the country's first repertory cinemas in 1953, offering art, foreign, and classic films (see figure 3.59). In 1964 Harvey converted the basement into an indoor bazaar occupied by small shops selling crafts and jewelry (see chapters 3 and 8).

The Colonial Club, organized in 1890 by Thomas Wentworth Higginson, Chester Kingsley, Daniel Chamberlin, Alvin Sortwell, and President Charles Eliot of Harvard, was conceived as a citywide gentlemen's social club and had 400 members at its peak. The members purchased the former home of Henry James Sr. at 20 Quincy Street and remodeled it in the Colonial Revival style, adding a dining hall, an assembly room, and a bowling alley (figure 7.44; see also figure 4.250). The university purchased the building in 1928 and replaced it two years later with the present Harvard Faculty Club. A sister organization, the Cantabrigia Club, built a brick clubhouse on Winthrop Square that was repurposed as a church in 1956 and razed in 1998.

Three clubs in succession provided recreational opportunities to Old Cambridge families. Ernest Longfellow, Samuel Batchelder, Charles Vaughn, and several other "prominent society leaders" incorporated the Cambridge Casino in 1882 and invested $10,000 to build a boathouse, bowling alley, and tennis courts on 1.6 acres of riverfront land purchased from the poet's heirs (*Chronicle*, May 12, 1888; see figure 2.20). Membership was limited to 100. The Casino disbanded in 1895 after the Cambridge Park Commission took its building and river frontage by eminent domain, and some members organized the Cambridge Skating Club in 1897. Neighborhood opportunities for safe skating diminished after 1887, when Dictionary Lake (between the Longfellow and Worcester houses) was filled in. Mrs. Thorp's field—a former salt marsh cut off from the Charles River by Mt. Auburn Street—offered a new venue for adults as well as for the Longfellow grandchildren and their friends

FIGURE 7.44 Colonial Club, 20 Quincy Street (1856; 1882 alterations by Peabody & Stearns, 1890 addition by Longfellow, Alden & Harlow; demolished 1930). Photo ca. 1907–8.

after the water board's 1899 decision to ban skating on Fresh Pond. The relocated casino bowling alley served as a warming hut until 1930, when a new generation of skaters purchased the property from Mrs. Thorp and built a proper clubhouse. They instructed Allen W. Jackson, a former club member who had designed many homes in Old Cambridge, to "make it unique and remembering that no one has to live in it, make it gay" (LaMond, "Allen Jackson," 3). The brightly painted Norwegian-style building was planned around a large, two-story room with a huge stone fireplace (figure 7.45).

The Thorps and the Danas, along with Stoughton Bell, Arthur H. Brooks, and Robert Walcott organized the Cambridge Boat Club in 1909. They leased a site near the old Casino and held an architectural competition for a clubhouse. Robert S. Peabody selected the design of John Worthington Ames, architect of several fashionable residences in Old Cambridge, for a stucco building "of the same general style … as the new Weld boathouse" (*Chronicle*, Dec. 4, 1909). The Metropolitan District Commission moved the clubhouse to Gerry's Landing in 1947 before it extended Memorial Drive to the Eliot Bridge (see figure 5.56).

FIGURE 7.45 Cambridge Skating Club, 183 Mt. Auburn Street (1930, Allen W. Jackson, architect). Architect's rendering, 1930.

SCHOOLS

> And by the side of the Colledge a faire Grammar Schoole, for the training up of young Schollars, and fitting of them for Academicall Learning, that still as they are judged ripe, they may be received into the Colledge: of this Schoole, Master Corlet … has very well approved himselfe for his abilities, dexterity and painfulnesse in teaching and education of the youth under him. *(New England's First Fruits,* 12, in Paige, 365)

Cambridge is notable for the diversity of its elementary and secondary schools. In Old Cambridge both public and private schools reflect the community's devotion to education. Only a few of the countless short-lived educational ventures established by widows, spinsters, dissatisfied parents, and impoverished Harvard graduates survived to maturity.

PUBLIC SCHOOLS

Elijah Corlett, an Oxford graduate, started Cambridge's first school in 1641 to prepare boys for admission to Harvard. A private venture, it probably operated out of his house on Dunster Street, but Harvard president Henry Dunster soon took responsibility on behalf of the town and erected a schoolhouse on Holyoke Street. Dunster's contract with the masons specified that they use 150 loads of stone from Charlestown to construct a two-story building with stepped gables, 12- to 18-inch-thick walls, and a tile roof: "the 2 gable endes of the forsaide wals or scholehouse shall be wrought up in battlement fashion … and the masons … wil lath the roofe of the aforesaid scholehouse and tile the same" (Paige, 371). Dunster was partially reimbursed with grants of land, but the town did not gain title to the building until after his death in 1659. In spite of the school's stone construction, which was exceptional for early Cambridge, it did not last long.[13] In October 1669, the town fathers contracted "to take downe the scholehouse, and set it up againe" (Town Records, 180).

The town took over Corlett's school in 1647 after the General Court required towns to provide public education. He taught both English and Latin curricula and earned a subsidy from the colony for preparing Native American boys for admission to Harvard (although only one ever graduated from the college). The selectmen set the teacher's salary, but Corlett was responsible for collecting it through student fees; when attendance fell, the town had to make up the difference. He taught for almost fifty years until his death in 1687. Thereafter, a progression of young men just out of Harvard kept the school, but few stayed very long or chose teaching as a profession. After 1737, when the legislature required towns to provide free public education for boys, the town had to pay the teachers.

In 1700 the town voted to replace the schoolhouse with a new one, 26 by 20 feet and probably built of wood, on the same site. The first school committee was established in 1744 "to inspect the Grammar School in this town, and to inquire … what proficiency the youth and children make in their learning" (Paige,

375). The Holyoke Street school was demolished in 1769; its replacement was on Garden Street opposite the Common. A watercolor from about 1781 shows the nearly square one-room school with a hip roof, although not the belfry mentioned in documents (figure 7.46). The cellar was used for storing wood, and the boys were expected to attend every Saturday long enough to split the next week's supply.

Cambridge was divided into school districts in 1794 when a new settlement grew up near the West Boston Bridge. The 19th century was a period of almost continuous expansion. Cambridge erected fifty-six school buildings between 1830 and 1930, mostly in the new neighborhoods east of the village. Although slightly more than one-third of the town's 12,490 inhabitants lived in Ward 1 (Old Cambridge) in 1845, it had only two elementary schools, in contrast to eleven in the rest of town. The city built small wooden primary schools in rapidly growing immigrant communities until 1883, while established neighborhoods received more substantial brick schools beginning in 1852. Middle-class neighborhoods received the most modern schools, such as the Agassiz in 1875 and the Peabody in 1888. In 1890 the city operated thirty-three elementary (primary and grammar) schools for 11,217 pupils; in 2010–11, eleven buildings sufficed for 4,249 elementary students.[14]

In 1802 the Old Cambridge district maintained a year-round grammar school for boys on Garden Street and a four-month "school for female children" in a rented building on the corner of Winthrop and Eliot streets, now 106 Winthrop Street (Paige, 376). The town remodeled the Garden Street school in 1828 so girls could share classrooms with boys but sold it four years later.[15] A new Latin Grammar School opened in 1833 on the same site. Later renamed the Washington School, it combined beginning and intermediate instruction for both boys and girls. In 1845 the upper room contained a grammar school (the grades just below high school) for boys, while the lower room had a mixed school of 100 primary and middle students taught by one female teacher and an assistant. In 1852 the students moved into a new Washington School on Farwell Place, and the old building was used as a gymnasium until it burned a year later.

FIGURE 7.46 Cambridge grammar school, Garden Street near Christ Church (1769), as seen in a 1781 watercolor of Cambridge Common (see figure 5.2). This is the earliest visual record of a school in Cambridge.

The Auburn School was built in 1838 on the corner of Brattle Street and Farwell Place on the same plan as the 1833 Washington School. In 1845 it accommodated the Female High School with ninety-six seats in the upper room and a mixed class of primary and alphabet students downstairs. The city moved it in 1851 to an empty corner of the burying ground while the new Washington School was completed, but a public outcry over this use of the cemetery resulted in its further move to Massachusetts Avenue opposite Lancaster Street. In 1857 the building was moved again to Concord Avenue, where it served as the Dunster School until St. Peter's parish purchased it for a parochial school. It was finally razed in 1927.

The new Washington School was one of the city's first brick schools, and its provisions for heating and ventilation were considered advanced for the period (figure 7.47). It was designed to accommodate the system of instruction then current in all city grammar schools. The lower floors each contained two class-rooms with adjacent recitation rooms; the third had one large (50-foot-square) schoolroom and two recitation rooms. From 100 to 225 pupils in four different grades spent most of the day in one room, where the teacher, sometimes with the help of an assistant, would attempt to instruct each grade of about fifty students "over the heads of the army stationed in this immense hall." Each grade in turn would leave the room to recite their lessons in an adjoining recitation room.

> The present arrangement brings under the control of one teacher, so many pupils that he or she is in danger of being overpowered by the mere force of numbers. The energy and strength necessary to preserve order in such a mass of rebellious humanity, as these crowds sometimes prove to be, wear out the vitality of the teachers. (Report of the Superintendent of Schools, *Cambridge Annual Documents,* 1869, 160–61)

After this the school committee reorganized the grammar schools into smaller rooms with teachers in charge of a single class averaging fifty-six pupils. The Washington School was thus remodeled in 1870, and the primary students were transferred to the new Holmes School on Hilliard Street. The building was razed in 1905 and replaced by the Washington Court apartments at 51 Brattle Street (see figure 6.222).

The thirty years following the Civil War saw the construction of five new public schools in Old Cambridge (compared to twenty-one in faster-growing neighborhoods). The brick Quincy Primary on Mason Street was erected in 1866; its two teachers had nearly 120 students in their charge (figure 7.48). The school committee put up the two-story frame Holmes Primary in 1870 at 12–20 Hilliard Street to serve the tradesmen's families who were populating the Marsh and Half Crown neighborhoods. Although the building measured only 35 by 65 feet, it contained four classrooms on each floor and accommodated up to 224 pupils. The Lowell School at 25 Lowell Street supplemented the Holmes School and eventually replaced it. Designed in 1883 by James Fogerty, this simple building was the last wooden school

FIGURE 7.47 Washington School, Brattle Street and Farwell Place (1852, Michael Norton, builder; demolished 1905). Photo 1905.

TABLE 7.1 CAMBRIDGE ELEMENTARY SCHOOLS

Name before 2003	Address	Name in 2011
Agassiz	28 Sacramento St.	Baldwin
Fitzgerald	70 Rindge Ave.	Peabody
Fletcher	89 Elm St.	Cambridgeport
Graham & Parks (formerly Webster)	15 Upton St.	Amigos
Haggerty	110 Cushing St.	Same
Harrington	850 Cambridge St.	King Open
Kennedy	158 Spring St.	Kennedy-Longfellow
King	100 Putnam Ave.	Same
Longfellow	389 Broadway	Closed
Morse	40 Granite St.	Same
Peabody	44 Linnaean St.	Graham & Parks
Roberts	225 Windsor St.	Fletcher-Maynard
Tobin	197 Vassal Lane	Same

FIGURE 7.48 Quincy Primary School, 14 Mason Street (1866, Albert Stevens, builder). Radcliffe College purchased the school in 1899 and demolished it in 1904 for Agassiz House. Photo 1876–77.

FIGURE 7.49 Lowell School, 25 Lowell Street (1883, James Fogerty, architect). The school is on the right; behind the fence is a playground built in 1924. Photo 1924–25.

built in Cambridge and cost an economical $12,943 for the land, construction, and furnishings (figure 7.49). Remarkably, the Lowell served until 1979; it is now the last frame schoolhouse in Cambridge. Still city-owned, it retains its original interior finishes and should be preserved as a landmark.[16]

The city built the first Agassiz School in 1875 to serve the children of Harvard faculty living on Professors Row and suburban families settling along Oxford Street. The brick primary school was one of the first in Cambridge designed for classroom-based instruction; each room was about 25 feet square and seated forty-two students. Architect Joseph H. Littlefield incorporated advances in ventilation and central heating previously seen in the 1871 Harvard School on Broadway. The building was named for Professor Louis Agassiz, who founded the Museum of Comparative Zoology on Oxford Street in 1859.

Maria Baldwin, the principal for many years, was born in Cambridge of Haitian descent in 1856 and attended the Cambridge High School and the city's teacher training course. Refused a position in Massachusetts, she taught in Maryland until she was hired to teach at the Agassiz in 1882. After seven years she became the first principal of her race in the state. When the second Agassiz School opened in 1916, she was designated "master," a position held by few women, let alone African Americans. Miss Baldwin served until her death in 1922 and was remembered with great respect by President Eliot, E.E. Cummings, and other former students.

The second Agassiz School, designed by Edward McGirr in "West Point Gothic" style, had twelve classrooms, an auditorium/gymnasium, and a deck for open-air sessions on the roof (*Chronicle,* Jan. 2, 1915).[17] Buttresses allowed window openings that were 25 percent larger than usual, reflecting contemporary educational theory and health concerns (figures 7.50–7.51). The third Agassiz was completed in 1995 on the same site. While intended to recall the scale of the older school, the new building was much larger and decidedly contemporary. The interior incorporates elements of the old building, including a Gothic doorway and beams from the ceiling of the auditorium (figure 7.52). Professor Agassiz's 19th-century racial views became

FIGURE 7.50 Second Agassiz School, 32 Sacramento Street (1915, Edward B. McGirr, architect; demolished 1993). Photo ca. 1993.

FIGURE 7.51 Sacramento Street entrance, Second Agassiz School. The 1915 limestone jambs and paneled doors were reused inside the present school. Photo ca. 1993.

FIGURE 7.52 Third Agassiz (now Maria L. Baldwin) School, 32 Sacramento Street (1995, HMFH Architects). Photo ca. 1995.

objectionable to the school community, and the building was renamed in 2002 to honor Miss Baldwin.

The first Peabody School, begun in 1888 on the corner of Linnaean and Avon streets, was named for Reverend Andrew Preston Peabody, Harvard's chaplain from 1860 to 1881 and a member of the school committee for twelve years. The *Cambridge Tribune* wrote that this prime residential neighborhood called "for something rather more than the conventional plain style of school buildings" (May 19, 1888). James Fogerty's design closely resembled his Putnam School, built the year before in East Cambridge, but with different window treatments and rusticated brownstone trim (figure 7.53). This was the first school in the city to have indoor sanitary facilities (although in the basement) and a hot-air heating system.

In 1960 the city demolished the old building and five adjacent houses for a new two-story Peabody School designed by Hugh Stubbins & Associates (figure 7.54). Like other Cambridge schools of its generation, notably the Morse (1955, Carl

FIGURE 7.54 Peabody School, 44 Linnaean Street (1960, Hugh Stubbins & Associates). This building currently houses the Graham & Parks School. Photo ca. 1962.

FIGURE 7.53 Peabody School, Linnaean and Avon streets (1888, James Fogerty, architect), as originally constructed. The school was expanded in 1899 and razed in 1960. Photo ca. 1890.

Koch), Fitzgerald, and Harrington (1955 and 1959, M.A. Dyer & Co.), the Peabody's architecture reflected a humanist strain of Modernism, characterized by an intimate scale, warm materials and colors, and generous windows. Old Cambridge escaped the school committee's subsequent infatuation with Brutalist architecture, as reflected in the Martin Luther King Jr. School (1970, Sert Jackson & Associates; demolished 2013), the John M. Tobin School (1970, Pietro Belluschi and Sasaki Associates), and the high school addition (1975, Eduardo Catalano).

The last location selected for a public school in Old Cambridge lay between Grozier and Larch roads, where the city completed the Russell School in 1897 to serve the developing streets off Huron Avenue (figure 7.55). Boston architect Aaron Gould won the 1895 design competition. The school originally contained ten rooms; in 1923 Charles R. Greco added two classroom wings and a gymnasium. The building was torn down in 1979 after neighbors objected to a proposal for adaptive reuse as affordable housing (see chapter 4).

In 2003 falling enrollment resulted in a consolidation and renaming of Cambridge elementary schools. The Peabody faculty

FIGURE 7.55 Russell School, 111 Larch Road (1895–96, Aaron Gould, architect). Wings added in 1923 largely obscured the original building. Photo 1896.

and students moved to the Fitzgerald School in North Cambridge and the Graham & Parks School, formerly of Cambridgeport, moved to the Peabody building. This unilateral action by the school committee caused lasting confusion among residents who identified with their neighborhood schools (see table 7.1, p. 645).

PRIVATE SCHOOLS

Public schools were not the only option for 19th-century families. Many small private schools operated in a teacher's home for only a few years. Some added classroom wings to their houses, while the most successful founded independent schools that long outlived them.

Dame schools, typically run by older women in their own homes, were a common choice for families able to give their children an early start. Tax records for the house at 106 Winthrop Street refer in 1801 to a "tenement lately used as a school room"

and in 1806 as a "school house improved for female scholars," but it is not known who taught there. Miss Jennison's dame school operated in Deacon Moore's old house at Garden and Mason streets in the 1840s and '50s for "the daughters and small sons of the best families," such as Thomas Wentworth Higginson, James Russell Lowell, and Charlie and Ernest Longfellow (figure 7.56). College students or recent graduates taught older children. Richard Henry Dana Jr. attended a school in Cambridgeport kept by Ralph Waldo Emerson (Harvard class of 1821) about 1820, and Lowell, Higginson, and Dana continued their education at William Wells's boarding school at 175 Brattle Street (see figure 4.62).

FIGURE 7.56 Miss Jennison's School occupied the 1718 Abraham Hill (later Deacon Moore) house at 11 Garden Street. This daguerreotype was taken for Henry Wadsworth Longfellow, whose son Charlie is sitting on the fencepost dressed in black. Behind him on the right is Elizabeth Ellery ("Lily") Dana; among the seven boys and eleven girls are Ernest Longfellow, Benjie Peirce, the Dixwell sisters, one of Winslow Homer's brothers, and future admiral Charles Henry Davis Jr. Miss Jennison died a year or two after the photo was taken, and the house was demolished in 1863. Photo 1851–52.

Elizabeth Cabot Cary Agassiz operated the Agassiz School for Girls from 1855 to 1863 in her home at 36 Quincy Street. Professor Agassiz himself lectured in the school, which was one of the first to offer a scientific education for women. Mrs. Agassiz was one of seven ladies who in 1879 published a circular offering women collegiate instruction by members of the Harvard faculty, and in 1883 she became the first president of the Society for the Collegiate Instruction of Women, soon renamed Radcliffe College.

Lyman Richards Williston, principal of the Cambridge High School, founded a private school for girls on Irving Street in 1862. A Hawaii-born adopted son of Samuel Williston, a wealthy manufacturer and philanthropist in western Massachusetts, Lyman built a large Italianate house at 15 Berkeley Street

FIGURE 7.57 Berkeley Street School students Margaret James, Susie Lovering, Constance Hall, Frances Kittredge, and Jessie Peirce in front of the one-story school wing on the west side of 15 Berkeley Street. All but Lovering were daughters of Harvard professors. Photo ca. 1897.

with a one-story classroom wing in 1863 (figure 7.57; see also figure 6.75). The Berkeley Street School operated from 1863 to 1912, when it merged with the Cambridge School for Girls; it was directed by others after Williston returned to the high school in 1870. The wing was detached from the house in 1900 and remodeled into the present house at 17 Berkeley in 1912.

Three schools founded in private homes in the 1880s—Browne & Nichols, Buckingham, and the Cambridge School for Girls—built campuses in Old Cambridge. In 1883 George Browne and Edgar Nichols, both 1878 graduates of Harvard, announced the opening of a college preparatory school for boys in a rented house at 11 Appian Way. By 1886 Browne & Nichols also occupied a house at 8 Garden Street, and it soon built a gymnasium. In 1894, with an enrollment of seventy-five, the school erected its first new academic building, a three-story shingled structure with a high gambrel roof (figure 7.58).

By 1897 Browne & Nichols needed additional space. Radcliffe College wanted to expand, so the institutions exchanged properties. B&N erected a three-story Georgian Revival building at 20 Garden Street designed by Minerva Parker Nichols, a Philadelphia architect who was Edgar Nichols's sister-in-law (figure 7.59). Smaller boys studied on the first floor, older boys on the second, and an assembly hall and laboratories occupied the third. Dr. John White Webster's 1837 house at 22 Garden Street became a dormitory, and James Hayden Wright, a young M.I.T.-trained architect, designed George Browne's residence next door (see figure 4.116). Radcliffe occupied the old B&N buildings on Appian Way until Longfellow Hall replaced them in 1929.

In 1912 Browne & Nichols purchased part of the Coolidge farm, a former salt marsh at Gerry's Landing recently protected from the tides by the Charles River Dam. The school leveled a drumlin to raise the grade of Nichols Field, constructed a locker building and a baseball cage, and added a woodworking shop known as the Sloyd Building in 1932.[18] B&N announced in 1928 that it planned to relocate to Gerry's Landing to conform to the country day school model popular at the time, but it did not begin to develop the site until twenty years later. Between 1949

FIGURE 7.58 Browne & Nichols School, 11 Appian Way. The original building, the John Warland Jr. house (1804), is at right. The gymnasium (1887) behind 11 Appian Way is in the center. A new academic building (1894, Browne & Stearns, architects) is on the left; it was divided into a preparatory department for younger boys, who entered from Appian Way, and an upper school entered from Garden Street. All were demolished by 1929. Photo ca. 1895.

and 1962, Henry Kennedy and Kilham & Hopkins designed a gymnasium, middle school, lower school, and auditorium, creating a new campus on the southeast corner of the field. Architectural Resources Cambridge designed the Almy Library and School Center (1979) and the Smith Science Wing (1984) in the manner of the firm's 1977 Kennedy School of Government. Renaissance Hall (2005, Centerbrook Architects) completed the academic campus. In 1997 a 162,000-square-foot athletic center designed by Chan Krieger Associates and the Office of Peter Rose replaced a 1966 ice hockey rink. The massive aluminum-and-glass-block facility, which dominates the Gerry's Landing campus, required the demolition of a significant 1946 house by Carl Koch (see figure 6.200). The Sloyd Building, which was saved from demolition in 1996, has been relocated twice and is a comfortable anachronism on an otherwise modern campus (figure 7.60).

FIGURE 7.59 Browne & Nichols School, 20 Garden Street (1897, Minerva Parker Nichols, architect; demolished 1967). B&N sold its Garden Street properties in 1948 when it consolidated at the Gerry's Landing campus. Photo 1967.

FIGURE 7.60 Buckingham Browne & Nichols School. The academic buildings in the foreground include Renaissance Hall (2005, Centerbrook Architects and Planners), enclosing a courtyard with Almy Library and School Center (1979) and the Smith Science Wing (1984, both Architectural Resources Cambridge). The Nicholas Athletic Center (1997, Chan Krieger Associates and the Office of Peter Rose, architects) lies across the baseball diamond. The Shady Hill School campus is at left, and Mount Auburn Hospital is in the background. Photo 2011.

Jeanette Markham, founder of the Buckingham School, was a Radcliffe scholarship student from Atchison, Kansas, who lived with Thomas Wentworth Higginson's family and cared for their young daughter. Miss Markham's School began in 1889 in a private house on Buckingham Street. After a year, Mrs. Richard Henry (Edith Longfellow) Dana bought a lot on the corner of Buckingham Place and lent Miss Markham money to build what is now the oldest private school building in Cambridge (figure 7.61). After a decade Miss Markham resigned to marry,

FIGURE 7.61 Miss Markham's School, 10 Buckingham Street (1888, Andrews, Jacques & Rantoul, architects). The building contained a single large classroom and an apartment above for Miss Markham. It was altered in 1917 by Allen W. Jackson and again in 1996. Architect's rendering, 1888.

FIGURE 7.62 Buckingham School, 16 Buckingham Street (1920, Andrews, Rantoul & Jones, architects). Photo ca. 1925.

and in 1902 parents and neighbors incorporated the Buckingham School to continue as before. The building remains in use but was altered in 1917 and again in 1996.

In 1920 Buckingham erected a Georgian Revival building at the corner of Parker Street that contained an assembly hall and a two-story gymnasium with a fine trussed ceiling (figure 7.62). A 1980 addition incorporated the exterior of the gym, including the cornice and part of the roof, into an atrium designed by Architectural Resources Cambridge. In 1967 Ashley/Myer/ Smith designed a new lower school at 19 Craigie Street that introduced charming irregularities in room shapes, floor levels, and ceiling heights to create a varied and stimulating environment. In spite of its modern design, the building's mass, use of gables, and placement on the lot respect the residential character of the neighborhood (figure 7.63). Meanwhile, the school had acquired the 1858 Deane residence at 80 Sparks Street in

FIGURE 7.63 Buckingham School (now BB&N Lower School), 19 Craigie Street (1967, Ashley/Myer/Smith Architects). Photo ca. 1970.

1949 and was continually adapting it for its upper school for girls (see figure 4.31). A previous owner had remodeled the Second Empire mansion in 1932 with brick veneer and Georgian Revival detail. Buckingham had Ames, Child & Graves and its successor firm, Griswold, Boyden, Wylde & Ames, design additions in 1949, 1954, and 1960. Ashley/Myer/Smith designed the Marian Vaillant wing in 1968, and in 2014–15 Austin Architects replaced the ell of the old house with a new structure that united the disparate additions.

Browne & Nichols and Buckingham merged to become Buckingham Browne & Nichols in 1974. The upper schools were consolidated at Gerry's Landing, the middle schools at 80 Sparks Street, and the lower schools on Buckingham Place. BB&N acquired several adjoining houses for redevelopment of the latter campus but instead entered into a community planning process that resulted in partial restoration of 15 Craigie Street (1870–71, formerly St. Anne's Convent) for a headmaster's residence and construction of a striking new science building designed by Ann Beha Associates.

Arthur Gilman (1836–1909), who had been instrumental in founding Radcliffe College in 1879, established the Cambridge School for Girls in 1886 "to give to girls and young women thorough and well-ordered instruction … thus fitting them for a college course or for any sphere of life which the future may bring to them" (*Cambridge Chronicle Semi-Centennial Souvenir,* 57).[19] Gilman had grown up in New York, retired from business there, and arrived in Cambridge in 1870 with a growing family of daughters and a strong interest in education and popular history. The Cambridge School soon outgrew the ca. 1770 Josiah Mason house at 20 Mason Street (now the site of the Radcliffe Gymnasium). Gilman purchased a lot at 77 Brattle Street in 1888 but waited until 1893 to hire E.N. Boyden to design a building that contained four large classrooms on the first floor and a library and recitation rooms upstairs (figure 7.64).

In 1889 Gilman commissioned a dormitory, Margaret Winthrop Hall, at 21 Chauncy Street (see figure 4.139), and in 1896 he erected a classroom building at 34 Concord Avenue (figure

FIGURE 7.64 Gilman Hall, Cambridge School for Girls, 77 Brattle Street (1893, E.N. Boyden, architect). The Radcliffe Gymnasium is visible in the background. Radcliffe moved Gilman Hall to 8 Garden Street in 1907 to make way for Schlesinger Library, and then moved it again to 73 Brattle Street in 1930 for Byerly Hall. It was demolished in 1932. Photo ca. 1905.

7.65). As the school grew it acquired three residences next door and in 1925 moved two of them to build a playground. In 1931 the upper school relocated to the suburbs and became the Cambridge School of Weston. The lower school remained and in 1948 became Lesley College's Ellis School for Children. Radcliffe College acquired the campus in 1984, and in 1986 Graham Gund Architects restored the complex to house the Mary I. Bunting Institute.

A few Harvard families founded the Cooperative Open-Air School (now the Shady Hill School) in 1915, during construction of the second Agassiz School. Six boys and girls began taking lessons on a sleeping porch at 16 Quincy Street, the home of philosophy professor William Ernest Hocking and his wife, Agnes Boyle O'Reilly, whose children comprised half the student

FIGURE 7.65 Cambridge School for Girls, 34 Concord Avenue (1896, E.N. Boyden, architect). This classroom building and the three houses at 36, 38, and 40 Concord Avenue (1854, 1871, and 1877) have been used successively by the Cambridge School for Girls, Lesley College, and the Radcliffe Institute for Advanced Study. Photo ca. 1920.

FIGURE 7.66 Professor Edward Tyrrel Channing house, 16 Quincy Street (1832, Oliver Hastings, builder; demolished 1945). Harvard University built the sleeping porch for Professor William Ernest Hocking and his family in 1914; it became the first home of the Cooperative Open-Air School a year later. The site is now occupied by Harvard's Dana-Palmer House. Photo ca. 1938.

body (figure 7.66). After a successful year the parents bought a lot on the corner of Holden and Scott streets, and in August 1916 the city issued permits for five buildings measuring 16 by 30 feet designed by one of their number, James H. Wright. Four were completed by the fall of 1917; an assembly hall came later (figure 7.67).

The Open-Air School began with no defined educational theory, and many of its methods were experimental. The school became known for using parents in the classroom, for a teaching approach called "central subject" that organized the year's curriculum, an emphasis on learning through first-hand experience rather than textbooks, and above all for holding open-air classes. In the low, open-sided buildings in their wooded setting

Miss Gould

THE COÖPERATIVE OPEN-AIR SCHOOL

SHADY HILL SQUARE

CAMBRIDGE, MASSACHUSETTS

FIGURE 7.67 Cooperative Open-Air School, 45 Holden Street. Prospectus for 1919–20. The school stood on the corner of Scott Street facing Shady Hill Square.

the children worked through the winter wearing layers of heavy woolen clothes, mittens, and padded bags that came over their shoulders.[20] Some public schools adopted the fresh-air concept to inhibit the spread of tuberculosis, but few carried it to these lengths.

In 1925 and 1926, when enrollment reached about 135, the Open-Air trustees purchased land between Coolidge Hill and Cambridge Cemetery adjoining Nichols Field and adopted the name Shady Hill to recall the school's original site. Parent-architect David Barnes helped replicate its original layout. Samuel Mead of Cabot, Everett & Mead designed five hip-roof buildings with long banks of windows, each containing two homerooms, two project rooms, washrooms, and lockers. These were ready for occupancy by the fall of 1926; only a workshop was moved from Holden Street (figure 7.68). A parabolic-roofed athletic building constructed in 1938 specifically for badminton extended the school's unconventional architectural tradition.

The first conventional structures at Shady Hill were a science building (1962, Kilham, Hopkins, Greeley & Brodie) and a field house (1965, Ashley, Myer & Associates). More recent buildings include a library called the Beehive (1974) and the Beginners Building (1990; figure 7.69). In 1998 the school razed the 1926 Grade 5 and 8–9 buildings, renovated and expanded the Grade 7 building, and put up three new frame replacements designed by Perry Dean Rogers Partners. In spite of these larger structures, the campus retains its informal, camp-like character.

FIGURE 7.68 The new Shady Hill School under construction at Coolidge Hill (1926, Samuel W. Mead of Cabot, Everett & Mead, architect). The house facing the camera in the right background is 173 Coolidge Hill. Photo ca. 1926.

The Cambridge Nursery School is thought to be the oldest continuously operated parent cooperative nursery school in the country. Founded in 1923 by five Cambridge mothers who had held informal playgroups in their homes, it adopted English principles recently brought to America by movement pioneer Abigail Adams Eliot, a 1914 Radcliffe graduate. The school first met in a private home at 4 Shady Hill Square. The experiment proved successful, and parents erected a small schoolhouse around the corner (now 20 Farrar Street). In 1928 they put up a building at 6 Hillside Place designed by Derby & Robinson of Boston; the Farrar Street branch closed in 1977. Another cooperative, the Parents Nursery School, originated as the private venture of Althea Teele in a house on Farwell Place. When she retired in 1947, the parents leased the ground floor of the 1902 Alvin Sortwell stable at 40 Reservoir Street, where the school remained until 2012.

The Caryl Peabody Nursery School would have gained international attention if it had built the facility it commissioned from Walter Gropius in 1937. The origins of the school are unclear. Peabody, a daughter of Harvard archeologist Charles Peabody, grew up at 197 Brattle Street. A champion sled-dog racer and breeder before her marriage to Frederick Lovejoy in 1928, she was involved with the Avon Home and the Nursery Training School of the Child Welfare Society but died in 1934. Three years later the school commissioned Gropius to design a building on her parents' property at the corner of Lexington Avenue, but it was never built, and the school relinquished its incorporated status in 1939 (figure 7.70).

The Manter Hall School had a symbiotic relationship with Harvard University. William W. Nolen, an 1884 graduate known to students as "Widow" Nolen, expanded his undergraduate tutoring job into a full-fledged school with "a corps of assistants" in his rooms at Manter Hall, a private dormitory at 4 Holyoke Street (*Cambridge Tribune,* Oct. 16, 1926). After his death in 1923, Nolen's colleagues incorporated the Manter Hall School and later erected a building at 71–77 Mt. Auburn Street (figure 7.71). Manter Hall specialized in preparing students

FIGURE 7.69 Shady Hill School, Beginners' Building, 178 Coolidge Hill (1990, James W. Freeman of Freeman/Brigham/Hussey Ltd., architect). Photo ca. 1990.

FIGURE 7.70 Proposed Caryl Peabody Nursery School, 205 Brattle Street (1937, Walter Gropius, architect; not built). Architect's rendering.

FIGURE 7.71 Manter Hall School, 71–77 Mt. Auburn Street (1927, Charles H. Way, architect). Photo 1968.

for college and ran review sessions before every Harvard exam period. During World War II, the entire school was devoted to preparing candidates for the aviation cadet examination. After the war, Manter Hall became a boarding school for special-needs students until it closed in 1996.

The Fayerweather Street School was founded in 1967 by parents and teachers interested in exploring child-centered educational methods. They found a landlocked parcel in a ravine behind 74 Fayerweather Street. In this unlikely setting, William Barton Associates built a three-story building with flexible interior spaces that could be adapted to changes in the curriculum (figure 7.72). Since the premises were small, the school built a monumental exterior stairway to reach a rooftop play space added by Benjamin Thompson & Associates. In 1999 the school moved to larger quarters at 765 Concord Avenue, and a new owner commissioned architect Maryann Thompson to convert the building into a single-family home.

FIGURE 7.72 Fayerweather Street School, 320 Huron Avenue (1968, William Barton Associates, architects). Photo 1972, before conversion to a single-family residence.

COLLEGES, INSTITUTES, AND PROFESSIONAL SCHOOLS

Old Cambridge has been a rich environment for advanced educational institutions. Some established a strong architectural presence, while others adapted preexisting buildings. Radcliffe College, in particular, pursued an architectural identity that was subtly distinct from Harvard's and remains so.

Episcopal Divinity School

An Episcopal seminary was first attempted in 1831, when Bishop Alexander Griswold purchased a house "about a quarter mile from Harvard College on the high road to Boston sufficiently near to the city to enjoy its benefits and escape its disadvantages" (Muller, 4). This failed after a year, and nothing more materialized until the Episcopal Theological School was established in 1867. The founders wished to establish a stronger presence for their faith in this bastion of Unitarianism. They purchased part of the present campus at 99 Brattle Street in 1868 and consecrated St. John's Chapel in 1869 (see figure 7.19). This was "intended to be not only the chapel of the school but also a center of church life for the academic community in Cambridge" (Muller, 36).

The school accepted Ware & Van Brunt's master plan for the campus quadrangle in 1871 while the architects were still working out the design of Harvard's Memorial Hall (figure 7.73). Lawrence Hall, a dormitory, was begun in 1872. Reed Hall, containing the library and recitation rooms, was built in 1873–75, and Burnham Hall, the refectory, in 1879 (figure 7.74). The chapel dominates the campus; the quadrangle was built of the same Roxbury puddingstone, although with red brick trim. The later buildings were more inventive, with stepped gables, accents of Panel Brick decoration, and a polychromatic use of black brick, another indication of Ruskin's influence. The dean's residence on Mason Street was a particularly exuberant example of the style (see figure 6.113).

The tight logic of the master plan made it difficult for later architects to expand the campus. Winthrop Hall, a stone and brick dormitory designed by Longfellow, Alden & Harlow in 1892, stands northwest of the quadrangle and is fairly compatible with it, but three academic buildings built in the 20th century are either weak echoes or aggressive antagonists of the original Ruskinian designs. Wright Hall (1911, Shepley, Rutan & Coolidge), originally a library and later an administration building, was executed in a pallid English Gothic manner. Washburn Hall (1961, Larsen, Bradley & Hibbard), containing a dining hall and meeting rooms, is a delicate International Style building that ignores its surroundings, while Sherrill (1965, Campbell & Aldrich) is an assertive Brutalist building with a library, classrooms, and offices (figure 7.75). Sherrill displaced both the Deanery and the 1852 Regency-style Judge Daniel Wells house at 2 Phillips Place. Hostility to Victorian romanticism was palpable during the 1960s, and after Professor Kenneth Conant, an architect and historian, dismissed the Deanery as unworthy of preservation it was razed with no apparent regret. The plain lines of the Wells house appealed to modern sensibilities, and it was relocated to 170 Brattle Street.

Reverend William Lawrence, later Bishop of Massachusetts, acquired the Oliver Hastings house at 101 Brattle Street as his private residence when he became dean of ETS in 1889 and made the two properties "as one, by the removal of fences, regrading the grounds, and laying out new walks" (*Chronicle*, Nov. 3, 1888). A later owner gave it to Harvard, which sold the property piecemeal to ETS in 1924 and 1949 (see figure 6.62).

After World War II the school acquired a pasture behind Henry Wadsworth Longfellow's barn and extended St. John's Road to create an enclave of faculty housing. Hugh Stubbins designed two modern houses there in 1954. Changing direction, in 1959 and 1963 ETS moved in three Federal and Greek Revival houses that were displaced by Harvard projects on Brattle Street and Appian Way, plus a 1901 Queen Anne of its own from Phillips Place (see figure 6.42). The school's president revealed that its "primary motive in moving the houses was not to preserve historical landmarks so much as to obtain charming and useful houses for our faculty" (James Garfield to Albert B. Wolfe, Feb. 12, 1964). ETS also acquired several houses in its

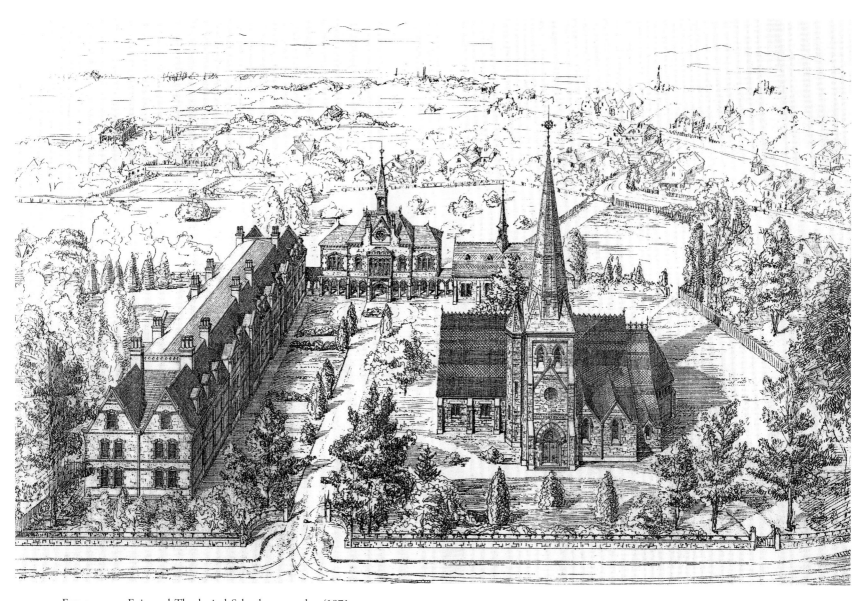

FIGURE 7.73 Episcopal Theological School master plan (1871,
Ware & Van Brunt, architects).

FIGURE 7.74 Episcopal Theological School. From left to right are Lawrence Hall (1872), a dormitory, Reed Hall (1873–75), and Burnham Hall (1879, all by Ware & Van Brunt, architects. Photo 2015.

FIGURE 7.75 The Episcopal Theological School campus in 1967, showing Washburn Hall (1961, Larsen, Bradley & Hibbard) and Sherrill Hall (1965, Campbell & Aldrich, architects).

immediate vicinity, including Richard Henry Dana Jr.'s house at 4 Berkeley Street, Reverend William Newell's at 6 Phillips Place (demolished 1960), and Harvard librarian John Langdon Sibley's at 9 Phillips Place (see figure 6.73). Neighborhood objections thwarted an attempt to build garden apartments for married students behind 168 Brattle Street (see chapter 4).

In 1974 ETS merged with the Philadelphia Divinity School and became the Episcopal Divinity School. For a few years EDS shared its library and chapel with the adjacent Weston School of Theology, which occupied houses at 3 and 5 Phillips Place, but that Jesuit institution moved to the Boston College campus in 2008. By this time EDS had only ninety-seven students and was actively seeking a partner to share its campus. Harvard was focused on expanding in Allston, so EDS and Lesley University entered into a $33.5 million condominium agreement in 2008. EDS sold seven buildings to Lesley and retained thirteen; the institutions share Sherrill Library and Washburn Hall.

The movement to create opportunities for higher education for women in Cambridge achieved success in the last quarter of the 19th century, well after the opening of Vassar in 1861 and Smith and Wellesley in 1875 as colleges for women, and Bates College (1855), Cornell University (1868), and Boston University (1869) as coeducational institutions. From 1840 to 1845, the city's Auburn Female High School on Farwell Place offered girls a classical secondary education, and in 1848 a coeducational public high school opened with more girls than boys. In 1849 Reverend William A. Stearns of the First Evangelical Congregational Church in Cambridgeport, a member of the school committee and a Harvard Overseer who became president of Amherst College in 1854, called for the establishment of a school "in which our daughters could obtain advantages for improvement approximating those which our sons enjoy at the University" (in Gilman, 1896, 175–76). Stearns's own daughters had to pursue their educations outside of Cambridge. Except for Elizabeth Agassiz's short-lived school, advanced instruction for girls depended on tutors or Harvard professors who were willing to take private pupils (see chapter 7).

President Eliot seemed to offer some hope to women in his inaugural address in 1869. While the Corporation would not "receive women as students into the College proper," the university would maintain "a cautious and expectant policy." He noted that "equality between the sexes, without privilege or oppression on either side, is the happy custom of American homes," but described the grave difficulties involved in bringing "hundreds of young men and women of immature character and marriageable age" into close proximity; "the necessary police regulations [would be] exceedingly burdensome." He concluded that "upon a matter concerning which prejudices are deep, and opinion inflammable, and experience scanty, only one course is prudent or justifiable when such great interests are at stake—that of cautious and well-considered experiment." Although few did so, women would be allowed to enroll in a new series of lectures

in 1869–70 that would fit them for teaching, "the one learned profession to which women have already acquired a clear title" (in Morison, *Development,* lxx–lxxi). Several women who had already earned degrees elsewhere applied to the schools of medicine, law, and divinity, but none were admitted.

It fell to the editor and popular historian Arthur Gilman and his wife, Stella, to advance the cause of women's education in Cambridge. The Gilmans had five daughters at home, and Grace, the oldest, turned sixteen in 1878. Her parents were opposed to coeducation and did not want her to commute to school in Boston. At his wife's urging and in consultation with his neighbor, classics professor James Greenough, Gilman wrote to President Eliot about his plan to "afford women opportunities for carrying their studies systematically forward further than it is possible for them now to do it in this country, except possibly at Smith College." Women would be required "to pass an examination not less rigid than that now established for the admission of young men" and would receive equivalent instruction. He asked Eliot to confirm that Harvard professors, many of whom already took private students, would be free to teach outside the university under such conditions (Gilman, "Radcliffe College," 55).

President Eliot called on Gilman the next day and gave his general consent in January 1879. Mr. and Mrs. Gilman selected a founding committee that consisted of seven prominent Cambridge women, most of whom were wives, daughters, or widows of Harvard professors. Elizabeth Cabot Cary Agassiz was the widow of Louis Agassiz. Stella Gilman, an author, was already active in her family's educational activities. Ellen Hooper Gurney was the wife of Harvard dean Ephraim Gurney and a sister of Edward Hooper, the treasurer. Mary Greenough's husband was Professor Greenough, and Mary Cooke's was Professor Josiah Parsons Cooke of the chemistry department. Lillian Horsford's father, Eben Norton Horsford, had been Rumford Professor and dean of the Lawrence Scientific School. Alice Longfellow stocked the library and offered her home for college functions. According to one source: "President Eliot had suggested naming the women's institution Longfellow College, after the poet, but

Alice … protested that surely it should be named after someone more concerned with women's education than her father" (Bunting, *Harvard*, 128).

The committee polled Harvard faculty members about whether they would be interested in teaching female students; Professors William Byerly (mathematics) and William James (psychology and philosophy) were among the forty-four who responded favorably. In May 1879 the committee announced that about fifty courses in thirteen subjects would be offered the first year. Entrance examinations were held in September in two rented rooms at 6 Appian Way, and twenty-seven students registered for the first term.

The Harvard Annex, as it was popularly known, was incorporated as the Society for the Collegiate Instruction of Women in 1882. The trustees chose Elizabeth Agassiz as the first president, and in 1894 renamed the college after Lady Ann Radcliffe Moulson, an early benefactor of Harvard College. Arthur Gilman served as regent until his death in 1909.[21] The first building they acquired was the 1807 Ireland-McKean house, a handsome brick Federal mansion facing the Common that they named for a more recent owner, Judge Samuel P.P. Fay (see chapters 4 and 6; figure 7.76). Over the next thirty years Radcliffe acquired about twenty adjoining properties—including the Quincy elementary school and the original buildings of the Cambridge School for Girls and the Browne & Nichols School—to form Radcliffe Yard (see chapter 7; figure 7.77). The west end of the future Radcliffe Yard was cleared first, and construction of the campus began in 1898 with Hemenway Gymnasium (renamed Knafel Center in 2013).[22] Agassiz Hall, which contained a theater and an elegant second floor room for college functions, followed in 1904, and in 1907 a grant from Andrew Carnegie funded the library.

Harvard professor Le Baron Russell Briggs began teaching at Radcliffe in 1880, served as dean from 1891 to 1902, and succeeded Mrs. Agassiz as president in 1903. Briggs was a part-time president until 1923, simultaneously serving as dean of the Faculty of Arts and Sciences at Harvard. During his term, Radcliffe asked to be made a college within Harvard, but President Lowell

FIGURE 7.76 Fay House, showing the third story and additions designed by A.W. Longfellow in 1890–92 (see also figure 4.111). Photo 2015.

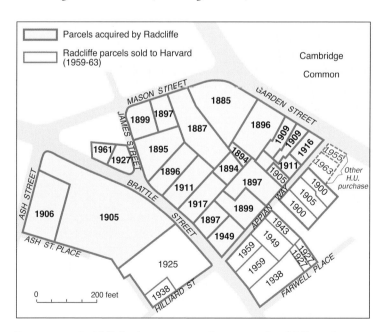

FIGURE 7.77 Radcliffe land acquisition in the vicinity of Radcliffe Yard, 1885–1959. Radcliffe sold the light-colored parcels to Harvard University in 1959, 1961, and 1963; they are now occupied by the Graduate School of Education and the Loeb Drama Center. Harvard bought the two parcels at the corner of Appian Way directly from their owners.

refused; he felt his professors were burdened by their extra teaching duties and wanted to cut Radcliffe loose entirely. Radcliffe's first full-time president, Ada Louise Comstock (1923–43), prevented this but agreed to limit the size of the college and did not pursue an expanded relationship with Harvard until after Lowell retired.

Although Radcliffe shared some architects with Harvard, it developed a distinct identity based on the tight grouping of buildings around its Yard and the light touch its designers employed; compare, for example, McKim's Radcliffe Gymnasium (1898) with the Harvard Union (1900), and Longfellow's Agassiz House (1904) with his design for Harvard's Semitic Museum (1900). In 1926 President Comstock entrusted Radcliffe's master plan to the Boston firm of Perry, Shaw & Hepburn, a significant statement of independence given President Lowell's devotion to Charles A. Coolidge. The "Master Plan for Radcliffe" called for enclosing the Yard with a series of Neo-Georgian buildings (figure 7.78)[23]. Longfellow Hall (1929, Perry, Shaw & Hepburn) and Byerly Hall (1931, Coolidge & Carlson) replaced the remaining houses on Garden Street and Appian Way. Two houses at 69 and 77 Brattle Street were slated for demolition, but by the time Radcliffe acquired the corner lot on Brattle Street in 1949 integration with Harvard had begun and the college had no need for the laboratory planned there.

Radcliffe also acquired several houses across Brattle Street; James Greenleaf's became the president's residence in 1913 (see figure 6.83). The 1926 plan envisioned a graduate center and a fine arts building east and west of Greenleaf, but only the Cronkhite Graduate Center was built on the corner of Ash Street in 1955. Harvard acquired the land east of Greenleaf for the Loeb Drama Center in 1959, leaving a handsome landscaped garden between the two buildings.

In the early years students lived at home or with local families. There was no space near the Yard for dormitories and playing fields, and the trustees probably felt that the girls should be housed as far away from Harvard men as possible. In 1900 Radcliffe purchased the Phillips and Bemis properties between Linnaean and Shepard streets and announced a new approach

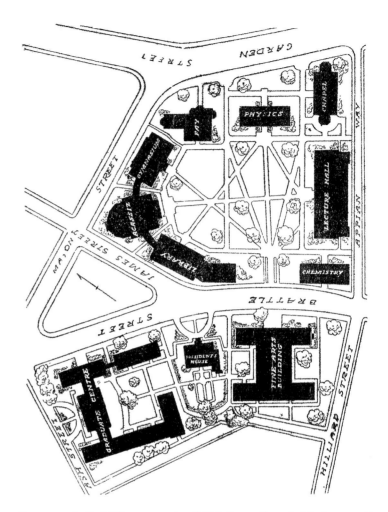

FIGURE 7.78 Radcliffe campus plan (1926, Perry, Shaw & Hepburn, architects). The proposed chapel, chemistry building, and fine arts building never materialized, but the Cronkhite Graduate Center was built in 1955 almost exactly as rendered here.

FIGURE 7.79 Radcliffe Yard, ca. 1935. The development of Radcliffe Yard ended with the construction of Longfellow and Byerly halls in 1929–31. Radcliffe razed the 1896 house at the corner of Appian Way for a parking lot in 1960.

to college housing that would avoid the isolation of students from one another in buildings without common rooms or dining facilities. "The fundamental idea ... will be to furnish the girls with the 'home' influence, and to this end the buildings will be so constructed that each girl will have full freedom of the whole house" (*Cambridge Tribune,* June 2, 1900).

Architect Guy Lowell laid out the quadrangle in 1902, and over the next thirty-five years four firms not notably favored by Harvard designed six Georgian Revival residence halls. A.W. Longfellow's Bertram and Eliot halls (1901 and 1907) established the lower edge of the quadrangle along Shepard Street (figure 7.80). Barnard and Whitman halls (1911 and 1912, Kilham & Hopkins), Briggs Hall (1923, Blackall & Elwell), and Cabot Hall (1936, Ames & Dodge) framed the quadrangle

behind them. Moors Hall closed the northern end in 1947, and Holmes and Comstock halls formed a further courtyard in 1951 and 1957. By this time all the energy had gone out of the Georgian Revival, and the later buildings are banal and formulaic examples of the style.

Harvard-trained historian Wilbur Kitchener Jordan became president in 1943. The absence of so many young men in the war made separate classes impractical, and Radcliffe women were allowed to attend Harvard for the first time. In 1952 President Conant remarked: "Harvard is not co-educational in theory, only in practice" (Howells, *A Century to Celebrate,* 27). Some buildings became redundant, and in 1961 the trustees agreed to sell Longfellow Hall and several properties on the east side of Appian Way to Harvard for the Graduate School of Education.

FIGURE 7.80 The Radcliffe Quad illustrates the gradual decline of the collegiate Georgian Revival style. The earliest buildings, A.W. Longfellow's Bertram and Eliot halls on Shepard Street (not shown), are delicate and graceful. Here, Briggs (1923, Blackall & Elwell, architects, left), and Cabot (1936, Ames & Dodge, right) frame Moors (1947, Maginnis, Walsh & Kennedy), to which Holmes (1951) and Comstock (1957, both the Maginnis firm) appear as appendages. Wolbach (1938, E.F. Heenan) to the right of Moors was built as an apartment house and acquired by Radcliffe in 1962. Photo 1973.

Mary I. Bunting, a microbiologist who served as president from 1960 until 1972, put Radcliffe on a new course. Recognizing the advantages of Harvard's residence system, she reorganized the Quad residences into houses, at first by painting their doors different colors and then by appointing house masters to revitalize student life. Women received Harvard degrees for the first time in 1963, although they were barred from Lamont Library until 1967.

Bunting retained Nelson Aldrich, a GSD-trained Modernist architect specializing in academic buildings, for a facilities study that recommended building a new library and dormitory complex on Garden Street. Radcliffe had been landbanking residential property near the Quad since the 1930s, and Bunting razed six Queen Anne houses along Garden Street for this purpose in 1964 (see figure 4.151). For Hilles Library, Radcliffe once again embraced a distinct identity by hiring Max Abramovitz of New York, who practiced a much more romantic form of Modernism than Gropius and Sert.[24] Hilles was surrounded by a deep garden moat and imaginative landscaping designed by Zion & Breen, the landscape architects responsible for Manhattan's 1967 Paley Park. The deeply recessed windows and organic forms expressed in bronze-tinted glass, limestone, and concrete were bordered by broad brick terraces behind a low brick wall along Garden Street (figure 7.81). The four pavilions of Currier House, designed in 1969 by Harrison & Abramovitz, are interconnected through a series of sunken courtyards separating them from a paved mall that runs through the block. The townhouse complex along Linnaean Street known as Faculty Row (1970, Gourley & Richardson), once praised for mediating between the Quad and the neighborhood to the north, now seems dark and dated.

Harvard and Radcliffe established coeducational residences in 1972, and in 1977 signed an agreement that gave Harvard responsibility for educating Radcliffe women. The institutions fully merged in 1999, and President Rudenstine announced the creation of a new Radcliffe Institute for Advanced Study as part of Harvard University. The Quad dormitories became undergraduate houses on a par with the River Houses, and in 2006

FIGURE 7.81 Hilles Library (1965, Harrison & Abramovitz, architects). Photo 1968.

Hilles Library was converted to a student activity center. The Radcliffe Institute retained control of Radcliffe Yard, as well as Greenleaf House, the Cronkhite Center, and the Bunting quadrangle on Concord Avenue.[25] The Institute has invested heavily in these buildings and maintains a distinct architectural identity.

SARGENT SCHOOL FOR PHYSICAL EDUCATION

Dr. Dudley Allen Sargent, a graduate of Bowdoin College and Yale Medical School, founded the Sargent School for Physical Education (now Sargent College of Boston University) in 1881. President Eliot hired Sargent in 1879 to be director of Harvard's Hemenway Gymnasium, whose previous directors had had no academic training and only given instruction in boxing, fencing, and gymnastics. Despite opposition from faculty members who disliked organized athletics, Eliot enthusiastically supported Sargent's appointment as Assistant Professor of Physical Training, a position he retained until 1919.

In 1881 Elizabeth Agassiz asked Sargent to establish a program for students of the Society for the Collegiate Instruction of

Women. Since women could not share Hemenway with Harvard men, Sargent started the Normal School of Physical Training in the old courthouse on Palmer Street. In 1883 the school occupied a stable loft on the corner of Palmer and Church streets, and Sargent convinced the landlord to construct a Mansard roof to accommodate the physical training machines, ropes, and bars that he had introduced at Harvard; he later recalled that "our old gymnasium on Church Street used to sway and vibrate so much during our exercises that parents were much alarmed for the safety of their children" (Ellis & Andrews archives, June 6, 1909; see figure 9.12). Sargent called this the "'Sanatory Gymnasium' to connote the curative as well as the more common implications of good health."

> Soft-coal smoke, the smells coming from our next-door neighbor, the livery stable, and the odors of burning leather, of horses' hoofs and old paint pots from our handy blacksmith shop were not the most pleasant aromas in the world; nor did the noises rising from the machinists' files, the carpenter's saw, and the smith's hammer form the most dulcet accompaniment to my lectures. But all these incidentals of trade had a significant bearing on the work at hand. These young people were learning that all kinds of manual labor and various physical activities had been the foundation, not only of the wealth of the republic, but also of the health and development of the majority of our people. (Sargent, in Makechnie, 39)

The Sargent School of Physical Education (as it became in 1916) trained teachers in that specialty just as Lesley College trained elementary school teachers. Sargent's relationship with President Eliot facilitated the purchase of property on Everett Street near Massachusetts Avenue, where he erected a five-story brick building in 1904 (figure 7.82). Sargent also acquired houses at 6, 15, and 19 Everett Street, 14–16 Mellen Street, 3 Sacramento Street, and 1593–1595 Massachusetts Avenue for dormitories (see figure 4.196). In 1929 Dr. Sargent's son gave the school to Boston University, which erected Lennox Hall, a dormitory, at the latter site in 1931. In 1958 BU relocated the Sargent School to its Boston campus and sold the buildings to Harvard. Lennox

FIGURE 7.82 Sargent School for Physical Education, 8 Everett Street. From right to left, the Frances Saunders house, 6 Everett Street (1875); the classroom building (1904, George Tilden, architect); and the gymnasium (1913, Kendall, Taylor & Co.). The gymnasium and classroom building maximized the constrained site by taking advantage of Jarvis Field for light and air. Harvard University razed all of these buildings to build a parking garage in 1968. Photo 1968.

became the Law School's Wyeth Hall, and 3 Sacramento Street became a cooperative dormitory. Harvard razed the gymnasium in 1968 for the Everett Street Garage and Wyeth Hall in 2007 for the new Wasserstein Hall law school building.

LESLEY UNIVERSITY

Lesley University was founded as a privately owned training school for kindergarten teachers. Edith Lesley (1874–1953) arrived from Maine in 1891. She learned Friedrich Fröbel's doctrine of kindergarten education in Boston and studied philosophy as a special student at Radcliffe before becoming principal of the Houghton elementary school. She started the Lesley Normal School in 1909 with nine students who met in her parents' rented house at 29 Everett Street. Following city policy, she had to resign as principal in 1912 when she married Merl Wolfard, a mechanical engineer and graduate of the Lawrence Scientific School, but her thriving school graduated forty-three young women in 1913.

Lesley purchased her parents' home in 1915 and added a brick classroom wing in 1926 (figure 7.83). The school expanded by acquiring nearby houses, and by 1930 it owned four contiguous properties at the corner of Oxford Street that became the core of its future campus. The Lesley School incorporated as a nonprofit institution in 1941 and began to grant baccalaureate degrees in 1944; as Lesley College it awarded its first graduate degrees in 1955. The focus of the all-female student body remained on teacher training. In 1949 the school purchased the Concord Avenue campus of the Cambridge School of Weston and opened

the Lesley-Ellis School as demonstration schools, where student teachers could experiment with new educational methods.[26]

The city rezoned the Agassiz neighborhood in 1942 to allow buildings up to 85 feet high. Lesley razed two houses to put up its first new building, Trentwell Mason White Hall, in 1957 (figure 7.84).[27] The college targeted the Everett-Mellen-Wendell blocks as its future campus and accelerated its purchases after a 1962 rezoning removed the height limit and increased the allowable density. In 1967 the school received permission from the city to close the Oxford end of Mellen Street, and the next year it demolished eight houses to make way for two dormitory and classroom buildings that were the first phase of a planned "urban academic village" (*Chronicle*, Sept. 30, 1971; figure 7.85).

FIGURE 7.83 Edith Lesley house, 29 Everett Street (1869). Edith Lesley's parents rented this house about 1893 and may have added the side porch in 1897. Photo 2015.

FIGURE 7.84 Lesley University, Trentwell Mason White Hall, 31 Everett Street (1957, William L. Galvin, architect). Photo 1962.

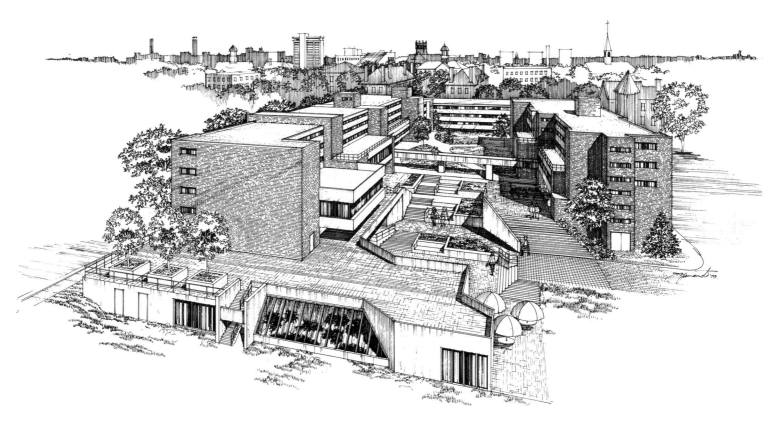

FIGURE 7.85 Lesley University, proposed National Center of Economic Education of Children (1979). The National Center (left foreground) would have joined Wolford House and Mackenzie House (1971, Smith Barker & Hanssen, architects), Trentwell Mason White Hall (center), and Doble House (1971) to create an "urban academic village" that was originally intended to include a glassed-in atrium extending from Everett to Wendell streets.

By 1978 Harvard and Lesley owned over 70 percent of the properties between Everett and Wendell streets. Encouraged by a successful downzoning north of Wendell Street in 1974 and provoked by Harvard's sale to Lesley of four houses on Mellen and Wendell streets, several residents filed a petition to reduce the height limit to 35 feet. Lesley offered to dispose of properties beyond its intended campus if Cambridge would recognize its development rights, but the city council enacted the more restrictive zoning in 1979. Lesley eventually adapted to the constraints on its core campus, embracing the Victorian character of its thirty 19th-century houses and painting them in historically appropriate colors.

In 1994 Lesley purchased the former Sears, Roebuck building in Porter Square and named it University Hall. The college merged with the Art Institute of Boston in 1998 and broadened its offerings

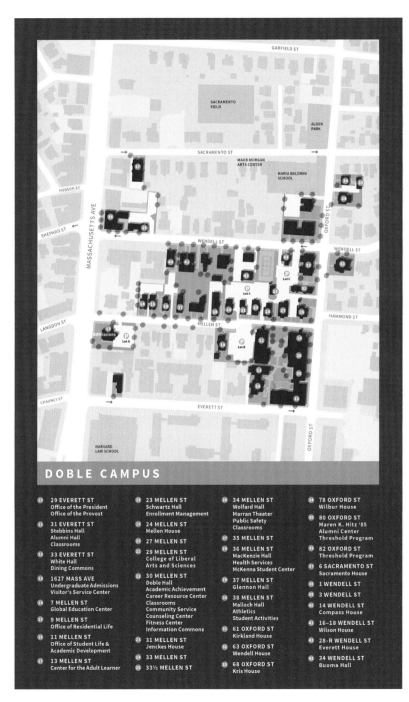

FIGURE 7.86 Lesley University's core campus in 2010.

FIGURE 7.87 Lesley University, Lunder Arts Center, 1801 Massachusetts Avenue (2011, Bruner/Cott & Associates, architects). The former North Prospect Congregational Church was lowered to the height of its original foundation, moved to one side, and restored to its earlier appearance with a replica of the 1906 cupola and restoration of long-absent acroteria, finials, and column capitals (see figures 4.178 and 7.16). The interior was repurposed as a library and given a glass and steel link to a new studio and art gallery building. Photo 2015

to include programs in counseling, human services, art therapy, and management. When it became Lesley University in 2000 about 2,600 undergraduates were enrolled in Cambridge along with about 6,000 graduate students at locations in fifteen states.

Lesley received a transformational bequest of $136 million in 2007, and a year later entered into a $33.5 million condominium agreement with the Episcopal Divinity School. In 2008 Lesley built its first new dormitories in many years at 1 and 3 Wendell Street. In 2011 it obtained city approval to move the former North Prospect Congregational Church on Massachusetts Avenue on its lot and construct a new classroom and studio wing for the Art Institute of Boston. The Lunder Arts Center opened in 2015 (figure 7.87).

CAMBRIDGE SCHOOL OF ARCHITECTURE AND LANDSCAPE ARCHITECTURE

The Cambridge School of Domestic Architecture and Landscape Architecture was founded in 1916 to provide professional training for women. When Katherine Brooks, a 1915 Radcliffe graduate, was denied admission to Harvard's School of Architecture, Professor James S. Pray recruited Henry Frost, a 1905 Harvard graduate who was Professor Langford Warren's assistant, to tutor her. A year later, Frost began the Cambridge School with six students who followed a three-and-a-half-year curriculum and then served apprenticeships. By 1918 seventeen young women were "studying to learn how to build an ideal small house and surround it with the ideal grounds" (*Boston Globe,* Feb. 24, 1918). The early emphasis on domestic architecture soon faded, the name of the school was simplified, and courses on town planning and urban housing were added in 1918.

Frost received his master's degree in architecture in 1918 and took on Eleanor Raymond, a recent Cambridge School graduate, as a partner in Frost & Raymond in 1919. Frost recalled that the school's approach reflected a movement among younger members of the profession who sought to break down barriers between architects, landscape architects, and structural engineers; it was "caught up in a small eddy of a greater movement in which women were beginning to demand equal educational rights with their brothers" (Anderson, 9).

Frost and Bremer Pond, an instructor in landscape architecture, initially held classes in their office at 5 Kennedy Street. In 1928 alumna Faith Bemis purchased the Torrey Hancock House at 53 Church Street from the Cantabrigia Club and leased it to the school for a nominal sum. Frost & Raymond designed a two-story brick addition with drafting rooms that accommodated up to sixty students and fifteen faculty, most of whom also taught at Harvard or M.I.T. (figure 7.88).

The Cambridge School began to seek affiliation with another institution in 1928. Most trustees favored a relationship with Radcliffe, but President Comstock was reluctant to proceed without the approval of President Lowell. The school instead

FIGURE 7.88   Cambridge School of Architecture (1928, Frost & Raymond, architects), and the Torrey Hancock house, 53 Church Street (1827). Benjamin Thompson Associates renovated both buildings for the Harvard Division of Continuing Education in 2001. Photo 2009.

affiliated with Smith College, which granted professional degrees to all its past graduates in 1934. In 1938 the trustees sought an outright merger. This time President Conant was amenable, but Smith's trustees were impatient, and the Cambridge School became a program of its graduate school. In 1942 a new administration in Northampton demanded that the Cambridge School raise a substantial sum or close at once. Harvard agreed to admit its students to the Graduate School of Design, and the school closed before the end of the year.

Cambridge School graduates achieved great success in what was still considered a man's profession. Katherine Brooks, Henry Frost's first student, graduated in 1919 and returned for a master's degree in landscape architecture in 1934; known as Katherine Brooks Norcross, she lectured and designed gardens for many years. Eleanor Raymond, who grew up on Ellery Street and graduated from Wellesley College in 1909, established her own practice in 1928; she designed several houses in Cambridge, as well as an early Bauhaus-derived house in Belmont in 1931 and a solar house in Dover, Massachusetts, in 1948 (see figure

6.193). Grace Kirkwood taught at the Rhode Island School of Design and had an international practice as a landscape architect; she designed the serpentine garden wall at the corner of Brattle Street and Fresh Pond Parkway in 1956. Sarah Pillsbury Harkness became a principal of The Architects Collaborative.

Longy School of Music

Georges Longy (1868–1930), principal oboist of the Boston Symphony Orchestra, founded the Longy School of Music in Boston in 1915. He returned to France in 1925, and the school continued under his daughter, Renée Longy-Miquelle, who in 1930 relocated it to a now-demolished house at 44 Church Street; faculty and students gave concerts at Brattle Hall. The school purchased the Edwin Abbot house at 1 Follen Street in 1937 (see figure 6.152). In 1965 Huygens & Tappé designed the adjacent Pickman Hall in a contemporary style but made it compatible with the old building by cloaking it with a rich tapestry of tawny orange brick (figure 7.89). Longy restored the 1905 Erasmus D. Leavitt house at 33 Garden Street (now the Rey-Waldstein Building) for additional classrooms and studios in 1998. The school merged with New York's Bard College in 2011.

Figure 7.89 Edward M. Pickman Concert Hall, Longy School of Music, 27 Garden Street (1968, Huygens & Tappé, architects). The design was published in 1966, but it was not built until 1968. Rendering 1965.

The Massachusetts legislature chartered the American Academy of Arts and Sciences in 1780 to "cultivate every art and science which may tend to advance the interest, honor, dignity and happiness of a free independent and virtuous people" (Province Laws, 1779–80, ch. 46). Like similar organizations devoted to promoting agriculture, navigation, and other practical arts, the academy declined during the 19th century as the initiative for research shifted to universities. Dr. Edwin Land, founder of the Polaroid Corporation, assumed the presidency in 1951 and made it a prestigious clearinghouse for interdisciplinary communication among its approximately 2,000 elected members. In 1976 the Academy announced that it would move from Jamaica Plain to a new building at Science Park, next to the Museum of Science. When this proved impractical it secured a ninety-nine-year lease of the Norton's Woods at Shady Hill, where Harvard's development plans had been stymied since it demolished the Charles Eliot Norton house in 1955 (see chapter 4).

The Academy's building, which was funded by Dr. and Mrs. Land and their Rowland Foundation, was designed by Boston's Kallman, McKinnell & Wood, architects of Boston's Brutalist City Hall (1968). The Academy asked for a design that would "respect old and new aesthetics, combine the traditional with the innovative, and correspond to the character of the academy, devoted to the exploration of past, present and future values"— a charge that Ada Louise Huxtable pointed out would have caused an architect "in the days of High Modernism ... to fall flat on his face" (*New York Times,* Sept. 20, 1981). The architects responded by combining traditional materials of wood, brick, and copper to create a design embodying great warmth and suitability for its function. Set in a landscape designed by Carol R. Johnson, the design won the Boston Society of Architects' prestigious Harleston Parker award in 1982 (figure 7.90).

Figure 7.90 American Academy of Arts and Sciences, 136 Irving Street (1980, Kallman, McKinnell & Wood, architects). Photo 1980.

CHARITABLE INSTITUTIONS AND HOSPITALS

In the early years of settlement the parish provided charitable assistance to the needy, but after about 1663 the town paid to board poor and distressed individuals with private families. This arrangement prevailed until 1779, when the town decided that paupers could be more effectively served if they were gathered into one facility.[28] The selectmen purchased a dwelling at 64 Kennedy Street for a workhouse in 1779 but sold it in 1785 and built a "Poor's House" at the corner of Cedar and Harvey streets (Paige, 219). Later poorhouses were located in Cambridgeport, Riverside, and North Cambridge but never again in Old Cambridge proper (see chapter 9 and *Report Five: Northwest Cambridge*, 131–33).

In 1874 James Huntington, a jeweler in Harvard Square, established a home for destitute children on Avon Hill Street. Preference was given to orphans and foundlings; boys over seven and girls over twelve were not admitted. The Avon Home had room for ten children under the care of a matron; in 1879 an addition increased its capacity to twenty-five (figure 7.91). In 1891 the trustees purchased a lot facing Mount Auburn Hospital and built an orphanage that accommodated forty children (figure 7.92). The Avon Home began placing children in foster homes in 1902, and the success of this approach prompted the board to close the orphanage in 1913. The organization continued as a child placement agency now known as Cambridge Family & Children's Services. The building burned in 1919 and was replaced by twelve two-family houses on Longfellow Road in 1923–25.

In 1896 the Trustees of the Cambridge Homes for Aged People acquired land on Mt. Auburn Street to replace their outmoded Old Ladies' Home at 185 Hancock Street. Construction began in 1898 on a building with separate wings for men and women (figure 7.93). The wings enclosed a sun porch and a south-facing garden for the enjoyment of residents. The isolated location offered peace and quiet, cool breezes from the river, and a hospital next door, but the extension of Gerry's Landing Road

FIGURE 7.91 The Avon Home, 32 Avon Hill Street (1874). The original building was indistinguishable from a typical Italianate house; the side gabled wing was added in 1879. Image ca. 1886.

FIGURE 7.92 The Avon Home, 309 Mt. Auburn Street (1891, Andrews Jaques & Rantoul, architects; demolished 1919). The Lowell School is visible in the right background. Photo ca. 1895.

FIGURE 7.93   Cambridge Homes for Aged People, 360 Mt. Auburn Street (1898, William E. Chamberlin and Stickney & Austin, architects; addition at right, 1912, W.D. Austin). Gerry's Landing Road now runs in the foreground. Photo 1944.

up the grassy swale from the river in 1951 made the site considerably less attractive (see figures 5.44–5.45). Wards and small bedrooms with shared baths were converted to self-contained apartments when the building became an assisted living facility in 1997.

Mount Auburn Hospital, the city's first, was originally the Cambridge Hospital. Emily Parsons, a granddaughter of Chief Justice Theophilus Parsons of the Massachusetts Supreme Judicial Court, had served as a nurse during the Civil War. In 1867 she opened a private charity hospital for women and children on Prospect Street but closed it in 1872 for lack of funds. The legislature incorporated the Cambridge Hospital in 1871, but it existed only on paper until 1881. By that time the population had increased by 20,000, and the physicians of the city "were sending more than a hundred patients annually to a single Boston hospital" (*Dedication,* 10). Fundraising resumed, and the trustees led by Dr. Morrill Wyman examined sites on Reservoir Hill, at Fresh Pond, and at Captain's Island before settling on a nine-acre plot on the Charles River near Gerry's Landing in

1881.[29] This remnant of Symonds' Hill was about 25 feet above the river and well positioned to catch the westerly breezes (see chapter 4). Construction of the first building began in 1884.

Designed by William E. Chamberlin of Cambridge and opened in 1886, the hospital initially consisted of a three-story center pavilion (now the Parsons Building) flanked by one-story, sixteen-patient wards connected by loggias that were glassed in during the winter (figure 7.94). The first floor of the main block held offices, a staff dining room, and an emergency room. Private rooms filled the second floor, while nurses and house physicians lived on the third; underground passageways connected the wards to the morgue and the kitchen. Chamberlin collaborated with Wheelwright & Haven of Boston to design a surgical wing in 1897. It used the same brick, slate, and granite as the Parsons Building, but its special function was expressed by the large north-facing window that lighted the operating room. In 2006 the wards, which had not been used for patients since 1961, were truncated to allow construction of a parking garage. The massing and proportions of these 19th-century buildings, the color and texture of their masonry, and their location in a park-like setting at the crest of a low hill are felicitous, and they remain the most handsome part of the complex.

In 1891 an isolated two-story brick and stone "pest house" for patients with infectious diseases was placed near the river, as far from the main buildings as possible (figure 7.95). For some years this was the only place in the city where patients with serious contagious diseases could be cared for safely.[30] The Nurses' Home, now the Clark Building, was constructed in three stages. The present east block, designed by Chamberlin in 1896, repeats the broad eaves and blocky shape of the Parsons Building. Establishment of a school of nursing in 1904 required substantial enlargement. The present central block, designed by Charles Cogswell in 1917, is considerably larger than the original but continues the projecting eaves, size and spacing of windows, and shortened attic story of the 1896 building. The west and south wings, designed by Kendall, Taylor & Company in 1928, completed the building.

FIGURE 7.94 Cambridge (now Mount Auburn) Hospital, 330 Mt. Auburn Street (1884–86, William E. Chamberlin, architect). Photo ca. 1896.

FIGURE 7.95 Cambridge Hospital isolation ward, 330 Mt. Auburn Street (1891, Chamberlin & Austin, architects). The isolation ward was demolished in 1959 for an extension of Wyman House. Photo ca. 1900.

Mount Auburn Hospital, as it became in 1946, expanded throughout the 20th century. Charles Cogswell designed the three-story Fisk Building in 1912 and an outpatient building in 1916 (figure 7.96). The five-story Wyman House of 1928 received a six-story wing in 1959 and a one-story laboratory in 1963, both by Markus & Mocka. Further expansion in 1969 required demolition of the east end of the campus. These

FIGURE 7.96 Aerial view of the Mount Auburn Hospital complex, ca. 1950. The Cambridge Homes is at the lower-right-hand corner; Harvard's Stillman Infirmary is at the upper left. The photo predates the extension of Memorial Drive and the construction of Gerry's Landing Road.

FIGURE 7.97 Mount Auburn Hospital in 2011. The Stanton Building and garage (2005, Tsoi/Kobus & Associates, architects) in the center of the complex were completed in 2008. Photo 2011.

facilities, designed by Perry, Dean & Stewart, provided a garage for 500 cars, a three-story office building for ninety doctors, and a ten-story medical support building on stilts.

A challenging national health care environment in the early 1990s led many hospitals to seek economies of scale through mergers and consolidation of services. Mount Auburn, which had become the dominant community hospital in Cambridge and surrounding towns, merged with Boston's Beth Israel and Deaconess hospitals in 1996. This alliance was soon restructured and the hospital remains an independent entity. The 2005 Stanton Building, the hospital's first new addition since 1971, replaced four-bed units with single-occupancy patient rooms and consolidated cardiac services in one location (figure 7.97).

Brewer's Block, 28–32 Brattle Street (1868; demolished 1930), ca. 1875.
See figure 8.18.

8 COMMERCIAL ARCHITECTURE

Harvard Square has been the business center of Old Cambridge for over 350 years. The earliest commerce took place in buildings that combined living spaces with shops for trade and industry; single-purpose business blocks appeared after the Civil War. Today the Square's commercial character dates largely from the late 19th and early 20th centuries. Most late 20th century development took place on the outskirts of the historic village, on former marshland once devoted to transportation and industry and along Massachusetts Avenue toward Central Square. By the end of the century, historic preservation measures steered developers toward more intensive use of existing sites and incremental replacement of less-significant buildings.

INNS, TAVERNS, AND HOTELS

The earliest known commercial establishment in Old Cambridge was Deacon Thomas Chesholm's tavern on the corner of Winthrop and Dunster streets, next to the meetinghouse. His license, granted by the General Court on September 8, 1636, allowed him "to keepe a house of intertainmente at Newe Towne." In 1637–38, Nicholas Danforth, a selectman and representative to the General Court, was "allowed to sell wine and strong water," or spirits, at his house on Bow Street, but he soon died, and a similar license was granted to Deacon Nathaniel Sparhawke on Kennedy Street in 1639 (Paige, 223). All three were considered "grave and respectable persons" whose probity

assured the community that intoxicating drinks would be dispensed responsibly, including at selectmen's meetings where the town paid for the food and drink (Hurd, 193).

In 1652 Andrew Belcher was licensed to sell "beer and bread for the entertainment of strangers and the good of the town" (Paige, 224). Unlike most such establishments, which came and went with their owners, Belcher's Blue Anchor Tavern remained in business for nearly 200 years and was long the favored venue for selectmen's meetings, whose "patronage of the bar ... probably paid for the use of the rooms" (Paige, 225). The first location of the Blue Anchor is not known; the second, after 1671, was at the northeast corner of John F. Kennedy and Mt. Auburn streets. Joseph Bean, a Boston innkeeper, took over in 1731. In 1737 he moved across the street into a square, low-studded, wood-frame house built in 1699, with a broad gambrel roof facing the street and a formidable many-flued chimney; a back door opened onto a stable yard off Brattle Street (figure 8.1). Successive owners added a two-story range of rooms to the south and a small shop to the north. Israel Porter, Bean's bartender, bought the place in 1796 and in 1820 built a brick house on the corner facing the Square. The Blue Anchor closed after Porter died in 1837, and the building became a notorious tenement that was "successfully fired by an incendiary" in 1850 (*Cambridge Chronicle*, Jan. 8, 1850).[1] The stable was rebuilt in 1887 to extend from Kennedy to Brattle streets and was adapted for retail use in the early 20th century (see figures 3.36 and 3.54).

FIGURE 8.1 Blue Anchor (Porter's) Tavern, 17 John F. Kennedy Street (1699). This site was occupied by Corcoran's Department Store after 1948 and by Urban Outfitters after 1987. Photo ca. 1856–59.

Other taverns, notably Steadman's (1731–90) to the south on Kennedy Street and the Brattle Square Inn (1699–1727) clustered nearby. Further away, the Red Lion Inn (1794) stood on the north side of Cambridge Common at the corner of Waterhouse Street and Massachusetts Avenue; an 1809 view shows a structure indistinguishable from a substantial house of the period (see figure 4.130). Opened a year after the West Boston Bridge, the Red Lion was a stop for the daily Boston stagecoach. The building was moved to 10 Wendell Street in 1863 and demolished in 1929.

Willard's Tavern, the most celebrated hostelry of the early 19th century village, opened on Massachusetts Avenue at the corner of Dunster Street in 1797. In contrast to the Blue Anchor's location on the old road to Boston via Roxbury, Willard's stood on the road to the West Boston Bridge. The first proprietor, Major John Brown, came into the property through his marriage to Elizabeth, a daughter of Zechariah Bordman, whose ancestors had settled there in 1668. Abel and Charles Willard, natives of Ashburnham, bought the tavern in 1826. One 19th century observer characterized the difference between it and the Blue Anchor:

Willard's was the resort of the moderns … men whose memories were of General Bonaparte, of the Embargo and the last war. Porter's tavern was the presumable resort of the ancients, whose remembrance might reach back to Bunker Hill, or possibly to the massacre at Fort William Henry. (John Holmes, in Hurd, 3)

The location was ideal for a transportation-related business. Abel Willard ran the Cambridge Stage Company's omnibuses from the tavern from 1839 until 1857, after which it served as a street railway waiting room until 1912. Willard's and the neighboring brick store were demolished for the Cambridge Savings Bank in 1923 (see figure 9.28).

In the 19th century the scarcity of overnight accommodations in Old Cambridge was widely noted. In 1825 the Harvard Corporation discussed building a hotel where College House now stands, but nothing came of it. Willard's operated as a hotel for a few years, but by 1847 the *Chronicle* commented that visitors had to stay at "the notorious Porter's" in North Cambridge or seek accommodation in a neighboring village (Aug. 26).[2] John Langdon Sibley concurred: "the want of some kind of a public house has been felt very seriously for eight or ten years, there not having been a place during that time where a stranger could apply for a meal of victuals or a lodging" (*Journal,* June 29, 1850).

Old Cambridge celebrated when Lyman Willard, proprietor of a popular summer resort at Fresh Pond, opened the Brattle House hotel in 1850 (figure 8.2). Constructed of wood "sanded and blocked in imitation of Jersey freestone," it contained 106 rooms in a massive square structure three stories tall that loomed over Brattle Square (Middlesex Deeds 550/344). Richly decorated and elegantly finished, it had separate entrances, reception rooms and parlors for men and women, a dining room with a 17-foot ceiling, and a spacious kitchen. The bathing facilities were "fitted up in good style and … constantly supplied with hot and cold water" that was pumped from a "never failing spring on the premises" (*Chronicle,* May 16, 1850).

The Brattle House closely resembled Boston's Tremont House, designed in 1828 by Isaiah Rogers, but did not share its

FIGURE 8.2 Brattle House hotel, Brattle Square (1849, J.B. Merrick, architect). Photo before 1865.

only transient hotel in Old Cambridge was the Packard at 12–14 Eliot Street (figure 8.3).[3] A widow, Mrs. Jennie Packard, took over a rooming house in 1897 in a tenement that was already two decades old. Such was the demand for respectable lodgings that she built an annex at 14A Eliot in 1900, giving her more than 100 rooms to rent (see figure 3.18). The English novelist Arnold Bennett was not impressed; in 1911 he observed that Cambridge "must be the only city of its size and amenity in the United States without an imposing hotel" (Bennett, 63).

Civic boosters considered a modern hotel desirable, not only for business travelers and college visitors but also for the role it could play in the city's social life. The extension of streetcar service over the new Harvard Bridge in 1890 made Back Bay establishments like the Vendome a magnet for Cambridge society. However, the university still valued the city's relative isolation from urban distractions and discouraged such initiatives. Promoters hoping to build a hotel on Massachusetts Avenue opposite Beck Hall asserted that it would be "conducted on no-license principles" (*Chronicle*, May 18, 1901). Their plans called for a

success. Although it was reported in 1851 that the hotel "is now recovering from its reverses and bids fair to become all that its projectors and friends have desired," it never prospered (*Chronicle,* Jan. 2, 1851). Harvard University bought it in 1857 for a law school dormitory and "let the basement for a restaurant to [Joshua Bowen] Smith, the colored man who is so celebrated throughout Massachusetts for serving excellent dinners on public occasions" (Sibley, *Journal*, Apr. 22, 1857). This arrangement did not work out either, and Harvard sold the property in 1865. A printing firm occupied the building until it was demolished in 1896 (see chapter 9).

For many years, no other hotels operated in Old Cambridge, and the passage of a no-license law in 1886 crippled the hospitality business. Some visitors patronized boarding houses, but most travelers chose modern accommodations in Boston, only a half-hour horsecar ride away. At the turn of the century, the

FIGURE 8.3 Hotel Packard, 12–14 Eliot Street (1869). Photo 1909.

seven-story "structure of Florentine design" with 200 rooms, elevators, banquet halls, private dining rooms, and "the usual accessories of a high-class modern hotel providing for transient as well as permanent guests" (figure 8.4). Hedging their bets, the proponents announced that "if for any reason it should not succeed as a hotel, [it] could be successfully used as a [private] dormitory" (ibid., Apr. 13, 1901). The *Chronicle's* warning that the promoters would have trouble overcoming "the Cambridge 'hoodoo' … which is an active participant in all movements in the city which are in any way a departure from the staid and ordinary methods in vogue" came true (June 15, 1901). The backers withdrew after the mayor, the school superintendent, and Harvard's President Eliot announced their opposition.

After World War I, Cambridge builder John J. Shine overcame the hoodoo and built three hotels in quick succession, the Commander in 1926 and the Continental and the Ambassador in 1928–29. The Commander and the Continental, two blocks apart on Garden Street north of the Common, were intended to operate jointly and serve both a residential and transient clientele (early plans included a connecting tunnel); the Ambassador, at 1737 Cambridge Street, was primarily a residential hotel. All three were nondescript brick blocks with banal Georgian Revival details, but Shine gave the Commander a historic theme by installing a replica of Mount Vernon's facade at the entrance (figures 8.5–8.6). A later owner, Frank A.K. Boland, acquired a copy of Houdon's statue of George Washington for the courtyard and commissioned a bas-relief of the general taking command of the troops in 1775; the plaster original was installed in the lobby and a bronze casting placed on Cambridge Common (see figure 5.21). The Commander became affiliated with the Sheraton hotel chain in 1955 and was acquired by the Guleserian family in the 1960s.

The Continental, operated by hotelier Chauncey Depew Steele Jr., became the preferred venue for weddings and community functions in part because it had a 140-car parking garage. Harvard University purchased both the Ambassador and the Continental in the 1970s. The Ambassador became Coolidge Hall, which Harvard razed in 2003 for the Center for Government and

FIGURE 8.4 Proposed Imperial Hotel, 1190 Massachusetts Avenue (1901, Little, Browne & Moore, architects). This site is now occupied by the Longfellow Court apartments, erected in 1916.

International Studies (figure 8.7). Architect Jonathan Levi adapted the Continental for graduate student apartments in 2004.

In 1960 a new type of hotel, the motor lodge, appeared in Eliot Square. John Briston Sullivan constructed a seventy-three-room, four-story, red brick Treadway Inn on piers over a municipal parking lot on the site of the City Building, which had been demolished in 1935 (see chapter 2). A year later the Harvard Square Motor House, an independent venture that operated as a Holiday Inn, was built at 1637–1653 Massachusetts Avenue. This six-story brick and metal-clad structure designed by local architect Maurice A. Reidy also stood over a parking lot; it became a Harvard Law School dormitory in 1992. Steele intended to build a three-story motel called the Continental Motor Gardens at 14 Concord Avenue in 1963 but instead put up a fourteen-story luxury apartment house (see figure 6.238). Community opposition stopped a proposed eighteen-story Holiday Inn on Mt. Auburn Street in 1972, and the site was eventually developed as University Place (see figure 3.84).

FIGURE 8.5 Commander Hotel, 16 Garden Street (1926, Silverman, Brown & Heenan, architects). Photo 1935.

FIGURE 8.6 Commander Hotel entrance, with a replica of the facade of George Washington's Mount Vernon. Photo 1927.

FIGURE 8.7 Ambassador Hotel, 1737 Cambridge Street (1928, Edward Heenan, architect; demolished 2003). Photo 1937.

FIGURE 8.8 The Inn at Harvard, 1201 Massachusetts Avenue (1990, Graham Gund Architects). The delicate Postmodern details of the facade echo McKim, Mead & White's Georgian Revival Harvard Union across Harvard Street. Photo 2009.

FIGURE 8.9 Veritas Hotel, 1131 Massachusetts Avenue (2007, Boyes-Watson Architects). The original Mansard house of 1869, which was remodeled with bow windows and an additional floor by Little, Browne & Moore in 1893, was razed in 2008 and replaced with this partial replica. Photo 2014.

A luxury hotel finally opened at Charles Square in 1985. Designed by Cambridge Seven Associates, the Charles Hotel contains 300 rooms in a brick and glass building that steps back from Eliot Square (see figure 3.81). In 1990–91, Harvard University built The Inn at Harvard, a 116-room, four-story hotel on the former site of Beck Hall (figure 8.8). Graham Gund Associates' original design was a muscular five-story building that, like Beck Hall, would have provided a visual terminus for this section of Massachusetts Avenue, but a contentious community review process diminished the design. The hotel was designed to allow for eventual conversion to faculty offices, but in 2013–14 Harvard adapted it for dormitory use during the renewal of the River Houses.

The Veritas Hotel at 1131 Massachusetts Avenue, completed in 2010, reflected a trend toward boutique hotels. A large Mansard house on the site had been updated in the Colonial Revival style in 1893. The Cambridge Historical Commission rejected a contemporary design, but it allowed the building to be replaced by a replica with an additional floor and a modern wing (figure 8.9).

The initial focus of commerce in Cambridge was Water (now Dunster) Street, which led from the ferry landing past the First Meetinghouse. After construction of the Great Bridge in 1660, trade moved to Kennedy Street. Harvard College's purchase of its first building north of the village in 1638, the relocation of the meetinghouse in 1650, and the construction of the courthouse in 1708 encouraged a further shift toward Harvard Square. The completion of the West Boston Bridge in 1793 introduced a new route through the village and reinforced the drawing power of the meetinghouse, courthouse, and college. Only in the 20th century did trade expand significantly beyond Harvard and Brattle squares.

The earliest commercial buildings were constructed of wood, had a distinctly domestic character, and often served multiple purposes. Among the town's first retailers were Andrew Bordman, who kept a store in his father's house on the east corner of Dunster Street and Massachusetts Avenue beginning about 1640, and his brother Aaron, who had a locksmith and clock shop on the west corner. Also on Dunster Street were Edward Marrett's tailor shop and Edmund Angier's woolen-draper's shop. In each case the proprietor conducted business and lived on the premises. Joseph Stacy Read's three-story house (1782–90) contained a shop and a post office. Similar buildings, including Willard's Tavern (1797) and the Read-Bartlett-Beals house and store on Farwell's Corner (ca. 1792–1800), were constructed east and west of the Read house in the prosperous years after the opening of the West Boston Bridge (figure 8.10; see also figure 3.33). Later in the 19th century home and workplace separated, as students and junior faculty rented upper floors and retail stores expanded behind plate-glass storefronts. A demand for offices, such as those occupied by the Union Railway in Whitney's Block, developed after the Civil War; the first office buildings in the modern sense were put up by banks in the early 20th century.

One frame building survives from this early period of commercial development. Levi Farwell put up a row of three stores

FIGURE 8.10 Massachusetts Avenue looking east from Farwell's Corner, ca. 1870. From right to left are the broad-gabled Read-Bartlett-Beals house and store (ca. 1792–1800, here as remodeled in 1855); the Joseph Read house (ca. 1782–90); Willard's Tavern (1797); and William Brown's store (ca. 1816). All but the last of these buildings would be remodeled as the Read Block in 1896 (see figure 3.34). The brick building on the opposite corner of Dunster Street is Little's Block (1854; see figure 3.14).

on Brattle Street in 1829 that completed the cluster of commercial buildings ringing Harvard Square. Thomas Russell, a furniture dealer, detached a two-bay section of the building in 1847 and moved it to the corner of Plympton Street so he could build a new brick store next to Lyceum Hall (see figure 3.15). In 1868 he moved it again to the back yard of his house on Massachusetts Avenue, where it still stands at 12 Bow Street.

Brick construction began about 1816 with William Brown's store on the corner of Dunster Street (figure 8.11). The Federal style house that Levi Farwell built at 12 Kennedy Street in 1820 and rented to Thomas Russell retains an original entrance arch and fanlight between two later storefront windows (figure 8.12). The opening of the Granite Railway in Quincy in 1826 reduced the cost of dressed granite, which was used to frame the storefronts of mercantile buildings such as Thomas Warland's block at 1320–1324 Massachusetts Avenue, designed by Boston architect William Sparrell in 1829 (figure 8.13). In 1832 Sparrell used the same plans for the first phase of College House, which Harvard built for students at its fledgling law school (figure 8.14). Here and at Holyoke House (1869), the university erected taxable mixed-use structures that were not easily distinguishable from those put up by private investors. College House was extended in 1845 and 1859 in the same Federal manner until it stretched 260 feet to Church Street (figure 8.15). A fourth story and a Mansard roof were added in 1870 (figure 8.16).

Levi Farwell's store on the corner of Kennedy Street replaced (or was remodeled from) the 1792–1800 Read-Bartlett-Beals house sometime between 1820 and 1833 (figure 8.17). The broad pediment that faced the meetinghouse predicted the coming Greek Revival style, but the fanlight, the narrow corner boards, and the absence of a frieze reflected the Federal details of the Professors Row houses built between 1822 and 1831 (see figure 6.45). Farwell's store survived until 1895, when it was remodeled with several others in a street-widening project (see figure 3.34).

Figure 8.11 William Brown store, 1372 Massachusetts Avenue (ca. 1816). William Brown operated a grocery and served as a licensed auctioneer until his death in 1862. The marker mounted between the second floor windows commemorated the site of Cambridge's first schoolhouse.

Figure 8.12 Thomas Russell house and store, 12 Kennedy Street (ca. 1820). The Russell store was restored by the Cambridge Savings Bank in 1997. Photo 2009.

FIGURE 8.13 Thomas Warland block, 1320–1324 Massachusetts Avenue (1829, William Sparrell, architect). The Warland Block originally extended to the corner of Holyoke Street, but the last bay burned in 1873 and was rebuilt by James M. Hilton in 1875. The remainder was replaced by the Porcellian Club in 1890. Photo ca. 1885–90.

FIGURE 8.15 College House, 1408–1446 Massachusetts Avenue, as extended in 1845 and 1859. Photo 1867.

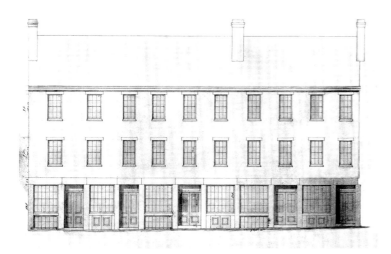

FIGURE 8.14 College House I, 1408–1414 Massachusetts Avenue (1832, William Sparrell, architect). For this commission Sparrell essentially repeated the design he had used for Warland's project three years previously.

FIGURE 8.16 College House, with the Mansard roof added in 1870. Photo ca. 1875.

FIGURE 8.17 Farwell's Store, 1384–1392 Massachusetts Avenue (ca. 1830). Kennedy Street is at right. Photo ca. 1870.

FIGURE 8.18 Brewer's Block, 28–32 Brattle Street (1868; demolished 1930). Brattle Street is in the foreground; Mt. Auburn Street is at right. Photo ca. 1875.

The Mansard style that became ubiquitous in residential architecture after the Civil War also appeared in commercial buildings. Thomas Brewer's exuberant 1868 Mansard block at 28 Brattle Street featured a panoply of elegant finishes, including flush-boarding sanded and scored to imitate masonry, storefronts with tall, narrow windows in stilted arches, and a fish-scale shingled roof with multiple dormers that demonstrated the great flexibility available to designers working with wood construction (figure 8.18). Richard Dolton, a merchant tailor, put up a restrained brick Mansard that featured Neoclassical pediments over the windows and the cast-iron piers and entablatures that replaced granite after the Civil War (figure 8.19). On a smaller scale, baker William Wright built an "elegant and substantial brick building" at the corner of Mt. Auburn and Dunster streets in 1870 "fitted up in a superb and artistic manner with every convenience for a bread and fancy cake store" (*Chronicle,* Nov. 26, 1870; figure 8.20). The university followed with the much larger Holyoke House, designed by Boston architects Ryder & Harris in a manner that, if executed in granite rather than brick, would have been at home in downtown Boston (see figure 3.14).

FIGURE 8.19 Dolton Block, 1300–1306 Massachusetts Avenue at the corner of Linden Street (1869). Merchant tailor Richard Dolton put up this three-story Mansard on the corner of Linden Street with stores on the ground floor and rooms above, but he died before it could be completed. The building survives as part of Fairfax Hall. The photo was taken before 1879, when James M. Hilton acquired the building and replaced Dolton's name with his own.

FIGURE 8.20 William Wright building, 82 Mt. Auburn Street (1870; demolished 1929). The long facade faced Dunster Street, while the bakery faced Mt. Auburn. A foundation stone at the corner commemorating the location of the First Meetinghouse was recovered from a West Cambridge landfill and reinstalled on the sidewalk in 2014. Photo ca. 1875.

The Mansard era in mercantile architecture ended when the great Boston fire of 1872 demonstrated the hazard of wood-framed roofs in dense commercial districts. In Cambridge it was followed by the Ruskinian Gothic style, first at Harvard with Memorial, Weld, and Matthews halls (1870–71) and then in the City Building (1875) and Beck Hall (1876). The largest commercial example was the four-story brick block at 13–25 Brattle Street, begun in 1875 and completed in 1877 as a joint venture by William L. Whitney, a Cambridge businessman, and Ivory Estes, a hardware dealer (figure 8.21). The brick and sandstone facade was enriched with brick belt courses, diamond-shaped panels, and a corbelled cornice. The upper floors housed a mixture of offices, flats, and light industrial uses, as well as a function hall. Nine bays of the building were demolished in 1936, but the eastern section survives, although remodeled with inappropriate replacement windows (see figure 8.43).

The Queen Anne style arrived in the prosperous 1880s with a new generation of architects that included William P. Richards and William P. Wentworth. In 1885 William Read's executors hired Richards to design "a large three-story brick block [with] four stores on the ground floor and six flats above" at 18–28 Kennedy Street (*Chronicle,* Oct. 17, 1885). Four massive Syrian arches supported a facade designed in the Panel Brick mode of the Queen Anne style (figure 8.22). As described in chapter 6, the Richards firm specialized in the Queen Anne style during this decade, designing the Stanstead apartments at 19 Ware Street in 1887 and the Jarvis at 27 Everett Street in 1890 (see figures 6.217–6.218). The firm also modernized the Read Block in 1896.

Vermont native William P. Wentworth (1839–96) trained as an architect in New York City before opening a practice in Boston in 1870; he designed many churches and the state hospital in Medfield. His most important Cambridge client was James Manter Hilton, a stove dealer turned developer of commercial blocks and private dormitories. Hilton transformed the Dolton building, which he acquired in 1879, into Hilton's Block. In 1883, 1885, and 1889 Hilton built additions at 1310–1312 and 1316 Massachusetts Avenue and 3 Linden Street, all executed in the Panel Brick mode with corbelled cornices and brownstone or Nova Scotia sandstone trim. Only 3 Linden can be definitely ascribed to Wentworth, but all the additions bear a strong resemblance to one another. For example, Manter Hall (1885), a small private dormitory at 4 Holyoke Street, shares Panel Brick detailing and Nova Scotia sandstone voussoirs with 50 Kennedy Street, which Wentworth designed in 1892. Hilton's Block was remodeled again and renamed The Fairfax in 1900 (figure 8.23; see also figure 3.25).

FIGURE 8.21 Whitney-Estes Block, 13–25 Brattle Street (1875). The left half of the building was taken down to one story in 1936. The brick wall below the bay window on the left side was exposed during renovations of the adjoining store at 27 Brattle Street in 2008. Photo March 1907.

FIGURE 8.22 Read Hall, 18–28 Kennedy Street (1885, Joseph R. and William P. Richards, architects). The arches had all been destroyed or obscured by the mid-20th century, but three were restored in 1990, 2004, and 2015. Photo ca. 1900.

FIGURE 8.23 The Fairfax, 1300–1316 Massachusetts Avenue (1869, with additions in 1883, 1885, 1889, and 1900). The original Dolton Building is at left (see figure 8.19). William P. Wentworth was probably the architect responsible for the Panel Brick additions at right and in the center. The firm of Coolidge & Carlson added two stories at the corner and unified the buildings with a continuous copper cornice in 1900. Photo ca. 1902–4.

A momentous shift to the Colonial and Georgian Revival styles occurred in the 1890s. The first commercial example in Harvard Square was John H.H. McNamee's 1894 bookbindery at 18–24 Brattle, a pastiche of Classical themes by Cambridge architect George Fogerty (figure 8.24). After Cambridge recovered from the Panic of 1893, private dormitories, not commercial buildings, attracted the most capital, and architects began exploring the Georgian Revival vocabulary of dark red brick with marble, limestone, or cast stone accents. Hampden Hall, one of the few that included stores on the ground floor, was a particularly florid example (figure 8.25).

FIGURE 8.25   Hampden Hall, 1246–1260 Massachusetts Avenue (1902, Coolidge & Carlson, architects). Built by University Associates as a private dormitory, Hampden Hall contained storefronts as well as single and double suites for about fifty students. Photo April 1909.

FIGURE 8.24 McNamee Building, 18–24 Brattle Street (1894, George Fogerty, architect). This early Colonial Revival facade with large, north-facing windows lighting workrooms was destroyed by fire in 1922. Newhall & Blevins designed a sober red brick Georgian replacement that has masonry spandrels and smaller three-part windows; natural light was no longer essential after the introduction of electricity. Photo March 1909.

The first purely commercial Georgian Revival building in Harvard Square was Edwin Abbott's 1909 project at 1 Kennedy Street, a refined expression of the style that prefigured many later projects (figure 8.26). The architects, Newhall & Blevins, were a young firm later known for their apartment houses (see chapters 2 and 6). In 1913 a committee considering the future development of Harvard Square recommended adopting the Georgian Revival style to reflect the prestige of Harvard University and establish a new architectural character for the business district (see chapter 3). George L. Dow's Brattle Building at 1–8 Brattle Street, designed by Newhall & Blevins in 1913, expressed these ideals, although the normally generous proportions of the style were subordinated to the building's commercial functions (figure 8.27).

FIGURE 8.27 Brattle Building, 1–8 Brattle Street (1913, Newhall & Blevins, architects). None of the original storefronts with fanlight transoms and broken-scroll pediments survived the 20th century. Photo ca. 1930.

FIGURE 8.26 Abbott Building, 1–7 Kennedy Street (1909, Newhall & Blevins, architects). The upper floors were designed for professional offices. Photo ca. 1910.

The Harvard Square Post Office at 38B Brattle Street, designed in 1919 by Boston architect George Nelson Jacobs, illustrated how quickly the Georgian Revival idiom began to degrade in the hands of some designers (figure 8.28; see figure 3.52). Sage's Market on the corner of Brattle and Church streets continued this trend with a plethora of inexpensive cast stone detailing: composite capitals, architrave and cornice, and a parapet with urns cluttered the design (figure 8.29). In the right hands, cast stone could have a pleasing effect, as in the pre-Moderne store that John Whouley built at 8–10 Holyoke Street in 1927, but it was more often used to construct inexpensive stores along major arteries (see figure 4.183).

The finest Georgian Revival building in Harvard Square is the Harvard Cooperative Society, designed by Perry, Shaw &

FIGURE 8.29   Sage's Market, 45 Brattle Street (1926, R. Currie Grovestein, architect). Edwin R. Sage (1884–1955) started in business in Brattle Square in 1898 and by the early 20th century had become one of Cambridge's leading grocers; the market continued in the family until 2000, when it closed. Photo ca. 1953.

FIGURE 8.28   Harvard Square Post Office, 38B Brattle Street (1919, George Nelson Jacobs, architect). Post offices in Harvard Square have always been in leased quarters. Everett contractor and investor John F. Coleman built this building to government specifications. Photo ca. 1930.

Hepburn in 1924 (figure 8.30). Established in 1882 by students dissatisfied with high prices at local shops, the Coop first operated in a basement rented from the university and sold secondhand books, stationery, furniture, and coal to heat students' rooms. The society acquired Lyceum Hall in 1904 when Harvard became concerned about protecting its tax-exempt status, but it soon found the building inadequate.

Perry, Shaw & Hepburn were notable practitioners of the Georgian Revival, and the Coop was one of their first commissions. The senior partner, William Graves Perry (1883–1975), was a Harvard graduate who had studied architecture at M.I.T. and the École des Beaux-Arts. Perry, Shaw went on to supervise

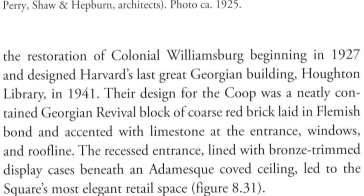

FIGURE 8.30 Harvard Cooperative Society, 1400 Massachusetts Avenue (1924, Perry, Shaw & Hepburn, architects). Photo ca. 1925.

FIGURE 8.31 Harvard Cooperative Society vestibule. Photo ca. 1925.

the restoration of Colonial Williamsburg beginning in 1927 and designed Harvard's last great Georgian building, Houghton Library, in 1941. Their design for the Coop was a neatly contained Georgian Revival block of coarse red brick laid in Flemish bond and accented with limestone at the entrance, windows, and roofline. The recessed entrance, lined with bronze-trimmed display cases beneath an Adamesque coved ceiling, led to the Square's most elegant retail space (figure 8.31).

Major changes were also taking place next door at College House, which Harvard sold in 1916. The Charles River Trust Company razed the three bays next to Lyceum Hall, and Loren Towle, a Boston investor, acquired the rest.[4] Over the next five

years the property changed hands several times. One owner announced that he would take it all down and build a new two-story structure with a 100-car garage on Church Street. Edward A. Barnard acquired the property in February 1920 with plans for a movie theater and a hotel, but he committed suicide a month later. Brookline investor Charles A. Newhall bought the building out of foreclosure in 1921. He sold the seven bays closest to the bank to Frank Brock, a hardware store owner, who remodeled them with florid Georgian details in 1922; known as the Palmer Building, this section was demolished by the Harvard Trust Company in 1956 (see figure 8.49).

Newhall remodeled the remainder into a modern office building, leaving its exterior "practically identical with its aspect in 'the Sixties'" (*Cambridge Tribune,* Mar. 29, 1924). In 1925 the city razed 23 feet of the north end to widen Church Street, and Newhall converted a storefront into a lobby for the new University Theater, designed by Boston architects Mowll & Rand for both vaudeville and moving pictures (see figure 3.45). The featureless side of the fly tower reinforced the back-street character of Church Street until 1982, when it became the main theater entrance with a *trompe l'oeil* facade. Newhall held the property until his death in 1970 and made no other major alterations except for a stainless steel canopy that was removed about 1980. New owners donated a preservation restriction to the city in 1983 and gradually restored the exterior to its appearance at the beginning of the 20th century. The theater closed in 2012.

The New England Telephone & Telegraph Company's building at 10 Ware Street was a major corporate expression of the Georgian Revival style. Built in 1932 to accommodate the large electromechanical switches associated with the introduction of dial telephones, it replaced an earlier manual exchange at 51 Inman Street (1911). The firm of Densmore, LeClear & Robbins, the designers, was founded by two Harvard engineering graduates. They initially specialized in factories, but after Harvard-trained architect Henry C. Robbins joined in 1914 they turned to department stores and office buildings. New England Telephone was a frequent client, and in 1930 the firm designed the Moderne exchange building at the head of Cambridge Street in Boston. For the Cambridge project they adopted the Georgian Revival mode of Harvard's River Houses, with an H-shaped plan, a white-painted cupola, elaborate cornices, and applied details (figure 8.32). Successive additions in 1939, 1947, and 1967 are little more than decorated boxes wrapped with red brick and given small-paned sash.

Cambridge architect William Galvin's impact on Harvard Square in the 1930s and '40s was similar to that of Newhall & Blevins in the teens and twenties.[5] His 1930 replacement for Brewer's 1871 store at 28–36 Brattle Street, known as the Hadley

FIGURE 8.32 New England Telephone & Telegraph Co., 10 Ware Street (1932, Densmore, LeClear & Robbins, architects). Photo 2015.

Building, featured Georgian appliqué that seemed to parody the sophisticated Harvard clubs nearby (figure 8.33). Only a year later, Galvin applied the neutral surfaces and light colors of the modern movement to a dry cleaning store on Dana Hill (figure 8.34). Commissions were scarce during the Depression, and his next significant commercial project came in 1936, when he remodeled an 1894 carriage factory at 23-25 Church Street by removing the upper floors and rebuilding the facade in the Art Moderne style (see figure 9.18). Internally illuminated bands outlined stepped-back panels and converged at the entrance. The dramatic lighting was an advertisement for the tenant, the Cambridge Electric Light Company, which sold appliances as well as utility service (figures 8.35–8.37).

Galvin participated in the renewal of Brattle Square by its major property owner, George L. Dow. As described in chapter 3, Dow and his partner, Harry Stearns, owned a ragged mélange of buildings between Palmer and Church streets and from 1936 to 1941 remodeled most of them into a single, unified commercial block. At 17–25 Brattle, the partners removed the upper

FIGURE 8.33 Hadley Building, 28–36 Brattle Street (1930, William L. Galvin, architect). The Hadley Building burned in 1972 and was replaced in 1974.

FIGURE 8.34 Shea Cleaners, 1016–1030 Massachusetts Avenue (1931, William L. Galvin, architect). Architect's rendering, 1931.

FIGURE 8.35 Cambridge Electric Light Co. showroom, 23–25 Church Street (1936, William L. Galvin, architect). Photo ca. 1936.

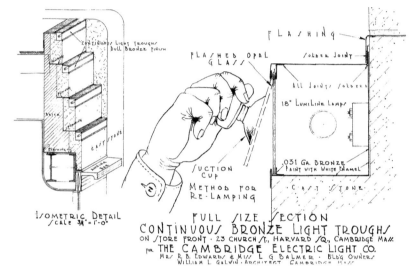

FIGURE 8.37 William L. Galvin designed the innovative lighting system using General Electric's incandescent Lumiline bulbs.

FIGURE 8.36 Cambridge Electric Light Co. showroom at night. Photo ca. 1936.

floors of Whitney's four-story brick building and had Galvin reface the remainder with a cast stone Moderne facade that set the tone for the rest of the project (figure 8.38). Boston architects Bowman Graton and Christian Born's 1938 design for the second phase at 33–37 Brattle maintained Galvin's overall horizontality but used a slightly more classical idiom. The central section at 27–31 Brattle Street, by the same architects, was completed in 1941 (see figure 3.52).

Three of Galvin's Moderne projects, the Cambridge Federal Savings & Loan building at 38A Brattle Street (1937; see figure 8.53), the Chez Dreyfus restaurant at 44 Church Street (1944), and the former Harvard Square Post Office at 38B Brattle Street that he remodeled as a Touraine's department store in 1954, are no longer standing. The Putnam Furniture building at 1045 Massachusetts Avenue, built immediately after World War II in response to the pent-up demand for home furnishings, employed glass block and neon signage to striking effect, but the exterior has since been remodeled (figure 8.39).

FIGURE 8.39 Putnam Furniture Co., 1045 Massachusetts Avenue (1946, William L. Galvin, architect). Galvin designed the present third story addition in 1957. Photo ca. 1948.

Aside from Corcoran's store at 14–16 Brattle/13–25 Kennedy streets (1949) and the 1956 addition to the Harvard Trust Company discussed below, little commercial construction occurred in the Square until 1966, when the Brattle-Mt. Auburn-Story block began to be redeveloped (see chapter 3). The great retailing innovation of the period was the "urban marketplace" concept of many small stores sharing an enclosed space. Bryant Haliday and Cyrus Harvey rented the basement of the Brattle Theater to small shops selling crafts, candles, gifts, and textiles in 1964. Adopting this idea, in 1972 Max Wasserman converted the former Union Railway stable and two 1920s parking garages into The Garage, leaving the automobile ramps in place to access three levels of small shops designed by Philip Briggs and Wilson Pollock of ADD Architects (see figure 3.64). This concept came to national attention in 1974–78 with the success of Boston's Faneuil Hall Marketplace, designed by Benjamin Thompson & Associates (BTA).

BTA's "bright glass prism on Brattle Street" was widely considered one of the best retail buildings of the 20th century (*Architectural Record*, May 1970). Winner of the 1970 Harleston Parker Medal of the Boston Society of Architects, the Design Research (D/R) building was made to showcase Thompson's contemporary furnishings store. Fully glazed walls resting on thin concrete slabs created an open architecture that minimized the traditional demarcation of exterior from interior (figure 8.40). No subsequent mixed-use building has approached this level of quality. When the Hadley Building at 28–36 Brattle burned in 1972, its owners also took advantage of an incentive in the 1962 zoning code that encouraged split-level retail space, but there the basement shops were cramped and proved difficult to rent. The brick facade and strip windows—one of the less appealing characteristics of late International Style architecture—were heavy and dark where the D/R building was light and airy. Only the curved facade alleviates the design (figure 8.41).

Although the early urban marketplace projects generated excitement among shoppers and retailers, later schemes were

FIGURE 8.40 Design Research, 46–48 Brattle Street (1969, Benjamin Thompson & Associates, architects).

FIGURE 8.41 New Hadley Building, 28–36 Brattle Street (1974, Symmes, Maini & McKee Associates, architects). Photo 2009.

unimaginative and suffered by comparison. The Galeria at 55 Kennedy Street, designed by Childs Bertram Tseckares Cansendino in 1974, was a halfhearted variant. The Atrium, designed by Sert Jackson & Associates for Louis DiGiovanni in 1978, was a more ambitious project that involved renovation and new construction to unify a number of contiguous buildings on Church and Brattle streets, but it would have been more successful had it provided a through-block passageway (figure 8.42). DiGiovanni preserved the Estes building, but Sert's new facades were awkward attempts at contextual design (figure 8.43). An enclosed shopping mall was proposed for Charles Square, but in the face of community opposition the final design included an open courtyard instead of an atrium. It remained a disappointing retail venue until the shops closed in the mid-1990s.

The public's growing appreciation for traditional urban values supported a Postmodern contextual movement in architecture that influenced many Cambridge projects in the 1980s, at least as far as cladding them in red brick. Architects began to

FIGURE 8.43 The Atrium, 9–15 Brattle Street. Photo 2009.

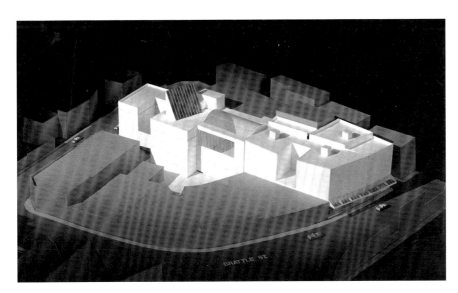

FIGURE 8.42 The Atrium, 50 Church Street and 9–15 Brattle Street (1978, Sert Jackson & Associates, architects). Model photo ca. 1978.

reject the austerity of the International Style and to give facades a greater variety of planes and fenestration; decorative elements appeared for the first time since the 1930s.[6] Where context was a primary concern, as at 1280 Massachusetts Avenue (1983), the buildings fitted comfortably into the streetscape (figure 8.44). At 104 Mt. Auburn Street, a 40,000 square foot mixed-use building facing Eliot Square, the initial design by Dimnaz Associates mimicked the strip windows of the Hadley Building. This proposal attracted the scrutiny of community groups, and a marginally better but still non-contextual design by DiMeo Associates featured a sloping, glazed facade for the top floor, red brick, and punched windows (figure 8.45). The recessed storefronts, a byproduct of the Modernist 1962 zoning code, were built out to the sidewalk in 2006.

No amount of contextual detailing was able to mitigate the size of One Brattle Square. The battle over this development in 1985–91 is discussed in chapter 3. Under the zoning then in effect—a 4.0 FAR and an 80-foot height limit—the 29,000 square foot site allowed a far more massive building than many thought desirable. Although the Harvard Square Defense Fund did manage to negotiate setbacks and other concessions from the developers, an exemption for rooftop mechanical enclosures allowed the building to exceed the height limit, and the freestanding site exposed the building to distant views that emphasize its bulk (see figure 3.95).

The contextual movement continued in 1987 with less controversy at One Mifflin Place, a five-story office building erected by Louis DiGiovanni's Trinity Realty Trust. The Architects Collaborative's use of Kane-Gonic red brick on the exterior made the design acceptable to local activists. The Poorvu family continued this approach with a building at 125 Mt. Auburn Street that replaced the post office they had built in 1953. Using the same materials, Elkus Manfredi Architects refined the residual Brutalism of One Mifflin into a more delicate and complex facade that was largely repeated at 114 Mt. Auburn Street, a 2008 design constructed in 2014–15 (figure 8.46).

FIGURE 8.44 Niles Building, 1280 Massachusetts Avenue (1983, Symmes Maini & McKee Associates, architects). Photo 1986.

FIGURE 8.45 Coolidge Bank Building, 104 Mt. Auburn Street (1983, DiMeo Associates, architects). Photo 2009.

FIGURE 8.46 Mt. Auburn-Story Building, 125 Mt. Auburn Street (2001, Elkus Manfredi Architects). Photo 2009.

BANKS

Central Square had already surpassed the old village as the town's commercial center when the Cambridge Bank was established there in 1826. Old Cambridge men such as bookseller William Hilliard, printer Eliab Metcalf, and tavernkeeper Israel Porter joined the board. Levi Farwell, the prominent Harvard Square merchant, served as president from 1828 until 1832, when he founded the Charles River Bank with Metcalf and Porter. Other investors in the new bank included Abel Willard, the omnibus proprietor, James Brown, the publisher, and Asahel Stearns, a former law professor.

The Charles River Bank issued its own currency, handled foreign and domestic exchange, held deposits of gold and silver bullion, and made loans to its shareholders to support their business activities. It initially operated from Whitney's Block in Brattle Square but soon moved to College House, on a site where its successors have done business ever since. Bank president Farwell was also steward of Harvard College, and students paid their term bills at the bank (figure 8.47).

In 1834 Farwell, William Hilliard, and others incorporated the Institution for Savings in Cambridge, now the Cambridge Savings Bank. As an early passbook stated:

FIGURE 8.47 Charles River Bank $3.00 banknote, with a vignette of Harvard Yard and the First Parish Church, 1859.

the design of this institution is to afford to those who are desirous of saving their money, but who have not acquired sufficient to purchase a share in the banks, ... the means of employing their money to advantage, without running the risk of losing it, as they are too frequently exposed to do, by lending it to individuals, who either fail or defraud them. (Allen, 2)

In its early years the Institution for Savings moved frequently, depending on who was treasurer. Depositors would go to William Hilliard's office, John Owen's University Book Store, or to William Whitney's office in Brattle Square. At various times the treasurer of the savings bank was also the cashier of the Charles River Bank, which then accommodated the customers of both institutions.

In 1864 the Charles River Bank reorganized under a federal charter and became the Charles River National Bank. It reorganized again in 1914 as the Charles River Trust Company but continued to do business in the same storefront in College

FIGURE 8.48 Harvard Trust Co., 1408 Massachusetts Avenue (1916, Charles N. Cogswell, architect). The Harvard Cooperative Society is at left; the Palmer Building (formerly part of College House) is on the right. Photo ca. 1921.

House that it first occupied in 1832. In 1916 the bank put up a one-story building on the site. Designed by Charles N. Cogswell, a Cambridge architect trained at M.I.T. and the École des Beaux-Arts, the new bank was a compact, decorative essay in the Georgian Revival style. When the Charles River Trust merged with Central Square's Harvard Trust Company in 1921, the bank's new name was spelled out in illuminated metal letters atop the parapet (figure 8.48).

Two years after the merger, the Harvard Trust Company decided to move its offices to Harvard Square and had one of its directors, Albert Blevins, design an addition. Cogswell's facade became an elaborate base for the heavily articulated brick and limestone upper stories. The new building was clumsier but more assertive than its neighbor, the Harvard Coop, and created a rank of pediments along the west side of the Square. In 1956 Harvard Trust undertook a major expansion, razing the Palmer Building, constructing a new office building and banking hall on that site, and converting the old building into retail space that it leased to the Coop (figure 8.49). Perry, Shaw, Hepburn & Dean (the firm that had designed the Coop thirty years before) unified the two buildings behind an aluminum screen that was restored by Fleet Bank in 2002 (figure 8.50).

The Institution for Savings became the Cambridge Savings Bank in 1868 and in 1873 took over a storefront in College House. In 1897 the bank constructed an opulent Renaissance Revival building designed by Clarence H. Blackall at 11–21 Dunster Street. Named Dana Chambers in honor of the bank's first salaried president, John B. Dana, it had private dormitory suites on the three upper floors (figure 8.51). In 1923 the bank acquired the corner lot and constructed its current five-story brick and limestone Georgian Revival structure. As in the earlier building, the bank initially occupied only a small portion of the ground floor (figure 8.52).

Judge Edward Counihan headed a group of investors that founded the Inman Cooperative Bank in 1913. In 1937 it reorganized as the Cambridge Federal Savings & Loan Association and hired William L. Galvin, one of its directors, to design a new

The Harvard Trust

ESTABLISHED 1860

Ten Locations in Cambridge, Arlington, Belmont and Concord

| Volume I Number 2 | Cambridge, Massachusetts | February, 1957 |

THE CHANGING SCENE IN HARVARD SQUARE

New Main Office Building Growing Into Handsome Landmark for Old Square

The Bank and the "Coop" in 1908

Palmer Building acquired in '55 for razing

Ready for expansion   Spring '56

Shape of things to come   Summer '56

The new blends with the old   Fall '56

Our hope for early Summer this year

FIGURE 8.49 Evolution of the Harvard Trust Co. buildings, 1908–56. The upper right image shows Albert Blevins's two-story addition to Charles Cogswell's one-story Charles River Bank. The bottom images depict Perry, Shaw, Hepburn & Dean's new structure, whose facade extended across the older building.

FIGURE 8.50 Harvard Trust Co., 1414 Massachusetts Avenue (1956, Perry, Shaw, Hepburn & Dean, architects). Photo ca. 1957.

FIGURE 8.51 Dana Chambers, 11–21 Dunster Street (1897, Clarence H. Blackall, architect). Dana Chambers also functioned as a private dormitory for Harvard students. Rendering ca. 1897.

FIGURE 8.52 Cambridge Savings Bank, 1372–1376 Massachusetts Avenue (1923, Albert H. Blevins with Newhall & Blevins associated architects). Photo ca. 1925.

headquarters at 38A Brattle Street. Galvin produced what was arguably his best commercial work, a two-story, Art Moderne limestone bank with a bowed front (figure 8.53).

The Cambridge Safe Deposit Company opened in 1889 in Hilton's Block, on Massachusetts Avenue at the corner of Linden Street (see figure 8.19). It was reorganized in 1891 as the Cambridge Safe Deposit & Trust, a full-service bank with a diverse group of local investors that included civil engineer E.D. Leavitt, future mayor Alvin Sortwell, and several Boston bank executives; Henry White, a New York businessman whose sons were attending Harvard, became president. Cambridge Trust moved in 1899 to Holyoke House, at the corner of Massachusetts Avenue and Holyoke Street, and retained that location when the university completed Holyoke Center in 1966. In 2013 the bank moved its executive offices out of Harvard Square and relinquished its sumptuous banking hall, which may have

FIGURE 8.53 Cambridge Federal Savings & Loan building, 38 Brattle Street (1937, William L. Galvin, architect). The Cambridge Historical Commission salvaged the etched glass transom when the building was demolished in 1990; the beaver (left) and eagle in the porthole windows did not survive. Photo ca. 1939.

FIGURE 8.54 Cambridge Trust Co. banking hall, 1336 Massachusetts Avenue (1966, Griswold, Boyden, Wylde & Ames, architects). Photo 2013.

been one of the finest International Style commercial interiors in the Boston area (figure 8.54).

The Coolidge Bank & Trust Company was founded in Watertown in 1960 and a few years later purchased a derelict filling station and garage at 104 Mt. Auburn Street (see figure 9.23). In 1968 the bank rented the building to industrial designer Michael Sands, who converted it into an ad hoc apartment and studio. This adaptive reuse was so appealing that Coolidge took back the building in 1970 and remodeled it as a branch bank (figure 8.55). A bright blue exterior and white supergraphics designed by Peter Forbes enlivened the corner until 1983, when the bank partnered with Intercontinental Developers of Boston to become the prime tenant of a new office building (see figure 8.45). Although Coolidge was years ahead of the competition when it introduced ATM machines in 1972, it closed in 1991.

FIGURE 8.55 Coolidge Bank & Trust Co., 104 Mt. Auburn Street (1930, Ralph T.C. Jackson, architect). The conversion into a branch bank was designed by Peter Forbes of PARD Team architects in 1971. Photo 1974.

The growth of architecture as a profession in postwar Cambridge can be traced to the influence of Walter Gropius at Harvard's Graduate School of Design (see chapter 10). While many practitioners preferred makeshift ateliers in old buildings, some firms created a recognizable category of Cambridge commercial architecture, the architects' office building.

The first firm to erect its own office building was The Architects Collaborative (TAC), which Gropius and seven young associates established in 1945. In the early 1960s the firm occupied six rented spaces, each of which "functioned as a studio under the direction of one or two principals" (*Architectural Record*, Sept. 1967, 160). TAC was known for such projects as the Harvard Graduate Center (1949) and the John F. Kennedy Federal Building in Boston (1961); with a staff of 150, it was one of the largest firms in New England. Gropius insisted that TAC remain near Harvard Square, rather than build in the suburbs, and it put up 46 Brattle Street (TAC I) in 1966 and 8–12 Story Street (TAC II) in 1969. TAC I's courtyard, the nucleus from which Brattle Walk evolved, was a response to its dense urban setting. TAC I and TAC II featured the firm's signature sandblasted concrete panels, with punched, deeply recessed window openings. The endless repetition of such forms could be deadening, but the firm's own buildings are small enough to retain an interesting scale (figure 8.56). TAC closed in 1995 after all but two of its original partners had died or retired.

Hugh Stubbins Jr. (1912–2006) was about four years older than the founders of TAC. He was educated in the Beaux-Arts tradition at Harvard's School of Architecture in 1933–35 and was one of the few in his generation who successfully absorbed the new principles of Modernist design from Gropius and Breuer. He founded his own firm in Cambridge in 1949 and taught at Harvard until 1972. One of his most recognizable buildings in Cambridge is the Loeb Drama Center (1960). The firm also designed the Federal Reserve Bank of Boston (1976) and Citigroup Center in New York (1977). Stubbins & Associates rented space in

FIGURE 8.56 TAC I, 46 Brattle Street, and TAC II, 8–12 Story Street (1966–1969, The Architects Collaborative). Photo 2009.

Central Square for many years, but in 1968 the firm designed a professional office building for architects and engineers at 1033 Massachusetts Avenue that was more striking in a rendering than in reality (figure 8.57). A speculative office building at 1100 Massachusetts Avenue is much more successful, in part because its prominent site forced a more dramatic design (see figure 2.65).

Earl Flansburgh (1932–2009) received an architecture degree from M.I.T. in 1957 and worked at TAC before founding his own firm in 1963. Flansburgh & Associates designed hundreds of schools throughout the country and abroad. Their 1970 office building at 14–16 Story Street shares some features with Sert, Jackson & Gourley's 44 Brattle Street but suffers from its cramped location (figure 8.58).

Josep Lluis Sert (1902–83) studied architecture in Barcelona and developed a successful practice there before moving to New York City in 1939. In 1953 he became dean of the Graduate School of Design and in 1955 founded a practice in Cambridge. He added GSD-trained architects Huson Jackson (1913–2006) and Ronald Gourley (1919–99) in 1958 to form Sert, Jackson & Gourley. The firm designed Holyoke Center in 1958, Peabody

FIGURE 8.58 14–16 Story Street (1970, Earl Flansburgh & Associates, architects). Photo 2009.

FIGURE 8.57 1033 Massachusetts Avenue (1968, Hugh Stubbins & Associates, architects). Architect's rendering, 1968.

Terrace apartments in 1962, and the Harvard Science Center in 1969. Sert's buildings in this period often displayed exposed concrete floor slabs infilled with concrete panels faced with purple crushed stone. Perhaps in deference to the adjoining D/R store, the firm's own office building at 44 Brattle Street downplayed these features in favor of floor-to-ceiling windows. An overhanging concrete upper story seems slightly menacing and gratuitous (figure 8.59).

Three TAC alumni, Paul Dietrich (1926–2001), Lou Bakanowsky, and Terry Rankine, and four recent Yale and Harvard architecture graduates, including Peter and Ivan Chermayeff, founded Cambridge Seven Associates (C7A) in 1962. Dietrich was highly influential in Cambridge, where he served twenty-eight years on the planning board, including ten as chair. The firm set out to combine architecture with graphic design and public art. Among its first projects were aquariums in Boston and Baltimore and the U.S. pavilion at Expo '67 in Montreal. In Cambridge, C7A designed Charles Square and the Porter Square MBTA station (1979–84). Cambridge Seven also created graphic standards for the MBTA, including the "T" logo and color coding of the mass transit lines. The north-facing skylights of C7A's sleek office building at Putnam Square, designed in 1973, reveal its function as an atelier (figure 8.60).

Symmes, Maini & McKee Associates (SMMA) was founded in 1958 by three M.I.T. graduates, engineers Parker Symmes and Walter Maini and architect Jon McKee. Early projects included warehouses and light manufacturing facilities, but in the 1970s SMMA began to win commissions for suburban office buildings and institutional projects. Its favored approach in this period is typified by the strip-windowed Hadley Building (1974) and its own office building at 1000 Massachusetts Avenue (1982; figure 8.61), but the firm also designed the critically acclaimed Niles Building at 1280 Massachusetts Avenue (1983) and the restoration of the Read Block (1997; see figures 3.88 and 8.44).

Figure 8.59 44 Brattle Street (1970, Sert, Jackson & Associates, architects). The Design Research building (1969) is at right. Photo 2014.

FIGURE 8.60 1050 Massachusetts Avenue (1973, Cambridge Seven Associates, architects) Photo 2009.

FIGURE 8.61 1000 Massachusetts Avenue (1982, Symmes, Maini & McKee Associates, architects). Photo 2009.

FIGURE 9.1 Schooners in the coasting trade carried lumber, firewood, coal, stone, bricks, and other cargoes to wharves up and down the Charles River. Most captains hired steam tugs to help negotiate the drawbridges and the narrow, tidal channel. John W.A. Scott's, "On the Banks of the Charles River, Cambridgeport, Mass.," shows the Magazine Wharf at Captain's Island in the foreground and "Maplewood Farm," a Brookline estate, in the 1850s.

9 TRANSPORTATION AND INDUSTRY

Old Cambridge's singular circumstances inhibited commerce and industry. The absence of streams that could be harnessed for waterpower, the scarcity of timber for fuel and building material, and the lack of raw materials (except clay) meant that manufacturing was slow to develop. On the other hand, the presence of Harvard College ensured that farmers found a ready market for produce and livestock and that tanners had a ready supply of hides; building tradesmen found steady employment; and printing and publishing would thrive. The distance from railroad connections encouraged waterborne commerce. The ability of small seagoing vessels to navigate the Charles River at high tide meant that firewood, lumber, granite, and coal could be carried cheaply to the edge of the village, and some processing and wholesaling of these materials took place. During the suburban period Harvard Square became a transit hub, and facilities for vehicle storage, horses, and power generation were established on the edge of the village (figure 9.1).

TRANSPORTATION

OLD CAMBRIDGE AND THE CHARLES RIVER

The Charles River was a major artery for commercial traffic until the end of the 19th century. By June 1631, only six months after settlement, John Masters had dug out the Town Creek as far as South Street, creating a "canal" 12 feet wide and 7 feet deep (see figure 1.4). At the end of 1635 a landing stage was built at the foot of Dunster Street, and in January 1636 Joseph Cooke was authorized to operate a ferry. In 1651 the Proprietors of Common Lands allowed William Manning to "make a wharffe out of the head of ye Cricke … and build a [ware]house on it to come as high as the great pine stump, and range with Mr. Pelhams house next the high street in to Towne" (Town Records, 94). Six years later, the selectmen authorized the owners of the ketch *Triall* to fell timber for another warehouse on the east side of Dunster Street, a little closer to the river than Manning's.

In the 17th century the town's residents owned a variety of watercraft. The assessors in 1647 listed a "barke" (a three-masted ocean sailing vessel) worth £50, a half share of another bark worth £140, and a "hoy" (a sailing vessel used in coastal trade) worth £50. The tax rolls also included a half share in a "shallup" (a light, open vessel that could be sailed or rowed) worth £5, and half a share in a "boate" worth £2 (ibid., 352–53). Several vessels were built in town, probably on the Ship Marsh, downstream from the Town Creek, where another canal had been dug near the foot of present DeWolfe Street. In 1670 the selectmen "granted to the owners of the Ketches that are to [be] builded in the town liberty to fell timber on the common" (Paige, 96). Two years later Daniel Gookin, Walter Hastings, and Samuel Champney brought suit against William Carr for poor workmanship on

FIGURE 9.2 This early schooner appears on the below-ground portion of the 1737 headstone of John Dickson in the Old Burying Ground. Vessels with this two-masted rig first appeared in Boston port records in 1715, and this sketch (about 3" long) may have been made from direct observation by a stone carver in Charlestown. The Dicksons were farmers near Alewife Brook and had no apparent involvement in maritime trade. Photo 2014.

these two-masted vessels, which were described as of 28 and 35 tons burden.[1]

The 1696 Massachusetts register of shipping recorded five vessels built in Cambridge since 1674. As a shipbuilding town, Cambridge was comparable to Milton, another inland village on a tidal river, but was far outclassed by Charlestown, which built eleven vessels in the same period. Cambridge vessels included the brigantines *Dove* and *William & John,* both 40 tons, built in 1694–95 and 1696, and the brig *Return*, 30 tons, built in 1696, all for Boston merchants. The *Dove* sailed to Connecticut ports and the *William & John* to Jamaica. The last ship built in Cambridge, the sloop *Rose* (1697), was the only early vessel known to list the town as its home port. Her master and owner, John Bonner, was a master mariner and a "Gentleman very skillful

and ingenious in many arts and sciences, especially in navigation, drawing, moulding of ships, etc.," who was "one of the best acquainted with the Coasts of North America, of any of his time" (*Boston News-Letter,* Feb. 3, 1726). Bonner had already enjoyed a distinguished career in the colony when he married a daughter of Jonas Clark about 1687 and settled on the east side of Dunster Street near the creek. The *Rose* was an 18-ton sloop, which would have made it one of the smallest vessels capable of transoceanic travel. Bonner moved to Boston in 1705 and made his well-known map of that town in 1722.

In 1727 the Proprietors granted six townsmen 30-foot-deep lots on the Town Creek between Manning's Wharf and the river. The owners included Andrew Bordman, the college steward; John Bradish, the college glazier; John Hicks, a carpenter; Abraham Watson, a tanner; and Deacon Samuel Whittemore, a leather dresser. Twenty years later Judge Edmund Trowbridge owned all these parcels and combined them into Trowbridge's Wharf. In 1751 the Proprietors granted Edward Marrett Jr. land at the mouth of the creek, where he constructed a wharf directly on the river. He imported cloth, hardware, and lumber on his own account and charged wharfage for cargoes of "beef, bricks, firewood, boards, rails and posts, dung, [and] mud" landed by others (Trautman, 98).[2] During the Revolution, he stored bricks, lumber, and timber for the barracks, and cannon, carriages, ammunition, firewood, and foodstuff of all sorts in his warehouses. Josiah Whittemore acquired Marrett's Wharf in 1803 and extended it to include 170 feet of frontage on the creek and 60 feet on the channel.

The most important cargoes delivered to the village were building materials and fuel. Christ Church bought rafts of lumber during its construction in 1760, and Harvard's accounts for building Stoughton Hall in 1804–5 include a substantial sum for wharfage. The American army stripped the countryside of all available timber during the winter of 1775–76, and for the next half century the scarcity of fuel was a constant concern. By this time, most of the firewood consumed by coastal Massachusetts came from Maine; Harvard owned about 7,000 acres of woodland east of

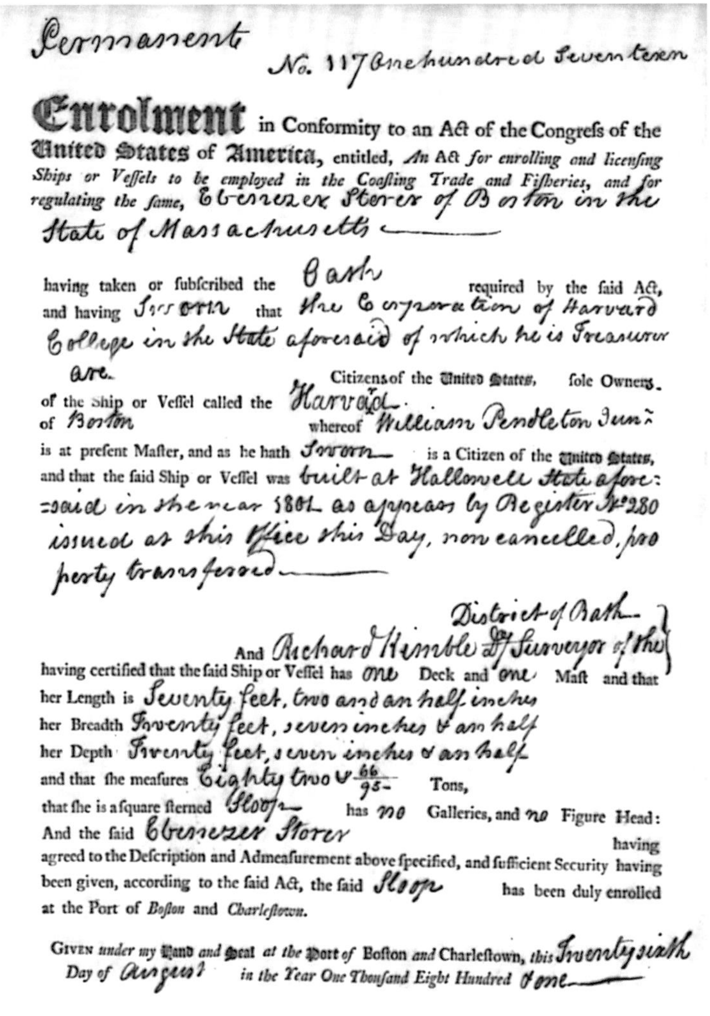

Permanent
No. 117 One hundred Seventeen

Enrolment in Conformity to an Act of the Congress of the United States of America, entitled, *An Act for enrolling and licensing Ships or Vessels to be employed in the Coasting Trade and Fisheries, and for regulating the same*, Ebenezer Storer of Boston in the State of Massachusetts ——

having taken or subscribed the Oath required by the said Act, and having Sworn that the Corporation of Harvard College in the State aforesaid of which he is Treasurer are Citizens of the United States, sole Owners of the Ship or Vessel called the Harvard of Boston whereof William Pendleton Jun. is at present Master, and as he hath Sworn is a Citizen of the United States, and that the said Ship or Vessel was built at Hallowell State aforesaid in the year 1801 as appears by Register No 280 issued at this Office this Day, now cancelled, property transferred ——

District of Bath

And Richard Kimble Dy Surveyor of the having certified that the said Ship or Vessel has one Deck and one Mast and that her Length is Seventy feet, two and an half inches her Breadth Twenty feet, seven inches & an half her Depth Twenty feet, seven inches & an half and that she measures Eighty two & 66/95 Tons, that she is a square sterned Sloop has no Galleries, and no Figure Head: And the said Ebenezer Storer having agreed to the Description and Admeasurement above specified, and sufficient Security having been given, according to the said Act, the said Sloop has been duly enrolled at the Port of Boston and Charlestown.

Given under my Hand and Seal at the Port of Boston *and* Charlestown, *this* Twenty sixth *Day of* August *in the Year One Thousand Eight Hundred* & one

Figure 9.3 Enrollment certificate for the sloop Harvard, Port of Boston and Charlestown, August 27, 1801. The Harvard was built at Hallowell, Maine, in 1801. She was 70 feet long, had one mast, a square stern, a capacity of 82 66/95 tons, and (regrettably) no figurehead

Penobscot Bay and turned to that source when its woodlot in Arlington and farm in Waltham no longer met its needs.

The college reorganized its procurement practices soon after the war, expanding its wood yard behind University Hall to hold 300 cords (about a year's supply) and securely fencing it against theft. In 1792 the college entered "the wood-coasting business" when it purchased a half interest in the *Cyrus*, a 59-foot sloop built in 1790 in Falmouth (now Portland), Maine, which brought about thirty cords of wood from down east every two and a half weeks (Bowditch, 28). Harvard's partner in this venture was William Winthrop, a 1770 graduate, gentleman farmer, and selectman who was the only ship-owning merchant in town. In 1795 the college acquired Winthrop's interest in the sloop, but in 1799 it was still buying about four times as much wood from him as it brought on its own vessel, although the price was the same—$3.58 per cord delivered to Winthrop's Wharf. Wharfage, carting, and stacking in the college wood yard brought the cost per cord to $4.42. Fuel was a significant expense; annual tuition was $20, but a student's fireplace might consume three cords over the course of a winter.

In October 1800, in a season of "great scarcity," the Corporation authorized the steward to contract with Winthrop "for building and completing [a] sloop upon as good terms, in all respects, as he engages one to be built and completed for himself" (Corporation Records, IV, 593, and IV-2, 28; figure 9.3). The sloop *Harvard*, launched at Hallowell the following September, made ten or twelve trips a year, but by 1807 students were paying $6.96 a cord. Harvard eliminated wharfage fees by purchasing Marrett's Wharf in 1812, but it was still a difficult and expensive business.

Harvard's involvement in the coasting trade ended after it was deprived of a subsidy it had been receiving from the Commonwealth since 1814. During a period of financial retrenchment Nathaniel Bowditch, the navigator, a new member of the Harvard Corporation, discovered irregularities in the accounts of the treasurer, John Davis, and the steward, Stephen Higginson. Instead of the small annual profit Davis had reported, the *Harvard* had accumulated a deficit of $4,400, and the college's wood cost the students $1 a cord more than if it had been obtained by contract. Lax management (other vessels in the coasting trade made up to sixteen trips a year) and the high cost of repairs in Boston contributed to the problem. In 1828 the Corporation reported to the Board of Overseers:

> Experience has shown that the manner in which the students were formerly provided with fuel, though adopted with a view to economy, is not in fact economical. The sloop *Harvard*, which was owned by the college and employed as a coaster, has accordingly been sold, and contracts have been made for furnishing the students with wood at a much lower rate than formerly. (Corporation Records VII, 56)

Ownership of the College Wharf was still advantageous, and between 1826 and 1845 Harvard purchased four adjoining marsh lots to accommodate a new trade in coal from Nova Scotia (figure 9.4).[3] William T. Richardson, foreman of the wharf, set up his own wood and coal business in 1840, and for many years the treasurer collected his charges with the students' term bills. Richardson leased the wharf for fifty-six years; the 360-foot-long coal shed of Richardson & Bacon was a landmark on the river until 1901, when the Cambridge Park Commission razed it and filled in the Town Creek (see figure 5.54).

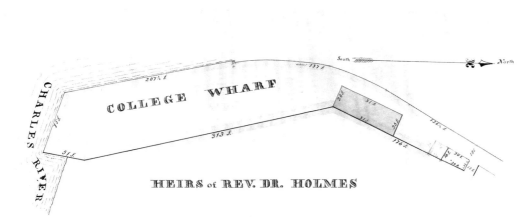

FIGURE 9.4 The College Wharf and sheds on the Town Creek at the foot of Dunster Street, as surveyed in 1841.

FIGURE 9.5 Charles River navigation chart, with soundings taken in 1861. The measurements show the distance above or below low water (shown as a dotted line) during spring tides. Although there was a turning basin below the Great Bridge, ebb tides left vessels resting on the flats at every wharf on the river.

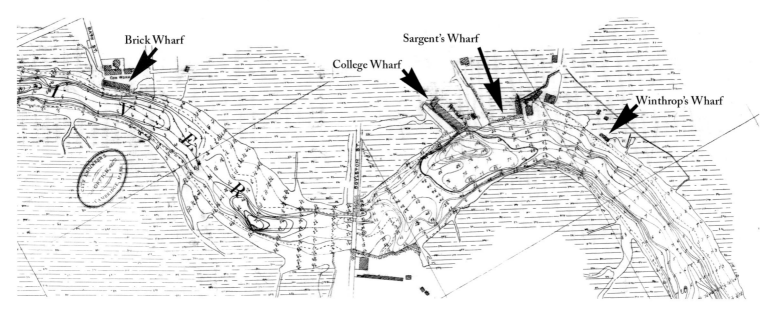

Several other wharves were active throughout the century. William Stearns and Solomon Sargent bought Winthrop's Wharf in 1854 and extended it about 200 feet south from the foot of DeWolfe Street. In 1856 they purchased another parcel from the Winthrop estate and developed Sargent's Wharf along Mill Street (figure 9.6). By 1875 masts lined the riverfront as coasting vessels unloaded fuel for the college and timber for builders' yards and planing mills (figure 9.7). The ancient Brick Wharf at the foot of Ash Street was probably named after the cargoes that were shipped from it in colonial times; between 1853 and 1874 the Cambridge Gas-Light Company received coal for its works there (figure 9.8; see also figure 2.20). Alexander McDonald's Monument Wharf near the foot of Sparks Street received shipments of granite that were carved into tombstones, shaped for foundations, or split for curbing. Gerry's Landing, near the foot of Coolidge Hill, served local farmers (see chapter 4). Downstream, the Cambridge Electric Light Company and The Riverside Press maintained wharves between Western Avenue and River Street (figure 9.9).

FIGURE 9.6 Wharves near Harvard Square, ca. 1862. Sargent's Wharf is piled with lumber; four two-masted schooners are tied up beyond the College Wharf.

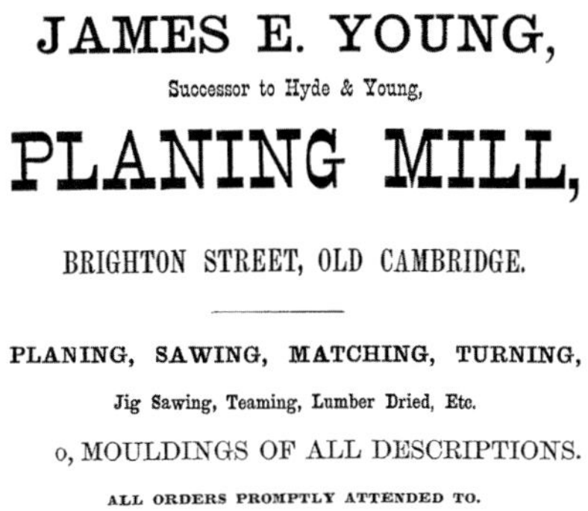

JAMES E. YOUNG,

Successor to Hyde & Young,

PLANING MILL,

BRIGHTON STREET, OLD CAMBRIDGE.

PLANING, SAWING, MATCHING, TURNING,

Jig Sawing, Teaming, Lumber Dried, Etc.

o, MOULDINGS OF ALL DESCRIPTIONS.

ALL ORDERS PROMPTLY ATTENDED TO.

N. N. STICKNEY & CO.

DEALERS IN

Rough and Dressed Lumber,

LIME, CEMENT, HAIR, AND PLASTER.

Also Gutters, Conductors, Mouldings, Laths, Shingles, Pickets, C. Posts, etc.

WINTHROP WHARF,

DE WOLF STREET, - - - OLD CAMBRIDGE.

N. N. STICKNEY.   WILLIAM E. SAUNDERS.

FIGURE 9.7 Advertisements for James Young's steam-powered planing mill on John F. Kennedy Street, just below South Street (1868) and Nathaniel Stickney's lumber yard on Winthrop's Wharf, at the foot of DeWolfe Street (1874).

FIGURE 9.8 The view upstream from the Great Bridge shows the Brick Wharf and the gasholder of the Cambridge Gas-Light Co. at the foot of Ash Street. Photo ca. 1890.

FIGURE 9.9 The view downstream from the Great Bridge, ca. 1900. Richardson & Bacon's coal shed occupies the College Wharf, followed by Sargent's Wharf and Winthrop's Wharf.

The specialized wooden vessels that evolved in the 19th century for carrying lumber, firewood, coal, and granite along the New England coast were mostly two-masted schooners from 75 to 130 feet long; flat-bottomed, two-masted scows or lighters were used for local deliveries within Massachusetts Bay (figure 9.10). In tidal streams like the Charles strong currents made navigation difficult, and until steam tugs came into use in the 1840s local knowledge was required to negotiate the channel safely. The proliferation of bridges was an annoyance.[4] In 1824 Harvard protested to the General Court against the construction of the Western Avenue bridge, noting that "it keeps constantly in its employ a Sloop, plying to and from [the College] Wharf, and that any destruction of the Navigation of the River must be injurious" (Corporation Records, VI, 118).

The volume of waterborne traffic in Old Cambridge declined toward the end of the century, but as late as 1893 sixty-four sailing vessels and sixty-one barges called at wharves in Old Cambridge and Watertown. In September 1899 five schooners, each carrying between 75,000 and 100,000 vitrified paving bricks

that the city had ordered from yards on the Hudson River, discharged their cargoes at Richardson & Bacon's and the Electric Light Company's wharves. The former received cargoes of coal and wood until the end of 1900, when the Park Commission terminated its lease (figure 9.11). Construction of the Longfellow Bridge excluded masted vessels after June 10, 1904. All commercial traffic on the upper river ceased in 1910, when barges stopped delivering coal to the Brighton abattoir, although East Cambridge canals continued to receive cargos of lumber, coal, fuel oil, molasses, and construction materials well into the 20th century. Schooners were employed in the lumber trade until at least 1927; the last commercial shipment of any kind was a delivery of fuel oil to the Broad Canal in the 1980s.

FIGURE 9.11 The industrial waterfront of Old Cambridge, seen from the chimney of the Boston Elevated Railway's power plant in 1897. Richardson & Bacon's coal shed is in the foreground. A schooner is unloading bulk cargo at Sargent's Wharf. The Cambridge Park Commission has moved the Cambridge Casino from the foot of Hawthorn Street to the flats near DeWolfe Street. Harvard had moved its boathouses downstream below Winthrop's Wharf in the 1870s to escape the city's sewer outfall at the foot of Dunster Street.

FIGURE 9.10 A schooner at the Riverside Press wharf, ca. 1890, as seen from the River Street Bridge. The houses at right face Daye Avenue and were removed as the plant expanded (see figure 9.46).

BLACKSMITH AND CARRIAGE SHOPS

The infrastructure of early overland transportation left few traces. Blacksmithing and wagon building were common trades but required little specialized construction until the mid-19th century. Blacksmith Torrey Hancock built a house and a smithy at 54 Brattle Street in 1808 (see figure 4.7). He sold both to Dexter Pratt of Framingham about 1827, and the two did business together long enough to cause confusion about whom Henry Wadsworth Longfellow had in mind when he wrote "The Village Blacksmith" in 1839.

Carriage building was a significant business in Old Cambridge for most of the 19th century. The general improvement of roads after the construction of the West Boston Bridge in 1793 and the growing prosperity of Cambridge as a suburb demanded wheeled vehicles and sleighs of all kinds. Carriage builders in Harvard Square worked on a craft basis and were eventually displaced by large manufacturers like Henderson Brothers in North Cambridge. The old firms then specialized in repairs and custom work until they disappeared around the turn of the century.

Carriage builders shared Palmer and Church streets with blacksmiths, wheelwrights, carpenters, and building tradesmen. The nature of this quarter had been established before the Revolution. Caleb Prentice bought 2½ acres there in 1747, and by his death in 1772 possessed "a pot house, pot kiln and accoutrements for potters work [and] a potash house and two large potash kettles and accoutrements for potash work" (Middlesex Probate Records 54/39, 88).[5] The ground behind College House was already occupied by the college wood yard and carpenter's shop, so when William Whitney laid out Palmer Street in 1845 the lots were attractive mostly to tradesmen (figure 9.12).

FIGURE 9.12 Palmer Street in 1910, with sheds and workshops dating from the mid-19th century. Abraham Lavash's two-story carpentry shop (on the left with the double arched window) occupied a remnant of the 1758 courthouse, which had been displaced from Harvard Square in 1841 (see figures 3.11 and 7.34). The brick buildings were constructed after a disastrous fire in 1856 leveled most of the street. The large Mansard-roofed building on the skyline at right housed Professor Sargent's Normal School of Physical Training.

The earliest known carriage builder in Old Cambridge was Edmund A. Chapman, who started in 1829 in a shed in the middle of the Brattle-Palmer-Church streets block. His brother Francis continued the firm until his death in 1893, nearly spanning the existence of the trade (figure 9.13). James White had a more substantial workshop in the old police and fire stations after the city vacated them in 1875 (figure 9.14). Wheelwright Amos Hurd, who came to Cambridge from Maine in the 1830s, put up a brick workshop and residence on Palmer Street in 1848 and engaged in carriage and sleigh building until he retired about 1878 (figures 9.15–9.16). Chapman's workshops were replaced by a storage warehouse in 1913, while Hurd's shop survived until 1965.

FIGURE 9.14 James White's carriage shop occupied the former fire and police stations at 27 and 31 Church Street from 1875 to 1896. Carriages were very light, and the improvised ramp and platform afforded additional workspace. Photo ca. 1890.

FIGURE 9.13 The Chapman Carriage Company occupied a 10,000 square foot parcel in the interior of the Brattle-Palmer-Church streets block that was entered from this alley at 11 Brattle Street. George O. Rollins and George M. Church operated the business from 1893 until 1901. Photo 1907.

FIGURE 9.15 Amos Hurd's workshop and residence (18–20 Palmer Street, 1856). Hurd used the proceeds of a public subscription to rebuild in brick after a fire destroyed his original shop. It remained a carpentry shop until it was demolished by the Harvard Cooperative Society in 1965. Photo 1964.

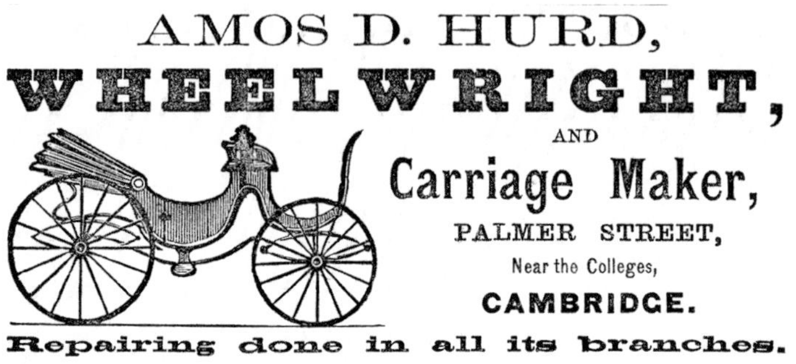

AMOS D. HURD,

WHEELWRIGHT,

AND

Carriage Maker,

PALMER STREET,

Near the Colleges,

CAMBRIDGE.

Repairing done in all its branches.

FIGURE 9.16 Amos Hurd's advertisement in the 1870 *Cambridge Directory* recalled the carriages of an earlier day.

Carriage makers competed to make their vehicles as light as possible, and some offered seasonal storage to their customers. Their buildings could be tall and lightly framed, with cranes and loading bays on each floor. Andrew Jackson Jones came from Maine in 1841 and apprenticed as a blacksmith. The four-story factory he put up on Church Street in 1857 included a smithy and workrooms in which he built all kinds of carriages and wagons, including gun carriages during the Civil War (figure 9.17; see figure 3.16). William Balmer, a blacksmith, built a three-story brick factory behind the Unitarian Church in 1894; he operated a forge and blacksmith shop on the first floor and rented the upstairs. He added the top floor in 1907 for the exclusive use of Harry Eldredge Goodhue, a maker of stained glass windows with a national clientele (figure 9.18). This homely building was reduced to one story in 1936 and given an Art Deco storefront.

FIGURE 9.17 Andrew Jones carriage factory, 26 Church Street (1857). By 1896 the upper floors were used for furniture storage; later the building became a book bindery operated by John McNamee, whose painted sign is still faintly visible high on the south elevation. The Church Street facade was rebuilt after the street was widened in 1926. Photo 2014.

FIGURE 9.18 William Balmer factory, 23–25 Church Street (1894, Marshall N. Stearns, builder). The large doors on the upper floors could accommodate wagons or cabinetwork; the top floor was added in 1907. The first story still exists behind the 1936 Art Deco facade shown in figure 8.35. The Motor Mart garage replaced the Cambridge 1 firehouse in 1922. Photo before 1936.

From the time of settlement, the village contained facilities for travelers and their mounts. Inns could not operate without stables, and some of these became independent businesses. Similar activities often persisted in the same location when new forms of transportation arrived. The stable of Willard's tavern was used by omnibus lines and then expanded by the Union Railway, one of whose buildings was adapted as an electric auto charging station and then as a parking garage (see figure 9.28). The service stations that displaced many homes and businesses in the 1930s and '40s were more ephemeral, and most were replaced by commercial development in the late 20th century.

Horses were the only means of personal transportation until the introduction of bicycles in the late 19th century. A few well-to-do families maintained private stables, but others shared the expense; President Eliot, for example, kept his horse in a club stable in the old Harvard Branch Railroad station.[6] Boarding stables for private mounts were often located in middle-class neighborhoods, while livery stables (with horses and carriages for hire) were found on the perimeter of the Square and near Porter's Station. Residents of Hubbard Park and Garfield Street, two planned neighborhoods that excluded private stables, depended on boarding stables provided by the developers.

The Oxford Street Stable on Eustis Street was one of the largest in Cambridge when it burned and was rebuilt in 1890. The two-story wooden building had room for at least thirty-five horses belonging to a cross-section of prosperous business and professional men from the neighborhood. Such facilities were not popular with their neighbors, but the stable was rebuilt after the fire and lasted until 1928, when it was replaced by a service garage that was itself supplanted by townhouses in 1994 (figure 9.19).

At the end of the century Harvard Square had three large livery stables: Blake's at 35 Church Street, the University Stables (the old Blue Anchor tavern stables, also known as Gwynne's) at 14–16 Brattle Street, and the Quincy Square Stables at 1230

FIGURE 9.19 Oxford Stables, 6 Eustis Street (1890, C. Herbert McClare, architect). Advertisement 1905.

Massachusetts Avenue. Blake's was the oldest and maintained over 100 horses and carriages. The Quincy Square Stables merged with Blake's to form the Cambridge Coach Company and moved to 35 Church Street in 1902. Gwynne's, in the heart of Harvard Square, was forced to close for public health reasons in 1903 (see chapter 3).

Automobile owners who had been accustomed to boarding their horses adopted similar habits for their machines. Early autos were difficult to maintain, and facilities where they could be kept out of the weather and repaired by skilled mechanics were a necessity. Safety concerns precluded conversion of wooden livery stables, so buildings designed specifically to display, store, and service automobiles soon followed. Some workshops near Harvard Square also produced custom-made autos for wealthy Harvard undergraduates (see figure 3.29). In 1906 the University Associates, developers of several Gold Coast dormitories, erected a two-story Classical Revival garage for the Harvard Automobile Company on the site of the Quincy Square stable (figure 9.20). Frederick Furbish put up the Church Street

FIGURE 9.20 Harvard Automobile Co., 1230 Massachusetts Avenue (1906, Coolidge & Carlson, architects). This reinforced concrete building was restored, expanded by two floors, and redeveloped for offices in 2002. Photo ca. 1907.

Garage next door to the Cambridge Coach stable in 1912 and added a second story in 1916 (figure 9.21). Later garages, such as the 1923 Harvard Square Garage on Kennedy Street, had no architectural pretensions whatever and resembled factories of the period (figure 9.22; see also figure 3.64).

Home garages proliferated during the early part of the century. Allen W. Jackson's house at 202 Brattle Street incorporated a garage in 1903, but freestanding private garages were far more popular (see figure 6.178). The city granted the first permit for one to a homeowner at 176 Upland Road in 1900, but very few were built until the 1920s, when hundreds were erected in backyards all over the city every year until the Depression. In June 1924 alone, thirty-six permits were issued for home garages (and five to raze stables); two-thirds were concrete-block and cost about $900. Prefabricated metal garages, a popular alternative, typically cost $500.

The spread of home garages reduced the need for seasonal storage and allowed service stations to become more compact. Activity shifted to busy street corners, where through traffic

FIGURE 9.21 Church Street Garage, 41 Church Street (1912, Wisner Martin; upper floor 1916, Martin & Freethy, architects). The Church Street Garage replaced the Cambridge Coach Co. stable; it was demolished in 1978 to expand a surface parking lot. Photo 1973.

FIGURE 9.22 Harvard Square Garage, 34–40 Kennedy Street, corner of Mt. Auburn Street (1923, E.B. Stratton, architect). William Read's three-story store and apartment building at 30 Kennedy Street (1869) with its unusual cornice was razed in 1936. Photo ca. 1930.

generated gasoline sales. Many service stations were standardized designs produced by large national oil companies, which could be attractive examples of their kind but often clashed with the traditional architecture of Old Cambridge. An Amoco service station at 104 Mt. Auburn Street and a Socony station opposite by the bus ramp blighted Eliot Square for decades before they were replaced by mixed-use buildings. At Quincy Square, Beck Hall fell in 1940 for a filling station that was itself replaced by a hotel in 1990 (figures 9.23–9.24). In this instance, the Gulf Oil Company acknowledged the context and designed a building with Georgian details and a cupola that mimicked those on Harvard's River Houses.

Kennedy Street alone had three service stations by 1930. The first, on the corner of Winthrop Street, appeared in 1912 and was extensively remodeled in 1940; it was replaced by the Galeria in 1974. A station occupied the northeast corner of Kennedy Street and Memorial Drive until Harvard built Eliot House in 1930. Cambridge developer Louis DiGiovanni razed a service station at the corner of Eliot Street and built the Harvard Square Garage in 1984. The zoning code allowed a much taller building, but community intervention in the development process and a subvention by Harvard University resulted in a lower structure clad in red brick for this important entrance to Harvard Square (figure 9.25).

FIGURE 9.23 American Oil Co. garage and filling station, 104 Mt. Auburn Street (1930, Ralph T.C. Jackson, architect). The parking garage under this service station was incorporated into the office building that replaced it in 1983. Photo 1964.

FIGURE 9.24 Gulf Oil Corp., 1201 Massachusetts Avenue (1940; demolished 1988). Photo 1956.

FIGURE 9.25 Harvard Square Parking Garage, 65 Kennedy Street (1984, Arrowstreet, architects). Photo 2009.

Railroad stations were a matter of pride and architectural excess in many towns, but in Cambridge they were generally modest structures serving distant neighborhoods. Most were illustrated in *Report Five: Northwest Cambridge,* but the subsequent discovery of a photograph of Cambridge's first station, built by the Fitchburg Railroad at Porter Square in 1844, contrasts with the more elaborate structure put up by the Harvard Branch Railroad across from Cambridge Common in 1849 (figure 9.26). The station at Porter's, erected at the dawn of passenger service on a line that was built to carry freight, was little more than a shelter, while the Harvard Branch station, clearly intended to support the real estate goals of its promoters, featured a portico, an oval domed waiting room, and a covered train shed about 50 feet long (figure 9.27).

The Union Railway, a horse-drawn street railroad, opened in March 1856 with fifteen cars that it left outside in all weather;

FIGURE 9.27 The Harvard Branch Railroad station and train shed on Holmes Place (1849, "Mr. Parker," architect), with the Gamage-Richardson-Morse house at right (1717; demolished 1883). Charles E. Parker was listed in the Boston directories as an architect from 1847 to 1884. He is said to have trained with Richard Bond; his best-known surviving building is 52 Broad Street in Boston. After the line closed, Harvard used the station as a lecture room and dining hall; the train shed (the gabled structure behind the station) became a dormitory for Memorial Hall waiters and a stable. Both were demolished for Austin Hall in 1883.

FIGURE 9.26 Cambridge's first railroad station, built by the Fitchburg Railroad in 1844 on Somerville Avenue and seen here as remodeled in 1851. It served until 1887, when it was sold and moved to the corner of Cedar and Dudley streets; this photo was taken ca. 1865 (see figure 2.13). Later stations are documented in *Report Five: Northwest Cambridge,* pp. 138–40.

horses were initially kept in Cambridgeport and in a former omnibus stable on Upland Road near Massachusetts Avenue (see figure 2.13). In 1857 the company took over Abel Willard's stable on Dunster Street and remodeled his tavern into a waiting room and office, and in 1860–63 it built a workshop, a barn for car storage, and a brick stable (figures 9.28–9.30). Another carbarn and stable went up on Mt. Auburn Street opposite the cemetery in 1860. By this time the railway had 54 cars and 305 horses and was already carrying 2.8 million passengers a year. In 1871 it purchased 1½ acres of the Ox Marsh west of Kennedy Street. When the West End Street Railway acquired the Union's successor, the Cambridge Railroad, in 1887, its stables there

FIGURE 9.28 Union Railway waiting room, 1378 Massachusetts Avenue (1797; demolished 1923). Formerly Willard's Tavern, this was one of several buildings in Harvard Square constructed after the opening of the West Boston Bridge in 1793. The hip roof seen in early views was replaced by this flat one after a fire in the 1870s. The building housed offices and a streetcar waiting room until the completion of the subway in 1912. Photo 1876, with Centennial decorations.

FIGURE 9.30 Union Railway shop and carbarns, 12–28 Dunster Street (1863, 1876). The building in the foreground was a carbarn and "horse car manufactory" (Sanborn 1868, plate 18). The gabled section in the distance was another carbarn. The two buildings were joined when the repair shops were expanded in 1876. The Cambridge Railroad constructed an experimental battery-powered car here in 1887. Photo 1891.

FIGURE 9.29 Union Railway stable, 25–33 Dunster Street (1860). This building accommodated about 125 horses. It became a charging station for battery-powered automobiles in 1900, but only the walls remained after a fire in 1907. Rebuilt as a garage with a full third floor in 1916, in 1924 it was joined to another garage at the corner of Kennedy and Mt. Auburn streets. A fourth floor was added to the combined structures in 1972, when they became the Garage, a complex of retail shops. Photo 1897.

FIGURE 9.31 West End Street Railway carbarn, 75 Kennedy Street (1888). Street railways required huge storage buildings to protect their wooden cars; this carbarn measured 70 feet by 300 feet. Photo November 1910.

accommodated 224 horses and 40 cars. The West End added a barn for 32 cars in 1888 (figure 9.31; see also figure 2.34). After electrification the company put the Dunster Street facilities up them for sale in 1892. The car shop was demolished for a private dormitory, the Dunster, and the Cambridge Savings Bank took down Willard's old stable to build Dana Chambers in 1897 (see figures 3.22 and 8.51). The stable at the northwest corner of Dunster and Mt. Auburn streets still stands, although much altered.

The West End initially purchased power for its streetcars from the Cambridge Electric Light Company but soon built its own generating stations in Allston and East Cambridge. In May 1897, just before it was leased by the Boston Elevated Railway, the company broke ground for a power station on the Charles River at Kennedy Street. The West End engineers designed the initial plant in consultation with the Cambridge Park Commission to minimize its effect on the new parkway. A 1907 addition designed by Robert S. Peabody reflected the Boston Elevated's higher standards in architecture but included a second massive chimney (figure 9.32). In 1913, with Widener Library under construction, Harvard arranged to buy steam from the company and began to build the utility tunnel network that eventually connected almost all university buildings. The Elevated put the generators on standby about 1927 and sold the facility to Harvard in 1929. The university tapped the Cambridge Electric Light Company's Blackstone Station instead of building its own steam plant near the business school as it once planned. Harvard demolished the complex to build Eliot House in 1930.

FIGURE 9.32 West End Street Railway generating station, 100 Kennedy Street (1897). The first brick chimney (right) was 223 feet high—a foot higher than the Bunker Hill Monument—and the building initially contained three cross-compound steam engines coupled to direct-current generators with a capacity of 3,600 kilowatts. Coal was delivered by dump cars that traveled on streetcar tracks from the company's wharf on the Miller's River. The addition (the larger building in the foreground) was designed by Peabody & Stearns in 1907. Harvard's Eliot House now occupies this site. Photo November 1909.

FIGURE 9.33 Cambridge Electric Light Co. power station, 46 Blackstone Street (1901, Sheaff & Jaastad, engineers and architects). The Neoclassical structure at left contained the steam engines and generators; the low building at right may have been the original generating station of 1888. The cornice and balustrade were removed in 1959. Photo ca. 1915.

The Cambridge Electric Light Company (CELCO) began operating on Main Street in 1886, but two years later—after considering sites in Brattle Square and on Putnam Avenue at Green Street—built its first power station on the Charles River next to the Riverside Press. This initially operated only at night, although the company would power up the system if an industrial customer needed light on an overcast day. Demand grew exponentially, and the company, having escaped both municipal ownership and acquisition by Boston's Edison Electric Illuminating Company, invested in a new central station on Western Avenue in 1901 (figure 9.33). Designed with elaborate Classical details to complement its prominent site, the Blackstone Station was Cambridge's main source of electricity until 1947, when the Kendall Station came on line. CELCO relegated Blackstone's generators to standby status but provided steam to the university until Harvard purchased the facility in 2009. Harvard refurbished the steam plant and began generating electricity for university use in 2015.

The planning and construction of the Cambridge Subway is described in chapters 2 and 3. Tracks entered Harvard Station on two levels and passed under Brattle Square to the yards near the river. A second, parallel "surface subway" carried streetcar tracks from Mt. Auburn Street to Flagstaff Park, while short connecting passages separated opposing streams of commuters and allowed them to transfer easily between modes (figures 9.34–9.35). The first headhouse (or kiosk, as Cantabrigians called it) was a simple brick structure with an oval plan and colonnades on the east and west sides (see figures 2.46 and 3.44). One critic lauded its restrained Georgian design:

Architects, painters and designers among Harvard graduates have often complained that the university authorities have violated aesthetics in admitting the present hocus-pocus of architectural styles to the college grounds. Now comes a public-service corporation with an object lesson at the university's doors. (*Boston Sunday Herald,* Mar. 24, 1912)

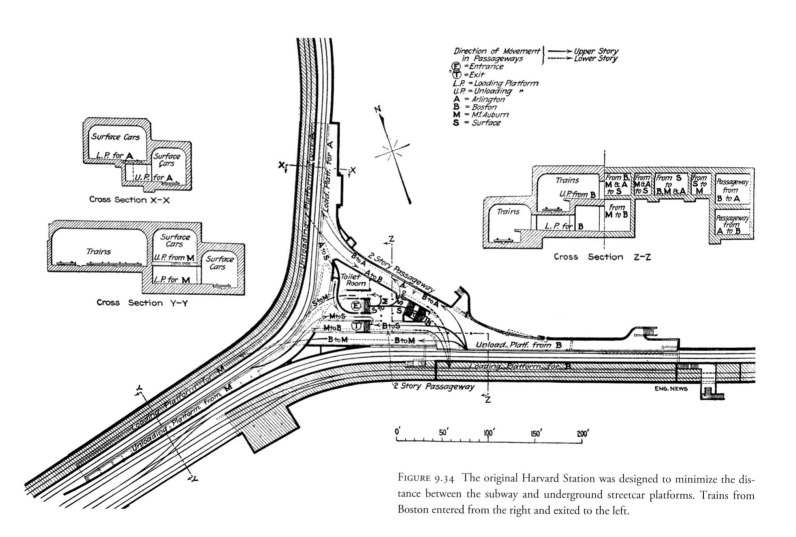

FIGURE 9.34 The original Harvard Station was designed to minimize the distance between the subway and underground streetcar platforms. Trains from Boston entered from the right and exited to the left.

FIGURE 9.35 Harvard Station, outbound subway platform. The exit ("Out to College Yard") led to the Porcellian Gate, opposite Holyoke Street. Photo 1912.

FIGURE 9.36 Second Harvard Station headhouse (1928, Blackall, Clapp & Whittemore, architects). The new kiosk was designed to be safer for pedestrians and more transparent to converging vehicles. Photo ca. 1935.

While the underground station was praised for its efficient handling of crowds, the surface structure was a serious hazard in the age of the automobile, and the Harvard Square Business-men's Association began calling for its removal in 1919. The streetcar tracks on each side left little room for other traffic, drivers could not see vehicles approaching on converging streets, and there was no sidewalk for pedestrians cutting across the Square. A replacement followed the concept, if not the plans, of Professor Charles B. Breed of M.I.T. to be transparent to oncoming traffic. Constructed in 1928, the new kiosk had a thin copper roof of shallow, intersecting barrel vaults supported by piers of alternating waterstruck brick and limestone in a pattern similar to that of Harvard's Class of 1877 Gate behind Widener Library (figure 9.36). Bearing signs promising "Eight Minutes to Park Street," this structure symbolized Harvard Square to generations of students and visitors (see figure 3.56).

The yards and shops of the Boston Elevated occupied 10½ acres between Eliot Square and Memorial Drive, from Kennedy Street to University Road (figure 9.37; see also figure 3.71). The company already owned the carbarns inherited from the West End Street Railway and took the rest of the site by eminent domain. A contractor excavated a third of the area to about 10 feet below street level and drove 12,000 piles to support an inspection and repair shop, storage tracks for 122 subway cars, and a loop track for turning trains. The perimeter of the loop along Kennedy Street served a platform known as Stadium Station, which was opened for Harvard football games (figure 9.38). The Elevated built a brick office building for the surface lines, 144 feet long but only 20 feet deep, on Mt. Auburn Street opposite the streetcar tunnel in 1912. This last remaining structure from the period when transit activities dominated the southwest sector of Harvard Square was restored as a restaurant in 2015–16 (figure 9.39).

FIGURE 9.37 The Boston Elevated shop and yards complex nearing completion in 1912. From left to right are the power station on the east side of Kennedy Street; the Eliot Square subway yards and shop buildings; a few remaining stables and houses on Murray Street; and the streetcar barns and workshops at Bennett Street. The printing plant of the University Press is at far right on University Road.

FIGURE 9.38 Crowds exiting Stadium Station, Kennedy Street at Memorial Drive, after a game on November 19, 1921. On this occasion Harvard beat Yale, 10 to 3.

FIGURE 9.39 Boston Elevated Railway, Division Seven headquarters, 112 Mt. Auburn Street (1912, F.F. Snow, architect). Placed between the carbarns and the entrance to the "surface subway," the building on the right provided lockers and recreation facilities for motormen and conductors, offices for administrators, and a vault for cash fares. Trackless trolleys were introduced in 1936. Photo May 1939.

The high quality of the Boston Elevated Railway's structures was not achieved by accident. Beginning about 1906, the company retained Robert S. Peabody, one of the best-known architects in New England, to advise its chief engineer, George A. Kimball. Peabody & Stearns had designed Matthews Hall (1871), Hemenway Gymnasium (1878), and the Weld Boat House (1906) for Harvard University, as well as city halls in Worcester and Chelsea and Boston's South Station. Working with Peabody was an advisory committee that included Edmund M. Wheelwright, designer of the Longfellow Bridge; Ralph Adams Cram, an early advocate of the Gothic style; Charles A. Coolidge of Shepley, Rutan & Coolidge, successor to H.H. Richardson's practice; Charles D. Maginnis of Maginnis & Walsh, designer of Boston College's earliest buildings at Chestnut Hill; and Clarence H. Blackall of Blackall, Clapp & Whittemore, a designer

of theaters and commercial buildings and secretary of the Cambridge Municipal Art Society.

This committee gathered "from time to time at Mr. Peabody's office for discussion of plans and elevations of forthcoming transit projects," which included the stations of the Washington Street subway, the Lincoln Wharf and South Boston power stations, the Charles River viaduct, and the Forest Hills terminal (*Boston Sunday Herald,* Mar. 24, 1912). For Cambridge, the committee reviewed the Kendall, Central, and Harvard stations and the tunnel entrances near the Longfellow Bridge and at Flagstaff Park. The company showed a remarkable sensitivity to context, providing robust Georgian Revival designs in Harvard Square but Beaux-Arts–influenced stair enclosures in Central Square.

The Massachusetts Bay Transportation Authority began the extension of the Cambridge Subway to Alewife in 1978 and completed it in 1986. The disused carbarns and storage yards on Bennett Street were cleared for temporary parking, but the subway turning loop and car shop remained in use until a new facility was completed in South Boston in 1976. A temporary station, Harvard-Brattle, was constructed at the mouth of the tunnel and served until the new Harvard Station was completed in 1983.[7] The MBTA intended to build a new headhouse designed by the Chicago office of Skidmore, Owings & Merrill, but the Cambridge Historical Commission nominated the 1927 kiosk for the National Register of Historic Places, and the firm designed a much smaller entrance that allowed the older structure to be restored as a newsstand (see figure 3.86).

INDUSTRY

To speak of the industrial development of Old Cambridge today seems like an oxymoron, but in the 19th century the area's preeminence in printing was on a par with East Cambridge's dominance of the glass and furniture industries. Easy communication between authors, printers, and proofreaders was essential in this period and constituted Old Cambridge's locational advantage in this competitive field. By the late 19th century, the trade was dominated by a few close associates at the center of a complex community of booksellers, authors, editors, proofreaders, printers, and bookbinders. The two most important printers in Old Cambridge—the University Press and The Riverside Press— were among the best known in America.

Old Cambridge experienced some early effects of industrialization, with print shops emerging in the heart of the village and a growing community of white- and blue-collar workers, but few other factories followed. The rest of the city developed a diversified industrial base; one commentator, writing in 1930, noted a 300 percent gain in manufactures in ten years and characterized the city as famous for "its factories, rather than its educational institutions." Cambridge was "as much an industrial boom town as Akron, Ohio, or Detroit, Michigan, though a much more artistic community because of its unusually attractive Charles River frontage" (Stone, 773). Most development took place in the Kendall Square area, but until zoning was adopted in 1924 factories could be built in any neighborhood.

Printing and Publishing

Cambridge had the first press in British North America. Harvard University served as a general printer of religious and legal tracts for the colony until 1692, when the enterprise was abandoned in favor of commercial printers in Boston (see chapter 1). Printing resumed in Cambridge in 1800. When Reverend Timothy Hilliard, minister of the First Parish Church, died in 1790, his widow could not afford to send their son William to Harvard with his two older brothers and apprenticed him to a printer in Boston. William returned to Cambridge to open a printing office and immediately secured the college's patronage. In 1802, when the corporation voted to procure its own press and type and engage a printer, President Joseph Willard turned to Hilliard, who operated the college's press alongside his own and published books under the University Press imprint. Eliab Metcalf, a printer from Wrentham, became a partner in 1808, and in 1823 Hilliard & Metcalf persuaded the college to construct a new print shop on Holyoke Street.

William Hilliard became a bookseller and publisher as well as a printer. He opened the University Bookstore on the corner of Holyoke Street in 1808, and about 1812 he partnered with Jacob Cummings, proprietor of the Boston Bookstore and author of some of the textbooks Hilliard was printing. Cummings & Hilliard published many of the books that were required for admission to Harvard College. Such was Hilliard's prominence that in 1824 Thomas Jefferson sent him a draft for $15,000 and engaged him to procure books in America and abroad for the library of the University of Virginia. In 1829 he and James Brown collaborated with Thomas Warland to put up a new brick building "occupied by Hilliard & Brown as a book store" and printing office (Middlesex Deeds 297/476). The store remained on the corner of Holyoke Street until 1859 (see figure 3.14).

Hilliard employed several young men who became important in the trade. John Bartlett joined Hilliard & Brown as an apprentice bookbinder in 1836 and owned the bookstore from 1849 to 1858. Bartlett was a relentless collector of quotations and trivia and in 1851 published *A Collection of College Words and Customs,* a compilation by graduating senior Benjamin Homer Hall. Four years later he published *Familiar Quotations,* which went through nine editions before his death in 1905 and made him a wealthy man with an estate at 165 Brattle Street.

In 1827, in the spate of economizing that eliminated the sloop *Harvard,* the corporation sold its interest in the University Press to Eliab Metcalf. After he died in 1835, the press continued under Charles Folsom and then passed to Metcalf's brother Charles. Folsom was the firm's proofreader, and his three years as University Librarian in the 1820s gave the press an academic character that was greatly appreciated by its authors. A constantly changing roster of partnerships maintained the imprint until Albion K.P. Welch and Marshall Bigelow took over in 1859. In 1867 Welch, Bigelow & Co. moved from Harvard's old printing plant on Holyoke Street into the remodeled Brattle House hotel (see figure 8.2). Welch died in 1870, leaving a mansion at 24 Craigie Street (see figure 4.30), but the firm continued until James R. Osgood & Company, its chief client, failed in 1878. Osgood was the leading Boston publisher of the day, and books by Holmes, Palfrey, Longfellow, Hawthorne, Whittier, Emerson, and Lowell all came out under the University Press imprint.[8] After Osgood and Welch failed, Henry Houghton acquired Osgood's list and published many of his authors at The Riverside Press.

A Boston firm, John Wilson & Son, moved into Harvard's old plant on Holyoke Street in 1865. In 1879 Wilson acquired Welch, Bigelow's University Press imprint and its Brattle Square facility, where it operated with over 300 employees and fifty-eight presses (figure 9.40). The connection with Harvard remained strong, although the college had established its own printing office in 1871 as a secure means of printing examination booklets. After reorganizing in 1895, the University Press built a large plant on University Road facing the Charles River (figures 9.41–9.42). The literary connection that had been severed in 1878 was never fully restored, and the company became a contract printer, producing books for various publishers and advertisements for direct mail campaigns. A merger in 1929 with Tolman Print, a Brockton firm specializing in shoebox labels, reinforced this trend. In 1966 the University Press gave up its presses, moved to Winchester, and became a printing broker.

After 1872 the single press that President Eliot installed on the second floor of Wadsworth House took on more and more work of the university's work, from job printing to books and journals, and the operation eventually filled the basement of University Hall. Charles Eliot Norton promoted the idea that Harvard should establish a publishing arm for scholarly works, and in 1906 he showed Eliot plans for a new building designed by H. Langford Warren's architectural firm, Warren & Smith, for the College Wharf property that then bordered Memorial Drive (figure 9.43). Two years later Eliot appointed Charles Chester Lane, a former executive with the East Cambridge textbook publisher Ginn & Co., as publications agent. In 1913 Lane became the first head of the Harvard University Press, which took over Randall Hall on Kirkland Street in 1916. The Harvard University Press and the Printing Office separated in 1942, but the latter remained at Randall until William James Hall replaced it in 1962.

FIGURE 9.40 The Brattle House failed as a hotel but succeeded as a printing plant for the University Press, which added a boiler house, steam engine, plate foundry, and fireproof annex for storage (see figure 8.2). The William Brattle house at right has not received the entrance vestibule added by the Cambridge Social Union in 1889. Photo ca. 1867–1873.

FIGURE 9.41 University Press, 33 University Road (1895, Morton D. Safford, architect). The complex occupied a prominent site overlooking the Charles River until 1970. The Society of St. John the Evangelist acquired the Memorial Drive frontage in 1924. The large Mansard at right is William L. Whitney's 1860 mansion at 126 Mt. Auburn Street, which was razed in 1908. Photo ca. 1900.

FIGURE 9.42 University Press, 33 University Road. Although clad with brick, this was one of the earliest reinforced concrete factories in New England. The site was cleared in 1970 and is now occupied by the University Green condominium complex. Photo 1969.

FIGURE 9.43 Proposed plant for the Harvard University Press, Memorial Drive (1906, Warren & Smith, architects). The plans do not specify a location, but the site plan matches the shape and dimensions of Harvard's College Wharf property.

Two of William Hilliard's clerks, Charles Little and James Brown, founded one of the most important publishing firms in America and fostered the greatest printing house in Cambridge, The Riverside Press. Charles C. Little (1799–1869) was born in Maine, worked as a clerk at Hilliard's Boston store, and became a partner in 1827. James Brown (1800–55) was born in Acton, clerked in the Cambridge store, and was made a partner there in 1826. Brown then became Little's partner in the Boston store, and in 1837 they formed a new partnership that became Little & Brown (later, Little, Brown & Company). Little married William Hilliard's daughter Sarah in 1829 and acquired John Appleton's Federal mansion and estate at 163 Brattle Street in 1840. He joined Gardiner Hubbard and Estes Howe in establishing the Cambridge Railroad and the Water Works and built Little's Block, the first private dormitory for undergraduates, in 1854.

Brown moved to Boston in 1829 but remained active in literary circles. He purchased the former William Winthrop mansion in 1849, and within a few years he and Little controlled most of the riverfront downstream to Western Avenue (see chapter 4). Like many Boston booksellers of the day, Little & Brown was also a publisher and had close relationships with printing firms.

Henry O. Houghton (1823–1895), a University of Vermont graduate, came to Boston in 1846 to work as a journalist and proofreader. In 1848 he purchased a partnership in the printing firm of Freeman & Bolles and moved the business to a new building that Little & Brown were erecting on Remington Street (figure 9.44). This was described as "a large and handsome wooden building, for the printing office and bindery, and two smaller brick buildings, one for the steam engine and the safe, and the other for a fireproof warehouse" (*Boston Daily Evening Traveler,* in Ballou, 24).

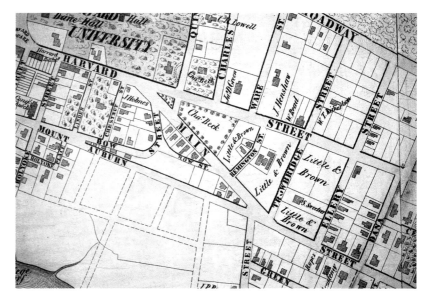

FIGURE 9.44 The original Little & Brown plant on Remington Street in 1854. The plant was rented to another printer, Allen & Bowles, after Houghton relocated in 1852. Charles Little bought out James Brown's heirs after his death in 1855 and subdivided the property for residential development.

Growing labor unrest among Boston's ninety-odd printing firms made this a fortuitous move; when the printers went on strike in November 1849 Cambridge was outside union territory. Although a young woman who set type for Houghton during the strike was attacked by Boston printers, he:

> went about amongst some teachers and other well-educated young women in Cambridge, persuaded them to put themselves under his tuition, privately trained them to set type, and, when the battle seemed to have gone against him, suddenly appeared with his reinforcements. … He was one of the first to demonstrate on a considerable scale the practicability of the employment of women in this capacity. (Scudder, *Houghton,* 73)

In 1851 the city disposed of its almshouse property on the Charles near River Street, advertising a three-story brick building 75 by 40 feet, with a hospital, a barn, sheds and about 15 acres of land "ten feet above high water mark, making it one of the most beautiful sites for … houses of the first class" and containing "a large number of young and vigorous fruit trees … several acres of strawberry vines in excellent condition, besides a large quantity of currant and raspberry plants" (*Chronicle,* May 3, 1851). Little and Brown may have felt that the isolated site would offer security against labor unrest and purchased it for $24,000. They announced that the location would be known as "Riverside," and within a year Houghton's firm had fifty hands setting type and twenty more operating five steam-powered presses. Another partnership operated a stereotype foundry, and a bindery employed forty men and women who used 15,000 sheepskins to bind 50,000 volumes a year.

Houghton initially printed all the work of Little & Brown, Ticknor & Fields, and G. & C. Merriam & Co. on a contract basis. During this period he developed relationships with many authors.[9] When the tide served, Dr. Oliver Wendell Holmes was known to sail his boat from its mooring at the foot of Beacon Hill up the river for lunch, while James Russell Lowell, editor of *The Atlantic Monthly* from 1857 to 1861, often walked down from Elmwood to check proofs. Houghton purchased the plant

from Little & Brown in 1867 and entered a new partnership with Melancthon Hurd, a Connecticut bookseller with New York connections; the firm then became a publisher as well as a printer, with offices in Boston. George Harrison Mifflin was admitted to partnership in 1872, and the firm became Houghton, Mifflin & Co. in 1880. The firm's excellence in typography and printing earned medals at the Philadelphia Centennial Exposition in 1876 and the Paris Exposition in 1878. After Houghton died in 1895, Mifflin placed even greater emphasis on artistic design and fine printing, producing the firm's well-known Riverside Press Editions of literary classics designed by artist Bruce Rogers (figure 9.45).

Houghton began the plant's first major expansion in 1867, building a three-story factory and several houses along Daye Court for his workmen, creating the nucleus of the Riverside neighborhood (figures 9.46–9.47).[10] The Riverside Press evolved into a major industrial complex with fifteen multistory brick and concrete buildings. The firm favored prestigious architects better known for their residential work. Bradlee, Winslow & Wetherell designed a building for lithography in 1886, C. Herbert McClare and George Fogerty received commissions in 1902 and 1904, and Newhall & Blevins designed four buildings between 1907 and 1917 (figures 9.48–9.49). The last major expansion was a four-story reinforced concrete factory built in 1946 (figure 9.50). Houghton, Mifflin sold the Riverside Press name, machinery, and equipment to Rand McNally in 1970; the plant closed in 1971, and the company cleared the site in 1973. Houghton sold 1½ acres to Orion Research, which put up a building designed by ADD Inc. of Cambridge, and donated the remainder to the city for Riverside Press Park.

The Press was an important source of employment for intelligent workers of both sexes. Until well into the 20th century young hands began with a four- or five-year apprenticeship. Although the work was generally clean and required a high level of skill, conditions were not easy. The Cambridge Typographical Union won a reduction in the ten-hour, six-day week to an eight-hour, six-day week in 1906, before the eight-hour day

FIGURE 9.45 Houghton, Mifflin's colophon, shown here on a decorative mural on the second floor of the Thomas Jefferson Building of the Library of Congress. Designed by Sidney L. Smith in 1884, it appeared in many versions until the mid-20th century. The firm's motto, "tout bien ou rien," means "all done well or not at all."

The Riverside Press

Cambridge, Mass

Frank Myrick Del

F.T.Stuart Sc

FIGURE 9.46 The Riverside Press about 1875. Houghton built the Mansard-roofed factory in 1867. The attached building on the right with four dormers was the city's almshouse of 1838, with a fireproof extension built in 1851. The building at right rear is a fireproof warehouse built in 1859. The workers' houses at left are on Daye Court.

became usual in other trades. In 1921 the company's resistance to a union demand for a forty-four-hour week and a return to previous pay levels triggered a strike. During the Depression, business was so slow that workers were called in for three days every other week, but none were laid off. When Houghton, Mifflin closed the plant it was the last major book publisher to operate its own presses. The company had maintained an intimate connection with Cambridge authors and printing tradespeople longer than any other firm.

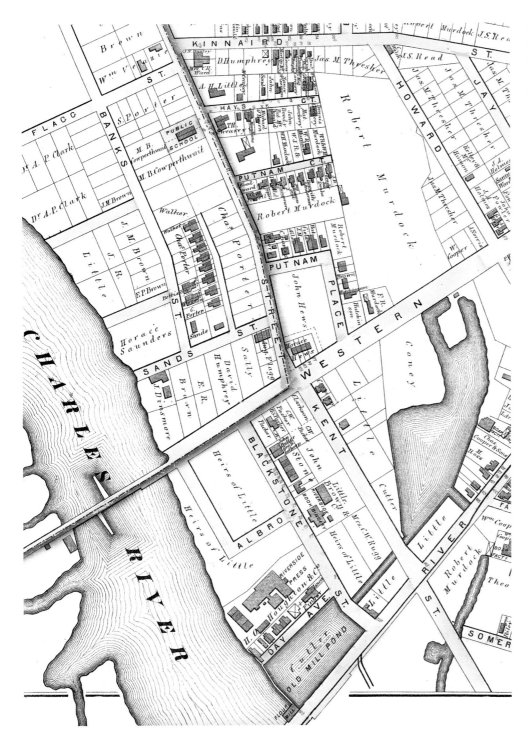

FIGURE 9.47 Riverside in 1873, showing Houghton's Riverside Press, the company's houses on "Day Ave." (Daye Court), and Little, Brown's bindery across Blackstone Street. The "old mill pond" powered a flour mill on the current generated by falling tides.

FIGURE 9.48 Riverside Press book storage building (1907, Newhall & Blevins, architects). Houghton, Mifflin's interest in architecture is evident in this otherwise functional warehouse, with a frieze of moulded brick, colored tiles, and stucco medallions bearing the firm's colophon.

FIGURE 9.49 Riverside Press addition (1910, Newhall & Blevins, architects). The building extended 122 feet along Blackstone Street; the saw-tooth roof and large steel sash windows afforded the greatest possible amount of natural light.

FIGURE 9.50 Riverside Press storage and manufacturing building, 349 River Street (1946, Ganteaume & McMullen, architects). The last addition to the Riverside Press complex was a throwback to the reinforced concrete factories that proliferated in Cambridge from about 1895 to 1930; the unnecessary brick infill reflected the traditional architectural preferences of the client. Photo 1947.

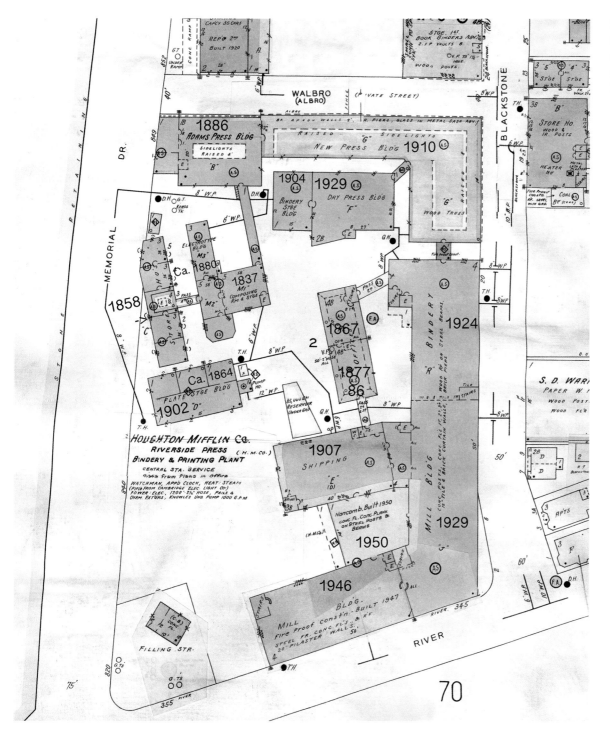

Several buildings of related firms survive nearby. Little & Brown built a bindery across Blackstone Street in 1863; the oldest remaining section, the plant's fireproof brick warehouse, is now surrounded by later structures (figures 9.52–9.53). Little, Brown & Co. chose the prestigious Boston firm of Hartwell & Richardson as the architect for at least three projects; their 1902 brick factory at 237 Putnam Avenue is a model of refined understatement. The Cambridgeport Diary Company (later Standard Diary) made a similar choice in 1889 when it commissioned a stylish four-story brick printing plant from Chamberlin & Whidden, another firm noted for its fine Queen Anne and Colonial Revival residences (figure 9.54). All of these buildings now house offices.

FIGURE 9.53 Riverside Bindery, 237 Putnam Avenue (1902, Hartwell, Richardson & Driver, architects). The availability of electric lights allowed the architects to revert to an earlier pattern of mill construction. The many small windows and finely detailed brickwork complement the residential scale of Putnam Avenue, whereas a more cost-conscious client might have intruded on the neighborhood with a reinforced-concrete building and large factory sash. Photo 2015.

FIGURE 9.52 Riverside Bindery, 19–23 Blackstone Street (1892, Hartwell & Richardson; 1920, Hartwell, Richardson & Driver, architects). The Little, Brown & Co. bindery incorporated several buildings designed by the Hartwell firm, which was better-known for its residential commissions. The patterned brick building at left was a fireproof storehouse; the 1920 warehouse at right replaced the firm's original 1863 building. Photo 2013.

FIGURE 9.54 Cambridgeport Diary Co., 24–26 Blackstone Street (1889, Chamberlin & Whidden, architects). Edwin Dresser, who had worked for Harper & Brothers, a New York publisher, began printing pocket diaries in Cambridgeport in 1850. The firm moved to this location in 1890 and became the Standard Diary Company in 1906. Architects' rendering, ca. 1890.

A third important printing venture failed at an early date but left a significant architectural legacy. When Houghton & Bolles moved to Riverside in 1851, Little & Brown leased the shop on Remington Street to Boston printers John Allen and John Farnham. They bought land on Arrow Street in 1860 and with the help of a $10,000 loan from Harvard University erected a printing plant complete with steam boiler, engine, and shafting to drive the presses. In 1865 Allen & Farnham sold the plant to Frederick Dakin and Eliab W. Metcalf, whose further improvements doubled the value of the property; in 1867 the complex consisted of a frame factory, a brick engine house, and a residence for the engineer.[11] When Dakin & Metcalf failed, Albion Welch and Marshall Bigelow partnered with a Boston firm to acquire the complex. The new owners sold the property out of the printing business, probably in order to suppress competition.

The plant's new owner was the Reversible Collar Company. In 1862 George K. Snow of Boston invented a method of making detachable paper collars for men's shirts. A further improvement that involved mating paper and cloth from continuous rolls "enabled the company to produce the most perfect fabric for machine-made collars that had been discovered" (Gilman, 376). In 1870 the company added a superintendent's office and expanded the factory on Mt. Auburn Street. More construction took place in 1875, and in 1889 the company rebuilt part of the Arrow Street frontage into a new structure 130 feet long (figure 9.55). Still pressed for space, Reversible erected a larger factory on Putnam Avenue in 1895 (figure 9.56). That year, the company produced more than 11 million shirt collars and cuffs as well as 1,400 tons of coated paper stock. Although changing fashions reduced the demand for its primary product, the company continued for many years as a supplier of coated paper; a successor firm in Davenport, Iowa, still produced paper collars on the original machinery in 2008. Harvard University razed the Putnam Avenue factory in 1960 to build Peabody Terrace. The Boston Bookbinding Company bought the Arrow Street

FIGURE 9.55 Allen & Farnham/Dakin & Metcalf/Reversible Collar Co. plant, 8–12 Arrow Street (1860–1907). From left to right are the superintendent's office (1870) and a factory addition (1889, S.S. Woodcock, architect). Adaptive reuse of the complex for professional offices began in 1965. Photo 2014.

building in 1898; it continued to serve various manufacturing purposes until 1966, when it was renovated for offices.

In 1912 the Sterling Knit Goods Company built a three-story concrete factory at 917 Memorial Drive, and two years later the Hingham Knitting Company put up another nearby (see figure 4.269). The location was advantageous because cheap labor was available in the Marsh and Riverside neighborhoods; the Hingham mill, for example, employed over a hundred workers producing seamless hosiery until it relocated to Lowell in 1929. The building became a landmark of the women's liberation movement after the feminist group Bread & Roses occupied it for ten days in 1971; their protest led to the founding of the Cambridge Women's Center. Harvard razed the Sterling mill in 1962 and the Hingham building in 1971 (figure 9.57).

FIGURE 9.56 Reversible Collar Co. factory, 111 Putnam Avenue (1895, Arthur F. Gray, architect; demolished 1960). Photo ca. 1938.

Industrial activity has completely vanished from Old Cambridge, and the mariners, street railway men, printers, and craftsmen who once labored among the more visible academicians, professionals, and businessmen have been long forgotten. Many industrial buildings remain, however, whether in disguise or adapted to new uses, and they contribute to the distinctive layering of periods and styles in Old Cambridge.

FIGURE 9.57 Hingham Knitting Company mill, 45 Hingham Street/888 Memorial Drive (1914, Wisner Martin, architect; demolished 1971). This two-story reinforced concrete mill was characteristic of many modern manufacturing buildings in New England. Narrow in proportion to its length, the floor-to-ceiling windows maximized natural light. Harvard razed the building after its occupation by radical feminists in 1971. Photo 1968.

FIGURE 10.1 Harvard Bicentennial Celebration, September 9, 1836. From left to right, Stoughton II (1804), Holden (1742), Hollis (1762), Harvard III (1764), University (1813), Massachusetts (1718), and Dane (1832) halls and the First Parish Church (1833).

10 Development of Harvard University

Cambridge at any time is full of ghosts; but on that day the anointed eye saw the crowd of spirits that mingled with the procession in the vacant spaces, year by year, as the classes proceeded; and then the far longer train of ghosts that followed the company, of the men that wore before us the college honors and the laurels of the State—the long winding train reaching back into eternity. (Ralph Waldo Emerson's description of the Harvard Bicentennial Celebration, in *Journals,* September 13, 1836)

The relationship between town and gown pervades Old Cambridge. Newtowne was founded as the capital of Massachusetts, but once the General Court moved to Boston in 1634 the village had no *raison d'etre* until the legislature created Harvard College in 1636. From the outset, the President and Fellows and the Board of Overseers of Harvard College included the most important ministers and political leaders of the colony, and the early college buildings were some of the most impressive in New England.[1] Cambridge's well-known sense of exceptionalism derives from this felicitous event.

For two centuries Harvard generally confined itself to today's Old Yard. In the 19th century the university (as it was designated by the legislature in 1780) began to expand, acquiring 64 acres north of the Yard, establishing outposts at the Botanic Garden, the Observatory, Divinity Hall, and the University Museum, and laying out a faculty enclave along Kirkland Street. After 1900 Harvard's expansion began to collide with Cambridge's own growth, setting the stage for a century of conflict.

Until well into the suburban period, Harvard determined the social composition of Old Cambridge. At the beginning of the 19th century, professors were mostly parochial, untraveled men who lived in college buildings or in the village. A few achieved distinction, but in 1801 an alumnus characterized them as "little better than Monks [filled with] enmity and suspicion of one another. The crew of a Privateer displays more social benevolence than so many Presidents and Professors collected" (George Minot to William Minot, in Channing, 196; in Story, 80). This began to change under President John Kirkland (1810–28). Some of the new faculty, such as Henry Wadsworth Longfellow and Europeans Charles Follen and Louis Agassiz, married daughters of wealthy Boston merchants; others, like James Russell Lowell, were members of the emerging Brahmin class. All brought Cambridge international renown. Later in the century it was common for well-to-do parents of undergraduates to settle in Cambridge while their sons attended school and for graduates to return to build elaborate homes and invest in real estate. Old Cambridge became an appealing suburb for families with intellectual sympathies and a fertile ground for architects. Hundreds of support staff—carpenters, glaziers, housekeepers, and waiters—lived unrecorded lives in the village and in the nearby neighborhoods of Lewisville, the Marsh, Kerry Corner, and Riverside.

Harvard students were noted for their habitually riotous and often arrogant behavior which adversely affected life in the village. President Everett recalled the "incendiary outrages" of the 1830s, when "every outhouse, shed, workshop and wooden fence near the Yard was marked for destruction" (Frothingham, 278). Students sometimes entertained prostitutes in their rooms and frequently battled "West Cambridge bullies" and "Port toughs" (or muckers, as the students called local youth in the early 20th century [K. Porter, 82]).[2] The majority lived in town, patronizing boarding houses, private dormitories, clubs, and exclusive stores. Student riots in 1927, 1932, and 1937 provoked Cambridge police to respond with billy clubs, tear gas, and mass arrests, but property damage was usually minor until the antiwar riots of the 1970s (see chapter 3). In the late 20th century, Harvard Square became a mecca for young adults, and many merchants came to depend on their patronage.

Architecture and planning in Cambridge have been strongly influenced by the university. Some Harvard buildings introduced novel stylistic features, while many professors retained notable architects for their own residences. Faculty at the School of Architecture, from Langford Warren to Walter Gropius and Josep Lluis Sert, also practiced and along with their students made Cambridge a national center of the profession in the 1960s. While dean of the Graduate School of Design, Sert accepted commissions for academic, public, and commercial buildings in Cambridge and served as chairman of the Cambridge Planning Board during a particularly critical period in the 1950s (see chapter 2).

Harvard has never been unresponsive to local affairs, although it has often feigned indifference. In the 18th century faculty members served as representatives in the General Court and county registers of deeds, and the administrative officers of the college were often influential townsmen. President Edward Everett designed the city seal and spoke at high school graduations. President Eliot encouraged faculty members to run for elected offices; university chaplain Reverend Andrew Preston Peabody served for many years on the Cambridge School Committee,

which named a school for him. In the 1930s Dean James M. Landis of the Law School masterminded the adoption of proportional representation in local elections. In recent times, Harvard graduates have served lengthy terms on the city council and joined the city's professional staff.

While President Eliot constructively engaged the city administration, President Lowell (1909–33) was dismissive and condescending. By Lowell's time city hall was largely controlled by Irish-Americans, and their mutual antipathy was sharpened by Harvard's destruction of Kerry Corner, home of many politicians. City Councillors like Michael ("Mickey the Dude") Sullivan (1936–49) and Alfred Vellucci (1955–89) found it rewarding to taunt the university with threats of paving the Yard for parking or making the Lampoon a public toilet. In the last third of the century, Cambridge began to exercise real power over the university through more restrictive zoning and other legislative measures. The resolution of several long-standing conflicts at the beginning of the 21st century came at a high price for Harvard and encouraged the school to expand beyond Cambridge.

EARLY HARVARD

The scituation of this Colledg is very pleasant, at the end of a spacious plain, more like a bowling green than a Wilderness, neer a fair navigable river, environed with many Neighbouring Towns of note; … the building thought by some to be too gorgeous for a Wilderness, and yet too mean in other apprehensions for a Colledg, it is at present inlarging by purchase of the neighbour houses; it hath conveniences of a fair Hall, comfortable studies, and a good Library. (Edward Johnson, *Wonder-working Providence of Sions Savior in New England,* 1651, 201)

Harvard's earliest building was a simple dwelling built by William Peyntree about 1633 and sold to the Overseers in 1637 or 1638. The house served as the residence of the first master, Nathaniel Eaton, and the first president, Henry Dunster, until it was replaced in 1644 by a new president's residence. In 1651 the college purchased an adjacent house from Edward Goffe as living quarters for students. Both were probably gone by the 1670s; their foundations are marked by bronze plaques in Massachusetts Avenue near Wadsworth House (figure 10.2).

The college began constructing its first building in 1638 and completed it in time for commencement in 1642. Set in the middle of the long, narrow Peyntree lot, Harvard Hall faced south toward the village, with wings extending toward the stock pens on Cow Yard Row (figure 10.3; see figure 1.8).[3] A brewhouse and the Indian College (ca. 1655) completed the early campus. The latter, Harvard's first brick building, was intended to house twenty Indian scholars, but when no more enrolled after 1665, it accommodated ordinary undergraduates, and, after 1677, the college printing press. Demolished in 1698, its bricks were used to build Stoughton Hall the next year.

Harvard Hall deteriorated quickly, and by 1671 a new building was being planned for a site opposite the burying ground. Harvard Hall II was a substantial brick structure, probably the most impressive in New England in the 17th century. The master builder, Samuel Andrew (1621–1701), was a local man who had been a mariner like his father and was "well skilled in mathematics" (Paige, 480). Measuring 99 by 42 feet, the structure required tremendous timbers to span its width, a huge quantity of bricks, and the services of many carpenters, masons, and laborers during the six years it took to finish it. The building's great hall (which served as chapel, dining hall, lecture hall, and commencement venue), library, and rooms for two tutors and fourteen students formed an academic community similar to an English university.

The placement of Harvard Hall II at a distance from the village and the formation of quadrangles facing the burying ground became the organizing principle of the college throughout the next century. Harvard Hall II faced the third president's house, built in 1680 on the current site of Massachusetts Hall. Stoughton Hall, a dormitory for thirty students and a tutor, completed Harvard's first quadrangle in 1698. Privies, hog pens, and a brewhouse were in what is now the Old Yard (between

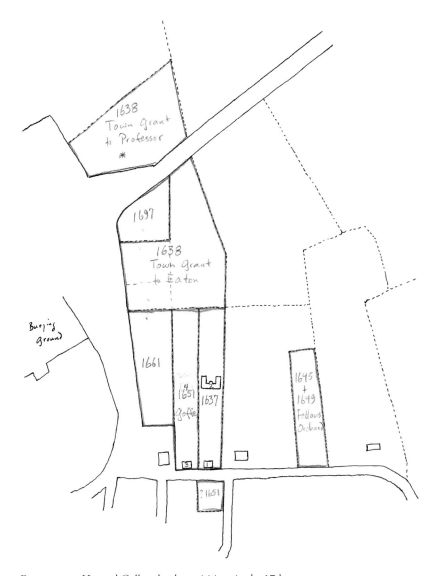

FIGURE 10.2 Harvard College land acquisitions in the 17th century.

Figure 10.3 "The old college from the yard," a conjectural view of the north elevation of Harvard Hall I drawn in 1933 for historian Samuel Eliot Morison by architect Harold R. Shurtleff, who was head of the research department at Perry, Shaw & Hepburn when that firm designed the restoration of Colonial Williamsburg.

Massachusetts and University halls), near a brook that flowed through Brattle and Eliot streets to the river.

Siting the college north of the village had a magnetic effect on local institutions. The original core at Dunster and Mt. Auburn streets dissolved in 1651 when the community erected the Second Meetinghouse on Watch House Hill next to the college. The earliest known courthouse (ca. 1707–8) faced the meetinghouse, ensuring Harvard Square's future as the center of the village.

EIGHTEENTH CENTURY HARVARD

The five buildings that Harvard put up in the 18th century created a series of courtyards facing Peabody Street and the Common. Massachusetts Hall, now Harvard's oldest building, was begun in 1718 and opened in 1720, completing a brick quadrangle with Harvard Hall II and Stoughton I (figure 10.4). As Bainbridge Bunting noted, it possessed "the simple dignity of an Early Georgian building in a provincial town where the budget was limited and sponsors were uninterested in external show" (Report Four, 151). Its present appearance is the result of many remodelings and changes in use, including an interior reconstruction in steel and concrete after a 1924 fire.

In the mid-18th century Harvard's four professors resided nearby, while the tutors, librarian, and proctors lived in college halls with the students. In 1726 the legislature appropriated funds for an official residence for President Benjamin Wadsworth, a fine example of early Georgian design that clearly influenced William Brattle's 1727 mansion at 42 Brattle Street (see figures 6.5 and 6.7). The president's house, like its neighbors the parsonage and the Wigglesworth house, faced the village. Unlike the earlier Eaton and Goffe houses, it had a generous lawn that emphasized the social standing of the president. (This disappeared when Massachusetts Avenue was widened in the 19th century.)

The college staked out a second quadrangle in 1742 with its first religious building, about 100 feet north of Harvard Hall. More advanced architecturally than anything Harvard had built before, Holden Chapel introduced the High Georgian mode

A Prospect of the Colledges in Cambridge in New England

Figure 10.4 "A Prospect of the Colledges in Cambridge in New England," by William Burgis, 1726. This earliest known view (apart from the 1693 Franquelin vignette, figure 1.13) shows Harvard's first complete open quadrangle, with (from left to right) Harvard Hall II (1671, destroyed by fire 1764), Stoughton I (1698, demolished 1781), and Massachusetts Hall (1718).

that was reflected in the loyalist mansions of the 1760s (figure 10.5). Its principal facade faced the road and was crowned by a pediment displaying the floridly carved crest of the Holden family, which provided a handsome motif for Harvard's Georgian Revival River Houses two centuries later. The original entrance was sealed in 1880; a copy of the Holden crest was added to the east pediment in the 1920s.

In 1762 the legislature funded Hollis Hall, a dormitory whose design is credited to master builder Thomas Dawes of Boston. The placement of Hollis between Harvard Hall II and Holden Chapel completed the second quadrangle. Harvard Hall burned to the ground in 1764; the present building, Harvard Hall III, was designed by Sir Francis Bernard, the royal governor, and erected by Dawes on the same site as its predecessor (figure 10.6). The first college building with no living quarters,

FIGURE 10.5 Holden Chapel (1742, attributed to John Smibert) about 1860, looking toward Cambridge Common and showing the new entrance in the east facade. By this time the windows had been lowered about two feet and cone-shaped skylights added to provide better light for lectures and recitations.

FIGURE 10.6 Harvard College in 1764, showing Holden, Hollis, Harvard III, Stoughton I, Massachusetts Hall, and the roof of the parsonage at the extreme right.

it contained a kitchen and dining hall on the ground floor, a hall above, and classrooms on the third floor.

The orientation of the college toward Massachusetts Avenue was reinforced in 1772, when Harvard converted the 1770 Daniel Wiswall house into a dormitory called College House. After the Revolution the school bought more property in the village, including a house next to Wiswall's that was rented to Professor Samuel Webber (see figure 1.17). Acquisition of President Leverett's 3½-acre pasture in 1786 and Professor Edward Wigglesworth's 4½-acre homestead in 1794 almost doubled the college's

FIGURE 10.7 Harvard land and buildings in 1799. The blue line indicates holdings in 1700.

1. Brewhouse (1668), burned 1814
2. Stoughton I (1699), razed 1781
3. Massachusetts Hall (1718)
4. Wadsworth House (1726)
5. Holden Chapel (1742)
6. Hollis Hall (1762)
7. Harvard Hall III (1764)
8. College House I (Wiswall's Den, 1770), acquired 1772, razed 1845
9. College House II (Webber House, 1750), acquired 1790, razed 1844
10. Wigglesworth house (ca. 1633), acquired 1794, razed 1844
11. College House III (Andrew Bordman House (by 1656), acquired 1794
CH. Courthouse III (1758–1841)
III. Third Meetinghouse (1704–1757)
IV. Fourth Meetinghouse (1756–1833)

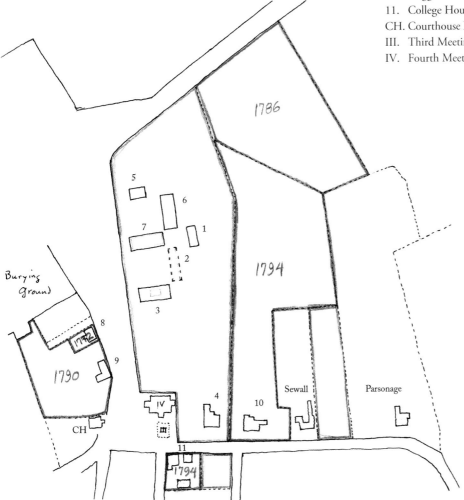

holdings and made possible the development of the Old Yard (figure 10.7).

By the end of the 18th century Harvard had nearly 200 students. Housing was scarce, and most freshmen boarded in private homes. Stoughton Hall had been so abused by troops quartered there during the Revolution that it was taken down in 1781. A lottery in 1795–96 funded Stoughton II, but construction did not begin until 1804. Designed by Charles Bulfinch with a three-part composition echoing Hollis, Stoughton II also faced the road, and its placement in line with Hollis defined a third quadrangle that was finally completed by Philips Brooks House in 1898. The site of old Stoughton was left open, upsetting the pattern of courtyard development but anticipating University Hall in 1813.

NINETEENTH CENTURY HARVARD BEFORE PRESIDENT ELIOT

Two early 19th century presidents, John Kirkland (1810–28) and Josiah Quincy (1829–45), propelled Harvard forward with vision and energy. Kirkland, a Unitarian minister, liberalized the curriculum, attracted students from all parts of the country, and founded the Divinity School (1816) and the Law School (1817). His strong ties with Boston's Federalist establishment helped win financial support from the legislature, enabling him to build University Hall in 1813–15 and acquire 64 acres of the Foxcroft estate north of Kirkland Street in 1816. Stephen Higginson, Kirkland's steward, or chief administrative officer, took office in 1819 and started to enclose and beautify the Yard by planting deciduous trees within it and pines around the perimeter.

Kirkland realized that the land along Peabody Street acquired in the 17th century would not suffice much longer. The meetinghouse and its parsonage on Massachusetts Avenue interrupted the evolving Yard, while to the east Judge Dana's heirs were not ready to sell their vast holdings. The Foxcroft estate on Kirkland Street, although much larger than immediately required, offered opportunities for long-term growth and profit. Virtually

all subsequent expansion occurred in the Yard or north of it until President Lowell turned his attention toward the river in 1909.

Kirkland's good relations with the legislature facilitated Harvard's expansion. The charter of 1650 had capped the value of its real estate at £500, but after repeated petitions, the General Court allowed the university to acquire "lands, tenements, and hereditaments" to the limit of $12,000 "in addition to the Public Buildings occupied by the students and for other public purposes" (Corporation Records, May 10, 1814). The legislature also granted Harvard $10,000 a year for ten years, the lion's share of the revenue from a tax on the Massachusetts Bank.

Harvard cherished its isolation and had helped block the construction of bridges to Boston in 1713 and 1738. The Corporation relented in 1785 when it was promised a portion of the tolls from the Charlestown Bridge to replace an ancient subsidy from the proceeds of the ferry. Harvard resisted the West Boston (today's Longfellow) Bridge in 1793 because of concerns that it would bring urban temptations within easy reach of the students; its fears were realized when a theater opened in Boston the following year. This led to talk of relocating the college to a more rural area, a threat that became explicit when the Cambridge & Concord Turnpike Corporation asked the legislature for permission to lay out Broadway from the Common to Kendall Square.

A Harvard official testified against the turnpike because it would end the "seclusion and retirement [that] are wisely sought for by a literary society."

> The true policy of the college has always been to promote the quiet and retirement of the students. These are greatly interrupted by the noise and bustle of travelers. … Cambridge has been considered by many serious friends of the university to be too near the metropolis for so considerable a seminary of learning—and proposals have been several times stirred for transferring the college to a more inland and secluded situation. The multiplying and shortening [of] the passages between Cambridge and Boston have increased the painful apprehensions in this regard, and are contemplated by grave and judicious persons as a circumstance of unpleasant aspect on the morals and diligence of the students. (College Papers V, Nov. 26, 1805)[4]

In addition, the college would no longer be able to extend its quadrangles north toward Kirkland Street.

> The [Corporation] had fondly contemplated the ground intersected by this new road as the area of future buildings, which would give a unity and an elegance to the whole not yet to be boasted of. By cutting off this prospect such new buildings as may be wanted … must now be placed without beauty or order, on the miry ground in the rear of the present buildings … for to extend them south of Massachusetts Hall would so far insert them into the town as greatly to increase the [illegible] and inconvenience of their situation. (Ibid.)

Harvard could not stop the road, but it did manage to have it diverted at today's Felton Street to a route "not approaching nearer than ninety feet to any part of [Stoughton Hall]" (Mass. Acts of 1804, Ch. 77). The decision to place Holworthy Hall at right angles to Stoughton in 1811 made a virtue of necessity by making the Yard an enclosed space rather than an undefined service area for buildings facing Massachusetts Avenue.

The controversy over Broadway was a catalyst for Harvard's next attempt at campus planning. In 1806 treasurer Ebenezer Storer proposed building houses for professors along Massachusetts Avenue near Wadsworth House and suggested that "Mr. Bulfinch or some other celebrated artist should be employed to draw a plan" (College Papers V, 29–30). In 1812 the Corporation appointed a committee "to devise the form and site of a Building on the College grounds to include a Common Hall" (College Papers V, in Kirker, 273). Charles Bulfinch prepared three plans that abandoned the college's traditional courtyard orientation. The earliest, most radical scheme imagined an extension of the campus to the east on land that Harvard did not yet own, with University Hall anchoring an enormous half-circular colonnade with nine south-facing entries. Two later plans showed how University Hall might someday be the centerpiece of a large open space surrounded by buildings. In the adopted plan, the broad side of University Hall faced the gate between Harvard and Massachusetts halls (figure 10.8).

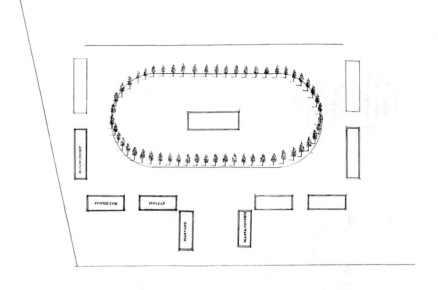

Figure 10.8   Final Bulfinch plan for Harvard Yard, ca. 1812–13. University Hall was to be the centerpiece of a quadrangle enclosed by buildings, only five of which existed at the time. Another plan had University Hall at a right angle to its present position.

Storer's program for University called for "a convenient Hall in the middle a Chapel over it & a kitchen under the Hall with a row of Chambers at each end two on a Story" (in Kirker, 274). Bulfinch produced two designs, one with a dome that anticipated his Massachusetts General Hospital of 1818. The accepted version was distinguished by its use of white Chelmsford granite, a state-of-the-art material made available by the opening of the Middlesex Canal in 1803. The privies were relocated, and the college brewhouse went up in flames just as University was completed (figure 10.9). Hollis and Stoughton were reoriented to face the Yard, and their rather plain back entries, which originally faced the privies, became the only doors in use. Much as Bulfinch envisioned, University Hall linked the Yard's two most important public spaces. The east facade (which originally faced the relocated privies) was as elaborately detailed as the west and lacked only the steps that were added in 1916.

FIGURE 10.9 The 1668 Harvard brewhouse in flames, August 3, 1814, looking northeast with University Hall at right.

FIGURE 10.10 Stephen Higginson Jr. (1770–1834), steward of Harvard College. Higginson was the son of a prominent Boston merchant who had been a delegate to the Continental Congress. A successful merchant himself, he was ruined by the Embargo of 1807. In 1818 his Federalist friends obtained an appointment for him as steward of Harvard College, where he landscaped the Yard and participated in the enclosure of Cambridge Common. He lived with his family on Professors Row (see figure 6.43). Charles Hayter (1761–1835), an English artist, painted this portrait in 1820.

FIGURE 10.11 Harvard Yard, seen from the northeast in 1821. In this view University Hall is on the left, Holworthy on the right, and the intersection of Cambridge Street and Broadway is in the foreground. Stephen Higginson began planting the pines around the perimeter of the Yard in 1816.

Kirkland was a capable and determined president, but he was careless about finances and resigned in 1828 after a painful confrontation with mathematician Nathaniel Bowditch, a member of the Corporation who had audited the college's accounts. The next president, Josiah Quincy (1829–45), a former mayor of Boston, was a skilled administrator with a strategic vision. One of his goals was to consolidate Harvard Yard and position the university for further growth. In 1833 the turmoil surrounding the disestablishment of the Congregational church and the doctrinal split between Unitarians and Trinitarians allowed him to acquire the Fourth Meetinghouse; the parsonage lot that came with it left only two parcels along Quincy Street in private hands.

Most 19th-century Harvard buildings originated with donors who dictated their function, design, and location. The first major edifice of Quincy's term was a gift from a Federalist politician, attorney Nathan Dane, to the fledgling law school. Dane Hall (1832), the only "'Grecian temple'" built by the university, was a radical departure from most Harvard buildings before University Hall and marked the first appearance of the Greek Revival style in Old Cambridge.[5] The two-story Ionic portico faced the Samuel Webber house, the Law School's original quarters across the Square (figure 10.12). The placement of Dane about 75 feet from Massachusetts Hall anticipated another small quadrangle fronting the road, but Matthews Hall, built in 1871, had such a large footprint that Dane was moved about 70 feet south onto the old site of the meetinghouse. Dane burned in 1918 and was replaced by Lehman Hall ten years later.

Harvard's first library was a Gothic building modeled after King's College Chapel in Cambridge, England (figure 10.13). Gore Hall was designed in 1838 by Boston architect Richard Bond and built of Quincy granite. For fear of fire, it stood alone in the open expanse east of University Hall (on the present site of Widener Library's front steps) and faced Massachusetts Avenue almost 150 feet away (see figure 10.25). Gore was much admired in its day; Jacob Bigelow modeled the original Mount Auburn Cemetery Chapel on it, and President Edward Everett placed it on the seal he designed for the city in 1846 (see figure 5.69). The

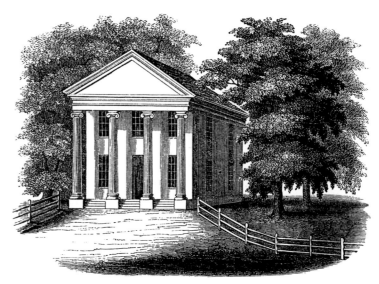

DANE HALL, ERECTED IN **1832**.

FIGURE 10.12 Dane Hall (1832, architect unknown), before a transverse wing was added by Isaac Melvin in 1844.

library opened in 1841 with 41,000 volumes and a capacity for new books that was expected to last for seventy-five years, but by 1863 the building was already full and the college built a sizable wing in 1876. The architects, Ware & Van Brunt, and the librarian, John Langdon Sibley, invented a metal book stack that transferred the weight of each tier of books to the foundation rather than through the frame of the building, an innovation that was widely adopted. Widener Library replaced Gore in 1913.

Appleton Chapel (1856) and Boylston Hall (1857) were designed by Paul Schulze, a German immigrant (see figure 7.17). The latter contained what may have been the first chemistry laboratory in the United States. Constructed of stone in accordance with the donor's bequest, its quarry-faced-granite exterior was closely related to contemporary mercantile buildings in Boston

FIGURE 10.13 Gore Hall (1838, Richard Bond, architect). Gore is seen from the southeast in 1844, with the Yard's perimeter planting of pine trees in the foreground. The four octagonal towers, which here are 83 feet high, deteriorated and were rebuilt at a somewhat lower height in 1850. Josiah Parsons Cooke, the photographer, began experimenting with the new Talbotype process in 1842, when he was 15; he graduated in 1848 and was appointed Professor of Chemistry in 1851.

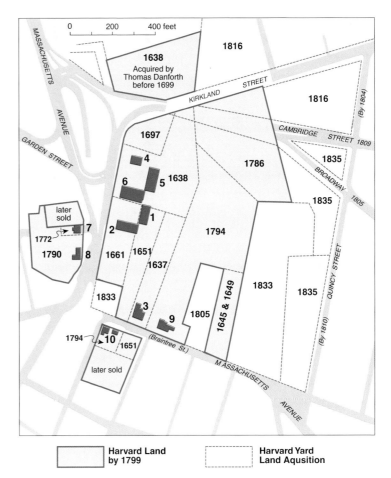

FIGURE 10.14

1. Old Stoughton, 1699
2. Massachusetts Hall, 1718
3. Wadsworth House, 1726
4. Holden Chapel, 1742
5. Hollis Hall, 1762
6. Harvard Hall III, 1764
7. College House I (Wiswall's Den), acquired 1772
8. College House II (Webber House), acquired 1790
9. Wigglesworth House, acquired 1794
10. College House III, acquired 1794

(figure 10.15). Successive modifications, including a Mansard roof added by Peabody & Stearns in 1871 and the installation of plate glass windows by The Architects Collaborative in 1959, did not alter the massive masonry shell. When Boylston was again remodeled in 1997, the Cambridge Historical Commission sanctioned new windows that recalled the precedent-setting TAC renovation.

Harvard's first building outside the Yard was Divinity Hall in 1825. Religious instruction had always been part of the undergraduate curriculum, but in 1816 the legislature chartered the Society for the Promotion of Theological Education in Harvard College to train Unitarian clergy. The society placed its building at the far end of Divinity Avenue on 20 acres of the recently purchased Foxcroft estate, a location intended "to protect the young divines from the pernicious influences of the secular Yard" (Peter Gomes, in Harvard Divinity School, *Foundations*, 14). The Society retained Solomon Willard, but when he started work on the Bunker Hill Monument he turned the project over to Boston architect Thomas Waldron Sumner.[6] Divinity Hall is a clear descendant of Hollis and Stoughton, but its austere Federal simplicity is somewhat relieved by the forward-looking Doric porticoes, which anticipated their wider use in vernacular domestic architecture (figure 10.16).

The Harvard Botanic Garden, the Observatory, the Lawrence Scientific School, and the Museum of Comparative Zoology were all donor-funded affiliated institutions (figure 10.17). Harvard had just purchased the 8-acre "summerhouse lot" of the Vassall-Craigie estate when the fortuitous appearance of a great comet in 1843 generated donations from Boston merchants interested in celestial navigation (see figure 4.119). Boston architect Isaiah Rogers designed the observatory's Sears Tower in 1843 with a central domed section and flanking end pavilions, one of which contained living quarters for astronomy professor William Bond (see figure 2.30). In 1847 textile magnate Abbott Lawrence endowed a new school for advanced studies in physical and natural sciences. Lawrence Hall, the only full-blown Italianate building at Harvard, was planned as a five-part

FIGURE 10.15 Boylston Hall (1857, Schulze & Schoen, architects), looking southeast toward Massachusetts Avenue. Photo ca. 1865.

FIGURE 10.16 Divinity Hall (1825, Solomon Willard and Thomas W. Sumner, architects). Photo ca. 1865.

FIGURE 10.17 The Harvard Observatory and the Botanic Garden in 1888.

composition like the Observatory, although the balancing wing was never built (figure 10.18). A bequest from Francis Calley Gray endowed the Museum of Comparative Zoology in 1859. Louis Agassiz's collections of minerals, fossils, and natural specimens already overflowed every available basement and attic, and he secured an astonishing number of grants from the Commonwealth to expand the building.[7]

Only a few projects in this period benefited undergraduates. Edward C. Cabot, first president of the Boston Society of Architects, designed Rogers Gymnasium, Harvard's earliest athletic building, on the Cambridge-Quincy-Broadway triangle in 1859 (figure 10.19). Rogers had no showers or toilets and was used only until 1878, when Hemenway Gymnasium opened; it was replaced in 1933 by the city's fire headquarters, after Harvard exchanged the site for Holmes Place. Although the student body had nearly doubled to 442, Grays Hall (1862) was the first new dormitory since Holworthy in 1812. Harvard closed the dining rooms in University Hall in 1848, and students took meals at

FIGURE 10.19 Rogers Gymnasium (1859, Edward C. Cabot, architect). Rogers stood at the intersection of Cambridge Street (left) and Broadway (right), now the site of the Central Fire Station (1933). Photo 1876.

FIGURE 10.18 Lawrence Scientific School (1847, Richard Bond, architect; 1871, remodeled by Ware & Van Brunt). The site is now occupied by the Harvard Science Center. Photo 1963.

their lodgings or in the village until Nathaniel Thayer, a Boston financier, sponsored the conversion of the Harvard Branch Railroad station into Thayer Commons in 1865 (see figure 9.27).[8]

PRESIDENT ELIOT (1869–1909)

Charles W. Eliot made Harvard an institution of national importance by reforming undergraduate education and expanding the graduate and professional schools. During his forty-year presidency, enrollment in the college grew to 2,200, graduate students increased from 200 to over 1,100, and the faculty grew from 31 to 182.[9] In its first 230 years, Harvard had accumulated thirty-four substantial structures; Eliot built (or enlarged) twenty-five in Cambridge and ten more in Boston.

Eliot's first new buildings were dormitories, but soon his focus shifted to the graduate schools. He believed that German universities, which provided no housing, dining halls, or athletic facilities, offered the best model for personal growth and academic excellence, and he gave undergraduates the freedom to live as they chose. In the 1890s, alumni concerned about the self-segregation of students by wealth and social background urged him to encourage sports and offer more dining and recreational opportunities. Eliot authorized two new dormitories, a dining hall, a student union, an infirmary, and athletic facilities, but he never intended to accommodate every undergraduate on campus.

Eliot was criticized for his seeming indifference to planning and for tolerating the eclectic styles favored by donors and their architects. In fact, he was sensitive to matters of design and appointed one of his strongest critics, his cousin Charles Eliot Norton, as the university's first professor of fine arts in 1874. In 1893 he hired H. Langford Warren, an M.I.T.-trained architect who had been H.H. Richardson's chief draftsman, to teach architecture at the Lawrence Scientific School. Under Warren and Norton, the two departments became close collaborators, sharing facilities in Hunt Hall and courses in drawing and architectural history. In 1901 Eliot retained Frederick Law Olmsted Jr. and Arthur Shurtleff to establish a program in landscape architecture.[10]

A follower of Ruskin, Warren helped found the Society of Arts and Crafts in Boston in 1897. Despite his interest in modernism, which in that period connoted an American approach that employed the latest technology and allowed the exterior to express the program for the building, he looked to the École des Beaux-Arts for a professor of design. Désiré Despradelle came from M.I.T. in 1910, and Eugene Joseph Armand Duquesne, a former French government architect and holder of the Grand Prix de Rome, taught in 1911–15. The École's curriculum, based on the study of Classical and Renaissance precedents with an emphasis on connoisseurship and skill in rendering, dominated American architectural education from the 1890s to the 1930s. The new orthodoxy swamped the imaginative and often eclectic

visions of American-trained architects, but Warren retained an emphasis on technology and collaboration with other design fields (including city planning, which was first taught at Harvard in 1909). Warren's tenure at the School of Architecture (as it was renamed in 1914) ended with his death in 1917, but his influence remained strong until the 1930s.

Early graduates of the department of architecture played important roles in the architectural development of Cambridge. Albert H. Blevins (S.B. 1898), William H. Mowll (1899), and Edward T.P. Graham (1900) designed numerous apartment buildings, houses, churches, and schools. Henry R. Shepley (A.B. 1910) became a partner in Coolidge, Shepley, Bulfinch & Abbott in 1924, and worked on Harvard's River House commissions in the 1930s. Arthur Graham Carey (A.B. 1914), who attended the school of architecture in 1919–21, was Warren's protégé in the Arts & Crafts movement. Henry Atherton Frost (M.Arch. 1918) founded the Cambridge School of Architecture and taught at Harvard until 1949 (see chapter 7).[11]

HARVARD YARD

In his first two years Eliot built four new dormitories (Thayer, Weld, and Matthews halls and Holyoke House), enlarged one (College House), and remodeled three others (Hollis, Holworthy, and Stoughton). He completed Memorial Hall, rebuilt Lawrence, added a Mansard roof to Boylston, and had all the old brick buildings in the Yard given a coat of red paint (figure 10.20). As Bunting noted, "nothing in prior presidential reports or Corporation minutes indicates that the previous administration had laid the groundwork for this sudden burst of construction" (*Report Four,* 162).

Careful thought was given to siting the new buildings, as these would be the final structures defining the Old Yard. Setting Thayer behind University's west facade emphasized the earlier building's prominence and maintained an opening through which to view Memorial Hall, then in the planning stages. Eliot's description of his first encounter with the building's donor,

FIGURE 10.20 Harvard Yard in 1875, as seen from the tower of Memorial Hall. President Eliot's initial projects included construction of Thayer Hall (1869, foreground), Weld Hall (1870), and Matthews Hall (1871, left background). He gave College House an extra floor with a Mansard roof (1870, center background) and added an extra floor on Holworthy Hall (1871, right).

Nathaniel Thayer, characterized many of Harvard's development decisions in the late 19th century:

> A few weeks after I became President, Mr. Thayer told me ... that he thought the College ought to have another dormitory [and] that he meant to see that it was shortly built. ... Mr. Thayer [selected the architects], made all the contracts and paid all the bills himself. ... I never knew the exact cost of the whole work. (Ellis, "Memoirs of Nathaniel Thayer")

In 1870 the same architects, Ryder & Harris, designed Holyoke House (on the present site of Holyoke Center), with stores and a restaurant on the ground floor and forty-seven suites above to "be let by the year to professional students, undergraduates, or other gentlemen" (*Annual Report of the President*, 1869–70, 24, 27). When Massachusetts Hall was renovated for classrooms

in 1869, the loss of twenty-two student rooms was made up by adding "a French-roof story" with twenty-six rooms to College House (ibid.; see figures 3.14 and 8.16).

Two other donor-funded dormitories completed the Old Yard. While Ware & Van Brunt advanced to the Queen Anne style for Weld Hall (1870), Peabody & Stearns continued with the Ruskinian Gothic for Matthews (1871). Although superficially different, both Weld and Matthews have complex Victorian massing, bay and oriel windows, and intricate Panel Brick details, quite unlike anything else in the Yard but foreshadowing the residential architecture of the following decade (figure 10.21).

Eliot also improved sanitary facilities in the Yard. The Cambridge Water Works laid mains in Harvard Square in 1857, but

FIGURE 10.21 Weld Hall (1870, Ware & Van Brunt, architects). Photo 2015.

it was not until 1870 that "water-trough privies" were installed in the basements of University and Holworthy halls. These at last allowed the removal of "the offensive and uncomfortable privies which so long stood in the centre of the College Yard" and "the scrubby evergreens which surrounded them" (ibid., 23–24). It was 1880 before all the dormitories in the Yard were equipped with basement water closets and 1898 before all had bathrooms with hot and cold water.

FIGURE 10.22 H.H. Richardson's proposed design for the east side of Harvard Yard, ca. 1878–79, with Sever Hall in the right foreground. The three buildings facing Quincy Street were never built.

Eliot also addressed the future development of the Yard:

The Corporation are following a carefully considered plan in locating new buildings in the College Yard. The rectangle between Holworthy Hall and Grays Hall is considered to be now completed. … For the rest of the Yard the Corporation are proceeding upon the plan of keeping the space between the Library, the Chapel, and University Hall forever open. A building may be placed on the eastern side of the avenue which leads to the southern door of the Library, to match Boylston Hall on the western side, and a continuous, or nearly continuous structure, may stretch along Quincy Street, from Harvard Street to Broadway. (*President's Report,* 1871, 31)

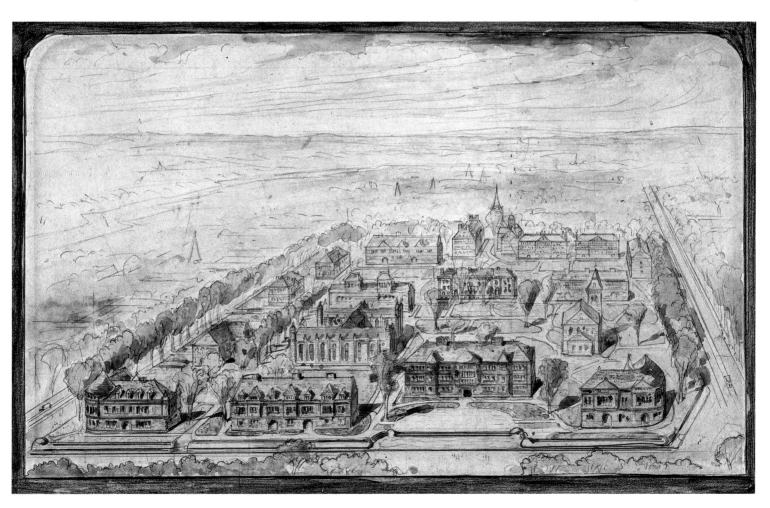

Sever Hall, the first important structure on the east side of the Yard, precluded Eliot's idea of a long building on Quincy Street and foretold the displacement of the faculty homes there (see chapter 4). Henry Hobson Richardson of the class of 1859 was appointed architect in October 1878. Displaying his distinctive blend of quiet monumentality and lavish ornamentation, Sever, like University, had two major facades, one facing inward to the Yard and one outward to Quincy Street (figure 10.23). Two decades later, Robinson (1900, McKim, Mead & White) and Emerson halls (1904, Guy Lowell) defined the Sever quadrangle.

Richard Morris Hunt, architect of the Breakers in Newport and the Biltmore estate in North Carolina, designed the original Fogg Museum (later known as Hunt Hall) on Broadway in 1893. Although Harvard awarded Hunt an honorary degree in 1892, the building's limestone cladding and rigid classical form were out of place in the Yard. Hunt was built in part to accommodate Charles Eliot Norton's lectures, but he was not consulted about the design and called it "beneath contempt" (*Chronicle*, Oct. 10, 1896; figure 10.24). Infamous for its bad acoustics, Hunt was demolished without regret and replaced by Canaday Hall, a freshman dormitory, in 1974.[12]

One of Eliot's most visible accomplishments was the enclosure of the Yard. The proximity of the campus to Harvard Square had troubled college administrators for centuries. Samuel Eliot Morison noted Nathaniel Eaton's 1639 account of "fencing the yard with pale[s] 6 foot and ½ high" and documented the efforts of proctors and tutors to keep student in the Yard and interlopers out ("Restoration of Old College," 131). The 1726 Burgis view shows a high enclosure, but if this ever existed it was replaced by a low wall supporting an ornamental picket fence with decorative gateposts (see figure 5.3). In 1841 the Corporation appointed a committee "to cause a suitable and substantial fence to be erected in front of the College" (Corporation Records 8, 140). The new granite post and rail fence kept livestock out but was completely ineffective for security. President Everett offered in 1847 to pay for police protection against "the

FIGURE 10.23 Sever's innovative carved and molded bricks were produced by John L. Sands & Son of North Cambridge and versions later appeared in several Boston-area buildings of the period. Photo 2014.

FIGURE 10.24 Hunt Hall (1893, Richard Morris Hunt, architect). Built originally to house the William Hayes Fogg Museum of Art, Hunt was altered in 1912–13 with a north-facing skylight above the central core and demolished in 1973. Photo before 1912.

multiplication of thefts from the rooms of the students, and the frequent appearance of prostitutes in the college yard" (President's Papers, Sept. 9, 1847).

Among the improvements hereafter to be made, that of an effectual enclosure of the College grounds is among the most needed. In connection with the discipline of the Institution the facility of entering and leaving the College grounds and buildings has ever been the source of great evil. … But the establishment of thoroughfares for the public in fact, if not in law, is the evil most to be apprehended. So long as the land northeast and southeast of the Colleges was comparatively unoccupied, there were few persons to whom it was of any convenience to pass through our grounds. Compact settlements are now growing up in both directions, and the time has already arrived when a numerous and rapidly increasing population passes habitually through the College Yard. … Servants with parcels and dogs, noisy school-boys at their sports, workmen crossing on their way to and from their places of labor are very frequently seen within the enclosure. Vagrants, hand-organists, beggars, and characters still more objectionable are not as rare as could be wished. At no remote period the College Square will form the centre of the population of Old Cambridge and will be traversed by all the direct lines of communication on foot. (Corporation Records, Aug. 14, 1847)

The Corporation directed Ebenezer Francis, Superintendent of College Buildings, "to close the passages through the grounds for one day, by placing a plank across them, firmly fixed with screws. … In this manner the right of the Corporation to close the passages was asserted" (ibid.). The practice of closing the Yard to outsiders continues on commencement day each year.

Fifty years passed before the university began to build a formal enclosure. Designs by Henry Van Brunt in 1870 and H.H.

FIGURE 10.25 Harvard's post and rail fence along Massachusetts Avenue west of Quincy Street, ca. 1876–85, before the university gave up a twelve-foot-wide strip of land to allow the street to be widened. Boylston Hall with its new Mansard roof is in the center, and Gore Hall is at right.

Richardson in 1878 went unrealized, but in 1889 the Corporation received a bequest from Chicago investor Samuel Johnston for "a gateway at the main entrance of the College Yard" (*Treasurer's Statement,* 1888–89, 9). Eliot gave the commission to Charles McKim of McKim, Mead & White, who had spent an unhappy year at the Lawrence Scientific School in 1866–67 before dropping out to attend the École des Beaux-Arts. McKim glorified the colonial heritage of the College with an improbably ornate English Georgian design, but he specified the same coarse, wood-fired, water-struck, hand-made brick that appeared on Massachusetts Hall, Harvard's oldest surviving building (figures 10.26–10.27).

FIGURE 10.26 Johnston Gate (1889, Charles H. McKim of McKim, Mead & White, architect), showing the gate as designed and the simpler version that was actually constructed.

This was the first use of the coarse brick masonry that characterized collegiate Georgian Revival architecture in the 20th century (figure 10.28). The New England Brick Company, a 1900 amalgamation of the five major brickyards in Cambridge and twenty-five firms elsewhere, marketed these variegated common brick and glazed headers as "Harvard Brick," and they appeared in most university buildings until the 1950s. Similar bricks were used in commercial projects until the 1970s.

The Memorial Fence was undertaken ten years after Johnston Gate, when the Corporation accepted McKim's initial design and acknowledged that it would "be glad to have any of the College Classes provide for the erection of the gates and adjoining sections of the fence" (Corporation Records 16, 320, in Hammond, "Enclosure"). The alumni responded with enthusiasm, and by 1936 various classes had donated funds for twenty-seven unique gates and the wrought-iron fencing between them.

Figure 10.27 Johnston Gate, ca. 1930.

Beginning in the Federal period, brickmakers had concentrated on making bricks "of a uniform smoothness, and a dead evenness of color. Care was taken to have the joints as even as possible, and as inconspicuous as they could be made ... the result was ... buildings whose surfaces were so smooth as to suggest paint" (New England Brick Co., *The Brick Kiln,* Oct. 1930, 22–24). For Johnston Gate, one of the architects recalled:

We selected the best of the old cast-off "rough-arch" brick, or "benchers," from the refuse heap where they had been thrown. Their varied coloring and irregularity of line was most artistic and produced the effect we were striving for. ... These bricks, which had been thrown away because they were thought to be too imperfect for the trade were being sold for $6.50 a thousand, immediately became the rage and sold for $18.00 a thousand and upwards. Very soon the demand exceeded the supply and they had to be manufactured specially so as to look as like the original ones as possible. (Hill, 35)

Figure 10.28 The brick masonry of Johnston gate represented the first use for decorative purposes of the distinctive glazed (or vitrified) headers that had been directly exposed to the intense heat of a wood-fired "clamp" of brick. The stacking pattern and the gradation of heat within the clamp gave the bricks their distinctive "flash," a variegated color impossible to duplicate in a modern kiln. Photo 2009.

When Eliot became president, the area north of the Yard was a poorly drained expanse bordering the abandoned right-of-way of the Harvard Branch Railroad. President Kirkland and his successors had sold most of the Foxcroft land, retaining only a relatively small tract at the end of Divinity Avenue for Divinity Hall and the Museum of Comparative Zoology (figure 10.29). Eliot eventually repurchased some of these properties, but in the meantime he acquired Jarvis and Holmes fields "at very low prices, upon opportunities not likely to recur, and with very substantial aid from generous friends." The university had

> acquired more than twenty acres of well-situated land in Cambridge, an acquisition which is already worth two or three times as much as it cost, and which has secured the University, so far as security can be devised, against any future necessity of abandoning its historical site. (*Annual Report,* 1871–1872, 37)

Harvard rounded out its contiguous campus by purchasing the Palfrey estate on Oxford Street in 1919 and continued to reacquire Foxcroft land until 1955.

The first and most important building erected north of the Yard was Memorial Hall. The movement to commemorate Harvard's Union Civil War dead originated in 1863, and a "Committee of Fifty" organized in 1865 chose not only the architects and the design, but also the location, an athletic field between Kirkland and Cambridge streets known as the Delta (figure 10.30). Eliot released the Delta for construction once the committee had purchased Jarvis Field as a substitute. After a competition open to alumni, the committee chose the firm of William Ware (class of 1852) and Henry Van Brunt (an 1855 graduate and a navy veteran). Work began in the fall of 1870, and the magnificent polychromatic brick and stone structure with its great banqueting hall, memorial transept, theater, and 195-foot tower was completed in 1878. Closely related to English buildings embodying John Ruskin's architectural theories, Memorial Hall represented "both a milestone in American architectural history and the first

large cooperative fund-raising project by Harvard alumni" (Bunting, *Report Four,* 168). For many generations it was a focus of Harvard life: its bell called students to classes, the dining hall accommodated over half the student body, and its clock, installed in 1897, kept time for much of the city until the tower burned in 1956 (figure 10.31; see also figure 10.82).

Eliot sketched an orderly plan for North Yard, but donors dictated another outcome (figure 10.32). Three large North Yard buildings—Hemenway Gymnasium (1876), Austin Hall (1881), and Jefferson Physical Laboratory (1882)—differed widely in style and bore no functional relationship to one another. When Augustus Hemenway of Boston asked the Corporation in 1876 to designate a site on which to build a gymnasium, the president's brother-in-law Robert S. Peabody had already drawn the plans. The Corporation chose the corner of Holmes Place and Kirkland Street, which had been vacated by the Old Cambridge Baptist Church in 1867. The project reflected post–Civil War interest in physical fitness, and when Hemenway opened in 1878 it was the first building in America with special rooms devoted to rowing, baseball, and fencing (figure 10.33).[13]

The location and design of Austin Hall were determined by donor Edward Austin, a China-trade merchant who wished to construct a memorial to his deceased brother Samuel. In 1882 Austin, having already hired H.H. Richardson and approved a design, offered Harvard $135,000 to construct his building, on the condition that no other structure stand within 60 feet of it. Thayer Commons (formerly the Harvard Branch Railroad station) and the ca. 1717 Moses Richardson house were razed immediately (see chapter 4). Directly in front of the new building, however, sat the venerable 1737 Hastings-Holmes house, headquarters of General Artemas Ward during the Siege of Boston and birthplace of Oliver Wendell Holmes, the prominent physician and author (see figure 4.192). Austin insisted that the house be sacrificed and offered Harvard an additional $3,000 to have it removed.[14] This brought the first public criticism of the university for demolishing an historic landmark. The elimination of Holmes Place in 1936 left Austin Hall with no

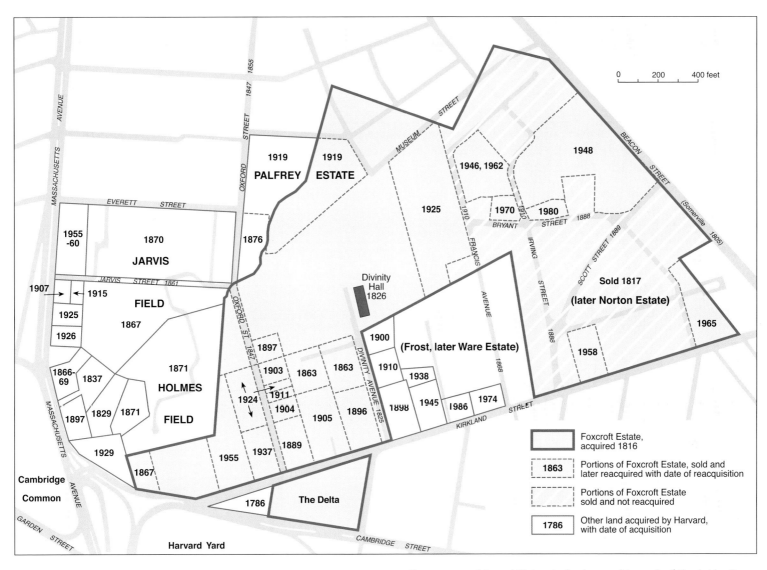

FIGURE 10.29 Harvard University land ownership north of Cambridge Street.

Map labels:

1919
1919
PALFREY   ESTATE

1946, 1962
1948

1925
1970   1980
BRYANT   STREET   1888

1876

1955
-60
1870
JARVIS

1955
-60

1907   1915
FIELD
1925
1926
1867

Divinity
Hall
1826

Sold 1817
(later Norton Estate)

1958
1965

1871
1866-
69   1837
HOLMES
FIELD
1897   1829   1871
1929
1867

1897
1903
1924   1911
1904
1905
1955   1937   1889

1863   1863
1900   (Frost, later Ware Estate)
1910
1938
1898   1945   1986   1974
1896

KIRKLAND   STREET

1786   The Delta

Cambridge
Common

Harvard Yard

CAMBRIDGE   STREET

Streets:
MASSACHUSETTS AVENUE, EVERETT STREET, OXFORD STREET, 1847, 1855, JARVIS STREET 1861, OXFORD ST. 1847, DIVINITY AVENUE 1826, MUSEUM STREET, FRANCIS AVENUE, IRVING STREET 1888, 1910, SCOTT STREET 1889, BEACON STREET, (Somerville 1805), 1868, GARDEN STREET

Legend:
Foxcroft Estate, acquired 1816

1863 Portions of Foxcroft Estate, sold and later reacquired with date of reacquisition

Portions of Foxcroft Estate sold and not reacquired

1786 Other land acquired by Harvard, with date of acquisition

0   200   400 feet

Figure 10.30 The Delta before 1868, with Kirkland Street at left, Cambridge Street at right, and the Treadwell-Sparks house in the distance.

FIGURE 10.31 Memorial Hall (1866–78, Ware & Van Brunt, architects). This view shows the tower as modified in 1878 with additional cresting and lancet dormers; this was the version restored in 2000. Photo ca. 1884–93.

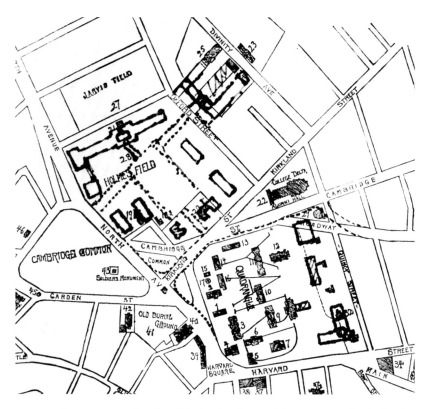

FIGURE 10.32 President Eliot's ideas for possible expansion, sketched in his copy of a Harvard guidebook published in 1878. He thought Cambridge Street could be extended through Flagstaff Park to Massachusetts Avenue, allowing a westward expansion of the Yard. The University Museum could be built out to Oxford Street, while a massive structure—possibly for the law school—could occupy the north end of Holmes Field.

FIGURE 10.33 Hemenway Gymnasium (1876, Robert S. Peabody, architect). Hemenway occupied the former site of the Old Cambridge Baptist Church, facing Harvard Square at the end of Peabody Street (see figure 7.15). Photo 1938.

particular orientation to its surroundings, and, since 1938, partially obscured by Littauer Hall (see figure 10.76).

The University Museum combined Louis Agassiz's Museum of Comparative Zoology, begun in 1859, and the Peabody Museum of Anthropology, begun in 1876. These institutions were separately chartered and independently funded but came under university control in 1876 and 1897 and expanded repeatedly. Agassiz died in 1873, but his son, Alexander, carried on his work and was "Harvard's most liberal benefactor" at the time of his death in 1910 (Morison, *Development,* 410). The museum now occupies a vast, six-story, U-shaped building completed in 1913 (see figure 10.72).

Langdell Hall was Harvard's only Neoclassical building in Cambridge, apart from the original Fogg Museum (Hunt Hall). By 1900 law school enrollment had more than tripled since the opening of Austin Hall in 1882. Harvard already occupied almost every available site in the North Yard, but most of the

FIGURE 10.34 The North Yard as seen from the tower of Memorial Hall, 1885. Clockwise from the left are the Lawrence Scientific School (1847–1970), Hemenway Gymnasium (1878–1938), Austin Hall (1881), and the Jefferson Physical Laboratory (1882). Professors Row houses built by Levi Frisbie (1822; demolished 1963) and Stephen Higginson (1822; demolished 1970) are in the foreground. The first Harvard-Epworth Methodist Church (1857, moved here in 1868) is visible beyond Jefferson.

FIGURE 10.35   Harvard Yard and the North Yard in 1887, as drawn by students at the Lawrence Scientific School.

Massachusetts Avenue frontage up to Everett Street remained in other hands until 1960, forcing the university to build on Holmes Field. Langdell Hall (1906, Shepley, Rutan & Coolidge) dominates the quadrangle with imperial grandeur and closely resembles the Harvard Medical School in Boston, designed by the same firm and under construction at the same time.

The Andover Theological Seminary (ATS) commissioned Andover Hall from Allen & Collens in 1909. Founded in 1807 by orthodox Congregationalists offended by Harvard's appointment of Unitarian Henry Ware as Hollis Professor of Divinity, ATS shared a campus and trustees with Phillips Academy in Andover until 1908. When the Supreme Judicial Court invalidated its merger with the Harvard Divinity School in 1931, ATS joined the Newton Theological Institute, leaving Andover Hall and its library in Harvard's possession. Andover Hall is Harvard's only Collegiate Gothic building.

The debate in Cambridge between advocates of the Georgian and Gothic styles first took place not at Harvard but at the First Parish Church in Harvard Square, where Eliot—a parishioner—fought to replace Isaiah Rogers's 1833 Gothic design with a "Colonial" building (see chapter 7). The controversy was still simmering in 1908 when Boston College built Gasson Hall (Maginnis & Walsh), the prototype for dominant Gothic towers at Princeton (1913) and Yale (1917). The issue arose at Harvard in 1913 when Shepley, Rutan, & Coolidge was planning the first dormitories along the river. Charles Coolidge instructed Herman Voss, the firm's chief designer, "to use Gothic castle architecture for guidelines in the preparation of his sketches" for the new Gore Hall, but when Coolidge was away another partner, George Shattuck asked Voss to search for an alternate concept. Voss prepared a design inspired by Christopher Wren's Hampton Court Palace, "which pleased Mr. Shattuck very much but which neither he nor Mr. Voss could persuade Mr. Coolidge to accept wholeheartedly" (Clapp, 1). At Shattuck's urging, Coolidge gathered a group of Boston architects to evaluate the two schemes—Scottish Gothic or English Renaissance. The overwhelming choice, even by Gothicists Ralph Adams Cram

and Charles Maginnis, was the Hampton Court design. With Coolidge at last persuaded and President Lowell a staunch advocate of the Georgian Revival, Harvard avoided the Collegiate Gothic style so many universities adopted in the early 20th century. Schools such as Dartmouth, Amherst, and Williams stood with Harvard in the Georgian camp. Andover Hall remained an anomaly on the campus.

Harvard's Housing Policies and the Rise of the Gold Coast

Harvard's academic and housing policies during the administration of President Eliot strongly influenced the development of Old Cambridge. Eliot liberalized the college's parietal rules and gave students unprecedented freedom to live as and where they wished. Yard dormitories were generally reserved for seniors; underclassmen had to find rooms off campus. Some families moved to Cambridge so their sons could live at home, but the university also cultivated a specialized housing market that included dozens of college-sanctioned boarding houses and private dormitories. The most desirable accommodations coalesced into the Gold Coast, an elite precinct of dormitories and student clubs on Mt. Auburn Street between Kennedy and Bow streets. Stores catering to students clustered along Massachusetts Avenue, while garages sprang up on the periphery to accommodate the automobiles that students adopted with enthusiasm. Under Eliot's successor, A. Lawrence Lowell (1909–33), the university's relationship with its undergraduates took a different turn, with drastic consequences for Cambridge property owners, restaurateurs, and lodging house keepers.

In 1891 the *Cambridge Chronicle* noted that the "growth of the college population has been met by the erection of private dormitories … which have absorbed students of the kind willing to pay from $200 to $400 a year in rent. Their departure from private houses has enabled poorer men to be housed with reasonable comfort, but now the time has come when the poor student has to walk a mile from the college yard in order to secure a $50 [per year] room for himself" (Feb. 7, 1891). This situation forced Harvard to build dormitories for the first time since 1872. Eliot acknowledged that "the Corporation desires very much to be enabled to offer students a large number of plain rooms, simply furnished, at a price not much exceeding fifty dollars a year, including the daily care of the rooms. … Cheap board and cheap rooms in Cambridge are necessary means for building up here a great, popular institution" (*Annual Report,* 1890–91, 36–37). He believed that the university should be a meritocracy accessible to all and admitted African Americans as well as the sons of immigrants who could pass the admissions examination.[15] Eliot favored admission of women to Harvard's graduate schools but was unable to convince the corporation.

The private sector met student needs in a number of ways. Lodging houses, which had existed throughout the history of the college, were typically dwellings relatively close to the campus where students could rent rooms, and, in some cases, have meals. A 1902 directory of 214 student boarding and lodging houses identified nearly all proprietors as "Mrs.," and city directory listings suggest that many were widows. Students did not mingle with the families; most ate at their clubs, Memorial Hall, or the Foxcroft Club on Oxford Street, where the university provided meals for an average of 40¢ a day. In 1902 there were about 760 sanctioned accommodations in houses around the university, most near the college but some as far away as Central Square. Buildings with more than ten students fell under university supervision, and by the 1890s a parietal board offered standardized leases for students renting off-campus. Available at local bookstores, these forms stipulated that students were subject to university regulations and would be evicted if expelled or suspended. A landlord using this lease could rent only to students and had to provide a room rent-free to a proctor.

Owners upgraded old properties to meet the demand. Theodore Seavey, a Central Square grocer, remodeled the 1798 Samuel Flagg Sawyer house at 24 Holyoke Street in 1867 and repeatedly enlarged it (figure 10.36). In 1886 Obed Shepherd, a carpenter, remodeled a tenement he had originally built in 1869 into flashy student accommodations he called Shepherd's Block (figure 10.37). Similarly, 5–7 Linden Street originated as a double house in 1839. Its owners upgraded and expanded it in 1868, 1890, and 1901, when it had six single rooms renting for $200–260 per year and three suites at $350–550, as well as an apartment for the owner. Others built special-purpose residences. In 1887 William Wilson, a foreman at the University Press, put up a two-story duplex at 94 Prescott Street for his family and included four suites for students. Mary Galvin, a widow, built "a house suitable for students" next door at 96 Prescott, behind her own house at 1734 Cambridge Street (*Tribune,* June 18, 1887; figure 10.38).

A second type of private student housing was the mixed-use block containing commercial space as well as suites and rooms designed for students. Harvard built the first of these, College House, in 1832, followed by Holyoke House in 1869. Mixed-use blocks were generally built as investments, and their owners often upgraded them to meet competition from newer buildings (see chapter 8).[16]

The third and most significant type of student accommodation was the private dormitory. In the 1890s the most luxurious of these charged as much as $700 per year, compared to $50 for university housing. A competitive market required owners to provide a high level of amenities, since "student needs and desires … are often peculiar and sometimes inexplicable to the outsider" (*Chronicle* May 2, 1896). Private dormitories were more advanced than most apartment buildings of the period. The most expensive had interior courtyards and multiple bay windows, because rooms with views and cross-ventilation commanded higher rents. Internally, the arrangement of rooms varied little. A suite generally contained one or more bedrooms and a study, but no kitchen. The *en suite* bathrooms that appeared about 1890 were a great attraction at a time when none existed on campus. Private dormitories were among of the earliest Cambridge buildings to offer electric lights, steam heat, and elevators. Some provided valet and maid service, round-the-clock doormen and elevator operators, room service, and bellhops.

FIGURE 10.36 Samuel Flagg Sawyer house, 24–26 Holyoke Street (1798–99; left section added 1867; top story added ca. 1887). The Sawyer house was remodeled several times to accommodate student rooms. The Dunster House Book Shop opened here in 1920 to serve the cultivated undergraduate's desire for fine first editions and English magazines. In 1923 the *Harvard Crimson* reported that this building had become "the intellectual centre of gravity of the university" with the bookstore, the Harvard Advocate, the Dramatic Club, and "an almost Johnsonian smoke shop [with] tiled floors, robin's egg blue walls and a samovar" around the corner at 69½ Mt. Auburn Street (Oct. 5). The building was razed in 1927 for the Manter Hall School (see figure 7.71). Photo 1926.

FIGURE 10.37 Shepherd's Block, 29–33 Holyoke Street (1869, Obed Shepherd, housewright). Shepherd's Block was given an elaborate makeover in 1886, but by the time it was razed in 1945 the *Crimson* characterized it as "one of the University's most secluded eyesores … a nest of old furniture, leaky radiators, creaking stairways, and falling plaster" (Mar. 9, 1945). Photo ca. 1900.

FIGURE 10.38 Mary Galvin's student lodging house, 96 Prescott Street (1887, James Fogerty, architect). Harvard moved this building to 18 Sumner Road in 2003. Photo before 1903.

Many offered common rooms and athletic facilities, such as the swimming tank at Craigie Hall and the squash and racquetball courts at Randolph. Breakfast service was standard, but students took their main meals elsewhere.

Anna Moëring, the widowed daughter of Professor Charles Beck, built Beck Hall, the first luxury dormitory, in 1876. Designed by Boston architect N.J. Bradlee, Beck's inset tiles, brownstone trim, and tarred brick accents echoed the Ruskinian Gothic details of Memorial Hall (figure 10.39). Conveniently located on Quincy Square, Beck became the preferred residence for affluent students like John Jacob Astor '88, J.P. Morgan '89, and William K. Vanderbilt '01. So prestigious was

it that Morgan was rumored to have reserved a place for his son at birth. Walter Cabot Baylies, vice president of Edison Electric, purchased the property in 1911 reportedly to secure a suite for his son, Lincoln. Felton Hall, a fanciful Stick Style building on Cambridge Street designed by Peabody & Stearns for Henry Bigelow Williams of the class of 1871, followed Beck in 1877. Felton was just far enough from the Yard that its residents were exempt from daily chapel attendance, but its popularity declined when this requirement was abolished in 1886 (figure 10.40).

The emergence of the Gold Coast upended the social geography of the university. At one time, any location within easy walking distance seemed acceptable for student lodgings. This changed dramatically in the 1890s, when a critical mass of luxury dormitories appeared along Mt. Auburn and Bow streets, where undergraduate clubs had already begun to occupy some older houses (table 10.1). The owners were a mixture of local investors and wealthy alumni who seemed motivated as much by school spirit as by the prospect of a good return. For example, Charles D. Wetmore, an ambitious young New Yorker, received

FIGURE 10.39 Beck Hall, 1201 Massachusetts Avenue (1876, Nathaniel J. Bradlee, architect). As the first really luxurious private dormitory, Beck established a precedent for private investment in student housing. It was demolished for a filling station in 1940. Rendering 1876.

FIGURE 10.40 Felton Hall, 1640 Cambridge Street (1877, Peabody & Stearns, architects). Felton became an apartment hotel before it was replaced by Cambridge's War Memorial building in 1952.

TABLE 10.1 PRINCIPAL PRIVATE DORMITORIES

Name	Address	Architect	Date	Sold to Harvard	Razed
Harvard Hall	1358–62 Mass. Ave.	William Sparrell	1854	1918	1964
Little's Block	1350–54 Mass. Ave.	unknown	1869	1918	1964
Beck Hall	Quincy Square	Nathaniel J. Bradlee	1876		1940
Felton Hall	1640 Cambridge St.	Peabody & Stearns	1877		1952
Manter Hall	4 Holyoke St.	unknown	c.1882	1978	
Shepherd's Hall	29–33 Holyoke St.		1886	1918	1945
Read Hall	18–28 Kennedy St.	J.R. Richards	1886		
Quincy Hall	1218 Mass. Ave.	George Fogerty	1891		
Claverly Hall	63 Mt. Auburn St.	George Fogerty	1892	1921	
Ware Hall	383 Harvard St.	George Fogerty	1893		
Trinity Hall	114–120 Mt. Auburn St.	W.H. & J.A. McGinty	1893		2014
Prescott Hall	472–474 Broadway	Arthur Bowditch	1893	1975	
Dunster Hall	16 Dunster St.	Little, Browne & Moore	1895	1918	1964
Dana Chambers	11–21 Dunster St.	Charles H. Blackall	1897		
Craigie Hall	2–6 University Rd.	Josephine Chapman	1897	1967	
Apley Court	16 Holyoke St.	John Howe	1897	1920	
Randolph Hall	12 Linden St.	Coolidge & Wright	1897	1917	
Westmorly Court	11–21 Bow St.	Warren & Wetmore	1898	1920	
Russell Hall	41 Bow St.	George Fogerty	1899	1925	1931
Brentford Hall	1137 Mass. Ave.	George Fogerty	1899		
Fairfax Hall	1300–1316 Mass. Ave.	Coolidge & Carlson	1900	1978	
Dolton's Block	1300 Mass. Ave.	unknown	1869	1978	
Hilton's Block	1310–12 Mass. Ave.	unknown	1883	1978	
"	1316 Mass. Ave	unknown	1885	1978	
"	3 Linden Street	W.P. Wentworth	1889	1978	
Drayton Hall	48 Kennedy Street	George McLean	1901		
Hampden Hall	1246–56 Mass. Ave.	Coolidge & Carlson	1902	1978	
Waverly Hall	115 Mt. Auburn St.	Nathan Douglass	1902		
Belmont Hall	119–123 Mt. Auburn St.	Nathan Douglass	1903		1987
Ridgely Hall	65 Mt. Auburn St.	George McLean	1904		

Source: building permits and contemporary descriptions specifying dormitory use.

a building permit to construct one of the earliest dormitories on Mt. Auburn Street in August 1892, weeks after he graduated from the Law School; Claverly Hall had fifty-five one- and two-bedroom suites, as well as a swimming pool, squash court, and reading and reception rooms (figure 10.41). Newspaper publisher Linn Boyd Porter gambled that he could outdo Claverly when he erected Ware Hall on Harvard Street; despite its remote location he sold it almost immediately to Edward Holbrook, president of the Gorham Silver Company, whose son was dissatisfied with his rooms at Beck (figure 10.42). The Dunster, built by New York merchant John Albro Little in 1895, had real grandeur. Designed by Boston architect Arthur Little on the model of a Renaissance palazzo, it had an inner courtyard that rose four stories to a glazed skylight (figures 10.43–10.44).

Wetmore took up the practice of law in New York City after graduating in 1892. In 1897 he returned to build Apley Court, a five-story Georgian Revival brick and limestone dormitory at 16 Holyoke Street. The architect was John Howe, an 1884 Harvard graduate who had worked for Hartwell & Richardson and Andrews & Jaques in Boston and McKim, Mead & White in New York. A year later, Whitney Warren, another architect with McKim, asked Wetmore to give up his law practice and enter an architectural partnership. When Howe joined Warren & Wetmore one of his first projects was Westmorly Court (1898), designed in a Medieval Revival style featuring diamond-paned windows and Tudor detailing. Westmorly's standing was assured when William K. Vanderbilt gave up his rooms in Beck for a suite that he furnished with antique tapestries, portraits by Dutch masters, a Turner landscape, and a library of rare folios. Warren & Wetmore went on to design the New York Yacht Club (1899), Grand Central Station (1903–1913), and the Ritz-Carlton (1911), Vanderbilt (1912), and Biltmore (1914) hotels in New York, as well as the Iroquois Club at 74 Mt. Auburn Street (1916).

The brothers Harold, Joseph, and Archibald Coolidge formed another prominent alumni investment group. Harold was the financier; Joseph, an architect with Coolidge & Wright and Coolidge & Carlson, designed Randolph, Hampden, and Fairfax

FIGURE 10.41 "One of the more luxurious rooms" in Claverly Hall, 1897.

FIGURE 10.42 Ware Hall, 383 Harvard Street (1893, George Fogerty, architect). Ware accommodated ninety-four students in what was "practically … a European plan hotel, with the most complete service ever used in a college building" (*Chronicle,* May 11, 1895). It was converted into fifty-five apartments in 1914. Photo ca. 1907–8.

FIGURE 10.43 The Dunster, 16 Dunster Street (1895, Little, Browne & Moore, architects). "No expense [was] spared in its erection to make it a first-class, thoroughly-constructed building" with fourteen single and twenty double suites (*Chronicle,* Apr. 4, 1896). The building was renamed Dudley Hall after Dunster House opened in 1930; Harvard razed it in 1964 to make way for Holyoke Center. Photo ca. 1929.

FIGURE 10.44 The Dunster's courtyard. Each level was treated in a different classical order, and all were ornamented with splendid wrought-iron balustrades befitting the social status of its undergraduate residents. Photo 1964.

FIGURE 10.45 The Gold Coast in 1912. From left to right, Ridgely Hall, 65 Mt. Auburn Street (1904, George S.R. McLean); Claverly Hall, 63 Mt. Auburn (1892, George Fogerty); Randolph Hall, 12 Linden (1897, Coolidge & Wright); Russell Hall, 41 Bow (1899, George Fogerty); and Westmorly Court, 11–21 Bow (1898, Warren & Wetmore). The Harvard Lampoon (1909, Wheelwright & Haven) is at right. Photo ca. 1907–8.

FIGURE 10.46 Randolph Hall. Randolph was designed so that the entries faced the discreetly enclosed courtyard fronting Apthorp House; there was no direct access from the street. After the formation of Adams House in 1931 Harvard constructed a tunnel under Linden Street to access the dining room in Russell Hall.

halls; and Archibald, a professor of history and director of the university library, supervised from his apartment in Randolph. As the Randolph Trust they built Randolph Hall (1897), and as the University Associates they acquired Manter and Hilton halls about 1900 and built Hampden Hall in 1902. The imaginatively designed Randolph oriented its Jacobean-gabled facade toward an intimate courtyard and the elegant 18th-century East Apthorp house in the center of the block (figure 10.46). Hampden, an opulent Classical Revival building at 1246–1256 Massachusetts Avenue, contained fifty student suites above a row of granite-trimmed storefronts, making it similar to The Fairfax, which the brothers created by remodeling the Hilton block (see figure 8.23).

Local investors were also active. Future mayor John H.H. McNamee, a bookbinder, developed Quincy Hall, a twelve-suite Queen Anne building in 1891 (figure 10.47). Peter Burns, a Kerry Corner resident with a keen eye for real estate, put up Russell Hall at 41 Bow Street in 1899. Isaac McLean, a local builder, erected Drayton Hall at 48 Kennedy Street in 1901 and Ridgely Hall at 65 Mt. Auburn Street in 1904; both were designed by his son, George S.R. McLean, a 1900 graduate.

A dozen more private dormitories lay outside the Gold Coast. West of the village on University Road, Harvard Square stationer Charles H. Thurston built the Craigie, the first important commission of Josephine Wright Chapman, a young architect who had

FIGURE 10.47 Quincy Hall, 1218 Massachusetts Avenue (1891, George Fogerty, architect). Photo 2014.

FIGURE 10.48 The Craigie, 2–6 University Road (1897, Josephine Wright Chapman, architect). The Craigie's swimming pool was removed when the building was converted to apartments in the 1920s. The building became known as Chapman Arms about 2010. Photo 2015.

apprenticed with Clarence H. Blackall in Boston (figure 10.48). Cambridge builder Henry Green put up Waverly Hall at 115 Mt. Auburn Street, designed by English architect Nathan Douglas in 1902 with a glazed-brick well that reflected light into the interior rooms; like the Craigie, it offered residents a swimming pool.[17] Trinity Hall at 114–120 (1893) and Belmont Hall at 119–123 Mt. Auburn (1903) were built of wood, but provided amenities such as breakfast service and tennis courts (figure 10.49). The appeal of these buildings evaporated in 1912 when the Boston Elevated Railway expanded its Bennett Street yards and began running streetcars past them into the new subway station.

The many clubhouses along Mt. Auburn Street reinforced the desirability of the Gold Coast. Student organizations had

FIGURE 10.49 Trinity Hall, 114–120 Mt. Auburn Street (1893, W.H. & J.A. McGinty, architects). A storefront built in the front yard in 1929 was the home of Cronin's, a legendary bar and grille, from 1960 until 1978. Trinity was replaced by an office building in 2014. Photo 1902.

existed since the 18th century, but they became a focus of college life after the Civil War, when undergraduates increasingly differentiated themselves by class and income. Club membership was characterized by arcane distinctions that entranced socially conscious students. "'Final'" clubs such as the Porcellian and the A.D. were the most exclusive. "'Waiting'" clubs were created by the final clubs around 1900 in order to maintain places for eligible sophomores. Specialized clubs included literary societies, journalistic endeavors like the Crimson and the Lampoon, and theatrical organizations like the Hasty Pudding and Pi Eta.

Clubs initially occupied rented quarters, but some began acquiring houses in the village in the 1880s. Delta Phi erected one of the first purpose-built clubs at 72 Mt. Auburn Street on the nascent Gold Coast in 1887 (figure 10.50). Most clubhouses were designed by distinguished alumni; for example, the Signet Society (a literary association, not a club) bought a simple 1820 Federal house on Dunster at the corner of Mt. Auburn Street in 1899 and in 1902 remodeled it with Georgian ornamentation designed by Bertram Goodhue (a partner of Ralph Adams Cram) and heraldist Pierre LaRose ('95).

Clubs considered Mt. Auburn Street opposite Claverly and Randolph halls an ideal location, except from about 1899 until 1906 while the city debated the route of a proposed elevated railroad between Harvard Square and Boston (see chapter 2). During this period the A.D. built at 1268 Massachusetts Avenue (1899), the Delphic at 9 Linden Street (1902), and Phi Delta Psi at 30 Holyoke Street (1905) (figures 10.51–10.52). Once the decision had been made to build a subway, the Fox Club replaced an old house at 44 Kennedy Street with a Georgian Revival building by Guy Lowell. The Phoenix-S.K, Iroquois, Spee, and D.U. all built single-purpose clubhouses on Mt. Auburn Street between 1915 and 1931 (figure 10.53). The D.U. had put up a building at 396 Harvard Street in 1914, but in 1930 felt compelled to build a new one on the Gold Coast. The Porcellian and the A.D. retained their highly visible sites on Massachusetts Avenue, where they had the only clubhouses with storefronts (figures 10.54–10.55).

Figure 10.50 Delta Phi Club, 72 Mt. Auburn Street (1887, James Fogerty, architect). Delta Phi was known as the "Gas House" because the steward kept every room brilliantly lit; the club was renamed the Delphic when it put up a more formal clubhouse on Linden Street in 1902. The Phoenix/S.K. Club was built on this site in 1915. Photo 1900.

FIGURE 10.51 Phi Delta Psi (now Owl) Club, 30 Holyoke Street (1905, James Purdon, architect). Purdon, a member of the class of 1895, gave the club a stiffly formal exterior that enclosed a luxurious array of public rooms. Photo 2015.

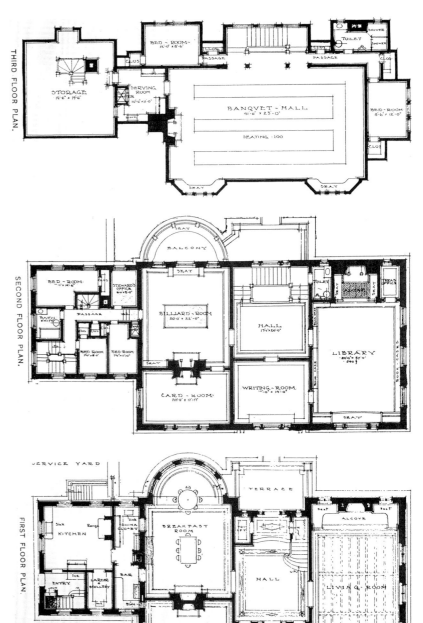

FIGURE 10.52 Floor plans of the Phi Delta Psi Club. Facilities included a living room and breakfast room on the ground floor, a card room, billiard room, writing room and library on the second, and a banquet hall seating 100 on the third. Students were not supposed to live at their clubs, so the bedrooms were probably meant for alumni.

Figure 10.53 Clubs on the Gold Coast. From left, Phoenix-S.K. Club, 72 Mt. Auburn Street; Iroquois Club, 74 Mt. Auburn; Spee Club, 76 Mt. Auburn; Kappa Gamma Chi, 78 Mt. Auburn; Signet Society, 46 Dunster Street; and D.U. Club, 45 Dunster. See table 10.2 for architects and dates. Photo 1973.

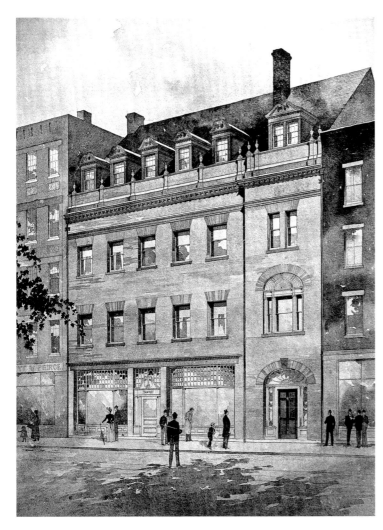

FIGURE 10.54 Porcellian Club, 1324 Massachusetts Avenue (1890, William Y. Peters, architect). Despite the Porcellian's place at the pinnacle of student clubs, the ground floor was prudently designed to be rented (see figure 8.13 for the previous building on this site).

FIGURE 10.55 A.D. Club, 1268 Massachusetts Avenue (1899, Parker & Thomas with Charles K. Cummings, architects). The grandiose A.D. Club contrasted with the restrained Porcellian. J. Harleston Parker (class of 1893 and a club member) studied at M.I.T. and the École des Beaux-Arts; he went on to a distinguished career in Boston, designing the Harvard Club (1912) and Boston's Art Deco United Shoe Machinery Building (1929). Photo 1900.

Among the specialized clubs, the Hasty Pudding built a theater at 12 Holyoke Street in 1887, and the Pi Eta put up another on Winthrop Street in 1896 (figure 10.56). The Harvard Crimson's restrained Georgian building on Plympton Street carries the paper's logotype above the entrance but cannot compete architecturally with the Lampoon, which occupies a key site at the heart of the Gold Coast. Established in 1876 to publish a college humor magazine, the Lampoon benefited from the business acumen of William Randolph Hearst and the literary efforts of Owen Wister, George Santayana, Robert Benchley, and John Updike. In 1909 founding member Edward M. Wheelwright designed a whimsical mock-Flemish castle in the form of a crouching lion whose helmet is surmounted by an ibis, the peripatetic symbol of the club (figure 10.57).

The Gold Coast changed the tenor of university life by making wealth the mark of distinction within the student body; residence and club membership dictated friendships and social standing. In response, Eliot authorized the construction of Perkins and Conant halls on Oxford Street in 1893, except for Hastings Hall (1888) the first new dormitories since 1872 (figure 10.58).[18] He also provided unprecedented amenities for undergraduates, including Randall Commons on Kirkland Street in 1898 and Stillman Infirmary and the Harvard Union in 1900 (figures 10.59–10.60). The Union's donor, Henry Lee Higginson, intended it to be as lavish as any finals club. The Stadium and associated facilities across the river replaced Jarvis and Holmes fields in 1903.

None of these projects except the Stadium appear to have made much difference to the undergraduates. In 1900 only 27 percent were housed in college halls. The new dormitories were too distant, meals were still too expensive, and the Union could not overcome the cachet of the clubs. Professor A. Lawrence Lowell described his concerns to Eliot in 1902:

It seems to me that there is a growing feeling among some members of the faculty that the tendency of the wealthier students to live in private dormitories outside the Yard involves great danger of a snobbish separation of the students on lines of wealth, and is thereby bringing about a condition of things that would destroy the chief value of the College as a place for the training of character. (In Cooney, "Dormitories," 11–12)

Figure 10.56 Hasty Pudding Club, 12 Holyoke Street (1887, Peabody & Stearns, architects). Photo ca. 1896.

FIGURE 10.57 Harvard Lampoon, 44 Bow Street (1909, Edward Wheelwright of Wheelwright & Haven, architect). Student Robert Goelet retrieves a shroud that Harvard Crimson members had wrapped around the Lampoon's ibis. Photo 1946.

TABLE 10.2 CLUBHOUSES AT HARVARD: BUILDINGS BUILT OR SIGNIFICANTLY RENOVATED BY UNDERGRADUATE ORGANIZATIONS

Name	Address	Architect	Date	Razed
Hasty Pudding	12 Holyoke St.	Peabody & Stearns	1887	
Delta Phi\Delphic	72 Mt. Auburn St.	James Fogerty	1887	1915
Porcellian	**1324 Mass. Ave.**	**William Y. Peters**	**1890**	
Zeta Psi	44 Church St.	Peabody & Stearns	1894*	1944
Pi Eta (theater)	91 Winthrop St.	W.P. Richards	1896	1997
Alpha Delta	46 Dunster St.	Peabody & Stearns	1895*	
Alpha Delta Phi\Fly	**2 Holyoke Place**	**Herbert D. Hale**	**1896**	
A.D.	**1268 Mass. Ave.**	**Cummings & Parker**	**1899**	
Digamma\Fox	**66 Winthrop St.**	**Shaw & Hunnewell**	**1899***	**1949**
Signet	46 Dunster St.	Cram, Goodhue & Ferguson	1902*	
Theta Delta Chi	54 Dunster St.	A.J. Russell	1900	
Delphic	**9 Linden St.**	**James Purdon**	**1902**	
Zeta Psi	15 Holyoke St.	Guy Lowell	1904	1962
Phi Delta Psi\Owl	**30 Holyoke St.**	**James Purdon**	**1905**	
Digamma\Fox	**44 Kennedy St.**	**Guy Lowell**	**1906**	
Pi Eta (house)	89 Winthrop St.	Putnam & Cox	1908	
Harvard Rowing Club	39 Holyoke St.	James Purdon	1908	1928
Harvard Lampoon	44 Bow St.	Wheelwright & Haven	1909	
Delta Upsilon	396 Harvard St.	R. Clipston Sturgis	1914	
Kappa Gamma Chi	78 Mt. Auburn St.	Harold O. Warner	1914*	
Harvard Crimson	14 Plympton St.	Jardine, Hill & Murdock	1915	
Phoenix/SK	**72 Mt. Auburn St.**	**Coolidge & Shattuck**	**1915**	
Iroquois	74 Mt. Auburn St.	Warren & Wetmore	1916	
Speakers	45 Mt. Auburn St.	Harry J. Carlson	1928*	
Sigma Alpha Epsilon	60 Kennedy St.	Smith & Walker	1929	
Delta Upsilon	45 Dunster St.	Perry, Shaw & Hepburn	1930	
Spee	**76 Mt. Auburn St.**	**William T. Aldrich**	**1931**	
Harvard Advocate	21 South Street	Eric Kebbon	1956	

Final clubs in boldface.

* Renovation of preexisting building.

FIGURE 10.58 Jarvis Field, ca. 1895. The principal facade of Perkins Hall (1893, Shepley Rutan & Coolidge, architects), seen in the distance, faced the field where Harvard football teams played before the completion of the stadium in 1904. Photo ca. 1895.

FIGURE 10.59 Stillman Infirmary, 270 Mt. Auburn Street (1900, Shepley, Rutan & Coolidge, architects). Students with infectious diseases were isolated in a ward connected to the infirmary by a loggia. Harvard sold Stillman in 1962; 1010 Memorial Drive, a private apartment building, replaced it in 1963. Photo ca. 1910.

FIGURE 10.60 Harvard Union (1900, McKim, Mead & White, architects). The Union was originally furnished as a men's club, with eighteen pool tables in the basement under the supervision of "a well-known professional" (*Crimson,* May 3, 1957). Theodore Roosevelt (class of 1880) contributed elk-horn chandeliers and more than thirty animal heads to decorate the great hall, which became the freshman dining room in 1930. The Union was restored and repurposed as the Barker Center, a faculty office building, in 1996–97. Photo ca. 1915.

FIGURE 10.61 Harvard University in 1906, near the end of Eliot's presidency.

CONSTRAINTS AND OPPORTUNITIES IN THE 1890S

Concerns about the tax-exempt status of its property discouraged Harvard from expanding too rapidly. A statute adopted in 1836 and confirmed in 1860 exempted from local taxation "the personal property of all literary, benevolent, charitable and scientific institutions incorporated within this Commonwealth, and such real estate belonging to such institutions, as shall actually be occupied by them, or by the officers of said institutions, for the purposes for which they were incorporated" (Greene, 9). When Eliot took office the Cambridge assessors were attempting to tax houses that Harvard rented to its professors, and for the rest of his tenure he worried that the favorable status of charitable corporations might be revoked at any time. In 1874 a legislative commission acknowledged that Harvard's "largest endowments, as well as those of other colleges, [had] come from private benefactions" that had reduced the state's need to tax its citizens in support of higher education (ibid., 54). Soon, however, the legislature diminished the university's ability to hold land for future development. One measure ended the tax exemption for property whose income was not used for academic purposes, and another put property back on the tax rolls that had been owned for two years but not occupied for educational purposes.[19] Attempts to tax dormitories and other income-generating, noninstructional buildings made Eliot reluctant to provoke the city, even though the legislature removed restrictions on investments in taxable real estate in 1889. He sold surplus property and evicted the Harvard Cooperative Society from Dane Hall in 1904 to protect the building's tax-exempt status.

Eliot worried about accepting gifts of land in Cambridge, but Boston seemed to be another matter. Harvard gained a bridgehead there in 1870 with Longfellow's gift of 70 acres of marsh in Brighton. Henry Lee Higginson gave 31 adjoining acres to create Soldiers Field in 1890. In 1903 Harvard received a bequest of $2 million from Gordon McKay, a wealthy inventor who lived near the Yard (see chapter 4).[20] Eliot used the windfall to promote a merger of Massachusetts Institute of Technology (then located

in the Back Bay) with the Lawrence Scientific School and solicited a gift from Andrew Carnegie to purchase more land across the river. M.I.T.'s trustees favored the merger, despite vigorous opposition from faculty and alumni, and only a decision of the Supreme Judicial Court prevented it. M.I.T. instead moved to its own campus in Cambridge in 1916, and Carnegie's site was occupied by the Harvard Business School in 1924.

With only meager resources for construction and no assistance from the state after 1833 (except for grants to the Museum of Comparative Zoology), Harvard depended on donors or quasi-independent committees to raise money for specific projects. Of the thirty-five buildings Harvard erected in Boston and Cambridge during Eliot's presidency, twenty-two were gifts of individuals, six were financed by special fund drives, and only three—Holyoke House, an addition to the library, and an addition to the University Museum—were built with university funds. Some donors, like Nathaniel Thayer and Edward Austin, selected their own architects and presented the finished buildings to the university, while others made unrestricted gifts or legacies like those that paid for Sever Hall and Johnston Gate. This practice resulted from the financial policies that Eliot announced in the 1880s: schools should spend all their income every year; the highest priority for fundraising should be to build endowments, particularly for professorships; and university funds should not be used for construction because "experience has shown that new buildings will be provided by gift nearly as fast as they are needed" (Eliot, *Annual Report,* 1882–83, in Coquillette, 565)

The architectural diversity that stemmed from relying on donors began to attract critical attention in the 1890s. The president's cousin, fine arts professor Charles Eliot Norton, told a national audience that

> If some special benefactor of the University should arise, ready to do a work that should hand down his name in ever-increasing honor with posterity, he might require the destruction of all the buildings erected in the last half-century, and their reconstruction in simple and beautiful design, in mutually helpful, harmonious and effective relation to each other. ("Harvard University in 1890," *Harper's New Monthly Magazine,* Sept. 1890, 591)

The president's son, landscape architect Charles Eliot, agreed: "This permitting donors of buildings and gates to choose their sites is fatal to general effect. Outside the quadrangle the Yard is already a jumble of badly placed buildings and roads" (Dec. 31, 1890, in Eliot, 292). The trade press joined the chorus, mocking Harvard for its "Neo-Grec-Romanesque-Queen Anne-Puginesque-Elizabethan-Richardsonian-Victorian Gothic-Anglo-Hellenic-Colonial conglomeration of buildings in and about the college yard" (*American Architect and Builder,* in the *Cambridge Tribune,* July 28, 1900).

During the Eliot years thirteen firms designed buildings for Harvard in Cambridge. Peabody & Stearns led the list with five commissions; McKim, Mead & White and Shepley, Rutan & Coolidge had four each; A.W. Longfellow had three; Ware & Van Brunt had two and at least three important remodelings; and Shaw & Hunnewell, Ryder & Harris, H.H. Richardson, and Guy Lowell each had two. Almost all of these firms also designed residences or public buildings in Cambridge. Robert Peabody (class of 1866), Eliot's brother-in-law, enjoyed Harvard's patronage from 1871 until 1907. Charles McKim received an honorary degree in 1890; his influence was paramount between 1890 and 1903 with the highly visible Johnston Gate, memorial fence, union, and stadium. Richardson's successor firm, Shepley, Rutan & Coolidge, obtained its first Harvard commission in 1893 but only achieved real influence in the next administration.

The emergence of the City Beautiful movement in the 1890s excited forward-looking architects and alumni. Visitors to the World's Columbian Exposition in Chicago in 1893 found an environment that expressed the ideals of the Progressive era in a form dictated by the Neoclassical principles of the École des Beaux-Arts: well ordered, sanitary, and spacious, starkly different from the chaotic nature of American cities—or the eclectic Harvard campus.

Cambridge's acquisition of its entire riverfront for parkland in 1892 allowed critics to imagine starting over in the manner proposed by Professor Norton. Faced with deliberate inaction by the president and corporation, an ad hoc subcommittee of Overseers consisting of Robert Peabody, Augustus Hemenway, and George Shattuck asked Olmsted, Olmsted & Eliot to prepare a master plan in 1896 (figure 10.62). The firm patched together a sequence of axial corridors involving nineteen proposed or enlarged buildings in and north of the Yard. No account was taken of the private land between the Yard and the river other than a 70-foot-wide, tree-lined boulevard along Plympton Street (an alignment that became impractical with the construction of Randolph Hall in 1897).

Late in 1901 several alumni led by Edward Waldo Forbes began acquiring property near the river for the future use of the university. Forbes (who later became director of the Fogg Museum) enlisted Harold Coolidge, who had used straws to buy land cheaply for Boston's South Station. After two years working *sub rosa,* Forbes and five other alumni filed a Declaration of Trust creating the Harvard Riverside Associates. They raised $400,000 from alumni and mortgaged the land they had already purchased for $485,000 more. One of the principals described the enterprise to J.P. Morgan Jr.:

> At the time the College had been growing with marked rapidity. Private dormitories were being built and the character of the territory between … Massachusetts Avenue and Mt. Auburn Street had changed very markedly in comparatively few years. The district immediately south of Mt. Auburn Street was a very decided eyesore. I believed … that it was a mistake for the College to try to force the dormitory development on the north side of the Yard, because I did not believe … that the college boys wanted to live [there] and I believed that the proper development for the college was toward the river. (Thomas Nelson Perkins, Aug. 11, 1908, in Cooney, "Riverside," 3)

President Eliot was ambivalent about Forbes's activities. Privately, he supported the effort, but he had recently assured the General Court that the university's interest was only in beautifying the area and that no land would be removed from taxation. When the purchases became public knowledge in March 1903, the newspapers were positive, but the city was bitter about the potential loss of taxable property and raised the assessments on

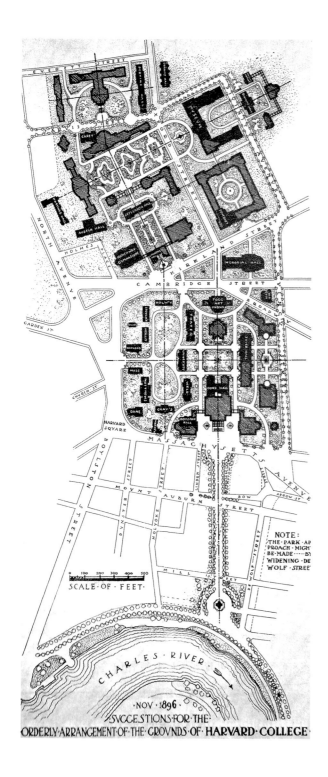

SCALE·OF·FEET·

·NOV·1896·
·SVGGESTIONS·FOR·THE·
ORDERLY·ARRANGEMENT·OF·THE·GROVNDS·OF·HARVARD·COLLEGE·

FIGURE 10.62 Olmsted, Olmsted & Eliot's unofficial plan "for the orderly arrangement of the grounds of Harvard College" (1896).

the 78 parcels acquired thus far (figure 10.63). The Associates had projected that rents would cover the mortgage and return a dividend to the investors, but higher taxes made that impossible. When the five-year trust expired in 1908 the Associates reorganized as the Harvard Riverside Trustees. The university contributed $300,000, but the city's opposition inhibited Harvard from taking title to the land, and bankruptcy ensued in 1918.

The university's first move to improve the riverfront lands occurred in January 1902, when Harvard College, President Eliot ("acting as a citizen of Cambridge … interested in the development of the park system"), the University Associates, and Richard Henry Dana III petitioned the city to widen DeWolfe Street into a tree-lined extension of Memorial Drive (*Chronicle*, Jan. 11, 1902; see figure 4.267). This proposal failed: it would have required taking the future site of St. Paul's Church as well as Quincy Hall, which belonged to future mayor John H.H. McNamee. Once the activities of the Associates became known, alumni-sponsored plans proliferated. The Olmsteds' plan for the Associates expanded on their 1902 proposal for DeWolfe Street, with buildings facing an open lawn called the New Yard. Charles Wetmore's grandiose Beaux-Arts scheme had a great quadrangle and nine Neoclassical buildings reminiscent of McKim, Mead & White's 1894 plan for Columbia University (figure 10.64). President Eliot, nearing the end of his forty-year term, ignored them all and left the field to his successor.

Charles W. Eliot transformed a small and tradition-encrusted New England college into a leader of American higher education without disrupting life in Cambridge, his lifelong home. He respected the city's elected officials and won their respect in turn. By taking care to expand where there was little resistance, he avoided the controversies that dogged later presidents. Eliot's reluctance to adopt a master plan or a uniform style, as his critics demanded, preserved the university's rich architectural heritage.

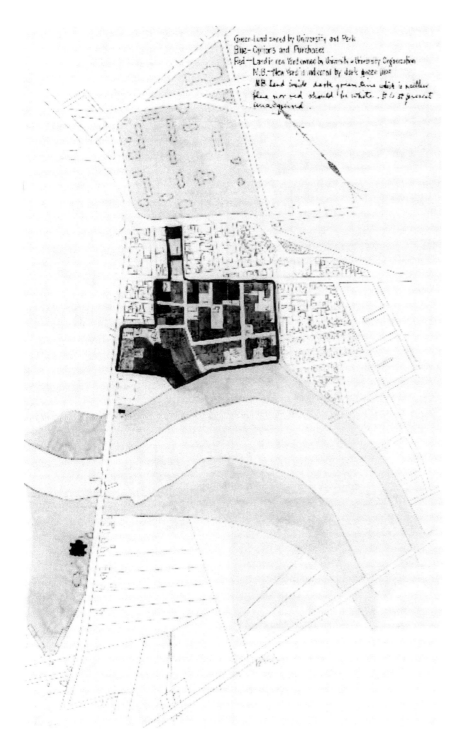

Green land owned by University and Park

Blue—Options and Purchases

Red—Land in use Yard owned by University & University Organization
N.B.—Then Yard is colored by dark green line
N.B. Land inside dark green line which is neither
blue nor red should be white. It is at present
unadquired

FIGURE 10.63 Purchases by the Harvard Riverside Associates, as of March 30, 1903. Edward Waldo Forbes sent this sketch map to Eliot after the Associates' activities became public knowledge.

The English essayist Arnold Bennett adopted a forgiving tone in 1912:

All the [Harvard] buildings are artistically modest; many are beautiful; scarcely one that clashes with the subtle and sober attractiveness of the whole aggregation. Nowhere is the eye offended. One looks upon the crimson facades with the same lenient love as marks one's attitude toward those quaint and lovely English houses … that are all picturesqueness and no bath-room. (*Your United States,* 158)

FIGURE 10.64 Charles Wetmore's 1903 scheme for the riverfront land envisioned a boulevard along Holyoke Street that would bypass Kennedy Street and the Great Bridge. This version, published in *Harper's Weekly* in 1909, omitted a Neoclassical domed building not unlike Columbia's Low Library that would have been inconsistent with Harvard's Georgian traditions.

A. Lawrence Lowell dedicated himself and his personal fortune to the university for thirty-six years. In 1902, while still a professor of government, he was the anonymous donor of what became known as Lowell Lecture Hall, and more buildings went up during his twenty-four year presidency than in all previous administrations combined. Lowell believed in long term planning; vacant land was diminishing, the university was beginning to encroach on the city, and it was no longer feasible to consider each new building as an independent entity.

Lowell understood architecture and enjoyed supervising Harvard's construction projects, which facilitated his close relationship with Boston architect Charles A. Coolidge, a graduate of the class of 1881 who joined H.H. Richardson's office after two years at M.I.T. Coolidge was made responsible for executing Richardson's design for the Converse Memorial Library in Malden in 1883–1885, although both Langford Warren and A.W. Longfellow were senior to him and consequently left the firm. He went on to design Stanford University's campus plan and early buildings (1886–1903), as well as the Art Institute of Chicago (completed 1893), the John Carter Brown Library at Brown University (1904), Harper Library at the University of Chicago (1912), and many others.[21] Lowell "had a fixed idea that Charles Coolidge was the only architect who understood university needs" (Julian Coolidge, 11). By the time Lowell left office, Coolidge, Shepley, Bulfinch & Abbott had been involved in almost thirty major Harvard projects; the sole exception was the business school, which McKim, Mead & White won in a blind competition.

Lowell nurtured Harvard's departments of architecture, landscape architecture, and city planning. George Edgell, an architectural historian whom he appointed dean in 1922, continued Langford Warren's reliance on European teachers and selected the École-trained Jean-Jacques Haffner as professor of design. Edgell was open to contemporary trends in design, but Lowell's attitude was expressed in a note scribbled on a 1925 announcement of an exhibit of contemporary German architecture that "it might be useful in instructing students what to avoid" (Alofsin, 82). Nevertheless, a student organization mounted the first American exhibit of Bauhaus architecture at Harvard in 1930, and the School of Architecture and the Fogg Museum co-sponsored the Museum of Modern Art show that introduced the International Style in 1932. Despite Lowell's personal antipathy, the ground was prepared during his presidency for the revolution in architectural instruction that would occur in the 1930s.

Lowell brought undergraduates fully into the life of the college by requiring them to live in Harvard buildings. As early as 1907 he proposed organizing undergraduate "houses," each with a library and dining hall modeled after the college system at Oxford and Cambridge. In his 1909 inaugural address he pledged to build dormitories for freshmen to give entering students an opportunity to meet their classmates on equal terms and alleviate the stratifying effects of private dormitories and clubs: these opened in September 1914 (Morison, *Founding,* 252). From then until 1930 seniors roomed in the Yard while sophomores and juniors remained in private accommodations. At the same time, the college became more exclusionary. Lowell placed a quota on Jewish admissions, barred African Americans from college housing, and established residency requirements that excluded local undergraduates who could not afford to live away from home.[22]

The Harvard Riverside Trustees had a new plan by William Ralph Emerson waiting when Lowell took office in 1909, but he asked Shepley, Rutan & Coolidge to prepare a design that accorded with his own ideas. Charles Coolidge's 1910 site plan for the freshmen dormitories avoided the quadrangles and malls of earlier plans and proposed instead a series of buildings grouped around courtyards open to the river (figure 10.65). In 1912 the trustees transferred a third of their holdings to the university. Gore and Standish halls, permitted in July 1913 and constructed over the next year, were the first dormitories built to the new plan; both faced the river. Smith Hall, permitted the same day, surrounded a closed courtyard off Kennedy Street. All three buildings were Georgian Revival in style, setting a precedent for the River Houses. Freshmen were required to reside in the halls beginning with the 1914–15 school year.

FIGURE 10.65 Standish Hall (1913, Shepley, Rutan & Coolidge, architects). Standish was remodeled in 1930 when it was incorporated into Winthrop House. The cupola and brick gable with twin chimneys at left belong to Smith Hall, also 1913. Photo ca. 1915.

As the freshmen dormitories were nearing completion Lowell designated five buildings in the Yard for seniors and had electric lights and bathrooms installed on each floor. On January 31, 1914, 334 men in private dormitories registered to move to the Yard in September. The *Chronicle's* headline, "Seniors Quit Gold Coast," forecast ruin for the operators of private dormitories. The profits from Randolph Hall dropped from $18,250 in 1914 to $892 in 1915. While Lowell noted the difficulty this caused the owners, especially Harold Coolidge, he did not want to provoke the city by taking more property off the tax rolls. Under the cover of a wartime housing shortage, Harvard purchased Dunster Hall and Little's Block and acquired the rest of the Riverside Trustees

property when they declared bankruptcy in 1918. In 1920 the university bought Apley Court, Westmorly Court, and Claverly Hall from Wetmore's Claverly Trust. The owners of Craigie, Waverly, and Ware halls converted them into apartment houses; only Drayton, Ridgely, and Beck continued to operate as before.

In 1920 Lowell appointed a "Committee on Plans for the Future Development of Harvard University" that included Guy Lowell, Charles Coolidge, and Henry Hubbard of the School of Landscape Architecture. Coolidge's firm prepared a comprehensive scheme to cloister the Yard with new buildings and erect dormitories arranged in quadrangles facing the river (figure 10.66).[23] The realization of this plan would be Lowell's most spectacular achievement. His vast building program and the accompanying creation of the house system preserved the Old Yard, established the Georgian Revival as Harvard's preeminent style, altered the university's relationship with its undergraduates, and decimated the Kerry Corner neighborhood (see chapter 4).

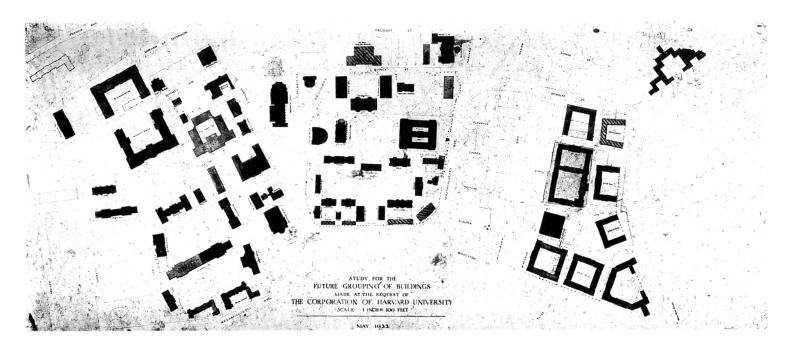

FIGURE 10.66 Charles A. Coolidge's 1922 plan for building the River Houses, cloistering the Yard, and erecting laboratories on Divinity Avenue. This comprehensive plan, the first in the history of the university, was followed until after World War II.

FIGURE 10.67 A view from the tower of St. Paul's Church, ca. 1922. The Gold Coast dormitories face the still largely intact neighborhood south of Mt. Auburn Street. The chimneys of the Boston Elevated Railway power station dominate the skyline beyond Gore, Standish, and Persis Smith halls (all 1913).

A détente with the city eased Lowell's path. Cambridge depended on property taxes for over 80% of its income, yet the proportion of tax-exempt property rose from 22% in 1900 to 45% in 1934. In 1928, when Harvard was about to purchase the highly assessed generating station of the Boston Elevated Railway on Kennedy Street, the university assured the city that it had "no present intention of acquiring more land," but it promised to pay a sum in lieu of taxes on any property it might acquire over the next twenty years (Buckley, 55; see figure 9.32). This averted a certain confrontation in the legislature, but forecast the rows that occurred in 1948, 1968, and every subsequent year in which the payment in lieu of taxes (PILOT) agreement was renewed.

Lowell's plan required a huge infusion of funds, which came in the form of a $13.2 million gift from Standard Oil heir Edward Harkness. Harkness was interested in creating residential halls on the English model and had originally offered his gift to Yale, his alma mater. When Yale hesitated, Harkness turned to Lowell. Since Harvard already owned land along the river, the project could begin almost immediately. Dunster, Lowell, and Eliot houses were built as self-sufficient complexes for upperclassmen in 1929–30. Three others—Kirkland, Winthrop, and Leverett—were created by expanding the freshman dormitories. Adams House incorporated an assortment of structures dating from 1760 to 1898; the East Apthorp house became the master's residence, and Claverly, Westmorly, and Randolph were remodeled to squeeze in more students. Harvard razed Russell Hall, a private dormitory on the corner of Bow Street—"neither comely without nor comfortable within"—and used the last of the Harkness funds to replace it with a new Russell that provided a handsome Georgian Revival focus for the complex (*Crimson,* Jan. 9, 1931).

When upperclassmen moved into the River Houses in September 1930, the freshmen took their place in the Yard; at the end of the school year, the *Boston Globe* headlined "Harvard's Gold Coast Passes into History" (July 5, 1931). The tradition of undergraduates living and eating in town ended for good. A contemporary observer noted the "cannibalization of real estate and 'homes'; ladies who ran boardinghouses for students were being

FIGURE 10.68 Harvard's newly completed River Houses, as seen from the tower of Lowell House looking toward McKinlock Hall. Photo 1930.

done out of their livelihoods, and hash houses where undergraduates used to feed were closing down" (Schlesinger, 174).

Harvard Yard achieved its current form during this period. Widener Library, erected in 1913, was the largest building the university had yet undertaken (figures 10.69–10.70). Eleanor Elkins Widener of Philadelphia gave it in memory of her son, Harry Elkins Widener, a 1907 graduate who went down with the *Titanic,* on the condition that she choose the architect and approve the design; once again, a donor made the decisions, paid the bills, and presented the university with a completed building. Unlike Gore, which it replaced, Widener turns its back on Massachusetts Avenue. Across the Tercentenary Theater Memorial Church, with its extraordinary 170-foot bell tower completed in 1932, balances Widener's overwhelming mass (see figure 10.75).

In 1923 the Committee on Plans adopted the principle of "cloistering" the Yard by constructing buildings along Massachusetts

FIGURE 10.69 Widener Library (1913, Horace Trumbauer, architect). Photo ca. 1915.

FIGURE 10.70 Stone carvers and masons during the construction of Widener Library, ca. 1915.

Avenue to screen out the traffic and bustle of Harvard Square, hoping to accomplish this "without producing an exterior appearance of monastic or snobbish exclusion" (*President's Report,* 1923–24, 26). Lionel and Mower halls (1924) are two

and a half stories high, in deference to the small scale of Holden Chapel, while Straus (1926) is similar in height to nearby Massachusetts Hall. Three sections of Wigglesworth erected in 1930 completed the enclosure. Lehman Hall (1924), the centerpiece of the project, was a disappointment, and this corner—which looked directly onto Harvard Square and was occupied by successive Cambridge meetinghouses until 1833 and by Dane Hall from 1871 until it burned in 1918—might have been better left open (figure 10.71; see figure 9.36).

Quincy Street saw substantial construction during Lowell's presidency. The president commissioned his cousin, Guy Lowell, to design a new official residence (now Loeb House) that he erected at his own expense in 1911. On the east side, the new Fogg Museum displaced four houses in 1925 and completed the Sever quadrangle, while the Faculty Club replaced the Colonial Club in 1930. A proposal to incorporate Quincy Street into the Yard surfaced periodically throughout the 20th century but never received serious consideration from the city.

The North Precinct also saw a great deal of activity, although the new buildings showed little consistency with one another. In 1911 Lowell commissioned Alexander Longfellow to design a science campus between Divinity Avenue and Oxford Street but built only two of the eight proposed laboratories, Wolcott Gibbs (1911) and T. Jefferson Coolidge (1912); he allocated much of the site to the Busch-Reisinger Museum in 1914 (figure 10.72).[24] The refined character of Longfellow's buildings contrasted with the uncharacteristically crude appearance of Coolidge, Shepley, Bulfinch & Abbott's Mallinckrodt Laboratory (1927), whose mill-like exterior was barely disguised by a superfluous portico. Across Oxford Street, Cruft (1913) and Lyman (1930) laboratories linked Jefferson (1882) and Pierce (1900) to enclose Holmes Field. The 1922 Coolidge plan proposed Mallinckrodt as the termination of a mall extending west toward the Common. Gannett House was turned to face Mallinckrodt's portico, but the temptation of so much open space was irresistible, and Gordon McKay broke the connection in 1951.

FIGURE 10.71 The former site of the Fourth Meetinghouse and Dane Hall, and the future site of Lehman Hall. Matthews (left) and Grays (right) frame the tower of Memorial Hall. Photo ca. 1920–24.

FIGURE 10.72 The North Precinct in 1934, dominated by the University
Museum on the left and the Biological Laboratories on the right. The Wolcott
Gibbs and Jefferson Coolidge laboratories stand adjacent to the Peabody
Museum, with the Busch-Reisinger Museum occupying most of A.W. Longfel-
low's proposed science campus.

The Biological Laboratories designed by the Coolidge office in 1930 are a striking contrast to the Georgian Revival buildings that characterized the Lowell administration. The vertical bays of factory sash separated by wide pylons of traditional red brick relate to Moderne buildings like the Central Square Post Office and the Rindge Technical School (both 1932). Katherine Ward Lane's magnificent birds, animals, and fish carved into the facade represent a humanizing tendency in American modern architecture that was quashed by proponents of the International Style in the 1940s. One the last projects of Lowell's presidency, it anticipated several future architectural developments at Harvard (figures 10.73–10.74).

FIGURE 10.73 Biological Laboratories (1930, Coolidge, Shepley, Bulfinch & Abbott, architects). The sculptor, later known as Katherine Lane Weems, created the intricate frieze, the double doors depicting plants, insects, and invertebrates, and the two life-size rhinoceroses installed at the main entrance in 1937. Photo 2015.

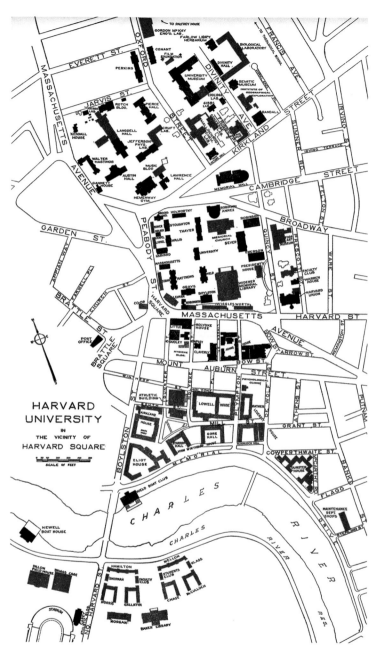

FIGURE 10.74 Harvard University in 1936. Buildings in red were acquired or constructed during A. Lawrence Lowell's presidency.

PRESIDENT CONANT (1933–53)

Chemistry professor James Bryant Conant became president in 1933, during a pause in Harvard's expansion that coincided with radical changes in architectural theory and practice. Lowell's great Georgian building program was complete, and few new buildings appeared until after World War II.

By the early 1930s the Neoclassical principles of the École des Beaux-Arts had dominated architectural education for forty years with an approach that emphasized fidelity to classical design, refined presentation techniques, and design problems that usually ignored modern conditions. President Conant thought that the schools of architecture, landscape architecture, and city planning should be closely integrated, and that they "should move away from archeology and toward engineering and a greater contact with economics and politics" (Alofsin, 118). To implement this agenda, he appointed Joseph Hudnut as dean of the school of architecture in 1935. Hudnut was a 1909 graduate

FIGURE 10.75 Harvard Yard in 1933.

of the college who had studied architecture at the University of Michigan, practiced briefly in New York City, and recently been appointed dean of the program at Columbia University. At Harvard he reorganized the school of architecture as the Graduate School of Design (GSD) and began a painful transition away from the educational methods of the École.

Hudnut's reforms stressed integration of design with practical training, replaced courses in architectural history and freehand drawing with instruction relevant to professional practice, and promoted collaboration with the landscape architecture and city planning programs. He considered this to be a return to the earlier American methods of William Ware and Langford Warren, "before the French influence became predominant" (Alofsin, 121). Courses that did not support professional education were transferred to the college.

Jean-Jacques Haffner's resignation in 1936 presented Hudnut with an opportunity to hire a new professor of design. The obvious course was to turn to the Bauhaus, the school founded on socialist principles at Dessau in Germany in 1919 that had been closed by the Nazis in 1933. Founders of the Bauhaus denounced the use of ornamentation, decorative detail, and expensive materials, and rejected principles of symmetry and proportion that had been accepted wisdom since Classical times. They believed architectural education should nurture concepts of advanced design and de-emphasize artistic skills in rendering and presentation. The study of architectural history was proscribed, and the iconic studio problem became the production of housing for the masses. The revolutionary fervor of the Bauhaus resonated with young American architects and design theorists such as Alfred Barr, Henry-Russell Hitchcock, and Philip Johnson, all of whom had strong Harvard connections. They promoted the new movement as an antidote to the ostensibly bankrupt principles of establishment architecture and as superior to indigenous expressions of modernity such as Art Deco and Art Moderne.

Hudnut decided to hire Walter Gropius (instead of Mies van der Rohe or the Dutch architect J.J.P. Oud) because of his experience as director of the Bauhaus in 1919–28, although he had accomplished little in the field since leaving Germany in 1934. Gropius arrived in April 1937 with Marcel Breuer and took over Haffner's design course. The first problem he set his students was to design public housing around Fresh Pond; every unit was to have a view and receive at least two hours of sunlight each day. The program dictated rows of tall buildings, all oriented at the same angle to the sun and isolated from the community at large, comprising an uncannily accurate forecast of the nearby Rindge Towers project of 1968–70.

The new orthodoxy that Hudnut and Gropius introduced at GSD was painful for many.

> The *realpolitik* of the modernist curriculum required the defamation of the preceding generation, which consisted largely of the claim that the Beaux-Arts had nothing to offer the modern design professions. … One kind of teacher was on the way out and along with this departure went a whole tone and atmosphere. The conservative gentleman scholar who often had deep Harvard or New England roots was being replaced by the teacher as ideologue: a fervent disciple, often from "outside" (meaning New York or Europe) who dispensed with tradition and orthodoxy in the pursuit of a social commitment and the implementation of a curriculum based on actual practice. (Alofsin, 154)

Gropius had hoped to recreate the architect-centered Bauhaus curriculum at Harvard, but Hudnut had also revitalized the city planning and landscape architecture programs, and for a time he achieved a partnership among the disciplines to an extent not seen since Langford Warren's time (or later). "The vision of an integrated response to modern problems, built around the principle of collaboration, flourished from 1945 to 1950 with unprecedented impact. … The students who attended during this fruitful period ultimately became a Who's Who of American and international architecture, landscape architecture, and planning" (Alofsin, 202).[25] In 1952 Gropius retired to The Architects Collaborative, the firm he had founded in 1945. Hudnut remained as dean until 1953, when Conant appointed Josep Lluis Sert to replace him.

Although Dean Hudnut had initiated the Modernist revolution at GSD, the charismatic Gropius got the credit. Gropius was also believed to have introduced the International Style at Harvard, but that process was actually underway when he arrived. Coolidge, Shepley, Bulfinch & Abbott (CSBA) had already broken with the past at the Biological Laboratories and reinterpreted Charles Bulfinch's 1818–23 Massachusetts General Hospital for the Conant administration's first large building, Littauer Center, in 1938 (figure 10.76).[26] The firm produced important modern work with the B+B Chemical complex at 780 Memorial Drive (1937) and the George White Building at Massachusetts General Hospital (1939). After World War II, CSBA designed two International Style buildings at Harvard, the Cyclotron (1946–51) and the Computation Laboratory (1946; figure 10.77). At Lamont Library (1947), Harvard's first contemporary building in the Yard, the firm used brick and limestone but omitted entirely the elaborate cornices and double-hung windows of its Georgian neighbors.

FIGURE 10.76 Littauer Hall (1938, Coolidge, Shepley, Bulfinch & Abbott, architects). At right, Mower and Lionel halls (1924–25, Coolidge, Shepley, Bulfinch & Abbott, architects) were part of the cloistering project to enclose the Yard. Photo 1949.

FIGURE 10.77 Howard Hathaway Aiken Computation Laboratory, 33 Oxford Street (1946, Coolidge, Shepley, Bulfinch & Abbott, architects; demolished 1997). Photo ca. 1947.

FIGURE 10.78 Harvard Graduate Center (1949, Walter Gropius/The Architects Collaborative, architects).

The Graduate Center, a cluster of seven dormitories and a dining commons on Everett Street, is Gropius's legacy at Harvard (figure 10.78). Much has been made of Conant's presumed neglect in denying Gropius a commission until so late in his tenure, but the Graduate Center was Harvard's first substantial venture after the war. Some celebrated its expression of Modernist principles, but the design was not ground-breaking; as Bainbridge Bunting noted, "it merely brought Harvard and New England abreast of European practice of about 1930" (*Harvard Architecture,* 222). With its severe geometry, flat roofs, strip windows, elimination of ornament, and straightforward use of iron, concrete, brick, and glass, the complex is a more orthodox example of the International Style than Lamont. The art works by Josef Albers, Jean Arp, Herbert Bayer, and Joan Miró in Harkness Commons were noteworthy as an expression of the collaborative process Gropius favored.[27] The dormitories resembled the postwar housing projects that were at the core of the

Bauhaus ethos. Intended to combine "simplicity and economy with maximum comfort and utility," their Spartan accommodations became less popular with every passing year (*Boston Globe,* Oct. 21, 1948).

CSBA's Allston Burr Lecture Hall expressed a more humanistic strain of Modernism. Conant was committed to science education, and project architect Jean-Paul Carlhan incorporated two specialized lecture halls and a number of classrooms in Burr's complex composition of bold massing, strip windows, and flat roofs (figure 10.79). R. Clipston Sturgis of the class of 1881, architect of the Georgian Revival Cambridge Fire Headquarters (1933), characterized Harvard's postwar building program in general and Allston Burr in particular as lacking in beauty. Gropius's students attacked Sturgis for his elitism but also disdained the lavish complexities of Burr, "which they considered to be in defiance of the puritanical principles of good modern architecture that they were attempting to implement in the low cost and

FIGURE 10.79 Allston Burr Lecture Hall, 483 Broadway (1951, Jean-Paul Carlihan of Coolidge, Shepley, Bulfinch & Abbott, architect). Burr was made redundant by the Science Center in 1970 and was razed for the Sackler Museum in 1982. Note William James Hall under construction. Photo 1964.

FIGURE 10.80 Holyoke Center and Forbes Plaza, as seen from the Class of 1857 Gate. Photo ca. 1968.

restrained design of the Graduate Center" (*Harvard Architecture,* 228). Sturgis's protest did not sway the university; Harvard was now committed to Modernism.

PRESIDENT PUSEY (1953–71)

Nathan Pusey's presidency was an era of prolific building, surpassing even Lowell's in square footage and cost. Harvard abandoned Georgian orthodoxy and indulged visionary architects, each with a singular approach to planning and design. Twenty-three projects went to several different firms, not just Shepley, Bulfinch, Richardson & Abbott (as CSBA became in 1952), and included Harvard's first high-rises. The university's first permanent planning office influenced Cambridge's approach to zoning and traffic issues.

The pressure of rising postwar enrollments overcame Harvard's reluctance to take property off the tax rolls, and the first

twenty-year PILOT agreement was renegotiated in 1948. In 1957 President Pusey embarked on a fundraising campaign that sought an unprecedented $82.5 million, about half of which was for construction. The proceeds funded the Loeb Drama Center, the Carpenter Center for the Visual Arts, Holyoke Center, William James Hall, and three new undergraduate houses. The university acquired over 120 properties in Cambridge and "landbanked" them for eventual development, a practice with severe adverse effects:

> When Harvard landbanks, it buys property with an eye to razing it, creating a site for construction of new university facilities. Such property is usually permitted to run down, because there's no sense in paying steep maintenance costs if the building will eventually be torn down. Landbanking can potentially turn an owner into a slumlord; the building is only secondary to the property value. (*Harvard Crimson,* June 8, 1978)

The 1950s and '60s were a stressful time in Cambridge, and Harvard often seemed to be fishing in troubled waters. Ballooning enrollments pressured neighborhoods during the postwar housing shortage, even as the city's population declined. Rising rents displaced local families and led to the imposition of rent controls in 1970. Student demonstrations against the Vietnam War caused major property damage in Harvard Square and along march routes from Boston, and the city was torn by a proposal to locate the John F. Kennedy presidential library in Harvard Square. Community protests at commencement in 1970 produced a brief moratorium on expansion in Cambridge and started a chain of events that led the university to shift its focus to Allston in the 1990s.

GSD dean Josep Lluis Sert (1902–83) amassed considerable power at the university and in Cambridge. A disciple of the Swiss Modernist LeCorbusier, Sert had moved to the United States at the end of the Spanish Civil War in 1939. He established a consulting firm in New York, taught city planning at Yale in 1944–45, and founded Sert, Jackson & Gourley in Cambridge in 1955. While Gropius was primarily a theoretician, Sert was a practicing architect who was the first dean of GSD to become involved in the university's planning and design decisions. He became an influential adviser to President Pusey and received three of the university's most prestigious commissions: Holyoke Center (1960–64), Peabody Terrace (1963), and the Science Center (1970). His position with Harvard's planning office led to his appointment to the Cambridge Planning Board, which elected him chair in 1956 and 1957. During this period he participated in a zoning study tailored to Modernist planning principles. The new code adopted in 1962 gave Harvard a district with no height limits that ran from Western Avenue to Garfield Street and from Story Street to Ellery Street (see figure 2.59).

The Modernists had nearly completed their revolution when Sert arrived at GSD. The new dean represented a humanist strain of the International Style and reestablished courses in architectural history and drawing that Hudnut and Gropius had abandoned. He strengthened the school's professional credentials and influence in the community by appointing practicing architects to teaching positions. Among these were Serge Chermayeff, Alfred Szabo, Wilhelm von Moltke, Jerzy Soltan (a former employee of Corbusier), Huson Jackson, and Ronald Gourley. Gerhard Kallmann and Michael McKinnell won the competition for Boston's City Hall while teaching at GSD. Hideo Sasaki, chair of the landscape architecture program, founded his own firm in 1953, as did William W. Nash and François Vigier of the city planning faculty a few years later. Sert's firm designed projects at Harvard, M.I.T., and Boston University as well as office buildings in Harvard and Central squares and the Martin Luther King Jr. elementary school on Putnam Avenue (demolished by the city in 2014).

The dogmatism often associated with the Modern movement was absent in Sert's vision for the university. He noted that congestion, lack of parking, and deteriorating neighborhoods had an adverse effect on the institution and could be solved only by close cooperation with the city. Harvard should make more efficient use of land it already owned and promote greater density. Tall buildings should be placed "on fringe areas and … along the Charles River," where they would not "spoil the unity of scale of existing groups of buildings." Buildings should not be merely utilitarian, but "dignified, serene, and harmonious … an expression of our times" and able to "live side by side with buildings of the past." He was tolerant of buildings "that we would call ugly by the standards of taste of 1957":

> Should they be demolished or streamlined to today's taste and the clichés of fashion? Of course not, especially those that are a genuine expression of their time. [The campus] is more alive because of [them], and sometimes it is more important to be more alive than to be more beautiful. (Sert, "Harvard—An Urban Problem," 7–10)

Sert was less tolerant of urban conditions in Cambridge, and in 1960 the Harvard Planning Office documented the school's inexorable need to expand in the midst of a congested city. The authors of *An Inventory for Planning* quoted a study that described the street pattern as "hopelessly incapable" and welcomed the proposed Inner Belt (3–8). Projected improvements in local roads included separating north–south from east–west arteries by putting Cambridge Street in an underpass below Cambridge Common and depressing Kennedy Street through Harvard Square. A ring road for local traffic would connect Putnam Avenue, Ware Street, Francis Avenue, Mellen Street, and Craigie Street. Parking garages would be developed in Kerry Corner, on the Delta, at the end of Francis Avenue, on Sacramento Field, and under Cambridge Common, as well as at the MBTA yards (figure 10.81).

The report advocated an increase in residential densities by abolishing the 120-foot (twelve-story) height limit and noted that the university might benefit from the city's urban renewal program. "If, in fact, the areas surrounding the university … are going to be developed eventually into multi-family living, it would be best to allow freedom from height restrictions and other arbitrary design restrictions" (ibid., 3–14).[28]

> High-rise buildings logically belong [along the river] and they will require plenty of open space between them. They should not be clustered like downtown office buildings, but widely spaced like the bell towers of old churches. Between high buildings, lower walk-up structures with sunny courts can maintain the scale of the old Cambridge unchanged. The old can, and should, live with the new. (Ibid., 4–20)

Of the fifteen sites described in the report, the five slated for university housing were the most controversial. Projects proposed for Observatory Hill (190 units), Sacramento Field (40), Shady Hill (191), and Western Avenue (82) surfaced again in the 1970s, but all were eventually defeated; a site in Allston was not fully built out until the completion of One Western Avenue in 2003.

Harvard's 1960 plan, unlike that of 1922, provided a flexible framework for growth. When architectural historian and Fogg Museum director John P. Coolidge criticized the campus as the product of "an endless succession of ad hoc decisions," Associate Dean for Resources and Planning Arthur Trottenburg replied

that such decisions had produced Harvard's most sacred spaces. Master planning of the sort that Harvard's critics had always wanted could create a dehumanizing environment; using the 1960 inventory and guidelines, Harvard ought to be flexible in its search for both greater density and create "as much openness, greenery, and open space around the base of these buildings as we possibly can" (Coolidge and Trottenburg, 160–62).

One of the most dramatic events of the Pusey administration was the fire that nearly destroyed Memorial Hall in 1956. Despite popular disdain for Victorian architecture, Alumni Hall (now Annenberg Hall) was the only suitable space for large functions, and Sanders Theater was one of the best performance spaces in the region. When a workman's torch ignited a blaze in the tower that was beyond the reach of the Cambridge Fire Department, President Pusey prophesied a bleak future (figure 10.82):

> And now perhaps the failure, through fire, of the recent effort to rehabilitate Memorial Hall points unmistakably to a time not too distant when we may have to find an appropriate replacement for this important historic building. (Pusey to the Board of Overseers, 1956. *Boston Globe,* Feb. 19, 1996)

The Architects Collaborative modernized Boylston Hall in 1959 and updated the Yard dormitories in 1961. Outside the Yard, Harvard constructed five important buildings, all different in scale and style from anything that preceded them. Some were quite disruptive, while others showed varying degrees of responsiveness to their surroundings.

The Carpenter Center for the Visual Arts (1961) attracted wide attention. As Bunting noted ten years after its completion: "Critical opinions … vary widely, depending upon whether one looks at the building as a historical document, an independent work of art, or an adjunct of an urban environment" (*Report Four,* 190–91). It is the only building in the United States designed by Le Corbusier. Carpenter Center was a creative, dynamic composition, but the choice of materials, restless composition, and angled placement disregarded its surroundings,

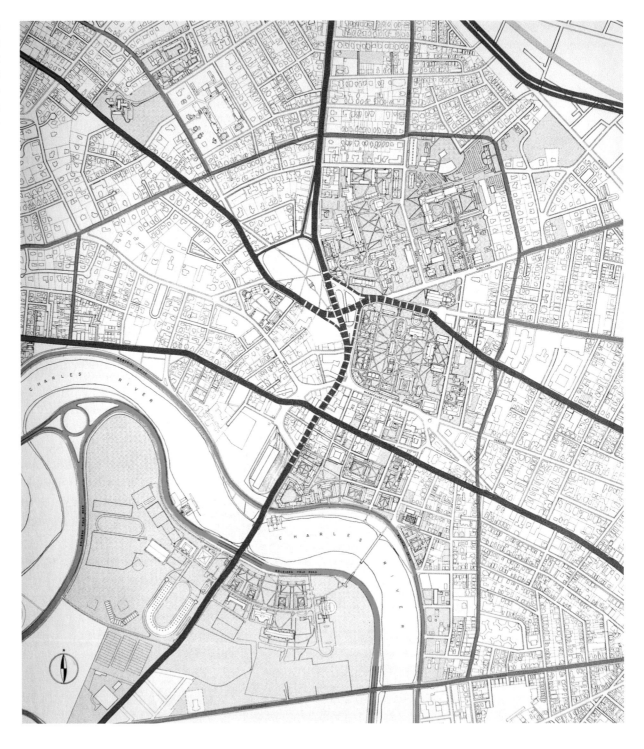

Figure 10.81 Harvard's 1960 proposed reorganization of Cambridge streets. A new ring road would divert traffic away from the campus, while major north–south and east–west arteries would be depressed through Harvard Square and under Cambridge Common (dashed lines).

FIGURE 10.82 Memorial Hall's tower burned on September 6, 1956. The Cambridge Fire Department, whose headquarters were across the street, saved most of the building from destruction. Photo 1956.

and it presented no ideas the architect had not already explored. This unique project had no discernible influence on later structures at Harvard.

Sert, Jackson & Gourley (after 1963, Sert, Jackson Associates), associate architects for Carpenter Center, designed several Modernist complexes for the university. Proposals for a new medical facility on Mt. Auburn Street emerged before World War II.[29] Plans to clear the entire block and build Holyoke Center as an infirmary and administration building were announced in 1957; the first permits were issued in 1960, and the project was completed in 1967. The architects set the highest elements back from the two main streets, lined the side streets with low-scale retail shops, and designed an open pedestrian arcade through the building. The arcade, the plazas on Massachusetts Avenue and Mt. Auburn Street, and even the store interiors were paved in brick that flowed in from the sidewalks (figures 10.83–10.84).

Peabody Terrace (1963) is a twenty-two-story, three-tower complex grounded by three-, five-, and eight-story blocks with 500 graduate student apartments (figure 10.85). Bainbridge Bunting considered this "one of the most successful contemporary buildings at Harvard and perhaps Sert's best work" (*Report Four,* 199). Many critics agreed with him, although it has never been popular in the community. A garage on Putnam Avenue walled off the neighborhood, and the Modernist superblock created by closing off Banks Street reinforced the perception of an exclusionary, self-contained environment. One study found that the same number of units could have been contained in four-story buildings and that the parking could have been accommodated without a garage. "High towers, street closings, and garage construction were not, in fact, necessities, but Modernist preferences" (Tod Aufiero, in Dixon, n.p.).

In 1965 Harvard asked Cambridge for permission to place Cambridge Street in an underpass next to Memorial Hall, as envisioned in 1960. The city closed the end of Kirkland Street, and Harvard gained a pedestrian mall between the Yard and the Law School as well as a site for the Science Center, which displaced the Lawrence Scientific School in 1970. This was the

FIGURE 10.83 Holyoke Center and Forbes Plaza, 1350 Massachusetts Avenue (1960–64, Sert, Jackson & Gourley, architects). Photo ca. 1970.

FIGURE 10.84 Holyoke Center arcade, open to the elements as originally designed; it was enclosed in 1992. Photo 1966.

FIGURE 10.85 The towers of Peabody Terrace (1963, Sert, Jackson & Gourley) and Mather House (1967, Shepley, Bulfinch, Richardson & Abbott), with the Riverside neighborhood in the foreground. Photo 2014.

least successful of Sert's Harvard commissions, perhaps because the program required such a massive volume. The Science Center intruded on the city by blocking Kirkland Street, and its jumble of receding upper floors, blocky roofscape, and "scramble of exposed roof girders, boxes for mechanical equipment, and projecting exit bays" has never settled into the comfortable familiarity of the architect's other buildings (*Report Four,* 194). Landscape architect Peter Walker's superb Tanner Fountain (1985), an arrangement of boulders exuding periodic bursts of mist, helps soften the building's setting.

William James Hall, the fifteen-story skyscraper towering above Divinity Avenue, was designed in 1963 by Minoru Yamasaki, architect of the 1965 World Trade Center in Manhattan. Most of Yamasaki's buildings were characterized by white precast concrete exterior finishes and landscaped settings that would convey "serenity and delight," but William James's vacant terraces, dry pools, and empty gardens emphasize how completely it ignored its context (*Crimson,* Oct. 13, 1962). The Graduate

School of Design's Brutalist George Gund Hall joined the architectural menagerie on Quincy Street in 1969–72. Canadian architect John Andrews designed the building with five "trays" of glass-roofed drafting space. Sert was still dean of GSD, and Andrews had been his student, so both bear responsibility for the building's ungainly composition and awkward relationship with Memorial Hall (see figure 10.94).

For a long time the North Yard accumulated buildings with little thought to architectural compatibility or long-term planning. Harvard gradually acquired the Massachusetts Avenue frontage up to Everett Street, and the Law School used its piecemeal acquisitions to build a series of disjointed additions to Langdell Hall rather than plan an effective use of all the territory it could have reasonably expected to acquire. Pound Hall (1968, Benjamin Thompson Associates) turned a blank wall to Massachusetts Avenue, while the Everett Street garage (1968, Sert, Jackson & Associates) blighted the avenue until it was razed for Wasserstein Hall in 2007.

Harvard's gradual integration with Radcliffe College allowed it new opportunities for expansion in the Pusey era. The Loeb Drama Center, designed in 1959 by Hugh Stubbins & Associates, was Harvard's first building on former Radcliffe property. The combination of concrete and brick and relatively low height on Brattle Street helped it blend into its setting. Harvard acquired Radcliffe's Longfellow Hall for the Graduate School of Education in 1962 and built Larsen Hall across Appian Way in 1964. Although Larsen's brick was familiar, the building's mysterious bulk occasioned much controversy at the time (figure 10.87). The zigzag footprint of Gutman Library (1970) allowed the creation of a garden on the corner of Appian Way. Harvard preserved the Read and Nichols houses as part of this project but buried them in an artificial setting at the back of the site (see chapter 4).

FIGURE 10.86 William James Hall (1963, Minouru Yamasaki, architect); Church of the New Jerusalem (1903, Warren Smith & Biscoe, architects); and Gund Hall (1969, John Andrews of Anderson & Habile, architects). Photo ca. 1972.

FIGURE 10.87 Larsen Hall, 14 Appian Way (1964, Caudill, Rowlett & Scott, architects). Photo before 1967.

To accommodate a larger student body Pusey converted three 1920s apartment buildings on Harvard and Prescott streets into freshman dormitories in 1956–58 and built three new houses on the river: Leverett and Quincy in 1958–60 and Mather in 1967–68. While spatially related to the original River Houses and designed by the same firm, they made a clear stylistic break with the earlier Georgian Revival designs.[30] Quincy House (1958) was anchored on the Gold Coast and incorporated Mather Hall (1930). Leverett (1958–59) was Harvard's first venture into high-rise construction. The decision to build twin twelve-story buildings and a separate library instead of a single four-story dormitory with a larger footprint allowed more space around the buildings but required demolishing thirty houses on Grant and Cowperthwaite streets (see chapter 4). Ten years later the Shepley firm designed Mather House. Harvard had originally hoped to build Mather on air rights over the Eliot Square subway yards, but the Kennedy Library claimed that site in 1966 (see chapter 3; figure 10.88).

FIGURE 10.88 Shepley, Bulfinch, Richardson & Abbott designed two high-rise River Houses during the Pusey administration. The towers of Leverett House (1959, left) and Mather House (1967) bracket Dunster House, designed by the same firm in 1929. Photo 2013.

Harvard's expansion created many points of friction with Cambridge. Shortly after the assassination of Martin Luther King Jr. in 1968, President Pusey created a "Committee on the University and the City" that was chaired by Professor James Q. Wilson and included Daniel Patrick Moynihan of the Joint Center for Urban Studies. The authors acknowledged that "we impinge upon many communities and some of them—perhaps most—are deeply suspicious of Harvard's intentions and capabilities." In the popular imagination, Harvard had a "master plan," was "territorially ambitious," secretive, committed to using straws to purchase properties and keep prices down, and acted no differently than any real estate speculator. Actually, they claimed, Harvard lacked a master plan ("or, in reality, much of any plans at all"), needed Corporation approval to buy property beyond Putnam Avenue and Garfield Street, and never employed "straws or front men in Cambridge real estate transactions" (*Preliminary Report,* 13, 31–32).

The authors foresaw three possible futures for Harvard and Cambridge. Harvard could maintain its historic isolation; it could support the "Harvardization" of Cambridge ("gentrification" was not yet a familiar term); or it could try to "maintain a diverse and heterogeneous community" (ibid., 42–43). "The natural forces of supply and demand … are such that it is only necessary for Harvard to do nothing for Cambridge to become a predominantly upper-middle-class community—that is to say, a community very much like Harvard itself." The authors urged Harvard "to ally itself with those who wish to preserve, for as long as possible, a measure of diversity and heterogeneity," to provide housing for students and faculty "with minimum injury to the community," and to help increase the supply of affordable housing. Its real estate practices needed to be reassessed: "the university, because of its visibility, its symbolic importance, and the standards of conduct to which it is held by its own students and faculty, has a special obligation to behave in exemplary ways" (ibid., 36).[31]

The report sent a strangely mixed message to the administration: congratulations on its supposed restraint, coupled with a warning against inaction that actually forecast a reassuring future in a gentrified Cambridge. It did little to alleviate the cynicism of the Cambridge community, which remembered the secret purchases of land by Harvard alumni and could see for itself the deteriorating condition of landbanked residential properties. Wilson complained about Pusey's lukewarm response, but by the time the report reached him Harvard was overwhelmed by protests that culminated in the demonstrations and occupation of commencement in 1970.

President Pusey's administration ended in turmoil. Student protests against American involvement in Vietnam reached a climax with the occupation of University Hall in April 1969. Protests spilled out into the community where marches and riots caused major damage. A red clenched fist, silk-screened by GSD students in the basement of Robinson Hall, became a widely recognized symbol of protest, and junior faculty and students worked with community groups to protest Harvard expansion. In June 1970 Riverside activists led by Saundra Graham, an African American resident of a nearby public housing project, shook Harvard to its foundations when they infiltrated commencement and commandeered the public address system to condemn a proposed affiliate housing project on Memorial Drive. Graham later served on the city council and in the state legislature and was among those who blocked Harvard's plans for a museum on the same site thirty years later (see figure 10.95).

PRESIDENT BOK (1971–91)

Derek Bok was dean of the law school before becoming Harvard's twenty-fifth president in 1971. For security reasons he was not allowed to live at 17 Quincy Street but instead resided at Elmwood, the residence of all later presidents. President Bok calmed many controversies and implemented some major reforms. He expanded Pusey's minimalist administrative structure and created three new vice presidencies, including one for community relations. The controversy over the Kennedy Library was resolved in 1975 when the family abandoned Cambridge for Dorchester (see chapter 3). Harvard's focus shifted to sites within the campus, and the university restored some of its most significant buildings.

Cambridge also began to function more effectively. In 1970 the city council adopted rent control to address an affordable housing crisis caused in part by Harvard's growing student body. The council began to roll back the permissive, unlimited-height zoning districts established in 1962 and secured legislation in 1981 that ended Harvard's exemption from use restrictions. The city manager professionalized the city's workforce, and relations with Harvard staff became discussions among equals. A 1986 protocol with the Cambridge Historical Commission marked a significant shift in Harvard's attitude toward historic preservation.

Harvard's response to the commencement protests of 1970 was a "Report to the Cambridge Community" written by Charles U. Daly, its first vice president for community affairs. The report cited Harvard's "moral commitment, enlightened self-interest, and … knowledge that today urban institutions neither can nor should live in isolation," and pledged that, pending completion of another "comprehensive study of its physical assets and needs, … neither Harvard University nor its agents will purchase a single piece of residential property in Cambridge" outside a defined area (1–2). The adoption of this so-called "red line" effectively halted Harvard's expansion and signaled a retreat to boundaries closer to the traditional campus.

The study promised in the Daly report appeared as a draft in 1974. As in 1960, traffic improvements were a particular focus. By this time the Inner Belt had been halted, and the MBTA was considering an extension of the Cambridge subway. Harvard proposed that the line be rerouted under Mt. Auburn Street to a new station near Winthrop Square. The old tunnel would become a vehicular underpass, most of the Square would be made into a pedestrian mall, and Quincy and lower Oxford streets would be absorbed into the campus. The final report committed Harvard to respect the red line until 1980 but still showed plans to build in several areas outside it (figure 10.89).

Most Old Cambridge neighborhoods eventually filed downzoning petitions to roll back the 1962 code and limit Harvard's ability to develop sites it had been landbanking. The Agassiz neighborhood scored the first success in 1974, winning a reduction of allowable density from 144 to 36 dwelling units per acre and a height limit of 35 feet. Residents of Observatory Hill filed a downzoning petition for their neighborhood, and in 1977 Mayor Alfred Vellucci called for a state of emergency: "*Finito.* No more buildings" (*Crimson,* Sept. 30). Harvard abandoned proposals for Shady Hill, Sacramento Field, and Observatory Hill but remained committed to projects in Riverside and Kerry Corner. In 1979 Mayor Thomas Danehy wrote the Overseers to complain about "the consistent poor judgment and insensitivity" of administrators. City Manager James Leo Sullivan observed that he had never seen a period of worse relations: "Harvard seems to pretend that the city doesn't exist. It seems to go on about its business as if it was located in the middle of a cow pasture in North Dakota" (*Crimson,* June 7, 1979). Finally Cambridge appealed to the General Court for relief.

The Massachusetts Constitution of 1780 had confirmed that the President and Fellows of Harvard College would forever enjoy "all the powers, authorities, rights, liberties, privileges, immunities, and franchises" that they possessed under the Province of Massachusetts Bay, and the university was once considered to be largely exempt from local regulation (Ch. V, §1, Art. 1). Its position was reinforced by a 1950 provision of the state zoning enabling act, the so-called Dover Amendment, which barred municipalities from restricting the use of land for educational or religious purposes, subject only to "reasonable regulations concerning the bulk and height of structures and determining yard sizes, lot area, setbacks, open space, parking and building coverage" (M.G.L. Ch. 40A, §3).[32] In 1980 the legislature accepted Cambridge's argument that it was uniquely affected by institutional expansion and exempted the city from this provision. Harvard's presumed constitutional protection at first gave the legislature pause, but as City Councillor David Sullivan noted: "the university would have felt mighty uncomfortable having a statewide referendum about its prerogatives" (*Crimson,* Nov. 4, 1980).

FIGURE 10.89 A "red line" defined Harvard University's self-imposed limits on property acquisition and future development. Harvard's 1975 long-range plan identified thirty-seven locations for future development in Cambridge, including sites in the Observatory Hill, Sacramento Field, Shady Hill, and Kerry Corner neighborhoods. These projects would have required razing forty-eight houses (fourteen of which were later listed on the National Register of Historic Places) and sixteen academic buildings.

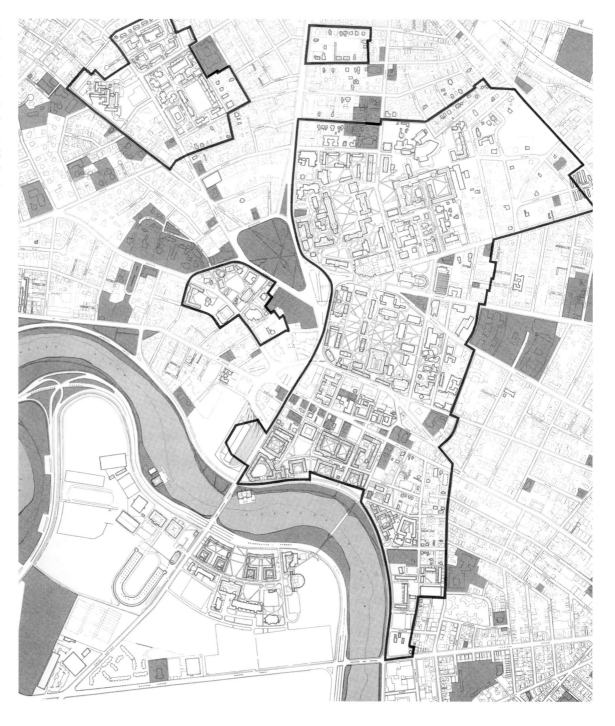

Harvard also confronted Cambridge in the area of historic preservation. Several Harvard properties had been listed on the National Register of Historic Places since the 1960s.[33] In 1979 Harvard tried to block the inclusion of about sixty additional buildings in a citywide nomination of 800 properties. The Planning Office claimed that many of the structures were "marginal" and that the nomination would obstruct compliance with building codes, create "irreconcilable environmental issues for the future," and "exacerbate the orderly renewal processes of the university" (UPO to CHC, Mar. 24, 1980). Quoting the criteria for inclusion on the Register, Vice President Joe Wyatt contended that Harvard Yard itself was ineligible:

> The area is not as a district associated with any "'… events that have made a significant contribution to the broad patterns of our history … or with any lives of persons significant to our past.'" And … the district does not "'… embody the distinctive characteristics of a type, period or method of construction or … represent a significant and distinguishable entity whose components may lack individual distinction.'" (Wyatt to Patricia Weslowski, State Historic Preservation Officer, Oct. 6, 1980)

The university claimed that the nomination constituted "a substantial interference with [its] property rights," denied it due process and equal protection, and was "arbitrary and capricious and constituted an abuse of discretion" (*President and Fellows of Harvard College v. Secretary of State for the Commonwealth of Massachusetts and the Massachusetts Historical Commission,* Suffolk Superior Court Civil No. 45717). The Cambridge Historical Commission pointed out that Harvard had not objected to earlier nominations; had received federal funds for restoration of its historic properties; had benefited from a National Register review of a proposed subway extension; and was seeking nomination of a property to secure an investment tax credit.

The court had not yet ruled when Harvard called a truce in 1982. A new vice president, Robert Scott, acknowledged that "the historical significance of University property must play an important role in our physical development plans" (Scott to Valerie Talmage, Acting SHPO, Dec. 8, 1982). Harvard retained architectural historian Cynthia Zaitzevsky to evaluate 1,300 structures within a three-quarter-mile radius of Harvard Square, and with the university's consent the CHC nominated twelve districts and twenty-two individual properties, including the entire Harvard Square business district, or about 50 percent more properties in Old Cambridge than it had proposed in 1979.

In February 1986 Vice President Scott assured the Historical Commission that Harvard "intended to rely on the National Register study in our planning process," affirmed "the suitability of the National Register as a planning tool," and agreed to consult Commission staff prior to undertaking "fundamental changes" to its National Register buildings (Scott to Robert G. Neiley, CHC chair, Feb. 10, 1986). In response, the commission agreed that "local designations do not necessarily follow National Register nominations," but reserved its right to protect significant buildings "threatened by development or unacceptable change" (Neiley to Scott, Feb. 11, 1986). The planning office hired preservation specialists to monitor university activities, and CHC staff began advising on projects ranging from ordinary maintenance and paint colors to major construction.

Given the climate of the times, Harvard's development undertakings were unadventurous and mostly confined to the campus. In the Yard, Canaday Hall, which resembled commercial architecture of the period, replaced Hunt Hall in 1974. Pusey Library, designed in 1973 by Hugh Stubbins & Associates, was Harvard's first underground project and represented an ingenious solution to the problem of housing archives and special collections adjacent to Widener Library without visibly connecting to it. Harvard's largest projects in this period, the Kennedy School of Government and its Belfer Center expansion, were executed by Architectural Resources Cambridge with more regard for context than would have been shown in the 1960s. Harvard had historically declined to invest in local real estate, but a steep increase in values in the late 1970s created profitable opportunities to put up office buildings that could be converted to academic use, as at University Place on Mt. Auburn Street (see chapter 3).

President Bok gave up Pusey's habit of seeking prominent architects to design signature buildings. The Sackler Museum on Quincy Street was his administration's one notable venture into internationalism and its least successful project overall. Initially, the Fogg planned to take over Allston Burr, but when a donor surfaced the museum selected British architect James Stirling to design a new building for the site. The plans included a 150-foot long bridge over Broadway, bearing an oculus "like a Cyclops staring at the neighborhood," in the words of one city councillor (*Crimson,* June 24, 1984; figure 10.90). Harvard had neglected to seek the city's permission until construction was underway, and the idea was deeply unpopular. While museum officials gamely asserted that the Sackler was designed to function independently, the lack of a direct connection made it less useful and eventually something of an orphan. The university suffered repercussions from this episode for many years.

Harvard had mixed success with other projects. Observatory Commons (1989, Woo & Williams), a faculty housing project on Concord Avenue, was described in the *Boston Globe* as "a superb example of sensitive integration of an institution and a neighborhood" (Sept. 19, 1990), but Goody, Clancy & Associates' 1989 graduate student dormitory darkened lower DeWolfe Street and walled off the Kerry Corner neighborhood. TAC's Taubman Building at the Kennedy School, the first Postmodern design at Harvard, illustrated the rapidly failing grip of the International Style (figure 10.91).

PRESIDENT RUDENSTINE (1991–2002)

President Neil Rudenstine was deeply interested in nurturing contemporary architecture. GSD dean Peter Rowe worked with the president to engage renowned architects such as Henry Cobb, Hans Hollein, Raphael Moneo, Renzo Piano, Rodolfo Machado, and Jorge Silvetti. Dean Jeremy Knowles of the Faculty of Arts and Sciences (FAS) facilitated the restoration of many historic buildings. Landbanked houses outside the red line were sold to faculty members, and some apartment buildings went to affordable housing organizations. Recognizing that obstacles to expanding in Cambridge were becoming insurmountable, the university began secretly purchasing property in Allston.

Soon after taking office President Rudenstine confirmed the university's protocol with the Cambridge Historical Commission. The Law School's Hauser Hall was consequently built with a smaller footprint and sited on axis with Holmes Field to preserve the setting of the Harvard Graduate Center (figure 10.92). Restoration of the three-quarter-mile fence around Harvard Yard required a special commitment in 1990–93 because no faculty or school had responsibility for it; the university covered the $2.3 million cost and established a dedicated maintenance reserve fund. The formal enclosure of the Yard was completed

FIGURE 10.90 Sackler-Fogg connector (James Stirling, architect). Cambridge residents felt that the proposed bridge over Broadway would symbolize the university's dominance over the city; the *Crimson* called it "monstrous" (May 1, 1984).

FIGURE 10.91 Kennedy School of Government. The four buildings comprising the Kennedy School illustrate the progression from the late International Style to Postmodernism. Counterclockwise from the left foreground are Rubenstein (1982), Littauer (1974), and Belfer (1982, all Architectural Resources Cambridge, architects); and Taubman (1990, The Architects Collaborative, architects). Photo 2011.

Figure 10.92 Hauser Hall (1992, Kallmann McKinnell & Wood, architects). As originally designed, Hauser would have spread across the north end of Holmes Field, blocking the southern exposure of Gropius's Harvard Graduate Center. Photo 2014.

when brick and steel replaced twenty-five year old chain link in the gap left by the demolition of Hunt Hall.

Restoration of the freshman dormitories, a $66 million project, began with Weld Hall in 1992 and continued until 1995. The project involved some of Boston's best architects, including Goody, Clancy & Associates Ann Beha, Childs Bertman Tseckares (CBT), and Finegold Alexander. Windows and roofs were replaced, and woodwork was painted in historically appropriate colors for each building, in place of the uniform white that was a holdover from the Georgian Revival period. A landscape master plan by Michael Van Valkenburg removed foundation plantings and the ivy that covered many buildings and introduced new varieties of high-branching, deciduous trees that complemented the Yard's remaining elms.[34]

The Rudenstine administration completed the restoration of Memorial Hall, which had begun under President Bok. After the fire in 1956 Harvard let the building languish, although a few devotees worked behind the scenes to protect it. The planning office prepared a feasibility study for restoration in 1976, and

a National Park Service grant supported work on the roof. Ten years later, the masonry was cleaned and repaired, and restoration of 5,000 square feet of stained glass was completed in 1992. Work on the interior depended on finding a use that would justify the expense. Dean Knowles realized that returning the building to its previous function as a dining hall would allow the Union to be converted to faculty offices. The firm of Venturi, Scott Brown & Associates designed a discreet kitchen addition, and Alumni Hall became a freshman dining room. Memorial Hall's interior finishes were restored to their original splendor for the reopening in 1996.

The miraculous restoration of the tower was due to the persistence of Katherine Loker, a strong-minded donor who agreed to underwrite the air conditioning of Widener Library if the university would accept a challenge grant of $2 million to rebuild the tower. With this incentive, the development office raised the balance, and Harvard began to consider which version to restore. The original architects had designed three iterations: the original "bare Mansardic envelope, with slate sheathing, copper crockets at ridges, and iron cresting"; an 1878 project that added "a 'skyline package' with heavier cresting, finials, and dormers"; and an 1897 adaptation that had clock faces on all sides and copper sheathing in place of patterned slate (Floyd, "Historic Structure Report," 26; see figure 10.31). Some alumni had fond memories of the clock, but most parties agreed that the 1878 version was closest to the architects' original intent. By early 2000 Memorial Hall was once again the most prominent landmark on the Cambridge skyline (figure 10.93).

The conversion of the Harvard Union into offices attracted significant opposition. The Union had served meals to freshman since 1930, and many alumni were strongly attached to the great dining room with elkhorn chandeliers donated by Theodore Roosevelt and a 40-foot-high coffered ceiling stained by decades of catapulted butter pats. GSD faculty censured the project, a preservationist chained himself to a nearby gate, and an alumni committee obtained a restraining order, but the university prevailed and the interior was lost.

FIGURE 10.93 Memorial Hall tower, as restored in 2000. Photo 2014.

Preservation efforts during the Rudenstine era concluded with the 2001 restoration of University Hall. The original dining facilities on the ground floor had long since been occupied as offices. Architects Bruner/Cott restored the original clay tile floors and oval openings between the rooms.[35] On the second floor they returned the Faculty Room (originally a chapel) to its appearance in 1898, when Pierre LaRose, an English instructor with an interest in aesthetic design, redecorated it.

President Rudenstine's desire to place the university at the forefront of contemporary design "after multiple decades of 'non-confrontational' architecture" was countered by growing constraints on its ability to build in Cambridge (*Crimson,* Oct. 17, 2000). While Agassiz residents worked to ensure that development along Hammond Street would be compatible with their neighborhood, community groups in Mid Cambridge, Kerry Corner, and Riverside were ablaze with resentment.

In 1996 Harvard announced plans for a new Center for Government and International Studies. An early study showed a mid-rise building occupying the lawn behind Gund Hall, bizarrely grafted onto Greek Revival houses at 30 and 34 Kirkland Street. Architect Henry Cobb of Pei Cobb Freed & Partners, who had been chair of the department of architecture in 1980–85, recognized the importance of the open space. In 1998 he devised a plan for two five-story buildings connected by a tunnel under Cambridge Street that would replace both Coolidge Hall (the former Ambassador Hotel) and the University Information Center (an office building built by IBM in 1958). This satisfied some opponents, but others complained that a tunnel would inappropriately transfer public property to the university and disrupt the neighborhood during construction. Their fury intensified when city boards approved a revised scheme four stories high. The university offered land for a new park, money for neighborhood projects, and a five-year moratorium on construction, but it abandoned the idea when the city council demanded more. Dean Knowles remarked that "sometimes the phrase 'cutting off one's nose to spite one's face' has a sadly clear meaning" (*Crimson,* Jan. 31, 2003; figure 10.94).[36]

During this period an even more intense controversy was brewing in Riverside, where resentment toward Harvard still festered thirty years after the occupation of commencement in 1970. In 1998 James Cuno, director of the University Art Museums, told the *Boston Globe* that he planned to build an art museum on the corner of Memorial Drive and Western Avenue, on property that Harvard had leased to a succession of garden centers since 1941. As head of an affiliated institution, Cuno reported directly to President Rudenstine and had bypassed the university's planners, who were considering whether to build a

FIGURE 10.94 Center for Government and International Studies (1998, Henry N. Cobb of Pei Cobb Freed & Partners, architect). CGIS was built without the pedestrian tunnel originally proposed. Photo 2011.

conference center, a hotel, or student housing on the site. Italian architect Renzo Piano, who had been working on a new project to connect the Fogg and Sackler museums, prepared the plans. The complex as originally proposed would have consisted of two buildings 45 and 55 feet tall, connected underground to preserve views to the river (figure 10.95). Neighbors were furious at Harvard's apparent *fait accompli,* and the City Council enacted an eighteen-month moratorium on development. At about the same time, Harvard announced plans to build a twenty-one-story dormitory directly across the river in Allston; this cutting-edge design by GSD faculty members Rodolfo Machado and Jorge Silvetti was reduced to fifteen stories, but activists were further enraged by what they imagined Harvard would build in Riverside if it were free to do so.

FIGURE 10.95   Proposed Harvard University Modern Art Museum (2001, Renzo Piano Building Workshop, architects).

In the midst of these controversies Harvard retained Hans Hollein, a Pritzker Prize–winning Expressionist architect from Vienna, to design a conservation laboratory at 90 Mt. Auburn Street (figure 10.96). The site contained an 1895 three-decker that had once housed several distinguished architects, including Buckminster Fuller, and would have been the first construction since 1930 on the low-rise blocks between Mt. Auburn Street and the River Houses, except for Moshe Safdie's modestly contextual 1993 Rosovsky Center for Harvard-Radcliffe Hillel. Despite guidelines encouraging contemporary architecture in the newly established Harvard Square Conservation District, the Historical Commission rejected the design as "incongruous because of its aggressive indifference to its surroundings" (Charles Sullivan to CHC, Apr. 2, 2001). Hollein resigned the commission, and Harvard retained the firm of Leers Weinzapfel Associates to design a more conventional four-story building.

FIGURE 10.96 Proposed Harvard University Libraries Building, 90 Mt. Auburn Street (2000, Hans Hollein, architect). Hollein's building was almost twice the height of surrounding structures and had a sloping, undulating wire-mesh facade overhanging a recessed first floor.

In the 1990s Harvard began to think about developing the north edge of the campus. The Palfrey estate had become an ugly industrial precinct of random science facilities and associated storage sheds, shipping containers, greenhouses, and parking lots. The first to go was the Cyclotron, which had been used since the 1950s for medical research and radiation treatment. Despite efforts to preserve it as an historic scientific instrument, state regulations required that it be razed after it was taken out of service in 2002. After a quiet negotiation with the Agassiz neighborhood, Harvard moved the Palfrey house to a new site on Hammond Street and excavated a five-level garage.[37] A new information systems building at 60 Oxford Street went up in 2001, and the massive Northwest Science building filled the rest of the site in 2005. The latter deftly enclosed the north end of the Museum of Natural History quadrangle and diminished in height to create a pleasing transition to the neighborhood. These projects were not without controversy, but they showed that a large architectural program could be undertaken successfully within the existing campus.

HARVARD AT THE BEGINNING OF THE TWENTY-FIRST CENTURY

When President Rudenstine announced his resignation in 2000, Harvard was engaged in its most dramatic physical expansion in a century. In 1997 the university disclosed that for the previous ten years it had been employing a private real estate firm to purchase industrial and commercial property in Allston. Kathy Spiegelman, associate vice president for planning and real estate, justified the acquisition: "The university began to understand that its history was a million to a million and a half square feet [of growth] a decade. ... Since most of the campus in Cambridge is surrounded by residential neighborhoods, and displacement of those neighborhoods was not in the university's interests or in the realm of possibility, it was necessary to look in other places" (Lewis Rice, "Cambridge v. Allston." *Harvard Law*

Bulletin, Summer 2002, 20). By 2009 Harvard owned 359 acres in Allston versus 210 in Cambridge.

Harvard's stated willingness to engage in an open planning process and its donation of a new branch library initially placated the Allston community. By the summer of 2000, planners had identified three scenarios for development: a professional school campus; a science complex; and cultural facilities and housing. An urban design study proposed "a pedestrian-friendly urban center, vibrant and interesting, though not simply a clone of nearby Harvard Square" (*Harvard Gazette,* Nov. 14, 2002). Transportation consultants disregarded Dutch architect Rem Koolhas's suggestion that the Charles River be relocated to join the Allston campus to Cambridge and studied the possibility of a moving sidewalk or a monorail to overcome the bottleneck at the Anderson Bridge.

In October 2003 Harvard's new president, Lawrence Summers, announced a set of "working hypotheses" to guide further planning. The Allston campus should be "an integral part of Harvard's academic enterprise, as magnetic in its drawing power as other key parts of our campus" and should "engage and be a part of the surrounding community, rather than an enclave that sets the university apart." Harvard "should recognize the reality that [its] long-term physical development capacity in and around its major academic precincts … is finite, and that we would not be serving Harvard's long-term interests if we planned as though the reality were otherwise." The Allston campus would serve the sciences, accommodate the Graduate School of Education and the School of Public Health (leaving the schools of Law, Design, Divinity, and Government in Cambridge) and "incorporate a variety of features essential to a lively and welcoming residential urban community." Some museums might be relocated from Cambridge, and there was a "possibility of new undergraduate houses close to the Charles River" that would allow the Radcliffe Quad to house graduate students (Harvard University, "President's Letter to the Harvard Community," 2–3).

The Allston venture came to an abrupt halt with the financial crisis of 2008, when the endowment plunged by 30 percent, free cash evaporated, and projects predicated on continued investment growth were suspended. President Drew Faust, who took office in 2007, was preoccupied with keeping the university afloat and had the massive, unfinished Allston Science Complex capped at ground level. The Allston planning staff dispersed, and the handful of projects announced in 2011 bore little resemblance to the grand vision of a few years earlier.

President Summers shelved the museum project on Memorial Drive in 2001. At the end of 2004 the university received planning board approval to build 328 units of housing in Riverside and Kerry Corner. In effect, the city returned to the 1924 height limits of six stories along the river and four stories inland (figure 10.97). Development at the Cambridge Electric Light Company's Blackstone Station, which Harvard purchased in 2002, occurred within the existing buildings.

FIGURE 10.97 Harvard's final build-out of the riverfront land that the alumni began to acquire in 1901 added 500 beds in graduate and affiliate housing. The community benefited by thirty-nine units of affordable housing and a three-quarter-acre park along the river. Harvard's 151-unit 10 Akron Street building (2009, Kyu Sung Woo, architect) overlooks the new Riverside Neighborhood Park (Halvorson Design Partnership), which was constructed by the university and conveyed to the city in 2011. Photo 2015.

Only two significant projects were carried out during the recession. Construction of the Law School's Wasserstein Hall began in 2007 with the relocation of the two significant Mansard houses and a carriage house to the corner of Mellen Street (see figure 4.187). This project required demolition of the Everett Garage, Wyeth Hall, and the east wing of Pound Hall, the latter to create a forecourt for the new building (figure 10.98). Renewal of the Fogg Museum began in 2008. Emptying the building of its contents required eighteen months, after which all of the post-1927 accretions, including Werner Otto Hall and the entire interior (except for the first two floors of the Montepulciano courtyard) were removed.[38] The outer shell of the original building was carefully restored, and an entirely new museum designed by Renzo Piano was built within it. A massive glass pyramid over the courtyard was carefully shaped to be minimally visible from Harvard Yard (figure 10.99).

Planning for the renewal of the twelve undergraduate houses began in 2007 "when administrators noted that a system originally designed to accommodate 3,900 students was housing 4,900" and that ageing mechanical systems would soon have to be replaced (*Harvard Magazine,* Sept.–Oct. 2012). Following a detailed assessment of student needs and expectations, the university announced a capital campaign in 2011 for a 15-year, one billion dollar project. Construction began in June 2012 with a prototype project at Old Quincy, a 1930 dormitory on Plympton Street, where Philadelphia architects Kieran Timberlake's modernization program improved circulation, restructured suites, and captured underutilized spaces for student facilities. A further demonstration project at McKinlock Hall renovated a kitchen, dining hall, and common room. In June 2014 Dunster House—three times the size of Old Quincy—closed for a complete rebuilding that took fifteen months. The renewal of Winthrop House will include construction of a five-story Neo-Georgian dormitory wing designed by Beyer Blinder Bell of New York as well as restoration of two survivors of Kerry Corner, the Michael O'Sullivan houses at 101 Plympton Street and 11 Riverview Avenue (see figure 4.268).

President Faust launched a Common Spaces Initiative in 2009 that initially sought to alleviate the formality of the Old Yard by setting out chairs for everyone to use. This proved immensely popular. When the Cambridge Street underpass needed to be renovated and waterproofed, the university seized the occasion to replace the unsustainable lawn with two acres of stark white pavers designed by Stoss Landscape Urbanism in 2011 and completed in 2013. While popular with patrons of food trucks, the new plaza was a jarring intrusion on the carefully groomed landscapes and restored buildings nearby.

The Common Spaces Initiative continued in 2013 with the announcement that Holyoke Center would be renamed the Richard A. and Susan F. Smith Campus Center and remodeled to accommodate new facilities for students and the public. Hopkins Architects of London (with Bruner/Cott of Cambridge) designed a new glass-enclosed space for Forbes Plaza and a student activity center that required the demolition of the shops on Holyoke Street, while Michael Van Valkenburgh Associates designed a new urban landscape for the center.

The college that began in a single house on the outskirts of the village had grown by the 21st century into a sprawling institution spread over hundreds of acres in Cambridge and Allston. The university's plans for this vast territory will not be realized for many years. Further growth in Cambridge will involve filling in open spaces, going underground, or replacing existing buildings. If most new Harvard initiatives are realized elsewhere, the future will hold fewer challenges but less excitement for Cambridge.

FIGURE 10.98 Wasserstein Hall (2007, Robert A.M. Stern Architects). Photo 2013.

FIGURE 10.99 Fogg Museum (1925, Coolidge, Shepley, Bulfinch & Abbott; renovations and addition, 2009, Renzo Piano Building Workshop, architects). A historic preservation review of the project gave the architect a free hand for the new wing but ensured that the exterior of the 1925 building would be restored and that the new glass roof would not overwhelm the composition. Photo 2014.

Notes

INTRODUCTION

1. U.S. Census Bureau, 2008–2010 American Community Survey. "Tenure by Year Householder Moved into Unit."

CHAPTER 1

1. The glaciated landscape of Massachusetts Bay is characterized by drumlins (isolated hills) and moraines (ridges) composed of till (glacial deposits of gravel), interspersed with kettle-hole ponds and vast, poorly drained beds of clay.

2. In lieu of footnotes, authors of direct quotations are identified by reference to the bibliography.

3. Throughout this book, geographic features, places, streets, and squares are identified by their current names.

4. The governor's assistants, or counselors, were magistrates who were elected by the colony's freemen. They were predecessors of the nine-member Governor's Council established by the Massachusetts Constitution in 1780.

5. Puritans relied on ministerial guidance in their search for salvation and believed that outward moral behavior was a sign of inward grace. Hutchinson and her followers held that God's grace flowed directly to individuals without the mediation of a pastor—prayerful self-examination would reveal God's presence. Puritan ministers objected violently to this subversive theology and excommunicated Hutchinson in 1638. She moved to Rhode Island, but continued threats by Massachusetts leaders drove her to Dutch territory in New York where she was murdered by Indians in 1643.

6. In Congregational Puritan usage, the word *church* referred to the people in covenant, not the edifice.

7. On March 28, 1631, Dudley wrote of recent fires and added, "for the prevention whereof in our new town, intended this summer to be builded, we have ordered that no man there shall build his chimney of wood, nor cover his house with thatch" (Paige, 18, n. 2).

8. Charlestown erected a much more elaborate fort "with palisadoes and flankers" designed by Thomas Graves on Town Hill in 1630 and maintained it until after 1670 (Frothingham, 97).

9. According to John Langdon Sibley, who interviewed many old residents, the grade of Massachusetts Avenue had been raised "probably five feet at least, & Dunster Street three or four feet; so that the meetinghouse, before the present, stood on a high elevation" (*Diary,* Nov. 16, 1847).

10. Until well into the 19th century the road systems of Charlestown and Cambridge had only one other connection, at present Beech Street in North Cambridge.

11. Initially the ministers lived in the Hooker-Shepard-Wigglesworth house, which was privately owned and passed from one minister to the next.

12. Peabody Street runs from Harvard Square to Cambridge Street and bounds Harvard Yard on the west.

13. As late as 1814, Sibley relates, "there were two justices of the peace constantly in session throughout [commencement], before whom offenders were brought to be disposed of" (*Diary,* June 27, 1870).

14. Towne's remarkable will freed his three slaves and left them each £10 and required a relative to free his own slave if he wished to receive an inheritance (Middlesex Probate 22675).

15. Coincidentally, Zachariah Porter (no relation of Israel) took over the Cambridge Market Hotel in North Cambridge in 1837 and renamed it the Porter House.

16. Cambridge tax valuation sheets exist only for 1749 and for the years after 1794. The records show that there were eight slaves in the Second Parish (Arlington) and thirteen in the Third Parish (Brighton).

17. Tories have been defined as "citizens who in thought, word, or deed recognized and preferred British rule to home rule" (Maas, 125). In common usage the term is synonymous with *loyalist*.

18. East Apthorp, the first rector of Christ Church, conceded that his parishioners possessed "a politeness and elegance which to a censorious eye may look worldly and voluptuous," but the Puritan majority considered them to be "often exceedingly loose, profligate, vain, and censorious" (Batchelder, "Vassall," 28 n. 3).

19. Mandamus—a command issued in the name of the sovereign authority.

20. "The argument of the cudgel."

21. Report of the Cambridge Committee of Correspondence, 1776, in Maas, 289; cf. Paige, 169.

22. General Friedrich Adolf Riedesel, a hereditary baron in the service of the Duke of Bruswick, was not entitled to use the "von" attributed to him by American historians.

CHAPTER 2

1. Justice Lemuel Shaw construed the Proprietors' grant as meaning that the Common could not be appropriated to private use, and that alterations to the landscape must not conflict with its use as a training field (Wellington et al. petitioners, 16 Pickering 87).

2. The chosen location at the corner of Norfolk and Harvard streets was equally inconvenient to all three villages, and after the building burned in 1853 municipal offices were relocated to Central Square.

3. Dwight based *Travels in New-England and New-York* on journeys he made between 1792 and 1815.

4. Green (1798–1882) was reelected for one-year terms in 1846, 1847, 1853, and 1860. He established the police and fire departments and implemented street paving and drainage works for the fledgling city.

5. See figure 2.19 for the political divisions of the town from 1846 to 1854, and figure 2.42 for the ward boundaries after 1857.

6. After a short but highly successful career as a railroad car builder, Davenport turned to developing the shores of the Charles River in Cambridgeport (see chapter 5).

7. When the Grand Junction Railroad finally built this connection in 1855, it ran along the river and offered no passenger service.

8. "Later the 'Tudor,' small as it was, had to be discarded for a Tea Canister car [presumably self-propelled] and even that was succeeded by horses drawing the two cars to the Fitchburg junction" (*Chronicle*, Oct. 8, 1921). See figure 9.27 for the station on Holmes Place.

9. The Boston Gas Company had served parts of that city since 1822.

10. The Walling map of 1854 is accurate in every known respect except for the placement of the reservoir, which was east of Reservoir Street (see figure 4.65). The foundation stones of the reservoir are still visible.

11. The first house to receive power from the company's distribution system belonged to Colonel Samuel Sleeper at 1785 Massachusetts Avenue in December 1888.

12. Horsford invented an improved form of baking powder and established the Rumford Chemical Works in Rhode Island to manufacture it. Baking powder is still sold under this brand, which Horsford named after his professorship. Remains of an actual Norse settlement were discovered in Newfoundland in 1960.

13. Sources: Oscar Handlin, *Boston's Immigrants* (1959); *Cambridge Directory,* 1856, pp. 29–30 (for Old Cambridge).

14. One writer recalling life on Brattle Street around 1800 observed: "In those days most wealthy families had one or more black servants who had formerly been slaves, but who, unwilling to accept their freedom, preferred living with [their former] masters and mistresses" (**O [probably Ann Stone Orne], *Chronicle*, Aug. 29, 1850).

15. Sources: Benton; Handlin, *Boston's Immigrants*; U.S. Census; Cambridge city directories. Direct comparisons are difficult because early enumerations counted all whites but only African Americans over age 16.

16. Minor Walker (b. 1758) may have been a sister of Quock Walker, whose successful suit against his master ended slavery in Massachusetts in 1783.

17. For more information on the Lewis family, see Ann Clifford, "Notes on the Lewis Family of Lewisville" (1999) in the files of the Cambridge Historical Commission.

18. Cambridge's first switchboard opened in 1879, but calls could be made only within the city until 1891. Service expanded rapidly to about 1,600 subscribers in 1901 and 11,200 in 1916. In 1905 the *Chronicle* observed that it was already "scarcely possible to conceive how the most simple business and social relations could be carried on without it" (Sept. 9).

19. Boston mayor James Michael Curley "caused a small sensation" in 1925 when he predicted to the Kendall Square Manufacturers' Association that Boston and Cambridge would someday merge (*Globe,* Dec. 4). The editors of the *Chronicle* shuddered, but nothing came of it.

20. This was perhaps the origin of the saying that one had to get up early in Cambridge to avoid the house movers.

21. Greco was underage when he won the competition and had to partner with an established architect who could sign the contract for him.

22. Hederstedt tried other architects, notably commissioning three-deckers from Newhall & Blevins (16 Chilton Street, 1910) and Charles H. McClare (20 Chilton Street, 1912) but gave Mowll almost all his business.

23. The Cambridge Historical Commission's collection of Ellis & Andrews correspondence, 1890–1935, illuminates the operations of the real estate market in the early 20th century.

24. The niche occupied by the Reliance Bank can be illustrated by the composition of its board of directors. In 1923, for example, the president, Fred Beunke, was a stationer, and the members included a general contractor, a plumber, a roofer, and a real estate investor.

25. Cambridge's small population and proximity to Boston has always inhibited local media. Boston's first newspaper appeared in 1690. Charlestown, a much larger community than Cambridge, had a paper by 1785, while more distant towns like Salem, Worcester, and Dedham had newspapers in 1768, 1775, and 1799. Eleven daily papers and thirty-three weeklies were published in Boston in 1845, so Cambridge needed a critical mass of readers before a local weekly could be successful.

26. The single known instance of a racial restriction involved a property on the former Craigie estate sold by the Foster family of New York in 1844 (see chapter 4).

27. The Massachusetts Department of Public Safety (MDPS) reviewed plans for places of public assembly, factories, department stores, hotels, multifamily dwellings, and schools from 1877 until the enactment of a statewide building code in 1975.

28. Tenements were defined as any structure containing more than two units.

29. The fireproofing requirement was not adopted, although in 1925 Walden Street resident Napoleon Bernier patented a process for spraying stucco on building facades. Bernier founded California Stucco Products in Cambridgeport in 1926, which later became the first New England manufacturer of latex paint.

30. Nolen resigned after eight months and appears to have had little effect on the direction of the board.

31. Automobile-related activities proliferated so quickly in Cambridge that by 1937 the city directory listed eighty filling stations and 189 establishments categorized as "automobile accessories, dealers, garages, and repairers."

32. The company obtained permission in 1888 to install a cable system on the Harvard Square route but never acted on it.

33. The line was extended down Aberdeen Avenue to Mt. Auburn when that street opened in 1896.

34. Sectional affiliations did not influence mayoral attitudes toward parks. Mayors Willard, Sargent, Harding, and Houghton lived in Cambridgeport, while Saunders and Alger lived in Old Cambridge.

35. The similarity of names can be confusing. President Charles W. Eliot (1834–1926) served from 1869 to 1909. Charles Eliot (1859–97), the landscape architect, was President Eliot's son. Charles W. Eliot [2nd] (1899–1993), an urban planner, was President Eliot's grandson by another son, Samuel A. Eliot (1862–1950).

36. In 1919 the legislature merged the MPC with the Metropolitan Water & Sewer Commission to form the Metropolitan District Commission (MDC). The MDC was a regional parks agency until 2003, when it became a unit of the Massachusetts Department of Environmental Management.

37. See "The Millers River Controversy" in *East Cambridge,* 205–206.

38. After Charles Eliot died in 1897 the firm was known as Olmsted Brothers until it closed in 1980. Its contract with the park commission lapsed in 1903. The firm consulted with the Cambridge Water Board at Fresh Pond from 1894 until 1908.

39. Jacobs's lasting accomplishment was her transcription of the earliest town and proprietors records, which were published by the city in 1896 and 1901.

40. Only 24,000 of 600,000 eligible women actually voted; critics took this as an absolute rejection of suffrage. Old Cambridge men and women gave the measure substantially less support than it received in Cambridgeport and North Cambridge (*Tribune,* Nov. 9, 1895).

41. The Cambridge Women's Heritage Project profiles many notable women; see http://www2.cambridgema.gov/historic/cwhp.

42. The poet's sons, Charles (1844–93) and Ernest (1845–1921), lived in his shadow. After serving with distinction in the Civil War, Charles spent the rest of his life traveling. A room at Craigie House is decorated with souvenirs of a lengthy residence in Japan. Ernest was a successful landscape painter who studied in Paris; his father built a house nearby for him in 1871 (108 Brattle), but he soon moved to New York and summered in Manchester, Massachusetts.

43. Fraternal and sororal lodges were well represented in other neighborhoods, but none had a physical presence in Old Cambridge (see chapter 7).

44. Arthur Gilman, ed., *The Cambridge of Eighteen Hundred and Ninety-Six.* Cambridge, 1896.

45. This promising trend did not last much longer. After Franklin H. Wright of Riverside served in 1921–23, there were no blacks on the city council until Thomas Coates was elected in 1964.

46. The common council, the lower house of Cambridge's old bicameral system, had been an entry point for aspiring politicians. When it was abolished the school committee assumed that function.

47. In 1938 the General Court established five types of city charters, Plans A through E. Cambridge's strong mayor and unicameral council of 1916–40 was essentially a Plan B charter.

48. Proportional representation (PR) is a system in which voters vote for candidates in order of preference. The National Municipal League included PR in a model charter in 1914, and by 1940 about two dozen cities (including Cincinnati, Cleveland, and New York) had adopted it. Political parties played on fears that it facilitated representation of Communists and African Americans. Boston voters rejected a Plan E charter in 1949, and by 1962 PR had been abandoned everywhere in the United States except Cambridge.

49. Floor-Area Ratio is a measure of development density. An FAR of 1.0 allows construction of a building with a floor area equal to the area of the lot it occupies.

50. John Briston Sullivan, Michael Sullivan and his descendants, who populated the City Council from 1936 until 2007, City Councillor David Sullivan, and James Leo Sullivan were not related to each other, or to the author.

51. The CCA coalition included the first blacks and women to serve on the city council since the 1920s. Pearl Wise, Cornelia Wheeler, and Barbara Ackermann all lived in Old Cambridge. Ackermann became the first female mayor of Cambridge in 1972.

52. Rent controls were established as a national war emergency measure in 1942 and remained in effect until January 1, 1956.

53. City Council approval of curb cuts is a remnant of the previous system of complete local control of public ways.

54. CDD published a pioneering urban design study of East Cambridge in 1976. Rezoning and public investment in infrastructure near the Lechmere Canal encouraged developers to build offices and an enclosed mall. In 1979 the department published a similar study of the Alewife area that anticipated the extension of the subway, and in 1983 a third study set the stage for the 2.3 million square foot University Park development in Cambridgeport.

55. A study of two apartment buildings on Craigie Circle found that both rents and assessed valuations more than doubled between 1996 and 1998. A fifth of the eighty-two units were vacated in the same period as young professionals replaced white collar workers and elderly tenants (Keogh, 19).

56. Cambridge's first million-dollar sale of a residence occurred in 1986, when 3 Channing Place sold for $1,200,000. The property sold for $2 million in 1989 and $3.2 million in 1994 and was offered for $7.9 million in 2004 (but sold for $5.9 million in 2005). Modest houses appreciated at much higher multiples (*Boston Globe,* Sept. 12, 2004).

CHAPTER 3

1. Harvard Square proper is the intersection of Massachusetts Avenue with Kennedy and Brattle streets. Today, the term "Harvard Square" refers more generally to the commercial district within several blocks of this intersection.

2. The block maintained a mostly residential character until the early 20th century, when the corners on Kennedy Street proved irresistible to filling station operators. These were replaced by the Galeria mall in 1974 and the Harvard Square garage in 1984. The last resident of 98 Winthrop Street left about 1986, and her house was converted to a restaurant. Winthrop Street west of Kennedy became a pedestrian precinct in 2007 and a popular entertainment district after licensing rules were relaxed a year later.

3. Occasionally tides rose above 13 feet; the record high tide in the 19th century, 15.66 feet, occurred in 1851.

4. This term was apparently first used in a 1905 Class Day oration, but it quickly came into general use—sometimes interchangeably with "millionaires' row" (*Cambridge Tribune,* June 24 and Sept. 30, 1905).

5. Real estate trusts were a common form of commercial property ownership in the Square. In contrast with other forms of tenure, a family trust tends to sustain older commercial buildings as long as they produce a reliable return. The increasingly numerous beneficiaries are likely to resist making capital investments, so properties may be held until they attract an irresistible offer.

6. Mrs. Fraser remarried and as Esther Stevens Brazer was well known as an author and lecturer on early American decorative arts.

7. The university placed no restrictions on undergraduate car ownership until 1958.

8. An experiment with one-way rotary traffic in 1936 failed because two-way streetcar and trolley bus lines remained in place. The 1949 trial lasted two months.

9. This caused Holyoke Center to be built with a greater setback from Mt. Auburn Street than originally planned. The five-foot setback on Kennedy Street required a fourth-story addition at 28–30 to be built with a corresponding setback. These measures were repealed in 1966.

10. Bunting, who was survey director of the Cambridge Historical Commission from 1964 until 1974, began his graduate work in art history at Harvard in 1937.

11. After thirty-seven years in a basement shop in the same building, Felix's shoe repair business was allowed to return to its original location in 2008.

12. The completion of the Red Line extension brought a spate of articles on this topic. See "Out with the Old: Harvard Square Goes Squaresville" (*Boston Phoenix,* Feb. 19, 1985); "The New Version of Harvard Square: A Suburban Quincy Market?" (*Crimson,* May 13, 1985); "The Square: Perfection Achieved, Serenity Restored" (*Harvard Magazine,* May-June 1985); "Red Brick Mania" (*Boston Magazine,* Nov. 1985); and "The Death of Harvard Square: or Maybe it's a Rebirth in Brick" (*Boston Globe Magazine,* Dec. 6, 1987).

13. Cambridge Booksmith, a branch of the regional Paperback Booksmith chain, opened at 37A Brattle Street in 1962. It was renowned in the 1970s for staying open 24 hours a day, seven days a week.

14. Rai Okamoto (1927–93) was a Philadelphia native with degrees in architecture and city planning from M.I.T. and Yale. His firm's master plan for the redevelopment of downtown Oakland won a national award in 1966, and he served as planning director in San Francisco in 1975–80.

15. The subsequent demand for coarse water-struck bricks similar to those specified by McKim, Mead & White in the 1890s for Harvard's Georgian Revival buildings supported the Kane-Gonic Brick Co.'s traditional yard in New Hampshire until 1994 (see chapter 10).

16. Under the 1962 code there were no height limits and an FAR of 3.0 in this district (see chapter 2).

17. See chapter 4 for the early history of this area.

18. The presence of so many architects attracted specialized services. The Charrette Corporation, founded by Lionel Spiro and Blair Brown, opened in 1964 as an offshoot of the student store they operated at Harvard's Graduate School of Design. In 1965 Charrette acquired the reproduction business of Cambridge photographer Fred Stone and was soon serving architects throughout the northeast from its headquarters at 44 Brattle Street.

CHAPTER 4

1. Some families with small children, concerned about unsafe milk, kept one or two cows in backyard barns until the city stopped licensing them in 1929.

2. The ancient way to the river at Windmill Hill was known as Bath Lane until 1847, when Samuel Batchelder petitioned the common council to have it renamed Ash Street.

3. See "West End Homesteads along Garden Street" for Brattle's land north of Brattle Street.

4. See "John G. Palfrey Estate" for a discussion of Edward Everett's earlier land purchase.

5. The house Leonard Vassall built in 1730–31 was confiscated during the Revolution and acquired by John and Abigail Adams in 1787. "Peacefield" is now part of the Adams National Historical Park in Quincy.

6. Until the late 18th century an undergraduate's class rank was determined by his family's social status.

7. Free adult males were assessed a poll tax that entitled them to vote in elections and at town meetings.

8. Amos Marrett then bought a farm in Watertown, which his heirs sold to Tory merchant George Ruggles in 1764.

9. The National Park Service discovered the foundations of the Marrett house in the course of an archeological survey. While the Vassall house faces Brattle Street, the Marrett house was placed at an angle to face south.

10. The United Kingdom's Public Record Office became the National Archives in 2003. This source is subsequently cited as PRO.

11. Craigie also purchased nine acres on upper Sparks Street from a former slave, Mark Lewis, in 1792; Lewis in turn farmed 29 acres that he rented from Craigie from at least 1796 until 1808 (see "Lewisville," below).

12. See "Wyeth and Hill Homesteads" for Berkeley Place and the west end of Berkeley Street.

13. By accepting this somewhat assertive modern design the commission acknowledged that contemporary architecture could be appropriate in a historic district.

14. Deed restrictions prohibiting obnoxious trades or requiring minimum expenditures on new houses were common, but exclusions based on race have not been found elsewhere in Cambridge. This unusual language may have represented New York practice.

15. A generous house lot at the time might have been 100 feet square, so Hubbard must have expected purchasers to subdivide these tracts.

16. The original course of this brook appears on a plan by James Hayward in 1837. Foster apparently buried it in a drain when he laid out lots on Willard Street in the early 1840s. Hubbard disclaimed responsibility for it in 1849, and in 1853 the aldermen ordered the superintendent of streets to build a proper culvert under Mt. Auburn Street. See Howe, "The Story of a Lost Brook."

17. Many such houses do not sit as high as they once did. When the city raised the streets to promote drainage some homeowners opted to fill in their lots rather than elevate their houses.

18. After Hubbard's death the street was straightened and the trees removed so it could be developed like the rest of the Marsh.

19. The traditional spelling of the Vassall family name was here abbreviated as early as 1854.

20. Attorney General Sewall handled the case of *James v. Lechmere,* in which one of Lechmere's slaves claimed that under the Massachusetts Charter all persons born or residing in the province were free. The case was settled in James's favor. Sewall also secured a verdict freeing James's mother, Margaret, in a jury trial in 1770.

21. Highland from Reservoir to Appleton opened in 1852 and was accepted by the city in 1870.

22. An 1808 deed (177/437) refers to horse chestnut trees along the Watertown road, a few of which still exist between 153 and 163 Brattle Street (see figure 6.11).

23. "West Cambridge" has had a fluid identity. The Third Parish of Cambridge became the town of West Cambridge in 1807, but changed its name to Arlington in 1867. The name reappeared in 1886, when the Fitchburg Railroad gave the name "West Cambridge" to its Brick Yards station at the Sherman Street crossing. Through the 1920s the name was attached to the surrounding neighborhood of Dublin and to the Race Course subdivision along Rindge Avenue. Later in the 20th century the designation was applied to the industrial area off Concord Avenue and to the Fresh Pond neighborhood along Huron Avenue.

24. The location of the reservoir is easily confused because H.F. Walling's otherwise excellent *Map of Cambridge* (1854) places it between Reservoir and Fayerweather streets.

25. Ellen Gurney's sister, Marian (Clover), married Henry Adams in 1872 and committed suicide in 1885.

26. There may have been other slaves for whom Oliver did not claim compensation; the list is accompanied by a note that "most of my Slaves I carried with me from the West Indies and were Patrimonial property. These few have no Conveyance [written title] of them."

27. Gerry is remembered for redrawing electoral districts to give his Democratic-Republican party control of the state senate, whereupon the Federalists dubbed a long, narrow Essex County venue a "gerrymander" for its resemblance to a salamander.

28. Remains were found in a utility trench near the corner of Mt. Auburn and Channing streets in 1876 and during construction of houses at 15 Channing in 1899 and 17 and 19 Channing in 1922.

29. "Elmwood Junior" was demolished in 1894 and replaced by the present house at 182 Brattle Street.

30. The remainder of the farm, a strip 130 feet wide at Brattle Street and 1,600 feet long, passed through a relative to Cambridge real estate man Frederick Fish, who laid out Larch Road along its length in 1883.

31. In 1937 nurseryman Harold A. Ryan laid out Old Dee Road as a cul-de-sac behind the 1882 Dee house (now 36 Larchwood Drive), creating lots for seven houses that were erected between 1937 and 1950.

32. Sorkin obtained a building permit days before the adoption of Cambridge's zoning ordinance and doubled his investment when the neighbors bought him out. The Larches and the Birches, two 16-unit apartment buildings with a frontage of 355 feet on Brattle Street opposite Larchwood, also received permits in the last rush before enactment, but their construction proceeded without incident (see figure 6.232).

33. Hederstedt's house was moved to 242 Lake View Avenue in 1929 to make way for the extension of the parkway; the present house at 139 Larch was built in 1971.

34. James Sturgis Pray and Henry V. Hubbard had studied at Harvard in the 1890s and spent their early careers in the Olmsted office; Hubbard studied under Frederick Law Olmsted Jr. at Harvard, and in 1901 he received one of the first degrees in landscape architecture granted in the United States.

35. Fresh Pond Lane's linearity made it unacceptable to the landscape architects, who redirected the street in a series of curves; only the section between Larchwood Drive and Meadow Way follows the original road.

36. Morrison and Nichols were also active in Brookline, where they hired the Olmsted firm to plan the Hillside subdivision off Warren Street in 1926.

37. The location of this windmill is not known. The mill initially erected on Windmill Hill is said to have been taken to Boston in 1632; no others were recorded.

38. See Michael Kenney, "The Long-Ago Squadrons of Cambridge," for the origins of this early surveyor's term, which was apparently unique to Middlesex County and its immediate surroundings.

39. The snuffbox is now in the possession of Countway Library at the Harvard Medical School.

40. Follen was one of several immigrants credited with introducing the German custom of decorated Christmas trees to the United States, as described by Harriet Martineau in 1838.

41. A relationship between this family and the Mark Lewis who was Andrew Craigie's tenant farmer cannot be established.

42. Hatch moved to 57 Avon Hill Street in 1895, but he rebuilt his stable in 1901 to accommodate teams that made deliveries for Boston department stores. Neighbors must have objected, because it was converted to a two-family house in 1903.

43. Anthony left another parcel to Darby Vassall, who in 1827 reerected the frame of his Boston house there and hired Billings Briggs, a housewright, to add a second floor.

44. See "The Agassiz Neighborhood" for more information on Clarke's property.

45. The frequency of executions in Cambridge is uncertain. The most notorious occurred in 1755, when two slaves were executed for poisoning their master in Charlestown; Mark was hanged and Phyllis burned at the stake. Oliver Wendell Holmes Sr. recalled attending the last hanging on Gallows Hill about 1816; thereafter, executions were held at the new jail in East Cambridge. A public way, Stone Court, reaches the site, now a parking lot behind 1780 Massachusetts Avenue.

46. Arlington was first called Chapel Street after the North Avenue Congregational Society moved its building to the corner in 1857 (see chapter 7). The street was renamed in 1866 for the military cemetery recently established on the Custis-Lee estate in Virginia.

47. The Niles Brothers' 1878 slaughterhouse—permission for which was "one of the most wicked things one municipality ever did to another"—was the direct cause of Cambridge's annexation of 570 acres from Belmont in 1880. The Fresh Pond watershed was not fully protected until the slaughterhouse was connected to the Metropolitan Sewer in 1895 (*Chronicle,* Mar. 19, 1881).

48. A few years later, Brooks commissioned Cambridge builder Harrison Simpson to put up 18 and 24 Agassiz (1889 and 1888) and 16 Lancaster (1892).

49. William A. Saunders described it as "an old house just below Mr. Willis' estate occupied by several colored families" (Jan. 5, 1875). Enoch Lewis rented it from about 1823 to 1827; his brother Joseph, sister Sophia, and her husband, John Levi, a frequent correspondent for *The Liberator* in the 1840s, also lived there.

50. Saunders was a committed antiquarian and recorded his vivid memories of presuburban Cambridge in a scrapbook now held by the Cambridge Historical Society.

51. Cattle were driven down the avenue to the Brighton abattoir well into the 1920s.

52. The Wood house was moved to 3 Sacramento Street in 1925. Harvard University acquired it from Boston University in 1958 (see chapter 7).

53. The Hartwell firm designed James Mellen's house 33 Washington Avenue in 1887. Edwin commissioned his own house from them after he inherited his father's interest in Curtis, Davis & Co., in 1896. Three years later he sold the company to Lever Brothers of England.

54. The boundaries of Charlestown originally extended as far as present-day Stoneham and Burlington. Somerville was set off from Charlestown and became a separate municipality in 1842.

55. The Hastings family operated a tanyard on Holmes Place for three generations. Tanning involved steeping fresh animal hides in open pits filled with chemicals extracted from oak or hemlock bark, a trade that often appeared as a prohibited activity in 19th-century deeds.

56. A 1730 graduate, Hastings preceded Caleb Gannett as college steward, serving from 1750 until 1779. He reportedly served the worst college food "in the course of … three centuries," provoking the Bad Butter Rebellion of 1766 (Sibley, VIII, 721, and Morison, *Three Centuries,* 117–18).

57. Although property ownership had recently been abolished as a requirement for holding office in Massachusetts, Everett may have appreciated its symbolic value to the electorate.

58. Adams must have long regretted this favor, since he paid taxes on the unimproved property until his death thirty-five years later.

59. Mayor Edward W. Quinn wanted the surplus building for a municipal auditorium, but Undersecretary of the Navy Franklin D. Roosevelt secured the property for Harvard in 1919.

60. "Office" in this case probably meant a stable or cowshed (OED).

61. William E. Frost relocated to California in the 1870s and was a builder in Monterey and Oakland until his death about 1910.

62. Grovestein's source for this name was a young woman who had called at his Harvard Square office. He remarked that he needed a name for a new street he was developing, and she told him about the Hotel Traymore, where she had recently stayed in Atlantic City. That "filled the bill and was at once accepted," Grovestein reported (Cambridge City Engineer street files).

63. Frost sold his unfinished house (now 10 Frost Street) to his sister and brother and moved to Haverhill.

64. Higginson's career as a ship owner and merchant ended in bankruptcy during the War of 1812, but his friends arranged for his employment by the college in 1819.

65. Frisbie's widow married James Hayward, who laid out Oxford Street through their side yard.

66. Norton's local reputation suffered when in a widely reported speech at the conclusion of Charles Dickens's American tour he referred to Cambridgeport as "an abomination of desolation" (*Chronicle*, Apr. 28, 1868).

67. Olmsted lived on Kirkland Street with Edwin Godkin, editor of *The Nation*, while moving his home and office from New York to Brookline during the summer of 1878.

68. The proposed extension of Everett Street appears on city atlases as late as 1903. In 1888 Harvard offered to "exchange triangles [and] build Everett Street from the Norton line to Divinity Avenue" if the Palfreys would extend it to Oxford Street (Charles Eliot to John C. Palfrey, May 18, 1888). Perhaps Palfrey's daughters objected to having a street pass in front of their home.

69. The site of Goffe's first house is now marked by bronze plaques in Massachusetts Avenue opposite Holyoke Center; see figure 1.7.

70. Webster's house was one of several that were lost to arson in 1868.

71. The exceptions were Wadsworth House (1726), the Professor of Natural History's Botanic Garden residence (1810), and a matron's house behind the Divinity School (1825).

72. Sparks's heirs sold the Treadwell-Sparks house in 1887 to the New Church Theological School, which moved it to the southeast corner of the property to make way for the Church of the New Jerusalem. In 1968 Harvard moved the house to 21 Kirkland Street, where it became the residence of the minister of Memorial Church (see figure 6.60).

73. The Ambassador became Harvard's Coolidge Hall, which was razed in 2002 for the north building of the Center for Government and International Studies.

74. The Gothic Revival James Walker house, for example, was moved three times: a few hundred feet on Quincy Street for Emerson Hall in 1904, to a field behind Divinity Hall when the new President's house was built in 1911, and finally to 26 Divinity Avenue when the Biological Laboratory was built in 1930. It was demolished when its site was needed for the Electron Accelerator in 1952.

75. Little Neck, a glacial esker that paralleled the Charles as far as River Street, was known in the 17th century as Wigwam Neck for a seasonal Indian settlement; Putnam Avenue follows an ancient path along the ridge.

76. Sir William (1651–95) began life as an illiterate shepherd in Maine. In 1687 he salvaged £300,000 from a Spanish treasure ship and was knighted by James II. He was appointed the first royal governor of Massachusetts in 1692, but was recalled to London and died awaiting trial on charges of maladministration.

77. DeWolfe Street was named for this family; the current spelling is incorrect.

78. The house at 37 Putnam Avenue was razed in 1966 to make room for a Mansard displaced by the Putnam Square Apartments at 2 Mt. Auburn Street.

79. Malaria began to appear in the Charles River watershed in the 1880s and was epidemic in some Cambridge neighborhoods by the mid-nineties. Although the disease was not associated with mosquitoes until 1898, scientists correctly associated it with standing water and began to promote drainage of fresh and saltwater marshes, reclamation of the riverbanks, and construction of sewers as public health measures.

CHAPTER 5

1. Military service was required of all able-bodied men over 16; until about 1686, when retirement was allowed at 60, some served to a great age, unwilling or unable to pay a five shilling fee to be released from the obligation of drilling two to four times a year during peacetime.

2. The narrow, triangular park at Waterhouse Street and Massachusetts Avenue (known as the Little Common) is not part of the Common and was not enclosed until 1860.

3. The last of these trees, the so-called Stone Elm near the corner of Bond Street, was cut down in 1935.

4. At Harvard University, the opposite occurred; proponents of a memorial hall, led by Charles Eliot Norton, prevailed over those who wished to see a triumphal monument.

5. The original stands in Chicago's Lincoln Park.

6. Bridge also commissioned Daniel Chester French to make the bronze statue of John Harvard now in Harvard Yard.

7. The Daughters of the Revolution and the Daughters of the American Revolution were separate organizations. The DAR was founded in 1890 by descendants of soldiers of all ranks; the DR, which admitted only descendants of officers, seceded from the DAR in 1891. The Boston chapter of the DR had a handful of Cambridge members; the Hannah Winthrop Chapter of the DAR had dozens (see chapter 2).

8. The Cambridge Park Commission took this tract in 1894. The Metropolitan District Commission extended Memorial Drive across it in 1948 and no longer maintains a view corridor from the house.

9. French was a childhood friend of Richard Henry Dana III, the poet's grandson. He lived in Cambridge for only a few years (about 1860–64, between the ages of 10 and 14), but he formed lasting bonds with his contemporaries, Dana and William Brewster, the future ornithologist.

10. A cutting from this willow, which had been uprooted by a storm, was planted on the east property line in 1985.

11. This movement is described in chapter 2.

12. The Memorial Drive trees are actually "a hybrid of long standing between an American and Eurasian" plane tree known to botanists as *Platanus acerifolia* or London plane tree (*Crimson,* Nov. 25, 1964).

13. The commissioners considered running the parkway inland along Blackstone Street; the final route involved filling in some of the channel and constructing a seawall.

14. The Metropolitan District Commission was established in 1919 in a merger of the Metropolitan Park Commission and the Metropolitan Water and Sewer Commission. When the MDC was dissolved by the legislature in 2003 its open space and recreational functions were assumed by the Massachusetts Department of Conservation and Recreation.

15. In many New England towns the burying ground was placed next to the meetinghouse, but here the cemetery preceded the churches.

16. Remains found on Channing Street in the 1920s were reinterred in Cambridge Cemetery (see chapter 4).

17. Mount Auburn Cemetery has been thoroughly described by Blanche Linden-Ward in *Silent City on a Hill: Picturesque Landscapes of Memory* (2007).

18. Subsequent purchases by the cemetery increased the grounds to 175 acres, of which only 11 are in Cambridge.

19. Four statues were commissioned for the chapel: John Winthrop (by Richard S. Greenough), James Otis (Thomas Crawford), John Adams (Randolph Rogers), and Joseph Story (William Wetmore Story). All were given to Har-

vard in 1934. Story's statue is now at the Law School; Adams and Winthrop are in the freshman dining room at Memorial Hall; and Otis is in Sanders Theater opposite a statue of Josiah Quincy, also by Story.

CHAPTER 6

1. The society's 2010 publication, *Rediscovering the Hooper-Lee-Nichols House,* expands on Anne Grady and Sarah Zimmerman's pioneering 1979 study and is the most authoritative analysis of the structure to date.

2. Batty Langley (1696–1751) was an English garden designer whose pattern books contained loose interpretations of Classical and Gothic designs. Although popular among the gentry in the colonies and used by George Washington at Mount Vernon, his books were considered rather middle-class in England.

3. First Period houses often had solid exterior shutters for security. Paired shutters appear to have been introduced in New England in the late 18th century.

4. Early carpenters often tapered ("skived") the ends of clapboards to make an overlapping joint for greater weather resistance. This practice disappeared during the 1840s.

5. What is referred to as "the sample House" was the 1838 double house at 347–51 Cambridge Street in East Cambridge, now severely defaced.

6. Hastings's design closely resembles Harrison Gray Otis's country home in nearby Watertown, where an 1809–10 remodeling, most likely the work of Charles Bulfinch, added a similar central elliptical bay, triple-sash windows, and low hip roof.

7. Although Smith was building up-to-date Stick Style houses, such as 88 Lake View (1874), at the same time, he continued to build Mansards on Lake View until 1878 and lived in one himself until 1882. Of the twelve houses that he erected on the street in the 1870s, seven had Mansard roofs.

8. Littlefield was listed in the Cambridge directory as an architect for the first time in 1873. It was a common practice for builders to erect houses on lots they subdivided and sold, and Littlefield may have been the designer of Laughlin's house.

9. Professor Kenneth Conant, a historian of medieval architecture who evaluated the Deanery at the request of the Cambridge Historical Commission, declared himself "more than ever convinced that [it] has no claim to preservation" (to Albert B. Wolfe, Mar. 31, 1964).

10. Niles may have been influenced by the lighthouse stair tower and observatory of "Thirlstane," an elaborate shingled ocean-front cottage at Bar Harbor designed by W.R. Emerson in 1881 and published to much acclaim in *The Builder* in 1886.

11. Sands supplied the decorative and wire-cut brick for H.H. Richardson's Sever Hall and Trinity Church rectory, as well as other Back Bay buildings.

12. Scully credits Emerson with achieving the first fully shingled exterior and characteristic open interior plan in a Shingle Style house he designed at Mount Desert in 1879.

13. A comparison with the relatively stiff late Shingle Style house at 13 Berkeley Street (1898, Dwight & Chandler, architects) reveals the skill and flexibility with which Emerson handled his shingled surfaces.

14. The fireproof roof consists of terra-cotta tiles supported by steel rafters and purlins (stamped "Carnegie") infilled with hollow terra-cotta blocks.

15. Whidden returned to Oregon in 1889, where he practiced until he retired in 1920.

16. Peters's only other Cambridge building was Harvard's Porcellian Club at 1320-1324 Massachusetts Avenue (1890; see figure 10.54).

17. Warren's best known Cambridge building is the Church of the New Jerusalem at 50 Quincy Street (1901), designed in the form of an English country parish church in the Late Gothic Revival style (see figure 7.27).

18. Their partner, George R. Martin, died in 1928, but the name of the firm did not change.

19. The Horsley Company had won a prize for designing small prefabricated houses for mass production and manufactured some for the government after the war.

20. Johnson had met Mies in Berlin in 1930 and commissioned him to design the interior of his Manhattan apartment.

21. Sert's work as Harvard's master planner and his major university buildings, Holyoke Center (1961–65) and Peabody Terrace (1963), are discussed in chapter 10.

22. Balconies were a hallmark of postwar high-rise apartment buildings; the city's first example appeared in 1949 at 100 Memorial Drive, but 29 Concord Avenue was the earliest in Old Cambridge.

CHAPTER 7

1. Benjamin's plans have not survived. Rogers's plans were redrawn twice to satisfy President Quincy.

2. Students ceased attending weekly services in the meetinghouse in 1815, after Harvard completed a new chapel in University Hall.

3. Seam-faced granite is quarried along the natural fractures in the stone and was valued in this period for the rusty surfaces discolored by the "sap" or groundwater that permeated the stone. Richards (1855–1925) was formerly a partner with his father in the firm of J.R. & W.P. Richards (see chapter 6).

4. Farwell had helped First Baptist acquire its present commanding site in Central Square in 1817. The town's Baptists had had considerable difficulty establishing themselves, not being "considered a desirable addition to the religious institutions of Cambridge" (*First Baptist Church,* 4).

5. Schulze trained in Berlin and Vienna before arriving in Boston in 1849. He lived in Cambridgeport for two years before going to New York in 1858. In 1877 he moved to Washington, D.C., where he designed several public buildings with his fellow refugee, Adolph Cluss.

6. St. James's Episcopal Church at 1991 Massachusetts Avenue (1888, Henry M. Congdon, architect) has a similar plan, but the interior there features the Low Church (pulpit centered) layout seen at Richardson's Trinity Church in Boston.

7. Seventy-five years later, Catholics in these towns were served by "forty churches, seventeen schools, thirteen convents, two hospitals, ninety-one priests [and] 278 sisters" *(Boston Evening Transcript,* Dec. 13, 1923).

8. The chapel was moved to 251 Hampshire Street, where it became the Inman Square Baptist Church; it was razed in 1932.

9. According to the *Crimson,* "MIT Lutherans persuaded [the building committee] to adopt a less conventional building with modern lines" (Dec. 15, 1950).

10. Throughout the colonial period, justices of the peace working from their homes dealt with minor crimes and civil cases. Superior Court justices traveled from courthouse to courthouse on a fixed schedule. Lawyers and court clerks accompanied them, staying in local inns while the court was in session.

11. William Hunneman (1769–1856) was a blacksmith and former apprentice of Paul Revere whose firm manufactured fire engines in Boston from 1805 until 1883.

12. A municipal police court was authorized by the legislature in 1854 with powers that were originally held by twenty-five justices of the peace. The court sat in City Hall and then upstairs in Station 1 until the City Building opened in 1875. The Third District Court of Eastern Middlesex, which replaced the municipal court in 1882, moved to East Cambridge in 1913.

13. Walls built of irregular slabs of ledgestone can be unstable without a strong mortar to hold them in place. Early masons burned clamshells to

obtain lime, an essential ingredient, but such mortar lacked strength and could not resist severe weather.

14. While the permanent population of Cambridge in 1890 was slightly larger than in 2010 (91,886 vs. 88,066), in the earlier period the city was growing rapidly, and family sizes were much larger. Private school enrollment is difficult to quantify. In 2011 about half the children born in Cambridge five years earlier entered first grade in the public schools (Cambridge School Dept. FY 2012 Annual Budget, 115).

15. The new owner moved it to the corner of Eliot and Kennedy streets, where it served as a dwelling until it was razed in 1911.

16. The Tarbell School on Callender Street in Riverside was built to the same plan but was radically altered in 1973 by the Cambridge Community Center.

17. Fresh air was considered the best preventive for tuberculosis. Agassiz parents founded the Shady Hill School on this principle while the new Agassiz was under construction (see below).

18. Sloyd is a Swedish method of teaching manual skills to primary schoolchildren.

19. One of the school's best-known students was Helen Keller, who took a preparatory course in 1896–97 before entering Radcliffe College.

20. By 1919 the school had softened slightly. The buildings were glazed and heated, but children were still required to have "special open air clothing" furnished by a supplier in Boston (*The Co-operative Open Air School,* 8). Classes would be canceled when the temperature fell below 5° F.

21. The Gilmans founded the Cambridge School for Girls in 1886 and presumably educated their younger daughters there, although only one subsequently attended Radcliffe (see chapter 7).

22. The donor was Mrs. Augustus Hemenway, whose husband had given a gymnasium to Harvard twenty years before.

23. Perry, Shaw & Hepburn, best known for its restoration of Colonial Williamsburg in Virginia in the 1920s, remained committed to the Georgian Revival style for a long as willing clients could be found. Their one building for Harvard was Houghton Library (1941).

24. Harrison & Abramovitz designed the United Nations headquarters in Manhattan (1947–53) and the Empire State Plaza complex in Albany (1959–76). Abramovitz was responsible for the Three Chapels at Brandeis University (1953) and Avery Fisher Hall at Lincoln Center (1962).

25. Radcliffe purchased the former Cambridge School for Girls and three 19th century houses on Concord Avenue from Lesley College in 1984 (see figure 7.65).

26. Lesley sold its demonstration schools in 1981, when they were reorganized under the auspices of the Schools for Children, Inc., and moved to Arlington.

27. Lesley's endowment was very small in this period, and the college could expand only by borrowing on the value of its real estate. Less restrictive zoning enhanced property values and made loans easier to obtain.

28. Under the Elizabethan Poor Law of 1601, which provided the conceptual basis for the constantly evolving welfare laws of Massachusetts, the "impotent poor" were eligible to be supported by towns in poorhouses or with outdoor relief (assistance administered by the parish overseers of the poor).

29. The prerequisites of a healthy site were exposure to prevailing winds and good drainage. Land around Fresh Pond was too expensive, and noise from the railroad yards across the Charles made Captain's Island undesirable. "The high grounds to the north [on Reservoir Hill] … command an excellent prospect, are well exposed to the sun and air, but … the soil is of clay, cold and damp, and difficult to drain" (*Dedication,* 10–11).

30. In 1908 the city addressed a tuberculosis epidemic by establishing a sanatorium on Concord Avenue near Fresh Pond. This became a full-fledged hospital, which the city sold to the Archdiocese of Boston in 1966.

CHAPTER 8

1. Coincidentally, Zachariah Porter (no relation of Israel) took over the Cambridge Market Hotel in North Cambridge in 1837 and renamed it the Porter House.

2. There were three hotels in East Cambridge and two in Central Square in 1849.

3. There were many apartment buildings called "hotels" in this period, but these did not cater to transients (see chapter 2). Most boardinghouse keepers in Old Cambridge restricted their clientele to students.

4. A story that Harvard traded College House to the Coolidge brothers in return for Randolph Hall and Apthorp House, private dormitories that are now part of Adams House, could not be substantiated. (The Coolidges were longtime supporters of the university whose buildings were devalued by President Lowell's requirement that undergraduates live in university housing.)

5. Newhall & Blevins, or Albert Blevins working alone, were responsible for six buildings in Harvard Square between 1905 and 1924, while Galvin designed or remodeled nine between 1930 and 1946 (see chapter 2).

6. The gradual relaxation of Modernist conventions is illustrated at the Kennedy School of Government, which consists of four buildings designed by different architects between 1978 and 1989 during the transition to Postmodernism (see figure 10.91).

CHAPTER 9

1. The unit of measurement was the tun, a cask containing 252 gallons and weighing 2,240 pounds. Small oceangoing vessels might have a capacity of 20 to 100 tons; a large full-rigged ship, 350 to 1,000 tons.

2. Mud dug from the riverbanks was sold to farmers as fertilizer.

3. According to Sibley, fireplaces in dormitory rooms were converted to coal after 1830.

4. Barges appeared in the Chesapeake Bay coal trade in the 1870s. A coasting schooner capable of navigating the Charles might have a capacity of 300 tons, but a steel "whaleback" barge that arrived at Richardson & Bacon's wharf in 1892 carried 1,400. A two-masted lighter that ran aground off Magazine Beach in 1902 carried 1,140 tons.

5. Potash, a potassium compound, was produced by boiling wood ashes (which student fireplaces produced in quantity). In its unrefined form potash was an ingredient of lye and soap; when purified in a kiln it became pearl ash, a leavening agent used in baking.

6. Individuals often joined together to rent a stable and hire a groom or stable boy to live on the premises. A stable with more than four horses had to be licensed by the board of health.

7. The tunnels and platforms for surface lines were retained, but the subway station was replaced with a concourse that led to new platforms running north along the extension.

8. So great was the interchange that in 1869 the General Court gave permission for a private telegraph line between Osgood's office in Boston and the Brattle Square plant.

9. Houghton's elegant 1857 Mansard at 1000 Massachusetts Avenue overlooking the plant is described in *Report Three: Cambridgeport,* figure 122.

10. Houghton named Daye Court for Stephen Daye, the first printer in the colonies.

11. Metcalf was the original Eliab's nephew; his father, Charles R. Metcalf, sold the University Press to Welch, Bigelow & Company in 1859.

CHAPTER 10

1. Two boards govern Harvard. The corporation, a self-perpetuating body known as the President and Fellows of Harvard College, has functioned since 1650 as a board of trustees; until 2010 it included the president, treasurer, and five external members, or fellows, who served indefinite terms. The corporation now has thirteen members who serve terms of twelve years. The overseers, who once included the ministers of Cambridge, Boston, Watertown, Charlestown, Roxbury, and Dorchester, as well as the Governor, Lieutenant Governor, the Governor's Council, and the entire Massachusetts Senate, are now an advisory body elected by the alumni.

2. In 1875 a writer for the *Magenta* (predecessor of the *Harvard Crimson*) summarized student attitudes. "Cambridgeport, indeed! What would it be without Harvard? A collection of slaughterhouses, a pig-killing village. Whoever heard of Cambridge but as the seat of Harvard University, from which it got its very name!" (*Crimson,* Feb. 14, 1927).

3. This association with the cow yards is the origin of Harvard's distinctive nomenclature for its core campus.

4. Talk about relocating the college diminished about this time as the administration adopted a more open world view and accepted its dependence on the intellectual and financial resources of Boston—what Professor Sidney Willard called the "intercommunity of the learned" (Willard, 328; in Simpson, 503).

5. Cambridge erected a Greek Revival town hall designed by Asher Benjamin on Norfolk Street in Cambridgeport in the same year.

6. Willard's only other Cambridge project was the nearby Phillips-Norton house at Shady Hill (see figure 4.230). Sumner's best-known surviving building is the East India Marine Hall in Salem (1925).

7. See chapter 5 for a history of the Botanic Garden.

8. After 1865 the university provided the facilities, and the student-run Harvard Dining Association managed the food service. Harvard took over the dining halls in 1924 and instituted mandatory meal plans in 1931.

9. Morison, *Three Centuries of Harvard,* 490. These figures do not include medical students.

10. Charles W. Eliot [2nd], the president's grandson, was born two years after his uncle, the landscape architect, died in 1897. He told one of the authors that his grandfather had decreed that his next grandson would be named after his recently deceased son and that the young man would be trained a landscape architect—and then started Harvard's program in that field. Arthur Shurtleff changed his last name to Shurcliff in 1930.

11. Harvard offered only undergraduate degrees in architecture and landscape architecture until 1906.

12. Professor Wallace Sabine established the field of architectural acoustics with experiments that compared Hunt's lecture hall to Sanders Theater, but he was unable to resolve its deficiencies. Sabine—who discovered that six Sanders seat cushions decreased reverberations as much as one human body—helped McKim, Mead & White design Boston's Symphony Hall in 1900.

13. The present Hemenway Gymnasium (1938) stands on a different site.

14. Treasurer Edward Hooper privately acknowledged Austin's gift as "vandalism money" (Treasurer's letterbooks, Hooper to Austin, Nov. 1, 1884).

15. Harvard abolished admission requirements for proficiency in Greek in 1886 and for Latin in 1898 to broaden its pool of applicants.

16. John Albro Little built the Big Tree swimming pool on Holyoke Street in 1900 for the exclusive use of the students living in Little's Block, which his father had erected in 1854.

17. Green (1875–1920) was one of several opportunistic investors who entered this specialized market. He came to America from Russia as an 11-year-old and became one of Cambridge's most prolific tenement builders in the 1890s. After going bankrupt in 1904 he had a successful second career as a builder in Roxbury and Dorchester.

18. Hastings Hall (1888) was convenient for law students, but was open to all who could afford it. Perkins was the first building in the Georgian Revival style that would dominate Harvard for the next fifty years. Charles Coolidge was said to have based the design on Hollis Hall (1762), "the best-looking of all the College buildings" (Eliot, *Harvard Memories,* 84).

19. Acts of 1874, chap. 375, sec. 8, and Acts of 1878, chap. 214.

20. The balance of McKay's estate, estimated at $20 million in 1903 (approximately $546 million in 2013 dollars), did not arrive until after the death of his last heir in 1949.

21. Following Richardson's death in 1886, Coolidge and his associates reorganized as Shepley, Rutan & Coolidge. Shepley died in 1903. After Rutan died in 1914, the firm was known as Coolidge & Shattuck until Shattuck's death in 1923. It was Coolidge, Shepley, Bulfinch & Abbott until 1952, Shepley, Bulfinch, Richardson & Abbott until 2000, and then became Shepley Bulfinch.

22. Lowell also disbanded Memorial Hall's corps of African American waiters, replacing them with white waitresses in 1924.

23. The blocks between Mt. Auburn and Winthrop streets were to be reserved for "clubs and semi-collegiate activities" (*Chronicle,* July 4, 1925). The only aspect of the study never achieved was a formal connection between the River houses and the Yard.

24. Plans for the Busch-Reisinger were drawn in Dresden by Professor German Bestelmeyer and adapted for the site by Langford Warren. The museum was unfinished when the United States entered World War I and did not open until 1921.

25. Among the notable graduates of this period were architects I.M. Pei, Ulrich Franzen, and Henry Cobb, as well as Ian McHarg, the landscape architect, and Martin Meyerson, the city planner.

26. At the same time and right next door, the firm designed the second Hemenway Gymnasium in a stripped-Georgian style, completing—with Austin, Hastings, and Gannett—one of the wildly disparate *mélanges* for which Harvard is famous.

27. Dean Elena Kagan had the Arp and Bayer works covered over or removed during a 2004 renovation.

28. At various times the entire adjoining Riverside neighborhood was slated for urban renewal, as was Harvard Square itself (see chapters 2 and 3).

29. The university established a satellite clinic on Holyoke Street in 1932. The original location of Stillman Infirmary next to Mount Auburn Hospital became less advantageous as medical advances reduced the need to isolate infectious patients.

30. Harvard's last Georgian Revival building in Cambridge was an addition to Paine Hall in 1955.

31. With hindsight, Harvard's problems seem small compared to the difficulties faced by Yale in New Haven, Columbia in Morningside Heights, or the University of Chicago in Hyde Park.

32. See chapter 2 regarding Harvard's assistance to the Holy Trinity Armenian Church in a Dover Amendment test case.

33. The National Register of Historic Places is a federal program administered by the states that recognizes places, buildings, and districts that are significant in American history, architecture, archeology, and culture on the local, state, or national level. Projects affecting listed properties that involve federal or state funds or permits are subject to review by the Massachusetts Historical Commission.

34. John Langdon Sibley recorded ceremonial plantings of ivy as early as 1844. In 1865 senior classes borrowed a tradition said to have originated at Yale and began planting ivy around buildings in the Yard.

35. The openings had once facilitated communication between the classes, as memorialized in 1818:

Nathan threw a piece of bread,
And hit Abijah on the head.
The wrathful Freshman, in a trice,
Sent back another bigger slice;
Which, being butter'd pretty well,
Made greasy work where'er it fell.
And thus arose a fearful battle …

(Augustus Peirce, *Rebelliad … A Poem in Four Cantos,* 14–15)

36. Harvard performed the mitigation it had promised the Mid Cambridge Neighborhood Conservation District Commission by relocating 96 Prescott Street to Sumner Road and restoring four Greek Revival houses adjacent to the site.

37. Advances in slurry-wall construction made going underground easier and sometimes less expensive than creating above-ground space.

38. Werner Otto Hall (1988, Gwathmey Siegel, architects) was built to house the Busch-Reisinger collection of Germanic art. Ineffective climate controls caused its steel skin to rust, and in 2007 it was judged to be beyond repair.

Bibliography

Adams, C.F. *Richard Henry Dana, Jr.: A Biography*. Boston, 1890.

Alduino, Therese. "The Cambridge Main Street Subway: Its History, Planning and Construction." Unpublished paper for the Cambridge Historical Commission, 1984.

Alduino, Therese. "Parks, Politics, and City Planning: The Design for the Cambridge River Front, 1893–1909." Unpublished thesis, Harvard University, 1984.

Allen, Glover M. "William Brewster, 1851–1919." *Cambridge Historical Society Publications* 24 (1938): 83–98.

Allen, T. Prentiss. "The 'Oxford Cap Rows' of 1842." *Harvard Graduates' Magazine* 8, no. 29 (September 1899).

Allyn, Alice C. "A History of Berkeley Street, Cambridge." *Cambridge Historical Society Publications* 21 (1935): 58–71.

Almy, Charles. "The History of the Third District Court of Eastern Middlesex." *Cambridge Historical Society Publications* 17 (1931): 16–27.

Alofsin, Anthony. *The Struggle for Modernism: Architecture, Landscape Architecture and City Planning at Harvard*. New York, 2002.

Ames, Carolyn Stetson. "Radcliffe's First Century." *Cambridge Historical Society Publications* 44 (1985): 139–57.

Ames, James B. "The Founding of the Mount Auburn Hospital." *Cambridge Historical Society Publications* 39 (1964): 39–49.

Amory, Thomas C. *Old Cambridge and New*. Boston, 1871.

Amory, Thomas C. "The Old Hooper-Lee House." *Cambridge Historical Society Publications* 16 (1930): 21–25.

Anburey, Thomas. *Travels Through the Interior Parts of America, 1771–1781*. Brooklyn, 1923.

Anderson, Dorothy May. *Women, Design and the Cambridge School*. West Lafayette, Ind., 1980.

Anesko, Michael. *Letters, Fictions, Lives: Henry James and William Dean Howells*. New York, 1997.

Austin, William D. "A History of the Boston Society of Architects in the 19th Century." Unpublished manuscript, 1942.

Ayer, Hannah Palfrey. *A Legacy of New England. Letters of the Palfrey Family*. Privately printed, 1950.

Ayres, Linda. *Harvard Divided*. Cambridge, 1976.

Bail, Hamilton V. *Views of Harvard*. Cambridge, 1949.

Bailey, Hollis Russell. "The Beginning of the First Church in Cambridge." *Cambridge Historical Society Publications* 10 (1924): 86–115 and 17 (1931): 92–97.

Bailyn, Bernard, and Lotte Bailyn. *Massachusetts Shipping 1697–1714: A Statistical Study*. Cambridge, 1959.

Baker, Christina Hopkinson. *The Story of Fay House*. Cambridge, 1929.

Ballou, Ellen B. *The Building of the House: Houghton Mifflin's Formative Years*. Boston, 1970.

Barker, Jeanette Palache. "A School for All Seasons." *Cambridge Historical Society Publications* 42 (1978): 123–35.

Bartlett, John. *A Collection of College Words and Customs*. Cambridge, 1851.

Bastlund, Knud. *Jose Luis Sert, Architecture, City Planning, Urban Design.* New York, 1967.

Batchelder, Samuel Francis. *Bits of Harvard History.* Cambridge, 1924.

Batchelder, Samuel Francis. *Christ Church, Cambridge, Some Account of Its History and Present Condition, Especially Prepared for Visitors.* Cambridge, 1893.

Batchelder, Samuel Francis. "Col. Henry Vassall and His Wife Penelope Vassall, With Some Account of His Slaves." *Cambridge Historical Society Publications* 10 (1917): 5–85.

Batchelder, Samuel Francis. "The Washington Elm Tradition." *Cambridge Historical Society Publications* 18 (1926): 46–75.

Bates, Jacob Hill. Papers. Cambridge Historical Society.

Beale, Joseph H. "The History of Local Government in Cambridge." *Cambridge Historical Society Publications* 22 (1937): 17–28.

Belknap, Jeremy. *The History of New-Hampshire.* Dover, N.H., 1812.

Bell, Mabel Hubbard. "Reminiscences." Bell Papers. Volta Bureau, Washington, D.C.

Bennett, Arnold. *Your United States, Impressions of a First Visit.* New York, 1912.

Bentinck-Smith, William. *The Harvard Book.* Cambridge, 1953.

Bentley, William. *The Diary of William Bentley, D.D., Pastor of the East Church, Salem, Massachusetts.* Salem, 1904.

Benton, Josiah H. Jr. *Early Census Making in Massachusetts, 1643–1765.* Boston, 1905.

Bergengren, Ralph. "Norton's Woods." *The House Beautiful.* (November 1915): 165–69.

Berkin, Carol. *Jonathan Sewell: Odyssey of an American Loyalist.* New York, 1974.

Bigelow, Jacob. *A History of the Cemetery of Mount Auburn.* Boston, 1859.

Billias, George Athan. *Elbridge Gerry.* New York, 1976.

Binford, Henry C. *The First Suburbs: Residential Communities on the Boston Periphery, 1815–1860.* Chicago, 1985.

Birket, James. *Some Cursory Remarks Made by James Birket in his Voyage to North America—1750–51.* New Haven, 1916.

Blodgett, Geoffrey. *The Gentle Reformers: Massachusetts Democrats in the Cleveland Era.* Cambridge, 1966.

Bond, Elizabeth L. "The Observatory of Harvard College and Its Early Founders." *Cambridge Historical Society Publications* 25 (1939): 75–85.

Bond, Henry. *Genealogies of the Families and Descendants of the Early Settlers of Watertown, Massachusetts.* Boston, 1860.

Bond, William. *Annals of the Astronomical Observatory of Harvard College.* [Cambridge?], 1856.

Boothe, Roger. "MCAIA Awards for the Built Environment." Cambridge Community Development Department. May 11, 1990.

Boston Elevated Railway Company. Cambridge Main Street Subway scrapbooks. 3 vols. February 9, 1907–May 15, 1912.

Boston Elevated Railway Company. *Fifty Years of Unified Transportation in Metropolitan Boston.* Boston, 1938.

Boston Transportation Planning Review. *Northwest [Sector] Preliminary Environmental Analysis [and] Preliminary Location Report.* Boston, 1973.

Boudinot, Elias. *Journey to Boston in 1809.* Princeton, 1955.

Bowditch, Nathaniel. "College History." Unpublished manuscript, ca. 1829. Harvard College Archives.

Bowen, Maria. "Reminiscences of Follen Street." *Cambridge Historical Society Publications* 20 (1934): 91–101.

Bowen, Maria, Mary Deane Dexter, and Rosalba Smith Proell. "Sparks Street." *Cambridge Historical Society Publications* 22 (1936): 46–57.

Boyd, John Taylor Jr. "Professor H. Langford Warren." *The Architectural Record* 42, no. 6 (December 1917): 590.

Brewster, Edwin T. *Life and Letters of Josiah Dwight Whitney.* Boston, 1909.

Brewster, William. "The Birds of the Cambridge Region of Massachusetts." *Memoirs of the Nuttall Ornithological Club.* Vol. 4. Cambridge, 1906.

Bridenbaugh, Carl. *Peter Harrison, First American Architect.* Chapel Hill, 1949.

Brooks, Charles. *History of the Town of Medford, Middlesex County, Massachusetts: from its first settlement in 1630 to 1855.* Revised ed. by James M. Usher. Boston, 1886.

Brooks, Van Wyck. *The Flowering of New England.* Boston, 1936.

Brown, Frank Choteau. "Tendencies in Apartment House Construction." *The Architectural Record* 49, no. 6–51 (June 1921–May 1922).

Brown, John Perkins. "Christ Church, Cambridge." *Cambridge Historical Society Publications* 23 (1937): 17–23.

Buckley, Daniel J. "Tax Exemption in Cambridge." BA/Honors thesis, Harvard University, April 14, 1937.

Bull, Mrs. Ole [Sara Thorp Bull]. "The Cambridge Conferences." *The Outlook* (August 7, 1897). [Cambridge, 1897?].

Bunting, Bainbridge. *Harvard, An Architectural History.* Completed and edited by Margaret Henderson Floyd. Cambridge, 1985.

Burton, John D. "Philanthropy and the Origins of Educational Cooperation: Harvard College, the Hopkins Trust, and the Cambridge Grammar School." *History of Education Quarterly* 37, no. 2 (1997): 141–61.

Burton, John D. "Puritan Town and Gown: Harvard College and Cambridge, Massachusetts, 1636–1800." Unpublished dissertation, 1996.

Calkins, Raymond. *The Life and Times of Alexander McKenzie.* Cambridge, 1935.

Cambridge Committee for Plan E. Scrapbooks, 1937–45. Cambridge Historical Commission.

Cambridge, Massachusetts, Directory. Various dates and publishers, 1848–1972.

Cambridge Firemen's Relief Association. *History of the Fire Service, Cambridge, Massachusetts.* 1888.

Cambridge Historical Society. *A City's Life and Times: Cambridge in the Twentieth Century.* Edited by Daphne Abeel. Cambridge, 2007.

Cambridge Historical Society. *Rediscovering the Hooper-Lee-Nichols House.* Cambridge, 2010.

Cambridge Historical Society. *Saving Cambridge: Historic Preservation in America's Innovation City.* Cambridge, 2013.

Cambridge No-license Citizens' Committee. *Ten No-license Years in Cambridge.* Cambridge, 1898.

Cambridge Rail Road Company. Records [Minutes of the Board of Directors, June 6, 1871, to April 20, 1888]. Handwritten ledger. Cambridge Historical Commission.

Cambridge Redevelopment Authority. *Harvard Square Development Area Technical Reports.* 6 vols. Prepared by Okamoto/Liskamm, Inc. Cambridge, May 1968.

Cambridge Skating Club. *Cambridge Skating Club, 1898–1948.* Cambridge, [1948?].

Cambridge Water Works. *The Cambridge Water Works.* Cambridge, [1858?].

Cambridge, City of. "Address of the Mayor Upon the First Organization of the City Government, May 4, 1846." Cambridge, 1846.

Cambridge, City of. *Annual Documents.* Cambridge, 1846–2014.

Cambridge, City of. *Cambridge in the Centennial.* Cambridge, 1875.

Cambridge, City of. *Cambridge Revolutionary Memorial.* Cambridge, 1870.

Cambridge, City of. *The Records of the Town of Cambridge (Formerly Newtowne) Massachusetts 1630–1703.* Cambridge, 1901.

Cambridge, City of. *The Register Book of the Lands and Houses in the "New Towne" and the Town of Cambridge, with the Records of the Proprietors of the Common Lands.* Cambridge, 1896.

Cambridge, City of. "Report of the Committee on Gerry's Landing." *The Mayor's Address at the Organization of the City Government … and the Annual Reports Made to the City Council.* Cambridge, 1884.

Cambridge, City of. *Report of the Committee on Public Parks.* Cambridge, 1892.

Cambridge, City of. *Report of the Committee on Rapid Transit.* Cambridge, September 28, 1904.

Cambridge, City of. *The Soldiers Monument in Cambridge.* Cambridge, 1870.

Cambridge, City of. "Soldiers' Monument, Cambridge, Mass. Dedication of the Memorial Tablets, May 30, 1927, with a History of the Monument." Cambridge, 1927.

Cambridge, City of. *Special Laws Enacted by the Legislature of Massachusetts for the City of Cambridge,* 1781–1890. Boston, 1890.

Cambridge, City of. *Zoning Law and Building Code.* Cambridge, 1924.

Cambridge, City of. *Zoning Ordinance.* Cambridge, 1943.

Cambridge, City of. *Zoning Ordinance.* Cambridge, 1962.

Cambridge, City of. Community Development Department. "Harvard Square Development Guidelines." Cambridge, 1986.

Cambridge, City of. Harvard Square Development Task Force. "Response of the Harvard Square Development Task Force to: 'A Long Range Plan for Harvard University and Radcliffe College in Cambridge and Allston.'" December 12, 1974.

Cambridge, City of. Historical Commission. *Final Report … Regarding the Proposed Harvard Square Conservation District.* November 29, 2000.

Cambridge, City of. Park Commission. *Annual Reports.* Cambridge, 1893–1941.

Cambridge, City of. Planning & Development Department. "CDP: Harvard Square, Vol. 1: Critique of Prior Plans and Proposals" (preliminary draft). Cambridge, April 1972.

Cambridge, City of. Planning & Development Department. "Status of Kennedy Library and Planning Activities in the Harvard Square Area." Cambridge, January 14, 1972.

Cambridge, City of. Planning Board. *The City Plan.* Cambridge, 1957–58.

Cambridge, City of. Planning Board. "How to Get Out of Harvard Square in a Train." Cambridge, November 1973.

Cambridge, City of. Planning Board. "Improvement of Traffic Conditions in Harvard Square." Cambridge, 1920.

Cambridge, City of. Planning Board. "Observations on the Development of the Bennett Street Yards." Cambridge, 1963.

Cambridge, City of. Planning Board. *Post-War Cambridge: Report to the City Council on Post-War Plans.* Cambridge, 1945.

Cambridge, City of. Planning Board. "Proposed Amendment to the Zoning Ordinance of the City of Cambridge." Cambridge, November 1958.

Cambridge, City of. Planning Board. "Zoning for Cambridge." Cambridge, 1920.

Cambridge Hospital, The. "Dedication of the Cambridge Hospital, April 29, 1886." Cambridge, 1886.

Cambridge Women's Heritage Project. Database of women and women's organizations. http://www2.cambridgema.gov/Historic/CWHP/.

Chadbourne, Christopher, and François Vigier. "Development in the Harvard Square Overlay District." Harvard University, Graduate School of Design. Cambridge, February 10, 1984.

Chamberlain, Gen. Joshua L., LLD. *Harvard University: Its History, Influence, Equipment and Characteristics.* Boston, 1900.

Chamberlain, Joseph. "The First Church in Cambridge, Congregational: Some Events in Its Life." *Cambridge Historical Society Publications* 43 (1980): 111–26.

Channing, Katherine Minot. *Minot Family Letters, 1773–1871.* Sherborn, Mass., 1957.

Charles River Railway. *Charles River Railway vs. Union & Cambridge Railroads.* Boston, 1882.

Chase, Philip Putnam. "Some Cambridge Reformers in the Eighties." *Cambridge Historical Society Publications* 20 (1934): 24–52.

Chase, Theodore. "Harvard Student Disorders in 1770." *The New England Quarterly* 61, no. 1 (March 1988): 25–54.

City Realty Company. "Coolidge Hill." Cambridge, n.d.

Clapp, James F. Jr. "Gore Hall Design as related to me by H.J. Vose." Shepley Bulfinch archives, n.d.

Clarke, John Spencer. *The Life and Letters of John Fiske.* Boston, 1917.

Clifford, Ann. "Notes on Lewisville and the Lewis Family in Cambridge." Unpublished paper for the Cambridge Historical Commission, 1999.

Coburn, Frederick William. "From Stagecoach to Subway." *Harvard Graduate's Magazine* 20, no. 78 (December 1911).

Cole, Doris. *Eleanor Raymond, Architect.* Philadelphia, 1981.

Committee Appointed by the President of Harvard University at the Request of the Mayor of Cambridge. "The Future Development of Harvard Square." Cambridge, 1913.

Cook, George E., ed. *The Cambridge Annual for 1887.* Boston, 1887.

Coolidge, John P., and Arthur D. Trottenberg. "Harvard Architecture Before the Bar." *Harvard Alumni Bulletin* (November 7, 1964).

Coolidge, Julian. "Lawrence Lowell, President." *Cambridge Historical Society Publications* 34 (1954): 7–18.

Coolidge, Rosamond. "The History of Coolidge Hill." *Cambridge Historical Society Publications* 32 (1949): 96–103.

Cooney, Sharon. "The Harvard Riverside Associates." Unpublished paper for the Cambridge Historical Commission, August 1990.

Cooney, Sharon. "Private Dormitories in Cambridge." Unpublished paper for the Cambridge Historical Commission, October 1990.

Cooney, Sharon. "Social Clubs at Harvard." Unpublished paper for the Cambridge Historical Commission, October 1990.

Cooperative Open-Air School, Shady Hill Square, Cambridge, Massachusetts [prospectus for 1919–20].

Coquillette Daniel R., and Bruce A. Kimball. *On the Battlefield of Merit: Harvard Law School, the First Century.* Cambridge, 2015.

Craigie, Andrew, Papers. American Antiquarian Society.

Cram, Ralph Adams. "Noteworthy Houses by Well-Known Architects." *The House Beautiful* 46 (September 1919).

Crane, Edward A. "Observations on Cambridge City Government Under Plan E." *Cambridge Historical Society Publications* 44 (1985): 87–103.

Cresson, Margaret French. *Journey into Fame: The Life of Daniel Chester French.* Cambridge, 1947.

Cromley, Elizabeth Collins. *Alone Together, A History of New York's Early Apartments.* Ithaca, 1990.

Crothers, Mrs. Samuel McChord. "Reminiscences of Cambridge." *Cambridge Historical Society Publications* 31 (1948): 7–21.

Cubbison, Diane. "Impact of the Cambridge Subway on Housing and Business Development in Cambridge, Arlington and Belmont." Unpublished paper for the Cambridge Historical Commission, 1985.

Cummings, Abbott Lowell. *The Framed Houses of Massachusetts Bay, 1625–1725.* Cambridge, 1979.

Cushing, Thomas. "Almost A Riot." *Harvard Graduates' Magazine* 8, no. 29 (September 1899).

Cushman, Esther Lanman. "Where the Old Professors Lived." *Cambridge Historical Society Publications* 42 (1978): 14–30.

Cutting, Nathaniel. "Extracts from the Diary of Nathaniel Cutting." *Proceedings of the Massachusetts Historical Society, 1871–1873.* Boston, 1873.

Dall, Caroline. *In memoriam, Alexander Wadsworth.* Washington, D.C., 1898.

Dana, Henry Wadsworth Longfellow. "Allston at Harvard, 1796–1800." *Cambridge Historical Society Publications* 29 (1948): 13–33.

Dana, Henry Wadsworth Longfellow. "Chronicles of the Craigie House: The Coming of Longfellow." *Cambridge Historical Society* Publications 25 (1939): 19–60.

Dana, Henry Wadsworth Longfellow. "The Dana-Palmer House." *Cambridge Historical Society Publications* 33 (1949–1950): 7–36.

Dana, Richard Henry Jr. *The Journal of Richard Henry Dana Jr.* Edited by Robert F. Lucid. Cambridge, 1968.

Dankers, Jaspar, and Peter Sluyter. *Journal of a Voyage to New York and a Tour of Several American Colonies in 1679–1680.* Brooklyn, 1867.

Daughters of the American Revolution, Hannah Winthrop Chapter. *An Historic Guide to Cambridge.* Cambridge, 1907.

Day, Gardiner M. *The Biography of a Church.* Cambridge, 1951.

Degou, David. *Cambridge Police Department.* Charleston, S.C., 2009.

DeRagon, Lionel, and Arlene (McNamee) DeRagon. *John McNamee's Union Marble and Granite Works, 1858–1905.* Privately printed, 2005.

DeVoto, Bernard. "Hell's Half Acre, Mass." *Harper's Magazine* 211, no. 1264 (September 1955).

Dixon, John Morris. "Yesterday's Paradigm, Today's Problem." *Progressive Architecture* (June 1994).

Dowling, Linda. *Charles Eliot Norton: The Art of Reform in Nineteenth Century America.* Durham, N.H., 2007.

Drake, Samuel Adams. *Historic Fields and Mansions of Middlesex.* Boston, 1874.

Duberman, Martin. *James Russell Lowell.* Boston, 1966.

Dudley, Laura Howland. "Thomas Dudley, Founder of Cambridge." *Cambridge Historical Society Publications* 30 (1944): 28–47.

Dwight, Timothy. *Travels in New-England and New-York.* Edited by Barbara Miller Solomon. Originally published New Haven, 1821–23. Cambridge, 1969.

Edelstein, Tilden G. *Strange Enthusiasms: A Life of Thomas Wentworth Higginson.* New Haven, 1968.

Egerton, Hugh Edward, ed. *The Royal Commission on the Losses and Services of the American Loyalists, 1783 to 1785.* New York, 1971.

Electric Railway Journal. "The Cambridge Subway." *Electric Railway Journal* 39, no. 19 (May 11, 1912).

Electric Railway Journal. "Recent Improvements of the Boston Elevated System." *Electric Railway Journal* 41, no. 10 (March 8, 1913).

Electrical World. "Use of Electricity in the Construction of the Cambridge Subway." *Electrical World* 56 (July 28, 1910).

Eliot, Charles. Papers. Loeb Library, Harvard Graduate School of Design.

Eliot, Charles W. "The Agassiz House on Quincy Street." *Harvard Alumni Bulletin* 19, no. 26 (March 29, 1917): 492–95.

Eliot, Charles W. *Charles Eliot, Landscape Architect.* Boston, 1902.

Eliot, Charles W. *Harvard Memories.* Cambridge, 1923.

Eliot, Charles W. 2nd. "Around the Top of the Hill: Houses and Neighbors." *Cambridge Historical Society Publications* 43 (1980): 7–31.

Eliot, Samuel Atkins (1798–1862). *A Sketch of the History of Harvard College.* Boston, 1848.

Eliot, Samuel Atkins (1862-1950). "All Aboard the 'Natwyethum.'" *Cambridge Historical Society Publications* 28 (1943): 35–54.

Eliot, Samuel Atkins (1862-1850). *A History of Cambridge, Massachusetts.* Cambridge, 1913.

Eliot, Thomas H. *Two Schools in Cambridge, The Story of Browne & Nichols and Buckingham.* Cambridge, 1982.

Ellis & Andrews. Correspondence, 1910–1926. Cambridge Historical Commission.

Ellis, George. "Memoirs of Nathaniel Thayer." *Publications of the Colonial Society of Massachusetts* 2 (1886). Series 2.

Emerson, Edward Waldo. *Early Years of the Saturday Club: 1855–1870.* Boston, 1919.

Emerson, Ralph Waldo. *Journals of Ralph Waldo Emerson, 1820–1872.* Boston, 1909–14.

Emerson, William. *Dairies and Letters of William Emerson, 1743–1776, Minister of the Church in Concord, Chaplain in the Revolutionary Army.* Arranged by Amelia Forbes Emerson, 1972.

Enebuske, Sarah McKean Folsom. "Charles Folsom and the McKeans." *Cambridge Historical Society Publications* 25 (1939): 97–112.

Episcopal Theological School. "A Statement of the Trustees of the Episcopal Theological School, Cambridge, Mass." Cambridge, 1873.

Everett, Edward. "An Oration delivered at Cambridge on the Fiftieth Anniversary of the Declaration of Independence of the United States of America." Boston, 1826.

Falb, Karen Forslund. *Cultural Landscape Report for the Hooper-Lee-Nichols House Site.* Cambridge, 2004.

Farlow, Mrs. William G. "Quincy Street in the Fifties." *Cambridge Historical Society Publications* 17 (1931): 27–45.

Fielding, Henry. *The History of John The Orangeman.* Boston, 1892.

First Baptist Church. *A Brief History of the First Baptist Church in Cambridge.* Cambridge, 1870.

[First Parish in Cambridge]. *An Account of the Controversy in the First Parish in Cambridge 1827–1829.* Boston, 1829.

[First Parish in Cambridge]. *Controversy Between the First Parish in Cambridge and The Rev. Dr. Holmes, Their Late Pastor.* Cambridge, 1829.

First Parish in Cambridge. *In the Matter of a New Meetinghouse.* Boston, 1900.

First Parish in Cambridge. *Report on the Connection at Various Times Existing Between the First Parish in Cambridge and Harvard College.* Cambridge, 1851.

Fiske, John. *The Letters of John Fiske.* New York, 1940.

Fiske, John, Papers, 1850–1901. Huntington Library.

Floyd, Margaret Henderson. *Architecture After Richardson.* Chicago, 1994.

Floyd, Margaret Henderson. *Architectural Education and Boston: Centennial Publication of the Boston Architectural Center, 1889–1989.* Boston, 1989.

Floyd, Margaret Henderson. *Henry Hobson Richardson, A Genius for Architecture.* New York, 1997.

Floyd, Margaret Henderson. *Historic Structure Report on the Replacement of the Tower Roof, Memorial Hall, Harvard University.* [Cambridge], September 22, 1995.

Fogg Art Museum. *Edward Waldo Forbes, Yankee Visionary.* Cambridge, 1971.

Follet, Jean. "The Hotel Pelham: A New Building Type for America." *American Art Journal* 15 (Autumn 1983): 58–73.

Forbes, Abner. *The Rich Men of Massachusetts.* Boston, 1852.

Forbes, Allan. *Ebenezer Francis (1775–1858): Including a Final Report of the Trustees.* Francis Real Estate Trust, 1946.

Forbes, Edward Waldo. "The Agassiz School." *Cambridge Historical Society Publications* 35 (1955): 35–51.

Ford, James, and Katherine Morrow Ford. *The Modern House in America.* New York, 1940.

Fowler, Frances. "Kirkland Place." *Cambridge Historical Society Publications* 23 (1935): 76–94.

Francis, Convers. *An Historical Sketch of Watertown from the First Settlement of the Town to the Close of Its Second Century.* Cambridge, 1830.

Francis, Mark. "Urban Impact Assessment and Community Involvement: The Case of the John Fitzgerald Kennedy Library." *Environment and Behavior* 7, no. 3 (September 1975).

Fraser, Esther Stevens. "The John Hicks House." *Cambridge Historical Society Publications* 20 (1934): 110–24.

Fresh Pond Parkway Realty Company. "Larchwood in Old Cambridge." Cambridge, n.d.

Friedman, Karen. "Victualling Colonial Boston." *Agricultural History* 47, no. 3 (July 1973).

Frothingham, Paul Revere. *Edward Everett, Orator and Statesman.* Boston, 1925.

Frothingham, Richard Jr. *The History of Charlestown, Massachusetts.* Boston, 1845.

Garrett, Wendell. *Apthorp House, 1760–1960.* Cambridge, 1960.

Gatell, Frank Otto. *John Gorham Palfrey and the New England Conscience.* Cambridge, 1963.

Gilman, Arthur, ed. *The Cambridge of Eighteen Hundred and Ninety-Six.* Cambridge, 1896.

Gilman, Arthur, ed. *Theatrum majorum. The Cambridge of 1776 … with which is incorporated the diary of Dorothy Dudley, now first published; together with an historical sketch.…* Cambridge, 1876.

Gilman, Roger. "Victorian Houses of Old Cambridge." *Cambridge Historical Society Publications* 26 (1941): 37–48.

Gilman, Roger. "Windmill Lane to Ash Street." *Cambridge Historical Society Publications* 31 (1948): 22–36.

Goldman, Guido. *A History of the Germanic Museum at Harvard University.* Cambridge, 1989.

Goodwin, William Warren. *Memoir of Henry Warren Torrey, LL.D.* Cambridge, 1894.

Gould, Benjamin Jr., and Joseph Winlock. "Cloverden Observatory and the Shelby Equatorial." *Proceedings of the American Association for the Advancement of Science* 8 (May 1854): 83–88.

Gozzaldi, Mary Isabella. "The Bates-Dana House." *Cambridge Historical Society Publications* 20 (1934): 60–62.

Gozzaldi, Mary Isabella. "A Child in a New England Colonial Garden." *Cambridge Historical Society Publications* 31 (1948): 37–43.

Gozzaldi, Mary Isabella. "Elmwood and its Owners." *Cambridge Historical Society Publications* 15 (1929): 41–45.

Gozzaldi, Mary Isabella. "Extracts from the Reminiscences of Isabella (Batchelder) James." *Cambridge Historical Society Publications* 23 (1937): 49–61.

Gozzaldi, Mary Isabella. "A Few Old Cambridge Houses." *Cambridge Historical Society Publications* 6 (1920): 17–26.

Gozzaldi, Mary Isabella. "Gerry's Landing and Its Neighborhood." *Cambridge Historical Society Publications* 13 (1927): 81–88.

Gozzaldi, Mary Isabella. "The Hooper-Lee-Nichols House." *Cambridge Historical Society Publications* 16 (1930): 18–20.

Gozzaldi, Mary Isabella. "Lieutenant George Inman." *Cambridge Historical Society Publications* 17 (1931): 46–79.

Gozzaldi, Mary Isabella. "The Ruggles-Fayerweather House." *Cambridge Historical Society Publications* 17 (1931): 54–59.

Gozzaldi, Mary Isabella. "Some Letters from Tory Row." *Cambridge Historical Society Publications* 9 (1923): 5–37.

Gozzaldi, Mary Isabella. *Supplement and Index* [to Lucius Paige, *History of Cambridge* 1630–1877]. Cambridge, 1930.

Gozzaldi, Mary Isabella, Elizabeth Dana, and David T. Pottinger. "The Vassall House." *Cambridge Historical Society Publications* 21 (1935): 78–118.

Grady, Anne, and Sarah J. Zimmerman. "The Hooper-Lee-Nichols House." Unpublished paper for Boston University Historic Preservation Studies Program, 1981.

Gras, N.S.B. *Harvard Co-operative Society Past and Present, 1882–1942.* Cambridge, 1942.

Graustein, Jeannette E. "Natural History at Harvard College, 1788–1842." *Cambridge Historical Society Publications* 38 (1960): 69–86.

Gray, Roland. "The William Gray House in Cambridge." *Cambridge Historical Society Publications* 14 (1928): 104–6.

Green, James D. *Remarks on the Connection of the City of Cambridge with the Cambridge Water Works.* Cambridge, 1858.

Greene, Jerome D. *Exemption from Taxation.* Boston, 1910.

Greenough, Hamilton Perkins. *Some Descendants of Captain William Greenough of Boston, Mass.* Santa Barbara, privately printed, 1969.

Greenough, Henry, and Frances Boott Greenough. Letters. Archives of American Art-Smithsonian Institution.

Gruskin, Nancy. *Building Context: The Personal and Professional Life of Eleanor Raymond, Architect (1887–1989).* Ann Arbor, 1997.

Hail, Christopher. *Cambridge Buildings and Architects.* Cambridge, 2001.

Hales, John G. *A Survey of Boston and its Vicinity, Showing the Distances from the Old State House … to All the Towns and Villages Not Exceeding Fifteen Miles Therefrom …* Boston, 1821.

Hall, David D. *A Reforming People: Puritanism and the Transformation of Public Life in New England.* New York, 2011.

Hall, Edwin Herbert. "Historical Sketch of Charitable Societies in Cambridge." *Cambridge Historical Society Publications* 17 (1931): 11–26.

Hall, Max. "Cambridge As Printer and Publisher." *Cambridge Historical Society Publications* 44 (1985): 63–83.

Hammond, Mason. "The Enclosure of Harvard Yard." *Harvard Library Bulletin* 31, no. 4 (Fall 1983).

Handlin, Oscar. *Boston's Immigrants.* New York, 1969.

Harris, Richard. "The Birth of the North American Home Improvement Store." *Enterprise & Society* 10, no. 4 (July 2009): 687–728.

Harris, William Thaddeus. *Epitaphs from the Old Burying-Ground in Cambridge.* Cambridge, 1845.

Harvard College. *Class Reports.* Cambridge, various years.

Harvard Divinity School. *Foundations for a learned ministry: catalogue of an exhibition on the occasion of the one hundred seventy-fifth anniversary of the Divinity School, Harvard University.* Cambridge, 1992.

Harvard Law School Association. *The Centennial History of the Harvard Law School.* [Cambridge], 1918.

Harvard Square Business Men's Association. *Bulletin of the Harvard Square Business Men's Association.* April 1911–.

Harvard Square Business Men's Association. *Report of Committee on Future Development of Harvard Square.* Cambridge, 1913.

Harvard University. *Annual Report of the President of Harvard College to the Overseers on the State of the University for the Academic Year…* [1825–1877]. Harvard University Archives.

Harvard University. *Annual Reports of the President and Treasurer of Harvard College …* [1877–1929]. Harvard University Archives.

Harvard University. *Education, Bricks and Mortar: Harvard Buildings and Their Contribution to the Advancement of Learning.* Cambridge, 1949.

Harvard University. *Growth and Change at Harvard: Ten Years in Statistical Summary.* Cambridge, 1964.

Harvard University. *Harvard University and Radcliffe College in Cambridge.* Cambridge, n.d., ca. 1971.

Harvard University. "List of Boarding and Lodging Houses." [Cambridge], 1901 and 1905.

Harvard University. "Notes on Harvard College: Graphic and Statistical." Cambridge, 1955.

Harvard University. "Notes on the Harvard Tercentenary." Cambridge, 1936.

Harvard University. *Preliminary Report of the Committee on the University and the City.* Cambridge, 1968.

Harvard University. "President's letter to the Harvard Community on Allston Planning." October 21, 2003.

Harvard University. *A Program for Harvard College: Three Announcements.* New York, February 13, 1957.

Harvard University. *Quinquennial Catalogue of the Officers and Graduates,* 1636–1930. Cambridge, 1930.

Harvard University. Records relating to the sloop Cyrus, 1793–1798, and the sloop Harvard, 1801–1827. Harvard University Archives.

Harvard University. *Report of the Office of Government & Community Affairs.* June 1976.

Harvard University. *Report to the Cambridge Community from the Office of Government and Community Affairs.* Cambridge, October 1972.

Harvard University. *Reports and Letterbooks of the Treasurer,* 1678–1990. Harvard University Archives.

Harvard University. *Reports of the President and the Treasurer of Harvard College …* 1903–1929. Harvard University Archives.

Harvard University. *Venture for American Education: The Current Crisis and a Program for Harvard College*. Cambridge, [1957].

Harvard University. College Papers. Harvard University Archives.

Harvard University. Corporation Records. Harvard University Archives.

Harvard University. Harvard College Records. *Publications of the Colonial Society of Massachusetts* 15 (1925).

Harvard University. Office of the President. *The University and the City*. Cambridge, 1969.

Harvard University. Planning Office. *Harvard University 1960, An Inventory for Planning*. Cambridge, 1960.

Harvard University. Planning Office. *A Long Range Plan for Harvard University and Radcliffe College in Cambridge and Allston*. Cambridge, 1974.

Harvard University. Planning Office. *Long Range Planning Inventory, Policies, and Recommendations, 1975: Harvard University and Radcliffe College, Cambridge and Allston*. Cambridge, 1975.

Harvard University. School of Architecture. Alumni Association. *First Report of the Alumni in Architecture of Harvard University, 1932*. Cambridge, 1932.

Hastings, Lewis M. "The Streets of Cambridge." *Cambridge Historical Society Publications* 14 (1926): 31–78.

Hay, Ida. *Science in the Pleasure Ground: A History of the Arnold Arboretum*. Boston, 1995.

Hayden, Dolores. *The Grand Domestic Revolution*. Cambridge, 1981.

Hayward, James. *Report of the Survey of the Roads in Cambridge*. Cambridge, 1838.

Herring, James, ed. "A Sketch of the Life of Jared Sparks." *The National Portrait Gallery of Distinguished Americans*. New York, 1834–39.

Higginson, Mary Thacher. *Thomas Wentworth Higginson, The Story of His Life*. Boston, 1914.

Higginson, Thomas Wentworth. *Cheerful Yesterdays*. Boston, 1898.

Higginson, Thomas Wentworth. *Old Cambridge*. New York, 1899.

Hilgenhurst, Charles G. & Associates. *Harvard Square Development Alternatives*. Boston, October 1975.

Hill, Frederick. *Charles F. McKim, The Man*. Francestown, N.H., 1950.

Hill, Thomas. Letters from Thomas Hill to Family, 1821–1827. Harvard University Archives.

Hillard, George Stillman. "Memoir of Cornelius Conway Felton, LL.D." Reprint from *Proceedings of the Massachusetts Historical Society for 1867–1869*. Cambridge, 1869.

Hillard, George Stillman. *Memoir of James Brown*. Boston, 1856.

Hirshson, Paul. "The Death of Harvard Square." *Boston Sunday Globe Magazine*. December 6, 1987.

Hitchcock, Henry-Russell, and Philip Johnson. *The International Style: Modern Architecture since 1922*. New York, 1932.

Hodges, Maud deLeigh. *Crossroads on the Charles: A History of Watertown, Massachusetts*. Canaan, N.H., 1980.

Holden, Wheaton. "The Peabody Touch: Peabody & Stearns of Boston, 1870–1917." *Journal of the Society of Architectural Historians* 32, no. 2 (May 1973).

Hollister, Susan. "Rare Species Identified: A Discussion of the Life and Work of Hartley Dennett." Unpublished paper, 1985.

Holmes, Abiel. "A Description of Cambridge, in Middlesex County." Manuscript, not before 1816.

Holmes, Abiel. *The History of Cambridge*. Boston, 1801.

Holmes, Abiel. "Memoir of Cambridgeport," appended to a sermon on the ordination of Reverend Thomas B. Gannett. January 19, 1814.

Holmes, John. "Cambridge." *History of Middlesex County, Massachusetts*. Edited by D. Hamilton Hurd. Philadelphia, 1890.

Holmes, John. "Harvard Square." *The Harvard Book*. Edited by F.O. Vaille and H.A. Clark. Cambridge, 1875.

Holmes, John. *Letters of John Holmes to James Russell Lowell and Others*. Edited by William Roscoe Thayer. Boston, 1917.

Holmes, Oliver Wendell. "The Gambrel-Roofed House and Its Outlook." *Poetic Localities of Cambridge*. Edited by W. J. Stillman. Boston, 1876.

Holmes, Oliver Wendell. *A Mortal Antipathy* (1886). Cambridge, 1981.

Holton, Gerald. "How the Jefferson Physical Laboratory Came to Be." *Physics Today* (December 1984).

Homans, J. Smith. *Sketches of Boston Past and Present*. Boston, 1851.

Hoppin, The Reverend Nicholas. *A Sermon on the Re-opening of Christ Church, Cambridge, Mass*. Boston, 1858.

Horton, James Oliver, and Lois E. Horton. *Black Bostonians: Family Life and Community Struggle in the Antebellum North*. New York, 1979.

Howe, Archibald Murray. "The State Arsenal and the Identification of the Cannon on the Cambridge Common." *Cambridge Historical Society Publications* 6 (1920): 5–15.

Howe, Lois Lilley. *Details of Old New England Houses, Measured and Drawn by Lois L. Howe and Constance Fuller.* New York, 1913.

Howe, Lois Lilley. "Dr. Estes Howe: A Citizen of Cambridge." *Cambridge Historical Society Publications* 25 (1939): 122–141.

Howe, Lois Lilley. "Harvard Square in the Seventies and Eighties." *Cambridge Historical Society Publications* 30 (1944): 11–27.

Howe, Lois Lilley. "The History of Garden Street." *Cambridge Historical Society Publications* 33 (1953): 37–57.

Howe, Lois Lilley. "Memories of Nineteenth-century Cambridge." *Cambridge Historical Society Publications* 34 (1952): 59–76.

Howe, Lois Lilley. "A Problem in Remodeling." *The House Beautiful* (January 1916).

Howe, Lois Lilley. Howe, Manning & Almy papers, 1883–1973. Massachusetts Institute of Technology. Institute Archives and Special Collections.

Howe, Lois Lilley, and Mrs. Edward S. King. "The Story of a Lost Brook." *Cambridge Historical Society Publications* 31 (1948): 44–60.

Howells, Dorothy Elia. *A Century to Celebrate: Radcliffe College 1879–1979.* Cambridge, 1978.

Howells, William Dean. *April Hopes.* New York, 1887.

Howells, William Dean. *Suburban Sketches.* Boston, 1875.

Hurd, D. Hamilton, ed. *History of Middlesex County, Massachusetts, with Biographical Sketches of Many of Its Prominent Men.* Philadelphia, 1890.

Huthmacher, J. Joseph. *Massachusetts People and Politics, 1919–1933.* Cambridge, 1959.

Hyman, Isabelle. "Marcel Breuer and the Franklin Delano Roosevelt Memorial." *Journal of the Society of Architectural Historians* 54, no. 4 (December 1995): 455.

Jackson, Allen W. *Building the half-timber house; its origin, design, modern plan, and construction, illustrated with photographs of old examples and American adaptations of the style.* New York, 1929.

Jackson, Allen W. "The Alterations to the First Parish Church in Cambridge, Mass." *Architecture* 31, no. 4 (April 1915): 112–16.

Jacobus, John M. *Philip Johnson.* New York, 1962.

James, Henry (1843–1916). *The Bostonians* (1886). New York, 1991.

James, Henry (1879–1947). *Charles W. Eliot.* Boston, 1930.

Johnson, Edward. *Wonder-working Providence of Sions Saviour in New England* (London, 1654). Introduction by William Frederick Poole. Andover, Mass., 1867.

Johnson, Philip. *Mies van der Rohe.* New York, 1947.

Jones, Bessie Z., and Lyle Gifford Boyd. *The Harvard College Observatory.* Cambridge, 1971.

Jones, E. Alfred. *The Loyalists of Massachusetts: Their Memorials, Petitions and Claims.* London, 1930.

Josselyn, John. *Colonial Traveler: A Critical Edition of Two Voyages to New England.* Edited by Paul J. Lindholdt. Hanover, N.H., 1988.

Kenney, Michael. "The Long-Ago Squadrons of Cambridge." Unpublished paper for Cambridge Historical Commission, 2015.

Keogh, Robert. "A New Lease: How Rent Control is Transforming One Block in Cambridge." *Boston Globe Magazine* (March 1, 1998).

Kermes, Stephanie. "'I wish for nothing more ardently upon earth, than to see my friends and country again': The Return of Massachusetts Loyalists." *Historical Journal of Massachusetts* 30, no. 1 (Winter 2002).

King, Moses. *Cambridge Vest-Pocket Guide.* Cambridge, 1883.

King, Moses. *Hand Book of Cambridge and Mount Auburn.* Cambridge, 1883.

King, Moses. *Harvard and Its Surroundings.* Cambridge and Boston, 1878, 1880, 1882, 1883, and 1886.

Kirker, Harold. *The Architecture of Charles Bulfinch.* Cambridge, 1969.

Koch, Carl. *At Home with Tomorrow.* New York, 1958.

Koocher, Glenn. "The Never-Boring Political History of Cambridge in the Twentieth Century." *A City's Life and Times: Cambridge in the Twentieth Century.* Edited by Daphne Abeel. Cambridge Historical Society. Cambridge, 2007.

Kutler, Stanley I. *Privilege and Creative Destruction: The Charles River Bridge Case.* Philadelphia, 1971.

Kyper, Frank. "T Launches Massive Red Line Extension." *New England Construction* (December 24, 1979).

LaMond, Annette. "Allen W. Jackson: Cambridge Architect." Cambridge [2015].

LaMond, Annette. *A History of the Cambridge Skating Club, 1897–2001.* Cambridge, 2002.

LaMond, Annette. "A Portrait of a 125-Year Friendship: The Arnold Arboretum and the Cambridge Plant & Garden Club." Cambridge, [2014].

Land, W.G., ed. *Harvard University Handbook: An Official Guide.* Cambridge, 1936.

Lancaster, Southworth. "Fire in Cambridge." *Cambridge Historical Society Publications* 36 (1957): 75–92.

Lane, William Coolidge. "The Building of Holworthy Hall." *Cambridge Historical Society Publications* 7 (1921): 63–69.

Lane, William Coolidge. "The Building of Massachusetts Hall, 1717–1720." Reprinted from *The Publications of the Colonial Society of Massachusetts*, vol. 24. Cambridge, 1920.

Lane, William Coolidge. "Dr. Benjamin Waterhouse and Harvard University." *Cambridge Historical Society Publications* 4 (1918): 5–22.

Lane, William Coolidge. "Nehemiah Walter's Elegy on Elijah Corlet." *Cambridge Historical Society Publications* 2 (1916): 13–20.

Lawrence, Bishop William. *Memories of a Happy Life.* Boston, 1936.

Lawrence, Bishop William. *Seventy-three Years of the Episcopal Theological School, Cambridge.* Cambridge, 1940.

Lewis, Paul J. "The Historical Development of Cambridge Common." *Cambridge Historical Society Publications* 43 (1973–75): 67–82.

Linden-Ward, Blanche. *Silent City on a Hill: Landscapes of Memory and Boston's Mount Auburn Cemetery.* Columbus, Ohio, 1989.

Lindgren, James M. *Preserving Historic New England.* New York, 1995.

Little, Arthur. *Early New England Interiors: Sketches in Salem, Marblehead, Portsmouth and Kittery.* Boston, 1878.

Little, Brown & Co. *One Hundred and Fifty Years of Publishing 1837–1987.* Boston, 1987.

Livermore, Isaac. *An Account of Some of the Bridges Over the Charles River.* Cambridge, 1858.

Longfellow, Henry Wadsworth. *The Letters of Henry Wadsworth Longfellow.* Edited by Andrew Hilen. Cambridge, 1982.

Loring, William. "The Residential Population of Cambridge." Cambridge, 1957.

Lotman, Mo. *Harvard Square: An Illustrated History Since 1950.* New York, 2009.

Lovett, Robert W. "The Harvard Branch Railroad, 1849–1855." *Railway & Locomotive Historical Society Bulletin* 113 (October 1965).

Lowe, Charles U. "The Forbes Story of the Harvard Riverside Associates: How Harvard Acquired the Land on which Lowell House Was Built." http://lowell.harvard.edu/land-which-lowell-was-built. [Cambridge, 2002]

Lowell, James Russell. "Cambridge Thirty Years Ago." *Fireside Travels.* Boston, 1864.

Lowell, James Russell. *Letters of James Russell Lowell.* Edited by Charles Eliot Norton. Boston, 1904.

Lurie, Edward. *Louis Agassiz: A Life in Science.* Baltimore, 1988.

Maas, David Edward. *The Return of the Massachusetts Loyalists.* New York, 1989.

MacLeod, William G. *The Dunvegan and Montrose.* Cambridge, 1899.

Maguire, Mary Hume. "The Curtain-Raiser to the Founding of Radcliffe College." *Cambridge Historical Society Publications* 38 (1961): 23–39.

Makechnie, George K. *Optimal Health: The Quest, A History of Boston University's Sargent College of Allied Health Professions.* Boston, 1979.

Marchione, William. *Allston-Brighton in Transition: From Cattle Town to Streetcar Suburb.* Charleston, S.C., 2007.

Marchione, William. *The Bull in the Garden: A History of Allston-Brighton.* Boston, 1986.

Mason, R.M. *A Sketch of the Life of the Late Ebenezer Francis of Boston.* New York, 1859.

Massachusetts Committee for the Preservation of Architectural Records. *Boston Architects and Builders, Compiled from the Boston Directory, 1749–1846.* Cambridge, 1989.

Massachusetts Committee for the Preservation of Architectural Records. *Directory of Boston Architects, 1846–1970.* Cambridge, 1984.

Massachusetts, Commonwealth of. *An Act to Establish the City of Cambridge.* Boston, 1846.

Massachusetts, Commonwealth of. *Opinion of the Supreme Judicial Court… in Relation to the Cambridge Common.* Boston, 1835.

Massachusetts, Commonwealth of. *Report of the Commission on Metropolitan Improvements.* Boston, 1909.

Massachusetts, Commonwealth of. *Report of the Joint Board … Upon the Improvement of the Charles River*. Boston, 1894.

Massachusetts, Commonwealth of. *Report Relating to the Enclosure of Cambridge Common*. Senate Documents No. 23. Boston, February 21, 1832.

Massachusetts, Commonwealth of. *Report Submitted to the Legislative Research Council Relative to the Establishment of Historic Districts Within the Commonwealth*. Boston, 1957.

Massachusetts, Commonwealth of. Joint Board for Metropolitan Master Highway Plan. *The Master Highway Plan for the Boston Metropolitan Area*. Boston, 1948.

Massachusetts, Commonwealth of. Metropolitan Park Commission. [*Annual Reports*]. Boston, 1894–1921.

Massachusetts, Commonwealth of. Metropolitan Park Commission. *Report of the Board of Metropolitan Park Commissioners, House No. 150*. Boston, 1893.

Massachusetts, Commonwealth of. Special Commission on the Charles River Basin. *Report on Proposed Improvements of the Charles River Basin*. Boston, January 2, 1929.

Massachusetts Bay, Province of. *Register of All Ships and Vessels*, vol. 3, 1697–1714.

Massachusetts Society for Promoting Agriculture. Trustee Records. Massachusetts Historical Society.

May, Ralph. "The Cambridge Boat Club." *Cambridge Historical Society Publications* 39 (1964): 125–43.

Mayo, Lawrence Shaw. *The Winthrop Family in America*. Boston, 1948.

McAlester, Virginia, and Lee McAlester. *A Field Guide to American Houses*. New York, 1984.

McCaughey, Robert A. *Josiah Quincy, 1772–1864: The Last Federalist*. Cambridge, 1974.

McIndoe, Heather. "Jacob Hill Bates, 1788–1861." Unpublished paper for the Cambridge Historical Commission, 1991.

McKenzie, Alexander. *Lectures on the History of the First Church in Cambridge*. Boston, 1873.

Meany, Eileen G. "The Avon Home." *Cambridge Historical Society Publications* 38 (1961): 121–29.

Meister, Maureen. *Architecture and the Arts and Crafts Movement in Boston: Harvard's H. Langford Warren*. Hanover, N.H., 2003.

Meister, Maureen. "An Uncommonly Good Design: H. Langford Warren's 1906 Drawings for a Proposed Press at Harvard." *Harvard Library Bulletin* 16, no. 4 (Winter 2005): 45–65.

Merrill, Joshua. "Sketch of the Life of Benjamin Pierce." *Contributions of the Old Residents Historical Association, Lowell, Mass.* 3 (1887): 1–12.

Meyer, Anne A. "Benjamin Waterhouse, An American Medical Doctor and Scientist." Unpublished paper, January 2001.

Mock, Elizabeth. *Built in USA, 1932–1944*. New York, 1944.

Monacelli Associates. *Harvard Square Planning and Design Analysis*. Cambridge, May 1976.

Monacelli Associates. "Investigations in Urban Design." Cambridge, 1974.

Moore, L.E. "The Cambridge Subway." *Engineering News* 67, no. 5 (February 1, 1912).

Moore, Mrs. James Lowell. "The Fayerweather House." *Cambridge Historical Society Publications* 25 (1939): 86–94.

Moran, Susan Drinker. *Gathered in the Spirit: Beginnings of the First Church in Cambridge*. Cleveland, 1995.

Morgan, Keith N. "Held in Trust: Charles Eliot's Vision for the New England Landscape." *National Association of Olmsted Parks Workbook* 1 (1991).

Morison, Samuel Eliot. *The Development of Harvard University Since the Inauguration of President Eliot, 1869–1929*. Cambridge, 1930.

Morison, Samuel Eliot. *The Founding of Harvard College*. Cambridge, 1935.

Morison, Samuel Eliot. "The Great Rebellion in Harvard College, and the Resignation of President Kirkland." *Publications of the Colonial Society of Massachusetts* 37 (1929).

Morison, Samuel Eliot. "Restoration of Old College." *Old Time New England* 72.

Morison, Samuel Eliot. *Three Centuries of Harvard*. Cambridge, 1936.

Muller, James Arthur. *The Episcopal Theological School 1867–1943*. Cambridge, 1943.

Murphy, Reverend Francis V. *St. Peter's Church, Cambridge, Massachusetts, One Hundred Years 1848–1948*. Cambridge, 1948.

Museum of Modern Art. *Modern Architecture: International Exhibition, Museum of Modern Art, February 10 to March 23, 1932*. New York, 1932.

Muzzey, Henry W. "Argument Before the Joint Committee on Street Railways of the Legislature, February 3, 1871." In Foster M. Palmer, "Horse Car, Trolley, and Subway." *Cambridge Historical Society Publications* 39 (1964): 78-107.

National Archives and Records Administration. Certificates of Registry, Enrollment, and License [of vessels] Issued at Boston, Massachusetts 1801–28.

Nathans, Sydney. *To Free a Family: The Journey of Mary Walker*. Cambridge, 2012.

Neighborhood Ten Association. *Cambridge, Harvard Square, and the Kennedy Memorial*. Cambridge, 1974.

Neighborhood Ten Association. *Newsletter*. Cambridge, 1979–83.

New England Brick Co. "The Great Building Program of Harvard, Creator of Precedents." *The Brick Kiln* (October-December 1930): 1–21.

New England Brick Co. "Harvard Brick, Too, Has a History." *The Brick Kiln* (October-December 1930): 22–31.

Newell, William. *The Christian Citizen: A Discourse Occasioned by the Death of Charles Beck, LL.D. Delivered March 25, 1866 Before the First Parish in Cambridge*. Cambridge, 1866.

Norris, Dr. Albert P. "Cambridge Land Holdings Traced from the Proprietors Records of 1635." *Cambridge Historical Society Publications* 22 (1933): 58–79.

Norton, Andrews. *A Collection of the Miscellaneous Writings of Professor Frisbie with Some Notices of his Life and Character*. Boston, 1823.

Norton, Andrews, Papers, 1768–1890. Harvard University Archives.

Norton, Charles Eliot. "Harvard University in 1890." *Harper's New Monthly Magazine* 81, no. 484 (September 1890): 581 -92.

Norton, Charles Eliot. "Reminiscences of Old Cambridge." *Cambridge Historical Society Publications* 1 (1915): 11-23.

Norton, Charles Eliot, Papers. Houghton Library, Harvard University.

Noyes, Penelope Barker. "From Lover's Lane to Sparks Street." *Cambridge Historical Society Publications* 41 (1970): 156–70.

O'Gorman, James F. *H.H. Richardson: Architectural Forms for an American Society*. Chicago, 1987

O'Gorman, James F. *Isaiah Rogers: Architectural Practice in Antebellum America*. Amherst, Mass., 2015.

Okamoto/Liskamm, Inc. *Final Preliminary Report: Harvard Square Development Area*. San Francisco, 1968.

Olmsted Associates. Records of the Olmsted Associates, 1863–1971. Library of Congress.

Olmsted, Frederick Law Jr. "Harvard and the Charles River." *Harvard Graduates' Magazine* 7, no. 26 (December 1898).

O'Malley, Thomas Francis. "Gallows Hill, the Ancient Place of Execution." *Cambridge Historical Society Publications* 17 (1931): 46–53.

Osterby-Benson, Krisan. "Longfellow Memorial Park: A Room With a View." Unpublished paper, 1983.

Paige, Lucius R. *History of Cambridge, 1630–1877*. Cambridge, 1877.

Palfrey, John G. *A Discourse on the Life and Character of the Reverend Henry Ware, D.D., A.A.S., Late Hollis Professor of Divinity in the University of Cambridge*. Pronounced in the First Church of Cambridge, September 28, 1845. Cambridge, 1845.

Palfrey, John G. "Notice of Professor Farrar." Boston, 1853.

Palfrey, John G., Palfrey Family Papers. Houghton Library, Harvard University.

Palfrey, John G., Papers. Harvard University Archives.

Palmer, Foster M. "Horse Car, Trolley and Subway." *Cambridge Historical Society Publications* 39 (1964): 78–107.

Parsons, William Barclay. *Report on the Location of Stations of the Boston-Cambridge Subway*. Unpublished typescript. N.Y., May 16, 1907.

Paterson, Stanley C., ed. "The Five of Clubs: Henry Wadsworth Longfellow and His Friends." Unpublished transcription of Longfellow diaries and correspondence [vol. I], 1836–50. Nahant, Mass., 1997.

Paterson, Stanley C., ed. "'The Second Act of Life's Drama': Longfellow and His Friends." Unpublished transcription of Longfellow diaries and correspondence [vol. II], 1850–61. Nahant, Mass., 1997.

Patterson, Bryan. "Louis Agassiz and the Founding of the Museum of Comparative Zoology." *Cambridge Historical Society Publications* 43 (1980): 53–65.

Patterson, L.G. "History and Guide to St. John's Chapel." Cambridge, 1978.

Peabody, Andrew Preston. *Harvard Graduates Whom I Have Known*. Boston, 1890.

Peabody, Andrew Preston. *Harvard Reminiscences*. Boston, 1888.

Peabody, Francis G. *Harvard in the Sixties: A Boy's Eye View.* Cambridge, 1935.

Peabody, Robert S. "Georgian Homes of New England." *American Architect & Building News* 2 and 3 (October 1877 and January 1878).

Peabody, Robert S. "A Talk About `Queen Anne.'" *American Architect & Building News* 2 (April 1877).

Peabody, W. Rodman. "The Browne and Nichols School." *Cambridge Historical Society Publications* 22 (1937): 105–12.

Pearlman, Jill. *Inventing American Modernism: Joseph Hudnut, Walter Gropius and the Bauhaus Legacy at Harvard.* Charlottesville, Va., 2007.

Peirce, Augustus. *The Rebelliad; or, Terrible Transactions at the Seat of the Muses, a Poem in Four Cantos.* Boston, 1842.

Perry, Bliss. *Richard Henry Dana, 1851–1931.* Boston, 1933.

Perry, Lilla Cabot, Perry Family Papers. Archives of American Art-Smithsonian Institution.

Petrone, Ann. "16 Chauncy Street, Cambridge, Massachusetts." Cambridge, 2010.

Pinanski, A. E. *The Street Railway System of Metropolitan Boston.* New York, 1908.

Piper, Elizabeth B. "Memories of the Berkeley Street School." *Cambridge Historical Society Publications* 32 (1949): 30–48.

Pizzo, Charlene. "MBTA's Red Line Northwest Extension." *Tunneling Technology* 44 (December 1983).

Porter, Kenneth Wiggins. "The Oxford Cap War at Harvard." *The New England Quarterly* 14, no. 1 (March 1941): 77–83.

Porter, Lucy Kingsley. "The Owners of Elmwood." *Cambridge Historical Society Publications* 33 (1953): 58–93.

Pottinger, David T. "Thirty-Eight Quincy Street." *Cambridge Historical Society Publications* 23 (1937): 24–48.

Power, Ethel B. *The Smaller American House: Fifty-five Houses of the Less-Expensive Type Selected from the Recent Work of Architects in All Parts of the Country.* Boston, 1927.

Pratt, Frederick Haven. "The Craigies." *Cambridge Historical Society Publications* 27 (1942): 43–86.

Process: Architecture. *TAC: The Heritage of Walter Gropius.* Tokyo, October 1980.

Proell, Rosalba Peale Smith. "Notes on Sparks Street." *Cambridge Historical Society Publications* 22 (1937): 49–57.

Pusey, Nathan M. *Cambridge and Harvard.* Cambridge, 1959.

Quinan, Jack. "The Transformation of an Asher Benjamin house." *The Magazine Antiques* (August 1982): 288–92.

Quincy, Josiah. *Figures of the Past.* Boston, 1896.

Quincy, Josiah. *The History of Harvard University.* Boston, 1860.

Rand, Christopher. *Cambridge, U.S.A.* New York, 1964.

Read, William. *First Parish in Cambridge, In the Matter of a New Meeting-House.* Boston, 1900.

Reeves, James Arthur. "Looking Backward." *The Browne & Nichols Bulletin* (March 1959).

Reinhardt, Elizabeth W. "Lois Lilley Howe, F.A.I.A., 1864–1964." *Cambridge Historical Society Publications* 43 (1980): 153–72.

Reps, John W. *The Making of Urban America, A History of City Planning in the United States.* Princeton, 1965.

Rettig, Robert B. *Guide to Cambridge Architecture: Ten Walking Tours.* Cambridge, 1969.

Reynolds, Deborah. "The Harvard Square Business Association: The Past Seventy-Five Years." Unpublished paper for the Cambridge Historical Commission, 1985.

Rhoads, William B. *The Colonial Revival.* New York, 1977.

Rice, Lewis. "Cambridge v. Allston." *Harvard Law Bulletin* 20 (Summer 2002).

Riedesel, Mrs. General Friedrich Adolf [Baroness Frederika Charlotte Luise Riedesel]. *Letters and Journals Relating to the War of the American Revolution.* (Reprint of 1867 edition). Translated by William L. Stone. Gansevoort, N.Y., 2001.

Robinson, Harriet J.H. *Massachusetts in the Woman Suffrage Movement.* Boston, 1881.

Rodgers, Patricia H. "Lake View Avenue: Early History, Architecture, and Residents." *Cambridge Historical Society Publications* 44 (1985): 159–69.

Roper, Laura Wood. *FLO: A Biography of Frederick Law Olmsted.* Baltimore, 1973.

Ross, Miriam I. "Planning Powers of Massachusetts Departments." *Journal of Social Forces* 2, no. 1 (November 1923).

Roth, Leland M. *McKim, Mead & White Architects*. New York, 1983.

Russell, Charles Theodore Jr., ed. *Speeches and Addresses of William E. Russell*. Boston, 1894.

Russell, Foster W. *Mount Auburn Biographies*. Cambridge, 1953.

Ryan, Father John J. *St. Paul's Church*. Cambridge, 1924.

Saint Peter's Parish. "Service Flag Exercises, March 17, 1918." Cambridge, 1918.

Saunders, William A. "The Old Menotomy Road Before it was modernized, From General Ward's Head Quarters on June 17th, 1775 to the Ancient Tavern, Northerly, and return to the Camp Ground of 1775." Handwritten manuscript, 1875. Cambridge Historical Society.

Schlesinger, Marian Cannon. *I Remember: A Life of Politics, Painting and People*. Cambridge, 2012.

Schlesinger, Marian Cannon. *Snatched from Oblivion*. Cambridge, 1979.

Schmertz, Mildred. "Getting Ready for the John F. Kennedy Library: Not Everyone Wants to Make It Go Away." *Architectural Record* (December 1974).

Schulze, Franz. *Philip Johnson: Life and Work*. New York, 1994.

Scott, Mel. *American City Planning Since 1890*. Berkeley, 1971.

Scudder, Horace. *Henry Oscar Houghton*. Boston, 1897.

Scudder, Horace. "St. George's Company." *The Atlantic Monthly* 42, no. 249 (July 1878).

Scudder, Winthrop S. *The Longfellow Memorial Association, 1882–1922*. Cambridge, 1922.

Scully, Vincent. *The Shingle Style and the Stick Style: Architectural Theory and Design from Richardson to the Origins of Wright*. New Haven, 1971.

Sert, Josep Lluis. "Harvard—Urban Problem and Opportunity." *Harvard Today* (November 1957).

Sert, Josep Lluis. "Introduction to the Urban Design Conference," April 9, 1956. Loeb Library, Harvard Graduate School of Design, Sert Archives D92.

Sewell, Jonathan, and Family *Fonds*. Library and Archives Canada. Manuscripts Division. MG23 GII10. Vol. 14 (1650–1788): 7627–37.

Shurtleff, Nathaniel B. *A Topographical and Historical Description of Boston*. Boston, 1871.

Shurtleff, Nathaniel B., ed. *Records of the Governor and Company of Massachusetts Bay, Printed by Order of the Legislature*. 5 vols. Boston, 1853.

Sibley, John Langdon. *Sibley's Private Journal, 1846–1882*. Edited by Brian A. Sullivan. http://hul.harvard.edu/lib/archives/refshelf/Sibley.htm.

Sibley, John Langdon, Clifford Kenyon Shipton, and Conrad Edick Wright. *Biographical Sketches of Graduates of Harvard University, in Cambridge, Massachusetts*. Vols. 1–18, 1873–1999.

Simpson, Lewis P. "'The Intercommunity of the Learned': Boston and Cambridge in 1800." *The New England Quarterly* 23, no. 4 (December 1950): 491–503.

Simpson, Sophia S. *Two Hundred Years Ago; or, a Brief History of Cambridgeport and East Cambridge*. Boston, 1859.

Sinclair, Jill. *Fresh Pond: The History of a Cambridge Landscape*. Cambridge, 2009.

Skidmore, Owings & Merrill. *Environmental Impact Report on Mixed Use Development of Parcel 1B, Harvard Square*. Boston, September 1981.

Sleeper, Moses. "Diary of a Revolutionary War Soldier." Transcribed by Frances Dickerson Ackerly. Friends of the Longfellow House. Cambridge, n.d.

Sparks, Jared. College letters. Vol. 3, 1849–53. Harvard University Archives.

Stachiw, Myron. "Culture Change in 19th Century Cambridge, Mass.: The Cooper-Frost-Austin House and Its Occupants." Unpublished paper, 1979.

Stark, James H. *The Loyalists of Massachusetts and the Other Side of the American Revolution*. Boston, 1910.

Steele, Chauncey Depew Jr. "A History of Inns and Hotels in Cambridge." *Cambridge Historical Society Publications* 37 (1959): 29–44.

Stevens, Levi Merriam. *Guide Through Mount Auburn, A Hand-Book for Passengers over the Cambridge Railroad*. Boston, 1859 (eighth edition, 1867).

Stillman, W.J. *Poetic Localities of Cambridge*. Boston, 1876.

Stone, Edward Durell. *The Evolution of an Architect*. New York, 1962.

Stone, Orra. *History of Massachusetts Industries: Their Inception, Growth and Success*. Boston, 1930.

Stone, William E. "A Petition of Dr. Daniel Stone, March 4, 1672/3, and Some Account of His Family and Ancestors." *Cambridge Historical Society Publications* 7 (1921): 70–77.

Story, Joseph. "An Address Delivered at the Dedication of the Cemetery at Mount Auburn, September 24, 1831." Boston, 1831.

Story, Ronald. *Harvard and the Boston Upper Class: The Forging of an Aristocracy, 1800–1870*. Middletown, Conn., 1980.

Sturges, Walter Knight. "Arthur Little and the Colonial Revival." *Journal of the Society of Architectural Historians* 32, no. 2 (May 1973).

Sturgis, R. Clipston. "Sir Christopher Wren." *Journal of the American Institute of Architects* 11, no. 3 (1923).

Tharp, Louise Hall. *Adventurous Alliance: The Story of the Agassiz Family in Boston*. Boston, 1959.

Thayer, William Roscoe. "Extracts from the Journal of Benjamin Waterhouse." *Cambridge Historical Society Publications* 4 (1909): 22–37.

Thompson, Roger. *Cambridge Cameos: Stories of Life in Seventeenth-Century New England*. Boston, 2005.

Thornton, Tamara Plakins. *Cultivating Gentlemen: The Meaning of Country Life Among Boston's Elite, 1785–1860*. New Haven, 1989.

Thwing, Walter Eliot. *The Livermore Family in America*. Boston, 1902.

Townsend, Kim. *Manhood at Harvard*. New York, 1996.

Trautman, Patricia Anne. *Captain Edward Marrett: A Gentleman Tailor*. Ann Arbor, Mich., 1983.

Treadwell, Daniel, Papers. Harvard University Archives.

Turner, James. *The Liberal Education of Charles Eliot Norton*. Baltimore, 1999.

Tyack, David B. *George Ticknor and the Boston Brahmins*. Cambridge, 1967.

United Kingdom. Public Record Office. American Loyalist Claims. Audit Office classes 12 and 13, Series I and II.

U.S. Department of the Interior. *Final Report of the Boston National Historic Sites Commission*. Washington, D.C., 1961.

U.S. Department of the Interior. National Park Service. *Cultural Landscape Report for Longfellow National Historic Site*, Vol. 1: Site History and Existing Conditions. Boston, 1993.

U.S. Department of the Interior. National Park Service. *Cultural Landscape Report for Longfellow National Historic Site*, Vol. 2: Analysis of Integrity and Significance. Boston, 1998.

U.S. Department of the Interior. National Park Service. *Cultural Landscape Report for Longfellow National Historic Site*, Vol. 3: Treatment. Boston, 1997.

U.S. Department of Transportation. Urban Mass Transportation Administration. *Final Environmental Impact Statement, Red Line Extension, Harvard Square to Arlington Heights*. 3 vols. September 1977.

U.S. General Services Administration. *Draft Environmental Impact Statement for the John F. Kennedy Library*. Washington, D.C., 1975.

Updike, D.B. *The Harvard Boathouse Memorial*. Boston, 1928.

Vaille, F.O., and H.A. Clark, eds. *The Harvard Book: A Series of Historical, Biographical and Descriptive Sketches by Various Authors*. Cambridge, 1875.

Vanderbilt, Kermit. *Charles Eliot Norton: Apostle of Culture in a Democracy*. Cambridge, 1959.

Varg, Paul A. *Edward Everett: The Intellectual in the Turmoil of Politics*. Selinsgrove, Penn., 1992.

von Mehren, Joan. *Minerva and the Muse: A Life of Margaret Fuller*. Amherst, 1994.

Vosburgh, Maude B. "The Disloyalty of Benjamin Church, Jr." *Cambridge Historical Society Publications* 30 (1945): 48–71.

Vose, George L. "A Sketch of the Life and Works of Loammi Baldwin, Civil Engineer." Read before the Boston Society of Civil Engineers, September 16, 1885. Boston, 1885.

Walcott, Charles F. "Changes in Bird Life in Cambridge, Massachusetts from 1860 to 1964." *The Auk* 91 (January 1974): 151–60.

Walcott, Dr. Henry P. "Some Cambridge Physicians." *Cambridge Historical Society Publications* 16 (1930): 110–31.

Walter, Cornelia W. *Mount Auburn Illustrated in Highly Finished Line Engraving, from Drawings Taken on the Spot by James Smillie*. New York, 1847.

Ware, John. *Memoir of the Life of Henry Ware, Jr.* Boston, 1946.

Ware, William Rotch. *The Georgian period; a collection of papers dealing with "colonial" or XVIII-century architecture in the United States, together with references to earlier provincial and true colonial work*. Boston, 1899–1902.

Warnecke, John C., and Robert Hart. Interview by Tom Page. "The President Selects His Library Site: Report at the White House; The Visit to Harvard; The President's Views on Architecture." December 4, 1963.

White, Norman Hill Jr. "Printing in Cambridge Since 1800." *Cambridge Historical Society Publications* 15 (1931): 16–23.

Whiting, Charles F. "Francis Avenue and the Norton Estate: The Development of a Community." *Cambridge Historical Society Publications* 41 (1967–69): 16–39.

Wilder, Catherine F. "Eighty-five Aromatic Years in Harvard Square." *Cambridge Historical Society Publications:* 41 (1970): 105–16.

Willard, Joseph. "Reminiscences of John Bartlett." *Cambridge Historical Society Publications* 1 (1915): 68–77.

Willard, Sidney. *Memories of Youth and Manhood*. Cambridge, 1855.

Williams, Carroll M. *The Jubilee of the Harvard Biological Laboratories*. Cambridge, 1982.

Wills, Jeffrey. *The Catholics of Harvard Square*. Petersham, Mass., 1993.

Wilson, James Q. "The University and the City: the Wilson Report." *Harvard Alumni Bulletin* 71 (February 3, 1969): 7.

Wines, E.C. *A Trip to Boston, in a series of letters to the editor of the* United States Gazette. Boston, 1838.

Winslow, Ola. *A Destroying Angel: The Conquest of Smallpox in Colonial Boston*. Boston, 1874.

Winsor, Justin, ed. *The Memorial History of Boston*. Boston, 1880.

Winthrop, John. *The History of New England from 1630 to 1649*. Boston, 1853.

Winthrop, John. *The Journal of John Winthrop, 1630–1649*. Edited by James Savage, Richard S. Dunn, and Laetitia Yeandle. Cambridge, 1996.

Withey, Henry F., and Elsie R. Withey. *Biographical Dictionary of American Architects*. Los Angeles, 1970.

Wood, William. *New-Englands Prospect*. [London, 1634]. Publications of The Prince Society. Boston, 1865.

Works Progress Administration. National Archives Project. Ship Registers and Enrollments for Boston and Charlestown, 1789–1795. Boston, 1942.

Wright, George Grier. "The Schools of Cambridge, 1800–1870." *Cambridge Historical Society Publications* 13 (1925): 89–112.

Wyman, Morrill Jr. *A Brief Record of the Lives and Writings of Dr. Rufus Wyman and Dr. Morrill Wyman*. Cambridge, 1913.

Yeomans, Edward. *The Shady Hill School: The First Fifty Years*. Cambridge, 1979.

Yeomans, Henry A. *Abbott Lawrence Lowell*. Cambridge, 1948.

Young, Alexander. *Chronicles of the First Planters of the Colony of Massachusetts Bay From 1623 to 1636*. Boston, 1846.

Zaitzevsky, Cynthia. *The Architecture of William Ralph Emerson, 1833–1917*. Cambridge, 1969.

Zaitzevsky, Cynthia. "Paul R. Frost of Cambridge: An Introduction to His Life and Work." *Journal of the New England Garden History Society* 2 (Fall 1992).

Zobel, Hiller B. "Jonathan Sewall: A Lawyer in Conflict." *Cambridge Historical Society Publications* 40 (1967): 123–36.

Pattern Books

Benjamin, Asher. *The American builder's companion: or, A system of architecture, particularly adapted to the present style of building; illustrated with seventy copperplate engravings*. Boston, 1827.

Benjamin, Asher. *The builder's guide: or, Complete system of architecture*. Boston, 1838.

Benjamin, Asher. *The country builder's assistant: containing a collection of new designs of carpentry and architecture which will be particularly useful to country workmen in general*. Greenfield, Mass., 1797.

Benjamin, Asher. *The practical house carpenter. Being a complete development of the Grecian orders of architecture*. Boston, 1830.

Benjamin, Asher. *Practice of architecture. Containing the five orders of architecture and an additional column and entablature, with all their elements and details explained and illustrated, for the use of carpenters and practical men*. Boston, 1833.

Benjamin, Asher, and Daniel Raynard. *The American builder's companion, or, A new system of architecture: particularly adapted to the present style of building in the United States of America*. Boston, 1806.

Campbell, Colen. *Vitruvius Britannicus; or, The British architect*. First published, London, 1715–25. New York, 1967–72.

Davis, Alexander Jackson, and other architects. *Rural residences: consisting of designs, original and selected, for cottages, farm-houses, villas, and village churches, with brief explanations, estimates, and a specification of materials, construction, etc*. First published 1837. New York, 1980.

Downing, Andrew Jackson. *The architecture of country houses: including designs for cottages, farm houses, and villas, with remarks on interiors, furniture, and the best modes of warming and ventilating*. New York, 1859.

Downing, Andrew Jackson. *Cottage residences: or, a series of designs for rural cottages and cottage-villas, and their gardens and grounds, adapted to North America.* New York, 1842, 1856 (fourth edition).

Gibbs, James. *A book of architecture, containing designs of buildings and ornaments.* London, 1728.

Hills, Chester. *The builder's guide. A practical treatise on Grecian and Roman architecture, together with specimens of the Gothic style … Revised and improved, with additions of villa and school house architecture, by H. Austin and H. Barnard.* Hartford, 1847.

Holly, Henry Hudson. *Modern dwellings in town and country adapted to American wants and climate.* New York, 1878.

Lafever, Minard. *The modern builders' guide.* New York, 1833 and 1846.

Langley, Batty. *The city and country builder's and workman's treasury of designs; or, The art of drawing and working the ornamental parts of architecture … To which are prefixed, the five orders of columns, according to Andrea Palladio.* London, 1756.

Palladio, Andrea. *The four books of Andrea Palladio's architecture: Wherein, after a short treatise of the five orders, those observations that are most necessary in building, private houses, streets, bridges, piazzas, xisti, and temples are treated of.* London, 1738.

Shaw, Edward. *Rural architecture: consisting of classic dwellings, Doric, Ionic, Corinthian and Gothic, and details connected with each of the orders; embracing plans, elevations parallel and perspective, specifications, estimates, framing, etc. for private houses and churches.* Boston, 1843.

Shaw, Edward. *The modern architect: or, Every carpenter his own master; embracing plans, elevations, specifications, framing, etc., for private houses, classic dwellings, churches, &c. to which is added a new system of stair-building.* Boston, 1854.

Sheldon, George W. *Artistic Country-Seats: Types of Recent American Villa and Cottage Architecture.* First published 1886–87. New York, 1979.

Stuart, James, and Nicholas Revett. *Antiquities of Athens.* London, 1762–1816.

Woodward, George E. *Woodward's architecture and rural art.* New York, 1868.

CREDITS

CHAPTER 1

Frontispiece: Library of Congress. Lt. John Hills, "Boston, with the surroundings, &c.," n.d., detail

1.1 Edwin Raisz, "Map of Boston, Cambridge and Their Environs in the Seventeenth Century," in Morison, *The Founding of Harvard College*

1.2 Image © The British Library Board. John Winthrop, "A chart of Boston and its vicinity, Massachusetts Bay; drawn on a scale of 2 1/3 Italian miles, by estimation, to an inch," n.d.

1.3 Courtesy of Massachusetts Archives

1.4 CHC. Robert H. Nylander

1.5 CHC. Robert H. Nylander

1.6 F.O. Vaille and H.A. Clark, eds., *The Harvard Book,* vol. II, 22

1.7 CHC. Charles Sullivan photo

1.8 CHC. Robert H. Nylander

1.9 Houghton Library, Harvard University, *AC6.E1452.663m. John Eliot, *Mamusse wunneetupanatamwe Up-Biblum God naneeswe Nukkone Testament kah wonk Wusku Testament. Ne quoshkinnumuk nashpe Wuttinneumoh Christ noh asoowesit* (Cambridge, 1663), title page

1.10 CHC

1.11 CHC. MapWorks

1.12 CHC. Robert H. Nylander

1.13 Bibliotheque Nationale de France. Jean-Baptiste Louis Franquelin, "Carte de la Ville, Baye, et Environs de Baston …" 1693, detail

1.14 Courtesy of Massachusetts Archives. "Land in Charlestown and Watertown whose owners wish to be set off to Cambridge," 1754, detail, rotated and cropped for clarity

1.15 CHC. Robert H. Nylander

1.16 Harvard University Archives, UAI 15.740 pf. ["Plan of Cambridge town."], n.d., retouched for clarity

1.17 Harvard University Archives, HUC 8782.514 no. 60, olvwork371815. William Boyd, "A North East View of The House of Samuel Webber, A.A.S, and of The Court House in Cambridge"

1.18 CHC. Photo © 1976 Steve Rosenthal

1.19 CHC. MapWorks. Based on predictive archeology map prepared by Robert H. Nylander with the support of a grant from the Massachusetts Historical Commission

1.20 Harvard Art Museums/Fogg Museum, Gift of Catherine Coolidge Lastavica, M.D., 2004.219. Katya Kallsen photo © President and Fellows of Harvard College. *Ralph Inman*, by Robert Feke

1.21 Harvard Art Museums/Fogg Museum, Gift of Catherine Coolidge Lastavica, M.D., 2004.220. Katya Kallsen photo © President and Fellows of Harvard College. *Susannah Speakman Inman*, by Robert Feke

1.22 CHC. Photo © 1976 Steve Rosenthal

1.23 Harvard University Archives, HUC 8782.514 no. 203. William A. Warner, "A Perspective Representation of Craigie's House," mathematical thesis, 1815

1.24 Boston Athenæum. *Massachusetts Magazine,* July 1792

1.25 Courtesy of Historic New England, Digital ID# rs2051. Halliday Photograph Company photo

1.26 Courtesy of Dr. Philip G. Levendusky. Image provided by Meredith Tufts, Coldwell-Banker Realty, Manchester, Mass.

1.27 Courtesy of Harvard Map Collection, Cambridge, Mass. Henry Pelham, "A plan of Boston in New England with its environs including Milton, Dorchester, Roxbury, Brooklin [sic], Cambridge, Medford, Charlestown, parts of Malden and Chelsea with the military works constructed in those places in the years 1775 and 1776" (London, 1777)

1.28 New York Public Library/Alden Lenox and Tilden Foundations, Spencer Collection. Archibald Robertson, "A View of the Country from the Town of Boston … taken from the Epaulement of the Citadel at Charles Town [sheet A]," January 4, 1776

1.29 New York Public Library/Alden Lenox and Tilden Foundations, Spencer Collection. Archibald Robertson, "A View of the Country from the Town of Boston … taken from the Epaulement of the Citadel at Charles Town [sheet B]," January 4, 1776

1.30 Detail of figure 1.29

1.31 Susannah S. Simpson, *Two Hundred Years Ago, or, a Brief History of Cambridgeport and East Cambridge*, frontispiece

1.32 Harvard University Archives, HUV 2180. Charles Warren, "View of the Colleges &c at Cambridge," ca. 1780–81

CHAPTER 2

2.1 Harvard University Archives, HUV 2196. Andrew Croswell (class of 1798), "A view of Harvard College without title"

2.2 Robert Gilmor, "Memorandums Made in a Tour to the Eastern States in the Year 1797," in *Boston Public Library Historical Manuscripts and Reprints, no. 2* (1892) and *Cambridge Historical Society Publications* 16 (1931): opp. 84

2.3 Library of Congress. Historic American Buildings Survey. Frank O. Branzetti photo

2.4 Cambridge Engineering Department

2.5 Daguerreotype courtesy of Matthew R. Isenburg

2.6 CHC. John G. Hales, "Plan of Cambridge from Survey Taken in June 1830," additions by CHC

2.7 CHC. Cambridge Chamber of Commerce collection

2.8 Private collection, courtesy of Hirschl & Adler Galleries

2.9 Courtesy of Neal Auction Company, New Orleans, La. *Francis Dana*, by James Sharpless Jr.

2.10 Merrill Department of Rare Books and Special Collections, Franklin Trask Library, Andover Newton Theological School. *Deacon Levi Farwell*, artist and date unknown but before 1875. Charles Sullivan photo

2.11 Merrill Department of Rare Books and Special Collections, Franklin Trask Library, Andover Newton Theological School. *Prudence Farwell*, artist and date unknown but before 1875. Charles Sullivan photo

2.12 Cambridge Historical Society. Harvard Class Album, 1862. George K. Warren photo

2.13 Boston Athenæum. [*Porter's Station, Cambridge, Mass.*], hand-colored lithograph, n.d.

2.14 Harvard Law School Library, Historical & Special Collections. *Dane Law-School, Cambridge, Mass.* Artist, lithographer, and publisher unknown

2.15 CHC. S.N. Dickinson, "Map of the Vicinity of Boston engraved for *The Boston Guide Book*" (Boston, 1848)

2.16 Edward Waldo Emerson, *Early Years of the Saturday Club: 1855–1870* (Boston, 1919)

2.17 National Geographic Creative. Kets Kemethy photo

2.18 Cambridge Historical Society

2.19 Courtesy of Harvard Map Collection, Cambridge, Mass. H.F. Walling, *Map of the City of Cambridge, Middlesex County, Massachusetts* (Boston, 1854)

2.20 CHC

2.21 Cambridge Historical Society

2.22 CHC. Stereographic view, C.W. Woodward (Rochester, N.Y.)

2.23 CHC. Gift of Dwayne Warren, 1996

2.24 CHC. J.G. Chase, "Rail Road Map showing the Street Rail Road Routes in and leading to Boston" (Boston, 1865)

2.25 Courtesy of National Park Service, Longfellow House-Washington's Headquarters National Historic Site. N. Vautin, untitled watercolor

2.26 Courtesy of National Park Service, Longfellow House-Washington's Headquarters National Historic Site

2.27 Cambridge Historical Society

2.28 "Cambridge in 1824," artist unknown, in Ferris Greenslet, *James Russell Lowell: His Life and Work* (Boston, 1905)

2.29 Courtesy of the Ohio History Connection

2.30 CHC. Robert Sears, *A Pictorial Description of the United States* (New York, 1860), 71

2.31 CHC. Marion Colby collection

2.32 Harvard University Archives, HUPSF Memorial Hall waiters (1a) olvwork361339

2.33 CHC. Roberta Hankamer collection of Lewis family photographs

2.34 CHC. Harry Hansen collection

2.35 Courtesy of Historic New England, Negative #51728-A [Original in Album 215]

2.36 F.O. Vaille and H. A. Clark, eds., *The Harvard Book*, vol. I (Cambridge, 1875)

2.37 CHC. *The Cambridge Chronicle Semi-Centennial Souvenir*, 1896

2.38 CHC. *Cambridge Directory*, 1889: 651

2.39 The Boston Post. *The Boston Post Book of Homes* (Boston, 1925), 97

2.40 CHC

2.41 City of Cambridge. "Zone Map to Accompany Building Code, As Approved January 7, 1924", additions by CHC

2.42 CHC. MapWorks. Based on W.A. Greenough & Co., *Map of the City of Cambridge* (Boston, 1889)

2.43 CHC. Frank Cheney collection

2.44 Courtesy of Historic New England, Digital ID# rs2429

2.45 *Cambridge Chronicle*, Mar. 25, 1905. Horace G. Simpson, delineator

2.46 Library of Congress. Detroit Publishing Co. collection

2.47 Charles W. Eliot, *Charles Eliot, Landscape Architect*, vol. I (Boston, 1903), frontispiece

3.46 CHC. *Boston Evening Transcript*, Sept. 22, 1928

3.47 CHC

3.48 Courtesy of Historic New England, Negative #51608-A [Original in Album 1, Book 5]

3.49 CHC. Charles Sullivan photo

3.50 CHC

3.51 CHC. Richard A. Dow collection

3.52 CHC. Richard A. Dow collection

3.53 CHC. Courtesy of Frank Cheney. Massachusetts Transit Authority photo

3.54 CHC. Paul Corcoran collection. The Marshall Studio photo

3.55 CHC. *The Boston Traveler*, Sept. 30, 1961

3.56 The Schlesinger Library, Radcliffe Institute, Harvard University, LC 52-2-3

3.57 Harvard University Archives, HUV 80 (10-8)

3.58 CHC. Daniel Reiff collection

3.59 CHC. Robert E. Smith collection

3.60 CHC. Rick Stafford photo

3.61 CHC. Lois Bowen collection

3.62 CHC. William L. Galvin collection

3.63 CHC. Staff photo

3.64 CHC. Richard Cheek photo

3.65 CHC

3.66 CHC. *Boston Herald*. Julian Carpenter photo

3.67 The Schlesinger Library, Radcliffe Institute, Harvard University, LC 21-3-2

3.68 CHC. *Boston Herald*

3.69 CHC. Postcard, Plastichrome by Colourpicture Inc. (Boston)

3.70 CHC. Photo May 13, 1976

3.71 CHC. Eastern Aerial Surveys, Inc.

3.72 CHC. G.M. Hopkins, *Atlas of the City of Cambridge, Massachusetts* (Philadelphia, 1873), detail

3.73 CHC. Cambridge Subway scrapbooks. *The Boston Post*, Feb. 15, 1910

3.74 CHC. Cambridge Engineering Department collection, Edward Carney photos, digitally combined by CHC

3.75 Pei Cobb Freed & Partners

3.76 Pei Cobb Freed & Partners. Photo © Thorney Lieberman

3.77 Cambridge Redevelopment Authority. Okamoto/Liskamm, Inc., "View Looking South from Harvard Square Toward Charles River"

3.78 Cambridge Redevelopment Authority. Okamoto/Liskamm, Inc., "Harvard Square Development Area, Section-Elevation Pedestrian Path, Scheme A, Section A-A"

3.79 CHC. Metropolitan District Commission, "Site Plan for the Proposed John Fitzgerald Kennedy Park," December 28, 1983

3.80 CHC. John Landers photo

3.81 Photo © 1984 Steve Rosenthal

3.82 CHC. Patriquin collection

3.83 CHC. Daniel Reiff photo

3.84 *Cambridge Chronicle*, Nov. 23, 1972. Jan Corash photo

3.85 CHC. Hines Industrial, "University Green" [marketing brochure], n.d.

3.86 Photo © 1979 Steve Rosenthal

3.87 CHC. Richard Cheek photo

3.88 CHC. Charles Sullivan photo

3.89 CHC. Charles Sullivan photo

3.90 CHC. Cambridge Planning Board collection

3.91 CHC. Lois Bowen collection

3.92 CHC. Richard Cheek photo

3.93 CHC. Charles Sullivan photo

3.94 CHC. Cambridge Geographic Information System

3.95 CHC. Charles Sullivan photo

CHAPTER 4

4.1 CHC. MapWorks

4.2 Courtesy of Harvard Map Collection, Cambridge, Mass. Henry Pelham, "A plan of Boston in New England …" (London, 1777), detail

4.3 Harvard Art Museums/Fogg Museum. Partial gift of Mrs. Thomas Brattle Gannett and partial purchase through the generosity of Robert T. Gannett, an anonymous donor, and the Alpheus Hyatt Purchasing Fund. Imaging Department photo © President & Fellows of Harvard College. *William Brattle Jr.*, by John Singleton Copley

4.4 Courtesy of Harvard Map Collection, Cambridge, Mass.

4.5 Courtesy of Harvard Map Collection, Cambridge, Mass. Alexander Wadsworth, "Plan of the Village in Old Cambridge" (Boston, Jan. 1833), detail, additions by CHC

4.6 CHC. MapWorks

4.7 Courtesy of National Park Service, Longfellow House-Washington's Headquarters National Historic Site

4.8 *Homes of American Statesmen* (Hartford, 1855)

4.9 Cambridge Historical Society

4.10 CHC. B. Orr photo

4.11 CHC. Charles Sullivan photo

4.12 Courtesy of Boston Public Library, Leslie Jones Collection

4.13 CHC

4.14 CHC. H.F. Walling, *Map of the City of Cambridge, Middlesex County, Massachusetts* (Boston, 1854), detail

4.15 Paul Frost, "A Garden in Cambridge," *House Beautiful* (June 1924)

4.16 Cambridge Historical Society. *Henry Vassall*, attributed to John Single-ton Copley

4.17 Cambridge Historical Society. *Penelope Royall Vassall*, attributed to John Singleton Copley

4.18 Courtesy of Historic New England, Digital ID# rs235101. George K. Warren photo

4.19 CHC. G.W. Bromley & Co., *Atlas of the City of Cambridge* (Philadel-phia, 1916), detail

4.20 CHC. Roger Gilman photo

4.21 Courtesy of National Park Service, Longfellow House-Washington's Headquarters National Historic Site

4.22 CHC. MapWorks

4.23 Robert Sears, *Pictorial History of the American Revolution* (New York, 1846)

4.24 CHC. MapWorks

4.25 Houghton Library, Harvard University, MS Am 1340. Henry Longfel-low, Craigie House journal

4.26 Courtesy of National Park Service, Longfellow House-Washington's Headquarters National Historic Site

4.27 CHC. Bertram Adams photo

4.28 Courtesy of National Park Service, Longfellow House-Washington's Headquarters National Historic Site

4.29 CHC. H.F. Walling, *Map of the City of Cambridge, Middlesex County, Massachusetts* (Boston, 1854), detail

4.30 Cambridge Historical Society

4.31 Cambridge Historical Society

4.32 CHC. Roger Gilman photo

4.33 CHC. G.M. Hopkins, *Atlas of the City of Cambridge, Massachusetts* (Philadelphia, 1873), detail

4.34 CHC. Roberta Hankamer collection of Lewis family photos

4.35 CHC. Dwight Andrews collection

4.36 Middlesex County Registry of Deeds, Plan Book 57: 6. Aspinwall & Lincoln, "Plan of Partition of the Estate of Henry W. Longfellow, October 16, 1888"

4.37 CHC. B. Orr photo

4.38 Courtesy of Harvard Map Collection, Cambridge, Mass. "Plan of the Craigie Estate in Cambridge To Be Sold at Public Auction … June 27, 1850," surveyor unknown

4.39 CHC. G.M. Hopkins, *Atlas of the City of Cambridge, Massachusetts* (Philadelphia, 1873), detail

4.40 CHC. Charles Sullivan photo

4.41 CHC. Charles Sullivan photo

4.42 CHC. B. Orr photo

4.43 CHC. Cambridge Engineering Department collection

4.44 National Geographic Creative. Dr. Gilbert H. Grosvenor photo

4.45 CHC. Edwin F. Bowker, surveyor, "Mercer Circle and Hubbard Park," *Cambridge Tribune Souvenir*, June 1890

4.46 CHC. Roger Gilman photo

4.47 CHC. G.W. Bromley & Co., *Atlas of the City of Cambridge* (Philadel-phia, 1916), detail

4.48 Courtesy of Historic New England, Digital ID# rs2022. Soule Art Company photo

4.49 Courtesy of National Park Service, Longfellow House-Washington's Headquarters National Historic Site

4.50 CHC. H.F. Walling, *Map of the City of Cambridge, Middlesex County, Massachusetts* (Boston, 1854), detail

4.51 CHC

4.52 CHC. MapWorks

4.53 Courtesy of Historic New England, Negative # 15329-B. Album 41-B

4.54 Courtesy of Historic New England, Digital ID# rs231642. Album 41-A

4.55 CHC. Roger Gilman photo

4.56 Collection of Massachusetts Historical Society. Peter Tufts Jr., Manu-script plan of Mr. Joseph Lee's farm [in Cambridge], January 20, 1803

4.57 CHC. Charles Sullivan photo

4.58 Courtesy of Harvard Map Collection, Cambridge, Mass. W.A. Mason & W.A. Barbour, surveyors, "Plan of Land in Cambridge belonging to the Estate of the Late Mrs. Deborah Carpenter to be sold at Public Auction May 16, 1861"

4.59 CHC. G.M. Hopkins, *Atlas of the City of Cambridge, Massachusetts* (Philadelphia, 1894), detail

4.60 CHC. B. Orr photo

4.61 Courtesy of Historic New England, Digital ID# rs32525. Peter Har-holdt photo

4.62 Courtesy of Edward Kania family. Charles Sullivan photo

4.63 Courtesy of Harvard Map Collection, Cambridge, Mass. Alexander Wadsworth, "Plan of a Part of Cambridge Showing the Location of the Fayerweather Estate" (Boston, 1852)

4.64 CHC. Ed James photo

4.65 CHC. G.M. Hopkins, *Atlas of the City of Cambridge, Massachusetts* (Philadelphia, 1873), detail

4.66 CHC. Charles W. Eliot 2nd collection

4.67 *Cambridge, Mass., Busy and Beautiful,* 19

4.68 Courtesy of Stephen Jerome

4.69 Charles W. Eliot 2nd, "Around the Top of the Hill: Houses and Neigh-bors," Cambridge Historical Society Publications, 43 (1980): 16

4.70 CHC. Cambridge Planning Board collection

4.71 CHC. Courtesy of Al Hamel

4.72 CHC. Ellis & Andrews collection

4.73 *Cambridge Sentinel Industrial Supplement,* July 1924

4.74 CHC. Cambridge Engineering Department collection

4.75 Courtesy of Historic New England, Digital ID# rs233339

4.76 Courtesy of Harvard Map Collection, Cambridge, Mass. Henry Pelham, "A Plan of Boston in New England with its environs …" (London, 1777), detail

4.77 CHC. MapWorks

4.78 CHC. G.W. Bromley & Co., *Atlas of the City of Cambridge* (Philadelphia, 1916), detail

4.79 CHC. Staff photo

4.80 Middlesex County Registry of Deeds, Plan Book 19-B: 62

4.81 CHC

4.82 Courtesy of Deborah Fennimore, C. Brendan Noonan Realty

4.83 CHC. G.W. Bromley & Co., *Atlas of the City of Cambridge* (Philadelphia, 1916), detail

4.84 CHC. Charles Sullivan photo

4.85 Courtesy of Historic New England, Digital ID# rs209727

4.86 CHC. *Boston Traveler,* Oct. 19, 1945

4.87 Cambridge Historical Society

4.88 CHC. G.M. Hopkins & Co., *Atlas of the City of Cambridge, Massachusetts* (Philadelphia, 1886), detail

4.89 CHC. Courtesy of Carola Govansky

4.90 CHC. Charles Sullivan photo

4.91 CHC. Charles Sullivan photo

4.92 CHC. G.W. Bromley & Co., *Atlas of the City of Cambridge* (Philadelphia, 1916), detail

4.93 *Architectural Forum* 26 (1917): 158

4.94 CHC. Cambridge Engineering Department. Cambridge City Engineer, Plan No. 1504

4.95 CHC. Richard Cheek photo

4.96 CHC. Gift of Dr. John C. Coolidge

4.97 Courtesy of Historic New England, Digital ID# rs209781. William Brewster photo

4.98 Cambridge Historical Society

4.99 CHC. G.W. Bromley & Co., *Atlas of the City of Cambridge* (Philadelphia, 1930), detail

4.100 CHC. Richard Cheek photo

4.101 CHC. Cambridge Planning Board collection

4.102 Fanny Winchester Hotchkiss, *Winchester Notes* (New Haven, 1912)

4.103 Library of Congress. "Christ Church, Cambridge, Mass." Artist unknown

4.104 CHC. MapWorks

4.105 CHC. MapWorks

4.106 Courtesy of Historic New England, Negative #51611-A [Original in Album 1, Book 5]

4.107 Courtesy of Harvard Map Collection, Cambridge, Mass. Alexander Wadsworth, "Plan of the Village in Old Cambridge" (Boston, Jan. 1833), detail

4.108 W.J. Stillman, *Poetic Localities of Cambridge* (1876), opp. 23

4.109 CHC. Daniel Reiff photo

4.110 Harvard University Archives, HUV 15 (BP97). View from Memorial Hall tower, detail.

4.111 Justin Winsor, *The Memorial History of Boston,* vol. III (Boston, 1883), 110

4.112 Cambridge Historical Society

4.113 CHC. Stereographic view, Miller & Brown (Boston)

4.114 CHC. *Cambridge Illustrated* (Gardner, Mass., ca. 1889–93)

4.115 CHC. Charles F. Binney, *The History and Genealogy of the Prentice or Prentiss Family in New England from 1631 to 1852* (Boston, 1852), frontispiece

4.116 CHC. Charles Sullivan photo

4.117 CHC. G.W. Bromley & Co., *Atlas of the City of Cambridge* (Philadelphia, 1916), detail

4.118 Harvard University Archives, HUC 8782.514 (96). Charles Saunders, "The Survey of a Tract of Land in Cambridge and a perspective delineation of the Summer house thereon," 1802

4.119 Harvard University Archives, UAI 15.740 pf, 24. William A. Mason, "Plan of Lot Purchased of the Heirs of Dr. Craigie by Harvard University," October 29, 1841

4.120 Harvard University Archives, UAI 15.740 pf, 26. Alexander Wadsworth, "Plan of the Summer House Lot in Cambridge Belonging to Harvard College," December 26, 1842

4.121 Courtesy of Historic New England, Negative #51729-A [Original Album 215]

4.122 CHC. Roger Gilman photo

4.123 Harvard University Archives, HUV 1020 (BP1)

4.124 CHC. Charles Sullivan photo

4.125 CHC. Staff photo

4.126 CHC. G.M. Hopkins, *Atlas of the City of Cambridge, Massachusetts* (Philadelphia, 1873), detail

4.127 Courtesy of James Stoutamire. H. Langford Warren photo

4.128 Courtesy of National Park Service, Frederick Law Olmsted National Historic Site

4.129 Courtesy of National Park Service, Frederick Law Olmsted National Historic Site

4.130 Harvard University Archives, HUV 2208.5, olvwork224077. D. Bell, *Cambridge Common from the Episcopal Church,* ca. 1808–09, detail

4.131 CHC. MapWorks

4.132 CHC. H.F. Walling, *Map of the City of Cambridge, Middlesex County, Massachusetts* (Boston, 1854), detail

4.133 Courtesy of Archives of First Church in Cambridge, Congregational, United Church of Christ

4.134 CHC. Roger Gilman photo

4.135 Harvard University Archives, HUV 1124 (1-5)

4.136 Harvard University Archives, HUV 1124 (1-1B)

4.137 CHC. G.M. Hopkins, *Atlas of the City of Cambridge, Massachusetts* (Philadelphia, 1873), detail

4.138 CHC

4.139 CHC. Frederick Hastings Rindge collection

4.140 CHC. Charles Sullivan photo

4.141 CHC. Courtesy of Charlotte Moore

4.142 CHC. Ed James collection

4.143 W.A. Mason & Son, "Estate of Thomas Stearns formerly Peter Lewis," Middlesex County Registry of Deeds, Plan Book 32, Plan 9, surveyed 1869, recorded 1878

4.144 CHC. Charles Sullivan photo

4.145 CHC. B. Orr photo

4.146 CHC. Charles Sullivan photo

4.147 CHC. Charles Sullivan photo

4.148 CHC. Charles Sullivan photo

4.149 CHC

4.150 [Harvard University Archives]

4.151 The Schlesinger Library, Radcliffe Institute, Harvard University, LC 37-1-6

4.152 CHC. G.W. Bromley & Co., *Atlas of the City of Cambridge* (Philadelphia, 1916), detail

4.153 Courtesy of Historic New England, Digital ID# rs86528. Pencil drawing, artist unknown

4.154 CHC. *Report Five: Northwest Cambridge,* figure 12, detail

4.155 CHC. H.F. Walling, *Map of the City of Cambridge, Middlesex County, Massachusetts* (Boston, 1854), detail

4.156 CHC. G.M. Hopkins, *Atlas of the City of Cambridge, Massachusetts* (Philadelphia, 1873), detail

4.157 CHC. Cambridge Engineering Department collection

4.158 CHC. Charles Sullivan photo

4.159 CHC. Gift of Ellen Spaethling

4.160 CHC

4.161 CHC. Patricia Hollander photo

4.162 CHC. G.M. Hopkins & Co., *Atlas of the City of Cambridge, Massachusetts* (Philadelphia, 1886), detail

4.163 CHC. Charles Sullivan photo

4.164 CHC. W. A. Mason & Son, "Plan of Land in Cambridge, Mass. belonging to the Austin Estate," March 25, 1886

4.165 CHC. Curtis Mellen collection

4.166 CHC. Curtis Mellen collection

4.167 CHC. Laverty-Lohnes collection

4.168 CHC. Roger Gilman photo

4.169 CHC. Gift of S. Bernard Pare

4.170 CHC. *Cambridge Directory,* 1897: 788

4.171 Harvard University Archives, HUV 199 (1-7b)

4.172 Cambridge Historical Society. William A. Saunders collection

4.173 CHC. Courtesy of Frank Buda

4.174 CHC. Chris McAuliffe collection

4.175 CHC. H.F. Walling, *Map of the City of Cambridge, Middlesex County, Massachusetts* (Boston, 1854), detail

4.176 Courtesy of Norman B. Leventhal Map Center, Boston Public Library. W.A. Mason, "Plan of Building Lots and Land in Cambridge and Somerville Belonging to Mr. Ozias Morse" (Boston, 1861), detail

4.177 Cambridge Historical Society

4.178 Courtesy of Historic New England, Copy negative # 7661B. Thomson & Thomson photo

4.179 Courtesy of Historic New England, Copy negative # 15383-B

4.180 CHC. Curtis Mellen collection

4.181 Harvard University Archives, HUV 199 (1-6)

4.182 CHC

4.183 CHC. Boston Elevated Railway collection

4.184 CHC. G.W. Bromley & Co., *Atlas of the City of Cambridge* (Philadelphia, 1894 and 1930), composite image

4.185 CHC. Courtesy of John F. Bromley

4.186 CHC. Charles Sullivan photo

4.187 CHC. Charles Sullivan photo

4.188 CHC. MapWorks

4.189 CHC. United States Coast Survey Office, "Boston Harbor, Massachusetts, from a Trigonometrical Survey by A. D. Bache, Superintendent of the Survey of the coast of the United States" (Washington, D.C., 1857), detail

4.190 Harvard University Archives, HUV 2196.10. Watercolor, ca. 1796, possibly by William Jenks (class of 1797)

4.191 Courtesy of Harvard Map Collection, Cambridge, Mass. Alexander Wadsworth, "Plan of the Village in Old Cambridge" (Boston, Jan. 1833), detail

4.192 CHC

4.193 CHC. Paul Flynn collection

4.194 Cambridge Historical Society

4.195 Courtesy of Harvard Map Collection, Cambridge, Mass. James Hayward, "Mellen Estate Sale, 1847"

4.196 CHC. Gift of Stephen Jerome

4.197 Harvard University Archives, HUV 15_BP 98_01

4.198 CHC. H.F. Walling, *Map of the City of Cambridge, Middlesex County, Massachusetts* (Boston, 1854), detail

4.199 CHC. Staff photo

4.200 CHC. G.W. Hopkins & Co., *Atlas of the City of Cambridge* (Philadelphia, 1873), detail

4.201 CHC. Charles Sullivan photo

4.202 CHC. G.W. Bromley & Co., *Atlas of the City of Cambridge* (Philadelphia, 1894), detail

4.203 CHC

4.204 CHC. *Report Two: Mid Cambridge,* figure 14

4.205 CHC. W.A. Mason, "Plan of Building Lots in Cambridge Belonging to Mr. Charles F. McClure," June 1851

4.206 CHC. Charles Sullivan photo

4.207 CHC. Charles Sullivan photo

4.208 CHC. Cambridge Planning Board collection

4.209 CHC. Cambridge Planning Board collection. Hansen-Cambridge photo

4.210 CHC. G.M. Hopkins, *Atlas of the City of Cambridge, Massachusetts* (Philadelphia, 1873), detail

4.211 Harvard University Archives, HUV15_BP98_01, detail

4.212 CHC. Charles Sullivan photo

4.213 CHC. H.F. Walling, *Map of the City of Cambridge, Middlesex County, Massachusetts* (Boston, 1854), detail

4.214 Middlesex County Registry of Deeds. Gideon Frothingham, "Plan of Land in Cambridge," original survey by Whitney S. Babbitt, June 1858

4.215 CHC. Charles Sullivan photo

4.216 CHC. Curtis Mellen collection

4.217 CHC. B. Orr photo

4.218 CHC. Charles Sullivan photo

4.219 CHC. Cambridge Engineering Department collection. Mason & Barbour, "Plan of Building Lots in Cambridge and Somerville belonging to Ozias Morse and Others," surveyed 1861, digitally reformatted to show correct scale and location of Somerville portion

4.220 CHC. Cambridge Engineering Department collection

4.221 CHC. *Report Two: Mid Cambridge,* figure 14, detail

4.222 CHC. Harvard Class Album, 1870

4.223 Courtesy of Harvard Map Collection, Cambridge, Mass. Alexander Wadsworth, "Plan of the Village in Old Cambridge" (Boston, Jan. 1833), detail

4.224 Harvard University Archives, HUV 286 (1-2)

4.225 Harvard University Archives, HUV 290 (1-1)

4.226 Courtesy of Historic New England, Digital ID# rs31364

4.227 CHC. H.F. Walling, *Map of the City of Cambridge, Middlesex County, Massachusetts* (Boston, 1854), detail

4.228 CHC. G.M. Hopkins, *Atlas of the City of Cambridge, Massachusetts* (Philadelphia, 1873), detail

4.229 Courtesy of Boston Public Library, Leslie Jones Collection

4.230 Cambridge Historical Society

4.231 CHC. Roger Gilman photo

4.232 Courtesy of Harvard Map Collection, Cambridge, Mass. Olmsted, Vaux & Co., *Preliminary Study Prepared for Charles E. Norton Esq.*

4.233 CHC. "Norton Estate, Cambridge Mass., Showing New Streets and Lots for Sale" [Mar. 1888]. A similar plan dated 1887–88 was published in Eliot, *Charles Eliot, Landscape Architect,* opp. 214

4.234 Southwest Harbor Public Library. Henry Rand Collection

4.235 Southwest Harbor Public Library. Henry Rand Collection

4.236 Ralph Bergengren, "Norton's Woods," *The House Beautiful* (Nov. 1915): 166

4.237 Southwest Harbor Public Library. Henry Rand Collection

4.238 CHC. Courtesy of Jane Rabe

4.239 CHC. G.W. Bromley & Co., *Atlas of the City of Cambridge* (Philadelphia, 1930), detail

4.240 Courtesy of MIT Museum. "Harvard University Housing Proposal – Sachs Estate, Cambridge," 1969

4.241 Harvard University Archives, HUV 130 (1-1)

4.242 Harvard University Archives, HUC 8782.514 (126). "Perspective View of the Seat of the Hon. Francis Dana, Cambridge"

4.243 Courtesy of Harvard Map Collection, Cambridge, Mass. Peter Tufts, Jr., "A Plan of part of the land belonging to Francis Dana, Esqr. lying in Cambridge," 1810

4.244 CHC. Harvard Class Album, n.d.

4.245 Cambridge Engineering Department. Plan 868

4.246 Harvard University Archives, UAI.15.740 pf, 19. Alexander Wadsworth, "Untitled plan for the west side of Quincy Street" (Boston, Sept. 15, 1843), detail

4.247 Courtesy of Historic New England, Digital ID# rs2049. Stereographic view

4.248 CHC. Harvard Class Album, n.d.

4.249 CHC. Roger Gilman photo

4.250 *Cambridge Chronicle,* Nov. 16, 1889

4.251 CHC. G.M. Hopkins, *Atlas of the City of Cambridge, Massachusetts* (Philadelphia, 1873), detail

4.252 Courtesy of Boston Public Library, Leslie Jones Collection

4.253 CHC. Boston Elevated Railway collection

4.254 Harvard University Archives, HUV 15 (27-6)

4.255 CHC. William A. Mason, "A Plan of the Farm Belonging to William Winthrop Esq. of Cambridge," ca. 1800, copied 1847

4.256 Daughters of the American Revolution, Hannah Winthrop Chapter. *An Historic Guide to Cambridge* (Cambridge, 1907)

4.257 CHC. Charles Sullivan photo

4.258 CHC. Joseph Bennett, "Plan of Land belonging to Heirs of Mr. Winthrop," 1844, Copy by J.B. Henck, 1857

4.259 CHC. MapWorks

4.260 *Cambridge Chronicle,* Apr. 10, 1858

4.261 CHC. G.M. Hopkins, *Atlas of the City of Cambridge, Massachusetts* (Philadelphia, 1873), detail

4.262 CHC. *Harvard Illustrated* (1900)

4.263 CHC. Charles Sullivan photo

4.264 Harvard University Archives, HUV 657E (1-3)

4.265 Cambridge Historical Society

4.266 CHC. Boston Elevated Railway collection

4.267 "Proposed Avenue from the River Parkway to Quincy Square, Cambridge," *Cambridge Chronicle*, Feb. 2, 1907

4.268 CHC. Charles Sullivan photo

4.269 CHC. Cambridge Planning Board collection. Bradford Washburn photo

4.270 Courtesy of Historic New England, Digital ID# rs209760

4.271 Courtesy of Harvard Map Collection, Cambridge, Mass. Alexander Wadsworth, "Plan of the Village in Old Cambridge" (Boston, Jan. 1833), detail

4.272 Harvard University Archives, HUA 900.13, Envelope 1; olvwork417641

4.273 CHC. G.W. Bromley & Co., *Atlas of the City of Cambridge* (Philadelphia, 1903), detail

4.274 Courtesy of Historic New England, F1151. Halliday Historic Photograph Company photo

4.275 Harvard University Archives, HUV 570 (1-3)

4.276 Harvard University Archives, HUV 15 (3-5)

4.277 CHC. Associated Press photo, Sept. 15, 1930

CHAPTER 5

5.1 Library of Congress. John Hills, manuscript map of Boston Harbor, n.d., detail

5.2 Harvard University Archives, UA1.15.740pf; olvwork400303. Joshua Green Jr., *A Plot of Cambridge Common with a View of the Roads and a principal part of the Buildings thereon,* ca. 1781

5.3 Harvard University Archives, HUV 2010pf; olvwork224079. D. Bell, *Cambridge Common from the Seat of Caleb Gannet, Esq., Comprehending a View of Harvard University,* ca. 1808–09

5.4 Harvard University Archives, HUV 2010 pf; olvwork224077. D. Bell, *Cambridge Common from the Episcopal Church,* ca. 1808–09

5.5 Courtesy of Massachusetts Archives. James Hayward, *A Plan of Cambridge Common as surveyed August 17th, 1830*

5.6 CHC. Harvard Class Album, 1862

5.7 CHC. *Ballou's Pictorial* 9, no. 1 (July 7, 1855)

5.8 Houghton Library, Harvard University, MS Am 2832

5.9 *Boston Post,* Oct. 27, 1923

5.10 CHC

5.11 Courtesy of Archives of First Church in Cambridge, Congregational, United Church of Christ. Competition design for a soldiers monument. "W.P.P. Longfellow Inv. et Del./Martin & Longfellow 18 Pemb'ton Sq."

5.12 Cambridge Engineering Department. Cambridge City Engineer, *Public Property* I (14)

5.13 CHC. Postcard, publisher unknown

5.14 CHC

5.15 Harvard University Archives, HUV 182 (1-2)

5.16 Plan of the Radio School barracks on Cambridge Common. *Cambridge Chronicle*, May 18, 1918 5.17 National Archives

5.18 Isabelle Hyman, "Marcel Breuer and the Franklin Delano Roosevelt Memorial," *Journal of the Society of Architectural Historians* 54, no. 4 (Dec. 1995): 455

5.19 CHC. Cambridge Planning Board collection. Bradford Washburn photo

5.20 CHC. Symmes, Maini & McKee, Inc., "Feasibility Study for Proposed Underground Garage [at] Cambridge Common," December 1972

5.21 *Cambridge Chronicle,* July 16, 1970

5.22 CHC. Mason & Frey, landscape architects, "Proposed Cambridge Common," November 15, 1972, revised February 8, 1973

5.23 Cambridge Engineering Department. Cambridge City Engineer, *Public Property* I (23)

5.24 Courtesy of National Park Service, Frederick Law Olmsted National Historic Site. Olmsted, Olmsted & Eliot, "City of Cambridge Park Commission, Winthrop Square Planting Plan," May 1, 1897

5.25 Brown, Richardson & Rowe. Nina Brown photo

5.26 Cambridge Historical Society

5.27 Courtesy of National Park Service, Frederick Law Olmsted National Historic Site

5.28 The Schlesinger Library, Radcliffe Institute, Harvard University, Ellis Gray Loring Papers, A160-19v-115

5.29 Library of Congress. Detroit Publishing Co. collection

5.30 Boston Public Library Print Department. Leon Abdalian photo

5.31 CHC. William Cullen Bryant, ed., *Picturesque America* (New York, 1872–74), 246

5.32 CHC. United States Coast Survey, "Boston Harbor, Massachusetts" [Washington, D.C.], 1857

5.33 Courtesy of Harvard Map Collection, Cambridge, Mass. Charles Davenport, "New Boston and Charles River Basin" (Boston, 1875), detail

5.34 Boston Athenæum

5.35 CHC. Photocopy of original formerly in the collections of The Bostonian Society

5.36 CHC. *Cambridge Park Commission Annual Report*, 1894. Olmsted, Olmsted & Eliot, "General Plan Showing Existing and Proposed Riverside Reservations on the Banks of the Charles River"

5.37 CHC. *Cambridge Park Commission Annual Report*, 1896

5.38 Courtesy of Historic New England, F1155. Samuel N. Wood photo

5.39 CHC. *Cambridge Park Commission Annual Report*, 1897. F.L. & J.C. Olmsted, "Charles River Parkway—Section G"

5.40 Courtesy of National Park Service, Frederick Law Olmsted National Historic Site

5.41 CHC. Cambridge Planning Board collection

5.42 CHC. Rice-Mank collection

5.43 CHC. Cambridge Planning Board collection

5.44 Library of Congress. Detroit Publishing Co. collection. Digitally restored by John Dalterio

5.45 CHC. Photo Aug. 4, 1958. Morris Ostroff photo

5.46 Courtesy of Ellen Moot. Jacek von Hennenberg, artist

5.47 CHC

5.48 CHC. Postcard, Leighton & Valentine Co. (New York)

5.49 Library of Congress. Detroit Publishing Co. collection

5.50 CHC. International Newsreel photo, May 17, 1927

5.51 CHC. *Cambridge Park Commission Annual Report*, 1924–25

5.52 CHC. *Boston Traveler*. Photo May 28, 1930

5.53 Moses King, *Harvard University: Eighty Photographic Views* (Boston, 1893; 2nd ed.)

5.54 Cambridge Historical Society

5.55 CHC. Cambridge Chamber of Commerce collection

5.56 CHC

5.57 CHC. G.W. Stadly Co., *Atlas of Middlesex County, Massachusetts* (Boston, 1900), detail

5.58 Library of Congress. Detroit Publishing Co. collection

5.59 Cambridge Historical Society

5.60 CHC. Charles Sullivan photo

5.61 Library of Congress. Detroit Publishing Co. collection

5.62 Cambridge Engineering Department. Cambridge City Engineer, Plan No. 5312

5.63 CHC. Charles Sullivan photo

5.64 CHC. Thomas Lewis photo

5.65 Courtesy of American Antiquarian Society. "Old Burying Ground Committee" [pamphlet], 1934

5.66 James Smillie, "View from Mount Auburn," in Cornelia W. Walter, *Mount Auburn Illustrated … by James Smillie* (New York, 1847)

5.67 CHC. *American Railroad Journal,* II, no. 39 (Aug. 17, 1833), after Alexander Wadsworth, "Plan of Mount Auburn" (Boston, 1831)

5.68 James Smillie, "Entrance to the Cemetery," in Cornelia W. Walter, *Mount Auburn Illustrated … by James Smillie* (New York, 1847)

5.69 CHC. Ray Day collection. George P. Thresher photo

5.70 CHC

5.71 CHC. Richard Cheek photo

5.72 Courtesy of Historic New England, Negative # 50296-A [Original in Album 162]

5.73 Courtesy of Harvard Map Collection, Cambridge, Mass. *Map of Cambridge Cemetery,* author and date unknown

5.74 Cambridge Engineering Department. Cambridge City Engineer, Plan No. 1504, detail

5.75 CHC. Postcard, Hugh C. Leighton Co.

5.76 CHC. Charles Sullivan photo

5.77 Courtesy of Mount Auburn Cemetery, Historical Collections. "Sketch of Vicinity of Mount Auburn Taken from Map of Mt. Auburn (1867) … Cambridge 1854 … Watertown 1850," detail

5.78 *Cambridge Directory*, 1869: 10

5.79 CHC

5.80 CHC. Courtesy of Lionel and Arlene (McNamee) DeRagon

5.81 CHC. Charles Sullivan photo

5.82 Boston Street Railway Association

5.83 Courtesy of Mount Auburn Cemetery, Historical Collections. Fairchild Aerial Surveys, Inc.

5.84 Harvard University Archives, HUC 8782.514 (164). Nathaniel L. Frothingham [class of 1811]

5.85 Cambridge Historical Society. Harvard Class Album, 1867

5.86 Harvard University Archives, HUV 1200 (1-3). Notman, Montreal photo

CHAPTER 6

6.1 Courtesy of Historic New England, Digital ID# rs225086. Halliday Historic Photograph Company photo.

6.2 CHC. Robert H. Nylander

6.3 CHC. Susan Maycock, delineator

6.4 Courtesy of Historic New England, Digital ID# rs177109. Halliday Historic Photograph Company photo

6.5 Harvard University Archives, HUV 46 (2-2)

6.6 CHC. Susan Maycock, delineator

6.7 Library of Congress. Historic American Buildings Survey. Arthur C. Haskell photo

6.8 Library of Congress. Historic American Buildings Survey. Arthur C. Haskell photo

6.9 Courtesy of Historic New England, Negative #2329-B [Original in Album 7]. Wilfred A. French photo

6.10 Cambridge Historical Society. Lois Lilley Howe, delineator

6.11 Cambridge Historical Society

6.12 Samuel Adams Drake, *Historic Fields and Mansions of Middlesex* (Boston, 1874)

6.13 Courtesy of Historic New England, Negative #AH10376. Arthur Haskell photo

6.14 Courtesy of Historic New England, Negative #AH1317a. Arthur Haskell photo

6.15 CHC. Boston Elevated Railway collection

6.16 Batty Langley, *The City and Country Builder's and Workman's Treasury of Designs* (London, 1740)

6.17 CHC. Charles Sullivan photo

6.18 CHC. Susan Maycock, delineator

6.19 Courtesy of National Park Service, Longfellow House-Washington's Headquarters National Historic Site. David Bohl photo

6.20 CHC. Richard Cheek photo

6.21 Yale University, Beinecke Rare Book & Manuscript Library. *Ezra Stiles Itineraries*, vol. 1: 125

6.22 M.I.T. Institute Archives and Special Collections

6.23 M.I.T. Institute Archives and Special Collections

6.24 Courtesy of Historic New England, Digital ID# rs2097575. Halliday Historic Photograph Company photo

6.25 CHC. Ray Day collection. George P. Thresher photo

6.26 Lois Lilley Howe, *Details of Old New England Houses* (New York, 1913)

6.27 CHC. B. Orr photo

6.28 Library of Congress. Historic American Buildings Survey. Jack Boucher photo

6.29 Courtesy of Historic New England, Digital ID# rs209758. H.C. Dean photo

6.30 Courtesy of Historic New England, Digital ID# rs209759. George Brayton photo

6.31 Cambridge Historical Society

6.32 Courtesy of Historic New England, Digital ID# rs2054

6.33 Batty Langley, *The City and Country Builder's and Workman's Treasury of Designs* (London, 1740)

6.34 CHC. B. Orr photo

6.35 Lois Lilley Howe, *Details from Old New England Houses* (New York, 1913), plate 1

6.36 CHC

6.37 Harvard University Archives, HUD 267. 1867 Class Album

6.38 CHC. Richard Cheek photo

6.39 CHC. Charles Sullivan photo

6.40 Cambridge Historical Society. Lois Lilley Howe photo

6.41 Library of Congress. Historic American Buildings Survey. James F. and Jean B. O'Gorman photo

6.42 The Schlesinger Library, Radcliffe Institute, Harvard University, LC56-1-8

6.43 Mary Thatcher Higginson, *Thomas Wentworth Higginson, the Story of His Life* (Boston, 1914), opp. 30

6.44 CHC. Daniel Reiff photo

6.45 Library of Congress. Charles H. Currier photo

6.46 Boston Public Library, Department of Rare Books and Manuscripts. *Plans and Elevations of a House proposed to be built at Cambridge*, 1832, ms.f.Am.2331. "Front Elevation drawn/from a scale of 8 feet to one/Inch by A Benjamin 1832," plate 1

6.47 Harvard University English Department

6.48 Harvard Art Museums, Fogg History Drawer, Shady Hill Exterior Photographs file

6.49 CHC. Cambridge Engineering Department House Book 2: 43

6.50 CHC. B. Orr photo

6.51 James Stuart and Nicholas Revett, *The Antiquities of Athens and Other Monuments of Greece* (London, 1827), vol. I, plate VI

6.52 CHC. Boston Elevated Railway collection

6.53 CHC. Charles Sullivan photo

6.54 CHC. Charles Sullivan photo

6.55 CHC. Susan Maycock, delineator

6.56 CHC. Charles Sullivan photo

6.57 CHC. Charles Sullivan photo

6.58 CHC. Ed James photo

6.59 CHC. Roger Gilman photo

6.60 CHC. *Cambridge Illustrated* (Gardner, Mass., [ca. 1890])

6.61 CHC. Charles Sullivan photo

6.62 CHC. Charles Sullivan photo

6.63 CHC. D. Wetherell photo

6.64 CHC. Ed James photo

6.65 CHC. Mrs. Ruth P. Gray collection

6.66 CHC. B. Orr photo

6.67 Chester Hills, *The Builder's Guide* (Hartford, 1847, 2nd ed.)

6.68 CHC. Richard Cheek photo

6.69 CHC. Roger Gilman photo

6.70 [Harvard University Archives]

6.71 CHC. Ed James photo

6.72 Cambridge Historical Society. Lois Lilley Howe photo

6.73 Massachusetts Historical Society

6.74 CHC. Charles Sullivan photo

6.75 CHC. Charles Sullivan photo

6.76 Alexander Graham Bell Association for the Deaf and Hard of Hearing (formerly the Volta Bureau)

6.77 Cambridge Historical Society. Lois Lilley Howe photo

6.78 Library of Congress. Charles H. Currier photo

6.79 [Harvard University Archives]

6.80 Courtesy of Historic New England, Digital ID# 2053. William Brewster photo

6.81 CHC

6.82 Smithsonian Institution. James. F. O'Gorman, ed., *Aspects of American Printmaking, 1800–1850* (Syracuse, N.Y., 1988)

6.83 CHC

6.84 CHC. Roger Gilman photo

6.85 Boston Public Library. Department of Rare Books and Manuscripts. *Plans and Elevations of a House proposed to be built at Cambridge*, 1832, ms.f.Am.2331. Watercolor, by Joseph R. Richards

6.86 CHC. Richard Cheek photo

6.87 Library of Congress. Historic American Buildings Survey. George Cushing photo

6.88 Library of Congress. Historic American Buildings Survey. George Cushing photo

6.89 CHC

6.90 Courtesy of Historic New England, Digital ID# rs224831

6.91 CHC. Charles Sullivan photo

6.92 Library of Congress. Historic American Buildings Survey. Jack Boucher photo

6.93 Library of Congress. Historic American Buildings Survey. George Cushing photo

6.94 CHC. Courtesy of Mrs. John Blitzer

6.95 CHC. Roger Gilman photo

6.96 CHC. Roger Gilman photo

6.97 Library of Congress. Historic American Buildings Survey. George Cushing photo

6.98 CHC. Richard Cheek photo

6.99 CHC. Charles Sullivan photo

6.100 CHC. Courtesy of Lawrence Eliot

6.101 CHC. Roger Gilman photo

6.102 CHC. B. Orr

6.103 CHC. Charles Sullivan photo

6.104 CHC. Roger Gilman photo

6.105 CHC. Susan Maycock, delineator

6.106 CHC. Roger Gilman photo

6.107 CHC. B. Orr photo

6.108 CHC. Charles Sullivan photo

6.109 CHC. Charles Sullivan photo

6.110 CHC. Richard Cheek photo

6.111 CHC. Charles Sullivan photo

6.112 Courtesy of Historic New England. *American Architect & Building News*, July 7, 1877

6.113 Episcopal Divinity School

6.114 CHC. Courtesy Mrs. A. Calvert Smith

6.115 CHC. Charles Sullivan photo

6.116 CHC. Courtesy of Jill Costello

6.117 CHC. Charles Sullivan photo

6.118 CHC. Charles Sullivan photo

6.119 CHC. Susan Maycock, delineator

6.120 CHC. Roger Gilman photo

6.121 CHC. Roger Gilman photo

6.122 CHC. B. Orr photo

6.123 CHC. B. Orr photo

6.124 Courtesy of Historic New England, Digital ID# rs215149. Soule Art Co. photo

6.125 CHC. Charles Sullivan photo

6.126 CHC. Roger Gilman photo

6.127 Courtesy of Historic New England, Digital ID# rs209706

6.128 CHC. Roger Gilman photo

6.129 CHC. Charles Sullivan photo

6.130 CHC. Charles Sullivan photo

6.131 CHC. Charles Sullivan photo

6.132 CHC. Charles Sullivan photo

6.133 CHC. Roger Gilman photo

6.134 CHC. Gift of Stephen Sacks

6.135 CHC. Roger Gilman photo

6.136 *Cambridge Tribune Souvenir*, June 1890

6.137 CHC. Charles Sullivan photo

6.138 Library of Congress. Historic American Buildings Survey. George Cushing photo

6.139 Library of Congress. Historic American Buildings Survey. George Cushing photo

6.140 CHC. Roger Gilman photo

6.141 CHC. Charles Sullivan photo

6.142 CHC. Charles Sullivan photo

6.143 CHC. Charles Sullivan photo

6.144 Courtesy of Historic New England, Digital ID# rs2428

6.145 Library of Congress. Historic American Buildings Survey. George Cushing photo

6.146 CHC. Elsa Craig photo

6.147 CHC. Charles Sullivan photo

6.148 CHC. Susan Maycock, delineator

6.149 CHC. B. Orr photo

6.150 CHC. B. Orr photo

6.151 Courtesy of Historic New England, Negative # 4098-B

6.152 CHC. Charles Sullivan photo

6.153 *The Engineering and Building Record* (Apr. 27, 1889)

6.154 Courtesy of Historic New England, Digital ID# rs1607

6.155 Courtesy of Historic New England, Digital ID# rs159181. *The American Architect & Building News*, Oct. 27, 1888

6.156 Library of Congress. Historic American Buildings Survey. *American Architect & Building News* 21 (Jan. 1, 1887): 575De

6.157 CHC. B. Orr photo

6.158 CHC. Courtesy of Arthur Brooks

6.159 CHC. Courtesy of Arthur Brooks

6.160 CHC. B. Orr photo

6.161 CHC. Courtesy of Sandy Ritchie, Lamb & Ritchie Co.

6.162 CHC. Curtis Mellen collection

6.163 CHC

6.164 CHC. Richard Cheek photo

6.165 Courtesy of Historic New England, Digital ID# rs971

6.166 Courtesy of Historic New England, Digital ID# rs17844. Album 31

6.167 Cambridge Historical Society. Lois Lilley Howe collection

6.168 CHC. Charles Sullivan photo

6.169 CHC. B. Orr photo

6.170 Cambridge Historical Society. Lois Lilley Howe photo

6.171 Courtesy of Richard Joslin, Patterson-Smith collection

6.172 CHC. B. Orr photo

6.173 CHC. Charles Sullivan photo

6.174 CHC. Charles Sullivan photo

6.175 CHC. Charles Sullivan photo

6.176 Samuel Howe, *American Country Houses of Today* (New York, 1912)

6.177 CHC. B. Orr photo

6.178 Allen W. Jackson, *The Half-Timber House: Its Origin, Design, Modern Plan, and Construction* (New York, 1912), 58

6.179 CHC. Charles Sullivan photo

6.180 CHC. Charles Sullivan photo

6.181 CHC. Charles Sullivan photo

6.182 University of Wisconsin Digital Collections. *The Craftsman,* 24, no. 1 (Apr. 1913): 73

6.183 CHC. B. Orr photo

6.184 CHC

6.185 CHC. Wm. C. McConnell Co. Catalogue B (Cambridge, 1925)

6.186 CHC. Richard Cheek photo

6.187 Ethel Power, *The Smaller American House* (Boston, 1927), 68

6.188 CHC. Charles Sullivan photo

6.189 CHC. Charles Sullivan photo

6.190 CHC. Charles Sullivan photo

6.191 CHC. B. Orr photo

6.192 CHC. Richard Cheek photo

6.193 Courtesy of Historic New England, Digital ID# rs17844. Paul J. Weber photo

6.194 CHC. Christopher Hail photo

6.195 *Architectural Forum* (Jan. 1939). Ezra Stoller photo © Ezra Stoller/Esto

6.196 CHC. Charles Sullivan photo

6.197 CHC. Charles Sullivan photo

6.198 Image © J. Paul Getty Trust. Getty Research Institute, Los Angeles (980060)

6.199 Ezra Stoller photo © Ezra Stoller/Esto

6.200 CHC. Richard Cheek photo

6.201 CHC. Gift of Peter Wasserman

6.202 CHC. Charles Sullivan photo

6.203 CHC. Lisanti Inc. photo

6.204 CHC. Richard Cheek photo

6.205 Courtesy of the Francis Loeb Library, Harvard Graduate School of Design. Phokion Karas photo

6.206 CHC. Charles Sullivan photo

6.207 CHC. Charles Sullivan photo

6.208 CHC. Charles Sullivan photo

6.209 CHC. Charles Sullivan photo

6.210 CHC. Charles Sullivan photo

6.211 CHC. Richard Cheek photo

6.212 CHC. Courtesy of Fenton Hollander

6.213 Graham Gund Associates

6.214 Graham Gund Associates

6.215 Ann Beha Architects. Eric Roth photo

6.216 Anmahian Winton Architects. Jane Messinger photo

6.217 CHC. Charles Sullivan photo

6.218 CHC. Charles Sullivan photo

6.219 CHC. Charles Sullivan photo

6.220 CHC. "The Dunvegan and The Montrose …" (Cambridge, 1905)

6.221 CHC. Charles Sullivan photo

6.222 *The American Architect* (Dec. 22, 1909)

6.223 CHC

6.224 CHC

6.225 CHC

6.226 CHC. Charles Sullivan photo

6.227 Courtesy of Historic New England, Digital ID# rs215125

6.228 CHC. Charles Sullivan photo

6.229 *The American Architect* 113, no. 2203 (Mar. 13, 1918)

6.230 *The American Architect* 113, no. 2203 (Mar. 13, 1918)

6.231 CHC. Cambridge Engineering Department photo

6.232 CHC. Charles Sullivan photo

6.233 CHC. Charles Sullivan photo

6.234 CHC. Acme Newspictures photo

6.235 CHC. William L. Galvin collection. Clarke & Marks photo

6.236 CHC. Courtesy of E.T. Steffian

6.237 CHC. Edward F. Carney photo

6.238 CHC. Charles Sullivan photo

6.239 CHC. Charles Sullivan photo

6.240 CHC. Charles Sullivan photo

6.241 CHC. Edward Pacheco photo

6.242 CHC. Charles Sullivan photo

6.243 CHC. Charles Sullivan photo

CHAPTER 7

7.1 Biblioteque Nationale, Paris. Jean-Baptiste Louis Franquelin, "Carte de la Ville, Baye, et Environs de Baston … ," 1693, detail

7.2 Courtesy of American Antiquarian Society. William Burgis, "A Southeast View of Ye Great Town of Boston …." (Boston, 1743)

7.3 Harvard University Archives, HUC 8782.514 (114). Benjamin R. Nichols, "Front View of the Meetinghouse in Cambridge," Harvard mathematics thesis drawing, 1803

7.4 Lucius Paige, *History of Cambridge, Massachusetts* (Boston, 1877). "Plan of the Meetinghouse Erected in Cambridge in 1756," 292ff, additions by CHC

7.5 Harvard University Archives, HUV 82 (1-3)

7.6 CHC. Cram, Goodhue & Ferguson, "Perspective Scheme B, Proposed Meeting House, First Parish, Cambridge," *The Architectural Record* 6, no. 10 (1899): plate 66

7.7 CHC. Chase & Ames, "Competition design for the First Parish Church, Cambridge, Mass.," *The Architectural Record* 6, no. 10 (1899), plate 64

7.8 *Cambridge Tribune,* Apr. 28, 1900

7.9 CHC. *Boston Herald,* Sept. 3, 1954. Calvin Campbell photo

7.10 CHC. Charles Sullivan photo

7.11 Henry Francis du Pont Winterthur Museum. "Christ's Church in Cambridge Massachusetts." Watercolor drawing

7.12 Courtesy of Historic New England. Halliday Historic Photograph Company photo

7.13 Christ Church, Cambridge

7.14 Courtesy of Archives of First Church in Cambridge, Congregational, United Church of Christ. Raymond Calkins, *The Life and Times of Alexander McKenzie* (1935), opp. 154

7.15 Harvard University Archives, HUV 171 (1-3a). Harvard Class Album, n.d.

7.16 CHC

7.17 CHC. Harvard Class Album, n.d.

7.18 CHC. Harvard Class Album, n.d.

7.19 CHC. Harvard Class Album, n.d.

7.20 Harvard University Archives, HUV 991 (1-1). Harvard Class Album, 1875

7.21 CHC. Reproduction, courtesy of Paul Feloney. St. Peter's Church, "St. Peter's Church and Rectory," E.R. Howe lithograph, n.d.

7.22 William A. Leahy, *The Catholic Churches of Boston and Vicinity* (Boston, 1891)

7.23 CHC. Charles Sullivan photo

7.24 CHC. Daniel Reiff photo

7.25 CHC. Charles Sullivan photo

7.26 CHC. Charles Sullivan photo

7.27 CHC. Charles Sullivan photo

7.28 CHC

7.29 CHC. Charles Sullivan photo

7.30 Courtesy of Historic New England, Negative 15326-B

7.31 CHC. Charles Sullivan photo

7.32 CHC. Charles Sullivan photo

7.33 CHC. [*Boston Herald*], photo Dec. 26, 1959

7.34 Harvard University Archives, HUC 8782.514 (82). Robert Hallowell, "Northeasterly Perspective View of Cambridge Court House Taken from the Stone Bridge"

7.35 CHC. Courtesy of Captain Steve Persson

7.36 Courtesy of The Bostonian Society, Boston Historical Library & Special Collections

7.37 Courtesy of Historic New England, Negative 6592-B

7.38 CHC. Courtesy of Lieutenant William R. Skelley

7.39 CHC. Charles Sullivan photo

7.40 CHC. William L. Galvin collection

7.41 Courtesy of Harvard Map Collection, Cambridge, Mass.

7.42 Harvard University Archives, HUV 80 (BP17) Box 49

7.43 CHC. *Cambridge Tribune,* Jan. 25, 1890

7.44 CHC. Paul Flynn collection

7.45 Cambridge Skating Club

7.46 Harvard University Archives, UA1.15.740 pf. Joshua Green Jr., *A Plot of Cambridge Common with a View of the Roads and a principal part of the Buildings thereon,* ca. 1781, detail

7.47 Library of Congress. Image © J.F. Olsson & Co., ca. 1905

7.48 Courtesy of Historic New England

7.49 CHC. *Cambridge Park Commission Report,* 1924–25

7.50 CHC. Gift of Deborah Baskin

7.51 CHC. Gift of Deborah Baskin

7.52 HMFH Architects, Inc.

7.53 *Cambridge Tribune, Harvard Bridge Souvenir,* June 1890

7.54 Courtesy of the Frances Loeb Library, Harvard University Graduate School of Design. David Hirsch photo

7.55 CHC. *Annual Documents of the City of Cambridge,* 1896

7.56 Courtesy of Historic New England, Digital ID# rs2052

7.57 The Schlesinger Library, Radcliffe Institute, Harvard University, Reel 9, Image 8688

7.58 Courtesy of Buckingham Browne & Nichols School

7.59 CHC. Elsa Craig photo

7.60 CHC. Charles Sullivan photo

7.61 Courtesy of Buckingham Browne & Nichols School, "Sketch of Proposed School for Miss Markham"

7.62 Courtesy of Buckingham Browne & Nichols School

7.63 Jonathan Green photo © Esto

7.64 The Schlesinger Library, Radcliffe Institute, Harvard University, RG 20-6-1v-15

7.65 Lesley University Archives

7.66 CHC. Roger Gilman photo

7.67 CHC

7.68 Courtesy of Shady Hill Archives. Edward Yeomans, *The Shady Hill School: The First Fifty Years* (Cambridge, 1979), 32–33

7.69 CHC. Freeman/Brigham/Hussey Ltd. photo

7.70 Harvard Art Museums/Busch-Reisinger Museum, BRGA.81.1. Gift of Walter Gropius. Imaging Department photo © President and Fellows of Harvard College

7.71 CHC. Richard Cheek photo

7.72 CHC. Edward Jacoby photo

7.73 Ware & Van Brunt, "Design of Buildings for Protestant Episcopal Theological School, Cambridge, Mass.," in *Statement by the Trustees of the Episcopal Theological School* (Cambridge, 1873)

7.74 CHC. Charles Sullivan photo

7.75 Episcopal Divinity School. Bradford Washburn photo

7.76 CHC. Charles Sullivan photo

7.77 CHC. MapWorks

7.78 *Boston Evening Transcript,* May 15, 1926

7.79 CHC

7.80 CHC. Richard Cheek photo

7.81 CHC. Richard Cheek photo

7.82 CHC. Daniel Reiff photo

7.83 CHC. Charles Sullivan photo

7.84 CHC. Paul Allard photo

7.85 CHC

7.86 Lesley University. *Town-Gown Report,* 2010

7.87 CHC. Charles Sullivan photo

7.88 CHC. Jeffrey F. Pike photo

7.89 CHC. Courtesy Huygens & Tappé

7.90 Photo © 1980 Steve Rosenthal

7.91 George F. Crook, *The Cambridge Annual for 1887* (Boston, 1887)

7.92 Courtesy of Historic New England

7.93 CHC. *Cambridge Directory,* 1944: 37

7.94 Arthur Gilman, *The Cambridge of 1896* (Cambridge, 1896), opp. 276

7.95 Cambridge Historical Society

7.96 CHC. *Cambridge Chronicle-Sun* photo

7.97 CHC. Charles Sullivan photo

CHAPTER 8

8.1 Boston Athenæum

8.2 [Harvard University Archives]

8.3 CHC. Boston Elevated Railway collection

8.4 *Cambridge Chronicle,* May 18, 1901

8.5 CHC. Cambridge Engineering Department collection

8.6 CHC. Photo Sept. 21, 1927

8.7 CHC. Cambridge Engineering Department collection

8.8 CHC. Charles Sullivan photo

8.9 CHC. Charles Sullivan photo

8.10 Courtesy of Historic New England, Negative 12041-B

8.11 CHC. Cambridge Engineering Department collection

8.12 CHC. Charles Sullivan photo

8.13 Courtesy of Historic New England, Negative #50290-A. William T. Clark photo

8.14 Harvard University Archives, UAI 15.25 pf Box 4. William Sparrell, elevation drawing

8.15 Harvard University Archives, HUV 81 (BP7)

8.16 Harvard University Archives, HUV 81 (1-9)

8.17 Cambridge Historical Society

8.18 CHC. Richard A. Dow collection

8.19 Cambridge Public Library

8.20 Cambridge Historical Society

8.21 Courtesy of Historic New England, Negative 11082-B

8.22 CHC. Harvard Class Album, 1905

8.23 Harvard University Archives, HUV 101 (1-4). Notman Photographic Co.

8.24 CHC. Boston Elevated Railway collection

8.25 CHC. Boston Elevated Railway collection

8.26 CHC. Richard A. Dow collection

8.27 CHC. Richard A. Dow collection

8.28 CHC. William L. Galvin collection

8.29 CHC. Robert E. Stevens photo

8.30 CHC. Cambridge Chamber of Commerce collection

8.31 CHC. Cambridge Chamber of Commerce collection

8.32 CHC. Charles Sullivan photo

8.33 CHC. William L. Galvin collection

8.34 CHC. William L. Galvin collection

8.35 CHC. Courtesy of Richard Duncan, First Church of Christ, Scientist, Cambridge

8.36 CHC. Cambridge Electric Light Co. collection

8.37 CHC. William L. Galvin collection

8.38 CHC. William L. Galvin collection

8.39 CHC. Courtesy of Carl Barron

8.40 Benjamin Thompson & Associates. Ezra Stoller photo © Esto

8.41 CHC. Charles Sullivan photo

8.42 Photo © 1978 Steve Rosenthal

8.43 CHC. Charles Sullivan photo

8.44 Photo © 1986 Steve Rosenthal

8.45 CHC. Charles Sullivan photo

8.46 CHC. Charles Sullivan photo

8.47 Courtesy of American Antiquarian Society

8.48 CHC. Cambridge Chamber of Commerce collection

8.49 "The Changing Scene in Harvard Square," *The Harvard Trust,* 1, no. 2 (Feb. 1957)

8.50 CHC. Harvard Trust Co. collection. Ralph H. Hutchins Jr. Co. photo

8.51 Cambridge Historical Society

8.52 CHC

8.53 CHC. Roy J. Jacoby photo

8.54 Harvard Planning & Project Management. David Kurtis photo

8.55 CHC. Richard Cheek photo

8.56 CHC. Charles Sullivan photo

8.57 Hugh Stubbins & Associates. Rendering, by Michael Gebhart

8.58 CHC. Charles Sullivan photo

8.59 CHC. Charles Sullivan photo

8.60 CHC. Charles Sullivan photo

8.61 CHC. Charles Sullivan photo

CHAPTER 9

9.1 John Wilmerding, *History of American Marine Painting* (Boston, 1968), figure 113. *On the Banks of the Charles River, Cambridgeport, Mass.,* by John W.A. Scott

9.2 Charles Sullivan photo

9.3 National Archives. Port of Boston, Enrollment, No. 117

9.4 Harvard University Archives, UAI 15.740 pf, 31. William A. Mason, surveyor

9.5 Harvard Map Collection, G3762.C5 1875.H3. Lewis Hastings, City Engineer, undated plan with soundings from an 1861 U.S. Coast Survey chart, detail, additions by CHC

9.6 Harvard University Archives, HUPSF Crew (BP 39). Sophomore Class Boat, 1862, detail. Black & Batchelder photo

9.7 CHC. *Cambridge Directory,* 1868 (Hyde & Young) and 1874 (N.N. Stickney)

9.8 CHC. Nathaniel L. Stebbins photo

9.9 CHC. Cambridge Engineering Department collection

9.10 Courtesy of Houghton Mifflin Harcourt Publishing Company

9.11 Harvard University Archives, HUV 2297.10

9.12 Courtesy of Historic New England, Digital ID# rs233695

9.13 CHC. Boston Elevated Railway collection

9.14 CHC. Courtesy of Stephen F. Andrew

9.15 CHC. Bertram Adams photo

9.16 CHC. *Cambridge Directory,* 1870

9.17 CHC. Charles Sullivan photo

9.18 CHC. Courtesy of Richard Duncan, First Church of Christ, Scientist, Cambridge

9.19 CHC. *Cambridge Directory,* 1905

9.20 CHC. Postcard, publisher unknown

9.21 CHC. Richard Cheek photo

9.22 CHC

9.23 CHC. Daniel Reiff photo

9.24 CHC. Daniel Reiff photo

9.25 CHC. Charles Sullivan photo

9.26 Cambridge Historical Society. William A. Saunders collection

9.27 Harvard University Archives, HUV 176 (1-5)

9.28 Cambridge Historical Society

9.29 CHC. Frank Cheney collection

9.30 CHC. Frank Cheney collection

9.31 CHC. Boston Elevated Railway collection

9.32 CHC. Boston Elevated Railway collection

9.33 CHC. Cambridge Electric Light Co. collection

9.34 *Engineering News* (Feb. 1, 1912)

9.35 CHC. Boston Elevated Railway collection

9.36 CHC. Boston Elevated Railway collection

9.37 CHC. Frank Cheney collection. Boston Elevated Railway photo

9.38 CHC. Frank Cheney collection. Boston Elevated Railway photo

9.39 CHC. Boston Elevated Railway collection

9.40 Harvard University Archives, HUV 705

9.41 CHC. Postcard, publisher unknown

9.42 CHC. Daniel Reiff photo

9.43 Courtesy of the Frances Loeb Library, Harvard University Graduate School of Design

9.44 CHC. H.F. Walling, *Map of the City of Cambridge, Massachusetts* (1854), detail

9.45 Library of Congress, Prints and Photographs Division

9.46 CHC. Gift of Suzanne R. Weinberg via M.I.T. Historical Collections

9.47 CHC. G.M Hopkins & Co., *Atlas of Cambridge, Massachusetts* (Philadelphia, 1873), detail

9.48 CHC. Gift of Suzanne R. Weinberg via M.I.T. Historical Collections

9.49 CHC. Thomas Ellison photo

9.50 CHC. Gift of Suzanne R. Weinberg via M.I.T. Historical Collections

9.51 CHC. Sanborn Map Company, Insurance Maps of Cambridge, Massachusetts, 1934, updated to 1962, annotated by CHC

9.52 CHC. Charles Sullivan photo

9.53 CHC. Charles Sullivan photo

9.54 B.F. Sturtevant Co., *500 Representative Buildings Heated and Ventilated by The Sturtevant System* (Boston, ca. 1890)

9.55 CHC. Charles Sullivan photo

9.56 CHC. Roger Gilman photo

9.57 CHC. Richard Cheek photo

CHAPTER 10

10.1 Josiah Quincy, *The History of Harvard University* (Boston, 1840), frontispiece, George Gridley Smith, engraver

10.2 CHC. Robert H. Nylander

10.3 Harvard Art Museums/Fogg Museum. Harold Robert Shurtleff, "The Old College from the Yard," 1934. Transfer from the Harvard Union, 1966.64. Imaging Department photo © President and Fellows of Harvard College

10.4 Collection of Massachusetts Historical Society. William Burgis, "A Prospect of the Colledges in Cambridge in New England," engraving attributed to John Harris after William Burgis, 1726

10.5 CHC. Harvard Class Album, ca. 1860

10.6 The Library Company of Philadelphia. Pierre Eugene DuSimitière, [View of Harvard College about 1764]

10.7 CHC. Robert H. Nylander

10.8 Harvard University Archives, UAI 15.10.5 Box 1, Folder 51, http://nrs.harvard.edu/urn-3:HUL.ARCH:16731712

10.9 Cambridge Historical Society. William Thaddeus Harris collection

10.10 The Colonial Society of Massachusetts, gift of Mrs. Augustus Vincent Tack (Agnes Gordon Higginson Fuller Tack). *Stephen Higginson* (1770-1834), by Charles Hayter (1761-1835), pastel on parchment, 1820. Matthew Hamilton photo, Williamstown Art Conservation Center. Photo restoration, by John Dalterio

10.11 Harvard Art Museums/Fogg Museum. Harvard University Portrait Collection, 1823, L4. Alvan Fisher, "College Yard: A View of the Colleges Taken from the Craigie Road [Cambridge Street]," 1821, presented for the use of Harvard College by Henry Pickering, 1823. Imaging Department photo © President and Fellows of Harvard College

10.12 Josiah Quincy, *The History of Harvard University*, vol. II (Boston, 1860), 441

10.13 Harvard Art Museums/Fogg Museum. Museum collection, P1979.19. Josiah Parsons Cooke IV, "Gore Hall, Harvard College," ca. 1844. Imaging Department photo © President and Fellows of Harvard College

10.14 CHC. MapWorks

10.15 CHC. Harvard Class Album, 1867

10.16 CHC. Harvard Class Album, n.d.

10.17 Harvard University Archives, UAI 15.740, 51. Students in Engineering 2, "Map of Harvard Botanic and Observatory Grounds, 1888"

10.18 CHC. Daniel Reiff photo

10.19 Harvard University Archives, HUV 2276

10.20 F.O. Vaille and H.A. Clarke, eds., *The Harvard Book* (Cambridge, 1875)

10.21 CHC. Charles Sullivan photo

10.22 Harvard University Archives, HUV 2278; olvwork616459

10.23 CHC. Charles Sullivan photo

10.24 CHC

10.25 Cambridge Historical Society

10.26 CHC. *Harper's Weekly* (Feb. 22, 1890)

10.27 CHC. Courtesy of John Booras. Leon Abdalian photo

10.28 CHC. Charles Sullivan photo

10.29 CHC. MapWorks

10.30 CHC. Harvard Class Album, before 1868

10.31 CHC. Ray Day collection. George P. Thresher photo

10.32 Harvard University Archives, UAI 15.740 pf 1860-1899. Moses King, *Harvard and Its Surroundings* (1878), detail

10.33 CHC. Photo Oct. 3, 1938

10.34 Courtesy of Historic New England, ID# rs215209

10.35 Harvard University Archives, UAI 15.740 pf, 54. Students in Engineering 2, "Map of Harvard University Property in the Vicinity of Harvard Square, Cambridge, Mass., Fall 1887"

10.36 Courtesy of Historic New England. William Sumner Appleton photo

10.37 Harvard University Archives, HUV 593 (1-1)

10.38 CHC. Gift of the Society for the Preservation of Long Island Antiquities

10.39 Harvard University Archives, HUB 1200pf. Nathaniel J. Bradlee, *The Centennial, Erected 1876* [Boston, 1876]

10.40 Harvard University Archives, HUV 438 (1-3)

10.41 CHC. *Scribner's Magazine* 21, no. 5 (May 1897): 543

10.42 CHC. Paul Flynn collection

10.43 Harvard University Archives, HUV 612 (1-3)

10.44 Harvard University Archives, HUV 612 (1-5). Historic American Buildings Survey. James F. and Jean B. O'Gorman photo

10.45 Courtesy of Historic New England, Negative # NS21207. Nathaniel L. Stebbins photo

10.46 Harvard University Archives, 376.UAI.5.160 1909-1914. Lowell Papers, Harvard Archives

10.47 CHC. Charles Sullivan photo

10.48 CHC. Charles Sullivan photo

10.49 [Harvard University Archives]

10.50 Harvard University Archives, HUV 635 (1-1). W.B. Swift photo

10.51 CHC. Charles Sullivan photo

10.52 *The Brickbuilder* 15, no. 3 (1906): plate 36

10.53 CHC. Richard Cheek photo

10.54 CHC. Architect's rendering, by William Y. Peters, 1890

10.55 CHC. *The American Architect* 1367 (Mar. 8, 1900)

10.56 Moses King, *Harvard University: Eighty Photographic Views* (Boston, 1896, 2nd Ed.)

10.57 CHC. International News Photo

10.58 CHC. Ray Day collection. George P. Thresher photo

10.59 Courtesy of Historic New England. Thomson & Thomson photo

10.60 Harvard University Archives, HUD 3298.5000.6. Harvard Cooperative Society, *Harvard University [Views]* (Brooklyn, ca. 1915)

10.61 Harvard University Archives HUV 2306; olvwork374318. *Harvard University*, by Richard Rummell, photogravure, by A.W. Elson Co., Boston.

10.62 Olmsted, Olmsted & Eliot, "Suggestions for the Orderly Arrangement of the Grounds of Harvard College," in Julius Gy. Fabos, Gordon T. Milde & V. Michael Weinmayr, *Frederick Law Olmsted, Sr.: Founder of Landscape Architecture in America* (Boston, 1968)

10.63 Charles U. Lowe, "The Forbes Story of the Harvard Riverside Associates"

10.64 CHC. Warren & Wetmore, "The New Plans for the Extension of Harvard University," *Harper's Weekly* (Dec. 18, 1909)

10.65 Library of Congress. Detroit Publishing Co. collection

10.66 Coolidge & Shattuck, "Study for the Future Grouping of Buildings made at the Request of the Corporation of Harvard University," May 1922

10.67 CHC. Courtesy of John Booras. Leon Abdalian photo

10.68 CHC. Photo June 1, 1930

10.69 CHC. Henry Deeks collection

10.70 CHC

10.71 Courtesy of Boston Public Library, Leslie Jones Collection

10.72 CHC. Wide World photo, Oct. 25, 1934

10.73 CHC. Charles Sullivan photo

10.74 CHC. "Harvard University in the Vicinity of Harvard Square," ca. 1936

10.75 CHC

10.76 CHC. Louis Baker photo

10.77 Courtesy of Shepley Bulfinch

10.78 CHC. Fred Stone photo

10.79 CHC. Daniel Reiff collection

10.80 CHC. Sert, Jackson & Associates. David Hirsch photo

10.81 Harvard University. *Harvard University 1960, An Inventory for Planning*, "Proposed Street Classification," plate 3–9

10.82 CHC. Associated Press Wirephoto, published Sept. 7, 1956

10.83 CHC. Sert, Jackson & Gourley via Harvard University News Office

10.84 CHC. Sert, Jackson & Gourley. Phokion Karas photo

10.85 CHC. Charles Sullivan photo

10.86 CHC. Photo © Edward Jacoby, 1973

10.87 CHC

10.88 CHC. Charles Sullivan photo

10.89 Harvard University Planning Office. *A Long Range Plan for Harvard University and Radcliffe College in Cambridge and Allston*, "Real Estate Acquisition Restrictions in Cambridge," June 1974, plate P-1

10.90 CHC. Hugh Russell collection. "Fogg Museum Connector Proposal," n.d. [1984]

10.91 CHC. Charles Sullivan photo

10.92 CHC. Charles Sullivan photo

10.93 CHC. Charles Sullivan photo

10.94 CHC. Charles Sullivan photo

10.95 CHC. Cambridge Planning Board collection

10.96 CHC. Harvard Planning and Real Estate. "90 Mount Auburn Street, February 2001. Architects' rendering, by Hans Hollein and Bruner/Cott"

10.97 CHC. Charles Sullivan photo

10.98 CHC. Charles Sullivan photo

10.99 CHC. Charles Sullivan photo

Architects and Builders Index

Includes architects, landscape architects, and city planners, as well as builders, carpenters, housewrights, and masons.

Downing, Andrew Jackson, 494, 498, 501, 850n18
Duguid & Martin, 203, 206, 248, 271, 576; (4.42)
Duguid, Mary, 206, 572, 576, 593, 634
Duguid, William A., 206, 219–221, 357, 572–573, 576, 593, 634; (6.191)
Duquesne, Eugene Joseph Armand, 143–144, 769; (3.43)
Dwight & Chandler, 549, 850n13

Earl Flansburgh & Associates, 172
Earp, Edwin, Jr., 598
Eayres, Joseph, 464; (6.13, 6.14)
Eisenberg, S.S., 152; (3.62)
Eliot, Charles, 89–92, 351–352, 410–411, 417–420, 432, 801, 843n35, 843n38; (2.47, 5.27, 5.36)
Eliot, Charles W., 351, 843n35; (4.231)
Eliot, Charles W., 2nd, 107, 843n35, 853n10
Elkus Manfredi Architects, 704–705; (8.46)
Elston, Thomas, 513
Emerson, William R., 199, 352, 517, 544, 549, 552–553, 557, 805, 850n12; (4.235, 6.146, 6.157)
Epps, Thomas B., 572
Estes, Ivory, 502; (4.207)
Esty, Alexander R., 626–627; (7.18)

F.A. Stahl Associates, 610–611; (6.241)
F.L. & J.C. Olmsted, 420; (5.39)
Feloney, Paul, 109; (2.63)
Fillebrown, James, 385
Fillmore, Wellington, 293
Finegold, Alexander, 832
Fisher, Clarence S., 564
Fisher, Howard T., 250, 577; (4.101, 6.192)
Fisher, Richard Arnold, 565–566; (6.176)
Flansburgh, Earl, 711; (8.58)
Fogerty, George, 74, 139, 286, 329, 368, 694, 742, 787, 791; (3.37, 4.252, 8.24, 10.45, 10.47)
Fogerty, James, 74, 285, 381, 516, 525–526, 534, 540–541, 645–646, 648, 785, 792, 797;

(4.266, 6.99, 6.115, 6.116, 6.131, 6.142, 7.49, 7.53, 10.38, 10.50)
Forbes, Peter, 709; (8.55)
Ford, Patrick W., 629–631; (7.21, 7.22, 7.24)
Francis, Ebenezer, 345, 773; (4.226)
Franzen, Ulrich, 853n25
Freeman/Brigham/Hussey Ltd., 657; (7.69)
Freeman, James W., 589, 657; (6.208, 7.69)
French, Daniel Chester, 411–413, 849n9; (5.30)
Frohman, Robb & Little, 634; (7.30)
Frost & Raymond, 271, 578, 672
Frost, Henry Atherton, 577–578, 672, 768
Frost, Paul, 187–188, 413; (4.15)
Frost, William E., 848n63
Frost, William, Jr., 305, 337–338, 848n63; (4.178, 4.216)
Furbish, Frederick, 74, 726–727; (2.38, 9.21)

Galvin, William E., 75, 138, 238, 577, 580–581, 608–609, 639–640, 669, 698–701, 706–709, 852n5; (4.86, 6.235, 7.40, 7.84, 8.33–8.39, 8.53)
Ganteaume & McMullen, 746; (9.50)
General Houses, Inc., 577
Geometrics, Inc., 590, 593
Gilman, Arthur, 250, 502, 594, 623, 626, 628; (4.102, 6.78)
Gilman, Frank F., 299; (4.169)
Glaser, Samuel, 608
Goodhue, Bertram Grosvenor, 562, 792
Goody, Clancy & Associates, 830, 832
Gould, Aaron, 648; (7.55)
Gourley & Richardson, 667
Gourley, Ronald, 586, 711, 818
Graham, Edward T.P., 75, 137, 318, 629–631, 769; (3.39, 7.21, 7.23)
Graton & Born, 149, 701; (3.52)
Graton, Bowman, 701; (3.52)
Graves, Thomas, 4–5
Gray & Blaisdell, 443
Gray, Arthur F., 750–751; (9.56)
Greco, Charles, 75, 101, 241, 244, 568–569, 572, 603–606, 648; (4.90, 4.93. 6.181, 6.229, 6.230)

Greeley, Roger, 607
Green, Henry, 791, 853n17
Greenough, Henry, 198, 266, 346, 366, 503–505, 625; (4.121, 4.249, 6.79, 6.80, 6.81, 7.14)
Griswold, Boyden, Wylde & Ames, 654, 709; (8.54)
Griswold, William, 200
Gropius, Walter, 171, 577–578, 584, 657, 710, 814–816, 818; (7.70, 10.78)
Grovestein, R. Currie, 75, 338, 848n62
Gulf Oil Corp., 728–729; (9.24)
Gund, Graham, 212, 591, 654, 686; (6.213, 6.214, 8.8)
Gwathmey Siegel, 854n38

Haffner, Jean-Jacques, 805, 814
Hale, Herbert D., 558, 797
Haley, Timothy F., 128; (3.18)
Halvorson Design Partnership, 406, 441, 837; (10.97)
Hansen, H.A., 243; (4.91)
Harkness, John, 359; (4.240)
Harlow, Hamilton, 75, 264, 599–603, 606; (4.140, 6.225)
Harrington, Eugene T., 267, 383; (4.125, 4.268)
Harris & Freeman, Inc, 610–611; (6.239)
Harrison & Abramovitz, 667, 851n24; (7.81)
Harrison, Peter, 385, 465, 622–623; (4.270, 7.11, 7.12)
Harrold, J. St. Clair, 309, 596–598; (4.182, 6.219)
Hartwell & Richardson, 295, 297, 306, 538–539, 544–547, 554–555, 748, 788, 847n53; (4.165, 4.180, 6.137, 6.138, 6.139, 6.147–6.150, 6.161, 6.162, 9.52)
Hartwell, Henry, 538
Hartwell, Richardson & Driver, 307, 748; (4.180, 9.52, 9.53)
Hastings, Oliver, 126, 147, 187, 195–196, 200, 252, 256, 257, 261, 302, 345, 349, 359, 363, 476, 479, 482–485, 487, 492, 506, 655, 849n6; (3.49, 4.109, 4.116, 6.40, 6.48, 6.49, 6.53, 6.62, 6.84, 7.66)
Hasty, John A., 299, 429, 560–561, 598, 606; (4.170, 5.55, 6.221, 6.231)

Hayden, Zebah, 533, 540–541; (6.142)

Heenan, Edward F., 606, 666, 684–685; (7.80, 8.7)

Hicks, Joseph, 121; (3.5)

Hill, George E.B., 580; (6.196)

Hill Miller Friedlander Hollander, 590–591

Hill, Walter L., 226

Himeon, Minor W., 516; (6.98)

Hines, R. A. & Son, 539

HMFH Architects, Inc., 590, 646–647; (7.52)

Hollander, Fenton, 590–591

Hollein, Hans, 174, 830, 836; (10.96)

Holmes, Joseph, 183, 185–186, 252, 477; (4.108)

Holt, William B., 74; (2.38)

Hopkins, Albert B., 74; (2.38)

Hopkins Architects, 838

Hopkins, James C., 585

Hovey & Ryder, 443–445; (5.73)

Hovey, William, Jr., 443, 492–493; (5.73, 6.63)

Howe & Manning, 271, 572; (6.187)

Howe, John, 787–788

Howe, Lois Lilley, 75, 97, 225, 233, 472, 499, 501, 518, 549, 551, 559, 562, 564, 566, 636; (6.167)

Howe, Manning & Almy, 572

Howells, Elinor Mead, 266, 512; (4.123)

Hubbard, Henry, 143, 806, 846n34; (10.66)

Hudnut, Joseph, 403, 577, 813–814, 818

Hugh Nawn Construction Co., 88–89

Hugh Stubbins & Associates, 110, 587, 609–610, 648, 710–711; (2.65, 6.237, 7.54, 8.57)

Humphrey, John, 143

Hunnewell, Charles, 491

Hunt, John, 461

Hunt, Richard Morris, 532, 722; (10.24)

Huygens & Tappé, 673; (7.89)

Jackson, Allen W., 99, 210, 218, 356, 566–567, 573, 620–621, 642–643, 653, 727; (6.178, 6.188, 7.45, 7.61)

Jackson, Huson, 711, 818

Jackson, Ralph T.C., 709, 728–729; (8.55, 9.23)

Jacobs, George Nelson, 696; (8.28)

Jardine, Hill & Murdock, 797

Johnson, Philip, 581–583, 814, 850n20; (6.198–6.199)

Kallman, Gerhard, 818

Kallman, McKinnell & Wood, 674, 830–831; (7.90, 10.92)

Kebbon, Eric, 797

Kelley, James T., 356; (4.237)

Kellogg, Harold Field, 568

Kelsey, Albert H., 514; (6.95)

Kendall, Taylor & Co., 668, 676; (7.82)

Kennebec Framing Co., 538

Kennedy, Henry, 651

Kenway, Herbert, 206

Kidder, Franklin E., 285; (4.148)

Kieran Timberlake, 838

Kilham & Hopkins, 651, 666

Kilham, Hopkins & Greeley, 607–608; (6.234)

Kilham, Hopkins, Greeley & Brodie, 656

Killam, Charles W., 79, 83

Kirkwood, Grace, 672–673

Koch, Carl, 200, 248, 578–579, 584, 648, 651; (4.101, 6.194, 6.195, 6.200)

Koetter Kim & Associates, 630–631; (7.25)

Koolhaas, Rem, 837

Lamson, Henry, 284; (4.146)

LaRose, Pierre, 366, 792, 833

Larsen, Bradley & Hibbard, 659, 661; (7.75)

Le Corbusier [Charles-Édouard Jeanneret-Gris], 819–821

Leers Weinzapfel Associates, 836

Levi, Jonathan, 684

Little, Arthur, 211, 554, 555–557; (4.49, 6.163, 6.164)

Little, Browne & Moore, 684, 686, 787; (8.4, 8.9)

Little, John Albro, 788; (10.43, 10.44)

Littlefield, Joseph H., 502, 510–511, 519, 638, 646, 850n8; (4.207, 6.91, 6.104, 6.105, 7.37)

Longfellow & Harlow, 547

Longfellow, Alden & Harlow, 208–210, 215–217, 276, 287, 547–549, 553–554, 557, 558–559, 640–641, 659; (4.151, 6.151, 6.152, 6.158, 6.159, 6.165, 6.166, 7.43)

Longfellow, Alexander Wadsworth, Jr., 95, 143, 202–203, 352, 462, 466, 476, 547, 566, 663–664, 666, 801, 805, 809; (3.41, 4.35, 6.7, 7.76, 10.71)

Longfellow, William Pitt Preble, 218, 398, 521–522, 524; (5.11, 6.109, 6.100, 6.114)

Lowell, Guy, 276, 364, 565–566, 666, 772, 792, 797, 801, 806, 809; (10.66)

M.A. Dyer & Co., 648

Machado, Ernesto M.W., 564; (6.174)

Machado, Rodolfo, 830, 835; (10.95)

Maginnis & Walsh, 629, 783

Maginnis, Charles D., 737, 783

Maginnis, Walsh & Kennedy, 666; (7.80)

Maini, Walter, 712

Malcolm, John L., 237

Mannos, Paul, 101

Markus & Mocka, 678

Marston, George W., 284, 495–496; (4.145, 6.65)

Martin & Freethy, 727; (9.21)

Martin, Abel C., 628; (7.20)

Martin, George R., 850n19

Martin, Wisner, 750–751; (9.57)

Mason & Frey, 407; (5.22)

Massachusetts Engineering Co., 572

McClare, Charles Herbert, 74, 318, 541, 550, 557–558, 560, 726, 742, 843n22; (9.19)

McDonald, Alexander, 398–400, 414, 447–448, 718; (5.10, 5.31, 5.78, 5.79)

McGinty, William H. & J. A., 787; (10.49)

McGirr, Edward, 646–647; (7.50, 7.51)

McHarg, Ian, 853n25

McKee, John, 712

McKim, Charles Follen, 550, 801

McKim, Mead & White, 427, 528, 532, 554, 564, 619–620, 664, 772–775, 788, 799, 801, 805, 845n15, 854n12; (5.50, 7.8, 10.26–10.28, 10.60)

McKinnell, Michael, 818

McLean & Graham, 137, 149; (3.39, 3.54)

McLean, George S.R., 137, 787, 790; (3.37, 10.45)

McLean, Isaac, 790

Saunders, William, 44, 183, 185, 251, 256, 264, 266, 472, 478, 487; (4.103, 4.122, 4.215 6.39, 6.42)

Saunders, William A., 281, 285, 302, 334, 336–338, 490, 491; (6.58, 6.60)

Sawyer, Samuel Flagg, 385

Schulze, Paul, 626, 764–766, 850n5; (7.17, 10.15)

Schwartz, David, 226

Sears, Roebuck & Co., 570

Sert, Jackson & Associates, 172, 703, 711–712, 821, 823; (3.92, 8.42, 8.43, 8.59)

Sert, Jackson & Gourley, 818, 821–823; (10.83, 10.84, 10.85)

Sert, Josep Lluis, 105, 150, 587, 711–712, 754, 814, 818–823; (6.204, 6.205)

Sewell, John, 534; (6.129)

Shattuck, George, 783

Shaw & Hunnewell, 560, 797, 801; (6.168)

Sheaff & Jaastad, 733; (9.33)

Shepard, Obed, 784; (10.37)

Shepley, Bulfinch, Richardson & Abbott, 817, 825, 853n21; (10.88)

Shepley, Henry R., 769

Shepley, Rutan & Coolidge, 543, 630, 659, 780–783, 798, 801, 805–806, 853n21; (10.58, 10.59, 10.65)

Shurcliff, Arthur (né Shurtleff), 79, 412, 769, 853n10

Shurtleff, Harold R., 756; (10.3)

Silverman & Brown, 264, 600, 606

Silverman, Brown & Heenan, 606, 684–685; (8.5, 8.6)

Silverman, David R., 606

Silvetti, Jorge, 830, 835; (10.95)

Simpson, Harrison, 847n48

Skidmore, Owings & Merrill-Boston, 168; (3.86)

Skidmore, Owings & Merrill-Chicago, 167, 612, 737; (3.85)

Smilie, Harold, 593

Smith & Walker, 797

Smith, Frank Hill, 624; (7.13)

Smith, Frank Warren, 509; (6.88)

Smith, William, 235, 512–513, 519, 525–527, 540, 849n7; (4.81, 6.117, 6.118)

Snell, George, 503, 623; (7.12)

Snow, F. F., 737; (9.39)

Soltan, Jerzy, 818

Sorkin, Jacob, 219, 241, 846n32

Sparrell, William, 125, 688, 787; (3.14, 8.13, 8.14)

Stearns, Marshall Ney, 283, 725; (9.18)

Stedman, John A., 534; (6.130)

Steele, Fletcher, 220, 577, 633

Stern, Robert A.M., 838–839; (10.98)

Stevens, Albert, 200, 645–646; (7.48)

Stewart, Erie, 208

Stickley, Gustav, 356, 569–570; (6.181, 6.182)

Stickney & Austin, 430–432, 675–676; (5.58, 7.93)

Stirling, James, 830; (10.90)

Stone, Edward Durrell, 578

Stoss Landscape Urbanism, 838

Stubbins, Hugh, Jr., 171, 237, 587, 589–590, 659, 710, 824, 829; (6.209)

Stull, Donald, 610

Sturgis & Brigham, 225, 517–518, 551–553, 554; (6.100, 6.154–6.156)

Sturgis Associates, 639; (7.39)

Sturgis, John Hubbard, 551

Sturgis, R. Clipston, 624, 639, 797, 816–817; (7.39)

Sumner, Thomas Waldron, 766; (10.16)

Symmes Maini & McKee Associates, 169, 405, 702, 712–713; (3.88, 5.20, 8.41, 8.44, 8.61)

Symmes, Parker, 712

Szabo, Alfred, 818

Techbuilt, 237

Thayer, Samuel J.F., 292, 532, 549; (4.159)

Thomas, Griffith, 514–515; (6.96)

Thomas, William F., 634–635; (7.32)

Thompson, Benjamin, 152–153, 172, 585; (3.61)

Thompson, Maryann, 658

Thouin, Gabriel, 452; (5.84)

Tidd, Ellsworth, 634–635; (7.32)

Tilden, George, 668; (7.82)

Town, Ithiel, 452, 478; (5.85, 6.37)

Tracey, Michael, 533

Trumbauer, Horace, 808–809; (10.69, 10.70)

Tsoi Kobus Associates, 170, 612, 679; (3.89, 6.242, 7.97)

Untersee, F. Joseph., 401; (5.13)

Van Brunt & Howe, 264, 529–530; (6.122, 6.123, 6.124)

Van Brunt, Henry, 228, 443, 528–530, 620, 623–624, 776; (6.121, 7.13)

Van Valkenberg, Michael, 831, 838

Vaughn, Henry, 628

Venturi, Scott Brown & Associates, 831

Vigier, François, 169, 818

von Moltke, Wilhem, 818

Voss, Herman, 783

Wadsworth, Hubbard & Smith, 575

Wainwright, William, 226–227, 590, 593; (4.70, 6.211)

Waitt, Andrew, 186

Walker & Best, 411–412; (5.30)

Walker, C. Howard, 411–412; (5.29)

Walker, Edward T.P., 449; (5.81)

Walker, Peter, 823

Walsh, Timothy F., 324, 560; (4.201)

Ware & Copeland, 207; (4.43)

Ware & Van Brunt, 521–524, 627–628, 659–661, 764, 768, 770, 776, 779, 801; (6.112, 6.113, 7.19, 7.73–7.74, 10.18, 10.21, 10.31)

Ware, William, 776, 814

Warland, John, 256

Warner, Harold O., 797

Warren & Smith, 739–741; (9.43)

Warren & Wetmore, 787, 797; (10.45)

Warren, H. Langford, 75, 92, 143, 269, 276, 363, 425, 482, 558, 562, 566–567, 632, 672, 769, 805, 814, 850n17, 853n24; (4.127, 6.171, 6.177, 7.27)

Warren, Smith & Biscoe, 824; (7.27, 10.86)

Warren, Whitney, 788

Way, Charles H., 657–658; (7.71)

Weems, Katherine Ward Lane, 812; (10.73)

Weld, John C., 285, 533; (4.148)

Wentworth, William P., 692–693, 787; (8.23)

West End Street Railway, 732–733; (9.32)

Wetmore, Charles D., 786–788, 802–804; (10.64)

Wheelock, Morgan, 227

Wheelwright & Haven, 676, 790; (10.45)

Wheelwright, Edmund M., 737, 796; (10.57)

Wheelwright, Haven & Hoyt, 427; (5.49)

Whidden, William M., 554, 850n15

White, Stanford, 550

Whiting, George C., 248, 250; (4.100)

Whitten & Gore, 606–607; (6.232)

Whitten, Roscoe, 604

Willard, Charles F., 533, 560–561; (6.169)

Willard, Solomon, 349–350, 479, 482, 486, 766, 853n6; (4.230, 6.48, 10.16)

William Barton Associates, 658; (7.72)

Williams, Morley, 437; (5.65)

Wills, Royal Barry, 575–576

Withey, Simeon, 256

Woo & Williams, 830

Woo, Kyu Sung, 837; (10.97)

Wood, F. W. Channing, 517; (6.102)

Woodcock, Shepard S., 750; (9.55)

Woodward, William E., 333, 534; (4.212)

Wright, James Hayden, 261, 650, 655; (4.116)

Wurster, William W., 403, 584

Yamasaki, Minouro, 823–824; (10.86)

Young, Ammi B., 440, 486

Zion & Breen, 667

Zwartz, Gerritt, 285; (4.147)

Street Address Index

Acacia Street
7: 549; (6.153)

Agassiz Street
19: 599, 602; (6.226)
32: 297, 540
33: 297, 540; (6.141)

Appian Way
6: 663
10: 256
11: 650, 651; (7.58)
14 (Larsen Hall): 824; (10.87)
22: 479, 480; (6.41)

Appleton Street
2: 219
6: 549
10: 219
71: 218, 521–522, 593; (6.109, 6.110)
88: 593; (6.215)
89: 218, 219; (4.57)

Arlington Street
1–9: 606, 607; (6.233)
16: 292
24: 292–293, 596
25: 560
26: 292, 293; (4.161)
28: 512
32: 291, 292; (4.160)
36: 512
37: 292, 513, 514; (6.95)

Arrow Street
0: 166, 174
8–12: 750; (9.55)
24 (St. Paul's): 630–631; (7.23)

Arsenal Square
1: 266, 267; (4.124)

Ash Street
5: 192, 553, 558, 560, 585
9: 581–583; (6.198, 6.199)
10: 187; (4.13)
13: 190
18: 186
19: 183, 190
34–36: 599, 600; (6.224)

Ash Street Place
6: 187, 494, 495; (6.65)
12: 187, 188; (4.15)

Athens Street
31: 382

Avon Hill Street
24: 502
32: 502, 675; (7.91)
71: 298, 570; (6.183)
109: 540

Avon Street
2–4: 602
32: 285, 502
38: 285, 502
42–44: 285, 498, 499; (6.71)

Banks Street
48: 379; (4.263)
112: 379
155: 379

Bates Street
17 and 21 (Charles Cook houses): 299

Beaver Street
8: 379; (4.262)

Bellevue Avenue
23: 540
48: 516; (6.98)

Bennett Street
Charles Square development: 165, 612, 686; (3.81)

Berkeley Place
1: 262
11: 580; (6.196)

Berkeley Street
3: 262, 264
4: 499, 500, 661; (6.73)
5: 499, 500; (6.74)
6: 499–500
7: 187
8: 485
11: 544
12: 197
15: 261–262, 500–501, 593, 650; (6.75, 7.57)
16: 566, 567–568; (6.179)
17: 650
20: 262, 506

21: 501

22: 514–515, 542; (6.96, 6.97)

Blackstone Street

19–23: 748; (9.52)

24–26: 748, 749; (9.54)

46: 732–733; (9.33)

Blanchard Road

12: 587

Bow Street

1: 166

11–21 (Westmorly Court): 787, 788, 790; (10.45)

12: 125, 126, 688; (3.13, 3.15)

30: 387; (4.272)

41 (Russell Halls): 387, 787, 790; (4.272, 10.45)

44 (Lampoon): 790, 796, 797; (10.45, 10.57)

Bowdoin Street

32: 541

35: 284, 285, 302, 330; (4.147)

Bradbury Road, 38: 256

Brattle Circle (William Galvin houses): 580–581

11–12: 238; (4.86)

14: 238; (4.86)

Brattle Square

1 (Brattle House): 126, 129, 180, 682–683, 738, 739; (3.15, 8.2, 9.40)

1 (One Brattle Square): 129, 169, 172, 173, 704; (3.95)

Brattle Street (nr. Kennedy St., I. Porter house): 139; (3.36, 3.37)

1–3 (Thomas Russell store): 125, 126; (3.13, 3.15)

1–8: 133, 144, 695; (3.27, 8.27)

9–15 (Atrium): 137, 703; (8.42, 8.43)

13–25 (Whitney-Estes): 129, 148, 692; (3.20, 3.51, 3.52, 8.21)

14–16: 726

17–37 (Dow buildings): 148, 698, 701; (3.51, 3.52, 8.38)

18–24 (McNamee bindery): 137, 139, 694; (3.37, 8.24)

27–31: 701

28–36: 690, 698, 699, 702; (8.18, 8.33, 8.41)

38A (Cambridge Federal S&L): 148, 149, 701, 706, 708, 709; (3.53, 8.53)

38B (Post Office): 148, 696, 701; (8.28)

40 (Brattle Hall/Theatre): 152, 171, 172, 558, 640–642; (3.59, 3.91, 3.92, 7.43)

42 (William Brattle house): 23, 171, 172, 178–182, 462, 756; (3.1, 3.92, 4.4, 6.7, 6.8)

44 (Sert, Jackson): 171, 172, 711–712; (3.91. 3.92, 8.59)

45: 148, 479, 696; (6.40, 8.29)

46 (rear of 48; TAC I): 153, 710; (8.56)

47–49: 252

48 (Brattle Inn): 171; (3.91)

48 (DR II): 172, 702; (3.92, 8.40)

51 (Washington Court): 92, 598–599; (6.222)

51 (Washington School): 644–645; (7.47)

52: 184; (4.9)

54: 180, 183, 184, 479, 640, 722; (4.7)

55 (James Read house): 254; (4.106)

57–61 (DR I): 152, 153; (3.61)

59: 256; (4.108)

60: 183, 184, 606, 608; (4.8)

62: 479, 480, 491, 659; (6.42)

63: 256, 257, 482–483; (4.109)

64 (Loeb Drama Center): 710

69 (Putnam House): 256, 490, 491, 664; (6.59)

76: 186, 506, 664; (6.83)

77 (Buckingham House): 256, 479, 654, 664; (7.64)

83 (Wadsworth Chambers): 206, 258, 599; (4.112)

85: 258, 495–496; (6.66, 6.67, 6.68)

90: 192, 542–543, 593; (6.144, 6.145)

92: 192, 519, 520; (6.106)

94: 188–192, 198, 463–465, 491; (4.18, 6.12–6.14)

96: 192; (4.20)

99 (St. John's Chapel): 624, 627–628, 659, 660; (7.19, 7.73)

100: 202

101: 484, 492; (6.62)

105 (Vassall/Craigie/Longfellow): 22, 62, 95, 193–198, 466–469; (1.23, 2.25, 4.23, 4.25, 6.15, 6.17–6.20)

106: 519

108: 197, 202; (4.27)

112: 203, 489, 490; (6.57)

113: 197, 532, 547, 550; (4.28, 6.127)

114: 564; (6.173)

115: 197, 547, 550, 553–554, 558, 585; (4.28, 6.158, 6.159)

120: 564

121: 198, 492; (6.61)

121A: 262

123: 262

124: 564; (6.173)

125: 262

126: 562

128: 205, 561, 562; (6.170)

132: 547

133: 590–591, 594; (6.212)

138: 210

140: 210

145: 532, 554

145 (Holy Trinity): 635; (7.33)

146: 208, 210, 501, 576; (4.44, 6.76, 6.191)

147: 547

149: 213–216; (4.51, 4.54)

152: 208

153: 217, 219, 472

154: 508, 510

155: 219, 547, 548

156: 511

157: 562–563; (6.172)

158: 211, 544, 552, 622; (6.157)

159: 217–19, 459–460, 463, 464, 472, 565; (6.11)

160: 211; (4.48)

161: 221

163: 217–18, 221, 594; (4.60)

164: 211, 511

165: 512, 738

167: 228, 527, 528–529, 593; (6.121)

168: 211–212, 555–557, 661; (4.49, 6.163, 6.164)

170: 260, 493, 659; (4.114)

175: 221–223, 228, 470, 567; (4.62, 6.24)

182: 544

183: 560
195: 562; (6.171)
199: 589–590; (6.209)
202: 566–567, 573, 727; (6.178)
205: 657; (7.70)
229: 567
240–244 (Larches): 606
245: 477
246–260 (Birches): 606, 607; (6.232)
Brewster Street
17–19: 215, 216, 531; (4.53)
23–25: 215, 216, 531, 532; (4.53, 6.126)
29–35: 215, 216, 531, 532; (4.53)
46: 549
Broadway
483 (Allston Burr): 816, 817; (10.79)
489–491: 639; (7.39)
Brown Street
7: 205
17: 23, 205, 206, 260; (4.40)
Bryant Street
1: 356
24: 356
Buckingham Place
4: 200
5: 200
7: 200
10: 200
Buckingham Street
4: 578–580; (6.194, 6.195)
9: 547, 548
10: 652–653; (7.61)
13: 200; (4.32)
16: 653; (7.62)
23: 200, 517, 519, 593; (6.104, 6.105)
29: 200, 528; (6.120)
34: 200
50: 200, 530, 531; (6.125)
60: 200

Cambridge Street
1640 (Felton Hall): 786; (10.40)
1689–1717: 489; (6.56)
1737 (Greenough house): 366, 368, 504; (4.252)

1737 (Ambassador Hotel): 77, 684, 685; (8.7)
1746: 516; (6.99)
Channing Place
3–5: 228, 560; (6.168)
6: 547, 548; (6.151)
10: 228
Channing Street
5: 233
7: 594
15: 550
Chapman Place
1–3: 186; (4.12)
Charles Square
Charles Hotel/Condos: 686
Chauncy Lane
1–10: 610, 612; (6.241)
Chauncy Street
1 (Norton house): 510; (6.89)
1–3: 279, 606
10: 279, 602
12: 276, 277; (4.136)
16: 279; (4.138)
18–26: 279, 280; (4.140)
21 (Margaret Winthrop Hall): 279, 654; (4.139)
21 (Elliott): 280, 602; (4.140)
Church Street
23–25: 67, 698, 700, 724, 725; (2.31, 8.35–8.37, 9.18)
26: 126, 637, 638, 724, 725; (7.35, 9.17)
27: 637, 638, 723; (7.36, 9.14)
31: 126, 723; (9.14)
35: 726
41: 727; (9.21)
50 (Atrium): 167, 703; (8.42, 8.43)
53: 96, 252, 672; (7.88)
Clement Circle
3: 568
Concord Avenue
3 (Concord Hall): 602; (6.227)
4: 275; (4.133)
5 (Lexington Hall): 602; (6.227)
7: 275; (4.133)
12: 550

14–16 (Continental Gardens): 609–610, 611; (6.238)
20–22: 264, 600
24–26: 264
29 (Continental Terrace): 264, 266, 492, 609, 610; (4.122, 6.237)
31: 264
34: 267, 654, 655, 669; (7.65)
35: 264, 528, 530, 531; (6.124)
36: 655, 669
37: 266, 512, 514; (4.123)
38: 655, 669
40: 655, 669
44: 267; (4.125)
54: 267
146 (St. Peter's): 628–629; (7.21)
Coolidge Avenue
16: 246
20: 576
34: 246; (4.95)
76 (Cambridge Cemetery): 443–446; (5.72–5.76)
Winchester house: 250, 502; (4.102, 6.78)
Coolidge Hill
110: 572
111: 572
115: 248, 250; (4.100)
116: 572
123: 250, 573; (4.100)
125: 250, 572; (4.100)
134: 572
144: 248, 256
148: 248, 572
178: 656, 657; (7.69)
197: 250, 577, 578; (4.101, 6.192)
Coolidge Hill Road
6: 245
8: 245
10: 244
20: 247
24: 234, 245
44: 247
Cowperthwaite Street
15R: 379

Frost Street
1: 340; (4.220)
10: 302, 338 478–479, 491; (4.215)
17: 339; (4.217)

Garden Street
0 (Christ Church): 23, 251, 622–624; (1.24, 4.103, 7.11–7.13)
1: 251, 256, 257, 472, 478, 479, 491; (4.103, 4.110, 6.39)
2: 251, 256, 257; (4.103, 4.110)
3: 257; (4.110)
8: 257, 650; (4.110)
10 (Fay House): 258, 476, 663; (4.111, 7.76)
11 (Hill house): 463, 649; (7.56)
11 (Shepard/First Church): 628, 629; (7.20)
14: 259, 260; (4.113, 4.115)
16 (Commander): 77, 684, 685; (8.5, 8.6)
17 (Whitfield Hall): 602
20: 650, 651; (7.59)
22: 261, 650; (4.116)
24: 261; (4.116)
26–28: 261; (4.116)
27: 673; (7.89)
29 (Hotel Continental): 77, 279, 684
33: 673–674
36–38: 266; (4.124)
40–42: 114, 266; (4.124)
45: 544, 549; (6.146)
50: 541
52: 264
57: 287, 558; (4.151)
58: 70, 264, 266, 504; (2.35, 4.121)
63: 505
84: 572
88: 269, 452–454, 478; (5.85, 6.37, 6.38)
99: 269
107: 269
Garden Terrace
6: 269, 566, 567; (4.127, 6.177)
7: 568
11: 573

Garfield Street
28: 534; (6.130)
31–33: 533, 534; (6.129)
34: 533
36: 534, 535; (6.131)
39: 333, 533; (4.212)
45: 333, 534; (4.212)
49: 333, 534, 535; (4.212, 6.132)
61: 602
75: 541
81: 513
Gerry Street
12: 186; (4.12)
Gerry's Landing Road
30: 248, 250, 565; (4.101, 6.175)
42: 248, 250, 584, 585; (4.101, 6.200)
44: 248, 250; (4.101)
46: 584
Gibson Street
26–38 (Gibson Terrace): 607–608
Gorham Street
2–4: 324
Gracewood Park
1–8: 237
Grant Street
25 1/2–25 1/3: 379
27: 379
Gray Gardens East
16: 271, 573–575; (6.189, 6.190)
17: 272
22: 272
Gray Gardens West
4: 572, 573; (6.187)
20: 272
Gray Street
8–14: 286
26: 286, 302, 330, 478
31: 286
Grozier Road
44: 591
46–64: 591
Gurney Street
16: 590

Hammond Street
55: 324; (4.201)
65: 324; (4.201)
Harvard Square
0 (kiosk): 153, 155, 735, 737; (3.60, 3.65, 9.36)
0 (newsstand): 158; (3.70)
Harvard Street
383 (Ware Hall): 78, 787, 788; (10.42)
396 (D.U.): 792, 797
398: 626–627; (7.18)
Hawthorn Street
11: 192
15: 203
41: 81, 192, 602
49: 192, 559, 564, 567
Hemlock Road
2: 594; (6.216)
5: 585
9: 215
15: 584
Highland Street
1: 215–217, 558–559; (6.166)
2: 215
11: 547
45: 517
48: 218, 573; (6.188)
51: 517, 519
54: 225, 554; (4.66, 6.160)
61: 226, 227, 593; (4.67, 4.70)
64: 224, 226, 496; (4.64)
Hilliard Place
5–7: 185; (4.10)
Hilliard Street
6: 185
8: 185
9: 185
10: 185
11: 185
12–20: 185, 645; (4.11)
17: 493
Hillside Avenue
11: 549
14: 538
30: 560

Hillside Place
  6: 657
Holden Green
  All: 607–608
Holden Street
  45: 655–656; (7.67)
Holmes Place
  Harvard Branch RR Station: 730, 776; (9.27)
  Hastings-Holmes house: 63, 314–16, 463, 776; (2.27, 4.190, 4.192, 6.9, 6.10)
  Omen Keith house: 317, 487; (4.193)
  Moses Richardson house: 314, 776
Holyoke Street
  4: 692
  8–10: 131, 696; (3.24)
  12 (Hasty Pudding): 131, 796, 797; (10.56)
  16 (Apley Court): 131, 787, 788
  20: 385
  24–26: 784, 785; (10.36)
  29–33: 784, 785; (10.37)
  30 (Cooke-Winthrop house): 389; (4.274)
  30 (Phi Delta Psi/Owl): 792, 793, 797; (10.51, 10.52)
  34: 389; (4.275)
  48: 382
Hubbard Park
  3: 208
  8: 208
  12: 210
  14: 210, 558; (6.165)
  15: 210, 566
  19: 210
  20: 210, 558
Hudson Place
  4–6: 283
  46: 302
Humboldt Street
  9–11: 502, 533
  10: 502, 533
  12: 533
  15: 502, 533
Hurlbut Street
  3: 533
  9: 285, 533; (4.148)

17: 285; (4.148)
24–26: 285, 598
25: 285, 533; (4.148)
28: 285, 598
33: 533, 541
39: 533
Huron Avenue
  40: 593
  294: 229; (4.73)
  320: 658; (7.72)
  333: 227; (4.71)
  342–356: 229; (4.74)

Irving Street
  95 (William James house): 352, 366, 544, 557
  99 (Jabez Fox house): 354, 557; (4.235)
  103 (Josiah Royce house): 557
  104 (Edward Cummings house): 354; (4.235)
  105 (Alphonse Van Daell house): 352, 354, 557; (4.235)
  110 (Mrs. Julia Davis house): 352, 544, 557
  114 (E.F. Scheibe house): 356, 569–570; (6.182)
  136 (Shady Hill): 349–350, 482, 484; (4.230, 6.48)
  136 (American Academy): 674; (7.90)
  138: 356

Kennedy Road
  1: 559; (6.167)
  4: 589
  11: 221
  13: 589; (6.208)
Kennedy Street
  1–7 (Abbott Building): 137, 144, 695; (3.44, 8.26)
  10–14: 136, 688; (8.12)
  13–25 (McNamee block): 137, 139, 149; (3.37, 3.54)
  17 (Blue Anchor/Porter's): 18, 121, 139, 681–682; (3.36, 8.1)
  18–28 (Read Hall): 692, 693; (8.22)
  29–41: 152, 153; (3.62)
  34: 133; (3.28)

34–40 (The Garage): 110, 147, 152, 154, 167, 702, 727, 728; (3.50, 3.64, 9.22)
40: 133; (3.28)
44 (Fox): 792, 797
48 (Drayton Hall): 787, 790
50: 692
55: 703
64 (John Hicks house): 23, 121, 124, 145–146, 463, 473–474; (3.5, 3.47, 6.31)
64 (Joseph Hicks house): 23, 463; (1.25)
65: 167, 728, 729; (9.25)
72–74 (Viking Co.): 133; (3.29)
100: 732, 733, 808; (9.32)
Kenway Street
  5: 593
Kirkland Place
  4: 505; (6.81)
  14: 345, 346
Kirkland Street
  1: 625–626; (7.15, 7.16)
  7 (Higginson house): 342, 480, 481, 781; (6.43, 10.34)
  13 (Frisbie house): 349, 480, 481, 781; (4.229, 6.44, 10.34)
  21: 344, 480, 491; (6.60)
  25: 344; (4.225)
  29: 346
  34: 489
  37: 349
  38: 345, 349, 484, 487; (6.53)
  59–61: 357
  61: 351; (4.231)
  67: 351
  72–74: 77

Lake View Avenue
  12: 234, 246; (4.79)
  68: 235
  77: 512
  87: 235
  88: 235, 519
  94: 235, 508, 513, 525
  97: 235; (4.81)
  107: 235; (4.81)

117: 568; (6.180)
128: 525–526, 527; (6.117, 6.118)
234: 239

Lancaster Street
7: 534
8–10: 295
9: 533; (6.128)
13: 533
15: 533
17: 295, 533; (4.163)
18: 528, 533; (6.119)
19: 295, 533; (4.163)
29: 554
37: 538, 544–547; (6.147–6.150)

Langdon Court
28–30: 280
55: 280

Langdon Street
15: 280, 516
20: 280
30: 280
37: 280
41–51: 280
44: 280
50: 280
55: 280
59: 280
65: 280

Larch Road
22: 239, 242, 476–477; (6.35, 6.36)
36: 238, 242
40: 593
71: 239
77: 239
93–107: 591
111: 648; (7.55)
126: 241–242; (4.91)

Larchwood Drive
17: 244; (4.93)
20: 572
54: 572

Lexington Avenue
23: 586–587; (6.203)
33 (Lowell): 237, 598; (6.221)

58–140: 237; (4.84)
61: 235
95–99: 237
115–117: 235
167: 235, 638–639; (7.38)
168: 235; (4.82)

Linden Street
3: 692
5–7: 784
9 (Delphic): 792, 797
10 (Apthorp house): 384–85, 466, 468–470; (4.270, 6.21–6.23)
12 (Randolph Hall): 387, 787, 790; (4.272, 10.45, 10.46)

Linnaean Street
3–5 (Linnaean Hall): 599, 600; (6.223)
7 (Humboldt): 602
21: 297, 327, 335, 457–459; (6.1–6.4)
24: 513
25: 297; (4.167)
26: 513
27–31: 606
28: 541; (6.143)
32: 286, 510
36: 286
38: 286
44: 648; (7.53, 7.54)
45: 608
49: 298, 453
41–43: 600; (6.225)
48–54 (Faculty Row):
  Botanic Garden Apartments: 586, 667
  608, 609; (6.236)

Longfellow Park
4 (LDS): 634, 635; (7.32)
5 (Friends Center): 634
6: 202
7: 197, 202; (4.26, 4.35)
16: 577–578, 579; (6.193)

Lowell Street
5: 591–592; (6.213, 6.214)
7: 211
19: 203; (4.37)
25: 645–646; (7.49)

Manassas Avenue
21: 267

Martin Street
10: 285, 303; (4.173)
18: 285, 541; (6.142)
20: 285, 540, 541; (6.142)
31: 285
43: 560
51: 284; (4.146)
52: 284; (4.145)

Mason Street
3 (Deanery): 260, 523, 659; (4.114, 6.113)
6–12: 505
14: 645, 646; (7.48)

Massachusetts Avenue
Dana mansion: 180, 360; (4.242)
878: 57
1000: 712, 713; (8.61)
1016–1030: 698, 699; (8.34)
1033: 710, 711; (8.57)
1045: 701; (8.39)
1050: 110, 712, 713; (8.60)
1075: 110, 612, 613; (6.243)
1100: 110, 710; (2.65)
1105: 110, 610, (2.65)
1131: 686; (8.9)
1201 (Beck Hall/Gulf/Inn): 145, 166, 169, 686, 728, 729, 786; (8.8, 9.24, 10.39)
1218 (Quincy Hall): 110, 787, 790, 791; (10.47)
1230: 133, 147, 174, 726, 727; (9.20)
1246–1260 (Hampden Hall): 694, 787, 790; (8.25)
1268 (A.D.): 792, 795, 797; (10.55)
1280: 166, 171, 704; (8.44)
1300–1306 (Dolton Block): 690, 601; (8.19)
1300–1316 (Fairfax Hall): 690, 691, 692, 693, 708, 787, 790; (8.19, 8.23)
1304 (storefront): 131–132, 155; (3.26, 3.66)
1320–1324 (Warland Block): 125, 688, 689; (3.14, 8.13)
1324 (Porcellian): 792, 795, 797; (10.54)
1326: 155; (3.67)
1336 (Cambridge Trust): 708–709; (8.54)

1336–1346 (Holyoke House): 125, 130, 151, 690; (3.14, 3.21, 3.57)

1341 (Wadsworth house): 20, 23, 461, 756; (6.5, 6.6)

1350 (Holyoke Center): 107, 150–151, 817, 821, 822; (2.60, 3.58, 10.80, 10.83, 10.84)

1350–1362 (Little's Block): 125, 130, 151; (3.14, 3.21, 3.57)

1372: 136, 688; (3.33, 8.11)

1372–1376 (Cambridge Savings): 144, 706, 708; (8.52)

1378 (Williard's Tavern): 124, 136, 682, 726, 730; (3.11, 3.33, 9.28)

1380–1382 (Joseph Read house): 124, 136; (3.11, 3.33)

1380–1392 (Read Block): 136–137, 143, 167, 170, 174, 687; (3.33, 3.34, 3.42, 3.87, 3.88, 8.10)

1384–1392 (Read-Farwell Store): 124, 138, 688, 690; (3.11, 3.35, 8.17)

1400 (Courthouse): 636; (7.34)

1400 (Lyceum): 124, 125, 144, 640, 641; (3.11, 3.13, 3.44, 7.41, 7.42)

1400 (Coop): 144, 696–697; (8.30, 8.31)

1408–1414 (Harvard Trust): 144, 706, 704, 708; (3.44, 8.48, 8.49, 8.50)

1408–1446 (College House): 124, 125, 688, 689, 697–698, 706, 707, 770; (3.11, 3.13, 8.14–8.16, 8.48, 8.49)

1430 (University Theatre): 145; (3.45)

1450 (First Parish): 619–621, 783; (7.5–7.10)

1541: 317; (4.194)

1555 (Harvard-Epworth): 632; (7.26)

1569: 302; (4.172)

1572 (Bay State): 603; (6.228)

1580: 311; (4.186)

1581–1583: 508, 513, 514; (6.94)

1587: 514

1590 (Greycroft): 114, 307, 555; (4.180, 6.162)

1593–1595: 668

1600: 301, 311, 610; (4.171, 4.186)

1607–1615: 307

1610: 301; (4.171)

1610–1622: 279

1626: 301, 302, 507, 511, 517; (4.171)

1627: 507, 510–511, 512; (6.91, 6.92)

1636 (John Harvard): 77

1637 (Keen, orig. 1581–1583): 311; (4.187)

1640: 302, 305; (4.177)

1648 (Montrose): 78, 307, 309, 596–598; (4.182, 6.219)

1653 (Holiday Inn): 310, 311; (4.187)

1654 (Dunvegan): 78, 307, 309, 596–598; (4.182, 6.219, 6.220)

1674: 283

1675–1679: 307

1676–1686: 505

1696: 303; (4.173)

1702: 302, 303; (4.173)

1705: 286, 302

1715–1727 (Clarke house/barn): 331–332, 333; (4.211)

1718: 306, 534; (4.179)

1722: 306, 534; (4.179)

1728: 306, 534; (4.179)

1734: 536; (6.134)

1760–1770 (stores): 309; (4.183)

1764 (Brooks house): 293

1771: 303; (4.174)

1776: 534, 536; (6.133)

1799: 338; (4.215)

1801 (Lunder Arts): 671; (7.87)

1803 (N. Ave. Cong. Church): 305, 626–626, 671; (4.178, 7.16, 7.87)

1804–1818 (Oxford Court): 606, 607; (6.233)

1815 (Sears/Lesley): 311, 670; (4.185)

Meadow Way

7: 572

Mellen Street

7: 318, 519, 520; (6.108)

9: 318, 519, 520; (6.108)

11: 318

13: 318

14–16: 668

31: 318

33: 318

35: 318

Memorial Drive

888 (Hingham Mill): 422, 750, 751; (9.57)

917 (Sterling Mill): 422, 750

980 (Conventual Church): 633; (7.29)

983–984 (Radnor Hall): 603–605; (6.229, 6.230)

985–986 (Hampstead Hall): 603–605; (6.229, 6.230)

987–988 (Barrington Court): 604

992–993 (Strathcona): 110, 603

1010: 105, 610, 611; (6.240)

Mercer Circle

1: 531

3: 531

4: 531

6: 531

8: 531

9: 547

Mifflin Place

1: 167, 704

12–14: 172

Mt. Auburn Place

3: 167; (3.85)

Mount Auburn Street

2: 610

9–11: 491

29: 630–631; (7.24, 7.25)

43: 370–374; (4.256)

47: 152, 153; (3.63)

63 (Claverly Hall): 130, 787, 788, 790; (10.41, 10.45)

65 (Ridgely Hall): 787, 790; (10.45)

71–77 (Manter Hall): 657–658; (7.71)

72 (Delta Phi): 792, 797; (10.50)

72 (Phoenix-S.K.): 792, 794, 797; (10.53)

74 (Iroquois Club): 788, 790, 792, 794, 797; (10.53)

75 (Shepard Cong./St. Paul's #1): 145, 147, 625, 630; (7.14, 7.22)

76 (Spee): 792, 794, 797; (10.53)

77 (Marrett house): 23, 463, 473, 474; (1.26, 6.29, 6.30)

78 (Willard/Kappa Gamma Chi): 491, 794, 797; (10.53)

82: 690, 691; (8.20)

90: 174, 836; (10.96)

96: 128

100: 121; (3.4)

102 (Chapman heirs): 170; (3.89)

104: 169, 487, 704, 709, 728, 729; (6.52, 8.45, 8.55, 9.23)

110 (City Building): 638, 639; (7.37)

110 (Treadway): 109

112 (Conductors building): 174, 704, 735, 737; (9.39)

114–120 (Trinity Hall): 174, 787, 791; (10.49)

115 (Waverly Hall): 791

117: 496, 497; (6.70)

119–123 (Belmont Hall): 787, 791

124 (University Place): 166–167; (3.85)

125: 172, 174, 704; (8.46)

127: 492–493; (6.63)

130 (University Green): 167, 491, 612; (3.85)

134: 167, 491; (3.85)

145: 186

151: 186

153: 502

154: 186

156–158. 186, 499, 501

183: 642, 643; (7.45)

185–199: 414; (5.31)

221 (Riverview): 207, 589, 610, 611; (6.239)

233: 207; (4.43)

270 (Stillman Infirmary): 105, 798; (10.59)

309: 675; (7.92)

330 (Mt. Auburn Hospital): 676–679; (7.94–7.97)

360: 675–676; (7.93)

380: 449; (5.80)

457: 449; (5.81)

575–581: 449; (5.82)

580 (Mount Auburn Cemetery: 438–442; (5.66–5.71)

583: 442; (5.70)

Mt. Vernon Street

48: 291; (4.157)

Newport Road

1–7: 606; (6.231)

2–8: 606; (6.231)

12: 606

Nutting Road

2: 186; (4.12)

4: 186; (4.12)

6: 186; (4.12)

8–10: 484

Old Dee Road

6: 593

7: 576

11: 585

12: 593

18: 584, 585; (6.201)

19: 576

Oxford Street

8: 344; (4.224)

12: 346

15: 346, 349; (4.229)

19: 349; (4.229)

20: 346

23: 346

50 (Hazelwood): 321–322, 324, 325, 480, 481; (4.203, 6.45)

60: 836

64: 606

114: 338, 339; (4.218)

121: 513

124: 598

135–137: 508

Palmer Street

18–20: 723,724; (9.15, 9.16)

Parker Street

47: 69, 200, 201; (2.33, 4.34)

Phillip's Place

2: 260, 493; (4.114)

3: 661

5: 489, 661

6: 661

9: 661

Plympton Street

14 (Crimson): 796, 797

101: 381, 383, 838; (4.268)

Potter Park

1: 284, 286; (4.149)

Prentiss Street

6: 302, 490; (6.58)

35: 517, 518, 526; (6.102)

42: 513

Prescott Street

94: 784

96: 784, 785; (10.38)

Putnam Avenue

5: 380, 381; (4.266)

22: 374; (4.257)

37: 380

111: 750, 751; (9.56)

237: 748; (9.53)

Quincy Street

12 (Beck-Warren house): 362, 482, 483; (6.47)

14–16 (Dana-Palmer house): 362, 364, 491; (4.244)

16 (Edward Tyrrel Channing house): 359, 362, 484, 485, 654–655; (4.241, 6.49, 7.66)

17: 364, 365, 565; (4.248)

20: 366, 642; (4.250, 7.44)

25: 496; (6.69)

28: 482, 506, 507, 508; (4.46, 6.85)

31: 365; (4.247)

36: 94, 505, 650

38: 366, 504; (4.249)

42: 503; (6.79)

Quincy Street

48: 491; (6.60)

50 (Swedenborg Chapel): 632, 633; (7.27)

Raymond Street

57: 593

60: 270, 575

79: 298, 593; (4.168)

87: 298

90: 560, 561; (6.169)

103–105: 561

Remington Street
   10–14: 602
Reservoir Street
   1: 226; (4.68)
   11: 226, 590; (6.210)
   12: 222, 522–523; (6.112)
   14: 226, 593
   18: 226, 593
   25: 225, 517, 551; (6.100)
   26: 226, 227, 593
   27: 57; (2.21)
   30: 226
   33: 566
   40: 657
   43: 566
   46: 229; (4.73)
   48: 229; (4.73)
   54: 229; (4.73)
   56: 229; (4.73)
   58: 229; (4.73)
   60: 229; (4.73)
Revere Street
   5: 168
   7: 168
Riedesel Avenue
   2: 532
   4: 532
   5: 215, 216, 531, 532; (4.53)
   6: 532
   7: 215, 216, 531, 532; (4.53)
   9: 215, 216, 531, 532; (4.53)
River Street
   349: 742, 746; (9.50)
Riverview Avenue
   11: 381, 383, 421, 838; (4.268)
Robinson Street
   Botanic Garden Apartments: 608
Rutland Street
   2: 281
   9: 280, 541; (4.141)

Sacramento Street
   3: 306, 329, 555, 668
   5: 329

9–13: 505
12: 513
15–19: 505
16: 528, 529–530; (6.122, 6.123)
20: 328, 329; (4.206)
32: 646–648; (7.50–7.52)
41: 65, 328–29, 502; (4.207)
42: 541
46: 328
Scott Street
   7: 352, 557
Shady Hill Square
   1–12: 356, 357; (4.238)
   4: 657
Shaler Lane
   1–33: 607–608; (6.234)
   2–24: 607–608; (6.234)
Shepard Street
   3–5: 305; (4.177)
   7–9: 305; (4.177)
   10–12: 281
   11: 305; (4.177)
   15–17: 281
   24: 281
   27–29: 281, 498
   38–44: 281; (4.142)
   46: 599, 602
   52: 519, 520; (6.107)
   56–58: 510
   57: 517, 518; (6.101)
South Street
   17: 146–147, 478; (3.49)
   20: 146; (3.48)
Sparks Place
   1: 587
Sparks Street
   45: 210
   47: 210
   49: 210; (4.46)
   61–67: 215, 505, 522; (6.111)
   70: 199, 521, 524, 525; (6.114)
   76: 199, 544
   77: 215; (4.55)
   80: 199, 267, 506, 653–654; (4.31)

85: 215
St. John's Road
   8: 587
   10–12: 587
   11: 659
   13: 256
Story Street
   4: 171, 585
   6: 171, 585
   8–12 (TAC II): 710; (8.56)
   11: 602
   14–16: 172, 711; (8.58)
   18: 493; (6.64)
Sumner Road
   18: 785; (10.38)

Traill Street
   15: 233
   17: 233

University Road
   2–6 (Craigie Hall/Chapman Arms): 787, 790, 791; (10.48)
   33: 165, 739, 740; (3.83, 9.41, 9.42)
Upland Road
   73: 291; (4.158)
   79: 291; (4.158)
   140: 374, 539–540; (4.257, 6.140)
   144: 587, 588; (6.206, 6.207)
   150–152: 560
   169: 299, 561; (4.170)
   176: 727
   182: 561
   186–188: 561
   196: 561
   226: 99

Walker Street
   26: 283
   30: 283; (4.144)
   33: 283
   34–36: 283; (4.144)
   44: 283, 525–526; (6.115, 6.116)
   57–59: 283, 508

68–70: 283, 513
69: 283
107: 550

Walnut Avenue
5: 510
6: 292, 536–537; (6.135)
9: 292, 536–538; (6.136)

Ware Street
10: 698; (8.32)
12: 87, 369; (4.253)
19–21 (Stanstead): 594, 595–596; (6.217)

Washington Avenue
4–6 (Stratford Manor): 607
5–7: 297; (4.166)
26: 295, 538, 554–555; (6.161)
33: 295, 297, 538, 546, 555; (4.165)
49: 295, 297, 525, 538–539, 541; (4.165, 6.137–6.139)
78: 512
81: 291, 512, 513; (6.93)
86–88: 292
92: 512, 513
99: 292; (4.159)
101: 291, 292, 513; (4.159)
107: 292; (4.159)

Waterhouse Street
1: 259; (4.113)
1 (Mather Court): 599, 602
5: 275
7: 272, 274, 474–75; (4.130, 6.32)
9: 275, 554, 560
11: 275; (4.134)
13 (Christ, Scientist): 632–633; (7.28)

Wendell Street
1: 671
3: 671
18: 502
20: 502
87: 322; (4.199)

Whittier Street
3: 299; (4.170)

Willard Street
4: 206, 564, 567; (6.174)
8: 206, 258; (4.112)
27: 585

Winthrop Square
Winthrop Park condos: 166, 170, 174, 612; (3.89, 6.242)

Winthrop Street
41: 126, 489, 490
44: 391; (4.277)
45: 391; (4.277)
66 (Univ. Lutheran): 634, 635; (7.30, 7.31)
80 (William Manning house): 17, 123, 134; (3.7, 3.20)
89: 484
91 (Pi Eta): 170, 796, 797; (3.89)
96: 126
98: 121, 123; (3.8)

General Index

Architects are listed in the General Index if they are mentioned in the text for reasons other than the buildings attributed to them. Refer to the Architects and Builders Index for a complete listing.

Georgian vs. Gothic, 619–621, 783
Gothic Revival, 224, 446, 494–497, 619–621,
    646–647, 659; (4.64, 5.76, 6.65–6.70, 7.5,
    7.6, 7.9, 7.50, 7.51)
Greek Revival, 126, 203, 302, 486–491;
    (6.52–6.59)
International Style, 226, 248, 272, 577–578,
    580–586, 659, 661, 702, 704, 709, 805, 812,
    815–817, 818, 830–831; (6.192–6.202, 7.75,
    10.77–10.79, 10.91)
Jacobean, 524, 598–600, 790
Mansard/Second Empire, 198, 261–262, 368,
    504–516, 690–692; (4.252, 6.81–6.99)
Mid-Century Modern (20th century), 225–226
Mid-Century Romanticism (19th century),
    493–504; (6.65–6.80)
Modern, 248, 576–594, 816–818;
    (6.192–6.216)
Panel Brick, 281, 505, 521–522, 525–526, 659,
    692–693, 770; (6.109, 6.111, 6.115, 6.116,
    8.23, 10.21)
Postmodern, 683, 703–705, 830–831, 852n6;
    (8.8, 8.44, 8.46, 10.91)
Queen Anne, 285, 324, 333, 517, 524–541;
    (4.201, 4.212, 6.114–6.143)
Ranch, 272
Regency, 198, 345, 491–493; (6.60–6.64)
Ruskinian Gothic, 521–524, 776, 779, 786,
    892; (6.109–6.113, 8.21, 10.31, 10.39)
Shingle Style, 541–550; (6.144–6.153)
Spanish Eclectic, 593
Stick Style, 517–520; (6.100–6.108)
Tudor Revival, 299, 563, 566–567, 572–575,
    604, 788; (6.172, 6.178, 6.188–6.190, 6.229)
architecture, domestic
house plans
    center-entrance, 207, 379, 461–489, 501,
        505–513, 553, 558–561; (4.41, 4.263,
        6.5–6.55, 6.76, 6.77, 6.81–6.93, 6.158,
        6.165–6.169)
    side-hall, 74, 479–480, 488–491, 498, 502,
        505–506, 513–516, 519–520, 540–541;
        (6.41, 6.42, 6.57, 6.59, 6.95, 6.99, 6.107,
        6.108, 6.142)

pattern books
    Benjamin, Asher, 465, 477, 486
    Campbell, Colen, 465–466
    Davis, Alexander Jackson, 493–494
    Downing, Andrew Jackson, 494, 498, 501
    Gibbs, James, 465
    Hills, Chester, 495; (6.67)
    Lafever, Minard, 486
    Langley, Batty, 465, 467–468, 475, 849n2;
        (6.16, 6.17, 6.33, 6.34)
    Palladio, Andrea, 465, 482
    Shaw, Edward, 486
    Stuart and Revett, 486, 492; (6.51)
    Vaux, Calvert, 505
    Woodward, George, 505
Arensberg, Walter and Louise, 354
Arnold, John, 122; (3.6)
Ashburner, Anne and Grace, 351
Astor, John Jacob, 786
August, Dr. Albert, 598–599, 800; (6.222)
Austin, Edward, 316, 776
Austin, Henry, 495; (6.67)
Austin, Lucy, 293
Austin, Rev. Thomas, 335, 459
Austin, Susan, 291, 459
Austin, Thomas, 336

Bacon, Henry, 413; (5.30)
Baez, Joan, 153; (3.60)
Baird, Walter, 165
Baker, George Pierce, 562; (6.171)
Baldwin, James W., 337
Baldwin, Maria, 98, 646
Balmer, William, 724–725; (9.18)
Bancroft, William A., 71, 87–88, 92, 98, 369,
    380–381; (4.253, 4.266)
banks, 77, 705–709; (8.47–8.55)
    Cambridge Bank, 39, 44, 705
    Cambridge Federal Savings & Loan Assoc., 77,
        148, 701, 706–707; (8.53)
    Cambridge Savings Bank, 77, 144, 169, 682,
        688, 705–706, 708, 732; (8.51, 8.52)
    Cambridge Trust Co., 108, 708–710; (2.61,
        8.54)

Charles River Bank, 44, 222, 705–706; (8.47)
Charles River Trust Co., 144, 697, 705–706;
    (3.44, 8.48)
Charlesbank Trust Co., 77
Coolidge Bank, 169, 612, 604, 709; (8.45, 8.55)
Fleet Bank, 706
Harvard Trust Co., 77, 144, 697, 706–708;
    (8.48–8.50)
Reliance Cooperative Bank, 77, 843n24
Barnard, Edward A., 606, 697
Barr, Alfred, 814
Barry, Mayor J. Edward, 100
Bartlett, A.S., 333, 534–535; (4.212, 6.132)
Bartlett, John, 512, 738
Bascom, Catherine (Mrs. William Bascom), 185
Bascom, William, 185
Bassett, William, 282; (4.143)
Batchelder, John, 180
Batchelder, Marianna, 185
Batchelder, Samuel (1784–1879), 54, 180, 183,
    190, 260, 464, 491, 496–497, 845n2; (4.18,
    6.70)
Batchelder, Samuel F., 97, 189–190, 398
Batchelder, Samuel, Jr., 185, 190, 640, 642
Bates, Jacob Hill, 44, 148, 192, 252, 479, 483;
    (6.40)
Bates, Joseph, 273–275; (4.131)
Bates, William, 256
Baxter, Sylvester, 90–91
Bayliss, Walter Cabot, 786
Beal, Rhoda, 259, 276; (4.113, 4.133)
Bean, Joseph, 18, 681
Beck, Charles, 362, 482–483; (6.47)
Belcher, Andrew, 179, 188
Belcher, Gov. Jonathan, 188, 273
Belknap, Jeremy, 16–17
Bell, Alexander Graham, 54, 208
Bell, Stoughton, 92, 100, 262, 642
Bemis, Dr. Jonathan, 287
Bemis, Faith, 672
Benchley, Robert, 796
Bennett, Arnold, 683, 804
Bennett, Joseph, 374
Bennett, Spencer. *See* Phips, Spencer

Benson, Mrs. Ruth, 560
Bent, Newell, 211
Berkeley, Bishop George, 261
Bernard, Gov. Francis, 465
Bernays, Edward L., 423–424
Bernier, Napoleon, 571, 843n29
Best, Herbert, 411–412; (5.29)
Beunke, Fred, 843n24
Bigelow, Jacob, 439–441, 764; (5.67–5.69)
Bigelow, Marshall, 738, 750
Bigelow, William, 528
Biglow, Abraham, 359, 362
Birkhoff, Garrett and Ruth, 225, 580–581;
    (6.197)
Bishop, Charles S., 329
Bishop, Joel Prentiss, 329
Bitter, Francis, 248, 250, 584; (4.101)
Blackall, Clarence, 75, 92, 279–280, 425, 542;
    (4.138). *See also Architects and Builders Index*
Blackman, Horace, 297, 540; (6.141)
Blaikie, Suther, 211
Blakey, John, 429; (5.53)
Blatchford, Mary, 432
Blevins, Albert, 75, 77. *See also Architects and
    Builders Index*
Blevins, John, 379; (4.263)
Blodgett, Emma and Abbie, 285, 533; (4.148)
Blodgett, Warren K., 549
Blowers, Capt. Pyam, 260
Blowers, Thomas, 260
Bok, President Derek, 167, 826–830; (10.89,
    10.90)
Boland, Frank A.K., 398, 684
Bond, George Phillips, 264
Bond, William Cranch, 364
Bonner, John, 716
books and periodicals
    American Architect & Building News, 521,
        524–525
    Architectural Record, 525, 584, 586, 589, 702,
        710
    The Cambridge of 1776, 397
Bordman, Aaron, 436, 687
Bordman, Andrew, 123, 254, 272–273, 687, 716;
    (4.105, 4.131)

Bordman, Elizabeth (Mrs. John Brown), 682
Bordman, Moses, 273
Bordman, Moses, Jr., 20
Bordman, Richard, 44
Bordman, Zechariah, 122, 682; (3.6)
Borland, Anna Vassall (Mrs. John Borland), 384
Borland, John, 25, 384–385; (Table 1.2)
Borland, John, Jr., 384
Borland, Leonard, 384, 845n5
Boucher, Ferdinand, 391
Bowditch, Nathaniel, 717, 764
Bowen, Francis, 276
Bowen, Maria, 276
Bowers, Elizabeth (Mrs. George Bowers), 334
Bowers, George, 334
Bowers, Jerathmeel, 334
Bowers, William and Rosamund Forbes, 248–
    250, 577–578; (4.101, 6.192)
Bowman, Hannah (Mrs. Samuel Bowman Jr.),
    335, 339
Bowman, Nathaniel, 339
Bowman, Noah, 339
Bowman, Samuel, 326, 335, 339
Bowman, Samuel, Jr., 335
Boynton, Morris, 280
Bradford, Gov. Robert M., 101
Bradish, Isaac, 18, 122; (3.6)
Bradish, John, 17, 716
Bradstreet, Anne (Mrs. Simon Bradstreet), 7
Bradstreet, Simon, 4, 7, 252–253; (4.104)
Brandeis, Louis, 225, 332–334
Brattle, Gen. William, 25–26, 122, 178–180,
    318; (3.6, 4.3, Table 1.2)
Brattle, Rev. William, 179
Brattle, Thomas, 25, 30, 121–122, 123, 179–183,
    252, 256, 428; (3.6, 4.108, Table 1.2)
Braybrook, Ezra, 499; (6.91)
Brazer, Esther Stevens (formerly Mrs. Cecil Fra-
    ser), 146, 844n6
Breed, Charles B., 735
Brewer, Thomas, 129
Brewster, John, 215–216, 218–219, 522, 531–
    532; (4.53, 6.111, 6.126)
Brewster, William, 95, 215–216, 532, 554, 635,
    849n9; (4.54)

Bridge, John, 401
Bridge, Samuel, 401
bridges
    Anderson Bridge, 425–427; (5.49)
    Charles River (Charlestown) Bridge, 35, 760
    Cottage Farm Bridge, 425
    Craigie's Bridge, 38, 394
    Eliot Bridge, 241, 422, 432; (5.42)
    Great Bridge, 7, 13, 92, 425–426, 428, 720;
        (5.47, 5.48, 9.8, 9.9)
    Harvard Bridge, 300, 683
    Longfellow Bridge, 30, 95, 425, 721, 760
    Menotomy Bridge, 9
    River Street Bridge, 430
    Weeks Bridge, 425–427; (5.50)
    West Boston Bridge, 35–40, 360, 394, 687,
        760; (2.6)
    Western Avenue Bridge, 417, 430, 721; (5.34)
Briggs, LeBaron Russell, 94, 663
Brigham, Thomas, 187
Brimmer, George, 47, 245, 248, 439
Brock, Frank, 697
Brooks, Arthur H., Jr., 585–586, 621. *See also Ar-
    chitects and Builders Index*
Brooks, Arthur H., Sr., 642
Brooks, Charlotte (Mrs. Edward Everett), 321
Brooks, John, 192, 202, 553
Brooks, Luther, 345, 359, 485
Brooks, Margaret, 202
Brooks, Peter Chardon, 321, 342
Brooks, Sumner A., 295
Brooks, Sumner J., 293–295, 297, 502, 527, 531–
    533; (6.128)
Brooks, Van Wyck, 362
Brown, Blair, 845n18
Brown, Daniel, 203, 205
Brown, Edward, 380
Brown, James, 373–376, 705, 738, 741–742;
    (4.259)
Brown, James heirs, 376–380
Brown, John M., 380
Brown, Maj. John, 682
Brown, Mary (Mrs. Joseph Cowperthwaite), 377,
    380

Brown, William, 687–688; (8.10, 8.11)

Browne, George, 261, 650; (4.116)

Bryant, Henry, 355; (4.236)

Bubier, John, 320; (4.196)

Buckingham, Ellen and Lucy, 200

Buckingham, Joseph, 200, 362, 480–482, 506–507; (6.46, 6.85)

building contracts, 482–484, 489–491

building materials
  brick, 2, 17, 39, 74–75, 164, 374, 571, 703–704, 714, 716, 721, 774–775, 845n15; (4.257, 6.184, 9.1, 10.28)
  clapboards, 39, 849n4
  columns, 488, 622–623
  concrete masonry units, 190, 198, 432–433; (5.60)
  concrete, reinforced, 78, 727, 740, 746, 751; (9.20, 9.42, 9.50, 9.57)
  granite, 447, 688, 762, 850n3
  Guastavino tile, 633
  ledgestone, 75, 446, 627, 628, 632–633, 851n13; (5.76, 7.18, 7.19, 7.27)
  lumber, 39, 75–76, 571, 714, 716, 719, 721; (9.1, 9.6, 9.7)
  marble, 447
  millwork, 571; (6.185)
  mortar, 75, 851n13
  prefabricated frames, 538
  roofing, terra-cotta, 850n14
  roughcast, 622
  shutters, 849n3
  stucco, 566–569, 571, 602, 622; (6.177–6.182)
  suppliers
    Cambridge Lumber Co., 76
    Dix Lumber Co., 76, 570, 572; (2.39, 6.186)
    Home Service Co., 76; (2.39)
    Kennebec Framing Co., 538
    Union Stone Co., 198
    Wm. C. McConnell Co., 571; (6.185)
  terra-cotta, 540; (6.140)
  timber, right to cut, 2, 318, 457, 460

building tradesmen, 73–74

building types

apartment houses, 145–146, 280, 318, 594–613; (3.46, 6.217–6.243)
  "pillboxes," 267, 570, 610

barns, 333; (4.211)

barracks
  Revolutionary War, 26, 276, 317, 394; (5.2)
  World War I, 403; (5.16, 5.17)

bathhouses, 428

boarding houses, 783–785, 808, 852n3; (10.38)

boathouses, 428–430; (4.53–4.56)

business blocks, 687–705; (8.10–8.46)

carbarns, shops, yards, 158–160, 447; (3.71–3.74, 5.77)

carriage houses, 264, 292, 334, 510, 514, 537, 538, 546; (6.89)

clubs and student organizations, 791–797; (10.50–10.57, Table 10.2)
  Hasty Pudding, 385, 796; (10.56)
  Lampoon, 790, 796–797; (10.45, 10.57)
  Phi Delta Psi, 389, 792–793; (10.51, 10.52)
  Pi Eta, 129, 170, 612, 796; (3.89, 6.242)

clubs and student organizations, 791–797; (10.50–10.57, Table 10.2)

courthouses, 636–637, 759; (10.7)

fire stations
  Cambridge 1 (Church Street), 637–638, 914; (7.36, 9.23)
  Central Fire, 316, 402–403, 639, 768; (7.39, 10.19)
  City Building, 638–639; (7.37)
  Lexington Avenue, 638–639; (7.38)
  Taylor Square, 639

French flats, 594, 595, 598

garages, commercial, 81, 147, 207, 300, 843n31; (4.43)

garages, home, 81, 567, 727, 852n3; (6.178)

garages, parking
  Amoco (104 Mt. Auburn Street), 728–729; (9.23)
  Harvard Square Garage (34–40 Kennedy Street, 133, 147, 154, 702, 727–728, 731; (3.50, 3.64, 9.22, 9.29)
  Harvard Square Garage (65 Kennedy Street), 728–729, 844n2; (9.25)

garages, service
  Church Street Garage, 726–727; (9.21)
  Harvard Automobile Co., 726–727; (9.20)
  Motor Mart Garage, 725; (9.18)
  Viking Company, 133; (3.29), 843n31

halls and clubhouses, 640–643; (7.41–7.45)

houses
  double houses, 235; (4.82)
  "large doubles," 298–299, 561; (4.170)
  "sixteen-footers," 207, 284; (4.41, 4.145)
  "ten-footers," 300, 317
  three-deckers, 79–80, 112, 128, 237; (2.40, 3.18)
  two-family houses, 219, 237, 269; (4.84)
  workers cottages, 205–207, 379; (4.41, 4.262)

market house, 116; (3.1)

meetinghouses, 615–621; (7.1–7.10)
  First, 5, 615–616, 691; (7.1, 8.20)
  Second, 13–14, 615–616; (1.13)
  Third, 14–15, 616–617, 759, 841n9; (1.15, 7.2, 10.7)
  Fourth, 15–17, 43, 116, 118, 395, 616–618, 759, 764; (1.18, 3.1, 3.3, 5.3, 7.3, 7.4, 10.7)
  Fifth, 619–621, 752; (7.5, 7.10, 10.1). *See also* First Parish Church

office buildings, 129, 166, 169, 172–173; (3.95)
  architectural offices, 710–713 (8.56–8.61)

police stations, 637–639, 914, 923; (7.37)

post offices, 115, 148, 696, 701, 812; (8.28)

power stations
  Blackstone Station, 733, 837; (9.33)
  Boston Elevated Railway, 134, 248, 390, 420, 732–737, 791, 807–808; (3.30, 4.276, 5.40, 9.32–9.39, 10.67)

private dormitories, 130–131, 783–791; (10.39–10.49, Table 10.1)
  Apley Court, 131, 806
  Beck Hall, 130, 145–146, 362, 594, 627, 686, 692, 728–729, 786, 806; (3.46, 7.18, 8.8, 9.24, 10.39)
  Belmont Hall, 171–172, 791; (3.90)
  Claverly Hall, 74, 130, 385, 788, 790, 806, 808; (10.41, 10.45)
  Craigie Hall (The Craigie), 165, 167, 786, 790–791, 806; (3.82, 10.48)

Gerry's Landing, 244–250; (4.94, 4.99)

Gold Coast, 130–135, 783–799, 806, 808, 844n4; (10.36–10.60)

Gray Gardens, 242, 247, 269–272; (4.129)

Hubbard Park, 204, 207–210; (4.45, 4.47)

Huron Village, 228–229; (4.74)

Kerry Corner, 66, 111, 114, 134, 374–383, 806–807, 827–828, 830, 833, 837; (4.259, 4.261, 4.269, 10.67, 10.89)

Larchwood, 239, 242–244, 248; (4.92)

Lechmere Triangle, 844n54

Lewisville, 67, 273–274, 281–283, 842n17; (4.132, 4.143)

Lower Common, 177, 251, 272–287; (4.131, 4.132, 4.137)

Lower Marsh. *See* Kerry Corner

Marsh (Upper Marsh), 66, 91, 203–207, 380; (2.48, 4.38, 4.39)

Mid Cambridge, 103, 111, 522, 833, 854n36

North Cambridge, xv, 48–49, 53, 75–76, 84, 89, 96, 99, 113, 115, 272, 289, 379; (2.13, 2.42, 4.155)

Observatory Hill, 105, 111, 114, 194, 263–272, 827–828; (4.126, 10.89)

Professors Row, 341–349, (4.222, 4.223, 4.227, 4.228)

Reservoir Hill, 226–227, 851n29; (4.69)

Riverside, 105, 111, 114, 742, 833–834, 837, 853n28

Shady Hill, 341, 349–358, 557, 819, 827–827; (4.232, 4.233, 4.236, 4.239, 10.89)

University Park, 844n54

Upper Marsh. *See* Marsh

West Cambridge, 212, 219, 846n23

newspapers, 77–78, 843n25

Cambridge Chronicle, 54, 77–78, 100

Cambridge Daily Telephone, 78

Cambridge Press, 77

Cambridge Sentinel, 77

Cambridge Tribune, 77–78, 298

parishes

First Parish (Cambridge), 14, 17, 20, 33, 37, 43, 118, 119, 494, 783; (2.4, 3.2)

Second Parish (Arlington), 10, 17, 38

Third Parish (Brighton), 11, 17, 38

parks movement, 89–93, 843n34

planning, Garden City Movement, 269, 356; (4.238)

politics

"Cambridge Idea," 97

Irish participation, 97–99, 205–206

population, 17, 33–34, 58, 61, 67–68, 70; (Table 2.2)

property values, 13, 34, 36, 71, 72, 78, 84, 112, 114–115, 169, 208, 212, 231, 242, 272, 332, 356, 364, 370, 421, 509, 510, 610, 829, 844n56, 851n27, 852n4

protests and demonstrations

anti-Catholic riots of 1834, 637

anti-Harvard, 111; (2.66)

anti-war, 111, 154–156; (2.67, 3.65)

save the sycamores, 423–424; (5.46)

Revolutionary War, 24–30, 394

roads

distance from Boston, 35–36, 38; (2.3, Table 2.1)

turnpikes, 36–40

social composition, 18, 20, 306, 818

squares

Arsenal Square, 276, 432

Brattle Square, 6, 126, 129, 148, 156; (3.15, 3.20, 3.68)

Central Square, 11, 44, 51, 77, 86, 103, 105, 113, 126, 142–144, 148

Eliot Square, 6, 148

Harvard Square, 6, 126, 148

Lafayette Square, 36, 39, 41; (2.7)

Porter Square, 289, 300, 307, 310, 313; (4.189)

Putnam Square, 110; (2.64, 2,65)

Winthrop Square. *See* Winthrop Park

topography, general, 1–4, 34, 212, 272, 841n1, 841n9

Agassiz neighborhood, 313; (4.189)

Avon Hill, 251, 272, 395; (4.130, 5.4)

Cambridge Heights, 288, 291. *See also* Avon Hill

Charles River, 4, 7, 413–431; (5.31–5.55)

clay pits, 227, 251, 267 372–374, 379, 841n1; (4.255)

"Craigie's Pond"/"Dictionary Lake"/"Smith Lake," 196, 198, 200, 205, 642; (4.25, 4.29)

Dana Hill, 11, 35, 272

drumlins, 4, 64, 211, 245, 247; (2.28, 4.94, 4.97)

Fresh Pond, 11, 12, 642; (1.11)

Gallows Hill (see also Avon Hill), 288

Gerry's Landing, 14, 414, 419, 428, 650–651; (5.31, 5.38, 5.51)

Gibbon's Creek, 9

Graves Neck, 12; (1.11)

Great Marsh, 12; (1.11)

Great Swamp, 11

Hell's Half Acre, 103, 423

"hill reserved for a fort," 389, 391; (4.277)

"Hollow, the," 200

Jones Hill, 288. *See also* Avon Hill

Lechmere's Point, 35, 38, 194, 213

"level plain, the," 272

Little Neck, 12, 370, 348n75; (1.11)

Long Marsh, 12; (1.11)

"Lost Brook"/"Atlantic Stream" (Follen-Willard streets), 9, 57, 198, 200, 205, 275, 846n16; (4.29)

Lower Marsh, 66

Millers River, 9, 312, 341, 843n37

Mount Auburn Cemetery, 439

Neck, The, 9, 11, 12, 33, 35; (1.11)

Observatory Hill, 66, 251, 272, 819

Ox Marsh, 12, 125, 158–159, 178–179, 420, 730; (1.11, 3.12, 3.72)

peat bogs (Parker Street), 200

Pelham's Island, 11, 35

pine swamps, 12, 185, 272, 312, 314, 318, 341; (1.11, 4.188)

ponds, unnamed, 29, 49, 177, 234, 313, 346, 375, 377; (2.13, 4.80, 4.189, 4.258)

Reservoir Hill, 57, 199, 212, 226–227, 851n29

Ship Marsh, 12, 715; (1.11)

Spring Hill, Somerville, 304

springs and wetlands, 4, 180, 194

Carey, Arthur Astor, 96, 200, 352, 551–552, 566; (6.154–6.156)

Carlton, Osgood, 72

Carnegie, Andrew, 800

Carpenter, Benjamin, 217

Carpenter, Deborah Lee (Mrs. Benjamin Carpenter), 217–219; (4.58)

Carpenter, Thomas, 122; (3.6)

Carr, Cornelia Crow, 219

Carr, Lucien, 219–221; (4.60)

Carr, William, 715

Carter, George E., 264, 530–531; (6.124)

Carter, George Putnam, 530–531; (6.125)

Carter, Silence (Mrs. William Carter), 298, 453

Carter, William, 298, 452–453; (5.86)

Cary, Sarah ("Sallie") and Emma, 192, 519–520; (6.106)

Casey, Thomas, 235; (4.82)

cemeteries
  burying place, original, 434
  Cambridge Cemetery, 244, 247, 250, 283, 443–446; (5.72–5.76)
  Cambridgeport Burial Ground, 436, 443
  Harvard burial ground, 434
  Lewisville tomb lot, 282–283; (4.143)
  Mount Auburn Cemetery, 238, 246, 438–442, 443, 447, 450; (5.66–5.71, 5.77, 5.83)
  Old Burying Ground, 26, 36, 193, 214, 251, 254, 434–436, 716; (2.3, 4.21, 4.105, 5.61–5.63, 9.2)
  Revolutionary War burials, 230–231, 436–437, 846n28, 849n16

Chadborne, Sarah, 133; (3.28)

Chadbourne, Christopher, 169

Chamberlin, Daniel, 232, 642

Chamberlin, John, 256

Chamberlin, William E., 233, 554. *See also Architects and Builders Index*

Champney, Martha, 384

Champney, Samuel, 715

Chandler, Samuel, 461

Chandler, Theophilus, 215

Channing, Edward Tyrrel, 45, 359, 362, 484–485, 655; (4.241, 6.49, 7.66)

Channing, William Ellery, 258

Chapin, Richard, 589; (6.208)

Chapman, Edmund A., 180, 487, 723; (6.52, 9.13)

Chapman, Francis, 129, 723

Chapman, John, 356

charitable institutions and hospitals, 675–679; (7.91–7.97)
  Avon Home, 233, 657, 675; (7.91, 7.92)
  Cambridge Children and Family Services, 675
  Cambridge Homes for Aged People, 244, 675–676; (7.93, 7.96)
  Cambridge Hospital. *See* Mount Auburn Hospital
  Mount Auburn Hospital, 105, 244, 428, 676–679; (5.52, 7.94–7.97)

Charles River
  commerce. *See* transportation
  dam, 377, 419–420, 430
  recreational facilities, 428–430; (5.51–5.56)
  tidal range, 844n3

Chase, Josiah, 443

Chase, William J., 109

Chauncy, Charles, 434

Chesholm, Deacon Thomas, 681

Child, Francis, 276, 351

Child, Julia, 557

Child, Samuel, Jr., 122; (3.6)

Childs, James, 186

Choate, Charles, 219; (4.58)

Church, Dr. Benjamin, 189

Church, George M., 723; (9.13)

churches
  Allen Congregational Church, 49, 304; (2.13, 4.176)
  Appleton Chapel, 626–627, 764; (7.17)
  Cambridge Society of the New Jerusalem (Swedenborgian), 586, 622–623, 824, 850n17; (7.27, 10.86)
  Christ Church, 22–23, 190, 251–252, 254, 256, 263–264, 384, 394, 395, 616, 622–624, 716; (1.24, 4.103, 4.105, 5.2, 5.4, 7.11–7.13)
  Church of Jesus Christ of Latter-Day Saints, 107, 192, 203, 634; (7.32)
  Conventual Church of St. Mary and St. John, 633; (7.29)

First Church in Cambridge, Congregational, 628–629; (7.20)

First Church of Christ, Scientist, 632–633; (7.28)

First Parish in Cambridge, Unitarian Universalist, 124, 619–621; (3.11, 7.5–7.10)

Friends Meeting at Cambridge, 203, 634

Harvard Epworth Methodist Episcopal Church, 317, 632, 781; (7.26, 10.34)

Holmes Chapel, 305

Holy Trinity Armenian Church, 107, 215, 635, 854n32; (7.33)

North Avenue Congregational Church, 305, 311, 339, 626, 671; (4.178, 7.16, 7.87)

Old Cambridge Baptist Church, 305, 315, 342–343, 346, 625–627, 630, 776; (4.178, 4.191, 4.223, 7.15, 7.18)

Shepard Congregational Church, 260, 380, 389; (4.114, 4.275). *See also* First Church in Cambridge, Congregational

St. James's Episcopal Church, 850n6

St. John's Chapel, 624, 627–628, 659–661; (7.19, 7.73, 7.75)

St. Joseph's Mission (Brighton), 429

St. Paul's Church, 145, 373, 374, 380, 382, 389, 628–629; (4.256, 4.267, 4.275, 7.21)

St. Peter's Church, 66, 267, 628–631; (2.30, 7.22–7.25)

University Lutheran Church, 634–635; (7.30, 7.31)

cities, towns, and political subdivisions
  Arlington, 10–11, 17, 38, 43, 89, 272, 846n23; (1.10)
  Barre, 67, 281
  Belmont, 89, 847n47
  Billerica, 10, 272; (1.10)
  Boston, 1, 2, 4–8, 10–11, 13, 18, 22, 27–28, 34, 35–38, 40, 46, 51, 52, 58, 60, 61, 66–67, 70–71, 89, 99, 102, 126, 130, 300, 760; (frontispiece, 1.2, 1.27, 1.28, 2.2, 2.6, 2.15, 2.24, Table 2.1)
  Brighton, 10, 11, 17, 38; (1.10)
  Cambridge Farms. *See* Lexington
  Cambridge Village. *See* Newton

Charlestown, 2–8, 10–12, 15, 26, 29, 34–35, 312, 342, 349, 715, 841n8, 841n10, 847n54; (1.2, 1.11, 1.14, 1.30, 4.188)

Duxbury, 272

Haverhill, 298; (4.169)

Lexington, 10, 14, 43; (1.10)

Little Cambridge. *See* Brighton

Marblehead, 231

Menotomy. *See* Arlington

Milton, 716

Newton, 10, 57, 141, 539; (1.10)

Salem, 3, 7–8, 217, 231, 239, 460, 477, 607, 843n25

Shawshine. *See* Billerica

Somerville, 1–2, 9, 15, 24, 26, 49, 54, 69, 73, 75, 79, 81, 97, 113, 304, 313, 330, 339, 352, 847n54; (1.14, 2.13, 2.37, 4.176, 4.189)

Southside. *See* Newton

Watertown, 4, 12, 14–15, 43, 141, 212ff, 244–250; (1.11, 1.14)

West Cambridge. *See* Arlington

Winchester, 250

Clark, Jonas, 716

Clarke, Henry M., 284–285, 331–334, 336, 527, 533–534; (4.210, 4.211)

Clarke, J. Milton, 98

Clarke, Jane Hurlbut (Mrs. Henry M. Clarke), 285

Clarke, Martha, 295

Cleary, Francis, 68

Clemens, Samuel, 410

Clendaniel, William, 441

clubs and voluntary associations

Bee, 96

Boston Watch & Ward Society, 155

Brattle Theater Company, 640–641

Cambridge Anti-Tuberculosis Association, 79

Cambridge Boat Club, 95, 244, 422, 429–430, 642; (5.56)

Cambridge Casino, 56, 96, 428–429, 642, 721; (2.20, 9.11)

Cambridge Civic Association, 103, 110, 114, 844n51

Cambridge Club, 96, 642

Cambridge Committee for Plan E, 100, 114

Cambridge Historical Society, 95, 97, 146, 197, 219, 276, 459, 636

Cambridge Housing Association, 79

Cambridge Liberian Emigrant Association, 67

Cambridge Municipal Art Society, 79, 92, 401, 425

Cambridge Plant & Garden Club, 96, 409, 432

Cambridge Skating Club, 95, 614, 642–643; (7.45)

Cambridge Social Dramatic Club, 96, 276, 640–641

Cantabrigia Club, 96, 170, 672

Colonial Club, 96, 366–369, 642; (4.250, 7.44)

Cooperative Housekeeping Association, 94

Daughters of the American Revolution, 96, 401, 849n7; (5.14)

Daughters of the Revolution, 401, 849n7; (5.13)

Friendly Fire Society, 637

Harvard Square Business Men's Association (Harvard Square Business Association), 136, 142–143, 147, 148, 735

Harvard Square Defense Fund, 164–170, 704

Hunneman Fire Company, 637–638; (7.35)

Ku Klux Klan, 99

Massachusetts Horticultural Society, 246, 439

Massachusetts Society for Promoting Agriculture, 194, 451–452

Neighborhood Ten Association, 163, 166

Newtowne Club, 96

Old Cambridge Photographic Club, 96

Riverside Boat Club, 428–430; (5.55)

Shepard Historical Society, 97

Society for the Collegiate Instruction of Women, 258, 476, 650, 662

Society for the Preservation of New England Antiquities (Historic New England), 95, 146, 197, 297, 459

Society for the Promotion of Theological Education at Harvard College, 344–345, 766

Society for the Propagation of the Gospel in Foreign Parts, 384, 622

Society of Arts and Crafts, Boston, 552, 562, 566, 769

South End House Association, 357

Temperance movement; No License, 68–69

Trustees of (Public) Reservations, 90

Coates, Thomas, 844n45

Cobb, Cyrus and Darius, 398–399; (5.10)

Coffman, Samuel, 160

Cohen, Bertha, 110, 152–153; (3.62)

Cohen, Sarah, 70; (2.35)

Cohen, Sheldon, 158; (3.70)

Cohen, Steven, 267

Cohn, Alfred, 284

Coleman, John F., 696; (8.28)

colleges, institutes, and professional schools

American Academy of Arts and Sciences, 674; (7.90)

Andover Theological Seminary/School, 314, 355, 783

Boston University, 667–668

Cambridge School of Architecture and Landscape Architecture, 672–673; (7.88)

Episcopal Divinity/Theological School, 256, 260, 480, 492, 523, 587, 624, 659–661, 671; (4.114, 6.42, 6.62, 6.113, 7.73–7.75)

Lesley Normal School. *See* Lesley University

Lesley University, 295, 311, 318, 492, 626, 661, 668–671; (6.62, 7.83–7.87)

Lincoln Institute of Land Policy, 532

Longy School of Music, 276, 673–674; (7.89)

National Center of Economic Education of Children, 670; (7.85)

Normal School of Physical Training. *See* Sargent School of Physical Education

Sargent School of Physical Education, 129, 310, 318, 667–668, 772; (3.20, 7.82, 9.12)

Smith College, 672–673

Weston School of Theology, 661

Collins, Thomas, 322; (4.199)

Colman, John, 24

Comey, Arthur, 81

Common Pales. *See* Newtowne, Town of, defenses

Comstock, Ada Louise, 664, 672

Conant, Kenneth, 583, 659

Conant, President James Bryant, 437, 666, 672, 813–817, 850n9; (10.75–10.79)
Connerton, Edward, 379
Connor, Maurice, 123; (3.9)
Cook, Charles W., 299
Cook, George, 7, 17
Cook, Joseph, 118
Cook, William, 218, 521–522; (6.109, 6.110)
Cooke, George and Joseph, 389, 715
Cooke, Joseph, Jr., 389
Cooke, Josiah Parsons, 369, 662, 765; (4.253, 10.13)
Cooke, Mary (Mrs. Josiah Parsons), 662
Coolidge brothers, 387, 852n4
Coolidge, Archibald, 387, 788–790, 852n4
Coolidge, Dr. Stephen, 384
Coolidge, Edward, 246
Coolidge, Harold, 387, 788–790, 801, 806, 852n4
Coolidge, John P., 819
Coolidge, Joseph (1666–1737), 384
Coolidge, Joseph G. (1820–87), 244, 246; (4.95, 4.96)
Coolidge, Joseph R., Jr. (1862–1926), 788–790, 852n4
Coolidge, Joshua (1759–1835), 231, 234, 244; (4.78, 4.80)
Coolidge, Joshua, Jr. (1785–1860), 234, 245
Coolidge, Josiah (1787–1874), 47, 234
Coolidge, Rosamund, 247
Coomaraswamy, Alice Richardson (Mrs. Francis Bitter), 248, 250, 585; (4.101)
Coon, Sarah B., 534–535; (6.131)
Cooney, Patrick, 267
Cooper family, 46, 312; (4.188)
Cooper, Hannah (Mrs. Samuel Cooper), 334
Cooper, John (1727–62), 334
Cooper, John (d. 1691), 326, 327
Cooper, John, Jr. (1656–1736), 327, 334
Cooper, Jonathan (1707–66), 302
Cooper, Samuel (1654–1718), 327, 458
Cooper, Samuel II (b. 1697), 327
Cooper, Sarah (Mrs. John Cooper Jr.), 334
Cooper, Walter (1697–1751), 458

Corcoran, Mayor John B., 101
Corcoran, Paul, 105
Corlett, Elijah, 643, 688; (8.11)
Cottrell, Adam, 180, 493; (6.64)
Counihan, Judge Edward, 706
Cowperthwaite, Joseph, 377
Cox, Allen H., 269, 454
Cox, George Howland, 92, 355; (4.236)
Cox, Susannah, 121
Crackbone, Benjamin, 274, 334
Crackbone, Gilbert, 300
Craigie, Andrew, 22, 36–38, 121, 194–195, 214, 217, 260, 262–263, 273, 359, 434, 452, 466–468, 845n11; (1.23, 4.23, 4.24, 4.119, 4.131, 6.15, 6.18)
Craigie, Elizabeth Shaw (Mrs. Andrew Craigie), 194–195, 214–215, 263; (4.118)
Crane, Mayor Edward A., 109–111
Crawford, Thomas, 849n19
Cromwell, Oliver, 7, 370, 389
Cronin, Daniel, 357
Crosby, Simon, 327
Crothers, Rev. Samuel McCord, 436
Cummings, Edward, 354, 402; (4.235)
Cummings, Jacob, 738
Cuno, James, 833
Curley, Mayor James Michael (Boston), 99, 843n19
Cushman, Charles, 269
Cutter, James, 387

Dakin, Frederick, 750
Daly, Charles U., 827
Daly, Mayor Augustus, 381
Dana, Chief Justice Francis (1743–1811), 35–36, 41, 44, 119, 359–361, 385, 387; (2.9, 3.2, 4.242)
Dana, Elizabeth (1789–1874), 362
Dana, Elizabeth Ellery (b. 1846), 649; (7.56)
Dana, Francis, Jr. (1777–1840), 121, 396
Dana, Henry Wadsworth Longfellow ("Harry") (1881–1950), 95, 97, 197
Dana, James (1811–90), 327, 330
Dana, John B. (1800–87), 222, 499, 706; (672)

Dana, Lydia (1755–1808), 360
Dana, Rev. Edmund (1729–1823), 360–362
Dana, Richard (1700–76), 360
Dana, Richard Henry III (1851–1931), 95, 97, 100, 183, 425, 532, 642, 802, 849n9; (6.127)
Dana, Richard Henry, Jr. (1815–82), 63, 67, 117, 180, 208, 261, 283, 398, 499–500, 649; (6.73)
Dana, Richard Henry Sr. (1787–1879), 44, 252, 362, 436
Dana, Sarah (1791–1866), 362
Dana, William (1776–1861), 362
Dane, Nathan, 764
Danehy, Mayor Thomas, 827
Danforth, Elizabeth (Mrs. Francis Foxcroft), 342
Danforth, Isaac, 501; (6.77)
Danforth, Nicholas, 681
Danforth, Samuel, 24, 25; (Table 1.2)
Danforth, Thomas, 341–342, 384
Daniels, Leonard, 185
Davenport, Charles, 50–51, 414–416, 842n6; (2.14, 5.33)
Davey, William H., 429
Davis, Adm. Charles Henry, 366, 649; (4.249, 7.56)
Davis, John (machinery dealer), 292–293; (4.161)
Davis, John (treasurer), 717
Davis, Julia, 352
Davis, Person, 234
Davis, T. Alfred, 234
Dawes, William, 26
Day, Rev. Gardiner, 436
Daye, Stephen, 8, 852n10
de Gerard, Victor and Alexandra, 576; (6.191)
de Gozzaldi, Mary Isabella Batchelder, 97, 190, 192; (4.20)
Deane, Charles, 199; (4.31)
Deane, George Clement, 199
Dearborn, Henry A.S., 439–440
Dee, Sarah, 239, 449
Dee, Thomas, 239–240, 447, 449–450; (4.88, 5.77, 5.83)
DeForest, Lockwood, 557; (6.164)
DeGuglielmo, John, 109–110, 112

Deming, David, 179
Demmon, Reuben, 234, 285, 303, 336–337; (4.174)
Derby, George, 318
DeRosay, Lewis, 338
Despradelle, Désiré, 769
Devens, Arthur Lithgow, 548
Devens, Mrs. Arthur L. (Agnes H. White), 219
Devi, Ratan. *See* Coomaraswamy, Alice Richardson
DeVoto, Bernard, 103, 423
DeWire, Thomas, 356
DeWolf, Dr. John J., 374, 376; (4.259)
Dexter, Lucy, 199
Dexter, D. Gilbert, 78, 290–292, 512, 514; (4.156, 4.159)
Dickson, John, 716; (9.2)
Diehl, Edward, 586–587; (6.203)
Dietrich, Paul, 712. *See also Architects and Builders Index*
Dietrick, Ellen Batelle, 94
Dietz, Sheldon and Annabel, 174, 587
DiGiovanni brothers (of Belmont), 267
DiGiovanni, John, 157, 174
DiGiovanni, Louis, 157, 167–168, 172, 261, 703, 704, 728–729; (8.42, 8.43, 9.25)
Dinsmore, James, 206
Dixwell sisters, 649; (7.56)
Dixwell, Epes Sargent, 70, 264, 266, 503; (2.35, 4.121)
Doane, Isaiah, 370
Dodge, Edward S., 199, 521, 524–525; (6.114)
Dodge, John C., 521, 524–525; (6.114)
Dolton, Richard, 130, 690–691; (8.19)
Dorrien, Carlos, 409
Dougherty, Rev. Manasses, 267, 381, 628–630
Douglass, Frederick, Jr., 147
Dow, George L., 144, 148, 695, 698–701; (3.51, 3.52, 8.38)
Dow, Richard (Tony), 148–149, 151
dower rights. *See* inheritance and dower
Dowling, Mark, 210; (4.47)
Downing, Antoinette, 108
Downing, Theodore, 338

Draper, J. Sumner, 210; (4.47)
Dresser, Edwin, 270, 276, 283, 749; (4.278, 9.54)
Drowne, Shem, 628
DuBois, W.E.B., 99
Dudley, Dorothy, 397
Dudley, Thomas, 4–5, 637
Duehay, Mayor Francis, 167
Duguid, William M. and Mary, 576, 634. *See also Architects and Builders Index*
Dunbar, Charles, 222, 224, 225; (4.64, 4.65)
Dunbar, Katherine Copeland (Mrs. William Dunbar), 225; (4.66)
Dunbar, William, 225
Dunlap, Frances (Mrs. James Russell Lowell), 232
Dunster, President Henry, 8, 252–253, 434–435, 643, 754; (4.104)
Duquesne, Eugene Joseph Armand, 769
Dwight, Timothy, 43–44, 842n3

Eagleson, Thomas, 379
Eastham, Melville, 269
Eaton, Nathaniel, 8, 20, 754, 772; (1.7)
economic cycles
    post-Revolutionary War, 26–30
    Embargo of 1807 and War of 1812, 36, 44, 256, 476
    Panic of 1873, 232, 235, 526
    Panic of 1893, 129, 561, 694
    Great Depression, 101–102; (Table 2.4)
    post-World War II, 101–103, 148
    1980s, 114–115
    1989 recession, 169
    1990s boom, 174
Edgell, George, 806
Edmunds, William, 108
Edwards, Abraham, 126
Ela, Alfred, Lucia, and Richard, 190
Eliot, Abigail Adams, 657
Eliot, Catharine (Mrs. Andrews Norton), 349–351
Eliot, Charles (1859–97), 89–93, 239, 351–353, 393, 410–412, 417–422, 557, 801, 843n35, 843n38; (4.233, 5.27, 5.29, 5.36, 5.37)
Eliot, Charles W. 2nd (1899–1993), 107, 843n35

Eliot, Mary Pitkin (Mrs. Charles Eliot), 369
Eliot, President Charles W. (1834–1926), 71, 92, 97, 241, 316, 350–351, 393, 410, 425, 430–432, 619–620, 642, 662, 667, 684, 726, 739, 754, 768–804, 843n35; (2.36, 4.89, 4.231, 10.20–10.64)
Eliot, Rev. Samuel Atkins, 225, 349–350
Eliot, Thomas Hopkinson, 99–100
Ellery, Elizabeth (Mrs. Francis Dana), 44, 360
Ellery, William, 360
Ellis & Andrews/Ellis & Melledge, 77, 108, 843n23; (2.61)
Ellis, Stearns, 334
Ellis, William Rogers, 77
Elston, Thomas, 513
Emerson, Ralph Waldo, 63, 649
Emerson, Rev. William, 26–27
Emory, Woodward, 211
entertainment
    Club 47, 152–153
    José Mateo Ballet Theatre, 627
Erikson, Leif, monument, 419, 842n12; (5.38)
Erinton, Ann, 434
Estabrook, Joseph, 534
estates
    Apthorp, 19, 384–388, 790; (1.19, 4.270, 4.271)
    Brattle, 19, 178–187; (1.19, 4.4–4.6, 4.14)
    Craigie, 194–212; (4.22, 4.24)
    Dana, Francis, 119, 312, 341, 359–369; (3.2, 4.188, 4.221, 4.242, 4.243, 4.245, 4.251)
    Deane, 199, 267; (4.31)
    Elmwood, 232–233, 430–431; (4.78, 5.57)
    Forbes, 247–250, 565, 577; (4.99, 4.101)
    Foxcroft, 13, 22, 177, 312, 341–358, 760, 777; (1.19, 4.188, 4.221, 10.29)
    Gray, 232, 238–244, 431, 449; (4.77, 4.88, 5.57)
    Inman, 13, 19, 22, 26, 29, 35, 177, 312; (1.19, 1.31, 4.188)
    Lechmere-Sewell, 19, 194–195, 212, 213–217; (1.19, 4.24, 4.51, 4.52)
    Lee, 19, 212, 214, 217–221; (1.19, 4.52, 4.56, 4.59)
    Longfellow, 196–198, 202; (4.25, 4.36)

Oliver-Gerry, 19, 212, 230–237; (1.19, 4.75–4.78)

Palfrey, 312, 321–326, 776, 836; (4.188, 4.198, 4.200, 4.202, 10.29)

Phips, David, 19; (1.19)

Phips, Spencer, 19, 370–383; (1.19, 4.254, 4.255)

Ruggles-Fayerweather, 19, 212, 214, 221–229; (1.19, 4.52, 4.62, 4.63)

Sachs, 357–359; (4.240)

Shady Hill (Norton), 242, 341, 349–358, 557, 674, 777, 819; (4.232–4.236, 4.239, 10.29)

Vassall, Henry, 19, 188–192, 194–194; (1.19, 4.19, 4.24)

Vassall, John, 19, 192–212; (1.19, 4.22)

Wendell, 204, 312, 313, 318–320, 321; (4.188, 4.195, 4.197, 4.198, 4.200, 4.202)

Winchester, 250, 443, 445; (4.102, 5.74)

Worcester, 195, 198–201, 261–262; (4.24, 4.29, 4.33, 4.117)

Estes, Ivory, 129, 139, 692; (3.20, 3.36, 8.21)

Eustis, Dr. William, 331

Eustis, Henry, 346

Eustis, Margaret, 317, 339; (4.218)

Everett, President Edward, 180, 185, 195, 258, 318, 321, 364, 397, 439, 754, 764, 772–773

Fales, Mary Ann, 484–485; (6.50)

Falxa, Dr. Martin and Madelon, 590–591; (6.212)

farms
  Bowers-Cooper, 312, 334; (4.188)
  Bowman, 312, 327; (4.188)
  Cooke, 389–391; (4.273, 4.276)
  Coolidge, 177, 245–248, 650; (4.94, 4.96–4.98)
  Cooper, 289, 293, 295–297, 312, 334; (4.164, 4.188)
  Cooper-Frost (east side Massachusetts Avenue), 312, 327–330; (4.188)
  Cooper-Frost-Austin, 272, 327, 334; (4.130)
  Frost (Kirkland Street), 312, 342, 345–348, 777; (4.188, 4.227, 4.228, 10.29)
  Frost, Edmund, 312, 335; (4.188)
  Frost, Gideon, 312, 334–340, 394; (4.188, 4.213, 5.2)
  Goffe, 360, 370

Haugh, 370

Hill, 258–262

Jackson-Bowman, 312, 339; (4.188)

Jarvis, 312, 317; (4.188)

Paddlefoot-Andrew-Bowman, 312, 334, 335–337; (4.188)

Parker-Hastings, 312, 327; (4.188)

Phips-Winthrop, 370–373; (4.255)

Stone, 244–246

Stratton, 237–244

Thatcher, 244–245

Wyeth, 258–262

Wyeth, Ebenezer, 238–239

Wyeth, Jonas, 237–238

Farnham, John, 750

Farquhar, Robert, 533

Farrar, John, 343–344, 480; (4.223)

Farwell, Levi, 39, 44–45, 136, 252, 625, 688–690, 692, 705; (2.10, 8.10, 8.17)

Farwell, Prudence Dockham Bordman (Mrs. Levi Farwell), 44–45; (2.11)

Faust, President Drew Gilpin, 837

Fay, Judge Samuel P.P., 258

Fayerweather, Thomas, 221–223, 371, 492; (4.61, 4.62, 4.254)

Felton, President Cornelius, 321, 362–364, 366; (4.249)

Fernald, Merritt, 269

Fessenden, Nathaniel, 273

Fessenden, William, 213

Fielding, Robert, 241

Fielding, Ruth, 241

Fillebrown, Edward, 273, 283, 302; (4.131)

Fillebrown, James, 385

Fillmore, Wellington, 293

Fish, Frederick, 239, 318, 846n30

Fisher, Clarence S., 564

Fiske, Ensign David, 72

Fiske, John, 192, 306, 430, 514–515, 542–543; (6.96, 6.97)

Fitzpatrick, Bishop John, 267

Flagg, Augustus, 380

Flax, Samuel, 308; (4.183)

Floyd, Margaret Henderson, 548, 552

Follen, Charles, 275; (4.134)

Folsom, Charles, 118, 339, 738

Forbes, Edward Waldo, 247–248, 250, 354, 565, 577–578, 584–585, 801, 803; (4.101, 6.175, 6.192, 6.200, 10.63)

Ford, James W., 79

Ford, Jonathan, 281, 330

Forrest, Lawrence, 380; (4.264)

Foster heirs, 202

Foster, Andrew (d. 1831), 195; (4.24)

Foster, Bossenger, 190, 194, 344

Foster, Charles C., 344

Foster, Dr. Thomas (d. 1831), 281, 362

Foster, George, 203, 211, 846n16

Foster, James, 203

Foster, Joseph, 194, 344

Foster, Samuel, 203

Fowler, Samuel, 349

Foxcroft heirs, 359

Foxcroft, Dr. Francis III, 342

Foxcroft, Francis, 20, 342

Foxcroft, John, 19, 22, 25, 146, 177, 274, 330, 331, 342; (1.19, Table 1.2)

Foxcroft, Judge Francis II, 342

Foxcroft, Phebe (Mrs. Samuel Phillips Jr.), 342

Francis, Convers, 212, 302

Francis, Ebenezer III, 356

Francis, Ebenezer, Jr., 283, 345, 773; (4.226)

Francke, Kuno, 262

Franquelin, Jean-Baptiste, 14, 616; (1.13, 7.1)

French, Daniel Chester, 95, 411–413, 849n6, 849n9; (5.30)

Friedman, Richard, 164

Friel, James, 327

Frisbie, Catherine Saltonstall Mellen (Mrs. Levi Frisbie), 318

Frisbie, Levi, 318, 344, 480–481, 781; (6.44, 10.34)

Frizzel, John (1713–47), 188

Frost family, 46

Frost, Benjamin, 337

Frost, David (1757–1787), 327, 330–331

Frost, Deborah (Mrs. Ebenezer Frost), 327

Frost, Ebenezer (1697–1798), 326, 327, 334

Frost, Edmund (1680–52), 326, 344

Frost, Edmund (b. 1803), 337

Frost, Edmund (d. 1672), 326

Frost, Elizabeth, 284–286, 302, 477; (4.147)

Frost, Elizabeth Allen (Mrs. David Frost), 330

Frost, Ephraim (1682–1753), 273

Frost, Frederick A. (b. 1820), 336–337

Frost, Gideon (1784–1803), 272–274, 295, 312, 326, 334–335, 339, 474–475; (4.130, 4.131, 4.188, 4.204, 6.32)

Frost, Dr. Gideon (b. 1755), 335

Frost, Hannah (Mrs. Samuel Bowman Jr.), 326, 335, 339

Frost, Hannah Cooper (Mrs. Edmund Frost), 326

Frost, Henry (b. 1817), 336–337, 672

Frost, Horace, 577–579; (6.193)

Frost, Dr. James (1732–70), 326, 327, 330, 331; (4.204)

Frost, James, Jr. (1754–1825), 326, 327, 330; (4.204)

Frost, Lucy (Mrs. Gideon Frothingham), 337

Frost, Martha (Mrs. Thomas Austin), 335, 345

Frost, Mary Prentiss (Mrs. James Frost), 327

Frost, Mary Teele (Mrs. William Frost), 313, 336–338; (4.213, 4.214)

Frost, Neptune (slave), 335, 436

Frost, Paul, 187–188, 413; (4.15, 5.30). *See also Architects and Builders Index*

Frost, Robert, 215

Frost, Sarah, 302, 335; (4.173)

Frost, Thomas, 336

Frost, Walter (1766–1818), 302, 335, 339, 345

Frost, William (1774–1832), 331, 335–336, 338; (4.215)

Frost, William E. (ca. 1825–1913), 338

Frost, William, Jr. (1801–87), 305, 335, 336–338, 478–479; (4.214–4.216)

Frothingham, Amos, 502

Frothingham, Francis, 572–573; (6.187)

Frothingham, Frederick, 337

Frothingham, Gideon, 337; (4.214)

fuel, home heating
coal, 718–721, 852n3; (9.11)
firewood, 716–718

Fuller, Abraham, 180

Fuller, Arthur Buckminster, 185

Fuller, Buckminster, 590

Fuller, Edith Davenport, 185

Fuller, Henry, 298

Fuller, Margaret, 117, 180

Fuller, Richard, 185

Fuller, Timothy, 180, 185

Galbraith, John Kenneth, 105

Galvin, Mary, 784–785; (10.38)

Galvin, William L., 75, 77, 238, 577, 580–581, 639–640, 698–701, 852n5. *See also Architects and Builders Index*

Gamage, William, 122; (3.6)

Gannett, Rev. Caleb, 252, 314–315; (4.191)

Gannett, Thomas B., 228, 560; (6.168)

Gardner, Thomas, 24

Gass, Mary (Mrs. Frederick Worcester), 536; (6.134)

Gates, William, 291

Gearner, Edmund, 122; (3.6)

Gerry, Elbridge, 230–234, 239, 846n27

Gibbs, James, 465

Gibson, John, 206

Giedion, Sigfreid, 577

Gifford, Gladys ("Pebble"), 166–167, 169

Giles, Joel, 287

Gilman, Arthur (architect). *See Architects and Builders Index*

Gilman, Arthur (educator), 94, 267, 275, 279, 397, 410, 654, 662–663; (4.139)

Gilman, Grace, 662

Gilman, Stella (Mrs. Arthur Gilman), 662

Glover, Elizabeth, 7–8, 252–253; (4.104)

Glover, Henry, 275, 510

Glover, Rev. Jose, 8

Goelet, Robert (1880–1941), 133

Goelet, Robert, Jr. (1921–89), 797; (10.57)

Goffe, Edward, 8, 13, 44, 360, 755; (1.7, 10.2)

Goldenberg, Harold, 210

Good, Mayor Timothy, 81, 381

Goodhue, Harry Eldredge, 724–725; (9.18)

Goodies (Harvard cleaners), 46; (2.12)

Goodridge, Charles F., 286, 330

Gookin, Daniel, 370, 715

Gookin, Samuel I and II, 274, 384

Gore, Christopher, 360

Gould, Benjamin, 276

Gould, Thomas Ridgeway, 401

Graham, Saundra, 111, 826; (2.66)

Grant, Christopher, 230

Graves, Thomas, 1, 5

Gray, Asa, 276, 453–454, 478; (5.85, 6.37, 6.38)

Gray, Francis Calley, 768

Gray, John Chipman, 239, 447, 449; (5.77)

Gray, Justin, 112

Gray, Roland, 239

Gray, William, 46, 232, 239, 476–477; (6.35, 6.36)

Greco, Charles, 75, 101, 568–569, 843n21; (6.181). *See also Architects and Builders Index*

Greely, Leander, 538

Greely, Mary Williams, 397

Green, Mayor James D., 47–48, 126, 393, 637, 842n4

Greene, George Washington, 196

Greene, Mrs. Harding, 108; (2.61)

Greene, Richard, 314

Greener, Richard T., 98

Greenleaf, James and Mary Longfellow, 183, 506; (6.83)

Greenleaf, Simon, 47, 183, 190

Greenough Horatio, 366, 503

Greenough, Henry, 366–368, 503–505, 625. *See also Architects and Builders Index*

Greenough, James, 662

Greenough, Mary (Mrs. James Greenough), 662

Greenough, Mrs. David, 503; (6.79)

Greenough, Richard S., 849n19

Griswold, Bishop Alexander, 659

Griswold, William, 200, 548

Grozier, Edwin, 212, 238

Guleserian family, 683

Gurney, Dean Ephraim, 225; (4.65)

Gurney, Ellen Hooper (Mrs. Ephraim Gurney), 225, 662, 846n25

Guyot, Arnold, 198, 504; (6.80)

Harvard Hall II, 13–14, 466, 637, 755–758;
  (1.13, 10.4)
Harvard Hall III, 30, 465, 752, 758–759, 765;
  (1.32, 10.1, 10.6, 10.7, 10.14)
Harvard Stadium, 425–426, 796; (5.48)
Harvard Union, 362, 369, 483, 769, 796, 799,
  832–833; (6.47, 10.60)
Hastings Hall, 317, 796
Hauser Hall, 831–832; (10.92)
Hemenway Gymnasium, 317, 766, 776, 780–
  781; (10.33, 10.34)
Hemenway Gymnasium II, 853n13, 853n26
Hicks House, 23, 30, 97, 121, 124, 145–146,
  463, 472–474; (1.35, 3.5, 3.10, 3.47, 6.31,
  Table 6.1)
Holden Chapel, 752, 756–759, 765; (10.1,
  10.5–10.7, 10.14)
Hollis Hall, 314, 466, 752, 758–759, 760,
  762, 765, 853n18; (4.190, 10.1, 10.6, 10.7,
  10.14)
Holworthy Hall, 761, 763, 769, 770–771;
  (10.8, 10.11, 10.20)
Holyoke Center, 150–151, 817–818, 821–
  822, 838, 845n9; (3.58, 10.80, 10.83,
  10.84)
Holyoke House, 125, 151, 688–690, 769–
  770, 800; (3.14, 3.58)
Houghton Library, 697, 851n23
Hunt Hall, 769, 772, 829, 832; (10.24)
Indian College, 13–14, 755
Indoor Athletic Building (see Malkin Center)
Jefferson Physical Laboratory, 349, 776, 781;
  (4.229, 10.34)
Kennedy School of Government, 829, 831;
  (10.91)
Kirkland House, 808
Kittredge Hall, 454
Lamont Library, 364
Langdell Hall, 349, 780–783; (4.229)
Larsen Hall, 256, 824; (10.87)
Lehman Hall, 16, 32, 116, 735, 764, 809,
  810; (2.1, 3.1, 9.36, 10.71)
Leverett House, 382, 808, 825; (10.88)
Lionel, Mower, and Wigglesworth Halls, 809,
  815; (10.76)

Littauer Hall, 346, 780, 815; (10.76)
Loeb Drama Center, 480, 817, 824; (6.42)
Loeb House, 809
Longfellow Hall, 824. See also Radcliffe
  buildings
Lowell House, 382, 391, 808; (4.277, 10.68)
Lowell Lecture Hall, 344, 806
Malkin Athletic Center, 382, 391; (4.277)
Mallinckrodt Hall, 316, 344, 809, 811
Massachusetts Hall, 17, 752, 756–759, 765,
  770, 774; (1.18, 10.1, 10.4, 10.6, 10.7,
  10.14)
Mather House, 372, 382, 825; (10.88)
Matthews Hall, 692, 764, 769–770, 810;
  (10.20, 10.71)
McKinlock Hall, 382–383, 838; (4.268)
Memorial Church, 808–809, 813; (10.75)
Memorial Hall, 68, 317, 517, 521, 659, 769,
  776–779, 784, 810, 819–821, 832–833,
  849n4, 849n19; (10.31, 10.71, 10.82,
  10.93)
Museum of Comparative Zoology, 317, 345,
  348, 503, 766–768, 776–780, 800; (4.228)
museum of modern art (proposed), 383, 826,
  833, 835, 837; (10.95)
Newell Boathouse, 429
Nichols House, 256–257, 824; (4.109)
Northwest Science Building, 324, 836
Observatory, 66, 268, 286, 766–768; (2.30,
  4.126, 4.150, 10.17)
Observatory (Quincy Street), 364, 371;
  (4.254)
Observatory Commons, 830
Old Quincy, 838
One Western Avenue, 819, 835
Paine Hall, 854n30
Palfrey House, 324, 480–481; (4.203, 6.45)
Peabody Museum, 780, 811; (10.72)
Peabody Terrace, 382, 383, 750, 821; (4.269)
Perkins Hall, 349, 796, 798; (4.229, 10.58)
Phillips Brooks House, 760
Pierce Hall, 349; (4.229)
Pound Hall, 823, 838
President's House I, 15

Presidents' houses II-III (Quincy Street), 364–
  366, 371, 809, 826; (2.48, 4.254)
privies, 755, 762, 771
Pusey Library, 829
Quincy House, 382, 825
Radio Hall, 324
Randall Hall, 346, 739, 796
Read House, 252, 254, 472, 475, 824; (4.106,
  6.33, 6.44, Table 6.1)
Richard A. and Susan F. Smith Campus Cen-
  ter. See Holyoke Center
river houses, 806–808; (10.65–10.68)
Robinson Hall, 369, 772
Rogers Gymnasium, 768; (10.19)
Roscoe Pound Hall, 310
Russell Hall II, 790; (10.46)
Sackler Museum, 366, 830; (4.249, 10.90)
Sanders Theater, 346, 849n19
Science Center, 819
Semitic Museum, 346
Sever Hall, 365, 369, 771–772, 850n11;
  (10.22–10.23)
Smith Hall, 382, 806; (10.65, 10.67)
Sparks House, 491, 505, 632, 778; (6.60,
  10.30)
Standish Hall, 382, 806; (10.65, 10.67)
Stillman Infirmary, 105, 610, 678, 769, 796,
  798, 821, 853n29; (7.96, 10.59)
Stoughton Hall I, 755, 756–760, 765; (10.4.
  10.6, 10.7, 10.14)
Stoughton Hall II, 716, 752, 760, 762; (10.1)
T. Jefferson Coolidge Laboratory, 809, 811;
  (10.72)
Taubman Building, 830
Thayer Commons, 730, 768, 776; (9.27)
Thayer Hall, 769–770; (10.20)
Thayer Herbarium, 453–454; (5.85)
University Hall, 752, 760–763, 768, 771, 826,
  833; (10.1, 10.8, 10.9, 10.11)
University Information Center I, 833
University Information Center II, 836
University Libraries Building, 836; (10.96)
University Museum, 780, 800, 811; (10.72)
Wadsworth House, 119, 461–462, 472, 759,
  765; (3.2, 6.5, 6.6, 10.7, 10.14, Table 6.1)

Hiam, Peter, 590–591; (6.211)

Hicks, Alonso, 324; (4.201)

Hicks, Elizabeth, 121, 123

Hicks, John (1725–75), 23, 26, 30, 97, 121, 123, 124, 145–146, 342, 436, 463, 472, 473–474, 715; (1.32, 3.5, 3.10, 3.47, 6.31, Table 6.1)

Hicks, Joseph (1661–1747), 23, 121, 463; (1.25, 3.5)

Higginson, Henry Lee, 425, 796, 800

Higginson, Stephen, 42, 342–343, 396, 480–481, 717, 760–763, 781; (4.222, 4.223, 6.43, 10.10, 10.11, 10.34)

Higginson, Thomas Wentworth, 43–44, 64, 93, 97, 117, 200, 205, 420, 430, 443, 528, 642, 649, 652; (6.120)

Hildreth, Abijah, 302

Hill, Aaron (1730–92), 23, 205–206, 217–218, 258, 260, 472; (4.40, 4.111, Table 6.1)

Hill, Abraham, 260, 463

Hill, Adam S., 522–523; (6.112)

Hill, Adam Sherman, 222

Hill, Dr. Aaron (1758–1830), 252, 267, 273, 287, 637; (4.131)

Hill, Edward B., 580; (6.196)

Hill, Hannah and Harriet, 260

Hill, Jacob (d. 1768), 258, 263, 472; (4.112, Table 6.1)

Hill, James, 318

Hill, Nathaniel, 314–315; (4.190, 4.191)

Hill, Susan, 267

Hilliard, Abraham, 302, 374

Hilliard, George S., 196, 221–222

Hilliard, Harriet (Mrs. William Peck), 452

Hilliard, Rev. Timothy, 738

Hilliard, Sarah (Mrs. Charles C. Little), 741

Hilliard, William, 124, 128, 183, 396, 483–484, 705, 738, 741

Hills, Chester, 495; (6.67)

Hills, John, 392

Hilton, James M., 180, 237, 519–520, 598, 689, 690, 692–693; (6.108, 6.221, 8.13, 8.19, 8.23)

Himeon, Minor W., 516

Hincks, Gen. Edward, 77, 91–92, 218, 227–228; (4.71, 4.72)

Hocking, William Ernest, 654–655; (7.66)

Hodges, Rev. Richard Manning, 275

Hoffman, Sidney, 449

Holbrook, Edward, 788

Holden, Samuel, 540

Holly, Patrick, 267

Holmes, Dr. Oliver Wendell (1809–1904), 63, 117, 180, 314, 316, 362, 410, 430, 742, 847n45; (2.27, 4.192)

Holmes, John, 56, 63–64, 314–316, 477; (2.27)

Holmes, Joseph, 183, 185–186, 252

Holmes, Olive, 166

Holmes, Oliver Wendell, Jr. (1841–1935), 63; (2.27)

Holmes, Rev. Abiel, 34, 43, 314–315, 625; (4.191)

Holyoke, President Edward, 389

Homer, Winslow, 256–257, 649; (4.110, 7.56)

Hooker, Rev. Thomas, 5, 7, 9–12, 30, 178; (1.6, 1.8, 1.32)

Hooper, Dr. Henry, 218, 460

Hooper, Dr. Richard, 217, 459–460

Hooper, Edward W., 225, 228, 517, 551; (4.65, 6.100)

Hooper, Fanny (Mrs. Edward W. Hooper), 225

Hopkinson, Charles, 98

Hoppin, Rev. Nicholas, 624

Horsford, Eben Norton, 64, 199, 436, 662, 842n12; (4.30)

Horsford, Lillian, 662

Hosmer, Harriet Goodhue, 219

Houghton, Mayor Henry O., 90, 443, 739, 741–745

house moving (not all houses listed), 190, 205–206, 212, 233, 242, 271–272, 285–285, 302, 317, 318, 338, 339, 346, 369, 379, 491, 838, 843n20; (4.215, 4.218, 6.60)

houses, named
  Apthorp, 384–387, 466, 468, 469–470, 472, 790; (4.270, 6.21–6.23, Table 6.1)
  Arborcroft, 369; (4.253)
  Brattle, William, 462, 472, 640, 739; (6.7, 6.8, 9.40, Table 6.1)
  Cloverden, 275–276, 484–485; (6.50)

Cooper-Frost-Austin, 288, 295–297, 327, 457–459, 472; (4.153, 4.167, 6.1–6.4, Table 6.1)

Elmwood, 230–233, 466, 470–472, 826; (4.75, 6.25, 6.26. Table 6.1)

Elmwood Junior, 232

Fern Hill, 250; (4.102)

First Parish parsonage (Hooker-Shepard-Wigglesworth house), 7, 30, 119, 457, 756, 759, 765, 841n11; (1.6, 1.32, 3.2, 10.7, 10.14)

Frost-Waterhouse, 272, 472, 474–475; (4.130, 6.31, Table 6.1)

Gray, Asa, 453, 478; (5.85, 6.37, 6.38)

Greycroft, 307, 310–311, 555, 610; (4.180, 4.186, 6.162)

Hastings-Holmes, 314–316, 394, 430, 463, 468, 776; (4.190–4.192, 5.2, 6.9, 6.10)

Hazelwood, 321, 480–481; (6.45)

Hooper-Lee-Nichols, 218–219, 276, 459–460, 463–464, 472; (4.58, 6.10, 6.11, Table 6.1)

Larches, 239–240, 243, 476–477; (4.88, 4.92, 6.35, 6.36)

Lechmere-Sewall-Riedesel, 213, 216, 472; (4.51, 4.54, Table 6.1)

Lee, Thomas, 468, 472

Longfellow House-Washington's Headquarters National Historic Site. See Vassall-Craigie-Longfellow House

Opposition House, 361; (4.243)

Parkway Bungalow, 241–242; (4.91)

Prentice-Webber, 17, 463; (1.17)

Richardson's Row, 359, 367, 489; (4.251, 6.56)

Riverview, 211–212, 555–557; (4.49, 6.163, 6.164)

Royall, Isaac (Medford), 464, 467

Ruggles-Fayerweather, 221, 223, 470–472; (4.62, 6.24, Table 6.1)

Shady Hill, 349–350, 476, 482, 484, 853n6; (4.230, 6.46)

Shirley-Eustis (Roxbury), 331, 467

Vassall, Henry, 190, 460, 463–464, 472, 491; (4.18, 6.12–6.14, Table 6.1)

Vassall-Craigie-Longfellow, 194–198, 466–470, 472; (4.23, 6.15–6.20, Table 6.1)

Howe, Dr. Estes, 53–56, 56, 158, 219, 232, 741; (2.16)

Howe, Elias, 443

Howe, J. Murray, 242

Howe, Julia Ward, 212, 410

Howe, Lois Lilley, 75, 97, 317, 463, 471, 477, 551, 559, 549, 551, 559, 636; (4.194, 6.10, 6.26, 6.35). *See also Architects and Builders Index*

Howe, Lois Lillie White (Mrs. Estes Howe), 219, 232, 549

Howe, Rosamund, 108

Howe, Sarah, 251, 256; (4.103)

Howe, William, 331

Howells, Elinor Mead (Mrs. William Dean Howells), 65, 266, 328–329, 510; (2.29, 4.123)

Howells, William Dean, 65–67, 264, 266, 306, 338, 350, 410, 430, 443, 595–596; (2.29, 4.123, 4.207)

Hubbard, Gardner Greene, 53–57, 203–210, 318, 501, 531, 558, 594, 741, 846n16; (2.17, 6.76)

Hubbard, John H., 595

Hubbard, Mabel (Mrs. Alexander Graham Bell), 54

Hudnut, Joseph, 403, 577, 814–814

Hunneman, William, 851n11

Hunnewell, Charles, 256, 491

Hunnewell, James, 187, 494–495; (6.65)

Hunnewell, Richard, 252

Hunt, Benjamin, 306, 534; (4.179)

Hunt, John, 213, 461

Hunt, Rebecca, 318

Huntington, Edward V., 218

Huntington, James, 302, 305, 675; (4.177)

Hurd, Amos, 723–724; (9.15, 9.16)

Hurd, Melancthon, 742

Hurley, Gov. Charles F., 112, 229, 269; (4.73)

Hutchinson, Anne, 5, 841n5

Hutchinson, Elizabeth (Mrs. Daniel Gookin), 370

Hutchinson, Gov. Thomas, 179, 214, 217

Hyatt, Alpheus, 558

Hyde, Edward, 232

industries

aircraft manufacturing, 133; (3.29)

bookbinding, 99, 128, 137, 694, 725, 742, 750; (8.24, 9.17)

brick manufacturing, 2, 372–374; (4.255, 4.257)

New England Brick Co., 571, 600, 774; (6.814)

Parry Bros. & Co., 539

Sands, Ivory, John, and Hiram, 374, 772; (10.23)

Sands, John L. & Co., 772; (10.23)

furniture

Braman, Shaw & Co. (Shaw, Applin & Co.), 329, 529–530; (6.122, 6.123)

ice harvesting, 46, 146–147, 239; (3.49)

ice tool manufacturing, 128

milling (windmill), 8, 252, 847n37

miscellaneous

Auto Wind Shield Co., 165; (3.81)

Baird-Atomic, Inc., 165

California (Stucco) Products Co., 571, 842n29

Hingham Knitting Co., 380, 383, 421, 750–751; (4.269, 9.57)

Reversible Collar Co., 374, 380, 383, 750–751; (4.269, 9.55, 9.56)

Somerville Dyeing & Bleaching Co., 329–330; (4.208, 4.211)

Standard Turning Works, 190

Sterling Knit Goods Co., 380, 383, 422, 750; (4.269)

Techbuilt, Inc., 586–587; (6.203)

printing and publishing, 8–9, 14, 128, 738–750; (9.40–9.55)

Allen & Farnham, 750; (9.55)

Cambridgeport Diary Co., 748–749; (9.54)

Cummings & Hilliard, 738

Dakin & Metcalf, 750; (9.55)

Freeman & Bolles, 741

Harvard Printing Office, 739

Harvard University Press, 739–741; (9.43)

Hilliard & Metcalf, 738

Houghton & Bolles, 742, 750

Houghton, Mifflin & Co., 742–746; (9.45–9.50)

James R. Osgood & Co., 738–739

John Wilson & Son, 739

Little & Brown/Little, Brown & Co., 741–742, 748; (9.44)

Rand McNally, 742

Riverside Press, 376, 417, 741–747; (5.34, 9.45–9.51)

Standard Diary Co., 748–749; (9.54)

Ticknor & Fields, 742

Tolman Print, 739

University Press, 165, 738–740; (3.83, 9.40–9.42)

Welch, Bigelow & Co., 738, 852n11

ship building, 12, 715–716; (1.11)

tanning, 252, 312, 334, 335, 338, 847n55

inheritance and dower, laws and practices, 312–313, 318, 327, 335, 349

Inman, Elizabeth Murray (Mrs. Ralph Inman), 21, 26; (1.20)

Inman, Ralph, 19, 21–22, 25, 29, 35, 177, 622; (1.19, 1.20, 1.31, Table 1.2)

Inman, Susannah Speakman (Mrs. Ralph Inman), 21; (1.21)

inns, taverns, and hotels, 13, 77, 145, 681–686; (8.1–8.9)

hotels

Ambassador, 77, 684–685, 833; (8.7)

Brattle House, 126, 180, 682–683, 739; (3.15, 8.2, 9.40)

Brattle Inn, 171–172; (3.91)

Charles, 164–165, 686; (3.81)

Commander, 77, 261, 684–685; (8.5, 8.6)

Continental, 77, 276, 684–685

Continental Motor Gardens (proposed), 683

Fresh Pond Hotel, 237, 239

Holiday Inn (1653 Massachusetts Avenue), 310–311, 683; (4.187)

Holiday Inn (proposed), 166–167; (3.84)

Hotel Packard, 128, 683; (3.18, 8.3)

Imperial Hotel (proposed), 683–684; (8.4)

Inn at Harvard, 145, 166, 169, 686; (8.8)

Mary Prentiss Inn, 302

Porter's [Cattle Market] Hotel, 63, 682, 841n15

Read & Lincoln's, 373

Red Lion Inn, 272, 274–275, 682; (4.130)

Lee, Caesar (slave), 218

Lee, Joseph, 218

Lee, Judge Joseph (1709–1802), 19, 22, 24, 25, 178, 212, 214, 217, 370; (1.19, Table 1.2)

Lee, Mark (slave). *See* Lewis, Mark

Lee, Thomas, 214

Lee, Thomas ("English" Thomas), 214, 219, 245; (4.58)

Lee, Thomas, Jr., 214, 217

Leiber, Matilda, 196

Lesley, Edith, 318, 668–669

Leverett, President John, 274

Levi, John, 847n49

Levy, Louis, 356

Lewis, Adam, 264, 281–283

Lewis, Azubah, 67

Lewis, Enoch, 67, 281–282, 330, 847n49; (4.143)

Lewis, George Washington, Jr., 68–69, 200–201, 283; (2.33, 4.34)

Lewis, Joseph, 281–282, 847n49

Lewis, Juno, 218

Lewis, Mark (slave), 218, 845n11, 847n41

Lewis, Minor Walker (Mrs. Peter Lewis), 67, 281–283, 842n16

Lewis, Nancy, 68–69; (2.33)

Lewis, Peter, 67, 274, 281–283

Lewis, Samuel, 281–282; (4.143)

Lewis, Sophia (Mrs. John Levi), 847n49

Lewis, Walker, 281–282

Lewis, William H., 98–99

Lincoln, Levi, 373

Little, Charles C., 57, 124, 130, 211, 212, 218, 222, 224, 376, 496, 741–742; (4.50, 4.64, 9.44)

Little, John Albro, 788, 853n16

Livermore, Isaac, 41, 57, 63

Livermore, Nathaniel, 41

Lockey, John, 339

Lodge, Henry Cabot, 430

Loker, Katherine, 832

Lonergan, Henry, 603

Long, Gov. John D., 292, 549; (4.159)

Longfellow House Trust, 197

Longfellow Memorial Association, 197, 410–413

Longfellow, Alexander Wadsworth, 95, 195, 202, 466–468; (4.25, 6.18)

Longfellow, Alexander Wadsworth, Jr., 547–548, 553–554, 566. *See also Architects and Builders Index*

Longfellow, Alice, 94–95, 197, 202–203, 466, 476, 662; (2.51, 4.36)

Longfellow, Anne Allegra (Mrs. Joseph Thorp), 94, 95, 197, 202–203, 553–554, 642; (4.28, 4.36, 6.158, 6.159)

Longfellow, Charles A., 62, 198, 202, 649, 843n42; (2.26, 4.36, 7.56)

Longfellow, Edith (Mrs. Richard Henry Dana III), 94, 95, 197, 200, 202, 532, 652; (4.28, 4.36, 6.137)

Longfellow, Ernest W., 62, 197, 202, 642, 649, 843n42; (2.26, 4.26, 4.27, 4.36, 7.56)

Longfellow, Fanny (Mrs. Henry Wadsworth Longfellow), 62, 195–196, 466; (2.26)

Longfellow, Henry Wadsworth, 61–63, 180, 195–198, 202, 232, 410, 430, 649, 662–663, 722; (2.26, 4.25, 4.35, 4.36)

Longfellow, William Pitt Preble, 398–399, 521, 524. *See also Architects and Builders Index*

Longy, Georges, 673

Longy-Miquelle, Renée, 673

Loomis, Eben, 328

Loring, Judge Edward G., 346, 505; (6.81)

Lovejoy, Frederick, 657

Lovell, Frederick, 339; (4:217)

Lovering, Joseph, 345, 487; (6.53)

Lovering, Susie, 650; (7.57)

Lovett, John "The Orangeman," 379, 381; (4.262)

Low, Horace, 285, 533; (4.148)

Lowell, James Russell, 53, 61–62, 64, 117, 123, 211, 230, 232–233, 274, 410, 430, 472, 649, 742, 846n29

Lowell, President A. Lawrence, 72, 143, 145, 364, 564–565, 663, 672, 754, 783, 796, 805–812; (10.65–10.74)

Lowell, Rev. Charles, 232

Loyalists, 18, 20, 25–26, 230–231, 342, 842n17, 842n18; (Table 1.2)

Loyalist claims, 193, 230–231, 263–264, 370

Lyon, George, 190

Lyons, Hugh, 108

Lyons, Mayor John W., 101

Lyons, Patrick J., 285, 598

MacKay, Barnard and Frances, 518; (6.103)

Mackay, Mungo, 35

Macomber, George A., 108; (2.61)

Malcom, John L., 237

Man, William, 317

Mann, Horace, 276

Mann, Jonathan, 398

Mann, Mary Peabody (Mrs. Horace Mann), 276

Manning, Capt. William (1700–79), 17, 122–123, 273; (3.6, 3.7, 4.131)

Manning, Dr. Samuel (1778–1822), 45–46, 387, 637

Manning, Samuel (1729–1825), 17, 122; (3.6)

Manning, William (1614–1691), 45, 123, 715; (3.7)

Mannos, Paul, 101

Marcy, William, 26, 436

Markham, Jeanette, 200, 652–653; (7.61)

Marrett, Amos (1638–1739), 192, 213, 221, 274, 845n8, 845n9

Marrett, Daniel, 192

Marrett, Edward, 23, 463, 472–474, 687, 715; (1.26, 6.29, 6.30, Table 6.1)

Marrett, Thomas, 192

Marston, George, 284; (4.145)

Martain, John C., 206

Mason, Charles, 72–73, 298

Mason, Nathaniel, 122; (3.6)

Mason, William A., 72–73, 190, 298, 377

Massachusetts Bay, Colony of
governance
    civil covenant, 5, 615
    governor and assistants, 3–6
    standing order, 5, 615, 625

Massachusetts Bay Company, 3–4; (1.3)

Massachusetts, Commonwealth of
    Arsenal, 259, 273–274 276–277, 394, 401, 432; (4.113, 4.132, 4.135, 4.136, 5.2)

Board of Health, 90, 417

Board of Railroad Commissioners, 86

Cambridge Bridge Commission, 425–426

Charles River Improvement Commission, 90

Department of Conservation and Recreation, 424, 849n14

Department of Environmental Management, 843n36

Department of Public Safety, 843n27

General Court, 3, 5, 7–8

Joint Board on the Improvement of the Charles River, 418–419; (5.36)

Metropolitan District Commission, 422–424, 430–432, 843n36, 849n14

Metropolitan Improvement Commission (MDC), 89

Metropolitan Park Commission, 90, 239, 414, 422–425, 430–432, 449, 449, 843n36, 849n14; (5.57, 5.80)

Metropolitan Parking Authority, 103, 403

Metropolitan Transit Authority, 160–163

Metropolitan Water & Sewer Commission, 843n36, 849n14

Master, James, 715

May, Abigail Williams, 432–433; (5.59)

May, Samuel, 432

McClure, Charles F., 327–331; (4.205–4.207)

McClure, David, 330

McColgan, Adam, 307

McDonald, Alexander, 207, 240, 398, 414, 447–448; (4.88, 5.31, 5.77–5.79)

McFarland, Andrew, 219

McGowan, William, 147

McIntyre, Mary, 94

McKay, Gordon, 374, 613, 800

McKean, Joseph, 258

McKenzie, Rev. Alexander, 97, 628, 640

McLean, Isaac, 790

McMillan, Priscilla, 166

McNamee, John (monument dealer), 448–449; (5.80)

McNamee, Mayor John H.H., 71, 92, 99, 128, 137, 381, 694, 725, 790–792; (2.54, 8.24, 9.17, 10.47)

Meacham, George, 126, 185–186, 199, 215, 293, 327, 374–376

Meane, Ann (Mrs. John Hastings), 314

Meane, John, 314

Meigs, Joe V., 86

Melendy, Henry, 290–292, 512–513; (4.156, 6.93)

Melledge, Benjamin, 77

Melledge, James, 208

Melledge, Robert, 77

Mellen, Edwin D., 96, 306–307, 555; (4.180, 6.162)

Mellen, James, 295–297, 538–539, 546; (4.165, 4.166)

Merrill, Estelle (Mrs. Samuel Merrill), 96, 298; (4.169). See also Kincaid, Jean

Merrill, John, 489; (6.57)

Merrill, Samuel, 298–299; (4.169)

Merriman, Roger, 228

Metcalf, Charles R., 738, 852n11

Metcalf, Eliab, 389, 705, 738, 750, 852n11

Middlesex County

    Court of Sessions (County Commissioners), 36, 38

    courthouses, 14–17, 38–39, 124, 636–637, 722, 759; (1.15, 1.17, 3.11, 7.34, 9.12, 10.7)

    courts, 8, 851n10, 851n11

    jail, 13, 18, 119, 121, 636–637; (3.4)

Mifflin, George Harrison, 742

Mifflin, Maj. Thomas, 179

Miller, Neil, 156

Mitchell, Rev. Jonathan, 436

Mitchelson, Edward, 384

Moëring, Anna, 130, 362, 786

Monroe, James, 185

Moore, Charles, 280–281

Moore, Golden, 260

Moore, Josiah, 260

Moot, John, 166, 424

Morgan, Clement, 98–99

Morgan, John P., Jr., 786, 801

Morgan, Mrs. Morris, 208

Moriarty, Patrick, 267

Morison, Samuel Eliot, 398, 437, 756, 772; (10.3)

Morris, Emory, 99

Morrison, Alva, 247–248, 269, 847n36

Morse, John, 121; (3.4)

Morse, Ozias Sr. and, Jr., 339–340; (4.219)

Morse, Royal, 314–315; (4.191)

Moulton, Helen, 77

Mower, Martin, 186

Mowll, William L., 74, 79, 769, 843n22. See also Architects and Builders Index

Moynihan, Daniel Patrick, 826

Munroe, Deacon James and Sarah, 258, 273, 472; (4.112, 4.131, Table 6.1)

Munroe, James, Jr., 493; (6.63)

Munroe, Rev. Charles, 345

Munroe, Susan and Mary, 258

Murdock, Asa, 267

Murray, James H., 572

Muzzey, Henry, 200; (4.32)

Mygate, Joseph, 314

Myles, Thomas F., 324; (4.201)

Nash, Nathaniel, 225; (4.68)

Neiley, Robert G., 829

Nelligan, Peter, 207; (4.41)

Newell, Elizabeth (Mrs. Samuel Newell), 373, 376

Newell, Frances, 228

Newell, Rev. William, 262, 506

Newell, Samuel, 373

Newhall, Charles A., 697

Newtowne, town of

    as capital, 4–5

    boundaries, 10; (1.10)

    building codes, 6, 78–83, 637

    defenses, 4, 5, 9–10, 19, 26–29, 188, 275, 312, 841n8; (1.19, 1.28–1.30)

    founding, 3–5

    government, 5

    land distribution, 11

    landscape, 1–3

    market town, 7, 408

    renamed Cambridge, 8

    roads, early, 5–6, 11; (1.4)

Nichols, Arthur Boylston, 247, 269, 847n36

Nichols, Dr. John, 256–257; (4.109)

Nichols, Edgar, 650
Nichols, Elizabeth, 218
Nichols, Eunice, 273; (4.131)
Nichols, George, 186, 218, 460
Nichols, Susan, 218
Niles Brothers, 292, 298, 561
Niles, Eugene M., 291, 536–538; (4.158, 6.136)
Niles, J. Harris, 292, 536–537, 561; (6.135)
Niles, S.N., 238
Niles, Stephen, 235, 237
Niles, Sullivan, 292, 299, 537; (4.170)
Niles, W. Harmon, 387
Nolen, John, 79, 81, 92, 143, 412, 843n30. *See also Architects and Builders Index*
Nolen, William W., 657
nonprofit organizations
  Cambridge Center for Adult Education, 179, 462, 640–642
  Cambridge Heritage Trust, 108
  Cambridge Social Union, 152, 180, 462, 640–641, 739; (7.43, 9.40)
  John F. Kennedy Presidential Library and Museum, 105, 111, 158–164, 432–433, 818, 826–827; (3.75, 3.76)
  Prospect Union, 71
Norcross, Katherine Brooks, 672
Norris, Forris, 228–229, 242–244, 247–248, 572, 603–606; (4.74, 4.92, 4.93)
Norton, Andrews, 349–350, 482, 484, 738; (6.48)
Norton, Charles Eliot, 65, 69, 97, 349–354, 566, 769, 772, 800, 801, 848n66, 849n4; (4.230)
Norton, Grace, 351, 356–357
Norton, Michael, 258, 284, 301–302, 495–496, 510, 645; (4.171, 6.66–6.68, 6.89, 7.47)
Nowell, Henry, 183
Noyes, James A. and Constance, 215–217, 558–559; (6.166)
Nuttall, Thomas, 452–453
Nutter, Charles, 356
Nutting, Elizabeth, 20
Nutting, John, 25, 317, 394, 470; (4.194, 5.2, Table 1.2). *See also Architects and Builders Index*
Nylander, Robert H., 6, 108, 436

Oakes, Urian, 434
O'Brien, Fr. John, 92
Oliver, Buff (slave), 231
Oliver, Cato (slave), 231
Oliver, Elizabeth (Mrs. John Vassall Jr.), 193, 230
Oliver, Jenny (slave), 231
Oliver, Jeoffrey (slave), 231
Oliver, Jerry (slave), 231
Oliver, Jude (slave), 231
Oliver, Mira (slave), 231
Oliver, Peter, 318
Oliver, Rebecca, 122; (3.6)
Oliver, Samuel (slave), 231
Oliver, Sarah (slave), 231
Oliver, Thomas, 19, 22, 24, 25–26, 29, 178, 230–231, 470–471, 622, 846n26; (1.19, 4.75, 6.25, 6.26, Table 1.2)
Oliver, Violet (slave), 231
Oliver, Young Jerry (slave), 231
Olmsted, Frederick Law, 242, 350–352; (4.232). *See also Architects and Builders Index*
Olmsted, Frederick Law, Jr., 92, 381, 769. *See also Architects and Builders Index*
O'Neill, Rep. Thomas P., Jr.,
O'Reilly, Agnes Boyle, 654–655; (7.66)
O'Reilly, Francis J., 400–401
Orne, John Gerry, 244
Orne, Sarah (Mrs. John G. Orne), 244
Orr, Fr. William, 381
Osgood, Benjamin, 297; (4.167)
Ossoli, Margaret Fuller. *See* Fuller, Margaret
O'Sullivan, Michael, 381–383, 421, 838; (4.268)
Otis, Harrison Gray, 360, 849n6

Packard, Jennie, 128, 683
Packard, William, 231–232
Paddlefoot, Jonathan, 335
Paige, Rev. Lucius, 64–65
Palfrey, Francis, 322
Palfrey, John (d. 1689), 317
Palfrey, John Carver (1839–1906), 322–324
Palfrey, John Gorham (1786–1881), 47, 321–325, 327, 346, 480–481; (6.45)
Palfrey, Mary Ann (Mrs. John Gorham), 324

palisade (pallysadoe). *See* Newtowne, defenses,
Palmer, Alice Freeman, 364
Palmer, George Herbert, 364
Palmer, John, 118
Palmer, Stephen, 187, 252
Papanti, Lorenzo, 640
Parke, George, 292–293
Parke, Richard, 314
Parker, Aaron, 274
Parker, George, 568; (6.179)
Parker, Joseph, 377–379
Parker, Josiah, 252
Parker, Judge Joel, 198, 489, 506; (6.82)
Parker, Robert, 318
Parker, Ruth E., 561–562; (6.170)
Parkman, George, 261
Parry, John E., 239, 534; (6.129)
Parry, Mrs. William A., 300
Parry, William, 539–540; (6.140)
Parsons, Emily, 676
Parsons, Sabra, 286, 505
Parsons, Theophilus, 264, 360, 480, 676
Parsons, William Barclay, 88
Partridge, Frank and Horace, 306, 534; (4.179)
Patrick, Capt. Daniel, 394
Peabody, Caryl (Mrs. Frederick Lovejoy), 657; (7.70)
Peabody, Charles, 657
Peabody, Rev. Andrew Preston, 648
Peak, Howard F., 324
Pearson, Eliphalet, 314, 321
Peck, William Dandridge, 452
Peirce, Benjamin, 364–365, 371; (4.247, 4.254)
Peirce, Benjie, 649; (7.56)
Peirce, Charles, 94
Peirce, Jessie, 650; (7.57)
Peirce, Melusina Fay (Mrs. Charles Peirce), 94
Pelham, Edward, 16
Pelham, Herbert, 13, 252–254; (4.104)
Perrin, Franklin, 264, 266; (4.124)
Perry, Ralph, 356
Perry, William Graves, 696–697
Petkin, Israel, 145
Pevey, Gilbert A.A., 285; (4.148)

Peyntree, William, 8, 754–755; (1.7)

Phillips, Harriet Hill, 267

Phillips, John (1770–1823), 46, 342, 359, 482

Phillips, Rev. John (b. 1609), 341

Phillips, Willard, 260, 286–287; (4.150)

Phips, David, 19, 24, 25, 370, 384, 622; (1.19, Table 1.2)

Phips, Elizabeth (Mrs. John Vassall), 188, 370

Phips, Mary (Mrs. Richard Lechmere), 213, 370

Phips, Rebecca (Mrs. Joseph Lee), 213, 217, 370

Phips, Sir William, 370

Phips, Spencer, 19, 22, 177, 188, 192, 213, 370, 618; (1.19, 7.4)

Pickett, Elizabeth, 436

Pickhall, Thomas, 328

Plympton, Dr. Sylvanus, 387

Plympton, Helen (Mrs. W. Harmon Niles), 387

Pollock, J.D., 156

Pomeroy, Ann, 349; (4.229)

Ponce, John H., 90

Pond, Bremer, 83, 672

Poorvu family, 172, 704

Poorvu, Harris and Sumner, 145

Popkin, John, 302

Porter, Arthur Kingsley, 232

Porter, Charles, 380

Porter, Isaac, 18

Porter, Israel, 118, 121, 123, 138, 139, 283, 396, 637, 681, 705, 841n15; (3.35–3.37)

Porter, Joseph, 281

Porter, Linn Boyd, 78, 788; (10.42)

Porter, Rev. William, 198

Porter, Zachariah, 327, 841n15

Potter, Alfred C, 559, 565; (6.167, 6.176)

Potter, H. Staples, 273, 286; (4.131, 4.149)

Potter, Henry, 286, 328, 330

Powers, John J., 237

Pratt, Daniel, 346

Pratt, Dexter, 46, 180, 184, 379, 722; (4.7)

Pratt, Patricia Ross, 432–433; (5.60)

Prentice, Benjamin, 231

Prentice, Caleb, 16–17, 722; (1.17)

Prentice, Daniel, 452

Prentice, Henry, 254, 260, 273; (4.105, 4.115)

Prentice, John, 256

Prentice, Sally, 256

Prentice, Solomon, 259, 273; (4.113)

Prentice, Stephen, 20

Prentice, Thomas, 263

Prentiss, Mary (Mrs. William A. Saunders), 302, 490; (6.58)

property development entities
  Carpenter & Company, 164–165; (3.81)
  Community Trust, 356–357; (4.238)
  Fresh Pond Parkway Realty Co., 242–244; (4.92)
  Garden Street Trust, 270
  Gerald Hines Interests, 167
  Gerry's Landing Associates, 247
  Harvard Housing Trust, 206, 356–357, 607–608; (6.234)
  Harvard Riverside Associates, 381, 801–805; (10.63)
  Intercontinental Developers, 170, 612, 704, 709; (3.89, 6.242, 8.45)
  Kavanos Enterprises, 166–167
  Marsh Associates, 207
  Massachusetts Engineering Co., 572
  Randolph Trust, 387, 788–790
  Shady Hill-Norton's Woods Enterprise, 356
  University Associates, 133, 694, 726–727, 788–790, 802; (8.25, 9.20)

property ownership, real estate trusts, 136, 844n5

Proprietors of Common Lands, 11–12, 42, 47, 118, 177, 252, 254, 272–274, 341, 393–394, 398, 408, 716; (4.105, 4.131)

Proprietors of the Market, 118

public transportation
  companies/agencies
    Boston Elevated Railway, 86–89, 142–144, 147, 158
    Broadway Railroad, 83
    Cambridge & South Boston Railroad, 86
    Cambridge Railroad, 49, 53, 57–60, 158, 377, 440, 730–731, 741; (2.13, 2.42)
    Cambridge Stage Co., 51, 58, 682
    Charles River Railroad, 83–86, 322; (2.42)
    Ebenezer Kimball, 49–50

    Massachusetts Bay Transportation Authority, 113, 163, 737
    Metropolitan Transit Authority, 158, 160; (3.74)
    New Line, 51, 264
    Union Railway, 53, 58–60, 126, 128, 158, 447, 730–731; (2.22, 2.23, 5.77, 7.28–7.30)
    West End Street Railway, 69, 83–86, 131, 730–733, 843n32; (2.34, 2.42, 3.22, 9.31, 9.32)

railroad passenger transportation, 53, 54–56, 289, 300, 313, 440, 730. See also railroad companies and stations

railroad stations
  Brighton (Boston), 51
  Cottage Farm (Boston), 51
  East Cambridge, 51
  Fresh Pond, 51
  Holmes Place, 54, 261, 313–315, 347, 402–403, 726, 730, 768, 776; (4.191, 4.227, 5.15, 9.27)
  Mount Auburn, 51, 447; (5.77)
  Park Street (Somerville), 51
  Porter's (Porter Square), 49, 51, 89, 303, 730; (2.13, 4.176, 9.26)
  West Cambridge (Brick Yards), 51, 846n23

rapid transit, elevated vs. subway, 87–89, 141–143; (3.40, 3.41)

routes and fares, 49, 51, 58, 60, 83–89, 112, 113, 141, 142, 149, 252, 313, 440; (2.24, 2.42)

routes (first mentioned, described)
  Alewife extension, 112–114, 168, 312, 338, 401, 402, 737, 827; (2.68)
  Beacon Street, Somerville, 84, 313, 322; (2.42)
  Boston via Charles River Railway, 83–84; (2.42)
  Brattle Street, 58, 60, 84; (2.24, 2.42)
  Broadway, 83–84; (2.42)
  Huron Avenue, 71, 84, 86, 112, 212, 235, 252, 561, 843n33; (2.42)
  Main Street-Massachusetts Avenue, 58, 60, 84; (2.24, 2.42)

Massachusetts Avenue (North Avenue), 49, 58, 60, 84; (2.13, 2.24, 2.42)

Mt. Auburn Street, 84; (2.42)

Cambridge Subway, 86–89, 113, 141–144, 307, 402, 404, 733–736; (3.42, 3.43, 5.19, 9.34–9.38)

street railways, electrification, 53, 57–60, 70, 83–86, 126, 137–141, 252, 307–308, 732–733; (2.42, 2.43, 4.181, 9.32)

subway stations

Central, 88

Davis, 113

Harvard, 88, 113, 141–144, 147, 733–735, 737; (2.46, 3.42–3.44, 9.34–9.36)

Harvard-Brattle, 737

Porter, 113

Stadium Station, 735–736; (9.38)

vehicles

buses, 112, 160

horsecars, 48, 58, 60, 62, 83, 85–86, 126, 130, 158; (2.13, 2.22, 2.24, 2.43, 2.44)

stage coaches, 49–50

streetcars, 112, 149

trackless trolleys, 112

Purcell, Hycent, 387

Pusey, President Nathan, 109, 817–826; (10.80–10.88)

Putnam, Gen. Israel, 29

Quigley, James, 205–206, 260; (4.40)

Quincy, Eliza, 119; (3.2)

Quincy, President Josiah, 34, 43, 119, 124, 263, 342, 362, 364, 396, 760–764ff, 850n1

Quinn, Mayor Edward W., 79

Racial and ethnic groups

African Americans, 18, 20, 24, 26, 34, 67–68, 98–99; (2.32)

covenants, preventing sale to, 78, 843n26

emigration movement, 67

Lewisville, 67, 264, 842n17

Memorial Hall waiters, 68, 730, 853n22; (2.32, 9.27)

Irish-Americans, 66–67, 91, 128, 203–207, 235, 267, 370, 377–383; (2.48, 4.268)

Native Americans, 2–4, 10, 16, 755, 848n75

Radcliffe College, 94, 256, 650, 654–655, 662–667, 672; (7.64, 7.65, 7.76–7.81)

buildings

Agassiz Hall, 663–664

Alumni House, 258; (4.112)

Buckingham House, 256, 506, 664–665; (6.83, 7.81)

Bunting Institute, 267, 654, 667

Byerly Hall, 664–665; (7.79)

Cronkhite Graduate Center, 664; (7.78)

Currier House, 287, 667

Daniels House, 287

Fay House, 258, 476, 663; (4.111, 7.76)

Greenleaf House, 664–665; (7.79)

Hemenway Gymnasium, 663–665; (7.79)

Hilles Library, 281, 287, 667; (7.81)

Longfellow Hall, 650, 664–665; (7.79). See also Harvard buildings

Putnam House, 256, 664–665; (7.76)

Schlesinger Library, 664–665; (7.79)

Quadrangle, 287, 666–667, 837; (4.152, 7.80)

Radcliffe Yard, 663–665; (7.77–7.79)

Radcliffe Institute for Advanced Study, 667. See also Radcliffe College

Rand, Jennie, 356

Rantoul, William Gibbons, 562–563

Raymond, Patrick H., 77

Raymond, Theodore H., 77

Rayne, George, 283

Read, James (1751–1814), 252, 254, 472; (4.105, Table 6.1)

Read, James (d. 1734), 252

Read, James (stableman), 327

Read, James B., 336

Read, John (1793–1871), 391; (4.277)

Read, Joseph Stacy (1754–1836), 124, 126, 136, 637, 687; (3.11, 3.33, 8.10, Table 6.1)

Read, Nathaniel, 373

Read, Sen. John, 71

Read, William (1800–84), 136–137, 692–693; (3.33, 3.34, 8.22)

Read, William, Jr. (1832–1927), 218–219, 225, 620; (4.57, 4.65)

Reed, Caleb, 215

Reed, Enos, 533

Reemie, Marcus, 317

Reeves, Addie (Mrs. Richard Fuller), 185

Reeves, Emma (Mrs. Arthur B. Fuller), 185

Reid, Andrew, 77

religious denominations

Anglican, 342

Baptist, 850n4

Congregational, 5, 615, 624

Episcopal, 622–624, 627–628

Protestant, 66

Puritan, 342, 841n5, 841n6

Roman Catholic, 66, 381–382, 628–630, 850n7

Unitarian-Trinitarian dispute, 43, 616–619, 625, 764

Remington, Judge Jonathan, 44, 360

Remington, Lt. Jonathan, 188, 460

Remington, Martha (Mrs. Edward Trowbridge), 360

restaurants

Au Bon Pain, 151

Chez Dreyfus, 701

Cronin's, 131, 791; (3.22; 10.49)

Dunster Café, 131; (3.22, 3.23)

Elsie's Lunch, 157

Hayes Bickford's Cafeteria, 154–155; (3.67)

Holly Tree Café, 139; (3.37)

Jimmie's Lunch, 131; (3.22, 3.23)

Rammy's Dairy Lunch, 131; (3.22)

The Tasty, 157, 169–170; (3.87)

Tommie's Lunch, 157

Wursthaus, 169–170; (3.87)

Young Lee, 149

retailers

bookstores

Amazon.com, 158

Barillari Books, 157

Barnes & Noble, 157

Cambridge Booksmith, 157, 845n13

Dunster House Book Shop, 146, 785; (3.48, 10.36)

Stearns, George, 283; (4.144)

Stearns, Harry, 148, 698–701; (8.38)

Stearns, Marshall Ney, 283, 525–526; (6.115, 6.116)

Stearns, Rev. William A., 662

Stearns, Thomas, 264, 281–283, 346, 374, 376–377, 519–520; (4.142, 4.259, 6.107)

Stearns, Thomas, and Solomon Sargent, 374–378; (4.259, 4.261)

Stearns, William G., 221–222, 224–227, 318; (4.63, 4.65)

Stedman, Cato (slave), 436

Stedman, Ebenezer and Samuel, 20, 146–147; (3.49)

Stedman, John, 7–8

Steele, Chauncey DePew, Jr., 609, 684

Stetson, Zephaniah, 283

Stickney, Nathaniel N., 719; (9.7)

Stiles, Ezra, 314, 469; (6.21)

Stiles, Ruth (Mrs. Caleb Gannett), 314

Stillman, Charles Chauncey, 145

Stockwell, Ellen, 70; (2.35)

Stone, Fred, 845n18

Stone, Gregory, 327, 334

Stone, Moses, 250

Stone, Simon, 250, 439

Storer, Ebenezer, 761–762

Storer, William B., 518; (6.101)

Story, Justice Joseph, 45, 47, 183, 439

Story, William Wetmore, 117, 849n19

Stoughton, Mary Fisk, 192, 542–543; (6.144, 6.145)

Stratton, Charles, 391; (4.277)

Stratton, John (d. 1691) and John, Jr., 232, 237–239; (4.77)

Stratton, Samuel, 237

Strawbridge, Jill, 166

streets (first mentioned, described)

  Aberdeen Avenue, 240, 448; (4.88)

  Acacia Street, 192

  Agassiz Street, 295–297; (4.164)

  Alewife Brook Parkway, 241, 422

  Appian Way, 118, 252–253, 255–257; (4.104, 4.107–4.109)

Appleton Road, 212, 219

Appleton Street, 212, 218

Arcadia Street, 338

Arlington Street, 290, 291–295, 847n46; (4.156, 4.162)

Arrow Street, 11, 124, 361, 372; (4.243, 4.255)

Ash Street, 186–187, 845n2

Ash Street Place, 187

Athens Street, 378, 388; (4.261, 4.273)

Avon Hill Street, 290, 294, 296, 298–299; (4.156, 4.162, 4.164)

Avon Street, 274, 281, 283, 285; (4.137)

Back Lane, 384, 385–387; (4.271). *See also* Arrow Street

Banks Street, 378, 383, 388, 745; (4.261, 4.273, 9.47)

Bates Street, 299

Bath Street (Lane), 420, 845n2; (5.39). *See also* Memorial Drive

Beacon Street, Somerville, 313, 322, 336, 337, 339–340, 344; (4.189, 4.213, 4.214, 4.219)

Beaver Street, 377–378, 388; (4.259, 4.273)

Beech Street, 289, 841n10

Bellevue Avenue, 294, 298–299; (4.162)

Bennett Street, 158

Berkeley Place, 262; (4.117)

Berkeley Street, 198, 261–262, 499; (4.29, 4.117)

Blackstone Street, 745; (9.47)

Blakeslee Street, 228

Blanchard Road, 585

Bond Street, 251, 265; (4.120)

Bow Street, 11, 124, 147, 363, 384–386; (4.243, 4.271)

Bowdoin Street, 278, 283–285; (4.137)

Boylston Street, 388; (4.273). *See also* Kennedy Street

Bradbury Park, 207

Braintree Street, 7, 384, 386; (4.271). *See also* Massachusetts Avenue

Brattle Arcade (passageway), 171–173; (3.93, 3.94)

Brattle Circle, 238, 431; (4.86, 5.57)

Brattle Street, 14, 46–47, 103, 107, 126, 149, 171, 177–178, 256, 431; (3.91, 4.108, 5.57)

  electrification controversy, 84–86

  truck traffic, 89, 113

Brattle Walk, 156; (3.68)

Brewer Street, 186

Brewster Street, 212, 215–216, 219; (4.53)

Brighton Street, 378; (4.261)

Broadway, 36, 38, 359, 760–761, 763; (10.11)

Brown Street, 205

Bryant Street, 353, 355; (4.233, 4.236)

Buckingham Street, 200–201; (4.33)

Buena Vista Park, 289, 290, 294; (4.156, 4.162)

Busby's Lane, 12; (1.11)

bypass roads, planned, 103, 149

Cambridge & Concord Turnpike, 36, 43, 66, 251, 359, 394, 760–761, 821; (2.30)

Cambridge Street, 36, 38, 359, 763, 778; (10.11, 10.30)

Carver Street, 322

Channing Place, 228

Channing Street, 232–233; (4.78)

Chapel Street, 847n46

Charles River Road, 388, 418–422; (4.273, 5.36, 5.39–5.41). *See also* Memorial Drive

Charles River Street, 378; (4.261). *See also* Plympton Street

Charlestown Road. *See* Kirkland Street

Charlestown-Watertown Path, 7, 11

Chauncy Street, 274, 276–281; (4.137, 4.138)

Chestnut Street. *See* Plympton Street

Church Street, 118, 124, 126, 132, 147, 252, 255, 722–725; (3.11, 4.107, 9.14, 9.17, 9.18)

Concord Avenue, 36, 38

Concord Road, 300. *See also* Massachusetts Avenue (North)

Concord Turnpike (Rt. 2), 430

Coolidge Avenue, 246

Coolidge Hill, 248–250; (4.99, 4.100)

Coolidge Hill Road, 247

Cow Yard Row, 7, 755

Cowperthwaite Street, 377–378, 383, 388, 825; (4.259, 4.273)

Craigie Circle, 198, 606

Craigie Street, 198

Creek Street. *See* Eliot Street

Crescent Street, 330

Crooked Street, 47, 118, 384–386; (4.271). *See also* Holyoke Street

Daye Avenue (Court), 721, 742, 744–745; (9.10, 9.46, 9.47)

DeWolfe Street, 377–378, 381–382, 388, 802; (4.259, 4.267, 4.273)

Dexter Avenue, 290; (4.156). *See also* Bellevue Avenue

Dinsmore Court, 206

Divinity Avenue, 321, 343, 345, 347, 348; (4.223, 4.227, 4.228)

Dunstable Road, 212, 219–221

Dunster Street, 6, 47, 123, 126, 131–132, 134, 146, 378, 388, 687, 841n9; (3.22, 3.30, 4.261, 4.273)

Dyke Street, 377–378; (4.259). *See also* Riverview Avenue

East Bellevue Avenue, 298

Eliot Street, 121, 135, 144, 378; (4.261)

Elmer Street, 380, 745; (9.47)

Elmwood Avenue, 38, 88, 233, 431; (4.78, 5.57)

Eustis Street, 334, 338

Everett Place, 186. *See also* Ash Street

Everett Street, 204, 318–319, 321, 353, 848n68; (4.195, 4.233)

Exeter Park, 337

Fallon Place, 380

Farrar Street, 353, 355, 357; (4.233, 4.236)

Farwell Place, 252, 256

Fayerweather Street, 212, 222, 224; (4.63)

Fernald Drive, 269, 608

Flagg Street, 372, 378, 380; (4.261)

Follen Street, 274–276, 745; (4.137, 9.47)

Forest Street, 337; (4.214)

Foster Street, 103, 203–204, 206

Francis Avenue, 345, 353, 355, 356; (4.226, 4.233, 4.236)

Fresh Pond Lane, 237, 239–241, 431–432, 847n35; (4.87, 4.88, 5.57)

Fresh Pond Parkway, 76, 233, 237, 239, 241, 244, 422, 424, 431–432, 846n33; (4.78, 4.90, 5.44, 5.45, 5.57, 5.58)

Frisbie Place, 346

Frost Street, 337; (4.214)

Fuller Place, 185, 187

Garden Street, 251–252, 254, 259, 263–270, 272, 287, 395, 398; (4.105, 4.113, 4.152, 5.4)

Garden Street Place, 283

Garden Terrace, 268–269; (4.126, 4.127)

Garfield Street, 332–334, 533–535; (4.212, 6.129–6.132)

Gerry Street, 186

Gerry's Landing Road, 241, 244, 248, 423–424, 678; (5.44, 5.45, 7.96)

Gibson Street, 206, 846n18

Gorham Street, 322

Gracewood Park, 237

Grant Street, 378, 383, 388, 825; (4.261, 4.273)

Gray Gardens East, 271–272, 298; (4.129)

Gray Gardens West, 268, 271; (4.126, 4.129)

Gray Street, 274, 283, 286

Great Road, 300. *See also* Massachusetts Avenue (North)

Greenough Boulevard, 423–424

Grozier Road, 212, 236–238, 431, 590; (4.83, 5.57)

Gurney Street, 212, 228

Hammond Street, 322

Hampshire Street, 36

Harris Street, 337, 338; (4.214)

Harvard Street, 36, 359, 361, 363; (4.242, 4.245)

Hawthorn Street, 192

Hawthorne Avenue, 431; (5.57). *See also* Grozier Road

Healy Street, 200–201; (4.33)

Hemlock Road, 215

Highland Street, 212, 215, 218, 846n21

Highway to Menotomy, 300. *See also* Massachusetts Avenue (North)

Highway to the Common Pales, 12; (1.11)

Highway to the Great Swamp, 12; (1.11)

Highway to the New West Field, 12; (1.11)

Hilliard Place, 185

Hilliard Street, 185

Hillside Avenue, 294, 296; (4.162, 4.164)

Holden Street, 353; (4.233)

Holmes Place, 312, 314–317, 395; (4.190, 4,191, 5.3, 5.4)

Holyoke Place, 118, 378, 388, 389; (4.261, 4.273)

Holyoke Street, 377–378, 384, 388, 390; (4.259, 4.273, 4.276)

Howland Street, 324

Hudson Street, 278, 283–284; (4.137)

Humboldt Street, 294, 295–297; (4.162, 4.164)

Hurlbut Street, 274, 283, 285, 332, 533; (4.148)

Huron Avenue, 76, 212, 219, 235, 289

Irving Street, 353, 355; (4.233, 4.236)

John F. Kennedy Street. *See* Kennedy Street

Kennedy Road, 218, 588

Kennedy Street, 7, 47, 134, 136–137, 139, 147, 149, 158, 164, 408, 687; (3.30, 3.80)

Kenway Street, 206

Kirkland Place, 346, 353; (4.233)

Kirkland Street, 32, 40, 177, 312, 341–349, 395, 778, 821; (2.1, 4.188, 4.221, 4.223, 4.227, 4.228, 5.3, 10.30)

Lake View Avenue, 212, 234–237, 431; (4.83, 5.57)

Lambert Avenue, 289, 290, 294; (4.156, 4.162). *See also* Upland Road

Lancaster Street, 290, 291–295, 296; (4.156, 4.162–4.164)

Langdon Street, 274, 276–281; (4.137)

Larch Road, 76, 212, 238–239, 241, 431, 591, 846n30; (5.57)

Lee Street, 103

Lexington Avenue, 212, 234–237, 431; (4.83, 5.57)

Liberty Street, 203. *See also* Willard Street

Linden Street, 118, 384, 386; (4.271)

Linnaean Street, 251, 272, 278, 287–288, 289, 290, 294, 296; (4.137, 4.146, 4.150, 4.152, 4.155, 4.162, 4.164)

Long Street. *See* Winthrop Street

Watertown Road, 12; (1.11). *See also* Brattle
  Street
Way to the Great Swamp. *See* Garden Street
Wendell Street, 204, 312, 318–319, 322;
  (4.195)
West Bellevue Avenue, 298
West Cambridge Road, 300. *See also* Massachu-
  setts Avenue (North)
Western Avenue, 36, 383, 745; (4.269, 9.47)
White Street, 289
Whitney Place, 294; (4.162). *See also* Buena
  Vista Park
Whittier Street, 298
Willard Street, 196, 203, 206
Winthrop Street, 121–123, 128, 134, 378, 388,
  391, 844n2; (3.6, 3.8, 3.9, 3.18, 3.30, 4.261,
  4.273, 4.277)
Wood Street. *See* Kennedy Street
Woodbine Lane, 185. *See also* Hilliard Street
Wright Street, 278, 283–284; (4.137)
Wyman Road, 212, 215
Sullivan, David, 827, 844n50
Sullivan, James (1744–1808), 35
Sullivan, James Leo, 827, 844n50
Sullivan, John Briston, 77, 108, 110, 160, 403,
  683, 844n50; (2.63)
Sullivan, Julia, 70; (2.35)
Sullivan, Michael A., 381, 754, 844n50
Sullivan, Timothy, 516
Sullivan, Walter J., 77, 110, 844n50
Summers, President Lawrence, 837
Sumner, Charles, 402
Sumner, William Hyslop, 345, 359
Swan, Olive (Mrs. J. Bertram Williams), 548;
  (6.141)
Swan, Sarah, 529

Taintor, Giles, 205–206, 245, 564
Talmage, Valerie, 829
Tamplin, James, 502
Tarbox, Joseph, 51
Taussig, Frank, 354
Taylor, William, 291
Teele, Althea, 657

Thackery, Emily, 200
Thatcher family, 231
Thaxter, Roland, 352
Thayer, Joshua and James, 374–375, 491; (4.258)
Thayer, Nathaniel, 454, 768, 800
Thomas, Griffith, 514
Thompson, Ann (Mrs. Elbridge Gerry), 231
Thompson, Benjamin, 152–153, 172, 585; (3.61,
  3.92). *See also Architects and Builders Index*
Thorp, Joseph G., 211, 555–557; (6.163, 6.164)
Thorp, Joseph G., Jr., 95, 211, 553–554; (6.158,
  6.159)
Thorpe, James G., 77, 211; (4.49)
Thouin, Gabriel, 452
Thurston, Mayor Charles, 92, 790
Ticknor, George, 45, 274
Toomey, John J., 100–101, 135
Toppan, Robert Noxon, 554; (6.160)
Tories, 20, 842n17. *See also* Loyalists
Torrey, Henry, 346
Tower, David, 200
Towle, Lauren, 697
Towne, Peter, 17, 20, 841n14
Tracy, Michael, 533
Tracy, Nathaniel, 189, 194, 263–264; (4.118)
trades, tradesmen, services, 17, 33
  blacksmith and carriage shops, 722–725;
    (9.12–9.18)
  boat builders, 429
  monument makers, 434–436, 447–450; (5.63,
    5.77–5.81, 5.83)
  Notman Photographic Co., 387
  real estate agents, 76–77
  surveyors, 72–73, 295; (2.37)
transportation
  automobiles, proliferation, and parking, 147,
    149, 843n31
  Charles River, commercial traffic on, 425
  Inner Belt, 103–104, 111, 819; (2.58)
  Middlesex Canal, 75–76, 121, 762
  Milestone, Old, 36; (2.3)
  railroad companies
    Boston & Albany, 51–52, 56; (2.15)
    Boston & Lowell, 51–52; (2.15)

Boston & Maine, 51, 56, 89
Charlestown Branch, 51–53, 300, 313, 337,
  339
Fitchburg, 49, 51–53, 56, 89, 313, 440, 730;
  (2.13, 2.15, 9.26)
Grand Junction, 51, 842n7
Harvard Branch, 53–56, 261, 313–316, 318,
  321–322, 347, 730, 842n8; (2.18, 4.227,
  9.27)
New York & Boston Air Line, 56
water
  ferries, 6, 11, 13, 34, 217, 687, 715, 760
  ships, shipping, 373, 425, 714–721, 852n4;
    (9.1–9.11)
wharves
  Brick Wharf, 187, 231, 414, 420, 428, 718–
    720; (5.31, 5.40, 9.5, 9.8)
  Cambridge Electric Light Co., 421, 429, 719,
    837, 842n11; (5.55)
  College Wharf, 124, 126, 378, 421, 717–721,
    741; (4.261, 5.41, 9.4–9.6, 9.9, 9.11)
  in Cambridgeport, 39
  Manning's Wharf, 716
  Marrett's Wharf, 716–717
  Monument Wharf, 207, 414, 420, 447, 718–
    719; (5.31, 9.5)
  Oliver's/Gerry's Landing, 244, 719
  Riverside Press, 417, 421, 429, 719, 721;
    (5.34, 5.55, 9.10)
  Sargent's Wharf, 126, 376, 378, 421, 718–
    720; (4.259, 4.261, 9.5, 9.6, 9.9)
  Town Wharf, 13
  Trowbridge's Wharf, 716
  Winthrop's Wharf, 373, 375, 376, 717–718,
    719–720; (4.258, 4.259, 9.5, 9.7, 9.9)
Treadwell, Daniel, 264, 266, 359, 491–493;
  (4.122, 6.60)
Treat, Marian (Mrs. Gordon McKay), 374
trees
  elms, Garden Street, 259, 849n3; (4.113)
  horse chestnuts, Brattle Street, 464, 846n22;
    (6.11)
  London plane trees ("sycamores"), 103, 849n12
  Norway maples, 403, 406

Siege of Boston, 26–29, 230, 314, 384, 716–717; (1.27–1.30)

Civil War, 276, 279, 398–401, 446; (4.138, 5.10, 5.11, 5.75)

Spanish-American War, 432, 611 (6.238)

Vietnam War, 154–155, 818, 826; (3.65)

War of 1812, 36

World War I, 247, 324–325, 403, 443, 853n24; (4.203, 5.16, 5.17)

World War II, 101–103, 109, 148, 403–404, 584, 608, 640, 658; (5.18)

Washington, Gen. George, 26, 179, 190, 194–195

Washington, Martha, 623

Wasserman, Max, 109–110, 152–154, 702; (3.63, 3.64)

Waterhouse, Dr. Benjamin, 273–276, 394, 452, 474–475, 847n39; (4.131, 5.2, 6.32)

Waterhouse, Louisa (Mrs. Benjamin Waterhouse), 276, 475, 488–489; (6.54, 6.55)

Watson, Abraham, 20

Watson, Daniel, 108, 233, 472–473; (2.61, 6.27, 6.28, Table 6.1)

Webb, Roger, 108

Webber, Samuel, 17, 34, 463, 759; (1.17, 10.7)

Webster, Dr. John White, 252, 261, 362, 369, 650; (4.116)

Webster, Mrs. Kenneth, 247

Weeks, John Wingate, 426

Weems, Katherine Ward Lane, 812

Welch, Albion K.P., 198, 432, 508–509, 738–739, 750; (4.30, 6.86, 6.87)

Weld, George, 428, 429; (5.54)

Wellington, Jeduthun, 36, 231–232

Wells, Ebenezer, 331

Wells, William, 46, 221, 228, 232

Wendell, John Mico, 179

Wendell, Katherine Brattle, 26, 179, 314, 318

Wendell, Oliver, 35, 314, 321

Wendell, Sarah (Mrs. Abiel Holmes), 314

Wentworth, Charles E., 211, 552–553; (6.157)

Wentworth, William P., 302, 692

Weslowski, Patricia, 829

Wesselhoeft, Dr. Walter, 261, 356; (4.116)

Wesson, William, 385

Weston-Smith, Robert, 558

Wetmore, Charles D., 786–788, 802, 804, 806; (10.64)

Wetmore, William, 35

Wheeler, Cornelia, 844n51

Whidden, William M., 554

Whipple, William, 336

White, Austin, 218

White, Henry, 708

White, James, 637, 723; (9.14)

White, Maria (Mrs. James Russell Lowell), 53, 232

White, Moses P., 547

White, Susannah (Mrs. Abel Whitney), 291

Whiting, Howard, 275, 554

Whitman, Ephraim, 344

Whitney, Abel, 291

Whitney, Anne, 402

Whitney, Augustus, 291, 308; (4.181)

Whitney, Hammond, 369

Whitney, Henry M., 83–85

Whitney, Josiah Dwight, 276, 346

Whitney, William L., 54, 56, 129, 165, 187, 692, 722, 740; (4.13, 8.21, 9.41)

Whittemore, Capt. Samuel (1696–1793), 24

Whittemore, Deacon Samuel (1693–1774), 18, 20, 122, 188, 716; (3.6)

Whittemore, Josiah, 716

Whittier, John Greenleaf, 410

Whouley, John, 696

Widener, Eleanor Elkins and Harry Elkins Widener, 808

Wilder, Cyrus D., 532

Willard, Abel, 51, 281, 682, 705

Willard, Charles, 682

Willard, Lyman, 180, 682

Willard, Mayor Sidney, 90, 389

Willard, President Joseph, 738

Williams, Bishop John J., 630

Williams, Henry, 202

Williams, Henry Bigelow, 786

Williams, J. Bertram, 548; (6.141)

Williams, John H., 572

Williams, Morley, 437

Willis, Stillman, 283–284, 286, 331; (4.149)

Williston, Lyman Richards, 94, 261–262, 500–501, 650; (6.75, 7.57)

Wilson, James Q., 826

Wilson, William, 784

Winchester, William P., 250, 443–445, 502, 503; (4.102, 5.74, 6.78)

Windship, Lucy, 256; (4.108)

Winlock, Joseph, 276

Winship, Edward, 288, 335

Winthrop, Hannah Tolman (Mrs. Prof. John Winthrop), 18

Winthrop, Harriet (of Providence), 374–376; (4.259)

Winthrop, James (1752–1821), 18, 35, 39, 123, 637; (3.28)

Winthrop, John (1587–1649), 3–5

Winthrop, John, Jr. (1747–1800), 373

Winthrop, Prof. John (1714–79), 18, 121, 138, 370, 408; (3.35)

Winthrop, William (1753–1825), 47, 125, 126, 359, 370–374, 389, 476, 630, 717; (3.12, 4.256, 4.274)

Winthrop, William heirs, 373–377; (4.259)

Wise, Henry, 100

Wise, Pearl, 844n51

Wister, Owen, 796

Wiswall, Daniel, 759, 765; (10.7, 10.14)

Withey, Robert, 168

Withey, Simeon, 183–184, 256; (4.9)

Wolford, Merle, 669

Wolfe, Albert B., 107–108

women
  Cambridge Women's Heritage Project, 843n41
  in politics and society, 93–96
  property rights, 93
  suffrage movement, 93–94, 843n40; (2.50)

Wood, Edward E., 534; (6.130)

Wood, Frederick and Evelyn, 518; (6.102)

Wood, James A., 306, 329, 555

Wood, William, 1, 6

Woodward, George, 505

Woodward, William, 534